MW01079671

*We support ASE
program certification
through*

ASE NATEF
Improving Programs
Through Certification

Automotive Engine Repair

Nicholas Goodnight
*Automotive Instructor, Ivy Tech
Fort Wayne, Indiana*

Kirk VanGelder
*ASE Certified Master Automotive Technician & L1 & G1
Technology Educators of Oregon – President
Certified Automotive Service Instructor
Vancouver, Washington*

JONES & BARTLETT
LEARNING

World Headquarters
Jones & Bartlett Learning
5 Wall Street
Burlington, MA 01803
978-443-5000
info@jblearning.com
www.jblearning.com

Jones & Bartlett Learning books and products are available through most bookstores and online booksellers. To contact Jones & Bartlett Learning directly, call 800-832-0034, fax 978-443-8000, or visit our website, www.jblearning.com.

Substantial discounts on bulk quantities of Jones & Bartlett Learning publications are available to corporations, professional associations, and other qualified organizations. For details and specific discount information, contact the special sales department at Jones & Bartlett Learning via the above contact information or send an email to specialsales@jblearning.com.

Copyright © 2018 by Jones & Bartlett Learning, LLC, an Ascend Learning Company

All rights reserved. No part of the material protected by this copyright may be reproduced or utilized in any form, electronic or mechanical, including photocopying, recording, or by any information storage and retrieval system, without written permission from the copyright owner.

The content, statements, views, and opinions herein are the sole expression of the respective authors and not that of Jones & Bartlett Learning, LLC. Reference herein to any specific commercial product, process, or service by trade name, trademark, manufacturer, or otherwise does not constitute or imply its endorsement or recommendation by Jones & Bartlett Learning, LLC and such reference shall not be used for advertising or product endorsement purposes. All trademarks displayed are the trademarks of the parties noted herein. *CDX Automotive: Engine Repair* is an independent publication and has not been authorized, sponsored, or otherwise approved by the owners of the trademarks or service marks referenced in this product.

There may be images in this book that feature models; these models do not necessarily endorse, represent, or participate in the activities represented in the images. Any screenshots in this product are for educational and instructive purposes only. Any individuals and scenarios featured in the case studies throughout this product may be real or fictitious, but are used for instructional purposes only.

Production Credits

General Manager: Douglas Kaplan
Executive Publisher: Vernon Anthony
Content Services Manager: Kevin Murphy
Senior Vendor Manager: Sara Kelly
Marketing Manager: Amanda Banner
VP, Manufacturing and Inventory Control: Therese Connell
Composition and Project Management: Integra Software Services Pvt. Ltd.

Cover Design: Scott Moden
Rights & Media Specialist: Robert Boder
Media Development Editor: Shannon Sheehan
Cover Image (Title Page): © 1001nights/E+/Getty
Printing and Binding: LSC Communications
Cover Printing: LSC Communications

Library of Congress Cataloging-in-Publication Data unavailable at time of printing.

6048

Printed in the United States of America
20 19 18 17   10 9 8 7 6 5 4 3 2 1

Source: NATEF Program Accreditation Standards, 2013, National Automotive Technicians Education Foundation (NATEF).

BRIEF CONTENTS

CONTENTS

NOTE TO STUDENTS

This book was created to help you on your path to a career in the transportation industry. Employability basics covered early in the text will help you get and keep a job in the field. Essential technical skills are built in cover to cover and are the core building blocks of an advanced technician's skill set. This book also introduces "strategy-based diagnostics," a method used to solve technical problems correctly on the first attempt. The text covers every task the industry standard recommends for technicians, and will help you on your path to a successful career.

As you navigate this textbook, ask yourself, "What does a technician need to know and be able to do at work?"

This book is set up to answer that question. Each chapter starts by listing the technicians' tasks that are covered within the chapter. These are your objectives. Each chapter ends by reviewing those things a technician needs to know. The content of each chapter is written to explain each objective. As you study, continue to ask yourself that question. Gauge your progress by imagining yourself as the technician. Do you have the knowledge, and can you perform the tasks required at the beginning of each chapter? Combining your knowledge with hands-on experience is essential to becoming a Master Technician.

During your training, remember that the best thing you can do as a technician is learn to learn. This will serve you well because vehicles keep advancing, and good technicians never stop learning.

Stay curious. Ask questions. Practice your skills, and always remember that one of the best resources you have for learning is right there in your classroom… your instructor.

Best wishes and enjoy!
The CDX Automotive Team

ACKNOWLEDGMENTS

▶ Editorial Board

Keith Santini
Addison Trail High School Addison, Illinois

Merle Saunders
Nyssa, Oregon

Tim Dunn
Sydney, New South Wales Australia

▶ Contributors

Daniel M. Kolasinski
Milwaukee Area Technical College

Jeffrey Rehkopf
Florida State College

Jack Ireland
Johnson County Community College

Jeffery A. Evans
Ivy Tech Community College

Sy Gammage
Somerset Community College

Fritz Peacock
Purdue University and Ivy Tech State College

Jerry DeLena
Middlesex County Vocational Technical High School

Damon Friend
Oakland Schools Technical Campus Southwest

Ronald Strzalkowski
Baker College of Flint

Justin Winebrenner
Western Technical College

Paul Kelley
Cypress College

Steve Levin
Columbus State Community College

CHAPTER 1

Strategy-Based Diagnostics

NATEF Tasks

- **N01001** Review vehicle service history.
- **N01002** Demonstrate use of the three C's (concern, cause, and correction).
- **N01003** Identify information needed and the service requested on a repair order.

- **N01004** Research vehicle service information including fluid type, vehicle service history, service precautions, and technical service bulletins.

Knowledge Objectives

After reading this chapter, you will be able to:

- **K01001** Describe the purpose and use of vehicle service history.
- **K01002** Demonstrate an understanding of the active listening process.
- **K01003** Demonstrate an understanding of the strategy-based diagnosis process.
- **K01004** Describe step one of the strategy-based diagnosis.

- **K01005** Describe step two of the strategy-based diagnosis.
- **K01006** Describe step three of the strategy-based diagnosis.
- **K01007** Describe step four of the strategy-based diagnosis.
- **K01008** Describe step five of the strategy-based diagnosis.
- **K01009** Explain how the three Cs are applied in repairing and servicing vehicles.
- **K01010** Describe the information and its use within a repair order.

Skills Objectives

After reading this chapter, you will be able to:

- **S01001** Use service history in the repair and service of vehicles.

- **S01002** Complete a repair order.

You Are the Automotive Technician

A regular customer brings his 2014 Toyota Sienna into your shop, complaining of a "clicking" noise when he turns the steering wheel. You ask the customer further questions and learn that the clicking happens whenever he turns the wheel, especially when accelerating. He tells you he has just returned from vacation with his family and has probably put 300 miles (482 kms) on the car during their trip.

1. What additional questions should you ask the customer about his concern, the clicking noise he hears when turning?
2. How would you verify this customer's concern?
3. What sources would you use to begin gathering information to address this customer's concern?
4. Based on what you know this far about the customer's concern, what systems might be possibly related to this customer's concern?

▶ Introduction

The overall vehicle service involves three major components. Those pieces are gathering information from the customer, the strategy-based diagnostic process, and documenting the repair. The flow of the overall service can be seen below.

1. Initial information gathering is often completed by a service advisor (consultant) and should contain details about the customer concern and pertinent history.
2. Verifying the customer concern begins the strategy-based diagnostic process. Technicians will complete this step to ensure that a problem exists and that their repair eliminated it.
3. Researching the possible cause will provide a list of possible faults. The technician will expand this list as testing continues.
4. Testing will focus on the list of possibilities. Technicians will start with broad, simple tests that look at an entire system or group of components. Testing will progressively become more narrowly focused as it pinpoints an exact cause.
5. Repairs will be made using suggested tools and recommended procedures. This is done to ensure a reliable repair and that manufacturer requirements are met.
6. Repairs must always be verified. This confirms that the technician has completed the diagnosis accurately and completely.

The repair must be documented. The technician has been doing this all along. When the customer concern is recorded, the tests are recorded, and the final repair procedure recorded, the repair has been documented.

▶ Vehicle Service History

K01001 Describe the purpose and use of vehicle service history.

N01001 Review vehicle service history.

S01001 Use service history in the repair and service of vehicles.

Service history is a complete list of all the servicing and repairs that have been performed on a vehicle (**FIGURE 1-1**). The scheduled service history can be recorded in a service booklet or owner's manual that is kept in the glove compartment. The service history can provide valuable information to technicians conducting repairs. It also can provide potential new owners of used vehicles an indication of how well the vehicle was maintained. A vehicle with a regular service history is a good indication that all of the vehicle's systems have been well maintained, and the vehicle will often be worth more during resale. Most manufacturers store all service history performed in their dealerships (based on the VIN) on a corporate server that is accessible from any of their dealerships. They also use this vehicle service history when it comes to evaluating warranty claims. A vehicle that does not have a complete service history may not be eligible for warranty claims. Independent shops generally keep records of the repairs they perform. However, if a vehicle is repaired at multiple shops, repair history is much more difficult to track and, again, may result in a denial of warranty claims.

Vehicle service history can be very valuable to the technician. This history is typically retrieved from service records kept by the shop, dealer network, **original equipment manufacturer (OEM)**, or **aftermarket** service center. This information often contains a list of services performed on a vehicle and the date and mileage at which they were completed. Not all service history contains the same information. Some histories may only contain repair information, while others include every customer concern and maintenance task performed. This information can be very helpful when diagnosing a concern. Service history may help technicians diagnose a vehicle and can also be used to prevent costly duplicated repairs.

Service history can also be used to guide repairs. Records of vehicle service history may indicate that the customer has recently been in for service and now has returned with a new concern. This all-too-common situation is usually found to be caused by error during the previous service. When working on a vehicle that has returned after a recent repair, the previous technician's work (whoever that may be) should be inspected meticulously.

FIGURE 1-1 Print outs of completed repair order as saved in the online repair order system.

The service history may also show that the customer is returning for the same issue due to a component failure. The history might indicate when the component was installed, help the customer get their vehicle repaired, and help the shop to get paid under the component warranty. A vehicle that returns more than once for the same repair could be an indicator that an undiagnosed problem is causing these failures. The service history allows technicians to determine if the vehicle has been well maintained. This can be extremely useful when a technician suspects that lack of maintenance may be the cause of the problem.

The vehicle's service history helps technicians determine what maintenance needs to be performed, and therefore helps customers save money over time by preventing future costly repairs. Routine maintenance is essential on today's modern automobile and prevents premature failures due to contamination and component wear.

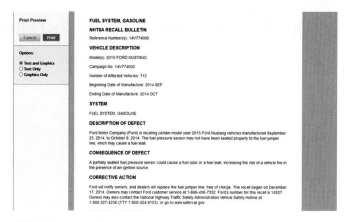

FIGURE 1-2 Recall notice example.

Today's vehicles also require regular software updates. There are many advanced computer systems on modern vehicles. From time to time, updates will be available to fix a bug or glitch in the computer programming. These updates are often designed to eliminate a customer concern, improve owner satisfaction, or increase vehicle life. This is very similar to an update for your PC or mobile device. Service history will indicate to the technician that the vehicle may need an update. The technician will inspect the vehicle's computer system and perform any needed updates as necessary.

Service history can also be used to keep customers safe. Occasionally, manufacturers may need to recall a vehicle for service due to a safety concern that has been identified for a vehicle (**FIGURE 1-2**). This means that the manufacturer has found that the potential exists for a dangerous situation to occur, and the vehicle must be serviced to eliminate it. Depending on the nature of the problem, recalls can be mandatory and required by law, or manufacturers may voluntarily choose to conduct a recall to ensure the safe operation of the vehicle or minimize damage to their business or product image. The service history would be used to verify that the vehicle is subject to the recall and has or has not had the recall service completed. The technician would perform the service, update the service history, and return the vehicle to the customer.

▶ TECHNICIAN TIP

Technicians and service advisors should check the vehicle service history against the manufacturer's service maintenance schedule to determine if the vehicle is due for scheduled maintenance. The maintenance schedule is a guide that indicates what service is due when; it can be found in the manufacturer's service information and often in the owner's manual. Keeping the vehicle well maintained can avoid a failure that strands the customer on the roadside.

Applied Science

AS-11 Information Processing: The technician can use computer databases to input and retrieve customer information for billing, warranty work, and other record-keeping purposes.

Dealership service departments have access to databases run by manufacturers for the purposes of accessing warranty information, tracking vehicle servicing and warranty repair history, and logging warranty repair jobs for payment by the manufacturer. When a customer presents their vehicle for a warranty repair, the customer service department staff begin by consulting the database to confirm that the vehicle is within its warranty period and that the warranty has not been invalidated for any reason. Once it is confirmed that the vehicle is still under a valid warranty, the repair order will be passed to the workshop for diagnosis and repair. Any parts required for the warranty repair must be labeled by the technician and stored for possible recall by the manufacturer.

For example, a young man comes in complaining that his vehicle is "running rough." The customer service staff confirms that the vehicle is nine months old and only has 14,500 miles (approx. 23,000 km), so it is within the manufacturer's 3-year/100,000 mile (160,000 km) warranty period. They check the manufacturer's database to confirm that the vehicle's warranty has not been invalidated before handing the repair order onto the workshop. Then a technician diagnoses the fault as a defective ignition coil and fills out a warranty parts form.

Once the repair has been completed and the parts labeled, the warranty parts form and any repair order paperwork is passed back to administrative staff for processing. Processing will include billing the manufacturer for the correct, pre-approved amount of time, logging the repair on the database for payment, and ensuring that all documentation is correct for auditing purposes.

Warranty Parts Form	
Customer concern: Vehicle running rough	Vehicle Information
Cause: #6 ignition coil open circuit on primary winding	VIN: IG112345678910111
Correction: Replaced #6 ignition coil	RO Number: 123456
Parts description: #6 ignition coil	Date of repair: 10/04/2016

SKILL DRILL 1-1 Reviewing Service History

1. Locate the service history for the vehicle. This may be in shop records or in the service history booklet within the vehicle glove compartment. Some shops may keep the vehicle's service history on a computer.

2. Familiarize yourself with the service history of the vehicle.
   a. On what date was the vehicle first serviced?
   b. On what date was the vehicle last serviced?
   c. What was the most major service performed?
   d. Was the vehicle ever serviced for the same problem more than once?

3. Compare the vehicle service history to the manufacturer's scheduled maintenance requirements, and list any discrepancies.
   a. Have all the services been performed?
   b. Have all the items been checked?
   c. Are there any outstanding items?

To review the vehicle service history, follow the steps in **SKILL DRILL 1-1**.

Active Listening Skills

Depending on the size of a shop, the first point of contact for the customer is the **service advisor** or consultant. This person answers the phone, books customer work into the shop, fills out repair orders, prices repairs, invoices, keeps track of work being performed, and builds customer relations with the goal of providing a high level of customer support. The service advisor also serves as a liaison between the customer and the technician who is working on the vehicle. A service advisor or consultant may advance to become a service manager. In smaller shops, a technician may perform these duties.

When the customer brings his or her vehicle in for service, the service advisor or technician should ask for more information than just the customer concern. It is important to let the customer speak while you use active listening skills to gather as many pertinent details as possible. Active listening means paying close attention to not only the customer's words, but also to their tone of voice and body language. Maintain eye contact with the customer throughout your conversation and nod to show you understand and are paying attention. Do not interrupt. Wait for the customer to finish speaking before responding, then ask open-ended questions to verify that you have heard the complaint clearly and understand the problem. An open-ended question is one that cannot be answered with a yes or no, but instead requires the customer to provide you with more information about the problem (**FIGURE 1-3**). If the shop is noisy, try to find a quieter location in which to speak with the customer. Excellent communication helps ensure that all relevant information is collected. It also makes a good first impression with customers; they are likely to feel that they were listened to and cared for.

Politely use open-ended questions to ask about any symptoms the customer may have noticed, such as:

- Under what circumstances does the concern occur or not occur?
- What unusual noises do you hear (e.g., squeaks, rattles, clunks, and other noises)?
- What odd smells or fluid leaks have you noticed?
- What recent work, service, or accessories have been added to the vehicle?
- What other recent changes or experiences have you had with the vehicle?
- What other systems seem to be operating improperly?

K01002 Demonstrate an understanding of the active listening process.

▶ **TECHNICIAN TIP**

A vehicle's service history is valuable for several reasons:

- It can provide helpful information to the technician when performing repairs.
- It allows potential new owners of the vehicle to know how well the vehicle and its systems were maintained.
- Manufacturers use the history to evaluate warranty claims.

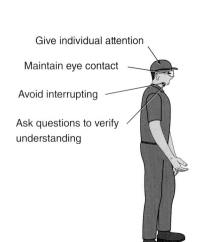

Give individual attention

Maintain eye contact

Avoid interrupting

Ask questions to verify understanding

Pay attention to nonverbal messages (e.g. tone of voice, body language)

FIGURE 1-3 The active listening process.

Although problems may seem unrelated initially, when multiple systems fail at the same time, the issues are frequently related. Open-ended questions can provide valuable information to the technician who is performing the diagnosis.

▶ Strategy-Based Diagnostic Process

Diagnostic problems can be very challenging to identify and correct in a timely and efficient manner. Technicians will find that having a plan in place ahead of time will vastly simplify the process of logically and systematically (strategically) solving problems. The plan should be simple to remember and consistent in its approach; yet it must work for the entire range of diagnostic problems that technicians will encounter. In this way, technicians will have one single plan to approach any diagnostic situation they may encounter, and will be confident in their ability to resolve it. This problem solving plan is called the **Strategy-Based Diagnostic Process**.

The strategy-based diagnostic process is focused on fixing problems correctly the first time. It is a scientific process of elimination, which is much the same process as a medical doctor uses for their diagnosis. It begins with identifying the customer's concern and ends with confirming that the problem has been resolved. The purpose of the problem-solving process is twofold: to provide a consistent road map for technicians as they address customer concerns that require diagnosis, and to ensure that customer concerns are resolved with certainty.

This process simplifies the problem-solving portion of the repair, making the job easier for the technician; it prevents technicians from having to work on the same job more than once; and it all but eliminates customer comebacks. While repeat customers are good for business, a customer coming back with the same problem is not. The customer is likely to be upset and the technician is likely to be working for free. In order to avoid this scenario, it is imperative to address customer concerns correctly the first time.

Proper diagnosis is important to consumers and to the federal government. Federal and state law protects consumers against the purchase of vehicles with significant persistent defects. Technicians are held to a standard of reasonable repair times and limited visits for the same concern. Although the law varies from state to state, this means technicians must not return a vehicle to a customer without addressing the customer's original concern. Also, technicians cannot make the vehicle unavailable to the customer for a long period while the vehicle is being repaired. The purpose of the state and federal laws is to protect consumers buying new vehicles.

Failure to comply with the state and federal law can be very expensive for the dealership and manufacturer. Although most state laws hold the manufacturer directly responsible, dealerships are also hurt by a loss in sales revenue, a loss in repair revenue, and irreparable damage to their customer and sometimes manufacturer relationships. Many state laws hold the manufacturer responsible for full purchase price, incurred loan fees, installed accessories, and registration and similar government charges. This can be a heavy cost on top of the value of the vehicle itself.

Need for the Strategy-Based Diagnostic Process

Finding the source of every customer concern can prove to be a challenge. Novice technicians frequently struggle with diagnostics situations. Even some veteran technicians have difficulty tackling diagnosis on some new technologies. However, if the strategy for solving a problem is generally the same every time, this greatly simplifies the process. Hopefully, by applying a strategy-based diagnostic process, technicians will resolve challenging customer concerns 100% of the time in an efficient manner.

Customer comebacks occur when the customer picks up the vehicle after service, only to bring it back shortly thereafter with the same concern. This situation is understandably upsetting to the customer. Typically, the end result is wasted labor time and a loss in shop productivity. The customer is left with one of the following impressions:

- The work was not performed;
- The shop is incompetent;
- Or, worse yet, the shop was trying to scam the customer.

K01003 Demonstrate an understanding of the strategy-based diagnosis process.

▶ **TECHNICIAN TIP**

Technicians need to do their best to find the issue and resolve it; otherwise, the vehicle may be required to be bought back from the customer, costing the dealership and manufacturer significant money.

▶ **TECHNICIAN TIP**

The diagnostic process makes the technician's job easier by providing a step-by-step strategy to solving the problem. It also answers the question: "Now what do I do?" As even the toughest job becomes easier, technicians will find their rate of diagnostic success increasing.

Customer comebacks are usually caused by one of two avoidable reasons:

1. The customer concern is misinterpreted or misunderstood. This results in the technician "fixing" a problem that does not exist or missing a problem altogether.
2. The technician failed to verify that the original concern was resolved. Technicians are often hurried; some will forget to ensure that the repair they had performed actually fixed the original customer concern.

Use of the strategy-based diagnostic process enables the technician and shop to make more money and satisfy more customers. This is a win-win situation for all involved. Using the strategy-based diagnostic process requires starting at the beginning and following it through to the end every time (**FIGURE 1-4**). This systematic approach will ensure the best results for each diagnostic situation.

Step 1: Verify the Customer's Concern

The first step in the diagnostic process is to verify the customer's concern. This step is completed for two main purposes:

- To verify that the vehicle is not operating as designed
- To guarantee that the customer's concern is addressed

Failure to complete this step may result in wasted time, wasted money, and, worst of all, an unhappy customer. The customer is probably not an experienced automotive technician. For this reason, the customer does not always accurately verbalize the problem that may be occurring. Therefore, it is very important that you have a complete understanding of the customer's concern before beginning the diagnosis. This will enable you to know with certainty that you have actually resolved the original concern after repairing the vehicle and before returning it to the customer. During this step, you may perform several of the following tasks, depending on the customer concern.

First, ask the customer to demonstrate the concern, if possible. This may necessitate a test drive (**FIGURE 1-5**). The customer should be encouraged to drive the vehicle while you ride along as a passenger and gather symptoms and details about the concern. Seeing the customer recreate the concern in real time will often provide some much needed context to the problem. Having the customer demonstrate the concern is ideal in most situations, though not always possible. In the event that the customer is not present, you must do your best to recreate the concern on your own based on the information obtained from the customer. With or without the customer present, be sure to document in writing any details about the scenario in which the concern arises.

Next, make sure that the customer concern doesn't fall outside the range of normal operation of the component or system. The manufacturer's service information provides

K01004 Describe step one of the strategy-based diagnosis.

FIGURE 1-4 The strategy-based diagnostic process.

Step 1 Verify the customer's concern

Step 2 Research possible faults and gather information

Step 3 Focused testing

Step 4 Perform the repair

Step 5 Verify the repair

FIGURE 1-5 Ask the customer to describe the concern.

system descriptions and expected operations; technicians can use these details, provided in the owner's manual or in the vehicle service manual, to become familiar with the system and then explain its operation to the customer. Especially on new cars with many amenities, customers may not be familiar with the controls and subsequent operation. This can cause a customer to bring a vehicle in for service unnecessarily, due to unfamiliarity with the system controls. Many shops use online service (shop) manuals where you can quickly access any information related to the customer's concern (**FIGURE 1-6**). Checking to make sure that the concern is really a fault, and not a normal operation, will avoid unnecessary diagnosis time. This is also an opportunity to provide excellent customer service by demonstrating the features and their controls to the customer.

Conducting a quick visual inspection to look for obvious faults can be very helpful (**FIGURE 1-7**). However, it does not replace the need for testing and is absolutely not intended as a shortcut to the diagnostic process. With that said, the visual inspection can provide valuable information that may speed up the testing processes. The visual inspection provides an opportunity for a quick safety check by the technician and may help to avoid some potentially dangerous situations during service.

While visual inspections can be very valuable, technicians must be careful not to jump to conclusions based on what they see. For example, a customer comes in with an illuminated and flashing overdrive light on the control panel. The technician has seen this problem before and it was caused by a bad solenoid pack in the transmission. If the technician decides that this problem is also caused by a bad solenoid pack, this determination is one that was reached solely on conjecture; no actual test was performed. Although the flashing light might indicate a fault with the solenoid pack, steps in the diagnostic process should never be skipped. This guess can lead to a very costly mistake when it is discovered that the new solenoid pack does not, in fact, fix the problem. In reality, the wiring harness to the transmission is frayed and shorting out. Had the technician performed a test, the cause of the customer concern could have been confirmed or denied before a solenoid pack was put in unnecessarily. While the visual inspection is very valuable, tests must always be performed to compare suspected faults against the expectations and specifications defined in the service information.

When recreating the customer concern, the technician should operate the system in question in all practically available modes. System operation should be checked to see if there are other symptoms that may have gone unnoticed by the customer. These other symptoms can be very valuable when determining which tests to perform; they could save the technician significant time during the diagnosis. When recreating the customer concern, it is important to check the entire system for symptoms and related faults.

Recreating **intermittent faults** can be a challenge. Intermittent symptoms often stem from a component or system that is failing or one where the nature of the fault is not yet clear. In these situations, the aforementioned check of system operation can prove to be highly valuable, as it may uncover previously unnoticed but consistent symptoms. Attempting to repair

FIGURE 1-6 A technician researching service information.

FIGURE 1-7 Performing a visual inspection.

an intermittent fault without consistent symptoms, data, or diagnostic trouble codes (DTCs) is a gamble, because a technician cannot be certain that the actual problem is isolated. This means that there would be no way to confirm with certainty that a repair was effective. The fault could appear again as soon as the vehicle is returned to the customer. To avoid such a situation, look for symptoms, data, or DTCs that are repeatable or consistent. Intermittent diagnosis may require the use of an oscilloscope (a specialized tool for looking at electrical waveforms), or a "wiggle" test (as the name implies, a test instrument is monitored as the electrical or vacuum harness is manipulated by hand). This can verify the customer concern and remove some of the challenge from the diagnosis of an intermittent fault.

Lastly, but notably, save DTCs and freeze frame data. **Freeze frame data** refers to snapshots that are automatically stored in a vehicle's power train control module (PCM) when a fault occurs; this is only available on vehicles model year 1996 and newer. Intermittent faults may be found by reviewing data stored just before, during, and after the fault occurred, similar to an instant replay. When working with computer controlled systems, it is very important to save the recorded data. It may become necessary to erase this information from the computer, though that should generally be avoided. This information is absolutely critical when the technician is trying to answer the questions, "When did this happen?" and "What was going on at the time?"

What will step one look like? When information is gathered and recorded for step one, it should contain the customer concern, any symptoms, and any retrieved DTCs. View the following example from a vehicle that has no reverse. The technician verified the customer concern and recorded:

1. Vehicle will not move when shifted into reverse
2. Vehicle operates normally in all forward gears in OD, D, L2, and L1
3. Current code P0868

Notice that the technician in this example verified and recorded the customer concern. The technician also tried other functions in the system. Specifically, the technician drove the vehicle and tested the other gears in each of the gear ranges and then recorded the results. The DTC data was also retrieved from the control module and recorded. Although it was short and concise, the information will be very useful in the next step.

Step 2: Researching Possible Faults and Gathering Information

The second step in the diagnostic process is to research possible faults that may be related to the customer's concern. The goal of this step is to create a list of possible faults. The list is created based on the information gathered in step one. The list will later be narrowed down by the tests performed in step three until the cause of the concern has been confirmed.

Before testing can begin, a technician must know what possible faults need to be tested. Researching possible faults should begin broadly. Especially when diagnosing electrical and electronic systems, this step should begin at the system level and work down to individual components. For example, if a vehicle engine cranks, but will not start, a technician would list these familiar possible faults: Air, Fuel, Ignition, Compression, and Security. These possible faults are not single components, but rather they are systems. This is where a diagnosis should begin. Starting a diagnosis by listing the dozens of components for each system will make the job unreasonably time intensive. However, once a test determines that there is a fault within a specific system, the list should be expanded to encompass that particular system's subsystems and components. This systematic elimination starts broadly and narrows, allowing technicians to work more efficiently.

In the second step of the diagnostic process, the technician creates a list to help focus their tests. The list may aid in a simple process of elimination by testing one possibility after the next. The list can also start broadly and narrow as testing continues. When starting a list, it may look similar to the following:

1. Air
2. Fuel

▶ TECHNICIAN TIP

All too often, the customer does not have symptoms to share and their only concern is that the malfunction indicator is illuminated. In this situation, the data stored in the computer is invaluable. Record it and do not clear it out unless directed to do so in the manufacturer's service procedure. Even then, you should capture the information before clearing the memory.

K01005 Describe step two of the strategy-based diagnosis.

N01004 Research vehicle service information including fluid type, vehicle service history, service precautions, and technical service bulletins.

3. Ignition
4. Compression
5. Security

This list is broad and starts at the system level. As you'll soon see in the next step, the technician would eliminate possible faults with a test that is focused on analyzing the whole system. When a system is located with a fault, in the ignition system for example, the list would become more specific:

1. Spark Plug
2. Coil on Plug
3. CKP
4. CMP
5. Sensor Triggers
6. Harness
7. Control Module

The technician would again focus his or her testing on the list, seeking to eliminate possible faults until one is confirmed, repaired, and verified.

Several great sources of information are available for researching possible faults, although the best source of information is usually the manufacturer's service information system. These systems are typically found online; however, some manufactures still publish paper service manuals. The manufacturer's service information contains definitions for diagnostic trouble codes, system description and operation, electrical wiring diagrams, diagnostic steps, repair procedures, and much more. Fault diagnosis should almost always begin with the factory service information.

Other resources for identifying faults can be used in conjunction with the factory service information. As previously discussed, the vehicle service history can provide valuable insight into the past maintenance or lack thereof. It can also provide information about recent or repeated repairs. **Technical service bulletins** (TSBs) are service notifications and procedures sent out by the manufacturers to dealer groups alerting technicians about common issues with a particular vehicle or group of vehicles (**FIGURE 1-8**). Some aftermarket sources also exist for the pattern failures addressed by TSBs (**FIGURE 1-9**). Additionally, both original equipment manufacturers (OEM) and aftermarket technician support services offer hotlines, or call-in support, that specifically provide technical support to professional technicians. Some of these hotlines offer subscriptions to searchable web-based components. These resources do not guarantee a repair; that is still the responsibility of the technician. However, all of the sources mentioned here can be a huge help as technicians research possible faults.

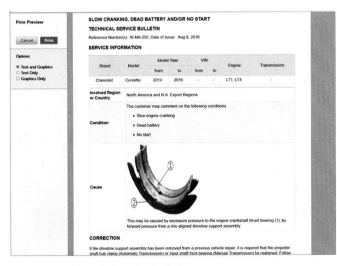

FIGURE 1-8 Technical service bulletin.

FIGURE 1-9 Aftermarket source.

While these resources are essential, the list of possible faults is just that: a list of possible faults. A technician must always be aware that steps in the diagnostic process cannot be skipped.

Step 3: Focused Testing

K01006 Describe step three of the strategy-based diagnosis.

Step three of the diagnostic process involves focused testing. In this step technicians use their testing skills to eliminate possible faults from the list they created in step two. Steps two and three work together; testing will start at a system level and work down to subsystems, then finally to individual components. The idea of focused testing should be to eliminate as many potential faults as possible with each test.

Focused testing is intended to eliminate possible causes with certainty. Each time a test is performed, the following three pieces of information must be recorded:

- a test description
- an expectation
- a result

These can be recorded on the repair order, electronic service record, or on an extra sheet of paper. Test records must be kept handy because they will become part of the documented record for this repair.

The three pieces of test information are recorded carefully for several reasons. Having an expectation before a test is performed makes each test objective and effective. The expectation is what the result is compared against, in order to determine if the vehicle passed or failed.

Many manufacturers, both original equipment and aftermarket, require that documented test results be submitted with each warranty claim. If the technician fails to document his or her work, the manufacturer will not pay the claim. The result is that the shop is out money for the parts and service, and the technician will not be paid for their work. Be sure to document the work properly (**FIGURE 1-10**).

FIGURE 1-10 The test record should include the test description, expectation or specification, and the result of measurement.

1. The test description is not long, or even a complete sentence; it is simply a brief description. It allows the reader to know what test was performed and on what component or system. The test description should be accurate enough that the reader could repeat the test with the same result.
2. The expectation should describe the expected result as if the system is operating normally. The expectation could come directly from the system specifications listed in the manufacturer's service information or from system description and operation.
3. The result is the third part that must be recorded for each test. This information should accurately reflect what happened when the test was performed.

In summary, the testing is focused on isolating a fault or faults from the list of potential faults, and the results are compared to the expectation.

Testing should begin broadly and simply. Consider the following example: A light bulb circuit is suspected of having a fault. If the light bulb is easily accessible, the first test might be to check the voltage drop (i.e., voltage used to push current through the bulb). If the result of the voltage drop measurement is as expected (i.e., within specification), then the problem is in the bulb or socket. In this test, the technician is able to check the integrity of the entire electrical circuit with one test. If the result of the measurement is outside of the expectation (i.e., out of specification), the technician would know that the bulb is not the source of the problem. Further testing would isolate the problem to the ground or power side of the circuit.

The technician in the example performed a simple test with an easy expectation. The test allowed the technician to quickly determine the state of operation for the entire system/circuit and move on. If a fault had been found, then the technician would have isolated the cause of the customer's concern to that particular system/circuit and would need to perform further testing to isolate the cause to a particular component. To do that, the technician would use the service information to determine what components comprise the system and adjust the list from step two to take into account the new information. Then testing would continue.

The next test might measure voltage supply at the bulb (i.e., available voltage). In this way, the technician would be testing the power supply, the conductors, and the switch (assuming a power-side switched circuit). The technician would have an expectation for the circuit voltage and compare his or her result to this expected voltage. As we saw earlier, the technician is testing more than one component with a single test, thereby operating in an efficient manner.

This strategy—starting with broad, simple tests and moving to more complicated, pinpoint tests—makes efficient use of the technician's time while still effectively testing the possible faults.

1. A technician is investigating a customer concern of "no heat from the dash." The technician's investigation might begin with a simple list.

    a. Engine cooling system
    b. HVAC duct and controls

2. The technician would then eliminate one or the other and expand the list. The technician might verify coolant level and temperature at the inlet and outlet of the heater core. The HVAC components controlling and delivering warm air could then be used to expand the list for the next round of testing.

    a. Doors and ducts
    b. Cables
    c. Servos
    d. HVAC control head
    e. Blower motor
    f. Harness
    g. In-cabin filter or debris

3. Notice that the technician has moved from broad system tests to individual components or component groups. The technician's test continues to become more specific as the possibilities are narrowed down.

FIGURE 1-11 Select tests that have simple expectations and are easy to perform.

Technicians commonly encounter vehicles with more than one customer concern. When these concerns both originate from the same or companion systems, technicians are inclined to search for one cause to both problems. Unfortunately, trying to diagnose two faults at once can quickly become problematic and confusing. Instead, select the easier customer concern and follow it through to the end. If both problems were caused by the same faults, then both were fixed. If they were caused by two separate faults, the technician is no worse off for having fixed one concern.

When selecting tests to perform, remember that they should be simple and easy (**FIGURE 1-11**). Except when following service procedures, you should select tests that have simple expectations, are easy to perform, and provide you with the maximum amount of information. This means simple tests that inspect an entire system or circuit are ideal ways to begin testing. Simple tests have expectations and results that are quickly understood and interpreted. They are short and involve basic tools and access to areas that are comfortable to reach.

When selecting tests, prioritize your testing. First choose tests that can be performed quickly and simply, even if they do not test an entire circuit. If a preferred test is in a difficult place to access, move to another test and come back to it, if needed. The answer may be found in the meantime and the time-consuming test can be avoided. Simple and easy tests are ideal, but they must be measurable or objective.

Yes, a visual inspection is a simple and valuable test, but a technician must determine what the issue is in an objective manner, with help from the service information. A guess based only on appearance is insufficient. If the service information says, "cracks in the serpentine belt indicate that it needs replaced," the belt can be visually and objectively (yes or no) tested. The belt will either have the indicated wear or it will not. If the service information states, "Chain deflection cannot exceed 0.75," then the deflection can be measured and compared to the specification. As testing continues, it may become necessary to use advanced tests, sophisticated equipment, additional time, or tests in areas difficult to access. Keeping initial testing simple and easy will produce the quickest, most reliable, and effective results.

When testing, use the recommended procedures and equipment. Manufacturers frequently recommend a particular procedure when testing one of their systems.

Failure to follow the specified service procedure can result in the warranty claim being denied by the manufacturer. In that case, both the shop and the technician lose money. Manufacturers may recommend a certain procedure because of the way their system is designed or monitored. Technicians must also be very careful to perform tests safely (**FIGURE 1-12**).

Beyond the mechanical dangers posed by automobiles, many of today's vehicles have dangerously high fluid pressures and deadly high voltage. It is of the utmost importance for the safety of the technician, and those working in the area, that safety procedures are always followed.

Proper test equipment and procedures are intended to test a particular component or system without causing any damage. Improper equipment or test procedures can create a second fault in the system being tested; making the technician's job even more difficult. For example, front probing an electrical terminal with the lead of a DMM can cause the terminal to spread or deform. This can create an intermittent high resistance or open within the circuit that was not there prior to the technician's test. Using the recommended equipment and procedures will help to ensure warranty claims are approved, people are safe, and testing goes smoothly.

When performing repairs, look beyond the obvious for the root cause. This simple suggestion can avoid customer comebacks. Novice technicians frequently have problems with misdiagnosing fuse-related issues. For example, a technician diagnoses a blown fuse as the cause of the customer concern. While replacing the fuse may have fixed the immediate fault, the technician did not look beyond the obvious. What causes a fuse to blow? Low

FIGURE 1-12 Always perform all tests safely.

resistance and increased amperage cause a fuse to blow. However, the technician did not test for one of these faults and the vehicle is likely to return with the same customer concern and the same blown fuse.

In another example of incomplete reasoning, a technician diagnoses a leaky transmission cooler line. The line is chaffed and leaking. This cooler line runs along the frame rail; the inner and outer tie rods are immediately below. The technician diagnoses the vehicle while it is on a lift and the suspension is unloaded (increasing the distance between the hose and steering linkage). The technician should have looked for the root cause of the chaffing, but instead the vehicle and customer come back some time later for the same concern. The technician notices several broken clips that held the flexible line into place on the frame rail. In both cases, the technician will work for free to repair the same vehicle, because time was not taken to ask the question: "Did something else cause this failure?" Testing must be focused beyond the obvious to identify the root cause of the problem and consequently avoid customer comebacks.

In summary, focused testing has several key elements. It picks up the possible faults identified in step two and begins testing each one broadly, narrowing down to more specific tests. Focused testing requires accurately documenting the tests performed, including a test description, expectation, and result, each and every time a test is performed. It should also be performed in a safe and proper manner, following manufacturers' guidelines and safety protocols. Focused testing is a safe, accurate, and repeatable method for isolating possible faults.

Step 4: Performing the Repair

The fourth step of the diagnostic process is to perform the repair. Although performing the repair is often the most straightforward step in the process, technicians must still avoid making several common mistakes. The following tips will help you to perform an effective and reliable repair.

K01007 Describe step four of the strategy-based diagnosis.

Use Proper Service Procedures

Manufacturers will often indicate what procedures are appropriate for their vehicles and components. Many design features and component materials require certain procedures be used and others avoided. Following the manufacturer's service information can prevent premature failure of the repair (**FIGURE 1-13**). For example, repair methods that are safe around the home may be unacceptable in the automotive industry. The use of twist-on wire connectors can create an unreliable and potentially dangerous electrical situation when used in a vehicle. Additionally, warranties, both original equipment and aftermarket, rely on the technicians' adherence to the manufacturer's service information. If technicians fail to do so, the warranty claim can go unpaid and the shop will lose money. Therefore, it is important for reliable repairs and warranty reimbursements that technicians follow the service information when performing repairs.

Use the Correct Tool for the Job

Failure to use the correct tool can lead to a customer comeback and injury to the technician. Proper tool selection is essential. If you are ever in doubt, refer to the manufacturer's service information. Improper tool use or selection can damage the component being installed or other components around it. For example, a technician may choose to install a pump busing with a hammer instead of using the recommended press and bushing driver. This incorrect tool selection can easily lead to misalignment, or damage to the bushing, pump, or torque converter. Using the wrong tool (or the right tool in the wrong manner) can also damage the tool and potentially injure those in the area. For example, if a technician is using a hardened chrome socket on an impact wrench, the socket may shatter, sending shrapnel flying. Using the correct tool for the job will produce better work and ensure the safety of the technician.

MAINTENANCE/SPECIFICATIONS

CHANGING YOUR WIPERS

The wiper arms can be manually moved when the ignition is disabled. This allows for ease of blade replacement and cleaning under the blades.

1. Disable the ignition before removing the blade.
2. Pull the arm away from the glass.
3. Left leading edge retaining block to release the blade. Swing the blade, away from with the arm, to remove it.
4. Swing the new blade toward the arm and snap it into place. Replace the

retaining block at the leading edge of the wiper arm. Lower the wiper arm back to the windshield. The wiper arms will automatically return to

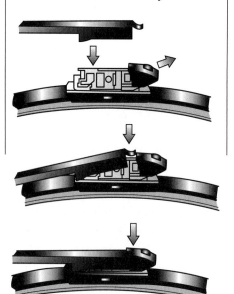

their normal position the next time the ignition is enabled.

Refresh wiper blades at least twice a year for premium performance.

Poor preforming wipers quality can be improved by cleaning the blades and the windshield. See *Windows and wiper blades* in the *Cleaning* chapter.

To extend the life of wiper blades, scrape off the ice on the windshield BEFORE turning on the wipers. The ice has many sharp edges and will damage and shred the cleaning edge of your wiper blade.

FIGURE 1-13 A typical shop manual page has a task description broken into steps and diagrams or pictures to aid the technician.

Take Time to Perform the Repair Properly

Because technicians are frequently paid by the job, or a flat rate, rather than paid hourly, it is possible for technicians to feel a rush to complete their current job. Rushing increases the likelihood of a mistake. If a mistake occurs, the customer will come back with the vehicle and the technician will work for free to repair the mistake. For example, if a technician replaces a water pump and fills the coolant without bleeding the system, a potentially damaging situation can occur. The trapped gas can affect the flow of coolant and create a hot spot in the cylinder head. This can lead to warning lights, poor performance, and possible engine damage. Take a little extra time to ensure that the work is performed correctly, with the right tools and the proper service procedures. Taking time to perform the repair will ensure fewer "comebacks" and more satisfied customers.

Make Sure the Customer Approves of the Repair

This may seem trivial, but it is extremely important. Most states' laws protect consumers by preventing unauthorized services from being charged or performed. This means that technicians cannot just repair a vehicle and charge the customer for the cost incurred. If the customer is paying, shops must receive a customer's approval prior to performing repairs.

> ▶ **TECHNICIAN TIP**
>
> It is very important to quote accurately and wait for approval before performing repairs on a customer's vehicle.

Check for Updates Prior to the Repair

It is also good practice to check for updated parts and software/firmware before performing a repair. It is possible that manufacturers have become aware of a problem with a particular component or software version and issued a software update or produced an updated component. When performing repairs it is a good idea to check for these sorts of updates (often found in TSBs), because it may prevent a customer comeback. Software updates are often downloaded from the manufacturer's website. For hard parts, the best resource is frequently the respective dealership's parts department.

Technical service bulletins also provide information related to unexpected problems, updated parts, or changes to a repair procedure on a particular vehicle system, part, or component. The typical TSB contains step-by-step procedures and diagrams on how to identify if there is a fault and perform an effective repair. Shops typically keep TSBs in a central location, or you may look them up online. Compare the information contained in the TSB with that of the shop manual. Note the differences and, if necessary, copy the TSB to take with you to perform the repair.

Pay Attention to Details

Performing the repair is straightforward but requires attention to detail. There are several things to keep in mind. Proper service procedures can be located in the manufacturer's service information. The correct tool for the job will lessen injury and ensure reliability. Use the necessary time to make sure that the repair was completed correctly. Document your work. These tips can greatly improve the likelihood of a successful repair, but the process does not stop with the repair.

Step 5: Verify the Repair

The most important step of the strategy-based diagnostic process is verifying the repair. The reason that this is the most important step is straightforward. The vehicle would never have been in the shop if the customer did not have a concern. If the technician fails to address the original concern, the customer may view the trip as ineffective, a waste of their time and money. Even when a valid repair that makes the vehicle safer and more reliable was performed, the customer will still be unsatisfied if his or her original concern was not addressed. For example, a customer brings the vehicle into the shop for a sticky glove box latch. The technician identifies and repairs a dangerous brake line leak, but fails to fix the glove box. Some customers may view this trip to the shop as unsuccessful because it failed to fix their original issue. When verifying the repair, technicians must always double check their work. This is a valuable confirmation that the repair performed did fix the identified problem.

K01008 Describe step five of the strategy-based diagnosis.

There are several ways to verify a repair, but generally, the simplest method is the best method. For example, a customer is concerned that the wipers stop moving when the switch is moved into the high position. In step one, the technician will verify that the customer concern and fault exist by turning the wiper switch to all positions. Then the technician uses the wiring diagram (step 2) to diagnose a fault (step 3) within the wiring harness and repairs it (step 4). The technician could then verify the repair by performing the last diagnostic test (from step 3) again. In most cases, the repair would be confirmed if the results had changed and were within expectation/specification.

But what if there was a second problem affecting the wipers such as worn brushes in the motor, or the wiper linkage fell off of the pivot on one side? The customer would still have issues with the wipers and would likely to be unhappy with the repair. So while performing the last diagnostic test (step 3) is a valid verification method, it is not foolproof. An easier method exists: simply return to the process used in step one to verify the customer concern. If the repair has eliminated the problem, the technician should now be able to turn the wiper switch to all positions (step 1) and confirm normal operation. Be certain to perform the same inspections used to verify the customer concern in step one after the repair is performed. This may include checking the entire system operation, not just a single function. This method of verifying that the customer concern is resolved is usually best in most scenarios because it is simple and it is exactly what the customer will do to check your work.

However, sometimes verifying the repair requires a more complicated means of verification. A common concern that falls into this scenario is as follows: The customer brings their vehicle in with a concern that the MIL (malfunction indicator lamp) or "check engine" light is illuminated. In this scenario, *NEVER* verify the repair by simply checking to see that the light is off. While this is what the customer will do to check your work, the failure of the MIL to light can often be misleading and result in a comeback for the exact same problem. This can occur because the MIL is illuminated when tests run by the computers in the vehicle fail. The computers are constantly running tests, but some tests require very specific conditions before they can be run and, hence, fail. Due to the requirements for the conditions to be right, simply checking to see if the light is illuminated is an inadequate method of verification.

For more complicated computer-controlled systems, the best method of verification is checking the test results stored on the vehicle's computer. This option will require an electronic scan tool that communicates with the vehicle's computer, along with a high level of diagnostic experience and service information to verify that the concern has been fully resolved. If the communication option is not available, the second best method of verification is repeating the last diagnostic test performed (in step 3) and confirming that the result has changed to now match the expectation/specification. Complicated computer-controlled systems require that the technician do more than verify the customer concern is eliminated. The technician will have to repeat a diagnostic test (step 3) or view test results stored on the vehicle's computer (this is the preferred method) in order to verify that the repair was effective.

Step five of the strategy-based diagnostic process is the most important. A vehicle should never be returned to a customer without this step completed.

▶ Documenting the Repair

The first two components, gathering information from the customer and the strategy-based diagnostic process, have already been described; this section discusses documentation. The repair is documented for several reasons: accurate vehicle history, returns or comebacks, and OEM or aftermarket warranties. Keeping accurate service records will help technicians to know what services and repairs have been performed on a vehicle when it needs any future services. This can be invaluable during the diagnostic process and can also help service advisors and technicians identify what maintenance or recall work still needs to be completed. Documenting the repair also helps technicians in the event that a vehicle returns, now or in the future, with the same customer concern or fault. This can help to identify defective parts or common problems.

Warranty work is another reason that all repairs must be documented. Whether the repair is submitted to an original equipment manufacturer or to an aftermarket warranty

---

▶ TECHNICIAN TIP

The job is not complete until you have verified that the repair resolved the customer's concern.

company for reimbursement, the repair must be well documented. Warranty clerks will review the repair order to ensure that proper testing and repair procedures have been followed. Technicians must document their work to ensure that the shop, and in turn the technician, get paid for the work performed.

Finally, documenting the work provides the shop with a record that the work was initiated and completed. This is important in case the vehicle is later involved in an accident or other mishap and the shop is involved in a lawsuit. It is important to have the customer sign or initial, depending on shop policy, the repair order, to verify that the customer accepted the repair.

The Three Cs of Documentation

When documenting a repair, technicians need to remember the **3 Cs: concern, cause**, and **correction** (**FIGURE 1-14**).

Concern

The main focus of the 3 Cs is the customer *concern*, which is also the focus of step one of the diagnostic process. Often the concern is documented on the repair order prior to the technician receiving the vehicle. If this is the case, the technician who works on the vehicle should take time to fully understand the concern, read the repair order, and possibly talk further with the customer to understand the nature of the problem. Think through the problem and develop a strategy to attack it. Other symptoms and diagnostic troubles codes are some examples of other information that should be included in the "concern."

Cause

The second C in the 3 Cs is *cause,* which details the cause of the customer concern. This correlates to the documentation done in step three of the diagnostic process. The technician should document any tests that they perform with enough detail that they can be repeated, as well as specifications/expectations, and results. This goes for all tests, even the simple ones.

Correction

The technician should then document the last C, the correction. This must include the procedure used as well as a brief description of the correction. This information comes from the fourth step of the diagnostic process. When documenting the repair order, technicians should include the customer concern and symptoms (DTCs are symptoms); brief descriptions of tests; expectations; and results, along with the procedure and repair that were performed. The technician should also include all parts that were replaced as well, and noted if they were new or used, OEM, or aftermarket.

Other Parts of Documentation

Additional service recommendations should also be documented on the repair order. While working on the vehicle, technicians should also be mindful of other work that may need to be performed. Technicians are obligated to make the customer aware of safety concerns that require attention. Customers may be unaware of a potential hazard or lack of maintenance. Bringing this to the attention of the customer right away can help the technician, as well as the customer. For example, if the technician is already working on the vehicle, they would not have to remove the vehicle from the service bay, bring in a new vehicle, and start all over. Repairing multiple issues in one trip to the service bay makes good use of the technician's time. It also improves customer relations by bringing the customer's attention to problems and thereby preventing possible failures.

K01009 Explain how the three Cs are applied in repairing and servicing vehicles.

N01002 Demonstrate use of the three C's (concern, cause, and correction).

FIGURE 1-14 The 3Cs of documenting the repair.

For example, a technician may be changing the fluid in a transmission and notice that the brake friction pads are extremely low. Bringing this to the attention of the customer can result in additional work for the technician and save the customer from a potentially more costly repair. For this reason, technicians should also note safety issues and maintenance items on the repair order.

Repair Order

K01010 Describe the information and its use within a repair order.

N01003 Identify information needed and the service requested on a repair order.

S01002 Complete a repair order.

A **repair order** is a key document used to communicate with both your customers and coworkers. Thoroughly document the information provided by the customer on the repair order; every bit of it may be helpful during the diagnosis (**FIGURE 1-15**). If you are not typing this information, make sure your handwriting is clear and easy for others to read. Unfortunately, if documentation of a complaint is not done well, the technician could be led on a much longer diagnostic path, wasting everyone's time. It can also be a time-consuming process for the diagnosing technician to make contact with the customer in order to get more information that was missed the first time. From time to time, it may be inevitable that the customer will need to be contacted for further inquiry after the initial visit. However, carefully gathering information from the customer on their initial visit will save time, prevent inconveniencing the customer, and aid in the diagnostic process.

To complete a repair order using the 3 Cs, follow the steps in **SKILL DRILL 1-2**.

▶ TECHNICIAN TIP

A repair order is a legal document that can be used as evidence in the event of a lawsuit. Always make sure the information you enter on a repair order is complete and accurate. The information required on a repair order includes: date; customer's name, address, and phone number; vehicle's year, make, model, color, odometer reading, and VIN; and description of the customer's concern. Store repair orders in a safe place, such as in a fireproof filing cabinet or electronically on a secure computer network. Finally, to prevent future complications, it is a good idea to have the customer sign or initial the repair order, indicating that they understand and agree to the needed repair. Having the customer's signature will help prevent the shop from being held liable in an accident involving the vehicle later.

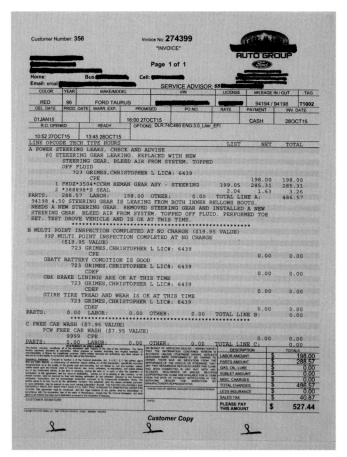

FIGURE 1-15 A repair order.

Applied Communications

AC-23: Repair Orders: The technician writes a repair order containing customer vehicle information, customer complaints, parts and materials used (including prices), services performed, labor hours, and suggested repairs/maintenance.

A repair order is a legal contract between the service provider and the customer. It contains details of the services to be provided by you and the authorization from the customer. To make sure everyone understands clearly what is involved, a repair order should contain information about the following aspects of the repair.

- Your company or service providers: The service provider section contains the company name, address, and contact details; the name of a service advisor who is overseeing the job; and the amount of time the service technician will have to service the vehicle.
- The customer: The customer section contains the customer's name, address, and contact phone numbers.
- The customer's vehicle: The vehicle section includes details about the vehicle to be serviced. Check the vehicle's license plate before starting work. The license plate numbers are usually unique within a country. You should also record information about the vehicle's make, model, and color. This information will make it easier for you to locate the vehicle on the parking lot. You may also need to know the manufacture date of the vehicle to be able to order the right parts. The odometer reading and the date will help keep track of how much distance the vehicle travels and the time period between each visit to the shop. The VIN is designed to be unique worldwide and contains specific information about the vehicle. Many shops do a "walk-around" with the customer to note any previous damage to the vehicle and to look for any obvious faults such as worn tires, rusted-out exhaust pipes, or torn wiper blades.
- The service operations: This section contains the details of the service operations and parts.

- The first part is the service operation details. For example, the vehicle is in for a 150,000 mile (240,000-km) service, which can be done in 3 hours and results in approximately $300 of labor costs. The information about the chargeable labor time to complete a specific task can be found in a labor guide manual. In some workplaces, this information is built into the computer system and will be automatically displayed.
- The second part of this section is the details of parts used in the service, including the descriptions, quantities, codes, and prices. The codes for each service and part are normally abbreviations that are used for easy reference in the shop. Some shops may have their own reference code system.
- As you do the vehicle inspection, you may discover other things that need replaced or repaired. These additional services can be recorded in another section. It is essential that you check with the customer and obtain their approval before carrying out any additional services.
- The parts requirements: This section lists the parts required to perform the repair.

Some repair orders also contain accounting information so they can be used as invoices.

SKILL DRILL 1-2 Completing a Repair Order

1. Greet the customer.
2. Locate a repair order used in your shop and obtain or verify the customer's name, address, and phone number.
3. Obtain details about the vehicle, including the year, make, model, color, odometer reading, and VIN.
4. Ask the customer to tell you more about the *concern* by using open-ended questions, such as "When does problem occur?" "At what speed(s)?" "How do you experience the problem?" "How long has this been occurring?" "How many passengers do you typically carry?" Type or clearly write the customer's responses on the repair order.
5. Ask the customer about other changes with the vehicle, such as recent work, or recent travel. Type or clearly write the customer's responses on the repair order.
6. Remembering the lessons learned regarding the proper diagnostic process, begin to verify the customer's *concern* by first performing a visual inspection.
7. If you see nothing unusual during your visual inspection, continue to verify the customer's concern by conducting a road test of the vehicle. The customer may ride along, if possible, to help identify the issue as it occurs, or you may conduct the test by yourself. Following the test drive, after verifying the customer's concern, record it on the repair order.
8. The second step of the diagnostic process is to research the possible faults, and gather information. Access the vehicle service history to determine if the vehicle has experienced a similar problem in the past, requires a routine service maintenance, or has been serviced recently. Document this information, if applicable, on the repair order.
9. Conduct research by accessing various sources of information related to the vehicle, such as the vehicle service

manual or the owner's manual. Check to see if a TSB related to the issue exists. As part of the process, rule out the possibility that the customer's concern is a normal operation of the vehicle.
10. Now that you have your broad list of possible faults related to the concern, begin step three, focused testing. Choose one of the possible broad faults you identified in step two. Now refer to the service manual to locate information that matches the concern. Service manuals usually contain diagnostic charts to aid in the focused testing process.
11. Conduct a test and record its description, your expectation, and the result on the repair order or another piece of paper. Continue to check each possible fault until you identify the *cause* of the concern.
12. Once you have identified the fault, you're ready for step four, performing the repair. You would inform the customer of your finding and obtain his or her approval to make the repair. Pending customer approval, you would then follow proper safety procedures and use the manufacturer's guidelines to correct the problem, being sure to use the correct tools and taking the time to complete the job properly.
13. Once you've made the repair, you are ready for step five, verifying the repair. The simplest way to verify that you have addressed and corrected the customer's concern is to repeat the test drive. Take the vehicle for a test drive and repeat the tests you initially performed. Is the issue gone? If so, you have verified the repair and can return the vehicle to the customer.
14. Document the correction on the repair order. If the issue is not resolved, you must return to your list of possible faults and continue testing after first alerting the customer that additional work and time will be necessary.

▶ Wrap-Up

Ready for Review

- Service history is typically retrieved from service records kept by the shop, dealer network, original equipment manufacturer (OEM), or aftermarket service center and contains a list of services performed on a vehicle and the date and mileage at which they were completed.
- The service history allows technicians to determine if the vehicle has been well maintained. This can be extremely useful when a technician suspects that lack of maintenance may be the cause of the problem.
- Failure to comply with the state and federal law can be very expensive for the dealership and manufacturer.
- Today's vehicles also require regular software updates made available to fix a bug or glitch in the computer programming. These updates are often designed to eliminate a customer concern, improve owner satisfaction, or increase vehicle life.
- The strategy-based diagnostic process is focused on fixing problems correctly the first time. It begins with identifying the customer's concern and ends with confirming that the problem has been resolved.
- The problem-solving process provides a consistent road map for technicians as they address customer concerns that require diagnosis and to make sure that customer concerns are resolved with certainty.
- Strategy-based diagnosis simplifies the problem-solving portion of the repair, making the job easier for the technician; it prevents technicians from having to work on the same job more than once; and it all but eliminates customer comebacks.
- Customer comebacks are usually caused by the customer concern being misinterpreted or misunderstood or failing to verify that the original concern was resolved.
- The strategy-based diagnostic process begins by gathering preliminary information from the customer and by reviewing the vehicle's service history.
- The first step in the diagnostic process is to verify the customer concern. This step is completed for two main purposes: verify that there is an actual problem present, and guarantee that the customer's concern is addressed.
- Visual inspections can be very valuable, but technicians need to be careful not to jump to conclusions.
- DTC's (Diagnostic Trouble Codes) and freeze frame data should always be saved and recorded on the repair order. Freeze-frame data provide a snapshot of the entire engine data when the DTC occurs, which allows for duplication of the condition so that the DTC can be replicated.
- The second step in the diagnostic process is to research possible faults. The goal of this step is to create a list of possible faults. The list will be created based on the information gathered in step 1 and narrowed down by the tests performed in step 3 until the cause of the concern has been confirmed.
- The best source of information is usually the manufacturer's service information system.
- Technical service bulletins (TSBs) are service notifications and procedures sent out by the manufacturers to dealer groups, alerting technicians to common issues with a particular vehicle or group of vehicles. Some aftermarket sources also exist for the pattern failures addressed by TSBs
- A technician must always be aware that steps in the diagnostic process cannot be skipped. A repair should never be performed unless the possible fault has been verified through testing.
- Step 3 of the diagnostic process involves focused testing, where technicians use their testing skills to eliminate possible faults from the list they created in step two. Steps 2 and 3 work together, because testing starts at a system level and works down to subsystems, then finally to individual components.
- When selecting tests prioritize your testing. First choose tests that can be performed quickly and simply, even if they do not test an entire circuit. If a preferred test is in a very difficult place to access, move to another test and come back to it, if needed.
- Following manufacturers' guidelines and safety protocols keeps technicians safe. Focused testing is a safe, accurate, and repeatable method for isolating possible faults. Once the fault has been isolated, it is time to perform the repair.
- The fourth step of the diagnostic process is to perform the repair. Performing the repair is often the most straightforward step in the process.
- Use proper service procedures when performing a repair. Manufacturers often indicate what procedures are appropriate for their vehicles and components.
- Use the correct tool for the job when performing a repair. Failure to use the correct tool for the job can lead to a customer comeback and injury to the technician.
- Take time to perform the repair properly. Technicians are frequently paid by the job, or flat rate, rather than paid hourly, it is possible for technicians to feel a rush to complete their current job. Rushing increases the likelihood of a mistake and the next time you may pay for it.
- The most important step of the strategy-based diagnostic process is verifying the repair. The reason that this is the most important step is straightforward. The vehicle would never have been in the shop if the customer did not have a concern.
- Verifying the original concern is the best method of double-checking your work and meeting your customers' expectations. The job is not complete until you have verified that the repair resolved the customer's concern.

- Documentation is key to effective and efficient repairs. Keeping all the information available to the service advisor, technician, and the customer allows for a more open dialogue which can limit the confusion of the repair process.
- The repair is documented for several reasons: accurate vehicle history, returns or comebacks, and warranties. Keeping accurate service records will help technicians to know what services and repairs have been performed on a vehicle when it needs any future services.
- When documenting a repair, technicians need to remember the three Cs: concern, cause, and correction.
- When documenting the repair order, technicians should include the customer concern and symptoms (Diagnostic Trouble Codes are symptoms) and a brief description of tests, expectations, and results, along with the procedure and repair that were processed.

Key Terms

Strategy-Based Diagnostic Process A systematic process used to diagnose faults in a vehicle.

service advisor The person at a repair facility that is in charge of communicating with the customer.

service history A complete listing of all the servicing and repairs that have been performed on that vehicle.

repair order The document that is given to the repair technician that details the customer concern and any needed information.

freeze frame data Refers to snapshots that are automatically stored in a vehicle's power train control module (PCM) when a fault occurs (only available on model year 1996 and newer).

technical service bulletin (TSB) Service notifications and procedures sent out by the manufacturers to dealer groups alerting technicians about common issues with a particular vehicle or group of vehicles.

original equipment manufacturer (OEM) The company that manufactured the vehicle.

aftermarket A company other than the original manufacturer that produces equipment or provides services.

intermittent faults A fault or customer concern that you can not detect all of the time and only occurs sometimes.

3 Cs A term used to describe the repair documentation process of 1st documenting the customer concern, 2nd documenting the cause of the problem, and 3rd documenting the correction.

concern Part of the 3Cs, documenting the original concern that the customer came into the shop with. This documentation will go on the repair order, invoice, and service history.

cause Part of the 3Cs, documenting the cause of the problem. This documentation will go on the repair order, invoice, and service history.

correction Part of the 3Cs, documenting the repair that solved the vehicle fault. This documentation will go on the repair order, invoice, and service history.

Review Questions

1. When a vehicle comes in for repair, detailed information regarding the vehicle should be recorded in the:
   a. service booklet.
   b. repair order.
   c. vehicle information label.
   d. shop manual.

2. The service history of the vehicle gives information on whether:
   a. the vehicle was serviced for the same problem more than once.
   b. an odometer rollback has occurred.
   c. the vehicle meets federal standards.
   d. the vehicle has Vehicle Safety Certification.

3. Which of the following steps is the last step in a strategy-based diagnostic process?
   a. Verifying the customer's concern
   b. Researching possible faults
   c. Performing the repair
   d. Verifying the repair

4. When possible, which of the following is the best way to understand the customer's concern?
   a. Asking the customer to guess the cause of the problem.
   b. Asking the customer to suggest a solution to the problem.
   c. Encouraging the customer to demonstrate the problem.
   d. Encouraging the customer to help you fix the problem.

5. The best way to address intermittent faults is to:
   a. look for symptoms, data, or DTCs that are repeatable or consistent.
   b. reverse the steps in the diagnostic process.
   c. ask the customer to bring back the vehicle when the fault occurs.
   d. take it up only when it is covered by warranty.

6. When the technician encounters a vehicle with more than one customer concern, and both originate from companion systems, the technician:
   a. should attempt to test for both faults at once.
   b. need not attempt to fix the second fault.
   c. should never choose those tests that might look at components of both systems.
   d. should isolate the faults and test them separately.

7. Choose the correct statement.
   a. When performing tests for an inspection under warranty, follow your intuition rather than the manufacturers' guidelines.
   b. Researching possible faults should begin with a specific cause in mind.
   c. For hard parts, the best resource is frequently the respective dealership's parts department.
   d. DTCs and freeze frame data need not be captured before clearing the memory.

8. All of the following will happen if the technician fails to document test results *except*:
   a. The manufacturer will not pay the claim.
   b. The shop is out money for the parts and service.

c. The technician will be unable to diagnose the fault.

d. The technician will not be paid for his or her work.

9. All of the following statements with respect to the 3 Cs are true *except*:

a. Customer concern is documented on the repair order prior to the technician receiving the vehicle.

b. The second C in the 3 Cs refers to the cause of the customer's concern.

c. Technicians should note safety issues and maintenance items on the repair order.

d. Additional service recommendations should never be documented on the repair order.

10. Which of the following is not one of the 3 Cs of vehicle repair?

a. Cause

b. Cost

c. Concern

d. Correction

ASE Technician A/Technician B Style Questions

1. Tech A says that when diagnosing a transmission problem, it is important to first verify the customer concern by taking the vehicle on a road test if possible. Tech B says that you should check for TSBs during the diagnostic process. Who is correct?

a. Tech A only

b. Tech B only

c. Both A and B

d. Neither A nor B

2. Tech A says that additional service recommendations should be documented on the repair order. Tech B says technicians are obligated to make the customer aware of safety concerns that require attention. Who is correct?

a. Tech A only

b. Tech B only

c. Both A and B

d. Neither A nor B

3. Tech A says the strategy-based diagnostic process is a scientific process of elimination. Tech B says the strategy-based diagnostic process begins with scanning the vehicle for DTCs. Who is correct?

a. Tech A only

b. Tech B only

c. Both A and B

d. Neither A nor B

4. Tech A says that manufacturers will often indicate what procedures are appropriate for their vehicles and components. Tech B says that the manufacturer's service information can avoid premature failure of the repair. Who is correct?

a. Tech A only

b. Tech B only

c. Both A and B

d. Neither A nor B

5. Tech A says that technicians are frequently paid by the job, or flat rate, rather than paid hourly. Tech B says rushing the repair is best for the customer, so they get their vehicle back quickly. Who is correct?

a. Tech A only

b. Tech B only

c. Both A and B

d. Neither A nor B

6. Tech A says that it is only necessary for dealerships to check for updated parts and software/firmware before performing a repair. Tech B says that it is possible that manufacturers have become aware of a problem with a particular component or software version and have issued a software update. Who is correct?

a. Tech A only

b. Tech B only

c. Both A and B

d. Neither A nor B

7. Tech A says that the customer concern is the focus of step 1 of the diagnostic process. Often the concern is documented on the repair order prior to the technician receiving the vehicle. Tech B says the technician who works on the vehicle should take time to fully understand the concern, read the repair order, and possibly talk further with the customer to understand the nature of the problem. Who is correct?

a. Tech A only

b. Tech B only

c. Both A and B

d. Neither A nor B

8. Tech A says that a repair order is only used in the shop and will be discarded when the vehicle is complete. Tech B says that the repair order is a legal document and could be used in a court. Who is correct?

a. Tech A only

b. Tech B only

c. Both A and B

d. Neither A nor B

9. Two technicians are discussing a transmission problem. Tech A says that it is important to test drive the vehicle because there may actually be no issue with the vehicle and the customer complaint is actually a normal operational characteristic of the transmission. Tech B says you should always check TSBs before performing any service of the transmission because the manufacturer may have updated a component. Who is correct?

a. Tech A only

b. Tech B only

c. Both A and B

d. Neither A nor B

10. Tech A says that experience will allow you to skip many of the steps of the diagnostic process because you will be familiar with the transmission. Tech B says that skipping steps of the diagnostic process can cause issues to be missed, or misdiagnosis of the problem. Who is correct?

a. Tech A only

b. Tech B only

c. Both A and B

d. Neither A nor B

CHAPTER 2

Safety

NATEF Tasks

- **N02001** Comply with the required use of safety glasses, ear protection, gloves, and shoes during lab/shop activities.
- **N02002** Identify and wear appropriate clothing for lab/shop activities.
- **N02003** Identify general shop safety rules and procedures.
- **N02004** Utilize proper ventilation procedures for working within the lab/shop area.

- **N02005** Identify the location and the types of fire extinguishers and other fire safety equipment; demonstrate knowledge of the procedures for using fire extinguishers and other fire safety equipment.
- **N02006** Identify the location of the posted evacuation routes.
- **N02007** Locate and demonstrate knowledge of safety data sheets (SDS).

Knowledge Objectives

After reading this chapter, you will be able to:

- **K02001** Describe the personal safety equipment and precautions for the workplace.
- **K02002** Describe the different kinds of hand protection.
- **K02003** Understand why it is important to wear headgear.
- **K02004** Describe the types of ear protection.
- **K02005** Describe the types of breathing devices.
- **K02006** Describe the types of eye protection.
- **K02007** Describe proper lifting techniques.
- **K02008** Comply with safety precautions in the workplace.
- **K02009** Describe how OSHA rules and the EPA impact the automotive workplace.
- **K02010** Explain how shop policies, procedures, and safety inspections make the workplace safer.

- **K02011** Describe the importance of demonstrating a safe attitude in the workplace.
- **K02012** Identify workplace safety signs and their meanings.
- **K02013** Describe the standard safety equipment.
- **K02014** Maintain a safe air quality in the workplace.
- **K02015** Describe appropriate workplace electrical safety practices.
- **K02016** Prevent fires in the workplace.
- **K02017** Identify hazardous environments and the safety precautions that should be applied.
- **K02018** Identify the proper method to clean hazardous dust safely.
- **K02019** Explain the basic first aid procedures when approaching an emergency.

Skills Objectives

After reading this chapter, you will be able to:

- **S02001** Maintain a clean and orderly workplace.
- **S02002** Use information in an SDS.

- **S02003** Properly dispose of used engine oil and other petroleum products.

You Are the Automotive Technician

It's your first day on the job, and you are asked to report to the main office, where your new supervisor gives you your PPE. Before you can begin working on the shop floor, you are given training on the proper use of PPE. Here are some of the questions you must be able to answer.

1. Which type of gloves should be worn when handling solvents and cleaners?
2. Why must safety glasses be worn at all times in the shop?
3. Why should rings, watches, and jewelry never be worn in the shop?
4. When should hearing protection be worn?
5. For what types of tasks should a face shield be worn?
6. Why must hair be tied up or restrained in the shop?
7. Which type of eye protection should be worn when using or assisting a person using an oxyacetylene welder?

▶ Introduction

Motor vehicle servicing is one of the most common vocations worldwide. Hundreds of thousands of shops service millions of vehicles every day. That means at any given time, many people are conducting automotive servicing, and there is great potential for things to go wrong. It is up to you and your workplace to make sure all work activities are conducted safely. Accidents are not caused by properly maintained tools; accidents are generally caused by people.

▶ Personal Safety

K02001 Describe the personal safety equipment and precautions for the workplace.

N02001 Comply with the required use of safety glasses, ear protection, gloves, and shoes during lab/shop activities.

Personal safety is not something to take lightly. Accidents cause injury and death every day in workplaces across the world (**FIGURE 2-1**). Even if accidents don't result in death, they can be very costly in lost productivity, disability, rehabilitation, and litigation costs. Because workplace safety affects people and society so heavily, government has an interest in minimizing workplace accidents and promoting safe working environments. The primary federal agency for workplace safety is the Occupational Safety and Health Administration (OSHA). States have their own agencies that administer the federal guidelines as well as create additional regulations that apply to their state.

Personal protective equipment (PPE) is equipment used to block the entry of hazardous materials into the body or to protect the body from injury. PPE includes clothing, shoes, eye protection, face protection, head protection, hearing protection, gloves, masks, and respirators (**FIGURE 2-2**). Before you undertake any activity, consider all potential hazards and select the correct PPE based on the risk associated with the activity. For example, if you are going to change hydraulic brake fluid, put on some impervious gloves to protect your skin from chemicals.

Protective Clothing

N02002 Identify and wear appropriate clothing for lab/shop activities.

Protective clothing includes items like shirts, vests, pants, shoes, and gloves. These items are your first line of defense against injuries and accidents, and clothing appropriate for the task must be worn when performing any work. Always make sure protective clothing is kept clean and in good condition. You should replace any clothing that is not in good condition, as it is no longer able to fully protect you. Types of protective clothing materials and their uses are as follows:

- Paper-like fiber: Disposable suits made of this material provide protection against dust and splashes.
- Treated wool and cotton: Adapts well to changing workplace temperatures. Comfortable and fire resistant. Protects against dust, abrasion, and rough and irritating surfaces.

FIGURE 2-1 Accidents are costly.

- Duck: Protects employees against cuts and bruises while they handle heavy, sharp, or rough materials.
- Leather: Often used against dry heat and flame.
- Rubber, rubberized fabrics, neoprene, and plastics: Provides protection against certain acids and other chemicals.

Source: PPE Assessment, Occupational Safety & Health Administration, U.S. Department of Labor.

Always wear appropriate work clothing. Whether this is a one-piece coverall/overall or a separate shirt and pants, the clothes you work in should be comfortable enough to allow you to move, without being loose enough to catch on machinery (**FIGURE 2-3**). The material must be flame retardant and strong enough that it cannot be easily torn. A flap must cover buttons or snaps. If you wear a long-sleeve shirt, the cuffs must be close fitting, without being tight. Pants should not have cuffs so that hot debris cannot become trapped in the fabric.

Always wash your work clothes separately from your other clothes to prevent contaminating your regular clothes. Start a new working day with clean work clothes, and change out of contaminated clothing as soon as possible. It is a good idea to keep a spare set of work clothes in the shop in case the ones you are wearing become overly dirty or a toxic or corrosive fluid is spilled on them.

The proper footwear provides protection against items falling on your feet, chemicals, cuts, abrasions, punctures, and slips. They also provide good support for your feet, especially when working on hard surfaces like concrete. The soles of your shoes must be acid and slip resistant, and the uppers must be made from a puncture-proof material such as leather.

Some shops and technicians prefer safety shoes with a steel toe cap to protect the toes. Always wear shoes that comply with your local shop standards.

FIGURE 2-2 Personal protective equipment (PPE) includes clothing, shoes, safety glasses, hearing protection, masks, and respirators.

> ▶ **TECHNICIAN TIP**

Each shop activity requires specific clothing, depending on its nature. Research and identify what specific type of clothing is required for every activity you undertake. Wear appropriate clothing for the activity you will be involved in, according to the shop's policies and procedures.

FIGURE 2-3 A. One-piece coverall. **B.** Shirt and pants.

Hand Protection

K02002 Describe the different kinds of hand protection.

Hands are a very complex and sensitive part of the body, with many nerves, tendons, and blood vessels. They are susceptible to injury and damage. Nearly every activity performed on vehicles requires the use of your hands, which provides many opportunities for injury. Whenever required, wear gloves to protect your hands. There are many types of gloves available, and their applications vary greatly as you will see below. It is important to wear the correct type of glove for the various activities you perform. In fact, when working on rotating equipment, it may be necessary for you to remove your gloves so that they don't get caught in the machinery and pull you into it.

Heavy-duty and impenetrable chemical gloves should always be worn when using solvents and cleaners. They should also be worn when working on batteries. Chemical gloves should extend to the middle of your forearm to reduce the risk of chemicals splashing onto your skin (**FIGURE 2-4**). Always inspect chemical gloves for holes or cracks before using them, and replace them when they become worn. Some chemical gloves are also slightly heat resistant. This type of chemical glove is suitable for use when removing radiator caps and mixing coolant.

Leather gloves protect your hands from burns when welding or handling hot components (**FIGURE 2-5**). You should also use them when removing steel from a storage rack and when handling sharp objects. When using leather gloves for handling hot components, be aware of the potential for **heat buildup**. Heat buildup occurs when the leather glove can no longer absorb or reflect heat, and heat is transferred to the inside of the leather glove. At this point, the leather gloves' ability to protect you from the heat is reduced, and you need to stop work, remove the leather gloves, and allow them to cool down before continuing to work. Also avoid picking up very hot metal with leather gloves, because it causes the leather to harden, making it less flexible during use. If very hot metal must be moved, it would be better to use an appropriate pair of pliers.

Light-duty gloves should be used to protect your hands from exposure to greases and oils (**FIGURE 2-6**). Light-duty gloves are typically disposable and can be made from a few different materials, such as nitrile, latex, and even plastic. Some people have allergies to these materials. If you have an allergic reaction when wearing these gloves, try using a glove made from a different material.

Cloth gloves are designed to be worn in cold temperatures, particularly during winter, so that cold tools do not stick to your

FIGURE 2-4 Chemical gloves should extend to the middle of your forearm to reduce the risk of chemical burns.

FIGURE 2-5 Leather gloves protect your hands from burns when welding or handling hot components.

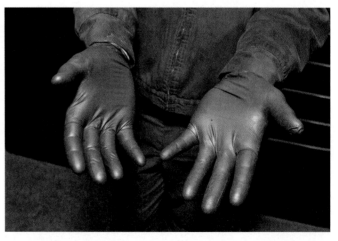

FIGURE 2-6 Light-duty gloves should be used to protect your hands from exposure to greases and oils.

FIGURE 2-7 Cloth gloves work well in cold temperatures, particularly during winter, so that cold tools do not stick to your skin.

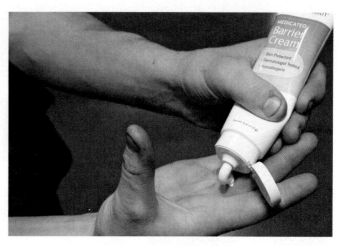

FIGURE 2-8 Barrier cream helps prevent chemicals from being absorbed into your skin and should be applied to your hands before you begin work.

skin (**FIGURE 2-7**). Over time, cloth gloves accumulate dirt and grime, so you need to wash them regularly. Regularly inspect cloth gloves for damage and wear, and replace them when required. Cloth gloves are not an effective barrier against chemicals or oils, so never use them for that purpose.

Barrier cream looks and feels like a moisturizing cream, but it has a specific formula to provide extra protection from chemicals and oils. Barrier cream prevents chemicals from being absorbed into your skin and should be applied to your hands before you begin work (**FIGURE 2-8**). Even the slightest exposure to certain chemicals can lead to dermatitis, a painful skin irritation. Never use a standard moisturizer as a replacement for proper barrier cream. Barrier cream also makes it easier to clean your hands because it can prevent fine particles from adhering to your skin.

When cleaning your hands, use only specialized hand cleaners, which protect your skin. Your hands are porous and easily absorb liquids on contact. Never use solvents such as gasoline or kerosene to clean your hands, because they can be absorbed into the bloodstream and remove the skin's natural protective oils.

Headgear

Headgear includes items like hairnets, caps, and hard hats. These help protect you from getting your hair caught in rotating machinery and protect your head from knocks or bumps. For example, a hard hat can protect you from bumping your head on vehicle parts when working under a vehicle that is raised on a hoist. Head wounds tend to bleed a lot, so hard hats can prevent the need for visiting an emergency room for stitches.

Some technicians wear a cap to keep their hair clean when working under vehicles, or to contain hair that reaches a shirt collar. Some caps are designed specifically with additional padding on the top to provide extra protection against bumps. If hair is longer than can be contained in a cap, then technicians can either use a ponytail holder or hairnet (**FIGURE 2-9**).

When in a workshop environment, watches, rings, necklaces, and dangling earrings and other jewelry present a number of hazards. They can get caught in rotating machinery, and because they are mainly constructed from metal, they can conduct electricity. Imagine leaning over a running engine with a dangling necklace; it could get caught in the fan belt and pull you into the rotating parts if it doesn't break; not only will it get destroyed but it could seriously injure you. A ring or watch could inadvertently short out an electrical circuit, heat up quickly and severely burn you, or cause a spark that might make the battery explode. A ring can also get caught on moving parts, breaking the finger bone or even ripping the finger out of the hand (**FIGURE 2-10**). To be safe, always remove watches, rings, and jewelry before starting work. Not only is it safer to remove these items but your valuables will not get damaged or lost.

K02003 Understand why it is important to wear headgear.

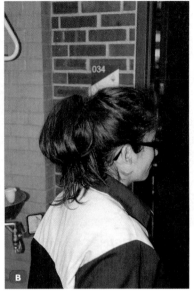

FIGURE 2-9 Containing hair. **A.** Ball cap. **B.** Pony tail.

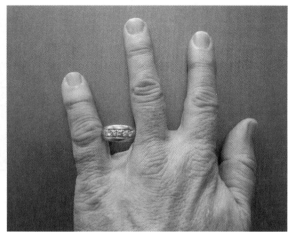

FIGURE 2-10 Finger missing because the wedding ring caught on rotating machinery.

Ear Protection

K02004 Describe the types of ear protection.

Ear protection should be worn when sound levels exceed 85 decibels, when you are working around operating machinery for any period of time, or when the equipment you are using produces loud noise. If you have to raise your voice to be heard by a person who is 2' (50 mm) away from you, then the sound level is about 85 decibels or more. Ear protection comes in two forms: One type covers the entire outer ear, and the other is fitted into the ear canal (**FIGURE 2-11**). Generally speaking, the in-the-ear style has higher noise-reduction ratings. If the noise is not excessively loud, either type of protection will work. If you are in an extremely loud environment, you will want to verify that the option you choose is rated high enough.

Breathing Devices

K02005 Describe the types of breathing devices.

Dust and chemicals from your workspace can be absorbed into the body when you breathe. When working in an environment where dust is present or where the task you are performing will produce dust, you should always wear an appropriate form of breathing device. When working in an environment where chemical vapors are present, you should always wear the proper respirator. There are two types of breathing devices: disposable dust masks and respirators.

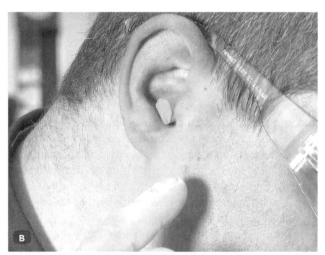

FIGURE 2-11 Ear protection comes in two forms: **A.** One type covers the entire outer ear. **B.** The other type is fitted into the ear canal.

A disposable dust mask is made from paper with a wire-reinforced edge that is held to your face with an elastic strip. It covers your mouth and nose and is disposed of at the completion of the task. This type of mask should only be used as a dust mask and should not be used if chemicals, such as paint solvents, are present in the atmosphere. It should also not be used when working around asbestos dust as the asbestos particles are too small for the filter to remove them, allowing then to be inhaled deeply into the lungs where their sharp tips pierce the lung's lining and become trapped. Over time, these create scar tissue in the lungs and can potentially cause cancer or other life-threatening diseases. Dust masks and respirators should fit securely on your face to minimize leaks around the edges. This can be especially difficult to prevent if you have a beard.

The **respirator** has removable cartridges that can be changed according to the type of contaminant being filtered. Always make sure the cartridge is the correct type for the contaminant in the atmosphere. For example, when chemicals are present, use the appropriate chemical filter in your respirator. The cartridges should be replaced according to the manufacturer's recommended replacement schedule to ensure their effectiveness. To be completely effective, the respirator mask must make a good seal onto your face (**FIGURE 2-12**).

FIGURE 2-12 To be completely effective, the respirator mask must make a good seal onto your face.

In some situations where the environment either contains too high a concentration of hazardous chemicals or a lack of oxygen, a fresh air respirator must be used. This device pumps a supply of fresh air to the mask from an outside location (**FIGURE 2-13**). Being aware of the environment you are working in allows you to determine the proper respirator or fresh air supply system.

Eye Protection

Eyes are very sensitive organs, and they need to be protected against damage and injury. There are many things in the workshop environment that can damage or injure eyes, such as high-velocity particles coming from a grinder or high-intensity light coming from a welder. In fact, the American National Standards Institute (ANSI) reports that 2000 workers per day suffer on-the-job eye injuries. Always select the appropriate eye protection for the work you are undertaking. Sometimes this may mean that more than one type of protection is required. For example, when grinding, you should wear a pair of safety glasses underneath your face shield for added protection.

K02006 Describe the types of eye protection.

The most common type of eye protection is a pair of **safety glasses**, which must be clearly marked with "Z87.1." Safety glasses have built-in side shields to help protect your eyes from the side. Approved safety glasses should be worn whenever you are in a workshop. They are designed to help protect your eyes from direct impact or debris damage (**FIGURE 2-14**).

FIGURE 2-13 Fresh air respirator.

FIGURE 2-14 Safety glasses are designed to protect your eyes from direct impact or debris damage.

The only time they should be removed is when you are using other eye protection equipment. Prescription and tinted safety glasses are also available. Tinted safety glasses are designed to be worn outside in bright sunlight conditions. Never wear them indoors or in low-light conditions because they reduce your ability to see clearly. For people who wear prescription glasses, there are three acceptable options that OSHA makes available:

- Prescription spectacles, with side shields and protective lenses meeting requirements of ANSI Z87.1
- Goggles that can fit comfortably over corrective eyeglasses without disturbing their alignment
- Goggles that incorporate corrective lenses mounted behind protective lenses

Safety goggles don't provide as much eye protection as safety glasses, but they do have added protection against harmful chemicals that may splash up behind the lenses of safety glasses (**FIGURE 2-15**). Goggles also provide additional protection from foreign particles. Safety goggles must be worn when servicing air-conditioning systems or any other system that contains pressurized gas. Goggles can sometimes fog up when in use; if this occurs, use one of the special antifog cleaning fluids or cloths to clean them.

A full face shield gives you added protection from sparks or chemicals over safety glasses alone (**FIGURE 2-16**). The clear mask of the face shield allows you to see all that you are doing and helps protect your eyes and face from chemical burns should there be any splashes or battery explosions. It is also recommended that you use a full face shield combined with safety goggles when using a bench or angle grinder.

The light from a welding arc is very bright and contains high levels of ultraviolet radiation. So wear a **welding helmet** when using, or assisting a person using, an electric welder. The lens on a welding helmet has heavily shaded glass to reduce the intensity of the light from the welding arc, allowing you to see the task you are performing more clearly (**FIGURE 2-17**).

Lenses come in a variety of ratings depending on the type of welding you are doing; always make sure you are using a properly rated lens for the welder you are using. The remainder of the helmet is made from a durable material that blocks any other light, which can burn your skin similar to a sunburn, from reaching your face. It also protects you from welding sparks. Photosensitive welding helmets that darken automatically when an arc is struck are also available. Their big advantage is that you do not have to lift and lower the helmet by hand while welding.

Gas welding goggles can be worn instead of a welding mask when using or assisting a person using an oxyacetylene welder (**FIGURE 2-18**). The eyepieces are available in heavily shaded versions, but not as shaded as those used in an electric welding helmet. There is much less ultraviolet radiation from an oxyacetylene flame, so a welding helmet is not required. However, the flame is bright enough to damage your eyes, so always use goggles of the correct shade rating.

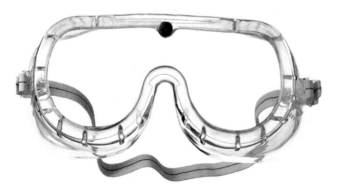

FIGURE 2-15 Safety goggles provide much the same eye protection as safety glasses, but with added protection against any harmful fluid that may find its way behind the lenses.

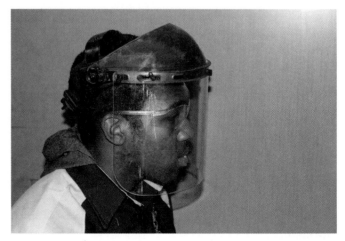

FIGURE 2-16 Full face shield.

FIGURE 2-17 The lens on a welding helmet has heavily tinted glass to reduce the intensity of the light from the welding tip, allowing you to see what you are doing.

FIGURE 2-18 Gas welding goggles can be worn instead of a welding helmet when using or assisting a person using an oxyacetylene welder.

Lifting

Whenever you lift something, there is always the possibility of injury; however, by lifting correctly, you reduce the chance of injuring yourself or others. Before lifting anything, you can reduce the risk of injury by breaking down the load into smaller quantities, asking for assistance if required, or possibly using a mechanical device to assist the lift. If you have to bend down to lift something, you should bend your knees to lower your body; do not bend over with straight legs because this can damage your back (**FIGURE 2-19**). Place your feet about shoulder width apart, and lift the item by straightening your legs while keeping your back as straight as possible.

▶ Shop Safety

The work environment can be described as anywhere you work. The condition of the work environment plays an important role in making the workplace safer. A safe work environment goes a long way toward preventing accidents, injuries, and illnesses. There are many ways to describe a safe work environment, but generally it would contain a well-organized shop layout, use of shop policies and procedures, safe equipment, safety equipment, safety training, employees who work safely, good supervision, and a workplace culture that supports safe work practices. Conversely, a shop that is cluttered with junk, poorly lit, and full of safety hazards is unsafe (**FIGURE 2-20**).

K02007 Describe proper lifting techniques.

SAFETY TIP

Never lift anything that is too heavy for you to comfortably lift, and always seek assistance if lifting the object could injure you. Always err on the side of caution.

K02008 Comply with safety precautions in the workplace.

N02003 Identify general shop safety rules and procedures.

FIGURE 2-19 Prevent back injuries when lifting heavy objects by crouching with your legs slightly apart, standing close to the object, positioning yourself so that the center of gravity is between your feet.

FIGURE 2-20 A. Relatively safe shop. **B.** Relatively unsafe shop.

Applied Science

AS-1: Safety: The technician follows all safety regulations and applicable procedures while performing the task.

Using a bench grinder to grind down a steel component is a simple everyday activity in shops. In terms of its potential safety implications, it carries significant risk of injury. Before beginning the task, you must ensure that the machinery is safe and ready to use. Inspect and/or adjust the guards/shields, grinding wheels, electrical cord, etc. From a personal perspective, you must make sure your clothing is suitable and safe for the task. Clothing cannot be loose, as it may get caught

in the grinder; it must be made of flame-retardant material because of the risk of ignition from sparks. Long hair must be tied back or contained within a hairnet or cap because of the risk of it getting caught in rotating machinery. Various items of PPE are required to safely carry out this task: safety goggles to protect against foreign objects entering the eyes, ear protection to guard against hearing damage due to excessive noise, steel-capped boots to prevent injury from falling heavy objects, and heavy-duty gloves to protect against skin contact with sharp or hot components.

OSHA and EPA

K02009 Describe how OSHA rules and the EPA impact the automotive workplace.

OSHA stands for the **Occupational Safety and Health Administration (OSHA)**. It is a U.S. government agency that was created to provide national leadership in occupational safety and health, and it works toward finding the most effective ways to help prevent worker fatalities and workplace injuries and illnesses. OSHA has the authority to conduct workplace inspections and, if required, fine employers and workplaces if they violate its regulations and procedures. For example, a fine may be imposed on the employer or workplace if a worker is electrocuted by a piece of faulty machinery that has not been regularly tested and maintained.

OSHA standard 29 CFR 1910.132 requires employers to assess the workplace to determine if hazards are present, or are likely to be present, which necessitate the use of PPE. In addition, OSHA regulations require employers to protect their employees from workplace hazards such as machines, work procedures, and hazardous substances that can cause injury. To do that, employers must institute all feasible **engineering and work practice controls** to eliminate and reduce hazards before using PPE to protect against hazards. This means that the employers have a responsibility not only to assess safety issues but to eliminate or reduce those that can be mitigated, and then provide PPE and training for those hazards that cannot be mitigated. At the same time, if you are injured, you are the one suffering the consequences, such as being out of work for a period of time, permanent disability, or death. So it is in your best interest to take responsibility for your own safety while on the job. Engineering controls means the employer has physically changed the machine or work environment to prevent employee exposure to the potential hazard. An example might be adding a ventilation system to an area where solvent tanks are used. Work practice controls means the employer changes the way employees do their jobs in order to reduce exposure to the hazard. An example of this might be requiring employees to use a brake wash station when working on brake systems.

EPA stands for the **Environmental Protection Agency**. This federal government agency deals with issues related to environmental safety. The EPA conducts research and monitoring, sets standards, conducts workplace inspections, and holds employees and companies legally accountable in order to keep the environment protected. Shop activities need to comply with EPA laws and regulations by ensuring that waste products are disposed of in an environmentally responsible way, chemicals and fluids are correctly stored, and work practices do not contribute to damaging the environment.

Applied Science

AS-2: Environmental Issues: The technician develops and maintains an understanding of all federal, state, and local rules and regulations regarding environmental issues related to the work of the automobile technician.

You need to keep up to date with local laws and regulations regarding environmental issues. There are large fines associated with disregarded environmental regulations. To remain informed, you can log on to local state websites to check the latest laws and regulations. The U.S. Environmental Protection Agency (EPA) website also has up-to-date information on environmental regulations (www.epa.gov/lawsregs/). More information can be found on the specific regulations for the automotive industry at www.epa.gov/lawsregs/sectors/automotive.html. This site has a full listing of laws and regulations, compliance measures, and enforcement tactics. For additional laws that are enforced by your local state environmental agencies, go to www.epa.gov/epahome/state.htm.

AS-3: Environmental Issues: The technician uses such things as government impact statements, media information, and general knowledge of pollution and waste management to correctly use and dispose of products that result from the performance of a repair task.

When you complete a job, you must be able to identify what to do with any waste products created from the repair task. This could be as simple as knowing where and how to recycle cardboard boxes or as complex as knowing what to do with brake components that may contain asbestos. Normally, there is a table posted in the garage that details the correct measures for disposing of and storing waste material. A sample table follows:

Component	Material/Parts	Removal and Safety Information	Recommended Storage
Air-conditioning gases (refrigerant)	R12, R134a	Use approved evacuation and collection equipment required. *Note:* Requires AC license.	Use approved storage containers—reused or recycled.
Batteries	Plastic, rubber, lead, sulfuric acid	Avoid contact between sulfuric acid and your skin, clothing, or eyes.	Store off the ground in a covered area for collection by recycler.
Brake fluid	Diethylene and polyethylene glycol-monoalkyl ethers	These are corrosive and highly toxic to the environment. Drain into pan or tray.	Store in a drum in a covered area for collection by a licensed operator.
Brake shoes and pads pre-2004	Asbestos	Fibers are dangerous if inhaled.	Put in a plastic bag in a sealed container for collection by contractor.
Coolant	Phosphoric acid, hydrazine ethylene glycol, alcohols	Radiator coolant can be toxic to the environment.	Store in sealed drums in a covered area for recycling or collection by a licensed operator.
Coverings for plastic parts, and plastic bags and containers for parts shipping	Plastic-made components	Plastic components that can be recycled bear a recycling symbol: this symbol has a number inside telling the recycling company what the product is made of.	If the plastic container has a recycle code, then put it in the recycle bin. If it does not, then put in general waste. Plastic oil containers cannot be recycled.
Fuel	Unleaded, diesel	Avoid fumes. Fire hazard; keep well away from ignition sources. Siphon from tank to avoid spillage.	Store in a drum in a covered area.
Metal	Brake discs, housings made of metal (gearbox/engine case and components), metal cuttings	Some metal products can be heavy, so lift with care.	All metal components can be recycled; keep waste metal in a separate recycle bin for sale or disposal.
Oil	Engine, transmission, and differential oils	Fire hazard; keep well away from ignition sources.	Store in a drum/container in a covered area for collection by a licensed operator.

(Continues)

Applied Science (Continued)

Component	Material/Parts	Removal and Safety Information	Recommended Storage
Oil filters	Steel paper fiber	—	Drain filter, then crush and store in a leakproof drum for collection.
Parts boxes and paperwork	Paper, cardboard	—	Store in a recycling bin to be taken away for recycling.
Tires	Rubber, steel, fabric	Keep away from ignition sources.	Store in a fenced area for collection by recycler.
Trim, plastic fittings, and seats	Plastic, metal, cloth	—	Store racked or binned for reuse, sale, or recycling.
Tubes and rubber components	Rubber hoses, mounts, etc.	Keep away from ignition sources.	Store in a collection bin, to be collected and recycled.
Undeployed airbags	Plastics, metals, igniters, explosives	Recommended specific training on airbags before attempting removal. Handle with care; accidental deployment can cause serious harm. If unit is to be scrapped, ensure that it is safely deployed first.	Store face up in a secure area.

Shop Policies, Procedures, and Safety Inspections

K02010 Explain how shop policies, procedures, and safety inspections make the workplace safer.

Shop policies and procedures are a set of documents that outline how tasks and activities in the shop are to be conducted and managed. They also ensure that the shop operates according to OSHA and EPA laws and regulations. A **policy** is a guiding principle that sets the shop direction, and a **procedure** is a list of the steps required to get the same result each time a task or activity is performed (**FIGURE 2-21**). An example of a policy is an OSHA document for the shop that describes how the shop complies with legislation, such as a sign simply saying, "Safety glasses must be worn at all times in the shop." An example of a procedure is a document that describes the steps required to safely use the vehicle hoist.

FIGURE 2-21 A. Policy. **B.** Procedure.

Each shop has its own set of policies and procedures and a system in place to make sure the policies and procedures are regularly reviewed and updated. Regular reviews ensure that new policies and procedures are developed and old ones are modified in case something has changed. For example, if the shop moves to a new building, then a review of policies and procedures will ensure that they relate to the new shop, its layout, and equipment. In general, the policies and procedures are written to guide shop practice; help ensure compliance with laws, statutes, and regulations; and reduce the risk of injury. Always follow your shop policies and procedures to reduce the risk of injury to your coworkers and yourself and to prevent damage to property.

It is everyone's responsibility to know and follow the rules. Locate the general shop rules and procedures for your workplace. Look through the contents or index pages to familiarize yourself with the contents. Discuss the policy and the shop

FIGURE 2-22 Shop safety inspection using a checklist.

rules and procedures with your supervisor. Ask questions to ensure that you understand how the rules and procedures should be applied and your role in making sure they are followed.

Shop safety inspections are valuable ways of identifying unsafe equipment, materials, or activities so they can be corrected to reduce the risk of accidents or injuries. The inspection can be formalized by using inspection sheets to check specific items, or they can be general walk-arounds where you consciously look for and document problems that can be corrected (**FIGURE 2-22**).

Here are some of the common things to look for:
Items blocking emergency exits or walkways

- Poor safety signage
- Unsafe storage of flammable goods
- Tripping or slipping hazards
- Faulty or unsafe equipment or tools
- Missing equipment guards
- Misadjusted bench grinder tool rests
- Missing or expired fire extinguishers
- Clutter, spills, unsafe shop practices
- People not wearing the correct PPE

Formal and informal safety inspections should be held regularly. For example, an inspection sheet might be used weekly or monthly to formally evaluate the shop, and informal inspections might be held daily to catch issues that are of a more immediate nature. Never ignore or put off a safety issue.

Housekeeping and Orderliness

Good housekeeping is about always making sure the shop and your work surroundings are neat and kept in good order. This habit pays off in a couple of ways. It makes the shop a safer place to work by not allowing clutter or spills to accumulate. It also makes the shop more efficient if everything is kept neat and orderly, by making it easier to find needed tools and equipment. Trash and liquid spills should be quickly cleaned up; tools need to be cleaned and put away after use; spare or removed parts need to be stored or disposed of correctly; and generally everything needs to have a safe place to be kept.

You should carry out good housekeeping practices while working, not just after a job is completed. For example, throw trash in the garbage can as it accumulates, clean up spills when they happen, and put tools away when you are finished working with them. It is also good practice to periodically perform a deep clean of the shop so that any neglected areas are taken care of.

S02001 Maintain a clean and orderly workplace.

K02011 Describe the importance of demonstrating a safe attitude in the workplace.

Safe Attitude

Develop a safe attitude toward your work. You should always think "safety first" and then act safely (**FIGURE 2-23**). Think ahead about what you are doing, and put in place specific measures to protect yourself and those around you. For example, you could ask yourself the following questions:

- What could go wrong?
- What measures can I take to ensure that nothing goes wrong?
- What PPE should I use?
- Have I been trained to use this piece of equipment?
- Is the equipment I'm using safe?

Answering these questions and taking appropriate action before you begin will help you work safely. If you don't know the answers to those questions, don't work! Stop and ask someone with more experience than yourself, or your supervisor. Also, don't count on others for your safety. You alone are primarily responsible for your own safety.

Also remember that the time to make a good decision is before an accident happens. Once the accident occurs, you will likely have very little to no control over the outcome. In fact, there are very few true accidents that happen all by themselves. Accidents are almost always caused by poor decisions or poor actions. Almost all accidents can be prevented with a little more thought, training, and practice.

Don't Underestimate the Dangers

Because vehicle servicing and repair are so commonplace, it is easy to overlook the many potential risks related to this field. Think carefully about what you are doing and how you are doing it. Think through the steps, trying to anticipate things that may go wrong and

FIGURE 2-23 Always think "safety first."

taking steps to prevent them. Also be wary of taking shortcuts. In most cases, the time saved by taking a shortcut is nothing compared to the time spent recovering from an accident.

Accidents and Injuries Can Happen at Any Time

There is the possibility of an accident occurring whenever work is undertaken. For example, fires and explosions are a constant hazard wherever there are flammable fuels. Electricity can kill quickly as well as cause painful shocks and burns. Heavy equipment and machinery can easily cause broken bones or crush fingers and toes. Hazardous solvents and other chemicals can burn or blind as well as contribute to many kinds of illness. Oil spills and tools left lying around can cause slips, trips, and falls. Poor lifting and handling techniques can cause chronic strain injuries, particularly to your back.

FIGURE 2-24 Clean up spills immediately.

Slip, Trip, and Fall Hazards

Slip, trip, and fall hazards are ever present in the shop, and they can be caused by trash, tools and equipment, or liquid spills being left lying around. Always be on the lookout for hazards that can cause slips, trips, or falls. Floors and steps can become slippery, so they should be kept clean and have antislip coatings applied to them. High-visibility strips with antislip coatings can be applied to the edge of step treads to reduce the hazard. Clean up liquid spills immediately, and mark the area with wet floor signs until the floor is dry (**FIGURE 2-24**). Make sure the workshop has good lighting, so hazards are easy to spot, and keep walkways clear from obstruction. Think about what you are doing and make sure the work area is free of slip, trip, and fall hazards as you work.

Accidents and Injuries Are Avoidable

Almost all accidents are avoidable or preventable by taking a few precautions. Think of nearly every accident you have witnessed or heard about. In most cases someone made a mistake. Whether caused by horseplay, neglecting maintenance on tools or equipment, or using tools improperly, these instances lead to injury. Most of these accidents can be prevented if people follow policies and develop a "safety first" attitude. By following regulations and safety procedures, you can make your workplace much safer. Learn and follow all of the correct safety procedures for your workplace. Always wear the right PPE, and stay alert and aware of what is happening around you.

Think about what you are doing, how you are doing it, and its effect on others. You also need to know what to do in case of an emergency. Document and report all accidents and injuries whenever they happen, and take the proper steps to make sure they never happen again.

Signs

Always remember that a shop is a hazardous environment. To make people more aware of specific shop hazards, legislative bodies have developed a series of safety signs. These signs are designed to give adequate warning of an unsafe situation. Each sign has four components:

K02012 Identify workplace safety signs and their meanings.

- Signal word: There are three signal words—danger, warning, and caution. Danger indicates an immediately hazardous situation, which, if not avoided, will result in death or serious injury. Danger is usually indicated by white text with a red background. Warning indicates a potentially hazardous situation, which, if not avoided, could result in death or serious injury. The sign is usually in black text with an orange or yellow background. Caution indicates a potentially hazardous situation, which, if not avoided, may result in minor or moderate injury. It may also be used to alert against unsafe practices. This sign is usually in black text with a yellow background (**FIGURE 2-25**).

FIGURE 2-25 Signs. **A.** Danger is usually indicated by white text on a red background. **B.** Warning is usually in black text with an orange background. **C.** Caution is usually in black text with a yellow background.

- Background color: The choice of background color also draws attention to potential hazards and is used to provide contrast so the letters or images stand out. For example, a red background is used to identify a definite hazard; yellow indicates caution for a potential hazard. A green background is used for emergency-type signs, such as for first aid, fire protection, and emergency equipment. A blue background is used for general information signs.
- Text: The sign will sometimes include explanatory text intended to provide additional safety information. Some signs are designed to convey a personal safety message.
- Pictorial message: In symbol signs, a pictorial message appears alone or is combined with explanatory text. This type of sign allows the safety message to be conveyed to people who are illiterate or who do not speak the local language.

Safety Equipment

K02013 Describe the standard safety equipment.

Shop safety equipment includes items such as:

- Handrails: Handrails are used to separate walkways and pedestrian traffic from work areas. They provide a physical barrier that directs pedestrian traffic and also offer protection from vehicle movements.
- Machinery guards: Machinery guards and yellow lines prevent people from accidentally walking into the operating equipment or indicate that a safe distance should be kept from the equipment.

- Painted lines: Large, fixed machinery such as lathes and milling machines present a hazard to the operator and others working in the area. To prevent accidents, a machinery guard or a painted yellow line on the floor usually borders this equipment.
- Sound-insulated rooms: Sound-insulated rooms are usually used when operating equipment makes a lot of noise, for example a chassis dynamometer. A vehicle operating on a dynamometer produces a lot of noise from its tires, exhaust, and engine. To protect other shop users from the noise, the dynamometer is usually placed in a sound-insulated room, keeping shop noise to a minimum.
- Adequate ventilation: Exhaust gases and chemical vapors are serious health hazards in the shop. Whenever a vehicle's engine is running, toxic gases are emitted from its exhaust. To prevent an excess of toxic gas buildup, a well-ventilated work area is needed, as well as a method of directly venting the vehicle's exhaust to the outside. It may only take a minute or two for a poorly running vehicle to fill the shop with enough carbon monoxide to affect people's health. Chemical vapors are also a hazard and need to be vented outside.
- Doors and gates: Doors and gates are used for the same reason as machinery guards and painted lines. A doorway is a physical barrier that can be locked and sealed to separate a hazardous environment from the rest of the shop or a general work area from an office or specialist work area.
- Temporary barriers: In the day-to-day operation of a shop, there is often a reason to temporarily separate one work bay from others. If a welding machine or an oxyacetylene cutting torch is in use, it may be necessary to place a temporary screen or barrier around the work area to protect other shop users from welding flash or injury.

Air Quality

Managing air quality in shops helps protect you from potential harm and also protects the environment. There are many shop activities, stored liquids, and other hazards that can reduce the quality of air in shops. Some of these are listed here:

K02014 Maintain a safe air quality in the workplace.

- Dangerous fumes from running engines
- Welding (gas and electric)
- Painting
- Liquid storage areas
- Air conditioning servicing
- Dust particles from brake servicing

Running engines produce dangerous exhaust gases including carbon monoxide (CO) and carbon dioxide (CO_2). Carbon monoxide in small concentrations can kill or cause serious injuries. Carbon dioxide is a greenhouse gas, and vehicles are a major source of carbon dioxide in the atmosphere. Exhaust gases also contain hydrocarbons (HC) and oxides of nitrogen (NOx). These gases can form smog and also cause breathing problems for some people.

Carbon monoxide in particular is extremely dangerous, as it is odorless and colorless and can build up to toxic levels very quickly in confined spaces. In fact, it doesn't take very much carbon monoxide to pose a danger. The maximum exposure limit is regulated by the following agencies:

- OSHA permissible exposure limit (PEL) is 50 parts per million (ppm) of air for an eight-hour period.
- National Institute for Occupational Safety and Health has established a recommended exposure limit of 35 ppm for an eight-hour period.

The reason the PEL is so low is because carbon monoxide attaches itself to red blood cells much more easily than oxygen does, and it never leaves the blood cell. This prevents the blood cells from carrying as much oxygen, and if enough carbon monoxide has been inhaled, it effectively asphyxiates the person. Always follow the correct safety precautions when running engines indoors or in a confined space, including over service pits,

FIGURE 2-26 Exhaust hoses should be vented to where the fumes will not be drawn back indoors.

as gases can accumulate there. The best solution when running engines in an enclosed space (shop) is to directly connect the vehicle's exhaust pipe to an exhaust extraction system hose that ventilates the fumes to the outside air. The extraction system should be vented to where the fumes will not be drawn back indoors, to a place well away from other people and other premises (**FIGURE 2-26**).

Do not assume that an engine fitted with a catalytic converter can be run safely indoors; it cannot. Catalytic converters are fitted into the exhaust system to help control exhaust emissions through chemical reaction. They require high temperatures to operate efficiently and are less effective when the exhaust gases are relatively cool, such as when the engine is only idling or being run intermittently. A catalytic converter can never substitute for adequate ventilation or exhaust extraction equipment. In fact, even if the catalytic converter were working at 100% efficiency, the exhaust would contain large amounts of carbon dioxide and very low amounts of oxygen, neither of which conditions can sustain life.

Proper Ventilation

N02004 Utilize proper ventilation procedures for working within the lab/shop area.

Proper ventilation is required for working in the shop area. The key to proper ventilation is to ensure that any task or procedure that may produce dangerous or toxic fumes is recognized, so measures can be put in place to provide adequate ventilation. Ventilation can be provided by natural means, such as by opening doors and windows to provide air flow for low-exposure situations. However, in high-exposure situations, such as vehicles running in the shop, a mechanical means of ventilation is required; an example is an exhaust extraction system. Parts cleaning areas or areas where solvents and chemicals are used should also have good general ventilation, and if required, additional exhaust hoods or fans should be installed to remove dangerous fumes. In some cases, such as when spraying paint, it may be necessary to use a personal respirator in addition to proper ventilation.

▶ **TECHNICIAN TIP**

Before starting a vehicle in the shop, make sure the correct ventilation equipment is connected properly and turned on. Also, if the system uses rubber hoses, make sure they aren't kinked.

Electrical Safety

K02015 Describe appropriate workplace electrical safety practices.

Many people are injured by electricity in shops. Poor electrical safety practices can cause shocks and burns as well as fires and explosions. Make sure you know where the electrical shutoffs, or panels for your shop, are located. All circuit breakers and fuses should be clearly labeled so that you know which circuits and functions they control (**FIGURE 2-27**).

In the case of an emergency, you may need to know how to shut off the electricity supply to a work area or to your entire shop. Keep the circuit breaker and/or electrical panel covers closed to keep them in good condition, prevent unauthorized access, and prevent accidental contact with the electricity supply. It is important that you do not block or obstruct access to this electrical panel; keep equipment and tools well away so emergency access is not hindered. In some localities, 3' (0.91 m) of unobstructed space must be maintained around the panel at all times.

There should be a sufficient number of electrical receptacles in your work area for all your needs. Do not connect multiple appliances to a single receptacle with a simple double adapter. If necessary, use a multi-outlet safety strip that has a built-in overload cutout feature. Electric receptacles should be at least 3' (0.91 m) above floor level to reduce the risk of igniting spilled fuel vapors or other flammable liquids.

If you need to use an extension cord, make sure it is made of flexible wiring—not the stiffer type of house wiring—and that it is fitted with a ground wire. The cord should be neoprene-covered, as this material resists oil damage.

Always check it for cuts, abrasions, or other damage. Be careful how you place the extension cord, so it does not cause a tripping hazard. Also avoid rolling equipment or vehicles over it, as doing so can damage the cord. Never use an extension cord in wet conditions or around flammable liquids. Portable electric tools that operate at 240 volts are often sources of serious shock and burn accidents. Be particularly careful when using these items. Always inspect the cord for damage and check the security of the attached plug before connecting the item to the power supply. Use 110-volt or lower voltage tools if they are available. All electric tools must be equipped with a ground prong or be **double insulated**.

If electrical cords don't have the ground prong or aren't double insulated, do not use them. Never use any high-voltage tool in a wet environment. In contrast, air-operated tools cannot give you an electric shock, because they operate on air pressure instead of electricity, and therefore, they are safer to use in a wet environment.

Portable shop lights/droplights have been the cause of many accidents over the years. Incandescent bulbs get extremely hot and can cause burns. They are also prone to shatter, which can cut skin and damage eyes or cause fires and electric shock. In fact, in some places incandescent portable shop lights cannot be used in automotive shops and must be replaced with less hazardous lights.

One such light is the fluorescent droplight. Although this type of light stays much cooler than incandescent lights, it still can shatter, causing cuts or damage to eyes. Because of this, droplights should be fully enclosed in a clear, insulating case. They may also contain mercury, which becomes dispersed when the bulb is shattered, creating a hazardous-materials situation.

The safest portable shop light to come on the market is the LED (light-emitting diode) shop light. It uses much lower voltage, and the LED is much less prone to shattering, so it is much safer to use. It also uses a small amount of electricity to produce a large amount of light, so many of them are cordless. They may also include a magnetic base, so the light can be attached to any steel surface and then adjusted to shine where needed.

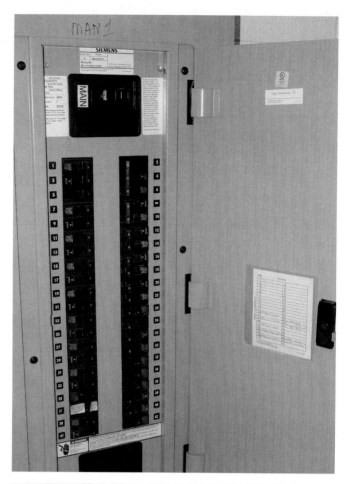

FIGURE 2-27 All electrical switches and fuses should be clearly labeled so that you know which circuits and functions they control.

Preventing Fires

The danger of a gasoline fire is always present in an automotive shop. Most automobiles carry a fuel tank, often with large quantities of fuel on board, which is more than sufficient to cause a large, very destructive, and potentially explosive fire.

In fact, 1 gallon of gasoline has the same amount of energy as 20 sticks of dynamite. So take precautions to make sure you have the correct type and size of extinguishers on hand for a potential fuel fire. Make sure you clean up spills immediately and avoid ignition sources, like sparks, near flammable liquids or gases. Being aware of the following topics will help you know how to minimize the risk of fires in the shop.

Extinguishing Fires

Three elements must be present at the same time for a fire to occur: fuel, oxygen, and heat (**FIGURE 2-28**). The secret of firefighting involves the removal of at least one of these elements. If a fire occurs in the shop, it is usually the oxygen or the heat that is removed to extinguish the fire. For example, a fire blanket when applied correctly removes the oxygen, and a water extinguisher removes heat from the fire. Fire extinguishers are used to extinguish the majority of small fires in a shop. Never hesitate to call the fire department if you cannot extinguish a fire quickly and safely.

In the United States, there are five classes of fire:

- Class A fires involve ordinary combustibles such as wood, paper, or cloth.
- Class B fires involve flammable liquids or gaseous fuels.

K02016 Prevent fires in the workplace.

▶ **TECHNICIAN TIP**

Try out the new LED flashlights or cordless LED shop lights. Good ones provide a lot of light, and the batteries last a long time. It is not unusual to hear about an LED flashlight that got dropped behind a toolbox while it was on, and was still illuminated days later.

N02005 Identify the location and the types of fire extinguishers and other fire safety equipment; demonstrate knowledge of the procedures for using fire extinguishers and other fire safety equipment.

FIGURE 2-28 Fire triangle.

FIGURE 2-29 Traditional labels on fire extinguishers often incorporate a shape as well as a letter.

N02006 Identify the location of the posted evacuation routes.

- Class C fires involve electrical equipment.
- Class D fires involve combustible metals such as sodium, titanium, and magnesium.
- Class K fires involve cooking oil or fat.

Fire extinguishers are marked with pictograms depicting the types of fires that the extinguisher is approved to fight (**FIGURE 2-29**):

- Class A: Green triangle
- Class B: Red square
- Class C: Blue circle
- Class D: Yellow pentagram
- Class K: Black hexagon

Unless the fire is very small, always sound the alarm before attempting to fight a fire. If you cannot fight the fire safely, leave the area while you wait for backup. You need to size up the fire before you make the decision to fight it with a fire extinguisher, by identifying what sort of material is burning, the extent of the fire, and the likelihood of it spreading. Also, if the fire is in electrical wires or equipment, make sure you won't be electrocuted while trying to extinguish it. To operate a fire extinguisher, follow the acronym for fire extinguisher use: PASS (pull, aim, squeeze, sweep).

- Pull out the pin that locks the handle at the top of the fire extinguisher to prevent accidental use. Carry the fire extinguisher in one hand, and use your other hand to:
- Aim the nozzle at the base of the fire. Stand about 8–12 feet (2.4–3.7 m) away from the fire, and
- Squeeze the handle to discharge the fire extinguisher. Remember that if you release the handle on the fire extinguisher, it will stop discharging.
- Sweep the nozzle from side to side at the base of the fire.

Continue to watch the fire. Although it may appear to be extinguished, it may suddenly reignite. Portable fire extinguishers only operate for about 10–25 seconds before they are empty. So use them effectively (**FIGURE 2-30**).

If the fire is indoors, you should be standing between the fire and the nearest safe exit. If the fire is outside, you should stand facing the fire, with the wind on your back, so that the smoke and heat are being blown away from you. If possible, get an assistant to guide you and inform you of the fire's progress. Again, make sure you have a means of escape, should the fire get out of control. When you are certain that the fire is out, report it to your supervisor. Also report what actions you took to put out the fire. Once the circumstances of the fire have been investigated and your supervisor or the fire department has given you the all clear, clean up the debris and submit the used fire extinguisher for inspection and service.

Fire blankets are designed to smother a small fire. They are ideal for use in situations where a fire extinguisher could cause damage. For example, if there is a small fire under the hood of a vehicle, a fire blanket might be able to smother the fire without running the risk of getting powder from the fire extinguisher down the intake system. They are also very useful in putting out a fire on a person. The fire blanket can be thrown around the person, smothering any fire.

Obtain a fire blanket and study the use instructions on the packaging. If instructions are not provided, research how to use a fire blanket, or ask your supervisor. You may require instruction from an authorized person in using the fire blanket. If you do use a fire blanket, make sure you return the blanket for use or, if necessary, replace it with a new one.

Evacuation Routes

Evacuation routes are a safe way of escaping danger and gathering in a prearranged safe place where everyone can be accounted for in the event of an emergency. It is important to have more than one evacuation route in case any single route is blocked during the

FIGURE 2-30 To operate a fire extinguisher, follow PASS. **A.** Pull. **B.** Aim. **C.** Squeeze. **D.** Sweep.

emergency. Your shop may have an evacuation procedure that clearly identifies the evacuation routes (**FIGURE 2-31**).

Often the evacuation routes are marked with colored lines painted or taped on the floors. Exits should be highlighted with signs that may be illuminated, and should never be chained closed or obstructed (**FIGURE 2-32**).

Always make sure you are familiar with the evacuation routes for the shop. Before conducting any task, identify which route you will take if an emergency occurs.

> ▶ **TECHNICIAN TIP**
>
> Never place anything in the way of evacuation routes, including equipment, tools, parts, cleaning supplies, or vehicles.

FIGURE 2-31 Your shop may have an evacuation procedure that clearly identifies the evacuation routes.

FIGURE 2-32 Exits should be marked, clear of obstructions, and not chained closed.

K02017 Identify hazardous environments and the safety precautions that should be applied.

N02007 Locate and demonstrate knowledge of safety data sheets (SDS).

S02002 Use information in an SDS.

▶ Hazardous Materials Safety

A **hazardous material** is any material that poses an unreasonable risk of damage or injury to persons, property, or the environment if it is not properly controlled during handling, storage, manufacture, processing, packaging, use and disposal, or transportation. These materials can be solids, liquids, or gases. Most technicians use hazardous materials daily, such as cleaning solvents, gasket cement, brake fluid, and coolant. In fact, there are likely to be hundreds of hazardous materials in a typical shop. Hazardous materials must be properly handled, labeled, and stored in the shop.

Safety Data Sheets

Hazardous materials are used daily and may make you very sick if they are not used properly. **Safety data sheets (SDS)** contain detailed information about hazardous materials to help you understand how they should be safely used, any health effects relating to them, how to treat a person who has been exposed to them, and how to deal with them in a fire situation. SDS can be obtained from the manufacturer of the material. The shop should have an SDS for each hazardous substance or dangerous product. In the United States, it is required that workplaces have an SDS for every chemical that is on site.

Safety data sheets (SDS) were formerly called material safety data sheets (MSDS). In 2012, OSHA changed the requirements for the hazard communication system (HCS) to conform to the United Nations Globally Harmonized System of Classification and Labeling of Chemicals (GHS). The MSDS needed to change its name and its format to fit the new standards. Whereas the original MSDS had 8 sections, safety data sheets are required to have 16 sections that provide additional details and make it easier to find specific data when needed. In addition, GHS requires all employers to train their employees in the new chemical labeling requirements and the new format for the safety data sheets.

Whenever you deal with a potentially hazardous product, you should consult the SDS to learn how to use that product safely. If you are using more than one product, make sure you consult all the SDS for those products. Be aware that certain combinations of products can be more dangerous than any of them separately.

SDS are usually kept in a clearly marked binder and should be regularly updated as chemicals come into the workplace. As of June 1, 2015, the HCS requires new SDS to be in a uniform format, and include the section numbers, the headings, and associated information under the headings below:

Section 1, Identification, includes product identifier; manufacturer or distributor name, address, and phone number; emergency phone number; recommended use; restrictions on use.

Section 2, Hazard(s) identification, includes all hazards regarding the chemical; required label elements.

Section 3, Composition/information on ingredients, includes information on chemical ingredients; trade secret claims.

Section 4, First-aid measures, includes important symptoms/effects, acute, delayed; required treatment.

Section 5, Firefighting measures, lists suitable extinguishing techniques, equipment; chemical hazards from fire.

Section 6, Accidental release measures, lists emergency procedures; protective equipment; proper methods of containment and cleanup.

Section 7, Handling and storage, lists precautions for safe handling and storage, including incompatibilities.

Section 8, Exposure controls/personal protection, lists OSHA's permissible exposure limits (PELs); threshold limit values (TLVs); appropriate engineering controls; personal protective equipment (PPE).

Section 9, Physical and chemical properties, lists the chemical's characteristics.

Section 10, Stability and reactivity, lists chemical stability and possibility of hazardous reactions.

Section 11, Toxicological information, includes routes of exposure; related symptoms, acute and chronic effects; numerical measures of toxicity.

Section 12, Ecological information*

Section 13, Disposal considerations*

Section 14, Transport information*

Section 15, Regulatory information*

Section 16, Other information, includes the date of preparation or last revision.

*Note: Since other Agencies regulate this information, OSHA will not be enforcing Sections 12 through 15 (29 CFR 1910.1200(g)(2)).

Source: https://www.osha.gov/Publications/HazComm_QuickCard_SafetyData.html.

To identify information found on an SDS, follow the steps in SKILL DRILL 2-1.

Cleaning Hazardous Dust Safely

Toxic dust is any dust that may contain fine particles that could be harmful to humans or the environment. If you are unsure as to the toxicity of any particular dust, then you should always treat it as toxic and take the precautions identified in the SDS or shop procedures. Brake and clutch dust are potential toxic dusts that automotive shops must manage. The dust is made up of very fine particles that can easily spread and contaminate an area. One of the more common sources of toxic dust is inside drum brakes and manual transmission bell housings. It is a good idea to avoid all dust if possible, whether it is classified as toxic or not. If you do have to work with dust, never use compressed air to blow it from components or parts, and always use PPE such as face masks, eye protection, and gloves.

K02018 Identify the proper method to clean hazardous dust safely.

After completing a service or repair task on a vehicle, there is often dirt and dust left behind. The chemicals present in this dirt usually contain toxic chemicals that can build up and cause health problems. To keep the levels of dirt and dust to a minimum, clean it up immediately after the task is complete. The vigorous action of sweeping causes the dirt and dust to rise; therefore, when sweeping the floor, use a soft broom that pushes, rather than flicks, the dirt and dust forward. Create smaller piles and dispose of them frequently. Another successful way of cleaning shop dirt and dust is to use a water hose. The

SKILL DRILL 2-1 Identifying Information in an SDS

1. Once you have studied the information on the container label, find the SDS for that particular material. Always check the revision date to ensure that you are reading the most recent update.
2. Note the chemical and trade names for the material, its manufacturer, and the emergency telephone number to call.
3. Find out why this material is potentially hazardous. It may be flammable, it may explode, or it may be poisonous if inhaled or touched with your bare skin. Check the threshold limit values (TLVs). The concentration of this material in the air you breathe in your shop must not exceed these figures. There could be physical symptoms associated with breathing harmful chemicals. Find out what will happen to you if you suffer overexposure to the material, either through breathing it or by coming into physical contact with it. This helps you to take safety precautions, such as wearing eye, face, or skin protection, or a

mask or respirator, while using the material, or like washing your skin afterward.
4. Note the flash point for this material so that you know at what temperature it may catch fire. Also note what kind of fire extinguisher you would use to fight a fire involving this material. The wrong fire extinguisher could make the emergency even worse.
5. Study the reactivity for this material to identify the physical conditions or other materials that you should avoid when using this material. It could be heat, moisture, or some other chemical.
6. Find out what special precautions you should take when working with this material. These include personal protection for your skin, eyes, and lungs, and proper storage and use of the material.
7. Be sure to refresh your knowledge of your SDS from time to time. Be confident that you know how to handle and use the material and what action to take in an emergency, should one occur.

FIGURE 2-33 Used oil and fluids often contain dangerous chemicals and need to be safely recycled or disposed of in an environmentally friendly way.

wastewater must be caught in a settling pit and not run into a storm water drain. Many shops also have floor scrubbers that use a water/soap solution to clean the floor. These shops usually vacuum up the dirty water and store it in a tank until it can be disposed of properly.

Various tools have been developed to clean toxic dust from vehicle components. The most common one is the brake wash station. It uses an aqueous solution to wet down and wash the dust into a collection basin. The basin needs periodic maintenance to properly dispose of the accumulated sludge. This tool is probably the simplest way to effectively deal with hazardous dust because it is easy to set up, use, and store. One system that used to be approved for cleanup of hazardous dust is no longer approved for that purpose. It is called a high-efficiency particulate air (HEPA) dust collection system and used a HEPA filter to trap very small particles. But these types of hazardous dust collection systems are no longer approved.

Used Engine Oil and Fluids

S02003 Properly dispose of used engine oil and other petroleum products.

Used engine oil and fluids are liquids that have been drained from the vehicle, usually during servicing operations. Used oil and fluids often contain dangerous chemicals and impurities such as heavy metals that need to be safely recycled or disposed of in an environmentally friendly way (**FIGURE 2-33**).

There are laws and regulations that control the way in which they are to be handled and disposed. The shop will have policies and procedures that describe how you should handle and dispose of used engine oil and fluids. Be careful not to mix incompatible fluids such as used engine oil and used coolant. Doing so makes the hazardous materials very much more expensive to dispose of.

Generally speaking, petroleum products can be mixed together. Follow your local, state, and federal regulations when disposing of waste fluids. Used engine oil is a hazardous material containing many impurities that can damage your skin. Coming into frequent or prolonged contact with used engine oil can cause dermatitis and other skin disorders, including some forms of cancer. Avoid direct contact as much as possible by always using impervious gloves and other protective clothing, which should be cleaned or replaced regularly. Using a barrier-type hand lotion also helps protect your hands and makes cleaning them much easier. Always follow safe work practices, which minimize the possibility of accidental spills. Keeping a high standard of personal hygiene and cleanliness is important so that you get into the habit of washing off harmful materials as soon as possible after contact. If you have been in periodic contact with used engine oil, you should regularly inspect your skin for signs of damage or deterioration. If you have any concerns, consult your doctor.

▶ First Aid Principles

K02019 Explain the basic first aid procedures when approaching an emergency.

The following information is designed to provide you with an awareness of basic first aid principles and the importance of first aid training courses. You will find general information about how to take care of someone who is injured. However, this information is only a guide. It is not a substitute for training or professional medical assistance. Always seek professional advice when tending to an injured person. One of the best things you can do is take a first aid class and periodic refresher courses. These courses help you stay current on first aid practices as they change. They also help remind you of the importance of preventing accidents so that first aid is less likely to be needed.

First aid is the immediate care given to an injured or suddenly ill person. Learning first aid skills is valuable in the workplace in case an accident or medical emergency arises. First aid courses are available through many organizations, such as the Emergency Care and Safety Institute (ECSI). It is strongly advised that you seek out a certified first aid course and become certified in first aid. The following information highlights some of the principles of first aid.

In the event of an accident, the possibility of injury to the rescuer or further injury to the victim must be evaluated. This means the first step in first aid is to survey the scene. While doing this, try to determine what happened, what dangers may still be present, and the best actions to take. Only remove the injured person from a dangerous area if it is safe for you to do so. When dealing with electrocution or electrical burns, make sure the electrical supply is switched off before attempting any assistance. Always perform first aid techniques as quickly as is safely possible after an injury. When breathing or the heart has stopped, brain damage can occur within four to six minutes. The degree of brain damage increases with each passing minute, so make sure you know what to do, and do it as quickly as is safe to do so.

Prompt care and treatment before the arrival of emergency medical assistance can sometimes mean the difference between life and death. The goals of first aid are to make the immediate environment as safe as possible, preserve the life of the patient, prevent the injury from worsening, prevent additional injuries from occurring, protect the unconscious, promote recovery, comfort the injured, prevent unnecessary delays in treatment, and provide the best possible immediate care for the injured person. When attending to an injured victim, always send for assistance. Make sure the person who stays with the injured victim is more experienced in first aid than the messenger. If you are the only person available, request medical assistance as soon as reasonably possible.

When you approach the scene of an accident or emergency, do the following:

1. Danger: Survey the scene to make sure there are no other dangers, and assist only if it is safe to do so.
2. Response: Check to see if the victim is responsive and breathing. If responsive, ask the victim if he or she needs help. If the victim does not respond, he or she is unresponsive.
3. Send for help: Have a bystander call 9-1-1. Always have the person with the most first aid experience stay with the victim. If alone, call 9-1-1 yourself.
4. Airway: Open the airway by tilting the victim's head back and lifting the chin.
5. Breathing: Check for normal breathing by placing one of your hands on the victim's chest, and lean down so your ear is near the person's mouth. Listen and watch for breathing. If the victim is breathing, monitor the victim for further issues. If the victim is not breathing normally, start CPR.
6. Circulation/CPR (cardiopulmonary resuscitation): If no pulse is present, start chest compressions at the rate of approximately 100 per minute. You can either give sequences of 30 compressions to two breaths, or just compressions if you are reluctant to give mouth to mouth resuscitation. Repeat the compression and breath cycles, or compression only cycles, until an automated external defibrillator (AED) is available or emergency medical system (EMS) personnel arrive.
7. Defibrillation: If a pulse is still not present once an AED arrives, expose the victim's chest and turn on the AED. Attach the AED pads. Ensure that no one touches the victim. Follow the audio and visual prompts from the AED. If no shock is advised, resume CPR immediately (five sets of 30 compressions and two breaths, or compressions by themselves). If a shock is advised, do not touch the victim and give one shock. Or shock as advised by AED. Follow the directions given by the AED.

▶ **TECHNICIAN TIP**

- Some vehicle components, including brake and clutch linings, contain asbestos, which, despite having very good heat properties, is toxic. Asbestos dust causes lung cancer. Complications from breathing the dust may not show until decades after exposure.
- Airborne dust in the shop can also cause breathing problems such as asthma and throat infections.
- Never cause dust from vehicle components to be blown into the air. It can stay floating for many hours, meaning that other people will breathe the dust unknowingly.
- Wear protective gloves whenever using solvents.
- If you are unfamiliar with a solvent or a cleaner, refer to the SDS for information about its correct use and applicable hazards.
- Always wash your hands thoroughly with soap and water after performing repair tasks on brake and clutch components.
- Always wash work clothes separately from other clothes so that toxic dust does not transfer from one garment to another.
- Always wear protective clothing and the appropriate safety equipment.

▶ **TECHNICIAN TIP**

Three important rules of first aid:

1. Know what you must not do.
2. Know what you must do.
3. If you are not sure what procedures to follow, send for trained medical assistance.

▶ Wrap-Up

Ready for Review

- Your employer is responsible for maintaining a safe work environment; you are responsible for working safely.
- Always wear the correct personal protective equipment, such as gloves or hearing protection.
- Personal protective equipment (PPE) protects the body from injury but must fit correctly and be task appropriate.
- Work clothing should be clean, loose enough for movement, but not baggy, and should also be flame-retardant.
- Footwear should be acid- and slip-resistant and made of puncture-proof material.
- Headgear can protect your head from bumps and should hold long hair in place.

- Hand protection includes chemical gloves, leather gloves, light-duty gloves, general-purpose cloth gloves, and barrier cream.
- Hazardous chemicals and oils can be absorbed into your skin.
- Wear ear protection if the sound level is 85 decibels or above.
- Breathing devices include disposable dust masks and respirators.
- Forms of eye protection are safety glasses, welding helmet, gas welding goggles, full face shield, and safety goggles.
- You may need two types of eye protection for some tasks.
- Before starting work, remove all jewelry and watches, and make sure your hair is contained.
- Lifting correctly or seeking assistance helps prevent back injuries.
- Thinking "safety first" will lead to acting safely.
- Accidents and injuries can be avoided by safe work practices.
- OSHA is a federal agency that oversees safe workplace environments and practices.
- The EPA monitors and enforces issues related to environmental safety.
- Shop policies and procedures are designed to ensure compliance with laws and regulations, create a safe working environment, and guide shop practice.
- Shop safety inspections ensure that safety policies and procedures are being followed.
- Safety includes keeping a clean shop with everything put where it belongs and all spills cleaned up.
- Safety signs include a signal word, background color, text, and a pictorial message.
- Shop safety equipment includes handrails, machinery guards, painted lines, soundproof rooms, adequate ventilation, gas extraction hoses, doors and gates, and temporary barriers.
- Air quality is an important safety concern.
- All shops require proper ventilation.
- Carbon monoxide and carbon dioxide from running engines can create a hazardous work environment.
- Electrical safety in a shop is important to prevent shocks, burns, fires, and explosions.
- Portable electrical equipment should be the proper voltage and should always be inspected for damage.
- Use caution when plugging in or using a portable shop light.
- Fuels and fuel vapors are potential fire hazards.
- Use fuel retrievers when draining fuel, and have a spill response kit nearby.
- Fuel, oxygen, and heat must all be present for fire to occur.
- Types of fires are classified as A, B, C, D, or K, and fire extinguishers match them accordingly.
- Do not fight a fire unless you can do so safely.
- Operating a fire extinguisher involves the PASS method: pull, aim, squeeze, and sweep.
- Every shop should mark evacuation routes; always know the evacuation route for your shop.
- Identify hazards and hazardous materials in your work environment.
- Safety data sheets contain important information on each hazardous material in the shop.
- Using a soap and water solution is the safest method of cleaning dust or dirt that may be toxic.
- Used engine oil and fluids must be handled and disposed of properly.
- First aid involves providing immediate care to an ill or injured person.
- Do not perform first aid if it is unsafe to do so.

Key Terms

barrier cream A cream that looks and feels like a moisturizing cream but has a specific formula to provide extra protection from chemicals and oils.

double insulated Tools or appliances that are designed in such a way that no single failure can result in a dangerous voltage coming into contact with the outer casing of the device.

ear protection Protective gear worn when the sound levels exceed 85 decibels, when working around operating machinery for any period of time, or when the equipment you are using produces loud noise.

engineering and work practice controls Systems and procedures required by OSHA and put in place by employers to protect their employees from hazards.

Environmental Protection Agency (EPA) Federal government agency that deals with issues related to environmental safety.

first aid The immediate care given to an injured or suddenly ill person.

gas welding goggles Protective gear designed for gas welding; they provide protection against foreign particles entering the eye and are tinted to reduce the glare of the welding flame.

hazardous material Any material that poses an unreasonable risk of damage or injury to persons, property, or the environment if it is not properly controlled during handling, storage, manufacture, processing, packaging, use and disposal, or transportation.

headgear Protective gear that includes items like hairnets, caps, or hard hats.

heat buildup A dangerous condition that occurs when the glove can no longer absorb or reflect heat, and heat is transferred to the inside of the glove.

Occupational Safety and Health Administration (OSHA) Government agency created to provide national leadership in occupational safety and health.

personal protective equipment (PPE) Safety equipment designed to protect the technician, such as safety boots, gloves, clothing, protective eyewear, and hearing protection.

policy A guiding principle that sets the shop direction.

procedure A list of the steps required to get the same result each time a task or activity is performed.

respirator Protective gear used to protect the wearer from inhaling harmful dusts or gases. Respirators range from single-use disposable masks to types that have replaceable cartridges. The correct types of cartridge must be used for the type of contaminant encountered.

safety data sheet (SDS) A sheet that provides information about handling, use, and storage of a material that may be hazardous.

safety glasses Safety glasses are protective eye glasses with built-in side shields to help protect your eyes from the front and side. Approved safety glasses should be worn whenever you are in a workshop. They are designed to help protect your eyes from direct impact or debris damage.

threshold limit value (TLV) The maximum allowable concentration of a given material in the surrounding air.

toxic dust Any dust that may contain fine particles that could be harmful to humans or the environment.

welding helmet Protective gear designed for arc welding; it provides protection against foreign particles entering the eye, and the lens is tinted to reduce the glare of the welding arc.

Review Questions

1. Neoprene gloves are ideal for protection from:
   a. dust.
   b. heavy materials.
   c. changing workplace temperatures.
   d. certain acids and other chemicals.
2. You can use a disposable dust mask to protect yourself against:
   a. asbestos dust.
   b. brake dust.
   c. brake fluid vapors.
   d. paint solvents.
3. When bending down to lift something, you should:
   a. bend over with straight legs.
   b. put your feet together.
   c. bend your knees.
   d. bend your back.
4. Which of the following works toward finding the most effective ways to help prevent worker fatalities and workplace injuries and illnesses?
   a. EPA
   b. FDA
   c. OSHA
   d. ASA
5. The list of steps required to get the same result each time a task or activity is performed is known as the:
   a. shop policy.
   b. shop regulations.
   c. shop procedure.
   d. shop system.
6. The signal word that indicates a potentially hazardous situation, which, if not avoided, could result in death or serious injury is:
   a. danger.
   b. caution.
   c. warning.
   d. hazardous.
7. Which of these should not be used in a shop?
   a. Incandescent bulbs
   b. Extension cords
   c. Low-voltage tools
   d. Air-operated tools
8. To operate a fire extinguisher, follow the acronym for fire extinguisher use: PASS, which stands for:
   a. Press, aim, squeeze, sweep.
   b. Pull, aim, shake, sweep.
   c. Press, aim, shake, sweep.
   d. Pull, aim, squeeze, sweep.
9. Which of these should never be used to remove dust?
   a. Floor scrubbers
   b. Water hoses
   c. Compressed air
   d. Brake wash stations
10. When disposing of used liquids:
    a. federal regulations need not be followed.
    b. incompatible liquids can be mixed together.
    c. impervious gloves are not needed.
    d. petroleum products can be mixed together.

ASE Technician A/Technician B Style Questions

1. Tech A says that personal protective equipment (PPE) does not include clothing. Tech B says that the PPE used should be based on the task you are performing. Who is correct?
   a. Tech A
   b. Tech B
   c. Both A and B
   d. Neither A nor B
2. Tech A says that rings, watches, and other jewelry should be removed prior to working. Tech B says that you should always wear cuffed pants when working in a shop. Who is correct?
   a. Tech A
   b. Tech B
   c. Both A and B
   d. Neither A nor B
3. Tech A says that one use of barrier creams is to make cleaning your hands easier. Tech B says that hearing protection only needs to be worn by people operating loud equipment. Who is correct?
   a. Tech A
   b. Tech B
   c. Both A and B
   d. Neither A nor B

4. Tech A says that tinted safety glasses can be worn when working outside. Tech B says that welding can cause a sunburn. Who is correct?
   a. Tech A
   b. Tech B
   c. Both A and B
   d. Neither A nor B

5. Tech A says that exposure to solvents may have long-term effects. Tech B says that accidents are almost always avoidable. Who is correct?
   a. Tech A
   b. Tech B
   c. Both A and B
   d. Neither A nor B

6. Tech A says that after an accident you should take measures to avoid it in the future. Tech B says that it is okay to block an exit for a shop if you are actively working. Who is correct?
   a. Tech A
   b. Tech B
   c. Both A and B
   d. Neither A nor B

7. Tech A says that both OSHA and the EPA can inspect facilities for violations. Tech B says that a shop safety rule does not have to be reviewed once put in place. Who is correct?
   a. Tech A
   b. Tech B
   c. Both A and B
   d. Neither A nor B

8. Tech A says that a safety data sheet (SDS) contains information on procedures to repair a vehicle. Tech B says that you only need an SDS after an accident occurs. Who is correct?
   a. Tech A
   b. Tech B
   c. Both A and B
   d. Neither A nor B

9. Tech A says that one approved way to clean dust off brakes is with compressed air. Tech B says that some auto parts may contain asbestos. Who is correct?
   a. Tech A
   b. Tech B
   c. Both A and B
   d. Neither A nor B

10. Tech A says that if you are unsure of what personal protective equipment (PPE) to use to perform a job, you should just use what is nearby. Tech B says that air tools are less likely to shock you than electrically powered tools. Who is correct?
    a. Tech A
    b. Tech B
    c. Both A and B
    d. Neither A nor B

CHAPTER 3

Basic Tools and Precision Measuring

NATEF Tasks

- **N03001** Demonstrate safe handling and use of appropriate tools.
- **N03002** Utilize safe procedures for handling of tools and equipment.
- **N03003** Identify standard and metric designation.

- **N03004** Demonstrate proper use of precision measuring tools (i.e., micrometer, dial-indicator, dial-caliper).
- **N03005** Demonstrate proper cleaning, storage, and maintenance of tools and equipment.

Knowledge Objectives

After reading this chapter, you will be able to:

- **K03001** Describe the safety procedures to take when handling and using tools.
- **K03002** Describe how to properly lockout and tag-out faulty equipment and tools.
- **K03003** Describe typical tool storage methods.
- **K03004** Identify tools and their usage in automotive applications.
- **K03005** Describe the type and use of wrenches.
- **K03006** Describe the type and use of sockets.
- **K03007** Describe the type and use of torque wrenches.
- **K03008** Describe the type and use of pliers.
- **K03009** Describe the type and use of cutting tools.
- **K03010** Describe the type and use of Allen wrenches.
- **K03011** Describe the type and use of screwdrivers.
- **K03012** Describe type and use of magnetic pickup tools and mechanical fingers.
- **K03013** Describe the type and use of hammers.
- **K03014** Describe the type and use of chisels.
- **K03015** Describe the type and use of punches.
- **K03016** Describe the type and use of pry bars.
- **K03017** Describe the type and use of gasket scrapers.

- **K03018** Describe the type and use of files.
- **K03019** Describe the type and use of clamps.
- **K03020** Describe the type and use of taps and dies.
- **K03021** Describe the type and use of screw extractors.
- **K03022** Describe the type and use of pullers.
- **K03023** Describe the type and use of flaring tools.
- **K03024** Describe the type and use of riveting tools.
- **K03025** Describe the type and use of measuring tapes.
- **K03026** Describe the type and use of steel rulers.
- **K03027** Describe the type and use of outside, inside, and depth micrometers.
- **K03028** Describe the type and use of telescoping gauges.
- **K03029** Describe the type and use of split ball gauges.
- **K03030** Describe the type and use of dial bore gauges.
- **K03031** Describe the type and use of vernier calipers.
- **K03032** Describe the type and use of dial indicators.
- **K03033** Describe the type and use of straight edges.
- **K03034** Describe the type and use of feeler gauges.
- **K03035** Describe the importance of proper cleaning and storage of tools.

Skills Objectives

There are no Skills Objectives for this chapter.

You Are the Automotive Technician

After finishing work on the last vehicle of the day, you are required to return your workstation back to order. You clean, inspect, and return tools and equipment to their designated place. You wipe up any spills, according to the shop procedure, and clear the floor of any debris, to avoid slips and falls. During your workspace inspection, you determine that the insulation on the droplight cord is frayed, and there are some tools that need to be cleaned and put away.

1. What needs to happen with the droplight?
2. What should you do to with a micrometer before storing it?
3. How do you check a micrometer for accuracy?
4. Describe a double flare and how it is different from a single flare.

▶ Introduction

In this chapter, we explore a variety of tool and basic shop equipment topics that are fundamental to your success as an automotive technician. They provide the means for work to be undertaken on vehicles, from lifting to diagnosing, removing, installing, cleaning, and inspecting. Nearly all shop tasks involve the use of some sort of tool or piece of equipment (**FIGURE 3-1**). This makes their purchase, use, and maintenance very important to the overall performance of the shop. In fact, most tool purchases are considered an investment because they generate income when they are used. For example, if you can buy a tool for $100 that saves you two hours of working time every time you use it, you only need to use it a couple of times in order to pay for it. Then, every time after that, it pays you a bonus. This means that you need to treat tools like your own personal moneymakers. One way to do that is to always use tools and equipment in the way they are designed to be used. Don't abuse them. Think about the task at hand, identify the most effective tools to do the task, inspect the tool before using it, use it correctly, clean and inspect it after you use it, and store it in the correct location. Doing all of these things ensures that your tools will be available the next time you use them and that they will last a long time.

▶ General Safety Guidelines

Although it is important to be trained on the safe use of tools and equipment, it is even more critical to have a safe attitude. A safe attitude will help you avoid being involved in an accident. Students who think they will never be involved in an accident will not be as aware of unsafe situations as they should be. And that can lead to accidents. So while we are covering the various tools and equipment you will encounter in the shop, pay close attention to the safety and operation procedures. Tools are a technician's best friend, but if used improperly, they can injure or kill (**FIGURE 3-2**).

Work Safe and Stay Safe

Whenever using tools, always think safety first. There is nothing more important than your personal safety. If tools (both hand and power) are used incorrectly, you can potentially injure yourself and others. Always follow equipment and shop instructions, including the use of recommended personal protective equipment (PPE). Accidents only take a second or two to happen but can take a lifetime to recover from. You are ultimately responsible for your safety, so remember to work safe and stay safe.

Safe Handling and Use of Tools

Tools must be safely handled and used to prevent injury and damage. Always inspect tools prior to use, and never use damaged tools. Check the manufacturer and the shop procedures, or ask your supervisor if you are uncertain about how to use tools. Inspect and clean tools when you are finished using them. Always return tools to their correct storage location.

To safely handle and use appropriate tools, follow **SKILL DRILL 3-1**.

Safe Procedures for Handling Tools and Equipment

Some tools are heavy or awkward to use, so seek assistance if required, and use correct manual handling techniques when using tools. To utilize safe procedures for handling tools and equipment, follow the steps in **SKILL DRILL 3-2**.

Tool Usage

Tools extend our abilities to perform many tasks; for example, jacks, stands, and hoists extend our ability to lift and hold heavy objects. Hand tools extend our ability to perform

N03001 Demonstrate safe handling and use of appropriate tools.

N03002 Utilize safe procedures for handling of tools and equipment.

K03001 Describe the safety procedures to take when handling and using tools.

FIGURE 3-1 Technicians rely on tools to perform work.

FIGURE 3-2 Tools used improperly can injure or kill.

SKILL DRILL 3-1 Safe Handling and Use of Tools

1. Select the correct tool(s) to undertake tasks.

2. Inspect tools prior to use to ensure they are in good working order. If tools are faulty, remove them from service according to shop procedures.

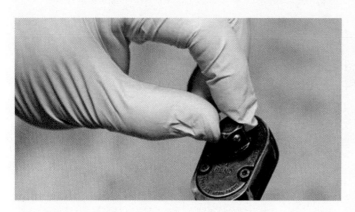

3. Clean tools prior to use if necessary.

4. Use tools to complete the task while ensuring manufacturer and shop procedures are followed. Always use tools safely to prevent injury and damage.

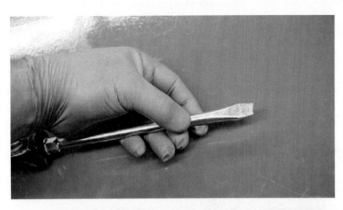

5. Ensure tools are clean and in good working order after use. Report and tag damaged tools, and remove them from service, following shop procedures.

6. Return tools to correct storage locations.

SKILL DRILL 3-2 Safe Procedures for Handling Tools and Equipment

1. Seek assistance if tools and equipment are too heavy or too awkward to be managed by a single person.

2. Inspect tools and equipment for possible defects before starting work. Report and/or tag faulty tools and equipment according to shop procedures.

Continued

3. Select and wear appropriate PPE for the tools and equipment being used.

4. Use tools and equipment safely.

5. Check tools for faults after using them and report and/or tag faulty tools and equipment according to shop procedures.

6. Clean and return tools and equipment to correct storage locations when tasks are completed.

fundamental tasks like gripping, turning, tightening, measuring, and cutting (**FIGURE 3-3**). Electrical meters enable us to measure things we cannot see, feel, or hear; and power and air tools multiply our strength by performing tasks quickly and efficiently. As you are working, always think about what tool can make the job easier, safer, or more efficient. As you become familiar with more tools, your productivity, quality of work, and effectiveness will improve.

FIGURE 3-3 Tools extend our abilities.

K03002 Describe how to properly lockout and tag-out faulty equipment and tools.

K03003 Describe typical tool storage methods.

Every tool is designed to be used in a certain way to do the job safely. It is critical to use a tool in the way it was designed to be used and to do so safely. For example, a screwdriver is designed to tighten and loosen screws, not to be used as a chisel. Ratchets are designed to turn sockets, not to be used as a hammer. Think about the task you are undertaking, select the correct tools for the task, and use each tool as it was designed.

Lockout/Tag-Out

Lockout/tag-out is an umbrella term that describes a set of safety practices and procedures that are intended to reduce the risk of technicians inadvertently using tools, equipment, or materials that have been determined to be unsafe or potentially unsafe, or that are in the process of being serviced. An example of lockout would be physically securing a broken, unsafe, or out-of-service tool so that it cannot be used by a technician. In many cases, the item is also tagged out so it is not inadvertently placed back into service or operated. An example of tag-out would be affixing a clear and obvious label to a piece of equipment that describes the fault found, the name of the person who found the fault, and the date that the fault was found, and that warns not to use the equipment (**FIGURE 3-4**).

Tool Storage

Typically, technicians have a selection of their own tools, which include various hand tools, air tools, measuring tools, and electrical meters (**FIGURE 3-5**). Often they add to their toolbox over time. These tools are kept in a toolbox that can be rolled around as needed but is typically kept in the technician's work stall. The shop usually has a selection of specialty tools and equipment that is available for technicians to use on a shared basis. These tools are located in specific areas around the shop, typically in a centralized location so they are relatively easy to access (**FIGURE 3-6**). They include specialized manufacturer tools, such as pullers or installation tools; high-cost tools such as factory scan tools; and tools that are not portable, such as hoists and tire machines. But because they are shared by everyone in the shop, it is critical that they are inspected for damage and put in their proper storage space after each use so they will be available to the other technicians.

FIGURE 3-4 A. An example of lockout would be physically locking out a tool or piece of equipment so that it cannot be accessed and used by someone who may be unaware of the potential danger of doing so. **B.** An example of tag-out would be affixing a clear and obvious label to a piece of equipment that describes the fault found and that warns not to use the equipment.

FIGURE 3-5 Typical technician's toolbox.

FIGURE 3-6 Manufacturer's special tools.

To identify tools and their usage in automotive applications, follow these steps:

1. Create a list of tools in your toolbox and identify their application for automotive repair and service.
2. Look through the shop's tool storage areas, and create a list of the tools found in each storage area; identify their application for automotive repair and service.

Standard and Metric Designations

Many tools, measuring instruments, and fasteners come in United States customary system (USCS) sizes, more commonly referred to as "standard," or in metric sizes. Tools and measuring instruments can be identified as standard or metric by markings identifying their size on tools or the increments on a measuring tool. **Fasteners** bought new have their designation identified on the packaging. Other fasteners may have to be measured by a ruler or **vernier caliper** to identify their designation. Manufacturer's charts showing thread and fastener sizing assist in identifying standard or metric sizing.

To identify standard and metric designation, follow these steps:

1. Examine the component, tool, or fastener to see if any marking identifies it as standard or metric. Manufacturer specifications and shop manuals can be referred to and may identify components as standard or metric (**FIGURE 3-7**).
2. If no markings are available, use measuring devices to gauge the size of the item and compare thread and fastener charts to identify the sizing. Inch-to-metric conversion charts assist in identifying component designation (**FIGURE 3-8**).

N03003 Identify standard and metric designation.

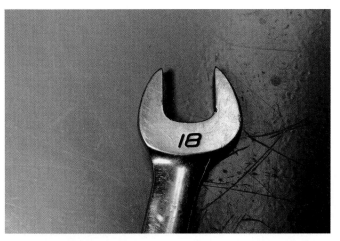

FIGURE 3-7 Manufacturer specifications and shop manuals can be referred to and may identify components as standard or metric.

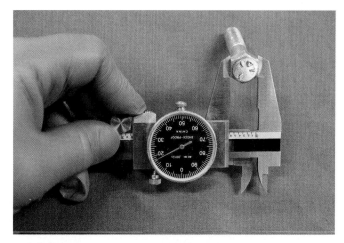

FIGURE 3-8 If no markings are available, use measuring devices to gauge the size of the item and compare thread and fastener charts to identify the sizing.

K03004 Identify tools and their usage in automotive applications.

▶ TECHNICIAN TIP

Invest in quality tools. Because tools extend your abilities, poor-quality tools affect the quality and quantity of your work. Price is not always the best indicator of quality, but it plays a role. As you learn the purpose and function of the tools in this chapter, you should be able to identify high-quality tools versus poor-quality tools by looking at them, handling them, and putting them to work.

K03005 Describe the type and use of wrenches.

▶ Basic Hand Tools

Like all tools, hand tools extend our ability to do work. Hand tools come in a variety of shapes, sizes, and functions (**FIGURE 3-9**). A large percentage of your personal tools will be hand tools. Over the years, manufacturers have introduced new fasteners, wire harness terminals, quick-connect fittings for fuel and other lines, and additional technologies that require their own different types of hand tools. This means that technicians need to continually add updated tools to their toolbox.

Speaking of toolboxes, technicians need to invest in a quality toolbox to keep their tools secure, so toolboxes should have enough capacity to hold all current and future tools. They should be built to last because a toolbox is in continuous use throughout the workday. A toolbox should have drawers that can handle the weight of the tools in it. Plus it should open and close easily; drawer slides that use bearings make them much easier to open and close (**FIGURE 3-10**). The toolbox should also be equipped with an easy-to-use locking system to secure the tools when they aren't being used.

Wrenches

Wrenches are used to tighten and loosen nuts and **bolts**, which are two types of fasteners. There are three commonly used wrenches: the **box-end wrench**, the **open-end wrench**, and the **combination wrench** (**FIGURE 3-11**). The box-end wrench fits fully around the head of the bolt or nut and grips each of the six points at the corners, just like a socket. This is exactly the sort of grip needed if a nut or bolt is very tight, and makes the box-end wrench less likely to round off the points on the head of the bolt than the open-end wrench. The ends of box-end wrenches are bent or offset, so they are easier to grip and have different-sized heads at each end (**FIGURE 3-12**). One disadvantage of the box-end wrench is that it can be awkward to use once the nut or bolt has been loosened a bit, because you have to lift it off the head of the fastener and move it to each new position.

The open-end wrench is open on the end, and the two parallel flats only grip two points of the fastener. Open-end wrenches usually either have different-sized heads on each end of the wrench, or they have the same size, but with different angles (**FIGURE 3-13**). The head is at an angle to the handle and is not bent or offset, so it can be flipped over and used on both sides. This is a good wrench to use in very tight spaces as you can flip it over and get a new angle so the head can catch new points on the fastener. Although an open-end wrench often gives the best access to a fastener, if the fastener is extremely

FIGURE 3-9 Hand tools.

FIGURE 3-10 Toolbox drawers need to open and close easily.

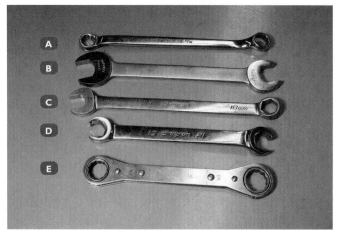

FIGURE 3-11 **A.** Box-end wrench. **B.** Open-end wrench. **C.** Combination wrench. **D.** Flare nut wrench. **E.** Ratcheting box-end wrench.

FIGURE 3-12 Box-end wrenches.

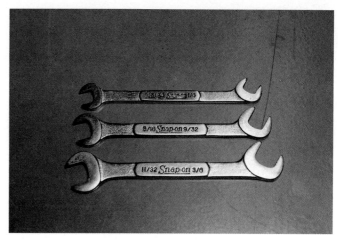

FIGURE 3-13 Types of open-end wrenches.

tight, the open-end wrench should not be used, as this type of wrench only grips two points. If the jaws flex slightly, the wrench can suddenly slip when force is applied. This slippage can round off the points of the fastener. The best way to approach a tight fastener is to use a box-end wrench to break the bolt or nut free, then use the open-end wrench to finish the job. The open-end wrench should only be used on fasteners that are no more than firmly tightened.

The combination wrench has an open-end head on one end and a box-end head on the other end (**FIGURE 3-14**). Both ends are usually of the same size. That way the box-end wrench can be used to break the bolt loose, and the open end can be used for turning the bolt. Because of its versatility, this is probably the most popular wrench for technicians.

A variation on the open-end wrench is the **flare nut wrench**, also called a flare tubing wrench, or line wrench. It gives a better grip than the open-end wrench because it grabs all six points of the fastener, not two (**FIGURE 3-15**). However, because it is open on the end, it is not as strong as a box-end wrench. The partially open sixth side lets the wrench be placed over the tubing or pipe so the wrench can be used to turn the tube fittings. Do not use the flare nut wrench on extremely tight fasteners as the jaws may spread, damaging the nut.

One other open-end wrench is the open-end adjustable wrench or crescent wrench. This wrench has a movable jaw that can be adjusted by turning an adjusting screw to fit any fastener within its range (**FIGURE 3-16**). It should only be used if other wrenches are not available because it is not as strong as a fixed wrench, so it can slip off and damage the head of tight bolts or nuts. Still, it is a handy tool to have because it can be adjusted to fit most any fastener size.

A **ratcheting box-end wrench** is a useful tool in some applications because it does not require removal of the tool to reposition it. It has an inner piece that fits over and grabs the points on the fastener and is able to rotate within the outer housing. A ratcheting mechanism lets it rotate in one direction and lock in the other direction. In some cases, the wrench just needs to be flipped over to be used in the opposite direction. In other cases, it has a lever that changes the direction from clockwise to counterclockwise (**FIGURE 3-17**). Just be careful to not overstress this tool by using it to tighten or loosen very

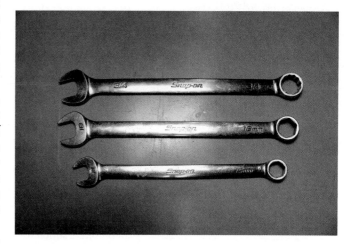

FIGURE 3-14 Combination wrenches.

FIGURE 3-15 Flare nut wrenches.

FIGURE 3-16 Open-end adjustable wrench.

FIGURE 3-17 Ratcheting box-end wrench.

tight fasteners, as the outer housing is not very strong. There is also a ratcheting open-end wrench, but it uses no moving parts. One of the sides is partially removed so that only the bottom one-third remains to catch a point on the bolt (**FIGURE 3-18**). When it is used, the normal side works just like a standard open-end wrench. The shorter side of the open-end wrench catches the point on the fastener so it can be turned. When moving the wrench to get a new bite, the wrench is pulled slightly outward, disengaging the short side while leaving the long side to slide along the faces of the bolt. The wrench is then rotated to the new position and pushed back in so the short side engages the next point. This wrench, like other open-end wrenches, is not designed to tighten or loosen tight fasteners, but it does work well in blind places where a socket or ratcheting box-end wrench cannot be used.

Specialized wrenches such as the **pipe wrench** grip pipes and can exert a lot of force to turn them (**FIGURE 3-19**). Because the handle pivots slightly, the more pressure put on the handle to turn the wrench, the more the grip tightens. The jaws are hardened and serrated, and increasing the pressure also increases the risk of marking or even gouging metal from the pipe. The jaw is adjustable, so it can be threaded in or out to fit different pipe sizes. Also, they come in different lengths, allowing you to increase the leverage applied to the pipe.

A specialized wrench called an **oil filter wrench** grabs the filter and gives you extra leverage to remove an oil filter when it is tight. These wrenches are available in various designs and sizes (**FIGURE 3-20**), and some are adjustable to fit many filter sizes. Also note that an oil filter wrench should be used *only* to remove an oil filter, never to install it. Almost all oil filters should be installed and tightened by hand.

▶ **TECHNICIAN TIP**

Wrenches (which are also known as spanners in some countries) will only do a job properly if they are the right size for the given nut or bolt head. The size used to describe a wrench is the distance across the flats of the nut or bolt. There are two systems in common use—standard (in inches) and metric (in millimeters). Each system provides a range of sizes, which are identified by either a fraction, which indicates fractions of an inch for the standard system, or a number, which indicates millimeters for the metric system. In most cases, standard and metric tools cannot be used interchangeably on a particular fastener. Even though a metric tool fits a standard sized fastener, it may not grip as tight, which could cause it to round the head of the fastener off.

FIGURE 3-18 Ratcheting open-end wrench.

FIGURE 3-19 Pipe wrench.

FIGURE 3-20 Oil filter wrenches.

Using Wrenches Correctly

Choosing the correct wrench for a job usually depends on two things: how tight the fastener is and how much room there is to get the wrench onto the fastener, and then to turn it. When being used, it is always possible that a wrench could slip. Before putting a lot of tension on the wrench, try to anticipate what will happen if it does slip. If possible, it is usually better to pull a wrench toward you than to push it away (**FIGURE 3-21**). If you have to push, use an open palm to push, so your knuckles won't get crushed if the wrench slips. If pulling toward yourself, make sure your face is not close to your hand or in line with your pulling motion. Many technicians have punched themselves in the face when the wrench slipped.

Sockets

Sockets are very popular because of their adaptability and ease of use (**FIGURE 3-22**). Sockets are a good choice where the top of the fastener is reasonably accessible. The **socket** fits onto the fastener snugly and grips it on all six corners, providing the type of grip needed on any nut or bolt that is extremely tight. Sockets come in a variety of configurations, and technicians usually have a lot of sockets so they can get in a multitude of tight places. Individual sockets fit a particular size nut or bolt, so they are usually purchased in sets.

K03006 Describe the type and use of sockets.

FIGURE 3-21 A. Pulling on a wrench is generally better than pushing on a wrench. **B.** Pushing regularly results in bruised or broken knuckles.

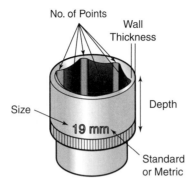

FIGURE 3-22 The anatomy of a socket.

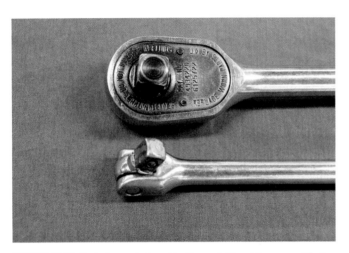

FIGURE 3-23 Sockets are designed to fit a matching drive on a ratchet.

FIGURE 3-24 A. Standard wall socket. **B.** Impact socket.

Because sockets are usually purchased in sets, with each set providing a slightly different capability, you can see why technicians could easily have several hundred sockets in their toolbox. Having a variety of sockets allows the technician to do jobs easier and quicker, which makes them an investment. Turning a socket requires a handle (**FIGURE 3-27**).

Sockets are classified by the following characteristics:

- Standard or metric
- Size of drive used to turn them: 1/2" (12.7 mm), 3/8" (9.525 mm), and 1/4" (6.35 mm) are most common; 1" (25.4 mm) and 3/4" (19.05 mm) are less common.
- Number of points: 6 and 12 are most common; 4 and 8 are less common.
- Depth of socket: Standard and deep are most common; shallow is less common.
- Thickness of wall: Standard and impact are most common; thin wall is less common.

Sockets are built with a recessed square drive that fits over the square drive of the ratchet or other driver (**FIGURE 3-23**). The size of the drive determines how much twisting force can be applied to the socket. The larger the drive, the larger the twisting force. Small fasteners usually only need a small torque, so having too large of a drive may make it so the socket cannot gain access to the bolt. For fasteners that are really tight, an impact wrench exerts a lot more torque on a socket than turning it by hand does. Impact sockets are usually thicker walled than standard wall sockets and have six points so they can withstand the forces generated by the impact wrench as well as grip the fastener securely (**FIGURE 3-24**).

Six- and 12-point sockets fit the heads of hexagonal-shaped fasteners. Four- and 8-point sockets fit the heads of square-shaped fasteners (**FIGURE 3-25**). Because 6-point and 4-point sockets fit the exact shape of the fastener, they have the strongest grip on the fastener, but they only can fit on the fastener in half as many positions as a 12- or 8-point socket, making them harder to fit onto the fastener in places where the ratchet handle is restricted.

Another factor in accessing a fastener is the depth of the socket. If a nut is threaded quite a way down a stud or bolt, then a standard length socket will not fit far enough over the stud to reach the nut (**FIGURE 3-26**). In this case, a deep socket will usually reach the nut.

The most common socket handle, the **ratchet**, makes easy work of tightening or loosening a nut where not a lot of pressure is involved. It can be set to turn in either direction and does not need much room to swing. It is built to be convenient, not super strong, so too much pressure could strip the ratchet mechanism. For heavier tightening or loosening, a breaker bar gives the most leverage. When that is not available, a **sliding T-handle** may be more useful. With this tool, both hands can be used, and the position of the T-piece is adjustable to clear any obstructions when turning it. The connection between the socket and the accessory is made by a square drive. The larger the drive, the heavier and bulkier the socket will be. The 1/4" (6.35 mm) drive is for small work in

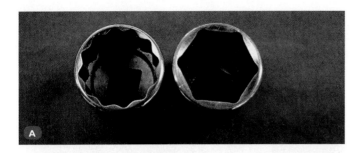

FIGURE 3-25 A. Six- and 12-point sockets. **B.** Four- and 8-point sockets.

FIGURE 3-26 A. Deep socket. **B.** Standard length socket.

difficult areas. The 3/8" (9.525 mm) drive accessories handle a lot of general work where torque requirements are not too high. The 1/2" (12.7 mm) drive is required for all-around service. The 3/4" (19.05 mm) and 1" (25.4 mm) drives are required for large work with high torque settings.

Many fasteners are located in positions where access can be difficult. There are many different lengths of extensions available to allow the socket to be on the fastener while extending the drive point out to where a handle can be attached. Because extensions come in various lengths, they can be connected together to get just the right length needed for a particular situation.

If an object is in the way of getting a socket on a fastener, a flexible joint is used to apply the turning force to the socket through an angle. This can allow you to still turn the socket even though you are no longer directly in line with the fastener. There are four common types of flexible joints: U-joint style, wobble extension, cable extension, and flex socket (**FIGURE 3-28**). The flex

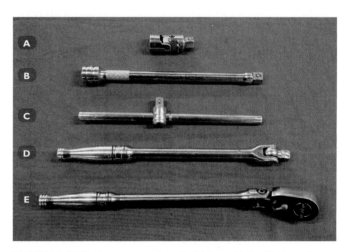

FIGURE 3-27 Tools to turn sockets. **A.** Universal joint. **B.** Extension. **C.** T-handle. **D.** Breaker bar. **E.** Ratchet.

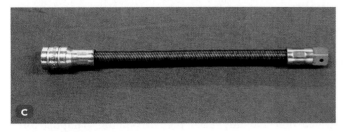

FIGURE 3-28 Flexible extensions. **A.** U-joint style. **B.** Wobble extension style. **C.** Cable extension style. **D.** Flex socket style.

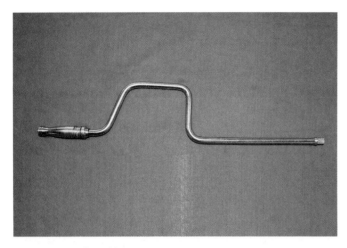

FIGURE 3-29 Speed brace.

FIGURE 3-30 Lug wrench.

socket has the universal built into it, so it's overall length is shorter, making it able to get into tighter spaces. In some situations, you may need to use more than one flexible joint to get around objects that are in the way. This is especially true when removing some bell housing bolts on some transmissions.

A **speed brace** or speeder handle is the fastest way to spin a fastener on or off a thread by hand, but it cannot apply much torque to the fastener; therefore, it is mainly used to remove a fastener that has already been loosened or to run the fastener onto the thread until it begins to tighten (**FIGURE 3-29**).

A **lug wrench** has special-sized lug nut sockets permanently attached to it. One common model has four different-sized sockets, one on each arm (**FIGURE 3-30**). Never hit or jump on a lug wrench when loosening lug nuts. If the lug wrench will not remove them, you should use an impact wrench. The impact wrench provides a hammering effect in conjunction with rotation to help loosen tight fasteners. *Never* use an impact wrench to tighten lug fasteners. Torque all lug fasteners to the proper torque with a properly calibrated torque wrench. And do it in the proper sequence.

Torque and Torque Wrenches

K03007 Describe the type and use of torque wrenches.

Bolt tension is what keeps a bolt from loosening and what causes it to hold parts together with the proper clamping force. **Torque** is the twisting force used to create bolt tension so that surfaces are clamped together with the proper force. The torque value is the amount of twisting force applied to a fastener by the torque wrench. A foot-pound is described as the amount of twisting force applied to a shaft by a perpendicular lever 1 ft (0.30m) long with a weight of 1 lb (0.45 kg) placed on the outer end (**FIGURE 3-31**). A torque value of 100 ft-lb (13.83 m-kg) is the same as a 100 lb (45.36 kg) weight placed at the end of a 1' (0.30m) long lever. A torque value of an inch-pound is 1 lb (0.45 kg) placed at the end of a 1" (25.40 mm) long lever. This means that 12 in-lb equals 1 ft-lb (0.14 m-kg) and vice versa. A newton meter (Nm) is described as the amount of twisting force applied to a shaft by a perpendicular lever 1 meter long with a force of 1 newton applied to the outer end. A torque value of 100 Nm is the same as applying a 100-newton force to the end of a 1 m long lever. One ft-lb is equal to 1.35 Nm. So torque is the measurement of twisting force.

Torque Charts

Torque specifications for bolts and nuts in vehicles are usually contained within service information. Bolt, nut, and stud manufacturers also produce torque charts, which contain the information you need to determine the maximum torque of bolts or nuts. For example, most charts include the bolt diameter, threads per inch, grade, and maximum torque setting for both dry and lubricated bolts and nuts (**FIGURE 3-32**).

A lubricated bolt and nut reach their maximum clamping force at a lower torque setting than if they are dry. In practice, most torque

Torque = 1 ft-lb

Force = 1 lb

Distance = 1 ft

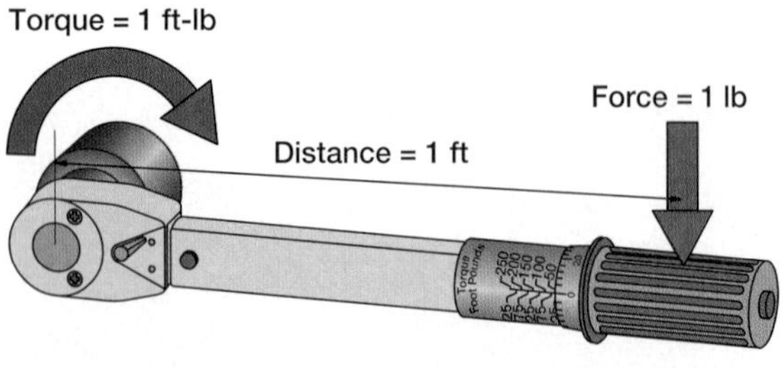

FIGURE 3-31 Torque is the measurement of twisting force. 1 ft-lb of torque.

specifications call for the nuts and bolts to have dry threads prior to tightening. There are some exceptions, so close examination of the torque specification is critical. Also remember that the bolt manufacturer's torque chart is a maximum recommended torque, not necessarily the torque required by the vehicle manufacturer for the specific application that the bolt is used for.

Torque Wrenches

A **torque wrench** is also known as a tension wrench (**FIGURE 3-33**) and is used to tighten fasteners to a predetermined torque. The drive on the end fits any socket and accessory of the same drive size found in ordinary socket sets. Although manufacturers do not specify torque settings for every nut and bolt, when they do, it is important to follow the specifications. For example, manufacturers specify a torque for head bolts.

The torque specified ensures that the bolt provides the proper clamping pressure and will not come loose, but will not be so tight as to risk breaking the bolt or stripping the threads. The torque value is specified in foot-pounds (ft-lb), inch-pounds (in-lb), or newton meters (N m).

Torque wrenches come in various types: beam style, clicker, dial, and electronic (**FIGURE 3-34**). The simplest and least expensive is the beam-style torque wrench, which uses a spring steel beam that flexes under tension. A smaller fixed rod then indicates the amount of torque on a scale mounted to the bar. The amount of deflection of the bar coincides with the amount of torque on the scale. One drawback of this design is that you have to be positioned directly above the scale so you can read it accurately. That can be a problem when working under the hood of a vehicle.

The clicker-style torque wrench uses an adjustable clutch inside that slips (clicks) when the preset torque is reached. You can set it for a particular torque on the handle

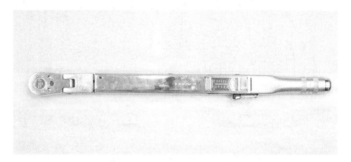

Bolt Size	TPI	Tensile Stress Area	Fastener Coating	Bolt Torque & Clamp Load	10,000 psi	25,000 psi	SAE J429- Grade 2	SAE J429- Grade 5	SAE J429- Grade 8
3/8 JNC	16	0.0775		Clamp Load (Lb)	775	1,937	3,196	4,940	6,974
			Lubricated		4	9	15	23	33
			Zinc Plated	Torque (Ft-Lb)	4	11	18	28	39
			Plain - Dry		5	12	20	31	44
3/8 JNF	24	0.0878		Clamp Load (Lb)	878	2,196	3,623	5,599	7,905
			Lubricated		4	10	17	26	37
			Zinc Plated	Torque (Ft-Lb)	5	12	20	31	44
			Plain - Dry		5	14	23	35	49
7/16 JNC	14	0.1063		Clamp Load (Lb)	1,063	2,658	4,385	6,777	9,568
			Lubricated		6	15	24	37	52
			Zinc Plated	Torque (Ft-Lb)	7	17	29	44	63
			Plain - Dry		8	19	32	49	70
7/16 JNF	20	0.1187		Clamp Load (Lb)	1,187	2,968	4,897	7,568	10,684
			Lubricated		6	16	27	41	58
			Zinc Plated	Torque (Ft-Lb)	8	19	32	50	70
			Plain - Dry		9	22	36	55	78
1/2	13	0.1419		Clamp Load (Lb)	1,419	3,547	5,853	9,046	12,77
			Lubricated		9	22	37	57	80

FIGURE 3-32 Bolt torque chart.

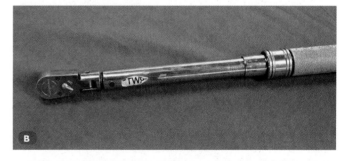

FIGURE 3-33 A torque wrench.

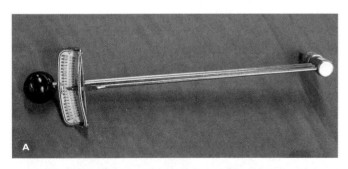

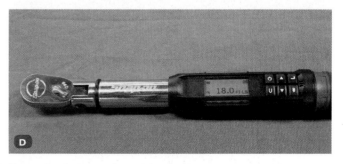

FIGURE 3-34 Torque wrenches. **A.** Beam style. **B.** Clicker style. **C.** Dial. **D.** Electronic.

(**FIGURE 3-35**). As the bolt is tightened, once the preset torque is reached, the torque wrench clicks. The higher the torque, the louder the click; the lower the torque, the quieter the click. Be careful when using this style of torque wrench, especially at lower torque settings. It is easy to miss the click and over-tighten, break, or strip the bolt. Once the torque wrench clicks, stop turning it, as it will continue to tighten the fastener if you turn it past the click point.

FIGURE 3-35 Torque setting scale on the handle.

FIGURE 3-36 Dial torque wrench reading torque.

The dial torque wrench turns a dial that indicates the torque based on the torque being applied. Like the beam-style torque wrench, you have to be able to see the dial to know how much torque is being applied (**FIGURE 3-36**). Many dial torque wrenches have a movable indicator that is moved by the dial and stays at the highest reading. That way you can double-check the torque achieved once the torque wrench is released. Once the proper torque is reached, the indicator can be moved back to zero for the next fastener being torqued.

The digital torque wrench usually uses a spring steel bar with an electronic strain gauge to measure the amount of torque being applied. The torque wrench can be preset to the desired torque. It will then display the torque as the fastener is being tightened (**FIGURE 3-37**). When it reaches the preset torque, it usually gives an audible signal, such as a beep. This makes it useful in situations where a scale or dial cannot be read.

Torque wrenches fall out of calibration over time or if they are not used properly, so they should be checked and calibrated on a periodic basis (**FIGURE 3-38**). This can be performed in the shop if the proper calibration equipment is available, or the torque wrench can be sent to a qualified service center. Most quality torque wrench manufacturers provide a recalibration service for their customers.

Using Torque Wrenches

The torque wrench is used to apply a specified amount of torque to a fastener. There are various methods used by torque wrenches to indicate that the correct torque has been reached. Some give an audible signal, such as a click or a beep, whereas others give a visual signal such as a light or a pin moving or clicking out. Some provide a scale and needle that must be observed while you are torquing the fastener. To help ensure that the proper amount of torque gets from the torque wrench to the bolt, support the head

FIGURE 3-37 Digital torque wrench displaying torque.

FIGURE 3-38 Checking torque wrench calibration.

of the torque wrench with one hand (**FIGURE 3-39**). When using a torque wrench, it is best not to use extensions. Extensions make it harder to support the head, which can end up absorbing some of the torque. If possible, use a deep socket instead.

Pliers

Pliers are a hand tool designed to hold, cut, or compress materials (**FIGURE 3-40**). They are usually made out of two pieces of strong steel joined at a fulcrum point, with jaws and cutting surfaces at one end and handles designed to provide leverage at the other. There are many types of pliers, including slip-joint, combination, arc joint, needle-nose, and flat-nose (**FIGURE 3-41**).

Quality **combination pliers** are one of the most commonly used pliers in a shop. They pivot together so that any force applied to the handles is multiplied in the strong jaws. Most combination pliers are designed so they have surfaces to both grip and cut. Combination pliers offer two gripping surfaces, one for gripping flat objects and one for gripping rounded objects, and one or two pairs of cutters. The cutters in the jaws should be used for softer materials that will not damage the blades. The cutters next to the pivot can shear through hard, thin materials, like steel wire or pins.

Most pliers are limited by their size in what they can grip. Beyond a certain point, the handles are spread too wide, or the jaws cannot open wide enough, but **arc joint pliers** overcome that limitation with a moveable pivot. Often, these are called Channel-locks™ after the company that first made them. These pliers have parallel jaws that allow you to increase or decrease the size of the jaws by selecting a different set of channels (**FIGURE 3-42**). They are useful for a wider grip and a tighter squeeze on parts too big for conventional pliers.

Another type of pliers is **needle-nose pliers**, which have long, pointed jaws and can reach into tight spots or hold small items that other pliers cannot (**FIGURE 3-43**). For example, they can pick up a small bolt that has fallen into a tight spot. **Flat-nose pliers** have an end or nose that is flat and square; in contrast, combination pliers have a rounded end. A flat nose makes it possible to bend wire or even a thin piece of sheet steel accurately along a straight edge. **Diagonal cutting pliers** are used for cutting wire or cotter pins (**FIGURE 3-44**). Diagonal cutters are the most common cutters in the toolbox, but they should not be used on hard or heavy-gauge materials because the cutting surfaces will be damaged. End cutting pliers, also called **nippers**, have a cutting edge at right angles to their length (**FIGURE 3-45**). They are designed to cut through soft metal objects sticking out from a surface.

Snap ring pliers have metal pins that fit in the holes of a snap ring (**FIGURE 3-46**). Snap rings can be of the internal or external type. If internal, then internal snap ring pliers compress the snap ring so it can be removed from and installed in its internal groove. If external, then external snap ring pliers are used to expand the snap ring so it can

K03008 Describe the type and use of pliers.

FIGURE 3-39 It may be necessary to support the torque wrench when using extensions.

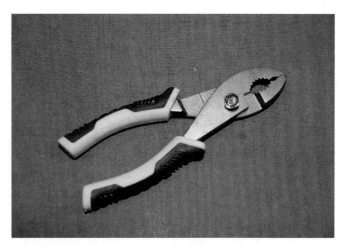

FIGURE 3-40 Pliers are used for grasping and cutting. These are slip-joint pliers.

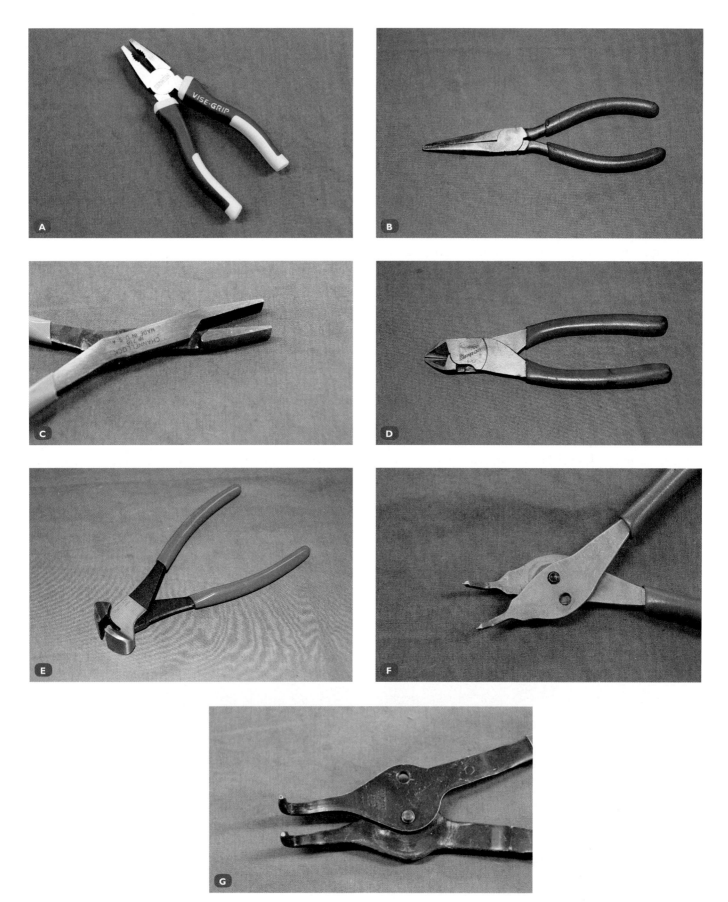

FIGURE 3-41 A. Combination pliers. **B.** Needle-nose pliers. **C.** Flat-nose pliers. **D.** Diagonal cutting pliers. **E.** Nippers. **F.** Internal snap ring pliers. **G.** External snap ring pliers.

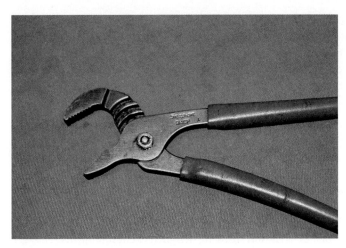

FIGURE 3-42 Arc joint pliers.

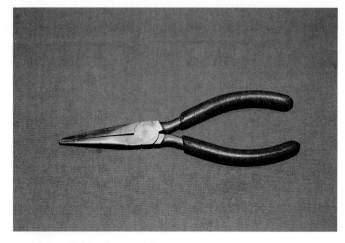

FIGURE 3-43 Needle-nose pliers.

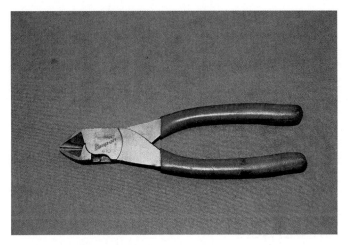

FIGURE 3-44 Diagonal side cutters.

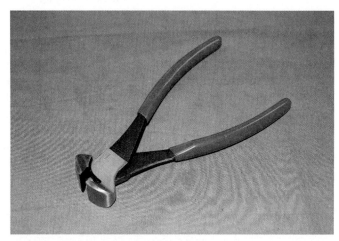

FIGURE 3-45 Nippers, or end cutting, pliers.

FIGURE 3-46 Snap ring pliers and snap ring.

FIGURE 3-47 Locking pliers.

remove and install the snap ring in its external groove. Always wear safety glasses when working with snap rings, as the snap rings can easily slip off the snap ring pliers and fly off at tremendous speeds, possibly causing severe eye injuries.

Locking pliers, also called vice grips, are general-purpose pliers used to clamp and hold one or more objects (**FIGURE 3-47**). Locking pliers are helpful by freeing up one or more of your hands when you are working, because they can clamp something and lock themselves in place to hold it. They are also adjustable, so they can be used for a variety of tasks. To clamp an object with locking pliers, put the object between the jaws, turn the screw until the handles are almost closed, then squeeze them together to lock them shut. You can increase or decrease the gripping force with the adjustment screw. To release them, squeeze the release lever, and they should open right up.

Cutting Tools

K03009 Describe the type and use of cutting tools.

Bolt cutters cut heavy wire, non-hardened rods, and bolts (**FIGURE 3-48**). Their compound joints and long handles give the leverage and cutting pressure that is needed for heavy gauge materials. **Tin snips** are the nearest thing in the toolbox to a pair of scissors. They can cut thin sheet metal, and lighter versions make it easy to follow the outline of gaskets. Most snips come with straight blades, but if there is an unusual shape to cut, there is a pair with left- or right-handed curved blades. **Aviation snips** are designed to cut soft metals. They are easy to use because the handles are spring-loaded in the open position and double pivoted for extra leverage.

Allen Wrenches

K03010 Describe the type and use of Allen wrenches.

Allen wrenches, sometimes called Allen or hex keys, are tools designed to tighten and loosen fasteners with Allen heads (**FIGURE 3-49**). The Allen head fastener has an internal hexagonal recess that the Allen wrench fits in snugly. Allen wrenches come in sets, and there is a correct wrench size for every Allen head. They give the best grip on a screw or bolt of all the drivers, and their shape makes them good at getting into tight spots. Care must be taken to make sure the correct size of Allen wrench is used, or else the wrench and/or socket head will be rounded off. The traditional Allen wrench is a hexagonal bar with a right-angle bend at one end. They are made in various metric and standard sizes. As their popularity has increased, so too has the number of tool variations. Now Allen sockets are available, as are T-handle Allen keys (**FIGURE 3-50**).

K03011 Describe the type and use of screwdrivers.

Screwdrivers

The correct screwdriver to use depends on the type of slot or recess in the head of the screw or bolt, and how accessible it is (**FIGURE 3-51**). Most screwdrivers cannot grip as securely as wrenches, so it is very important to match the tip of the screwdriver exactly with the slot or recess in the head of a fastener. Otherwise, the tool might slip, damaging the fastener or the tool and possibly injuring you. When using a screwdriver, always check where the screwdriver blade can end up if it slips off the head of the screw. Many technicians who have not taken

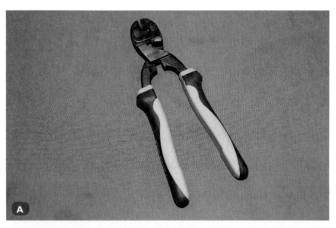

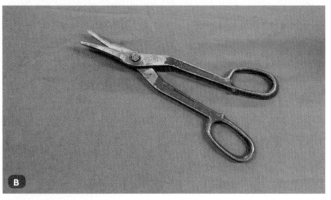

FIGURE 3-48 A. Bolt cutters. **B.** Tin snips. **C.** Aviation snips.

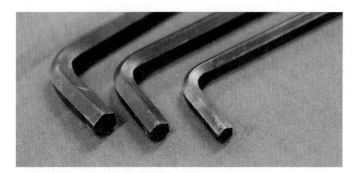

FIGURE 3-49 Typical Allen wrench head.

FIGURE 3-50 **A.** Allen socket. **B.** T-handle Allen wrench.

this precaution have stabbed a screwdriver into or through their hand, which can be painful as well as become infected or damage nerves.

The most common screwdriver has a flat tip, or blade, which gives it the name **flat blade screwdriver**. The blade should be almost as wide and thick as the slot in the fastener so that twisting force applied to the screwdriver is transferred right out to the edges of the head, where it has most effect. The blade should be a snug fit in the slot of the screw head. Then the twisting force is applied evenly along the sides of the slot. This guards against the screwdriver suddenly chewing a piece out of the slot and slipping just when the most force is being exerted. Flat blade screwdrivers come in a variety of sizes and lengths, so find the right one for the job. If viewed from the side, the blade should taper slightly to the very end where the flat tip fits into the slot. If the tip of the blade is not clean and square, it should be reshaped or replaced.

When you use a flat blade screwdriver, support the shaft with your free hand as you turn it (but keep it behind the tip). This helps keep the blade square in the slot and centered. Screwdrivers that slip are a common source of damage and injury in shops. A screw or bolt with a cross-shaped recess requires a **Phillips head screwdriver** or a Pozidriv screwdriver (**FIGURE 3-52**). The cross-shaped slot holds the tip of the screwdriver securely on the head. The Phillips tip fits a tapered recess, whereas the Pozidriv fits into slots with parallel sides in the head of the screw. Both a Phillips and a Pozidriv screwdriver are less likely to slip sideways, because the point is centered in the screw, but again the screwdriver must be the

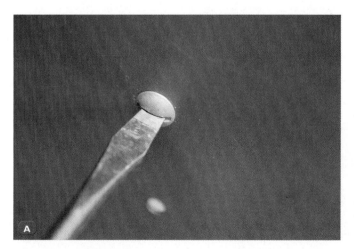

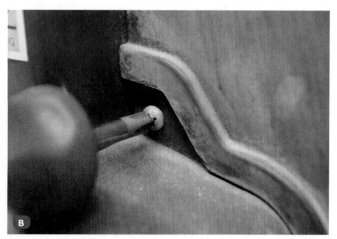

FIGURE 3-51 **A.** Slotted screw and screw driver. **B.** Phillips screw and screw driver.

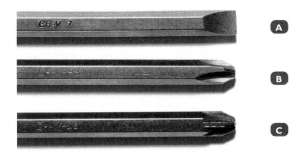

FIGURE 3-52 A. Flat blade screwdrivers. **B.** Phillips screwdriver. **C.** Pozidriv screwdriver.

FIGURE 3-53 Four sizes of Phillips screwdrivers.

right size. The fitting process is simplified with these two types of screwdrivers because four sizes are enough to fit almost all fasteners with this sort of screw head (**FIGURE 3-53**).

The **offset screwdriver** fits into spaces where a straight screwdriver cannot and is useful where there is not much room to turn it (**FIGURE 3-54**). The two tips look identical, but one is set at 90 degrees to the other. This is because sometimes there is only room to make a quarter turn of the driver. Thus the driver has two blades on opposite ends so that offset ends of the screwdriver can be used alternately.

The **ratcheting screwdriver** is a popular screwdriver handle that usually comes with a selection of removable flat and Phillips tips. It has a ratchet inside the handle that turns the blade in only one direction, depending on how the slider is set. When set for loosening, a screw can be undone without removing the tip of the blade from the head of the screw. When set for tightening, a screw can be inserted just as easily.

An **impact driver** is used when a screw or a bolt is rusted/corroded in place or over-tightened, and needs a tool that can apply more force than the other members of this family. Screw slots can easily be stripped with the use of a standard screwdriver. The force of the hammer forcing the bit into the screw while turning it makes it more likely the screw

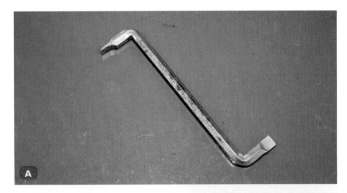

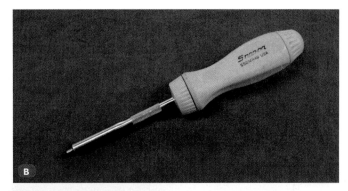

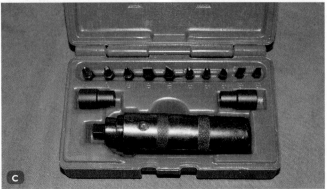

FIGURE 3-54 A. Offset screwdriver. **B.** Ratcheting screwdriver. **C.** Impact driver.

will break loose. The impact driver accepts a variety of special impact tips. Choose the right one for the screw head, fit the tip in place, and then tension it in the direction it has to turn. A sharp blow with the hammer breaks the screw free, and then it can usually be unscrewed normally.

Magnetic Pickup Tools and Mechanical Fingers

Magnetic pickup tools and **mechanical fingers** are very useful for grabbing items in tight spaces (**FIGURE 3-55**). A magnetic pickup tool typically is a telescoping stick that has a magnet attached to the end on a swivel joint. The magnet is strong enough to pick up screws, bolts, sockets, and other ferrous (containing iron, making it magnetic) metals. For example, if a screw is dropped into a tight crevice where your fingers cannot reach, a magnetic pickup tool can be used to extract it.

Mechanical fingers are also designed to extract or insert objects in tight spaces. Because they actually grab the object, they can pick up nonmagnetic objects, which makes them handy for picking up rubber or plastic parts. They use a flexible body and come in different lengths, but typically are about 12–18" (305–457 mm) long. They have expanding grappling fingers on one end to grab items, and the other end has a push mechanism to expand the fingers and a retracting spring to contract the fingers.

Hammers

Hammers are a vital part of the shop tool collection, and a variety are commonly used (**FIGURE 3-56**). The most common hammer in an automotive shop is the **ball-peen (engineer's) hammer**. Like most hammers, its head is hardened steel. A punch or a chisel can be driven with the flat face. Its name comes from the ball peen or rounded face. This end is usually used for flattening or **peening** a rivet. The hammer should always match the size of the job, and it is usually better to use one that is too big than too small.

Hitting chisels with a **steel hammer** is fine, but sometimes you only need to tap a component to position it. A steel hammer might mark or damage the part, especially if it is made of a softer metal, such as aluminum. In such cases, a soft-faced hammer should normally be used for the job. Soft-faced hammers range from very soft with rubber or plastic heads to slightly harder with brass or copper.

When a large chisel needs a really strong blow, it is time to use a **sledgehammer**. The sledgehammer is like a small mallet, with two square faces made of high carbon steel. It is the heaviest type of hammer that can be used one-handed. The sledgehammer is used in conjunction with a chisel to cut off a bolt where corrosion has made it impossible to remove the nut.

A **dead blow hammer** is designed not to bounce back when it hits something. A rebounding hammer can be dangerous or destructive. A dead blow hammer can be made

K03012 Describe type and use of magnetic pickup tools and mechanical fingers.

K03013 Describe the type and use of hammers.

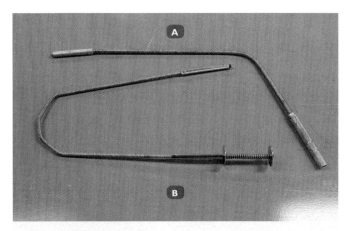

FIGURE 3-55 A. Magnetic pickup tools. **B.** Mechanical fingers.

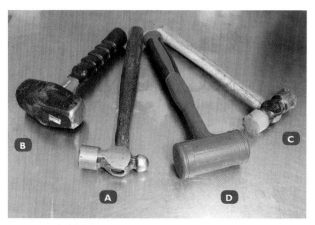

FIGURE 3-56 A. Ball peen hammer. **B.** Sledge hammer. **C.** Soft-faced hammer. **D.** Dead blow hammer.

K03014 Describe the type and use of chisels.

K03015 Describe the type and use of punches.

with a lead head or, more commonly, a hollow polyurethane head filled with lead shot or sand. The head absorbs the blow when the hammer makes contact, reducing any bounce-back or rebounding. This hammer can be used when working on the vehicle chassis or when dislodging stuck parts.

A **hard rubber mallet** is a special-purpose tool and has a head made of hard rubber. It is often used for moving things into place where it is important not to damage the item being moved. For example, it can be used to install a hubcap or to break a gasket seal on an aluminum housing.

Chisels

The most common kind of chisel is a **cold chisel** (**FIGURE 3-57**). It gets its name from the fact it is used to cut cold metals rather than heated metals. It has a flat blade made of high-quality steel and a cutting angle of approximately 70 degrees. The cutting end is tempered and hardened because it has to be harder than the metals it is cutting. The head of the chisel needs to be softer so it will not chip when it is hit with a hammer. Technicians sometimes use a cold chisel to remove bolts whose heads have rounded off.

A variation of the cold chisel is a spring-loaded cold chisel (**FIGURE 3-58**). This chisel works really well in tight spaces where a hammer can't be swung. The chisel is made up of three parts: the chisel, the weighted hammerhead, and a spring in tension, holding the other two components together. It is operated by holding the chisel end against the part you are working on, pulling back on the hammerhead, and allowing the spring to rapidly slam the hammerhead into the end of the chisel. The force of the hammerhead hitting the end of the chisel transfers a lot of energy to the chisel. This type of arrangement is also used on some spring-loaded center punches.

A **cross-cut chisel** is so named because the sharpened edge is across the blade width. This chisel narrows down along the stock, so it is good for getting in grooves. It is used for cleaning out or even making key ways. The flying chips of metal should always be directed away from the user.

Punches

Punches are used when the head of the hammer is too large to strike the object being hit without causing damage to adjacent parts. A punch transmits the hammer's striking power from the soft upper end down to the tip that is made of hardened high-carbon steel. A punch transmits an accurate blow from the hammer at exactly one point, something that cannot be guaranteed using a hammer on its own.

Four of the most common punches are the prick punch, center punch, drift punch, and pin punch (**FIGURE 3-60**). When marks need to be drawn on an object like a steel plate, to help locate a hole to be drilled, a **prick punch** can be used to mark the points so they will not rub off. They can also be used to scribe intersecting lines between given points. The

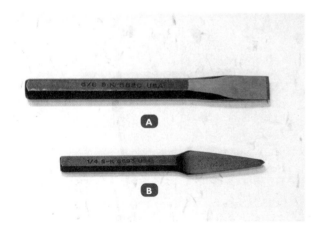

FIGURE 3-57 A. Cold chisel. **B.** Cross-cut chisel.

FIGURE 3-58 Spring-loaded chisels.

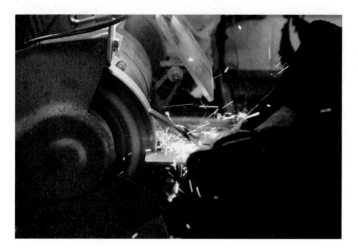

FIGURE 3-59 Dressing a chisel.

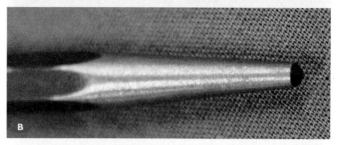

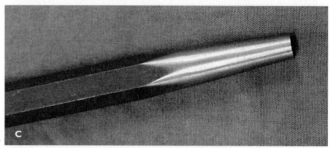

FIGURE 3-60 A. Prick punch. **B.** Center punch. **C.** Drift punch. **D.** Pin punch.

prick punch's point is very sharp, so a gentle tap leaves a clear indentation. The **center punch** is not as sharp as a prick punch and is usually bigger. It makes a bigger indentation that centers a drill bit at the point where a hole is required to be drilled.

Although most center punches are used with a hammer, some center punches operate automatically when the punch is pressed tightly up against the part you are punching. This type of punch has a spring and weighted hammer inside of the back end of the center punch. It is machined in such a way that pushing the center punch against a surface compresses a spring behind a movable weight (**FIGURE 3-61**). When pushed far enough, the weight is released, and the spring forces it against the center rod in the punch, causing it to indent the work surface.

A **drift punch** is also named a starter punch because you should always use it first to get a pin moving. It has a tapered shank, and the tip is slightly hollow so it does not spread the end of a pin and make it an even tighter fit. Once the starter drift has gotten the pin moving, a suitable pin punch will drive the pin out or in. A drift punch also works well for aligning holes on two mating objects, such as a valve cover and cylinder head. Forcing the drift punch in the hole aligns both components for easier installation of the remaining bolts. **Pin punches** are available in various diameters. A pin punch has a long slender shaft that has straight sides. It is used to drive out pins or rivets (**FIGURE 3-62**). A lot of components are either held together or accurately located by pins. Pins can be pretty tight, and a group of pin punches is specially designed to deal with them.

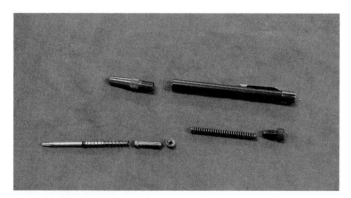

FIGURE 3-61 Internal workings of an automatic center punch.

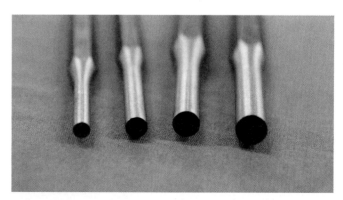

FIGURE 3-62 Various pin punches.

FIGURE 3-63 Wad punch.

FIGURE 3-64 Number and letter punches.

Many engine components are made of aluminum. Because aluminum is quite soft, it is critical that you use the gasket scraper very carefully so as not to damage the surface. This can be accomplished by keeping the gasket scraper at a fairly flat angle to the surface. Also, the gasket scraper should only be used by hand, not with a hammer. Some manufacturers specify using plastic gasket scrapers only on certain aluminum components such as cylinder heads and blocks.

Special punches with hollow ends are called **wad punches** or **hollow punches** (**FIGURE 3-63**). They are the most efficient tool to make a hole in soft sheet material like shim steel, plastic, and leather, or, most commonly, in a gasket. When being used, there should always be a soft surface under the work, ideally the end grain of a wooden block. If a hollow punch loses its sharpness or has nicks around its edge, it will make a mess instead of a hole.

Numbers and letters, like the engine numbers on some cylinder blocks, are usually made with number and letter punches that come in boxed sets (**FIGURE 3-64**). The rules for using a number or letter punch set are the same as for all punches. The punch must be square with the surface being worked on, not on an angle, and the hammer must hit the top squarely.

Pry Bars

K03016 Describe the type and use of pry bars.

Pry bars are tools constructed of strong metal that are used as a lever to move, adjust, or pry (**FIGURE 3-65**). Pry bars come in a variety of shapes and sizes. Many have a tapered end that is slightly bent, with a plastic handle on the other end. This design works well for applying force to tension belts or for moving parts into alignment. Another type of pry bar is the **roll bar**. One end is sharply curved and tapered, which is used for prying. The other end is tapered to a dull point and is used to align larger holes such as transmission bell housings or engine motor mounts. Because pry bars are made of hardened steel, care should be taken when using them on softer materials, to avoid any damage.

Gasket Scrapers

K03017 Describe the type and use of gasket scrapers.

A **gasket scraper** has a hardened, sharpened blade. It is designed to remove a gasket without damaging the sealing face of the component when used properly (**FIGURE 3-66**). On

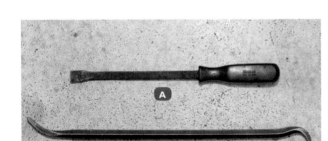

FIGURE 3-65 A. Pry bar. **B.** Roll bar.

FIGURE 3-66 A gasket scraper.

one end, it has a comfortable handle like a screwdriver handle; on the other end, a blade is fitted with a sharp edge to assist in the removal of gaskets. The gasket scraper should be kept sharp and straight to make it easy to remove all traces of the old gasket and sealing compound. The blades come in different sizes, with a typical size being 1" (25 mm) wide. Whenever you use a gasket scraper, be very careful not to nick or damage the surface being cleaned.

Files

Files are hand tools designed to remove small amounts of material from the surface of a workpiece. Files come in a variety of shapes, sizes, and coarseness depending on the material being worked and the size of the job. Files have a pointed tang on one end that is fitted to a handle. Files are often sold without handles, but they should not be used until a handle of the right size has been fitted. A correctly sized handle fits snugly without working loose when the file is being used. Always check the handle before using the file. If the handle is loose, give it a sharp rap to tighten it up, or if it is the threaded type, screw it on tighter. If it fails to fit snugly, you must use a different-size handle.

What makes one file different from another is not just the shape but how much material it is designed to remove with each stroke. The teeth on the file determine how much material will be removed (**FIGURE 3-67**). Because the teeth face one direction only, the file cuts in one direction only. Dragging the file backward over the surface of the metal only dulls the teeth and wears them out quickly. Teeth on a coarse-grade file are larger, with a greater space between them. A coarse-grade file working on a piece of mild steel removes a lot of material with each stroke, but it leaves a rough finish. A smooth-grade file has smaller teeth cut more closely together. It removes much less material on each stroke, but the finish is much smoother. On many jobs, the coarse file is used first to remove material quickly, and then a smoother file gently removes the remaining material and leaves a smoother finish to the work. The full list of grades in flat files, from rough to smooth, follows:

- **Rough files** have the coarsest teeth, with approximately 20 teeth per inch (25 mm). They are used when a lot of material must be removed quickly. They leave a very rough finish and have to be followed by the use of finer files to produce a smooth final finish.
- **Coarse bastard files** are still a coarse file, with approximately 30 teeth per inch (25 mm), but they are not as course as the rough file. They are also used to rough out or remove material quickly from the job.
- **Second-cut files** have approximately 40 teeth per inch (25 mm) and provide a smoother finish than the rough or coarse bastard file. They are good all-round intermediary files and leave a reasonably smooth finish.
- **Smooth files** have approximately 60 teeth per inch (25 mm) and are a finishing file used to provide a smooth final finish.
- **Dead smooth files** have 100 teeth per inch (25mm) or more and are used where a very fine finish is required.

Some flat files are available with one smooth edge (no teeth), called safe edge files. They allow filing up to an edge without damaging it. Flat files work well on straightforward jobs, but some jobs require special files. A **warding file** is thinner than other files and comes to a point; it is used for working in narrow slots (**FIGURE 3-68**). A **square file** has teeth on all four sides, so you can use it in a square or rectangular hole. A square file can make the right shape for a squared metal key to fit in a slot.

A **triangular file** has three sides. It is triangular, so it can get into internal corners easily. It is able to cut right into a corner without removing material from the sides. **Curved files** are typically either half-round or round. A half-round file has a shallow convex surface that can file in a concave hollow or in

K03018 Describe the type and use of files.

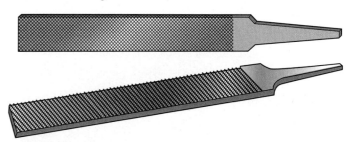

FIGURE 3-67 The teeth on a file determine how much material will be removed from the object being filed.

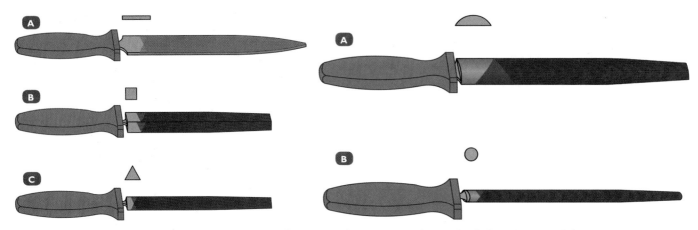

FIGURE 3-68 A. Warding file. **B.** Square file. **C.** Triangular file.   **FIGURE 3-69 A.** Half-round file. **B.** Round, or rat-tail, file.

an acute internal corner (**FIGURE 3-69**). The fully round file, sometimes called a rat-tail file, can make holes bigger. It can also file inside a concave surface with a tight radius.

The **thread file** cleans clogged or distorted threads on bolts and studs. Thread files come in either standard or metric configurations, so make sure you use the correct file. Each file has eight different surfaces that match different thread dimensions, so the correct face must be used (**FIGURE 3-70**).

Files should be cleaned after each use. If they are clogged, they can be cleaned by using a file card, or file brush (**FIGURE 3-71**). This tool has short steel bristles that clean out the small particles that clog the teeth of the file. Rubbing a piece of chalk over the surface of the file prior to filing makes it easier to clean.

Clamps

K03019 Describe the type and use of clamps.

There are many types of vices or clamps available (**FIGURE 3-72**). The **bench vice** is a useful tool for holding anything that can fit into its jaws. Some common uses include sawing, filing, or chiseling. The jaws are serrated to give extra grip. They are also very hard, which means that when the vice is tightened, the jaws can mar whatever they are gripping. To prevent this, a pair of soft jaws can be fitted whenever the danger of damage arises. They are usually made of aluminum or some other soft metal or can have a rubber-type surface applied to them.

When materials are too awkward to grip vertically in a plain vice, it may be easier to use an **offset vice**. The offset vice has its jaws set to one side to allow long components to be held vertically (**FIGURE 3-73**). For example, a long threaded bar can be held vertically in an offset vice to cut a thread with a die.

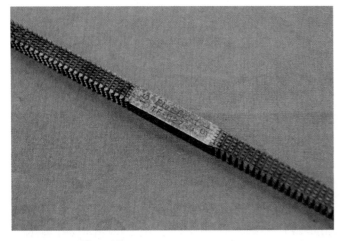

FIGURE 3-70 Thread file.

FIGURE 3-71 File card.

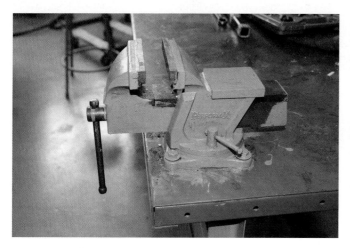

FIGURE 3-72 Bench vice.

FIGURE 3-73 Offset vice being used to hold a pipe.

A **drill vice** is designed to hold material on a drill worktable (**FIGURE 3-74**). The drill worktable has slots cut into it to allow the vice to be bolted down on the table, to hold material securely. To hold something firmly and drill it accurately, the object must be secured in the jaws of the vice. The vice can be moved on the bed until the precise drilling point is located and then tightened down by bolts to hold the drill vice in place during drilling.

The name for the **C-clamp** comes from its shape (**FIGURE 3-75**). It can hold parts together while they are being assembled, drilled, or welded. It can reach around awkwardly shaped pieces that do not fit in a vice. It is also commonly used to retract disc brake caliper pistons. This clamp is portable, so it can be taken to the work.

Taps and Dies

Taps and dies are used to form threads in metal so that they can be fastened together (**FIGURE 3-76**). The tap cuts female threads in a component so a fastener can be screwed into it. The die is used to cut male threads on a bolt so that it can be screwed into the female threads created by the tap. The tap and die are companion tools that create matching threads so that they can both be used to fasten things together.

K03020 Describe the type and use of taps and dies.

Taps

Various types of taps are designed to be used based on what you want to do and the material you are working with. The most common taps are the taper tap, intermediate tap (also called a plug tap), bottoming tap (also called a flat-bottomed tap), and the thread chaser (**FIGURE 3-77**). These are explored in more depth below.

FIGURE 3-74 Drill vice on a drill worktable.

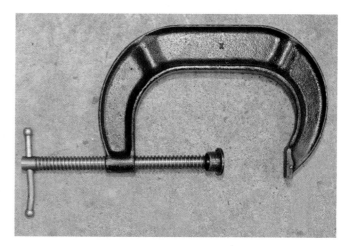

FIGURE 3-75 C-Clamp.

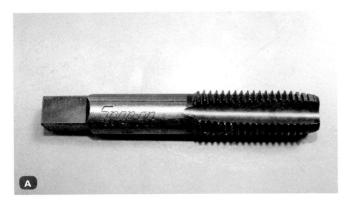

FIGURE 3-76 A. Tap. **B.** Die.

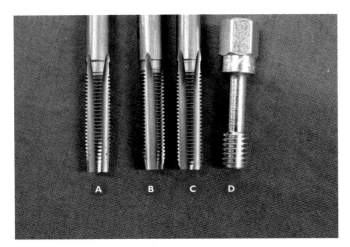

FIGURE 3-77 A. Taper tap. **B.** Intermediate tap. **C.** Bottoming tap. **D.** Thread chaser.

FIGURE 3-78 A. Die nut. **B.** Split die.

Taper Tap

A **taper tap** narrows at the tip, which makes it easier to start straight when cutting threads in a new hole. It also makes it less likely to break the tip off the tap because it removes metal in a less aggressive manner. Taps are very hard, which gives them good wear resistance but also makes them very brittle; they can break off easily. If a tap breaks in the hole, it can be very hard to remove. This makes taper taps good taps to use when starting a hole. Plus, they are easier to get started straight in the hole.

Intermediate Tap

The second type of tap is an **intermediate tap**, also known as a plug tap. It is more aggressive than a taper tap, but not as aggressive as a bottoming tap. This is the most common tap used by technicians. Although it is a bit more aggressive than the taper tap, it can be used as a starter tap for a new hole.

Bottoming Tap

The **bottoming tap** is used when you need to cut threads to the very bottom of a blind hole and in holes that already have threads started that just need to be extended slightly. It has a flat bottom. and the threads are the same all the way to the end. This type of tap is virtually impossible to use in a new, unthreaded hole.

Thread Chaser

Thread chasers are used to clean up the threads of a hole to make sure they are free from debris and dirt. They do not cut threads, but just clean up the existing threads so that the bolt doesn't encounter any excessive resistance.

Dies

A **die** is used to cut external threads on a metal shank or bolt. The threads in a die create the male companion to the female threads that have been cut into the material by a tap. Usually the dies come with a setscrew that allows the user to slightly adjust the size of the die so the threads can be cut to the right fit that matches the threaded hole. Loose-fitting threads strip more easily than they should and are not as secure. Tight-fitting threads increase the torque required to turn the bolt, thereby reducing the clamping force relative to bolt torque. So adjusting thread fit is typically accomplished by adjusting the die. Dies are hardened, which makes them very wear resistant, but very brittle. Die nuts do not have the split like the threading die does because they are used to clean up threads like the thread chasers (**FIGURE 3-78**).

Proper Use of Taps and Dies

The proper use of taps and dies is a major issue often overlooked in repairing a thread on a bolt or threads in a hole. Improper use of these two items causes the bolt not to thread into the hole properly, or it could even break the tool, which is something to avoid. Both of these tools are made of hardened steel, which makes them very wear resistant but also makes them very brittle. If they are used improperly they have a tendency to facture and break.

Because taps and dies both need to be rotated, special tools are used to turn them. A **tap handle** is used to turn taps. It has a right-angled jaw that matches the squared end of all the taps (**FIGURE 3-79**). The jaws are designed to hold the tap securely, and the handles provide the leverage for the operator to comfortably rotate the tap to cut the thread. To cut a thread in an awkward space, a T-shaped tap handle is very convenient (**FIGURE 3-80**). Its handle is not as long, so it fits into tighter spaces; however, it is harder to turn and to guide accurately.

To cut a brand new thread on a blank rod or shaft, a die held in a **die stock** is used (**FIGURE 3-81**). The die fits into the octagonal recess in the die stock and is usually held in place by a thumb screw. The die may be split so that it can be adjusted more tightly onto the work with each pass of the die as the thread is cut deeper and deeper, until the external thread fits the threaded hole properly.

When tapping a hole, the diameter of the hole is determined by a tap drill chart, which can be obtained from engineering suppliers. This chart shows what hole size has to be drilled and what tap size is needed to cut the right thread for any given bolt size (**FIGURE 3-82**).

Just remember that if you are drilling a 1/4" (6 mm) or larger hole, use a smaller pilot drill first. Once the properly sized hole has been drilled, the taper tap or intermediate tap can be started in the hole. Make sure to use the proper lubricant for the metal you are tapping. Also be sure to start the tap straight. The best way to do that is to start the tap about one turn, stop, and then use a square to check the position of the tap in two places 90 degrees apart. If it isn't perfectly straight, you can usually straighten it while turning it another half turn. Again stop and verify that it is straight in two positions, 90 degrees apart. If the tap is straight, turn the tap about one full turn, and then back it off about a quarter turn. Continue cutting and backing off the tap until either the tap turns easily or you are at the bottom of the hole. Remove the tap. If you are cutting threads in a blind hole, you need to use a bottoming tap to finish the threads off. If not, clean the threaded hole and test-fit a bolt in the hole to check the threads. The bolt should turn smoothly by hand.

Screw Extractors

Screw extractors are devices designed to remove screws, studs, or bolts that have broken off in threaded holes. A common type of extractor uses a coarse left-hand tapered thread formed on its hardened body (**FIGURE 3-83**). Normally, a hole is drilled in the center of the broken screw, and then the extractor is screwed into the hole. The left-hand thread grips the broken part of the bolt and unscrews it. The extractor is marked with two sizes: one showing the size range of screws it is designed to remove, and the other, the size of the hole that needs to be drilled. It is important to carefully drill the hole in the center of the bolt or

K03021 Describe the type and use of screw extractors.

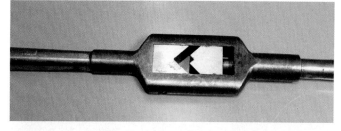

FIGURE 3-79 Tap handle.

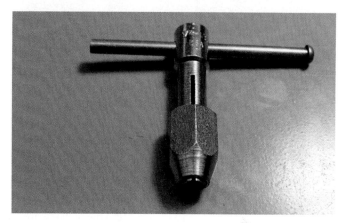

FIGURE 3-80 T-shaped tap handle.

FIGURE 3-81 Die stock.

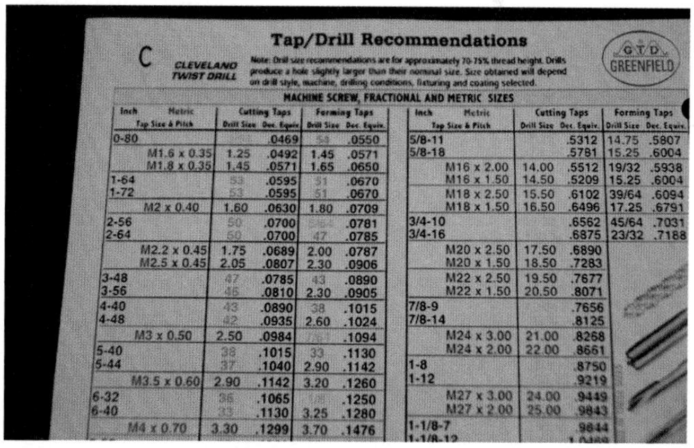

FIGURE 3-82 Tap drill chart.

FIGURE 3-83 Screw extractors.

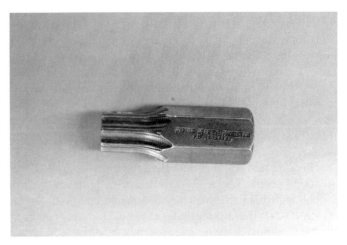

FIGURE 3-84 Straight-sided screw extractor.

stud in case you end up having to drill the bolt out. If you drill the hole off center, you will not be able to drill it out all the way to the inside diameter of the threads, as the hole is offset from center. This makes removal of the bolt much harder.

Some screw extractors use a hardened, tapered square shank that is hammered into a hole drilled into the center of the broken off bolt. The square edges of the screw extractor cut into the bolt and are used to grip it so it can be removed. Another type of screw extractor is the straight-sided, vertically splined, round shaft. The sides of the shaft have straight splines running the length of the extractor (**FIGURE 3-84**). It doesn't taper, so it is strong up and down its length. A straight hole of the correct diameter is drilled into the broken-off bolt. Then the extractor is driven into the newly drilled hole. The vertical splines, being larger than the hole, grab onto the bolt, allowing it to be unthreaded.

Pullers

K03022 Describe the type and use of pullers.

Pullers are a very common universal tool that can be used for removing bearings, bushings, pulleys, and gears (**FIGURE 3-85**). Specialized pullers are also available for specific tasks where a standard puller is not as effective. The most common pullers have two or three legs that grip the part to be removed. A center bolt, called a forcing screw or jacking bolt, is then screwed in, producing a jacking or pulling action, which extracts the part. **Gear pullers** come in a range of sizes and shapes, all designed for particular applications. They consist of three main parts: jaws, a cross-arm, and a forcing screw. There are normally two or three jaws on a puller. They are designed to connect to the component either externally or internally.

FIGURE 3-85 A. Puller. **B.** Gear puller.

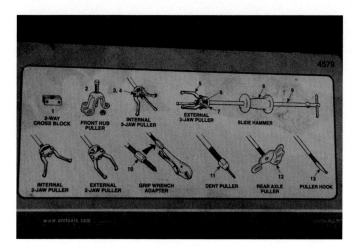

FIGURE 3-86 Interchangeable feet for the gear puller.

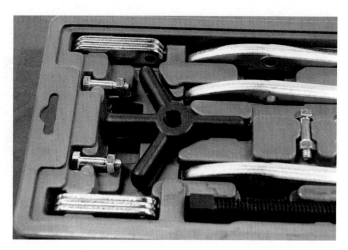

FIGURE 3-87 Four-arm puller.

The **forcing screw** is a long, fine-threaded bolt that is applied to the center of the cross-arm. When the forcing screw is turned, it applies a very large force to the component you are removing. The forcing screw typically has interchangeable feet (**FIGURE 3-86**). A tapered cone style of foot does a good job of centering the puller, but it also creates a very large wedging effect, which can distort the end of the shaft. A flat-style foot is very good for pushing against the end of a shaft, but doesn't center itself. In either situation, the wrong foot size can push on the internal threads of the shaft, damaging them. The cross-arm attaches the jaws to the forcing screw. If the **cross-arm** has four arms, three of the arms are spaced 120 degrees apart. The fourth arm is positioned 180 degrees apart from one arm (**FIGURE 3-87**). This allows the cross-arm to be used as either a two- or a three-arm puller.

Using Gear Pullers

Gear and bearing pullers are designed for hundreds of applications. Their main purpose is to remove a component such as a gear, pulley, or bearing from a shaft; or to remove a shaft from inside a hole. Normally these components have been pressed onto that shaft or into the hole, so removing them requires considerable force. To select, install, and use a gear puller to remove a pulley, follow the steps in **SKILL DRILL 3-3**.

Flaring Tools

A **tube flaring tool** is used to flare the end of a tube so it can be connected to another tube or component. One example of this is where the brake line screws into a wheel cylinder. The flared end is compressed between two threaded parts so that it seals the joint and withstands high pressures. The three most common shapes of flares are the **single flare**, for tubing carrying low pressures like a fuel line; the **double flare**, for higher pressures such as in a brake system; and the ISO flare (sometimes called a bubble flare), which is the metric version used in brake systems (**FIGURE 3-88**).

Flaring tools have two main parts: a set of bars with holes that match the diameter of the tube end that is being shaped, and a yoke that drives a cone into the mouth of the tube (**FIGURE 3-89**). To make a single flare, the end of the tube is placed level with the surface of the top of the flaring bars. With the clamp screw firmly tightened, the feed screw flares the end of the tube. Making a double flare is similar, but an extra step is added before flaring the tube, and more of the tube is exposed to allow for folding the flare over into a double flare. A double flaring button is placed into the end of the tube, and when it is removed after tightening, the pipe looks like a bubble. Placing the cone and yoke over the bubble allows you to force the bubble to fold in on itself, forming the double flare.

SAFETY TIP

■ Always wear eye protection when using a gear puller.
■ Make sure the puller is located correctly on the workpiece. If the jaws cannot be fitted correctly on the part, then select a more appropriate puller. Do not use a puller that does not fit the job.

K03023 Describe the type and use of flaring tools.

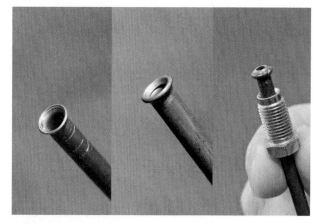

FIGURE 3-88 Single flare, double flare, and ISO flare.

SKILL DRILL 3-3 Using Gear Pullers

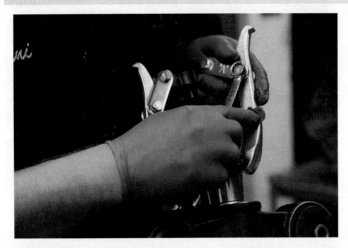

1. Examine the gear puller you have selected for the job. Identify the jaws; there may be two or three of them, and they must fit the part you want to remove. The cross-arm enables you to adjust the diameter of the jaws. The forcing screw should fit snugly onto the part you are removing. Finally, select the right wrench or socket size to fit the nut on the end of the forcing screw.

2. Adjust and fit the puller. Adjust the jaws and cross-arms of the puller so that it fits tightly around the part to be removed. The arms of the jaws should be pulling against the component at close to right angles.

3. Position the forcing screw. Use the appropriate wrench to run the forcing screw down to touch the shaft. Check that the point of the forcing screw is centered on the shaft. If not, adjust the jaws and cross-arms until the point is in the center of the shaft. Also be careful to use the correct foot on the end of the puller.

4. Tighten the forcing screw slowly and carefully onto the shaft. Check that the puller is not going to slip off center or off the pulley. Readjust the puller if necessary.

Continued

5. If the forcing screw and puller jaws remain in the correct position, tighten the forcing screw, and pull the part off the shaft.

6. You may sometimes have to use a hammer to hit directly on the end of the forcing screw to help break the part loose.

An ISO flare uses a flaring tool made specifically for that type of flare. The process is similar to that of the double-flare but differs in the use of the button, because an ISO flare does not get doubled back on itself. It should resemble a bubble shape when you are finished.

A **tubing cutter** is more convenient and neater than a saw when cutting pipes and metal tubing (**FIGURE 3-90**). The sharpened wheel does the cutting. As the tool turns

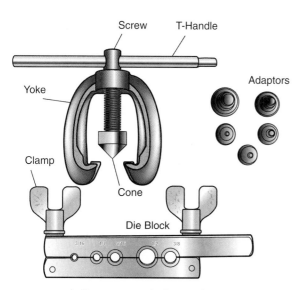

FIGURE 3-89 Components of a flare tool.

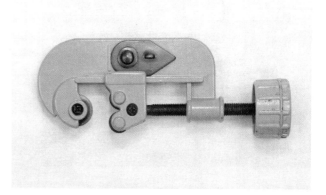

FIGURE 3-90 Tubing cutter.

K03024 Describe the type and use of riveting tools.

around the pipe, the screw increases the pressure, driving the wheel deeper and deeper through the pipe until it finally cuts through. There is a larger version that is used for cutting exhaust pipes.

Using Flaring Tools

To make a successful flare, it is important to have the correct amount of tube protruding through the tool before clamping. Otherwise, too much of the end will fold over and leave too small of a hole for fluid to pass through. Too little and there won't be enough tube to fold over properly, and the joint won't have full surface contact.

If you are making a double flare or ISO flare, make sure you use the correctly sized button for the tubing size. The button is also used to measure the amount of tube required to protrude from the tool prior to forming it. To prevent the tool from slipping on the tube and ruining the flare, make sure the tool is sufficiently tight around the tube before starting to create the flare.

To use a flaring tool to make a flare in a piece of tubing, follow the steps in **SKILL DRILL 3-4**.

Riveting Tools

There are many applications for blind rivets, and various rivet types and tools may be used to do the riveting. Rivets are used in many places in automotive applications where there is a need for a fastener that doesn't have to be easily removed. Some older window regulators,

SKILL DRILL 3-4 Using Flaring Tools

1. Choose the tube you will use to make the flare, and put the flare nut on the tube before creating the flare.

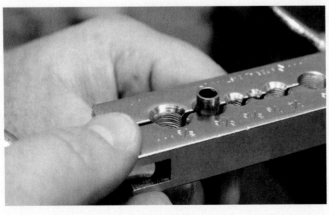

2. Match the size of the tube to the correct hole in the tubing clamp.

Continued

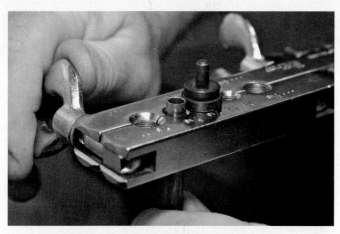

3. Holding the flaring tool, put the tube into the clamp. Position the tube so the correct amount is showing through the tool. If you are conducting a double flare, use the correctly sized button to ensure the proper amount of the tube is sticking up above the top of the clamp. Tighten the two halves of the clamp together using the wing nuts. Make sure the tool is tight enough to clamp the tube so it will not slip.

4. Put the cone and forming tool over the clamp, and turn the handle to make the flare. If you are doing a double flare or ISO flare, place the button in the end of the tube, install the cone and forming tool, and turn the handle to make the bubble. Remove the button from the tube.

5. If this is an ISO flare, inspect it to see if it is properly formed. If it is a double flare, put the cone and forming tool back on the clamp, and tighten the forming tool handle to create the double flare.

6. Remove the forming tool.

7. Remove the tube from the clamp, and check the flare to ensure it is free of burrs and is correctly formed.

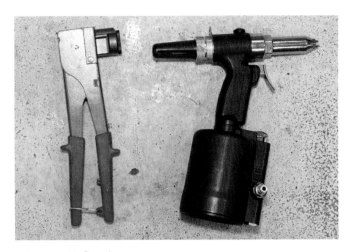

FIGURE 3-91 Pop rivet guns.

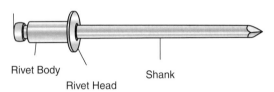

FIGURE 3-92 Anatomy of a rivet.

▶ **TECHNICIAN TIP**

A rivet is a single-use fastener. Unlike a nut and bolt, which can normally be disassembled and reused, a rivet cannot. The metal shell that makes up a pop rivet is crushed into place so that it holds the parts firmly together. If it ever needs to be removed, it must be drilled out or cut off.

SAFETY TIP

When compressing the rivet handles, be careful not to place your fingers between the handles as they could end up pinching your fingers when the mandrel on the rivet breaks.

N03004 Demonstrate proper use of precision measuring tools (i.e., micrometer, dial-indicator, dial-caliper).

---

body panels, trim pieces, and even some suspension members use rivets to keep them attached without vibrating loose. **Pop rivet guns** are convenient for occasional riveting of light materials (**FIGURE 3-91**).

A typical pop, or **blind rivet**, has a body that forms the **finished rivet** and a mandrel, which is discarded when the riveting is completed (**FIGURE 3-92**). It is called a blind rivet because there is no need to see or reach the other side of the hole in which the rivet goes to do the work. In some types, the rivet is plugged shut so that it is waterproof or pressure proof.

The rivet is inserted into the riveting tool, which, when squeezed, pulls the end of the **mandrel** back through the body of the rivet. Because the **mandrel head** is bigger than the hole through the body, the body swells tightly against the hole. Finally, the mandrel head will snap off under the pressure and fall out, leaving the rivet body gripping the two pieces of material together.

Using Riveting Tools

Rivet tools are used to join two pieces of metal or other material together—for example, sheet metal that needs to be attached to a stiffening frame. To perform a riveting operation, you need a rivet gun, rivets, a drill, a properly sized drill bit, and the materials to be riveted.

Rivets come in various diameters and lengths for different sizes of jobs and are made of various types of metals to suit the job at hand. When selecting rivets to suit the job, consider the diameter, length, and rivet material. Larger diameter rivets should be used for jobs that require more strength. The rivet length should be sufficient to protrude past the thickness of the materials being riveted by about 1.6 times the diameter of the rivet stem. Typically, you should select rivets that are made from the same material as that being riveted. For example, stainless steel rivets should be used for riveting stainless steel, and aluminum rivets should be used to rivet aluminum.

Pilot holes must be drilled through the metal to be riveted. Ensure that the hole is just large enough for the rivet to comfortably pass through it, but do not make it too large. If the hole is too large, the rivet will be loose and will not hold the materials securely together. When drilling holes for rivets, stay back from the material's edge to ensure that the rivets do not break through the edge of the materials being riveted. A good rule of thumb is to allow at least twice the diameter of the rivet stem as clearance from any edge.

Most rivet tools are capable of riveting various sizes of rivets and have a number of nosepiece sizes to work with different sizes of rivets. Make sure you select the properly sized nosepiece for the rivet you are using.

To use a riveting tool to rivet two pieces of material together, follow the steps in **SKILL DRILL 3-5**.

▶ Precision Measuring Tools

Technicians are required to perform a variety of measurements while carrying out their job. This requires knowledge of what tools are available and how to use them. Measuring tools can generally be classified according to what type of measurements they can make. A measuring tape is useful for measuring longer distances and is accurate to a millimeter or fraction of an inch (**FIGURE 3-93**). A steel rule is capable of accurate measurements on shorter lengths, down to a millimeter or a fraction of an inch. Precision measuring tools are accurate to much smaller dimensions, such as a micrometer, which in some cases can accurately measure down to 1/10,000 of an inch (0.0001") or 1/1000 of a millimeter (0.001 mm).

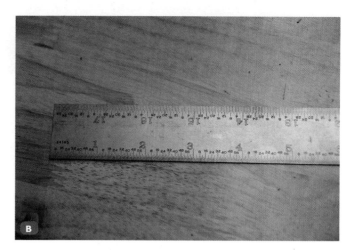

FIGURE 3-93 A. Measuring tape. **B.** Steel rule.

Measuring Tapes

Measuring tapes are a flexible type of ruler and are a common measuring tool. The most common type found in shops is a thin metal strip about 0.5" to 1" (13 to 25 mm) wide that is rolled up inside a housing with a spring return mechanism. Measuring tapes can be of various lengths, with 16' or 25' (5 or 8 m) being very common. The measuring tape

K03025 Describe the type and use of measuring tapes.

SKILL DRILL 3-5 Using Riveting Tools

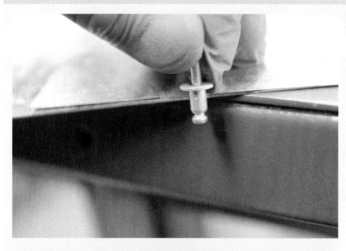

1. Select the correct rivet for the material you are riveting. Make sure the rivet is the correct length.

2. Drill pilot holes in the material to be riveted. Remove any burrs. Ensure that the pilot hole is the correct size—not too large or too small.

Continued

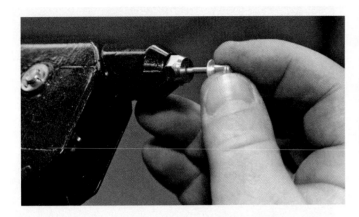

3. Make sure the correctly sized nosepiece for the rivet size is fitted to the rivet tool.

4. Insert the rivet into the gun, and push the rivet through the materials to be riveted. Hold firm pressure while pushing the rivet into the work.

5. Squeeze and release the rivet tool handle to compress the rivet. Continue this process until the rivet stem or shank breaks away from the rivet head.

6. Check the rivet joint to ensure the pieces are firmly held together.

is pulled from the housing to measure items, and a spring return winds it back into the housing. The housing usually has a built-in locking mechanism to hold the extended measuring tape against the spring return mechanism. The hooked end can be placed over the edge of the object you are measuring and pulled against spring tension to take the measurement (**FIGURE 3-94**).

Steel Rulers

K03026 Describe the type and use of steel rulers.

As the name suggests, a **steel rule** is a ruler that is made from steel. Steel rules commonly come in 12" (0.030 m), 24" (0.60 m), and 36" (0.91 m) lengths. They are used like any ruler to measure and mark out items. A steel rule is a very strong ruler, has precise markings, and resists damage. When using a steel rule, you can rest it on its edge so the markings are closer to the material being measured, which helps to mark the work more precisely

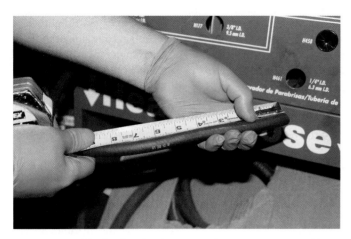

FIGURE 3-94 The hook makes it easy to take a measurement with one hand.

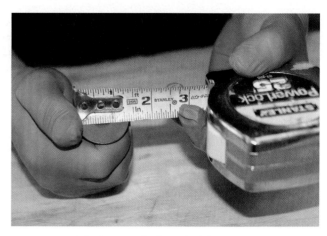

FIGURE 3-95 Tipping a steel rule on its side to get a more accurate reading.

(**FIGURE 3-95**). Always protect the steel rule from damage by storing it carefully; a damaged ruler will not give an accurate measurement. Never take measurements from the very end of a damaged steel rule, as damaged ends may affect the accuracy of your measurements.

Outside, Inside, and Depth Micrometers

Micrometers are precise measuring tools designed to measure small distances and are available in both inch and millimeter (mm) calibrations. Typically they can measure down to a resolution of 1/1000 of an inch (0.001") for a standard micrometer or 1/100 of a millimeter (0.01 mm) for a metric micrometer. Vernier micrometers equipped with the addition of a vernier scale can measure down to 1/10,000 of an inch (0.0001") or 1/1000 of a millimeter (0.001 mm).

K03027 Describe the type and use of outside, inside, and depth micrometers.

The most common types of micrometers are the outside, inside, and depth micrometers (**FIGURE 3-96**). As the name suggests, an **outside micrometer** measures the outside dimensions of an item. For example, it could measure the diameter of a valve stem. The **inside micrometer** measures inside dimensions. For example, the inside micrometer could measure an engine cylinder bore. **Depth micrometers** measure the depth of an item such as how much clearance a piston has below the surface of the block.

The most common micrometer is an outside micrometer and is made up of several parts (**FIGURE 3-97**). The horseshoe-shaped part is the frame. It is built to make sure the micrometer holds its shape. Some frames have plastic finger pads so that body heat is not

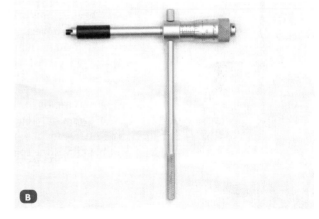

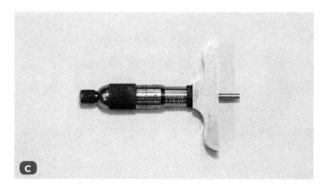

FIGURE 3-96 **A.** Outside micrometer. **B.** Inside micrometer. **C.** Depth micrometer.

The United States customary system (USCS), also called the standard system, and the metric system are two sets of standards for quantifying weights and measurements. Each system has defined units. For example, the standard system uses inches, feet, and yards, whereas the metric system uses millimeters, centimeters, and meters. Conversions can be undertaken from one system to the other. For example, I inch is equal to 25.4 millimeters, and I foot is equal to 304.8 millimeters. Tools that make use of a measuring system, such as wrenches, sockets, drill bits, micrometers, rulers, and many others, come in both standard and metric measurements. To work on modern vehicles, an understanding of both systems and their conversion is required. Conversion tables can be used to convert from one system to the other. The more you work with both systems, the easier it will be to understand how they relate to each other.

If the end of a rule is damaged, you may be able to measure from the I" mark and subtract an inch from the measurement.

transferred to the metal frame as easily, as heat can cause the metal to expand slightly and affect the reading. On one end of the frame is the anvil, which contacts one side of the part being measured. The other contact point is the spindle. The micrometer measures the distance between the anvil and spindle, so that is where the part being measured fits.

The measurement is read on the sleeve/barrel and thimble. The sleeve/barrel is stationary and has the linear markings on it. The thimble fits over the sleeve and has the graduated marking on it. The thimble is connected directly to the spindle, and both turn as a unit. Because the spindle and sleeve/barrel have matching threads, the thimble rotates the spindle inside of the sleeve/barrel, and the thread moves the spindle inward and outward. The thimble usually incorporates either a ratchet or a clutch mechanism, which is turned lightly by finger, thus preventing over-tightening of the micrometer thimble when taking a reading.

A lock nut, lock ring, or lock screw is used on most micrometers to lock the thimble in place while you read the micrometer. Standard micrometers use a specific thread of 40 TPI (threads per inch) on the spindle and sleeve. This means that the thimble rotates exactly 40 turns in 1' of travel. Every complete rotation moves the spindle one 40th of an inch, or 0.025" (1 ÷ 40 = 0.025). In four rotations, the spindle moves 0.100" (0.025 × 4 = 0.100). The linear markings on the sleeve show each of the 0.100" marks between 0 and 1 inch as well as each of the 0.025" marks (**FIGURE 3-98**). Because the thimble has graduated marks from 0 to 24 (each mark representing 0.001"), every complete turn of the thimble uncovers another one of the 0.025" marks on the sleeve. If the thimble stops short of any complete turn, it will indicate the number of 0.001" marks past the zero line on the sleeve (**FIGURE 3-99**). So reading a micrometer is as simple as adding up the numbers as shown below.

To read a standard micrometer, perform the following steps (**FIGURE 3-100**):

1. Verify that the micrometer is properly calibrated.
2. Verify what size of micrometer you are using. If it is a 0–1" micrometer, start with 0.000. If it is a 1–2" micrometer, start with 1.000". A 2–3" micrometer would start with 2.000", etc. (To give an example, let's say it is 2.000".)
3. Read how many 0.100" marks the thimble has uncovered (example: 0.300").
4. Read how many 0.025" marks the thimble has uncovered past the 0.100" mark in step 3 (example: 2 × 0.025 = 0.050").
5. Read the number on the thimble that lines up with the zero line on the sleeve (example: 13 × 0.001 = 0.013").
6. Lastly, total all of the individual readings (example: 2.000 + 0.300 + 0.050 + 0.013 = 2.363").

A metric micrometer uses the same components as the standard micrometer. However, it uses a different **thread pitch** on the spindle and sleeve. It uses a 0.5 mm thread pitch (2.0 threads per millimeter) and opens up approximately 25 mm. Each rotation of the thimble moves the spindle 0.5 mm, and it therefore takes 50 rotations of the thimble to move

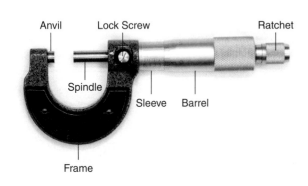

FIGURE 3-97 Parts of an outside micrometer.

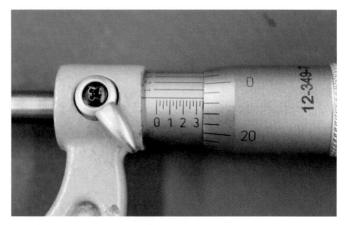

FIGURE 3-98 0.100" and 0.025" markings on the sleeve.

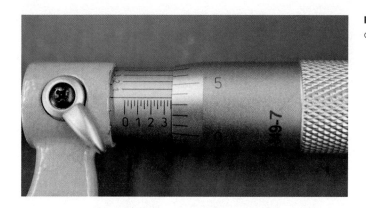

FIGURE 3-99 Markings on the thimble.

the full 25 mm distance. The sleeve/barrel is labeled with individual millimeter marks and half-millimeter marks from the starting millimeter to the ending millimeter, 25 mm away (**FIGURE 3-101**). The thimble has graduated marks from 0 to 49 (**FIGURE 3-102**).

Reading a metric micrometer involves the following steps:

1. Read the number of full millimeters the thimble has passed (To give an example, let's say it is 23.00 mm).
2. Check to see if it passed the 0.5 mm mark (example: 0.50 mm).
3. Check to see which mark on the thimble lines up with or is just passed (example: 37 × 0.01 mm = 0.37 mm).
4. Total all of the numbers (example: 23.00 mm + 0.50 mm + 0.37 mm = 23.87 mm).

If the micrometer is equipped with a vernier gauge, meaning it can read down to 1/10,000 of an inch (0.0001") or 1/1000 of a millimeter (0.001 mm), you need to complete one more step. Identify which of the vernier lines is closest to one of the lines on the thimble (**FIGURE 3-103**). Sometimes it is hard to determine which is the closest, so decide which three are the closest, and then use the center line. At the frame side of the sleeve will be a number that corresponds to the vernier line, numbered 1–0. Add the vernier to the end of your reading. For example: 2.363 + 0.0007 = 2.3637", and 23.77 + 0.007 = 23.777 mm.

For inside measurements, the inside micrometer works on the same principles as the outside micrometer and so does the depth micrometer. The only difference is that the scale on the sleeve of the depth micrometer is backward, so be careful when reading it.

Using Micrometers

To maintain accuracy of measurements, it is important that both the micrometer and the items to be measured are clean and free of any dirt or debris. Also make sure the micrometer is zeroed before taking any measurements. Never over-tighten a micrometer or store it with its measuring surfaces touching, as this may damage the tool and affect its accuracy. When measuring, make sure the item can pass through the micrometer surfaces snugly

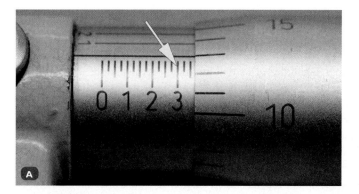

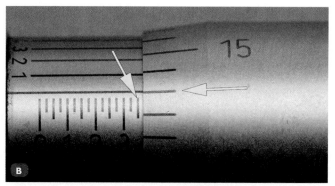

FIGURE 3-100 A. Read how many 0.100" marks the thimble has uncovered. **B.** Read the number on the thimble that lines up with the zero line on the sleeve.

FIGURE 3-101 Metric markings on the sleeve.

FIGURE 3-102 Markings on the thimble.

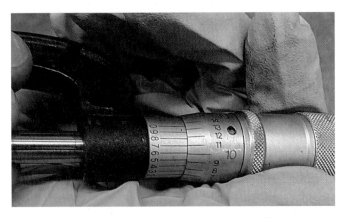

FIGURE 3-103 Vernier scale on a micrometer showing 7 on the sleeve lined up the best with a line on the thimble.

K03028 Describe the type and use of telescoping gauges.

K03029 Describe the type and use of split ball gauges.

K03030 Describe the type and use of dial bore gauges.

and squarely. This is best accomplished by using the ratchet to tighten the micrometer. Always take the measurement a number of times and compare results to ensure you have measured accurately.

To correctly measure using an outside micrometer, follow the steps in **SKILL DRILL 3-6**.

Telescoping Gauges

For measuring distances in awkward spots like the bottom of a deep cylinder, the **telescoping gauge** has spring-loaded plungers that can be unlocked with a screw on the handle so they slide out and touch the walls of the cylinder (**FIGURE 3-104**). The screw then locks them in that position, the gauge can be withdrawn, and the distance across the plungers can be measured with an outside micrometer or calipers to convey the diameter of the cylinder at that point. Telescoping gauges come in a variety of sizes to fit various sizes of holes and bores.

Split Ball Gauges

A **split ball gauge** or small hole gauge is good for measuring small holes where telescoping gauges cannot fit (**FIGURE 3-105**). They use a similar principle to the telescoping gauge, but the measuring head uses a split ball mechanism that allows it to fit into very small holes. Split ball gauges are ideal for measuring valve guides on a cylinder head for wear. A split ball gauge can be fitted in the bore and expanded until there is a slight drag. Then it can be retracted and measured with an outside micrometer.

Dial Bore Gauges

A **dial bore gauge** is used to measure the inside diameter of bores with a high degree of accuracy and speed (**FIGURE 3-106**). The dial bore gauge can measure a bore directly by using telescoping pistons on a T-handle with a dial mounted on the handle. The dial bore gauge combines a telescoping gauge and dial indicator in one instrument. A dial bore gauge determines if the diameter is worn, tapered, or out-of-round according to the manufacturer's specifications. The resolution of a dial bore gauge is typically accurate to 5/10,000 of an inch (0.0005") or 1/100 of a millimeter (0.01 mm).

Using Dial Bore Gauges

To use a dial bore gauge, select an appropriate-sized adapter to fit the internal diameter of the bore, and install it to the measuring head. Many dial bore gauges also have a fixture to calibrate the tool to the size you desire (**FIGURE 3-107**). The fixture is set to the size desired,

SKILL DRILL 3-6 Using Micrometers

1. Select the correct size of micrometer. Verify that the anvil and spindle are clean and that it is calibrated properly. Clean the surface of the part you are measuring.

2. In your right hand, hold the frame of the micrometer between your pinky, ring finger, and the palm of your hand, with the thimble between your thumb and forefinger.

3. With your left hand, hold the part you are measuring, and place the micrometer over it.

4. Using your thumb and forefinger, lightly tighten the ratchet. It is important that the correct amount of force is applied to the spindle when taking a measurement. The spindle and anvil should just touch the component with a slight amount of drag when the micrometer is removed from the measured piece. Be careful that the part is square in the micrometer so the reading is correct. Try rocking the micrometer in all directions to make sure it is square.

Continued

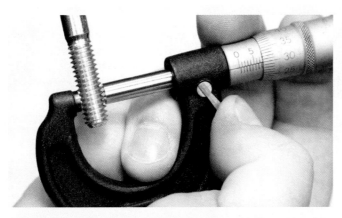

5. Once the micrometer is properly snug, tighten the lock mechanism so the spindle will not turn. Read the micrometer and record your reading.

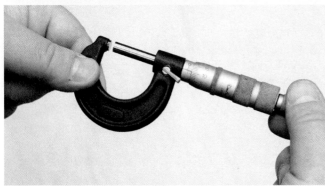

6. When all readings are finished, clean the micrometer, position the spindle so it is backed off from the anvil, and return it to its protective case.

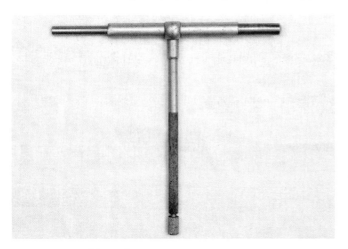

FIGURE 3-104 Telescoping gauge.

FIGURE 3-105 Split ball gauges.

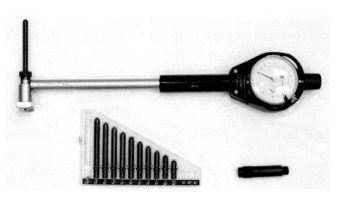

FIGURE 3-106 A dial bore gauge set.

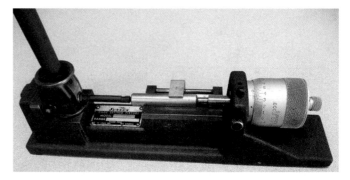

FIGURE 3-107 Dial bore gauge being calibrated to a predetermined size.

and the dial bore gauge is placed in it. The dial bore gauge is then adjusted to the proper reading. Once it is calibrated, the dial bore gauge can be inserted inside the bore to be measured. Hold the gauge in line with the bore, and slightly rock it to ensure it is centered. Read the dial when it is fully centered and square to the bore, to determine the correct measurement. It takes a bit of practice to get accurate readings.

Store a bore gauge carefully in its storage box and ensure the locking mechanism is released while in storage. Bore gauges are available in different ranges of size. It is important to select a gauge with the correct range for the bore you are measuring. When measuring, make sure the gauge is at a 90-degree angle to the bore and read the dial. Always take the measurement a number of times and compare results to ensure you have measured accurately.

To correctly measure using a dial bore gauge, follow the steps in **SKILL DRILL 3-7**.

Vernier Calipers

Vernier calipers are a precision instrument used for measuring outside dimensions, inside dimensions, and depth measurements, all in one tool (**FIGURE 3-108**). They have a graduated bar with markings like a ruler. On the bar, a sliding sleeve with jaws is mounted for taking inside or outside measurements. Measurements on older versions of vernier calipers are taken by reading the graduated bar scales, and fractional measurements are read by comparing the scales between the sliding sleeve and the graduated bar. Technicians often use vernier calipers to measure length and diameters of bolts and pins or the depth of blind holes in housings.

Newer versions of vernier calipers have dial and digital scales (**FIGURE 3-109**). The dial caliper has the main scale on the graduated bar, and fractional measurements are taken from a dial with a rotating needle. These tend to be easier to read than the older versions.

K03031 Describe the type and use of vernier calipers.

SKILL DRILL 3-7 Using Dial Bore Gauges

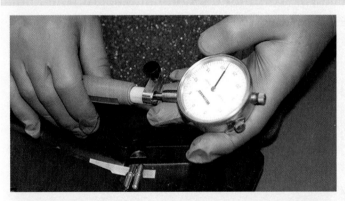

1. Select the correct size of the dial bore gauge you will use, and fit any adapters to it. Check the calibration and adjust it as necessary. Insert the dial bore gauge into the bore. The accurate measurement will be at exactly 90 degrees to the bore. To find the accurate measurement, rock the dial bore gauge handle slightly back and forth until you find the centered position.

2. Check the calibration and adjust it as necessary.

Continued

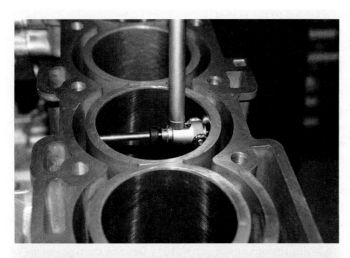

3. Insert the dial bore gauge into the bore. The accurate measurement will be at exactly 90 degrees to the bore. To find the accurate measurement, rock the dial bore gauge handle slightly back and forth until you find the centered position.

4. Read the dial to determine the bore measurement.

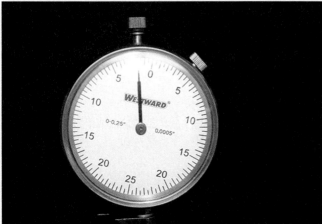

5. Always clean the dial bore gauge, and return it to its protective case when you have finished using it.

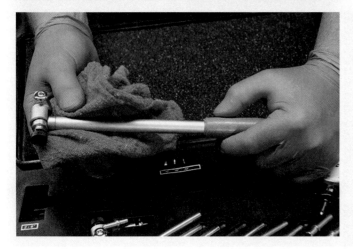

More recently, digital scales on vernier calipers have become commonplace (**FIGURE 3-110**). The principle of their use is the same as any vernier caliper; however, they have a digital scale that reads the measurement directly.

Using Vernier Calipers

Always store vernier calipers in a storage box to protect them and ensure the measuring surfaces are kept clean for accurate measurement. If making an internal or external measurement, make sure the caliper is at right angles to the surfaces to be measured. You should always repeat the measurement a number of times and compare results to ensure you have

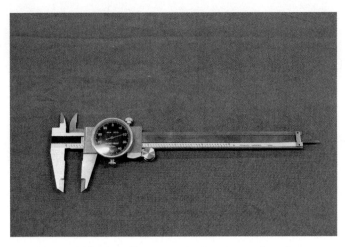

FIGURE 3-108 Vernier calipers can take three types of readings.

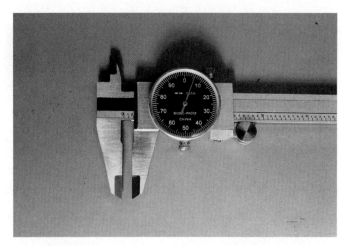

FIGURE 3-109 Dial vernier caliper.

measured accurately. To correctly measure using digital vernier calipers, follow the steps in **SKILL DRILL 3-8**.

Dial Indicators

Dial indicators can also be known as dial gauges, and as the name suggests, they have a dial and needle where measurements are read. They have a measuring plunger with a pointed or rounded contact end that is spring loaded and connected via the housing to the dial needle (**FIGURE 3-111**). The dial accurately displays movement of the plunger in and out as it rests against an object. For example, they can be used to measure the trueness of a rotating disc brake rotor. A dial indicator can also measure how round something is, such as a **crankshaft**, which can be rotated in a set of **V blocks** (**FIGURE 3-112**). If the crankshaft is bent, it will show as movement on the dial indicator as the crankshaft is rotated. The dial indicator senses slight movement at its tip and magnifies it into a measurable swing on the dial. Dial indicators normally have either one or two indicator needles. The large needle indicates the fine reading of thousandths of an inch. If it has a second needle, it will be smaller and indicates the coarse

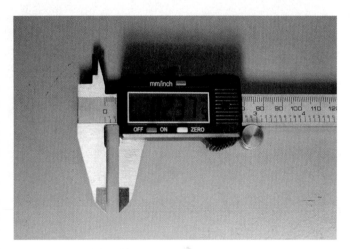

FIGURE 3-110 Digital caliper.

K03032 Describe the type and use of dial indicators.

SKILL DRILL 3-8 Using Vernier Calipers

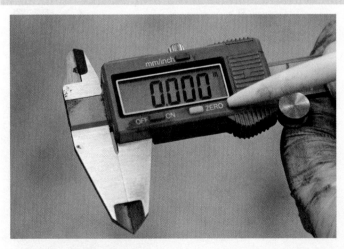

1. Verify that the vernier caliper is calibrated (zeroed) before using it.

Continued

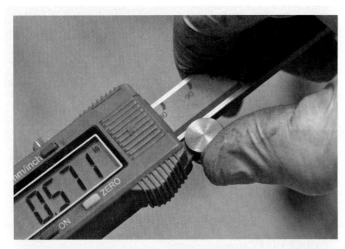

2. Position the caliper correctly for the measurement you are making. Internal and external readings are normally made with the vernier caliper positioned at 90 degrees to the face of the component to be measured. Length and depth measurements are usually made parallel to or in line with the object being measured. Use your thumb to press or withdraw the sliding jaw to measure the outside or inside of the part.

3. Read the scale of the vernier caliper, being careful not to change the position of the moveable jaw. If using a non-digital caliper, always read the dial or face straight on. A view from the side can give a considerable **parallax error**. Parallax error is a visual error caused by viewing measurement markers at an incorrect angle.

reading of tenths of an inch. The large needle is able to move numerous times around the outer scale. One full turn may represent 0.100" or 1 mm. The small inner scale indicates how many times the outer needle has moved around its scale. In this way, the dial indicator is able to read movement of up to 1" or 2 cm. Dial indicators can typically measure with an accuracy of 0.001" or 0.01 mm.

The type of dial indicator you use is determined by the amount of movement you expect from the component you are measuring. The indicator must be set up so that there

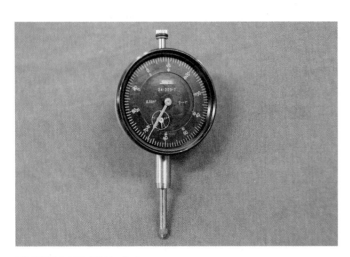

FIGURE 3-111 Dial indicator.

FIGURE 3-112 A dial indicator being used to measure crankshaft runout.

is no gap between the dial indicator and the component to be measured. It also must be set perpendicular and centered to the part being measured. Most dial indicator sets contain various attachments and support arms, so they can be configured specifically for the measuring task.

Using Dial Indicators

Dial indicators are used in many types of service jobs. They are particularly useful in determining runout on rotating shafts and surfaces. Runout is the side-to-side variation of movement when a component is turned. When attaching a dial indicator:

- Keep support arms as short as possible.
- Make sure all attachments are tightened to prevent unnecessary movement between the indicator and the component.
- Make sure the dial indicator plunger is positioned at 90 degrees to the face of the component to be measured.
- Always read the dial face straight on, as a view from the side can give a considerable parallax error.

The outer face of the dial indicator is designed so it can be rotated so that the zero mark can be positioned directly under the pointer. This is how a dial indicator is zeroed. To correctly measure using a dial indicator, follow the steps in **SKILL DRILL 3-9**.

SKILL DRILL 3-9 Using Dial Indicators

1. Select the gauge type, size, attachment, and bracket that fit the part you are measuring. Mount the dial indicator firmly to keep it stationary.

2. Adjust the indicator so that the plunger is at 90 degrees to the part you are measuring, and lock it in place.

Continued

3. Rotate the part one complete turn, and locate the low spot. Zero the indicator.

4. Find the point of maximum height and note the reading. This indicates the runout value.

5. Continue the rotation, making sure the needle does not go below zero. If it does, re-zero the indicator and remeasure the point of maximum variation.

6. Check your readings against the manufacturer's specifications. If the deviation is greater than the specifications allow, consult your supervisor.

BRAKE SPECIFICA

RER			ROTOR		
				Thickness	
CALIPER ILLUS.	Maximum Parallel Variation	Runout Limit	Nominal Thickness	Minimum Machining	Discard Or Und
	NS	.0029	NS	.937	.905
	NS	.0019	NS	.386	.354
			NS	935	90
			NS	1.015	98
			NS	.421	39

Straight Edges

Straight edges are usually made from hardened steel and are machined so that the edge is perfectly straight. A straight edge is used to check the flatness of a surface. It is placed on its edge against the surface to be checked (**FIGURE 3-113**). The gap between the straight edge and the surface can be measured by using feeler gauges. Sometimes the gap can be seen easily if light is shone from behind the surface being checked. Straight edges are often used to measure the amount of warpage the surface of a cylinder head has.

K03033 Describe the type and use of straight edges.

Feeler Gauges

Feeler gauges (also called feeler blades) are used to measure the width of gaps, such as the clearance between valves and rocker arms. Feeler gauges are flat metal strips of varying thicknesses (**FIGURE 3-114**). The thickness of each feeler gauge is clearly marked on each one. They are sized from fractions of an inch or fractions of a millimeter. They usually come in sets with different sizes and are available in standard and metric measurements. Some sets contain feeler gauges made of brass. These are used to take measurements between components that are magnetic. If steel gauges are used, the drag caused by the magnetism would mimic the drag of a proper clearance. Brass gauges are not subject to magnetism, so they work well in that situation. Some feeler gauges come in a bent arrangement to be more easily inserted in cramped spaces. Others come in a stepped version. For example, the end of the gauge might be 0.010" thick, while the rest of the gauge is 0.012" thick. This works well for adjusting valve clearance. If the specification is 0.010", then the 0.010 section can be placed in the gap. If the 0.012 section slides into the gap, then the valve needs to be readjusted. If it stops at the lip of the 0.012" section, then the gap is correct (**FIGURE 3-115**).

K03034 Describe the type and use of feeler gauges.

FIGURE 3-113 Straight edge being used to measure the flatness of a surface.

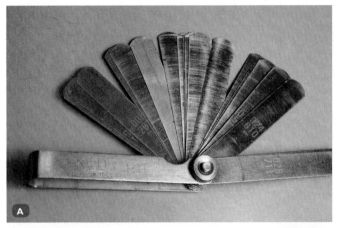

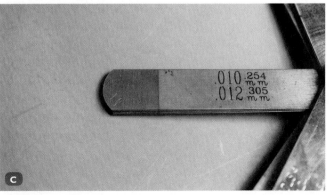

FIGURE 3-114 Feeler blade set. **A.** Straight. **B.** Bent. **C.** Stepped. **D.** Wire gauge.

FIGURE 3-115 Stepped feeler blade being used during a valve adjustment.

FIGURE 3-116 Wire feeler gauge used to check a spark plug gap.

Two or more non-stepped feeler gauges can be stacked together to make up a desired thickness. For example, to measure a thickness of 0.029 of an inch, a 0.017 and a 0.012 feeler gauge could be used together to make up the size. Alternatively, if you want to measure an unknown gap, you can interchange feeler gauges until you find the one or more that fits snugly into the gap and total their thickness to determine the measurement of the gap. In conjunction with a straight edge, they can be used to measure surface irregularities on a cylinder head.

Using Feeler Gauges

If the feeler gauge feels too loose when measuring a gap, select the next size larger, and measure the gap again. Repeat this procedure until the feeler gauge has a slight drag between both parts. If the feeler gauge is too tight, select a smaller size until the feeler gauge fits properly. When measuring a spark plug gap, feeler gauges should not be used because the surfaces of the spark plug electrodes are not perfectly parallel, so it is preferable to use wire feeler gauges (**FIGURE 3-116**).

Wire feeler gauges use accurately machined pieces of wire instead of flat metal strips. To select and use feeler gauge sets, follow the steps in **SKILL DRILL 3-10**.

SKILL DRILL 3-10 Using Feeler Gauges

1. Select the appropriate type and size feeler gauge set for the job you are working on.

2. Inspect the feeler gauges to make sure they are clean, rust-free, and undamaged, but slightly oiled for ease of movement.

Continued

3. Choose one of the smaller wires or blades, and try to insert it in the gap on the part. If it slips in and out easily, choose the next size up. When you find one that touches both sides of the gap and slides with only gentle pressure, then you have found the exact width of that gap.

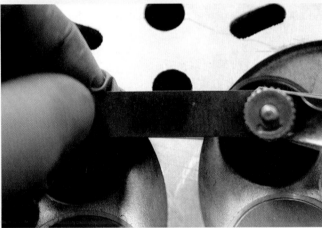

4. Read the markings on the wire or blade, and check these against the manufacturer's specifications for this component. If gap width is outside the tolerances specified, inform your supervisor.

5. Clean the feeler gauge set with an oily cloth before storage to prevent rust.

▶ Cleaning Tools and Equipment

Clean tools and equipment work more safely and efficiently. At the end of each working day, clean the tools and equipment you used and check them for any damage. If you note any damage, tag the tool as faulty and organize a repair or replacement. Electrical current can travel over oily or greasy surfaces. Be sure to keep electrical power tools clean. All shop equipment should have a maintenance schedule. Always complete the tasks described on the schedule at the required time. This helps to keep the equipment in safe working order.

N03005 Demonstrate proper cleaning, storage, and maintenance of tools and equipment.

K03035 Describe the importance of proper cleaning and storage of tools.

Store commonly used tools in an easy-to-reach location. If a tool or piece of equipment is too difficult to return, then it will likely be left on a workbench or on the floor, where it will become a safety hazard. Keep your work area tidy. This will help you work more efficiently and safely. Keep a trash can close to your work area, and place any waste in it as soon as possible. Dispose of liquid and solid waste, such as oils, coolant, and worn components, in the correct manner. Local authorities provide guidelines for waste disposal with fines for noncompliance. When cleaning products lose their effectiveness, they need to be replaced. Refer to the supplier's recommendations for collection or disposal. Do not pour solvents or other chemicals into the sewage system. This is both environmentally damaging and illegal.

Always use chemical gloves when using any cleaning material, because excessive exposure to cleaning materials can damage skin. Also, absorbing some chemicals through the skin over time can cause permanent harm to your body. Some solvents are flammable; never use cleaning materials near an open flame or cigarette. The fumes from cleaning chemicals can be toxic, so wear appropriate respirator and eye protection wherever you are using these products.

To keep work areas and equipment clean and operational, follow the steps in **SKILL DRILL 3-11**.

SAFETY TIP

Do not use flammable cleaners or water on electrical equipment.

SKILL DRILL 3-11 Tool and Equipment Cleaning

1. Clean hand tools. Keep your hand tools in good, clean condition with two types of rags. One rag should be lint-free to clean or handle precision instruments or components. The other should be oily to prevent rust and corrosion.

2. Clean floor jacks. Wipe off any oil or grease on the floor jack, and check for fluid leaks. If you find any, remove the jack from use, and have it repaired or replaced. Occasionally, apply a few drops of lubricating oil to the wheels and a few drops to the posts of threaded jack stands.

Continued

3. Clean electrical power tools. Keep power tools clean by brushing off any dust and wiping off excess oil or grease with a clean rag. Inspect any electrical cables for dirt, oil, or grease, and for any chafing or exposed wires. With drills, inspect the chuck and lubricate it occasionally with machine oil.

4. Clean air-powered tools. Apply a few drops of oil into the inlet of your air tools every day. Although these tools have no electrical motor, they do need regular lubrication of the internal parts to prevent wear.

5. Clean hoists and heavy machinery. Locate the checklist or maintenance record for each hoist or other major piece of equipment before carrying out cleaning activities.

6. You should clean equipment operating mechanisms and attachments of excess oil or grease.

▶ Wrap-Up

Ready for Review

- Tools and equipment should be used only for the task they were designed to do.
- Always have a safe attitude when using tools and equipment.
- Do not use damaged tools; inspect before using, then clean and inspect again before putting them away.
- Lockouts and tag-outs are meant to prevent technicians from using tools and equipment that are potentially unsafe.
- Many tools and measuring instruments have USCS or metric system markings to identify their size.
- Torque defines how much a fastener should be tightened.
- Torque specification indicates the level of tightness each bolt or nut should be tightened to; torque charts list torque specifications for nuts and bolts.
- Torque (or tension) wrenches tighten fasteners to the correct torque specification.
- Torque value—the amount of twisting force applied to a fastener by the torque wrench—is specified in foot-pounds (ft-lb), inch-pounds (in-lb), or newton meters (Nm).
- Torque wrench styles are beam (simplest and least expensive), clicker, dial, and electronic. Each gives an indication of when proper torque is achieved.
- Bolts that are tightened beyond their yield point do not return to their original length when loosened.
- Common wrenches include box end, open end, combination (most popular), flare nut (or flare tubing), open-end adjustable, and ratcheting box end.
- Box-end wrenches can loosen very tight fasteners, but open-end wrenches usually work better once the fastener has been broken loose.
- Use the correct wrench for the situation, so as not to damage the bolt or nut.
- Sockets grip fasteners tightly on all six corners and are purchased in sets.
- Sockets are classified as follows: standard or metric, size of drive used to turn them, number of points, depth of socket, and thickness of wall.
- The most common socket handle is a ratchet; a breaker bar gives more leverage, or a sliding T-handle may be used.
- Fasteners can be spun off or on (but not tightened) by a speed brace or speeder handle.
- Pliers hold, cut, or compress materials; types include slip-joint, combination, arc joint, needle-nose, flat, diagonal cutting, snap ring, and locking.
- Always use the correct type of pliers for the job.
- Cutting tools include bolt cutters, tin snips, and aviation snips.
- Allen wrenches are designed to fit into fasteners with recessed hexagonal heads.
- Screwdriver types include flat blade (most common), Phillips, Pozidriv, offset, ratcheting, and impact.
- The tip of the screwdriver must be matched exactly to the slot or recess on the head of a fastener.
- Magnetic pickup tools and mechanical fingers allow for the extraction and insertion of objects in tight places.
- Types of hammers include ball peen (most common), sledge, mallet, and dead blow.
- Chisels are used to cut metals when hit with a hammer.
- Punches are used to mark metals when hit with a hammer and come in different diameters and different points for different tasks; types of punches include prick, center, drift, pin, ward, and hollow.
- Pry bars can be used to move, adjust, or pry parts.
- Gasket scrapers are designed to remove gaskets without damaging surrounding materials.
- Files are used to remove material from the surface of an automotive part.
- Flat files come in different grades to indicate how rough they are; grades are rough, coarse bastard, second cut, smooth, and dead smooth.
- Types of files include flat, warding, square, triangular, curved, and thread.
- Bench vices, offset vices, drill vices, and C-clamps all hold materials in place while they are worked on.
- Taps are designed to cut threads in holes or nuts; types include taper, intermediate, and bottoming.
- A die is used to cut a new thread on a blank rod or shaft.
- Gear and bearing pullers are designed to remove components from a shaft when considerable force is needed.
- Flaring tools create flares at the end of tubes to connect them to other components; types include single, double, and ISO.
- Rivet tools join together two pieces of metal; each rivet can be used only once.
- Measuring tapes and steel rules are commonly used measuring tools; more precise measuring tools include micrometers, gauges, calipers, dial indicators, and straight edges.
- Micrometers can be outside, inside, or depth.
- Learn to read micrometer measurements on the sleeve/barrel and thimble; always verify the micrometer is properly calibrated before use.
- Gauges are used to measure distances and diameters; types include telescoping, split ball, and dial bore.
- Vernier calipers measure outside, inside, and depth dimensions; newer versions have dial and digital scales.
- Dial indicators are used to measure movement.
- A straight edge is designed to assess the flatness of a surface.
- Feeler blades are flat metal strips that are used to measure the width of gaps.
- Keep work area, tools, and equipment clean and organized.

Key Terms

Allen wrench A type of hexagonal drive mechanism for fasteners.

arc joint pliers Pliers with parallel slip jaws that can increase in size. Also called Channellocks.

aviation snips A scissor-like tool for cutting sheet metal.

ball-peen (engineer's) hammer A hammer that has a head that is rounded on one end and flat on the other; designed to work with metal items.

bench vice A device that securely holds material in jaws while it is being worked on.

blind rivet A rivet that can be installed from its insertion side.

bolt A type of threaded fastener with a thread on one end and a hexagonal head on the other.

bolt cutters Strong cutters available in different sizes, designed to cut through non-hardened bolts and other small-stock material.

bottoming tap A thread-cutting tap designed to cut threads to the bottom of a blind hole.

box-end wrench A wrench or spanner with a closed or ring end to grip bolts and nuts.

C-clamp A clamp shaped like the letter C; it comes in various sizes and can clamp various items.

center punch Less sharp than a prick punch, the center punch makes a bigger indentation that centers a drill bit at the point where a hole is required to be drilled.

cold chisel The most common type of chisel, used to cut cold metals. The cutting end is tempered and hardened so that it is harder than the metals that need to be cut.

combination pliers A type of pliers for cutting, gripping, and bending.

combination wrench A type of wrench that has a box-end wrench on one side and an open end on the other.

crankshaft A vehicle engine component that transfers the reciprocating movement of pistons into rotary motion.

cross-arm A description for an arm that is set at right angles or 90 degrees to another component.

cross-cut chisel A type of chisel for metal work that cleans out or cuts key ways.

curved file A type of file that has a curved surface for filing holes.

dead blow hammer A type of hammer that has a cushioned head to reduce the amount of head bounce.

depth micrometer A measuring device that accurately measures the depth of a hole.

diagonal cutting pliers Cutting pliers for small wire or cable.

dial bore gauge An accurate measuring device for inside bores, usually made with a dial indicator attached to it.

dial indicator An accurate measuring device where measurements are read from a dial and needle.

die Used to cut external threads on a metal shank or bolt.

die stock A handle for securely holding dies to cut threads.

double flare A seal that is made at the end of metal tubing or pipe.

drift punch A type of punch used to start pushing roll pins to prevent them from spreading.

drill vice A tool with jaws that can be attached to a drill press table for holding material that is to be drilled.

fasteners Devices that securely hold items together, such as screws, cotter pins, rivets, and bolts.

feeler gauge A thin blade device for measuring space between two objects.

finished rivet A rivet after the completion of the riveting process.

flare nut wrench A type of box-end wrench that has a slot in the box section to allow the wrench to slip through a tube or pipe. Also called a flare tubing wrench.

flat blade screwdriver A type of screwdriver that fits a straight slot in screws.

flat-nose pliers Pliers that are flat and square at the end of the nose.

forcing screw The center screw on a gear, bearing, or pulley puller. Also called a jacking screw.

gasket scraper A broad sharp flat blade to assist in removing gaskets and glue.

gear pullers A tool with two or more legs and a cross bar with a center forcing screw to remove gears.

hard rubber mallet A special-purpose tool with a head made of hard rubber; often used for moving things into place where it is important not to damage the item being moved.

hollow punch A punch with a center hollow for cutting circles in thin materials such as gaskets.

impact driver A tool that is struck with a hammer to provide an impact turning force to remove tight fasteners.

inside micrometer A micrometer designed to measure internal diameters.

intermediate tap One of a series of taps designed to cut an internal thread. Also called a plug tap.

locking pliers A type of pliers where the jaws can be set and locked into position.

lockout/tag-out A safety tag system to ensure that faulty equipment or equipment in the middle of repair is not used.

lug wrench A tool designed to remove wheel lugs nuts and commonly shaped like a cross.

magnetic pickup tools An extending shaft, often flexible, with a magnet fitted to the end for picking up metal objects.

magnetic pickup tools Useful for grabbing items in tight spaces, it typically is a telescoping stick that has a magnet attached to the end on a swivel joint.

mandrel The shaft of a pop rivet.

mandrel head The head of the pop rivet that connects to the shaft and causes the rivet body to flare.

measuring tape A thin measuring blade that rolls up and is contained in a spring-loaded dispenser.

mechanical fingers Spring-loaded fingers at the end of a flexible shaft that pick up items in tight spaces.

micrometer An accurate measuring device for internal and external dimensions. Commonly abbreviated as "mic."

needle-nose pliers Pliers with long tapered jaws for gripping small items and getting into tight spaces.

nippers (pincer pliers) Pliers designed to cut protruding items level with the surface.

nut A fastener with a hexagonal head and internal threads for screwing on bolts.

offset screwdriver A screwdriver with a 90-degree bend in the shaft for working in tight spaces.

offset vice A vice that allows long objects to be gripped vertically.

oil filter wrench A specialized wrench that allows extra leverage to remove an oil filter when it is tight.

open-end wrench A wrench with open jaws to allow side entry to a nut or bolt.

outside micrometer A micrometer designed to measure the external dimensions of items.

parallax error A visual error caused by viewing measurement markers at an incorrect angle.

peening A term used to describe the action of flattening a rivet through a hammering action.

phillips head screwdriver A type of screwdriver that fits a head shaped like a cross in screws.

pin punch A type of punch in various sizes with a straight or parallel shaft.

pipe wrench A wrench that grips pipes and can exert a lot of force to turn them. Because the handle pivots slightly, the more pressure put on the handle to turn the wrench, the more the grip tightens.

pliers A hand tool with gripping jaws.

pop rivet gun A hand tool for installing pop rivets.

prick punch A pinch with a sharp point for accurately marking a point on metal.

pry bar A high-strength carbon steel rod with offsets for levering and prying.

pullers A generic term to describe hand tools that mechanically assist the removal of bearings, gears, pulleys, and other parts.

punches A generic term to describe a high-strength carbon steel shaft with a blunt point for driving. Center and prick punches are exceptions and have a sharp point for marking or making an indentation.

ratchet A generic term to describe a handle for sockets that allows the user to select direction of rotation. It can turn sockets in restricted areas without the user having to remove the socket from the fastener.

ratcheting box-end wrench A wrench with an inner piece that is able to rotate within the outer housing, allowing it to be repositioned without being removed.

ratcheting screwdriver A screwdriver with a selectable ratchet mechanism built into the handle that allows the screwdriver tip to ratchet as it is being used.

roll bar Another type of pry bar, with one end used for prying and the other end for aligning larger holes, such as engine motor mounts.

screw extractor A tool for removing broken screws or bolts.

single flare A sealing system made on the end of metal tubing.

sledgehammer A heavy hammer, usually with two flat faces, that provides a strong blow.

sliding T-handle A handle fitted at 90 degrees to the main body that can be slid from side to side.

snap ring pliers A pair of pliers for installing and removing snap rings or circlips.

socket An enclosed metal tube commonly with 6 or 12 points to remove and install bolts and nuts.

speed brace A U-shaped socket wrench that allows high-speed operation. Also called a speeder handle.

split ball gauge A measuring device used to accurately measure small holes.

square file A type of file with a square cross section.

steel hammer A hammer with a head made of hardened steel.

steel rule An accurate measuring ruler made of steel.

straight edge A measuring device generally made of steel to check how flat a surface is.

tap A term used to generically describe an internal thread-cutting tool.

taper tap A tap with a tapper; it is usually the first of three taps used when cutting internal threads.

tap handle A tool designed to securely hold taps for cutting internal threads.

telescoping gauge A gauge that expands and locks to the internal diameter of bores; a caliper or outside micrometer is used to measure its size.

thread file A type of file that cleans clogged or distorted threads on bolts and studs.

thread pitch The coarseness or fineness of a thread as measured by either the threads per inch or the distance from the peak of one thread to the next. Metric fasteners are measured in millimeters.

tin snips Cutting device for sheet metal, works in a similar fashion to scissors.

torque Twisting force applied to a shaft that may or may not result in motion.

torque specifications Supplied by manufacturers and describes the amount of twisting force allowable for a fastener or a specification showing the twisting force from an engine crankshaft.

torque wrench A tool used to measure the rotational or twisting force applied to fasteners.

triangular file A type of file with three sides so it can get into internal corners.

tube flaring tool A tool that makes a sealing flare on the end of metal tubing.

tubing cutter A hand tool for cutting pipe or tubing squarely.

V blocks Metal blocks with a V-shaped cutout for holding shafts while working on them. Also referred to as vee blocks.

vernier calipers An accurate measuring device for internal, external, and depth measurements that incorporates fixed and adjustable jaws.

wad punch A type of punch that is hollow for cutting circular shapes in soft materials such as gaskets.

warding file A type of thin, flat file with a tapered end.

wrenches A generic term to describe tools that tighten and loosen fasteners with hexagonal heads.

Review Questions

1. Specialty tools:
   a. should not be shared among technicians.
   b. should have tag-out practices for regular storage.
   c. should be put in the proper storage space after each use.
   d. can be used for purposes they were not designed for.
2. A set of safety practices and procedures that are intended to reduce the risk of technicians inadvertently using tools that have been determined to be unsafe is known as:
   a. lockout.
   b. shop policy.
   c. equipment storage procedure.
   d. PPE maintenance.
3. Which of these wrenches can be awkward to use once the nut or bolt has been loosened a bit?
   a. Open-end
   b. Flare nut
   c. Combination
   d. Box-end
4. Oil filters should be installed using:
   a. an oil filter wrench.
   b. a flare nut wrench.
   c. your hand.
   d. arc joint pliers.
5. When tightening lug fasteners, an impact wrench should:
   a. always be used.
   b. never be used.
   c. be used in difficult-to-access positions.
   d. never be used in high-torque settings.
6. Which of these would you use for a wider grip and a tighter squeeze on parts too big for conventional pliers?
   a. Diagonal cutting pliers
   b. External snap ring pliers
   c. Arc joint pliers
   d. Combination pliers
7. When a large chisel needs a really strong blow, use a:
   a. sledgehammer.
   b. hard rubber mallet.
   c. dead blow hammer.
   d. ball-peen hammer.

8. Which style of torque wrench is the simplest and least expensive?
   a. Clicker
   b. Dial
   c. Beam
   d. Electronic
9. The depth of blind holes in housings can best be measured using a:
   a. measuring tape.
   b. steel rule.
   c. dial bore gauge.
   d. vernier caliper.
10. All of the following are good practices *except*:
    a. replacing cleaning products when they lose their effectiveness.
    b. discarding solvents into the sewage system immediately after use.
    c. using chemical gloves when using any cleaning material.
    d. wearing a respirator when using toxic cleaning chemicals.

ASE Technician A/Technician B Style Questions

1. Tech A says that knowing how to use tools correctly creates a safe working environment. Tech B says that a flare nut wrench is used to loosen very tight bolts and nuts. Who is correct?
   a. Tech A
   b. Tech B
   c. Both A and B
   d. Neither A nor B
2. Tech A says that lockout is designed to secure a vehicle after all work on it has been completed. Tech B says that tag-out is used when a tool is no longer fit for use and identifies what is wrong with it. Who is correct?
   a. Tech A
   b. Tech B
   c. Both A and B
   d. Neither A nor B
3. Tech A says that torque wrenches need to be calibrated periodically to ensure proper torque values. Tech B says that when using a clicker-style torque wrench, keep turning the torque wrench ⅛–¼ turn to make sure the bolt is properly tightened. Who is correct?
   a. Tech A
   b. Tech B
   c. Both A and B
   d. Neither A nor B
4. Tech A says that when using a micrometer, a "standard" is used to hold the part you are measuring. Tech B says that the micrometer spindle should be firmly closed against the anvil prior to storage. Who is correct?
   a. Tech A
   b. Tech B
   c. Both A and B
   d. Neither A nor B

5. Tech A says that a box-end wrench is more likely to round the head of a bolt than an open-end wrench. Tech B says that 6-point sockets and wrenches will hold more firmly when removing and tightening bolts. Who is correct?
   a. Tech A
   b. Tech B
   c. Both A and B
   d. Neither A nor B

6. Tech A says that it is usually better to pull a wrench to tighten or loosen a bolt. Tech B says that pushing a wrench will protect your knuckles if the wrench slips. Who is correct?
   a. Tech A
   b. Tech B
   c. Both A and B
   d. Neither A nor B

7. Tech A says that a feeler gauge is used to measure the diameter of small holes. Tech B says that a feeler gauge and straight edge are used to check surfaces for warpage. Who is correct?
   a. Tech A
   b. Tech B
   c. Both A and B
   d. Neither A nor B

8. Tech A says that a dead blow hammer reduces rebound of the hammer. Tech B says that a dead blow hammer should be used with a chisel to cut the head of a bolt off. Who is correct?
   a. Tech A
   b. Tech B
   c. Both A and B
   d. Neither A nor B

9. Tech A says that gaskets can be removed quickly and safely with a hammer and sharp chisel. Tech B says that extreme care must be used when removing a gasket on an aluminum surface. Who is correct?
   a. Tech A
   b. Tech B
   c. Both A and B
   d. Neither A nor B

10. Tech A says that when using a file, apply pressure to file in the direction of the cut and no pressure when pulling the file back. Tech B says that file cards are used to file uneven surfaces. Who is correct?
    a. Tech A
    b. Tech B
    c. Both A and B
    d. Neither A nor B

CHAPTER 4

Fasteners and Thread Repair

NATEF Tasks

- **N04001** Perform common fastener and thread repair, to include: remove broken bolt, restore internal and external threads, and repair internal threads with thread insert.

Knowledge Objectives

After reading this chapter, you will be able to:

- **K04001** Identify threaded fasteners and describe their use.
- **K04002** Identify standard and metric fasteners.
- **K04003** Describe how bolts are sized.
- **K04004** Describe thread pitch and how it is measured.
- **K04005** Describe bolt grade.
- **K04006** Describe the types of bolt strength required.
- **K04007** Describe nuts and their application.

- **K04008** Describe washers and their applications.
- **K04009** Describe the purpose and application of thread-locking compounds.
- **K04010** Describe screws and their applications.
- **K04011** Describe the torque-to-yield and torque angle.
- **K04012** Describe how to avoid broken fasteners.
- **K04013** Identify situations where thread repair is necessary.

Skills Objectives

- **S04001** Perform common fastener and thread repair.

You Are the Automotive Technician

The new intern was helping you disassemble a leaking water pump. All was going well until one of the bolts broke off while removing it. It is evident that the shank of the bolt had been narrowed considerably due to rust and corrosion over time. You know that removing this bolt could turn the job into a real nightmare if not performed properly and carefully. It is also an opportunity to teach the intern how to perform this important task. As you are thinking about this task, several questions come to mind.

1. If part of the bolt extends past the surface it is threaded into, what can be done to try to remove it without using a bolt extractor?
2. What processes can be tried on bolts that are stuck, before they are broken off?
3. Is it okay to use a replacement bolt of a different grade from the original bolt? Why or why not?
4. What is the purpose of a thread-locking compound? Give an example of when should it be used?
5. What is the purpose of antiseize? Give examples of when it should and shouldn't be used?

▶ Introduction

Fasteners come in two common types: threaded fasteners and non-threaded fasteners (**FIGURE 4-1**). Both types of **fasteners** are designed to secure parts. **Threaded fasteners** are primarily designed to clamp objects together. Non-threaded fasteners are designed to hold parts together, such as preventing a component from falling off a shaft by using C-clips, cotter pins, roll pins, or other retainers. They can also be used to clamp components together, for example, with rivets. Each type of fastener has a different purpose or application, so getting to know the various kinds will help you know how to disassemble and reassemble component assemblies. We cover the major types of threaded and non-threaded fasteners below.

▶ Threaded Fasteners and Torque

K04001 Identify threaded fasteners and describe their use.

Threaded fasteners are designed to secure parts that are under various tension and sheer stresses. The nature of the stresses placed on parts and threaded fasteners depends on their use and location. For example, head bolts withstand tension stresses by clamping the head gasket between the cylinder head and block so that combustion pressures can be contained in the cylinder (**FIGURE 4-2**). The bolts must withstand the very high combustion pressures trying to push the head off the top of the engine block in order to prevent leaks past the head gasket. In this situation, the pressure is trying to stretch the head bolts, which means they are under tension.

Some fasteners must withstand sheer stresses, which are sideways forces trying to shear the bolt in two (**FIGURE 4-3**). An example of fasteners withstanding sheer stresses is wheel lug studs and lug nuts. They clamp the wheel assembly to the suspension system, and the weight of the vehicle tries to sheer the lug studs. If this were to happen, the wheel would fall off the vehicle, likely leading to an accident.

To accomplish their job, fasteners come in a variety of diameters for different sized loads, and hardnesses, which are defined in grades. Threaded fasteners are designed to be tightened to a specified amount depending on several factors such as the job at hand, the grade or hardness of the material they are made from, their size, and the thread type. If a fastener is over-tightened, it could become damaged or could break. If it is under-tightened, it could work loose over time. Torque is a measure of twisting force around an axis, so it is a way of defining how much a fastener should be, or is, tightened to. Manufacturers print **torque specifications** in torque charts for virtually every fastener on a vehicle.

The idea of threaded fasteners has been around since approximately 240 B.C., when Archimedes invented the screw conveyor. The screw design was adapted to a straight pin to attach different materials together. As time progressed, the materials that the screw was made from became stronger, and the sizing became more precise. Whitworth created a thread profile that had a rounded crest and rounded root in England in 1841 (**FIGURE 4-4**). Then in 1864, in the United States, Sellers created a thread profile that had a flat crest and flat root (**FIGURE 4-5**).

In order to create the threaded fasteners we use today, the flat crest and rounded root is used along with a 60-degree pitch angle (**FIGURE 4-6**). Metric and standard size bolts use the same shape of threads, excluding specialty-use bolts, which are made for a particular purpose, such as the lead screw for a vice or gear puller. The square edges of this specialty thread (**square thread**) tend to exert force more in line with the screw, where a V-thread tends to push at a 90-degree angle to the thread, not the screw (**FIGURE 4-7**).

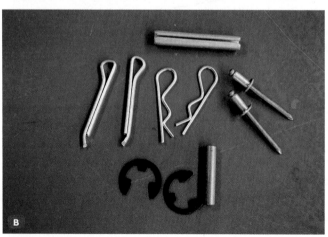

FIGURE 4-1 A. Threaded fasteners. **B.** Non-threaded fasteners.

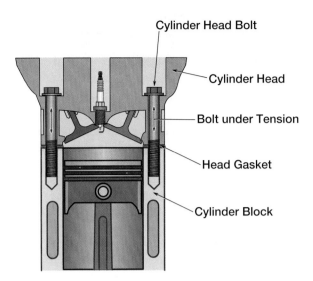

FIGURE 4-2 Bolts clamp parts together.

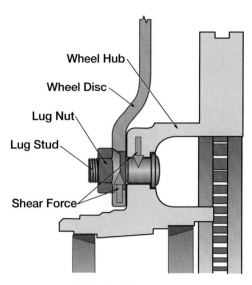

FIGURE 4-3 Bolt under sheer stresses.

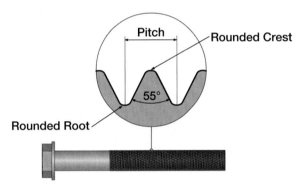

FIGURE 4-4 Whitworth thread.

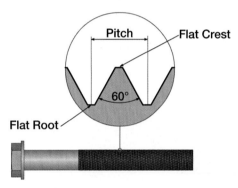

FIGURE 4-5 Sellers thread.

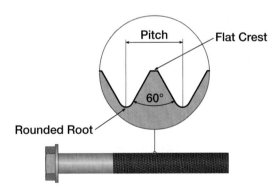

FIGURE 4-6 Current thread.

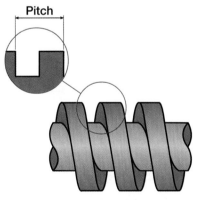

FIGURE 4-7 Square thread as used in a vice.

▶ Fastener Standardization

There are many different groups that monitor and set the standards that make the automotive industry conform to one universally recognized specification set. There are three main groups to know about. The American Society for Testing and Materials (ASTM) is a nongovernmental controlled group that tests and sets standards in all areas of industry. The International Organization for Standardization (ISO) is an independent developer of standards that are created to ensure a reliable, safe, and quality product. The Society of

K04002 Identify standard and metric fasteners.

Automotive Engineers (SAE) was initially started to standardize automotive production and has since grown to encompass a lot of engineering disciplines creating standards and best practices literature.

Metric Bolts

The metric bolt came about from the ISO standard 898, which defines mechanical and physical properties of metric fasteners. The ISO is an independent developer of voluntary international standards. In other words, any one government or group does not control them. The ISO develops standards that apply to many different industries in many different countries, using an unbiased logical approach. The metric decimal system has been around since the late 1600s and is sequential, so people can quickly see which number is larger. Many countries have adopted this standard for their weights and measure systems, but have also retained their own customary standards. Certain industries have required more precision in measurement, so they have adopted the metric system exclusively.

The automotive industry is one that deals in precise measurement and exact specifications in every aspect of automobile design. For this reason and because most automotive companies are worldwide, the automotive industry has embraced the metric measuring system. Uniformity is very important in the production environment, as it leads to efficiencies and conformity. Because of this, most vehicle manufacturers use metric fasteners almost exclusively, but not entirely. So you need to be able to distinguish between metric and standard fasteners. Most metric fasteners can be identified by the grade number cast into the head of the bolt (**FIGURE 4-8**).

FIGURE 4-8 Metric bolts can be identified by the grade number on the top of the bolt head.

Standard Bolts

The standard measurement of bolts is a combination of the Imperial and U.S. customary measurement systems. SAE standard J429 covers the Mechanical and Material Requirements that govern this standard for externally threaded fasteners. It combines the British measuring units and the U.S. measuring units created after the Revolutionary War. Based on the British units of measure, units have been developed over the past millennia to arrive at today's standards. Instead of using a decimal number–based system like the Metric units, they are fractional based. Because the measurement system is based on a fractional scale, people unfamiliar with fractions can find using it difficult. This system is falling out of favor with many industries. As technology becomes more demanding, more precision and standardization is required for both effectiveness and efficiency. Standard bolts can generally be identified by hash marks cast into the head of the bolt, indicating the bolt's grade (**FIGURE 4-9**).

FIGURE 4-9 Standard bolts can be identified by the hash marks on top of the bolt head.

▶ Bolts, Studs, and Nuts

Bolts, studs, and nuts are threaded fasteners designed for jobs requiring a fastener heavier than a screw and tend to be made of metal alloys, making them stronger (**FIGURE 4-10**). Typical **bolts** are cylindrical pieces of metal with a hexagonal head on one end and a thread cut into the shaft at the other end. The thread acts as an inclined plane; as the bolt is turned, it is drawn into or out of the mating thread. Hexagonal **nuts** thread onto the bolt thread. The hexagonal heads for the bolt and nut are designed

FIGURE 4-10 Bolts, studs, and nuts.

to be turned by tools such as wrenches and sockets. Note that other bolt head designs are used as well. These require special shaped tools as covered in the Hand Tools chapter.

A **stud** does not have a fixed hexagonal head; rather, it has a thread cut on each end. It is threaded into one part where it stays. The mating part is then slipped over it, and a nut is threaded onto the other end of the stud to secure the part. Studs are commonly used to attach one component to another, such as a throttle body to the intake manifold. Studs can have different threads on each end, to work best with the material they are threaded into. Coarse threads work well in aluminum; in such cases, one end of the stud may use a coarse thread to grip the threads in an aluminum intake manifold and to position the throttle body. On the other end, there may be a fine thread for pulling everything together tightly with a steel nut. Bolts, nuts, and studs have either standard or metric threads. They are designated by their thread diameter, thread pitch, length, and grade. The diameter is measured across the outside of the threads, in fractions of an inch for standard-type fasteners, and millimeters for metric-type fasteners. So a 3/8" (9.5 mm) bolt has a thread diameter of 3/8" (9.5 mm). It is important to note that a 3/8" (9.5 mm) bolt does not have a 3/8" (9.5 mm) bolt head.

FIGURE 4-11 Bolt diameter and length.

Sizing Bolts

Bolts are sized either by metric or standard measuring systems. A ½" (12.7 mm) bolt does not mean that the bolt has a head that fits into a ½" (12.7 mm) socket. It means that the distance across the outside diameter of the bolt's threads measures ½" (12.7 mm) in diameter. The same goes for the metric equivalent; an 8 mm bolt is the diameter of the outside diameter of the bolt's threads. The length of a bolt is fairly straightforward. It is measured from the end of the bolt to the bottom of the head and is listed in inches or millimeters (**FIGURE 4-11**).

K04003 Describe how bolts are sized.

Thread Pitch

The coarseness of any thread is called its **thread pitch** (**FIGURE 4-12**). In the standard system, bolts, studs, and nuts are measured in threads per inch (TPI). To determine the TPI, simply count the number of threads there are in 1" (25.4 mm). Each bolt diameter in the standard system can typically have one of two thread pitches, **Unified National Coarse Thread (UNC)** or **Unified National Fine Thread (UNF)**. For example, a 3/8–16 is coarse, and a 3/8–24 is fine. In the metric system, the thread pitch is measured in millimeters by the distance between the peaks of the threads. So course threads have larger distances, and fine threads have smaller distances. Each bolt diameter in the metric system can have up to four thread pitches (**FIGURE 4-13**). Consult a metric thread pitch chart, because there is no clear pattern of thread pitches for metric fasteners. These charts can be found in tap and die sets or on the Internet.

K04004 Describe thread pitch and how it is measured.

FIGURE 4-12 UNC and UNF standard bolt thread pitch.

FIGURE 4-13 Metric thread pitches.

Thread Pitch Gauge

Thread pitch gauges make identifying the thread pitch on any bolt quick and easy. Without a thread pitch gauge, technicians are stuck measuring the number of threads per inch, or the distance from peak to peak in millimeters, with a ruler. Each thread pitch gauge matches a particular thread pitch that is stamped or engraved on the gauge. To use a thread pitch gauge, find the gauge that fits perfectly into the threads on the bolt you are measuring. Just make sure you keep the gauge parallel to the shaft of the bolt; otherwise, you will get a wrong match (**FIGURE 4-14**).

Grading of Bolts

K04005 Describe bolt grade.

What is bolt grading? Bolt grade or class means that the fastener meets the strength requirements of that grade or classification. There are a variety of grades, so it is important to use the specified grade of bolt for each component. When bolts are tested for grade, the bolt is put in a testing tool and abused to the point of breakage so that the maximum readings can be determined to properly grade the fastener. We need to know a bolt's grade so that we are able to use the correct fastener for the application and avoid bolt failures down the road. Standard bolts are typically grade 1 to grade 8, with grade 8 being the strongest. The grade can be identified by counting the hash marks on the head of the bolt and adding two to that number. For example, there are three hash marks on the head of a grade 5 bolt and six on the head of a grade 8 bolt (**FIGURE 4-15**).

Metric bolt grades are typically grade 4.6 to grade 12.9, with grade 12.9 being the strongest. In metric bolts, the grade number is cast into the top of the bolt head. These numbers on metric bolts have specific meanings. The number before the decimal indicates its tensile strength in megapascals (MPa), which is found by multiplying the number by 100. For example a metric 12.9-grade bolt would have a tensile strength of 1200 MPa. The number to the right of the decimal, when multiplied by 10 indicates the yield point as a percentage of the tensile strength (**FIGURE 4-16**).

Just because the higher grades are stronger doesn't mean you should use those in all applications. There are times when lower-graded bolts are more appropriate for particular applications, such as with some head bolts that need to have a little bit of give in them to allow for expansion and contraction of the cylinder head when the head gasket is clamped in place. Otherwise, the head gasket seal could fail. In other situations, using the wrong grade of bolt could cause either the bolt to fail or the threads in the threaded hole to fail. So you should always use the specified grade bolt when replacing bolts with new ones.

FIGURE 4-14 Thread pitch gauge being used. **A.** Standard. **B.** Metric.

FIGURE 4-15 A. Grade 5 standard bolt. **B.** Grade 8 standard bolt.

FIGURE 4-16 A. Grade 8.8 metric bolt **B.** Grade 10.9 metric bolt.

Strength of Bolts

Tensile Strength

Tensile strength is the maximum tension (applied load) the fastener can withstand without being torn apart or the maximum stress used under tension (lengthwise force) without causing failure. Tensile strength is determined by the strength of the material and the size of the stress area. When a typical threaded fastener fails in pure tension, it usually fractures through the threaded portion, as that is the weakest area because it is also the smallest area of the bolt (**FIGURE 4-17**). Generally speaking, the higher the grade of bolt, the higher the tensile strength.

K04006 Describe the types of bolt strength required.

Shear Strength

Shear strength is defined as the maximum load that can be supported prior to fracture, when applied at a right angle to the fastener's axis. A load occurring in one transverse plane is known as single shear (**FIGURE 4-18**). Double shear is a load applied in two planes, where the fastener could be cut into three pieces. For most standard threaded fasteners, shear strength is not specified, even though the fastener may be commonly used in shear applications. Generally speaking, the higher the grade of bolt, the higher the shear strength.

FIGURE 4-17 Bolt failure (tension).

Proof Load

The proof load represents the usable strength range for certain standard fasteners. By definition, the proof load is an applied

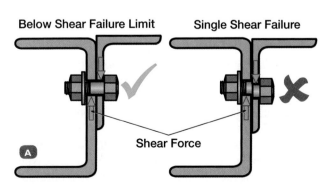

FIGURE 4-18 A. Single shear. **B.** Double shear.

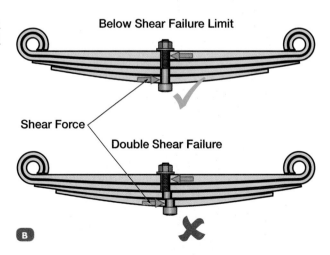

tensile load that the fastener must support without exceeding the elastic phase, which is the point up to which the bolt returns to its original point when tension is removed.

Fatigue Strength

A fastener subjected to repeated cyclic loads can suddenly and unexpectedly break, even if the loads are well below the strength of the material. The repeated cyclic loading weakens the fastener over time, and it fails from fatigue. The fatigue strength is the maximum stress a fastener can withstand for a specified number of repeated cycles before failing. Connecting rod bolts are an example of a situation where fatigue strength would need to withstand millions of cyclic loads.

Torsional Strength

Torsional strength is a measure of a material's ability to withstand a twisting load, usually expressed in terms of torque, in which the fastener fails by being twisted off about its axis. A fastener that fails due to low torsional strength typically fails during installation or removal. Generally speaking, the higher the grade, the higher the torsional strength of the fastener.

Ductility

Ductility is the ability of a material to deform before it fractures. A material that experiences very little or no plastic deformation before fracturing is considered brittle. Think of a piece of flat glass: If you try to bend it, it breaks easily. This is an example of a material with low ductility material. Most automotive fasteners need to have some measure of ductility to avoid catastrophic failure. A reasonable indication of a fastener's ductility is the ratio of its specified minimum yield strength to the minimum tensile strength. The lower this ratio, the more ductile the fastener, meaning that the more ductile the bolt, the more it can flex or stretch without breaking. Generally speaking, the higher the grade, the lower the ductility of the fastener. So a balance between tensile strength and ductility is needed that depends on the requirements of the application.

Toughness

Toughness is defined as a material's ability to absorb impact or shock loading. Impact strength toughness is rarely a specified requirement for automotive applications. In addition to its specification for various aerospace industry fasteners, ASTM A320 specification for alloy steel bolting materials for low-temperature service is one of the few specifications that requires impact testing on certain grades.

Nuts

K04007 Describe nuts and their application.

Nuts are screwed onto the threads of a bolt to hold something together. They have internal threads that match the threads on the same size bolt. The many different kinds of nuts are mostly application specific. We cover some of the more popular ones below. When you replace a nut with a new nut on a vehicle, you need to match the nut to the grade of bolt or stud that it is going to be screwed onto. For example, if the bolt is a grade 8, you need a grade 8 nut. By matching the grade of fasteners, you are keeping the integrity of the manufacturer's intended fastening system. If you mix different grades of bolts and nuts, one could prematurely fail, causing catastrophic failure of the component.

Locking Nuts

Locking nuts are used when there is a chance of the nut vibrating loose. Two common types of locking nuts are used in automotive applications: the nylon insert lock nut and the deformed lock nut (**FIGURE 4-19**). The nylon lock nut has a nylon insert with a smaller diameter hole than the threads in the nut. As the nut is threaded onto the bolt, the nylon insert is deformed by the bolt threads, which tends to lock the nut onto the thread of the bolt or stud so that it can't vibrate loose. In a deformed lock nut, the top thread of the nut is deformed, thus pinching the bolt threads so the nut can't vibrate loose. Both of these types of lock nuts are considered single use, meaning they should be replaced with new ones once they have been removed.

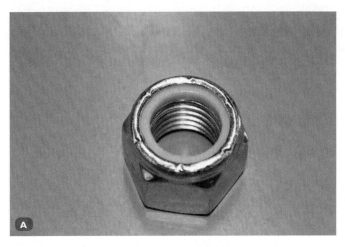

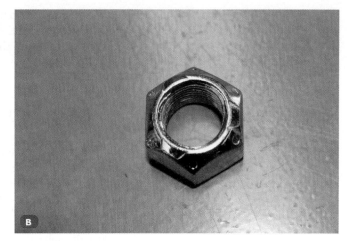

FIGURE 4-19 A. Nylon lock nut. **B.** Deformed lock nut.

Castle Nuts

Castle nuts, sometimes called castellated nuts, are used with a cotter pin to keep them from moving once they are installed. Protrusions and notches are machined into the top of the nut. The notches then can be lined up with a hole in the threaded bolt or stud (**FIGURE 4-20**). A cotter pin passes through the notch on one side of the nut, then through the hole in the stud and out the notch in the other side of the nut. The cotter pin physically prevents the castle nut from backing off the stud. These nuts are usually used on suspension components or other critical components so that they can't loosen up. It is good practice to always use new cotter pins and visually check to verify if they are installed in the castle nuts before finishing up a job (**FIGURE 4-21**).

Specialty Nuts

In the automotive industry. there are lot of specialty nuts with special characteristics—for example, an extended shoulder, a special head size, or a special material—required for a particular application. You must use the correct nut for the correct application (**FIGURE 4-22**). Sheet metal nuts are a cheap alternative to a regular nut that manufactures are using on different components. Sometimes called J nuts, these nuts are folded

FIGURE 4-20 Castle nut used on a ball joint.

FIGURE 4-21 New cotter pins installed in the castle nuts.

FIGURE 4-22 A variety of specialty nuts.

piece of sheet metal that fits over a hole in a piece of sheet metal; they are threaded to accept a fastener, and they usually do not need to be held as they are clipped to the component. Failure to use the proper fasteners for the proper uses usually results in failure of the component.

Washers

K04008 Describe washers and their applications.

Why are washers used underneath bolt heads and nuts? There are three main purposes of a washer:

- To distribute the force exerted on the component that it is pressing against evenly
- To prevent the surface around the hole from being worn down due to tightening of the head of the bolt or nut against a surface
- To provide a measure of locking force to keep the bolt or nut from loosening due to vibration

Not all applications require washers that provide all three functions, so make sure you know what the application requires. When selecting a washer for a bolt or nut, make sure you use the correct type, size, and grade.

Grades of Washers

Just as with nuts, you want to match the grade of washer to the nut and bolt so that you can maximize the clamping force on the component (**FIGURE 4-23**). Using dissimilar metals that have different hardness characteristics can cause the surface of the softer metal to wear away. This reduces the clamping force over time, which can cause the bolt or component to fail. Not all washers have grade ratings on them, so be careful to select the proper one when replacing a damaged or missing washer with a new one.

Flat Washers

A flat washer is a piece of steel that has been cut in a circular shape with a hole in the middle for the bolt or stud to fit through. Washers are sized and paired with a metric or standard bolt so that the pressure created by torquing the bolt down is spread out on the component that it is being used on (**FIGURE 4-24**). They prevent marring of the surface of the component around the bolt hole. They also act as a bearing surface so that the bolt achieves the expected clamping force at the specified torque. Flat washers are graded just like bolts, which means you need to match the grade on the washer with the fasteners that you are using them on.

Lock Washers

Lock washers are made from spring steel and have a slit cut in them to allow for the spring action to hold tension against the nut so that the nut will not loosen. Also, the slit is cut at an angle, with sharp edges on the top and bottom to cut into the bottom of the bolt head and the surface of the component being clamped (**FIGURE 4-25**). The sharp edges bite into the bolt and component if the bolt tries to loosen. These are used with conventional nuts and are usually used in applications that create a lot of vibration. Lock washers are usually considered to be single use and should be replaced rather than reused.

Star Washers

Star washers, also called toothed lock washers, are used sometimes to stop the rotation of the nut above. They work in a similar way to lock washers in that the teeth are at angles so that they bite into the bottom of the bolt head and the surface being clamped (**FIGURE 4-26**). If these washers are required for your application, they need to be reinstalled before the nut is installed. They also should be replaced with new ones rather than reused.

FIGURE 4-23 Washer with its grade rating marked on it.

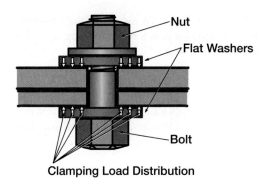

FIGURE 4-24 Flat washer spreading out the clamping force.

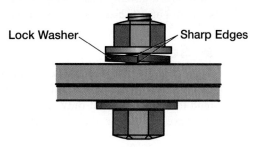

FIGURE 4-25 Lock washers prevent bolts and nuts from loosening. (Note: this nut and bolt is not fully tightened to show the action of the lock washer.)

FIGURE 4-26 Star washers prevent nuts and bolts from loosening.

▶ Threadlocker and Antiseize

Thread-locking compound is a liquid that is put on the threads of a bolt or stud to hold the nut that is threaded over it. The thread-locking compound acts like very strong glue. Once the compound between the nut and bolt cures, it bonds the two together so that they do not move. A popular thread-locking compound (threadlocker) that most automotive technicians prefer is Loctite®. The two main strengths of locking compound that are used in the automotive industry are blue and red (**FIGURE 4-27**). The blue allows for relatively easy removal of the nut or bolt with a socket and ratchet, whereas the red is much stronger. The red version usually requires a fair amount of heat to soften the compound so the nut or bolt can be removed. Thread-locking compound is a good safety item that technicians use on critical parts they do not want to come loose. In fact, the manufacturer may specify its use on certain fasteners, so be aware of situations that require thread-locking compound, and use the strength required.

Antiseize compound is the opposite of thread-locking compound as it keeps threaded fasteners from becoming corroded together or seized due to galling. One common use of antiseize compound is on black steel spark plug threads when the spark plug is installed into an aluminum cylinder head. Antiseize compound is a coating that prevents rust and provides lubrication so that the fastener can be removed in the future. Because of that, it should *not* be used on most fasteners in a vehicle; otherwise, they

K04009 Describe the purpose and application of thread-locking compounds.

FIGURE 4-27 Thread-locking compound.

could vibrate loose, causing damage or an accident. When you do use antiseize compound on specified fasteners, use a very light coating, as a little bit goes a very long way. In fact, a small can of antiseize lasts the average technician several years.

▶ Screws

K04010 Describe screws and their applications.

Many different types of screws are found in automotive applications (**FIGURE 4-28**). A screw is very similar to a bolt except for a couple of differences: They are not hardened and they tend to be used in light-duty applications where they need to hold together components that have a low shear or tensile strength.

Machine Screws

Similar to a bolt, a machine screw is used to fasten components together, but these are usually driven by a screwdriver with a Philips or slotted head. Machine screws are usually driven into a nut or threaded hole that has been tapped to the thread pitch of the screw. As vehicles become more complex, manufacturers have started to introduce new types of driving tools for these screws. Torx, square, and Allen head screws are becoming prevalent in this fastener group (**FIGURE 4-29**).

Self-Tapping Screws

Self-tapping screws are designed to create their own holes in the material they are being driven into. They have a fluted tip so you can drill a hole into the base material, without needing a pilot hole (**FIGURE 4-30**). The threads on a self-tapping screw are very similar to those on a sheet metal screw as they grip onto the metal as you drill through it. Usually they have a cap screw–type head so they can be driven with a screw gun, but they can have Phillips, square, Allen, or Torx heads as well.

Trim Screws

Trim screws are used in applications where there is a need to hold plastic and metal ornamentation to the vehicle. They are also used to hold door panels, trim pieces, and other small components to the vehicle. They are basic screws that are usually painted either the trim color or black so that they blend in with the material that they are used with (**FIGURE 4-31**).

Sheet Metal Screws

Sheet metal screws are used to attach things to sheet metal. They have a chip on the tip of the screw to push away material as it

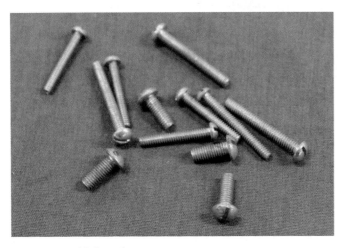

FIGURE 4-28 Variety of screws.

FIGURE 4-29 Machine screw heads.

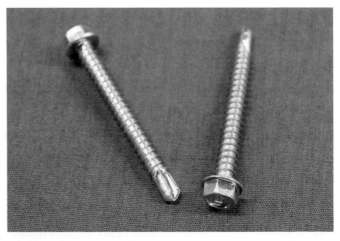

FIGURE 4-30 Self-tapping screws.

FIGURE 4-31 Trim screws.

FIGURE 4-32 Sheet metal screws.

comes off (**FIGURE 4-32**). These screws are usually threaded all the way up to the head so that they can be run down all the way, clamping the pieces together.

▶ Torque-to-Yield and Torque Angle

Torque is not always the best method of ensuring that a bolt is tightened enough as to give the proper amount of clamping force. If the threads are rusty, rough, or damaged in any way, the amount of twisting force required to tighten the fastener increases. Tightening the rusty fastener to a particular torque does not provide as much clamping force as a smooth fastener torqued the same amount. This also brings up the question of whether threads should be lubricated. In most automotive cases, the torque values specified are for dry, non-lubricated threads. But always check the manufacturer's specifications.

When bolts are tightened, they are also stretched. As long as they are not tightened too much, they will return to their original length when loosened. This is called **elasticity**. If they continue to be tightened and stretch beyond their point of elasticity, they will not return to their original length when loosened. This is called the **yield point**. As threaded fasteners are torqued, they go through the following phases:

- **Rundown Phase:** Free running fastener (may or may not have prevailing torque).
- **Alignment Phase:** Fastener and joint mating surfaces are drawn into alignment.
- **Elastic Phase:** *This is the third and final stage for normal bolts!* The slope of the torque/angle curve is constant. The fastener is elongated but will return to original length upon loosening.
- **Plastic or Yield Phase:** *Over-torqued condition for normal bolts. TTY bolts are tightened just into the beginning points of this phase.* Permanent deformation and elongation of the fastener and/or joint occur. Necking of the fastener occurs.

Torque-to-yield means that a fastener is torqued to, or just beyond, its yield point. With the changes in engine metallurgy that manufacturers are using in today's vehicles, bolt technology had to change also. To help prevent bolts from loosening over time and to maintain an adequate clamping force when the engine is both cold and hot, manufacturers have adopted **torque-to-yield (TTY) bolts**. TTY bolts are designed to provide a consistent clamping force when torqued to their yield point or just beyond. The challenge is that the torque does not increase very much, or at all, once yield is reached. So using a torque wrench by itself will not indicate the point at which the manufacturer wants the bolt tightened. TTY bolts generally require a new torquing procedure called torque angle. Also, it is important to note that in virtually all cases, TTY bolts cannot be reused because they have been stretched into their yield zone and would very likely fail if retorqued (**FIGURE 4-33**).

K04011 Describe the torque-to-yield and torque angle.

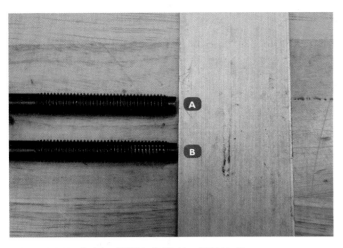

FIGURE 4-33 A. New TTY bolt. **B.** Used TTY bolt.

Torque angle is considered a more precise method to tighten TTY bolts and is essentially a multistep process. Bolts are first torqued in the required pattern, using a standard torque wrench to a required moderate torque setting. They are then further tightened one or more additional specified angles (torque angle) using an angle gauge, thus providing further tightening, which tightens the bolt to, or just beyond, their yield point. In some cases, after the initial torquing, the manufacturer first wants all of the bolts to be turned to an initial angle and then turned an additional angle. And in other cases, the manufacturer wants all of the bolts torqued in a particular sequence, then detorqued in a particular sequence, then retorqued once again in a particular sequence, and finally tightened an additional specified angle. So always check the manufacturer's specifications and procedure before torquing TTY bolts.

To use a torque angle gauge in conjunction with a torque wrench, follow the steps in **SKILL DRILL 4-1**.

SKILL DRILL 4-1 Using a Torque Angle Gauge with a Torque Wrench

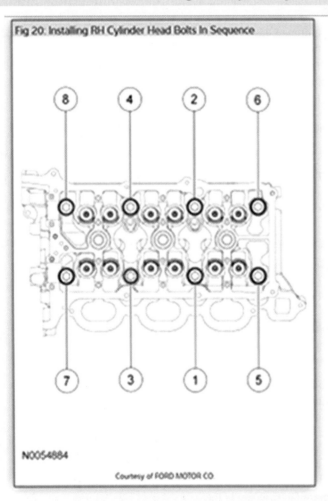

I. Check the specifications. Determine the correct torque value (ft-lb or N·m) and sequence for the bolts or fasteners you are using. Also, check the torque angle specifications for the bolt or fastener, and whether it involves one step or more than one step.

Continued

2. Tighten the bolt to the specified torque. If the component requires multiple bolts or fasteners, make sure to tighten them all to the same torque value in the sequence and steps that are specified by the manufacturer.

3. Install the torque angle gauge over the head of the bolt, and then put the torque wrench on top of the gauge and zero it, if necessary.

4. Turn the torque wrench the specified number of degrees indicated on the angle gauge.

5. If the component requires multiple bolts or fasteners, make sure to tighten them all to the same torque angle in the sequence that is specified by the manufacturer. Some torquing procedures could call for four or more steps to complete the torquing process properly.

▶ How to Avoid Broken Fasteners

Broken bolts can turn a routine job into a nightmare job by adding hours dealing with the broken bolt. In most cases, it is worth taking a bit of extra time doing whatever is needed to avoid breaking a bolt. One of the first things to do is to make sure that you are not dealing with a left-handed bolt (**FIGURE 4-34**). Left-hand bolts loosen by turning them clockwise. So trying to loosen them by turning them counterclockwise will actually tighten them, making it likely you will break them off.

Another cause of broken bolts is fasteners that are rusted or corroded in place. Although it is impossible to prevent all broken bolts in this case, there are several things you can do to minimize the percentage of bolts you break. One of the first things to do is use a good penetrating oil. Penetrating oil actually penetrates the rust between the nut and bolt and breaks it down, making it easier to break the nut or bolt loose. Once the penetrating oil has been given time to soak into the threads of the fastener, you may attempt, with the proper tool, to try to loosen the fastener. Note that you may want to try both loosening and tightening the bolt to help break it loose. It may be good to try using an impact wrench as well, because the hammering effect might assist in breaking it loose. Just try it a little at a time in each direction, and not with too much force.

If the fastener is still not loosening, you may need to heat up the component to help break up the rust or corrosion. The heat not only expands the metal components, it also expands the space between the nut and bolt. This also helps break the nut or bolt loose. The bolt or nut can be heated up in two primary ways. The first is with an oxyacetylene torch, but be careful because the flame from the torch also burns everything in its path. When heating up a bolt on a vehicle, there are almost always other things in the way that could be affected by the heat. The second is with an inductive heater, which uses electrical induction to heat up any ferrous metal that is placed in the inductive coil (**FIGURE 4-35**). The induction heater is preferred by many technicians for many applications, as it doesn't have a flame and it only heats up what is in the induction coil. Most induction heaters come with several sizes of induction coils that make them handy for most applications.

When heating a fastener to remove it, you usually heat it up to a dull orange color and then let it cool a bit before attempting to remove it. Once a heated fastener is removed, it must be replaced with a new bolt because the heat alters the strength of the fastener.

N04001 Perform common fastener and thread repair, to include: remove broken bolt, restore internal and external threads, and repaire internal threads with thread insert.

K04013 Identify situations where thread repair is necessary.

S04001 Perform common fastener and thread repair.

▶ Thread Repair

Thread repair is used in situations where it is not feasible to replace a damaged thread. This may be because the damaged thread is located in a large expensive component, such as the engine block or cylinder head of a vehicle, or because replacement parts are expensive or not available. The aim of thread repair is to restore the thread to a condition that restores

FIGURE 4-34 Left-hand lug nuts are installed on some vehicles.

FIGURE 4-35 Heating a stuck nut with an induction heater.

the fastening integrity (**FIGURE 4-36**). It can be performed on internal threads, such as in a housing, engine block, or cylinder head, or on external threads, such as on a bolt. However, it is usually easier to replace a bolt if the threads become damaged than repairing it.

Types of Thread Repair

Many different tools and methods can be used to repair a thread. The least invasive method is to reshape the threads. If the threads are not too badly damaged, such as when the end thread is slightly damaged from the bolt being started crooked (cross-threaded), then a thread file can be used to clean them up, or a restoring tool can be used to reshape them (**FIGURE 4-37**). Each thread file has eight different sets of file teeth that match various thread pitches. Select the set that matches the bolt you are working on, and file the bolt in line with the threads. The file removes any distorted metal from the threads. Only file until the bad spot is reshaped.

The thread-restoring tool looks like an ordinary tap and die set, but instead of cutting the threads, it reshapes the damaged portion of the thread (**FIGURE 4-38**). Threads that have substantial damage require other methods of repair.

A common method for repairing damaged internal threads is a thread insert. A number of manufacturers make thread inserts, and they all work in a similar fashion. There are two main types of thread inserts: helical thread inserts and sleeve-type thread inserts (**FIGURE 4-39**). A helical thread insert of the same internal thread pitch is used when the threads need to be replaced with the same size thread. The damaged threaded hole is drilled out bigger, tapped with a special tap to a larger size that matches the outside size of the helical insert, and then the threaded coil insert is screwed into place. The insert provides a brand new internal thread that matches the original size. A common name for this type is a HeliCoil®.

The solid sleeve type of insert also replaces the damaged thread with the same size thread as the original. The difference between this type of insert compared to the helical insert is that this one is a slightly thicker insert that resembles a sleeve or bushing, but with threads on both the inside and outside. It may also have a small flange at the top of the insert that prevents it from being installed too deeply in the hole. Like the previous insert, the damaged hole needs to be drilled out to the proper oversize. Then a special tap is used to cut new threads in the hole that match the external thread on the insert. The insert is then installed in the hole and locked into place with either thread-locking compound or keys that get driven down into the base metal. A common name for this type is a Time-Sert.

Self-tapping inserts are a type of insert that is driven in a similar way to a self-tapping screw, making its own threads and at the same time locking the insert into the base material. Bushing inserts are a type of threaded insert that is pressed into a blind hole with an arbor press. These types of inserts can be inserted in any material, so you must be aware of material that is soft as it may break if too much force is put to it. It has internal threads, so bolts and screws can be threaded into them.

The process of repairing a thread should first start with attempting to remove the broken bolt without damaging the threads. If this can be accomplished, then you will likely save time as well as avoid the possibility of making the problem worse, such as breaking off an

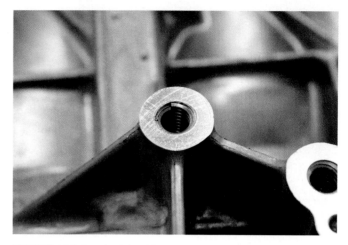

FIGURE 4-36 Repaired thread.

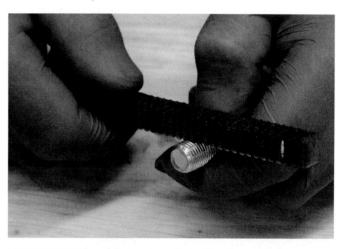

FIGURE 4-37 Threads being cleaned up with a thread file.

FIGURE 4-38 Thread-restoring tool being used.

FIGURE 4-39 Thread inserts. **A.** Heli-Coil. **B.** Time-Sert.

easy out in the broken bolt. If the bolt can't be removed without damaging the threads, then the use of a thread insert to repair an internal thread is probably needed.

To remove a broken bolt, inspect the site. If enough of the bolt is sticking out of the surface, then a pair of pliers or locking pliers may be enough to turn and remove the bolt. The author has had quite a bit of luck using a pair of special curved jaw Channellock pliers. The curved jaw tends to get a better grip on the broken-off bolt than regular straight jaw Channellock pliers (**FIGURE 4-40**). Using penetrant or heat may help coax the bolt out. If the bolt is broken off flush with the surface, and the bolt is large enough in diameter, then you may be able to use a small center punch to turn the bolt by tapping on the outside diameter of the bolt, but in the reverse direction (**FIGURE 4-41**). If that doesn't work, or the bolt is too small in diameter, then a screw or bolt extraction tool can be tried.

Use a center punch to mark the center of the bolt to assist in centering the hole to drill. Select the correctly sized **screw extractor**, and drill the designated hole size in the center of the broken bolt to accommodate the extractor. Once the hole is drilled, insert the extractor and turn it counterclockwise (**FIGURE 4-42**).

FIGURE 4-40 Using pliers to remove a broken bolt.

FIGURE 4-41 Removing a broken bolt with a center punch or cold chisel.

FIGURE 4-42 Removing a bolt with a screw extractor.

The flutes on the extractor should grab the inside of the bolt and hopefully enable you to back it out. Be careful not to exert too much force on the extractor if the bolt is extremely stuck in place. If the extractor breaks, it is almost impossible to remove it, as it is made of hardened steel that cannot be cut by most drill bits. Once the broken bolt is removed, run a lubricated tap or thread-restoring tool of the correct size and thread pitch through the hole, to clean up any rust or damage. If the screw extractor can't remove the broken bolt, then it will need to be drilled out. If the internal treads are damaged during the removal process, then the thread will have to be repaired with a thread insert, as described earlier.

To conduct thread repair, follow the steps in **SKILL DRILL 4-2.**

SKILL DRILL 4-2 Conducting Thread Repair

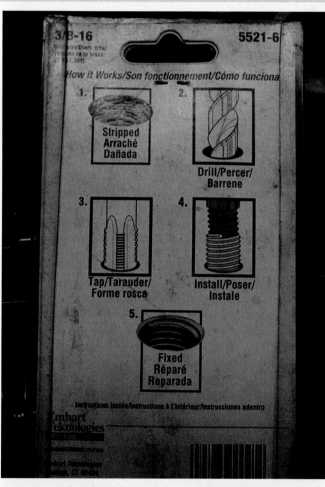

1. Always refer to the manufacturer's manual for specific operating instructions.

2. Inspect the condition of the threads, and determine the repair method.

Continued

3. Determine the type and size of the thread to be repaired. Thread pitch gauges and vernier calipers may be used to measure the thread.

4. Prepare materials for conducting the repair: dies and taps or a drill bit and drill; cutting oil, if required; and inserts.

5. Select the correctly sized tap or die if conducting a minor repair. Run the die or tap through or over the thread; be sure to use cutting lubricant.

6. If using inserts, select the correctly sized insert, based on the original bolt size. Drill the damaged hole, ensuring the drill is in perfect alignment with the hole.

Continued

7. Cut the new thread, using the proper size tap. Make sure you use cutting lubricant if required.

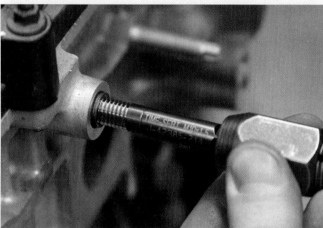

8. Using the insert-installing tool, install the insert by screwing it into the newly cut threads. Make sure the insert is secure or locked into the hole using the method specified by the manufacturer. Some inserts use a locking tab, whereas others use a liquid thread locker that hardens and holds the insert in place.

9. Test the insert to ensure it is secure and that the bolt will screw all the way in.

▶ Wrap-Up

Ready for Review

▶ Threaded fasteners include bolts, studs, and nuts, and are designed to secure vehicle parts under stress.

▶ Torque defines how much a fastener should be tightened.

▶ Bolts, nuts, and studs use threads to secure each part; these threads can be in standard or metric measures.

▶ Thread pitch refers to the coarseness of the thread; bolts, nuts, and studs are measured in threads per inch (TPI), classified as Unified National Coarse Thread (UNC) or Unified National Fine Thread (UNF).

▶ Fasteners are graded by tensile strength (how much tension can be withstood before breakage).

▶ The SAE rates fasteners from grade 1 to grade 8; always replace a nut or bolt with one of the same grade.

▶ Torque specification indicates the level of tightness each bolt or nut should be tightened to; torque charts list torque specifications for nuts and bolts.

▶ Torque (or tension) wrenches tighten fasteners to the correct torque specification.

▶ Torque value—the amount of twisting force applied to a fastener by the torque wrench—is specified in foot-pounds (ft-lb), inch-pounds (in-lb), or newton meters (N·m).

▶ Bolts that are tightened beyond their yield point do not return to their original length when loosened.

▶ Torque-to-yield (TTY) bolts can be torqued just beyond their yield point, but should not be reused.

▶ Torque angle can be used to tighten TTY bolts and requires both a torque wrench and an angle gauge.

▶ Thread repair is performed to restore fastening integrity to a damaged fastener.

▶ Threads can be reshaped with a file, or a thread insert may be used.

Key Terms

bolt A type of threaded fastener with a thread on one end and a hexagonal head on the other.

coarse (UNC) Used to describe thread pitch; stands for Unified National Coarse.

elasticity The amount of stretch or give a material has.

fasteners Devices that securely hold items together, such as screws, cotter pins, rivets, and bolts.

fine (UNF) Used to describe thread pitch; it stands for Unified National Fine.

nut A fastener with a hexagonal head and internal threads for screwing on bolts.

screw extractor A tool for removing broken screws or bolts.

square thread A thread type with square shoulders used to translate rotational to lateral movement.

stud A type of threaded fastener with a thread cut on each end rather than having a bolt head on one end.

tensile strength In reference to fasteners, the amount of force it takes before a fastener breaks.

threaded fasteners Bolts, studs, and nuts designed to secure parts that are under various tension and sheer stresses. These include bolts, studs, and nuts, and are designed to secure vehicle parts under stress.

thread pitch The coarseness or fineness of a thread as measured by either the threads per inch or the distance from the peak of one thread to the next. Metric fasteners are measured in millimeters.

thread repair A generic term to describe a number of processes that can be used to repair threads.

torque Twisting force applied to a shaft, which may or may not result in motion.

torque angle A method of tightening bolts or nuts based on angles of rotation.

torque specifications Supplied by manufacturers and describes the amount of twisting force allowable for a fastener or a specification showing the twisting force from an engine crankshaft.

torque-to-yield A method of tightening bolts close to their yield point or the point at which they will not return to their original length.

torque-to-yield (TTY) bolts Bolts that are tightened using the torque-to-yield method.

torque wrench A tool used to measure the rotational or twisting force applied to fasteners.

yield point The point at which a bolt is stretched so hard that it will not return to its original length when loosened; it is measured in pounds per square inch of bolt cross section.

Review Questions

1. Which of these are threaded fasteners?
   a. C-clips
   b. Trim screws
   c. Cotter pins
   d. Solid rivets

2. All of the following statements are true *except*:
   a. Metric bolts can be identified by the grade number on the top of the bolt heads.
   b. Measuring units of standard bolts use a fractional number–based system.
   c. Standard bolts can be identified by the hash marks on the top of the bolt heads.
   d. Measuring units of metric bolts use a roman number–based system.

3. In an 8 mm bolt, 8 mm refers to the:
   a. length of the bolt.
   b. size of the bolt head.
   c. threads' outer diameter.
   d. number of threads per inch.

4. The easiest way to identify the TPI is to:
   a. use a vernier caliper.
   b. count the number of threads.
   c. measure distance from peak to peak.
   d. use a thread pitch gauge.

5. A bolt has 3 hash marks on its head. What is its grade?
   a. 2
   b. 5
   c. 6
   d. 8

6. Which nut is made with a deformed top thread?
   a. Lock nut
   b. J nut
   c. Castle nut
   d. Specialty nut

7. When you want a nut or bolt to hold tight such that it needs heat to be removed with a socket and ratchet, you should use a(n):
   a. lubricant.
   b. blue thread-locking compound.
   c. antiseize compound.
   d. red thread-locking compound.

8. Which of these has a fluted tip to drill a hole into the base material so that there is no need for a pilot hole?
   a. Machine screw
   b. Self-tapping screw
   c. Trim screw
   d. Sheet metal screw

9. Torque-to-yield bolts:
   a. should be tightened using torque angle.
   b. can be reused multiple times.
   c. cannot be torqued beyond the elastic phase.
   d. do not get stretched.

10. All of the following are ways to avoid breaking a bolt when removing it *except*:
    a. using penetrating oil with bolts that are rusted or corroded in place.
    b. applying maximum force in both directions.
    c. first checking whether it is a left-hand bolt.
    d. as a last resort, you may heat up the bolt that is rusted or corroded in place.

ASE Technician A/Technician B Style Questions

1. Tech A says that most metric fasteners can be identified by the grade number cast into the head of the bolt. Tech B says that standard bolts can generally be identified by hash marks cast into the head of the bolt indicating the bolt's grade. Who is correct?
   a. Tech A
   b. Tech B
   c. Both A and B
   d. Neither A nor B

2. Two technicians are discussing bolt sizes. Tech A says that the diameter of a bolt is measured across the flats on the head. Tech B says that the length of a bolt is measured from the top of the head to the bottom of the bolt. Who is correct?
   a. Tech A
   b. Tech B
   c. Both A and B
   d. Neither A nor B

3. Tech A says that a standard grade 5 bolt is stronger than a standard grade 8 bolt. Tech B says that a metric grade 12.9 bolt is stronger than a metric grade 4.6 bolt. Who is correct?
   a. Tech A
   b. Tech B
   c. Both A and B
   d. Neither A nor B

4. Tech A says that torque-to-yield head bolts are tightened to, or just past, their yield point. Tech B says that the yield point is the torque at which the bolt breaks. Who is correct?
   a. Tech A
   b. Tech B
   c. Both A and B
   d. Neither A nor B

5. Tech A says that some locking nuts have a nylon insert that has a smaller diameter hole than the threads in the nut. Tech B says that castle nuts are used with cotter pins to prevent the nut from loosening. Who is correct?
   a. Tech A
   b. Tech B
   c. Both A and B
   d. Neither A nor B

6. Tech A says that antiseize compound is a type of thread-locking compound. Tech B says that thread-locking compounds acts like very strong glue. Who is correct?
   a. Tech A
   b. Tech B
   c. Both A and B
   d. Neither A nor B

7. Tech A says that flat washers act as a bearing surface, making it so that the bolt achieves the expected clamping force at the specified torque. Tech B says that lock washers are usually considered single use and should be replaced rather than reused. Who is correct?
   a. Tech A
   b. Tech B
   c. Both A and B
   d. Neither A nor B

8. Tech A says that a common method for repairing damaged internal threads is a thread insert. Tech B says that a thread file is used to repair the threads on the inside of a bolt hole. Who is correct?
   a. Tech A
   b. Tech B
   c. Both A and B
   d. Neither A nor B

9. Tech A says that if a bolt breaks off above the surface, you might be able to remove it using locking pliers or curved jaw Channellock pliers. Tech B says that a hammer and punch can sometimes be used to remove a broken bolt. Who is correct?
   a. Tech A
   b. Tech B
   c. Both A and B
   d. Neither A nor B

10. Tech A says that when using a Heli-Coil to repair a damaged thread, the Heli-Coil is welded into the bolt hole. Tech B says that when using a solid sleeve type of insert, the damaged threads need to be drilled out with the correct size drill bit. Who is correct?
   a. Tech A
   b. Tech B
   c. Both A and B
   d. Neither A nor B

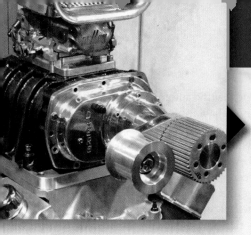

CHAPTER 5
Engine Design Fundamentals

NATEF Tasks

- **N05001** Inspect engine assembly for fuel, oil, coolant, and other leaks; determine needed action.

Knowledge Objectives

After reading this chapter, you will have:

- **K05001** Knowledge of what an internal combustion engine is used for.
- **K05002** Knowledge of the processes of combustion engines.
- **K05003** Knowledge of how temperature changes pressure in a sealed chamber.
- **K05004** Knowledge of the way engine's power potential is measured.

- **K05005** Knowledge of the process of creating power in an engine.
- **K05006** Knowledge of alternative combustion cycle engines.
- **K05007** Knowledge of the measurement of the engine.
- **K05008** Knowledge of spark ignition engines.

Skills Objectives

There are no Skills Objectives for this chapter.

You Are the Automotive Technician

You are working in the back shop when a salesman from the new car sales department asks if you could answer some questions for a customer. The customer's previous car was totaled in a parking lot accident, and he is very interested in a couple of cars on the lot. He has some technical questions that have to be answered, and the service manager has selected you to answer these. You greet the customer, and he asks you the following questions:

1. "I see a nice diesel pickup truck that I could use on the farm. How does a compression ignition engine operate differently from a spark ignition engine?"
2. "My son would like me to buy that RX8. How does a rotary engine operate differently from a piston engine?"
3. "As I am looking at specifications on the vehicles, what is the difference between horsepower and torque?"
4. "What is meant by camshaft lift and duration specifications?"

▶ Introduction

Engines come in many forms and sizes, the main one that the automobile uses is the internal combustion engine because of its versatility and reliability in the various conditions that vehicles operate. The internal combustion engine is an irreplaceable part of modern society. We rely on it to haul food and water, deliver passengers to their destinations, and even save lives. Over time, the internal combustion engine has seen many changes; however, the basics have remained about the same. In this chapter, we cover the fundamental principles of internal combustion engines and the types of spark-ignition engines that are available in the modern automobile, identify the components that make up the engine, and describe how these components operate together (**FIGURE 5-1**). Throughout this book, we break down all the components that make up an automotive internal combustion engine.

FIGURE 5-1 Chevy Corvette engine.

▶ Engine Principles

There are two types of combustion engines: internal and external. An internal combustion engine is one where combustion takes place inside the engine assembly, which then turns that explosive force into mechanical energy. An external combustion engine is one where the fuel is ignited outside the engine assembly and then directed into the engine to create mechanical power. Any internal or external combustion engine is developed to move an object from point A to point B efficiently. The design of an engine takes into account thermodynamics, chemistry, geometry, physics, and metallurgy to create a well-running machine. As you progress through this chapter, you will be exposed to the various aspects of an engine, the types of engines, and how we classify each one. In future chapters, this book breaks down each area into a more in-depth description so that the theory of these components can be understood.

Principles of Thermodynamic Internal Combustion Engines

Thermodynamics is the branch of physical science that deals with heat and its relation to other forms of energy, such as mechanical energy. In automotive applications, thermodynamics allows a vehicle to move down the road as well as provide motive (moving) power for all of the onboard systems. Engines used for motive power may be classified as external combustion or internal combustion engines. External combustion means that the fuel is burned outside the engine, whereas internal combustion means the fuel is burned inside the engine. Two examples of the external combustion engine are the steam engine and the Stirling engine (**FIGURE 5-2**).

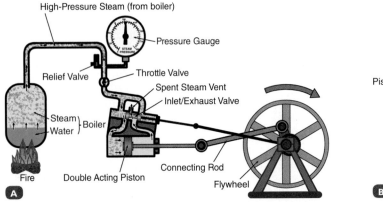

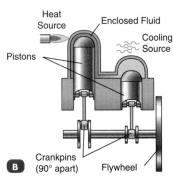

FIGURE 5-2 External combustion engines. **A.** Steam engine. **B.** Stirling engine.

At one time, external combustion engines, such as steam engines, were used to power almost all equipment. In a steam engine, steam is created in an external boiler (external combustion) and used to push a piston back and forth in a cylinder. Most steam engines applied steam alternately to each side of the piston, so the piston was powered in both directions. One problem with steam engines is that they take a relatively long time to generate steam pressure, so you could not simply hop in a steam-powered car and take off. The boilers also presented an explosion hazard if they generated too much pressure or if the boiler weakened due to rust. Steam engines have been used to power equipment such as farm tractors, railroad trains, automobiles, boats, ships, and more. Even a steam-powered airplane was produced, although it never became popular.

The Stirling engine is also an example of an external combustion engine. It holds promise as an alternative source of power but has not become popular for transportation because its output cannot be easily varied. Solar-powered Stirling engines are gaining popularity as home power sources because they are environmentally friendly. Because solar energy is used to provide the heat for the engine, there are no by-products of combustion to worry about. Stirling engines can run almost silently and therefore can be used near people without disturbing them.

The internal combustion engine (ICE) has almost completely replaced the external combustion engine today and has been around for well over a century. It is the favored mode of power for the transportation industry, whether for on-road applications (cars, trucks, buses, etc.) or for non-road applications (tractors, trains, ships, etc.). This chapter focuses on spark-ignition internal combustion engines, as they are the most widely used engines in modern automobiles. The reason that this type of engine is used in an automobile is that it is a self-contained power plant that takes chemical energy and converts it into mechanical energy to do work. The combustion chambers inside the engine cylinders create a high-pressure environment that uses the explosion of the fuel mixture to push on a moveable piston to create mechanical energy. The ICE can be classified in two ways: as a reciprocating piston engine or as a rotary engine. The gasoline piston engine uses a crankshaft to convert the reciprocating movement of the pistons in their cylinder bores into rotary motion at the crankshaft. The piston engine may be of the two-stroke or four-stroke design (**FIGURE 5-3**). The rotary engine uses a rotating motion rather than reciprocating motion. It uses ports rather than valves to control intake and exhaust flow (**FIGURE 5-4**). Both the piston and the rotary engine will be described in greater detail later in this chapter. Piston engines are either spark-ignition (SI) engines or compression-ignition (CI) engines. In SI engines, liquid fuels such as gasoline, ethanol, methanol, or butenol are compressed and ignited by an electrical spark, which jumps across the air gap of a spark plug in the combustion chamber. Timing of combustion is totally reliant on when the spark jumps across the electrodes of the spark plug (**FIGURE 5-5**). In diesel engines, air in the sealed combustion chamber is compressed so tightly that it becomes hot enough to ignite the fuel as soon as it is injected into the combustion chamber. Timing of the combustion process is reliant on when the fuel is injected; therefore, CI engines do not use spark plugs (**FIGURE 5-6**).

Principles of Engine Operation

Engines operate according to the unchanging laws of physics and thermodynamics. Understanding the physics and science involved with an engine will help you to diagnose engine problems. For example, knowing that pressure rises when the

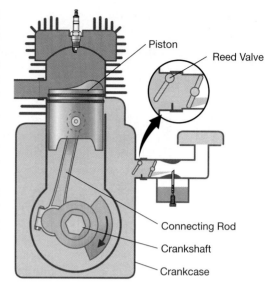

FIGURE 5-3 Two-stroke reed valve operation.

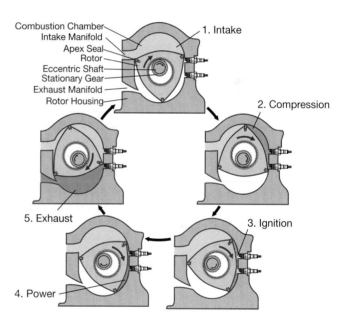

FIGURE 5-4 Operation of a rotary engine.

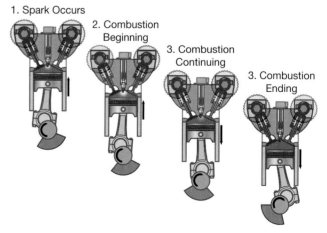

FIGURE 5-5 Combustion in an SI engine.

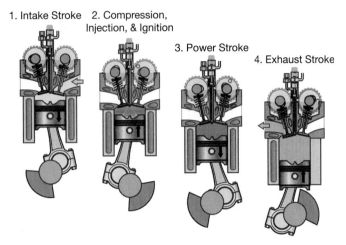

1. Intake Stroke   2. Compression, Injection, & Ignition

3. Power Stroke

4. Exhaust Stroke

FIGURE 5-6 Combustion in a CI engine.

volume of a sealed container is reduced helps you understand the need for sealing the chamber for maximum power. Realize too that when molecules are tightly packed together, they produce far more expansion pressure during combustion than when they are not. Valves and ports in the engine's cylinder head(s) provide a means of sealing the combustion chamber. If the valves leak, the pressure in the cylinder will not rise as it should during the compression stroke of the piston. If there is too little pressure squeezing the air-fuel mixture together in the cylinder, the mixture will not get packed tightly enough, and less engine power will be developed when it is ignited. A good example of the importance of compression is the burning of black powder in open air; it produces fire and smoke, but no explosion. If the same powder is wrapped tightly, it becomes a firecracker (or even a stick of dynamite)—exploding the wrapping and producing the bang. More power is produced when air and fuel are compressed into a tightly packed space.

Pressure and Temperature

K05003 Knowledge of how temperature changes pressure in a sealed chamber.

Charles's law states that in a sealed chamber, the pressure and temperature of a gas are directly related to each other (**FIGURE 5-7**). As pressure rises, so does temperature; as pressure decreases, so does temperature. For example, think of a portable propane bottle used when boiling water on a camp stove. The bottle has a fixed amount of gas inside it. As the propane is used, the metal propane bottle gets ice cold and frosts over due to the pressure being released. In contrast, think of a cylinder with a moveable plunger at one end (**FIGURE 5-8**). This plunger seals tightly in the cylinder so that no air can escape past the plunger. Installed on the other end of the cylinder are a pressure gauge and a thermometer. As we push the plunger in, the air pressure rises in the sealed cylinder as the air molecules are squeezed together. As the air molecules are squeezed together more tightly, the pressure and the temperature rise as a result of friction between the air molecules as they bounce off one another with greater force. The air in the cylinder heats up as this happens, so we see not only the pressure rise on the pressure gauge but also the temperature rise on the thermometer. The same amount of heat is in the cylinder as when uncompressed, but when it is compressed, the heat is concentrated; thus, the temperature rises.

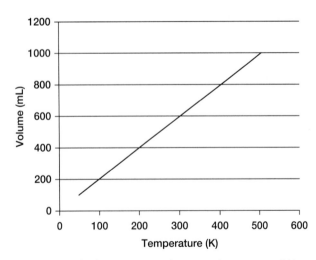

FIGURE 5-7 As the temperature increases the pressure within the container becomes higher and the inverse is also true as the temperature gets colder the pressure in the container contracts.

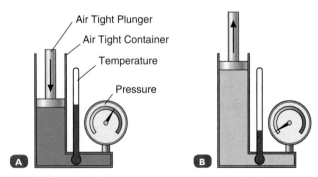

FIGURE 5-8 Pressure changes temperature. **A.** As pressure goes up, temperature goes up. **B.** As pressure goes down, temperature goes down.

A diesel engine uses this principle to ignite the fuel injected into an engine cylinder. The air is compressed so tightly that it becomes hot enough to ignite the fuel when it arrives; this is why diesel engines are called compression-ignition engines. Again using our plunger in a cylinder example, what happens when the plunger is pulled outward? Pulling out the plunger reduces gas pressure and gives the molecules more room to move; they affect one another less, and temperature decreases. Thus, a drop in pressure produces a lower temperature because even though the same amount of heat is contained in the cylinder, the heat is more spread out. Looking at a related scenario, what happens to pressure when the gas *temperature* changes? When a gas is heated, its molecules start to move more quickly and want more space. Heating a gas in a sealed container will increase the pressure in the container (thermal expansion) (**FIGURE 5-9**). Cooling a gas has the opposite effect. As the molecules slow down, they demand less space. As a result of cooling a gas in a sealed container, the pressure will drop.

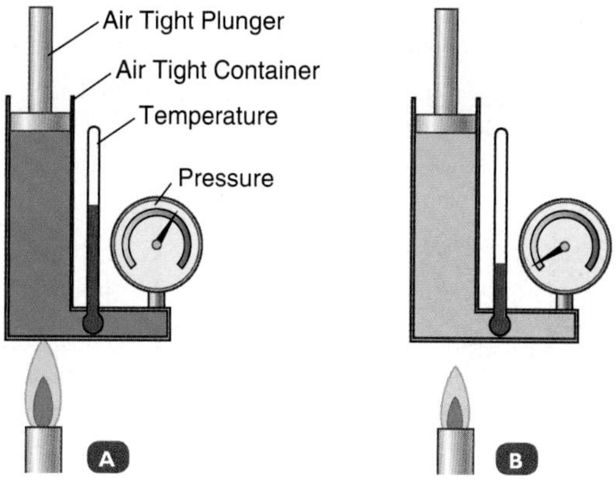

FIGURE 5-9 Temperature changes pressure. **A.** As temperature goes up, pressure goes up. **B.** As temperature goes down, pressure goes down.

Temperature and Energy

The temperature of a gas is one measure of how much energy it has. The more energy a gas has, the more work it can do. The heating of gas particles makes them move faster, which produces more pressure. This pressure exerts more force on the container in which the gas is located. This is how an ICE functions, pressure is first raised through compression and then through combustion of the air-fuel mixture. Burning the air-fuel mixture increases the heat temperature inside the container tremendously, which creates the necessary pressure to produce work. The more energy the air-fuel mixture has, the more force it exerts on the piston and the more work the piston can do (**FIGURE 5-10**). This principle takes place during the power stroke and pushes the piston down the sealed container.

Latent (stored) heat energy exists in various kinds of fuels; it is released to do work when the fuel is ignited and burned. Types of fuels that contain latent heat energy include liquid fuels such as gasoline, diesel, and ethanol; gaseous fuels such as natural gas, propane, and hydrogen; and solid fuels such as gunpowder, wood, and coal. Latent heat energy is often measured and expressed as British thermal units (Btu). One Btu equals the heat required to raise the temperature of 1 pound (lb) of water by 1°F. Gasoline has a comparatively high Btu per gallon rating of around 14,000 Btu. Diesel fuel is even more energy dense at around 25,000 Btu per gallon. Coal has a much lower Btu rating, 8000–12,700 based on the type of coal, which is one reason why both the home heating and the transportation (rail) industries have moved from coal to petroleum (i.e., home heating oil and diesel fuel) for better energy efficiency (transport and storage of a liquid fuel is also lots easier).

1. Compressing the air/fuel mixture raises its heat energy level.
2. Igniting the fuel increases the heat and pressure even higher.
3. The high combustion temperature causes high cylinder pressures which force the piston down the cylinder.

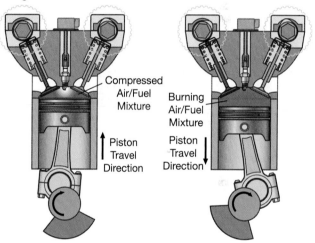

FIGURE 5-10 Burning a compressed gas increases temperature, producing more pressure and increased force.

Pressure and Volume

Pressure and volume are inversely related; as one rises, the other falls. A cylinder with a pressure gauge and a movable piston is a good example. The cylinder contains air, and as the piston is pushed in, the inside air is forced into a smaller volume. At the same time, the pressure gauge shows an increase in pressure. It is this increase in pressure that allows the pump to do its work. When the piston is pulled out, the volume occupied by the gas grows larger, and the pressure drops. A larger volume will have less gas pressure, and when the volume is reduced, the gas pressure will rise. Keep in mind that larger pressures are desirable to increase the amount of work done in an engine (**FIGURE 5-11**).

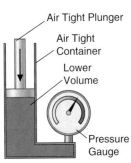

A: As the volume decreases,
the pressure increases.

B: As the volume increases,
the pressure decreases.

FIGURE 5-11 Volume affects pressure.

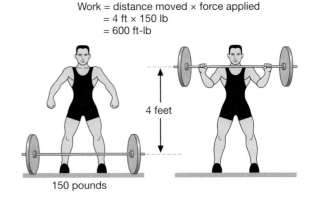

Work = distance moved × force applied
= 4 ft × 150 lb
= 600 ft-lb

4 feet

150 pounds

FIGURE 5-12 Work.

Force, Work, and Power

K05004 Knowledge of the way engine's power potential is measured.

Effort to produce a push or pull action is referred to as force. A compressed spring applies force to cause, or resist, movement. A tensioned lifting cable applies force to cause lifting movement. Force is measured in pounds, kilograms, or Newtons. When force causes movement, work is done (**FIGURE 5-12**). For example, when the compressed spring or the tensioned lifting cable causes movement, work is performed. Without movement, work cannot be performed even if force is applied. Work is equal to distance moved times force applied. If the lifting cable of a hoist lifts a 250-lb engine 4' in the air, the amount of work done is equal to 4' times 250 lb, or 1000 foot-pounds of work. Work is measured in foot-pounds (ft-lb), watts, or joules. The rate or speed at which work is performed is called **power** (**FIGURE 5-13**). The more power that can be produced, the more work can be performed in a given amount of time. Power is measured in ft-lb per second or ft-lb per minute. If an electric motor can lift a 600-lb weight 20' in 10 seconds, power used would be equal to 20 (feet) × 600 (lb) ÷ 10 (seconds) = 1200 ft-lb per second. One horsepower equals 550 ft-lb per second, or 33,000 ft-lb per minute. So 1200 ft-lb per second equals 2.18 horsepower. The watt or kilowatt (1000 watts) is the metric unit of measurement for power, where 746 watts equals 1 horsepower. So the electric motor in the example would be developing 2.18 (horsepower) times 746 (watts), which equals 1627 watts, or 1.627 kilowatts, of power.

Power = (distance moved × force applied)/time
= (4 ft × 150 lb)/2 seconds
= 300 ft-lb/second
= 0.54 HP

4 feet in
2 seconds

150 pounds

1 Horsepower (HP) = 550 ft-lb per second

FIGURE 5-13 Formula for power.

Power and Torque

Torque is described as a twisting force. Movement does not have to occur to have torque. Torque is applied before or during movement. When a twist cap on a water bottle is removed, maximum torque is applied just before the cap starts to turn. When the same cap is tightened, maximum torque is applied once the cap starts to get tight. The concept of "twisting force" should always come to mind when the term "torque" is used. When a piston is pushed down a cylinder during the power stroke, it applies force to a connecting rod linking the piston and crankshaft, causing the crankshaft to rotate. The rotational force applied to the crankshaft is called torque. The unit of measurement for torque in the imperial system is ft-lb; in the metric system it is Newton meters. If a force of 100 lb is applied to the end of a 1' long wrench (lever) attached to a bolt, the resulting torque applied to the wrench will be 100 ft-lb. The measurement of engine power is calculated from the amount of torque at the crankshaft and the speed at which it is turning in rpm.

The formula for engine horsepower is:

$$\text{Horsepower} = \text{rpm} \times \text{ft-lb} \div 5252.$$

For example, if an engine creates 500 ft-lb of torque at 4000 rpm, then the amount of horsepower is: 500 × 4000 ÷ 5252, or 380 horsepower at 4000 rpm.

Because horsepower would change with rpm, it is necessary to express not only the power value but to include the engine speed, in rpm, at which it occurs. Power can also be measured in kilowatts. A kilowatt (1,000 watts) is equivalent to 1000 Newtons per meter per second.

▶ **TECHNICIAN TIP**

Holding a heavy starter motor in place while trying to get the bolts started is not technically work; it is force. Although it seems like you are working hard, your arm muscles twitching as you stand under the vehicle and hold the part in place, you are not performing work in the true physics sense. It takes movement, along with force, to qualify as work. So lifting the starter from the ground to its position on the engine is work, but holding it there is not work. Understanding the difference between these two terms will give you a good foundation for understanding power.

The formula for computing an engine's horsepower might seem confusing since we said earlier that 1 horsepower equals 33,000 ft-lb per minute; yet we divide the product of torque × rpm by 5252. Why do we use 5252 instead of 33,000? The reason is a bit complicated, having to do with the definition of ft-lb. When relating to *work*, ft-lb means force times distance moved. That works well in a lifting situation but not so well in a twisting (torque) situation. In a *torque* situation, ft-lb means a twisting force applied to a shaft—that is, applied force times lever distance of the applied force. Thus, it is possible for torque to result in no movement, only an applied force. And we label that force in ft-lb even though for work or power to happen, movement must take place. To calculate the twisting power of a shaft, we need a way to add *distance moved* and *time* to the equation so that ft-lb = 1 horsepower when talking about torque. That is why rpm is included in the formula. Because rpm refers to a certain number of revolutions per minute, it includes both time and distance. But how much distance is 1 rpm? The answer relates to radians. A radian describes how many radius distances there are in the circumference of a circle (**FIGURE 5-14**). Because there are 3.14 diameters in the circumference of a circle, there are twice as many, or 6.28, radius distances (radians) in the circumference of any circle. The larger the circle, the longer the radians, but still only 6.28 of them fit within the total circumference. And that is where we get our distance.

Because torque relates to an equivalent amount of force a certain distance from the rotational center (radius), and there are 6.28 radians in the circumference of a circle, every revolution equals a distance of 6.28 radians. To convert torque ft-lb to work ft-lb, there has to be movement. We can either multiply the rpm by 6.28 and use the 33,000 (ft-lb per horsepower) factor, or divide the 33,000 ft-lb by 6.28 (distance around a circle in radians) and come up with a new factor, which is 5252, that we can use with the original "torque × rpm" numbers for calculating engine horsepower. To keep the numbers more manageable, most people go with the 5252 factor. Thus, if we multiply the ft-lb of torque × rpm and divide that number by 5252, we will have calculated the engine's horsepower at that particular rpm.

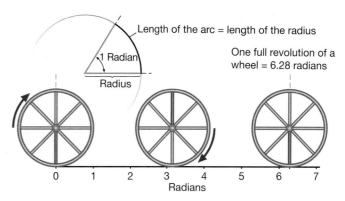

FIGURE 5-14 Radians in the circumference of a circle.

Applied Science

AS-50: Work: The technician can explain the relationship between torque and horsepower.

Two technicians are discussing the relationship between torque and horsepower during their break time at work. Al believes that torque is the turning force at the engine's crankshaft. Bob says that horsepower is the rate at which force is produced. Both technicians are correct as they discuss the unique relationship of torque and horsepower. One cannot exist without the other. When we compare a race car to a bulldozer, we can see two different applications of torque and horsepower. A bulldozer has lots of torque but the engine may be operating at 2000 rpm. A race car may be operating at 8000 rpm with a lower amount of torque. Low-speed torque is needed in some situations and high-rpm horsepower is needed in others.

Applied Science

AS-97: Torque: The technician can demonstrate an understanding of how torque relates to force and angular acceleration.

Newton's second Law of Motion states that the change in speed of an object over a given time is proportional to the force exerted on it. We know that a train is much slower to accelerate than a car, and once it is moving the train is far more difficult to stop. This is the basis for our understanding of the concept of torque relating to force and angular acceleration. Physics can tell us a lot about how engines react to forces. Consider a flywheel attached to the crankshaft of an engine, which is an example of rotational motion. The torque necessary for the assembly to rotate is the product of force multiplied times distance. In physics, torque can be thought of as a rotational force that causes a change in rotary motion. The term "twisting force" is used by most automotive technicians. To determine angular acceleration, which is measured in radians per second squared, we need to know several other items of information. We would need to know the initial and final angular velocities and time. Angular velocity describes the speed of rotation of an object that is following a specific axis. Angular acceleration is the rate of change of angular velocity with time and is measured in radians per second squared. The angular acceleration is caused by the torque, which produces the force to make it happen. This process is proportional as stated in Newton's second Law of Motion.

Engine Load Factor

Load factor or power range is typically used in regard to diesel engines and describes how long an engine can produce its maximum power output. An engine that is quite powerful may not be designed to produce its maximum power over long periods. A gasoline engine in a car may give good acceleration in short bursts, but it can overheat and/or fail if operated at maximum speed and power for too long. In contrast, due to its robust construction, a heavy-duty diesel engine in a large truck is designed to operate near or at its maximum speed and load for long periods without damage.

One way to describe the load factor of an engine is to give its power as an average over a certain period. This is stated as a percentage and is called load factor. An engine required to operate at maximum power over 10 hours is said to have a load factor of 100%. Using that as a standard, most car engines typically only operate at about 20% to 30% efficiency, as evidenced by the drive cycle of a typical automobile. A drive cycle is the operating range of an engine from start-up until shutdown when finished performing its job. A typical vehicle will accelerate, decelerate, and idle many times during a typical daily drive. It will never be run at 100% load for an entire drive cycle; in fact, it may never reach 100%.

Torque Versus Horsepower

As torque is a twisting or turning force, horsepower is the rate (in time and distance) at which that force (torque) is produced. Torque alone does not mean work has been accomplished. It takes movement and time to accomplish a given amount of work in a given amount of time (horsepower). At the same time, for an engine to produce torque, it has to be running. So the rotation of the crankshaft (torque × distance) in a running engine means that work and power are occurring since torque × rpm gives us power (**FIGURE 5-15**). Also, an engine will put out varying amounts of torque and power as it is operating. Thus, if it is producing torque, it is producing power. Factors that affect an engine's torque output include engine **volumetric efficiency** (the rate of air intake and exhaust) at various crankshaft speeds and internal component friction (**parasitic losses**). In a naturally aspirated engine (nonpressurized intake system), torque peaks at the rpm where the engine's cylinders fill the most with air. Torque starts to drop as engine speed increases past peak torque rpm. Actually, in a naturally aspirated (naturally breathing, nonpressurized) engine, air never completely fills the combustion chamber while the engine is running. Peak engine torque rpm occurs at the peak volumetric efficiency (somewhere around 85% in an unmodified engine). Peak torque usually occurs at some low- to mid-rpm engine speed, depending on bore and stroke of the engine, as well as intake and exhaust port size and valve timing. Since engine rpm tends to rise faster than torque falls off (above peak volumetric efficiency), an engine's maximum horsepower occurs at a higher rpm than the peak torque rpm. At some point in the rpm range, the torque on the crankshaft drops so low that the crankshaft can no longer do additional work and the horsepower actually starts to decrease. Remember, it is horsepower that does the work, but torque makes it happen. Engine torque (and therefore horsepower) increases can be achieved through any engine modifications that improve volumetric efficiency (**FIGURE 5-16**). In fact, a turbocharger or supercharger will increase an engine's volumetric efficiency well above 100%. For example, a 1.6-liter Volkswagen diesel engine when turbocharged to its rated 11 lb of boost would be theoretically equivalent, horsepower-wise, to a naturally aspirated 2.8-liter engine.

FIGURE 5-15 An automotive chassis dynamometer measures output of the engine at the wheels of the vehicle.

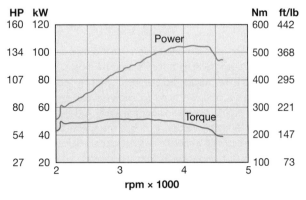

FIGURE 5-16 The relationship between torque and horsepower.

Four-Stroke Spark-Ignition Engines

The SI engine used in today's vehicles operates on the four-stroke cycle principle: It takes four strokes of the piston to complete one cycle. When the piston in a cylinder is at the position farthest away from the crankshaft, it is at top dead center (TDC). When the piston in the cylinder is at a position closest to the crankshaft, it is said to be at bottom dead center (BDC). When the piston moves from TDC to BDC or from BDC to TDC, one stroke has occurred (**FIGURE 5-17**). Two or more strokes are called reciprocating motion, meaning an up-and-down motion within the cylinder. Piston engines are therefore referred to as reciprocating engines. Piston engines can be simple, single-piston engines such as those on lawn mowers, or they can be much more complicated, multipiston engines, such as those in automobiles, trucks, and heavy equipment. Multi-cylinder engines come in various cylinder arrangements. Some automotive engines have cylinders arranged in a line (in-line engine), with pistons one behind another. Some automobile engines are flat, with opposed cylinders lying horizontally. This style of engine is called a boxer engine. Other automobile engines have cylinders at an angle (a V-type engine), with the pistons forming a "V" configuration.

K05005 Knowledge of the process of creating power in an engine.

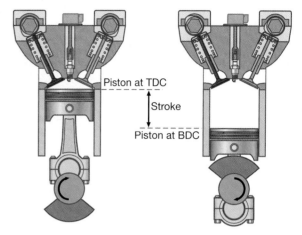

FIGURE 5-17 Piston movement from TDC to BDC or from BDC to TDC is one stroke.

Intake Stroke

On the intake stroke of a four-cycle engine, the intake valve is open, and the vacuum created by the downward motion of the piston in the cylinder sucks the air-fuel mixture into the cylinder. This portion of the process sees the piston go from TDC to BDC, causing the crankshaft to rotate 180 degrees.

Compression Stroke

The compression stroke starts once the air-fuel mixture is in the cylinder and the piston is at BDC. As the piston reaches BDC, the intake valve closes, and the piston comes back up toward TDC. As the piston is moving up in the cylinder, the air-fuel mixture is being compressed and directed toward the spark plug. The crankshaft rotates 180 degrees to complete this stroke.

Power Stroke

Once the piston reaches the top of the cylinder, maximum amount of compression has occurred, and the spark plug is sparked, causing the mixture to explode and starting to push the piston back down to BDC. The air-fuel mixture is ignited and burns rapidly at up to about 4500°F (2482°C). The heat of combustion causes burning gases to expand greatly (thermal expansion), which creates very high pressure in the combustion chamber. The crankshaft has rotated another 180 degrees once this occurs.

Exhaust Stroke

As the power stroke completes and the piston is back at the bottom of the cylinder, the exhaust valve opens up. The crankshaft is rotated another 180 degrees so that the piston is pushed back up to TDC. Along the way to TDC, the piston is pushing out to the exhaust system hot exhaust gases that are left in the cylinder through the open exhaust valve.

This is the 720-degree, four-stroke engine cycle; once this process is completed, it is restarted with the intake stroke (**FIGURE 5-18**). Note that the crankshaft has completed two full rotations during the four-stroke cycle. Thus, four complete strokes make one complete cycle. When this is coupled with multiple cylinders, it creates a very powerful engine that is able to be on multiple power strokes with every revolution. Similar to a piston engine is the rotary engine that also has four strokes but uses two rotors instead of pistons to create the combustion chambers (**FIGURE 5-19**).

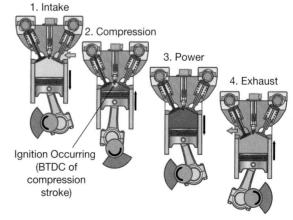

FIGURE 5-18 The basic four-stroke cycle.

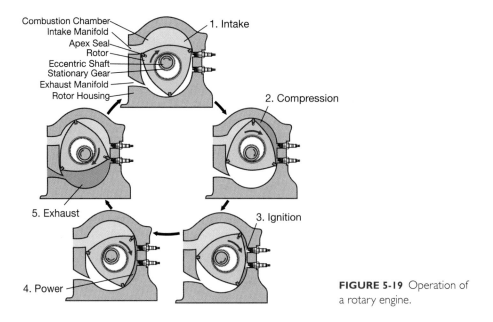

Combustion Chamber
Intake Manifold
Apex Seal
Rotor
Eccentric Shaft
Stationary Gear
Exhaust Manifold
Rotor Housing

1. Intake

2. Compression

3. Ignition

4. Power

5. Exhaust

FIGURE 5-19 Operation of a rotary engine.

Atkinson and Miller Cycle Engines

K05006 Knowledge of alternative combustion cycle engines.

The **Miller cycle engine** and the **Atkinson cycle engine** are both variations on the traditional four-stroke SI engine. These engines operate more efficiently but produce lower power outputs for the same displacement. In a conventional four-stroke cycle, the compression and the power (expansion) strokes are the same length. Increasing engine efficiency by increasing the stroke and raising the expansion ratio also raises the compression ratio. There is a limit to how high the compression ratio can be because raising it too much results in temperatures high enough to ignite the air-fuel mixture prematurely, before the ignition spark occurs. The Miller and the Atkinson cycles overcome this by using valve timing variations to make the effective compression stroke shorter than the expansion stroke. The effective compression stroke is shortened by delaying the closing of the intake valve at the beginning of the compression stroke. This shortens the distance that the piston has to compress the air-fuel mixture. The combustion chamber is slightly smaller so that the engine will still have a normal compression ratio. Thus, the compression pressure at ignition is still typically the same as that of a conventional four-stroke engine. The effective expansion stroke is lengthened by delaying the opening of the exhaust valve until closer to BDC, so more of the pressure created by the expansion of the burning gases can act on the piston longer, applying pressure to the crankshaft for a longer time and increasing efficiency. Because some of the intake gases are pushed back from the cylinder into the intake manifold, Miller and Atkinson engines can use a larger throttle opening for a given amount of power. This design results in lower manifold vacuum, reduced pumping (parasitic drag) losses, and increased fuel efficiency.

The Miller cycle engine adds an engine-driven supercharger to increase volumetric efficiency and boost power output when required. When the engine is operating at low load and speed, the supercharger is not needed. A clutch disengages the drive, so there is no unnecessary drag on the engine. When extra power is required, the clutch is engaged, and the supercharger boosts the amount of air drawn into the engine, supercharging the cylinder.

The Atkinson cycle engine is efficient within a specific operating range (the so-called engine "sweet spot" of peak torque rpm), typically between 2000 and 4500 rpm, but its overall power output and torque are lower than a conventional ICE. This type of engine is less useful as a primary power source, but it is ideal in applications such as a series-parallel hybrid vehicle, where it can work in tandem with a battery-driven electric motor as well as charge the high-voltage battery. Also, the lower maximum operating rpm allows engine components to be of lighter construction and weight as compared to a conventional ICE. Lighter and smaller components reduce friction and increase engine efficiency.

In addition, the crankshaft is mounted slightly off-center from the cylinder bores. This position reduces the thrust load on the piston, thereby reducing power loss due to friction.

Engine Measurement

Internal combustion engines (ICE) are designated by the amount of space (volume) their pistons displace as they move from TDC to BDC, which is called **engine displacement**. So, a 5.4-liter V8 engine has eight cylinders that displace a total volume of 5.4 liters. Displacement can be listed in cubic centimeters, liters, or cubic inches. To find an engine's displacement, you need to know the bore, stroke, and number of cylinders for a particular engine. The diameter of the engine cylinder is the cylinder bore. The bore is measured across the cylinder, parallel with the block deck, which is the machined surface of the block farthest from the crankshaft. Automotive cylinder bores can vary in size from less than 3" to more than 4". The distance the piston travels from TDC to BDC, or from BDC to TDC, is called the piston stroke. Piston stroke is determined by the offset portion of the crankshaft, called the throw. The crankshaft is described in greater detail later in this chapter. Piston stroke also varies from less than 3" to more than 4". Generally speaking, the longer the stroke, the greater the engine torque produced. A shorter stroke enables the engine to run at higher rpm to create greater horsepower. Engine specifications typically list the bore size first and the stroke length second (bore vs. stroke). The volume that a piston displaces from BDC to TDC is piston displacement. Increasing the diameter of the bore or increasing the length of the stroke produces a larger piston displacement. The formula for calculating piston displacement is (**FIGURE 5-20**):

> K05007 Knowledge of the measurement of the engine.

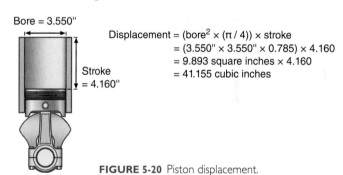

$$\text{Displacement} = (\text{bore}^2 \times (\pi / 4)) \times \text{stroke}$$
$$= (3.550" \times 3.550" \times 0.785) \times 4.160$$
$$= 9.893 \text{ square inches} \times 4.160$$
$$= 41.155 \text{ cubic inches}$$

Bore = 3.550"

Stroke = 4.160"

FIGURE 5-20 Piston displacement.

Cylinder bore squared × 0.785 × the piston stroke

This formula works for calculating both the standard displacement in cubic inches or the metric displacement in cubic centimeters (ccs) or liters. For example, a 5-4-liter (329-cubic-inch) V8 truck engine has a 3.55" bore, a 4.16" stroke, and eight cylinders. Using the formula for displacement:

$$3.55 \times 3.55 \text{ (bore 2)} = 12.6025 \times 0.785 \text{ (constant)} = 9.893 \times 4.16 \text{ (stroke)} =$$
41.155-cubic-inch piston displacement

Once you know the piston displacement, the next step to finding engine displacement is to multiply piston displacement times the number of cylinders in the engine (**FIGURE 5-21**). Continuing from the previous example:

41.155-cubic-inch piston displacement × 8 (number of cylinders) = 329.24-cubic-inch engine displacement

The displacement of an engine (also called engine size) can be altered by changing cylinder bore (diameter), piston stroke (length), or the number of cylinders.

Engine displacement = $(bore^2 \times (\pi / 4)) \times stroke \times number\ of\ cylinders$
= $(3.550" \times 3.550" \times 0.785) \times 4.160 \times 4$
= $9.893\ square\ inches \times 4.160 \times 4$
= $164.62\ cubic\ inches$

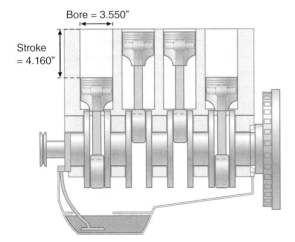

Bore = 3.550"

Stroke = 4.160"

FIGURE 5-21 Engine displacement.

FIGURE 5-22 A broken crankshaft from an unbalanced engine.

FIGURE 5-23 A broken harmonic balancer from an unbalanced engine.

Number of Cylinders

The number of cylinders that an internal combustion engine has depends on the intended use of the engine. The higher the power needs for the application, the higher the number of cylinders the engine has to meet the torque and horsepower requirements. Vibration is the enemy of any internal combustion engine, so to help minimize the amount of vibration in any engine, an even number of cylinders is used (**FIGURES 5-22** and **5-23**). By doing this, we are able to cancel out the vibrations that are being made by the combustion process on the opposing cylinder. In addition to vibration control, the sound and performance of the engine is heavily affected by the number of cylinders propelling the vehicle.

Compression Ratio

The accompanying picture is the piston at BDC and at TDC (**FIGURE 5-24**). Maximum cylinder volume is at BDC, and minimum cylinder volume is at TDC. The ratio is given as two numbers. A compression ratio listed as 8:1 (8 to 1) means that the maximum cylinder volume is eight times larger than the minimum cylinder volume. **Compression ratio** is affected by changing the size and shape of the top of the piston, changing the size of the combustion chamber, or altering valve timing. The higher the compression ratio, the higher the compression pressures within the combustion.

Cylinder Arrangement

In a piston engine, the way engine cylinders are arranged is called the engine configuration. Multi-cylinder internal combustion automotive engines are produced in four common configurations:

- **In-line:** The pistons are all in one bank on one side of a common crankshaft.
- **Horizontally opposed:** The pistons are in two banks on both sides of a common crankshaft.
- **V:** The pistons are in two banks on opposite sides, forming a deep V with a common crankshaft at the base of the V.
- **VR and W:** In a VR engine, the pistons are in one bank but form a shallow V within the bank. The W engine consists of two VR banks in a deep V configuration with each other.

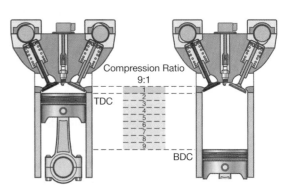

Compression Ratio
9:1

TDC

1
2
3
4
5
6
7
8
9

BDC

FIGURE 5-24 The compression ratio of an engine is found by taking the volume of the cylinder at BDC and comparing it to the volume at TDC. In this example, a 9:1 compression ratio is found.

Engineers design engines with tilted cylinder banks to reduce engine height. This can reduce the height of the hood as well, which allows a more streamlined hood line (**FIGURE 5-25**). Tilting can be carried to an extreme by designing the engine to lie completely on its side in the case of a horizontally opposed engine, also called a flat engine. As the number of cylinders increases, the length of the engine block and the crankshaft can become a problem structurally and space-wise. One way to avoid this problem is by having more than one row of cylinders, as in a horizontally opposed, V, or W configuration. These designs make the engine block and the crankshaft shorter and more rigid. In vehicle applications, the number of cylinders can vary, usually up to 12. Some examples are listed here:

FIGURE 5-25 Tilting cylinder banks can reduce both engine height and hood height, which allows for a more streamlined hood line.

- **In-line 4:** Compact, fairly inexpensive, easier to work on, and having better fuel economy than other types.
- **V8:** Approximately twice as powerful as the in-line 4 but having less than twice the space. Good power for its size and not overly complicated.
- **Flat 6:** Low-profile engine that fits well in vehicles with very low hood lines.
- **W12:** Most powerful compared to its overall dimensions, but more complicated and expensive than the other engines.

Common angles between the banks of cylinders are 180 degrees, 90 degrees, 60 degrees, and 15 degrees. Angles vary due to the number of cylinders and the manufacturer's design considerations.

- In-line cylinders arranged side by side in a single row identify the in-line engine and can be found in three-, four-, five-, and six-cylinder configurations (**FIGURE 5-26**). There have been in-line eight-cylinder engines, but they are too long to fit into the engine bay of a conventional modern car. In-line engines can be mounted longitudinally (lengthwise) or transversely (sideways) in the engine bay. In-line engines are generally less complicated to design and manufacture as they do not have to share components with a second bank of cylinders. This lack of shared components can mean extra working room in the engine compartment when performing maintenance and repairs. As a general rule of thumb, in-line engines are easier to work on than the other cylinder arrangements.
- Horizontally opposed engines are sometimes referred to as "flat" engines and are commonly found in four- and six-cylinder configurations (**FIGURE 5-27**). They are shorter lengthwise than a comparable in-line engine, but wider than a V type. Horizontally opposed engines have two banks of cylinders, 180 degrees apart, on opposite sides of the crankshaft. It is a useful design when little vertical space is available. A horizontally opposed engine is only fitted longitudinally.

FIGURE 5-26 Cylinders arranged side by side in a single row identify the in-line engine.

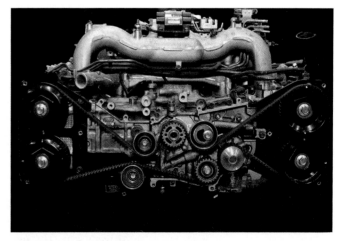

FIGURE 5-27 Horizontally opposed engines are commonly found in four- and six-cylinder configurations.

FIGURE 5-28 V-engines are shorter than in-line engines of equivalent capacity.

- V-engines have two banks of cylinders sitting side by side in a V arrangement, sharing a common crankshaft (**FIGURE 5-28**). This compact design allows for about twice the power output from a V-engine as an in-line engine of the same length. In automotive applications, V-engines can typically be found in 6-, 8-, 10-, and 12-cylinder configurations. A V6 will have two banks of three cylinders; a V8, two banks of four cylinders; etc. The angle of the V tends to vary according to the number of cylinders and can be found by dividing 720 degrees (two rotations of the crankshaft, which equals one complete cycle) by the number of cylinders. The natural angle for a V8 is 90 degrees. The natural angle for a V6 is 120 degrees, for a V10 is 72 degrees, and for a V12 is 60 degrees. Designing the engine around the natural angle means the engine can have a shorter length because each crankshaft throw can be shared between two cylinders. Some manufacturers vary their angles from those natural angles and use 90 degrees for a V6 and 15 degrees for a VR6 due to convenience or design requirements. Varying away from the natural angle means that the crankshaft must have one cylinder per crank throw, making the engine slightly longer.
- The VR engine uses a single bank of cylinders, but the cylinders are staggered at a shallow 15-degree V within the bank. This design not only allows the engine to be shorter than an in-line engine but also makes it narrower than a typical V-engine.
- The W engine consists of two VR cylinder banks in a deeper V arrangement to each other. This gives a very compact, yet powerful engine design.
- Rotary engines are very powerful for their size, but they do not use conventional pistons that slide back and forth inside a straight cylinder. Instead, a rotary engine uses a triangular rotor that turns inside an oval-shaped housing. The rotary engine has three combustion events for each rotation of the rotor. As the rotor turns, it carries the air-fuel mixture around the chambers, which are created between the tips of the rotor and the chamber wall. The rotor compresses the air-fuel mixture, and spark plugs ignite the mixture just like a conventional engine. The rotary engine does not have intake and exhaust valves like a traditional piston engine; instead, it has exhaust and intake ports that are covered and uncovered by the rotating rotor in the chamber. This design reduces the number of parts and makes it less complicated than a piston engine. Rotary engines generally have more than one rotor, with two being most common. The design of the rotary engine provides a very compact power unit.

Engine Rotation Direction

The engine in a modern automobile turns counterclockwise when viewed from the driver's seat. The reason that this happens is that rotational force is put on the drive wheel that is nearest to the driver. In theory, this helps increase traction to that wheel. In front wheel drive applications the engine rotates clockwise when looking at the front crankshaft pulley.

Variable Displacement Engines

Some engines have the ability to turn off a portion of their cylinders to save on fuel and increase mileage and are called variable displacement engines. Most **variable displacement engines** use oil pressure to shut off lifters to the cylinders that they are trying to disable so that the intake and exhaust valves do not open (**FIGURE 5-29**). At the same time this is happening, the injector and spark plug is shut off, which allows for a lower load on the engine electrical system. For example, taking a V-8 engine and turning off four cylinders allows the owner to only use the power of a V-8 when it is needed, thus allowing it to turn into a more fuel-efficient four cylinder most of the time (**FIGURE 5-30**). The speed at which the conversion takes place is within 300 ms assuming that the engine is in good operating shape and the proper oil is used.

▶ Spark-Ignition Engine Components

The SI engine is the most widely used engine to power passenger vehicles in the United States. It is the vehicle's main power plant, providing power to drive the vehicle down the road and operate the many accessories that drivers have come to expect, such as power steering, air-conditioning, entertainment systems, and other features.

N05001 Inspect engine assembly for fuel, oil, coolant, and other leaks; determine needed action.

K05008 Knowledge of spark ignition engines.

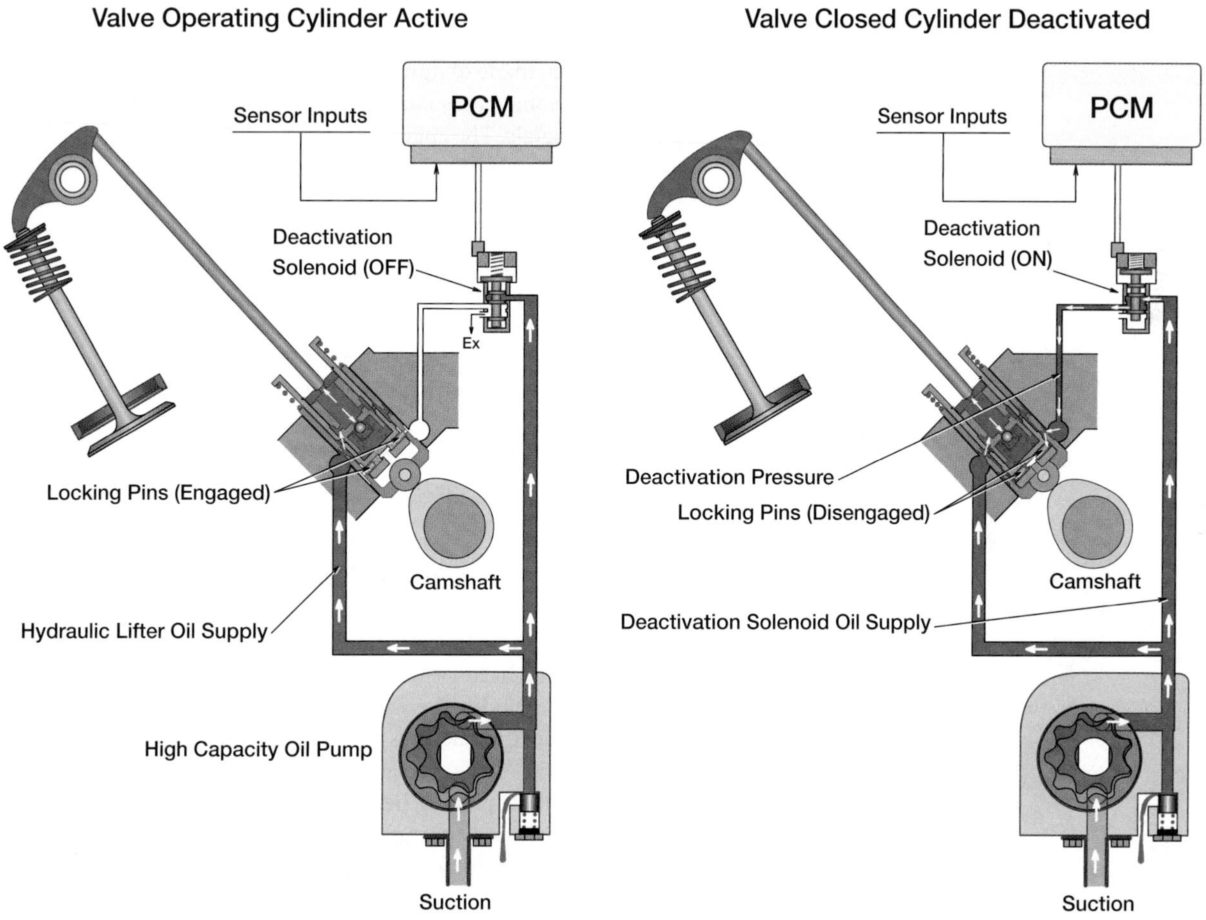

Valve Operating Cylinder Active

PCM

Sensor Inputs

Deactivation Solenoid (OFF)

Ex

Locking Pins (Engaged)

Camshaft

Hydraulic Lifter Oil Supply

High Capacity Oil Pump

Suction

Valve Closed Cylinder Deactivated

PCM

Sensor Inputs

Deactivation Solenoid (ON)

Deactivation Pressure

Locking Pins (Disengaged)

Camshaft

Deactivation Solenoid Oil Supply

Suction

FIGURE 5-29 How displacement-on-demand deactivates each valve.

FIGURE 5-30 Displacement-on-demand lifter.

Components of the Spark-Ignition Engine

SI engines have evolved over their 125-year life, but the fundamental principles are still the same: an air-fuel mixture is brought into the cylinder, compressed to increase its energy, and ignited by a high-voltage spark; the mixture burns rapidly, causing the thermal expansion needed to push the piston down, and the exhaust gases are pushed out of the cylinder. Modern materials, machining processes, and lubricants have made these engines longer lasting, more powerful, and more environmentally friendly than ever. Manufacturers have made incredible gains in the manufacturing of engines and engine components, which are due to new technologies that have found their way into the automotive field. Engine blocks and cylinder heads are commonly manufactured from lightweight aluminum; valve covers and intake manifolds are being made of durable plastic materials; pistons are made of newer aluminum alloys; and in some cases connecting rods are manufactured from powdered metals. The engine can be divided into a couple of main assemblies: the bottom end and the top end. The engine's so-called "bottom end" is the crankcase where the crankshaft, bearings, and connecting rod "big ends" reside. They also make up what is called the rotating assembly. The so-called "top end" is where the cylinder heads and combustion chambers reside. The engine block contains the pistons and connecting rods, crankshaft, and flywheel; if it is a cam-in-block configuration, it also contains the camshaft. The cylinder head(s) contains the overhead valves and valvetrain; if it is a cam-in-head configuration (overhead cam), it also contains the camshaft. Each of these assemblies and components is explored further.

Short Block and Long Block

If a rebuilt engine is needed, an engine subassembly may be purchased. A short block replacement includes the engine block from below the head gasket to above the oil pan. A cam-in-block engine also includes the camshaft and timing gears. An overhead-cam short block does not include the camshaft or timing gears. A long block replacement engine includes the short block, plus the cylinder head(s), new or reconditioned valvetrain, camshaft and timing chain, and/or gears (or timing belt) (**FIGURE 5-31**). A long block engine replacement still requires swapping parts from the original engine to the long block, including the intake and exhaust manifolds, fuel injection system, the starter, alternator, power steering pump, and air-conditioning compressor.

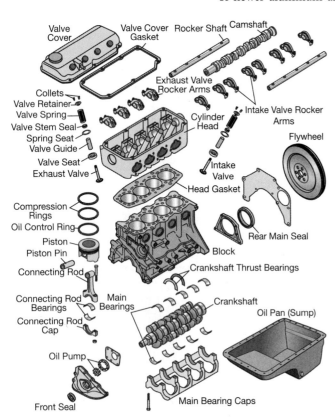

FIGURE 5-31 The engine contains many parts that work together to power the vehicle.

Cylinder Block, Crankshaft, and Flywheel

The cylinder block is the single largest part of the engine. The block can be made of cast iron or aluminum, which is much lighter. The block casting includes the cylinder bore openings, also known as cylinders, which are machined into the block to allow for the fitting of pistons. The block deck is the top of the block and is machined flat. The cylinder head bolts to the block deck. Passages for the flow of coolant and lubrication are machined or cast into the block. Holes machined into the bottom of the block, called main bearing bores, have removable main caps and are used to hold the crankshaft in place. Each cap is held in place with two or more bolts. Reinforcements for strength and attachment points for related parts are also machined into the block. The lowest portion of the block is called the crankcase because it houses the crankshaft. The oil pan completes the crankcase. On most modern engines, the main bearing caps are now a part of the engine girdle, also called a bedplate. The use of a girdle provides an even stronger design, as all main bearing caps are connected and reinforce one another. The crankshaft can be made of cast iron or forged steel, or can be machined out of a solid piece of steel. The crankshaft converts the reciprocating motion of the moving rod and piston assemblies into mechanical force.

Connecting Rod and Piston

The **connecting rod** is what connects the piston to the crankshaft. Connecting rods are made out of forged steel or high-strength aluminum so that they are highly resistant to stretch (**FIGURE 5-32**). The connecting rod is the main piece in an engine that transfers the energy created by the explosion above the **piston** and moves that potential energy to the crankshaft, which then converts it into rotational energy (**FIGURE 5-33**). The piston is usually made out of cast or forged aluminum, which allows for a lighter rotating assembly. Pistons create a sliding combustion that can change size to gain a mechanical advantage when combustion does occur (**FIGURE 5-34**). The piston is attached to the connecting rod with a wrist pin so that it is allowed to pivot on the rod to compensate for the movement of the crankshaft. The piston rings are made of spring steel and go around the piston to seal the combustion gases above the piston so the engine is able to convert force from combustion to create mechanical force. With temperatures reaching up to 1200°F (649°C), the piston must be allowed to expand and handle the temperature change, or it could end up breaking the cylinder wall. Once the piston is installed on the connecting rod, it is then considered a piston-and-rod assembly (**FIGURE 5-35**).

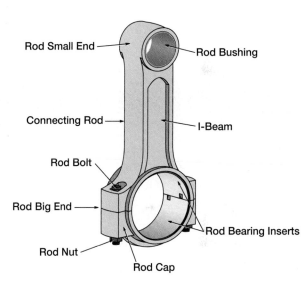

FIGURE 5-32 The different parts of a connecting rod.

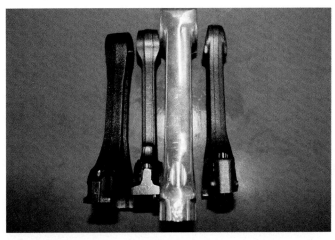

FIGURE 5-33 Various connecting rods.

FIGURE 5-34 Piston, piston rings, wrist pin clips, and wrist pin.

FIGURE 5-35 Piston installed on connecting rod with wrist pin holding it together.

FIGURE 5-36 Windage tray and one-piece sheet metal oil pan.

The Oil Pan

The oil pan on an engine, or the sump, is used to catch the oil that is dripping down from the rest of the engine components inside the engine. The oil pan is an integral part of the engine that protects the engine from losing all of the oil inside the engine. Often a windage tray is part of the oil pan, which helps keep the oil in the sump part of the oil pan, so the oil pump can pick it up and circulate it through the rest of the engine (**FIGURE 5-36**). By directing the oil to a certain place in the sump, engine designers are able to make sure that the engine is not starving for oil. The windage tray also helps to lower the amount of pressure created by a rotating crankshaft in an enclosed space and cuts the excess oil that is slinging off the crankshaft and being held there by centrifugal force. Losing the excess oil that is being collected on the crankshaft and lowering the pressure increases the power the engine can make. Baffling, which is using sheet metal to create a compartment in the oil pan to stop the oil from sloshing around, allows the oil to be trapped in the sump so the oil pump strainer can pick up the oil more easily because it is all in one place (**FIGURE 5-37**). Newer model engines have started to use a more rigid pan and have designed the engine to use the strength of the pan to help strengthen the engine (**FIGURE 5-38**). Some oil pans are made in two pieces, an upper and lower component, which allows for easier installation and inspection of the bottom end of the engine (**FIGURE 5-39**).

FIGURE 5-37 Sheet metal oil pan with built-in baffle to keep oil around the oil pump pickup.

FIGURE 5-38 Cast aluminum oil pan installed on engine.

FIGURE 5-39 Two-piece oil pan—there is an upper and lower oil pan to this application.

The Cylinder Head

The cylinder head is constructed of cast iron or aluminum. Most engines are now constructed using an aluminum cylinder head, which reduces the weight of the engine. The cylinder head contains the valves and valvetrain (valve actuating components) of the engine. The head also includes intake and exhaust ports to which intake and exhaust manifolds are attached. The head forms the top of the cylinder and is sealed in place with the use of a head gasket. The cylinder head has a combustion chamber either cast or machined into it. Combustion chambers in the cylinder head come in several different designs, such as the wedge or the hemispherical combustion chamber, a variation that is used in most engines now (**FIGURE 5-40**).

Engine Cam and Camshaft

The ICE uses so-called "poppet" valves. These are somewhat mushroom-shaped parts that slide up and down in the valve guides. When not actuated (closed), the valves, under pressure from the valve springs, rest on seats of hardened material such as Stellite®. Valves need a system to make them open and close. Control of the valves is accomplished through the use of cams on a common shaft. A cam is an egg-shaped piece (lobe) mounted on the camshaft (**FIGURE 5-41**). The egg shape of the cam lobe is designed to lift the valve open, hold it open, and let it close. The camshaft is timed to the rotation of the crankshaft to ensure that the valves open at the correct position of the piston. Timing the valve opening to the piston position is critical to ensure proper power output and low-emissions operation of the engine. The camshaft is turned either by gears, a toothed belt, or a chain that is driven by sprockets.

Up until the 1950s, many engines had their valves installed in the engine block. Such engines are called flathead engines. Some manufacturers still place the camshaft in the center of the block, but the valves are installed in the cylinder head(s). So-called cam-in-block engines use pushrods to transfer the camshaft's lifting motion to the valves by way of rocker arms on top of the cylinder head. Tappets, or "lifters," ride on the camshaft lobes to actuate the pushrods, rocker arms, and valves. In most automotive engines today, however, the camshaft is mounted on top of the cylinder head. These engines are called overhead cam (OHC) engines (**FIGURE 5-42**).

FIGURE 5-40 Combustion chambers can be designed in several configurations (wedge combustion chamber shown).

FIGURE 5-41 Cam lobes on a camshaft.

FIGURE 5-42 A. Cam-in-block engine. **B.** Overhead cam (OHC) engine.

Intake and exhaust valves may be actuated by a single camshaft or two camshafts per head, called dual overhead cam (DOHC) engines. One camshaft may be used to actuate all of the intake valves and another to actuate all of the exhaust valves. When separate intake and exhaust camshafts are used, there is no need for rocker arms. Most manufacturers use a lifter, called a "bucket lifter," placed right on top of the valve and valve spring to actuate the valve directly from the camshaft. Camshaft lobes are designed, as described previously, to open the valve, hold it, and allow it to close to ensure that the engine operates correctly. In designing the cam lobe, engineers seek a proper compromise for the application of the engine. If the engine is designed to operate at one engine rpm, then the camshaft can be designed to provide optimal power, economy, and emissions. Automotive engines do not operate at one rpm, however, so a camshaft must be designed to provide the best balance of all requirements. High-performance engines built for racing use camshafts designed for high rpm power but would not work well for use on the street where engines rarely stay above 3000 rpm. Newer engine designs have overcome some of these limitations by using variable valve timing.

Valves

A valve is used to open and close a port in a cylinder head. The intake controls the flow of air and/or fuel into the combustion chamber. The exhaust valve controls the flow of exhaust gases out of the combustion chamber and cylinder. The exposed intake port area usually must be larger than the exhaust port area to make it easier for the piston to pull air into the engine on the intake stroke. Engine vacuum created by the piston on the intake stroke is not as effective at moving air into the engine as the pressure created by the piston on the exhaust stroke is at pushing exhaust gases from the engine. The exposed port area can be increased by making the intake valve larger than the exhaust valve, or the manufacturer can use multiple intake valves.

In the case of a three-valve engine, there would be two intake valves and one exhaust valve, but the intake valves would be smaller than the exhaust valve in this case. The valve head is disc shaped, and the top of the valve head faces the combustion chamber. A machined surface on the back of the valve head is the valve face (**FIGURE 5-43**). The valve face seals on a hardened valve seat in the cylinder head. Located between the valve head and the valve face is a flat surface on the outer edge of the valve head, called the valve margin. The margin helps to prevent the valve head from melting under the heat and pressure of combustion. A shaft attached to the valve head is the valve stem, which operates in a valve guide in the cylinder head. The valve stem and guide work together to maintain valve alignment as the valve slides open and closed. Grooves machined into the opposite end of the stem receive locking pieces, sometimes referred to as valve keepers, that hold a valve spring retainer and spring on the valve. Keepers hold the retainer, preventing it from coming loose while under tension from the valve spring, and preventing the parts from coming loose under normal use. Engines may have two to five valves per cylinder.

FIGURE 5-43 The parts of a valve.

Intake and Exhaust Valves

Intake and exhaust valves, in conjunction with the camshaft(s), are the controlling mechanism of the ICE. If the valves do not open and seal at the proper times, combustion will be irregular, weak, or nonexistent. The valves are an incredibly important part of the four-stroke ICE. The intake valve tends to run much cooler than the exhaust because it is always passing cool air and fuel past it when it lifts off its seat. The exhaust valve, in contrast, runs very hot, because when it lifts off its seat, it is surrounded by extremely hot exhaust gases. Because the exhaust valve runs hotter than the intake valve, some manufacturers use sodium-filled valves, which transfer heat away from the head of the valve more quickly. The valve face may also be coated in a material called Stellite, which is a mixture of chromium and cobalt that can hold up to higher heat. The problem with getting the exhaust valve too hot is that it can either melt or deform the sealing surface of the face as it slams closed. The need for new, stronger materials will persist as engines are pushed for maximum power and minimum fuel consumption.

Scavenging

Scavenging is the process of using a column of moving air to create a low-pressure area behind it to assist in removing any remaining burned gases from the combustion chamber and replacing these gases with a new charge. As the exhaust stroke ends and the intake stroke begins, both valves are open for a short time. The time that both valves are open is called valve overlap. As the exhaust gases leave the combustion chamber, the flow tends to continue, creating a low pressure behind it that helps to draw the intake air and fuel charge in. At the same time, the flow of the air and fuel charge being pushed (by atmospheric pressure) into the combustion chamber also helps to push the remaining exhaust gases out. The flow effect during this valve overlap is called scavenging. Valve overlap has a desirable effect during high power/high rpm demand, as more air and fuel are able to be pulled into the engine; however, during engine idling, valve overlap produces a rougher idle as exhaust gases are moving slowly and tend to be drawn back into the intake manifold, diluting the incoming air. The rpm at which the most efficient scavenging occurs contributes to peak volumetric efficiency and engine peak torque. Better exhaust scavenging and induction system (intake) breathing work together to improve volumetric efficiency. This is achieved by smoothing intake and exhaust passages, using tuned intake and exhaust runners (to maximize ram effect and scavenging), and using a low back-pressure exhaust.

Valve Arrangement

Valves may be arranged in one of two methods: the L-head arrangement and the overhead valve, or I-head, arrangement (**FIGURE 5-44**). L-head engines have not been used in automobiles for many years due to inefficiency and exhaust emissions. You will find them on automobile engines up through the early 1950s and on older lawn and garden equipment engines. The L-head engine's valves are located in the block beside the piston. The "flathead Ford" is a well-known V8 engine that used this L-head style of valve arrangement until 1954. The term "flathead" is appropriate, as the head is very thin, acting essentially as a cap to the cylinders. It does not have to be very thick, as the valves are in the block and not in the head. In the I-head arrangement, the valves are placed in the cylinder head above the piston. This design allows a better porting arrangement for air to flow smoothly into and out of the engine for better power and improved fuel economy. Today, the I-head is the design found on all automotive engines.

FIGURE 5-44 In the L-head valve arrangement, valves are placed beside the piston in the engine block, whereas in the I-head, valves are in the head.

Mechanical and Hydraulic Valvetrain

The valvetrain is the combination of parts that work together to open and close the valves of the engine. The valvetrain operates off the camshaft, and the part that rides against the cam lobe is the valve lifter. The lifter transfers motion from the cam lobe to a pushrod, or may directly act on the valve and spring, depending on whether the cam is in the engine block or on the cylinder head. The valve lifter works as a mechanical spacer, providing a hardened bearing surface that slides across the cam lobe. If the lifter is a mechanically solid piece, it is said to be a mechanical lifter, and therefore the engine is said to have a mechanical valvetrain. If the lifter has a hydraulic plunger in its center, it is a hydraulic lifter, and the engine is said to have a hydraulic valvetrain. The hydraulic plunger allows for the expansion and contraction of components during engine warm-up and cooldown. With a hydraulic valvetrain, valve adjustment is made by the hydraulic lifter, which takes up any clearance automatically. If a mechanical valvetrain is used, valve adjustments will be necessary at periodic intervals to ensure proper clearance is maintained as parts in the valvetrain wear.

FIGURE 5-45 This roller rocker with a roller lifter compared to the standard rocker and flat lifter.

Roller Rockers and Lifters

Roller-equipped rocker arms are used on many new engines because they reduce friction and increase engine efficiency. They may also be used to replace the cast or stamped steel rocker arms that have been used for many years as part of a standard valvetrain (**FIGURE 5-45**). A typical rocker arm has a fulcrum, a half-round bearing, or a shaft that the rocker moves on as a bearing surface. One end of the rocker touches the top of the valve stem, and the metal slides across the valve as it pushes the valve open and then lets it close. The other end of the rocker arm connects with the pushrod. The rocker's sliding motion across the valve stem and center pivot results in friction, and friction creates loss of power and wear. To remedy this, needle bearings and a roller may be added to the end of the rocker where it contacts the valve stem, and needle bearings are added to the pivot point where the fulcrum is. This system greatly reduces friction and results in a more powerful and reliable valvetrain. Rocker arms are designed to increase the amount of lift designed into the cam lobe because they work off-center as a lever. A typical rocker arm has the center pivot closer to the push-rod end. This design causes the valve end of the rocker arm to move more than the pushrod end. Many rocker arms have a 1.5:1 lift ratio, which means that the valve moves 1.5 times farther than the pushrod. High-performance rockers have even higher ratios, such as a 1.6:1 or 1.7:1. These rockers increase the lift of the valve even more than a standard rocker arm. The other friction loss point in the valvetrain is at the lifter as it rides upon the cam lobe. To reduce this friction loss, rollers with needle bearings are added to the base of the lifter on some engines. The lifter now rolls on the cam lobe profile rather than sliding on it. This modification further reduces friction in the valvetrain, resulting in more power delivered to the engine flywheel and less wasted as heat. The use of rollers on the lifters also allows the use of more aggressive cam lift profiles. Such profiles would rapidly wear an ordinary flat lifter and cam lobe. This difference between cam profiles used with flat tappets versus roller lifters means camshafts and tappets should never be interchanged. Also, the roller lifter must be held in position so that it does not turn in the lifter bore and scrape on and wear the cam lobe. To prevent this, a retainer keeps the lifter from turning sideways.

Valve Clearance

Valve clearance is the amount of slack between the rocker arm or cam follower and the valve stem, or the cam and the lifter if it is a bucket-style OHC engine (**FIGURE 5-46**). If valve clearance is too large, the valves will tick and make enough noise to irritate the operator and increase wear of the valvetrain. If valve clearance is too small, the valve can be held open

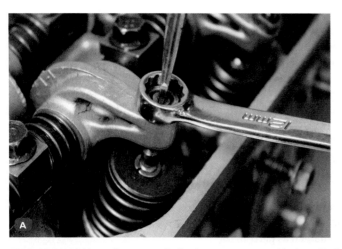

FIGURE 5-46 Valve adjustments. **A.** Rocker arm screw and locknut. **B.** Rocker arm center bolt.

longer than it should be. As the cylinder head and valvetrain parts heat, they expand, so adequate clearance is needed to allow for this expansion. Insufficient valve clearance could result in burned valves. Some valves are adjustable through the use of adjusting screws, nuts, or metal shims. Other valves are nonadjustable, and the rocker arm simply bolts to the head, or the valve lifter is a preset dimension before it is installed under the camshaft if it is a bucket setup. Bucket lifters contain solid metal discs (shims) of different thicknesses. These shims are used to preset the proper valve clearance during cylinder head assembly or during a major tune-up.

Valve Timing

Valve timing is critical to the proper operation of the ICE. Many performance gains can be made by simply changing valve timing, but it all depends on what range of rpm (i.e., maximum power) is desired. Valve timing is a mechanical setting, and once set, it cannot be changed without physically changing the timing components in some way (FIGURE 5-47). For standard-performance engines, the technician sets timing components to marks the factory has made on the engine. The camshaft is usually driven by a chain, tensioners, guides and gears, or a toothed timing belt. The timing chain is typically designed to last the life of the engine, whereas the timing belt is a required maintenance part that must be changed on a regular scheduled maintenance plan. In some vehicles, not doing so results in damage to the engine if the belt breaks. It is critical that the technician take care when reinstalling the belt or chain to ensure that the timing marks are lined up correctly.

FIGURE 5-47 Valve timing marks.

The intake and exhaust valves must also open at the correct point in the rotation of the crankshaft so that the pistons will be in the correct position and not strike the valves. When the piston is sitting at TDC and preparing to go down, the intake valve opens, and air is drawn in with fuel (unless direct injected). The intake valve closes at BDC, and the air-fuel is compressed as the piston moves back up to TDC, where ignition happens. Once fuel is ignited, the piston is driven back down to BDC, where the exhaust valve opens, and the piston moves back to TDC, pushing the exhaust out of the cylinder. In reality, the valves open and close sooner or later than in this description. Because of inertia and other forces, the valves need enough open time to allow gases to flow in and out of the engine. If the valves opened and closed as described in the preceding paragraph, the valves would have 180 degrees of cam duration (TDC to BDC, and BDC to TDC). Although this would be fine for very low-rpm engines, it would not work for high-rpm engines. Thus, we begin the intake stroke by opening the intake valve as the piston is still moving up and the exhaust valve is still slightly open, but closing (FIGURE 5-48). As air flows into the cylinder, it gains velocity, which creates a column of air that has inertia and keeps the airflow moving, or racing, into the cylinder. If we keep the intake valve open after BDC, air continues to rush in because of the inertia of the airflow. This is called column inertia; as a column of air flows into the combustion chamber, it creates inertia, which keeps air flowing until its inertial energy is spent.

This principle of airflow allows the intake valve to be left open even when the piston is starting back up in the cylinder. The inertia causes air molecules to pack together more tightly, especially at higher engine rpm, thus creating a ram-air effect. As the cam allows the valve spring to close the intake valve, the piston continues moving toward TDC and squeezes the air and fuel into a small package. Sometime near TDC, the spark plug ignites the fuel and air. Doing so early allows enough time for the air-fuel mixture to be ignited and burn, which produces power. Air-fuel has a fairly constant burn time, so as engine rpm increases, the spark will have to occur earlier (in degrees) before top dead center (BTDC) to make sure maximum pressure is developed shortly after top dead center (ATDC). As air-fuel burns, it heats and expands the air, which pushes the piston down. As the piston moves down, the exhaust valve begins to open shortly before the piston reaches BDC. This timing allows the pressure in the cylinder to escape before the piston starts moving back up. More importantly, it allows time

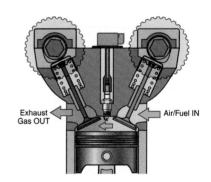

FIGURE 5-48 The intake valve starts to open while the piston is still moving up on the exhaust stroke. The exhaust valve is closing, but it is not closed until the piston starts moving back down.

to open the exhaust valve far enough so that at higher rpm there is enough time to effectively evacuate the cylinder. When the piston travels back toward TDC, the intake valve begins to open slightly before TDC. The exhaust valve is still open past TDC, with exhaust gases rushing out; this helps provide the scavenging effect discussed earlier. The exhaust valve will hang open on some engines a small amount after the piston begins to move down on the intake stroke, in order to allow maximum scavenging effect. All airflow that happens in the engine, whether in or out, is helped by the column inertia effect.

Consider again the definition of valve overlap described earlier. In the real world, even standard camshaft grinds (valve timing) include some degree of valve overlap at BDC and TDC. Yet in traditional engine designs, camshaft design and valve timing are a compromise for street engine use. Racing engines are designed with greater valve lift, longer valve duration (valve open time in degrees of camshaft rotation), and increased valve overlap to maximize the effect of fuel and air inertia encountered at higher rpm. At cranking speeds, there is not much column inertia, so having the valve open for a long time reduces engine intake vacuum and makes the engine difficult to start; this is because the intake air would move back out past the intake valve as the piston travels up on the compression stroke. With no column inertia to speak of, leaving the intake valve hanging open during the initial portion of the compression stroke lowers engine compression. The other problem that can result with large overlap is that at cranking speeds the intake is opening during the exhaust stroke, allowing exhaust gases still burning to work their way out the intake valve and create a backfire in the intake manifold (not a desirable effect).

When the engine starts and the speed of airflow increases, column inertia starts to increase, reducing the problems experienced while cranking. The timing of the valvetrain is basically controlled by the physical shape of the cam lobes. We can move the entire cam forward or backward in relation to the crankshaft position to make the events happen sooner or later in the piston stroke.

Advancing or retarding cam timing should not be confused with ignition timing, however, which is when the spark occurs. Cam timing can be controlled in fixed valve timing engines by installing different gears and a chain or belt. Aftermarket performance companies manufacture cam gears that can be advanced or retarded manually to gain additional power at the desired rpm. Advancing cam timing closes the intake valve sooner, giving more cranking compression, again because of low column inertia. This results in more torque and power in the low rpm range. If we retard cam timing, then the intake valve closes later and gives us more torque and power at a higher rpm range. Because the column inertia is greater at high rpm, more air can be pushed into the engine if the valve is held open later in the four-stroke cycle. Cam duration (valve open time) is built into the cam lobe profile and cannot normally be changed. Duration determines how long the valves remain open and closed. By advancing or retarding the cam opening or closing time, we can affect how long the valves stay open or closed; that is, the point at which they open and close in the cycle can be designed for a distinct engine purpose (peak torque rpm range). Serious valve overlap is typically not used on turbocharged or supercharged engines, as air forced into the engine by the turbo or supercharger would be forced out of the exhaust during overlap.

Variable Valve Timing

We can see from the previous section that the ability to control the advance and retard of the cam timing is a huge benefit to engine performance. Retarded timing provides greater engine efficiency when large amounts of air are flowing into the engine at higher rpm. Advanced timing is useful when the engine needs high torque during lower engine rpm operations. In past applications, an engine designer would have to decide which valve timing best served the operating range of the engine and then design the camshaft for that purpose.

For optimum engine performance in a vehicle used both for commuting and for rallying or racing, what if an electronic module could manage optimum valve timing for such widely differing engine demands? Well, today's automobiles do almost that by using electronically controlled, hydraulically assisted variable valve timing while the engine is operating. Twin camshafts are advanced or retarded through the use of **cam phasers**, or actuators. The phaser typically takes the place of the standard cam gear or pulley and uses oil pressure from the engine oil pump to move (some advance, some retard) the camshafts when commanded by the powertrain control module (PCM). One type of actuator, or phaser, uses a twisted gear arrangement and a return spring. When oil pressure pushes against the gear mechanism, the cam rotates and advances. When oil pressure is released, the return spring brings the cam back to the fully retarded position. At rest, these types of actuators may be either fully retarded or fully advanced (**FIGURE 5-49**). The other type of actuator used is the vane-type phaser. This phaser uses vanes similar to what is used in a vane-type oil pump to move the camshaft (**FIGURE 5-50**). Oil pressure moves into the phaser and pushes on one side of the vane to advance the cam timing. When oil pressure is switched to the other side of the vane, the camshaft is retarded. Cam timing is adjusted according to what the PCM desires based on its input sensors. If oil pressure is held constant, the cam phaser will likewise hold cam timing constant. The cam phaser uses a mechanical stop to limit maximum valve timing advance or retard. Cam phasers can be used on any camshaft arrangement, such as cam-in-block or OHC engines. If the cam is a single cam with exhaust and intake lobes, then both intake and exhaust will be affected by rotating the camshaft to the advanced or retarded position. In a DOHC engine, some engine designers use a phaser on the exhaust camshaft only. The phaser used with this type of engine is not intended for increased engine power, but rather for better exhaust gas recirculation. If the exhaust valve is held open later in the exhaust stroke, then it will also hang open later into the intake stroke, which can result in exhaust gases being pulled back into the engine. The exhaust gases pulled back into the engine dilute the incoming air-fuel mixture with an inert gas to help reduce oxides of nitrogen emissions. Because inert gas does not react chemically, it cools the combustion chamber to reduce oxides of nitrogen or NOx. Controlling NOx in this way allows for the elimination of the exhaust gas recirculation (EGR) valve on some vehicles. In other DOHC engines, the phaser can be installed only on the intake camshaft for greater engine power, or it can be installed on both the intake and the exhaust camshafts.

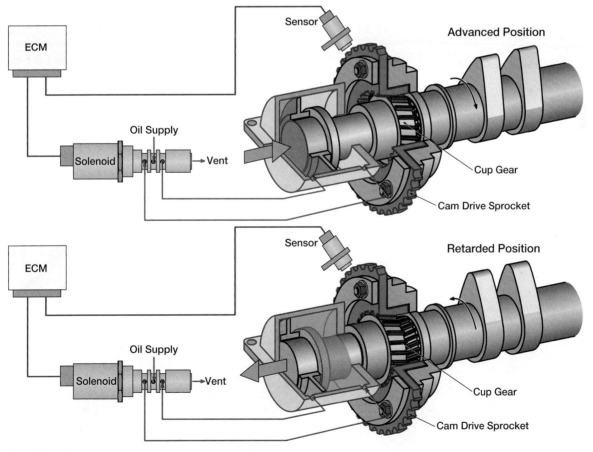

FIGURE 5-49 Spline-type camshaft phaser.

FIGURE 5-50 Vane-type camshaft phaser.

FIGURE 5-51 Phaser oil control solenoid.

The newest cam phaser in use relies on an electric motor-driven phaser to vary the cam timing; this type of phaser is more accurate, as it does not rely on the oil being a consistent viscosity or squeaky clean. Variable cam timing is controlled by the PCM. Several inputs are used to ensure that the PCM is able to control the timing accurately. These inputs are the same inputs used by the PCM to control fuel delivery and ignition system timing. The PCM also must know oil temperature to ensure that the oil viscosity is not too thick or thin. Based on input from an oil temperature sensor, the PCM will either allow or disable variable valve timing; the viscosity of the oil must be correct for accurate valve timing. The PCM must know the amount of engine load to determine the need for an advance or retard of cam timing. To calculate engine load, the PCM primarily uses the following inputs: mass airflow sensor or manifold absolute pressure sensor, throttle position sensor, intake air temperature sensor, engine coolant temperature sensor, and crankshaft position sensor. The PCM relies on feedback to ensure that the cams are rotating as commanded; the cam position sensor (CMP) is used for this function. The output of the PCM is delivered to the cam timing solenoid. The cam solenoid allows oil pressure to move into the cam phaser (**FIGURE 5-51**). The solenoid is turned on and off with a pulse-width modulation (PWM) signal. PWM is the variable rapid (in milliseconds) time-based on/off switching of a DC signal. The longer the solenoid device is turned off, the less it opens; the longer it is turned on, the more it opens. In this way, the solenoid can regulate the amount, and direction, of oil flow to the cam phaser to alter camshaft/valve timing.

Valvetrain Drives

The valvetrain is driven by the camshaft, which in turn is driven by a chain or belt (depending on the engine design) driven by the crankshaft (**FIGURE 5-52**). In older engine designs, the camshaft was driven by a gear-to-gear arrangement like that found in small lawnmower engines. The trouble with a gear-to-gear design is that it tends to be a bit noisy compared to a chain or belt, and the camshaft has to be relatively close to the crankshaft. In any four-cycle engine design, the camshaft must rotate at half of crankshaft speed. This may be accomplished by using a camshaft gear or pulley that has twice the number of teeth as the crankshaft gear. The ratio of the crank to the cam gear is 2:1; thus it takes two turns of the crankshaft to turn the camshaft one turn.

FIGURE 5-52 Cam drives. **A.** Belt-driven OHC. **B.** Chain-driven OHC.

The timing chain drive is louder than a belt, but the belt will not last as long as the timing chain, and if exposed to fluids or dirt, will wear out more quickly. The timing chain must have a constant supply of engine oil to lubricate the chain to keep it from wearing out quickly. Timing gears rarely jump time, but if the timing chain or belt breaks, serious engine damage could result, depending on whether it is a freewheeling engine or an interference engine. A freewheeling engine will not be damaged, but in an interference engine, the valves will be tap-dancing on the piston crowns, bending the valves, with the valves possibly punching holes in the pistons. The freewheeling engine has enough clearance between the pistons and the valves so that in the event the timing belt breaks, any valve that is hanging all the way open will not contact the piston, thus preventing engine damage. A broken timing belt is an inconvenience to the customer. The engine dies and will not restart; the good news is that no mechanical engine damage occurs. By contrast, the interference engine has minimal clearance between the valves and pistons during normal operation. When the timing belt breaks, the pistons keep moving and hit the remaining open valves. A broken timing belt on an interference engine means a huge repair expense, and in some cases the entire engine must be replaced. The manufacturer's service information normally tells you if the engine is an interference engine.

The timing chain camshaft drive used in a cam-in-block engine is very different from that used in the OHC engine. The pushrod engine typically uses a chain behind a timing chain cover located on the front of the engine. This type of timing chain is fairly short, as the camshaft is close to the crankshaft. Some pushrod engines use a timing chain tensioner to ensure that the correct timing chain tension is maintained; however, most designs do not use a tensioner. The timing chain tensioner applies pressure against the chain; as the chain wears and gets longer, the tensioner takes up play in the chain. As the timing chain stretches, cam timing may become retarded. Slack of the chain affects the positioning of the cam gear in relation to the crank gear. Retarded cam timing in this case can create undesirable engine performance problems. The OHC engine requires a longer timing chain or belt, and in this design one or more tensioners are required. The timing chain in an OHC engine typically has hard plastic–type guides for the chain to slide on and assist the tensioner(s) with correct tracking and tension of the timing chain. The OHC timing chain must run in oil to ensure that the chain is lubricated. Without oil, the chain would wear out rapidly. A belt system uses a toothed or cogged belt to turn toothed or cogged pulleys on the camshaft. The belt is a scheduled maintenance replacement item and should be replaced at the mileage or time recommended by the manufacturer (e.g., 60,000 miles [100,000 kilometers] or five years, whichever occurs first).

Intake Manifold

The intake manifold is the main component of the engine that allows the cylinders to suck in fuel and air so that combustion can occur. Without this vital component, the engine would not function, as it could not draw in the fuel and air mixture to sustain combustion in the cylinders. The manifold also acts as a coolant transfer between both cylinder heads on a V-engine and also holds a majority of the engine management sensors. The intake manifold could be a configured differently from the various applications that it is asked to operate in. The design of the runners of the manifold dramatically affects the amount of power the engine has, the mileage that it can sustain, and the space limitations that the vehicle has. For weight savings, the intake could be made out of plastic (**FIGURE 5-53**), or it could be made out of aluminum (**FIGURE 5-54**). Most vehicle manufacturers are incorporating some type of weight-saving material into the intake because it is an area that does not have the stress that would require a steel component. The complexity of machining an intake manifold causes the design to be multi-piece so that the ports and dynamics can be created the way that best suits the engine. When this happens, the upper intake, or plenum, is a separate piece that is bolted onto the lower intake to complete the intake manifold (**FIGURE 5-55**).

FIGURE 5-53 Plastic intake manifold.

FIGURE 5-54 Aluminum lower intake manifold.

FIGURE 5-55 This is a two-piece intake, the lower is aluminum and the upper plenum is plastic.

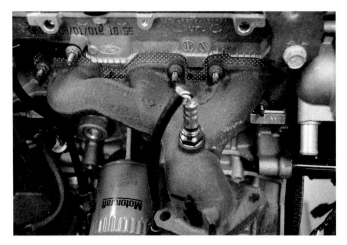

FIGURE 5-56 Cast iron exhaust manifold.

FIGURE 5-57 Tubular exhaust manifold.

Exhaust Manifold

An exhaust manifold is usually made of cast iron or tubular steel and directs the exhaust from the engine toward the back of the vehicle (**FIGURES 5-56, 5-57**). The manifold connects the cylinder head with the rest of the exhaust system so that the fumes will not harm the occupants of the vehicle. As the engine runs, the manifold gets super-heated from the hot combustion that is happening in each cylinder. The manifold also protects the rest of the engine compartment from the sparks, backfires, and raw fuel that goes out the exhaust valves. Without these manifolds, an internal combustion engine, in an enclosed engine compartment, would not be feasible.

▶ Wrap-Up

Ready for Review

▶ An internal combustion engine is one where combustion takes place inside the engine assembly, which then turns that explosive force into mechanical energy. An external combustion engine is one where the fuel is ignited outside the engine assembly and then directed into the engine to create mechanical power, like a steam engine.

▶ Thermodynamics is the branch of physical science that deals with heat and its relation to other forms of energy, such as mechanical energy. In automotive applications, thermodynamics allows a vehicle to move down the road as well as provides motive (moving) power for all of the onboard systems.

▶ Engines operate according to the unchanging laws of physics and thermodynamics.

▶ Pressure rises when the volume of a sealed container is reduced helps you understand the need for sealing the chamber for maximum power.

▶ When molecules are tightly packed together, they produce far more expansion pressure during combustion than when they are not.

▶ Valves and ports in the engine's cylinder head (s) provide a means of sealing the combustion chamber. If the valves leak, the pressure in the cylinder will not rise as it should during the compression stroke of the piston.

▶ If there is too little pressure squeezing the air-fuel mixture together in the cylinder, the mixture will not get packed tightly enough, and less engine power will be developed when it is ignited.

▶ Charles's law states that in a sealed chamber, the pressure and temperature of a gas are directly related to each other. As pressure rises, so does temperature; as pressure decreases, so does temperature.

▶ A diesel engine uses Charles's law to ignite the fuel injected into an engine cylinder. The air is compressed so tightly that it becomes hot enough to ignite the fuel when it arrives; this is why diesel engines are called compression-ignition engines.

▶ The temperature of a gas is one measure of how much energy it has. The more energy a gas has, the more work it can do. The heating of gas particles makes them move faster, which produces more pressure. This pressure exerts more force on the container in which the gas is located. This is how an internal combustion engine works, pressure is first raised through compression and then through combustion of the air-fuel mixture. Burning the air-fuel mixture increases the heat temperature inside the container tremendously, which creates the necessary pressure to produce work.

▶ The more energy the air-fuel mixture has, the more force it exerts on the piston and the more work the piston can do and takes place during the power stroke and pushes the piston down the cylinder.

▶ Pressure and volume are inversely related; as one rises, the other falls. The cylinder contains air, and as the piston is pushed in, the inside air is forced into a smaller volume. This causes an increase in pressure. It is this increase in pressure that allows the engine/pump to do its work. When the piston is pulled out, the volume occupied by the gas grows larger, and the pressure drops, which would allow atmospheric pressure to push more air into the cylinder.

▶ Effort to produce a push or pull action is referred to as force. Force is measured in pounds, kilograms, or Newtons.

▶ Work is equal to distance moved times force applied. Work is measured in foot-pounds (ft-lb), watts, or joules. The rate or speed at which work is performed is called power (Horsepower). The more power that can be produced, the more work can be performed in a given amount of time. Power is measured in ft-lb per second or ft-lb per minute.

▶ One horsepower equals 550 ft-lb per second, or 33,000 ft-lb per minute. So 1200 ft-lb per second equals 2.18 horsepower. The watt or kilowatt (1000 watts) is the metric unit of measurement for power, where 746 watts equals 1 horsepower.

▶ Torque is described as a twisting force. Movement does not have to occur to have torque. Torque is applied before or during movement. It is a force that tries to turn or twist something around, and is defined as the product of a force and the perpendicular distance between the line of action of the force and the axis of rotation.

▶ Horsepower = rpm × ft-lb ÷ 5252. The number 5252 is a constant that is 33,000 divided by two times π 3.1416 or 6.2832.

▶ Brake or shaft horsepower is the power delivered at the shaft of the engine. One horsepower would be produced when a horse walked 165 feet in one minute pulling a 200-pound weight, or 165 ft. x 200 lb. = 33,000 ft-lb.

▶ Newton's second Law of Motion states that the change in speed of an object over a given time is proportional to the force exerted on it. Force = mass times acceleration.

▶ Volumetric efficiency (the rate of air intake and exhaust) at various crankshaft speeds and internal component friction. It is the ratio of the weight of air that actually enters the cylinder to the weight of air that could enter the cylinder, measured at ambient conditions, if the piston-displaced volume were completely filled.

▶ An automotive chassis dynamometer measures output of the engine at the wheels of the vehicle.

▶ The four-stroke or Otto cycle strokes are: intake, compression, power, and exhaust.

▶ On the intake stroke of a four-cycle engine, the intake valve is open, and the vacuum created by the downward motion of the piston in the cylinder sucks the air-fuel mixture into the cylinder. This portion of the process sees the piston go from TDC to BDC, causing the crankshaft to rotate 180 degrees.

▶ The compression stroke starts once the air-fuel mixture is in the cylinder and the piston is at BDC. As the piston reaches BDC, the intake valve closes, and the piston comes back up toward TDC. As the piston is moving up in the cylinder, the air-fuel mixture is being compressed and directed toward the spark plug. The crankshaft rotates 180 degrees to complete this stroke.

▶ Once the piston reaches the top of the cylinder, maximum amount of compression has occurred, and the spark plug is sparked, causing the mixture to explode and starting to push the piston back down to BDC. The air-fuel mixture is ignited and burns rapidly at up to about 4500°F (2482°C). The heat of combustion causes burning gases to expand greatly (thermal expansion), which creates very high pressure in the combustion chamber. The crankshaft has rotated another 180 degrees once this occurs.

▶ As the power stroke completes and the piston is back at the bottom of the cylinder, the exhaust valve opens up. The crankshaft is rotated another 180 degrees so that the piston is pushed back up to TDC. Along the way to TDC, the piston is pushing out to the exhaust system hot exhaust gases that are left in the cylinder through the open exhaust valve.

▶ The Miller cycle engine and the Atkinson cycle engine are both variations on the traditional four-stroke spark-ignition engine. These engines operate more efficiently but produce lower power outputs for the same displacement.

▶ The Miller and the Atkinson cycles use valve timing variations to make the effective compression stroke shorter than the expansion stroke. The effective compression stroke is shortened by delaying the closing of the intake valve at the beginning of the compression stroke. This shortens the distance that the piston has to compress the air-fuel mixture. This design results in lower manifold vacuum, reduced pumping (parasitic drag) losses, and increased fuel efficiency.

▶ Bore is the diameter of the engine cylinder and also the piston diameter. The bore is measured across the cylinder, parallel with the block deck, which is the machined surface of the block farthest from the crankshaft.

▶ Stroke is the distance the piston travels from TDC to BDC, or from BDC to TDC. Piston stroke is determined by the offset portion of the crankshaft, called the throw.

▶ Generally speaking, the longer the stroke, the greater the engine torque produced. A shorter stroke enables the engine to run at higher rpm to create greater horsepower.

▶ Engine specifications typically list the bore size first and the stroke length second (bore vs. stroke). The volume that a piston displaces from BDC to TDC is piston displacement. Increasing the diameter of the bore or increasing the length of the stroke produces a larger piston displacement.

▶ Internal combustion engines (ICE) are designated by the amount of space (volume) their pistons displace as they move from TDC to BDC, which is called engine displacement. To find an engine's displacement, you need to know the bore, stroke, and number of cylinders for a particular engine. A 5.4-liter V8 engine has eight cylinders that displace a total volume of 5-4 liters. A 5.4L (329-cubic-inch) V8 engine has a 3.55" bore, a 4.16" stroke, and eight cylinders. Using the formula for displacement: 3.55×3.55 (bore 2) $= 12.6025 \times 0.785$ (constant) $= 9.893 \times 4.16$ (stroke) $= 41.155$-cubic-inch piston displacement $\times 8 = 329$ cubic inches of displacement.

▶ An engine with the same size bore and stroke is referred to as a square engine. An engine with a larger bore than stroke is called an oversquare engine (shortstroke engine). An engine with a bore smaller than the stroke is called an undersquare engine (long-stroke engine). Oversquare engines tend to make their power at higher rpm, whereas undersquare engines tend to make their power at lower rpm.

▶ The term "compression ratio" is actually a volume ratio. In an internal combustion engine, compression ratio is the ratio of the total cylinder volume to the clearance volume. It is the volume of the cylinder at the beginning of the compression stroke divided by the volume of the cylinder at the end of the compression stroke.

▶ In a piston engine, the way engine cylinders are arranged is called the engine configuration. Multicylinder internal combustion automotive engines are produced in four common configurations: In-line: The pistons are all in one bank on one side of a common crankshaft. Horizontally opposed: The pistons are in two banks on both sides of a common crankshaft. V: The pistons are in two banks on opposite sides, forming a deep V with a common crankshaft at the base of the V. VR and W: In a VR engine, the pistons are in one bank but form a shallow V within the bank. The W engine consists of two VR banks in a deep V configuration with each other.

▶ Engineers design engines with tilted cylinder banks to reduce engine height. This can reduce the height of the hood as well, which allows a more streamlined hood line.

▶ In vehicle applications, the number of cylinders can vary, usually up to 12. Some examples are listed here: In-line 4, V8, Flat 6, and W12.

▶ Common angles between the banks of cylinders are 180 degrees, 90 degrees, 60 degrees, and 15 degrees. Angles vary due to the number of cylinders and the manufacturer's design considerations.

▶ Rotary engines are very powerful for their size, but they do not use conventional pistons that slide back and forth inside a straight cylinder. Instead, a rotary engine uses a triangular rotor that turns inside an oval-shaped housing. The rotary engine has three combustion events for each rotation of the rotor.

▶ The engine in a modern automobile turns counterclockwise when viewed from the driver's seat. It turns clockwise when viewed from the front of the vehicle. The reason that this happens is that rotational force is put on the drive wheel that is nearest to the driver. In theory, this helps increase traction to that wheel.

▶ Variable displacement engines use oil pressure to shut off lifters to the cylinders that they are trying to disable so that the intake and exhaust valves do not open. At the same time this is happening, the injector and spark plug is shut off, which allows for a lower load on the engine electrical system.

▶ Spark-ignition (SI) engines use an air-fuel mixture that is brought into the cylinder, compressed to increase its energy, and ignited by a high-voltage spark; the mixture burns rapidly, causing the thermal expansion needed to push the piston down, and the exhaust gases are pushed out of the cylinder.

▶ Engine blocks and cylinder heads are commonly manufactured from lightweight aluminum; valve covers and intake manifolds are being made of durable plastic materials; pistons are made of newer aluminum alloys;

and in some cases connecting rods are manufactured from powdered metals.

▶ The engine can be divided into a couple of main assemblies: the bottom end and the top end. The "bottom end" is the crankcase where the crankshaft, bearings, and connecting rod "big ends" reside. They also make up what is called the rotating assembly.

▶ The "top end" is where the cylinder heads and combustion chambers reside. The engine block contains the pistons and connecting rods, crankshaft, and flywheel; if it is a cam-in-block configuration, it also contains the camshaft.

▶ The cylinder head (s) contains the overhead valves and valvetrain; if it is a cam-in-head configuration (overhead cam), it also contains the camshaft.

▶ A short block replacement includes the engine block from below the head gasket to above the oil pan.

▶ A cam-in-block engine also includes the camshaft and timing gears.

▶ An overhead-cam short block does not include the camshaft or timing gears.

▶ A long block replacement engine includes the short block, plus the cylinder head(s), new or reconditioned valvetrain, camshaft and timing chain, and/or gears (or timing belt).

▶ The cylinder block can be made of cast iron or aluminum. The block casting includes the cylinder bore openings, also known as cylinders, machined into the block to allow for the fitting of pistons. The block deck is the top of the block and is machined flat. The cylinder head bolts to the block deck.

▶ Passages for the flow of coolant and lubrication are machined or cast into the block. Holes machined into the bottom of the block, called main bearing bores, have removable main caps and are used to hold the crankshaft in place. Each cap is held in place with two or more bolts.

▶ The lowest portion of the block is called the crankcase because it houses the crankshaft. The oil pan completes the crankcase. The main bearing caps are now a part of the engine girdle, also called a bedplate. The use of a girdle provides an even stronger design, as all main bearing caps are connected and reinforce one another.

▶ The crankshaft can be made of cast iron or forged steel, or can be machined out of a solid piece of steel. The crankshaft converts the reciprocating motion of the moving rod and piston assemblies into mechanical force.

▶ The connecting rod is what connects the piston to the crankshaft. They are made out of forged steel or high-strength aluminum. It is the main piece in an engine that transfers the energy created by the explosion.

▶ The piston moves potential energy to the crankshaft, which then converts it into rotational energy. It is made out of cast or forged aluminum. Pistons create a sliding combustion that can change size to gain a mechanical advantage when combustion does occur.

▶ The piston is attached to the connecting rod with a wrist pin so that it is allowed to pivot on the rod to compensate for the movement of the crankshaft. The piston rings are made of spring steel and go around the piston to seal the combustion gases above the piston so the engine is able to convert force from combustion to create mechanical force.

▶ Once the piston is installed on the connecting rod, it is then considered a piston-and-rod assembly.

▶ The oil pan on an engine, or the sump, is used to catch the oil that is dripping down from the rest of the engine components inside the engine.

▶ A windage tray is part of the oil pan, which helps keep the oil in the sump part of the oil pan, so the oil pump can pick it up and circulate it through the engine. It helps to lower the amount of pressure created by a rotating crankshaft in an enclosed space and cuts the excess oil that is slinging off the crankshaft and being held there by centrifugal force.

▶ Newer model engines have started to use a more rigid pan and have designed the engine to use the strength of the pan to help strengthen the engine.

▶ The cylinder head is constructed of cast iron or aluminum and contains the valves and valvetrain of the engine and includes intake and exhaust ports to which intake and exhaust manifolds are attached.

▶ The cylinder head forms the top of the cylinder and is sealed in place with the use of a head gasket. The cylinder head has a combustion chamber either cast or machined into it.

▶ Combustion chambers in the cylinder head come in several different designs, such as the wedge or the hemispherical combustion chamber.

▶ Poppet valves are used as the intake and exhaust valves that slide up and down in the valve guides.

▶ Valves need a system to make them open and close. Control of the valves is accomplished through the use of cams on a common shaft.

▶ The cam is an egg-shaped piece (lobe) mounted on the camshaft. The egg shape of the cam lobe is designed to lift the valve open, hold it open, and let it close. The camshaft is timed to the rotation of the crankshaft to ensure that the valves open at the correct position of the piston. Timing the valve opening to the piston position is critical to ensure proper power output and low-emissions operation of the engine.

▶ The camshaft is turned either by gears, a toothed belt, or a chain that is driven by sprockets.

▶ Some manufacturers still place the camshaft in the center of the block, but the valves are installed in the cylinder head(s). They use pushrods to transfer the camshaft's lifting motion to the valves by way of rocker arms on top of the cylinder head. Tappets, or "lifters," ride on the camshaft lobes to actuate the pushrods, rocker arms, and valves. In most automotive engines today, however, the camshaft is mounted on top of the cylinder head.

▶ Intake and exhaust valves may be actuated by a single camshaft or two camshafts per head, called dual overhead cam (DOHC) engines. One camshaft may be used to

- actuate the intake valves and another to actuate all of the exhaust valves.
- Most manufacturers use a lifter, called a "bucket lifter," placed right on top of the valve and valve spring to actuate the valve directly from the camshaft.
- High-performance engines built for racing use camshafts designed for high rpm power but would not work well for use on the street where engines rarely stay above 3000 rpm.
- Newer engine designs have overcome some of these limitations by using variable valve timing.
- The intake controls the flow of air and/or fuel into the combustion chamber. The exhaust valve controls the flow of exhaust gases out of the combustion chamber and cylinder.
- In the case of a three-valve engine, there would be two intake valves and one exhaust valve, but the intake valves would be smaller than the exhaust valve in this case.
- The valve face seals on a hardened valve seat in the cylinder head.
- The valve margin is located between the valve head and the valve face is a flat surface on the outer edge of the valve head, called. The margin helps to prevent the valve head from melting under the heat and pressure of combustion.
- A shaft attached to the valve head is the valve stem, which operates in a valve guide in the cylinder head. The valve stem and guide work together to maintain valve alignment as the valve slides open and closed.
- Grooves machined into the opposite end of the stem receive locking pieces, sometimes referred to as valve keepers that hold a valve spring retainer and spring on the valve.
- The intake valve tends to run much cooler than the exhaust because it is always passing cool air and fuel past it when it lifts off its seat. The exhaust valve, in contrast, runs very hot, because when it lifts off its seat, it is surrounded by extremely hot exhaust gases.
- Some manufacturers use sodium-filled valves, which transfer heat away from the head of the valve more quickly.
- The valve face may also be coated in a material called Stellite, which is a mixture of chromium and cobalt that can hold up to higher heat.
- Scavenging is the process of using a column of moving air to create a low-pressure area behind it to assist in removing any remaining burned gases from the combustion chamber and replacing these gases with a new charge.
- Valve overlap has a desirable effect during high power/high rpm demand, as more air and fuel are able to be pulled into the engine; however, during engine idling, valve overlap produces a rougher idle as exhaust gases are moving slowly and tend to be drawn back into the intake manifold, diluting the incoming air.
- Valves may be arranged in one of two methods: the L-head arrangement and the overhead valve, or I-head, arrangement.
- The valvetrain is the combination of parts that work together to open and close the valves of the engine. The valvetrain operates off the camshaft, and the part that rides against the cam lobe is the valve lifter. The lifter transfers motion from the cam lobe to a pushrod, or may directly act on the valve and spring, depending on whether the cam is in the engine block or on the cylinder head.
- The hydraulic plunger allows for the expansion and contraction of components during engine warm-up and cooldown. With a hydraulic valvetrain, valve adjustment is made by the hydraulic lifter, which takes up any clearance automatically.
- If a mechanical valvetrain is used, valve adjustments will be necessary at periodic intervals to ensure proper clearance is maintained as parts in the valvetrain wear.
- Roller-equipped rocker arms are used on many new engines because they reduce friction and increase engine efficiency.
- A typical rocker arm has a fulcrum, a half-round bearing, or a shaft that the rocker moves on as a bearing surface. One end of the rocker touches the top of the valve stem, and the metal slides across the valve as it pushes the valve open and then lets it close. The other end of the rocker arm connects with the pushrod.
- Many rocker arms have a 1.5:1 lift ratio, which means that the valve moves 1.5 times farther than the pushrod.
- High-performance rockers have even higher ratios, such as a 1.6:1 or 1.7:1.
- The use of rollers on the lifters also allows the use of more aggressive cam lift profiles. Such profiles would rapidly wear an ordinary flat lifter and cam lobe.
- Valve clearance is the amount of slack between the rocker arm or cam follower and the valve stem, or the cam and the lifter if it is a bucket-style OHC engine.
- If valve clearance is too large, the valves will tick and make enough noise to irritate the operator and increase wear of the valvetrain. If valve clearance is too small, the valve can be held open longer than it should be.
- Some valves are adjustable through the use of adjusting screws, nuts, or metal shims. Other valves are nonadjustable, and the rocker arm simply bolts to the head, or the valve lifter is a preset dimension before it is installed under the camshaft if it is a bucket setup. Bucket lifters contain solid metal discs (shims) of different thicknesses. These shims are used to preset the proper valve clearance during cylinder head assembly or during a major tune-up.
- Valve timing is critical to the proper engine operation of the ICE. It is a mechanical setting that cannot be changed without physically changing the timing components in some way
- For standard-performance engines, the technician sets timing components to marks the factory has made on the engine.
- The camshaft is usually driven by a chain, tensioners, guides and gears, or a toothed timing belt. It is critical that the technician take care when reinstalling the belt or chain to ensure that the timing marks are lined up correctly.

▶ The intake and exhaust valves must also open at the correct point in the rotation of the crankshaft so that the pistons will be in the correct position and not strike the valves. When the piston is sitting at TDC and preparing to go down, the intake valve opens, and air is drawn in with fuel (unless direct injected). The intake valve closes at BDC, and the air-fuel is compressed as the piston moves back up to TDC, where ignition happens, and keeps the airflow moving, or racing, into the cylinder.

▶ Well, today's automobiles do almost that by using electronically controlled, hydraulically assisted variable valve timing while the engine is operating.

▶ Twin camshafts are advanced or retarded through the use of cam phasers or actuators. The phaser typically takes the place of the standard cam gear or pulley and uses oil pressure from the engine oil pump to move (some advance, some retard) the camshafts when commanded by the powertrain control module (PCM).

▶ One type of actuator, or phaser, uses a twisted gear arrangement and a return spring. When oil pressure pushes against the gear mechanism, the cam rotates and advances. When oil pressure is released, the return spring brings the cam back to the fully retarded position. At rest, these types of actuators may be either fully retarded or fully advanced.

▶ The other type of actuator used is the vane-type phaser. This phaser uses vanes similar to what is used in a vane-type oil pump to move the camshaft. Oil pressure moves into the phaser and pushes on one side of the vane to advance the cam timing. When oil pressure is switched to the other side of the vane, the camshaft is retarded. Cam timing is adjusted according to what the PCM desires based on its input sensors. If oil pressure is held constant, the cam phaser will likewise hold cam timing constant. The cam phaser uses a mechanical stop to limit maximum valve timing advance or retard.

▶ Cam phasers can be used on any camshaft arrangement, such as cam-in-block or OHC engines. If the cam is a single cam with exhaust and intake lobes, then both intake and exhaust will be affected by rotating the camshaft to the advanced or retarded position.

▶ In a DOHC engine, some engine designers use a phaser on the exhaust camshaft only. The phaser used with this type of engine is not intended for increased engine power, but rather for better exhaust gas recirculation. If the exhaust valve is held open later in the exhaust stroke, then it will also hang open later into the intake stroke, which can result in exhaust gases being pulled back into the engine.

▶ In other DOHC engines, the phaser can be installed only on the intake camshaft for greater engine power, or it can be installed on both the intake and the exhaust camshafts.

▶ The newest cam phaser in use relies on an electric motor-driven phaser to vary the cam timing; this type of phaser is more accurate, as it does not rely on the oil being a consistent viscosity or squeaky clean. Variable cam timing is controlled by the engine management computer.

▶ The engine management computer relies on feedback to ensure that the cams are rotating as commanded; the cam position sensor (CMP) is used for this function.

▶ The valvetrain is driven by the camshaft, which in turn is driven by a chain or belt (depending on the engine design) driven by the crankshaft.

▶ The ratio of the crank to the cam gear is 2:1; thus it takes two turns of the crankshaft to turn the camshaft one turn.

▶ The timing chain drive is louder than a belt, but the belt will not last as long as the timing chain, and if exposed to fluids or dirt, will wear out more quickly. The timing chain must have a constant supply of engine oil to lubricate the chain to keep it from wearing out quickly.

▶ Timing gears rarely jump time, but if the timing chain or belt breaks, serious engine damage could result, depending on whether it is a freewheeling engine or an interference engine.

▶ A freewheeling engine will not be damaged, but in an interference engine, the valves will be tap-dancing on the piston crowns, bending the valves, with the valves possibly punching holes in the pistons. The freewheeling engine has enough clearance between the pistons and the valves so that in the event the timing belt breaks, any valve that is hanging all the way open will not contact the piston, thus preventing engine damage

▶ The interference engine has minimal clearance between the valves and pistons during normal operation. When the timing belt breaks, the pistons keep moving and hit the remaining open valves.

▶ The manufacturer's service information normally tells you if the engine is an interference engine.

▶ The timing chain camshaft drive used in a cam-in-block engine is very different from that used in the OHC engine. The pushrod engine typically uses a chain behind a timing chain cover located on the front of the engine. This type of timing chain is fairly short, as the camshaft is close to the crankshaft.

▶ Some pushrod engines use a timing chain tensioner to ensure that the correct timing chain tension is maintained; however, most designs do not use a tensioner.

▶ The timing chain tensioner applies pressure against the chain; as the chain wears and gets longer, the tensioner takes up play in the chain. As the timing chain stretches, cam timing may become retarded. Slack of the chain affects the positioning of the cam gear in relation to the crank gear.

▶ Retarded cam timing in this case can create undesirable engine performance problems.

▶ The OHC engine requires a longer timing chain or belt, and in this design one or more tensioners are required.

▶ The timing chain in an OHC engine typically has hard plastic–type guides for the chain to slide on and assist the tensioner(s) with correct tracking and tension of the timing chain.

- The OHC timing chain must run in oil to ensure that the chain is lubricated. Without oil, the chain would wear out rapidly.
- A belt system uses a toothed or cogged belt to turn toothed or cogged pulleys on the camshaft. The belt is a scheduled maintenance replacement item and should be replaced at the mileage or time recommended by the manufacturer (60,000 miles [100,000 kilometers] or 5 years, whichever occurs first).
- The intake manifold is the main component of the engine that allows the cylinders to suck in fuel and air so that combustion can occur. The manifold also acts as a coolant transfer between both cylinder heads on a V-engine and also holds a majority of the engine management sensors
- The exhaust manifold is usually made of cast iron or tubular steel and directs the exhaust from the engine toward the back of the vehicle.

Key Terms

Atkinson cycle engine Allows for all four events—intake, compression, power, and exhaust—to happen on one revolution of the engine.

cam phaser An assembly that allows for the advancement or retardation of the camshaft to adjust valve timing, which increases power and decreases emissions.

compression ratio The column of the cylinder with the piston at bottom dead center as compared to the volume of the cylinder at top dead center, given in a ratio such as 10:1 CR.

connecting rod Connects the piston to the crankshaft and is an integral part in converting the chemical energy of the fuel to the mechanical energy needed to rotate the engine.

engine displacement The size of the engine, given in cubic inches, cubic centimeters, and lifters. It is found by multiplying the piston displacement by the number of cylinders in the engine.

Miller cycle engine The intake valve is left open longer than the typical Otto cycle engine.

piston Part of the combustion chamber that is moveable and transfers the combustion energy to the connecting rod, which then creates mechanical energy by rotating the crankshaft.

power The rate or speed at which work is performed.

scavenging The process that uses a column of moving air to create a low pressure area behind it to assist in removing any remaining gases; this creates a vacuum.

valve timing The relationship between the crankshaft and the valve opening events, which is what allows combustion to happen properly.

variable displacement engine An engine that can change the cubic inches of displacement through cylinder deactivation.

volumetric efficiency The measurement of the amount of air-fuel mixture that is drawn into the cylinder as compared to the size of the cylinder.

Review Questions

1. When compared to internal combustion engines:
   a. the output of Stirling engines can be easily varied.
   b. steam engines take relatively less time to generate pressure.
   c. steam engines do not present an explosion hazard under too much pressure.
   d. Stirling engines run almost silently.
2. Choose the correct statement:
   a. As pressure increases, temperature decreases and volume increases.
   b. As pressure increases, temperature and volume increase.
   c. As pressure increases, temperature increases and volume decreases.
   d. As pressure increases, temperature and volume decrease.
3. The effort to produce a push or pull action is referred to as:
   a. force.
   b. power.
   c. work.
   d. torque.
4. Which event occurs when the piston reaches TDC of the compression stroke?
   a. Ignition
   b. Power stroke
   c. Exhaust
   d. Intake
5. The displacement of an engine can be altered by changing all of the below, *except* the:
   a. cylinder bore.
   b. type of fuel.
   c. piston stroke.
   d. number of cylinders.
6. In the Miller and Atkinson cycle engines
   a. compressor stroke is longer and expansion stroke is shorter.
   b. the combustion chamber is slightly bigger.
   c. the compression pressure at ignition is greater than in a conventional engine.
   d. compressor stroke is shorter and expansion stroke is longer.
7. Which of these converts the reciprocating movement of the pistons into rotary motion?
   a. Camshaft
   b. Flywheel
   c. Crankshaft
   d. Piston ring
8. Proper power output and low-emissions operation of the engine is ensured by:
   a. using pistons with an iron coating.
   b. timing the valve opening to the piston position.
   c. keeping the combustion pressure in check by letting it into the crankcase.
   d. increasing the number of valves per cylinder.
9. The two-stroke engine differs from the four-stroke engine in all the below aspects, *except*:
   a. the events involved in the operation of the engine.
   b. the emissions produced by the engine.

c. the method of air induction and exhaust.

d. their production costs and size.

10. Which of the below statements is true with respect to a rotary engine?

a. The rotor is mounted in a cylindrical housing.

b. Reciprocating motion need not be converted to rotary motion.

c. The engine will produce one power pulse per rotor rotation.

d. The engine produces more vibration when compared to other ICEs.

ASE Technician A/Technician B Style Questions

1. Technician A says that compression ratio is the comparison of the volume above the piston at bottom dead center (BDC) to the volume at top dead center (TDC). Technician B says that scavenging of the exhaust gases occurs once the exhaust valve closes. Who is correct?

a. Tech A

b. Tech B

c. Both A and B

d. Neither A nor B

2. Technician A says that the principle of thermal expansion is what pushes the piston down the cylinder on the power stroke. Technician B says that the piston is pulled down the cylinder on the intake stroke. Who is correct?

a. Tech A

b. Tech B

c. Both A and B

d. Neither A nor B

3. Technician A says that engines are classified by the number of cylinders that are present in the engine. Technician B says that engines are classified by the layout of the cylinders in the engine. Who is correct?

a. Tech A

b. Tech B

c. Both A and B

d. Neither A nor B

4. Technician A says that a long block includes the cylinder heads and intake manifold assembly. Technician B says that the short block assembly only includes cylinder block, crankshaft, connecting rods, and pistons. Who is correct?

a. Tech A

b. Tech B

c. Both A and B

d. Neither A nor B

5. Technician A says roller rocker arms increase the friction so that they contact the valve with increased pressure. Technician B says that less friction is created by metal-on-metal contact. Who is correct?

a. Tech A

b. Tech B

c. Both A and B

d. Neither A nor B

6. Technician A says that a hydraulic valvetrain compensates for any wear that might occur as the engine gains mileage. Technician B says that a nonadjustable valvetrain will not allow for adjustment. Who is correct?

a. Tech A

b. Tech B

c. Both A and B

d. Neither A nor B

7. Technician A says excessive valve clearance is the cause of a lot of valvetrain noise. Technician B says that a mechanical valvetrain compensates for the increase valve clearance. Who is correct?

a. Tech A

b. Tech B

c. Both A and B

d. Neither A nor B

8. Technician A says valve arrangement in the cylinder head is confined to the diameter of the cylinder. Technician B says that cylinder heads can be made out of cast iron or cast aluminum. Who is correct?

a. Tech A

b. Tech B

c. Both A and B

d. Neither A nor B

9. Technician A says a windage tray helps keep the oil in the sump of the oil pan. Technician B says that not all oil pans have a windage tray. Who is correct?

a. Tech A

b. Tech B

c. Both A and B

d. Neither A nor B

10. Technician A says the connecting rod can be made out of aluminum or forged iron. Technician B says that a piston pin can only be pressed in. Who is correct?

a. Tech A

b. Tech B

c. Both A and B

d. Neither A nor B

CHAPTER 6

Engine Mechanical Testing

NATEF Tasks

- **N06001** Research applicable vehicle and service information, such as internal engine operation, vehicle service history, service precautions, and technical service bulletins.
- **N06002** Perform cooling system pressure and dye tests to identify leaks; check coolant condition and level; inspect and test radiator, pressure cap, coolant recovery tank, and heater core; determine needed action.
- **N06003** Inspect, remove, and replace engine mounts.

Knowledge Objectives

After reading this chapter, you will have:

- **K06001** Knowledge of when to use mechanical tests in diagnosis of an engine.
- **K06002** Knowledge of how a compression test helps to diagnose the engine mechanical condition.
- **K06003** Knowledge of when to do a leak-down test.
- **K06004** Knowledge of how to diagnosis engine noises and vibrations.
- **K06005** Knowledge of the effect of mechanical issues on vacuum.
- **K06006** Knowledge of how to verify fluid consumption by the engine.
- **K06007** Knowledge of how the exhaust system affects the engine.

Skills Objectives

- **S06001** Perform a cranking sound diagnosis.
- **S06002** Test engine vacuum using a vacuum gauge.
- **S06003** Test engine vacuum using a pressure transducer and lab scope.
- **S06004** Perform a cylinder power balance test.
- **S06005** Perform a cranking compression test.
- **S06006** Perform a running compression test.
- **S06007** Perform a cylinder leakage test.
- **S06008** Perform spark plug removal.
- **S06009** Perform a relative compression test.
- **S06010** Perform an exhaust system backpressure test.
- **S06011** Test an engine for oil pressure.
- **S06012** Test for a dye leak.
- **S06013** Perform a chemical block test.
- **S06014** Test cooling system pressure.

You Are the Automotive Technician

A customer comes into the dealership complaining that her vehicle is not running as smoothly as before and that the check engine light is flashing, which indicates a potentially catalyst-damaging fault. As an experienced, certified technician, you explain to the customer that she did the right thing by bringing in the vehicle for diagnosis. First, you locate the customer's vehicle history and write up a repair order including the customers concerns. Second, you use a scan tool to retrieve the DTCs and find a P0304-cylinder 4 misfire detected code. Third, you hold the throttle to the floor, with the ignition switch in the off position, and then crank the engine over. The engine exhibits an uneven cranking sound indicating a compression-related fault. Next, you research the technical service bulletins (TSBs) and find one that relates to this code and low compression condition. The TSB indicates possible soft camshaft lobes, which can wear down and then do not open the valve(s) fully. To verify whether this is the case, the TSB directs you to perform a cranking compression test along with a running compression test on any misfiring cylinders. The TSB then lists the acceptable minimum pressures for each test.

1. Why did the engine have an uneven cranking sound?
2. What does the running compression test indicate?
3. How would you determine which cylinder is misfiring if the engine computer doesn't have that capability?

▶ Introduction

For an engine to operate efficiently and effectively, the mechanical condition of the engine must be in good working order. The pistons, piston rings, cylinder walls, head gasket, and valves must seal properly. If they do not, then the engine will not operate correctly, and all of the tuning in the world will not be able to fix it. So assessing the condition of the engine is a critical step in the diagnostic process before any parts are replaced. There are few things more dreaded than having to tell a customer that the $300 tune-up you just performed did not resolve the vehicle's misfiring problem caused by a burned valve and that the vehicle really needs a $1500 valve job, or a $4000 engine replacement. First, the customer will not be happy that the vehicle is not fixed. Second, the repair will now cost substantially more money than the customer expected. Third, the customer now has very good reason to doubt your competence and wonder if you are correct now, when you were wrong earlier. This is a no-win situation, but it can be avoided by always diagnosing the problem instead of throwing parts at it. Engine mechanical testing is also performed to diagnose more accurately what major engine work is needed, such as replacing a head gasket, rebuilding of the cylinder heads, or performing a full engine replacement. Understanding exactly what is wrong allows you to better advise the customer on the appropriate repairs. Also, by fully understanding the situation and clearly communicating it in a professional manner, you build credibility with your customers. This chapter helps you learn the skills and procedures for performing engine mechanical tests.

N06001 Research applicable vehicle and service information, such as internal engine operation, vehicle service history, service precautions, and technical service bulletins.

K06001 Knowledge of when to use mechanical tests in diagnosis of an engine.

▶ Engine Mechanical Testing

Engine mechanical testing uses a series of tests to assess the mechanical condition of the engine. The tests start off broad and narrow down as each test is performed. This process helps you identify first the location of the fault and then its cause. Having a good understanding of engine theory will help you evaluate the results of each test and provide you the information needed to know what path to follow after each step. Mechanical testing starts with a good visual inspection. A visual inspection of the engine assembly for leaks will affirm the ability of the seals and gaskets to contain each of the engine's fluids. Starting the engine and listening to its operation can indicate a host of problems, from loose belts to worn main bearings. It can also reveal if the engine is misfiring and how steady the misfire is. After a good inspection, it is time to pull out the tools and equipment to take a deeper look at the mechanical condition of the engine (**FIGURE 6-1**).

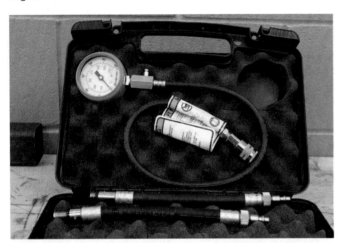

FIGURE 6-1 A compression tester.

When to Do Mechanical Testing

We determine to do mechanical testing when we receive a work order with a running issue. As a future technician, you should get into the habit early on of verifying the mechanical integrity of any engine that happens to come into your bay. If you fail to do this step and proceed to try to fix a customer's vehicle, you could be putting money into something that you cannot fix. Verifying **mechanical integrity** of an engine should be the number one thing that a technician does before moving on to anything else.

Cranking Sound Diagnosis Overview

S06001 Perform a cranking sound diagnosis.

Engine noises can give a technician valuable insight into the condition of the engine. As you have learned, compression is one of the five critical requirements for each cylinder to operate properly. If the compression in one or more cylinders is too low, then the affected cylinders will not create as much power as cylinders with the proper amount of compression. If one or more cylinders have low compression, the engine will run rough, in many cases misleading the customer to request a "tune-up." Yet, performing a tune-up by replacing spark plugs and any other related tune-up items will not fix the low compression issue,

Applied Science

AS-6: Operational: The technician can relate scientific terms to automotive system diagnosis, service, and repair.

The use of pressure gauges is a common procedure in most automotive repair facilities. When assigned to perform engine mechanical testing, the technician works with pounds per square inch (psi) as related to engine compression gauge readings and cylinder leakage tests. A vehicle with low compression produces a number of drivability problems including a rough idle condition. For a smooth-running engine, cylinder compression should be as uniform as possible between cylinders. Psi refers to the primary units of measure for pressure in the United States. The metric unit is the kilopascal, or kPa, and 10 psi is equal to approximately 68.95 kPa. Most manufacturers supply both units as technical information. If necessary, the technician can consult conversion charts to obtain the US standard or metric unit that is needed.

causing the engine to still run poorly after the tune-up. This results in an unhappy customer as well as technician. To help avoid that situation, a cranking sound diagnosis can identify whether the compression is similar across all of the cylinders. If compression is not similar across all cylinders, a tune-up will not fix the problem. If compression is similar across all cylinders, then compression is not likely causing the engine to run rough. When you perform a cranking sound diagnosis, you should disable the engine so that it will not start. Then crank the engine over, using the key, and listen to the cranking sounds. It might take a few times to isolate any noises. The noise could be from a misaligned starter, the clunk of a spun crankshaft bearing noise, an uneven cranking sound that a low-compression cylinder gives, or a fast cranking sound from a no-compression condition that is due to bent valves caused by a broken timing belt. Each of these noises can give you a clue as to where the problem may lie.

Cylinder Power Balance Test Overview

A **cylinder power balance test** (also called a power balance test for short) is used for two purposes. First, it identifies which cylinders are not operating properly when the vacuum test indicates a mechanical issue or when the engine is not running smoothly. Second, it is used as a general indication of each cylinder's overall health. Every cylinder in the engine should contribute equally to the engine's power output. When a mechanical, electrical, or fuel problem occurs within an engine, the affected cylinders will not produce as much, if any, power when compared to the other cylinders. We can test to see how much each cylinder is contributing to the engine's output by disabling one cylinder at a time and measuring the rpm drop. Disabling a cylinder that is not operating correctly does not produce much, if any, rpm drop. Disabling a cylinder that is working properly, however, produces a much larger rpm drop. The greater the difference in rpm drop, the greater the difference between each cylinder's ability to produce its share of the engine's power.

Many newer vehicles control the idle speed electronically through the **power control module (PCM)**. In these vehicles, if something loads the engine down, such as the air-conditioning compressor turning on, the PCM will allow more air and fuel into the engine so that the idle speed stays relatively the same. In the case of a manual power balance test, disabling one of the cylinders will not produce a drop in rpm because the PCM will compensate for it. In these cases, use the PCM's built-in power balance feature, if equipped. Alternatively, in some vehicles you can disconnect the electrical connector on the idle speed control system to prevent the PCM from changing the idle speed. Unfortunately, in some vehicles if you disconnect the connector on the idle speed control system, the engine will die. On these vehicles, you can usually perform the power balance test slightly above idle, as the PCM only controls engine speed at idle. Raising the rpm can be accomplished by wedging an appropriate tool between the throttle body and the throttle linkage or by having an assistant hold the throttle steady while you perform the test.

The purpose of the power balance test is to see whether the cylinders are creating equal amounts of power and, if not, to isolate the problem to a particular cylinder or cylinders. Once the problem is isolated, we can take the next step, which is to determine whether it is a mechanical issue related to compression, or an ignition or fuel-related issue.

S06004 Perform a cylinder power balance test.

Performing a Cylinder Power Balance Test

There are several ways that a power balance test can be performed. Knowing each of the options allows you to choose the easiest one for the vehicle you are diagnosing. Which is easiest is determined by the capabilities of the PCM, the ease of accessing the required components, and the tools available. For many OBDII vehicles, you can identify which cylinders are misfiring by using a scan tool to access stored diagnostic trouble codes (DTCs) in the PCM. Or you can access mode 6 data, which will give you information on how prevalent misfires are on each cylinder. In some cases, you can also use the scan tool to command the PCM to perform an automatic power balance test and report the results right on the scan tool. On most newer vehicles, using the scan tool is by far the best method of performing a power balance test.

If the system is not set up to perform the test automatically, you will have to do it manually. You need to determine whether to disable the ignition or the fuel to each individual cylinder. If the engine has port fuel injectors that are accessible, disconnecting the electrical connector from each injector, one at a time, will shut off the fuel to the cylinder. Shutting off the fuel to the cylinder is the preferred method because it stops injecting fuel in the cylinder. If the ignition system is disabled for a cylinder, the fuel will still be delivered but will not be burned in the cylinder. However, it will burn in the catalytic converter, which can cause the catalytic converter to overheat and possibly be damaged. Therefore, shutting down the fuel is preferable if it is an option on the engine you are working on.

If the engine has individual ignition coils on each spark plug, you can disconnect the primary electrical connector, which shuts off the spark to the spark plug. If the vehicle has coils that share cylinders (waste spark system), then you can place a 1" (25 mm) section of vacuum hose between each coil tower and spark plug wire. Then connect the alligator clip from a non-powered test light to a good engine ground, and touch the tip of the test light to each length of vacuum hose to short out each spark plug, one at a time. If the vehicle is equipped with a distributor, disconnect one spark plug at a time from the distributor cap (it is good to use a test lead to ground the spark at the distributor cap terminal to prevent the spark from damaging the ignition module in the distributor), which shuts down the spark for the cylinder being tested.

To perform a cylinder power balance test, follow the steps in **SKILL DRILL 6-1**:

SKILL DRILL 6-1 Performing a Cylinder Power Balance Test

1. Visually inspect the engine to determine the best method to disable the cylinders. If this involves connecting a scan tool, installing vacuum lines on each coil, or removing spark plug wires, prepare the engine accordingly. If necessary, disable the idle control system.

Continued

2. Start the engine and allow it to idle. Record the idle rpm.

3. Using the method chosen to disable cylinders, disable the first cylinder, and record the rpm. (Do not leave the cylinder disabled for more than a few seconds.)

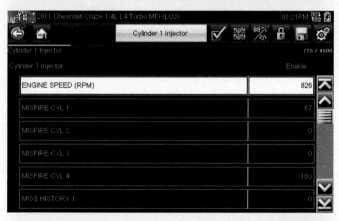

4. Reactivate the cylinder, and allow the engine to run for approximately 10 seconds to stabilize.

5. Repeat the steps on each of the cylinders, and record your readings. Determine any necessary actions.

S06008 Perform spark plug removal.

Spark Plug Removal and Reading

When you remove the spark plugs to install the various gauges explored in this chapter, you need to look at the spark plugs to verify that the engine is operating on all the cylinders. Wet or corroded plugs indicate an issue in that cylinder that needs to be explored further to verify what is causing it. White or broken porcelain on the spark plugs indicate burning oil or preignition, which needs to be explored before a complete diagnosis is reached. When removing plugs, make sure you keep them in order so that you are aware of which cylinders are having the issues; follow the steps in **SKILL DRILL 6-2**.

SKILL DRILL 6-2 Inspecting Spark Plugs

1. Remove the spark plugs, and line them up on a bench so that they can be compared.

2. Inspect the spark plugs, looking for damage and or contamination from coolant or oil.

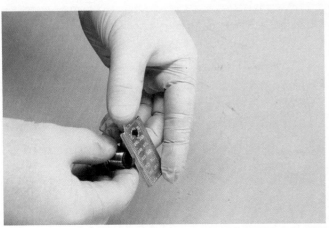

3. Once the spark plugs are out, the gap should always be checked.

Continued

4. Verify that the plug is reusable.

Cranking and Running Compression Tests

In a cranking or a running **compression test**, a high-pressure hose is hand-threaded in the spark plug hole of the cylinder to be tested and then connected to the compression gauge. The engine needs to be cranked over or started, depending on the test that is being performed. The compression gauge reads the amount of pressure that the piston is producing by compressing the air in the cylinder. You should always check factory specifications before performing the test so that you know what the results should be.

Performing a Cranking Compression Test

During a cranking compression test, the engine is cranked over but is not started by the starter. As the piston moves up, it compresses the air in the cylinder. The engine should crank until at least five compression pulses are observed on the compression gauge to get an accurate reading. If the final reading is low, there could be a problem with the valves, rings, pistons, or the head gasket.

The cranking compression test is performed when indications show a misfiring or dead cylinder that is not caused by an ignition or fuel problem. A compression test measures the air pressure as it is compressed in the cylinder. The cylinders should all measure within 10% to 15% of one another.

For the compression test to be completely accurate, it is recommended that the engine be at operating temperature; all of the spark plugs be removed; the battery be fully charged; the throttle be held wide open; and at least five compression pulses be made on each cylinder (the same number of pulses for each cylinder). All of these conditions help the engine create maximum compression and accurate readings. At the same time, if a technician suspects that only one or two cylinders have excessively low compression (because they failed the power balance test), then only the suspect spark plugs will be removed and a compression test made. If the compression is substantially low on that cylinder, then the engine has a compression problem, and further testing of the cylinder is required. If the compression is reasonably close to the specifications, then the compression is not causing the issue, and there is likely a fuel or ignition fault causing the problem.

To perform a cranking compression test, follow the steps in **SKILL DRILL 6-3**.

Many newer vehicles are programmed with a "clear flood" capability. This effectively shuts off the fuel injectors as long as the throttle is held to the floor before the ignition key is turned to the run or crank position. When the key is turned to crank (with the throttle still held down), the vehicle's powertrain control module (PCM) shuts off the fuel injectors. This allows the engine to crank without starting. If the engine starts, it means either that the vehicle is not equipped with clear flood mode or that fuel has leaked into the intake manifold, requiring a diagnosis. Using the clear flood mode is a quick way of performing a cranking sound diagnosis on these vehicles.

K06002 Knowledge of how a compression test helps to diagnose the engine mechanical condition.

S06005 Perform a cranking compression test.

SKILL DRILL 6-3 Performing a Cranking Compression Test

1. Remove any spark plug wires or ignition coils connected directly to the spark plugs.

2. Disable the ignition system by grounding the coil wire(s) or disconnecting the coil primary circuit(s).

3. Disable the fuel injectors, or remove the fuel pump fuse or relay.

4. Remove all spark plugs.

Continued

5. Install the compression tester.

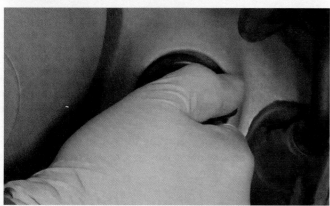

6. Hold the throttle down, and crank the engine over so that the compression tester needle jumps at least five times. Record the first and last needle readings. Repeat this procedure on the other cylinders.

7. Record the measurement on the gauge.

8. If any of the cylinders has low compression, perform a wet test by placing a couple of squirts of clean engine oil in the low cylinder, and retest the compression. If the compression pressure increases substantially, the piston rings are worn. If the compression doesn't change much, a valve, the head gasket, or the top of the piston has a leak. Determine any necessary action.

Applied Math

AM-16: Charts/Tables/Graphs: The technician can construct a chart, table, or graph that depicts and compares a range of performance characteristics of various system operational conditions.

A typical diagnostic test would be checking the compression of an engine. In this scenario, we have a four-cylinder engine that has the customer's concern of running rough at idle. A visual inspection did not reveal any problems that could easily be identified. A compression gauge is used to measure the compression on each cylinder. The technician records the information as the readings are taken from each cylinder, and the results could be recorded on the following chart. By consulting the manufacturer's specifications, the technician is able to determine whether the compression is satisfactory.

Cylinder	Cranking Compression in PSI	Running Compression in PSI
Cylinder 1		
Cylinder 2		
Cylinder 3		
Cylinder 4		

S06009 Perform a relative compression test.

Performing a Relative Compression Test with Lab Scope

A **lab scope** has the ability to graph the changes in a cylinders compression through the four-stroke cycle. By being able to graph the condition of the engine cylinder, the technician is able to explain to the customer what is happening in the engine, save that record for later use, and compare it to records of other cylinders they have similarly tested. Information about the internal cylinder integrity is critical to evaluating the condition of the engine before work is done on it. **SKILL DRILL 6-4** shows you, step by step, how to set up a compression test with a lab scope.

SKILL DRILL 6-4 Setting Up a Compression Test with a Oscilloscope Scope

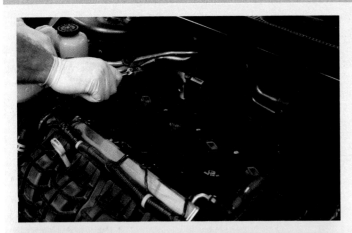

1. Remove any spark plug wires or ignition coils connected directly to the spark plugs.

2. Disable the ignition system by grounding the coil wire(s) or disconnecting the coil primary circuit(s).

Continued

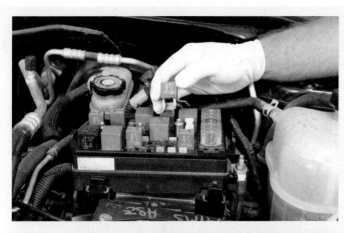

3. Disable the fuel injectors, or remove the fuel pump fuse or relay.

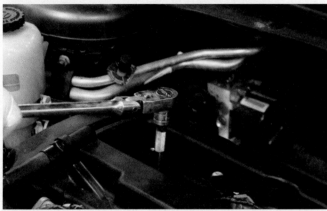

4. Remove all spark plugs.

5. Install the compression transducer.

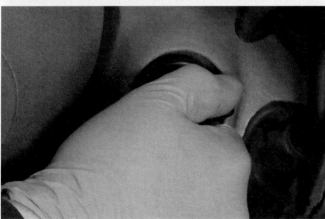

6. Hold the throttle down, and crank the engine over so that the compression tester needle jumps at least five times. Record the first and last needle readings. Repeat this procedure on the other cylinders.

Continued

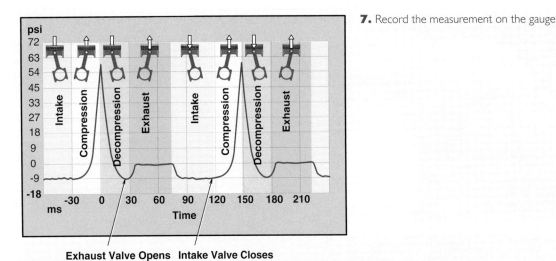

Exhaust Valve Opens   Intake Valve Closes

7. Record the measurement on the gauge.

8. If any of the cylinders has low compression, perform a wet test by placing a couple of squirts of clean engine oil in the low cylinder, and retest the compression. If the compression pressure increases substantially, the piston rings are worn. If the compression doesn't change much, a valve, the head gasket, or the top of the piston has a leak. Determine any necessary action.

Performing a Running Compression Test

S06006 Perform a running compression test.

In a **running compression test**, the engine is running during the test. Unlike the cranking compression test, which checks the sealing capability of the cylinder, the running compression test checks the engine's ability to move air into and out of the cylinder. This is referred to as the engine's ability to breathe. For example, if a camshaft lobe is badly worn, less air will enter or exit the cylinder, depending on which valve is affected. The running compression test helps a technician to evaluate this process.

The test is performed in two parts, idle and snap throttle. During idle, because the engine is running and the throttle is relatively closed, the compression pressure will be approximately half of the cranking compression pressure. The second part of the test is a snap throttle test. With the engine idling, the throttle is snapped open and then closed fairly quickly, which allows a big rush of air into the intake manifold. The idea is not to make the rpm change very much during the test. If the intake and exhaust system are operating correctly, then the compression tester needle will jump to about 80% of the cranking compression pressure. If the intake side of the system is restricted, then the reading will be lower than the 80% threshold. If there is a restriction on the exhaust side of the system, then the pressure will be substantially higher than the 80% threshold.

The running compression test is performed by leaving all of the spark plugs in the engine except for the one in the cylinder that you are testing. Most technicians leave the Schrader valve in the compression tester to hold pressure in the tester while performing the running compression test, although it can be hard on the Schrader valves. Always have a couple of spares handy. Also know that compression tester Schrader valves use lighter-weight springs than tire Schrader valves, so do not interchange them. The compression tester has to be installed in the cylinder to be tested, and then the engine can be started. This test can detect flat cam lobes, broken valve springs or rocker arms, carboned-up valves, or restricted intake and exhaust passageways in general. To confirm your diagnosis, do a visual inspection of the suspect components.

To perform a running compression test, follow the steps in **SKILL DRILL 6-5**.

SKILL DRILL 6-5 Performing a Running Compression Test

1. Remove the spark plug on the cylinder that you are testing, and ground the spark plug wire with a test lead. Unless the engine utilizes coil on plug design, unplug the ignition coil.

2. Install the proper hose and compression tester into the spark plug hole.

3. Start the engine, allow it to idle, press and release the bleed valve, and record the reading once the pressure stabilizes.

Continued

4. Have your partner quickly snap the throttle open for about 1 second, and then close it quickly. (Make sure the key can be turned off quickly if the throttle sticks.) Record the reading.

5. Repeat the process on the other cylinders. Determine any necessary action.

▶ Cylinder Leakage Test Overview

K06003 Knowledge of when to do a leak-down test.

The **cylinder leakage test** is performed on a cylinder with low compression to determine the severity of the compression leak and where the leak is located. Compressed air is applied to the cylinder through a tester that is calibrated to show the amount of cylinder leakage as a percent of air entering the cylinder. An ideal reading is close to 0%. But since piston rings have a small gap between their ends to allow for expansion as the engine heats up, a cylinder will not be sealed 100%. There will almost always be at least a small amount of leakage past the piston ring gaps (**FIGURE 6-2**). Typically manufacturers consider up to 20% cylinder leakage past the piston rings acceptable, but the smaller the leakage, the better. Although it is okay to have a small amount of leakage past the piston rings, it is not okay to have any leakage past one of the valves or the head gasket. Leaks at these places mean the engine likely has a major mechanical engine issue.

The point of this test is to measure how much air is leaking as well as to determine where it is leaking. The gauge tells you the percentage of air leaking from the cylinder, so that is straightforward. Determining where the air is leaking from is a bit more challenging. Because there is always some air leaking past the piston rings, you will be able to hear some air leaking out of the oil fill hole when the oil fill cap is removed. If that is the only leak that you end up diagnosing, then the gauge will indicate if the leakage past the piston rings is excessive.

FIGURE 6-2 Cylinder leak-down tester.

If an exhaust valve is burnt or warped, then you will hear leakage out of the exhaust pipe. If the intake valve is burnt or warped, then you will hear leakage out the air intake system. There should be no leakage past either of the valves, so any leak in the exhaust or intake is a bad leak. If the head gasket is blown, then you will either hear air coming out of an adjacent spark plug hole or see bubbles in the coolant when the radiator cap is removed.

Performing a Cylinder Leakage Test

A couple of critical steps are required to make sure the cylinder leakage test is accurate. First, the engine should be near operating temperature, which ensures that oil has been circulated to the piston rings to help them seal. Next, it is helpful to loosen each of the spark plugs about one turn for the cylinders you are testing, and then run the engine at 1500 rpm for 10 to 15 seconds. This process helps blow out any chunks of carbon straddling the spark plug to cylinder head gap that break off when the spark plugs are removed. If you do not do this, it is possible for one of these chunks of carbon to get stuck between a valve and valve seat, holding the valve open slightly and producing a false reading.

S06007 Perform a cylinder leakage test.

Because the cylinder leakage test is usually only performed on a cylinder with low compression, you must remove only the spark plug for the cylinder you are testing and the spark plug for each of the cylinders next to that one. If the suspect cylinder is in the middle of the bank, then you need to remove the spark plug on either side. If the suspect cylinder is at the end of the bank, then you need to remove only the nearest spark plug. It also helps to remove the air cleaner assembly and radiator cap for listening purposes during the test.

Cylinder leakage is measured when the piston is on top dead center on the compression stroke. This means that you have to turn the crankshaft to position each piston in this position before pressurizing the system. The challenge is that the piston, connecting rod, and crankshaft throw must be in near perfect alignment; otherwise, the pressure on the piston from the cylinder leakage tester will push the piston down, which turns the crankshaft. If this happens, then the intake or exhaust valve will open, depending on which way the piston ends up turning the crankshaft.

The hardest part is getting the piston exactly on top dead center. There are two primary ways to do so. One is to screw the cylinder leakage tester into the spark plug hole and then slowly turn the engine over by hand while lightly floating your thumb over the end of the hose to feel pressure and vacuum. When you feel the transition from pressure to vacuum, turn the engine in the opposite direction slightly, and stop right as the pressure stops and before the vacuum begins. It takes experience to get the feel for this. The second way is to use a plastic straw that fits down the spark plug hole and that can be pushed up by the piston without damaging the cylinder or piston. Rotate the engine by hand until the piston is as high as it will go, as indicated by the plastic straw. While the piston is on top dead center, you will not know if it is on the top of the compression stroke or the exhaust stroke until you pressurize the cylinder (unless the engine is equipped with a distributor and you can see where the rotor is pointing). If it is wrong, turn the engine one complete revolution, and try it again.

To perform a cylinder leakage test, follow the steps in **SKILL DRILL 6-6**.

Diagnosing Engine Noise and Vibrations

Running engines are fairly quiet, considering all of the mechanical activity that happens within them. But if something starts to go wrong, noises can be one of the first indicators. Noise issues can indicate something as simple to fix as a worn accessory belt or as complicated as a spun connecting rod bearing, which would generally require rebuilding the entire engine. Understanding the engine's theory of operation and how the individual components of an engine work gives you a good starting foundation.

N06003 Inspect, remove, and replace engine mounts.

K06004 Knowledge of how to diagnosis engine noises and vibrations.

Many sounds can be pinpointed through an experienced technician's previous knowledge, so investigate unusual noises and build your experience. A loud knocking noise could be from a bad main bearing or a connecting rod bearing with a worn or spun bearing. A main bearing noise is generally deeper sounding than a rod bearing. Also, a main bearing makes an evenly spaced single knock, whereas a rod bearing generally makes a double knock. A light ticking noise could be a valve lifter problem, which can be heard near the

SKILL DRILL 6-6 Performing a Cylinder Leakage Test

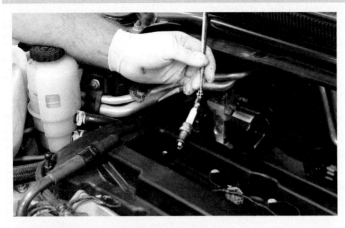

1. Remove the spark plug of the low-compression cylinder and any adjacent spark plugs.

2. Install the cylinder leakage tester adapter hose into the spark plug hole.

3. Position the piston for the cylinder being tested at top dead center on the compression stroke. You can do this by making sure you feel air escaping the cylinder leakage hose when you are turning the crankshaft by hand.

4. Connect the compressed air hose to the tester, and adjust the tester so it reads zero.

Continued

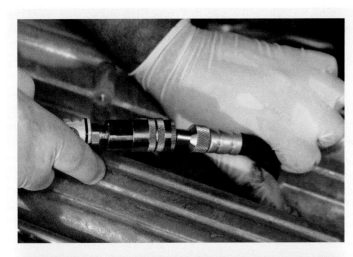

5. Connect the cylinder leakage adapter hose to the tester.

6. Make sure the engine does not turn over. If the engine turns over, you will need to reset the piston back to the compression stroke. Record the reading.

7. Listen for leakage from the oil fill hole, the throttle body, and the exhaust pipe, and look for bubbles in the radiator. Determine any necessary actions.

camshaft area. Or you might hear a light knocking noise that comes under slight rocking of the throttle that is caused by a collapsed piston skirt. A whirring noise can be caused by worn bearings in alternators, water pumps, and belt tensioners. One way to help locate any type of engine noise is to use a mechanic's stethoscope. Mechanical stethoscopes are the most common, but many electronic stethoscopes have settings that enhance selected sound frequencies while filtering out others, making them very handy. Place the stethoscope against engine components in a variety of positions around the engine, and listen to the noises. Generally, the louder the noise, the closer you are to its source.

Depending on the noise, a stethoscope may not be appropriate. In the case of a squeaky belt, spraying water on one belt at a time will make the noise go away temporarily when you spray the one that is squeaking. Squeaks and creaks that come from linkage and joints can sometimes be sprayed, one at a time, with a lubricant and operated until the offending joint is found.

Vibrations can be difficult to pinpoint. Vibrations can come from the engine or the drivetrain. The best clue is to determine if the vibration occurs only when the vehicle is being driven or if it occurs with the engine running irrespective of vehicle movement. If the vibration occurs only when the vehicle is moving, suspect a component within the drivetrain or drive line, the U-joints, or even the tire balance. A good way to isolate the drivetrain is to drive the vehicle up to the speed at which the vibration is noticeable. Then place the transmission in neutral and allow the engine to idle. If the vibration is still there, then the issue is probably associated with the wheels, tires, or axles. If the vibration goes away, then raise the engine rpm while still in neutral. If the vibration reoccurs, then the issue is most likely with the engine. If there is no vibration, reengage the appropriate drive gear and accelerate moderately. If the vibration reappears, then the issue is likely with the driveshaft, U-joints, or CV joints.

Internal Engine Noise

Internal engine noises are the first indicator that there is a problem inside the engine in the vehicle. These noises must be diagnosed properly and quickly if the owner has any hope of saving this engine. If misdiagnosed, then parts that were not need could be replaced; in addition, the engine could still be broken once its repairs are completed.

Main Bearing Knock

Main bearing noise is a constant noise that doesn't change with rpm and may cause the crankshaft to "walk" in the block, which will then cause a leak. This type of problem usually comes after a low oil pressure event, as these bearings are the first ones that are oiled after the oil exits the filter (**FIGURE 6-3**). These bearings are made of the same material as the rod bearings, which makes them susceptible to dry start events. The correction for this issue is bearing replacement and machining of the crankshaft.

Rod Bearing Knock

Rod bearing noise changes with rpm fluctuation and usually gets the loudest when you get close to the higher rpm range. These bearings are second in line to get oil from the filter, right after the main bearings, which makes killing them very difficult. Over-revving the engine or heavy cornering can starve the engine for the proper amount of oil, which could affect the rod bearings (**FIGURE 6-4**). You can determine which cylinder is faulty by doing a power balance test; when one of the cylinders changes the engine's sound when you are disabling it, you have found the problem cylinder. The correction for this condition is usually replacement of the bearing and reconditioning or replacement of the connecting rod.

FIGURE 6-3 Damaged main bearings.

FIGURE 6-4 Damaged connecting rod bearings.

Piston Pin Knock

Piston pin knock is usually caused by a loose wrist pin in one of the pistons, creating a noise or double tap every revolution. This condition is usually caused by lack of oiling, improper installation, or a heavily worn-out engine (**FIGURE 6-5**). The correction for this condition is usually replacement of the piston and piston pin, and reconditioning of the connecting rod.

Piston Slap

Piston slap is the piston striking the cylinder walls, causing a loud noise in the engine. To verify which cylinder is malfunctioning, you need to do a power balance test, and when the noise changes you have found the cylinder. This is usually caused by a worn-out cylinder wall, worn or broken piston, or worn-out wrist pin causing excess movement, or lack of oil pressure. To fix this issue, you need to replace the piston and pin and condition the connecting rod. You also have to machine the cylinder to accept the new piston.

Valvetrain Clatter

Valvetrain clatter is usually excess clearance between two valvetrain components, causing a noticeable tick. Because the valvetrain is located at the top of the engine, it is last to get oil from the oil pan, which makes it one of the first components to fail due to lack of oil. Along with lack of oil, these components are constantly changing direction, which causes wear, creating increased clearance between parts, which then results in a noise (**FIGURE 6-6**). Clearance is the biggest cause of top end noise but is usually caused by an external problem.

Timing Chain Noise

Timing chains are a simple chain and two sprockets (similar to a bicycle) that connect the camshaft and crankshaft. The purpose of the timing chain is to keep the camshaft in time with the crankshaft so that the valve events happen at the correct time. As the automotive engine has progressed throughout time, multiple camshafts, variable valve timing components, balance shafts, oil pump drives, and water pumps driven off the timing chain have been added. This causes a lot of extra stress on the chains, guides, sprockets, and oiling systems of these high-dollar engines. With all of these added components, the slightest lack of lubrication on the chain or guides causes huge problems. Once the timing chain has been damaged by a lack of oiling condition, the only proper way to fix it is to replace all of the components of the timing chain setup (**FIGURE 6-7**). The vehicle that has these issues will probably have others related to the lack of oil pressure over a period of time, so you must thoroughly check out the entire engine before presenting the repair to the customer.

Motor Mounts

Motor mounts connect the engine to the chassis so that the power from the engine can be used to propel the vehicle down the road. Typical motor mounts are made out of a reinforced rubber insulator that helps stop vibrations from the engine from transmitting into the passenger compartment (**FIGURE 6-8**). Some applications call for an oil-filled motor mount, which allows for more vibration absorption and greater flexibility for the high-torque engine. When diagnosing engine noises inspect the motor mounts first as they tend to wear out over time, causing the engine to come in contact with the chassis, which causes multiple different types of noises.

FIGURE 6-5 Damaged piston pin.

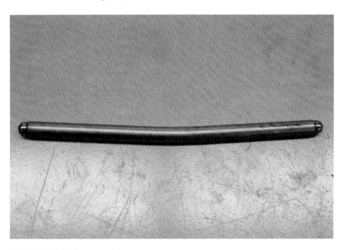

FIGURE 6-6 Broken valvetrain components.

FIGURE 6-7 Broken timing components.

FIGURE 6-8 Collapsed motor mount.

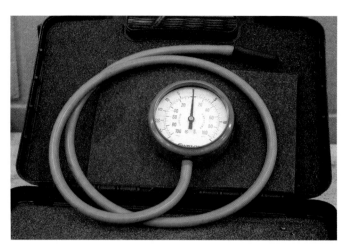

FIGURE 6-9 Using a vacuum gauge can help the technician determine an internal engine fault as a broken valve spring, bad cylinder, or timing issue which will affect the amount of reliable vacuum.

Vacuum Testing

K06005 Knowledge of the effect of mechanical issues on vacuum.

A **vacuum gauge** is used to determine the engine's general condition (**FIGURE 6-9**). The vacuum gauge reading shows the difference between outside atmospheric pressure and the amount of vacuum (manifold pressure) in the engine. The vacuum gauge is installed in a vacuum port on the intake manifold. Always select the largest and most centrally located vacuum port. This may require using a vacuum tee so that the vacuum gauge can be connected while vacuum can still be supplied to the existing component. The typical vacuum reading for a properly running engine at idle is a steady 17" to 21" of vacuum (57.6 to 71.1 kPa) (**TABLE 6-1**). A low reading could relate to a problem with ignition or valve timing. A sharp oscillation back and forth in the needle or a dip in the gauge reading could relate to a problem such as a bad valve. A low reading at a constant 2500 rpm could indicate a restricted exhaust system.

With the advent of lab scope diagnostics, many technicians are using a pressure transducer to measure the engine's manifold pressure and display it graphically on a lab scope. The pressure transducer is a very accurate measuring tool; when attached to a vacuum port and hooked up to a lab scope, it gives a pressure trace that shows the low pressure created by each piston's intake stroke (**FIGURE 6-10**). If the ignition pattern for cylinder 1 is monitored on a separate trace, the vacuum pulses can be tied to specific cylinders. Technicians can view these traces and see how well each cylinder is functioning at producing and maintaining a vacuum.

Using a Vacuum Gauge to Test Engine Mechanical Integrity

S06002 Test engine vacuum using a vacuum gauge.

During an engine vacuum test, all vacuum gauges are calibrated at sea level, and all instructions and readings are referenced to sea level. When testing above sea level, you need to compensate. For instance, if the gauge reads 18" of vacuum at sea level, it would drop to 17" at 1000' above sea level.

TABLE 6-1: Chart of Vacuum Readings—Vacuum Gauge

Reading	Indication
17" to 21", steady needle at idle.	Good reading
Needle oscillates back and forth about 4" to 8".	Burned or constantly leaking valve
A low and steady reading.	Possible late valve timing or late ignition timing
Snap acceleration needle drops to zero and then only reads 20" to 23" of vacuum; should be much higher, around 27".	Possible worn rings
Good reading at idle. As engine speeds up to a steady 2500 rpm, the needle slowly goes down and may continue to drop.	Possible restricted exhaust system

The vacuum gauge reading shows the difference between outside atmospheric pressure and the amount of vacuum in the engine in a non-turbo or non-supercharged engine. The average inches of vacuum for a good running engine at idle is a steady 17" to 21" of vacuum. The average inches of vacuum at idle for a performance camshaft with a high lift and large overlap duration is around 15". The amount of vacuum an engine creates relies on the piston rings, valves, ignition timing, and fuel.

To test engine vacuum using a vacuum gauge, follow the steps in **SKILL DRILL 6-7**.

Testing Engine Vacuum Using a Pressure Transducer

Using a **pressure transducer** and lab scope is a similar process to using a vacuum gauge, except it is much more accurate and allows you to look at the vacuum graphically. When paired with a second trace consisting of the ignition pattern for cylinder 1, any issues with the vacuum trace can be tied to a specific cylinder. By using a pressure transducer on a variety of vehicles with various issues, you will become familiar with the patterns of common faults

To use a pressure transducer and lab scope for testing engine vacuum, follow the steps in **SKILL DRILL 6-8**.

FIGURE 6-10 Waveform of the vacuum in an engine.

S06003 Test engine vacuum using a pressure transducer and lab scope.

SKILL DRILL 6-7 Testing Engine Vacuum Using a Vacuum Gauge

1. Connect the vacuum gauge to the intake manifold. You might have to use a vacuum tee.

2. Make sure the engine is at operating temperature. Start the engine, take a reading at idle, and record the reading.

Continued

3. Snap accelerate the engine by quickly opening and closing the throttle; record the highest vacuum reading obtained.

4. Hold the throttle steady at 2500 rpm, and record your reading.

SKILL DRILL 6-8 Using a Pressure Transducer and Lab Scope for Testing Engine Vacuum

1. Connect the pressure transducer to the intake manifold and the lab scope. You might have to use a vacuum tee.

2. Connect the second channel of the lab scope to the ignition system so it can identify cylinder 1.

Continued

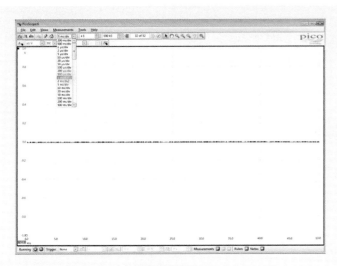

3. Start the engine and let it idle. Adjust the lab scope so that the screen captures the vacuum pulses for all of the cylinders.

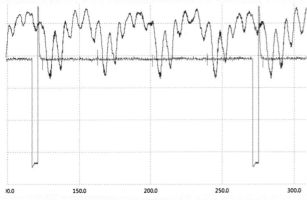

4. Observe the vacuum trace, and compare it to known good readings.

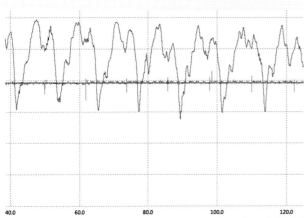

5. Snap accelerate the engine by opening and closing the throttle, and compare the trace to known good readings.

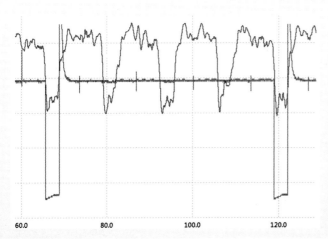

6. Hold the throttle steady at 1200–1500 rpm, and compare the trace to known good readings.

Continued

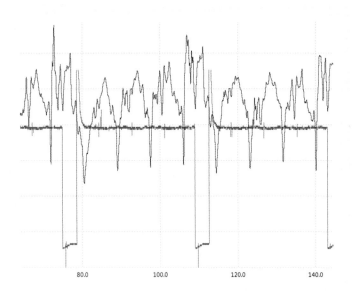

7. Hold the throttle steady at 2500 rpm, and compare the trace to known good readings.

Diagnosing Oil Consumption

N06002 Perform cooling system pressure and dye tests to identify leaks; check coolant condition and level; inspect and test radiator, pressure cap, coolant recovery tank, and heater core; determine needed action.

K06006 Knowledge of how to verify fluid consumption by the engine.

When there is a complaint about an engine consuming oil you first must do a visual inspection to determine if there are any external leaks on the engine. Once that is confirmed, then you must change the oil, put in the correct amount, document the mileage on the work order, and advise the customer to come back at three-mileage thresholds so that you can verify oil level. When the customer comes back check the oil and compare to the notes that you recorded earlier. If there is a significant drop in oil, level refer to the service information to verify the specification and determine if the usage is within that specification. Once that is verified, make your recommendations on those readings.

Oil Pressure Testing

S06011 Test an engine for oil pressure.

Oil pressure testing is a vital tool in diagnosing the integrity of the engine in the vehicle. If an engine has low oil pressure some of the systems may not work, causing a running issue or a check engine light issue. Oil pressure must be up to specification or engine damage will result, and anything that is fixed on the engine will have been a waste of time.

To test an engine's oil pressure, follow the steps in **SKILL DRILL 6-9**.

SKILL DRILL 6-9 Testing an Engine's Oil Pressure

1. Check the oil level in the engine.

Continued

2. Locate the oil pressure sending unit.

3. Remove the oil pressure sending unit.

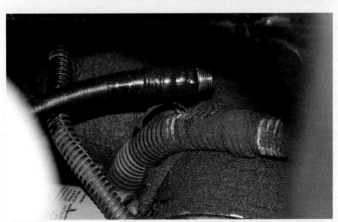

4. Install the oil pressure gauge hose in the oil pressure sending unit hole.

5. Start the engine and operate it within the specifications of the manufacturer's oil pressure checking procedure.

Continued

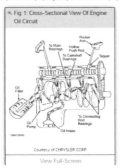

ENGINE LUBRICATION SYSTEM
System has a rotor-type oil pump and full-flow oil filter. Oil is forced by pump through a series of oil passages in engine to provide lubrication t

Crankcase Capacity
Oil Pressure
Oil pressure is 6 psi (.4 kg/cm²) at idle and 30-80 psi (2.1-5.6 kg/cm²) at 3000 RPM with engine at normal operating temperature.

Fig 1: Cross-Sectional View Of Engine Oil Circuit

Courtesy of CHRYSLER CORP.

View Full-Screen

6. Compare the readings with the service information.

S06012 Test for a dye leak.

S06013 Perform a chemical block test.

Oil Leak Diagnosis

The first step in diagnosing an oil leak is to visually inspect underneath the vehicle, inspect the engine, and inspect the place when the vehicle has been sitting. You may have to put the vehicle on a lift to inspect underneath of it, look for any wetness, pooling of oil, or any signs that oil may have leaked out of the engine (**FIGURE 6-11**). This is a pretty straightforward process as you should be able to see the oil leak if the engine has one.

Dye Testing

If the source of the leak cannot be found, most auto parts stores have access to dye that creates a fluorescent color on top of the leak so that a person with an ultraviolet light is able to see the source of the leak. This type of testing is great for verifying when the leak is coming from which allows the technician the ability to pinpoint the component that needs to be replaced. Dyes are made for all different types of fluids and usually vary in colors.

To test an engine for leakage using a dye, follow the steps in **SKILL DRILL 6-10**.

Diagnosing Coolant Consumption

The first step for any complaint is to verify that the vehicle is full of coolant and there are no external leaks on the engine. Once that is confirmed, you can continue on to diagnosing an internal problem that is allowing the coolant to be burned in the cylinders. The first procedure that we are going to do is called a cylinder leak-down test; this test is going to test the integrity of the cylinder so that we can determine whether the head gasket is leaking around this cylinder; the valves are leaking; or there is any other mechanical problem with

FIGURE 6-11 An engine with oil leakage is a major cause of engine failures.

SKILL DRILL 6-10 Testing for a Dye Leak

1. Determine which fluid is leaking from the engine, and acquire the necessary dye as they are made for different fluids.

2. Clean the engine off in the suspect area so that the dye can be easily spotted.

3. Dump the dye in to the particular system, and run the engine to allow the dye to find its way to the leaking component.

4. Once the engine has ran for an extended period of time, use a black light to shine in the target area to verify where the leak is coming from.

Continued

5. Replace gasket or component that is causing the issue so that the engine will not leak.

this cylinder (**FIGURE 6-12**). This test does not account for heat or expansion of the head or block; it merely gives you a snapshot of the cylinder at this moment in time. Once you have completed doing this on all the cylinders of the engine, if you still do not know the culprit of the coolant consumption, we can do another test called a block leak test. This test involves sucking out some of the coolant from the radiator, putting a special liquid into the tools, placing the tool on the radiator cap housing, and sucking up the vapors that the coolant puts out. If the liquid in the tool turns a color, there are exhaust vapors in the cooling system, which will lead you to an engine top-end teardown. If it does not change color, then you need to re-verify the integrity of the cooling system and pay attention to the plastic parts, as temperature can cause them to leak one moment and not the next.

To perform a chemical block test, follow the steps in **SKILL DRILL 6-11**.

Cooling System Pressure Testing

S06014 Test cooling system pressure.

Cooling system pressure testing is used to find a leak in a cooling system on a vehicle. By pressuring up the cooling system on a vehicle with the engine not running, we are able to see where the leak is coming from (**FIGURE 6-13**). Pressuring up the cooling system allows for checking the integrity of the hoses, fittings, clamps, plastic components, radiator, and related engine components (Skill Drill 6-12). This type of test is hard to do on an engine going down the road, which is why we have the ability to do this in the bay.

To test a vehicle's cooling system pressure, follow the steps in **SKILL DRILL 6-12**.

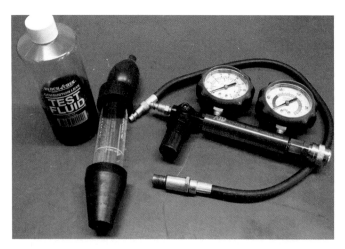

FIGURE 6-12 A leak-down test and a chemical block tester are used to check for internal cylinder leaks.

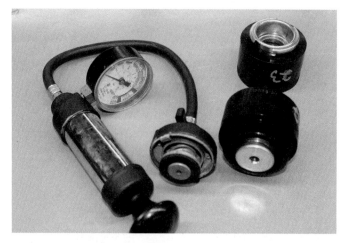

FIGURE 6-13 A cooling system pressure tester used to create pressure within the cooling system to pinpoint leaks for repair.

SKILL DRILL 6-11 Performing a Chemical Block Test

1. To do a bock chemical test, you need to remove about a quart of fluid from the surge tank or radiator tank.

2. Acquire the block testing tool, and fill it to the line on the tube with the chemical agent that is in the kit.

3. Attach the tool to the radiator cap or surge tank cap opening.

4. Using the suction ball, suck the exhaust fumes in the cooling system into the tube.

Continued

5. If the chemical changes color, then you have a cylinder head or gasket leaking into the cooling system.

SKILL DRILL 6-12 Testing Cooling System Pressure

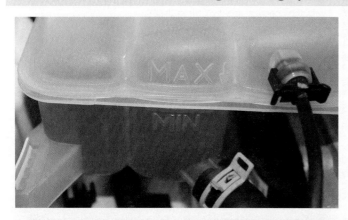

1. When you decide that you need to perform a cooling system pressure test, you must first verify that the cooling system has coolant in it.

2. Find the correct adapter to adapt the cooling system pressure tester to the surge tank or radiator tank.

3. Pump up or attach the air line to the regulator to pressure the system up to the pressure rating on the radiator cap.

Continued

4. Inspect the engine for leaks, and document and recommend repair procedures.

Exhaust System Testing

The exhaust system is a very important part of the internal combustion engine management systems, as it directs the burnt exhaust fumes away from the vehicle. If the exhaust system somehow gets damaged, it will cause performance issues and possibly be detrimental to the engine.

Exhaust Restriction Symptoms

Some symptoms of exhaust restriction are engine performance issues, starting issues, and emission issues (**FIGURE 6-14**). A restricted or partially restricted exhaust has major side effects for the operation of the vehicles engine. Without the ability to get rid of the exhaust created by combustion, the engine cannot take in new air to start the process over. At the same time, the emission sensors and components must work harder to maintain what little performance the engine has. **Catalytic converters** are the main cause of this restriction: as they age, they start to fall apart and become restricted, causing the engine to adjust and creating more problems for the owner of the vehicle. The first step in diagnosing a restricted exhaust is doing a complete visual inspection, looking for bent or broken piping, smashed mufflers or catalytic converters, and obvious problems with the exhaust plumbing.

Backpressure Testing

Backpressure testing is used to verify that the vehicle has a restricted exhaust. It is done by removing the oxygen sensor, screwing the adapter into the hole, and attaching the gauge to the adapter (**FIGURE 6-15**). Once connected, start the engine and take a reading (Skill Drill 6-13). Rev the engine up and take a reading. Compare. The reading should be very low—somewhere around 1–1½ psi max; if it is more than that, there is a restriction in the exhaust system.

To perform an exhaust system backpressure test, follow the steps in **SKILL DRILL 6-13**.

K06007 Knowledge of how the exhaust system affects the engine.

S06010 Perform an exhaust system backpressure test.

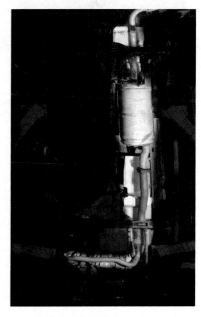

FIGURE 6-14 An exhaust system on the vehicle.

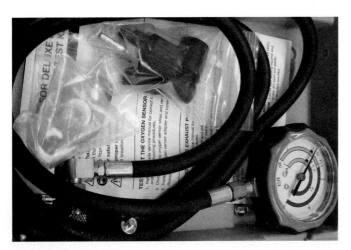

FIGURE 6-15 Exhaust backpressure gauge.

SKILL DRILL 6-13 Performing an Exhaust System Backpressure Text

1. Lift the vehicle with a vehicle lift so that you can access the undercarriage.

2. Locate the front oxygen sensor.

3. Remove the oxygen sensor.

4. Install the back pressure gauge in the oxygen sensor hole.

Continued

5. Start engine and ready the gauge—it should be very low under 1 psi.

6. Bring engine rpm up to 2000 and read the gauge; it still should be under 1 psi.

7. If a reading of more than 1 psi is found, check for a restriction in the exhaust system.

▶ Wrap-Up

Ready for Review

- ▶ For an engine to operate efficiently and effectively, the mechanical condition of the engine must be in good working order. The pistons, piston rings, cylinder walls, head gasket, and valves must seal properly.
- ▶ Engine mechanical testing uses a series of tests to assess the mechanical condition of the engine. Mechanical testing starts with a good visual inspection.
- ▶ A visual inspection of the engine assembly for leaks will affirm the ability of the seals and gaskets to contain each of the engine's fluids. Starting the engine and listening to its operation can indicate a host of problems, from loose belts to worn main bearings. It can also reveal whether the engine is misfiring and how steady the misfire is.
- ▶ Verifying the mechanical integrity of an engine is the number-one thing that a technician does before moving on to anything else.

- ▶ Compression is one of the five critical requirements for each cylinder to operate properly. If the compression in one or more cylinders is too low, then the affected cylinders will not create as much power as cylinders with the proper amount of compression.
- ▶ The cylinder power balance test (power balance test) is used for two purposes. First, it identifies which cylinder(s) are not operating properly when the vacuum test indicates a mechanical issue or when the engine is not running smoothly. Second, it is used as a general indication of each cylinder's overall health.
- ▶ The purpose of the power balance test is to see whether the cylinders are creating equal amounts of power and, if not, to isolate the problem to a particular cylinder or cylinders.
- ▶ To perform a power balance test, first visually inspect the engine to determine the best method to disable the cylinders. If this involves connecting a scan tool, installing

vacuum lines on each coil, or removing spark plug wires, prepare the engine accordingly. If necessary, disable the idle control system. Start the engine and allow it to idle. Record the idle rpm. Using the method chosen to disable cylinders, disable the first cylinder, and record the rpm. Reactivate the cylinder, and allow the engine to run for approximately 10 seconds to stabilize. Repeat the steps on each of the cylinders, and record your readings.

▶ When you remove the spark plugs, you need to look at them to verify that the engine is operating on all of the cylinders.

▶ Wet or corroded plugs indicate an issue in the cylinder that has to be explored further to verify what is causing it.

▶ White or broken porcelain on the spark plugs indicates burning oil or preignition, which has to be explored before a complete diagnosis is reached.

▶ When removing plugs, make sure you keep them in order.

▶ In a cranking or a running compression test, a high-pressure hose is hand-threaded in the spark plug hole of the cylinder to be tested, and then connected to the compression gauge.

▶ The compression gauge reads the amount of pressure that the piston is producing by compressing the air in the cylinder.

▶ A lab scope has the ability to graph the changes in a cylinder's compression through the four-stroke cycle.

▶ In a running compression test, the engine is running during the test.

▶ The running compression test checks the sealing capability of the cylinder and the engine's ability to move air into and out of the cylinder. This is referred to as the engine's ability to breathe. For example, if a camshaft lobe is badly worn, less air will enter or exit the cylinder, depending on which valve is affected.

▶ The running compression test is performed by leaving all of the spark plugs in the engine except for the one in the cylinder that you are testing.

▶ The cylinder leakage test is performed on a cylinder with low compression to determine the severity of the compression leak and where the leak is located. Compressed air is applied to the cylinder through a tester that is calibrated to show the amount of cylinder leakage as a percent of air entering the cylinder.

▶ An ideal cylinder leakage reading is close to 0%. But because piston rings have a small gap between their ends to allow for expansion as the engine heats up, a cylinder will not be sealed 100%. There is almost always at least a small amount of leakage past the piston ring gaps. Typically up to 20% cylinder leakage past the piston rings is acceptable. No valve leakage amount is acceptable.

▶ Many sounds can be pinpointed through an experienced technician's previous knowledge, so investigate unusual noises, and build your experience.

▶ A loud knocking noise could be from a bad main bearing or a connecting rod bearing with a worn or spun bearing.

▶ A main bearing noise is generally deeper sounding than a rod bearing. Also, a main bearing makes an evenly spaced single knock, whereas a rod bearing generally makes a double knock.

▶ A light ticking noise could be a valve lifter problem, which can be heard near the camshaft area.

▶ A light knocking noise that comes under slight rocking of the throttle that is caused by a collapsed piston skirt.

▶ A whirring noise can be caused by worn bearings in alternators, water pumps, and belt tensioners.

▶ One way you can locate any type of engine noise is to use a mechanic's stethoscope. Mechanical stethoscopes are the most common, but many electronic stethoscopes have settings that enhance selected sound frequencies while filtering out others, making them very handy.

▶ Place the stethoscope against engine components in a variety of positions around the engine, and listen to the noises. Generally, the louder the noise, the closer you are to its source.

▶ The best clue is to determine whether the vibration occurs only when the vehicle is being driven or if it occurs with the engine running irrespective of vehicle movement.

▶ If the vibration occurs only when the vehicle is moving, suspect a component within the drivetrain or drive line, the U-joints, or even the tire balance.

▶ A good way to isolate the drivetrain is to drive the vehicle up to the speed at which the vibration is noticeable. Then place the transmission in neutral, and allow the engine to idle. If the vibration is still there, then the issue is probably associated with the wheels, tires, or axles.

▶ If the driveline vibration goes away, then raise the engine rpm while still in neutral. If the vibration reoccurs, then the issue is most likely with the engine.

▶ Main bearing noise is a constant noise that doesn't change with rpm and may cause the crankshaft to "walk" in the block, which will then cause a leak.

▶ Main bearing noise usually comes after a low oil pressure event, as these bearings are the first ones that are oiled after the oil exits the filter.

▶ Rod bearing noise changes with rpm fluctuation and usually gets the loudest when you get close to the higher rpm range. These bearings are second in line to get oil from the filter, right after the main bearings, which makes killing them very difficult.

▶ Over-revving the engine or heavy cornering can starve the engine for the proper amount of oil, which could affect the rod bearings

▶ You can determine which cylinder rod bearing is faulty by doing a power balance test; when one of the cylinders changes the engine's sound when you are disabling it, you have found the problem cylinder.

▶ Piston pin knock is caused by a loose wrist pin in one of the pistons, creating a noise or double tap every revolution. This condition is usually caused by lack of oiling, improper installation, or a heavily worn-out engine.

▶ Piston slap is the piston striking the cylinder walls, causing a loud noise in the engine. To verify which cylinder is malfunctioning, you need to do a power balance test, and when the noise changes, you have found the cylinder.

- Piston slap is caused by a worn-out cylinder wall, worn or broken piston, or worn-out wrist pin causing excess movement, or lack of oil pressure.
- Valvetrain clatter is usually excess clearance between two valvetrain components, causing a noticeable tick. Clearance is the biggest cause of top end noise but is usually caused by an external problem.
- Timing chain noise is caused by the slightest lack of lubrication on the chain or guides, resulting in huge problems. Once the timing chain has been damaged by a lack of oiling condition, the only proper way to fix it is to replace all of the components of the timing chain setup.
- Motor mounts connect the engine to the chassis so that the power from the engine can be used to propel the vehicle down the road. Typical motor mounts are made of a reinforced rubber insulator that helps stop vibrations from the engine from transmitting into the passenger compartment.
- Some applications call for an oil-filled motor mount, which allows for more vibration absorption and greater flexibility for the high-torque engine.
- When diagnosing engine noises, inspect the motor mounts first as they tend to wear out over time, causing the engine to come in contact with the chassis, which causes multiple different types of noises.
- The vacuum gauge is used to determine the engine's general condition.
- The vacuum gauge reading shows the difference between outside atmospheric pressure and the amount of vacuum (manifold pressure) in the engine. It is installed in a vacuum port on the intake manifold.
- The typical vacuum reading for a properly running engine at idle is a steady 17" to 21" of vacuum (57.6 to 71.1 kPa).
- A low vacuum reading could relate to a problem with ignition or valve timing. A sharp oscillation back and forth in the needle or a dip in the gauge reading could relate to a problem such as a bad valve. A low reading at a constant 2500 rpm could indicate a restricted exhaust system.
- Using a pressure transducer and lab scope is a similar process to using a vacuum gauge, except it is much more accurate and allows you to look at the vacuum graphically.
- When there is a complaint about an engine consuming oil, you first must do a visual inspection to determine whether there are any external leaks on the engine.
- When there is a complaint about an engine consuming oil, you must change the oil, put in the correct amount, document the mileage on the work order, and advise the customer to come back at three-mileage thresholds so that you can verify oil level.
- If an engine has low oil pressure, some of the systems may not work, causing a running issue or a check engine light issue.
- Oil pressure must be up to specification or engine damage will result, and anything that is fixed on the engine will have been a waste of time.
- The first step in diagnosing an oil leak is to visually inspect underneath the vehicle, inspect the engine, and inspect the place when the vehicle has been sitting. You may have to put the vehicle on a lift to inspect underneath it. Look for any wetness, pooling of oil, or any signs that oil may have leaked out of the engine.
- Dye testing is adding a dye to the oil or fluid that creates a fluorescent color on top of the leak so that a person with an ultraviolet light is able to see the source of the leak. Dyes are made for all different types of fluids and usually vary in colors.
- When testing for coolant consumption in the engine, you first do a cylinder leak-down test; this test is going to test the integrity of the cylinder so that we can determine whether the head gasket is leaking around this cylinder; the valves are leaking; or there is any other mechanical problem with this cylinder.
- This cylinder leak-down test does not account for heat or expansion of the head or block; it merely gives you a snapshot of the cylinder at this moment in time.
- You can also do a block leak test for coolant consumption, which involves sucking out coolant from the radiator, putting a special liquid into a tool, placing the tool on the radiator cap housing, and sucking up the vapors that the coolant puts out. If the liquid in the tool turns a color, there are exhaust vapors in the cooling system, which will lead you to an engine top-end teardown.
- Cooling system pressure testing is used to find a leak in a cooling system on a vehicle. By pressuring up the cooling system on a vehicle with the engine not running, you can see where the leak is coming from.
- Pressuring up the cooling system allows for checking the integrity of the hoses, fittings, clamps, plastic components, radiator, and related engine components.
- Some symptoms of exhaust restriction are engine performance issues, starting issues, and emission issues.
- A restricted or partially restricted exhaust has major side effects for the operation of the vehicles engine. Without the ability to get rid of the exhaust created by combustion, the engine cannot take in new air to start the process over.
- Catalytic converters are the main cause of this restriction: as they age, they start to fall apart and become restricted, causing the engine to adjust and creating more problems for the owner of the vehicle.
- The first step in diagnosing a restricted exhaust is doing a complete visual inspection, looking for bent or broken piping, smashed mufflers or catalytic converters, and obvious problems with the exhaust plumbing.
- Backpressure testing is used to verify that the vehicle has a restricted exhaust. It is done by removing the oxygen sensor, screwing in the adapter to hole, and attaching the gauge to the adapter
- Backpressure testing: start the engine and take a reading. Rev the engine up and take a reading. Compare. The reading should be very low—somewhere around 1–1½ psi max, if it is more than that, there is a restriction in the exhaust system.

Key Terms

catalytic converters An emission device that helps oxidize the exhaust as it flows out of the engine, to help combat the hazardous fumes that are created by the combustion process.

compression test Test that checks the integrity of the cylinder by taking a reading on how much pressure is produced by complete events.

cylinder leakage test Test done by pressuring up the cylinder with compressed air and measuring the amount of air that is leaking past the piston rings, head gasket, or valves.

cylinder power balance test Test that helps the technician realize which cylinders are actually contributing to the running of the engine and those that are weak.

lab scope An electrical instrument used to measure the waveform of an electrical device and create a visual representation of the electrical performance of the component.

main bearing Supports the crankshaft.

mechanical integrity Determines the strength of the internal components of the engine, which should be the first step to any repair.

motor mounts Support the engine in the vehicle and isolate the vibrations from the chassis.

power control module (PCM) The computer that operates the fuel and ignition systems on later model vehicles.

piston slap Term used when the piston hits the cylinder wall, causing a loud noise every revolution; usually caused by excessive clearance between the cylinder wall and the piston.

pressure transducer Electrical device that creates an electrical signal based on a pressure input.

rod bearing Supports the connecting rod.

running compression test Test done with the engine running to see the compression of a particular cylinder under a load as it looks for a cylinder that is failing once the engine is operating.

vacuum gauge Measures the negative pressure that is present in the internal combustion engine as the pistons create suction as they move through the Otto cycle.

Review Questions

1. All of the below statements are true with respect to engine mechanical testing, *except*:
   a. It helps to determine what major engine work is needed.
   b. It is an integral part of preventive maintenance.
   c. The tests start off broad and narrow down as each test is performed.
   d. Testing needs to be done before tune-up parts are replaced.

2. Which of these measures engine vacuum or pressure and displays it graphically on a lab scope?
   a. Pressure transducer
   b. Cylinder leakage tester
   c. Vacuum gauge
   d. Stethoscope

3. When performing a cranking sound diagnosis, a no-compression condition produces:
   a. an even cranking sound.
   b. slow cranking sound.
   c. an uneven cranking sound.
   d. fast cranking sound.

4. When performing vacuum testing using a vacuum gauge, a steady reading of 17" to 21" of vacuum indicates:
   a. burned valve.
   b. possible worn rings.
   c. possible late valve timing.
   d. good reading.

5. All of the below are advantages of using a pressure transducer rather than a vacuum gauge, *except*:
   a. greater accuracy.
   b. easier identification of the specific cylinder.
   c. measuring higher pressures.
   d. ability to see the levels graphically.

6. During a cylinder power balance test, when a cylinder that is not operating correctly is disabled, it:
   a. produces a large rpm drop.
   b. does not produce much, if any, rpm drop.
   c. produces the same rpm drop as when disabling a correctly operating cylinder.
   d. will not be compensated for by the PCM.

7. For the cranking compression test to be completely accurate, it is recommended that the engine:
   a. be at operating temperature.
   b. spark plugs be connected.
   c. battery be fully discharged.
   d. throttle be closed.

8. When doing the cylinder leakage test, it is acceptable to have a small amount of leakage past the:
   a. head gasket.
   b. intake valve.
   c. exhaust valve.
   d. piston rings.

9. A light ticking noise could be caused by a problem in the:
   a. main bearing.
   b. connecting rod bearing.
   c. valve lifter.
   d. piston skirt.

10. All of the below are helpful in identifying the source of a liquid leak, *except*:
    a. the smell of the fluid.
    b. the part on which the fluid pool is formed.
    c. the addition of a fluorescent dye.
    d. the color of the fluid.

ASE Technician A/Technician B Style Questions

1. Technician A says that a vacuum gauge that oscillates back and forth about 4–8" could be a worn timing belt. Technician B says that a steady needle on a vacuum gauge that

reads 18" of vacuum indicates the mechanical integrity of the engine is acceptable. Who is correct?

a. Technician A
b. Technician B
c. Both A and B
d. Neither A nor B

2. While conducting a cylinder leakage test, the technician hears airflow out the throttle body. Technician A says that is an indication of a bad intake valve on that cylinder could be the cause. Technician B says that it indicates the exhaust valve is bad. Who is correct?

a. Technician A
b. Technician B
c. Both A and B
d. Neither A nor B

3. Technician A says that a compression test should be done to determine if the cylinder has a mechanical issue. Technician B says that a broken motor mount can cause a vehicle vibration. Who is correct?

a. Technician A
b. Technician B
c. Both A and B
d. Neither A nor B

4. Technician A says that when using a block tester to check for a bad head gasket the radiator tank or the surge tank should be full. Technician B says that using dye in the coolant allows for the technician to use a black light to see where it is leaking. Who is correct?

a. Technician A
b. Technician B
c. Both A and B
d. Neither A nor B

5. The engine has a light engine knocking noise during light engine loads, when a particular cylinder is disabled the sound disappears. Technician A says that the cause of the sound is the ignition coil on that cylinder. Technician B says that the technician should investigate that cylinder and look for a mechanical issue related to that cylinder. Who is correct?

a. Technician A
b. Technician B
c. Both A and B
d. Neither A nor B

6. Technician A says that when checking for backpressure in the exhaust system, the oxygen sensor must be removed to install the backpressure gauge. Technician B says you can tell if an engine has an exhaust restriction by installing a vacuum gauge and taking a reading. Who is correct?

a. Technician A
b. Technician B
c. Both A and B
d. Neither A nor B

7. Technician A says when pressuring up a cooling system, the pressure should be the highest the tester can go. Technician B says that the system should only be pressured up to the rating of the cap. Who is correct?

a. Technician A
b. Technician B
c. Both A and B
d. Neither A nor B

8. Technician A says that a cylinder balance test should be performed when a misfire is present. Technician B says that you should read the spark plugs prior to doing a cylinder head gasket replacement. Who is correct?

a. Technician A
b. Technician B
c. Both A and B
d. Neither A nor B

9. Technician A says that a rotary engine uses apex seals instead of piston rings to seal the combustion chamber. Technician B says that piston rings seal the combustion cylinder on a piston engine. Who is correct?

a. Technician A
b. Technician B
c. Both A and B
d. Neither A nor B

10. Technician A says that a pressure transducer converts a pressure measurement to an electrical signal a lab scope can read. Technician B says that using a scan tool to disable cylinders is not possible on all vehicles. Who is correct?

a. Technician A
b. Technician B
c. Both A and B
d. Neither A nor B

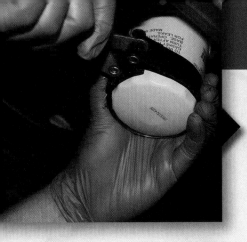

CHAPTER 7
Lubrication System

NATEF Tasks

- **N07001** Inspect auxiliary coolers; determine needed action.
- **N07002** Inspect oil pump gears or rotors, housing, pressure relief devices, and pump drive; perform needed action.
- **N07003** Perform oil and filter change.
- **N07004** Perform oil pressure tests; determine needed action.
- **N07005** Inspect, test, and replace oil temperature and pressure switches and sensors.

Knowledge Objectives

After reading this chapter, you will have:

- **K07001** Knowledge of the usage of engine oil in an internal combustion engine.
- **K07002** Knowledge of where oil comes from and how motor oil is created.
- **K07003** Knowledge of types of oil.
- **K07004** Knowledge of different types of oil additives.
- **K07005** Knowledge of the vehicle engine oil requirements.
- **K07006** Knowledge of lubrication system components.
- **K07007** Knowledge of how to maintain a lubrication system.

Skills Objectives

- **S07001** Check the engine oil.
- **S07002** Drain the engine oil.
- **S07003** Inspect the engine assembly for fuel, oil, coolant, and other leaks.
- **S07004** Replace a spin-on filter.
- **S07005** Replace a cartridge filter (replaceable element).
- **S07006** Refill the engine oil.
- **S07007** Test the oil pressure.
- **S07008** Inspect the oil sensors.
- **S07009** Inspect, test, and replace the oil temperature and pressure switches.

You Are the Automotive Technician

A customer brings his five-year-old vehicle into your shop for an oil and filter change. The vehicle is right at the recommended 7500-mile interval. He says he has noticed some oil spots on his garage floor, and the oil level was a bit below the "add" mark this morning when he checked it. He is concerned that he has an oil leak, and he would like to know why the oil pressure light on the dash didn't indicate that his oil level was low. You pull the vehicle onto the hoist. The oil light comes on when the key is turned to Run and goes off once the engine starts, proving that the oil pressure warning light circuit is working. With the engine running, you find that a drop of oil forms every so often on the end of the oil pressure switch, indicating it is leaking and needs to be replaced. None of the engine seals and gaskets show any signs of leakage.

1. What are the functions that oil performs inside an engine?
2. Why didn't the oil pressure light indicate that the oil was below the "add" line?
3. How often should the oil and filter be changed?

K07001 Knowledge of the usage of engine oil in an internal combustion engine.

K07002 Knowledge of where oil comes from and how motor oil is created.

▶ Introduction

Machinery, like our automobiles, relies on lubrication to keep the moving parts from wearing out quickly. Lubricating oil is processed from crude oil in a refinery with gasoline and diesel, along with many other beneficial and useful products. Oil is much more than simply crude oil dumped into our engine's crankcase; it is heavily processed to remove impurities, and many additives are put into the processed oil, which are designed in a lab to enhance its lubricating qualities.

Each moving part in the engine needs lubricating oil. The system that moves the oil through the engine is called the lubrication system. This chapter covers the theory of lubrication systems and the methods and specialized tools involved to ensure that you can properly diagnose and correct common problems associated with this system.

Oil

Oil originates from the ground as **crude oil** (**FIGURE 7-1**), varying in color from a dirty yellow to dark brown to black. It can be thin like gasoline or a thick oil- or tarlike substance. Crude oil is pumped from the ground and processed into many products such as fuel for use in diesel and gasoline vehicles. Crude oil is also broken down into other products used in plastics manufacturing as well as in kerosene, aviation fuel, asphalt, cosmetics, pharmaceuticals, and many others. Many of the products refined from crude oil are used in the transportation industry. For example, **lubricating oil** is distilled from the crude oil and used as a base stock. Additives are added to the base stock to make the lubricating oil useful in engines. Other additives, such as thickening agents, are added to the base stocks and used as lubricating grease in bearings. The additives that are added to the base stock perform a variety of tasks such as keeping acids from forming, cutting down on oxidation, and maintaining the correct viscosity over a broader temperature range.

Function of Lubricating Oil

Lubricating oil performs five main functions: lubricates, cushions, cools, cleans, and seals. Lubrication involves reducing friction, protecting against corrosion, and preventing metal-to-metal contact between the moving surfaces. Friction occurs between all surfaces that come into contact with one another. When moving surfaces come together, friction tends to slow them down. Friction can be useful, as in a brake system, but in the moving parts of engines, friction is undesirable and leads to serious damage. Friction can make metal parts so hot they melt and fuse together. When this happens, an engine is said to have seized.

Lubrication reduces unwanted friction and reduces wear on moving parts. Clearances, such as those between the crankshaft journal and crankshaft bearing, fill with lubricating oil so that engine parts move or float on layers of oil instead of directly on one another (**FIGURE 7-2**). By reducing friction, less power is needed to move these

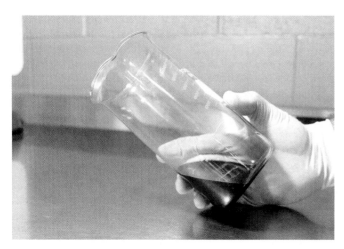

FIGURE 7-1 Crude oil straight from the ground.

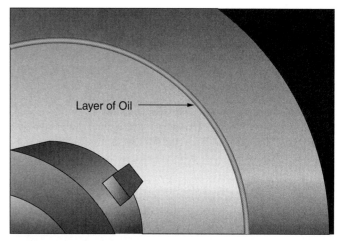

FIGURE 7-2 Clearances fill with lubricating oil so that engine parts move or float on layers of oil instead of directly on one another.

Applied | Science AS-92

AS-92: Friction: The technician can explain the need for lubrication to minimize friction.

Oil is a good lubricant in an engine because it has a low coefficient of friction. It creates a protective layer between two metal components, which both have a high coefficient of friction. The high coefficient of friction produces heat, causing the metal to expand, potentially creating engine wear and damage. Oil keeps the two metal components from rubbing against each other, thus preventing damage.

components, and more of the engine's power can be used to turn the crankshaft instead of wasted as heat; the result is increased power to move the vehicle and better fuel economy.

How long an engine lasts depends mostly on how well it is lubricated, especially at the points of **extreme loading**, or high-wear areas, such as between the cam lobe and cam follower. At the same time, the connecting rod and crankshaft bearings take large amounts of stress as the piston tries to break the crankshaft each time the cylinder fires. A power stroke can put as much as 2 tons of force on the main bearings. The lubricating oil between the surfaces helps to cushion these shock loads, similar to the way a shock absorber absorbs a bump in the road.

Lubricating oil also helps cool an engine. The lubricating oil collects heat from the engine's components and then returns to the sump, where it cools. The heat from the lubricating oil is picked up by the air moving over the oil sump. Many heavy-duty and high-performance vehicles have cooling fins on their oil pan or even a separate oil cooler to help the oil do its job of cooling critical engine components.

Lubricating oil also works as a cleaning agent. Additives in the lubricating oil allow it to collect particles of metal and carbon and carry them back to the oil sump. Larger pieces fall to the bottom of the oil sump, and smaller pieces are suspended in the oil and removed when the oil moves through the oil filter. When oil is changed, most of the particles are removed with the oil filter and old oil.

The last function of oil is that it seals. It plays a key role in sealing the piston rings to the cylinder walls. Without a small film of oil between the rings and cylinder walls, blowby gases would be much higher, resulting in diluted oil, lower compression, lower power, and lower fuel economy.

Viscosity

For oil to do all of the work that is expected of it, it must have special properties. Its viscosity is crucial. **Viscosity** is a measure of how easily a liquid flows. Low-viscosity liquid is thin and flows easily. High-viscosity liquid is thick and flows slowly (**FIGURE 7-3**). Lubricating oil must be thin enough to circulate easily between moving parts, but not so thin that it will be squeezed out easily. If it is too viscous, it moves too slowly to protect the moving parts, especially in a cold engine. As engine machining and metal technology have become more advanced, the clearances between lubricated parts have decreased. As a result, engine manufacturers have specified thinner oils for their engines so that oil can flow into the smaller clearances. The thinner oil also flows more easily, which increases fuel economy.

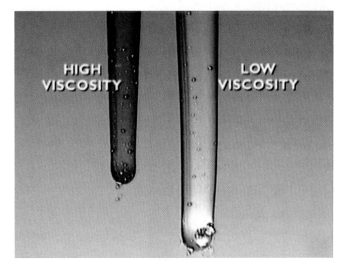

FIGURE 7-3 As you can tell from the picture, the weight of the oil does matter, and it does affect the ability of the oil to protect the vital engine components.

Types of Oil

There are three types of oil sold by oil manufacturers: conventional, synthetic, and synthetic blend. **Conventional oil** is processed from petroleum and uses additives to help the oil work properly in today's high-tech engines. **Synthetic oil** can be artificially made or highly processed petroleum. Synthetic oil has fewer impurities because it either is made in a lab rather than pumped from the ground, or, if it is pumped from the ground, is more highly refined and processed. **Synthetic blends** are used because they are cheaper to purchase and

K07003 Knowledge of types of oil.

Applied Science AS-103

AS-103: Viscosity: The technician can demonstrate an understanding of fluid viscosity as a measurement and explain how it impacts engine performance.

Viscosity is the measurement of a liquid's resistance to flow. This concept is often best understood by example. Imagine you have a small funnel that you fill with honey. You will find that the funnel drains quite slowly. If you filled the funnel with water, it would drain almost instantly. The difference is because honey has a higher viscosity than water.

▶ TECHNICIAN TIP

Be sure to use at least the minimum specified recommended oil by the manufacturer. Manufacturers of engines spend a lot of money and time designing engines that are efficient and long lasting. Always follow the manufacturer's recommendations.

FIGURE 7-4 The refining process from ground to quart.

FIGURE 7-5 Synthetic oil is an engineered product that is designed to last longer than conventional oil inside the harsh engine environment.

give the benefit of half synthetic. Manufacturers publish the required oil for each vehicle in the owner's manual.

Conventional

Conventional oil is processed from crude oil pumped from the ground (**FIGURE 7-4**). The crude oil contains many impurities that are removed during the refining process. One of the impurities found in all crude oil is wax. This wax is removed during refining and is used for candle wax; it also serves as an additive in some food and candy. Wax is not a good thing in oil because it creates a thickening effect when it gets cold, becoming too thick to flow through the engine. Crude is broken down into mineral oil, which is then combined with additives to enhance the lubricating qualities. Without the additives, conventional oil would not work well. It would foam easily, break down quickly, and corrode the engine parts after being in the engine for a short time.

Synthetic

There are two main categories of synthetic lubricating oils: type 3, which is not a true synthetic, and type 4 (PA O), which is a true synthetic. Both types of synthetics are more costly to manufacture, as the base stocks are more highly refined or are developed in a lab, and are therefore more costly to the customer. Synthetic lubricants have a number of advantages over conventional oils. They offer better protection against engine wear and can operate at the higher temperatures needed by performance engines. Synthetic oils have better low-temperature viscosity, which allows the oil to be circulated through the engine more quickly during low temperature engine start-ups. Synthetics have fewer wax impurities that coagulate at low temperatures; they are chemically more stable; and they are generally thinner, so they allow for closer tolerances in engine components without loss of lubrication (**FIGURE 7-5**). Modern high-performance engines run much tighter tolerances, so the need for a thinner oil that is able to hold up under higher temperatures is desirable. Some synthetics also last considerably longer, extending oil change intervals to 20,000 miles (30,000 km) or more, which benefits the environment by reducing the used oil stream and reducing the need for finding new sources of oil.

True synthetic oils are based on artificially made hydrocarbons, commonly **polyalpha-olefin (PAO)** oil, which is an artificial oil base stock—meaning it is not refined from crude oil. Synthetic oils were developed in Germany during World War II because of the lack of crude oil. Normal conventional oil would create heavy carbon deposits on bearings due to the extreme heat, which led to failures. Amsoil was the first synthetic to be approved by the API in 1972. Many companies now offer synthetic oils. Very few synthetic oils on the market are full PAO oils. Many of the oils allowed to be labeled as synthetic are in fact blends of processed mineral oil (highly refined base stock refined from crude oil) and PAO, or even just highly refined base stock, that possess lubrication qualities similar to PAOs.

High Mileage

High mileage oils have additives in them that swell the seals in the engine to help prevent leakage. Another feature of high mileage oils is that they are engineered to give that worn engine extra polymers to help extend the usage of the internal parts of the engine (**FIGURE 7-6**). These types of oil are geared more toward older engines.

Heavy-Duty Oils

Heavy-duty oils are designed for severe service that requires a type of oil that is engineered to take more abuse than conventional oils. A lot of the time you find these oils used in commercial applications in high-value equipment because of the cost of replacing that equipment (**FIGURE 7-7**). You should read the service information to determine which type of oil the engine needs to operate at in the environment that it is designed to work in.

Oil Additives

K07004 Knowledge of different types of oil additives.

Special chemicals called additives are added to the base oil by the oil companies. Different combinations of these additives allow the oil to do different jobs in an engine. A description of common additives follows:

- **Extreme-pressure additives** coat parts with a protective layer so that the oil resists being forced out under heavy load.
- **Oxidation inhibitors** stop very hot oil from combining with oxygen in the air to produce a sticky tarlike material, which coats parts and clogs the oil galleries and drainback passages. **Oil galleries** are the passageways that carry oil through the engine. They are either cast or drilled into the engine block and head(s).
- **Corrosion inhibitors** help stop acids from forming that cause corrosion, especially on bearing surfaces. Corrosion due to acid etches into bearing surfaces and causes premature wear of the bearings.
- **Antifoaming agents** reduce the effect of oil churning in the crankcase and minimize foaming. Foaming allows air bubbles to form in the engine oil, reducing the lubrication quality of oil and contributing to breakdown of the oil due to oxidation. Because air is compressible, oil with foam reduces the ability of the oil to keep the moving parts separated, causing more wear and friction. The antifoaming additives keep these conditions from occurring.
- **Detergents** reduce carbon deposits on parts such as piston rings and valves.
- **Dispersants** collect particles that can block the system; the dispersants separate the particles from one another, and keep them moving. They are removed when the oil is changed
- **Pour point depressants** keep oil from forming wax particles under cold-temperature operation. When wax crystals form, they result in the **gelling** of the oil and keep oil from flowing during cold start-up conditions. Gelling is the thickening of oil to a point that it will not flow through the engine; it becomes close to a solid in extreme cold temperatures.
- Base stock derived from crude oil will not retain its viscosity if the temperature gets cold enough, so viscosity improvers are added to the stock. A **viscosity index improver** is an additive that helps to reduce the change in viscosity as the temperature of the oil changes. Viscosity index improvers also keep the engine oil from becoming too thin during hot operation.

FIGURE 7-6 High-mileage oil is used to help stop oil leaks and restore engine combustion.

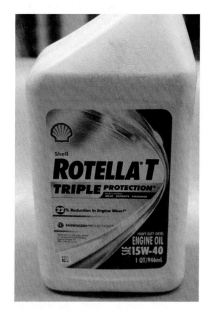

FIGURE 7-7 Heavy-duty engine oil is used for engines that will be operated in a harsh environment most of the time.

K07005 Knowledge of the vehicle engine oil requirements.

▶ Vehicle Specifications and Requirements

Automotive technicians should read the service information to determine what types of standards of fluids that the vehicles they repair need. These standards are designed by the engineers of the vehicles to maintain the integrity of the internal rotating parts of the engine. Deviating from these standards could cause the engine to become inoperable and the customer to be dissatisfied.

American Petroleum Institute (API)

The American Petroleum Institute (API) sets minimum performance standards for lubricants, including engine oils. The API has a two-part classification: service class and service standard. The API service class has two general classifications: S for spark-ignition engines and C for compression-ignition engines. Engine oil that meets the API standards may display the API Service Symbol, which is also known as the API "donut." This protocol is important to understand because oil rated S only cannot be used in compression-ignition engines unless they also carry the C rating, and vice versa. Be careful that the wrong oil is not used in a particular engine. The API service standard (SA) was used in

Applied Science

AS-25: Inhibitors: The technician can explain the need for additives in automobile lubricants.

Automotive lubricants are composed of base stock plus an additive package. In addition to engine oil, additives are used in lubricants for manual and automatic transmissions as well as differentials.

Oil additives are a very necessary part of modern lubricants. The improvements in modern automotive lubricants are one of the factors that enable vehicles to last longer than ever before. Oil additives consist of chemical compounds that have many beneficial functions.

Detergents are additives that help keep the oil clean. Corrosion- (or rust-) inhibiting additives work to prevent oxidation of engine parts. A corrosion inhibitor is a chemical compound that, when added to a liquid or gas, decreases the corrosion rates of a material, typically a metal or an alloy.

▶ TECHNICIAN TIP

In most cases, higher rated engine oils are backward compatible. This means you can use SM oil in a vehicle that requires SL. But there is one exception that some technicians have found. SN-rated oil has very low levels of phosphorus and zinc, which aids in flat tappet camshaft lubrication. So if you are working on an older engine that uses flat tappets, you probably do not want to use SN-rated oil, but SM instead.

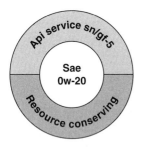

FIGURE 7-8 The API donut shows the API service class and service standard, the viscosity, the ILSAC performance rating, and the energy-conserving designation.

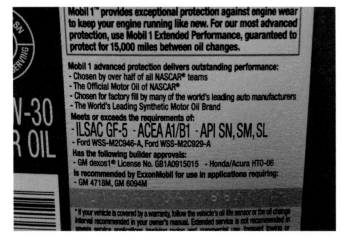

FIGURE 7-9 The location of the ILSAC emblem on an oil container.

engines up to 1930, which means pure mineral oil without any additives. As engine manufacturers improved engine technology—or as government regulations changed, such as requiring reduced amounts of phosphorus—engine oil with new qualities was required, and the API would introduce a new rating level. The API SN level was added in October 2010 for 2011 gasoline vehicles. API CJ-4 was added in 2010 to meet four-stroke diesel engine requirements. The API symbol is the donut symbol located on the back of the oil bottle (**FIGURE 7-8**). In the top half of the symbol is the service class—S or C—and the service standard that the oil meets. The center part carries the SAE viscosity rating for the oil. The API symbol may also carry an energy-saving designation if it is a fuel-saving oil. Be sure to use oil that has a correct API rating and also an energy-conserving designation in all North American vehicles.

Explanation

The API classifies oils into five groups:

1. Group 1 oils are produced by simple distillation of crude oil, which separates the components of the oil by their boiling point, and by the use of solvents to extract sulfur, nitrogen, and oxygen compounds. This method was the only commercial refinement process until the early 1970s, and the bulk of commercial oil products on the market are still produced by this process, such as conventional engine oils.
2. Group 2 and group 3 oils are refined with hydrogen at much higher temperatures and pressures, in a process known as **hydrocracking**. This process results in a base mineral oil with many of the higher performance characteristics of synthetic oils.
3. The more heavily hydrocracked group 3 oils have a very high viscosity index (above 120) and many, but not all, of the higher performance characteristics of a full polyalphaolefin (PAO) synthetic oil. Although not fully synthetic, these oils can be sold as synthetic oil in North America.
4. Group 4 oils are all of the full synthetic PAO group (most common true synthetic).
5. Group 5 includes all other types of synthetic oil.

International Lubricant Standardization and Approval Committee (ILSAC)

The International Lubricant Standardization and Approval Committee (ILSAC) works in conjunction with the API in creating new specifications for gasoline engine oil. However, ILSAC requires that the oil provide increased fuel economy over a base lubricant (**FIGURE 7-9**). These oils should reduce vehicle owners' fuel costs a small amount compared to an oil that does not meet the ILSAC standard. Like the API standard, ILSAC issues sequentially higher rating levels each time the standards are changed. ILSAC GF-5 replaced GF-4 and became the standard in September 2011. Engine oils that meet the GF-4 and GF-5 standard can display the API starburst symbol, which the API created to verify that the oil meets the highest ILSAC standard.

SAE

The **Society of Automotive Engineers (SAE)** set the standards that oil manufactures must meet to qualify for the viscosity rating for each particular oil. Engine oil with an SAE number of 50 has a higher viscosity, or is thicker, than an SAE 20 oil. Oils with low viscosity ratings, such as SAE 0W, 5W, and 10W (the "W" stands for winter viscosity), are tested at a low temperature—around 0°F (−17.8°C) (**FIGURE 7-10**). These ratings indicate how the oil will flow when started cold in cold climate conditions. Oils with high viscosity ratings, such as SAE 20, 30, 40, and 50, are tested at a high temperature—around 210°F (98.9°C). These ratings indicate how the oil will flow when the engine is being used under loaded conditions in hotter conditions.

Modern oils are blends of oils that combine different properties of each oil to create the desired outcome oil. The oils are blended with viscosity index improvers to form multi-grade, or multi-viscosity, oils. They provide better lubrication over a wider range of climatic conditions than monograde oils. These oils are classified by a two-part designation, such as SAE 0W-20. In this example, when the oil was tested at 0°F (−17.8°C), it met the specifications for a viscosity of 0W weight oil, and when the same oil was tested at 210°F (98.9°C), it met the viscosity specifications for 20 weight oil. Multi-viscosity oils flow easily during cold engine start-up but do not thin out as much as the engine and oil come up to operating temperature. These properties allow the oil to get to the components more quickly during start-up, while maintaining its ability to cushion components when it is hot. Although multi-viscosity oils extend the operating temperature range of the engine, always refer to the vehicle's service information to determine the correct oil viscosity to use for the climate the engine will be operated in.

JASO

The **Japanese Engine Oil Standards Implementation Panel (JASO)** standards set the classification for motorcycle engines, both two-stroke and four-stroke, as well as Japanese automotive diesel engines (**FIGURE 7-11**). For four-cycle motorcycle engines, the JASO T 903:2011 came into effect in October 2011 and designates different ratings for wet clutch (MA) and dry clutch (MB). For two-stroke motorcycles, JASO M 34:2003 came into effect in October 2003. And for automotive diesel engines, JASO M355:2008 came into effect in August 2008.

ACEA

The **European Automobile Manufacturers' Association (ACEA)**, classifications formulated for engine oils used in European vehicles and are much more stringent than the API and ILSAC standards (**FIGURE 7-12**). Some of the characteristics the ACEA-rated oil must score high on are soot thickening, water, sludge, piston deposits, oxidative thickening, fuel economy, and after-treatment compatibility. Although some of these may be tested by the API and ILSAC, the standards are set high to achieve ACEA certification ratings. This means that the engine oil provides additional protection or characteristics that API- or ILSAC-rated oils may not match. If you are servicing a European vehicle, it is advised that you do not go by any API recommendations; instead, make sure the oil meets the recommended ACEA rating specified by the manufacturer or the manufacturer's own specification rating.

FIGURE 7-10 The SAE symbol on a quart of oil.

FIGURE 7-11 The standards that the oil meets according to the manufacturer. The JASO lubrication standards are in use for Japanese manufactured automotive and diesel engines. This standard should be printed on the back label of the oil container.

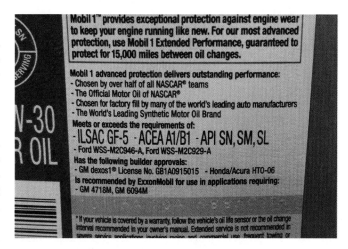

FIGURE 7-12 ACEA standard is stamped on the oil container in a similar location as the one pictured.

N07001 Inspect auxiliary coolers; determine needed action.

K07006 Knowledge of lubrication system components.

SAFETY TIP

The lubrication system contains pressures up to approximately 80 psi (552 kPa), which shoots oil a good distance. Be sure to wear safety glasses, and be careful if the engine oil is hot, as it could cause burns.

▶ Lubrication System Components

Lubrication system components are pieces that help disperse the oil throughout the engine block to lubricate the engine. The components that are a part of the lubrication system are engineered to handle the requirements of the engine efficiently, which means they must be precisely created to meet those requirements.

Lubrication Systems

The **lubrication system** is a series of engine components that work together to keep the moving parts inside an engine lubricated (**FIGURE 7-13**). Proper lubrication ensures that the engine runs cooler, produces maximum power, and gets maximum fuel efficiency. Lubrication also ensures that the engine will last. The lubrication system has many components that work together to deliver the oil to the correct locations in the engine. A typical lubrication system consists of an **oil sump**, an oil pump strainer (also called a pickup tube), an **oil pump**, a pressure regulator, oil galleries, an oil filter, and a low pressure warning system.

The oil is stored in the oil sump. Oil is drawn through the oil pump strainer from the oil sump by an oil pump. The oil travels from the oil pump to the oil filter, which removes particles of dirt from the oil. Then it is transferred throughout the engine to lubricate the various components required for it to operate. Without the oil feed, most of the components would overheat and fail. Oil may also be splashed from the connecting rods onto the cylinder walls, and the circulation of the oil assists with the cooling of the internal parts.

Pressure Fed

Modern vehicle engines use a **pressure,** or **force-feed, lubrication system**, where the oil is forced throughout the engine under pressure (**FIGURE 7-14**). In gasoline engines, oil will not flow up into the engine by itself, so the oil pump collects it through a pickup tube and strainer and forces it through an oil filter, then into passageways, called galleries, in the engine block. The galleries allow oil to be fed to the crankshaft bearings first, then through holes drilled in the crankshaft, to the connecting rods. The oil also moves from the galleries onto the camshaft bearings and the valve mechanism. After circulating through the engine, the oil falls back to the oil sump to cool. This design is called a wet sump lubrication system.

Some engines use a **dry sump lubrication system**, which uses all of the parts that make up a wet sump system and lubricates the engine in the same way. It differs from the wet sump system in the way the oil is collected and stored. In a dry sump system, the oil falls to the bottom of the engine into an oil collection pan. A **scavenge pump** then pumps it to an oil tank, where it is stored until the normal oil pump collects it and pumps it through the filter and engine in the normal way. Because there is no oil storage sump under the engine, the engine can be mounted much lower than in a wet sump system, which allows the vehicle to have a much lower center of gravity. The oil tank can be positioned away from the engine, where it can get best cooling, and the amount of oil in the system can be much greater than in the wet sump system because space is less of an issue.

Diesel engines are lubricated in much the same way as gasoline engines, but there are a few differences. Diesel engines typically operate at the top end of their power range, so their internal operating temperatures are usually higher than those in similar gasoline engines. Thus, the parts in diesel engines are usually more stressed. Because diesel fuel is ignited by the heat of compression, the compression pressures (and compression ratio) are much higher than in gasoline engines. Diesel fuel has more **British thermal units (BTUs)** of heat energy than gasoline, so it produces more heat when it is ignited, placing more stress on the engine's moving parts. Because of stress from the higher compression and combustion

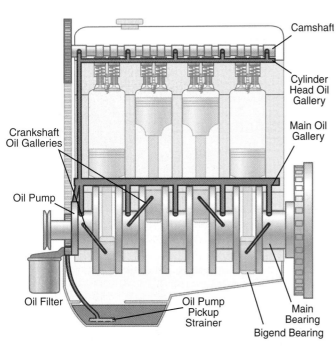

FIGURE 7-13 The lubrication system.

Camshaft

Cylinder Head Oil Gallery

Main Oil Gallery

Crankshaft Oil Galleries

Oil Pump

Oil Filter

Oil Pump Pickup Strainer

Main Bearing

Bigend Bearing

pressures/temperatures, parts have to be much heavier, and with heavier parts, oil must be able to handle higher shear forces. As a result, diesel oils need a different range of properties and are classified differently, usually with a C rating in the API system. It is also common for many diesel engines to use an oil-to-water cooler to cool the oil in the engine. The cooler and oil filter are usually on the same mounting on the cylinder block.

Splash

Not all lubricated engine components are lubricated by the pressure-fed system. Some are lubricated by the **splash lubrication** method (**FIGURE 7-15**). In this method, the oil is thrown around and gets into spaces that need lubrication. Automotive and diesel engines use splash lubrication for lubricating the cylinder walls, pistons, wrist pin, valve guides, and sometimes the timing chain. The oil that is splashed around usually comes from moving parts that are pressure-fed; as the oil leaks out of those parts as designed, it is thrown around and provides splash lubrication to the needed components. On horizontal-crankshaft engines, a **dipper** on the bottom of the connecting rod scoops up oil from the crankcase for the bearings. The dipper is also able to splash oil up to the valve mechanism. Alternatively, an **oil slinger** can be driven by the crankshaft or camshaft. A slinger is a device that runs half-submerged in the engine oil. The oil is slung from the slinger upward by centrifugal force to lubricate moving parts. A similar system is used in most small vertical-crankshaft engines. Oil is also splashed up to the valve mechanism from the centrifugal force of the slinger spinning at engine speed.

Oil Pan

The **oil pan** is located at the bottom of the engine (**FIGURE 7-16**). On a wet sump lubricating system, the oil pan holds the entire volume of the oil required to lubricate the engine. The lowest point of the oil pan is the oil sump. This is where the **oil pump pickup tube** is located. The deep point in the oil pan ensures that there should never be a shortage of oil for the oil pump to pick up if the correct amount of oil is in the engine. The oil pan is sealed to the engine with silicone or an oil pan gasket. The sump is equipped with a drain plug that allows the oil to be drained from the engine during oil changes (**FIGURE 7-17**).

High Performance Application Oil System Features

Some high-performance vehicles have a **windage tray**, which is a pan located close to the crankshaft, fitted to prevent churning of the oil by the rotation of the crankshaft (**FIGURE 7-18**). The windage tray can be made from stamped sheet metal or a one-way mesh screen that allows oil to flow down through the mesh, but not the other way. This design helps keep oil away from the rotating crank as much as possible. **Baffles** are flat pieces of steel placed around the oil pump pickup in the oil pan to prevent oil from surging away from the pickup during cornering, braking, and accelerating. Baffles are commonly used on vehicles that experience strong g-forces, such as rally cars, stock cars, and drag-racing cars.

Pickup Tube

Between the oil sump and oil pump is a pickup tube with a flat cup and a wire mesh strainer immersed in the oil (**FIGURE 7-19**). The pickup tube pulls oil from the oil sump by suction of the oil pump and atmospheric pressure. A strainer on the pickup tube stops large particles of debris from entering the oil pump and damaging it. The pickup tube leads to the inlet of the oil pump, on the low-pressure side of the oil pump. The pickup tube fits tightly into the oil pump and is usually bolted in place by a bracket to ensure that it does not fall out due to vibration. If the pickup tube were to fall out, the engine would not receive oil, as the pump would not reach down into the sump from which oil is drawn.

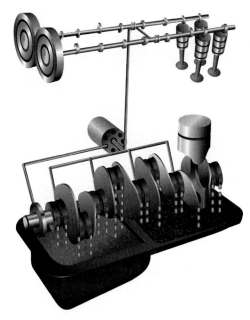

FIGURE 7-14 The cylinder block that houses the oil system.

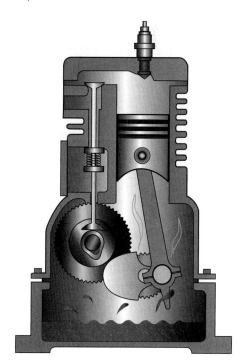

FIGURE 7-15 How a non-pressurized oil system lubricates the crankshaft and piston.

FIGURE 7-16 The oil pan.

FIGURE 7-17 A drain plug allows oil to be drained during oil changes.

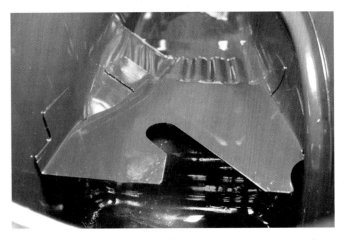

FIGURE 7-18 A windage tray. A windage tray is an integral part of some engine oil pans to cut down on windage that can be created by the turning of the crankshaft at high rpm.

FIGURE 7-19 The pickup tube and screen allows the oil pump to suck up oil from the oil pan sump.

N07002 Inspect oil pump gears or rotors, housing, pressure relief devices, and pump drive; perform needed action.

> ▶ **TECHNICIAN TIP**

What is the difference between a high-pressure oil pump and a high-volume oil pump? A high-pressure pump has a stiffer pressure relief spring, which allows the pump to create higher oil pressure. A high-volume pump has greater volume between the rotor or gear teeth, usually accomplished by making both the rotor/gear and the oil pump housing deeper. This design causes more oil to be drawn into the pump during each revolution, and therefore more oil is forced out of the pump each revolution. Generally speaking, a high-volume pump is more beneficial; because it can pump more oil, the pressure will not fall as quickly as the engine experiences wear and tear.

Oil Pump

Most oil pumps are the positive displacement type. This means that they move a given amount of oil from the inlet to the outlet each revolution. The faster the pump turns, the more oil that is pumped. Oil pressure is determined by two factors: (1) the bearing clearance of the main and rod journals and (2) the amount of oil flowing in the system. As you can imagine, an engine has a fairly consistent set of leaks. When the engine is new, the leaks are fairly small. When the engine has acquired many miles, the leaks are larger. This is why engine oil pressure falls over the life of the engine. In fact, low oil pressure can mean one of three things (other than a bad oil pressure gauge). Either the bearing clearance has gotten excessive (e.g., worn bearings); the oil pump is worn out and not creating as much flow as it needs to; or the oil is thinner than it should be (e.g., saturated with gasoline from a leaky fuel injector), which causes it to drain from the leaks faster than it should.

Oil pumps may be driven from the camshaft or the crankshaft. In a **rotor-type oil pump**, sometimes referred to as a gerotor pump, has an inner rotor drives an outer one; as they turn, the volume between them increases (**FIGURE 7-20A**). The larger volume created between the rotors lowers the pressure at the pump inlet, creating a vacuum. Outside atmospheric pressure, which is higher, forces oil into the pump, and the oil fills the spaces between the rotor lobes. As the lobes of the inner rotor move into the spaces in the outer rotor, oil is squeezed out through the outlet. In other words, oil is drawn into the spaces between the lobes on the inlet side and travels around with the lobes. The oil cannot get back to the inlet side because the lobes come together, and it is therefore forced out of the pump outlet.

The **crescent pump** uses a similar principle (**FIGURE 7-20B**). It is usually mounted on the front of the cylinder block and straddles the front of the crankshaft. The inner gear is then driven by the crankshaft directly. An external toothed gear meshes with the inner one. Some gear teeth are meshed, but others are separated by the crescent-shaped part of the pump housing. The increasing volume between gear teeth causes pressure to fall, creating a vacuum, and atmospheric pressure pushes oil into the pump. Oil is then carried around between the gears and crescent before being discharged to the outlet port.

In a **geared oil pump**, the driving gear meshes with a second gear (**FIGURE 7-20C**). As both gears turn, their teeth separate, creating a low-pressure area. Higher atmospheric pressure outside forces the oil up into the inlet, which fills the spaces between the gear teeth. As the gears rotate, they carry oil around the chamber. As the teeth mesh again, oil is forced from the outlet into the oil gallery and toward the oil filter, where it is filtered of any particles.

Pressure Relief Valves

A normal oil pump is capable of delivering more oil than an engine needs. Extra volume provides a safety measure to ensure the engine is never starved for oil. As the oil pump rotates and engine speed increases, the volume of oil delivered also increases. The fixed clearances between the moving parts of the engine slow the oil's escape back to the oil sump, and pressure builds up in the lubrication system. An **oil pressure relief valve** stops excess pressure from developing. It is like a controlled leak, releasing just enough oil back to the oil sump to regulate the pressure in the whole system. The oil pressure relief valve contains a spring calibrated to a specific pressure. When the pressure is reached, the oil pressure relief valve slides open just enough to bleed sufficient oil back to the pan to maintain the preset maximum relief pressure. If the engine speed and oil flow increase, the pressure relief valve will open farther and allow more oil to escape back to the sump. If the engine speed and oil flow decrease, the pressure relief valve will close an appropriate amount.

Factors That Affect Oil Pressure

Some factors affect oil pressure in the engine. Bearing clearance helps create oil pressure, oil pump output pressure, oil quality, oil filter quality, and engine rpm. The quality of the components used has a dramatic effect on the output of the lubrication system, and quality should not be compromised.

Bearing clearance must be maintained to keep the pressure up in the oiling system as it relies on the metered loss that the bearing clearance provides. The oil pump output

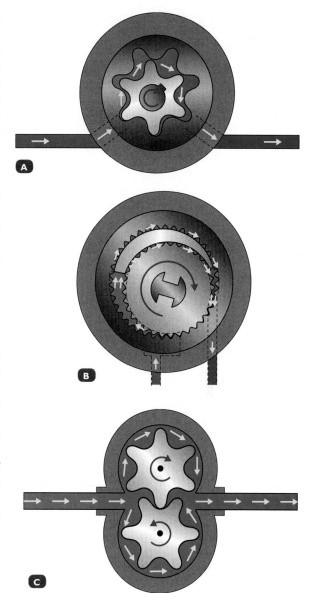

FIGURE 7-20 A. Rotor-type oil pump. **B.** Crescent pump. **C.** Geared oil pump.

Applied Math

AM-29: Volume: The technician can use various measurement techniques to determine the volume as applicable.

Two technicians are examining an engine oil pan as it is being cleaned. It is a standard automotive pan from a V6 engine and has a rectangular shape. Randy says that the volume of the pan could be calculated by multiplying the area of the base times the height. Tom agrees with this and adds that in the US system of measurement, the result would be in cubic inches, which can be converted into quarts.

At break time, they decide to measure the pan and calculate its volume in quarts. The pan measures 6 inches wide, 9 inches long, and 5.35 inches deep. The area of the base is 6 × 9, which is 54 square inches. Next, they multiply times the height of 5.35 inches for 288.9 square inches. This is approximately 5 quarts (considering one quart is equal to 57.750 cubic inches).

To calculate the example in metric units, the process is very similar. Centimeters are used for the linear units to determine the base × height. Cubic centimeters convert to liters.

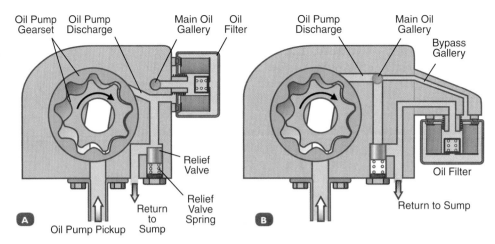

FIGURE 7-21 A. Full-flow filtering system. **B.** Bypass filtering system.

pressure is what drives the oiling system; without the continuous flow into the oil galleries, there would be nothing to create the pressure needed to keep the engine from failing. Oil and filter quality are two of the biggest issues that face the automotive repair industry today. As the price of oil fluctuates, manufacturers try to keep their profit margins, which then causes them to cut back on the quality of the materials they are using. This causes a snowball affect: most consumers already don't maintain their vehicle like they are supposed to, so when inferior products are used too, they fail sooner, increasing the likelihood of engine failure. Always recommend a quality filter and oil, as those are the lifeblood of any engine. Over-revving any engine on a regular basis will eventually cause that engine to fail. Manufacturers have remedied many of these types of problems by putting in electronic rev limiters that do not allow the engine to be over-revved.

Oil Filters

There are two basic oil-filtering systems: full-flow and bypass (**FIGURE 7-21**). The most common, **full-flow filters**, are designed to filter all of the oil before delivering it to the engine. The location of the filter right after the oil pump ensures that all of the oil is filtered before it is sent to the lubricated components. The bypass filtering system is more common on diesel engines and is used in conjunction with a full-flow filtering system. The bypass filter is discussed later in this section.

Oil filters use a pleated filter paper for the filtering medium (**FIGURE 7-22**). Oil flows through the paper, and as it does so, it filters out particles in the oil. Most full-flow oil filters catch particles down to 30 microns. A micron is 0.000039" (0.001 mm)—a very small particle. A human hair's thickness can be as small as 50 microns, for example. As the oil filter catches these fine particles, the paper filter element begins to clog, making it harder for the oil to flow through. As the engine is initially started cold for a few seconds, or if the filter becomes clogged, the bypass valve opens to let unfiltered oil flow to the lubricated components. The manufacturers believe it is better to have unfiltered oil flow to components than no oil at all. To prevent excessive engine wear, it is critical to change the oil filter at the manufacturer's recommended interval.

There are two common types of oil filters: spin-on and cartridge (**FIGURE 7-23**). The spin-on type is the most common. It uses a one-piece filter assembly with a crimped housing and threaded base. The pleated paper filter element is formed into the inside of the crimped housing. This kind of filter spins off with the use of an oil filter wrench and tightens by hand force only. A square-cut or round-cut rubber O-ring fits into a groove in the base of the filter and seals the base of the filter to the engine block. A new O-ring comes with the filter, so it gets replaced

FIGURE 7-22 Pleated oil filter paper.

FIGURE 7-23 A. Spin-on filter and O-ring. **B.** Cartridge paper filter, housing, and bolt.

with the filter. Be aware, though, that the old O-ring may stick to the filter adapter on the engine block. If you do not notice this and leave the old O-ring on along with the new O-ring, the old one will not be able to stay in place because it is not in any groove. As a result, it will get pushed out of place when the engine is started and most, if not all, of the engine oil will be pumped out onto the ground. Always check for the old O-ring when removing the oil filter.

The cartridge-style oil filter uses a separate reusable metal or plastic housing and a replaceable filter cartridge. It is typically held together in one of two ways: a threaded center bolt or screw-on housing. If it uses a center bolt, it will have a sealing washer between the bolt and the housing to prevent oil from leaking out. There is also a seal that fits either between the cylindrical housing and the filter adapter on the block or between the cylindrical housing and the end cap, depending on the design. Cartridge filters must be disassembled, the housing cleaned, and the paper filter element and any O-rings or seals replaced with new ones.

Most oil filters on diesel engines are larger than those on similar gasoline engines, and some diesel engines have two oil filters. Diesel engines produce more carbon particles than gasoline engines, so the oil filter can have a full-flow element to trap larger impurities and a bypass element to collect sludge and carbon soot. In a bypass system, the bypass element filters only some of the oil from the oil pump by tapping an oil line into the oil gallery. It collects finer particles than a full-flow filter. After this oil is filtered, it is returned to the oil sump. If the bypass filter were to clog

Applied Math

AM-30: Volume: The technician can determine whether the existing volume is within the manufacturer's recommended tolerance.

A technician was instructed to change the engine oil and filter on a late model automobile. In addition to this, he was also to change the automatic transmission fluid and filter. The technician has access to the manufacturer's service information, which he consulted before starting the tasks. The service information stated that 5.5 quarts of oil would be needed for an engine oil change with filter replacement. Concerning the automatic transmission fluid and filter change, the manual stated 9.5 quarts are needed for this service.

The technician begins working by draining the engine oil and filter. As he puts the new oil into the engine, the technician counts the number of quart containers. He discovers that after the engine was started, to fill the oil filter and shut off takes a total of 5.5 quarts to bring the oil level to the exact full mark on the dipstick. By this method, the technician is able to determine that the existing volume is within the manufacturer's tolerance.

At this point, the technician goes on to the transmission fluid and filter change. He drains the fluid and changes the filter. As before, the technician counts the number of quart containers necessary for filling the system properly. He pours in one quart at a time in order to take an accurate count. The technician observes that it takes 9.5 quarts to fill the system to the full line on the dipstick, with the engine running in Park. By this method, the technician is able to verify that the existing volume is within the manufacturer's tolerance.

and stop oil flow, the flow of oil lubricating the engine components would not be affected.

Anti-Drainback Valve

Anti-drainback valve is used to keep the oil filter full of oil once the engine is shut off so that at the next start-up the engine will not have to wait as long for oil pressure. This valve is built into the filter most of the time so that it gets regularly changed when the filter gets replaced. Failure to use the proper filter could cause catastrophic engine damage as the valve could be set to a different specification. Without this valve, the oil filter would drain every time that oil pressure was turned off, and the engine would have to refill the filter before it would make it to the crankshaft.

Using the Wrong Oil Filter

Oil filters are designed to work with the engine that they are meant for and are not supposed to be used on engines that they are not designed to work on. If the wrong filter is installed on the engine, it may create external leaks or lower the oil pressure, or it might explode from excess pressure. Always make sure you have the correct oil filter before you install it on the engine.

Spurt Holes and Galleries

Pistons, rings, and pins are lubricated by oil thrown onto the cylinder walls from the connecting rod bearings. Some connecting rods have oil spurt holes that are positioned to receive oil from similar holes in the crankshaft (**FIGURE 7-24**). Oil can then spurt out at the point in the engine cycle when the largest area of cylinder wall is exposed. This oil sprays from the connecting rod holes and lubricates the cylinder walls and piston wrist pin, and may help cool the underside of the piston.

Oil is fed to the cylinder head through oil galleries and on to the camshaft bearings and valvetrain. When oil reaches the top of the cylinder head and lubricates the valvetrain, it has completed its pressurized journey. The oil drains back to the oil sump through oil drainback holes located in the cylinder head and engine block.

Oil Coolers

Oil coolers are installed in line with the oil system so that the oil is pumped through a heat exchanger, a process similar to what happens in the cooling system (**FIGURE 7-25**). The oil cooler is usually part of the engine cooling system, and it uses coolant to help transfer heat to the outside air. Cooling the oil helps stop the breakdown of the

FIGURE 7-24 Some connecting rods have oil spurt holes, which are positioned to receive oil from similar holes in the crankshaft.

FIGURE 7-25 An oil to water cooler mounted underneath the oil filter to save space.

lubrication properties in the oil, which leads to an engine that runs cooler and has a better protective oil film on all of its bearing surfaces. Certain engines require oil coolers or the oil will become overheated and break down more quickly, which could result in increased wear inside the engine. Those types of engines usually are the ones that have a supercharger or turbocharged addition to the engine that causes increased heat. Along with boosted engines, trucks that have tow packages and other commercial vehicles are equipped with heavy-duty coolers for the transmission and oil, and bigger radiators to help lessen the impact of the extra heat that is generated by towing a trailer.

Oil Analysis

Oil will suspend particles as the engine wears. Analysis of the engine oil is a useful way to see what parts are wearing in the engine. The military as well as many companies use oil analysis to ensure that the engine oil is changed at the appropriate interval. A small tube is slipped down the oil dipstick tube all the way to the oil pan sump. A vacuum device is hooked to this tube to pull a sample of oil from the pan to a collection container. This sample is labeled with the vehicle information and sent to a lab. The lab thoroughly analyzes the oil and reports the findings back to the shop. The report lists physical properties such as viscosity, condensed water, fuel dilution, antifreeze, acids, metal content, and oil additives. Each of these attributes can be used to determine the condition of the oil as well as the engine. When oil analysis is performed for a particular engine on a regular basis, issues can usually be addressed before they become catastrophic. Oil analysis is typically used in heavy vehicle applications that may use 3 or more gallons (11.4 or more liters) of engine oil. Some race teams will analyze the engine oil to ensure that the engine is not being damaged.

As a technician, you can do a simple test to check for excessive engine wear. Take a white paper towel and wipe the oil from the dipstick on it. Hold the towel to the light and move it back and forth to see if light reflects from metal. If metal is in the oil, there is substantial wear happening inside the engine.

Oil Indicators and Warning Systems

A lubrication system failure can be catastrophic to the engine. Because of the damage that would happen if the lubrication system failed, a warning system is installed to let the driver know the system has failed. If oil pressure falls too low, a pressure sensor threaded into a gallery can activate a low oil pressure warning light, register pressure on a gauge, or turn on a low oil pressure warning message (**FIGURE 7-26**). The pressure sensor is also commonly called a sending unit because it sends a signal to the light, gauge, or message center in the dash. If the sending unit is designed as part of a warning lamp system, it is made up of a spring-loaded diaphragm and a set of switch contacts and is commonly called a pressure switch. Oil pressure is on the engine side of the diaphragm, and a spring is on the other. With the engine off and the ignition switch in the Run position, the oil pressure is zero, so the spring holds the diaphragm toward the engine, and the switch contacts are closed (i.e., making contact with each other). This

FIGURE 7-26 If oil pressure falls too low, a pressure sensor in a gallery can **A.** activate a warning light, **B.** register on a gauge, or **C.** turn on a warning message.

causes current to flow from the warning lamp in the dash through the closed switch contacts in the sending unit to ground, which turns on the warning light. When the engine is started, oil pressure increases above spring pressure, and the diaphragm is pushed away from the engine, opening the switch contacts and turning off the warning light. In some vehicles, the sending unit sends the electrical signal to the BCM, which is programmed to turn the light on below a certain pressure. This is how the system should work when everything is working normally. If the oil pressure drops below spring pressure while the engine is running, the light will come on, warning the driver of the low oil pressure condition.

If the sending unit is part of an oil pressure gauge system, it usually uses a variable resistor within the sending unit. The variable resistor is moved by the oil pressure moving the diaphragm against the spring pressure. As the pressure increases, the diaphragm is forced against spring pressure, changing the resistance of the variable resistor. In turn, this changes the amount of current flowing through the oil pressure gauge and causes it to read higher. If the engine oil pressure drops, then the spring pushes the diaphragm toward the engine, again changing the resistance of the variable resistor and the current flowing through the oil pressure gauge, decreasing the pressure reading on the gauge. Some factory-installed oil pressure gauges include a warning light to warn the driver of low oil pressure. In many instances, a driver may not notice that the oil pressure gauge reading has dropped and keeps driving the vehicle, leading to engine damage. But the warning light is designed to catch the driver's attention so that he or she can stop the vehicle and investigate the cause of the low oil pressure.

If the sending unit is part of a driver information system, then the sending unit could be the switch type or the variable resistance type. It usually also would include a sensor for low oil level monitoring and maybe even an oil temperature monitor. You need to investigate various manufacturers' driver information systems to familiarize yourself with the different systems and strategies each manufacturer uses.

Oil Monitoring Systems

Oil monitoring systems are used to inform the driver when to change the oil. There are several types of oil monitoring systems. Some oil systems are simply timers that keep track of mileage and activate a warning light to notify the driver when it is time to change the engine oil. Other systems are very sophisticated, analyzing the conductivity of the oil through a sensor in the oil pan and monitoring changes that indicate it is time to change the oil. Depending upon the feedback from the sensor, the monitoring system computer will activate the change oil light or message to warn the driver that it is time to change the oil.

Another monitoring system, called an oil-life monitor, calculates the expected life of the oil and displays it to the driver. The computer receives inputs from several sensors that take into account the number of start-ups, mileage, driving habits and conditions, temperature, length of run time, and other data to calculate the remaining life of the oil, which is displayed as a percentage. When the oil is freshly changed and the oil-life monitor is reset, it will indicate that the oil life is 100%. As the oil life wears out, the monitor reads closer to 0% oil life, informing the driver of the need to change the oil (**FIGURE 7-27**). Because it monitors the conditions the oil is operating under, the life of the oil can change drastically depending on the conditions. For example, if the vehicle were only driven in moderate temperatures for long distances, the oil would be good thousands of miles longer than a vehicle driven in stop-and-go traffic and with long periods of idling. Each vehicle equipped with an oil monitoring system has a specific reset procedure to turn the light or message off after an oil change.

FIGURE 7-27 An oil life monitoring system light that indicates the vehicle needs its oil changed.

▶ Lubrication System Procedures—Maintenance and Repair

K07007 Knowledge of how to maintain a lubrication system.

In this section we go through the various procedures that you need to complete on customer's vehicles so that they are in good running order. Without regular maintenance, an internal combustion engine will seize up and fail prematurely.

Checking the Engine Oil

S07001 Check the engine oil.

Checking the engine oil level regularly is necessary and should be performed during every fuel fill-up or every other fuel fill-up, depending on the age and condition of the vehicle. There is a danger of damaging the engine if the engine oil drops too low in the oil sump. The oil level can be low either because there is an oil leak or because the engine is consuming oil by burning it. Burning engine oil could be due to worn piston rings, worn valve guides, or a malfunction with the positive crankcase ventilation (PCV) system. Checking the oil level should also be part of any pre-trip check or part of a pre-delivery inspection on a new car at the dealership.

Always make sure the vehicle is on a level surface and the engine is off before taking a reading. If you do not, you will get inaccurate readings. Also, wipe the dipstick off and reinsert it fully before removing it and reading it. When reading it, hold the dipstick horizontal so the oil does not run down the stick. Typically, the amount of oil needed to raise the oil level from the bottom of the "safe" mark on the dipstick to the "full" mark is about a quart. This amount may vary, so always check the service manual to determine the correct quantity. Always install the recommended amount and type of oil given in the service manual. Although fresh oil is translucent, whereas oil that needs to be replaced often looks black and dirty, it is usually difficult to assess the condition of engine oil simply by its color. Oil loses its clean, fresh look very quickly but may still have a lot of life left in it.

The best guide to knowing when to change the oil is the vehicle's oil-life monitor, if it is so equipped. It tells you the percentage of oil life remaining before a change is needed. If the vehicle is not equipped with an oil-life monitor, check the oil change sticker on the windshield, or ask the owner for oil change records to determine if the oil needs to be changed. This can ensure that the oil is not changed too often, which would be an unnecessary expense for the customer. Our job as technicians is to provide high-quality work only when it is truly needed by the customer. Part of being a professional is letting customers know when they do and when they do not need a service performed. Informing the customer of what needs to be done and what does not, along with giving an explanation, helps to build trust with the customer and often results in the customer returning to your shop for future repairs.

If the oil on the dipstick is not blackish in color, but looks milky-gray, it is possible that there is water (or coolant) being mixed into the oil. This could indicate a serious problem somewhere inside the engine, such as a leaking intake manifold gasket, head gasket, or a cracked cylinder head. You should report this to your supervisor immediately. Engine operating conditions can also influence the oil's condition. For instance, continuously stopping and starting the engine with very short operating cycles can cause condensation to build up inside the engine. An extreme case of this will cause very rapid oil deterioration and require frequent oil changes. The oil of a vehicle that is running too rich or that has a leaking fuel injector smells like fuel and is very thin. These problems can ruin an engine quickly, as oil will not adequately lubricate the moving surfaces in the engine. If you had to add oil to the engine, do not forget to reinstall the filler cap after topping off the oil.

To check the engine oil, follow the steps in **SKILL DRILL 7-1**:

Draining the Engine Oil

S07002 Drain the engine oil.
S07003 Inspect the engine assembly for fuel, oil, coolant, and other leaks.

Draining the engine oil is a necessary task any time the oil and filter are to be changed or whenever the oil pan needs to be removed for service work. Draining the engine oil for an oil change is necessary after a certain time or mileage interval to remove the dirt and

SKILL DRILL 7-1 Checking the Engine Oil

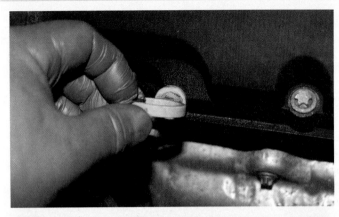

1. Locate the dipstick on the side or front of the engine block. It is usually very easy to find, with a distinctively shaped or brightly colored handle.

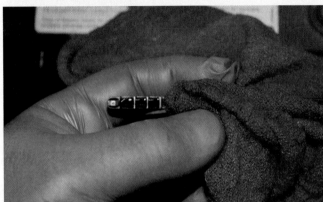

2. With the engine off, remove the dipstick, catching any drops of oil on a rag, and wipe it clean. Observe the markings on the lower end of the stick, which indicate the "full" and "add" marks or specify the "safe" zone.

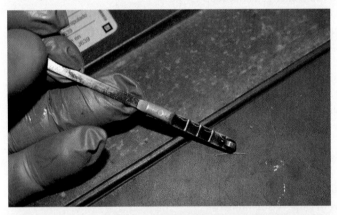

3. Replace the dipstick and push it back down into the sump as far as it will go. Remove it again, and hold it level while checking the level indicated on the bottom of the stick. If the level is near or below the "add" mark, then you will need to determine if the engine just needs to be topped off to the full level with fresh oil or replaced with new oil and oil filter.

4. Check the oil for any conditions such as unusual color or texture. Report these to your supervisor. Check the oil monitoring system, oil sticker, or service record to determine if the oil needs to be changed. (Some oil monitoring systems show the percentage of life left in the oil.)

Continued

5. If additional oil is needed, estimate the amount by checking the service manual guide to the dipstick markings. Unscrew the oil filler cap at the top of the engine, and using a funnel to avoid spillage, turn the oil bottle so the spout is on the high side of the bottle, and gently pour the oil into the engine. Recheck the oil level.

6. Replace the oil filler cap, and check the dipstick again to make sure the oil level is still correct.

particulates that are suspended in the oil. As the engine wears, the very small pieces of metal become suspended in the oil. Removing the old contaminated oil helps to make the engine last longer. Always follow the manufacturer's oil change interval, and remember that normal use and severe use have different oil change intervals.

When draining the oil, several precautions are necessary. First, the engine oil is normally changed after the engine is fully warmed up. This helps to stir up any contaminants, making them easier to flush out with the draining of the oil. However, that means that the oil can be 200–300°F (93–149°C), so use disposable gloves and don't burn yourself.

Second, make sure you locate the correct drain plug—or in some cases, the correct two drain plugs. Some vehicles have a drain plug on the transmission/transaxle that can be mistaken for the oil drain plug. If in doubt, look it up or ask your supervisor to point it out.

Third, many drain plugs are either angled off the bottom radius of the oil pan or almost sideways at the bottom side of the pan. This means when the drain plug is removed, hot oil will want to spray sideways. Always make sure you take into consideration what path the oil will take. Oil can shoot out pretty far. The lower the drain pan is compared to the drain plug, the harder it will be to judge the distance the oil will spray.

Fourth, the drain plug gasket can be of the integrated silicone, long-life style that rarely needs to be replaced. The gasket can also be a single-use gasket made of plastic, aluminum, or fiber. This type of gasket should be replaced during every oil change because it is crushed to conform to any irregularities of the pan and drain plug. Because it is crushed, it will not conform as easily the next time it is tightened. This means that someone may think it needs to be tightened excessively to prevent seepage. Over-tightening can strip the threads on the oil pan, especially if it is made of aluminum, or can strip the threads on the drain plug itself. Replace a non-silicone drain plug gasket every time it is removed.

To drain the engine oil, follow the steps in **SKILL DRILL 7-2**.

SAFETY TIP

If the engine has been running, be careful not to burn your hand or arm on the exhaust manifold or any other hot part of the engine when reaching for the dipstick. Remember, the dipstick and the oil on it will also be hot. Dripping oil from the dipstick will smoke or burn if it falls on any hot engine surfaces.

▶ TECHNICIAN TIP

Magnets are also used as a type of filter. They attract ferrous metal particles and hold them in place until they can be cleaned off. Some manufacturers use magnetic drain plugs, which then must be inspected and cleaned off as part of an oil change. Others place a magnet on the inside or outside of the oil pan. Although this style cannot readily be cleaned, it does hold the magnetic particles in place so they cannot travel freely.

SKILL DRILL 7-2 Draining the Engine Oil

1. Before you begin, clean up any oil spills; obtain the oil drain container (and make sure it has enough room for the oil to be drained); have enough new oil of the correct type to refill the engine later; and ensure that the engine oil is up to operating temperature before starting the oil change.

2. Set vehicle on lift, and lift the vehicle so that you can access the undercarriage.

3. Identify the location of the oil drain plug, which is low on the oil pan. Some vehicles have two drain plugs, draining separate sump areas. If the drain plug is leaking, damaged, or does not look right, inform your supervisor. To minimize the possibility of damage to the head of the bolt, you need a box wrench or socket to remove and replace the drain bolt. Be very careful that you do not remove the transmission drain plug by mistake.

4. Position the drain pan so it will catch the oil. Remove and inspect the drain plug and gasket. Replace the gasket if it is the replaceable type. If the threads are damaged, then the bolt may have to be replaced. Look for solid metal particles stuck to the bolt, and report these to your supervisor. They may indicate an undiagnosed problem with the engine.

Continued

5. Allow the oil to drain while you are dealing with the drain plug gasket and oil filter.

6. Screw in the drain plug all the way by hand, and then tighten it to the torque specified by the manufacturer. You can find this information in the vehicle service information. Wipe any drips from the underside of the engine.

7. Safely dispose of the drained oil according to all local regulations.

Replacing Oil Filters

Oil filters are designed to filter out particles that find their way into the oil. The filter catches particles that result from carbon from the combustion process that leaks past piston rings, or small metal flakes that result from normal engine wear. The engine oil suspends some of the particles, and the heavier particles fall to the bottom of the oil pan. The oil filter is designed to catch the particles and let the oil flow through. It is critical to change the oil filter at the manufacturer's recommended mileage to help ensure that it does not become clogged.

Some cartridge filters are near the bottom of the engine, and others are on top. Use the service information to help you locate the filter. If the filter is on the top of the engine, there is a good chance that you will need to prefill the cartridge before installing the filter end cap. Again, check the service information for the vehicle you are working on.

N07003 Perform oil and filter change.
S07004 Replace a spin-on filter.

Be careful with tightening a cartridge filter, as it is easy to crack or damage the housing—especially if it is plastic. Always follow the manufacturer's torque procedure.

Last, because the filter housing is being reused, it is important that it is clean before being reinstalled. You may need to wash it out in a clean solvent tank. Just be sure that you also remove any solvent residue before reinstalling it.

Replacing Spin-on and Cartridge Filters

S07005 Replace a cartridge filter (replaceable element).

To replace a spin-on filter, follow the steps in **SKILL DRILL 7-3**.

Refilling Engine Oil

S07006 Refill the engine oil.

It may also be necessary to refill the engine oil after a lubrication system part has been replaced, if the oil was drained. Always add the recommended grade and amount of oil listed in the service information. After adding the required amount of oil, be sure to start the engine to build oil pressure and fill the oil filter, and then shut the engine off to check for leaks and the level on the dipstick. Fill the oil to the max line and no farther.

To refill the engine oil, follow the steps in **SKILL DRILL 7-4**.

SKILL DRILL 7-3 Replacing a Spin-on Filter

1. Before removing an oil filter, refer to the service information for the vehicle, and identify the type of filter required. Make sure a suitable replacement filter is available.

2. The filter is usually located on the side of the engine block or at an angle underneath the engine but can be separate from the engine. Select the proper oil filter wrench.

3. Position a drain pan to catch any oil that leaks from the filter, and remove the filter.

Continued

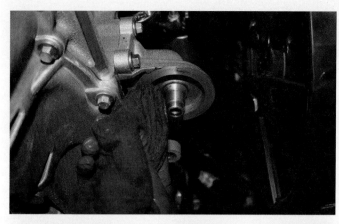

4. Clean the sealing area on the engine so that its surface and the surface of the new filter can seal properly. Make sure the O-ring from the removed filter is not still stuck to the filter mounting surface.

5. Confirm you have the correct replacement filter.

6. Smear a little oil on the surface of the new O-ring. This helps to make a tight seal and also prevents the gasket from binding and distorting while it is being tightened.

7. Screw in the filter until it just starts, and verify it cannot be pulled off. Then turn the filter by hand at least five turns until the filter lightly contacts the base.

Continued

8. To help judge how far to turn the filter to tighten it, mark the outside of the filter with a marker or a dab of oil (but remember to wipe the oil off when you have finished). Do not over-tighten the filter. Typically, three-quarters to a full turn is adequate torque for a seal that will not leak, but make sure to follow the tightening instructions for the filter, which are on the filter and/or the box it came in. Be careful not to cross-thread the oil filter on the threaded adapter fitting.

9. Replacing a cartridge filter requires the technician to unscrew the cap that is covering the cartridge.

10. Remove the old cartridge and replace with a new cartridge.

11. Then torque the cap to the manufacturer's torque specification.

SKILL DRILL 7-4 Refilling the Engine Oil

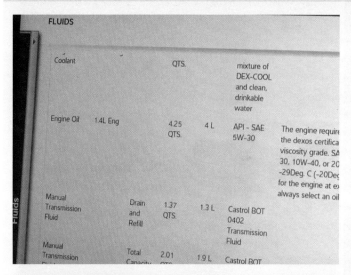

1. Using the service information, research the correct grade and the quantity of oil you need to fill the engine.

2. Turn the container of oil so that the spout is on the high side of the bottle. Pour the oil into the funnel carefully so that no oil is spilled onto the outside of the engine, and pour slowly enough to avoid the risk of blowback or overflow. Fill the engine only to the level indicated on the engine dipstick, not until the oil is coming out the top of the filler hole. Replace the filler cap.

3. Start the engine, and check the oil pressure indicator on the dash. If the oil pressure is inadequate, stop. Do not continue to run the engine.

4. If the oil pressure is good, turn the engine off, and check underneath the vehicle to make sure no oil is leaking from the oil filter or the drain plug.

Continued

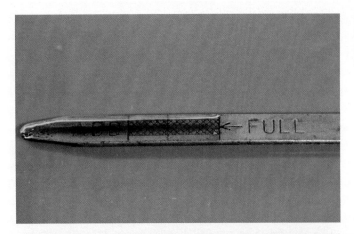

5. With the vehicle level, check the oil level again with the dipstick. It may be necessary to top off the engine by adding a small quantity of oil to compensate for the amount absorbed by the new filter. Do not overfill.

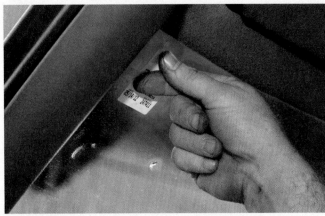

6. Refer to the owner's manual or the service information, and install an oil change sticker.

7. Reset the maintenance reminder system to remind the owner when the next oil change is due.

Vehicle Diagnosis

Changing the engine oil at the recommended time is the most important maintenance item the customer can have performed. Failure to change oil results in sludge formation, which clogs the oil passageways and keeps oil from lubricating critical parts. When bearings fail to get enough lubricant, they begin to wear and then will seize, resulting in the need for a new or rebuilt engine. An engine replacement is a vastly more expensive alternative to the relatively inexpensive oil change the customer did not want to pay for or did not have time for. As technicians, we need to educate customers on the importance of maintaining their vehicles.

Another common issue is oil leaks. You must be able to diagnose where that puddle of oil on the customer's garage floor is coming from. Oil will run down the engine from valve covers or the camshaft seals and may appear to be coming from a lower point. Remember to look over the engine closely and check all mating surfaces. Oil leaking from seals of rotating parts typically slings oil in a circle; for example, a crankshaft seal slings oil around the front of the engine in a circular pattern.

Another common area in which to check for leaks is on the oil pressure sending unit. The sending unit uses a diaphragm, which can develop a hole over time. When this happens, oil will typically leak out of the body either at the crimp or at the terminal end while the engine is running. If you watch it while it is running, you will usually see it drip. Just be aware that if the sending unit is at a downward angle, then oil from another location can possibly run down to it and then drip off it. So always look above the sending unit. If there is little to no oil above it, the sending unit is bad.

Noises are another lubrication issue found in the repair shop. Low oil pressure can result in valve lifters not pumping up, creating valvetrain noise. The use of an oil pressure gauge will show if the noise is related to low oil pressure or if it is a result of worn parts with improper running clearances. Low oil pressure can be caused by a low oil level or an oil that is too thin in the crankcase. It could also be caused by worn bearings or oil pump. Oil can be low for a couple of reasons: It may have leaked away, or it may have burnt off. An engine can leak its lubricating oil from seals or gaskets that are intended to seal the oil in. Burning the engine oil can be caused by worn piston rings or by worn valve guides that let oil into the combustion chamber or by an improperly operating PCV system. Some engines even use an automatic cut-out that turns off the engine if oil pressure falls too low.

Too little oil in the engine is a problem, but so is too much oil. The crankshaft can whip it into foam and cause leaks by flooding the seals. Another problem with excessive oil is the drag produced when the crankshaft hits the oil in the oil pan and tries to stop the crankshaft from turning. This condition causes a loss of power and results in more fuel consumption. Additionally, the foaming caused by the crankshaft hitting the oil results in the oil pump starving the engine of precious lubricating oil. Air in the oil causes problems, as the pump will send this air to the moving parts and cause damage.

Tools for Diagnosing the Lubrication System

The tools used for diagnosis of the lubrication system include the following:

- An oil pressure gauge, with various size adapters that screw into the pressurized oil passage, is used to measure the engine's oil pressure.
- A DVOM is used to test the electrical circuits of oil pressure sensors and gauges.
- Fluorescent dye and a black light are useful tools to find oil leaks. Fluorescent dye specially made for engine oil is added to the crankcase. The engine is run to circulate the oil, and then a black light is used to pinpoint the location of the leak.
- Oil pressure sending unit sockets are useful tools for removing and installing oil pressure sending units.
- A variable resistor is used to diagnose gauge problems by substituting precise resistances in the gauge circuit and comparing the gauge reading to the specifications.

Testing the Oil Pressure

Oil pressure testing has to be performed whenever low oil pressure is suspected and the oil level is within the "safe" range. If the oil pressure gauge in the dash of the vehicle shows low, you need to verify that it is correct with a manual test gauge. If the test gauge indicates a different pressure from the vehicle's gauge, you need to test the gauge according to the manufacturer's procedure.

(If an engine is noisy, it may be necessary to check oil pressure to verify that the engine is repairable. An engine that has been operated for long periods of time with no or low oil pressure will have extensive damage and in almost all cases will require complete engine replacement or overhaul. So if the noise is accompanied by low oil pressure, the low oil pressure must be diagnosed first. If the noise is accompanied by normal oil pressure, then further diagnosis of the noise is warranted.)

▶ **TECHNICIAN TIP**

Many vehicle manufacturers have moved to using a switch-type sending unit with a gauge. The switch is spring loaded so that it comes on below a predetermined pressure. But it also allows current to flow through a resistance that is in series with the switch. When the oil pressure is above the spring pressure, the resistor causes the oil pressure gauge to stay mid-scale. When oil pressure falls below this setting, the contacts open, and the gauge reads low. This can confuse drivers because the oil pressure remains very steady for many years, and all of a sudden, it drops to zero. As the engine clearances become larger, or if oil becomes thin, oil pressure drops. Once it falls low enough that spring pressure overcomes oil pressure, the gauge will read low or zero.

N07004 Perform oil pressure tests; determine needed action.
S07007 Test the oil pressure.

You need a quality oil pressure gauge of the correct pressure reading and correct threaded adapters. The oil pressure gauge is usually installed where the oil pressure sensor (sometimes called an oil pressure sending unit or oil pressure switch) is located. Remove the oil pressure sensor, and install the oil pressure gauge in its place. If oil pressure is lower than specifications, refer to service information for additional information. There may be excessive clearance in the engine bearings (which causes oil to bleed off and pressures to decline), and/or the oil pump may be worn. If the oil pressure is higher than specifications, suspect a sticking oil pressure regulator. Be sure to follow service information to troubleshoot this condition.

To perform oil pressure testing, follow the steps in **SKILL DRILL 7-5**.

SKILL DRILL 7-5 Testing the Oil Pressure

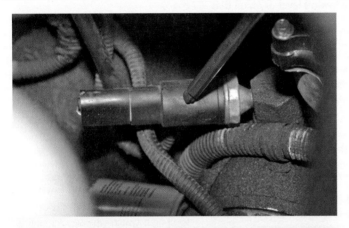

1. Locate the oil pressure sensor by using the component locator in your service information. It is often located near the oil filter.

2. Place an oil drain pan under the engine to catch any oil when you remove the oil pressure sensor.

3. Disconnect the wire harness connector, and remove the oil pressure sensor from the engine, using the recommended tool in the service information.

Continued

4. Match the adapter thread to the thread on the sending unit to ensure that the correct adapter will be screwed into the engine.

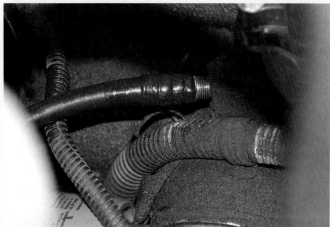

5. Carefully thread the adapter into the engine, ensuring that you do not cross-thread the adapter.

6. Connect the oil pressure gauge; then start and completely warm up the engine.

7. Compare the readings to the specifications in the service information. Your specifications may be at two different engine speeds; if so, you will need to check at both speeds.

Continued

8. Remove the manual pressure gauge and adaptor. Using a thread sealant, reinstall the oil sending unit, and torque to specifications.

9. Install the wiring and start the engine. Inspect for oil leaks and proper pressure gauge operation.

N07005 Inspect, test, and replace oil temperature and pressure switches and sensors.

S07008 Inspect the oil sensors.

▶ **TECHNICIAN TIP**

Some people erroneously refer to the low oil pressure warning system as a low oil level warning system. They think this because if the oil level gets really low, then the oil pump draws air into the lubrication system, and the oil pressure falls, turning on the low oil pressure warning light. Unfortunately, if the oil is allowed to get that low, it is doing damage to the engine. A true low oil level warning system is designed to alert the driver when the oil level approaches the "add" mark, which is well before engine damage is being done.

S07009 Inspect, test, and replace the oil temperature and pressure switches.

Inspecting Oil Sensors

Oil sensors feed oil pressure information back to the gauge or warning light to issue the operator a warning if oil pressure goes too low. Many oil sensors are typically variable resistors that change resistance based on pressure changes. The variable resistance causes the gauge to read differing amounts, depending on the variable resistance. Others have a fixed resistance in line with a spring-loaded switch. When oil pressure is above the spring pressure, the switch closes, and the gauge indicates a midpoint reading. When oil pressure is below the spring pressure, the switch opens, and the gauge reading falls toward the low-pressure side. Testing oil pressure sensors usually involves substituting the specified resistance in place of the sensor and observing the reaction of the oil pressure gauge. Be sure to follow service information to diagnose the sensor you are working with. Use care with hot engines, as serious burns can result.

Inspecting, Testing, and Replacing Oil Temperature and Pressure Switches

The oil temperature sensor or the oil pressure sensor or switches have to be inspected when there is an issue with a gauge or warning light. The driver of the vehicle may notice that the gauge or light does not operate correctly. It is your job to diagnose the gauge or light system. It may be that the gauge or light is operating as designed, and operator education is necessary. For the times when the gauges or lights are not operating as designed, following the manufacturer's troubleshooting procedure will assist you in proper diagnosis. The steps listed in Skill Drill 7-6 are a guide and should not take the place of the manufacturer's specifications. The diagnostics may reveal that a sensor or switch has to be replaced. Remember, some oil will run from the hole that the sensor is threaded into, so use a container or rag to catch any residual fluid.

To inspect, test, and replace the oil temperature and pressure switches, follow the steps in **SKILL DRILL 7-6**.

SKILL DRILL 7-6 Inspecting, Testing, and Replacing Oil Temperature and Pressure Switches

1. Locate the oil pressure switch or sensor. Use the manufacturer's service information to locate the component.

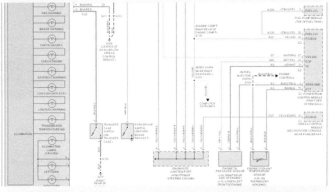

2. Disconnect the connector to the switch or sensor. If it is a sensor, determine which wire is the signal wire to the gauge or warning light. Use a wiring diagram to ensure that the correct wire is identified. You may need to use a connector end view to double-check that the correct wire is found. Refer to the manufacturer's service information.

3. Use a non-powered test light to ground the signal wire to see if the gauge or light responds. Providing you have the correct setup and the right wire, the gauge should move in one direction or the warning light should glow.

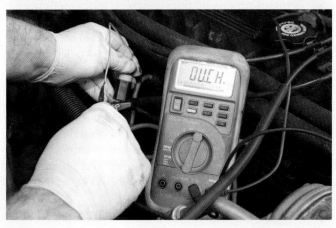

4. If the gauge or light does not respond, then use an ohmmeter to test the wiring to the gauge or light for an open or high resistance. If the gauge or light does respond, then the sensor or switch is bad.

Continued

5. Replace the oil pressure sensor or switch. Use the proper socket to remove the sensor or switch. If the new sensor does not come with thread sealant, use thread sealant on the threads, then install and torque the new sensor to the manufacturer's specifications. Remember to double-check the oil level after replacement, as the oil level may have dropped.

▶ Wrap-Up

Ready for Review

▶ Each moving part in the engine needs lubricating oil. The system that moves the oil through the engine is called the lubrication system.

▶ Lubricating oil is distilled from the crude oil and used as a base stock. Additives are added to the base stock to make the lubricating oil useful in engines. Other additives, such as thickening agents, are added to the base stocks and used as lubricating grease in bearings.

▶ Friction occurs between all surfaces that come into contact with one another and is undesirable because it leads to serious damage. Friction can make metal parts so hot they melt and fuse together. When this happens, an engine is said to have seized.

▶ Lubricating oil performs five main functions: lubricates, cushions, cools, cleans, and seals.

▶ Lubrication reduces unwanted friction and reduces wear on moving parts. Clearances, such as those between the crankshaft journal and crankshaft bearing, fill with lubricating oil so that engine parts move or float on layers of oil.

▶ How long an engine lasts depends mostly on how well it is lubricated, especially at the points of extreme loading, or high-wear areas, such as between the cam lobe and cam follower.

▶ Lubricating oil works as a cleaning agent.

▶ Engine oil plays a key role in sealing the piston rings to the cylinder walls. Without a small film of oil between the rings and cylinder walls, blowby gases would be much higher, resulting in diluted oil, lower compression, lower power, and lower fuel economy.

▶ Viscosity is a measure of how easily a liquid flows. Low-viscosity liquid is thin and flows easily. High-viscosity liquid is thick and flows slowly.

▶ There are three types of oils sold by oil manufacturers: conventional, synthetic, and synthetic blend.

▶ Conventional oil is processed from petroleum and uses additives to help the oil work properly in today's high-tech engines.

▶ Synthetic oil can be artificially made or highly processed petroleum and has fewer impurities because it is either made in a lab rather than pumped from the ground, or if it is pumped from the ground, it is more highly refined and processed.

▶ True synthetic oils are based on artificially created hydrocarbons, commonly polyalphaolefin (PAO) oil, which is a synthetic oil-based stock—meaning it is not refined from crude oil.

▶ High-mileage oils have additives in them that swell the seals in the engine to help prevent leakage.

▶ Heavy-duty oils are designed for severe service, which requires a type of oil that is engineered to take more abuse than conventional oils.

▶ Extreme-pressure additives coat parts with a protective layer so that the oil resists being forced out under a heavy load.

▶ Oxidation inhibitors stop very hot oil from combining with oxygen in the air to produce a sticky tarlike material, which coats parts and clogs the oil galleries and drain-back passages.

▶ Corrosion inhibitors help stop acids from forming that cause corrosion, especially on bearing surfaces.

▶ Antifoaming agents reduce the effect of oil churning in the crankcase and minimize foaming. Foaming allows air bubbles to form in the engine oil, reducing the lubrication quality of oil and contributing to breakdown of the oil due to oxidation.

▶ Detergents reduce carbon deposits on parts such as piston rings and valves.

- Dispersants collect particles that can block the system; the dispersants separate the particles from one another, and keep them moving. They will be removed when the oil is changed.
- Pour point depressants keep oil from forming wax particles under cold temperature operation.
- A viscosity index improver is an additive that helps to reduce the change in viscosity as the temperature of the oil changes. Viscosity index improvers also keep the engine oil from becoming too thin during hot operation.
- The American Petroleum Institute (API) sets minimum performance standards for lubricants including engine oils.
- The API has a two-part classification: service class and service standard. There are two general classifications: "S" for spark ignition engines and "C" for compression ignition engines.
- Engine oil that meets the API standards may display the API Service Symbol, which is also known as the API "donut." This protocol is important to understand because oil rated S only cannot be used in compression ignition engines unless they also carry the C rating and vice versa.
- The API symbol is the donut symbol located on the back of the oil bottle. In the top half of the symbol is the service class—S or C—and the service standard that the oil meets.
- The center part of the API symbol donut carries the SAE viscosity rating for the oil. The API symbol may also carry an energy saving designation if it is a fuel-saving oil.
- The API classifies oils into five groups.
- The International Lubricant Standardization and Approval Committee (ILSAC) works in conjunction with the API in creating new specifications for gasoline engine oil. However, ILSAC requires that the oil provide increased fuel economy over a base lubricant.
- The Society of Automotive Engineers (SAE) set the standards that oil manufactures must meet to qualify for the viscosity rating for each particular oil.
- Engine oil with an SAE number of 50 has a higher viscosity, or is thicker, than an SAE 20 oil.
- Oils with low viscosity ratings, such as SAE 0W, 5W, and 10W (the "W" stands for winter viscosity), are tested at a low temperature—around 0°F (−17.8°C).
- The Japanese Engine Oil Standards Implementation Panel (JASO) standards set the classification for motorcycle engines, both two-stroke and four-stroke, as well as Japanese automotive diesel engines.
- The European Automobile Manufacturers' Association (ACEA) classifications formulated for engine oils used in European vehicles are much more stringent than the API and ILSAC standards.
- The lubrication system is a series of engine components that work together to keep the moving parts inside an engine lubricated.
- Proper lubrication ensures that the engine runs cooler, produces maximum power, and gets maximum fuel efficiency.

- A typical lubrication system consists of an oil sump, an oil pump strainer (also called a pickup tube), an oil pump, a pressure regulator, oil galleries, an oil filter, and a low pressure warning system.
- The oil is stored in the oil sump, which is called a wet-sump systems because oil is stored in a sump or oil pan.
- Oil is drawn through the oil pump strainer from the oil sump by an oil pump. The oil travels from the oil pump to the oil filter, which removes particles of dirt from the oil. Oil moves from the filter to the oil galleries.
- Oil galleries are small passages in the cylinder block and head(s) that direct oil to the moving parts. Oil that has been pumped to the crankshaft main bearings travels through oil-ways to the connecting rods.
- Oil may also be splashed from the connecting rods onto the cylinder walls, and the circulation of the oil assists with the cooling of the internal parts.
- Modern vehicle engines use a pressure, or force-feed, lubrication system where the oil is forced throughout the engine under pressure.
- In a dry sump lubrication system, the parts are the same as a wet sump system and it lubricates the engine in the same way. The difference is the way the oil is collected and stored. In a dry sump system, the oil falls to the bottom of the engine into an oil collection pan. A scavenge pump then pumps it to an oil tank, where it is stored until the normal oil pump collects it and pumps it through the filter and engine in the normal way.
- Diesel engines are lubricated in much the same way as gasoline engines, with some differences.
- The oil pan is located at the bottom of the engine.
- On a wet sump lubricating system, the oil pan holds the entire volume of the oil required to lubricate the engine. The lowest point of the oil pan is the oil sump. This is where the oil pump pickup tube is located. The deep point in the oil pan ensures that there should never be a shortage of oil for the oil pump to pick up if the correct amount of oil is in the engine.
- The sump is equipped with a drain plug that allows the oil to be drained from the engine during oil changes.
- Some high-performance vehicles have a windage tray, which is a pan located close to the crankshaft, fitted to prevent churning of the oil by the rotation of the crankshaft.
- Baffles are flat pieces of steel placed around the oil pump pickup in the oil pan to prevent oil from surging away from the pickup during cornering, braking, and accelerating. Baffles are commonly used on vehicles that experience strong g-forces, such as rally cars, stock cars, and drag-racing cars.
- The pickup tube pulls oil from the oil sump by suction of the oil pump and atmospheric pressure. A strainer on the pickup tube stops large particles of debris from entering the oil pump and damaging it. The pickup tube leads to the inlet of the oil pump, on the low-pressure side of the oil pump.
- Most oil pumps are of the positive displacement type. This means that they move a given amount of oil from the inlet

to the outlet each revolution. The faster the pump turns, the more oil that is pumped.

▶ Oil pressure is determined by two factors: (1) the bearing clearance of the main and rod journals and (2) the amount of oil flowing in the system.

▶ In a rotor-type oil pump, an inner rotor drives an outer one; as they turn, the volume between them increases. The larger volume created between the rotors lowers the pressure at the pump inlet, creating a vacuum, which allows atmospheric pressure to move the oil.

▶ The crescent pump works like the rotor type pump. It is usually mounted on the front of the cylinder block and straddles the front of the crankshaft. The inner gear is then driven by the crankshaft directly. An external toothed gear meshes with the inner one.

▶ In a geared oil pump, the driving gear meshes with a second gear. As both gears turn, their teeth separate, creating a low-pressure area, allowing allows atmospheric pressure to move the oil.

▶ An oil pressure relief valve stops excess pressure from developing. It is like a controlled leak, releasing just enough oil back to the oil sump to regulate the pressure in the whole system.

▶ The oil pressure relief valve contains a spring that is calibrated to a specific pressure. When the pressure is reached, the oil pressure relief valve slides open just enough to bleed sufficient oil back to the pan to maintain the preset maximum relief pressure.

▶ There are some factors that affect the oil pressure in the engine. Bearing clearance helps create oil pressure, oil pump output pressure, oil quality, oil filter quality, and engine rpm.

▶ The quality of the components used has a dramatic effect on the output of the lubrication system and quality should not be compromised.

▶ There are two basic oil-filtering systems: full-flow and bypass.

▶ The full-flow filter is designed to filter all of the oil before delivering it to the engine. The location of the filter right after the oil pump ensures that all of the oil is filtered before it is sent to the lubricated components.

▶ The bypass filtering system is more common on diesel engines and is used in conjunction with a full-flow filtering system.

▶ Most full-flow oil filters will catch particles down to 30 microns. A micron is 0.000039″ (0.001 mm).

▶ There are two common types of oil filters: spin-on and cartridge.

▶ The spin-on type is a self-contained unit that just spins on the filter housing and you must following the tightening instructions to avoid leaks.

▶ The cartridge style of oil filter uses a separate reusable metal or plastic housing and a replaceable filter cartridge along with sealing O-rings.

▶ Most oil filters on diesel engines are larger than those on similar gasoline engines, and some diesel engines have two oil filters.

▶ Diesel engines produce more carbon particles than gasoline engines, so the oil filter can have a full-flow element to trap larger impurities and a bypass element to collect sludge and carbon soot.

▶ In a bypass system, the bypass element filters only some of the oil from the oil pump by tapping an oil line into the oil gallery. It collects finer particles than a full-flow filter.

▶ The anti-drainback valve is used to keep the oil filter full of oil once the engine is shut off so that the next startup the engine will not have to wait as long for oil pressure. This valve is built into the filter most of the time, so it gets regularly changed when the filter gets replaced.

▶ Oil filters are designed to work with the engine that they are meant for and are not supposed to be used on engines that they are not designed to work on.

▶ If the wrong filter is installed on the engine it may create external leaks, it may lower the oil pressure, or it may explode from excess pressure.

▶ Always make sure you have the correct oil filter before you install it on the engine.

▶ Some connecting rods have oil spurt holes that are positioned to receive oil from similar holes in the crankshaft. Oil can then spurt out at the point in the engine cycle when the largest area of cylinder wall is exposed and lubricates the cylinder walls and piston wrist pin, and may help cool the underside of the piston.

▶ Oil coolers are installed in line with the oil system so that the oil is pumped through a heat exchanger similarly to what happens in the cooling system; it is usually part of the engine cooling system and uses coolant to help transfer heat to the outside air.

▶ Analysis of the engine oil is a useful way to see what parts are wearing in the engine.

▶ The oil analysis report lists physical properties such as viscosity, condensed water, fuel dilution, antifreeze, acids, metal content, and oil additives. Each of these attributes can be used to determine the condition of the oil as well as the engine.

▶ As a technician, a simple test to check for excessive engine wear is to take a white paper towel and wipe the oil from the dipstick on it. Hold the towel to the light, and move it back and forth to see if light reflects from metal. If metal is in the oil, there is substantial wear happening inside the engine.

▶ Warning systems are used to warn of lubrication system failure. If oil pressure falls too low, a pressure sensor threaded into a gallery can activate a low oil pressure warning light, register pressure on a gauge, or turn on a low oil pressure warning message.

▶ Oil monitoring systems are used to inform the driver when the oil has to be changed.

▶ Some oil systems are simply timers that keep track of mileage and activate a warning light to notify the driver when it is time to change the engine oil. Other systems are very sophisticated, analyzing the conductivity of the oil through a sensor in the oil pan and monitoring changes that indicate it is time to change the oil.

▶ When the oil is freshly changed and the oil-life monitor is reset, it will say the oil life is 100%. As the oil life wears out, the monitor reads closer to 0% oil life, informing the driver of the need to change the oil.

▶ Checking the engine oil level regularly is necessary and should be performed during every fuel fill-up or every other fuel fill-up, depending on the age and condition of the vehicle. There is a danger of damaging the engine if the engine oil drops too low in the oil sump.

▶ Always make sure the vehicle is on a level surface and the engine is off before taking a reading. If you do not, you will get inaccurate readings. Also, wipe the dipstick off and reinsert it fully before removing it and reading it.

▶ When reading the oil dipstick, hold the dipstick horizontal so the oil will not run down the stick. Typically, the amount of oil needed to raise the oil level from the bottom of the "safe" mark on the dipstick to the "full" mark is about a quart. This amount may vary, so always check the service manual to determine the correct quantity.

▶ If the oil on the dipstick is not blackish in color, but looks milky-gray, it is possible that there is water (or coolant) being mixed into the oil.

▶ When draining the oil, several precautions are necessary. Engine oil is normally changed after the engine is fully warmed up, so use disposable gloves, and don't burn yourself.

▶ Make sure you locate the correct drain plug.

▶ Many drain plugs are either angled off the bottom radius of the oil pan or almost sideways at the bottom side of the pan. This means when the drain plug is removed, hot oil will want to spray sideways. Always make sure you take into consideration what path the oil will take. Oil can shoot out pretty far.

▶ The drain plug gasket can be of the integrated-silicone, long-life style that rarely needs to be replaced. The gasket can also be a one-time-use gasket made of plastic, aluminum, or fiber. This type of gasket should be replaced during every oil change because it is crushed to conform to any irregularities of the pan and drain plug.

▶ Over-tightening can strip the threads on the oil pan, especially if it is made of aluminum, or can strip the threads on the drain plug itself. Replace a non-silicone drain plug gasket every time it is removed.

▶ Before removing an oil filter, refer to the service information for the vehicle and identify the type of filter required. Make sure a suitable replacement filter is available.

▶ Changing the engine oil at the recommended time is the most important maintenance item the customer can have performed. Failure to change oil results in sludge formation, which clogs the oil passageways and keeps oil from lubricating critical parts.

▶ Oil will run down the engine from valve covers or the camshaft seals and may appear to be coming from a lower point.

▶ Oil leaking from seals of rotating parts typically slings oil in a circle; for example, a crankshaft seal slings oil around the front of the engine in a circular pattern.

▶ Another common area in which to look for leaks is on the oil pressure sending unit.

▶ Noises are another lubrication issue found in the repair shop. Low oil pressure can result in valve lifters not pumping up, creating valvetrain noise. The use of an oil pressure gauge will show whether the noise is related to low oil pressure or is a result of worn parts with improper running clearances.

▶ Oil pressure testing will have to be performed whenever low oil pressure is suspected and the oil level is within the "safe" range.

▶ You need to verify that the dash gauge is correct with a manual test gauge.

▶ If the test gauge indicates a different pressure from the vehicle's gauge, you need to test the gauge according to the manufacturer's procedure.

▶ Be sure to follow service information to diagnose the oil pressure sensor you are working with.

Key Terms

The American Petroleum Institute (API) Sets minimum performance standards for lubricants, including engine oils.

anti-drainback valve Used to keep the oil filter full of oil once the engine is shut off so that at the next start-up, the engine will not have to wait as long for oil pressure.

antifoaming agents Reduce the effect of oil churning in the crankcase and minimize foaming. Foaming allows air bubbles to form in the engine oil, reducing the lubrication quality of oil and contributing to breakdown of the oil due to oxidation. Because air is compressible, oil with foam reduces the ability of the oil to keep the moving parts separated, causing more wear and friction. The antifoaming additives keep these conditions from occurring.

baffles Panels constructed in the oil pan to direct the flow of oil regardless of the angle of the engine in relationship to the ground. So if you are driving on a hill, the oil pump will continue to be fully submerged because of the baffles keeping the oil from moving to the low end of the oil pan.

British thermal units (BTUs) The amount of work needed to raise the temperature of 1 lb of water by 1°F, which equals about 1055 joules.

conventional oil Type of oil that is processed from crude oil to the desired viscosity, after which additives are added to increase wear resistance.

corrosion inhibitors Help stop acids that cause corrosion from forming, especially on bearing surfaces. Corrosion due to acid etches into bearing surfaces and causes premature wear of the bearings.

crescent pump Usually mounted on the front of the cylinder block and straddles the front of the crankshaft. The inner gear is then driven by the crankshaft directly. An external toothed gear meshes with the inner one. Some gear teeth are meshed, but others are separated by the crescent-shaped part of the pump housing. The increasing volume between gear teeth causes pressure to fall, creating a vacuum, and atmospheric pressure pushes oil into the pump. Oil is then carried around between the gears and crescent before being discharged to the outlet port.

crude oil Oil that originates from the ground; it is then refined into a usable substance.

detergents Reduce carbon deposits on parts such as piston rings and valves.

dipper Used in a splash lubrication system. This scope, attached to the bottom of the connecting rod, dips into the oil and throws it up on the cylinder wall each revolution.

dispersants Collect particles that can block the system; the dispersants separate the particles from one another, and keep them moving. They are removed when the oil is changed.

dry sump lubrication system A type of lubricating system with an external reservoir that houses the oil until the pump needs it to pressurize and distribute it through the engine.

European Automobile Manufacturers' Association (ACEA) Creates classifications formulated for engine oils used in European vehicles; these classifications are much more stringent than the API and ILSAC standards.

extreme loading The areas in the engine that are high stress because of the location of the components.

extreme-pressure additives Coat parts with a protective layer so that the oil resists being forced out under heavy load.

full-flow filters Type of filters that are designed to filter all of the oil before delivering it to the engine.

geared oil pump The driving gear meshes with a second gear as both gears turn, and their teeth separate, creating a low-pressure area. Higher atmospheric pressure outside forces the oil up into the inlet, which fills the spaces between the gear teeth. As the gears rotate, they carry oil around the chamber. As the teeth mesh again, oil is forced from the outlet into the oil gallery and toward the oil filter, where it is filtered of any particles.

gelling The thickening of oil to a point that it will not flow through the engine; it becomes close to a solid in extreme cold temperatures.

hydrocracking Refining crude oil with hydrogen, resulting in a base oil that has the higher performance characteristics of synthetic oils.

The International Lubricant Standardization and Approval Committee (ILSAC) International body that rates gasoline and engine oils to meet the standards set forth by the manufacturers' requirements.

The Japanese Engine Oil Standards Implementation Panel (JASO) Japanese standards set for the classification of motorcycle engines, both two-stroke and four-stroke, as well as Japanese automotive diesel engines.

lubrication system Refers to the oil circuit that sends lubrication throughout the engine.

lubricating oil Oil distilled from crude oil and used as a base stock in the oil that you use in vehicles.

oil galleries The passageways that carry oil through the engine. They are either cast or drilled into the engine block and head(s).

oil monitoring systems Monitor engine running conditions to calculate the condition of the oil in the engine. When the condition of the oil falls below the specification, the oil monitoring system alerts the driver to change the oil.

oil pan Located at the bottom of the engine, this component usually covers the crankshaft and rods, commonly where the oil sump is located on a wet sump oil system.

oil pressure relief valve A calibrated spring-loaded valve that allows for pressure bleed-off if the oil pump creates too much pressure.

oil pump A positive pressure pump that produces oil flow within the engine and lubricates the internal moving components.

oil pump pickup tube Attached to the oil pump and fully submerged in the oil pan sump so that it is always submerged in oil. There is usually a strainer attached to it so that no debris can reach the oil pump.

oil slinger Usually attached to the crankshaft and half-submerged in oil, causing it to throw the oil onto the moving parts with every rotation.

oil sump The location of the engine where the oil collects after it runs off the rotating assembly and off the valvetrain.

oxidation inhibitors Stop very hot oil from combining with oxygen in the air to produce a sticky tarlike material that coats parts and clogs the oil galleries and drain-back passages.

polyalphaolefin (PAO) oil An artificially made base stock that is not refined from crude oil.

pour point depressants Keep oil from forming wax particles under cold-temperature operation.

pressure or force-fed lubrication system Type of oiling system that has a pump that creates positive pressure to shoot oil throughout the engine's moving parts.

rotor-type oil pump An inner rotor driving an outer one; as they turn, the volume between them increases. The larger volume created between the rotors lowers the pressure at the pump inlet, creating a vacuum. Outside atmospheric pressure, which is higher, forces oil into the pump, and the oil fills the spaces between the rotor lobes. As the lobes of the inner rotor move into the spaces in the outer rotor, oil is squeezed out through the outlet.

scavenge pump Type of pump used in a dry sump oil system to remove the oil from the oil reservoir and pump it through the engine.

The Society of Automotive Engineers (SAE) Body that started out with setting standards that oil manufacturers must meet to qualify for the viscosity rating for that particular grade of oil

splash lubrication Type of lubrication system that uses a dipper to throw oil up on the cylinder walls and onto the crankshaft to lubricate the internal components.

synthetic blend Type of oil that is cheaper than synthetic as it utilizes conventional oil along with synthetic to create an oil that has the best of both worlds.

synthetic oil Artificially made or heavily processed oil that has been engineered with enhanced lubricating properties.

viscosity The measurement of how easily a liquid flows; the most common organization that rates lubricating fluids is SAE.

viscosity index improver An additive that helps to reduce the change in viscosity as the temperature of the oil changes. Viscosity index improvers also keep the engine oil from becoming too thin during hot operation.

windage tray Component usually made out of sheet metal or plastic; it prevents the churning of oil by the rotation of the crankshaft.

Review Questions

1. Lubricating oil performs all of the below functions, *except*:
   a. cleaning.
   b. powering.
   c. sealing.
   d. cooling.
2. Which of these additives reduces carbon deposits on parts such as piston rings and valves?
   a. Oxidation inhibitors
   b. Corrosion inhibitors
   c. Detergents
   d. Dispersants
3. All of the below are advantages of synthetic oil over conventional oil, *except*:
   a. cost-effectiveness.
   b. better low-temperature viscosity.
   c. fewer wax impurities.
   d. operation at higher temperatures.
4. Choose the correct statement:
   a. A dry sump system collects and stores oil.
   b. A wet sump system collects and stores oil.
   c. The wet sump system is the best fit during aggressive driving conditions.
   d. The dry sump system is the best fit in low performance applications.
5. If oil pressure falls too low, a pressure sensor in a gallery can do any of the below, *except*:
   a. adding oil from the gallery.
   b. activating a warning light.
   c. registering on a gauge.
   d. turning on a warning message.
6. Which of the following statements is true of a splash lubrication system?
   a. Oil that is splashed around usually comes from an oil pump.
   b. It can lubricate all of the parts on bigger engines.
   c. Diesel engines use only the splash lubrication system.
   d. Oil is thrown around and gets into spaces that need lubrication.

7. Which of these is the best guide to knowing when to change the oil?
   a. Dipstick
   b. Oil-life monitor
   c. Oil level sensor
   d. Pressure gauge
8. If the oil on the dipstick looks milky gray, it is possible that there is water (or coolant) being mixed into the oil. This could have been caused by any of the below, *except*:
   a. a bad head gasket.
   b. cracked head.
   c. leaky oil cooler.
   d. leaky fuel injector.
9. Choose the correct statement with respect to oil change.
   a. Normal use and severe use have the same oil change intervals.
   b. When draining oil, the oil should be cold.
   c. The drain plug should be tightened with maximum force to prevent oil leak.
   d. The engine should be fully warmed up when draining oil.
10. Excessive oil results in all of the below, *except*:
   a. low oil pressure.
   b. oil leak.
   c. drag.
   d. foaming.

ASE Technician A/Technician B Style Questions

1. Technician A says that oil with the API symbol is okay to run in automotive engines, without problems. Technician B says that bearing clearance must be maintained to keep the oil pressure up. Who is correct?
   a. Tech A
   b. Tech B
   c. Both A and B
   d. Neither A nor B
2. Technician A states that the SAE grading system allows for manufacturers and consumers to understand the abilities of specific types of oil. Technician B states that ACEA oil standards are less stringent than those of API or ILSAC. Who is correct?
   a. Tech A
   b. Tech B
   c. Both A and B
   d. Neither A nor B
3. Technician A says that a dry sump lubrication system is used when space is tight, as the oil pan on this type of system is very shallow. Technician B states that a wet sump oiling system is the most common system on the market today. Who is correct?
   a. Tech A
   b. Tech B
   c. Both A and B
   d. Neither A nor B

4. Technician A says that oil pumps are usually driven by the crankshaft or the camshaft. Technician B states that oil filters filter all of the oil before it goes into the oil galleys in the engine. Who is correct?
   a. Tech A
   b. Tech B
   c. Both A and B
   d. Neither A nor B

5. Technician A says that the anti-drain-back valve is located in the in the crankshaft galley. Technician B says using the wrong oil filter can cause internal engine component failure. Who is correct?
   a. Tech A
   b. Tech B
   c. Both A and B
   d. Neither A nor B

6. Technician A states that an oil pressure sensor is located in an oil gallery so that it can receive pressure from the oil pump the measure. Technician B says that the oil pressure sensor is usually located near the oil filter. Who is correct?
   a. Tech A
   b. Tech B
   c. Both A and B
   d. Neither A nor B

7. Technician A states when checking the oil in an engine the engine must be off. Technician B states that if you check the oil when the engine is running, it will be over full. Who is correct?
   a. Tech A
   b. Tech B
   c. Both A and B
   d. Neither A nor B

8. Technician A says when tightening the oil drain plug you should make it as tight as possible so it doesn't leak. Technician B says that the technician should tighten every bolt to the toque specification that the manufacture recommends. Who is correct?
   a. Tech A
   b. Tech B
   c. Both A and B
   d. Neither A nor B

9. Technician A says when refilling the engine after an oil change, you should over fill it so that you know that it has enough oil in it. Technician B says that you should fill the engine to the level recommend by the manufacturer. Who is correct?
   a. Tech A
   b. Tech B
   c. Both A and B
   d. Neither A nor B

10. Technician A says that there are usually multiple oil pressure specifications based on the rpm of the engine, and they all should be checked. Technician B says removing the oil pressure send usually requires a specialty socket. Who is correct?
    a. Tech A
    b. Tech B
    c. Both A and B
    d. Neither A nor B

CHAPTER 8
Engine Cooling Systems

NATEF Tasks

- **N08001** Inspect, remove, and replace water pump.
- **N08002** Identify causes of engine overheating.

Knowledge Objectives

After reading this chapter, you will have:

- **K08001** Knowledge of cooling systems on an internal combustion engine.
- **K08002** Knowledge of engine coolant types and characteristics.
- **K08003** Knowledge of different types of cooling systems.
- **K08004** Knowledge of coolant flow inside an engine.
- **K08005** Knowledge of cooling system components.
- **K08006** Knowledge of heater core, control valve, and actuators.

Skills Objectives

- **S08001** Test the heater control valve.

You Are the Automotive Technician

A customer brings his 2009 Honda Accord into your dealership, complaining about the coolant boiling over on hot days. The engine gauge gets higher than normal, but never to the red zone, when steam comes out from under the hood. You ask some clarifying questions, and he gives these answers: It happens most during stop-and-go traffic on his way home from work, which is the hot time of the day. He isn't sure whether or not the electric cooling fan is coming on, because he is focused on traffic. He says that the quick lube shop takes care of his fluids, so he doesn't know if it is using coolant or not. He agrees to let you diagnose it, so you take it back to the shop and verify that the coolant level is near the full mark. You then take a minute to plan your steps for diagnosis.

1. What are the possible causes for coolant that boils over below the red zone?
2. How can engine operating temperature be verified?
3. What two factors determine the boiling point of coolant?
4. What are some of the most likely causes of coolant that boils over when in the red zone?

K08001 Knowledge of cooling systems on an internal combustion engine.

▶ Introduction

Cooling systems play a critical role in the life span of the engine. Typically, a great deal of focus is placed on engine lubrication and the maintenance of the engine's lubrication system, but little focus is placed on the engine's cooling system. Yet, because the Department of Transportation has stated that cooling system failure is the leading cause of mechanical breakdowns on the highway, it deserves our attention. The cooling system can have a huge effect on the lubrication system and can also affect engine emissions and fuel economy, thus making its role a significant one.

This chapter explains the importance of modern cooling system maintenance. We cover coolant, what it is made of, how it works, and what will happen if the cooling system is not maintained. The chapter also discusses all the components of the cooling system and how each contributes to the function of cooling the engine.

▶ Cooling Fundamentals

Heat is thermal energy. It cannot be destroyed; it can only be transferred. It always moves from areas of higher temperature to areas of lower temperature. This principle is applied to the transfer of heat energy from engine parts to ambient air, using the coolant as a medium to carry it. To control this heat transfer, it is necessary to understand how heat behaves. Heat travels in three ways:

1. From one solid to another, by a process called **conduction** (**FIGURE 8-1**)
2. Through liquids and gases by a process called **convection**, whereby heat follows paths called convection currents (**FIGURE 8-2**)
3. Through space, by **radiation** (**FIGURE 8-3**)

Heat Transfer

The internal combustion engine relies on the heat of combustion to produce torque to move the vehicle and power accessories. Unfortunately, much of the heat produced during combustion is not used productively and must be removed to avoid overheating the engine. No matter how efficiently fuel burning occurs, and no matter the size of the engine, the heat energy generated never completely transforms into kinetic energy (**FIGURE 8-4**). Some heat energy remains unused for powering the vehicle and is typically wasted in three ways: (1) About 33% is wasted by being dumped straight out of the exhaust to the atmosphere (some of this wasted energy can be recovered by a turbocharger); (2) about 33% is wasted by the cooling system, which prevents overheating of the engine components; and (3) about

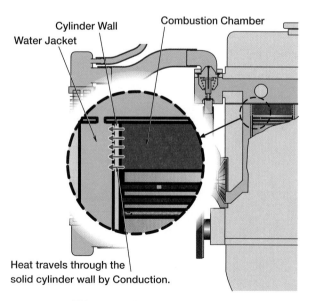

FIGURE 8-1 This process, known as conduction, allows heat to be conducted from one piece of matter to another, which it is usually touching.

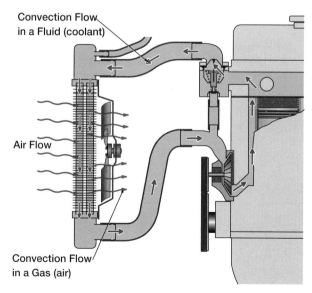

FIGURE 8-2 The convection process is the transfer of heat; hotter fluid rises to the top, and the denser colder fluid sinks under the influence of gravity.

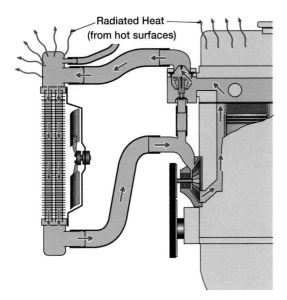

FIGURE 8-3 Radiation is the transfer of heat through molecules in the air to another object, which accepts those molecules and heats up as a result.

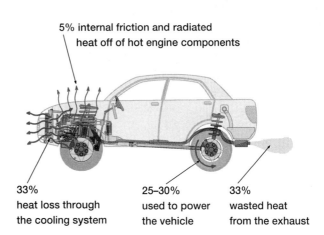

5% internal friction and radiated heat off of hot engine components

33% heat loss through the cooling system

25–30% used to power the vehicle

33% wasted heat from the exhaust

FIGURE 8-4 An internal combustion engine creates a lot of heat as it operates, which means it must dispel the heat from the components or risk failure of the components.

5% is wasted by internal friction and from radiating off hot engine components straight to the atmosphere. This leaves only about 25% to 30% of the original energy that is used for powering the vehicle and its accessories. However, turbocharged vehicles recover some of the energy lost from the exhaust, bringing engine efficiency up to near 35%.

Principles of Engine Cooling

From the **second law of thermodynamics**, we know that heat always moves from hot to cold. These principles are put to use in the automotive cooling system to keep everything working properly. The automotive cooling system provides a means of transferring heat from the hot parts of the engine to ambient air. This can be accomplished through a group of parts working together to circulate coolant throughout a sealed system to carry heat away from those engine parts. Heat can then be released to outside air or to air entering the passenger compartment for comfort purposes. Manufacturers use various cooling system configurations, but the basic concept is to transfer excessive heat from hotter to cooler environments or materials. Regardless of the parts used by the manufacturer, the job is the same. You might be thinking that if some engine cooling is good, then more must be better. But that is not the case. Engines have an ideal operating temperature somewhere around 200°F (93°C), give or take 20°F (11°C), depending on the vintage of the vehicle. The purpose of the cooling system is to allow the engine to warm up to its optimum temperature as quickly as possible, and then transfer any excess heat energy to the atmosphere, thereby maintaining that ideal temperature.

Most automotive engines are liquid cooled, although some manufacturers have used air-cooled engines. A liquid-cooled system uses coolant, a fluid that contains special antifreezing and anticorrosion chemicals mixed with water (**FIGURE 8-5**). In general terms, a water pump causes coolant to flow through passages in the engine, picking up heat along the way, and then through a cooler radiator where it gives up that heat. The radiator accepts hot coolant from the engine and lowers its temperature. As air moves over and through the radiator, the heat energy is transferred from the coolant to the ambient air. The lower-temperature coolant is returned to the engine to absorb more heat energy and continue the cycle. The circulation of the coolant is controlled by the thermostat, which opens and

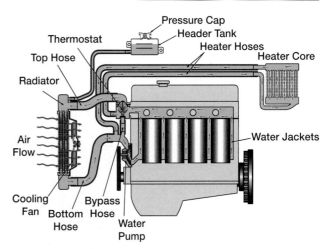

FIGURE 8-5 A basic layout of a cooling system on a modern automotive engine.

FIGURE 8-6 This container helps keep preheated coolant available to speed up the process of heating up the engine in the next engine cycle. This particular feature was only used on the Prius, but similar types of components are utilized on different vehicles.

▶ TECHNICIAN TIP

If you need to replace a pressure cap, use only a cap with the correct recommended pressure. If a cap with a lower pressure rating is installed, it will lower the boiling point of the coolant. Alternatively, a higher rated cap increases the boiling point and could result in a hose, radiator, or heater core bursting if pressures get too high.

SAFETY TIP

Because the pressurized coolant in the cooling system boils at a higher temperature than when the radiator pressure cap is removed, you should *never* remove a radiator pressure cap on a hot engine. If the coolant is above 212°F (110°C), all of the coolant will turn to steam as soon as the pressure is released, pushing superheated steam out the radiator, potentially scalding you.

K08002 Knowledge of engine coolant types and characteristics.

closes coolant flow from the engine to the radiator. When the engine is cold, coolant circulates through the engine (and heater core) only. Once the engine warms up, the thermostat opens and allows coolant from the engine to flow through the radiator.

Some newer vehicles use a coolant heat storage system (CHSS) like the one utilized in the early model Prius. This system uses a vacuum-insulated container, similar to a thermos bottle (**FIGURE 8-6**). The storage container holds an amount of hot coolant and maintains the temperature for up to three days when the engine is shut down. When the vehicle is started the next time, a small electric water pump preheats the engine by circulating this hot coolant through the engine, which greatly reduces hydrocarbon exhaust emissions during start-up and warm-up.

Air cooling is common on smaller internal combustion engines. Most engines use cooling fins. Their design makes the exposed surface area as large as possible, which allows more heat energy to radiate away and be carried off in convection currents in the air. Many small engines also use a fan to direct air through and over the cooling fins, which increases the cooling capacity. Air-cooled engines have fallen out of favor in passenger vehicles because they are harder to maintain at a stable temperature, thereby increasing emissions output of the engine (**FIGURE 8-7**).

Vehicle Coolant

Coolant is a mixture of water and antifreeze, which is used to remove heat from the engine. If an engine did not have the heat removed from it, it would fail very quickly. Coolant absorbs the heat from the engine by convection. Because coolant contacts the hot metal directly, it is a very effective heat sink. The coolant is important for three reasons: (1) It prevents an engine from overheating while in use; (2) it keeps the engine from freezing while not in use in cold climates; and (3) it prevents corrosion of the parts in the cooling system.

Water alone is by far the best coolant there is, as it can absorb a larger amount of heat than most other liquids. But water has some drawbacks. It freezes if its temperature drops below 32°F (0°C) (the temperature at which water becomes a solid). As water freezes, it expands into a solid. If it expands in the coolant passages inside the engine, these passages—typically made of cast aluminum or cast iron—will not flex to allow expansion and will break. This renders the engine inoperative and unrepairable in most cases.

FIGURE 8-7 An air-cooled engine cooling system, which is a finned type of system that is integrated with a cylinder block and works by dispersing the heat to the surrounding air. It was used in some early model vehicles but is now reserved for smaller engines like lawn mowers.

Another thing to realize about using water alone as a coolant is that water is corrosive and causes metal to rust. Think about a piece of unpainted metal that is lying outside in the rain. Rust and corrosion build up quickly on that metal simply because of the reaction (oxidation) of the metal, water, and oxygen. Antifreeze prevents corrosion and rusting through anticorrosion additives (called corrosion inhibitors) mixed into the solution. Another important note on water is that water contains minerals and will potentially lead to excessive deposits even when added to antifreeze. Because of this, most manufacturers recommend using distilled water for cooling systems.

Antifreeze is mixed with water to lower the freezing point of water and reduce the chances of cracking the engine block, cylinder heads, and other cooling system components. Antifreeze is made from one of two base chemicals—ethylene glycol or propylene glycol—plus a mixture of additives to protect against corrosion and foaming. Ethylene and propylene glycol may achieve a maximum very low freezing point of –70°F (–57°C) when mixed with the appropriate amount of water. **Ethylene glycol** is a chemical that resists freezing but is very toxic to humans and animals. **Propylene glycol** is another chemical that resists freezing but is not toxic and is used in nontoxic antifreezes. Either of these antifreezes actually freezes around 0°F (–18°C) if not mixed with water, so water is a necessary part of coolant. The freezing point of coolant varies depending upon how much water is added to the antifreeze (**FIGURE 8-8**). Because antifreeze does not absorb heat as effectively as water, it should not be mixed at a ratio higher than 65% antifreeze and 35% water. Using a higher proportion of antifreeze actually reduces the cooling quality of the mixture and raises the operating temperature of the engine.

The best coolant is a 50/50 balance of water and antifreeze, making it an ideal coolant for both hot and cold climates and providing adequate corrosion protection. Also, when antifreeze is added at a 50% mixture, the boiling point increases from 212°F (100°C) to around 228°F (109°C). As you can see, this is an extremely beneficial characteristic of antifreeze as manufacturers continue to build engines that are more powerful, create more heat, and operate at higher temperatures.

Antifreeze can be purchased as straight antifreeze (100%) or as a 50/50 premix with water. Straight antifreeze that you buy from the dealer or parts store consists of three parts: glycol (around 96%), corrosion inhibitors and additives (around 2–3%), and water (around 2%). Glycol, as discussed previously, keeps the freezing point low and the boiling point high. Corrosion inhibitors and additives prevent corrosion and erosion, resist foaming, ensure coolant is compatible with cooling system component materials and hard water, resist sedimentation, and balance the acid-to-alkaline content of the antifreeze. Water is added to blend the inhibitors with the glycol.

Antifreeze is an amazing chemical that performs a monumental task in the operation of our vehicles. It works so well that customers often overlook it in maintenance. However, because the additives wear out and become less effective over time, coolant does need to be changed at recommended intervals. Doing so reduces the possibility of engine damage and failure over time. Likewise, lubrication enhancers, which keep the water pump and seals functioning properly, wear out and need to be replaced.

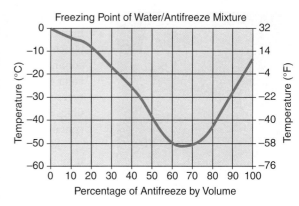

FIGURE 8-8 Freezing point of antifreeze and water solution.

Coolant Types

As mentioned earlier, water-cooled engines must be protected from freezing, boiling, and corrosion. Water absorbs a larger amount of heat than most other liquids, but it freezes at a relatively high temperature, and it is corrosive. Mixing antifreeze with water provides an adequate coolant solution by lowering the freezing point of water, raising the boiling point of water a bit, and providing anticorrosive properties.

Several types of coolants are available for use in the liquid-cooled automobile engine. The recommended coolant depends on the original equipment manufacturer's (OEM) recommendation. It may be influenced by the metallurgy of the engine parts and the length of time or mileage between scheduled services that the manufacturer has determined.

FIGURE 8-9 Inorganic Additive Technology antifreeze is the original engine coolant which is usually ethylene glycol or propylene glycol.

FIGURE 8-10 An OAT coolant that is engineered to last for much longer than IAT coolant and is usually an orangish-red color.

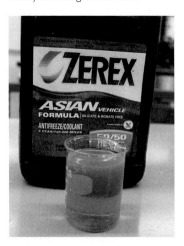

FIGURE 8-11 HOAT is a mixture of inorganic and organic coolant and is very intolerant to outside influences, which causes it to become acidic.

It is important to note that brands and types of coolant (antifreeze) differ from one manufacturer to another. Some believe coolant can be identified according to its color, which may be anything from green or purple to yellow/gold, orange, blue, or pink. OEM cooling system designs and coolant recommendations have changed in recent years, so the color of coolant is no longer a reliable way to identify a particular type of antifreeze. Mixing types of antifreeze can cause a reaction that turns the chemicals in antifreeze to sludge that plugs up the passages in the system, including the radiator and heater core. Always read the container label, and follow OEM coolant recommendations.

Most coolant types start with a base of ethylene glycol and add specific corrosion inhibitors, lubricants, and other additives, which all determine the type of coolant it is. Each coolant has antifoaming and antiscale additives. Maintaining the proper coolant acid/alkaline pH balance is also critical (which also determines when to perform coolant replacement).

Ethylene glycol is a toxic chemical that works very well as an antifreeze. Ethylene glycol mixes well with water and has a low viscosity, allowing it to circulate easily through the cooling system. Propylene glycol performs essentially the same as ethylene glycol except it is not as toxic. In fact, propylene glycol antifreeze is sold as a nontoxic coolant.

IAT

The first category of coolant, IAT, is an early designed chemical formula that became available in the 1930s and was green in color (**FIGURE 8-9**). This coolant is still in use today. It contains phosphate and silicate as corrosion additives. Phosphate protects iron and steel parts, and silicate keeps aluminum from corroding. IAT coolant needs to be changed every two years or 24,000 miles (39,000 km) because the additives break down. This coolant is old technology that has been used for many years in the automotive world and has now been phased out because of its lack of flexibility in usage.

OAT

The second category, OAT, is a longer-lasting coolant. Called extended-life coolant, it is designed to be changed at five years or 100,000–150,000 miles (160,934–241,000 km), a giant increase in the change interval from IAT coolant. OAT coolant was introduced in North America around 1994 and was intended for certain vehicles of that year and newer. One example of OAT is Dex-Cool®, the orange coolant used by GM (**FIGURE 8-10**). The anticorrosion additives in OAT coolant do not break down as quickly, which explains the longer service time. The primary additives in OAT coolant are organic acids, such as ethylhexanoic acid as a corrosion inhibitor. These coolants do not use the additives used in IAT coolants. Like the rest of the coolants explored in this chapter, lack of maintenance and contamination from the outside allow these coolants to breakdown, which causes problems with the plastics that are used in the engine.

HOAT

The third category, HOAT, is a coolant that contains a mixture of inorganic and organic additives. This type of coolant can use silicate and organic acid; it is the best of both worlds of coolants. Some manufacturers found that without silicate, problems arose if the system was not properly serviced, such as oxidation of the coolant, leading to breakdown of the corrosion inhibitors and, ultimately, failure of engine parts and gaskets. Other tests indicate that silicates cause premature water pump failures. Less silicate is present in HOAT coolant than in IAT coolants, so this coolant is still considered extended life and will have to be changed at five years or 100,000–150,000 miles (160,934–241,000 km). An example of this type of coolant is the yellow coolant used by Ford, pink coolant used by VW/Audi, and the blue coolant used by Honda (**FIGURE 8-11**). The key to keeping this coolant working in the engine is to keep the pH at 7 so that it does not become acidic and start dissolving engine components. What usually happens with type of coolant is that it gets contaminated with water that is not distilled, has a leak that allows air in it, or is not maintained like it is supposed to be. Once the coolant becomes exposed to this outside stimuli, it becomes acidic and starts destroying the engine gaskets.

PHOAT

The fourth category, PHOAT, is a relatively new coolant that contains a proprietary blend of corrosion inhibitors. PHOAT stands for phosphate hybrid organic acid technology, which is ethylene glycol based and is embittered so that pets do not drink it (**FIGURE 8-12**). It is a very long-life coolant, providing up to seven years or 250,000 miles (402,000 km) of protection. Check with manufacture information to see if it compatible with other types of coolant. This coolant is usually dark green in color and used in Mazda-based Fords 2008 and up.

Boiling Point and Pressure

The boiling point of a liquid is the temperature at which it begins to change from a liquid to a gas. Water at sea level atmospheric pressure 14.7 psi (101.4 kPa, or 1 atmosphere [atm]) boils at 212°F (100°C). Atmospheric pressure becomes lower as elevation is increased. Because atmospheric pressure is lower at higher elevations (such as in the mountains), the boiling temperature of a liquid in an unsealed system is lower. Think of it as lower pressure = lower boiling point. Conversely, raising the pressure has the opposite effect; it raises the boiling point of a liquid. Stated another way, a liquid in a vacuum has a lower boiling point than when that same liquid is at atmospheric pressure. A liquid under pressure higher than atmospheric pressure has a higher boiling point than when that liquid is at atmospheric pressure. Thus, the boiling point of a liquid varies depending upon the surrounding environmental pressure. For a given pressure, different liquids boil at different temperatures.

This principle is used to enable water in the engine's cooling system to remain a liquid at temperatures well above the normal boiling point of 212°F (100°C). The pressurized coolant in the cooling system boils at a higher temperature than when the radiator pressure cap is removed (or if the system has a leak). For every 1 psi of pressure, the boiling point is raised by 3 degrees Fahrenheit, so a 15 psi cap would add 45 degrees to the boiling point, which would put the coolant at 257°F.

Over the years, manufacturers intentionally have raised the operating temperature of their engines for more efficient combustion and reduced emissions. A pressurized cooling system can handle the extra heat without boiling over. Pressurizing the cooling system means that the cooling system can be downsized (for less weight and space requirement) and still cool the engine effectively. Also, with a higher temperature differential between the cooling system's operating temperature and the outside ambient air, the radiator is more effective at radiating excess heat from the coolant. In today's vehicles, most automotive cooling systems are pressurized at 13–17 psi (89.6–117.2 kPa). However, some factory radiator caps are rated as high as 24 psi (165.5 kPa), and high-performance systems can go as high as 34 psi (234.4 kPa).

FIGURE 8-12 PHOAT coolant is very similar to OAT coolant, but it has been mixed with phosphates to help lubricate the cooling system.

SAFETY TIP

When working around the cooling system, care must be taken, particularly if the engine is at operating temperature, as the coolant may be hot enough to scald. Always allow the system to cool before removing the radiator or pressure cap, and use extreme caution when removing the radiator cap. If you must remove the radiator cap from a hot system, wear protective gloves and eyewear, and place a cloth fender cover or other large rag on top of the radiator cap before releasing it slowly to the first (safety) point, to prevent the pressure inside from erupting.

Applied Science

AS-30: Fusion/Vaporization: The technician can demonstrate an understanding of how heat causes a change in the state of matter.

Vaporization and fusion are two ways in which the application of heat can cause matter to change states. Vaporization refers to the transitional phase from liquid to vapor, whereas fusion refers to the transitional phase from solid to liquid. Both concepts have applications in the shop.

Pressurized cooling systems in motor vehicles are designed to prevent vaporization, in this case from boiling. Water boils at 212°F (100°C) at atmospheric pressure at sea level. When coolant in the cooling system is pressurized, its boiling point is raised, allowing the system to continue to cool the engine at temperatures over 212°F (100°C). Vaporization must be avoided because, unlike liquids, vapors do not effectively remove heat from engine components. Most cooling systems have pressure limits of 14 to 15 lb per square inch (psi, or 97 to 103 kilopascals [kPa]), effectively raising the boiling point of the coolant by approximately 45°F (25°C).

In contrast, water turns from a liquid to a solid (freezes) at 32°F (0°C). When water freezes, it expands approximately 10%. Pressure from ice is strong enough to break cast iron, which would cause leaks in the cooling system, causing extensive damage to the engine. Antifreeze is used to lower the freezing point of water to prevent freezing of the water and antifreeze mixture, called coolant.

Applied Science

AS-101: Proportion Mixtures: The technician can correctly mix fluids using proportions.

As discussed earlier, engine coolant is composed of water and anti-freeze. The normally recommended mixture of these two liquids is 50/50—50% water and 50% antifreeze—which provides freeze protection to about −34°F (−37°C). Automotive cooling system capacity typically is given in quarts or liters, with smaller vehicles requiring perhaps 5 quarts (or liters) and larger SUVs with air conditioning requiring up to 20 or more quarts (or liters).

If a vehicle's specifications call for a total of 16 quarts of coolant, then a 50/50 mixture would consist of 8 quarts of antifreeze mixed with 8 quarts of distilled water. A 10-quart system would require

5 quarts of each, and so forth. The challenge in ensuring a 50/50 mix is the unknown mixture that remains in the cooling system, because not all of the coolant will drain out. If the system has been flushed with clean water and drained, then to end up with a 50/50 mix, the technician would first add the entire 50% of antifreeze and then top off the rest with clean water, leaving a 50/50 mix. If the coolant was flushed out with a 50/50 mix, then the technician can premix coolant and top the cooling system off with that. After topping off the cooling system, be sure to run the engine to circulate the coolant, and then check the mixture's freeze point with a hydrometer or refractometer. Coolant can now be purchased premixed for convenience, but you will be paying for 50% water, plus the cost of shipping it, so it is less expensive to mix your own coolant.

Freeze Point

The freeze point of coolant is determined by the ratio of water to antifreeze mixture. The more antifreeze that is added to the mixture, the lower the freezing point. That is true up until the point where the antifreeze solution goes above 70%, the freeze point starts to go back up, which means that you need to watch the mixture ratio. The purer the antifreeze, the more likely you will lose your freeze protection.

Electrolysis

Electrolysis is the process of pulling chemicals (materials) apart by using electricity or by creating electricity through the use of chemicals and dissimilar metals. Electrolysis is used in manufacturing to create some metals, gases, and chemicals. You may have performed electrolysis in a science class by passing electrical current through water to break the hydrogen out of the water. Electrolysis is what takes place in the automotive battery. Two dissimilar metals are submerged in an acid solution, resulting in the reaction that is called electricity. Another common experiment in science class is the potato battery, made from two different types of metal stuck into the potato and used to power a digital clock or a lightbulb.

Electrolysis can occur in places where it is not desired and can have undesirable effects. For instance, in automotive cooling systems, electrolysis is possible when the coolant breaks down and becomes more acidic. Many types of metal are used in the engine, such as cast iron, aluminum, copper, and brass. Introducing an acid solution into a mix of metals produces electricity. When this electricity is produced, the movement of the electrons begins to erode away the metal in the system. Eventually, pinholes are created in the thinner, softer cooling system components (typically, the heater core or aluminum cylinder head) (**FIGURE 8-13**). To combat electrolysis, the customer needs

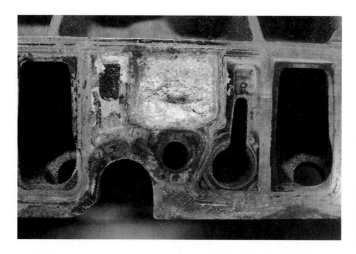

FIGURE 8-13 This is what happens when the pH is off, and the coolant has been too acidic.

to have regular scheduled maintenance of the coolant performed, including flushing out the old coolant and replacing it with new coolant. Electricity can also appear in the cooling system because of faulty grounds on accessories or even the starter motor circuit. Electricity is known to follow the path of least resistance and will be partially carried through the coolant, where it can erode metals, if that path is easier than its intended path. We discuss how to test for electrolysis later in this chapter and revisit bad grounds at that point.

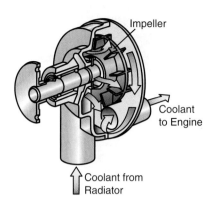

FIGURE 8-14 When coolant enters the center of this pump and the internal rotor spins, centrifugal force moves the liquid outward.

Centrifugal Force

Centrifugal force is a force pulling outward on a rotating body. For example, if you were to take a tennis ball and tie it to a string and swing it around you, centrifugal force would pull the tennis ball outward, making the string taut. Another example of centrifugal force occurs when a vehicle turns a curve. Centrifugal force resists the turning of the vehicle and tries to keep the vehicle moving in a straight line, creating a sliding condition if centrifugal force is great enough. Centrifugal force can be useful in some cases, such as in the water pump. When coolant enters the center of the water pump and the internal rotor spins, centrifugal force moves the liquid outward toward the outlet (**FIGURE 8-14**). Centrifugal force pushes the coolant into the engine block and head passageways that surround the cylinders. The coolant then travels through the radiator to be cooled.

▶ Cooling System Types

Almost all modern vehicles have engine cooling systems that use a liquid coolant to transfer heat energy from parts of the internal combustion engine to outside air. (*Note:* Other cooling systems, such as those used for turbocharger intercoolers/aftercoolers or hybrid high-voltage battery packs, may use air-to-air systems to cool the engine's intake air or high-voltage battery.) In the engine's liquid-cooled system, coolant is forced to flow around and through parts of the engine, to pick up excess heat and carry it through flexible hoses to the radiator. Engine heat is transferred from hotter components to cooler ones. The cooling fan forces air over the fins of the radiator, as necessary, to assist the transfer of heat energy from the coolant to the ambient air (**FIGURE 8-15**). The coolant also flows through coolant hoses to the heater core, which is located in the air box in the passenger compartment and provides heat for the passengers when needed. Cooling hoses (i.e., radiator hoses and heater hoses) are flexible rubber tubes that connect stationary components of the cooling system, such as the heater core and radiator, to the engine, which is allowed to move on its flexible mounts. Engine movement in its flexible rubber mounts causes nonflexible coolant hoses to break over time.

K08003 Knowledge of different types of cooling systems.

Air Cooling

Air engine cooling is common on smaller internal combustion engines and was used in the past on some automobiles like the early Volkswagen Beetle and Porsches. Air cooling an automobile was not ideal from an emissions standpoint, nor did it always provide sufficient cabin heat for the passenger compartment. All automobiles are now water cooled, although small engines can still be found in older automobiles that are air cooled. Air cooling uses heat-dissipating fins on the engine cylinders and heads to allow the movement of air to absorb heat and carry it away from the engine through special ducting. Because the air does the work of keeping the engine cool, an air-cooled system is very simple and light compared to a water-cooled one. This is one of several reasons why most small aircraft engines are air cooled. A major drawback to air cooling is that the engine has to be exposed to the airstream for best cooling. Many motorcycles were air cooled, but as the engines

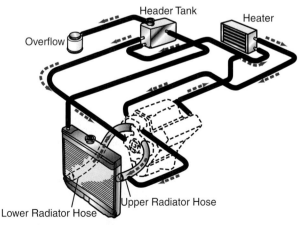

FIGURE 8-15 Coolant moves through the engine and then to the radiator to transfer heat to the air.

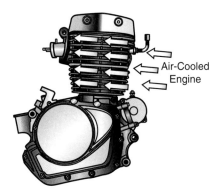

FIGURE 8-16 An air-cooled motorcycle engine uses fins to cool the engine and works by convection as air moves through the fins.

became more powerful, a more effective cooling system became necessary. Most motorcycle engines produced today are water cooled.

Air-cooled engines in automobiles usually are not exposed to the air; rather, the engine is housed in an enclosed engine bay. A cooling fan that is belt driven forces air across the engine so that it is being cooled. As the vehicle is moving at highway speed, airflow over the engine may be high enough to prevent overheating. At lower speeds or during idling, heat may build up, which is why there is a cooling fan continuing to push air over the engine so that the engine will not overheat. An engine that uses these components is called a "forced draft" air-cooled engine. Some air-cooled engines are "open draft" air-cooled, which require the engine to be moving through the air to have sufficient airflow (**FIGURE 8-16**).

Liquid Cooling

In modern vehicles, radiators are low and wide to allow the hood to sit lower to the ground for aerodynamics. Because of this design, modern vehicles use a water pump that pulls coolant from the radiator and forces it through passages, called water jackets, in the engine block and cylinder head. Coolant absorbs heat by conduction from the engine and becomes hotter. The heated coolant then moves to the radiator for cooling; air flowing over and through the radiator causes heat to be absorbed from the coolant by the air.

All engines operate best when they are at their full operating temperature, commonly referred to as the operating temperature. Most engine wear and high exhaust emissions occur during the warm-up period. Ideally, we want the engine to get to operating temperature as quickly as possible, but not overheat. In order to accomplish this, a thermostat is used to regulate the coolant temperature. The thermostat initially blocks coolant flow to the radiator, keeping coolant circulating in the engine, where it heats up quickly and does not pull heat from the warming engine. Once operating temperature is reached, the thermostat starts to open and allows coolant to flow to the radiator to remove excessive heat. The thermostat does not normally open completely, but adjusts between its fully closed or fully open position continually to maintain an optimum engine operating temperature, regardless of engine load.

Coolant Flow—Normal and Reverse Flow

K08004 Knowledge of coolant flow inside an engine.

In a water-cooled cooling system with normal flow, the flow of coolant starts at the water pump. Cold coolant is moved through the engine and starts to warm up as the engine begins to run. The coolant travels up through the engine, assisted by the water pump. The pump relies on centrifugal force of the impeller (rotor) to force coolant through the cooling passageways of the engine. The coolant flows around the cylinders, where combustion is taking place and picks up excess heat. Heat transfers from around the cylinders to the coolant as it moves past them. It then moves upward through the cylinder head, where it passes over the top of the combustion chamber in the head and flows around the valve guides, all the while picking up more heat as it passes those hotter surfaces.

From the head, it moves to the thermostat, which works like a trapdoor: If it is closed, the coolant will continue to circulate within the engine, flowing through a bypass hose or passage to move back down to the water pump again, which was the starting point of its

---

Applied Science

AS-27: Heat: The technician can demonstrate an understanding of the effect of heat on automotive systems.

The heat created by burning fuel in the internal combustion engine causes rapid expansions of pressure, which drives the pistons (see the Motive Power Types—Spark-Ignition (SI) Engines chapter). Some of the heat from the combustion process must be dissipated so that it does not overheat or melt engine parts. This is the job of the engine cooling system. The cooling system helps the engine to come up

quickly to its specified operating temperature and to maintain that temperature in spite of ambient weather conditions or engine load. If the engine is not allowed to warm up properly, other systems will not operate properly. For example, the engine coolant temperature greatly affects the engine air–fuel mixture (fuel trim) and thus fuel economy and emissions. Operation of the evaporative emission system and other systems is also affected by engine temperature, so it is important that the cooling system be maintained to operate correctly.

journey. The thermostat is meanwhile sensing the coolant's temperature, and at a specified temperature it begins to open. As the thermostat opens, the coolant begins to flow through the radiator hose and to the radiator. Coolant enters the radiator's inlet tank and then the radiator core, where it flows through small tubes that have heat-dissipating fins on the outside. The tubes act like fins on an air-cooled engine, to transfer the coolant's heat to the outside air. As it cools, coolant moves to the cool side of the radiator to begin its journey back to the engine through the other radiator hose. The coolant's return flow to the engine is aided by the suction created by the water pump impeller.

One problem with this normal-flow system was discovered on race cars, which develop more heat than a standard automobile. Because race car engines run hotter, and cylinder heads in general run hotter than engine blocks, the heads would get too hot and fail. The hottest part of any engine is the cylinder head, because this is where the combustion chamber is located. High cylinder head temperatures tend to increase chances of detonation and failure of head gaskets. As a cylinder head heats more than the cylinder block, it expands further and slides across the head gasket more. When the head does this many times, the gasket is more likely to fail.

In the normal-flow cooling system, coolant goes through the engine block first and then moves to the hottest part—the cylinder head. As a result, the cylinder head operates at a hotter temperature than the cylinder block. Engineers found that if they changed the flow design, they could keep the cylinder head and block closer to the same temperature by pushing coolant through the head first, thus making the head, valves, and head gaskets last longer. Therefore, in some reverse-flow cooling systems, coolant flows to the cylinder heads first and then through the engine block.

In the typical reverse-flow design, like that used in the Chevy Trailblazer's 4.2 L engine, coolant starts from the radiator and flows through the radiator outlet hose the cylinder head, into the cylinder block and, then to the thermostat, and finally to the radiator (**FIGURE 8-17**). Because the flow through the radiator is the same, it is simply the flow through the engine that has changed. This design differs only in the way coolant flows, block to head; all the components are generally the same.

One problem with the reverse-flow design was easily fixed: As coolant moved through the hottest part of the engine, steam tended to form and get stuck at the head cooling

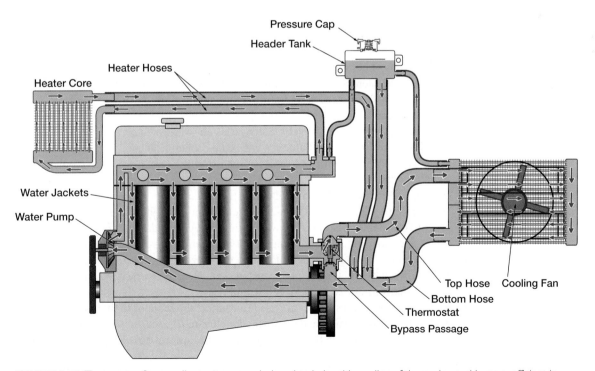

FIGURE 8-17 The reverse flow cooling system was designed to help with cooling of the engine and is more efficient in some applications.

FIGURE 8-18 A rotary engine cooling system, which is very similar to a typical engine cooling system.

passages, as this is the highest part of the engine. Because the engine will overheat if gas pockets get stuck in the water passageways, the solution was to drill holes in the head for steam to escape and to run a tube from the head back to a surge tank, where the steam turns back into coolant and is recycled through the system. The surge tank is discussed in greater detail later in the chapter.

Rotary Engine Cooling System

The cooling system of the rotary engine is not much different from the piston engine's cooling system. The engine itself is extremely different because it does not use pistons, but instead uses a triangular part called a rotor that moves with combustion and turns the crankshaft. The cooling system uses a standard radiator, thermostat, and radiator hoses. Water flows from the radiator to the water pump, then into the **rotor housing**, which is essentially the engine block of the rotary engine, where the rotor moves (**FIGURE 8-18**). Passageways (water jackets) cast and machined into the rotor housing go around the rotor housing and allow heat to be pulled from around the rotor, where combustion is taking place. To cool the rotors in this type of an engine, the design uses oil and an oil cooler to transfer the heat away from the rotors, extending the life of the Apex seals. After coolant moves through the water jackets, it finds its way to the thermostat, where it returns to the radiator.

▶ Cooling System Components

K08005 Knowledge of cooling system components.

The primary components of a vehicle cooling system are listed here:

- **Radiator**—The radiator is usually made of copper, brass, or aluminum tubes, with copper, brass, aluminum, or plastic tanks on the sides or top for coolant to collect in. Air is drawn over the radiator to transfer heat energy to ambient air. The fins on the tubes of the radiator give more surface area for heat dissipation—the spreading of heat over a large area to ease heat transfer.
- **Thermostat**—The thermostat regulates coolant flow to the radiator. It opens at a predetermined temperature to allow coolant flow to the radiator for cooling. It also enables the engine to reach operating temperature more quickly for reduced emissions and wear.
- **Recovery system**—The recovery system uses an overflow tank to catch any coolant that is released from the radiator cap when the coolant heats up.
- **Surge tank**—This pressurized tank is piped into the cooling system. Coolant constantly moves through it. It is used when the radiator is not the highest part of the cooling system. Remember, air collects at the highest point in the cooling system.
- **Water pump**—This pump is used to force coolant throughout the cooling system in order to transfer heat energy. The water pump is typically driven off the engine timing belt or accessory belt. On some engines, it is driven by the camshaft timing chain.
- **Cooling fan**—This fan forces air through the radiator for heat transfer. Cooling fans can be driven by a belt or by an electric motor. The fan can be controlled by viscous fluid or thermostatic sensors, switches, and relays.
- **Radiator hoses**—These hoses are used to connect the radiator to the water pump and engine. They are usually made of formed, nylon-reinforced rubber. In some radiator hoses, coiled wire inside them is used to prevent hose collapse as the cooling system temperature fluctuates.
- **Heater hoses**—These hoses connect the water pump and engine to the heater core. They carry heated coolant to the heater core to be used to heat the passenger compartment.

- **Drive belts**—These belts provide power to drive the water pump and other accessories on the front of the engine. Three types are used: V-belts, serpentine (also called multi-groove) belts, and toothed/cogged belts.
- **Temperature indicators**—Temperature indicators provide information to the operator about engine temperature. The temperature gauge indicates engine temperature continuously. A temperature warning indicator comes on only when the engine is overheating, to warn the operator that engine damage will occur if the vehicle is driven much farther.
- **Water jackets**—Water jackets are passages surrounding the cylinders and head on the engine, where coolant can flow to pick up excess heat. They are sealed by replaceable core plugs.
- **Heater core**—The heater core is a small radiator used to provide heat to the passenger compartment from the hot coolant passing through it. The amount of heat can be controlled by a heater control valve.
- **Coolant**—Coolant is the liquid used to prevent freezing, overheating, and corrosion of the engine.
- **Auxiliary coolers**—Auxiliary coolers are used to cool automatic transmission fluid, power steering fluid, EGR gases, and compressed intake air.

Each of these coolers transmits heat either to the cooling system or directly to the atmosphere. Because there is such a wide variety of auxiliary coolers, refer to the manufacturer's service information for how to properly inspect the auxiliary cooler for leaks and proper operation.

Radiator

The radiator is located in a convenient position under the hood of the vehicle, where maximum airflow can pass through it. Its actual location under the hood depends on the engine configuration, the available space, and the shape or line of the hood itself. The radiator consists of top and bottom tanks or side tanks and a core. The radiator core allows the coolant to pass through it in either a vertical or a horizontal cross-flow direction. In addition, the radiator core serves as a good conductor of heat away from the engine.

The materials used in the radiator must be good heat conductors, such as brass, copper, or aluminum. Brass or copper is often used for tanks when combined with a brass or copper core. Late model vehicles starting in the late 1980s and early 1990s often use plastic tanks combined with an aluminum core. This design saves weight and cost while still providing good heat transfer.

The core consists of a number of cooling tubes that carry coolant between the two tanks. The tubes can be in a horizontal (cross-flow) design or a vertical (downflow) design (**FIGURE 8-19**). In a **downflow radiator**, the cooling tubes run top to bottom, with the tanks on the top and bottom. In a **cross-flow radiator**, the cooling tubes are arranged horizontally, with one tank on each side. Because of this arrangement, the same amount of cooling area can be achieved without the need for a very tall radiator; instead, it is wide and short. This design feature allows the hood profile to be lower to allow for better aerodynamics, which improves fuel economy and safety by increasing the driver's vision in front of the vehicle. The function of both types of radiator configurations is the same, which is to cool the coolant before it reenters the engine.

Cross Flow Radiator   Down Flow Radiator

FIGURE 8-19 Two different types of radiators used in automotive applications.

AS-32: Radiation: The technician can demonstrate an understanding of heat transfer that involves infrared rays.

At one end of the light spectrum, just beyond visibility, lies the infrared portion of light. Infrared is a form of heat energy and can be detected by special instruments. Thermography involves the use of heat-sensing instruments to detect heat sources. The amount of radiation emitted by an object increases with temperature; therefore, thermography allows one to see variations in temperature. In the automotive trade, an infrared "temp gun" is pointed at objects to determine their temperature. This method is useful for detecting cylinders that are contributing less power to the engine, finding leaks in air-conditioning systems, and so forth. On the dashboard of many vehicles lies an infrared-sensing "sun-load sensor," which helps automatic HVAC systems to regulate cabin temperature and enables automatic headlight dimming.

FIGURE 8-20 A surge tank removes air and gases from the coolant. This is where you normally fill the cooling system.

FIGURE 8-21 A radiator with an overflow tank.

Surge Tank/Overflow Tank

Some vehicles are equipped with a surge tank/expansion tank. The surge tank has coolant constantly running through it and is located higher than the top of the radiator. If the radiator sits lower than any other part in the cooling system, then steam will collect in whatever component is highest. On some vehicles this may be the heater core. To solve this problem, engineers have installed a surge tank and placed it so it is the highest component in the system. Thus, any gas in the system will make its way to this tank, ensuring that only liquid coolant circulates through the system. The surge tank has at least one line in and one line out. It is usually made of hardened plastic, which allows for visually checking the fluid level through the plastic. This tank is usually where the cooling system is filled or topped off with coolant. In many vehicles with a surge tank, the pressure cap is mounted on the surge tank instead of the radiator (**FIGURE 8-20**).

Recovery System

The coolant recovery system maintains coolant in the system at all times. The recovery system consists of an overflow bottle, a sealed radiator pressure cap, and a small hose connecting the bottle to the radiator neck (**FIGURE 8-21**). As engine temperatures rise, the coolant expands. Pressure builds against a valve in the radiator cap until, at a preset pressure, the valve opens. Hot coolant flows out of the radiator, through the connecting hose, and into an overflow bottle. As the engine cools, coolant contracts, and pressure in the cooling system drops below atmospheric pressure. Atmospheric pressure in the overflow bottle opens the vacuum valve in the radiator cap, and overflow coolant flows back into the radiator. Like water, air contains oxygen, which reacts with metals to form corrosion. With use of a recovery system, no coolant is lost, and excess air is kept out of the system.

Thermostat and Housing

N08001 Inspect, remove, and replace water pump.

The thermostat is located under the thermostat housing, which can be located in many different places, depending on the engine application. The thermostat regulates the flow of coolant, allowing coolant to flow from the engine to the radiator when the engine is running at its operating temperature. The thermostat prevents coolant from flowing to the radiator when the engine is cold, to allow the engine to warm up more rapidly so as to reduce engine wear and emissions.

The thermostat is a spring-loaded valve that is controlled by a wax pellet located inside the valve (**FIGURE 8-22**). As the temperature of the coolant rises, the wax pellet melts and expands, forcing the spring-loaded valve open at a preset temperature. As the valve opens, coolant is allowed to flow through it. The thermostat works like a door to control movement of coolant. When the engine is cold, the door is closed; when hot, the door opens. Some dashboard temperature gauges show a slight swing of engine temperatures as the thermostat cycles slightly toward open or closed.

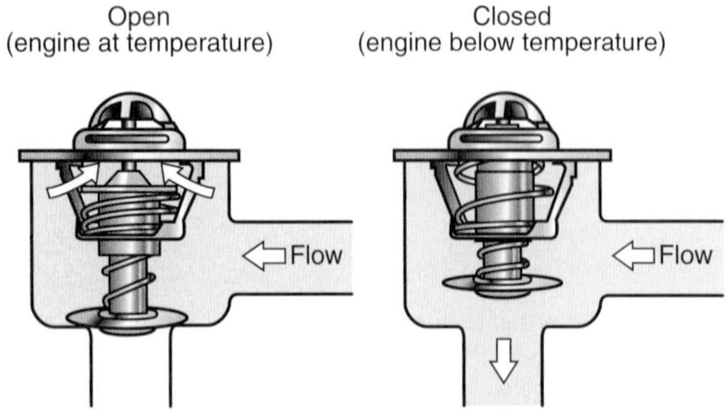

Some engines are designed such that the coolant bypass passage is directly under the thermostat. In those situations, the thermostat may have a flat disc attached to the bottom of it, which moves along with the thermostat. When the thermostat fully opens, the flat disc blocks off the bypass passage so that all coolant must flow through the radiator. But when the thermostat partially closes, the bypass passage is partially open. This helps give more effective cooling when the thermostat is fully open.

Most thermostats have a small hole on one side of the thermostat valve that allows any air in the system to move past the closed thermostat when the valve is closed. This is especially helpful when the cooling

Open
(engine at temperature)   Closed
(engine below temperature)

⇐ Flow   ⇐ Flow

FIGURE 8-22 The thermostat has a moving valve that is controlled by a wax pellet. When the wax is cool, the valve stays closed; as temperature increases, the wax melts and forces the valve open.

system has been drained and is being filled. The hole usually contains a little pin, called a jiggle valve or jiggle pin, to help break the surface tension of the coolant and allow any air to flow slowly through the hole. Air trapped in the cooling system is thus able to slowly find its way to the uppermost part of the cooling system, where it can be bled. When installing the thermostat, the jiggle valve should be in the uppermost position so that as much air as possible can be bled from the system.

The thermostat and housing are normally located on the outlet side of the coolant flow from the engine. However, on some engines they are located on the inlet side of the engine. The thermostat is identified by being located in the housing connected to the inlet radiator hose. The reason for installing the thermostat on the inlet side is to better control the amount of cold water that rushes into the engine, which can create a temperature shock to the engine.

Some vehicles include a manual bleed valve on the thermostat housing or within a high part of the cooling system. After the vehicle cooling system has been serviced and refilled, the technician should carefully open the bleed valve to vent any trapped air to the atmosphere. It is good practice to bleed the system again once the engine has warmed up.

What Can Cause Failure?

A thermostat could fail for a number of reasons, but most of the time thermostats fail because the wax that changes from a solid to a liquid simply wears out. You can only thermocycle materials so many times before they fail, which then would cause the thermostat not to open at all, overheating the engine. Another reason that thermostats fail is because electrolysis from coolant has not been maintained in the vehicle's engine. When you are diagnosing this failure, you must evaluate the coolant and fix the pH balance in the cooling system. Failure of thermostats can also be because of using lower quality components, which fail because of the substandard materials.

Water Pump

The water pump is usually belt driven from a pulley on the front of the crankshaft. The engine drives the water pump, using an accessory belt or the timing belt. Some newer vehicles use an electrically driven water pump. Internally, the water pump has fan like blades on an impeller or rotor, which is turned by a shaft connected to the pulley. The shaft rides on a heavy-duty double-row ball bearing for long life and to withstand belt tension. The shaft is sealed where it enters the pump chamber. Most water pumps have a small weep hole that sits between the seal and the bearing and vents any coolant that leaks past the seal to be drained to the outside of the engine (**FIGURE 8-23**). Checking this hole for signs of coolant leakage is part of the process of inspecting the engine for leaks.

The water pump is usually located at the front of the engine block; a hose typically connects it to the output of the radiator, where the relatively cool coolant emerges. Coolant enters the center of the pump. As the impeller rotates, it catches the coolant and flings it outward with centrifugal force. This type of water pump is called a centrifugal pump, meaning that it creates movement of the coolant due to centrifugal force, but does not cause much buildup of pressure. Coolant is driven through the outlet into the water jackets of the engine block and to the cylinder heads. Coolant can be directed to critical hot spots, such as around the exhaust ports in the cylinder head, to stop localized overheating. The cylinder head gasket has holes of various sizes to help determine how much coolant should flow to these and other locations of the head. If the head gasket is not properly installed, cylinder head damage may result from localized overheating.

Replacing a water pump is a fairly common task that used to be performed mostly as a result of noise or leak issues on accessory-belt-driven water pumps (**FIGURE 8-24**). But now with many water pumps being driven by timing belts, it is common to replace the water pump along with the timing belt at the belt's recommended replacement schedule (**FIGURE 8-25**). When changing this type of pump, the timing belt will have to be removed, so following the manufacturer's procedure will be necessary to prevent damage to the valves and pistons. Once the drive belt is removed from either style

N08002 Identify causes of engine overheating.

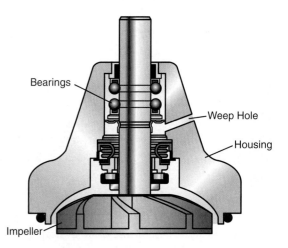

FIGURE 8-23 Cutaway view of water pump and weep hole.

FIGURE 8-24 Replacing a water pump.

FIGURE 8-25 Water pumps are typically driven by timing belts.

of water pump, the removal of the pump involves the unbolting of the pump, carefully prying it off the mating surface, cleaning the mounting surface, and rebolting it back in place with the appropriate gasket or O-ring.

Cooling Fan

Cooling fans are used to provide airflow through the radiator core for engine cooling. This is most needed during slow driving or stop-and-go driving. There are two main categories of cooling fans: engine driven and electric. Engine-driven cooling fans may be located on the water pump shaft or in a few cases may be attached to a dummy shaft that's whole purpose is to drive the cooling fan. Most vehicles today use one or more electrically driven engine cooling fans, which are mounted directly to the radiator. On a fan that is driven by the engine, engine horsepower is directly needed to drive the fan, requiring extra fuel even when the fan is not needed. Such fans are also noisy and dangerous to work around.

It takes a fair amount of energy to turn a fan, which ultimately comes from the crankshaft, consuming energy that could be used to drive the vehicle down the road. Yet, the fan is not needed during cold engine operation. It is also not needed when the vehicle is traveling above about 35 mph (56 kph) and the airflow is strong enough to cool the radiator without using the fan. For years, vehicle manufacturers have sought ways to reduce the energy the fan uses. One type of fan design (called a flex fan) uses flexible steel or plastic blades that straighten out and lessen their pitch as engine speed increases. This design increases fuel economy and reduces noise.

Mechanical

A mechanical fan is simply a fan that is attached to the water pump with four bolts and runs any time the engine is running (**FIGURE 8-26**). This is the most basic cooling fan as there are no parts other than the fan blades that could fail. The problem with this type of fan is it robs engine horsepower and decreases fuel mileage because it is turning all the time, even when the engine does not need cooled. These fans fell out of favor in the late 1960s to early 1970s, because of the increased emphasis on fuel mileage and emission-related savings. Performance wise this fan will always work as there is nothing to fail.

Thermostatic

Another type of engine-driven fan uses a viscous coupler to connect the water pump pulley to the cooling fan. The viscous coupler is called a fan clutch because it can engage and disengage the fan from the pulley (**FIGURE 8-27**). The fan clutch typically uses

FIGURE 8-26 A conventional mechanical fan setup, mostly found on rear-wheel drive vehicles.

two discs that have closely fitted interwoven rings and grooves. When viscous silicone oil is allowed to fill the small spaces between the rings and the grooves, it transmits torque from one disc to the other, and is used to transmit torque across the two halves of the hub. A bimetallic spring on the front moves as air temperature from the radiator changes. This spring is attached to a valve that turns and allows more silicone oil to flow into the coupler, thereby transmitting more of the pulley's speed to the fan to move more air. As air temperature decreases from air flowing through the radiator, the bimetallic spring turns the valve, and the silicone oil moves out of the coupler back to the reservoir located in the clutch body. This causes the fan to slow and move less air. This type of fan is driven at all times by the accessory belt. The benefit of using a viscous clutch is to increase fuel economy by being able to cycle on and off.

A variation of the clutch fan is the solenoid-controlled fan clutch, which operates in the same manner as the thermostatic fan clutch. The clutch uses oil to control the speed of the fan in relation to engine speed (allows slip to slow fan down) and temperature of the air moving across the radiator. The only difference in the operation is that the bimetallic spring is removed, and an electric solenoid is installed on the front of the clutch. This solenoid is controlled by the powertrain control module (PCM), based on engine coolant temperature. As temperature increases, more oil is allowed to flow to the viscous coupler and fan speed increases. As temperature decreases, oil is directed back to the reservoir in the body of the clutch and fan speed decreases. On this type of fan, a feedback sensor provides actual fan speed or rpm information back to the PCM.

Hydraulic

Another type of cooling fan is the hydraulically operated fan. In many cases, it uses power steering fluid from the power steering pump to power the fan (**FIGURE 8-28**). Because the power steering pump can create substantial power, hydraulically driven fans can be used to draw a large amount of air through the radiator. They are sometimes used on vehicles with heavy trailer towing capacities, as well as ordinary vehicles. The system consists of the power steering pump, a fluid control device, the hydraulic fan motor, and high-pressure connecting hoses. The fan is typically controlled by a pulse-width-modulated solenoid valve. The solenoid controls how much hydraulic fluid is directed to the fan motor. That way the PCM can vary the signal to the solenoid valve, which controls the amount of hydraulic fluid to the fan motor, which determines how fast it spins. One benefit of the hydraulically controlled fan is that it can be operated at near full speed and force even at idle, similar to an electric fan. Yet it can tap into more engine power than the electric fan, so it can be more heavy duty.

Electric

As fan designs evolved to increase efficiency, and as more vehicles moved to front-wheel drive, which turns the front of the engine away from the radiator, the electric fan was introduced. Now it is by far the most common and simple type of cooling fan (**FIGURE 8-29**). It can be turned on and off easily whenever it is needed, and it can operate at full speed even though the engine is idling. This versatility makes it very efficient. It only runs when the engine is above the

FIGURE 8-27 A thermostatic fan clutch allows the fan to disengage when it is not needed so that it is not a drag on an engine.

FIGURE 8-28 A hydrostatic fan clutch is run off the power steering pump so that it is not a drag on the engine.

FIGURE 8-29 An electric fan does not drag on the engine, which helps with increasing fuel economy.

ideal operating temperature. In addition, because it can run at full speed independent of the engine, it can move plenty of air to cool the engine effectively.

Electric fans use an electric motor to turn an attached fan. In most cases, the fan blades are made of plastic, making them safer than metal blades. The blades can be designed to either push or pull air through the radiator, so mounting options are increased. The electric fan is controlled by one of two methods: A control module, such as the PCM, is used to energize a fan relay to turn the fan on and off, or a thermo-control switch is used. The PCM knows the temperature of the engine by means of the coolant temperature sensor. The PCM can then supply either power or ground to the fan relay, energizing the relay and fan.

The thermo-control switch is a temperature-sensitive switch that is mounted into the radiator or into a coolant passage on the engine. When engine temperature gets hot enough (say, 215°F [102°C]), the thermo-control switch closes and either send power directly to the fan or cause a relay to be activated, which turns on the fan. Once the engine coolant temperature cools back down, the switch opens and the fan stops.

Thermo-control switches often operate on the bimetallic strip principle. These consist of two different metals or alloys laminated back to back. As different metals and alloys heat and cool, they expand and contract at different rates. That means that if two different metals are joined, and then heated, the greater expansion of one will force the whole strip to flex into a curved shape. As the strip changes shape, it can be designed to complete an electric circuit by closing a switch, which turns the fan on.

With an electric fan, the electricity to run it comes from the alternator, which comes from the engine, which comes from the gasoline fuel. Because an electric fan typically needs to operate only part of the time, fuel is saved whenever it is off. Some manufacturers use multiple fans and control them separately, whereas others use multi-speed fans to provide only enough fan operation to keep the coolant at the proper temperature.

Radiator Hoses

On most vehicles there are two radiator hoses: the upper hose and the lower hose, also called the inlet hose and the outlet hose. Radiator hoses are rubber hoses that are subject to high pressure; they are therefore reinforced with a layer of fabric, typically nylon, to give them strength and prevent them from ballooning, and yet still be flexible. They are often molded into a special shape to suit the particular make and model of vehicle. Some radiator hoses, especially lower hoses, have a spiral wire inside to keep the hose from collapsing during heavy acceleration when the water pump is drawing a lot of water from the radiator.

The top radiator hose is typically attached to the thermostat housing, which allows the heated coolant to enter the inlet side of the radiator. The bottom or lower radiator hose is connected between the outlet of the radiator and the inlet of the water pump. The radiator hoses are held in position by clamps. These can be spring clamps, wire-wound clamps, or worm drive clamps. Radiator hoses deteriorate over time and use. They can also be damaged by oil or fuel leaking on them. Thus, they need to be inspected and changed periodically. Many vehicle manufacturers recommend radiator and heater hose replacement approximately every four to five years or 48,000 to 60,000 miles (77,000 to 97,000 km). When servicing hoses, be sure to reinstall the clamps correctly, or the seal between the hose and the component will leak. Every component has a raised ridge built into it. The hose clamp has to clamp on the inside of this ridge, but not on top of it. If the hose clamp is on top of the ridge, the hose is likely to come unattached once the cooling system becomes pressurized (**FIGURE 8-30**).

Heater Hoses

The heater hoses carry a smaller volume of coolant than do the radiator hoses. Some heater coolant hoses have special shapes and must be ordered specially for the vehicle being serviced. Other heater hoses are straight and can be replaced by heater hose that is supplied on a roll. The construction of the heater hose is the same as the radiator hose, with a reinforcing material embedded into it.

There are two hoses for the heater core: one inlet hose and one outlet hose. The heater hose directs hot coolant to the heater core to provide heat to the inside of the passenger

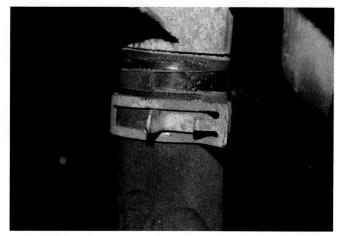

FIGURE 8-30 On the left is a correctly installed hose clamp, and on the right is an incorrectly installed one.

compartment. Some vehicles use a coolant control valve in line with the heater core hose. The coolant control valve controls the flow of hot coolant to the heater core as requested by the driver. The fittings on the valve, like other fittings in the cooling system, usually have a raised ridge to aid in sealing and keeping the hose from blowing off. The heater hoses are sealed and retained by the use of a hose clamp. As with radiator hoses, be sure to install hose clamps correctly. All hoses are subject to hot coolant and high underhood temperatures, and they will deteriorate and fail over time. Some coolant hoses are made of silicone, which is designed to withstand heat better and last longer than the standard rubber hose. Be sure to inspect hoses whenever you are servicing the customer's vehicle.

Coolant Hoses

Additional coolant hoses that carry hot coolant through the cooling system are often ignored when checking hoses (**FIGURE 8-31**). As part of a maintenance inspection, the technician inspects the upper and lower radiator hoses along with the heater hoses, but may forget about

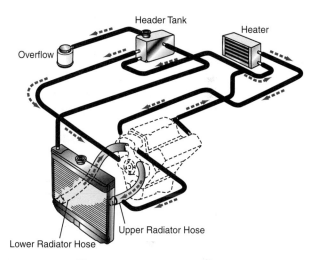

FIGURE 8-31 The cooling system may have multiple flexible coolant hoses, as seen in this cooling system schematic.

these other hoses, which can fail if neglected. It is critical that these hoses be checked. Any break in the system will dump the coolant and cause the engine to quickly overheat.

One of the additional hoses is the bypass hose. The bypass hose is typically located on the water pump and connects to the intake manifold on many V-configured engines, such as a V6 or V8. This hose allows the water pump to circulate the water in the engine when the thermostat is closed. This hose is made of the same materials as the radiator hoses and heater hoses. Another coolant hose that may be used is a throttle body coolant line. This hose runs from the intake up to the throttle body to keep the throttle body from freezing during cold outside temperatures when there is high moisture content in the air. The cold wet air being pulled through the throttle plate may create ice, restrict airflow, and cause the throttle to stick. Running coolant through the throttle body eliminates this problem. There are many possible configurations of additional cooling system hoses, such as to remote oil coolers, turbochargers, or even some alternators. In a compressed natural gas vehicle, coolant hoses are routed to the CNG pressure regulator under the vehicle to keep the regulator warm. A similar setup may be used for the engine's idle air control motor and more. The point is to be sure to inspect all of the coolant hoses used on the vehicle.

Drive Belts

Typically, the water pump is turned by a belt that is driven by the crankshaft. This belt may be part of the accessory drive belt system found on the front of the engine. If the belt

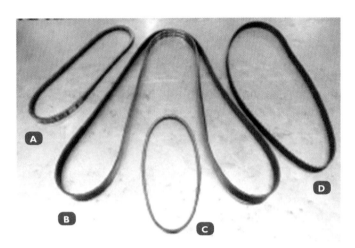

FIGURE 8-32 Belts. **A.** V-belt. **B.** Serpentine belt. **C.** Stretch belt. **D.** Timing belt.

is located on the front of the engine, it may be tensioned by a separate tensioner or by simply moving a component such as the alternator on slotted bolt holes. Some engines use the camshaft timing belt or chain as the drive for the water pump.

There are four types of drive belts (**FIGURE 8-32**).

- **V-type**—A V-type belt has a wedge-shaped interior and sits inside a corresponding groove in the pulley. The sides of the V-belt wedge in the sides of the pulley.
- **Serpentine**—A serpentine-type belt, also called a multi-groove V-belt, has a flat profile with a number of small V-shaped grooves running lengthwise along the inside of the belt. These grooves are the exact reverse of the grooves in the outer edge of the pulleys; they increase the contact surface area as well as prevent the belt from slipping off the pulley as it rotates. The serpentine belt is used to drive multiple accessories and to save underhood space forward of the engine. It winds its way around the crankshaft pulley, water pump, alternator, air-conditioning compressor, and tensioner. Most serpentine belts use a spring-loaded tensioner to maintain proper tightness of the belt and prevent it from slipping.
- **Stretch belt**—A stretch belt looks like an ordinary serpentine belt but is found on vehicles without a tensioner. It is made of a special material that allows it to stretch just enough to be installed over the pulleys but then shrink back to its original size, which is shorter than the distance around the pulleys. This stretchiness keeps the belt properly tensioned. Stretch belts require special tools to install and are usually cut off when being removed.
- **Toothed belt**—The toothed (also known as a cogged belt) belt has teeth on the inside that are perpendicular to the belt and fit inside the teeth of a gear. Timing belts are always toothed belts to keep the camshaft running exactly half the speed of the crankshaft. To save on labor cost, these belts are generally replaced whenever a water pump replacement is required. And the water pump is generally replaced whenever the timing belt is changed.

The technician must be careful when replacing drive belts to avoid tensioning them too much or too little. If excessive tension is placed on the belt, the water pump bearing can be overloaded, get hot, and fail due to excessive working load. Follow the manufacturer's service information for correct tensioning.

Drive Belt Pulleys and Tensioners

Tensioners are used to keep the drive belt tight around the pulleys to ensure the least amount of slippage without causing damage to component bearings. Tensioners can be either manual or automatic. Manual tensioners come in a wide variety of configurations. One type uses a pulley that is adjusted by turning a tensioning bolt. When the bolt is tightened, the pulley moves against the belt with increased tension; if the bolt is rotated the other direction, tension decreases. The tensioner is locked in place by tightening the nut on the front of the pulley.

A spring-loaded automatic tensioner is typically used with serpentine accessory belts (**FIGURE 8-33**). This type of tensioner is very simple to operate and adjusts itself, so there is no chance of getting it too tight. However, be sure to note the routing of the serpentine belt when servicing it; there are many pulleys to route around, and it can become confusing if you do not have a routing picture. Automatic tensioners can wear out and cause belt slippage or become noisy. Also, a seized front engine drive component such as a tensioner can cause a no-crank, or slow crank, engine condition that mimics a seized engine. Simply loosening or removing the belt may help to diagnose the problem.

If the water pump is driven by the timing belt, one of two types of tensioners may be used. One type is the spring-loaded tensioner, in which a spring sets the tension, and a bolt locks the tensioner into position (**FIGURE 8-34**). The other type is the oil-actuated tensioner

FIGURE 8-33 A spring-loaded automatic tensioner is typically used with serpentine accessory belts.

FIGURE 8-34 A timing belt tensor that is spring loaded, keeping tension by means of spring pressure.

(**FIGURE 8-35**). The oil-actuated tensioner uses oil pressure from the engine to provide additional tension on the belt. Regardless of the style of tensioner, belt tension can be checked with a belt tension tool and compared to specifications, which are typically published in the service information.

Temperature Indicators

Temperature indicators can come in two forms: a temperature gauge or a temperature light located in the instrument cluster (**FIGURE 8-36**). The two forms are sometimes used in conjunction. Overheating can heavily damage an engine, so a warning indicator is necessary. A temperature warning light is a good indicator of an overheating condition, but it cannot indicate a condition where the engine stays below operating temperature, which causes excess engine wear, increased emission output, and decreased fuel economy. A temperature gauge indicates to the driver whether the temperature is normal, below normal, or

FIGURE 8-35 An oil-metered orifice tensioner that keeps tension on the timing belt by the pressure built up in the tensioner.

above normal. But drivers can forget to monitor it, which means that the engine could overheat without the driver noticing. Thus, a warning light in addition to a temperature gauge gives the best of both worlds.

Temperature gauges and warning lights both operate from a signal sent from a coolant temperature sensor located on the engine in a coolant passage. When engine coolant gets

FIGURE 8-36 **A.** Temperature gauge. **B.** Temperature warning lamp.

hotter than it should, the sensor causes the warning light or message to turn on to alert the driver that the engine is overheating. The temperature gauge also uses a sensor, which is designed to continuously indicate the temperature of the engine. The sensor for either type of warning device sits in engine coolant so that an accurate reading is always given—that is, as long as there is no air in the cooling system.

There may also be a low coolant indicator that shows when engine coolant level is low. This system works by having a low-level sensor in the surge tank or overflow bottle that turns on a warning light in the instrument cluster if the coolant level falls below an acceptable level. If the low coolant indicator illuminates, there is a good chance that the cooling system has a leak that must be found.

Water Jackets

Coolant passages such as water jackets are cast into the block and heads during the manufacturing process. They are designed to allow coolant to circulate around the tops and sides of the cylinders and are critical for the transfer of excess heat energy. It is crucial to the efficiency of heat transfer to keep the coolant passages free of scaling and buildup that can restrict heat transfer and coolant flow by ensuring proper cooling system maintenance. As part of proper maintenance, the technician must drain, flush, and refill the cooling system according to the recommended maintenance intervals. (Also see earlier reference to head gasket design.)

Core Plugs

Core plugs are also known as soft plugs or expansion plugs. These aluminum, brass, or steel plugs are designed to seal the openings left from the casting process where the casting sand was removed (**FIGURE 8-37**). Under some conditions, the core plugs might pop out if the engine coolant is allowed to freeze—that is, if the proper mixture of antifreeze was not used. Because water expands when it freezes, the block or heads can crack internally or externally near the coolant passages. Sometimes the core plug will be pushed out, and the coolant will leak out before the block cracks; however, that is not what they are designed for, so do not rely on soft plugs to protect the engine from freezing. Also, core plugs can rust out and start leaking coolant, so do not forget to inspect them when trying to locate a coolant leak.

Heater Core

K08006 Knowledge of heater core, control valve, and actuators.

The heater core is simply a small radiator that is mounted inside the heater box in the passenger compartment. As air is blown past the fins of the core, heat energy is radiated to the air and used to heat the passenger compartment for comfort. The heater core connects to the engine's cooling system and is supplied with hot water by circulation of the water pump (**FIGURE 8-38**). Typically, hot water enters the bottom of the radiator and exits the top; thus,

FIGURE 8-37 Core plugs are designed to seal the openings left from the casting process of the block and heads.

FIGURE 8-38 A heater core used to create heat inside the vehicle.

the hot water flows from the bottom to the top of the heater core, so more heat can be pulled from the coolant. Heater cores are typically constructed of aluminum, brass, or copper.

Heater Control Valve

If used, the heater control valve is mounted in one of the heater hoses that supply coolant to the heater core. This valve controls the flow of coolant to the heater core to control the temperature of the air desired by the operator. The climate control panel, which is adjusted by the operator, controls this valve. This feature is discussed further in the Electronic Climate Control chapter.

Inspecting and Testing Heater Control Valves

Heater control valves control the flow of coolant to the heater core so that the operator can control heater output. If this valve becomes stuck open, the operator will not be able to turn down the heat, or the air conditioning will not be as cold as before. If the valve sticks shut, the customer will complain of no heat in the vehicle. The problem can be with the valve or the control system. The valve can get plugged up with contaminants in the coolant, or the lever can slip on the shaft that turns the valve. If it is cable operated, the cable can slip or even corrode in place. If it is vacuum operated, the diaphragm can get a hole in it; the vacuum hose can leak or fall off; or the vacuum controller can quit working. If it is electrically operated, the motor can seize, or the circuit can go bad. Heater control valves can also leak coolant, so they need to be inspected for leaks. In fact, one of the first indicators of low coolant in a vehicle is that the heater stops blowing hot air or blows hot air intermittently. Always verify that the coolant is full before spending too much time tracking down any kind of heater issues.

    To test the heater control valve, follow the steps of the **SKILL DRILL 8-1**.

S08001 Test the heater control valve.

SKILL DRILL 8-1 Testing the Heater Control Valve

1. Verify that the coolant level is full. Bring the engine up to operating temperature by running the engine for the appropriate amount of time.

2. Locate the heater control valve in line with the heater hose running to the heater core.

Continued

3. Have an assistant turn the temperature selector to hot, and observe whether the control valve lever is moving and the vent temperature is becoming hot.

4. Have an assistant turn the temperature selector to cold, and observe whether the control valve lever is moving and the vent temperature is becoming cold. If the lever is not moving, determine whether it is actuated by vacuum, cable, or electricity. Follow service information to diagnosis. One helpful tip is that both heater hoses will be hot if coolant is flowing through the heater core. One will be hot and the other cooler if it is not running through the heater core. This could be due to a heater control valve that is stuck closed or a plugged-up heater core. Determine necessary action.

5. Once you have determined that the valve is working, you must use a temperature gun to verify the temperature going in and out of the valve to see if it is stuck internally.

FIGURE 8-39 A heater/evaporator box, which directs heat and air-conditioning into the cabin.

Air Doors and Actuators

The heater box consists of many air doors, which are plastic or metal flaps that seal off parts of the air box to control airflow (**FIGURE 8-39**). The air doors are moved by one of three methods: cable, vacuum actuator, or electric actuator, called a stepper motor. The actuator is a device that is electrically or vacuum controlled and is used to physically move doors within the heater box to control airflow. This system is discussed in detail in the Electronic Climate Control chapter.

The layout and function of the doors depend on the design of the system. Most systems flow air through the evaporator at all times, and air can be diverted around the heater core when heat is not wanted. Also, for best defrost operation, the air is directed first over the evaporator to remove any moisture from the air. Then it is directed over the heater core to warm it up. This process results in dry, warm air to defog or defrost the windshield.

Wrap-Up

Ready for Review

- The Department of Transportation has stated that cooling system failure is the leading cause of mechanical breakdowns on the highway.
- Heat is thermal energy. It cannot be destroyed; only transferred. It always moves from areas of higher temperature to areas of lower temperature. This principle is applied to the transfer of heat energy from engine parts to ambient air, using the coolant as a medium to carry it.
- Heat travels in three ways: from one solid to another, by a process called conduction; through liquids and gases by a process called convection, whereby heat follows paths called convection currents; and through space, by radiation.
- Some heat energy is wasted in three ways: 33% is wasted by being dumped straight out of the exhaust; 33% is wasted by the cooling system, which prevents overheating of the engine components; and 5% is wasted by internal friction and from radiating off hot engine components straight to the atmosphere.
- Only about 25% to 30% of the original energy is used for powering the vehicle.
- The automotive cooling system provides a means of transferring heat from the hot parts of the engine to ambient air. This can be accomplished through a group of parts working together to circulate coolant throughout a sealed system to carry heat away from those engine parts.
- Heat can then be released to outside air or to air entering the passenger compartment for comfort purposes.
- The purpose of the cooling system is to allow the engine to warm up to its optimum temperature as quickly as possible and then transfer any excess heat energy to the atmosphere, thereby maintaining that ideal temperature.
- A liquid-cooled system uses coolant, a fluid that contains special antifreezing and anticorrosion chemicals mixed with water.
- Some vehicles use a coolant heat storage system (CHSS). This system uses a vacuum-insulated container, similar to a Thermos bottle. The storage container holds an amount of hot coolant and maintains the temperature for up to three days when the engine is shut down.
- Coolant is a mixture of water and antifreeze, which is used to remove heat from the engine.
- The coolant is important for three reasons: prevents an engine from overheating while in use, keeps the engine from freezing when not in use in cold climates, and prevents corrosion of the parts in the cooling system.
- Water alone is by far the best coolant there is, as it can absorb a larger amount of heat than most other liquids. But water has some drawbacks. It freezes if its temperature drops below 32°F (0°C).
- The problem with using water alone as a coolant is that water is corrosive and causes metal to rust.

- Antifreeze prevents corrosion and rusting through anti-corrosion additives (called corrosion inhibitors) mixed into the solution.
- Antifreeze is mixed with water to lower the freezing point of water and reduces the chances of component cracking.
- Ethylene glycol is a chemical that resists freezing but is very toxic to humans and animals.
- Propylene glycol is another chemical that resists freezing but is not toxic and is used in nontoxic antifreeze.
- The freezing point of coolant varies depending upon how much water is added to the antifreeze; because antifreeze does not absorb heat as effectively as water, it should not be mixed at a ratio higher than 65% antifreeze and 35% water.
- The best coolant is a 50/50 balance of water and antifreeze, making it an ideal coolant for both hot and cold climates and providing adequate corrosion protection.
- It is important to note that brands and types of coolant (antifreeze) differ from one manufacturer to another.
- Original equipment manufacturer (OEM) cooling system designs and coolant recommendations have changed in recent years, so the color of coolant is no longer a reliable way to identify a particular type of antifreeze.
- Mixing types of antifreeze can cause a reaction that turns the chemicals in antifreeze to sludge that plugs up the passages in the system, including the radiator and heater core. Always read the container label, and follow OEM coolant recommendations.
- IAT (inorganic acid technology) coolant is an early designed chemical formula that became available in the 1930s, was green in color, and is still in use today. It contains phosphate and silicate as corrosion additives.
- OAT (organic acid technology) is a longer-lasting coolant designed to be changed at five years or 150,000 miles (241,000 km). It was introduced in North America around 1994 and was intended for certain vehicles of that year. Dex-Cool, the orange coolant used by GM is an OAT coolant.
- HOAT (hybrid organic acid technology) is a coolant that contains a mixture of inorganic and organic additives. This type of coolant can use silicate and organic acid; it is the best of both worlds in coolants.
- PHOAT (phosphate hybrid organic acid technology) is a relatively new coolant that contains a proprietary blend of corrosion inhibitors. It is ethylene glycol based and is embittered so that pets do not drink it. It is a very long-life coolant, providing up to seven years or 250,000 miles (402,000 km) of protection.
- PHOAT is believed to be compatible with most other types of coolant, but check the manufacturer's current service information. This coolant is usually dark green in color and used in Mazda-based Fords 2008 and up.
- Water at sea level atmospheric pressure 14.7 psi (101.4 kPa, or 1 atmosphere [atm]) boils at 212°F (100°C). Atmo-

spheric pressure becomes lower as elevation is increased. Because atmospheric pressure is lower at higher elevations (such as in the mountains), the boiling temperature of a liquid in an unsealed system is lower.

▶ A liquid under pressure higher than atmospheric pressure has a higher boiling point than when that liquid is at atmospheric pressure.

▶ Pressurizing the cooling system enables an engine's cooling system to remain a liquid at temperatures well above the normal boiling point of 212°F (100°C).

▶ The pressurized coolant in the cooling system boils at a higher temperature than when the radiator pressure cap is removed (or if the system has a leak).

▶ For every 1 psi of pressure, it raises the boiling point by 3°F, so a 15 psi cap would add 45 degrees to the boiling point, which would put the coolant at 257°F (125°C).

▶ The freeze point of coolant is determined by the ratio of water to antifreeze mixture.

▶ Electrolysis is the process of pulling chemicals (materials) apart by using electricity or by creating electricity through the use of chemicals and dissimilar metals.

▶ Electrolysis is possible when the coolant breaks down and becomes more acidic.

▶ Many types of metal are used in the engine, such as cast iron, aluminum, copper, and brass. Introducing an acid solution into a mix of metals produces electricity. When this electricity is produced, the movement of the electrons begins to erode away the metal in the system.

▶ Centrifugal force is a force pulling outward on a rotating body.

▶ Centrifugal force is used in the water pump. When coolant enters the center of the water pump and the internal rotor spins, centrifugal force moves the liquid outward toward the outlet.

▶ Centrifugal force pushes the coolant into the engine block and head passageways that surround the cylinders.

▶ In the engine's liquid-cooled system, coolant is forced to flow around and through parts of the engine to pick up excess heat and carry it through flexible hoses to the radiator.

▶ In a water-cooled cooling system with normal flow, the flow of coolant starts at the water pump and proceeds through the engine to carry away the heat, and then back to the radiator.

▶ In the typical reverse-flow design, coolant starts from the radiator and flows through the radiator outlet hose to the water pump, through the water jackets, to the cylinder head, then to the thermostat, and finally to the radiator.

The radiator is usually made of copper, brass, or aluminum tubes with copper, brass, aluminum, or plastic tanks on the sides or top for coolant to collect in. Air is drawn over the radiator to transfer heat energy to ambient air. The fins on the tubes of the radiator give more surface area for heat dissipation—the spreading of heat over a large area to ease heat transfer.

▶ The thermostat regulates coolant flow to the radiator. It opens at a predetermined temperature to allow coolant flow to the radiator for cooling. It also enables the engine to reach operating temperature more quickly for reduced emissions and wear.

▶ Most thermostats have a small hole on one side of the thermostat valve that allows any air in the system to move past the closed thermostat when the valve is closed. This is helpful when the cooling system has been drained and is being filled. The hole usually contains a little pin called a jiggle valve or jiggle pin to help break the surface tension of the coolant and allow any air to flow slowly through the hole.

▶ The recovery system uses an overflow tank to catch any coolant that is released from the radiator cap when the coolant heats up.

▶ This pressurized surge tank is piped into the cooling system. Coolant constantly moves through it. It is used when the radiator is not the highest part of the cooling system. Remember, air collects at the highest point in the cooling system.

▶ The water pump is used to force coolant throughout the cooling system in order to transfer heat energy. The water pump is typically driven off the engine timing belt or accessory belt. On some engines, it is driven by the camshaft timing chain.

▶ The cooling fan forces air through the radiator for heat transfer. Cooling fans can be driven by a belt or an electric motor. The fan can be controlled by viscous fluid or thermostatic sensors, switches, and relays.

▶ Radiator hoses are used to connect the radiator to the water pump and engine. They are usually made of formed, nylon-reinforced rubber. Some radiator hoses use coiled wire inside them to prevent hose collapse as the cooling system temperature fluctuates.

▶ Some radiator hoses, especially lower hoses, have a spiral wire inside to keep the hose from collapsing during heavy acceleration when the water pump is drawing a lot of water from the radiator.

▶ Heater hoses connect the water pump and engine to the heater core. They carry heated coolant to the heater core to be used to heat the passenger compartment.

▶ As part of a maintenance inspection, you inspect the upper and lower radiator hoses along with the heater hoses, which can fail if neglected. It is critical that these hoses be checked. Any break in the system will dump the coolant and cause the engine to quickly overheat.

▶ The bypass hose is typically located on the water pump and connects to the intake manifold on many V-configured engines, such as a V6 or V8. This hose allows the water pump to circulate the water in the engine when the thermostat is closed.

▶ Drive belts provide power to drive the water pump and other accessories on the front of the engine. Three types are used: V-belts, serpentine (also called multi-groove) belts, and toothed belts.

- Temperature indicators provide information to the operator about engine temperature. The temperature gauge indicates engine temperature continuously.
- A temperature warning indicator comes on only when the engine is overheating, to warn the operator that engine damage will occur if the vehicle is driven much farther.
- Water jackets are passages surrounding the cylinders and head on the engine, where coolant can flow to pick up excess heat. They are sealed by replaceable core plugs.
- The heater core is a small radiator used to provide heat to the passenger compartment from the hot coolant passing through it. The amount of heat can be controlled by a heater control valve.
- Auxiliary coolers are used to cool automatic transmission fluid, power steering fluid, EGR gases, and compressed intake air.
- In a downflow radiator, the cooling tubes run top to bottom, with the tanks on the top and bottom.
- In a cross-flow radiator, the cooling tubes are arranged horizontally, with one tank on each side.
- A thermostat could fail for a number of reasons, but most of the time thermostats fail because the wax that changes form from a solid to a liquid simply wears out.
- Most water pumps have a small weep hole that sits between the seal and the bearing and vents any coolant that leaks past the seal, to be drained to the outside of the engine. Checking this hole for signs of coolant leakage is part of the process of inspecting the engine for leaks.
- Replacing a water pump is performed mostly as a result of noise or leak issues on accessory-belt driven water pumps. But now, with many water pumps being driven by timing belts, it is common to replace the water pump along with the timing belt at the belt's recommended replacement schedule.
- Core plugs are also known as soft plugs or expansion plugs. These aluminum, brass, or steel plugs are designed to seal the openings left from the casting process where the casting sand was removed. Under some conditions, the core plugs might pop out if the engine coolant is allowed to freeze.
- When working around the cooling system, care must be taken, particularly if the engine is at operating temperature, as the coolant may be hot enough to scald.
- Always allow the system to cool before removing the radiator or pressure cap, and use extreme caution when removing the radiator cap.
- If you must remove the radiator cap from a hot system, wear protective gloves and eyewear, and place a cloth fender cover or other large rag on top of the radiator cap before releasing it slowly, to the first (safety) point, to prevent the pressure inside from erupting.

Key Terms

auxiliary coolers Used to cool automatic transmission fluid, power steering fluid, EGR gases, and compressed intake air.

Each of these coolers transmits heat to either the cooling system or directly to the atmosphere. Because there is such a wide variety of auxiliary coolers, refer to the manufacturer's service information for how to properly inspect the auxiliary cooler for leaks and proper operation.

conduction Heat transfer from one solid to another when there is a difference of temperature or of electrical potential without movement of the material.

convection The movement caused within a fluid by the hotter and therefore less dense material to rise and colder material to sink, which results in the transfer of heat.

coolant The liquid used to prevent freezing, overheating, and corrosion of the engine.

cooling fan Forces air through the radiator for heat transfer. Cooling fans can be driven by a belt or by an electric motor. The fan can be controlled by viscous fluid or thermostatic sensors, switches, and relays.

cross-flow radiator Type of radiator that has the coolant flow from left to right and is more conformable to the low hood designs of today's vehicles.

downflow radiator Type of radiator that has the cooling tubes from top to bottom, so the surface area needed becomes taller than the cross flow radiator, which is why they are used mostly in trucks or vehicles that have a higher hood line.

drive belts Provide power to drive the water pump and other accessories on the front of the engine. Four types are used: V-belts, serpentine (also called multi-groove) belts, stretch belts, and toothed belts.

ethylene glycol An organic material that has properties that do not allow it to freeze until it is below the freezing point of water. It is usually infused with anticorrosive additives and rust inhibitors so that it conditions the materials that it flows through.

heater core A small radiator used to provide heat to the passenger compartment from the hot coolant passing through it. The amount of heat can be controlled by a heater control valve.

heater hoses Connect the water pump and engine to the heater core. They carry heated coolant to the heater core to be used to heat the passenger compartment.

propylene glycol An organic material that is taking the place of ethylene glycol as it is nontoxic and still has most of the properties that are needed to use in an automotive application.

radiation The emission of energy as electromagnetic waves that excite molecules in the objects they come in contact with.

radiator hoses Used to connect the radiator to the water pump and engine. They are usually made of formed, nylon-reinforced rubber. Some radiator hoses use coiled wire inside them to prevent hose collapse as the cooling system temperature fluctuates.

recovery system Uses an overflow tank to catch any coolant that is released from the radiator cap when the coolant heats up.

rotor housing Houses the rotors in a Wankel/rotary engine. This is the base for the engine, similar to the engine block.

second law of thermodynamics The **second law of thermodynamics** also states that the entropy (measurable coordinates that characterize a system) of an isolated system can only increase over time. It can remain constant in ideal cases where the system is in a steady state (equilibrium) or undergoing a reversible process. There is an upper limit to the efficiency of conversion of heat to work in a heat engine.

serpentine belt Also called a multi-groove V-belt, with a flat profile that has a number of small V-shaped grooves running lengthwise along the inside of the belt. These grooves are the exact reverse of the grooves in the outer edge of the pulleys; they increase the contact surface area, as well as prevent the belt from slipping off the pulley as it rotates. The serpentine belt is used to drive multiple accessories and to save underhood space forward of the engine. It winds its way around the crankshaft pulley, water pump, alternator, air-conditioning compressor, and tensioner. Most serpentine belts use a spring-loaded tensioner to maintain proper tightness of the belt and prevent it from slipping.

stretch belt Looks like an ordinary serpentine belt but is found on vehicles without a tensioner. It is made of a special material that allows it to stretch just enough to be installed over the pulleys but then shrink back to its original size, which is shorter than the distance around the pulleys. This stretchiness keeps the belt properly tensioned. Stretch belts require special tools to install and are usually cut off when being removed.

surge tank A pressurized tank that is piped into the cooling system. Coolant constantly moves through it. It is used when the radiator is not the highest part of the cooling system. (Remember, air collects at the highest point in the cooling system.)

temperature indicators Provide information to the operator about engine temperature. The temperature gauge indicates engine temperature continuously. A temperature warning indicator comes on only when the engine is overheating, and warns the operator that engine damage will occur if the vehicle is driven much farther.

thermostat Regulates coolant flow to the radiator. It opens at a predetermined temperature to allow coolant flow to the radiator for cooling. It also enables the engine to reach operating temperature more quickly for reduced emissions and wear.

toothed belt Has teeth on the inside that are perpendicular to the belt and fit inside the teeth of a gear. Timing belts are always toothed belts to keep the camshaft running exactly half the speed of the crankshaft. To save on labor cost, these belts are generally replaced whenever a water pump replacement is required. And the water pump is generally replaced whenever the timing belt is changed.

V-type Has a wedge-shaped interior and sits inside a corresponding groove in the pulley. The sides of the V-belt wedge in the sides of the pulley.

water jackets Passages surrounding the cylinders and head on the engine where coolant can flow to pick up excess heat. They are sealed by replaceable core plugs.

water pump A pump that is drivenby the engine to move coolant through the cooling system so that heat can be extracted from the engine and transferred to the air through radiation.

Review Questions

1. The coolant heat storage system:
   a. uses a condenser.
   b. maintains the temperature of the coolant for a day.
   c. increases hydrocarbon exhaust emissions.
   d. preheats the engine when the vehicle is started the next time.
2. A coolant serves all of the below purposes, *except*:
   a. preventing an engine from overheating while in use.
   b. keeping the engine from freezing while not in use in cold climates.
   c. reducing friction in the moving parts of the engine.
   d. preventing corrosion of the parts in the cooling system.
3. Draining and refilling the coolant will be necessary in all of the below cases, *except* when:
   a. a customer requests for it.
   b. the system is corroded.
   c. the coolant is contaminated.
   d. the coolant level is low.
4. When using a pressurized coolant:
   a. its boiling point increases.
   b. the cooling system becomes heavier.
   c. the radiator becomes bigger.
   d. engine efficiency decreases.
5. Which of these is used to force coolant throughout the cooling system in order to transfer heat energy?
   a. Water pump
   b. Thermostat
   c. Radiator
   d. Cooling fan
6. The surface area that dissipates heat is increased by the use of:
   a. radiator shrouding.
   b. heat-dissipating fins.
   c. hood insulation.
   d. drain plugs.
7. The surge tank:
   a. stores the coolant.
   b. prevents coolant leak.
   c. reduces engine noise.
   d. removes gas from the system.
8. Which hose allows the water pump to circulate the water in the engine when the thermostat is closed?
   a. Bypass hose
   b. Throttle body coolant line
   c. Heater hose
   d. Radiator hose
9. The engine's operating temperature can be verified using all of the below, *except* a:
   a. dash gauge.
   b. thermometer.
   c. scan tool.
   d. temperature gun.

10. If the vehicle only overheats while stopped, it could be an issue with the:
    a. radiator.
    b. thermostat.
    c. cooling fan.
    d. coolant.

ASE Technician A/Technician B Style Questions

1. Technician A says that when replacing the thermostat, you should replace it with one that opens up at a lower temperature, to cure an overheating problem. Technician B says that electric cooling fans do not drag on the engine as much as a thermostatic clutch fan. Who is correct?
   a. Tech A
   b. Tech B
   c. Both A and B
   d. Neither A nor B

2. Technician A says that when refilling a cooling system, you must use the same coolant that was in the system before. Technician B says that when refilling the cooling system, you must use the manufacturer's recommend coolant. Who is correct?
   a. Tech A
   b. Tech B
   c. Both A and B
   d. Neither A nor B

3. Technician A states that after you fill the cooling system with coolant, you must bleed the system. Technician B says that bleeding the system is only required when there is a bleeder valve in the system somewhere. Who is correct?
   a. Tech A
   b. Tech B
   c. Both A and B
   d. Neither A nor B

4. Technician A states that when mixing antifreeze with water, the water should be distilled, not from a tap. Technician B says that a radiator cap with a 16 psi marking indicates that the system operates at 16 psi. Who is correct?
   a. Tech A
   b. Tech B
   c. Both A and B
   d. Neither A nor B

5. Technician A says that fan shrouds that are on the vehicle do not need to be reinstalled if removed, as they are not needed to have the cooling system function properly. Technician B states that cooling hoses should be checked for sponginess or oil contamination on a periodic basis. Who is correct?
   a. Tech A
   b. Tech B
   c. Both A and B
   d. Neither A nor B

6. Technician A states that IAT coolant is typically green in color and contains phosphate and silicate as corrosion inhibitors. Technician B says when adding pressure to a cooling system it increases the boiling point. Who is correct?
   a. Tech A
   b. Tech B
   c. Both A and B
   d. Neither A nor B

7. Technician A states that a faulty ground wire could electrify the coolant causing electrolysis to rapidly corrode the metals that it touches. Technician B says that using the wrong coolant will not cause any harm to the engine or the components it touches. Who is correct?
   a. Tech A
   b. Tech B
   c. Both A and B
   d. Neither A nor B

8. Technician A states that water pump could be driven by a camshaft, timing belt, or accessory belt. Technician B states that when changing the timing belt, it is good practice to replace the water pump if it is driven by the timing belt. Who is correct?
   a. Tech A
   b. Tech B
   c. Both A and B
   d. Neither Technician

9. Technician A says a cooling system with a surge tank has no overflow tank. Technician B says that a cooling system with an overflow tank will leak coolant on the ground when there is a fault. Who is correct?
   a. Tech A
   b. Tech B
   c. Both A and B
   d. Neither A nor B

10. Technician A states that a mechanical cooling fan can be operated by a thermostatic clutch. Technician B says that a hydraulic cooling fan is powered by the power steering pump. Who is correct?
    a. Tech A
    b. Tech B
    c. Both A and B
    d. Neither A nor B

CHAPTER 9

Cooling System Maintenance and Repair

NATEF Tasks

- **N09001** Inspect and test coolant; drain and recover coolant; flush and refill cooling system with recommended coolant; bleed air as required.
- **N09002** Inspect, replace, and adjust drive belts, tensioners, and pulleys; check pulley and belt alignment.
- **N09003** Inspect engine cooling and heater systems hoses; perform needed action.
- **N09004** Remove, inspect, and replace thermostat and gasket/seal.
- **N09005** Inspect and test fan(s) (electrical or mechanical), fan clutch, fan shroud, and air dams.
- **N09006** Remove and replace radiator.
- **N09007** Perform cooling system pressure and dye tests to identify leaks; check coolant condition; inspect and test radiator, pressure cap, coolant recovery tank, and heater core; determine needed action.

Knowledge Objectives

After reading this chapter, you will have:

- **K09001** Knowledge of proper maintenance and repair of cooling system.
- **K09002** Knowledge of how to test engine coolant.
- **K09003** Knowledge of how to check and adjust the coolant in a vehicle.
- **K09004** Knowledge of how to evaluate an engine drive belt.
- **K09005** Knowledge of how cooling fans operate.
- **K09006** Knowledge of cooling system diagnosis and repair procedures.
- **K09007** Knowledge of proper procedure to check a cooling system issue.

Skills Objectives

- **S09001** Use a hydrometer to measure the freeze point of coolant.
- **S09002** Use a refractometer to measure the specific gravity/freeze point of coolant.
- **S09003** Test the coolant pH.
- **S09004** Test the coolant for electrolysis problems.
- **S09005** Check coolant level.
- **S09006** Drain and refill coolant.
- **S09007** Flush coolant.
- **S09008** Replace engine drive belt.
- **S09009** Replace an engine coolant hose.
- **S09010** Remove and replace a thermostat.
- **S09011** Inspect the shroud/air dam and test the electric cooling fan.
- **S09012** Removing and replacing the radiator.
- **S09013** Removing, inspecting and reinstall the heater core.
- **S09014** Pressurizing cooling system to check for leaks.
- **S09015** Inspecting and testing cooling fan.

You Are the Automotive Technician

A customer brings her 2014 Ford Focus into your repair facility, complaining about the temperature gauge going into the red when the vehicle is at a stoplight. The exhaust smoke is very white in color, and your customer estimates that she uses about a quart of coolant every week. What should you do first as the technician?

1. Check the coolant level.
2. Conduct a leak down test to verify a fault.
3. Check the oil in the vehicle.
4. Check the timing belt.

▶ Maintenance and Repair

K09001 Knowledge of proper maintenance and repair of cooling system.

Maintenance and repair of a cooling system is very important for the longevity of the engine in the vehicle. Without a properly operating cooling system, the engine will not last very long and will cost the customer considerably more money in the long run.

EPA Guidelines

As discussed in the coolant section of this chapter, ethylene glycol antifreeze, the most common antifreeze, is highly toxic to humans and animals. Because of this, the Environmental Protection Agency (EPA) has strict regulations for the handling and disposal of vehicle coolant. Coolant should never be dumped into a storm drain or down a shop floor drain. Coolant is a poison and should only be poured into an approved container and either be recycled in house or removed by a licensed recycler.

Care must be taken when a spill occurs when servicing a vehicle; it should be cleaned up promptly according to EPA regulations. Taking a little extra time to place a catch pan under the component being removed can prevent a spill and save time in the long run. Also, coolant should never be mixed with oil or other liquids; separate catch pans should always be used and marked accordingly.

Coolant Testing

K09002 Knowledge of how to test engine coolant.

Coolant testing is done to ensure that the vehicles cooling system is able to withstand the abuses that the weather puts on it. The coolant must be tested yearly to determine the abilities of it to protect the engine from the possibility to freeze and crack the block. Without testing, the engine could operate with substandard coolant, causing multiple problems throughout the cooling system when the temperature gets below freezing.

Measuring Freeze Protection

The use of a hydrometer or refractometer is necessary when testing the freeze protection of the coolant in the cooling system. The customer may request this service as part of a winterization package performed by the shop. Any time coolant is replaced in the cooling system, the freeze point should be verified.

The hydrometer is a tool that measures the specific gravity of a liquid. When coolant is drawn into the hydrometer, a float will rise to a certain level depending upon the density of the coolant. Antifreeze has a higher specific gravity than water, so the higher the float rises in the liquid, the greater the percentage of antifreeze in the mix. One drawback to hydrometers is that they are typically antifreeze specific. This means you need one for ethylene glycol and one for propylene glycol, as the specific gravities of the two chemicals are different. Another drawback is that as the temperature of the coolant goes up, the specific gravity goes down. Some hydrometers have a built-in thermometer and a chart, allowing you to compensate for the temperature of the coolant.

A refractometer can also tell the proportions of antifreeze and water in the coolant mix (or the level of freeze protection) by measuring a liquid's specific gravity. It works by allowing light to shine through the fluid. The light bends in accordance with the particular liquid's specific gravity. The bending of the light displays on a scale inside the tool, indicating the specific gravity of the fluid. One nice thing about a refractometer is that it has a scale for both types of antifreeze and reads the freeze point accurately.

Using a Hydrometer to Test the Freeze Point

S09001 Use a hydrometer to measure the freeze point of coolant.

To use a hydrometer to test the freeze point of the coolant, follow the steps in **SKILL DRILL 9-1**.

Using a Refractometer to Test the Freeze Point

S09002 Use a refractometer to measure the specific gravity/freeze point of coolant.

To use a refractometer to test the freeze point of the coolant, follow the steps in **SKILL DRILL 9-2**.

Testing the Coolant pH

Testing pH is performed whenever cooling system maintenance service is requested or if there is reason to suspect the coolant has outlived its useful life. It can be accomplished with test strips that turn color based on the level of acidity in the coolant, or electronic testers that measure the pH of the coolant directly can be used. Testing the pH of coolant is a great way to determine if the corrosion inhibitors are still working in the antifreeze. As corrosion inhibitors break down over time, the solution of water and antifreeze becomes more acidic. As the acid level builds, so does corrosion and electrolysis in the cooling system. If the coolant is left in this acidic condition, it will create permanent erosion to component surfaces that may require replacement of affected components.

S09003 Test the coolant pH.

SKILL DRILL 9-1 Using a Hydrometer to Test the Freeze Point of Coolant

1. Remove the pressure cap. Be sure the cooling system is cool before removing the cap.

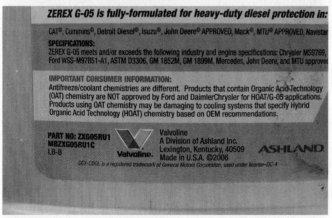

2. Determine the type of antifreeze, and verify that the hydrometer is designed to be used with it.

3. Place the hydrometer tube into the coolant, and squeeze the ball on top of the tool.

Continued

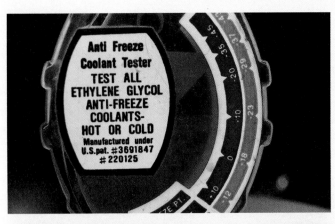

4. Release the ball to draw in a sample of coolant. Make sure the level of coolant drawn in is above the minimum line.

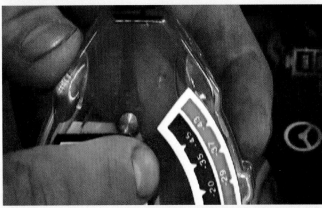

5. Read the scale on the tool to verify the freeze protection of the coolant.

6. Return the coolant sample to the radiator or surge tank.

SKILL DRILL 9-2 Using a Refractometer to Test the Freeze Point of Coolant

1. Remove the pressure cap. Be sure the cooling system is cool before removing it.

Continued

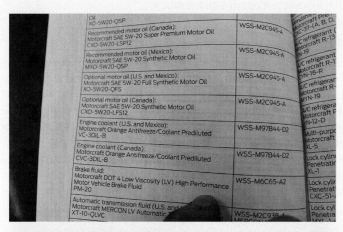

2. Determine the type of antifreeze, and verify that the refractometer is designed to be used with it.

3. The refractometer is a tool that is used to find the specific gravity of a fluid.

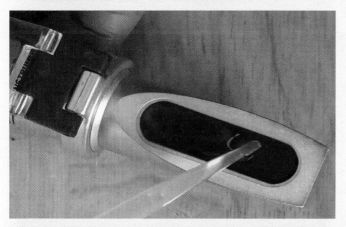

4. Place a few drops of coolant on the sample plate on the top of the tool.

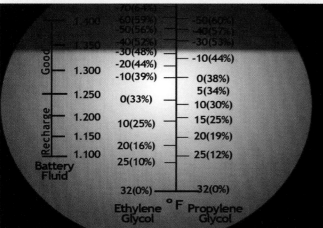

5. Hold the refractometer roughly level under a light, look through the viewfinder, and read the scale to verify the freeze protection of the coolant.

To test the coolant pH, follow the steps in **SKILL DRILL 9-3**.

Testing for Electrolysis

As the search for greater fuel efficiency continues and lighter-weight nonconductive materials find their way into our engines and vehicles, problems have arisen that result in the need for new training of technicians. Electrolysis, described earlier in chapter 8, is the reaction of different metals to an acid solution to produce electricity. It can result in negative effects on the cooling system, sometimes eroding metals from the inside of the cooling system and leading to damage.

Electrolysis can also be due to faulty grounds in the electrical system. If a circuit has a faulty ground, the current will try to find its way back to the battery in whatever way it can.

SKILL DRILL 9-3 Testing Coolant

1. Ensure that the coolant is relatively cool before removing the radiator cap.

2. If using a pH test strip kit, read the instructions to know how long to dip the strip in the coolant and how long to wait to compare the color of the test pad to the chart. Also, some strips have a second test pad on the strip that indicates the percentage of antifreeze in the coolant, so verify the time for that also.

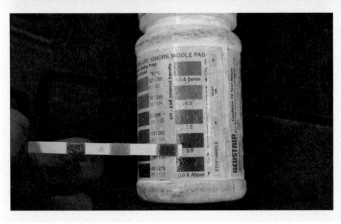

3. Dip litmus paper into the coolant, and wait the amount of time directed by the instructions. Compare the color of the litmus paper to the color scale on the kit.

Continued

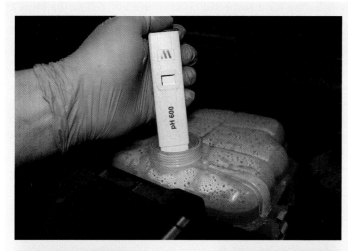

4. If using an electronic pH tester, turn on the tester and immerse it in the coolant.

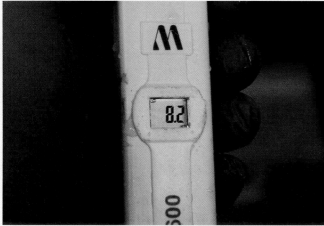

5. Read the meter.

6. Some cooling system experts suggest performing a coolant flush if the pH level is below 8.5.

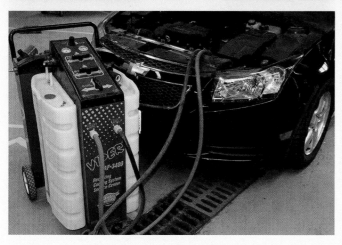

And that can include sending some of the current flow through the coolant. For example, if the engine ground is dirty and has an excessive voltage drop, then when the engine is cranked over, some of the current could flow through the coolant to another ground. Current flowing through the coolant can erode metal surfaces in the cooling system. In this case, the coolant is not at fault, and flushing will have little to no effect on the condition. Repairing the failed ground is the solution in this case. To verify that electricity is finding its way into the cooling system, voltage can be measured when various electrical loads are operated to see if there is any stray voltage in the coolant. If voltages are over 0.3 volt when the load or loads are activated, then you will have to perform electrical diagnosis of the circuit being tested.

To perform electrolysis testing for a suspected coolant problem, follow the steps in **SKILL DRILL 9-4**.

Recycling Coolant

Used coolant that has been removed from a vehicle is very hazardous to the environment and local wildlife. By law the technician is responsible for proper disposal of used engine coolant mixture, which must be collected and disposed of properly or the company may face legal fines. Most areas have companies that deal in recycling oil and antifreeze so that it can be reused instead of dumping it into the ground. As an ethical technician you must practice proper removal and disposal procedures so that the environment is not affected by your businesses operation.

SKILL DRILL 9-4 Performing Electrolysis Test for a Suspected Coolant Problem

1. Connect the black lead of the voltmeter to a good engine ground.

2. Hold the red lead of the voltmeter in the coolant in the radiator.

3. Observe the voltage reading. If it is greater than 0.3 volt (300 millivolts), flush the cooling system, refill, and retest. If less than 0.3 volt, there is no problem found. Determine necessary action.

Checking and Adjusting Coolant

Checking and adjusting coolant implies two separate tasks. First, is the level at the full mark? Second, is the level of freeze protection appropriate for the climate the vehicle is operated in? Checking coolant level should be part of every oil change so that any leaks can be identified before they become more serious. You may also need to check or adjust coolant level if the customer's low coolant indicator comes on. There are usually two correct level marks on the reservoir because the coolant in the system expands and contracts according to changes in its temperature. The coolant level should not be below the lower mark when the vehicle is cold. It should be near the upper mark when the coolant is hot. If the coolant is indeed low, testing for a coolant leak will be necessary.

Verification of coolant condition can be performed by checking its pH level with a test strip or electronic tester. Its freeze protection level can be tested with a coolant hydrometer or refractometer. If either of these tests shows that the coolant does not meet specifications, it will need to be flushed and replaced.

To check and adjust coolant, follow the steps in **SKILL DRILL 9-5**.

K09003 Knowledge of how to check and adjust the coolant in a vehicle.

S09005 Check coolant level.

Draining and Refilling Coolant

Draining and refilling coolant will be necessary if the customer requests a preventive maintenance service to flush the cooling system. Another reason you may need to perform this task is if corrosion is discovered in the system or if the coolant was contaminated by an incorrect fluid being added to the radiator, such as mistakenly adding power steering fluid to the coolant reservoir. Any time you have to replace a part of the cooling system, you will have to drain and refill the coolant. The discovery of electrolysis in the radiator also requires flushing the cooling system.

N09001 Inspect and test coolant; drain and recover coolant; flush and refill cooling system with recommended coolant; bleed air as required.

S09006 Drain and refill coolant.

SKILL DRILL 9-5 Checking and Adjusting Coolant

1. Most modern vehicles have a coolant system that uses a transparent recovery or surge tank as a coolant reservoir.

2. Check the level of coolant in this reservoir; if the engine is hot, the level should be visible near the upper mark. If the engine is cold, it should be at or above the lower mark.

Continued

3. Before adding new coolant, check the specific gravity of the coolant in the system with a coolant hydrometer or refractometer.

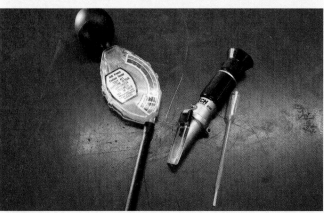

4. Draw some coolant up into the hydrometer, or place a couple of drops onto the sample plate, and read the freeze protection level on the gauge. These tools indicate the freezing point of the coolant mixture in the system, so you can tell if it has the right proportions of antifreeze and water.

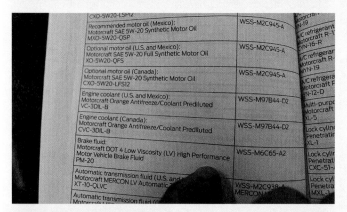

5. Check the service information for the recommended type and mixture of coolant that will produce an appropriate level of protection for the conditions where the vehicle will be used. Use a funnel to add enough coolant to bring the level up to the appropriate mark.

6. Replace the coolant reservoir cap. If the level was low, find the cause of the loss.

Your shop may have a coolant flushing machine, which will change the steps of the following Skill Drill. If you are using a flushing machine, follow the directions for the machine you are using.

To drain and refill coolant, follow the steps in **SKILL DRILL 9-6**.

SKILL DRILL 9-6 Draining and Refilling Coolant

1. Locate the cooling system drain plug or valve on the bottom tank of the radiator, if equipped. Place a clean catch pan, large enough to contain all the coolant, underneath the drain valve

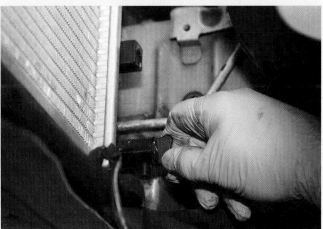

2. Carefully remove the pressure cap. This allows air into the cooling system so that it can drain quickly and completely. Open the drain valve so that the coolant can drain into the pan below. When all the coolant has drained out, close the drain valve.

3. Carefully remove the block drain plugs, and allow the coolant to drain into the catch pan.

Continued

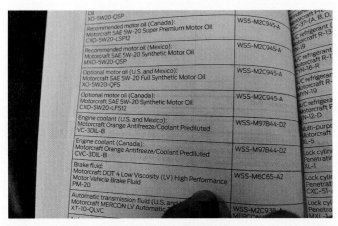

4. Check the shop service information for the capacity of the system and the recommended type and mixture of coolant for the operating conditions of the vehicle.

5. Measure the recommended amount of coolant. Using a funnel, pour it in through the top of the radiator or surge tank, and squeeze the upper hose to help push out any excess air.

6. Start the engine, and verify the proper level. Air can be trapped in the cooling system, so leave the radiator cap off to allow it to escape, and run the engine until the thermostat opens to allow the coolant to circulate and get rid of trapped air. Some vehicles will need to follow a cooling system bleed procedure following the service manual recommendations.

7. Fill the radiator; then replace the radiator cap and again bring the engine up to operating temperature. Check the coolant level in the reservoir, and top it off to the high or hot engine mark.

Continued

8. Dispose of waste. Antifreeze is toxic, so dispose of the waste coolant carefully and in an environmentally recommended way.

Flushing the Coolant

Coolant flushing is necessary either as a preventive maintenance service performed by most shops or because the coolant is worn out or contaminated. It will be necessary if the corrosion inhibitors in the coolant are found to be worn out or if some type of contamination is found. Flushing the coolant is performed in one of two ways: manually or with a flushing machine. Most shops have a coolant flushing machine; if you are using this machine, follow the directions on the machine as they are all different. In this example, we perform the manual flush.

To flush the coolant, follow the steps in **SKILL DRILL 9-7**.

S09007 Flush coolant.

SKILL DRILL 9-7 Flushing Coolant

1. Locate the radiator drain plug, if the vehicle is so equipped, and place a coolant catch pan under the drain plug. Be sure you know which direction to turn it to open. Some drain plugs are quarter-turn valves and are plastic. If turned too far, these drain plugs will break off. These drain plugs cannot always be found as a replacement part, and replacement of the entire radiator may be necessary.

2. Drain the coolant into the catch pan. Loosen and remove the pressure cap so coolant can flow out more freely.

Continued

3. Remove drain plugs located on the engine block, if it is so equipped. Be sure to check the service manual for the location of these plugs. Allow the coolant to drain from the block.

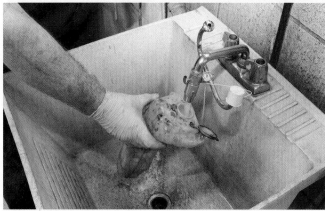

4. Remove the overflow or surge tank, drain coolant into the catch pan, and using hot water, clean the container until all deposits are removed.

5. Reinstall the tank and all drain plugs.

6. Refill the radiator with clean water, and start the engine.

7. Allow the engine to reach full operating temperature. The water will cycle through the engine and wash out any remaining coolant and debris. A cooling system flush additive may be used by some shops.

Continued

8. Drain water from the cooling system, remembering to remove any drain plugs in the engine to remove water from the engine block.

9. Refill the cooling system with a 50/50 mix of the required antifreeze and distilled water. Refer to the manufacturer's service information for the correct antifreeze to use in the vehicle you are servicing. Distilled water is recommended because it has no minerals in it, which would result in deposits in the cooling system. If the vehicle has heavy deposits in the cooling system, the cleaning process may have to be repeated several times to remove all the deposits. If the cooling system has been contaminated with some type of oil, a soapy solution must be used to remove the oil residue. This cleaning may need to be repeated until all traces of oil are removed.

10. Unless vacuum filling the cooling system, make sure to run the engine with the radiator cap removed until the thermostat opens to remove all trapped air. Then top off the radiator, and fill the overflow tank to the full mark.

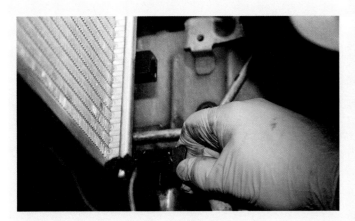

Replacing an Engine Drive Belt

Replacement of an engine drive belt may be necessary when the belt is cracked, glazed, separating, and getting ready to fail. Verifying that the pulley system is not damaged is the first step if noise is a problem. Perform a pulley alignment check as part of inspecting the drive belt system if noise is a concern or if belts are being thrown off. Checking pulley alignment is done with a straightedge across the face of the pulleys or with a special laser that fits in the grooves of the pulley. If it is a serpentine belt system, the pulley edges should be within 1/16" (1.6 mm) of alignment with each other.

Another reason to replace belts is if the customer requests belt replacement as part of the vehicle's preventive maintenance.

To replace a standard engine drive belt, follow the steps in **SKILL DRILL 9-8**.

N09002 Inspect, replace, and adjust drive belts, tensioners, and pulleys; check pulley and belt alignment.

K09004 Knowledge of how to evaluate an engine drive belt.

S09008 Replace engine drive belt.

SKILL DRILL 9-8 Replacing a Standard Engine Drive Belt

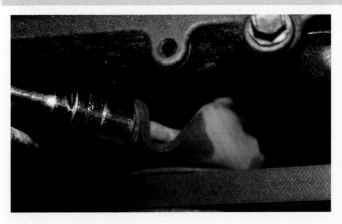

1. On a manually adjusted belt, locate the locking fastener and loosen it. It is usually on the alternator mounting or on a separate pulley. Move the adjusting mechanism in far enough to allow you to remove the belt.

Continued

2. On an automatic belt tension system, rotate the tensioning device back so that you can remove the belt. This is done with a breaker bar when a square opening is provided in the adjuster or with a special automatic adjuster tool for all others.

3. Look for cracks and other forms of damage in the belt. Inspect the pulleys for sideways movement, which indicates worn bearings, and spin the pulleys by hand to check that the bearings are rotating freely, without noise.

4. Check the pulleys for alignment with a straightedge or pulley laser tool. Also check the tensioner alignment.

5. Obtain the correct size and type of replacement belt specified in the service information, and compare it with the belt you have just removed. They should be very similar, although the old belt may have stretched and worn in use.

Continued

6. On a V-belt, install the new belt, making sure it is properly seated in the V-shape groove in the pulley.

7. If the belt is a serpentine type, make sure it is the correct width and squarely aligned in the pulley grooves. If it is not correctly aligned, the belt will be damaged and may be thrown off the pulleys.

8. Correctly tension the new belt. To do so, use the proper tools, and then check the belt with a tension gauge. With automatic tension systems, gently allow the automatic tensioner to apply the tension to the belt. A common recommendation at this point is to replace the automatic tensioner, as by this point in its life it is worn and can cause issues if it fails.

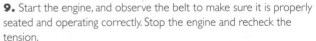

9. Start the engine, and observe the belt to make sure it is properly seated and operating correctly. Stop the engine and recheck the tension.

Checking and Replacing a Coolant Hose

N09003 Inspect engine cooling and heater systems hoses; perform needed action.

S09009 Replace an engine coolant hose.

Checking and replacing coolant hoses is a very important job of the technician. If the hose is deteriorating, it will eventually burst and coolant will be pumped out of the engine, resulting in overheating. Coolant hoses should be checked anytime the vehicle is in the shop for a maintenance inspection. If you find one defective radiator hose, the chances are that the other hose(s) may be deteriorating in the same way and will soon need to be replaced. For this reason, most technicians will generally replace both radiator hoses at once as a sensible precaution. Do not forget that there may be many hoses in the cooling system and you will need to inspect all of them to ensure proper function of the cooling system. You may need to use a flashlight to inspect the coolant hoses so that you can clearly see if the surface is starting to crack. Radiator hose problems include:

- **Swollen hose:** This hose has lost its elasticity and is swelling under pressure. It may soon rupture; typically you will see a bubble protruding from the side of this hose. Replace this hose immediately (**FIGURE 9-1**).
- **Hardened hose**—This hose has become brittle and will break and leak. Verify hardening by squeezing the hose and comparing it to a known good hose (**FIGURE 9-2**).
- **Cracked hose**—This hose has cracked and will soon start to leak. Verify cracking by a visual inspection (**FIGURE 9-3**).
- **Soft hose**—This hose has become very weak and is in danger of ballooning or bursting. Verify softening by squeezing the hose and comparing it to a known good hose (**FIGURE 9-4**).

Hose clamps come in several forms and will require different tools to properly remove or replace. These clamps secure the hose to the component it is connected to. Be sure to follow proper installation instructions to prevent future leaks from this seal. Types of clamps include:

- **Gear or worm clamp**—Adjust with a screwdriver or nut driver (**FIGURE 9-5**).
- **Banded or screw clamp**—Adjust with a screwdriver (**FIGURE 9-6**).

FIGURE 9-1 Swollen hose.

FIGURE 9-2 Hardened hose.

FIGURE 9-3 Cracked hose.

FIGURE 9-4 Soft hose.

FIGURE 9-5 Worm-type hose clamp.

FIGURE 9-6 Band/screw clamp.

- **Wire clamp**—This spring clamp is not adjustable. It is fitted and removed with special hose clamp pliers, which have grooved jaws (**FIGURE 9-7**).

Clamps are not expensive, so it is good practice to fit new ones at the same time as new hoses. Even if not corroded, the old clamps may have become distorted when being removed from an unserviceable hose. The time and money associated with replacing clamps are very small when thinking of the results of your customer losing a hose and becoming stranded.

To check and replace a coolant hose, follow the steps in **SKILL DRILL 9-9**.

FIGURE 9-7 Wire clamp.

SKILL DRILL 9-9 Checking and Replacing a Coolant Hose

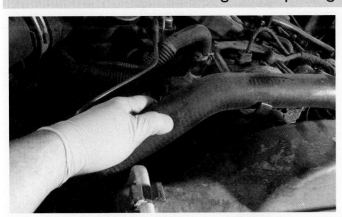

1. Locate both the hoses that carry coolant between the radiator and the engine. One is at the inlet and the other is at the outlet of the radiator. Squeeze each hose. It should feel pliable and springy. If it feels very soft and weak or very hard and brittle, it will need to be replaced. Look for signs of swelling or cracking, particularly near the hose clamps. Check that the clamps are holding the hoses firmly in position and are not damaged or corroded.

2. Drain the coolant from the system before removing either of the hoses. Remove the clamp using the appropriate tool. If the hose is stuck and will not pull off easily, be careful to not damage the radiator fitting by using too much force. It is better to cut the hose in several places so that you can peel it away from the radiator fitting. Clean the hose fittings thoroughly on both the engine and the radiator with fine sandpaper or emery cloth so that a good seal is made with the new hose.

Continued

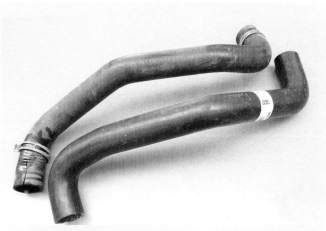

3. Obtain new hoses and compare them with the removed hoses to make sure they are the same length and diameter. If the hose is a molded type, the new one must also have the same preformed curve. Note that some hoses must be cut to length. Use the original hose as a guide.

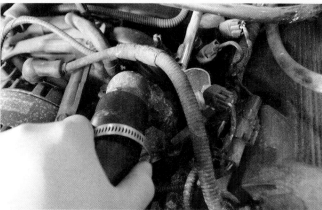

4. Place new loosened clamps over the hose ends and then slide the hose fully into position on the engine and radiator fittings. Position the clamps about 1/4" [6 mm] from the end of the hose. Be careful not to over-tighten and damage the hoses, but it is important that they do not fall off once the pressure in the cooling system increases. Spring clamps will apply the proper tightness if the clamp is installed correctly and the clamp is not damaged.

5. Refill the cooling system, pressure check the system, and then run the engine for a few minutes. Check the hose connections to make sure there are no leaks. When the engine is at its normal operating temperature, check the tightness of the clamps again, as the clamps and hoses will both expand at different rates as they heat up.

Removing and Replacing a Thermostat

N09004 Remove, inspect, and replace thermostat and gasket/seal.

S09010 Remove and replace a thermostat.

It will be necessary to remove and replace a thermostat in the event that the thermostat is found to be faulty, creating either an overheating concern or an overcooling concern. You may want to suggest to the customer a thermostat replacement during a cooling system flush or water pump replacement as a precautionary maintenance step. Before starting a repair or service task on the cooling system, allow sufficient time for the system to cool adequately before opening the pressurized system.

Drain at least 50% of the coolant in the system to avoid spills. Once the thermostat has been removed, clean any old gasket material and corrosion that has built up on both sealing surfaces where the thermostat seats. Properly position the thermostat air bleed valve (if equipped). Always install a new gasket and/or O-ring seal when installing the thermostat. Make sure the thermostat is fully seated in the groove and stays there before installing the housing. In most cases, if the thermostat falls out of its recessed groove, one of the thermostat housing ears will break off when the bolts are tightened, and the thermostat itself is likely to be damaged. Tighten the housing bolts to the correct torque. Use the manufacturer's procedure to properly bleed all air from the cooling system.

To remove and replace a thermostat, follow the steps in **SKILL DRILL 9-10**.

SKILL DRILL 9-10 Removing and Replacing a Thermostat

1. Drain the coolant from the cooling system using an approved catch container.

2. Unbolt the thermostat housing from the engine. Be very careful not to damage the housing, as it is generally made from aluminum or a similar fragile material. Remove the thermostat.

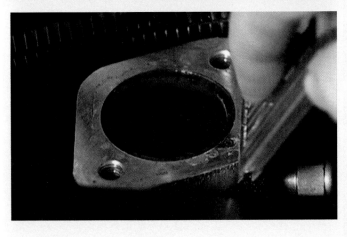

3. Inspect the mating surfaces. Inspect the thermostat housing and remove any gasket material from the mating surface of the housing. Inspect the other mating surface and remove any gasket material from its surface. Also be sure the recessed grove is clean and free from any debris.

Continued

4. Inspect the new thermostat to ensure that the part number and temperature rating are correct.

5. Install the new thermostat, ensuring that the air bleed hole is in the correct position (toward the top, vertically). Check that the thermostat is fully seated in its groove.

6. Fit the correct type of gasket or O-ring for the vehicle you are working on.

7. Carefully install the thermostat housing to the engine and torque it into place.

8. Refill the cooling system with coolant. Run the engine to circulate the coolant and remove any air trapped in the system. Check that the temperature indicator gauge shows that the coolant temperature is in the normal operational range. Top off the radiator or reservoir with coolant if necessary.

Inspecting and Testing Fans, Fan Clutch, Fan Shroud, and Air Dams

The need to inspect and test fans and fan shrouds will arise when the customer complains of overheating. Air dams are located under the vehicle and are designed to direct airflow into the radiator as the vehicle is moving down the road. If the air dam is damaged or missing, the engine temperature may be higher than originally designed while driving on the highway. If the vehicle only overheats while stopped, it could be an issue with the fan shroud, which directs airflow through the radiator. The shroud is what surrounds the cooling fan and allows a maximum amount of air to be moved by the cooling fan. If the shroud is missing, air will be pulled from around the fan blades rather than pulling air through the radiator. A visual inspection of these components will verify whether they are in proper position and operating as designed.

A mechanical or electric fan can fail, which will also result in air not being pulled through the radiator. A quick test to verify that air is moving through the radiator is to hold a piece of paper in front of the radiator and see if suction pulls the paper in. If it does not, then air is not being pulled through the radiator. Follow the service manual information on diagnosing the fan equipped on your vehicle.

To inspect the shroud/air dam and test the electric cooling fan, follow the steps in **SKILL DRILL 9-11**.

N09005 Inspect and test fan(s) (electrical or mechanical), fan clutch, fan shroud, and air dams.

K09005 Knowledge of how cooling fans operate.

S09011 Inspect the shroud/air dam and test the electric cooling fan.

SKILL DRILL 9-11 Inspecting the Shroud/Air Dam and Testing the Electric Cool Fan

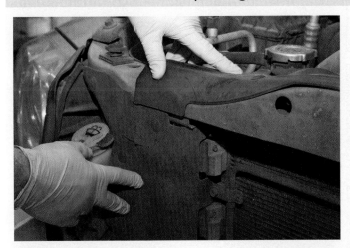

1. Visually inspect all shrouds, ducts, and air dams around the radiator and fan for damaged or missing pieces.

2. If equipped with a fan clutch, rotate the fan and check it for looseness, play, or binding. If bad, replace the fan clutch.

Continued

3. If the fan clutch feels free, place cardboard in front of most of the radiator. Start the engine, and monitor the engine temperature with a temperature gun. Verify that it cycles on at the proper temperature. If not, replace the fan clutch.

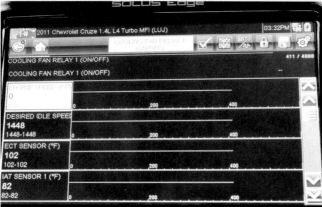

4. If equipped with an electric fan, connect a scan tool to the data link connector under the dash.

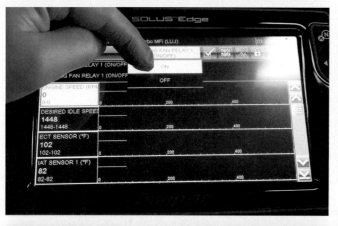

5. Locate the bidirectional command menu, and command the cooling fan on. This activates the relay and should send power to the fan.

6. Verify that the fan runs by visually inspecting that the fan is turning.

Continued

7. Verify that air is flowing across the radiator. Use a piece of paper to ensure airflow is strong enough to pull the paper to the radiator.

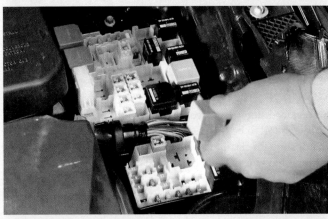

8. If the fan is not operating, locate the cooling fan relay, remove the relay, and check for the presence of power and ground at the appropriate terminals in the relay block. Two terminals should have battery positive voltage, one terminal should have a ground all the time and one should be a switched ground that is controlled by the PCM.

9. If all terminals read properly, test the relay winding for continuity. If out of specifications, replace the relay.

10. If the relay winding is okay, install a relay socket tester, and reinstall the relay into the relay box, then activate the electric fan. Measure the voltage drop on each leg of the circuit and the relay contacts themselves.

Continued

11. Trace the path that indicated a problem, and locate the voltage drop or defective component. Determine the necessary actions based on your findings.

Removing and Replacing a Radiator

N09006 Remove and replace radiator.

S09012 Removing and replacing the radiator.

A radiator may need to be replaced due to an overheating condition traced to partially plugged radiator tubes. If this is found to be the case, the radiator will have to be removed and can be sent out to a radiator shop for cleaning. A good flush of the entire cooling system is necessary as further clogging is likely, especially in the heater core.

Another reason to remove the radiator is for leaks traced to the radiator through the use of the coolant pressure tester or coolant dye and an ultraviolet light. Some radiators can be repaired by a radiator shop, but a cost analysis must be performed to see if doing so is more cost effective for the customer than buying a new radiator.

When replacing the radiator, make sure the coolant catch tray is large enough to catch any spills and has the capacity to hold all the system coolant. If you are replacing the coolant, dispose of the old coolant properly in accordance with environmental and legislative requirements. If reusing the old fluid, keep it stored in a covered and uncontaminated container. Most situations will require replacement of the coolant. If, for example, the vehicle just had new coolant installed, you may want to catch and reuse the coolant.

Inspect the cooling system hoses and clamps. Replace them if worn or damaged. When removing the hose from the radiator fitting, do not twist it; doing so can damage the fitting or even rip it out of the radiator. If it does not easily release, carefully work a tool between the hose and the fitting, breaking it loose all the way around. If the hoses are to be replaced, you can carefully slit them with a knife or hose-cutting tool, and peel them off the fitting, which is less likely to damage the fitting.

When replacing hoses, reinstall them all the way onto the fittings. Make sure the clamps are installed just beyond the flared or barbed segment, not on top of it. Placing a clamp on top of the flare or barb will likely result in the hose being blown off the fitting. Many vehicles have automatic transmission cooler lines attached to the radiator. Remember to disconnect these lines when removing the radiator, and always reinstall them before refilling the system with coolant. Remember, when you disconnect these lines that transmission fluid will leak out. Do not mix coolant and oil! Using a separate catch container will ensure that coolant and oil are not mixed.

Refill the system with the correct coolant at the proper antifreeze/water ratio. It is advisable to pressure test the system to check for leaks upon completion of the job. Start the engine, warm it up until the thermostat has opened, and check for proper operation of the cabin heater. Check for proper coolant level after it cools sufficiently.

To remove and replace a radiator, follow the steps **SKILL DRILL 9-12**.

SKILL DRILL 9-12 Removing and Replacing a Radiator

1. Place a catch pan below the radiator, and remove the drain plug, if the vehicle is so equipped. Drain the coolant from the system. Replace the drain plug, and dispose of the drained coolant in an environmentally approved manner.

2. Carefully remove any hoses and tubes that are attached to the radiator, being careful not to damage the radiator fittings.

3. Unscrew any shrouds or covers from the radiator.

4. Remove the bolts or screws that hold the radiator in position in the engine bay, and lift the radiator from its location.

Continued

5. Visually inspect the radiator to ensure that it is suitable for reinstallation in the vehicle. If the radiator fins are blocked by debris, carefully clean the fins with a dry brush or garden hose. If the radiator is damaged, advise your supervisor so a decision can be made about whether to repair it or replace it.

6. Place the radiator into position, and replace the securing bolts or screws. Reinstall the shrouds or covers. Rotate the fan and belts by hand to check that the covers do not restrict movement. Attach the hoses and tubes to the radiator.

7. Refill the system with new coolant of the correct type. Run the engine to circulate the coolant and remove any air trapped in the system. Check that the temperature indicator gauge shows that the coolant temperature is in the normal operational range. Top off the radiator or reservoir with coolant, if necessary.

Removing, Inspecting, and Reinstalling the Heater Core

S09013 Removing, inspecting and reinstall the heater core.

Removal of a heater core may become necessary if the customer notices a puddle of coolant on the carpet in the vehicle, usually on the passenger side. Typically, the heater core will leak, fill the air box, and drip onto the floor inside the vehicle. The other concern the customer may have is the smell of coolant inside the vehicle, or the complaint of a film on the inside of the windshield, which upon inspection is coolant that is being discharged with the air when the customer uses the defroster. The removal of a heater core is not an easy task, as sometimes it may be necessary to pull the entire dash from the vehicle. It is highly recommended to take pictures of the process as you go, to make reassembly easier. Follow the manufacturer's service information to perform this task. The procedure in the following Skill Drill is generic and may be substantially different than on the vehicle you are working on.

To remove, inspect, and reinstall the heater core, follow the steps in **SKILL DRILL 9-13**.

SKILL DRILL 9-13 Removing, Inspecting, and Reinstall the Heater Core

1. Find service information on the removal and replacement of the heater core for the vehicle you are working on. Determine if the air-conditioning refrigerant needs to be recovered.

2. Drain the coolant from the radiator.

3. If the air-conditioning evaporator needs to be removed, recover the air-conditioning refrigerant.

4. Remove necessary dash panels and covers, making sure to collect screws in a magnetic tray or plastic bag. Mark screws to remind you where they were removed. This becomes more critical the longer the vehicle is apart; it can be hard to remember after a couple weeks have gone by.

Continued

5. Remove heater core hoses (and remove air-conditioning lines to the evaporator, if necessary).

6. Locate all bolts securing the air box to the bulkhead of the vehicle and remove, if necessary.

7. Pull the air box from the vehicle, if necessary.

8. Remove the bolts holding the air box halves together, and separate the halves.

9. Remove the heater core.

Continued

10. Now is a good time to clean the air box of any debris or gunk in the bottom around the drain; doing so could prevent a vehicle from coming back at a later date for an air-conditioning odor complaint. Inspect all air box doors to ensure there are no cracks or dry-rotting rubber or foam. If found, the doors will have to be replaced.

11. Install the new heater core, and reverse the steps to reinstall the air box. Properly refill the cooling system, and recharge the air-conditioning system.

Cooling System Procedures

The cooling system is an often overlooked part of the automobile. It does its job very effectively and is rarely thought of until problems arise. The lack of periodic service of the cooling system according to OEM maintenance schedules is the leading reason that cooling systems fail. Properly performed cooling system maintenance ensures that the cooling system continues to perform as designed.

Common failures of the cooling system can require repairs ranging from simple to complex. An example of a failure that requires a simple repair is a radiator hose clamp that has not been installed properly and is creating a leak. The customer notices the leak and brings the vehicle in for service. An example of a more complex repair is a vehicle that needs a new head and block because a severe pH imbalance in the cooling system has heavily corroded the internal metal. Corrosion can build up to the point that normal cooling system operation cannot be restored without replacing multiple parts, including the engine itself, due to corrosion pitting of the engine block or cylinder head, leading to an internal coolant leak. Corrosion can also coat and/or block coolant passages and lead to an engine that runs hotter than normal or overheats.

Another common customer complaint is that the heater does not produce heat when turned on. This issue can result from a group of problems that have to be diagnosed by the technician, but often the culprit is a stuck-open thermostat that will not let the engine come up to operating temperatures. If the thermostat fails, it can fail in either the open position or the closed position. If it sticks closed, the result will be an overheating condition because coolant cannot get to the radiator to be cooled. If it sticks open, the engine will not warm up fully, leading to excessive engine wear, higher emissions, and reduced fuel economy.

Overheating conditions can have several causes, such as low coolant level due to a leak, a stuck-closed thermostat, a faulty radiator cap, clogged radiator tubes or fins, an inoperative cooling fan, a water pump impeller that is eroded or slipping on the shaft, or a blown

K09006 Knowledge of cooling system diagnosis and repair procedures.

head gasket, to name a few. Understanding how the cooling system works, as well as the manufacturer's test procedures, is necessary to successfully diagnose and repair the vehicle.

When diagnosing a cooling system problem, you need to use all of your senses to help determine what is wrong. Your sense of touch can allow you to feel for hot and cold parts in the system. For example, if the engine is overheating, but the upper radiator hose is cold, that could indicate a thermostat that is stuck closed. Your sense of smell could pick up the scent of antifreeze leaking into the passenger compartment from a leaky heater core. Your sense of hearing can tell you that the accessory belt is loose and the water pump is slipping. And your sense of sight could see the telltale stream of coolant leaking out of the water pump weep hole or a rusted-through soft plug. It is advisable not to use your sense of taste when diagnosing cooling system issues.

If the problem cannot be determined by your senses alone, you may have to resort to tools or equipment to help you locate the issue. A cooling system pressure tester allows you to pressurize the cooling system and radiator cap and check for any visible leaks. Starting the engine and using an exhaust analyzer to sniff the vapors coming out of the neck of the radiator can indicate if there is a small leak from one of the combustion chambers that is leaking combustion gases into the cooling system. Using a cylinder leakage tester and pressurizing each cylinder can help locate which cylinder has the combustion leak, due to either a blown head gasket or a cracked head. If the leak is a small external leak and the source cannot be located easily, you may need to use a fluorescent dye and black light to help make it stand out better.

An infrared temperature gun is a useful tool that can be used to measure the operating temperature of the engine to verify whether the engine really is overheating. Or it can be used to check the radiator for cold spots, which would indicate blockage within the core of the radiator. A scan tool can be a quick way to monitor the operating temperature, verify any cooling system diagnostic trouble codes (DTCs), or command the electric fan to come on. As you can see, understanding how cooling systems operate, as well as observing what is happening and having a few tools available, can take you a long way toward diagnosing customers' cooling system concerns.

Tools for Servicing the Cooling System

A properly trained and experienced technician use special tools for diagnosing and servicing the engine cooling system. These tools include:

- **Coolant system pressure tester**—Used to apply pressure to the cooling system to diagnose leakage complaints. Under pressure, coolant may leak internally to the combustion chamber, intake or exhaust system, or the engine lubrication system. It can also leak externally to the outside of the engine (**FIGURE 9-8**).
- **Hydrometer**—Used to test coolant mixture and freeze protection by testing the specific gravity of the coolant. You must use a hydrometer specifically designed for the antifreeze you are testing (**FIGURE 9-9**).

FIGURE 9-8 Cool system pressure tool.

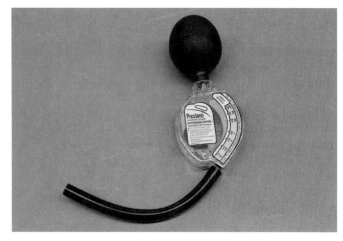

FIGURE 9-9 Hydrometer.

FIGURE 9-10 Refractometer.

FIGURE 9-11 pH testing strips.

- **Refractometer**—Used to test coolant mixture and freeze protection by testing the fluid's ability to bend light. This tester can be used with any type of antifreeze (**FIGURE 9-10**).
- **Coolant pH test strips**—Used to test the acid-to-alkalinity balance of the coolant (**FIGURE 9-11**).
- **Coolant dye kit**—Used to aid leak detection by adding dye to coolant and using an ultraviolet light source (black light) to trace to the source of the leak; the dye glows fluorescent when a black light is shined on it (**FIGURE 9-12**).
- **Infrared temperature sensor**—A noncontact thermometer used to check actual temperatures and variations of temperature throughout the cooling system to help pinpoint faulty parts and system blockages (**FIGURE 9-13**).
- **Thermometer**—Used to check the temperature of air exiting the heating ducts (**FIGURE 9-14**).
- **Voltmeter**—Used to check for electrical problems such as cooling fan and temperature gauge issues (**FIGURE 9-15**).
- **Belt tension gauge**—Used to check belt tension (**FIGURE 9-16**).

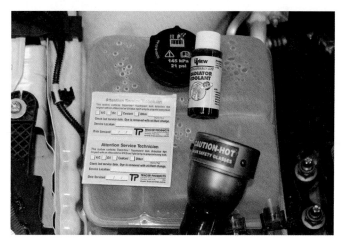

FIGURE 9-12 Coolant dye test kit.

FIGURE 9-13 Infrared thermometer.

FIGURE 9-14 Thermometer.

FIGURE 9-15 Voltmeter.

FIGURE 9-16 Belt tension gauge.

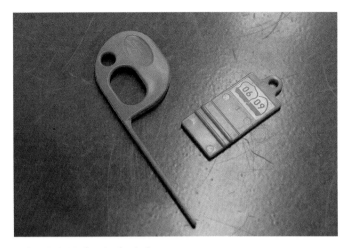

FIGURE 9-17 Serpentine belt wear gauge.

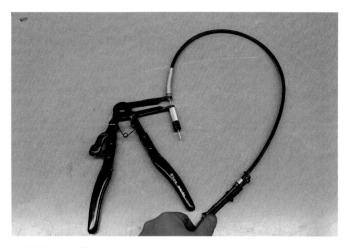

FIGURE 9-18 Radiator clamp pliers.

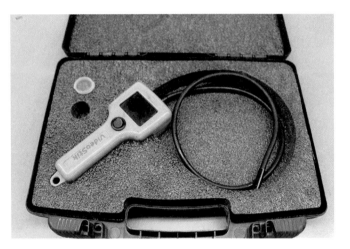

FIGURE 9-19 Borescope.

FIGURE 9-20 Scan tool.

- **Serpentine belt wear gauge**—Used to check if the serpentine belt grooves are worn past their specifications (**FIGURE 9-17**).
- **Radiator clamp pliers**—Used to safely remove spring-type radiator clamps (**FIGURE 9-18**).
- **Borescope**—Used for examining internal passages for evidence of a coolant leak (**FIGURE 9-19**).
- **Scan tool**—Used to activate the cooling fan through bidirectional controls for testing; to monitor cooling sensor operation and to command air door actuators when testing low heat complaints; and to read DTCs related to cooling system operation (**FIGURE 9-20**).
- **Cooling system flush machine**—Used to flush coolant backward through the system with cleaners that remove corrosion buildup and old coolant. Most of these machines have their own pump so the vehicle does not have to run to perform the flush (**FIGURE 9-21**).
- **Exhaust gas analyzer**—Used to detect exhaust gases that are finding their way into the cooling system due to a leaking head gasket or damaged head or block. Be careful not to allow liquid coolant to be picked up by the analyzer probe (**FIGURE 9-22**).

FIGURE 9-21 Cooling system flush machine.

FIGURE 9-22 Gas analyzer.

Visual Inspection of the Cooling System

Many times a visual inspection of the cooling system will give you a good indication of any issues. Check the level of the coolant in the overflow bottle and radiator. At the same time, check the condition of the coolant to see if it is cloudy or contaminated. Also check the belt condition and for the proper tension, and check hoses for any leaks or wear. If the sweet aroma of coolant is detected when the engine is first started, check for leaking coolant at the heater box drain, which would indicate a possible cracked or rotted leaking heater core. Check the engine exhaust for white smoke. A head gasket failure or a cracked head or valve seat may cause coolant to leak into the exhaust manifold and be seen as white smoke, especially when combustion pressures are high when accelerating. Also start the engine with the radiator cap off and look for bubbles from combustion in the radiator. Bubbles indicate a leak in the combustion chamber, likely at the head gasket. Disassembly and inspection must happen to verify that it is the head gasket, not a cracked head or block.

Testing the Cooling System for Leaks

Pressure testing the cooling system for leaks is usually an effective way to locate leaks because it causes coolant to leak out much more quickly, making leaks easier to locate. But before you pressurize the system, make sure it is topped off with coolant or water. Otherwise, the leak could be above the coolant level and only leak air, which is much harder to observe. Topping off leads to quicker pressurization because it removes air, which is compressible. Also, if the system is full of liquid, the pressure reading on the gauge will fall faster if there is a leak.

The pressure tester puts pressure on the cooling system, and with pressure applied, leaks generally show up easily as identified by coolant coming from the source. The use of a droplight and a mirror may be necessary to see behind the engine or in tight areas. Don't forget to check the heater core in the passenger compartment. If the pressure gauge is losing pressure, ensure that the tester is installed correctly; if it still loses pressure, ensure that the tool is working properly. Once the tool is verified and you cannot find an external leak, you know that the cooling system may be leaking internally into the engine. Check engine oil for evidence of coolant. It will have a milky appearance on the dipstick. If coolant is not leaking into the oil, it could be leaking into the cylinder. Remove the spark plugs, and look for coolant being burned in the cylinders, as evidenced by a color-stained spark plug insulator; instead of it being white, it could be a dark brown or blackish color. A combustion chamber experiencing a coolant leak will

N09007 Perform cooling system pressure and dye tests to identify leaks; check coolant condition; inspect and test radiator, pressure cap, coolant recovery tank, and heater core; determine needed action.

S09014 Pressurizing cooling system to check for leaks.

appear to be steam cleaned. A borescope can be used to inspect the cylinders through the spark plug holes.

Normally, the engine should be off when carrying out any visual inspection of the system or when you connect test equipment such as the pressure tester. However, it is possible that the leak only occurs when the engine is running, such as around the water pump seal, making it necessary to run the engine while testing. If you do have to run the engine after the tester has been installed and pressurized, make sure to watch the pressure gauge, and release excess pressure as the engine heats up. When the engine is running, make sure you keep well away from any rotating or hot parts.

Also remember to pressure test the radiator cap, as a leak at the cap will prevent the cooling system from building pressure. Low pressure on the coolant leads to a lower boiling point, which can cause coolant to boil at normal operating temperatures. Many a technician has been fooled into thinking that the vehicle had a serious overheating problem after changing the thermostat, water pump, and so on, when all it needed was a radiator cap.

A pressure tester is normally used to test the cooling system for both internal and external leaks. Most pressure testers are hand operated and come with a number of adapters to fit a variety of cooling systems. Adapters are used to connect the tester to the radiator, surge tank, or radiator cap.

To test the cooling system pressure, follow the steps in **SKILL DRILL 9-14**.

SKILL DRILL 9-14 Testing the Cooling System Pressure

1. Before pressure testing the system, inspect it for any obvious signs of leaks. These may show up as puddles under the vehicle or on the engine. Check for obvious leaks at the radiator core, radiator tanks, coolant and heater hoses, water pump seal and weep hole, heater box drain, and all accessible engine core plugs. Also inspect the cooling fan, drive belt, and radiator cap and seals.

2. The operating pressure should be indicated on the outside of the radiator cap. Refer to the service information or vehicle owner's manual to check that the pressure cap installed has the correct pressure rating. Attach the radiator cap to the tester with an adapter, and pump up the pressure. The pressure should hold just below the relief pressure setting. If the cap will not hold or cannot reach pressure, or if it does not vent at that pressure, then replace it with a new cap of the correct type and pressure rating.

Continued

3. Before pressure testing the integrity of the cooling system, top off the coolant level. Attach the cooling system tester to the radiator. Pump up the system pressure to slightly above the specified radiator cap pressure.

4. Observe the pressure reading over a few minutes. During this time, inspect the entire cooling system for any signs of leakage. If the pressure drops, and there is no visible external leak, then the leak is probably internal.

5. Once you have determined that the leak is not external to the vehicle, you must be able to recommend the next steps that will help you determine what has failed in the engine.

Dye Testing

Dye testing a cooling system consists of acquiring a vial of fluorescent dye and adding that dye to the cooling system (**FIGURE 9-23**). Once it is in the cooling system, you must run the engine up to operating temperature so that the dye has time to circulate throughout the system. The dye will seep out the area where the coolant is leaking, causing it to stain that spot. The technician now is able to use an ultraviolet light to locate the component that is leaking so that he or she can replace it to stop the leak.

Flow Restriction Issues

With the debris that can come from electrolysis or other scaling, there is an increased possibility for a clogged radiator or heater core. The tubes that run through the radiator and the heater core are very small, so any type of debris could restrict the follow. Once the flow is restricted, there is no way of cleaning it or removing the debris, and the component must be replaced. This is becoming a larger problem, as coolant change intervals are becoming longer; the debris in the system builds up, creating more of a chance for it to end up causing a restriction.

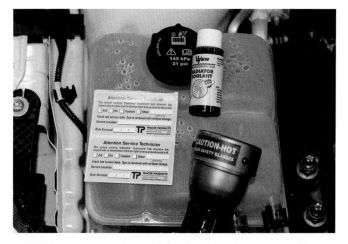

FIGURE 9-23 Coolant dye is used to find a leak that is in a difficult position to see; the dye leaks out of the area, and then the technician can use a blacklight to see where it is coming from.

Coolant Mixture Issues

Mixing water and coolant must be precisely done, or you could end up with a coolant mixture that is not able to withstand the temperatures that it is operating in. Improper coolant mixture could void the warranty on most vehicles as well as cause massive engine damage from freezing or overheating.

Oil Contamination

As you are evaluating the coolant in an engine's cooling system, you must be aware if it has been contaminated by engine oil. Vehicle manufactures have increasingly been trying to control the temperature of the engine oil in the engine by running it through the radiator to cool it down. This is a good idea: It helps make the oil last longer and causes less wear on the engine, as the oil can protect it better if it is not broken down. A problem occurs when you have a gasket or cooler leak into the engine cooling system, causing oil to mix with coolant. When this happens, the oil coats the heat transfer surfaces, causing the coolant not to absorb the heat from the engine efficiently (**FIGURE 9-24**). Another problem happens when the coolant gets into the crankcase, where it gets sucked into the oiling system, allowing it to be moved throughout the engine in place of oil. Coolant is not a lubricant like oil and will cause rapid degradation of the bearing surfaces in the engine if not removed.

Transmission Contamination

In a situation similar to oil contamination, the automatic transmission fluid also gets cooled by the radiator, which gives it a way to enter the cooling system if there is a failure (**FIGURE 9-25**). Transmission fluid is oil based and causes the coolant to lose its heat transfer capabilities, which could cause the engine to eventually overheat. Along with engine damage, you could potentially have transmission damage, as coolant does not have the same properties that transmission fluid does, which can cause friction clutch and servo failures. The first step to diagnosis this type of issue is to find the cause of the contamination. After fixing it, you must flush out the transmission.

Air in the System

One of the main causes of overheating issues in today's vehicles is air trapped in the cooling system. This air can come from a few places. Usually, it is from a leak in the engine, where, as the engine cools, it causes an air pocket to form in the cooling system, which doesn't allow for cooling of the engine. Then a large bubble in the cooling system moves through the system, causing the overheating condition that the customer complains of. A cooling system operates best in a pressurized environment, and when you have a hole in that system, the system cannot adapt. Once air is introduced in the system, you must get it out to return the system to the condition it needs to be in to cool the engine correctly.

FIGURE 9-24 When water/coolant mixture mixes with oil, it creates a milklike substance.

FIGURE 9-25 When coolant and transmission fluid mix, it creates a brownish slew of fluid.

What Are the Symptoms of Air Pockets in the Cooling System?

Some of the symptoms of air in a system are a temperature gauge that jumps from cold to hot, to cold again, very sporadically. No heat in the vehicle is another symptom of air in the system as the air bubble becomes trapped in the heat core, which doesn't allow for coolant flow through the core to create heat. Odd noises from the cooling system as the engine runs could be a sign that air has infiltrated the system.

How to Bleed the Air Out

Once air is in the cooling system, you must bleed it out, usually by attaching a funnel to the surge tank or radiator, filling it with coolant, and allowing the engine to run. As the engine runs, the air works its way up to the highest point of the system, which should be your funnel. In some vehicles, the place where the funnel attaches is not the highest point of the cooling system, which means the air gets trapped in the component that is. These systems usually have bleeder valves located throughout the system to remove the air from the system. Start the vehicle, get it up to operating temperature, and as it runs slowly, open the bleeder valves 1/8 of a turn to bleed out the air.

Airflow Restriction

As you are diagnosing an overheating issue, you must examine if the radiator has the ability to exchange the heat from the engine with the air outside the vehicle. If the radiator cannot exchange the heat, then the vehicle will not be able to cool itself down. This type of problem can be from a number of things, from a piece of cardboard in front of the radiator, to debris from trees impeding airflow, to missing shrouding. Air must be directed through the radiator so that this process can occur; without the airflow, the engine cannot cool itself down.

Radiator Fins Clogged

One type of airflow restriction occurs when the radiator fins are clogged. Usually this happens when outside debris finds its way into the fins of a radiator, thereby not allowing the radiator to exchange its heat with the outside air (**FIGURE 9-26**). The simple fix for this is to remove the debris from the radiator or replace the radiator with a new one that does not have debris.

Condenser Fins Clogged

The most overlooked area of air flow restrictions is the condenser, because it sits directly in front of the radiator, and any airflow restrictions it has also affect the condenser (**FIGURE 9-27**). Bent fins, clogged fins, missing fins, or damaged fins can all cause airflow restrictions that affect both the AC and the cooling systems. A visual inspection should be able to see if this type of situation does exist and should allow you to determine what it would take to fix it.

FIGURE 9-26 A radiator that has been clogged with debris in the fins, causing it not to cool correctly.

FIGURE 9-27 A picture of a condenser with debris in the fins, which causes it not to allow airflow to reach the radiator, which in turn may cause overheating.

Inspecting and Testing the Cooling Fan

S09015 Inspecting and testing cooling fan.

The cooling fan is a critical part in the cooling system. When coolant moves through the engine, it picks up heat. Even if the coolant is picking up the heat from the engine and moving it to the radiator, air still has to move across the radiator to remove the heat from the coolant. The cooling fan must operate to pull air across the radiator at times when airflow is low, such as when sitting in traffic. If the cooling fan stops working and the vehicle sits in traffic, engine heat will continue to build, possibly until the coolant's boiling point is reached. When this happens, the pressure relief valve in the radiator cap will vent, releasing steam from the radiator and producing a hissing sound. The customer may note that a temperature warning light has come on, and/or the temperature gauge has moved to its full hot position. If the engine is operated in this condition, it will be damaged. It is possible to even create damage to the automatic transmission if the engine gets too hot, as the transmission fluid is typically cooled through the cooler located in the radiator.

When testing the fan, start by determining what type of fan the vehicle is equipped with—mechanical, clutch, electric, or hydraulic. Mechanical fans are the easiest to inspect, typically requiring only a visual inspection. Check the condition and tension of the drive belt, the condition of the pulley, and the condition of the fan blades themselves. Especially look for cracks in any metal fan blades, as they can cause the blade to be ripped off and thrown with deadly force. It is also possible that someone previously installed the fan blades backward, which lowers the effectiveness of the fan.

A clutch fan is inspected in the same way as the mechanical fan, but the clutch also has to be tested. First, with the engine off, the bearings in the fan clutch are tested by trying to move the blades frontward and backward, and then rotating them to see if there is any play in the bearings in any direction. To test the operation of the fan clutch, some manufacturers specify placing cardboard in front of the radiator to block most of it. The engine is then started, with the vehicle in the shop, while monitoring the engine temperature and watching/listening to see if the fan clutch engages at the proper engine temperature. If it does not, it most likely will have to be replaced, although some fan clutches can be refilled with silicone oil.

Electric fans are quite reliable. If they do cause trouble, it is usually because they don't come on when they are supposed to. Because electric fans are electrically operated, diagnosing them is quite different from diagnosing mechanical fans. Be aware that some electric fans can come on automatically, even when the key is off, so be careful when working around them. In fact, you should unplug the fan's electrical connector before physically inspecting the fan assembly. Just be sure to reconnect it when you are finished. Once the fan is disconnected, check that the fan is free to turn and does not catch or bind on any of the shrouding. If it is not free to rotate, then the electrical system and the fan motor itself will have to be tested.

To inspect and test the cooling fan, follow the steps in **SKILL DRILL 9-15**.

SKILL DRILL 9-15 Inspecting and Testing the Cooling Fan

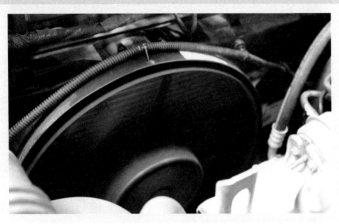

1. Refer to manufacturer's service information for proper operation of the cooling fan. For this example, we use an electric cooling fan on a 1996 or newer vehicle.

Continued

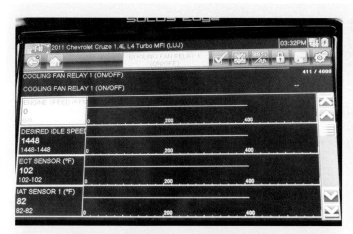

2. Install a scan tool to the data link connector, often located under the dash, and establish communication with the vehicle.

3. Find the bidirectional controls of the scan tool, and command the cooling fan on.

4. If the cooling fan comes on and runs, check for intermittent operation by wiggling connectors and wiring to the cooling fan. If the fan stops intermittently when you wiggle connectors, check for improper pin fit in the connector. You may have to replace the connector to repair this concern. If the fan continues to operate during the wiggle test, move to the next step.

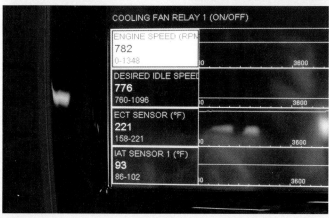

5. Pull up cooling temperature sensor data on the scan tool. Point an infrared temperature gun at the thermostat housing to verify that engine operation temperature is nearly the same as that displayed on the scan tool. If the temperature is off excessively, then you will have to test the coolant temperature sensor and wiring.

Continued

6. If the fan does not operate, wiggle test the fan wires. If it still does not work, measure the voltage drop to the input terminal of the fan. If there is no voltage, then using a wiring diagram of the fan circuit diagnose the cause.

7. If voltage is present at the input terminal, check the voltage drop on the ground side of the fan circuit.

8. If the ground is good, check the continuity of the fan motor with an ohmmeter. If out of specs, replace the fan motor.

9. Once the repair is completed, verify that fan is operating.

Verifying Engine Operating Temperature

There are a few ways to verify that the engine is at operating temperature. First, you need to hook up a scan tool to the PCM and scroll down to the electronic coolant temperature (ECT) parameter identification (PID) to see what the temperature is of the coolant in the engine. We could also use an infrared temperature gun to see what the temperature is of the various surfaces of the engine. We could also use an actual thermometer to test the temperature of the coolant. Using a combination of a couple of ways will lead to the best result.

Diagnosing Operating Temperature Issues

If an engine is not operating at the correct temperature, a mechanical issue must be addressed before it is detrimental to the engine. The first step is to determine whether the cooling system is too hot or too cold. Then you can then go through a diagnostic procedure to ascertain the cause of the symptoms.

K09007 Knowledge of proper procedure to check a cooling system issue.

If the engine is too hot:

1. Is the cooling system filled with coolant?
2. If the thermostat working, then are the fans operating correctly?
3. Is the water pump drive feature working correctly?
4. Is the coolant flowing through the system correctly?
5. Is there air in the system, and does the radiator have the proper air flow through it?

If the engine is too cold:

1. Is the thermostat stuck open?
2. Is there a thermostat in the engine?
3. Is the cooling fan working more than it should?

▶ Wrap-Up

Ready for Review

- ▶ Ethylene glycol antifreeze, the most common antifreeze, is highly toxic to humans and animals.
- ▶ The Environmental Protection Agency (EPA) has strict regulations for the handling and disposal of vehicle coolant.
- ▶ Coolant should never be dumped into a storm drain or down a shop floor drain. Coolant is a poison and should only be poured into an approved container and either be recycled in-house or removed by a licensed recycler.
- ▶ The use of a hydrometer or refractometer is necessary when testing the freeze protection of the coolant in the cooling system.
- ▶ The hydrometer is a tool that measures the specific gravity of a liquid. When coolant is drawn into the hydrometer, a float rises to a certain level depending upon the density of the coolant. Antifreeze has a higher specific gravity than water, so the higher the float rises in the liquid, the greater the percentage of antifreeze in the mix.
- ▶ Hydrometers are typically antifreeze specific.
- ▶ A refractometer can also tell the proportions of antifreeze and water in the coolant mix by measuring a liquid's specific gravity. It works by allowing light to shine through the fluid. The light bends in accordance with the particular liquid's specific gravity. The bending of the light displays

on a scale inside the tool, indicating the specific gravity of the fluid.

- ▶ The pH testing of coolant is a way to determine whether the corrosion inhibitors are still working in the antifreeze, by using test strips, which are a litmus paper.
- ▶ Electrolysis can also be due to faulty grounds in the electrical system. If a circuit has a faulty ground, the current will try to find its way back to the battery in whatever way it can. And that can include sending some of the current flow through the coolant.
- ▶ To verify that electricity is finding its way into the cooling system, voltage can be measured when various electrical loads are operated, in order to see whether there is any stray voltage in the coolant. If voltages are over 0.3 volt when the load or loads are activated, then you will have to perform electrical diagnosis of the circuit being tested.
- ▶ Used coolant that has been removed from a vehicle is very hazardous to the environment and local wildlife.
- ▶ By law the technician is responsible for proper disposal of used engine coolant mixture, which must be collected and disposed of properly or the company may face legal fines.
- ▶ There are two correct level marks used to check or adjust coolant level reservoir because the coolant in the system expands and contracts according to changes in its temperature.

▶ The coolant level should not be below the lower coolant level mark in the recovery tank when the vehicle is cold. It should be near the upper mark when the coolant is hot.

▶ If the coolant level is low, testing for a coolant leak will be necessary.

▶ Verification of coolant condition can be performed by a checking its pH level with a test strip or electronic tester.

▶ The discovery of electrolysis in the radiator also requires flushing the cooling system.

▶ Coolant flushing is necessary either as a preventive maintenance or because the coolant is worn out or contaminated.

▶ Replacement of an engine drive belt may be necessary when the belt is cracked, glazed, separating, and getting ready to fail. Verifying that the pulley system is not damaged is the first step if noise is a problem.

▶ Coolant hoses should be checked anytime the vehicle is in the shop for a maintenance inspection. If you find one defective radiator hose, the chances are that the other hose(s) may be deteriorating in the same way and will soon need to be replaced.

▶ Most technicians will generally replace both radiator hoses at once as a sensible precaution.

▶ A swollen hose has lost its elasticity and is swelling under pressure. It may soon rupture; typically you will see a bubble protruding from the side of this hose. Replace this hose immediately.

▶ A hardened hose has become brittle and will break and leak. Verify hardening by squeezing the hose and comparing it to a known good hose.

▶ A cracked hose has cracked and will soon start to leak. Verify cracking by a visual inspection.

▶ A soft hose has become very weak and is in danger of ballooning or bursting. Verify softening by squeezing the hose and comparing it to a known good hose.

▶ Hose clamps come in several forms and require different tools to properly remove or replace.

▶ Types of clamps include the following: gear or worm clamp—adjust with a screwdriver or nut driver; banded or screw clamp—adjust with a screwdriver; and wire clamp—this spring clamp is not adjustable. It is fitted and removed with special hose clamp pliers, which have grooved jaws.

▶ It is necessary to remove and replace a thermostat in the event that the thermostat is found to be faulty, creating either an overheating concern or an under-heating concern.

▶ The need to inspect and test fans and fan shrouds arises when the customer complains of overheating.

▶ A mechanical or electric fan can fail, which also results in air not being pulled through the radiator. A quick test to verify that air is moving through the radiator is to hold a piece of paper in front of the radiator and see if suction pulls the paper in. If it does not, then air is not being pulled through the radiator.

▶ A radiator may have to be replaced due to an overheating condition traced to partially plugged radiator tubes. If this is found to be the case, the radiator will have to

be removed and can be sent out to a radiator shop for cleaning. A good flush of the entire cooling system will be necessary as further clogging will be likely, especially in the heater core.

▶ Removal of a heater core may become necessary if the customer notices a puddle of coolant on the carpet in the vehicle, on the passenger side.

▶ A heater core can leak, fill the air box, and drip onto the floor inside the vehicle. The other concern the customer may have is the smell of coolant inside the vehicle or a film on the inside of the windshield.

▶ The lack of periodic service of the cooling system according to maintenance schedules is the leading reason that cooling systems fail.

▶ Properly performed cooling system maintenance will ensure that the cooling system continues to perform as designed.

▶ Overheating conditions can have several causes, such as low coolant level due to a leak, a stuck-closed thermostat, a faulty radiator cap, clogged radiator tubes or fins, an inoperative cooling fan, a water pump impeller that is eroded or slipping on the shaft, or a blown head gasket.

▶ When diagnosing a cooling system problem, you need to use all of your senses to help determine what is wrong.

▶ Starting the engine and using an exhaust analyzer to sniff the vapors coming out of the neck of the radiator can indicate whether there is a small leak from one of the combustion chambers that is leaking combustion gases into the cooling system.

▶ Using a cylinder leakage tester and pressurizing each cylinder can help locate which cylinder has the combustion leak, due to either a blown head gasket or a cracked head.

▶ A coolant system pressure tester is used to apply pressure to the cooling system to diagnose leakage complaints. Under pressure, coolant may leak internally to the combustion chamber, intake or exhaust system, or the engine lubrication system. It can also leak externally to the outside of the engine.

▶ A hydrometer is used to test coolant mixture and freeze protection by testing the specific gravity of the coolant. You must use a hydrometer specifically designed for the antifreeze you are testing.

▶ A refractometer is used to test coolant mixture and freeze protection by testing the fluid's ability to bend light, and can be used with any type of antifreeze.

▶ Coolant pH test strips are used to test the acidity-to-alkalinity balance of the coolant.

▶ The coolant dye kit is used to aid leak detection by adding dye to coolant and using an ultraviolet light source (black light) to trace to the source of the leak; the dye glows fluorescent when a black light is shined on it.

▶ An infrared temperature sensor is a noncontact thermometer used to check actual temperatures and variations of temperature throughout the cooling system to help pinpoint faulty parts and system blockages.

▶ A thermometer is used to check the temperature of air exiting the heating ducts.

▶ A digital voltmeter is used to check for electrical problems such as cooling fan and temperature gauge issues.

▶ A belt tension gauge is used to check belt tension.

▶ A serpentine belt wear gauge is used to check whether the serpentine belt grooves are worn past their specifications.

▶ Radiator clamp pliers are used to safely remove spring-type radiator clamps.

▶ The borescope is used for examining internal passages for evidence of a coolant leak.

▶ The scan tool us used to activate the cooling fan through bidirectional controls for testing; to monitor cooling sensor operation and to command air door actuators when testing low heat complaints; and to read DTCs related to cooling system operation.

▶ The cooling system flush machine is used to flush coolant backward through the system with cleaners that remove corrosion buildup and old coolant. Most of these machines have their own pump, so the vehicle does not have to run to perform the flush.

▶ An exhaust gas analyzer is used to detect exhaust gases that are finding their way into the cooling system due to a leaking head gasket or damaged head or block. Be careful not to allow liquid coolant to be picked up by the analyzer probe.

▶ A visual inspection of the cooling system will give you a good indication of any issues. Check the level of the coolant in the overflow bottle and radiator. Check the condition of the coolant to see if it is cloudy or contaminated. Check the belt condition and for the proper tension, and check hoses for any leaks or wear. If the sweet aroma of coolant is detected when the engine is first started, check for leaking coolant at the heater box drain, which indicates a possible cracked or rotted leaking heater core.

▶ Pressure testing the cooling system for leaks is usually an effective way to locate leaks because it causes coolant to leak out much more quickly, making leaks easier to locate. But before you pressurize the system, make sure it is topped off with coolant or water.

▶ A gasket or cooler leak into the engine cooling system causes oil to mix with coolant. When this happens, the oil coats the heat transfer surfaces, causing the coolant not to absorb the heat from the engine efficiently.

▶ In a situation similar to oil contamination, the automatic transmission fluid also gets cooled by the radiator, which gives it a way to enter the cooling system if there is a failure.

▶ Once air is introduced in the system you must get it out to return the system to the condition it has to be in to cool the engine correctly.

▶ A symptom of air in a system is a temperature gauge that jumps from cold to hot to cold again, very sporadically.

▶ No heat in the vehicle is another symptom of air in the system, as the air bubble becomes trapped in the heat core, which doesn't allow for coolant flow through the core to create heat.

▶ Once air is in the cooling system, you must bleed it out, usually by attaching a funnel to the surge tank or radiator, filling it with coolant, and allowing the engine to run. As the engine runs, the air will work its way up to the highest point of the system, which should be your funnel.

▶ One type of airflow restriction occurs when the radiator fins are clogged. Usually this happens when outside debris finds its way into the fins of a radiator, thereby not allowing the radiator to exchange its heat with the outside air.

▶ A visual inspection of the A/C condenser fins should be able to detect whether they are bent, causing a restriction in airflow to the radiator.

▶ Today's electronically controlled cooling fans are diagnosed by using a scan tool.

▶ To verify that the engine is at operating temperature, you need to hook up a scan tool to the PCM and scroll down to the electronic coolant temperature (ECT) parameter identification (PID), and see what that says. That sensor tells the PCM what the temperature of the coolant is in the engine.

▶ You can use an infrared temperature gun to read the operating temperature of the various surfaces of the engine.

▶ If the engine is too hot, check to see whether the cooling system is full of coolant, the thermostat is working; the fans are operating correctly; the water pump drive feature is working correctly; coolant is flowing through the system correctly; there is air in the system; and the radiator has the proper air flow through it.

▶ If the engine is too cold, check to see whether the thermostat is stuck open; whether there is a thermostat in the engine; and/or whether the cooling fan is working more than it should.

Key Terms

banded or screw clamp Adjust with a screwdriver.

belt tension gauge Used to check belt tension.

borescope Used for examining internal passages for evidence of a coolant leak.

coolant dye kit Used to aid leak detection by adding dye to coolant and using an ultraviolet light source (black light) to trace to the source of the leak; the dye glows fluorescent when a black light is shined on it.

coolant pH test strips Used to test the acid-to-alkalinity balance of the coolant.

coolant system pressure tester Used to apply pressure to the cooling system to diagnose leakage complaints. Under pressure, coolant may leak internally to the combustion chamber, intake or exhaust system, or the engine lubrication system. It can also leak externally to the outside of the engine.

cooling system flush machine Used to flush coolant backward through the system; cleaners remove corrosion buildup and old coolant. Most of these machines have their own pump so the vehicle does not have to run to perform the flush.

cracked hose Hose that has cracked and will soon start to leak. Verify cracking by a visual inspection.

exhaust gas analyzer Used to detect exhaust gases that are finding their way into the cooling system due to a leaking head gasket or damaged head or block. Be careful not allow liquid coolant to be picked up by the analyzer probe.

gear or worm clamp Adjust with a screwdriver or nut driver.

hardened hose Hose that has become brittle and will break and leak. Verify hardening by squeezing the hose and comparing it to a known good hose.

hydrometer Used to test coolant mixture and freeze protection by testing the specific gravity of the coolant. You must use a hydrometer specifically designed for the antifreeze you are testing.

infrared temperature sensor A noncontact thermometer used to check actual temperatures and variations of temperature throughout the cooling system to help pinpoint faulty parts and system blockages.

radiator clamp pliers Used to safely remove spring-type radiator clamps.

refractometer Used to test coolant mixture and freeze protection by testing the fluid's ability to bend light. This tester can be used with any type of antifreeze.

scan tool Used to activate the cooling fan through bidirectional controls for testing; to monitor cooling sensor operation and to command air door actuators when testing low heat complaints; and to read DTCs related to cooling system operation.

serpentine belt wear gauge Used to check whether the serpentine belt grooves are worn past their specifications.

soft hose Hose that has become very weak and is in danger of ballooning or bursting. Verify softening by squeezing the hose and comparing it to a known good hose. Hose clamps come in several forms and require different tools to properly remove or replace. These clamps secure the hose to the component it is connected to. Be sure to follow proper installation instructions to prevent future leaks from this seal.

swollen hose Hose that has lost its elasticity and is swelling under pressure. It may soon rupture; typically, you will see a bubble protruding from the side of this hose. Replace this hose immediately.

thermometer Used to check the temperature of air exiting the heating ducts.

voltmeter Used to check for electrical problems such as cooling fan and temperature gauge issues.

wire clamp A spring clamp that is not adjustable. It is fitted and removed with special hose clamp pliers, which have grooved jaws.

Review Questions

I. All of the following statements with respect to the handling and disposal of coolants are true, *except*:
   a. Used coolants should be immediately disposed of by dumping them into drains.
   b. Coolants are highly toxic and should be poured only in the appropriate container.
   c. Coolants could be removed using a licensed recycler.
   d. Coolants should never be mixed with oil or other liquids.

2. A refractometer is used to test:
   a. coolant pH.
   b. the freeze protection of the coolant.
   c. for electrolysis.
   d. coolant level.

3. Which of the following is tested during coolant testing?
   a. Thickness of the coolant
   b. Temperature of the coolant
   c. Viscosity of the coolant
   d. pH value of the coolant

4. The best way to remove hoses is:
   a. to slit them and peel them off.
   b. pry them off with a screwdriver.
   c. twist the hose off.
   d. to heat them mildly.

5. A borescope is:
   a. used for examining internal passages for evidence of a coolant leak.
   b. used to check belt tension.
   c. used to check the temperature of air exiting the heating ducts.
   d. used to activate the cooling fan through bidirectional controls.

6. When testing the coolant system for leaks using a pressure tester:
   a. ensure there is only 50% coolant or water.
   b. the radiator cap need not be tested.
   c. do not adjust the pressure when the engine heats up.
   d. look for both internal and external leaks.

7. The engine's operating temperature can be verified using all of the below, *except* a:
   a. dash gauge.
   b. thermometer.
   c. scan tool.
   d. temperature gun.

8. When removing a radiator:
   a. do not disconnect automatic transmission cooler lines.
   b. inspect the cooling system hoses and clamps.
   c. do not drain the coolant.
   d. use the same container to hold transmission fluid and coolant.

9. Which of the following steps should be performed when removing and reinstalling a heater core?
   a. Drain the coolant from the radiator.
   b. Bleed any air from the cooling system.
   c. Inspect the belts and pulleys for wear and damage.
   d. Inspect the thermostat housing.

10. Odd noises from the cooling system as the engine runs could be a sign of:
    a. transmission contamination.
    b. clogging of radiator fins.
    c. air infiltration of the system.
    d. coolant mixture issues.

ASE Technician A/Technician B Style Questions

1. Technician A states that a loose drive belt could cause the water pump not to operate fast enough to cool the engine. Technician B says that water by itself is a good coolant. Who is correct?
   a. Tech A
   b. Tech B
   c. Both A and B
   d. Neither A nor B

2. Technician A states that guessing at the protection level of coolant is okay in the summer. Technician B says that using a hydrometer is a good way to check the freeze protection of the coolant mixture. Who is correct?
   a. Tech A
   b. Tech B
   c. Both A and B
   d. Neither A nor B

3. Technician A says when evaluating a serpentine drive belt, the technician should look at ribbed side of the belt for cracks. Technician B says that a serpentine belt should never be replaced. Who is correct?
   a. Tech A
   b. Tech B
   c. Both A and B
   d. Neither A nor B

4. Technician A says when verifying a cooling system issue you should first do a visual inspection on all the components on the engine. Technician B says that replacing the thermostat is the first step is fixing an overheating issue. Who is correct?
   a. Tech A
   b. Tech B
   c. Both A and B
   d. Neither A nor B

5. Technician A states that electric cooling fans never fail. Technician B says that the engine should not overheat without a cooling fan. Who is correct?
   a. Tech A
   b. Tech B
   c. Both A and B
   d. Neither A nor B

6. Technician A says that flushing engine coolant should be done every 30 days. Technician B says that the technician should verify the coolant should be replaced before replacing it. Who is correct?
   a. Tech A
   b. Tech B
   c. Both A and B
   d. Neither A nor B

7. Technician A says air in the cooling system may cause an overheating condition. Technician B says that pure water will stop an overheating condition. Who is correct?
   a. Tech A
   b. Tech B
   c. Both A and B
   d. Neither A nor B

8. Technician A states that clogged cooling fins on radiators must be cleaned before diagnosing an overheating problem. Technician B says that a condenser that has clogged fins could cause the radiator to overheat. Who is correct?
   a. Tech A
   b. Tech B
   c. Both A and B
   d. Neither A nor B

9. Technician A says that a vehicle with an automatic transmission could contaminate the cooling system. Technician B says that the cooling system could get contaminated with windshield washer fluid. Who is correct?
   a. Tech A
   b. Tech B
   c. Both A and B
   d. Neither A nor B

10. Technician A says that a spongy coolant hose should be replaced with a new hose. Technician B says that an oil-soaked hose should be replaced with a new one. Who is correct?
    a. Tech A
    b. Tech B
    c. Both A and B
    d. Neither A nor B

CHAPTER 10

Engine Removal and Installation

NATEF Tasks

- **N10001** Complete work order to include customer information, vehicle identifying information, customer concern, related service history, cause, and correction.

- **N10002** Remove and reinstall engine in an OBDII or newer vehicle; reconnect all attaching components, and restore the vehicle to running condition.

Knowledge Objectives

After reading this chapter, you will have:

- **K10001** Knowledge of when to remove an engine.
- **K10002** Knowledge of how to physically remove the engine from the vehicle.
- **K10003** Knowledge of what needs to be disconnected on the top of an engine when removing the engine.
- **K10004** Knowledge of fuel disconnection and safety with flammable liquids.
- **K10005** Knowledge of coolant capture and proper disposal.

- **K10006** Knowledge of what to disconnect underneath of the vehicle for engine removal.
- **K10007** Knowledge of what is needed to install the engine in a vehicle.
- **K10008** Knowledge of what to check before initial engine start-up.

Skills Objectives

- **S10001** Remove the engine in a vehicle.
- **S10002** Install an engine in a vehicle.

- **S10003** Set timing on a computer-controlled engine.

You Are the Automotive Technician

Today you will be removing and replacing the engine of a 2006 Ford Focus. Before you begin the job, you look at the customer work order. The customer has complained of dash warning lights illuminating and noises coming from under the hood. You confirm the customer complaints and diagnose the engine as having low oil pressure due to worn main bearings. The engine also exhibits a worn or spun connecting rod bearing, as evidenced by the "rod knock" noise the customer was hearing. These conditions verify the need to replace the engine. You gather the tools needed to remove and reinstall an engine, including special service tools, a vehicle lift, an engine hoist, jacks, and general shop hand tools.

1. What are the considerations prior to disconnecting the battery?
2. Why is it important to be organized, careful, and methodical when removing or repairing an engine?
3. What are the important checks to make before starting the engine after installation?

N10001 Complete work order to include customer information, vehicle identifying information, customer concern, related service history, cause, and correction.

K10001 Knowledge of when to remove an engine.

▶ Introduction

Once a major engine failure has been diagnosed, the engine often must be removed for repair or replacement. Typically, if well maintained, an engine will last many years and 200,000 miles (322,000 km) or more; however, abuse or defective components can severely shorten the life of an engine. If an engine has failed, the customer needs to get the vehicle to a clean, professional, and well-equipped shop for repair or replacement.

A major mistake made by technicians when removing and replacing an engine is rushing to get the job done. Completing the work order, looking up service history, and understanding what caused the engine to fail help ensure that the repair will not have to be done again. To perform this task well, technicians must be organized, careful, and methodical in their work. The very first step in the performance of this task is to reference the appropriate service information, preferably the manufacturer's service information. It is important to follow the steps listed in the service information in order and step-by-step. Keep in mind the cost of replacing damaged components caused by sloppy or hasty workmanship. Some of the electronically controlled components in today's vehicles can cost thousands of dollars.

▶ Preparation and Safety

There are many engine installation configurations, including front-wheel drive (FWD), rear-wheel drive (RWD), and all-wheel drive (AWD) designs. Although it is impossible to go into detail for every vehicle ever made, they all have similar engine removal procedures. In this chapter, a typical RWD and a typical FWD vehicle are used. Always refer to the service information for the specific vehicle for step-by-step disassembly procedures.

Most engines in RWD vehicles are best removed from the top of the engine compartment, but many engines in FWD vehicles can be removed from the top or the bottom of the engine compartment. If being removed from the top of the engine compartment, the engine can be separated from the transmission and removed by itself, or in some cases the engine and transmission are removed as a unit (**FIGURE 10-1**). If the engine is removed from the bottom of the engine compartment, the engine and transaxle are usually removed as a unit attached to the engine cradle, which bolts the engine and transmission to the vehicle (**FIGURE 10-2**). Some vehicles require that the cab or part of the passenger compartment be removed from the frame so that you are able to access the engine. When this is the case, you should be aware of an unbalanced vehicle assembly that may tip or fall off the lift. Engine removal and installation can be dangerous; therefore, it is important to put safety first in each step of the process. Vehicles and engines are heavy. During the removal and installation procedure, one of those heavy items will be lifted high enough to clear the other. If the engine slips, it can crush or pinch fingers, hands, and feet. Many parts have sharp edges that can cut through skin and tendons, which gloves can help protect. Fluids and chemicals can spray into your eyes and mouth, or they can be absorbed through your skin, so always use personal protective equipment. Fluids on the floor can cause slips and falls, so clean up messes quickly. It is important to follow the vehicle manufacturer's guidelines to the letter. Always respect and implement shop safety standards and regulations.

FIGURE 10-1 The engine is being removed for the vehicle from the topside.

FIGURE 10-2 Engine being removed from a FWD vehicle from below.

▶ Engine Removal Tools

The tools you need to remove and replace an engine include special service tools, a vehicle lift, an **engine stand**, jacks, and general shop hand tools. Additionally, a scan tool is important on all but vintage vehicles to check and clear trouble codes, relieve pressure from fuel systems, and monitor engine and transmission systems after starting the replacement engine.

An engine hoist is necessary if the engine will be pulled from the top of the engine compartment (**FIGURE 10-3**). Make sure the engine hoist is rated for the capacity you will be lifting. A strong chain is also required. Make sure the chain can exceed the weight capacity that it will be supporting. Some engines have pulling brackets that allow the chains to be attached by hooks when pulling the engine. The hooks too must exceed the weight capacity of the engine being pulled. If a vehicle hoist is not being used, a floor jack and jack stands are required to support the vehicle or the vehicle components (**FIGURE 10-4**).

If the engine is being removed by lowering it from underneath of the vehicle, as is recommended for many FWD vehicles, a scissor jack is required, along with a vehicle two-post hoist. Once the engine has been removed from the vehicle, an engine stand will make the procedure of taking the engine apart much easier (**FIGURE 10-5**).

▶ Topside Disconnection

The first step in the engine removal process is to remove the hood. With the hood removed, you have greater access to the engine compartment and greater visibility because more light can get in. If the vehicle is FWD and the engine is coming out from underneath the vehicle,

K10006 Knowledge of how to physically remove the engine from the vehicle.

S10001 Remove the engine in a vehicle.

K10002 Knowledge of what needs to be disconnected on the top of an engine when removing the engine.

FIGURE 10-3 To remove the engine from the vehicle, an engine crane must be used to support the weight of the engine assembly.

FIGURE 10-4 A floor jack and jack stands.

FIGURE 10-5 Once the engine is out of the vehicle it can then be mounted on a stand so that working on it will be easier for the technician.

FIGURE 10-6 Scribing the hood bracket.

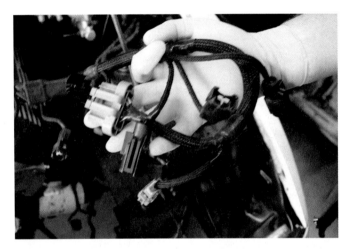

FIGURE 10-7 As the technician is disconnecting the engine wiring harness, he/she must document where the various connecters go for an easier reassembly.

FIGURE 10-8 A technician disconnecting the negative terminal of the battery.

K10003 Knowledge of fuel disconnection and safety with flammable liquids.

or if the hood opens at least 90 degrees, you may not need to remove the hood. Before removing the hood, scribe or otherwise mark the hood bracket (**FIGURE 10-6**) where the bolts attach the hood to the hinge. By doing this, you will have a reference mark showing the exact place to reinstall the hood.

After referencing the appropriate service information, begin the engine removal process from the topside of the engine. Disconnect everything necessary for engine removal that is within reach from the top of the engine (**FIGURE 10-7**). One of the first things to do is to disable the electrical system by disconnecting and removing the battery. Doing so reduces the risk of fire or explosion due to an inadvertent spark near exposed gases during the engine removal process. It also protects the electrical/electronic circuits from short-circuiting. Thinking ahead will save you extra work in cleaning up afterward: Before the fluids are properly drained, you need to avoid removing anything that would cause a fluid leak.

Battery

Most modern vehicles have 10 or more computers monitoring and controlling nearly every operational system of the vehicle. In fact, an automobile could have 50 separate microprocessors onboard. Considering the sophistication of the onboard electronics, it is easy to understand why the vehicle's electrical/electronic system is vulnerable to damage from short-circuiting or grounding during the removal and installation process. Disconnecting the battery before disconnecting any other component from the engine helps prevent damage. Some electronic components, such as radios and navigation devices, have an antitheft system built into them. If power is removed from the component, it will not work until the proper unlock code is keyed into it. Therefore, before disconnecting the battery, make sure you have the unlock codes available. These codes usually come with the owner's manual.

When disconnecting the battery, remove the negative terminal of the battery first (**FIGURE 10-8**). The negative side is always disconnected first because it is already grounded and is considered safe. After disconnecting the negative side of the battery, disconnect the positive terminal at the battery. As a note of caution, do not lay tools or anything else on the battery—an accidental connection could be made between the positive and the negative posts of the battery, which could cause the battery to explode. One option is to remove the battery so this is not even possible.

Fuel and Fuel Lines

Most vehicles are fuel injected. Typically, a fuel injection supply line stays under pressure even when the engine is not running; therefore, you need to relieve the pressure on the fuel system before disconnecting the lines. Check the service information for proper procedures to release the fuel system pressure.

If the vehicle is in running condition, one way to relieve the pressure is to remove the fuel pump fuse while the engine is running, and wait until the engine runs out of fuel. If the fuel-injected vehicle is not running, install a fuel pressure gauge, and relieve the pressure (**FIGURE 10-9**) by venting the extra fuel into a plastic bottle. Once the fuel pressure has been relieved, you can disconnect the fuel line. For most fuel-injected vehicles, you need a fuel disconnect tool (**FIGURE 10-10**). Be sure to block off and seal the fuel supply line from the fuel tank, as

FIGURE 10-9 A fuel gauge used to relieve fuel pressure.

FIGURE 10-10 To protect the end of the fuel line and not allow debris to enter the fuel system, the technician should plug the line with a plastic insert.

well as the port that goes to the fuel rail, so that no debris get into an injector. This can be accomplished by plugging the line with a plastic plug, acquiring a dedicated line cap that screws over the hole, or taping over the end of the line with duct tape.

Electrical Components

Before removing the engine from the vehicle, you must disconnect many electrical wires and connectors from the engine, bearing in mind that they must be reconnected after installation (**FIGURE 10-11**). This can be time-consuming and tedious work. Take your time; be methodical and careful during this process. If your work is rushed and sloppy, this job could become your worst nightmare.

To begin, look closely at the electrical wire harnesses, to evaluate the best area to disconnect them. Often, it is easier to disconnect main harnesses at their central connector instead of at the end of each branch, so you should investigate this option.

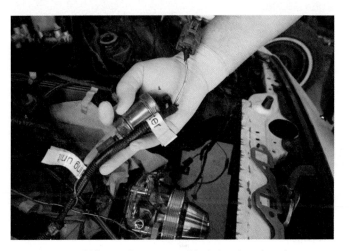

FIGURE 10-11 Wires and connectors labeled and ready to be disconnected.

Before disconnecting the electrical wire harness plug ends, it is a good idea to take pictures. If you take pictures for later identification, examine the pictures before disconnecting anything. You want to be sure you can identify connector and wire locations based on the pictures. For vehicles built in the 1980s and earlier, you might want to label the plug-in connectors (Figure 10-8). For late-model vehicles, the electrical plug ends are not interchangeable. However, pictures will work to help you remember the general locations. When in doubt, label them to save yourself time and aggravation later.

Front Accessories Disconnection

Continuing through the steps of engine removal, you next remove the radiator and accessories. The air-conditioning compressor, power steering pump, and related mounting brackets and components are included in the accessory section. After checking the appropriate service information, you can determine if the air-conditioning or power steering systems need to be disconnected for the engine to be removed. If the air-conditioning system has to be opened, the refrigerant will have to be removed and stored by a properly trained technician using the appropriate recycling machine. If the power steering circuit has to be opened, the fluid must be drained first.

Radiator

At the bottom of the radiator, there should be a drain valve or plug (**FIGURE 10-12**), but if not, you have to disconnect the lower radiator hose, place the drain pan underneath the

K10004 Knowledge of coolant capture and proper disposal.

FIGURE 10-12 Draining the radiator.

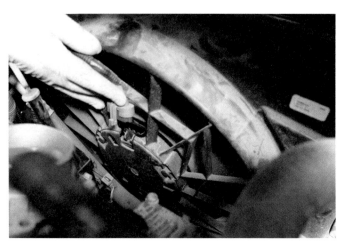

FIGURE 10-13 Removing the electric fans.

FIGURE 10-14 Removing the radiator.

K10005 Knowledge of what to disconnect underneath of the vehicle for engine removal.

valve, and open the valve. If there is no valve, place the pan under the lower radiator hose. Next, disconnect the lower radiator hose until all the coolant has been drained, and then disconnect the upper radiator hose. For RWD vehicles, disconnect the fan shroud, unbolt the radiator, and remove. For most FWD vehicles, disconnect the electric fan, determine whether there is enough room to remove the radiator without removing the electric fans, and if not, remove the electric fans (**FIGURE 10-13**), unbolt the radiator, and remove the radiator (**FIGURE 10-14**).

Brackets

Air-conditioning compressors and power steering pumps are examples of accessory components that are mounted to the engine. They are mounted with brackets. Often, these brackets have several pieces because they are not only used to mount, but also to adjust the mounted components (**FIGURE 10-15**). Therefore, if the brackets must be removed, keep as many of the components and attachment bolts together as possible to make reassembly easier.

Take off only the brackets that are necessary to remove the engine. Again, pictures are helpful in reminding you of the locations and positioning of the brackets. When removing the air-conditioning system, it is best to keep the system sealed, using mechanics' wire to secure the compressor and hoses up and out of the way (**FIGURE 10-16**). If you are removing the air-conditioning pump and you have to disconnect the air-conditioning, use the proper air-conditioning recovering equipment. It is best to leave all the air-conditioning lines intact and use mechanics' wire to hold the air-conditioning components off to the side of the engine. Remove the power steering pump, take it off the bracket, and wire it out of the way. It is usually not necessary to disconnect the hydraulic lines.

▶ Underside Disconnection

When preparing to raise the vehicle and make the necessary disconnections for removing the engine, start by reviewing the manufacturer's information. By following the steps for the specific vehicle you are working on, you can avoid missing components, bolts, hoses, and wires that must be disconnected before the engine can be removed. When the engine is loose, hanging from the **engine hoist** and unsupported by the vehicle, it is not the time to discover that you missed removing something under the vehicle. Remember to take your time and work carefully and methodically as you make the underside disconnections.

FIGURE 10-15 Accessory brackets should be removed to make removal of the engine easier for the technician.

FIGURE 10-16 Wiring the air-conditioning compressor and hoses out of the way.

Draining Remaining Fluids

Because most fluid drain points are located under the vehicle, now is the time to drain fluids not previously drained. Drain the engine oil (**FIGURE 10-17**). If the transmission or transaxle is coming out with the engine, you need to drain the transmission/transaxle fluid as well. If not already drained, drain the cooling system. Look for related units that may need to be drained, such as the power steering fluid if the pump is being removed from the lines.

Exhaust System

Exhaust systems are not quite as simple as they once were. Currently produced vehicles could have three or four oxygen sensors, a catalytic converter, resonator, muffler, and/or a turbocharger driven by the exhaust gases (**FIGURE 10-18**). Light-duty diesel-powered vehicles are now equipped with particulate filters. It is important to understand the exhaust system and related components on the vehicle before removing the exhaust system.

To begin the exhaust removal process, identify the oxygen sensors that have to be removed or disconnected. Disconnect the sensors. Check the exhaust pipe and component routing to determine the best places to disconnect the system, and be certain that the exhaust pipes will not restrict engine removal. Disconnect the exhaust pipe from the exhaust header, or manifold (**FIGURE 10-19**). On most vehicles, there usually is enough room to remove the engine with the stock exhaust header in place. Nonetheless, always follow the exhaust removal guidelines in the manufacturer's information, or other reliable service information.

Starter Removal

The **starter motor** is normally located where the engine and the transmission/transaxle are mounted together. That mounting point is called the bell housing, and the starter is usually bolted to it (**FIGURE 10-20**). The starter should be removed before the engine is removed so that it will not be damaged in the removal process. It is important to understand that the positive battery cable connects to a terminal on the starter; therefore, it is imperative that the battery be disconnected before removing the cable and wires from the starter. To remove the starter motor, disconnect the starter electrical wires and mark

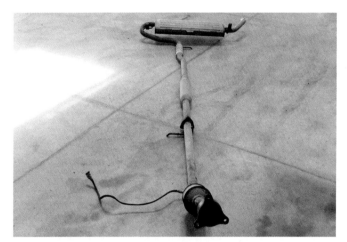

FIGURE 10-17 Exhaust assembly with oxygen sensors.

FIGURE 10-18 Removing the exhaust pipe from the vehicle.

FIGURE 10-19 Disconnecting the exhaust at the exhaust manifold allows the engine to come out of the vehicle easier, as well the technician will not have to fight removing the exhaust manifold in the vehicle.

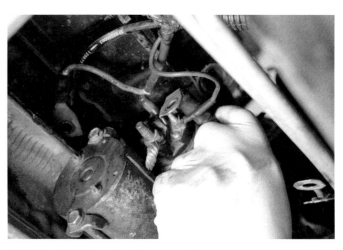

FIGURE 10-20 Removing the starter wires.

FIGURE 10-21 Removing the starter bolts.

FIGURE 10-22 The engine of a FWD vehicle strapped to a scissor jack.

> ▶ **NOTE**
>
> For the purposes of this text, the term "transmission" may include "transaxle" and vice versa, but not always. We will leave it up to the reader to determine its use, based on the vehicle being worked on.

where they go (**FIGURE 10-21**). Then, while holding the starter firmly (it is heavy), remove the starter bolts, and lower the starter from the engine or bell housing (**FIGURE 10-22**).

Automatic Transmissions: Torque Converter Disconnection

Remove the inspection cover on the bell housing to access the torque converter bolts on RWD and FWD vehicles, if the engine is being removed from the top. For FWD vehicles in which the engine is being removed from the bottom, the engine and **subframe**, also called a cradle, must be removed together. A subframe is a mount used to support the engine and transaxle assembly and is attached to the vehicle. Disconnecting the torque converter is not needed at this time, because the engine, transaxle, axles, and subframe are removed at the same time.

After the inspection cover is removed, turn the flexplate so that one of the torque converter bolts is accessible. If the bell housing does not have an inspection cover, then you may have to access the flexplate by going through the starter mounting hole. Turn the flexplate by hand to align the flexplate bolts or nuts for easy access, and unbolt the torque converter bolts or nuts, be sure to set these aside as they are specially sized and hardened to work with this application (**FIGURE 10-23**). If there is no inspection cover, you may have to turn the flexplate by turning the harmonic balancer in the front of the engine. Once the bolts or nuts have been removed, push the torque converter back into the bell housing so it will not fall out during engine removal.

Transmissions/Transaxles, Automatic and Manual

If the engine is being removed from the bottom of the vehicle with a subframe scissor jack, do not disconnect the transaxle at this time. If the engine is being removed from the top of the vehicle without the transmission/transaxle, you ultimately will need to unbolt the transmission/transaxle, but do not try to separate the transmission/transaxle from the engine until the transmission is supported and the engine is on the hoist. Removal of the linkage or shift cables will need to be investigated or they may end up breaking once the transmission is disconnected from the engine. If you are working on a manual transmission on a RWD vehicle, determine whether it can be separated from the bell housing or if the bell housing is integral with the transmission case. Determine if the bell housing should be unbolted from the engine or transmission. Support the transmission and then unbolt it or the bell housing at this time, but do not yet separate the two (**FIGURE 10-24**).

FIGURE 10-23 When removing the engine from an automatic equipped vehicle the technician must disconnect the torque converter from the flexplate.

▶ Engine Installation

In the engine removal process, have assistants help you install the engine. First, organize the work site. Begin by making sure the area is clean and clear of obstructions. To be prepared, conveniently arrange the bolts and engine mounts needed to secure the engine. Additionally, lay out tools that will be needed for the initial installation of the engine. Time spent organizing the work site will ensure a safe and smooth engine installation.

To reinstall the engine, basically, reverse the process used to remove it. However, there are some additional procedures. For vehicles equipped with automatic transmissions, it is a good idea to consider changing the front transmission seal while the torque converter is removed. It only takes a few minutes and will avoid having to remove the transmission again if it were to leak. Also be sure to fill the torque converter with the proper transmission fluid. Lay the torque converter down facing up and pour enough transmission fluid into the torque converter to fill it about halfway (**FIGURE 10-25**). When reinstalling the torque converter, push in and turn the torque converter, making sure it engages into the front

SAFETY TIP

Always put safety first in each step of the engine removal and installation process. Vehicles and engines are heavy. During the removal and installation procedure, one of those heavy items will be lifted high enough to clear the other. If the engine slips, it can crush or pinch fingers, hands, and feet.

N10002 Remove and reinstall engine in an OBDII or newer vehicle; reconnect all attaching components, and restore the vehicle to running condition.

K10007 Knowledge of what is needed to install the engine in a vehicle.

S10002 Install an engine in a vehicle.

FIGURE 10-24 When the engine is removed from the vehicle the front of the transmission could fall causing damage therefore it must be supported.

FIGURE 10-25 If the ignition timing is adjustable, make sure it is set close enough to start, and then hook up a timing light to make an adjustment when the engine first starts.

pump. You should feel three distinct clunks. If the torque converter is not being replaced, make sure it is engaged into the front pump. When mating the engine up to the transmission, make sure the torque converter does not bind against the flexplate. If it does, remove the engine, and reengage the torque converter into the transmission. Some converters have studs that protrude out and are connected with nuts. The converter must be rotated to match the holes in the flexplate for the two to mate up.

For vehicles equipped with manual transmissions, the clutch disc needs to be aligned with the clutch pilot hole, using a clutch alignment tool. First verify that the correct pilot bearing or bushing is installed in the rear of the crankshaft. Once you know the correct pilot bearing is in place, you can use an alignment tool that has the same splines as the clutch disc and fits snugly in the pilot bearing. Align the clutch disc, and install the pressure plate.

When installing a manual transmission to the engine, you sometimes need to turn the splined input shaft to align it with the clutch disc splines. A good way to do this is to leave the transmission in fourth gear and then turn the output shaft. Also, the front of the input shaft needs to align with the flywheel pilot bearing or bushing. Make sure the bell housing holes are aligned with the engine's dowel pins, and tighten all of the bell housing bolts evenly.

FIGURE 10-26 After the motor mount is installed in the vehicle, reattach it to the engine.

Engine Motor Mounts

After the transmission is bolted to the engine, the engine has to be mounted to the vehicle frame or cradle. To do so, attach the motor mounts that connect the engine to the frame or mounting platform (**FIGURE 10-26**). To mount the engine, lower the engine carefully, aligning the motor mounts. On some vehicles, the exhaust header must be aligned to the exhaust pipe at this time. Tighten the motor mounts when the engine and mounts are in place. Reinstall all parts and components in reverse order of disassembly.

You can make alignment pins by taking two bolts that are longer than the bell housing bolts, cutting off their heads, and chamfering the cut ends. Screw these by finger into two of the bell housing holes in the block. The pointed ends will guide the bell housing into alignment against the block. Once a couple of bell housing bolts are threaded into the block, remove the guide pins, and replace them with the proper bolts (either automatic or manual).

Engine Start-Up

Engine start-up after installation is a critical time for engine operation and longevity. It is important to make sure all fluid levels are checked and at the correct level. Keep your eyes and ears open, listening for unusual noises and looking for fluid leaks. Monitor the temperature and oil pressure gauges, and shut the engine down immediately if the gauges indicate overheating or low oil pressure. If the engine is not starting, do not crank the engine excessively, because the starter might be damaged from excessive heat. Also, the lack of proper lubrication from the slow-turning oil pump can cause premature engine damage. Crank the engine for 10 seconds or less at a time. Some new camshaft break-in procedures require the engine to start immediately and to run at 1200 to 2000 rpm for 20 or 30 minutes to provide proper lubrication and break-in.

Prestart Engine Checks

K10008 Knowledge of what to check before initial engine start-up.

Before starting the engine after installation, you need to make several checks, including the following:

1. Check all fluid levels, especially the engine oil and coolant levels. If a vacuum fill method of filling the cooling system was used, the cooling system will be full. If this method was not used, the system will look full but likely will have air pockets. If there is a vacuum pocket at the thermostat, it could prevent the thermostat from getting up to temperature and opening, potentially causing the brand-new engine to overheat.

2. Check that the battery terminals are connected firmly and the battery is charged.

3. Make sure the fuel is supplied to the injection system by turning the key to the Run position, and check that there are no fuel leaks at the connections and fittings.

4. If the ignition timing is adjustable, make sure it is set close enough to start and then hook up a timing light to make an adjustment when the engine first starts (**FIGURE 10-27**).

5. Check all of the auxiliary components, such as the air conditioner and the power steering pump, for proper installation and hose routing.

6. Check the serpentine belt and/or other belts and pulleys for proper installation.

7. Determine that electrical connectors and vacuum hoses are properly connected.

8. Connect the exhaust removal hose to the exhaust pipe.

9. Verify that the brake pedal is not spongy.

FIGURE 10-27 Using a timing light to set ignition timing.

Initial Break-In

To ensure that the piston rings are seated properly and that the camshaft and other internal components are not damaged, it is important to follow the manufacturer's break-in procedures of the various components. If required during the initial engine break-in period, run the engine at high idle (1200–2000 rpm). Observe the temperature and oil pressure gauges. If the engine begins to run hot or the oil pressure drops, shut the engine off immediately. Also, monitor the engine for external leaks. If any are found, shut the engine down, and repair the leak.

Run the engine at fast idle until it reaches and holds normal operating temperature or for the prescribed break-in time; then shut down the engine. Check the engine oil and oil level to ensure that there is no evidence of coolant in the oil. If the oil looks milky or the oil level has risen above the full line, there may be an internal coolant leak.

Engine Timing Adjustment and Diagnostic Trouble Code Inspection

After starting the engine, you need to determine whether the engine ignition timing is set correctly if it is adjustable. There are almost as many methods of setting the timing as there are vehicle models. Again, you need to consult the appropriate service literature to determine the correct method.

S10003 Set timing on a computer-controlled engine.

You will notice that there are significant differences in timing methods from one decade to another. On vehicles from the 1970s and earlier, the primary method for setting the timing is to adjust the distributor while using a timing light. For 1980s models, you might need to disconnect a computer spark control wire or ground a particular wire or disconnect a sensor, and then set the timing by adjusting the distributor while using a timing light. On most vehicles made since the mid to late 1980s, the computer controls the timing, and you do not need to manually set it.

Another important task to complete after you have started the engine is connecting a diagnostic scan tool to the **data link connector (DLC)** and checking for **diagnostic trouble codes (DTCs)**. If you find that a DTC was set during the engine break-in period, diagnose the condition. Once corrected, run the engine until it is fully warm again, and check for any DTCs.

Once the engine is timed properly and the engine runs without turning on the MIL, and the engine has reached operating temperature and there are no sign of leaks or other problems, take the vehicle for a test drive. Drive it for 30 minutes without exceeding 50 mph (80 kph) and 2000 rpm. This will allow the piston rings to seat and ensure good seating of other internal components such as cam lobes. Once back at the shop, recheck all of the fluid levels, and look for any leaks. Also check for any loose or missing components. If everything is in working order, clean the vehicle and return it to the customer.

SKILL DRILL 10-1 Setting Timing on a Computer Controlled Engine with a Distributor

1. Install distributor with rotor facing number one terminal.

2. Reinstall distributor cap.

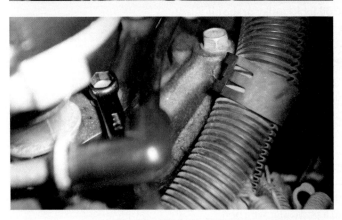

3. Snug distributor hold down bolt.

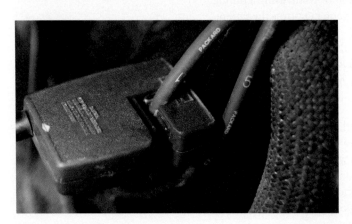

4. Start engine.

5. Attach Timing light to number one cylinder spark plug wire.

Continued

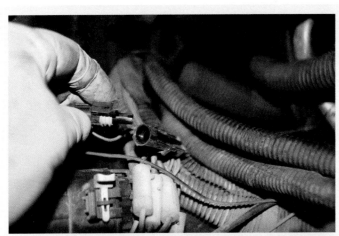

6. Put the engine in base timing mode, refer to service information.

7. Point timing light at the harmonic balancer and find the mark on the balancer.

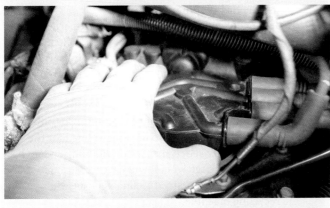

8. Rotate the distributor to move the timing mark to the specified timing degree.

9. Tighten down distributor hold down bolt.

Continued

10. Revert engine back to computer controlled timing mode.

▶ Wrap-Up

Ready for Review

▶ Once a major engine failure has been diagnosed, the engine often has to be removed for repair or replacement.

▶ Most engines in rear-wheel drive vehicles are best removed from the top of the engine compartment, whereas many engines in front-wheel drive vehicles can be removed from the top or the bottom of the engine compartment.

▶ If removing from the top of the engine compartment, the engine can be separated from the transmission and removed by itself, or in some cases, the engine and transmission are removed as a unit.

▶ If the engine is removed from the bottom of the engine compartment, the engine and transaxle are usually removed as a unit attached to the engine cradle, which bolts the engine and transmission to the vehicle.

▶ The first step in the engine removal process is to remove the hood. With the hood removed, you have greater access to the engine compartment and greater visibility because more light can get in.

▶ If the vehicle is front-wheel drive and the engine is coming out from underneath the vehicle, or if the hood opens at least 90 degrees, you may not need to remove the hood.

▶ One of the first things you will do is disable the electrical system by disconnecting the battery. Doing so reduces the risk of fire or explosion due to an inadvertent spark near exposed gases during the engine removal process.

▶ When disconnecting the battery, remove the negative terminal of the battery first.

▶ A good idea is to take a picture of the engine compartment before you begin, so you have a record where everything goes; or you should label all disconnects.

▶ Typically, a fuel injection supply line stays under pressure even when the engine is not running; therefore, you need to relieve the pressure on the fuel system before disconnecting the lines.

▶ Check the service information for proper procedures to release the fuel system pressure.

▶ To begin, look closely at the electrical wire harnesses to evaluate the best area to disconnect them. Often, it is easier to disconnect main harnesses at their central connector instead of at the end of each branch, so you should investigate this option.

▶ After checking the appropriate service information, you can determine whether the air-conditioning or power steering systems will have to be disconnected for the engine to be removed. If the air-conditioning system has to be opened, the refrigerant will have to be removed and stored by a properly trained technician using the appropriate recycling machine.

▶ If the power steering circuit has to be opened, the fluid must be drained first.

▶ To drain engine coolant, there should be a drain valve or plug at the bottom of the radiator, but if not, you will have to disconnect the lower radiator hose, place the drain pan underneath the valve, and open the valve.

▶ Air-conditioning compressors and power steering pumps are examples of accessory components that are mounted to the engine.

▶ When preparing to raise the vehicle and make the necessary disconnections for removing the engine, start by reviewing the manufacturer's information. By following the steps for the specific vehicle you are working on, you can avoid missing components, bolts, hoses, and wires that must be disconnected before the engine can be removed.

▶ When the engine is loose, hanging from the engine hoist and unsupported by the vehicle, it is not the time to discover that you missed removing something under the vehicle.

▶ Because most fluid drain points are located under the vehicle, now is the time to drain fluids not previously drained.

▶ Drain the engine oil, and if the transmission or transaxle will be coming out with the engine, you will have to drain the transmission/transaxle fluid as well.

▶ Currently produced vehicles could have three or four oxygen sensors, a catalytic converter, resonator, muffler, and or a turbocharger driven by the exhaust gases.

▶ Light-duty diesel-powered vehicles are now equipped with particulate filters. It is important to understand the exhaust system and related components on the vehicle before removing the exhaust system.

▶ To begin the exhaust removal process, identify the oxygen sensors that have to be removed or disconnected. Disconnect the sensors.

▶ Always follow the exhaust removal guidelines in the manufacturer's information or other reliable service information.

▶ Remove the inspection cover on the bell housing to access the torque converter bolts on rear-wheel drive and front-wheel drive vehicles. If the engine is being removed from the top.

▶ For front-wheel drive vehicles in which the engine is being removed from the bottom, the engine and subframe, also called a cradle, have to be removed together.

▶ A subframe is a mount used to support the engine and transaxle assembly and is attached to the vehicle.

▶ If the bell housing does not have an inspection cover, then you may have to access the flexplate by going through the starter mounting hole.

▶ If the engine is being removed from the bottom of the vehicle using a subframe scissor jack, do not disconnect the transaxle at this time.

▶ If the engine is being removed from the top of the vehicle without the transmission/transaxle, you ultimately will have to unbolt the transmission/transaxle, but do not try to separate the transmission/transaxle from the engine until the transmission is supported and the engine is on the hoist.

▶ Always put safety first in each step of the engine removal and installation process. Vehicles and engines are heavy.

▶ During the removal and installation procedure, one of those heavy items will be lifted high enough to clear the other. If the engine slips, it can crush or pinch fingers, hands, and feet.

▶ The tools you need to remove and replace an engine include special service tools, a vehicle lift, an engine hoist, an engine stand, jacks, and general shop hand tools.

▶ Just as in the engine removal process, have assistants help you install the engine. First, organize the work site. Begin by making sure the area is clean and clear of obstructions. To be prepared, conveniently arrange the bolts and engine mounts needed to secure the engine.

▶ When reinstalling the torque converter, push in and turn the torque converter, making sure it engages into the front pump. You should feel three distinct clunks.

▶ When mating the engine up to the transmission, make sure the torque converter does not bind against the flexplate. If it does, remove the engine and reengage the torque converter into the transmission.

▶ For vehicles equipped with manual transmissions, the clutch disc has to be aligned with the clutch pilot hole, using a clutch alignment tool. First verify that the correct pilot bearing or bushing is installed in the rear of the crankshaft.

▶ After the transmission is bolted to the engine, the engine needs to be mounted to the vehicle frame or cradle.

▶ Attach the motor mounts that connect the engine to the frame or mounting platform. To mount the engine, lower the engine carefully, aligning the motor mounts, and then tighten them to specifications.

▶ You can make alignment pins by taking two bolts that are longer than the bell housing bolts, cutting off their heads, and chamfering the cut ends. Screw these by finger into two of the bell housing holes in the block.

▶ Engine start-up after installation is a critical time for engine operation and longevity. It is important to make sure all fluid levels are checked and at the correct level.

▶ Keep your eyes and ears open, listening for unusual noises and looking for fluid leaks.

▶ Monitor the temperature and oil pressure gauges, and shut the engine down immediately if the gauges indicate overheating or low oil pressure.

▶ Some new camshaft break-in procedures require the engine to start immediately and to run at 1200 to 2000 revolutions per minute (rpm) for 20 or 30 minutes to provide proper lubrication and break-in.

▶ Before starting the engine after installation, you will need to do the following:

- Check all fluid levels, especially the engine oil and coolant levels. If a vacuum fill method of filling the cooling system was used, the cooling system will be full. If this method was not used, the system will look full but likely will have air pockets in the system. If there is a vacuum pocket at the thermostat, the air pocket may prevent the thermostat from getting up to temperature and opening, potentially causing the brand new engine to overheat.
- Check that the battery terminals are connected firmly and the battery is charged.
- Make sure the fuel is supplied to the injection system by turning the key to the run position, and check that there are no fuel leaks at the connections and fittings.
- Check all of the auxiliary components, such as the air conditioner and the power steering pump, for proper installation and hose routing.
- Check the serpentine belt and/or other belts and pulleys for proper installation.

- Determine that electrical connectors and vacuum hoses are properly connected.
- Connect the exhaust removal hose to the exhaust pipe.
- Verify that the brake pedal is not spongy.

▸ Another important task to complete after you have started the engine is connecting a diagnostic scan tool to the data link connector (DLC) and checking for diagnostic trouble codes (DTCs). If you find that a DTC was set during the engine break-in period, diagnose the condition.

Key Terms

data link connector (DLC) Located near the steering column and allows for a scan tool to interrogate the PCM in a vehicle for information.

diagnostic trouble code (DTC) A monitor code that shows that there is a fault with in the engine management system.

engine hoist A crane that allows for the engine to be removed, usually rated from 3 to 6 tons, to safely lift the heavy engines found in today's vehicles.

engine stand Supports the engine when it is removed from the vehicle so that the technician can disassemble and repair the various components.

exhaust system The piping and components that direct the flow of exhaust from the engine to out from underneath the vehicle.

starter motor The electric motor that, in conjunction with the flywheel, rotates the engine over to start the combustion process.

subframe A removal section of the frame that usually supports the drivetrain and suspension components.

Review Questions

1. Removing engines can pose all of the below safety hazards, *except*:
   a. crushing fingers due to engine slips.
   b. fluids and chemicals spraying into your eyes.
   c. sharp edges of parts causing cuts.
   d. shock from the electrical system.

2. During topside disconnection:
   a. always remove the hood irrespective of the degree to which it opens.
   b. maintain the fuel pressure in the fuel system.
   c. disable the electrical system by disconnecting the battery.
   d. retain the fluids in the engine.

3. When disconnecting a battery:
   a. Have the unlock codes of the antitheft system available.
   b. Remove the positive terminal of the battery first.
   c. Lay the tools on the battery for easy use.
   d. Ensure that all other components are connected.

4. When removing accessory components that are mounted to the engine:
   a. Remove all the brackets.
   b. Always disconnect the hydraulic lines.

c. Place all attachment bolts separate from the components.
   d. Take pictures to remind you of bracket locations and positions.

5. During the exhaust removal process, the exhaust pipe and component routing should be checked to:
   a. prevent leaks.
   b. improve their efficiency.
   c. determine the best places to disconnect.
   d. avoid emission of toxic gases.

6. For front-wheel drive vehicles in which the engine is being removed from the bottom, all of the below may be removed along with the engine, *except* the:
   a. transaxle.
   b. the inspection cover on the bell housing.
   c. cradle.
   d. axles.

7. Until the transmission is supported and the engine is supported by the hoist, do not try to:
   a. drain engine fluids.
   b. remove the radiator.
   c. separate the transmission from the engine.
   d. disconnect the battery.

8. When reinstalling the torque converter, push in and turn the torque converter. We can make sure it engages into the front pump when we feel:
   a. four distinct clunks.
   b. three distinct clunks.
   c. two distinct clunks.
   d. a single clunk.

9. Choose the correct statement:
   a. Layout diagrams are not helpful during reinstallation.
   b. Changing the front transmission seal is essential in manual transmission vehicles.
   c. The clutch disc needs to be aligned with the clutch pilot hole in manual transmission.
   d. After the transmission is bolted to the engine, the engine has to be mounted on the engine stand.

10. As part of prestart engine checks, it is essential to do all of the below *except*:
    a. Check all fluid levels, especially the engine oil and coolant levels.
    b. Check that the battery terminals are clean and connected firmly.
    c. Check all auxiliary components for proper installation.
    d. Check that the engine ignition timing is set correctly.

ASE Technician A/Technician B Style Questions

1. Tech A says that when replacing the engine with a used one, the technician must be well organized to complete the job efficiently. Tech B states that using the proper tools to remove an engine will help complete the task quickly. Who is correct?
   a. Tech A
   b. Tech B
   c. Both A and B
   d. Neither A nor B

2. Tech A states that removal of the engine from a vehicle may be easiest out of the bottom of the vehicle. Tech B says following the manufactures procedures on removal and installation will make the technician more efficient. Who is correct?
   a. Tech A
   b. Tech B
   c. Both A and B
   d. Neither A nor B

3. Tech A says labeling wires and hoses helps with reassembly, which saves a lot of wasted time in trying to find where they should be connected. Tech B states when replacing the fluids in the engine you must use the old fluids over again. Who is correct?
   a. Tech A
   b. Tech B
   c. Both A and B
   d. Neither A nor B

4. Tech A says that diagnosing the cause of the engine failure is the first step in repairing the vehicle because if you don't, you will be replacing the engine again. Tech B states that most engine failures are a result of lack of maintenance. Who is correct?
   a. Tech A
   b. Tech B
   c. Both A and B
   d. Neither A nor B

5. Tech A states that you can replace an engine with any engine that you find. Tech B says that the engine that you replace must match it exactly or there could be running issues. Who is correct?
   a. Tech A
   b. Tech B
   c. Both A and B
   d. Neither A nor B

6. Tech A says when doing engine work on a hybrid engine, you must disable the battery packs, or you face possible death. Tech B states that using the wrong coolant in the engine could cause premature hose and gasket failure. Who is correct?
   a. Tech A
   b. Tech B
   c. Both A and B
   d. Neither A nor B

7. Tech A says that using the wrong water pump on an engine that has reverse cooling flow will cause the engine to overheat. Tech B states that changing the radiator out for a smaller unit will save room and make the engine run cooler. Who is correct?
   a. Tech A
   b. Tech B
   c. Both A and B
   d. Neither A nor B

8. Tech A states that when removing the exhaust bolts, you should use heat so that the bolts will not break. Tech B states that the exhaust system should be inspected to make sure that it is in serviceable condition. Who is correct?
   a. Tech A
   b. Tech B
   c. Both A and B
   d. Neither A nor B

9. Tech A says that when using an engine hoist, you should make sure that it is rated for the weight of the engine, or you could potentially drop the engine. Tech B the use of jack stands and jacks can make the removal of the engine easier. Who is correct?
   a. Tech A
   b. Tech B
   c. Both A and B
   d. Neither A nor B

10. Tech A says that when installing the engine, you do not need to worry about the torque converter lining up. Tech B says that the transmission must be in the right position so that it will line up with the engine when it is installed and that failure to do so could result in a broken transmission housing. Who is correct?
    a. Tech A
    b. Tech B
    c. Both A and B
    d. Neither A nor B

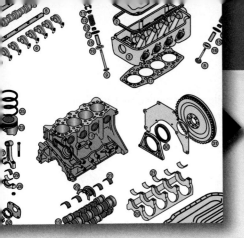

CHAPTER 11
Engine Disassembly

NATEF Tasks

- **N11001** Remove, inspect, or replace crankshaft vibration damper (harmonic balancer).
- **N11002** Disassemble engine block; clean and prepare components for inspection and reassembly.
- **N11003** Deglaze and clean cylinder walls.
- **N11004** Inspect engine block for visible cracks, passage condition, core and gallery plug condition, and surface warpage; determine needed action.
- **N11005** Inspect and measure cylinder walls/sleeves for damage, wear, and ridges; determine needed action.
- **N11006** Inspect crankshaft for straightness, journal damage, keyway damage, thrust flange and sealing surface condition, and visual surface cracks; check oil passage condition; measure end

play and journal wear; check crankshaft position sensor reluctor ring (where applicable); determine needed action.
- **N11007** Inspect main and connecting rod bearings for damage and wear; determine needed action.
- **N11008** Identify piston and bearing wear patterns that indicate connecting rod alignment and main bearing bore problems; determine needed action.
- **N11009** Inspect and measure piston skirts and ring lands; determine needed action.
- **N11010** Inspect and measure camshaft bearings for wear, damage, out-of-round, and alignment; determine needed action.
- **N11011** Determine piston-to-bore clearance.

Knowledge Objectives

After reading this chapter, you will have:

- **K11001** Knowledge of how to set up the engine so that it can be disassembled.
- **K11002** Knowledge of how to remove timing components.
- **K11003** Knowledge of the different types of cylinder heads.
- **K11004** Knowledge of disassembly of engine block.
- **K11005** Knowledge of cylinder ridge removal.
- **K11006** Knowledge of proper labeling and part organization.
- **K11007** Knowledge of engine component inspection.

Skills Objectives

- **S11001** Mount the engine to an engine stand.
- **S11002** Deglaze an engine cylinder.
- **S11003** Inspect the engine block for visible cracks.
- **S11004** Inspect the crankshaft.
- **S11005** Inspect the main and connecting rod bearings.
- **S11006** Identify main, connecting rod, and cam bearings wear issues.
- **S11007** Inspect and measure cylinder walls/sleeves for damage and wear.
- **S11008** Inspect and measure piston skirts.
- **S11009** Identify main, connecting rod, and cam bearings wear issues.

You Are the Automotive Technician

Today you are disassembling an engine that has more than 250,000 miles on it. The vehicle still runs well, but doesn't have as much power as it used to. The fuel economy is also not as good as it once was, and the vehicle is burning more oil than specified. The owner would prefer that this engine be rebuilt rather than replaced, because it has lasted so long, but only if that makes economic sense. He has agreed to pay you to disassemble the engine, measure the critical components of the engine, compare them to specifications, and estimate the cost to rebuild it.

1. What measurements will you need to perform on the block and its internal components?
2. How will you determine whether the block and heads have any cracks?
3. What precautions should be taken when disassembling an engine in which the major components may be reused?

K11001 Knowledge of how to set up the engine so that it can be disassembled.

▶ Introduction

Engine disassembly is a very in-depth area of automobile maintenance that is often overlooked with today's throwaway culture. The technician must be aware of a lot of areas and must know what to do when they come across problems in these areas. Throughout this chapter, we explain in depth the procedures that the technician must know and perform when disassembling an engine.

▶ Engine Disassembly

Engine disassembly is an important procedure in the rebuilding of an engine as it allows you to verify which components failed, which are good to be reused, and what will need to be done to the engine to put it back in service. This procedure should be meticulously done, as any small problem in this area could cause a larger issue when the engine is reassembled and fired up.

Mounting the Engine to an Engine Stand

S11001 Mount the engine to an engine stand.

When you are going to mount the engine that you are disassembling to an engine stand, you must be careful on how you attach it to the stand. The rating of the engine stand must be high enough to hold the weight of the engine with all of its accessories attached to it. As well, you must inspect the engine stand to verify that it is in good condition to be used in this way. Different lengths and sizes of bolts must be available to attach the engine to the engine stand, and you should have these ready before you try to mount the engine to the stand. Once on the engine stand, disassembly and reassembly will go quickly because you are able to manipulate the engine to the exact position that you need to in order to remove and reinstall the components.

To mount an engine to an engine stand, follow the steps of the **SKILL DRILL 11-1**.

SKILL DRILL 11-1 Mounting an Engine to an Engine Stand

1. Gather your engine, engine stand, and attachment bolts together in one area.

2. Verify that the engine stand will hold the weight of the engine.

Continued

3. Line the engine up with the engine stand.

4. Adjust the mounting arms to match up with the bell housing mounting points.

5. Once the mounting arms are positioned, find the appropriate bolts to attach the stand to the engine.

6. Once the engine is bolted to the stand, you can lower the crane to remove the chain.

Draining the Engine Block

The first step in disassembling the engine is to remove any remaining fluids, such as the oil and the coolant, from the engine block. It is not uncommon to find some leftover oil and coolant inside the engine block once the heads have been removed. The coolant often becomes trapped inside the water jacket passages, especially if you were unable to remove one of the drains plugs earlier in the disassembly process (**FIGURE 11-1**). Leftover oil is also frequently found in trapped oil passageways. It is a good idea to always place a catch tray underneath the engine when it is rolled over, to catch these fluids as they drain out of the engine (**FIGURE 11-2**).

Removing the Oil Pan

To gain access to the rotating assembly of the engine, the oil pan has to be removed. If the engine has a lot of miles on it, was poorly maintained, or had extensive damage, there will probably be a layer of oil sludge and possibly metal particles or other foreign objects in the bottom of the oil pan. In order to keep this evidence intact, do not rotate the engine block upside down yet.

To remove the oil pan, you need to remove the bolts holding the oil pan, or sump, onto the block and store them in a bin or bag. If you are removing the oil pan with the engine side up, leave two bolts in opposite corners threaded in about halfway. Insert a putty knife or gasket scraper between the engine block and the oil pan, and start to pry the pan loose (**FIGURE 11-3**). Use care to avoid bending the pan while prying. When you separate the oil pan enough to rest on the catch bolts, support the oil pan from the bottom, and remove those remaining two bolts. Pull the oil pan away carefully, working around any obstructions such as the oil pump or baffles.

Removing the Oil Pump and Tray

Some oil pumps are located inside the crankcase and have to be removed before the pistons, whereas others are located on the front of the block and have to be removed along with any timing components. On a crankcase-mounted oil pump, you may be able to unscrew one bolt and simply pull off the oil pump. Other oil pumps have two bolts and may also have a few other bolts that hold the pickup tube and screen in place (**FIGURE 11-4**). As the oil

FIGURE 11-1 A water jacket drain plug.

FIGURE 11-2 Unbolt and remove the oil pump and pickup tube.

FIGURE 11-3 To remove the oil pan on an engine that is attached to a stand, rotate the engine over so that the oil pan is easily accessible.

FIGURE 11-4 The oil pickup tube is sometimes attached to the engine block when the oil pump is not in the oil pan.

pump is removed, you may see the plastic collar that holds the oil pump drive rod onto the oil pump. If the collar is broken, you will need to replace it.

If the engine has a windage tray (to prevent oil from splashing onto the crankshaft), remove it now, along with any dipstick tube or extension that might be inside the oil pan area. With the oil pan removed, it is easier to check for evidence of engine problems. If there were knocking noises heard coming from deep inside the engine, then it may be visible or apparent that one of the rod bearings has disintegrated and/or spun.

Removing the Timing Components

When you start to disassemble the timing components, you must be aware of how those components went together. Using the harmonic balancer, line up the timing marks on the balancer and the timing cover. Remove the cover, and then check the **timing marks**, as this will orient you to how the pieces go together, which will help with reassembly once your internal engine work is complete. As you disassemble the timing components. you must pay close attention to all the guides, tensioners, chains, belts, and gears, to see if any of those components must be replaced (**FIGURE 11-5**). Normal procedure when rebuilding an engine is to replace the timing components as a kit so that you know that they will be functional once the engine is run. If you are reusing the chain, when you remove it, make sure you mark the direction of the chain, along with the direction the gears are to be installed, on the engine (**FIGURE 11-6**) Timing chains create a wear pattern on the chain and the sprockets, causing them to be matched, and if you change the pattern, the chain will end up trying to create a new one, which may cause a component to fail. Timing belts are very similar to chains as they create a wear pattern in the belt, which means you must keep the direction the same as it was when it was installed on the engine. Another issue with the timing belt is that you must inspect it for cracking, fraying, or liquid degradation (**FIGURE 11-7**). If the belt is damaged in any way, it must be replaced as it cannot be trusted to last.

N11001 Remove, inspect, or replace crankshaft vibration damper (harmonic balancer).

K11002 Knowledge of how to remove timing components.

FIGURE 11-5 Some timing chain setups are very complicated and require proper procedures in removal and reassembly.

Removing the Cylinder Heads

Once the timing components, intake, and exhaust manifolds are removed, it is time to remove the cylinder heads. The first step in removing the cylinder heads is to refer to your information system to verify the correct procedure for removal of the cylinder head (**FIGURE 11-8**). Sometimes a detorquing procedure must be followed so that the cylinder head will not become warped as the head bolts are removed. Once the proper procedure is found, follow it so that the cylinder head can be reconditioned and reinstalled on the assembled engine. Once the cylinder head is removed, it must be checked for cracks and flatness, as it is imperative that the head is in good working order to be reinstalled. This process is usually handled by a local machine shop because they have the equipment to check the cylinder head out, unlike most automotive repair shops.

K11003 Knowledge of the different types of cylinder heads.

OHV

The **OHV** designation means that the engine has **overhead valves**, usually actuated by a pushrod (**FIGURE 11-9**). This information is very important when ordering parts for vehicles that have the same engine sizes but different engine configurations. Most of the time, the OHV parts will not interchange with the OHC parts because the design of these

FIGURE 11-6 Marking the timing chain with a paint marker allows for easier reassembly of the timing components.

FIGURE 11-7 Contaminated timing belts are susceptible to failure, which means if you find a contaminated one, it will have to be replaced.

FIGURE 11-8 A typical cylinder head that has been removed from an engine for service.

FIGURE 11-9 This cylinder head is set up to use a pushrod valvetrain for valve actuation.

FIGURE 11-10 This cylinder head has the camshaft installed in it, which means it is an overhead camshaft engine.

engines is completely different. The camshaft is located in the cylinder block, which requires a shorter timing chain or belt, as well the external covers that support this type of design.

OHC

An **overhead cam engine (OHC)** is one that has the camshaft mounted on the cylinder head so that there are no pushrods or lifters in the engine block like the OHV engine (**FIGURE 11-10**). This type of engine has vastly different components from the OHV engine, which means that when you are purchasing parts or looking up information on this type of engine, you must make sure that you are referencing the proper engine. This design was used to simplify the valvetrain by reducing the number of moving parts related to it. By moving the camshaft to the cylinder head the lifter, pushrod and many components can be eliminated or reduced in size.

K11004 Knowledge of disassembly of engine block.

N11002 Disassemble engine block; clean and prepare components for inspection and reassembly.

▶ Disassembly of the Engine Block Components

Disassembling an engine is a meticulous process where the technician must be highly organized to do this process efficiently. Organization is key to making the correct decisions on part replacement and reuse. Errors in this stage of the process can cause problems throughout the engine reassembly.

Applied Math

AM-20: Place Value: The technician can interpret standard or metric units when conducting precision measurements.

A technician and his helper are rebuilding an automotive engine. It has been disassembled, and the task is to measure the components with micrometers. The helper is familiar with use of a micrometer, which can measure parts to within one-thousandth of an inch. The micrometer set that is being used is capable of measuring parts to within 1/10,0000 of an inch.

To assist the helper, the technician mentions the term "place value." Place value is the value of the position of a digit in a number. For example, in the measurement 2.4137 inch, the "3" represents thousandths of an inch. Most automotive engine specifications will be listed with four numbers to the right of the decimal, indicating the ten-thousandths position. In our example, the "7" is four numbers to the right of the decimal, which is the ten-thousandths position.

Concerning the metric system, the unit of linear measurement is the millimeter or centimeter. Understanding place value of this system is essential. A typical specification in the metric system would be 45.428 mm, which is equal to 1.7885". In metric units, engine specifications would extend three numbers to the right of the decimal for linear measurement in millimeters.

Disassembling the Block Underside

The block underside refers to the area located in the oil pan and timing chain part of the engine cylinder block assembly (**FIGURE 11-11**). These areas are fully covered by the timing chain cover and the oil pan cover, which are stamped sheet metal assemblies or cast aluminum assemblies.

Cylinder Ridge Removal

The ridge at the top of the cylinder is too big if, after the carbon has been scraped off, it catches a fingernail. If the ridge is significant, and you are planning on reusing the pistons, you will need to remove the ridge with a tool called a **ridge reamer** (**FIGURE 11-12**). The ridge reamer is a cutting tool used to cut into the metal ridge and carbon buildup at the top of the cylinder and remove the lip. If the ridge is not removed, the piston rings could break as they move across the ridge. The piston itself could be damaged if it is forced over the ridge when you are removing the piston.

K11005 Knowledge of cylinder ridge removal.

If the pistons are going to be reused, any excessive ridge will have to be removed first, and then the pistons can be tapped out carefully. Also, care needs to be taken not to damage the connecting rod journal on the crankshaft when removing the piston. Using rod bolt covers will help protect the connecting rod journal.

Labeling the Connecting Rods and Caps

The connecting rod caps must be replaced in the same orientation as they are removed. If they are not already labeled, label them in two places: above and below the parting line of the cap and rod body. It is a good idea to also label the main caps

K11006 Knowledge of proper labeling and part organization.

FIGURE 11-11 The lower end of the engine block is where the rotating assembly and most of the engine internals are housed.

FIGURE 11-12 Position a piston at BDC, and remove the connecting rod nuts.

FIGURE 11-13 Marking the connecting rod caps to correspond to the connecting rods allows for correct and easy reassembly.

FIGURE 11-14 To remove the main cap, loosen the two bolts that keep it tight to the cylinder block. The main cap is what holds the crankshaft into the cylinder block.

FIGURE 11-15 When the main cap is removed, the crankshaft bearing may be stuck to the main cap and must be removed to be checked.

of the block in the same way. One way to label these components is with a number punch set, but you could use a regular center punch. *Note: Do not* stamp or center punch powdered metal rods; doing so could destroy them. Clean the side of a powdered metal rod with a solvent, and use paint to mark it instead (**FIGURE 11-13**).

You will have to rotate the crankshaft over during disassembly, so you may want to use a crankshaft turning tool that allows you to turn the crankshaft assembly. Or you can also reinstall the harmonic balancer and turn the engine over by grabbing the harmonic balancer and turning the engine over by hand. Do not use pliers or vise grips because they will damage the crankshaft and/or Woodruff key.

Removing the Pistons

Removing the pistons is a multistep process that requires making some decisions before starting the process. The two most basic decisions are deciding whether the pistons are going to be reused or replaced and whether the ridge at the top of the cylinder needs to be reamed off. The answer to those questions will determine the order at which you perform the steps and the amount of care you use to remove the pistons.

It may be obvious that the pistons will have to be replaced, such as when the cylinders are worn enough that they will have to be bored oversize or when the engine exhibits enough wear requiring piston replacement. When a motor is running, the piston rings slowly wear away the cylinder wall where they ride, and create what is called a ridge at the top of the cylinder. Higher mileage and harder worked engines develop more severe ridges than other engines. Carbon buildup also adds thickness to the ridge of a cylinder, but this can be removed with a razor blade. A thick ridge makes it more difficult to push the piston out.

Removing the Crankshaft and Bearings

Before removing the **main bearing caps**, make sure they are marked for reinstallation. To do so, use a number punch or marking paint. To remove the crankshaft bearing caps, you may need some additional leverage to loosen the bolts that hold the crankshaft caps. Some engine blocks have two bolts per cap. Others have four. Remove the bolts (**FIGURE 11-14**). The cap may not come away easily, especially if it has long alignment dowels. Make sure the bolts are not threaded in at this point. Hold them up halfway out of their bolt holes, and tap lightly side to side on the bolt heads. You will need to alternate sides until the cap is clear to be removed. The lower half of the main bearing inserts may come away with the cap as you remove it, or they may stick to the crankshaft journal (**FIGURE 11-15**).

To remove the crankshaft on an application with a one-piece rear main seal, you first need to remove the rear main seal and housing (**FIGURE 11-16**). This may require removing the engine from the engine stand to gain access to the rear of the block. Depending on the maker of engine stand, and the engine block, sometimes the engine stand adapter will prevent the ease of removing the crankshaft assembly due to the end part of the

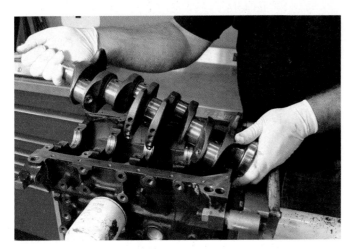

FIGURE 11-16 Lift out the crankshaft.

FIGURE 11-17 Remove the bearing inserts from the bearing saddles in the block.

crankshaft sticking out past the engine block and the adapter covering it. Crankshafts are both heavy and awkwardly shaped, so be very careful lifting a crankshaft out of the engine block, or ask for assistance (**FIGURE 11-17**).

When the **crankshaft** is removed from the engine cylinder block, sometimes the oil has become sticky and the crankshaft bearings may get stuck to the crankshaft assembly. In this case, you must examine the crankshaft thoroughly and remove the sticky bearings. Also examine the engine cylinder block saddles, where the crankshaft lies inside the block, to see if there are any bearings left inside the engine block. Next, remove any bearing inserts left in the engine cylinder block. Push each half-shell to the side from the center, with your fingers opposite the bearing tang (**FIGURE 11-18**). If necessary, use a wooden hammer handle to help remove the bearing. The thrust bearing is a special bearing for the crankshaft assembly. It is the largest bearing insert, and its purpose is to prevent the crankshaft from moving forward or backward during engine operation. This crankshaft movement is also known as lateral movement. In addition to being the largest bearing, the thrust bearing can be identified by its sides, whose purpose is to cover the engine cylinder block saddles and prevent bearing movement.

Bearings with visible wear patterns, especially if the copper core is showing through in some areas, are not reusable and should be replaced. If you are not sure of their reusability, take them to a machine shop specialist for advice. If the engine has a rope seal or a two-piece rear main seal, pull out both halves with needle-nose pliers, a scratch awl, or a flat-blade screwdriver.

Core Plus and Gallery Plugs Removal

Remove the water jacket **core plugs**. The water jacket core plugs cannot be easily pulled out, but they can usually be tilted so that Channellock pliers can grab them and pry them out. Use a punch to carefully drive one side of the core plug toward the water jacket. This should tilt them (**FIGURE 11-19**). If not, keep tapping one side in, but be careful to hang on to it, because some core plugs can fall into the water jackets and drop down out of sight. Grip one side of the plug with channel lock pliers, and pry it back out (**FIGURE 11-20**).

FIGURE 11-18 Carefully hammer one side of the core plug until it tilts or pushes into the water jacket.

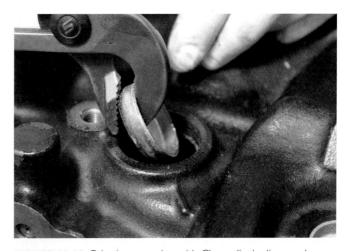

FIGURE 11-19 Grip the core plug with Channellock pliers, and pry it out.

FIGURE 11-20 Remove the block from the engine stand, and remove the adapter.

FIGURE 11-21 Remove the oil gallery plugs.

FIGURE 11-22 Remove the front oil plugs.

FIGURE 11-23 Place the components in a spray wash cabinet to be cleaned.

If you have a stuck water jacket drain plug, now is the time to remove it. Drill right through the plug, then heat it up and let it cool again to try to break some of the threads loose. Insert an extractor tool into the open hole and use a wrench to break it free and unthread it. Next, take the engine block off the stand. Lower the engine block carefully onto a bench and remove the engine stand adapter (**FIGURE 11-21**). Remove the oil gallery plugs (**FIGURE 11-22**). If they are square-type plugs, only use the proper hardened steel tool to remove them. Do not use the square part of a socket wrench. If they are stuck, do not force them to the point of stripping them. Use an oxyacetylene torch to heat up frozen plugs. Get them very hot, then let them cool, after which they may be loose enough to undo. If not, or if they strip, a machining specialist may have to remove them for you.

With the rear plugs out, you can pass a metal rod through the oil gallery and hammer out the front plugs from the rear, if they are the hammer-in type (**FIGURE 11-23**). Hammer-in types do not have any threads showing, but rather a smooth surface on the sides and top of the plug. A threaded plug has visible threads on the side and a square recessed area on top where a drive from a ratchet would be placed during installation or removal.

Each engine block has its own particular engine block plugs. The manufacturer of the engine cylinder block decides plug type based on the engine cylinder block application. Check the service information to locate all of the plugs. Go around the engine block, taking notes as you remove any plug, adapter, or fitting that might hinder the cleaning process.

Cleaning the Components

Before the parts are examined beyond a quick visual inspection, they should be cleaned. The cleaning process of the engine cylinder block can vary depending on what is available to the technician. Most shops use a spray wash cabinet, which operates much like a dishwasher and usually uses environmentally friendly degreasers and hot water (**FIGURE 11-24**). Some machine shops dip the major engine parts for several hours in a hot or cold caustic solution. The strong corrosive chemicals remove mineral deposits in the water jackets, carbon deposits, oil, greases, and paints.

FIGURE 11-24 Cleaning engine components is the first step in the rebuild process.

▶ **NOTE**

It is of utmost importance to remember that, after beading, all of the beads will have to be thoroughly cleaned out and off the parts. Beads will get stuck in parts with baffles and myriad other places and will quickly destroy a newly rebuilt engine when they become dislodged and circulate inside the engine.

Depending on the condition of the components, everything from the engine block and disassembled heads to the crankshaft and all the covers may have to be put into the spray wash for degreasing. After that, the heads and engine block will have to be hot tanked, blasted, or baked until they are perfectly clean, and any of the external covers must be bead blasted to be ready for paint later on. It is much easier to inspect and properly assess the condition of the parts when everything is clean.

Deglazing and Cleaning Cylinders

If the cylinder measures within specifications, it will have to be prepared for the new piston rings. The cylinder wall will probably have a polished "glaze" on its surface that must be removed. Removing the glazed surface with an abrasive stone of the proper grit will give the cylinder walls a nice crosshatch pattern, which allows a small amount of oil to be retained in the fine scratches. This oil helps to lubricate the piston rings during engine operation, and the fine crosshatched scratches allow the new piston rings to seat against the surface of the freshly honed cylinder wall. The recommended crosshatch for a cylinder wall is approximately 45 degrees.

A cylinder hone can be rigid, flexible, or ball style. A rigid hone uses fixed rectangular abrasive stones and is used on a cylinder after it has been bored to give a perfectly cylindrical shape with the proper finish. A flexible hone uses spring-loaded rectangular stones that can more easily follow the contours of a minimally used cylinder; thus, it is used to deglaze a cylinder that will be reused. A ball hone uses round abrasive stones on the ends of flexible metal spokes. A ball hone also works well on a minimally worn cylinder that will be put back into service.

To deglaze and clean a cylinder wall, follow the steps in **SKILL DRILL 11-2**.

S11002 Deglaze an engine cylinder.

N11003 Deglaze and clean cylinder walls.

SKILL DRILL 11-2 Deglazing and Cleaning a Cylinder Wall

1. Using a drill, attach the proper-sized **flex hone**.

Continued

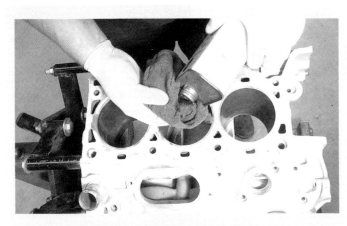

2. Apply honing oil to the cylinder walls.

3. Using the drill with the attached flex hone, stroke up and down in the cylinder that you are honing for approximately 10 to 15 seconds at a speed at which you get a good crosshatch. Be sure to pull the flex hone (ball hone) out of the bore before stopping the drill.

4. Use a rag to wipe the cylinder out so you can inspect the cylinder walls. Repeat as necessary to get a good crosshatch pattern.

5. For final cleaning, use brake cleaner or something similar.

Continued

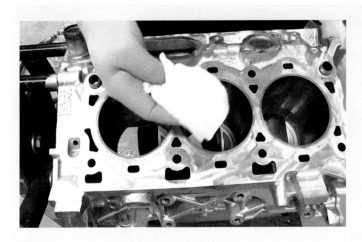

6. Use soap and water with a cylinder block brush for a final cleaning; rinse and blow-dry the cylinders. Ensure that the cylinders are completely clean. There should be no color when you wipe them with a white cloth. Wipe down the cylinders with an anti-rusting spray to prevent rust.

Inspecting the Engine Block

The engine block should be inspected for cracks after the cleaning process is finished and the block is thoroughly dried. You need to determine whether the block is cracked before performing any machining work so that the crack can be repaired or the block replaced; otherwise, time and materials will likely be wasted. Checking the cylinder walls for damage will determine if cylinder boring is required. Cracks can occur anywhere in the block, inside or outside, so you need to thoroughly test all of the surfaces of the block. This includes applying compressed air or a strong vacuum to the engine block water jackets and oil galleries to check for any internal leaks. Cracks in cast iron parts can be detected by a process called magnetic particle inspection, more commonly referred to as **magnafluxing**. In this process, an electromagnet is attached to the part, which is then sprayed with a special magnetic powder or liquid that will stick to the magnetic field created at any cracks, thereby making them visible.

Another option is to use a leak detection dye. The product used could be a fluorescent dye such as Zyglo™, which is sprayed on the surface being checked, soaks into cracks, and is wiped off. A special black light is then shone on the surface, and the dye appears in any cracks. Another type of dye detection system uses a two-part process. First the dye is applied and wiped off. Then a white developer is sprayed onto the surface. If the dye has soaked into any cracks, it will bleed out of the crack and stain the white developer. Leak detection dyes can be used on nonferrous metals such as aluminum. The purpose of the inspection is to make sure the engine block is still useable and can be rebuilt into an operating automotive engine.

To inspect the engine block for visible cracks, follow the steps in **SKILL DRILL 11-3**.

Inspecting the Crankshaft

A crankshaft can be faulty in several ways. First, it could be warped, which would cause the journals to be forced against the bearings, wearing them out prematurely. Second, the main and rod journals could be excessively worn, leading to too much bearing clearance, which would cause low engine oil pressure. Third, the bolt holes, keyways, and sealing surfaces could be damaged, causing their own set of issues. These situations mean that a thorough inspection along with precise measurements must be made to ensure the crankshaft can be put back in service.

To inspect the crankshaft, follow the steps in **SKILL DRILL 11-4**.

Inspecting Main and Connecting Rod Bearings

The main and connecting rod bearings must be inspected to determine whether they are in good condition or need replacing. Both normal wear and traumatic events can damage the bearings, resulting in a knocking noise and/or low oil pressure. Typically, a visual inspection is all that is needed to determine that they need to be replaced, as excessive wear will be apparent. If the bearings look to be in good shape, then the bearing clearance should be measured to determine if it meets the manufacturer's specifications. This is covered in a later Skill Drill.

To inspect main and connecting rod bearings, follow the steps in **SKILL DRILL 11-5**.

N11004 Inspect engine block for visible cracks, passage condition, core and gallery plug condition, and surface warpage; determine needed action.

N11005 Inspect and measure cylinder walls/sleeves for damage, wear, and ridges; determine needed action.

K11007 Knowledge of engine component inspection.

S11003 Inspect the engine block for visible cracks.

N11006 Inspect crankshaft for straightness, journal damage, keyway damage, thrust flange and sealing surface condition, and visual surface cracks; check oil passage condition; measure end play and journal wear; check crankshaft position sensor reluctor ring (where applicable); determine needed action.

S11004 Inspect the crankshaft.

N11007 Inspect main and connecting rod bearings for damage and wear; determine needed action.

S11005 Inspect the main and connecting rod bearings.

SKILL DRILL 11-3 Inspecting the Engine Block for Visible Cracks

1. Visually inspect the engine block for any damage, excessive wear, or cracks. If none are visible, it should be checked for hard-to-see hairline fractures or cracks by magnafluxing or a dye check method.

2. Check all core plug and galley plug areas for obstruction or blockage. You should also check the sealing surface of the plug holes for cleanliness and to make sure there are not any nicks or burrs.

3. Clean the deck surface, using a gasket scraper, wire brush, or bristle discs for cast iron. Use only nonmetallic and nonabrasive scrapers on aluminum sealing surfaces.

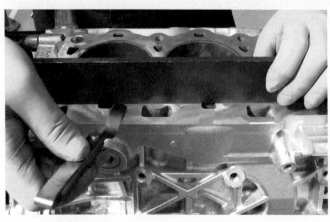

4. Using a straightedge and feeler gauge, check the deck surface for warpage across the top in several different angles. Most machine shops resurface an engine block with more than 0.0025" (0.064 mm) warpage. Check the manufacturer's specifications for maximum warpage.

SKILL DRILL 11-4 Inspecting the Crankshaft

1. Check the crankshaft for straightness. There are two methods you can use to check the crankshaft for straightness.

   a. Crankshaft in block: With the pistons and rods removed, make sure all main caps are numbered; the main caps must not be mixed up, because they must go back in the exact order in which they were removed. Pull the number one main cap, and clean the main journal on the crankshaft. Using a dial indicator with a 0.001" (0.025 mm) scale and a magnetic base, attach the dial indicator on the pan rail, and center the dial indicator over the number one main journal. Preload the dial indicator on the main journal, and move the face on the dial indicator to zero. Rotate the crankshaft one full rotation, watching the dial indicator, and record your findings. Repeat the process to check the center main, and record your findings. Determine any necessary actions based on your findings.

   b. Crankshaft out of block: With the crankshaft removed, make sure the main journals are clean. Position the crankshaft on two V-blocks, using the first main journal and the last main journal. Using a dial indicator with a 0.001" (0.025 mm) scale, attach the dial indicator on the bench with a magnetic base or clamp. Position the dial indicator over the number one journal. Preload the dial indicator on the main journal, and set the face on the dial indicator to zero. Rotate the crankshaft one full rotation, watching the dial indicator. Record your findings. Repeat the process on the center main, and record your findings. Determine any necessary actions based on your findings.

2. Visually inspect the journals for grooves. The journals should be smooth to the touch. Use an outside micrometer to measure the rod and main journals. Both rod and main journals should have measurements taken 90 degrees apart. Also, rod journals should be measured across the face of the journal to check for taper. Compare your findings to factory specifications, and determine the necessary action.

Continued

3. Visually inspect the square-cut or Woodruff key and keyway. If the square key or Woodruff key is out, make sure the keyway is straight with sharp edges. The square-cut or Woodruff key must fit snugly.

4. Visually inspect the thrust flange, bolt holes, and rear seal surface to make sure there are no nicks or scratches.

5. Visually inspect the crankshaft for cracks. If you need a more detailed inspection, the crankshaft should be checked by magnafluxing. Determine any necessary actions.

6. Probe the oil passages with a small plastic tube (a spray can nozzle extension works well), making sure the oil passages from the mains into the rod journals are clear. Determine any necessary actions.

7. Check the crankshaft position sensor **reluctor ring**, when applicable. Visually inspect the reluctor ring to make sure there is no damage.

SKILL DRILL 11-5 Inspecting Main and Connecting Rod Bearings

1. If you are considering reusing the main and rod bearing inserts, be sure to keep them together, and mark them once they are removed. The main caps and connecting rods should have already been marked with numbers to avoid mixing them up.

2. Remove each main bearing insert from the main cap and main housing support, one at a time. If the bearing insert will not come out using your fingers, use a wooden hammer handle to push the bearing on the opposite side of the tang at the parting line. The bearing should slip out.

3. Clean each main bearing, and mark the back of each half-shell with a permanent marker with the correlating bearing support number. It is important to know what journal the bearings were located on in order to identify any unusual wear patterns.

Continued

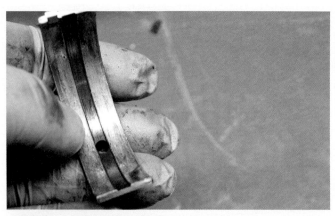

4. Visually check that there are no grooves or embedded foreign matter. Check with the bearing wear chart to see if the bearings are wearing normally or if the wear pattern indicates that the bearings need replacement. Repeat the process for the connecting rod bearings.

5. Before you inspect the thrust bearing, go back to your crankshaft end play findings. If end play was excessive, you should be able to determine why by checking for damage or wear on either the front or the rear thrust bearing surface.

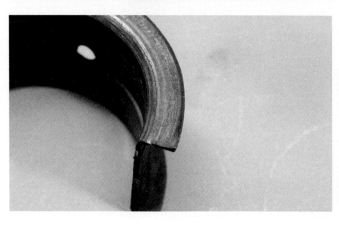

6. If the rear surface of the thrust bearing is worn and the vehicle is equipped with an automatic transmission, the wear is usually caused by a torque converter ballooning, which causes pressure on the thrust bearing. If it is a manual transmission, the wear could be caused by someone holding the clutch pedal down excessively or by a pressure plate with too much pressure.

Identifying Piston and Bearing Wear Patterns

N11008 Identify piston and bearing wear patterns that indicate connecting rod alignment and main bearing bore problems; determine needed action.

S11006 Identify main, connecting rod, and cam bearings wear issues.

Examining the piston and bearing wear patterns is useful because the patterns serve as a diagnostic tool for determining whether the parts are operating normally or if there are possible alignment issues or engine operating problems with the engine block and its internal components. The technician must compare the wear patterns with those provided in the manufacturer's wear chart. The wear chart correlates the wear pattern with the contributing problem, such as a component failure or a damaged crankshaft assembly, lubrication system, or cooling system.

To identify piston and bearing wear patterns that indicate connecting rod alignment and main bearing bore problems, follow the steps in **SKILL DRILL 11-6**.

Inspecting and Measuring the Cylinder Walls/Sleeves

S11007 Inspect and measure cylinder walls/sleeves for damage and wear.

The surfaces of the cylinder bores wear over time as the pistons travel up and down the cylinders millions of times over their life. The cylinder bore in both sleeved and nonsleeved engine blocks must be perfectly round and of a uniform diameter from top to bottom. Careful measurement is required to determine if the cylinders can be reused or if they will need

SKILL DRILL 11-6 Identifying Piston and Bearing Wear Patterns

1. Visually inspect the rod bearings. There should be an even wear pattern across the full face of the bearing. Greater wear on one side than the other is an indication of a bent connecting rod. A bent rod also typically shows an increased wear pattern on one side of the piston skirt. If uneven wear is observed, have a machine shop check the rod for straightness.

2. Inspect the main bearings. There should be an even wear pattern across the full face of the bearing. Greater wear on one side than the other is an indication that the main line that supports the crankshaft is no longer straight. If uneven wear is observed, inspect the crankshaft for straightness, and determine whether it needs to be straightened or replaced.

to be replaced (sleeves) or bored oversize. The tool that most quickly measures the cylinder bores is a dial bore gauge. It uses a dial indicator gauge connected to a handle. Once it is calibrated to a certain size, it can be inserted into the cylinder and a quick measurement made. Another tool that is just as accurate, but not as easy and quick, is the inside micrometer.

To inspect and measure cylinder walls/sleeves for damage and wear, follow the steps in **SKILL DRILL 11-7**.

Inspecting and Measuring Piston Skirts

Pistons, like cylinder walls, wear over time. If they are to be reused, they must be carefully inspected, measured, and compared to specifications first. It does no good to put new piston rings on a piston that has too much wear at the ring lands, as the rings will leak oil and compression. If the piston skirt is worn, the piston may make a knocking noise due to too much clearance between the skirt and the cylinder wall.

To inspect and measure piston skirts, follow the steps in **SKILL DRILL 11-8**.

Checking Main Bearing Saddles for Straightness

Before an engine can be reassembled, the technician must check the main bearing saddles for straightness. This can be done by taking the main caps off the engine block and using a true bar to verify that the main bearing saddles have not became warped (**FIGURE 11-25**). The crankshaft is going to spin in these saddles at a high rpm, which could lead to failure if they are not in a straight line. If the technician is uncomfortable with measuring this, the job can be sublet to the local machine shop.

Lifter Bores

Lifter bores inside the cylinder block must be checked for pitting, damage, and overheating, before the new lifters are installed (**FIGURE 11-26**). This is a very easy check as first you should do a visual inspection of the all the lifter bores. Then, using a telescoping

N11009 Inspect and measure piston skirts and ring lands; determine needed action.

S11008 Inspect and measure piston skirts.

SKILL DRILL 11-7 Inspecting and Measuring Cylinder Walls/Sleeves for Damage and Wear

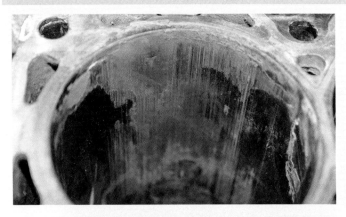

1. If the visual inspection showed obvious scoring or damage to the cylinder walls in the block, then the pistons cannot be reused, and the block will have to be machined.

2. If there are no cracks or scratches, then you can use a cylinder bore gauge or inside micrometer to measure the cylinders.

3. If using the dial bore gauge, set it to the original size of the cylinder. This way, you will be able to see whether the cylinders are oversize or out of round or if there is a taper from the bottom to the top of the cylinder. If using an inside micrometer, assemble the proper adapters to measure the bore.

4. Measure each cylinder at the top, center, and bottom, 90 degrees across the thrust side and pin side at each level. Compare the readings to specifications.

#1	3.223	3.223	3.223
#2	3.227	3.223	3.223
#3	3.223	3.223	3.223
4	(3.233)	3.230	3.223

SKILL DRILL 11-8 Inspecting and Measuring Piston Skirts

1. With the piston inverted, use a micrometer to measure the skirt just above the pin bore.

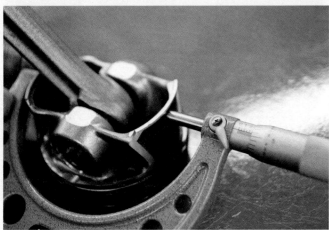

2. Measure the diameter of the bottom of the piston skirt. It should never be smaller than the measurement taken at the pin measurement area. If the measurement is smaller, then the piston has a collapsed skirt, and the piston must be replaced.

3. Measure the diameter of the piston skirt just below the oil ring groove, and compare the reading to the specifications. If it is found to be worn or there is too much clearance between the piston and the cylinder wall, the piston will have to be replaced.

gauge, you take a measurement inside the lifter bore, use a micrometer to measure the telescoping gauge, and then refer to the service manual to verify that the bore is within specification. If you find a lifter bore that is out of specification or damaged, the local machine shop should be able to install an oversized insert to fix the lifter bore problem.

Camshaft and Camshaft Bearings

The camshaft is the component that controls the timing of the valves in an internal combustion engine. The lobe that is on the camshaft determines how fast, how long, and how

N11010 Inspect and measure camshaft bearings for wear, damage, out-of-round, and alignment; determine needed action.

N11011 Determine piston-to-bore clearance.

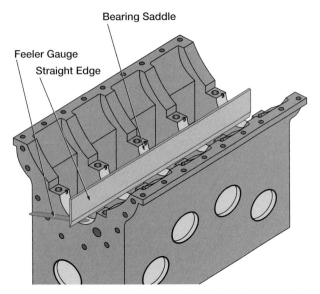

FIGURE 11-25 If the engine is severely overheated or starved of oil, the main bearing saddles may warp, which means they will have to be remachined to be returned to true status.

FIGURE 11-26 Component failure or lack of oil pressure can cause lifter bore damage.

FIGURE 11-27 A camshaft bearing that is used in the block camshaft application.

FIGURE 11-28 A camshaft bearing installed in a cylinder block.

S11009 Identify main, connecting rod, and cam bearings wear issues.

much the valves are open. When the engine is disassembled it must be checked for any wear, and if it is worn, it must be replaced. Anytime that the engine is disassembled for a rebuild, the camshaft bearings must be replaced. These bearings are located inside the cylinder block on OHV engines and in the cylinder head in OHC engines. These bearings are made of the same Babbitt material that the main and connecting rod bearings are made of, which makes them susceptible to same problems that the other bearings have (**FIGURE 11-27**). The camshaft bearings in the cylinder block are pressed in using a bearing installation tool, which allows the technician to press in each bearing to locate it in the correct position (**FIGURE 11-28**). The oil passage holes in the cylinder block must be lined up with the bearing to allow oil flow to the camshaft. The oiling system is an integral part of the bearings inside an automotive engine, which means that if the bearing clearance is not within specification, the oil pressure of the engine will not be within specification. When it comes to OHC engines, some engine designs incorporate bearings into the cylinder head, and other designs do not use bearings. As you disassemble these types of engines, you must pay attention to the condition of these bearings, as they can tell you what has happened to the engine before it required service.

▶ Wrap-Up

Ready for Review

- ▶ Engine disassembly is an important procedure in rebuilding an engine as it allows you to verify which components failed, which are good to be reused, and what needs to be done to the engine to put it back in service.
- ▶ The rating of the engine stand must be high enough to hold the weight of the engine with all of its accessories attached to it. As well you must inspect the engine stand to verify that it is in good condition to be used in this way.
- ▶ The first step in disassembling the engine is to remove any remaining fluids, such as the oil and the coolant, from the engine block.
- ▶ To gain access to the rotating assembly of the engine, the oil pan has to be removed.
- ▶ If the engine has a lot of miles on it, was poorly maintained, or had extensive damage, there will probably be a layer of oil sludge and possibly metal particles or other foreign objects in the bottom of the oil pan.
- ▶ Some oil pumps are located inside the crankcase and have to be removed before the pistons; others are located on the front of the block and have to be removed along with any timing components.
- ▶ On a crankcase-mounted oil pump, you may be able to unscrew one bolt and simply pull off the oil pump. Other oil pumps have two bolts and may also have a few other bolts that hold the pickup tube and screen in place.
- ▶ Be careful with oil pump vanes and gears falling out and the oil pump drive mechanism.
- ▶ If the engine has a windage tray (to prevent oil from splashing onto the crankshaft), remove it now, along with any dipstick tube or extension that might be inside the oil pan area.
- ▶ When you start to disassemble the timing components, you must be aware of how those components went together.
- ▶ Remove the cover, and then check the timing marks, as this will give you some orientation as to how the pieces go together, which helps with reassembly once your internal engine work is complete.
- ▶ As you disassemble the timing components, you must pay close attention to all the guides, tensioners, chains, belts, and gears to see whether any of those components must be replaced.
- ▶ Normal procedure when rebuilding an engine is to replace the timing components as a kit so that you know that they will be functional once the engine is run.
- ▶ Timing chains create a wear pattern on the chain and the sprockets, causing them to be matched. When you change the pattern, the chain ends up trying to create a new pattern, which may cause a component to fail.
- ▶ Timing belts are very similar to chains, as they create a wear pattern in the belt, which means you must keep the direction the same as it was when it was installed on the engine.

- ▶ The first step in removing the cylinder heads is to refer to your information system to verify the correct procedure for removal of the cylinder head.
- ▶ Sometimes a detorquing procedure must be followed so that the cylinder head will not become warped as the head bolts are removed.
- ▶ Once the cylinder head is removed, it must be checked for cracks and flatness as it is imperative that the head be in good working order to be reinstalled.
- ▶ The OHV designation means that the engine has overhead valves, usually actuated by a pushrod. This information is very important when ordering parts for vehicles with the same size engine but different engine configurations.
- ▶ In an overhead cam engine (OHC), the camshaft is mounted on the cylinder head so that there are no pushrods or lifters in the engine block like those in an OHV engine.
- ▶ The OHC engine has vastly different components from the OHV engine, which means that when you are purchasing parts or looking up information on this type of engine, you need to make sure that you are referencing the proper engine.
- ▶ The block underside refers to the area located in the oil pan and timing chain part of the engine cylinder block assembly. These areas are fully covered by the timing chain cover and the oil pan cover, which are stamped sheet metal assemblies or cast aluminum assemblies.
- ▶ The ridge at the top of the cylinder is too big if, after the carbon has been scraped off, it catches a fingernail. If the ridge is significant and you are planning on reusing the pistons, you will need to remove the ridge with a tool called a ridge reamer.
- ▶ The ridge reamer is a cutting tool that cuts into the metal ridge and carbon buildup at the top of the cylinder and removes the lip. If the ridge is not removed, the piston rings could break.
- ▶ The connecting rod caps must be replaced in the same orientation as they are removed. If they are not already labeled, label them in two places: above and below the parting line of the cap and rod body.
- ▶ It is a good idea to also label the main caps of the block in the same way. One method of labeling these components is with a number punch set.
- ▶ Removing the pistons is a multistep process that requires making some decisions before you start.
- ▶ The two most basic piston decisions are deciding whether the pistons are going to be reused or replaced and whether the ridge at the top of the cylinder has to be reamed off. The answers to those questions determines the order at which you perform the steps and the amount of care you use to remove the pistons.
- ▶ Before removing the main bearing caps, make sure they are marked for reinstallation. To do so, use a number punch or marking paint. To remove the crankshaft bearing

▶ caps, you may need some additional leverage to loosen the bolts that hold them. Some engine blocks have two bolts per cap; others have four.

▶ To remove the crankshaft on an application with a one-piece rear main seal, you must first remove the rear main seal and housing. This may require removing the engine from the engine stand to gain access to the rear of the block.

▶ Crankshafts are both heavy and awkwardly shaped, so be very careful lifting it out of the engine block, or ask for assistance.

▶ Bearings with visible wear patterns, especially if the copper core is showing through in some areas, are not reusable and should be replaced. If you are not sure of their reusability, take them to a machine shop specialist for advice.

▶ The crankshaft should *never* be stored standing upright. Never lay it down unless it is supported on the bearing throws by V-blocks.

▶ Remove the water jacket core plugs. The water jacket core plugs cannot be easily pulled out, but they can usually be tilted so that Channellock pliers can grab them and pry them out. Use a punch to carefully drive one side of the core plug toward the water jacket.

▶ Before the parts are examined beyond a quick visual inspection, they must d be cleaned.

▶ The cleaning process of the engine cylinder block can vary depending on what is available to the technician. Most shops use a spray wash cabinet, which operates much like a dishwasher and usually uses environmentally friendly degreasers and hot water.

▶ Some machine shops dip the major engine parts for several hours in a hot or cold caustic solution. The strong corrosive chemicals remove mineral deposits in the water jackets, carbon deposits, oil, greases, and paints.

▶ If the cylinder measures within specifications, it will have to be prepared for the new piston rings.

▶ The cylinder wall will probably have a polished "glaze" on its surface that must be removed.

▶ Removing the glazed surface with an abrasive stone of the proper grit will give the cylinder walls a nice crosshatch pattern, which allows a small amount of oil to be retained in the fine scratches.

▶ The recommended crosshatch for a cylinder wall is approximately 45 degrees.

▶ A rigid hone uses fixed rectangular abrasive stones and is used on a cylinder after it has been bored to give a perfectly cylindrical shape with the proper finish.

▶ A flexible hone uses spring-loaded rectangular stones that can more easily follow the contours of a minimally used cylinder; thus, it is used to deglaze a cylinder that will be reused.

▶ A ball hone uses round abrasive stones on the ends of flexible metal spokes. A ball hone also works well on a minimally worn cylinder that will be put back into service.

▶ The engine block should be inspected for cracks after the cleaning process is finished and the block is thoroughly dried.

▶ Cracks in cast iron parts can be detected by a process called magnetic particle inspection, more commonly referred to as magnafluxing.

▶ In the magnafluxing process, an electromagnet is attached to the part, which is then sprayed with a special magnetic powder or liquid that will stick to the magnetic field created at any cracks, thereby making them visible.

▶ Another option is to use a leak detection dye. The product used could be a fluorescent dye such as Zyglo™, which is sprayed on the surface being checked, soaks into cracks, and is wiped off. A special black light is then shone on the surface, and the dye appears in any cracks.

▶ Another type of dye detection system uses a two-part process. First the dye is applied and wiped off. Then a white developer is sprayed onto the surface. If the dye has soaked into any cracks, it will bleed out of the crack and stain the white developer.

▶ Leak detection dyes can be used on nonferrous metals such as aluminum. The purpose of the inspection is to make sure the engine block is still useable and can be rebuilt into an operating automotive engine.

▶ A crankshaft can be faulty in several ways. First, it could be warped, which would cause the journals to be forced against the bearings, wearing them out prematurely.

▶ There are two methods you can use to check the crankshaft for straightness. Crankshaft in block, where measurements are made, and Crankshaft out of block: With the crankshaft removed, make sure the main journals are clean and that you position the crankshaft on two V-blocks.

▶ Visually inspect the crankshaft journals for grooves. The journals should be smooth to the touch. Use an outside micrometer to measure the rod and main journals. Both rod and main journals should have measurements taken 90 degrees apart.

▶ The main and connecting rod bearings must be inspected to determine whether they are in good condition or need replacing. Both normal wear and traumatic events can damage the bearings, resulting in a knocking noise and/or low oil pressure.

▶ The technician must compare the piston and bearing wear patterns with those provided in the manufacturer's wear chart.

▶ The surfaces of the cylinder bores wear over time as the pistons travel up and down the cylinders millions of times over their life.

▶ The cylinder bore in both sleeved and nonsleeved engine blocks must be perfectly round and of a uniform diameter from top to bottom.

▶ Careful cylinder measurement is required to determine if the cylinders can be reused or if they will need to be replaced (sleeves) or bored oversize. The tool that most quickly measures the cylinder bores is a dial bore gauge.

▶ If the piston skirt is worn, the piston may make a knocking noise due to too much clearance between the skirt and the cylinder wall.

- Before an engine can be reassembled you must check the main bearing saddles for straightness. This can be done by taking the main caps off the engine block and using a true bar to verify that the main bearing saddles have not became warped.
- Lifter bores inside the cylinder block must be checked for pitting, damage, and overheating, before the new lifters are installed.
- When the engine is disassembled, the camshaft must be checked for any wear, and if it is worn it, must be replaced.
- Anytime that the engine is disassembled for a rebuild, the camshaft bearings must be replaced.

Key Terms

core plugs Made out of brass or steel; they seal the holes that are left after the casting process. The alternative purpose of these plugs is to help with freeze protection for the cylinder block.

crankshaft The component that transfers force from the connecting rod to the flywheel. This integral piece to the piston engine is the main component that allows the chemical explosion to be converted to mechanical motion that can be utilized to propel the vehicle.

flex hone Type of hone that has multiple balls attached to it on the flexible steel end, which allow it to move in the cylinder as it is being honed. This type of hone is the most common in the industry today.

lifter bore The hole in the cylinder block that the lifter rides in. This could have a bushing in it, but most are just machined into the casting.

magnafluxing The process that uses special fluorescent dye and a magnet to check for cracks in cast iron engine components. This process can only be used on ferrous material.

main bearing caps Keep the crankshaft attached to the cylinder block. This caps house half of the main bearing; the other half is housed in the cylinder block. They can be cross bolted and have either two or four bolts.

overhead valve engine (OHV) Acronym referring to an engine that has overhead valves, which means the valves are in the cylinder head, and the camshaft is located in the cylinder block.

overhead camshaft engine (OHC) Acronym for an engine that has a camshaft on the cylinder head over the valves. This type of engine has fewer valvetrain components than an OHV engine, which leads to a longer engine life.

reluctor ring A toothed ring that a crankshaft position sensor picks up to reference where the crankshaft is in its revolution. It is sometimes cast into the crankshaft and sometimes attached to the harmonic damper.

ridge reamer Used to remove the ridge that is developed at the top of the cylinder as the piston wears the cylinder, so that the piston can be removed.

timing marks Marks for assembly of the timing components so that the valve events will happen at the correct time in order to support combustion.

Review Questions

1. Choose the correct statement:
   a. The rating of the engine stand should be high enough to hold the engine along with all the accessories.
   b. There is no difference in the weight that engine stands can handle.
   c. The fasteners required to attach the engine are of the same size and lengths.
   d. The engine should be attached upside down on the stand.

2. Which of the following components should be removed in order to access the rotating parts of the engine?
   a. Drain plugs
   b. Oil pan
   c. Oil pump
   d. Timing components

3. All of the following statements with respect to the removal of timing components are true, *except*:
   a. It is important to be aware of how those components went together.
   b. Using the harmonic balancer, line up the timing marks on the balancer and the timing cover.
   c. Pay close attention to all the guides, tensioners, chains, belts, and gears to see if any of those components must be replaced.
   d. Timing belts, unlike timing chains, need not be marked for direction as they do not create a wear pattern on the chain and the sprockets.

4. All of the following damages are to be inspected in a timing belt, *except*:
   a. cracking.
   b. fraying.
   c. liquid degradation.
   d. swaying.

5. Choose the correct statement:
   a. Overhead valves are usually actuated by a timing chain.
   b. Overhead cam engine is used to simplify the valve train.
   c. In an OHC, lifter and pushrods are present in the engine block.
   d. Overhead valves have the camshaft located on the cylinder head.

6. Choose the correct statement regarding the proper labeling of the components during engine assembly:
   a. Cylinder rod caps don't need labeling as they can be replaced in any orientation.
   b. Punch labeling can be done on the powdered metal rods.
   c. Regular center punch can be used to label any component in the engine.
   d. Clean the side of a powdered metal rod with a solvent, and use paint to mark it instead.

7. If the ridge at the top of the cylinder is too big, and you are planning on reusing the pistons, you will need to remove the ridge using:
   a. a ridge reamer.
   b. Channellock pliers.
   c. machining.
   d. a solvent.

8. The contributing problem can be identified from piston and bearing wear patterns by:
   a. measuring the depth of the pattern.
   b. analyzing the frequency of the pattern.
   c. comparing them with the manufacturer's wear chart.
   d. using a gauge.
9. When the engine is disassembled for a rebuild, the camshaft bearings must be replaced:
   a. if they are worn.
   b. if the camshaft lobe is replaced.
   c. always.
   d. if the engine makes a rumbling noise.
10. All of the following statements with respect to deglazing the cylinder wall are true, *except*:
   a. It helps to lubricate the piston rings.
   b. The recommended crosshatch for a cylinder wall is approximately 45 degrees.
   c. It allows the new piston rings to seat against the surface of the freshly honed cylinder wall.
   d. It prevents cracking of the cylinder block.

ASE Technician A/Technician B Style Questions

1. Tech A states that an OHC engine has the camshaft in the cylinder block. Tech B says that engine using a ridge reamer on a cylinder allows for easy removal of the piston/rod assembly in that cylinder. Who is correct?
   a. Tech A
   b. Tech B
   c. Both A and B
   d. Neither A nor B
2. Tech A says that the timing marks allow for easy alignment of the crankshaft and the camshaft so that the valve events line up with the crankshaft strokes. Tech B states that some engine do not use timing marks and require special tools to align the camshaft and crankshaft. Who is correct?
   a. Tech A
   b. Tech B
   c. Both A and B
   d. Neither A nor B
3. Tech A says that before reassembly of the engine, the cylinders must be honed to break up any glaze or machining marks so that the piston rings have a consistent surface to seat to. Tech B states that all components must be checked for cracking or failures so that they can be replaced before they are reused. Who is correct?
   a. Tech A
   b. Tech B
   c. Both A and B
   d. Neither A nor B
4. Tech A says that core plugs are a result of misshaped cylinder block molds. Tech B states that an engine stand must be rated for the weight of a fully dressed engine. Who is correct?
   a. Tech A
   b. Tech B
   c. Both A and B
   d. Neither A nor B
5. Tech A says that when installing rod caps, the tangs must be on the same side of the rod. Tech B states that when installing rod caps on a rod, the tangs must be on opposite sides. Who is correct?
   a. Tech A
   b. Tech B
   c. Both A and B
   d. Neither A nor B
6. Tech A says that when rebuilding an OHV engine, the camshaft bearings must be replaced before the new camshaft is installed. Tech B says that OHC engines use a timing belt or timing chain. Who is correct?
   a. Tech A
   b. Tech B
   c. Both A and B
   d. Neither A nor B
7. Tech A states that to check for cracks on an aluminum engine component, you must use a form of dye, as there is no ferrous material in aluminum. Tech B says that engine painting must use a high-temperature paint to withstand the heat an engine creates. Who is correct?
   a. Tech A
   b. Tech B
   c. Both A and B
   d. Neither A nor B
8. Tech A says that resleeving an engine is an option to repair a damaged cylinder wall. Tech B states that engine coolant would make for a good assembly lube to reinstall components. Who is correct?
   a. Tech A
   b. Tech B
   c. Both A and B
   d. Neither A nor B
9. Technician A states that a damaged reluctor ring could cause a crankshaft not to be reused. Technician B says that you must reuse the crankshaft regardless of its condition. Who is correct?
   a. Tech A
   b. Tech B
   c. Both A and B
   d. Neither A nor B
10. Tech A says that using a certified cleaner is the best way to clean an engine block after it has been to a machine shop. Tech B says that using soap and water is the best way to clean an engine block after it has been to a machine shop. Who is correct?
   a. Tech A
   b. Tech B
   c. Both A and B
   d. Neither A nor B

CHAPTER 12

Engine Block Design and Usage

NATEF Tasks

There are no NATEF Tasks for this chapter.

Knowledge Objectives

After reading this chapter, you will have:

- **K12001** Knowledge of how the engine block is designed.
- **K12002** Knowledge of how the ending block is manufactured.

- **K12003** Knowledge of what types of materials engine blocks are made from.
- **K12004** Knowledge of the use of balance shafts in the engine.

Skills Objectives

There are no Skills Objectives for this chapter.

You Are the Automotive Technician

Today you are disassembling an engine that has more than 250,000 miles on it. The vehicle still runs well but doesn't have as much power as it used to. The fuel economy is also not as good as it once was, and the vehicle is burning more oil than specified. The owner would prefer that this engine be rebuilt rather than replaced, because it has lasted so long, but only if that makes economic sense. He has agreed to pay you to disassemble the engine, measure the critical components of the engine, compare them to specifications, and estimate the cost to rebuild it.

1. What measurements do you need to perform on the block and its internal components?
2. How will you determine whether the block and heads have any cracks?
3. What precautions should be taken when disassembling an engine in which the major components may be reused?

▶ Introduction

The engine block (also called the cylinder block or simply the block) is the main structural member of the internal combustion engine. Although many different engine designs are available, in all configurations the engine block acts as the framework for the entire engine and provides for the mounting of all the components. In the early days of the automobile, the distinct parts of the engine, such as the cylinders, intake and exhaust passages, and crankcase, were constructed as separate pieces that were then bolted or welded together. Today, engine blocks are cast in one piece with machined surfaces and holes added for the placement and attachment of the engine components. The process of constructing a single block into which all parts fit is more efficient from a manufacturing standpoint. It also gives the block more strength and rigidity. This chapter discusses the engine block as a whole, describes each component of the engine block and the procedures for inspecting it, and explains how all the components work together to generate the power that drives the vehicle.

▶ Engine Block

K12001 Knowledge of how the engine block is designed.

The engine block is the largest part of the engine; it is the main supporting structure for all of the engine parts (**FIGURE 12-1**). The block is also the main aligning structure for all parts of the engine. Within the engine block are the cylinders and pistons; the top of the piston and the matching cylinder head form the combustion chamber. When fuel and air are brought together in the combustion chamber, along with the presence of an ignition source, combustion occurs.

Combustion is carefully timed to occur when the piston is near the top of its travel on the compression stroke. The rapidly expanding gases produced by combustion pressurize the combustion chamber and push down on the piston during the power stroke, forcing it through the cylinder until it reaches the bottom of its travel. This movement causes the crankshaft to spin, which pushes the piston back up the cylinder in preparation for the next combustion event. The crankshaft also powers the rest of the drivetrain through the flywheel or flexplate and the accessories from the crankshaft pulley.

For optimum performance and engine life, the engine block must be designed, cast, and machined within precise tolerances, meaning that the components must be designed and connected together within narrow specifications. These precise specifications are critical to prevent leakage of air and fuel, withstand the thermal stresses of combustion, and accommodate shocks and vibration applied to the engine during the power pulses.

The upper section of the engine block contains the cylinders and pistons. The lower section of the engine block forms the crankcase, which supports the main bearings, crankshaft, camshaft (some engines), and balance shafts (some engines). A few engine designs, like the various Subaru models, have a horizontally opposed engine, sometimes called a boxer engine. In these engines, the cylinders are positioned side to side, rather than up and down, and the crankcase is located between the cylinders (**FIGURE 12-2**).

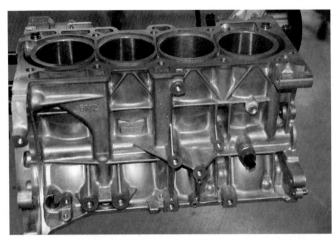

FIGURE 12-1 An in-line engine is one where all the cylinders are in line with one another.

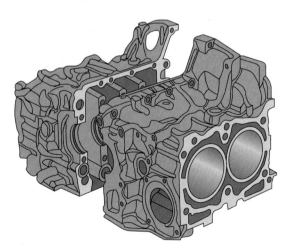

FIGURE 12-2 A boxer engine or opposed engine is one that has a split block where the pistons are opposite one another.

The various designs that are currently used in production include the following:

- The V-engine, which has the pistons at a 60- or 90-degree angle off the crankshaft.
- The in-line engine, where the pistons line up in a straight line so that each piston has its own rod throw on the crankshaft.
- The W engine, which has a Volkswagen (VW) design that positions pistons in different locations to help make the engine compact; VW is currently the only manufacturer that is using this design.
- The slant 4 or 6, a design utilized by Chrysler in the 1960s and 1970s for the benefit of an in-line engine and the low clearance of a V-engine.

The rotary engine is very different from the conventional engine as it has rotors instead of pistons that create the mechanical movement from the chemical explosions. The engine block for this type of engine is assembled from pieces that are bolted together to create the combustion chambers. There are no cylinder heads or valves for operation—just two different ports whose opening and closing are controlled by the rotors movement inside the chamber (**FIGURE 12-3**).

FIGURE 12-3 In a rotary engine, the rotor is in a rotor housing that also includes the water jacket.

Engine Block Manufacturing

In the metal casting foundry process, different types of materials and techniques are used to create steel or cast iron and aluminum engine blocks. The most common methods are the green sand, shell, and **lost foam** processes. In all three processes, hot molten metal is poured into a mold. The engine block can be cast in one piece from gray iron, or it can be alloyed with other metals such as nickel or chromium. The specific type of metals or metal used depends on many factors, including the intended use of the engine block, the type of environment it will be run in, and the cost.

The casting process begins by making the shapes for what will become water jackets and cylinders as sand cores or foam shapes, which are then fitted into molds. The term "water jacket" is used to describe the area created by the sand, shell, or foam shapes during the casting process. The water jackets create passageways around the cylinders and throughout the engine block that hold coolant to keep engine temperature in functional ranges. Molten metal is poured into the casting mold from a tub or ladle without the use of pressure, a process known as **gravity pouring**. Different engine block molds are used depending on the specific engine type desired, such as V8, V6, or four-cylinder in-line.

Core sand is used in the casting process to create cavities. It is a mix of fine-grit sand and oil that is highly moldable, yet holds its shape, making it great for sculpturing. During the casting process, molten metal is poured around the molded core sand and allowed to harden. Once the metal cools, the core sand is removed through holes in the sides and ends of the engine block casting, leaving cavities for the cooling and lubricating passages.

K12002 Knowledge of how the ending block is manufactured.

Applied Math

AM-19: Proper Operation: The technician can determine the sequence of arithmetic operations needed to arrive at a solution when comparing system measurements with the manufacturer's specifications.

An engine is being overhauled at an automotive repair facility. After the engine has been disassembled, the technician uses precision measuring tools to evaluate the components. The camshaft is being checked with an outside micrometer regarding the journal diameter. The technician finds that all journals are 1.7875" in diameter.

Using service information, it is discovered that the specifications for the journal diameter should be 1.7865–1.7885". The proper operation for this task would be to compare the technician's measurement of 1.7875" to the manufacturer's specification. The result shows a very good camshaft regarding the journal diameter. It is exactly between the minimum and maximum specifications. The manufacturer has allowed a measurement of 0.002" between the minimum and maximum diameters and this part is 0.001" between each specification.

FIGURE 12-4 When the engine is being machined to accept the pistons, a boring machine is used to get the cylinders close to the finished bore and then a hone is used to finish out the cylinder to specification.

FIGURE 12-5 As the engine is being machined, the holes are drilled and tapped to accept bolts that allow other components to attach to it.

K12003 Knowledge of what types of materials engine blocks are made from.

These holes are sealed with core plugs, which may also be called Welch plugs or soft plugs. The plugs are rounded discs or cups that are used to seal the openings created in the casting process for removal of core sand. The discs can be flat, concaved, or threaded to fit the particular opening. For years, the term **freeze plugs** has also been used; however, the term is inaccurate. The engine block was never designed to withstand freezing of the water in the cooling passages. Water expands approximately 10% as it freezes into ice. If the engine temperature drops below freezing, the pressure of the expanding ice may cause the block to crack, even if the core plugs pop out.

Once the engine block casting is inspected and cleaned, it goes through a series of machining processes to bore, flatten, and thread the various surfaces and holes (**FIGURE 12-4**). Parts of the engine block that typically require machining include the top of the engine block (also called the **deck**); cylinders; front of the block; rear of the block; bottom of the block, including the crankshaft main bearing and thrust areas; and any other area to which another engine part is attached, such as the cam bearing or balancer shaft journals. Other finishing processes include honing the cylinders, drilling holes, and cutting threads (**FIGURE 12-5**).

As more manufacturers try to make vehicles lighter and more fuel efficient, more engine blocks are being cast from aluminum. An engine block made of aluminum alloy is lighter than one made of cast iron. The lighter aluminum engine provides a higher power-to-weight ratio and also provides the vehicle with greater fuel efficiency.

Engine Block Construction and Crankshaft Support

The engine block assembly, or lower end as it is sometimes called, consists of the following: oil galleries and plugs (oil passage plugs), water jacket and plugs, pistons and rings, piston pins, connecting rods and caps, rod bearing inserts, main bearing caps, main bearing inserts, the thrust bearing, the crankshaft, rear seals (lip or rope seal), the camshaft (for overhead cam engines), and a vibration balancer. The engine block also has smooth surfaces in certain areas to which the mating parts, such as the cylinder heads, oil pan, timing cover, water pump, and transmission, are attached with a precise and tight fit.

The engine lubrication system also begins in the engine block assembly, with a system of oil passages that feed oil to the main and rod bearings, cam bearings, and cylinder heads. Oil pressure is developed by an attached oil pump, and the resistance to flow of the oil is provided by the tight spaces the oil is pumped into. The oil pump may be attached on either the front or the bottom of the block, generally near the crankshaft. The oil pump may be driven by the crankshaft or by a gear off the camshaft. Usually adjacent to the oil pump is a mounting surface for attachment of the oil filter.

In casting the engine block, ribs, webs, and fillets are used to provide rigidity to the casting while reducing overall engine weight (**FIGURE 12-6**). These structures are made of the same materials as the engine block but are constructed into the shape of a rib, web, or fillet. They are placed near areas that encounter high levels of stress and vibration, reinforcing and adding strength to the engine block without bulk.

The crankshaft is supported in the engine block's main bearing bores by main bearing caps. The main bearing bores and caps provide support for the crankshaft. The caps can be

FIGURE 12-6 Ribs, webs, and fillets.

FIGURE 12-7 In some applications, the main bearing caps are attached together to make a girdle that creates a stronger cylinder block.

fastened using a two- or four-bolt design. The shape is the same for each design; only the number of bolts—two or four—varies. The main bearing caps can be inset within the block. The bolts can be fastened through the top of the main cap, or they can be fastened with two bolts on top and two bolts on the side of the main bearing cap.

Some engines use an integrated **main cap girdle** (**FIGURE 12-7**) that has all the main caps cast in a single supporting structure. Others use a main cap girdle that is separate from the main caps. It acts as a cover to the main bearing caps and links the caps together by connecting each individual cap to all of the others in order to reinforce their strength. The girdle also helps position the main bearings in the engine block assembly, supplies engine block rigidity and structure, and prevents lateral or vertical movement.

Gray Cast Iron

Gray cast iron has been used for cylinder blocks for some time now because of its relative cheap cost and overall durability (**FIGURE 12-8**). The wear resistance of gray cast iron is one of the attributes that attracts OE manufactures to use this type of material to create their cylinder blocks. There are some problems with using this type of material, as it tends to fracture easily if subjected to forces other than those it is designed to handle. Weight is another issue, as when this material is used, it is used in large quantities, making the blocks very heavy but also allowing them to withstand both thermal cycles and increase the longevity of the engine block.

Compacted Graphite Cast Iron (CGI)

Compacted graphite cast iron is a type of iron that is between gray cast iron and ductile cast iron. It has the rigidness of cast iron, but with a higher psi rating so that it can handle more abuse than its gray cast iron counterpart can (**FIGURE 12-9**). This type of metal is used in high-stress environments, such as for diesel engine cylinder blocks, as

---

Applied Math

AM-31: Length/Volume/Weight: The technician can determine the degree of conformance to the manufacturer's specifications for length, volume, weight, and other appropriate measurements in the standard and metric systems.

An automotive engine is being overhauled in a repair facility. The technician takes various measurements to determine the degree of conformance to the manufacturer's specifications. The technician uses an inside micrometer to measure the diameter of the cylinders. The measurement is 3.8 inches (96.5 mm). This information verifies to the technician that the engine matches the specifications in the service information.

In order to measure the cylinders with a more exact procedure, a dial bore gauge is used. This gauge is a special tool used to mea-

sure cylinder bore for taper and out-of-round conditions. The dial bore gauge is able to measure cylinders to within 1/10,000 of an inch. Service information for this engine allows a maximum out-of-round of 0.0004". The maximum allowable taper is 0.0005". The metric units would be a maximum out-of-round of 0.010 mm and a maximum taper of 0.013 mm. If a cylinder is worn beyond these limits, the piston rings do not seal properly. When an engine is found to have excessive out-of-round and taper, the likely solution would be to bore the cylinders oversize. In some cases, this could be 0.030" or 0.060" oversize and larger pistons would be installed. By comparing the measurements to manufacturer's specifications, the technician is able to determine the degree of conformance.

FIGURE 12-8 A gray cast iron cylinder block is very popular within the automotive industry as it is very durable and fairly cheap to produce.

FIGURE 12-9 Compacted graphite cast iron cylinder blocks are used in high-stress applications as it has a higher psi rating than gray cast iron.

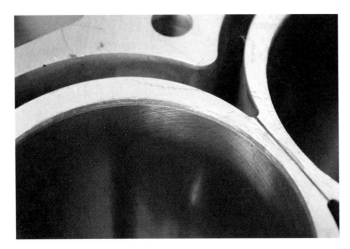

FIGURE 12-10 Aluminum cylinder blocks are used to help with weight reduction and increased heat dissipation. Because of the softness of aluminum, iron sleeves must be installed to resist the piston forces that attempt to destroy the cylinder block.

K12004 Knowledge of the use of balance shafts in the engine.

they are required to handle more pressures and vibrations than a standard engine block made out of gray cast iron. The problem with using CGI is that the creation of the piece must be monitored very closely because machining this type of metal is very expensive and causes tool problems because it is so dense.

Aluminum Alloy

Aluminum alloy has grown in popularity because of its light weight, which can drastically reduce the overall weight of the vehicle. The alloy is able to withstand increased resistance to failure because of the material that it is made from. Aluminum does not have the wear resistance of cast iron, which requires that iron sleeves be installed to increase the wear resistance of the cylinders. The weight reduction more than makes up for the increased machine work needed for the installation of the sleeves (**FIGURE 12-10**). The cost of the aluminum alloy is much more expensive than gray cast iron, but its features outweigh the increased costs. A problem with aluminum cylinder blocks is that they are not as forgiving in terms of overheating the engine, and they are more prone to electrolysis than their cast iron counterparts.

Balance Shaft(s)

Some in-line four-cylinder and 90-degree V6 engines use one or two balance shafts to reduce vibrations from engine operation. Their asymmetrical design, or lack of symmetry in cylinder configuration, causes these engines to have an inherent second-order vibration. The second-order vibration is at twice the engine rpm. It cannot be eliminated, no matter how well the internal parts are balanced. This vibration is produced because of the even firing of the four-cylinder and some 90-degree V6 engines. The descending and ascending pistons are not always completely opposed in their acceleration.

To address this problem, engine manufacturers have developed a balance shaft with counterweights spaced so as to cancel out inherent vibrations. The balance shafts are mounted in the engine block, either below the crankshaft, next to the crankshaft, or above the crankshaft, depending on design (**FIGURE 12-11**). The shafts are typically driven at twice the engine rpm, usually by a chain, gear, or belt from the crankshaft. The weights on the shaft are timed to cancel the second-order vibrations in the engine.

FIGURE 12-11 The balance shaft that is installed in an engine is used to lower the vibrations caused by the design of the engine.

▶ Wrap-Up

Ready for Review

- The engine block (also called the cylinder block or simply the block) is the main structural member of the internal combustion engine.
- The engine block is the largest part of the engine; it is the main supporting structure for all of the engine parts.
- The block is also the main aligning structure for all parts of the engine.
- Within the engine block are the cylinders and pistons; the top of the piston and the matching cylinder head form the combustion chamber.
- For optimum performance and engine life, the engine block must be designed, cast, and machined within precise tolerances, meaning that the components must be designed and connected together within narrow specifications.
- The upper section of the engine block contains the cylinders and pistons. The lower section of the engine block forms the crankcase, which supports the main bearings, crankshaft, camshaft (some engines), and balance shafts (some engines).
- In the V-engine, the pistons are at a 60- or 90-degree angle off the crankshaft.
- In the in-line engine, the pistons line up in a straight line so that each piston has its own rod throw on the crankshaft.
- The W engine is a Volkswagen design that positions pistons in different locations to help make the engine compact. VW is currently the only manufacturer that is using this design.
- The rotary engine has rotors, instead of pistons, that create the mechanical movement from the chemical explosions. The engine block for this type of engine is assembled from pieces that are bolted together to create the combustion chambers. There are no cylinder heads or valves for operation, just two different ports whose opening and closing are controlled by the rotors movement inside the chamber.
- In the metal casting foundry process, different types of materials and techniques are used to create steel or cast iron and aluminum engine blocks. The most common methods are the green sand, shell, and lost foam processes. In all three processes, hot molten metal is poured into a mold. The engine block can be cast in one piece from gray iron, or it can be alloyed with other metals such as nickel or chromium.
- The casting process begins by making the shapes for what will become water jackets and cylinders as sand cores or foam shapes, which are then fitted into molds.
- The term "water jacket" is used to describe the area created by the sand, shell, or foam shapes during the casting process.
- Molten metal is poured into the casting mold from a tub or ladle without the use of pressure, a process known as gravity pouring.
- Once the metal cools, the core sand is removed through holes in the sides and ends of the engine block casting, leaving cavities for the cooling and lubricating passages. These holes are sealed with core plugs, which may also be called Welch plugs or soft plugs.
- The term "freeze plugs" was used for core plugs, but the term is inaccurate. The engine block was never designed to withstand freezing of the water in the cooling passages. Water expands approximately 10% as it freezes into ice. If the engine temperature drops below freezing, the pressure of the expanding ice may cause the block to crack even if the core plugs pop out.
- Parts of the engine block that typically require machining include the top of the engine block (also called the deck).

▶ The engine block assembly, or lower end as it is sometimes called, consists of the following: oil galleries and plugs (oil passage plugs), water jacket and plugs, pistons and rings, piston pins, connecting rods and caps, rod bearing inserts, main bearing caps, main bearing inserts, the thrust bearing, the crankshaft, rear seals (lip or rope seal), the camshaft (for overhead cam engines), and a vibration balancer.

▶ The engine lubrication system also begins in the engine block assembly, with a system of oil passages that feed oil to the main and rod bearings, cam bearings, and cylinder heads. Oil pressure is developed by an attached oil pump, and the resistance to flow of the oil is provided by the tight spaces the oil is pumped into.

▶ The oil pump may be attached on either the front or the bottom of the block, generally near the crankshaft. The oil pump may be driven by the crankshaft or by a gear off the camshaft. Usually adjacent to the oil pump is a mounting surface for attachment of the oil filter.

▶ The crankshaft is supported in the engine block's main bearing bores by main bearing caps. The main bearing bores and caps provide support for the crankshaft.

▶ Some engines use an integrated main cap girdle that has all the main caps cast in a single supporting structure.

▶ Some in-line four-cylinder and 90-degree V6 engines use one or two balance shafts to reduce vibrations from engine operation. Their asymmetrical design, or lack of symmetry in cylinder configuration, causes these engines to have an inherent second-order vibration.

Key Terms

deck   The area that is machined on top of the cylinder block and is a gasket sealing area for the head gaskets. This area must be completely flat and must be checked when the head gaskets have failed.

freeze plug   A slang term used to describe the core plugs.

gravity pouring   The process used to pour the molten metal into a mold to create a cylinder block blank.

lost foam process   A casting process where foam spacers take up the space in a mold so that when molten metal is poured over them, they will keep their shape until the metal is cooled enough to retain its shape. Once that foam gets hot enough, it dissolves and exits the component.

main cap girdle   Location where all the main bearing caps are attached with a structure so that they combine to become a strong unit.

Review Questions

1. Which of these is the main aligning structure for all parts of the engine?
   a. Crankshaft
   b. Block
   c. Cylinder
   d. Transmission

2. Which of the following is *not* present in the engine block of a vehicle?
   a. Pulley belt
   b. Cylinder
   c. Piston
   d. Crankshaft

3. Designing engine blocks with narrow specifications and utmost precision serves all of the below functions, *except*:
   a. preventing leakage of air and fuel.
   b. withstanding the thermal stresses of combustion.
   c. accommodating shocks and vibration.
   d. increasing the vehicle's load-carrying capacity.

4. Which of the following designs has blended the benefits of an inline engine and low clearance of a V-engine?
   a. Boxer engine
   b. Rotary engine
   c. W engine
   d. Slant 4 or 6 engine

5. An engine made of which of these materials gives the vehicle greater fuel efficiency?
   a. Compacted CGI
   b. Gray cast iron
   c. Aluminum
   d. Steel alloy

6. Once the metal cools after casting, the holes are sealed with:
   a. lip seal.
   b. rope seal.
   c. bearing caps.
   d. core plugs.

7. An engine made of which of these materials is more suited for highly stressful environments?
   a. Compact graphite cast iron
   b. Gray cast iron
   c. Aluminum
   d. Steel

8. Which of the following parts is present in the top half of the engine block and requires a tight fit with the block?
   a. Water pump
   b. Piston ring
   c. Oil pan
   d. Cylinder head

9. All of the following are provided in the engine block for enhancing rigidity while reducing overall weight, *except*:
   a. fins.
   b. ribs.
   c. webs.
   d. fillets.

10. Choose the correct statement describing the use of balance shafts in an engine:
    a. They are developed and placed to cancel out inherent vibrations.
    b. They are mounted beside the pistons.
    c. They are driven at the same rpm as the engine.
    d. They are not attached to the crankshaft.

ASE Technician A/Technician B Style Questions

1. Tech A says that a cylinder block is where the rotating assembly is installed. Tech B says that an engine block can be made of cast iron or aluminum. Who is correct?
   a. Tech A
   b. Tech B
   c. Both A and B
   d. Neither A nor B

2. Tech A states that once a cylinder block is cast, it must be machined to the tolerances that it was designed for. Tech B says that the owner of the vehicle must decide what to make the engine block out of. Who is correct?
   a. Tech A
   b. Tech B
   c. Both A and B
   d. Neither A nor B

3. Tech A states that the cylinder block could be installed in a vehicle transversely or horizontally. Tech B states that a four-stroke engine has a different engine block from a two-stroke engine. Who is correct?
   a. Tech A
   b. Tech B
   c. Both A and B
   d. Neither A nor B

4. Tech A says that Volkswagen is the only manufacturer that utilizes the P engine. Tech B says that the V-engine design is used to help with increasing the size of the engine without making it take up excess space. Who is correct?
   a. Tech A
   b. Tech B
   c. Both A and B
   d. Neither A nor B

5. Tech A says that a balance shaft is used to increase the horsepower in the engine. Tech B states that the balance shaft must be timed to the engine. Who is correct?
   a. Tech A
   b. Tech B
   c. Both A and B
   d. Neither A nor B

6. Tech A says that an aluminum alloy engine block has the cylinder walls directly in the material without any extra support. Tech B says that the use of cast iron as an engine block material is ideal as it is very durable. Who is correct?
   a. Tech A
   b. Tech B
   c. Both A and B
   d. Neither A nor B

7. Tech A says that a rotary engine has an engine block whose components are bolted together. Tech B says that a rotary engine has coolant passages just like a piston engine. Who is correct?
   a. Tech A
   b. Tech B
   c. Both A and B
   d. Neither A nor B

8. Tech A states that opposed piston engines are also called boxer engines. Tech B says that a cylinder block should always be cleaned with soap and water after machining. Who is correct?
   a. Tech A
   b. Tech B
   c. Both A and B
   d. Neither A nor B

9. Tech A says that gravity pouring is the common method used to cast the cylinder block. Tech B states that core plugs are installed to protect from freezing. Who is correct?
   a. Tech A
   b. Tech B
   c. Both A and B
   d. Neither A nor B

10. Tech A says that CGI cylinder blocks are used in high-stress applications, such as heavy diesel engines. Tech B says that cylinder blocks are very solid and shouldn't crack. Who is correct?
    a. Tech A
    b. Tech B
    c. Both A and B
    d. Neither A nor B

CHAPTER 13

Crankshafts and Bearings

NATEF Tasks

There are no NATEF Tasks for this chapter.

Knowledge Objectives

After reading this chapter, you will have:

- **K13001** Knowledge of the crankshafts role in an engine.
- **K13002** Knowledge of the features of a crankshaft.
- **K13003** Knowledge of evaluating a crankshaft for straightness.
- **K13004** Knowledge of crankshaft and connecting rod bearings.
- **K13005** Knowledge of the connected components to the crankshaft.
- **K13006** Knowledge of how to balance the crankshaft externally.
- **K13007** Knowledge of the location of the crankshaft seals.

Skills Objectives

- **S13001** Check the crankshaft for straightness.
- **S13002** Measure out-of-round on a crankshaft journal.
- **S13003** Measure journal taper of a crankshaft journal.
- **S13004** Check bearings with Plastigage®.

You Are the Automotive Technician

You are disassembling an engine with over 200,000 miles on it, and as you take it apart, you notice that the crankshaft is hard to remove from the cylinder block. All of the main bearing caps have come off easily, but the crankshaft will not separate from that cylinder block. What do you suspect happened to the crankshaft?

1. The crankshaft is not made for this application and is stuck because it is wrong.
2. The crankshaft may be warped, causing it become lodged in the cylinder block.
3. The crankshaft still has a bolt holding it in.

K13001 Knowledge of the crankshafts role in an engine.

▶ Introduction

The crankshaft is an integral part of the internal combustion engine, and if it is not in working order, the engine cannot produce power. Vehicle power is transferred from the engine to the drivetrain so that it can be used to propel the vehicle through the crankshaft. If the engine is missing the crankshaft power transfer from the piston/connecting rod assemblies would not happen, thus no vehicle movement would happen.

▶ Crankshaft

The main role of the crankshaft is to transfer the up-and-down strokes of the pistons into rotary motion. It is situated in the **crankcase**, which is the lower part or bottom of the engine block. Connecting rods are attached to offset journals called **throws**. This is where the reciprocating motion of the piston is changed into a rotary motion. The rotary motion is then used to power the vehicle.

The crankshaft now also plays a role in creating the spark for the combustion process. In newer engine models, the crankshaft houses the reluctor for the crankshaft positioning sensor, which is a device that lets the engine computer know the position of the crankshaft in order to help produce high-voltage sparks at the right times for properly timed ignition (**FIGURE 13-1**). The crankshaft may also have teeth and notches embedded in it or have shields and windows to help create the Hall-effect signal that the computer uses to know the position of the crankshaft for a properly timed ignition.

The back end of the crankshaft serves as the mounting area for the flywheel or flexplate, and the front end serves as the drive for the camshaft and accessories. Many current engines also drive the oil pump off the front of the crankshaft.

Crankshafts are a one-piece casting or forging, or they can be machined out of a **billet**, which is a solid piece of metal (**FIGURE 13-2**). The raw crankshaft is then machined into the desired shape for the particular engine into which it will be installed. If the crankshaft journals are worn or damaged, they can generally be refinished to a smaller size and reused with undersized bearings—that is, bearings that are thicker.

▶ TECHNICIAN TIP

You might be wondering why bearings would be called undersized when in reality they are thicker than a standard-sized bearing. The reason is that the crankshaft journal is typically machined to give it a new wear surface; as a result, the journal becomes undersized. The matching bearings are then referred to as undersized bearings.

Crankshaft Assembly

The crankshaft assembly and related parts are responsible for transferring the power created inside the cylinder and combustion chamber to the external drives of the engine. The piston and connecting rod assembly inside the cylinder are connected to the crankshaft. The movement of the piston and connecting rod assembly driven by the force of combustion turns the crankshaft. Rotation of the crankshaft drives the flywheel/flexplate, and then the drivetrain, which rotates the wheels. The crankshaft also transmits power to the front of the crankshaft assembly, which drives the valvetrain assembly through a series of belts, chains, and gears. The power to the front of the crankshaft assembly also drives the pulley configuration that connects to the power steering pump, air-conditioning compressor, water pump, and alternator.

K13002 Knowledge of the features of a crankshaft.

Journals

Main bearing journals are the part of the crankshaft assembly that mate to the main bearings found at the bottom of the engine block. Main bearing journals are very smooth and perfectly round so that they can rotate inside the softer main bearings. The main bearing journals are positioned in a straight line down the center of the crankshaft and are used to position the crankshaft assembly into the lower part of the engine block. The **main journals** are ground to manufacturer specifications from the **crank core** (the rough, unfinished crankshaft assembly that has just left the foundry or forging area) or billet. The center of the main journals is referred to as the centerline of the crankshaft.

FIGURE 13-1 The reluctor wheel is cast into the crankshaft so that the crankshaft position (CKP) sensor can create a waveform to tell the powertrain control module (PCM) which piston is firing.

The crankshaft is held in the block by main bearing caps, which can be separate from one another or attached to one another by an assembly called a **girdle**. Main bearing caps mate to **journal saddles**, which are smooth, curved, machined areas located at the bottom of the engine block. The main bearing cap and the journal saddle create a perfectly round bore that clamps bearing inserts in place to support the crankshaft journals. The main bearing inserts are secured by main bearing caps and bolts.

As discussed earlier, the number of journal saddles in an engine is generally dependent on the length of the engine block. A common V8 has five main journals on the crankshaft, whereas many straight in-line six-cylinder engines have seven main journals, and a V6 typically has only four main journals.

The crankshaft main journals rotate in bearing inserts called main bearings. Cross-drilled passages in the crankshaft carry lubricant under pressure from the main bearings to the adjacent crank throws (rod throws). **Rod throws**, also called rod journals, are located in the **offset area** of the crankshaft assembly, as opposed to the main journals that sit in a straight line with the centerline of the crankshaft assembly. The crank throws are offset from the centerline of the crankshaft; the amount of offset determines the **piston stroke** (the distance the piston travels from TDC to BDC). The crankshaft design in some 90-degree V6 engines differs significantly from that of 60-degree V6 engines. In order for a 90-degree V6 to have evenly spaced power pulses, the crankshaft must have connecting rod journals that are splayed (**FIGURE 13-3**). A splayed journal is designed with two connecting rod journals, each one offset from the other. The crank pin, or journal, appears split, but both journals are actually located between the crankshaft throws or counterweights. This arrangement creates a 90-degree V6 engine with evenly spaced power pulses and is called an even fire V6. It is smoother running than an odd fire V6, which has uneven power pulses because it does not use splayed connecting rod journals.

Counterweights are formed on the crankshaft to balance the components of the rotating assembly that are mounted inside and attached to the engine block, including the rod journals, rod bearings, connecting rods, pistons, piston pin, and rings. The balancing of the rotating assembly is done by drilling out weight or by adding weight to the counterweights. A heavy metal called **Mallory metal** is added to the counterweights during manufacturing to balance the counterweights. Mallory is approximately 117% heavier than steel (that is, more than twice as heavy).

Some crankshafts are internally balanced, which means the crankshaft is balanced solely from the counterweights of the crankshaft. No external counterweights are needed. Other crankshafts are externally balanced, which means the crankshaft counterweights are not heavy enough, so counterweights need to be positioned on the flywheel or flexplate at the rear of the crankshaft and the harmonic balancer at the front. On an externally balanced engine, it is critical to use the proper externally balanced flywheel or flexplate and harmonic balancer for the engine, and they need to be installed in the proper orientation. Check the service information carefully.

Most crankshafts use **induction-hardened** journal surfaces to give good wear qualities. Induction hardening is a process for hardening the outer surface of a metal structure by rapid heating and cooling. Using the induction hardening process allows the crankshaft to be reground on the main and rod bearing surfaces without grinding through the hardened layer. Regrinding is used to smooth and polish the main and rod journals so they can be reused when the engine is being rebuilt. It is used as an alternative to replacing the entire crankshaft assembly.

Some heavy-duty and performance crankshafts use a nitridization process, which takes longer and is more costly but results in an extremely hard surface. **Nitriding** is a surface hardening heat treatment that introduces nitrogen into the surface of steel at a temperature range of approximately 930°F to 1020°F (499–549°C). Nitriding creates a surface that is harder than that produced by the induction hardening process, but the hardened layer is not as thick. The crankshaft will have to be re-nitrided if the main journals or connecting rod journals have to be reground due to wear.

FIGURE 13-2 The three different types of crankshafts: cast, forged, and billet.

FIGURE 13-3 Splayed crankshaft from a 90-degree V6 engine.

FIGURE 13-4 The counterweights are offset to the piston/connecting rod assembly so that the crankshaft has an opposing force to counteract the vibration of the rotating weight.

FIGURE 13-5 A fillet allows for the connecting rod to center itself on the journal, keep the connecting rod from rubbing on the counterweight, and increase the strength of the journal.

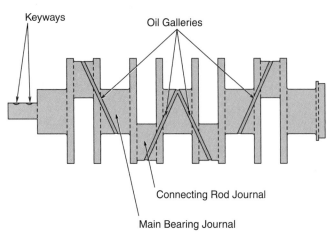

FIGURE 13-6 Holes drilled through the crankshaft allow oil to get from the main journals to the connecting rod journals to lubricate the connecting rod bearings.

Counterweights

The counterweights on a crankshaft mirror the weight of the piston rod assembly opposite the counterweight. Equaling out the rotating weight allows the engine to rotate with minimal vibration (**FIGURE 13-4**). If the counterweights did not weigh the same as the piston/rod assembly, then a severe rotational vibration would occur, which could then cause part failure. The counterweights are where the machinist either adds or subtracts weight to adjust for replacement rod and piston assemblies. This process is called balancing the rotating assembly and can only be completed by a trained machinist.

Fillets

Fillets are machined in to the crank pins where they meet the side of the rod throws so that the force of the connecting rod can be spread out (**FIGURE 13-5**). These fillets are rounded corners that allow the rod to self-center so that the force of combustion is being exerted in the center of the crankshaft, to maximize the use of that force. Without the fillets, the connecting rod could ride on the edge of the crank pin and might cause unneeded stress on the crankshaft, which could lead to premature failure. In addition to the excess stress, the side of the connecting rod would be rubbing against the side of the crank throw, which could cause wear, creating a potential place for failure.

Oil Passages

To feed the connecting rod and main bearings, the crankshaft has holes drilled through each throw to feed the bearings with the required lubrication so that they are not riding on the crankshaft itself. The film of oil allows for movement of the components without causing damage to the bearing (**FIGURE 13-6**). As the crankshaft rotates, the oil passages in the crankshaft line up with the oil passages in the block, which then allows the flow of oil through the crankshaft to the bearing surfaces (**FIGURE 13-7**). Using substandard oil or not having enough oil in the engine could starve the crankshaft and cause the engine to seize up.

FIGURE 13-7 The main bearing saddles is where the transfer of oil pressure from the cylinder block to the crankshaft takes place.

Seal Surfaces

The crankshaft has multiple sealing surfaces, which allows for movement of the crankshaft while keeping the oil inside the dirt out (**FIGURE 13-8**). When you are reconditioning the crankshaft, you must examine these surfaces as they can develop grooves or pitting because of age or abuse. Bypassing this crucial step could cause the technician to reinstall a component that has a high probability of leaking in the near future.

Bolt Holes and Keyways

The crankshaft has bolt holes that allow the attachment of the **flywheel/ flexplate** and the harmonic damper/pulley (**FIGURE 13-9 A** and **B**). These holes allow engine components to be added and removed so that they can be replaced, modified, or disassembled. The keyways that are machined into the crankshaft do not allow the pulley to rotate on the crankshaft, but it rotates with the crankshaft (**FIGURE 13-10**).

Internally and Externally Balance Engines

Engines are balanced either internally or externally, and the technician must be aware of how the engine is balanced. The reason that you must balance an engine is to stop the vibrations that are created by the movement of the internal components.

How to Measure Journals to See Whether the Crankshaft Is Serviceable

A crankshaft can be faulty in several ways. First, it could be warped, which would cause the journals to be forced against the bearings, wearing them out prematurely. Second, the main and rod journals could be excessively worn, leading to too much bearing clearance, which would cause low engine oil pressure. Third, the bolt holes, keyways, and sealing surfaces could be damaged, causing their own set of issues. These situations mean that a thorough inspection along with precise measurements must be made to ensure the crankshaft can be put back in service.

To inspect the crankshaft, follow the steps in **SKILL DRILL 13-1**.

Measuring Taper

Taper is a wear direction that goes from wide to narrow, causing the crank pin not to be the same size on both ends. The crankshaft is

FIGURE 13-8 A sealing surface of a front seal and a rear main seal. The seal rides on this flat surface, so it must be smooth and machined correctly to ensure sealing.

K13003 Knowledge of evaluating a crankshaft for straightness.

S13001 Check the crankshaft for straightness.

Ⓐ

FIGURE 13-10 A keyway on a crankshaft that drives the harmonic balancer.

Ⓑ

FIGURE 13-9 A. The rear of the crankshaft has a flange that allows for mounting of the flywheel or flexplate. **B.** The snout of the crankshaft, where the harmonic balancer is installed.

SKILL DRILL 13-1 Inspecting the Crankshaft

1. Check the crankshaft for straightness. There are two methods you can use to check the crankshaft for straightness.

   A. **Crankshaft in block:** With the pistons and rods removed, make sure all main caps are numbered; the main caps must not be mixed up because they must go back in the exact order in which they were removed. Pull the number one main cap, and clean the main journal on the crankshaft. Using a dial indicator with a 0.001" (0.025 mm) scale and a magnetic base, attach the dial indicator on the pan rail, and center the dial indicator over the number one main journal. Preload the dial indicator on the main journal, and move the face on the dial indicator to zero. Rotate the crankshaft one full rotation, watching the dial indicator, and record your findings. Repeat the process to check the center main, and record your findings. Determine any necessary actions based on your findings.

   B. **Crankshaft out of block:** With the crankshaft removed, make sure the main journals are clean. Position the crankshaft on two V-blocks, using the first main journal and the last main journal. Using a dial indicator with a 0.001" (0.025 mm) scale, attach the dial indicator on the bench with a magnetic base or clamp. Position the dial indicator over the number 1 journal. Preload the dial indicator on the main journal, and set the face on the dial indicator to zero. Rotate the crankshaft one full rotation, watching the dial indicator. Record your findings. Repeat the process on the center main, and record your findings. Determine any necessary actions based on your findings.

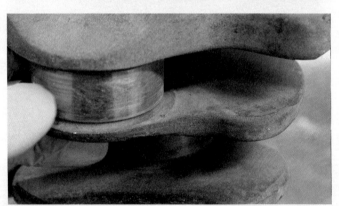

2. Visually inspect the journals for grooves. The journals should be smooth to the touch.

3. Use an outside micrometer to measure the rod and main journals. Both rod and main journals should have measurements taken 90 degrees apart. Also, rod journals should be measured across the face of the journal to check for taper. Compare your findings to factory specifications, and determine the necessary action.

Continued

4. Visually inspect the square-cut or Woodruff key and keyway. If the square key or Woodruff key is out, make sure the keyway is straight with sharp edges. The square-cut or Woodruff key must fit snugly.

5. Visually inspect the thrust flange, bolt holes, and rear seal surface to make sure there are no nicks or scratches.

6. Visually inspect the crankshaft for cracks. If you need a more detailed inspection, the crankshaft should be checked by magnafluxing. Determine any necessary actions.

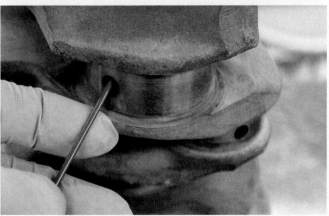

7. Probe the oil passages with a small plastic tube (a spray can nozzle extension works well), making sure the oil passages from the mains into the rod journals are clear. Determine any necessary actions.

Continued

8. Check the crankshaft position sensor reluctor ring, when applicable. Visually inspect the reluctor ring to make sure there is no damage.

constantly taking the abuse from the up-and-down movement from the piston/rod assembly, it will eventually wear out the crank pin that it rides on, and it will require machining to bring it back into spec. When rebuilding an engine, the technician must inspect this portion of the crankshaft, as it could cause premature failure of the connecting rod or main bearing.

Measuring Out-of-Round

S13002 Measure out-of-round on a crankshaft journal.

S13003 Measure journal taper of a crankshaft journal.

Measuring out-of-round on a crankshaft is another vital measurement when rebuilding an engine as a journal that is not a perfect circle can cause premature bearing failure. When measuring out-of-round, you need to use a micrometer to get the most precise measurement so that you can evaluate the needs of this particular component. Measurement at three different locations on the journal will determine if the journal is out-of-round and needs machining. To measure for taper and out-of-round, follow the steps in **SKILL DRILL 13-2**.

SKILL DRILL 13-2 Measuring for Out-of-Round and Taper

1. Stand crankshaft on its end so that you are able to access all the journals.

Continued

2. Starting with the top journal, measure each end of the journal in three spots with a micrometer.

3. Record measurements.

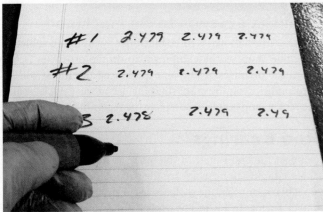

4. Start with the measurement at one end of the journal, and subtract from the measurement of the other end of the journal.

5. The difference between the two measurements is taper of the journal.

6. To determine whether the journal is out of round, take the measurements of the three locations and determine whether they are the same in all locations.

7. Once it is determined that the crankshaft needs to be reconditioned, it must be sent off to the machine shop to complete this task.

Warpage

Like any piece of metal that is exposed to high temperatures, the crankshaft may warp over its lifetime. When rebuilding this engine, you must check the crankshaft for straightness; if it were not straight, reusing it would cause the crankshaft to destroy the internals of the engine very quickly. If you are unable to determine whether the crankshaft is warped, you should send it out of the machine shop to get it checked.

Applied Math

AM-37: Mentally: When comparing the observed measurement with the manufacturer's specifications, the technician can mentally compute whether the observed measurement meets specifications.

A technician is assigned to overhaul a V8 engine. He is currently measuring the crankshaft, which has been removed from the block and cleaned. The manufacturer's service information lists the minimum diameter for the main bearing journals as 2.6576", a maximum taper of 0.0002", and maximum out-of-round of 0.0003'. While measuring each journal in four places with an outside micrometer, the techni-

cian compares each reading to the minimum diameter specification and mentally computes whether it meets specifications. Also, the technician compares the two readings used to measure the amount of taper and mentally computes the difference between them to come up with the amount of taper, which again is compared to specifications. The same process is performed with the out-of-round measurement. The two measurements are taken; the difference is calculated mentally; and that difference is compared to specifications. These measurements are then performed on each of the other crankshaft journals.

What to Do If Crankshaft Needs to Be Machined

If you have determined that the crankshaft needs to be machined, you should sublet that job out to a local trusted machine shop, as the equipment to do the processes is often expensive and large to have on the premises. Using an experienced machinist will help you expedite the process of reconditioning the crankshaft for use in the vehicle, making the customer happy when the repair shop is able to complete the repair in a timely fashion.

▶ Crankshaft/Rod Bearings

K13004 Knowledge of crankshaft and connecting rod bearings.

Bearings are used to help support the crankshaft in the block as well as the connecting rods on the crankshaft journals. Crankshaft bearings are the friction bearing type as compared to the antifriction type. This means that the surfaces are in sliding contact with each other rather than rolling contact, such as in a wheel bearing. Connecting rod bearings and the crankshaft main bearings are the split-sleeve type, which means they are in two halves, called **bearing inserts** or half-shell bearings (**FIGURE 13-11**).

Bearing inserts are made from Babbitt metal bonded to a steel shell. The shell gives rigidity to the bearing, and the Babbitt metal is relatively soft and provides the bearing wear surface. Bearings, along with lubricant, are used in engines to support and protect rotating parts and allow them to turn freely. Between the bearing insert and the journal is a very thin layer of oil that separates the bearing material from the surface of the crankshaft journals. The oil acts as a shock absorber and is designed to keep the journal from making contact with the surface of the bearing.

Crankshaft bearings are split into two halves so that they can be assembled over the corresponding journal. Each of the bearing shells has a built-in tang that fits into a matching machined notch in the bearing saddle and cap. The tang prevents the bearing from spinning inside the saddle and cap by butting up against the machined faces of the saddle

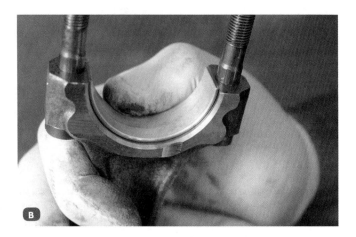

FIGURE 13-11 Bearing inserts. **A.** Main bearings. **B.** Rod bearings.

and cap. In a main bearing, the upper half of the bearing fits into a machined section of the cylinder block called the main bearing saddle. The main bearing saddle has a notch for the bearing tang to fit within and a drilled oil passage for supplying oil to the bearing and journal.

It is important to match the proper bearing half with its oil hole, as it must align to the oil passage in the main saddle. The lower half is carried in the main bearing cap. The bearing cap also has a notch for the bearing tang to fit into. The main cap is held in place on the main saddle by main bearing cap bolts. It is important that the bearing tang fits into the bearing slot; otherwise, the bearing will be pinched and cause excessive drag on the crankshaft journal, damaging both the bearing and the journal. Refer to the manufacturer's specifications for torque procedures.

In a connecting rod bearing, the bearing's upper half is carried in the big end of the connecting rod, which has a notch for the bearing tang. The lower half is carried in the connecting rod cap, which also contains a notch for the bearing tang. The cap is bolted to the connecting rod and torqued to specifications. Refer to the manufacturer's specifications for torque procedures.

The crankshaft requires a thrust bearing, which limits the end play movement of the crankshaft. These bearings can be in the form of bearing flanges that are part of one of the main bearings, giving each main bearing insert a U shape. This U-shaped bearing insert fits over a precisely machined main bearing saddle and cap (**FIGURE 13-12**). The thrust bearing will only fit on the specified bearing support. Alternatively, a separate two-piece **thrust bearing** can be fitted into a machined recess in each side of the bearing support and cap, and acts as the thrust bearing for the crankshaft. In the same way that the bearing-to-journal clearance is important, so is the clearance between the bearing flange (or thrust bearing) and the mating surface on the crankshaft. The thrust bearing clearance prevents excessive end play (forward or backward movement) of the crankshaft, especially in a vehicle equipped with a manual transmission/transaxle and clutch, because the crankshaft thrust surfaces bear all of the force of compressing the pressure plate springs when the operator pushes down on the clutch pedal.

Oil flows through an oil gallery in the cylinder block. Each main bearing receives its own oil under pressure from the oil hole in the main bearing saddle, which connects directly to the oil gallery. Some top bearing inserts have a groove around the middle. The groove provides a space for oil to flow around the journal, which helps provide more lubrication for the bearing. The grooved bearing also helps extend the time that the rod bearing receives pressurized oil, because the oil hole in the crankshaft lines up to the bearing groove for half of the rotation of the crankshaft. Passageways drilled in the crankshaft carry oil from the main bearing journals to the rod journals (**FIGURE 13-13**).

Oil flow maintains an oil cushion between the crankshaft and the bearing as the engine is operating. But when the engine is first started up, especially when it is cold, it takes a few seconds to pump oil to the bearings, which can result in the crankshaft touching the bearing surface for a short time. The oil flow also carries away heat and particles that could cause wear. If the cushion of oil did not exist, the bearing would overheat and fail. Engine manufacturers specify the clearance required between the bearing material and the crankshaft. This clearance specification helps maintain the balance between adequate oil pressure and adequate oil flow.

Main bearings and rod bearings come in various sizes. The most common bearing size is a standard size (std), which means that it fits the same size journal as originally manufactured. Undersized bearings can be purchased for many engines in the following

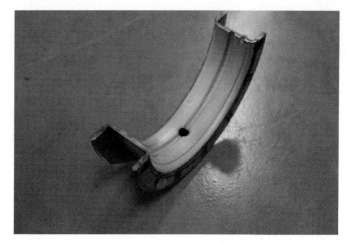

FIGURE 13-12 Thrust bearing.

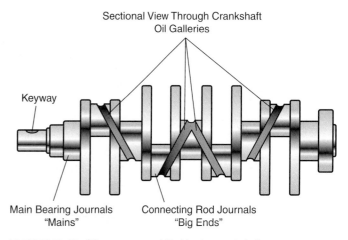

FIGURE 13-13 Oil passageway drilled in the crankshaft.

> ▶ **TECHNICIAN TIP**

In some high-performance and race applications, rather than using an oil groove in both halves of the bearings, the crankshaft is cross-drilled in the main journal of the crankshaft. This allows oil to be sent through the crankshaft to the rod journal during the full revolution of the crankshaft, while only using a groove in one of the two bearing inserts. This technique allows more bearing surface on the load side of the main bearing. By allowing more bearing surface on the load side of the bearing insert, the bearing can support a greater load.

FIGURE 13-14 A damaged bearing usually has foreign debris in it; this causes it to become out of tolerance, which then leads to failure.

sizes: 0.001" (0.025 mm), 0.010" (0.25 mm), 0.020" (0.51 mm), and 0.030" (0.76 mm). If you are replacing the crankshaft, it is important to measure the crankshaft journals and check to make sure they are within the specifications set out by the crankshaft supplier. The clearance between the crankshaft journal and the bearings is crucial and must be within the manufacturer's specifications. If there is too little clearance, the oil will not be able to flow through the clearance in the bearing, which can cause the bearing material to overheat and possibly seize to the journal. If the clearance is too large, the oil pressure will be lowered and the oil will be squished out of the clearance in the bearing, which allows the journal to come into direct contact with the bearing, creating a knocking noise and extreme wear.

Bearing Materials

Bearings require a difficult mix of properties; they must be hard enough to resist wear, but soft enough not to damage the crankshaft. One bearing material, called Babbitt metal, is an alloy that can include metals such as tin, lead, aluminum, and copper. This mix of metals creates a unique combination of hardness and softness.

The two most popular engine bearings in use are the trimetal and the bimetal types. Both bearings have their distinct advantages. Most trimetal bearings are made of a lead, tin, and copper overlay that rides next to the crankshaft, followed by a nickel barrier, and next a high-fatigue strength copper and lead lining, which is bonded to a steel backing. The biggest advantage of the trimetal bearing is that it has a higher load capacity; thus, it is ideal for high-performance and racing engines. Most bimetal bearings are made of an aluminum, tin, and silicon alloy that is bonded on a steel backing. There are also some aluminum bearings that are made of an aluminum alloy that contains tin and copper, which is bonded to a steel backing. Some of the advantages of the aluminum bearings are that they are less expensive and they contain no lead (which is an environmental concern).

Embedability

The material that the bearing is made out of allows it to be very forgiving when it comes in contact with the spinning parts in the engine. This same feature also allows the bearing to be susceptible to embedding of foreign objects into the material with relative ease (**FIGURE 13-14**). Once the bearing has a foreign object embedded in it, the properties of that bearing have changed, which could cause accelerated wear on the spinning component that is running on it. We must be aware of the possibility of foreign objects entering the engine so that this failure will not happen when you are repairing this vehicle.

Fatigue

Bearing fatigue is something that becomes more apparent as the vehicle ages and the engine gets more miles on it. Fatigue is when the material physically gives out and no longer can be utilized to be a bearing in this engine (**FIGURE 13-15**). When this happens, the only recourse is replacement of the failed component, which usually means an engine overhaul. Before you decide to proceed with this course of action, you must first consult with the owner of the vehicle and explain that this is a very costly repair so that he or she is not surprised at the bill when you are finished.

Bearing Crush

All main bearings and rod bearings are held in place by what is called **bearing crush** (**FIGURE 13-16**). Bearing crush is a term meaning that the bearing inserts are slightly larger than the bore they fit into and are therefore slightly crushed into position when tightened into place. The proper bearing crush is designed into the bearing when it is made, by allowing the bearing insert to slightly protrude from the parting line of the

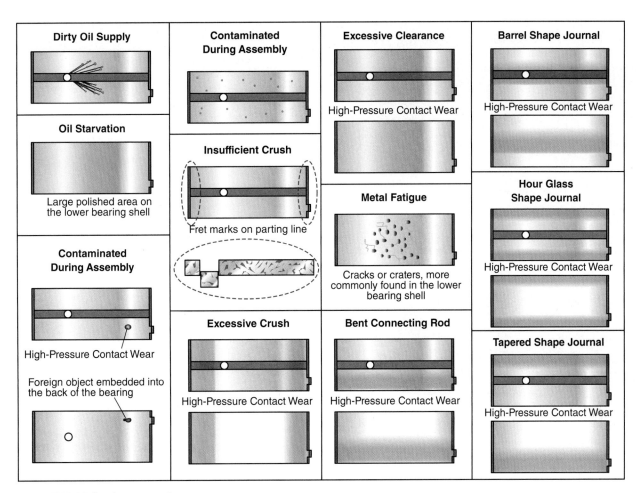

FIGURE 13-15 Bearing wear patterns.

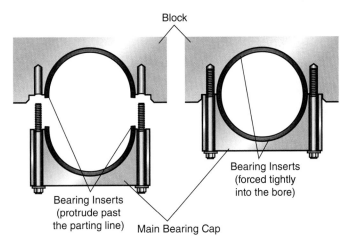

FIGURE 13-16 Bearing crush.

bearing support and cap. When the cap is tightened properly, the bearing inserts are forced very tightly into the bore, which helps hold them in place.

Checking Bearings with Plastigage

There is a way to check bearing clearance on main and rod bearings without using a micrometer or to double-check your micrometer measurement. Plastigage is a claylike substance that is engineered to flatten out, to create a reading that is easily gauged by the human eye. **SKILL DRILL 13-3** shows you how to effectively use Plastigage to check bearing clearance.

S13004 Check bearings with Plastigage®.

SKILL DRILL 13-3 Checking Bearing with Plastigage

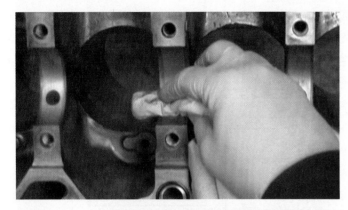

1. Make sure that the bearing, bearing cap, rod or crankshaft, and the bores they ride in are free from oil, dirt, or other contaminates.

2. Install the component like you are going to assemble on the final assembly.

3. Cut off a piece of Plastigage that is as wide as the journal on the component.

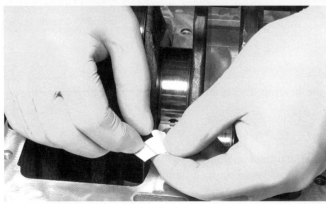

4. Open the paper backing, and take the clay out of its package.

Continued

5. Lay the piece of Plastigage on the journal that you want to measure.

6. Put the main or rod cap on the journal so that it is ready to be torqued.

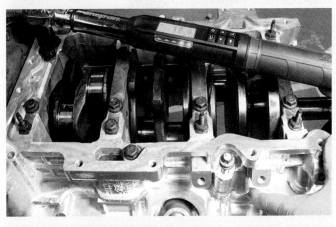

7. Torque the bolts on the cap to the specified torque.

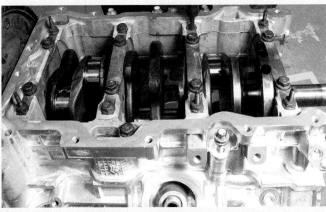

8. Loosen the cap.

Continued

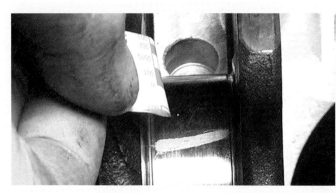

9. Use the gauge on the paper covering for the Plastigage to measure the bearing clearance.

10. Consult service information for specifications for this journal, and take corrective action if out of specs.

▶ Crankshaft-Connected Components

K13005 Knowledge of the connected components to the crankshaft.

The crankshaft is the base for the connected components that convert the chemical energy into mechanical energy that can be used to propel the vehicle. This engine component is under constant abuse, which means that the pieces attached to it must be in balance and correct for the application if the crankshaft is expected to survive. A thorough understanding of the frequencies and forces that are acting on the crankshaft must be had to ensure you are repairing it properly.

Flywheel

The flywheel is a heavy metal disc that bolts to the rear of the crankshaft of all engines equipped with a manual transmission/transaxle. The flywheel is very heavy, and its momentum helps smooth out engine operation. It maintains crankshaft momentum during the non-power strokes of the piston. Essentially, it stores up rotational energy, which ensures less fluctuation in crankshaft speed between the engine's power strokes. The flywheel is bolted to the rear of the crankshaft (**FIGURE 13-17**). It links the crankshaft to the manual transmission/transaxle, through the clutch assembly. The size of the flywheel varies based on the manufacturer's priorities. Heavier flywheels do a better job of smoothing out the power pulses but do not allow the engine to accelerate as quickly. Lighter flywheels allow much quicker engine acceleration, but they do not smooth out the power pulses as well.

The flywheel rim carries the ring gear. The teeth on the ring gear mesh with the **starter teeth** and are used to crank over the engine. The ring gear is typically attached to the flywheel by an interference fit, so no bolts or welds are used to hold it on. The ring gear is installed by heating it up until it has expanded enough to fit over the edge of the flywheel. Once it cools, it shrinks enough to firmly lock it in place. The face of the flywheel is machined smooth and flat and acts as one of the friction surfaces for the clutch.

FIGURE 13-17 A flywheel with the ring gear still installed. It is usually used on a manual transmission vehicle.

FIGURE 13-18 A flexplate that bolts the torque converter to the engine. It is usually used on an automatic-equipped vehicle.

Flexplate

In automatic transmission engines, a flexplate is used instead of a flywheel (**FIGURE 13-18**). Unlike the flywheel, the flexplate has a torque converter bolted to it. Like the flywheel, the flexplate is constructed as a round disc and mounted to the end of the crankshaft. The flexplate is lighter than a conventional flywheel because the weight of the torque converter performs the function of the flywheel. Since the torque converter is quite heavy, the flexplate can be constructed to be much lighter and thinner than a flywheel. The torque converter is bolted to the flexplate. The flexplate often has a ring gear welded to its edge because of the flexplate's light weight. If an interference fit were used, the flexplate would warp under the pressure created by the fit. Some manufacturers weld the ring gear to the outside of the torque converter and use a smaller flexplate.

Stock Balancer

The **harmonic balancer** is also known as the crankshaft damper. Located on the front of the crankshaft assembly, its function is to reduce vibration from the crankshaft and piston assembly. When the crankshaft deflects or twists slightly (vibrates) from the power pulses, the harmonic balancer absorbs the vibrations and reduces their severity. Minimizing vibration is critical in preventing damage to the crankshaft. Excessive torsional vibration can cause a crankshaft to break in two.

A harmonic balancer is composed of two elements—a mass and an energy-dissipating system, mounted to a central hub. The mass is a heavy circular steel disc that absorbs and releases the energy from the twisting of the crankshaft. A rubber or fluid dissipater is fitted between the circular mass and the hub (**FIGURE 13-19**). The dissipater allows the mass to rotate at a more constant speed than the crankshaft. This helps to even out the torsional vibrations of the crankshaft. Over time, the rubber material can get brittle and hard, letting the mass of the harmonic balancer slip. When the mass slips on the rubber, or if the rubber is brittle and cracked, the harmonic balancer cannot provide the needed dampening effect and needs to be replaced with a new or remanufactured one.

The harmonic balancer is attached to the crankshaft using a **Woodruff key** or a square key and center bolt. The Woodruff key is a metal half-moon–shaped piece that protrudes from a slot near the end of the crankshaft. It fits into a slot in the harmonic balancer center hub and prevents the harmonic balancer from spinning on the end of the crankshaft. Some manufacturers use a square-cut key instead of the Woodruff key. The center bolt is threaded so that it will clamp the front side of the harmonic balancer to the front of the crankshaft.

The accessory drive pulleys are bolted to the front hub of the harmonic balancer. In modern vehicles, there typically is one pulley and one serpentine drive belt attached to the balancer to operate the various accessories. The pulley and belt transfer the power output needed for various systems in the vehicle. Older vehicles generally contained multiple pulleys and belts to operate systems that are now powered electronically or through other means.

High-Performance Balancer

A stock harmonic balancer that is installed from the factory on an internal combustion engine is tuned to the frequency that is made from the combination of the components of the engine. As you change the engine components, the frequency changes, which may cause failure of the stock harmonic balancer (**FIGURE 13-20**). The balancer is spinning at the same rpm as the engine, which may cause it to fail and come apart, destroying the engine. As a technician, you must be aware of these types of issues and recommend or replace the harmonic

K13006 Knowledge of how to balance the crankshaft externally.

FIGURE 13-19 Harmonic balancer.

> ► **TECHNICIAN TIP**
>
> The harmonic balancer may have counterweights for an externally balanced engine. Be sure to replace it with the correct harmonic balancer, or the engine will be out of balance and have a bad vibration.

FIGURE 13-20 This is what happens when the stock damper has failed and has started to come apart.

FIGURE 13-21 A high-performance harmonic damper designed to withstand higher rpms when compared to a stock damper.

K13007 Knowledge of the location of the crankshaft seals.

balancer with a higher performance model for the application. A high-performance balancer is tuned to dampen the varying frequencies that is created by the combination of the engine components and is built with a more robust material so that it can resist the failure that happens to the stock one (**FIGURE 13-21**).

Crankshaft Seals

Crankshaft seals are located at each end of the crankshaft assembly where it projects through the crankcase. The seals help contain the lubricating oils inside the lower part of the crankcase and prevent them from leaking out. A rear main seal is located just after the rear main bearing (**FIGURE 13-22**). In engines that use a timing chain or timing gear, the front main seal is located in the front timing cover. In engines equipped with a timing belt, the front main seal is located in a housing bolted to the front of the engine block (**FIGURE 13-23**) and sits between the block and the timing belt. Most crankshaft seals today are a circular one-piece style with a sealing lip. Some seals use a small spring, called a garter spring, around the inside the sealing lip to tension the lip against the sealing surface of the crankshaft or harmonic balancer.

FIGURE 13-22 Rear main seal.

FIGURE 13-23 Front main seal.

▶ Wrap-Up

Ready for Review

▶ Vehicle power is transferred from the engine to the drivetrain through the crankshaft so that it can be used to propel the vehicle.

▶ The main role of the crankshaft is to transfer the up-and-down strokes of the pistons into rotary motion; the crankshaft is located in the crankcase or lower part or bottom of the block.

▶ Connecting rods are attached to the crankshaft offset journals, called throws. This is where the reciprocating motion of the piston is changed into a rotary motion, which is then used to power the vehicle.

▶ The back end of the crankshaft serves as the mounting area for the flywheel or flexplate, and the front end serves as the

drive for the camshaft and accessories. Many current engines also drive the oil pump off the front of the crankshaft.

▶ Crankshafts are a one-piece casting or forging, or they can be machined out of a billet, which is a solid piece of metal.

▶ Main bearing journals are the part of the crankshaft assembly that mate to the main bearings found at the bottom of the engine block.

▶ Main bearing journals are very smooth and perfectly round so that they can rotate inside the softer main bearings, and they are positioned in a straight line down the center of the crankshaft.

▶ The main journals are ground to manufacturer specifications from the crank core (the rough, unfinished crankshaft assembly or billet).

- ▶ The center of the main journals is referred to as the center-line of the crankshaft.
- ▶ The crankshaft is held in the block by main bearing caps, separated from or attached to one another by an assembly called a girdle.
- ▶ Main bearing caps mate to journal saddles, which are smooth, curved, machined areas located at the bottom of the engine block.
- ▶ The crankshaft main journals rotate in bearing inserts called main bearings. Cross-drilled passages in the crankshaft carry lubricant under pressure from the main bearings to the adjacent crank throws (rod throws).
- ▶ Rod throws, also called rod journals, are located in the offset area of the crankshaft assembly, as opposed to the main journals that sit in a straight line with the centerline of the crankshaft assembly.
- ▶ The crank throws are offset from the centerline of the crankshaft; the amount of offset determines the piston stroke (the distance the piston travels from TDC to BDC).
- ▶ A 90-degree V6 has to have evenly spaced power pulses, so the crankshaft must have connecting rod journals that are splayed. A splayed journal is designed with two connecting rod journals, each one offset from the other. The crank pin, or journal, appears split, but both journals are actually located between the crankshaft throws or counterweights.
- ▶ The balancing of the rotating assembly is done by drilling out or adding weight to the counterweights. A heavy metal called Mallory metal is added to the counterweights during manufacturing to balance the counterweights.
- ▶ Most crankshafts use induction-hardened journal surfaces to give good wear qualities. Induction hardening is a process for hardening the outer surface of a metal structure by rapid heating and cooling.
- ▶ Using the induction hardening process allows the crankshaft to be reground on the main and rod bearing surfaces without grinding through the hardened layer.
- ▶ Crankshaft regrinding is used to smooth and polish the main and rod journals so they can be reused when the engine is being rebuilt.
- ▶ Grinding is an alternative to replacing the entire crankshaft assembly.
- ▶ Nitriding is a surface-hardening heat treatment that introduces nitrogen into the surface of steel at a temperature range of approximately 930°F to 1020°F (499–549°C).
- ▶ Nitriding creates a surface that is harder than that produced by the induction hardening process, but the hardened layer is not as thick. The crankshaft will have to be re-nitrided if the main journals or connecting rod journals have to be reground due to wear.
- ▶ The counterweights on a crankshaft mirror the weight of the piston rod assembly opposite of the counterweight. Balancing the rotating weight allows the engine to rotate with minimal vibration.
- ▶ If the counterweights do not weigh the same as the piston/rod assembly, then a severe rotational vibration will occur, which could then cause part failure.

- ▶ The counterweights are where a machinist adds or subtracts weight to adjust for replacement rod and piston assemblies. This process is called balancing the rotating assembly and can only be completed by a trained machinist.
- ▶ Fillets are rounded corners that allow the rod to self-center so that the force of combustion is being exerted in the center of the crankshaft in order to maximize the use of that force that is machined into the crank pins where they meet the side of the rod throws.
- ▶ Fillets spread the force of the connecting rod.
- ▶ To feed the connecting rod and main bearings, holes drilled through each throw in the crankshaft feed the bearings with the required lubrication so that they are not riding on the crankshaft itself. If they did, the engine would seize.
- ▶ The crankshaft has multiple sealing surfaces that allow for movement of the crankshaft and keep the oil inside and the dirt out.
- ▶ When reconditioning the crankshaft, you must examine these surfaces, as they can develop grooves or pitting because of age or abuse. Bypassing this crucial step could cause you to reinstall a component that has a high probability of leaking in the future.
- ▶ The crankshaft has bolt holes that allow the attachment of the flywheel/flexplate and the harmonic damper/pulley.
- ▶ Keyways are machined into the crankshaft that do not allow the pulley to rotate on the crankshaft, but rotate with the crankshaft.
- ▶ Engines are balanced either internally or externally.
- ▶ A crankshaft can be faulty in several ways. First, it could be warped, which would cause the journals to be forced against the bearings, wearing them out prematurely. Second, the main and rod journals could be excessively worn, leading to too much bearing clearance, which would cause low engine oil pressure. Third, the bolt holes, keyways, and sealing surfaces could be damaged.
- ▶ You must carefully inspect the crankshaft during an engine rebuild.
- ▶ Taper is a wear direction that goes from wide to narrow, causing the crank pin not to be the same size on both ends.
- ▶ The crankshaft will eventually wear out the crankpin that it rides on and will require machining to bring it back into specification.
- ▶ Measuring crankshaft journal out-of-round is a vital measurement.
- ▶ A crankshaft journal that is not a perfect circle can cause premature bearing failure.
- ▶ When measuring out-of-round, you should use a micrometer to get the most precise measurement so that you can evaluate the needs of this particular component. Measurement at three different locations on the journal is needed to determine whether the journal is out of round and requires machining.
- ▶ When you are rebuilding this engine, you must check the crankshaft for straightness for reusing.

▶ If you are unable to determine whether the crankshaft is warped, you should send it out to the machine shop to get it checked.

▶ Crankshaft bearings are the friction bearing type, which means that the surfaces are in sliding contact with one another rather than rolling contact, such as in a wheel bearing.

▶ Connecting rod bearings and the crankshaft main bearings are the split-sleeve type, which means they are in two halves, called bearing inserts or half-shell bearings.

▶ Bearing inserts are made from Babbitt metal bonded to a steel shell. The shell gives rigidity to the bearing, and the Babbitt metal is relatively soft and provides the bearing wear surface.

▶ Crankshaft bearings are split into two halves so that they can be assembled over the corresponding journal. The bearing shells each have a tang built into them that fits into a matching machined notch in the bearing saddle and cap.

▶ The bearing tang prevents the bearing from spinning inside the saddle and cap by butting up against the machined faces of the saddle and cap.

▶ In a main bearing, the upper half of the bearing fits into a machined section of the cylinder block called the main bearing saddle. The main bearing saddle has a notch for the bearing tang to fit within and a drilled oil passage for supplying oil to the bearing and journal.

▶ It is important to match the proper bearing half with its oil hole, as it must align to the oil passage in the main saddle. The lower half is carried in the main bearing cap. The bearing cap also has a notch for the bearing tang to fit into.

▶ The main cap is held in place on the main saddle by main bearing cap bolts.

▶ Main bearing tangs fit into the bearing slot; otherwise, the bearing would be pinched and cause excessive drag on the crankshaft journal, damaging both the bearing and the journal.

▶ The crankshaft uses a thrust bearing, which limits the end play movement of the crankshaft and can be in the form of bearing flanges that are part of one of the main bearings, giving each main bearing insert a U shape. This U-shaped bearing insert fits over a precisely machined main bearing saddle and cap.

▶ The thrust bearing will only fit on the specified bearing support.

▶ A separate two-piece thrust bearing can be fitted into a machined recess in each side of the bearing support and cap, and acts as the thrust bearing for the crankshaft.

▶ Main and rod bearings come standard size, which means that they fit the same size journal as originally manufactured.

▶ Undersized main and rod bearings can be purchased in the following sizes for many engines: 0.001" (0.025 mm), 0.010" (0.25 mm), 0.020" (0.51 mm), and 0.030" (0.76 mm).

▶ If you are replacing the crankshaft, it is important to measure the crankshaft journals and check to make sure they are within the specifications set out by the crankshaft supplier.

▶ The clearance between the crankshaft journal and the bearings must be within the manufacturer's specifications. If there is too little clearance, the oil will not be able to flow through the clearance in the bearing, which can cause the bearing material to overheat and possibly seize to the journal. If the clearance is too large, the oil pressure will be lowered, and the oil will be squished out of the clearance in the bearing, which will allow the journal to come into direct contact with the bearing, creating a knocking noise and extreme wear.

▶ The two most popular engine bearings in use are the trimetal and bimetal types.

▶ Trimetal bearings are made of a lead, tin, and copper overlay that rides next to the crankshaft, followed by a nickel barrier and then a high-fatigue-strength copper and lead lining, which is bonded to a steel backing.

▶ Bimetal bearings are made of an aluminum, tin, and silicon alloy that is bonded on a steel backing.

▶ Embedability of the bearing allows it to be very forgiving when it comes in contact with the spinning parts and allows the bearing to be susceptible to embedding of foreign objects into the material.

▶ Bearing fatigue occurs when the material physically gives out and no longer can be utilized to be a bearing in the engine. When this happens, the only recourse is replacement of the failed component.

▶ "Bearing crush" is a term meaning that the bearing inserts are slightly larger than the bore they fit into and are therefore slightly crushed into position when tightened into place.

▶ To check clearance on main and rod bearings, you can use a micrometer or Plastigage, which is a claylike substance that is engineered to flatten out to create a reading between the bearing and the cap that is easily gauged by the human eye.

▶ The flywheel is a heavy metal disc that bolts to the rear of the crankshaft of all engines equipped with a manual transmission/transaxle.

▶ In automatic transmission engines, a flexplate is used instead of a flywheel, which has a torque converter bolted to it.

▶ The harmonic balancer or damper is located on the front of the crankshaft assembly and reduces vibration from the crankshaft and piston assembly.

▶ When the crankshaft deflects or twists slightly (vibrates) from the power pulses, the harmonic balancer absorbs the vibrations.

▶ The harmonic balancer is attached to the crankshaft using a Woodruff key or a square key and center bolt.

▶ Crankshaft seals are located at each end of the crankshaft assembly where it projects through the crankcase. The seals help contain the lubricating oils inside the lower part of the crankcase and prevent them from leaking out.

Key Terms

bearing crush Indicates a condition in which the bearings are slightly bigger than the journals, which cause them to crush on the ends when the cap is installed and torqued down.

bearing inserts Bearings for the crankshaft and the rod bearings. They come in two pieces and clamp around the components journal.

billet Type of component that is cut out of a large blank instead of being cast into a shape.

crank core Is the rough unfinished crankshaft assembly that has just left the foundry area.

crankcase The lower part of the engine block that houses the crankshaft and rotating assembly.

crank throws Pieces that make up the stroke of the engine and are where the connecting rods attach to the crankshaft.

flexplate A circular component that has the starter ring gear attached to it for starting purposes. It also transfers power from the engine to the torque converter on an automatic transmission.

flywheel A balanced component that has a machined surface where the clutch pressure plate attaches so that power can be transferred from the engine to the manual transmission.

girdle A subassembly of main caps all attached that attaches to the engine block to retain the crankshaft.

harmonic balancer Reduces the vibrations from the harmonics of the engine rotating and the explosions that happen inside the engine.

induction hardened Process done to harden steel by inducting a voltage through the steel to make it heat up, and then quenching it in a coolant.

journal saddles The machined areas in the engine block where the other half of the main bearings sit.

main journal The journals that support the crankshaft inside the cylinder block are called the main journals.

mallory metal Metal added to counterweights to balance them; it is 117% heavier than steel.

nitriding A surface hardening treatment that produces a thin, very hard surface on a steel object.

offset area The area where the rod journals are located.

piston stroke The distance the piston travels from TDC to BDC in the engine block.

rod throws The area where the connecting rod is attached to the crankshaft.

starter teeth The teeth that are a part of the Bendix in the starter and that mesh with the ring gear on the flywheel in order to turn the engine over.

thrust bearing Bearing that controls the forward and rearward movement of the crankshaft in the engine block.

woodruff key A piece of steel that has part of the key in a half moon and the other half straight. Used on shafts to spin a gear or component on the shaft.

Review Questions

1. Which of the following statements describes the basic purpose or main role of a crankshaft in an IC engine?
   a. It converts the reciprocating motion of pistons into rotary motion.
   b. It converts the linear motion of pistons into rotary motion.
   c. It converts the rotary motion of the throws into the reciprocating motion of pistons.
   d. It converts the rotary motion of the throws into the linear motion of pistons.

2. All of the following statements with respect to the crankshaft are true, *except:*
   a. The back end of the crankshaft serves as the mounting area for the flywheel or flexplate.
   b. The crankshaft is assembled from individually manufactured castings.
   c. The crankshaft now also plays a role in creating the spark for combustion.
   d. The crankshaft can also have teeth and notches embedded in it.

3. Which of the following components is driven by the power transmitted to the back of the crankshaft?
   a. Valve train assembly
   b. Camshafts
   c. Drive train
   d. Power steering pump

4. To which of the following components are weights added to or drilled with to balance a rotating assembly in an internally balanced crankshaft?
   a. Flywheel
   b. Harmonic balance
   c. Rod throws
   d. Counterweight

5. Which of the following hardening processes is used for most of the crankshafts?
   a. Induction hardening
   b. Flame hardening
   c. Nitriding
   d. Annealing

6. All of the following are measured to evaluate a crankshaft's straightness, *except:*
   a. taper.
   b. wobble.
   c. out of round.
   d. warpage.

7. Which of the following instruments is used to check the precise measurement in the case of an out of round condition on a crankshaft?
   a. Bevel angle protractor
   b. Spirit level
   c. Micrometer
   d. Radius gauge

8. The combination of metals which is used in constructing environment friendly crankshaft bearings is:
   a. lead, tin, and copper
   b. lead, tin, and aluminum

c. aluminum, silicon alloy, and copper

d. aluminum, tin, and silicon alloy

9. All of the following statements are true with respect to the components connected to the crankshaft, *except:*

   a. The flywheel maintains the crankshaft momentum during non-power strokes.

   b. A ring gear is attached to the flywheel through interference fit.

   c. An automatic transmission uses a flexplate instead of a flywheel.

   d. A flexplate is usually heavier than a flywheel.

10. Choose the correct statement with respect to the balancing of the crankshaft externally.

   a. The crankshaft is balanced externally with the help of a flywheel.

   b. The crankshaft is balanced with help of a flexwheel.

   c. A dissipater allows to balance the torsional vibration of the crankshaft.

   d. The harmonic balancer helps in reducing the effect of counterweight inside the crankshaft.

ASE Technician A/Technician B Style Questions

1. Technician A says that Mallory metal is used to help balance the counterweights on a crankshaft. Technician B states that the connecting rods are connected to the main bearings of the crankshaft. Who is correct?

   a. Tech A

   b. Tech B

   c. Both A and B

   d. Neither A nor B

2. Technician A states that bearing crush is a thing that should be avoided as it causes damage to the bearing. Technician B says that a thrust bearing controls the forward and rearward movement of the crankshaft in the cylinder block. Who is correct?

   a. Tech A

   b. Tech B

   c. Both A and B

   d. Neither A nor B

3. Technician A states that when utilizing a flexplate, the engine is meant to be in a vehicle that has an automatic transmission. Technician B says that the starter uses the ring gear that is a part of the flexplate or flywheel to start the vehicle. Who is correct?

   a. Tech A

   b. Tech B

   c. Both A and B

   d. Neither A nor B

4. Technician A says that oil passages in the crankshaft are fed by the pushrods in the valvetrain. Technician B states that the counterweights of the crankshaft help to offset the weight of the piston and connecting rod assembly. Who is correct?

   a. Technician A

   b. Tech B

c. Both A and B

d. Neither A nor B

5. Technician A says that a billet crankshaft is superior in strength to a cast crankshaft. Technician B says that the rod journals are offset to the main journals on a crankshaft. Who is correct?

   a. Tech A

   b. Tech B

   c. Both A and B

   d. Neither A nor B

6. Technician A says that when replacing a crankshaft, the technician should inspect the reluctor wheel to make sure it is the same as the original one. Technician B says that using the wrong crankshaft could cause the engine to go into an overspeed condition. Who is correct?

   a. Tech A

   b. Tech B

   c. Both A and B

   d. Neither A nor B

7. Technician A says that the crankcase is could be part of the engine block. Technician B says that an aluminum engine doesn't have engine bearings. Who is correct?

   a. Tech A

   b. Tech B

   c. Both A and B

   d. Neither A nor B

8. Technician A says that crankshafts that utilize fillets on the mains and rod bearing throws help strengthen the crankshaft and center the connecting rod. Technician B says that Plastigage is a good way to check crankshaft thrust. Who is correct?

   a. Tech A

   b. Tech B

   c. Both A and B

   d. Neither A nor B

9. Technician A says that checking for cracks in a crankshaft is done by pressure checking. Technician B says that you cannot machine crankshafts to bring them back into serviceable condition. Who is correct?

   a. Tech A

   b. Tech B

   c. Both A and B

   d. Neither A nor B

10. Technician A says that when measuring a crankshaft, you should measure each journal for taper. Technician B states that excess out-of-round requires machining to correct the issue. Who is correct?

   a. Tech A

   b. Tech B

   c. Both A and B

   d. Neither A nor B

CHAPTER 14

Pistons, Rings, and Connecting Rods

NATEF Tasks

- N14001 Inspect, measure, and install piston rings.

Knowledge Objectives

After reading this chapter, you will have:

- K14001 Knowledge of types of pistons.
- K14002 Knowledge of different applications of piston types.
- K14003 Knowledge of different types of piston pins.

- K14004 Knowledge of types of piston rings.
- K14005 Knowledge of different types of connecting rods.

Skills Objectives

- S14001 Fit piston rings.
- S14002 Fit pistons to connecting rods with full floating pins.

- S14003 Mark connecting rod caps to keep them with the main body.

You Are the Automotive Technician

You have disassembled the engine, and the machine shop has machined the cylinder bores 0.040" over. What type of piston rings must you get to install the pistons into the cylinder bore?

1. Standard piston rings, as the engine is not being used for performance applications.
2. Oversized piston rings because the bore is no longer the stock bore dimensions.
3. Ductile piston rings, as this engine will operate mostly on the street and will not see any racing action.

▶ Introduction

The piston and connecting rod assemblies are the main components of the engine that convert the chemical energy into mechanical energy to create a motorized vehicle. These parts are some of the most abused pieces in an internal combustion engine and must be utilized correctly to gain the most usage out of them. This chapter goes through the different aspects of the pistons and connecting rods so that you, as the technician, can use this information to assemble an engine that will stand the tests that the customer puts on it.

▶ Pistons

K14001 Knowledge of types of pistons.

The piston fits in the cylinder like a close-fitting, movable plug. The clearance between the piston and the cylinder wall is typically within a few thousandths of an inch, and on some current model engines it can be less than a thousandth of an inch. A good way to think of the piston is as the "movable floor of the combustion chamber." When the air-fuel mixture burns in the combustion chamber, it creates pressure that pushes the piston down on the power stroke. The job of the piston is to extract the thermal energy from the burning fuel and convert it into mechanical energy, which can be used to power the vehicle. Accordingly, it is critical that the piston fit the cylinder with close tolerance so that the pressurized gases cannot easily leak past it. The piston, with its connecting rod and bearing, transfers the force of the power stroke to the crankshaft.

Types of Pistons

K14002 Knowledge of different applications of piston types.

The three main types of pistons available for automotive use are cast, hypereutectic, and forged. The **cast piston** is the entry-level model that is usually utilized in stock applications that are not boosted, as these types of pistons will work for a naturally aspirated engine. If the engine is intended to have a some performance required of it, the builder could move up to the **hypereutectic** line, which has more silicon content, creating a harder piston that resists abuse better than a cast piston does. The problem with these pistons is that they are brittle when used out of their specification range. The **forged piston** is used with boosted applications where durability and heat are required to make the engine last. The forged piston is usually the most expensive of the pistons, as the production process is different and the material is more expensive (**FIGURE 14-1**).

FIGURE 14-1 Cast piston, hypereutectic piston, and forged piston.

Control of Heat in Pistons

The piston must stand up to great heat and pressure. All pistons expand as they heat up. Because there is more metal near the wrist pin, this area tends to expand more. To allow for this, many pistons are machined into a slightly oval shape in a process called cam grinding, and the piston is called a cam-ground piston. As an oval piston heats up to operating temperature, it expands and becomes round.

Other methods that allow, and help to control, piston expansion involve using steel struts or ribs, expansion slots in the skirt of the piston, or slots called heat dams that restrict movement of the heat. In the first method, steel struts or ribs are built into the piston assembly. Their sole purpose is to control expansion by slowing heat flow and stiffening the piston. However, they cause more piston weight. In the second method, expansion slots are cut vertically into the piston skirt. As the piston expands, the slots are slowly closed. The third method uses a horizontal slot cut directly beneath the piston head. The "T" slot acts like a dam or retardant, preventing heat from traveling down from the top of the piston.

Piston Head Shape

The shape of the top of the piston depends on the shape of its combustion chamber and its compression ratio. Combustion chambers vary in shape, depending on the manufacturer and type of engine for which it is intended. The top of the piston forms the bottom of the engine's combustion chamber. The compression ratio is the difference between the volume in the combustion chamber above the piston when the piston is at **bottom dead center (BDC)** and the volume of the combustion chamber above the piston when the piston is at **top dead center (TDC)**. The compression ratio can be changed by using a piston with a different head design or a cylinder head with a different chamber size. This is because the sizes of the piston head and chamber affect the ratio between the volume at BDC and the volume at TDC within the combustion chamber. A taller piston head takes up some of the available volume in the combustion chamber as compared to a shallower piston head. The automotive engineer or manufacturer selects the correct piston head shape for the performance level desired.

In designing an engine, the automotive engineer creates the design with a particular piston head in mind. The piston head must be able to work in accordance with the rest of the piston assembly, as well as with the structure of the combustion chamber and the valve-train assembly, because they all work together in obtaining the engineer's goals for engine output and performance. Different piston heads are used to accommodate variations in combustion chamber and valvetrain designs. Variations in piston head shapes can also be used to change the compression ratio. The top of the piston may be flat, concave, dome shaped, or recessed (**FIGURE 14-2**), and it can have one to five valve relief areas. Valve relief areas are used to prevent pistons from hitting the valves, or vice versa. Depending on the needs and shape of the engine, valve relief areas may be used on just one side of the piston head or on both.

There are two processes in manufacturing pistons: forging and casting. The forged piston is the stronger and more costly of the two. In forging a piston, metal molecules are compressed into a denser area. This makes the piston stronger and more desirable for diesel engines and

FIGURE 14-2 Piston shapes. **A.** Flat. **B.** Concave. **C.** Dome. **D.** Recessed.

racing applications. With the stronger forged piston, the higher compression ratios that create hotter exhaust gases and higher pressures can be used without piston damage.

There are two versions of the cast piston: (1) cast aluminum with steel struts and (2) cast aluminum with 16% to 19% silicon, which is called a hypereutectic piston. Steel struts are used to help control the flow of heat from the combustion process and can be embedded into the piston assembly to help control piston expansion. Hypereutectic pistons are stronger than 100% aluminum pistons and are used in many applications. Although the cost of hypereutectic pistons is considerably less than forged pistons, the trade-off is that forged pistons are stronger than hypereutectic pistons. Another advantage of hypereutectic pistons is that the clearance between the piston and the engine block cylinder is extremely small, which allows for a tighter fit of the piston assembly inside the cylinder as compared to all other piston types. The smaller clearance allows (requires) the use of lower viscosity oils that can provide lubrication between the closer running components.

Forced Induction

Forced induction engines require a special piston to handle the increased cylinder pressures that are a result of the intake pressurization. The type of pistons that are used in these applications are the forged aluminum alloy type as they have the molecular structure needed to handle the increased abuse. Besides having a stronger piston, the compression ratio is adjusted to compensate for the increase capacity that the engine is expected to handle.

Gasoline Direct Injection

A **gasoline direct injection (GDI)** engine has pistons that are not designed like your typical piston; they have to be made for the configuration that is present in that particular engine. A GDI engine has the injector pressed into the cylinder so that it is spraying the fuel directly into the cylinder at a precise time. Because the fuel has to be dispersed when it hits, the top of the piston is designed with a particular dish or dome to direct the fuel to the proper place in the cylinder so that complete combustion can occur (**FIGURE 14-3**). These engines can run from 11–14:1 compression ratio on 87 octane fuel, which allows for increased efficiency and decreased emissions. The reason that these types of engines can do this is because of the precise control of fuel injection, variable valve timing and ignition control. Replacing or removing the piston requires that you reinstall it in the correct cylinder and on the correct bank, or the engine may not run optimally.

Piston Coatings

It is not uncommon today to see pistons that have a coating. The most popular is a black moly, which is a molybdenum disulfide, coating on the piston skirt, which helps reduce friction between the piston skirt area and the cylinder wall (**FIGURE 14-4**). Ceramic coating is also

FIGURE 14-3 What differences in design between the GDI piston and the conventional cast piston can you distinguish?

FIGURE 14-4 A piston with a coating on the skirt to decrease the friction that is created as the piston moves in the cylinder bore.

available. Some manufacturers and aftermarket companies coat the top of the piston with a ceramic coating, which creates a thermal barrier. The ceramic coating prevents the piston metal from absorbing heat as quickly, thus allowing the piston to operate at a lower temperature and withstand greater combustion temperatures without deforming. It also increases the efficiency of the engine by retaining more heat in the combustion chamber rather than transferring it through the piston to the cooling system. Designing the exhaust system to take advantage of the faster exhausting of gases due to the increase in exhaust gas temperature can aid in the scavenging effect and help the engine breathe more efficiently.

Piston Pins

The piston pin (wrist pin) is made of steel and is hollow in the center to reduce weight, thereby reducing the engine's reciprocating mass (**FIGURE 14-5**). The wrist pin design can be a **floating pin** or a **press-fit pin**. In both cases, the pin is slightly smaller than the pin bore in the piston, and the piston is free to move on the pin. With the floating pin design, the piston pin floats in both the piston and the rod, with the piston pin being held in place by snap rings on each side of the piston.

FIGURE 14-5 The piston pin is installed to connect the piston with the connecting rod before it is installed inside the cylinder block.

K14003 Knowledge of different types of piston pins.

With the press-fit pin design, the piston is held in place by a wrist pin that is pressed into the connecting rod. The small end of the connecting rod uses an interference fit with the wrist pin to lock the pin firmly in place. The wrist pin is installed into the connecting rod by pressing it in or by heating the end of the rod with a rod heater. The rod heater heats up the small end of the connecting rod, expanding the size of the hole just enough for the pin to slide into the connecting rod. When it cools, the pin is firmly locked into the rod.

Full-Floating Pin

The full-floating pin is a slide fit in both the piston and the connecting rod bore. The pin is retained by a pair of snap rings. Note that some snap rings are directional, which means they must be installed with the correct side facing the wrist pin. Otherwise, the snap ring can work its way out of its groove and score the cylinder wall, destroying the engine. Install one snap ring on one side of the piston (**FIGURE 14-6**), and then lubricate the pin area of the piston, the connecting rod, and the pin. Next, slide the piston pin in place, and secure the pin with the other snap ring (**FIGURE 14-7**).

Semi-Floating

Most engines have semi-floating, or wrist, pins, in which case the machine shop will have already attached the pistons to the rods. The semi-floating pin moves freely in the piston

FIGURE 14-6 Installing the snap ring.

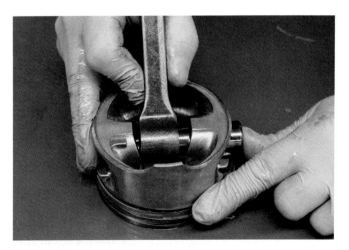

FIGURE 14-7 Sliding the piston pin into the piston and rod.

FIGURE 14-8 The fixture that helps you install the piston pin into the connecting rod.

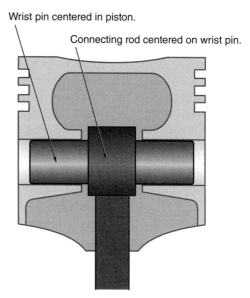

Wrist pin centered in piston.

Connecting rod centered on wrist pin.

FIGURE 14-9 The piston pin installed in the piston and the connecting rod. If it is installed incorrectly, engine damage could result.

bore but is press fit in the connecting rod bore. The preferred method for installing the wrist pin is to use a rod heater. Adjust the setting fixture where the piston pin needs to stop (**FIGURE 14-8**). When installed correctly, the wrist pin is centered in the connecting rod (**FIGURE 14-9**). Make sure the rod heater is hot; lubricate the piston pin bore with a thin film of automatic transmission fluid (ATF). The small end of the connecting rod will have a slight glow from heat; slide the piston pin in, using a mandrel or pin press, and let cool.

Pin Offset

Each piston has a major thrust face and a minor thrust face. The side of the piston that is forced into the cylinder wall on the power stroke is the major thrust face. The side of the piston that is forced into the cylinder wall on the compression stroke is the minor thrust face. Most piston pin bores are not centered in the piston, but are set slightly off-center of the piston. Having the pin offset preloads the piston toward the minor thrust side of the piston. The piston pin is offset because the connecting rod changes its angle as the piston transitions between the compression and power strokes, and the piston moves from the minor thrust face to the major thrust face. If the clearances between the piston and the cylinder wall become too great, the transfer from one piston skirt to the other can cause a condition known as piston slap. Piston slap causes an audible noise that is most noticeable when the pistons are cold and at their smallest diameter, and it also increases piston/cylinder wear. Piston slap occurs as the piston pivots on the pin near TDC, when the piston is forced to the thrust side of the cylinder at the top of the power stroke. Offsetting the wrist pin in the piston helps reduce piston slap.

Compression Ratio

Compression ratio relates to how tightly the air-fuel mixture is compressed in the combustion chamber. The tighter the air-fuel mixture, the more power that can be extracted from a given amount of air and fuel. Unfortunately, increased compression ratios can cause engine damage. Increased compression ratios increase compression pressures, thereby increasing the temperature of the mixture within the combustion chamber as it is being compressed. If the mixture gets too hot, it will ignite by itself before it should, which is known as preignition or detonation. This is very hazardous to the engine, so compression ratios must not be raised too high. Typical compression ratios for stock gasoline engines run between 8:1 and 10.5:1. High-performance vehicles can be around 12:1. Diesel engines run around 20:1.

To calculate the compression ratio, divide the volume of the combustion chamber above the piston at BDC by the volume of the combustion chamber above the piston at TDC. For example, a cylinder that has a total combustion chamber volume of 50 cubic inches at BDC and 5 cubic inches at TDC has a compression ratio of 50 to 5, or 10 to 1, which is written 10:1. In other words, the piston is compressing 50 units of volume into 5 units of volume (**FIGURE 14-10**).

Compression ratio can be raised in several ways. First, a taller piston or one with a dome will reduce the volume of the combustion chamber at both TDC and BDC, thus raising the ratio. Another option is to use cylinder heads with smaller chambers so that the mixture is squeezed into a smaller space. Likewise, machining the cylinder head surface or using a thinner head gasket increases the compression ratios slightly. Also, using a crankshaft with longer throws increases the engine's stroke, which increases how high and low the piston travels in the cylinder, raising the compression ratio but also changing engine size. Finally, boring out the cylinders and using larger pistons will make the cylinder volume larger so the compression ratio will be increased, but this method also changes engine size.

What we have just discussed is theoretical compression ratio, which does not take into consideration valve timing. We have assumed that the intake valve closed at BDC, which would mean that compression could start at BDC. In reality, intake valves close after BDC, so compression cannot start until the intake valve is fully closed. Complete closure could be substantially after BDC in the case of a high-performance camshaft, and the piston has already moved partially up the cylinder, lowering the effective compression ratio. So the effective compression ratio is the volume above the piston when the intake valve just closes, compared to the volume above the piston at TDC.

▶ Piston Rings

Piston rings are thin, metallic, C-shaped rings set into grooves located around the piston skirt that fill the space between the piston and the cylinder wall. Generally, three to four rings are used per piston. The first two rings are called **compression rings** and are designed to seal and create a close fit between the piston and the cylinder wall (**FIGURE 14-11**). The other rings are specially designed to hold a small amount of lubrication oil to lubricate the piston and cylinder walls. They also scrape excessive oil from the walls and release it back to the crankcase as needed. The compression rings are typically splash lubricated by the oil released onto the cylinder wall from the oil leaking out of the connecting rod bearing. Rings can be square, tapered, flat, or slanted on the ring surface. The different ring designs are available so that the best possible fit can be created between pistons and cylinder walls of different manufacturers.

The most common piston arrangement has two thin compression ring grooves and one larger oil ring groove; they are known collectively as **piston ring grooves**. The sides of the grooves, called **ring lands**, support the piston rings. The piston ring grooves are located between the top of the piston and the piston pin. The width and depth of the piston ring groove dictate the width and depth of the piston rings that should be used.

Oil rings have two rails separated by a groove around the outer surface of the ring, giving them a U-shaped cross section. The groove holds a small amount of oil and directs excess oil back to the crankcase. Because of this U-shaped cross section, oil rings can be a one-piece design or a three-piece design with two side rails and an expander. Both styles perform the same job; they just look different (**FIGURE 14-12**).

Compression Ring

Compression rings must seal against compression loss during the compression and power strokes. Compression loss results in low compression pressures and excessive amounts of

FIGURE 14-10 Break the oil pan loose.

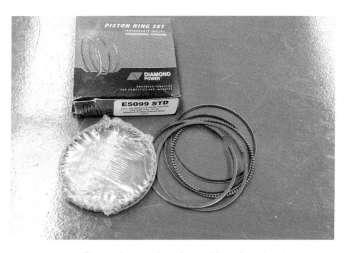

FIGURE 14-11 Piston rings ready to be positioned on the pistons before installation.

K14004 Knowledge of types of piston rings.

N14001 Inspect, measure, and install piston rings.

S14001 Fit piston rings.

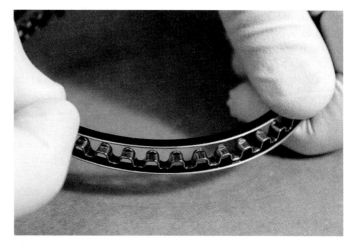

FIGURE 14-12 Oil rings. **A.** One-piece design. **B.** Three-piece design.

blowby gases into the crankcase, leading to reduced combustion efficiency, less engine power, more emissions, and poor fuel economy. The compression ring is typically made of cast iron. It is subject to wear due to its movement against the cylinder wall. To enhance the longevity of the compression rings, the rings may have a coating on the sealing surface. The ring coating could be made of chromium, nitride, plasma, molybdenum, or a ceramic material.

Piston rings are not a complete circle; they are split and must have a specified piston ring end gap. This **ring gap** allows the piston rings to be expanded so they can fit over the ring lands when the rings are being installed on the piston. The gap also allows the piston rings to expand when they heat up as the engine is operating. The small gap should almost close when the engine is up to full operating temperature, but should not close entirely. Insufficient end gap results in the compression ring binding, breaking, twisting, or scoring the cylinder walls when the compression ring expands as the engine warms up. Conversely, if the gap is too large, then compression pressure will be lost through the gap, which leads to excessive blowby and lost efficiency. Thus, technicians measure the piston ring end gap to make sure the gap is within the specified tolerances.

The piston ring end gaps should be staggered around the piston when the piston rings are installed. Staggering prevents a straight path for the compression or gases to escape. If the path is too straight and smooth, the speed of gas escape is far too rapid, increasing the blowby gases. There must also be side clearance between the compression rings and the ring lands. The clearance prevents the piston ring from becoming stuck in the groove when it expands due to combustion heat. The ring must also have back clearance inside the piston groove to accommodate heat expansion of the piston.

The compression ring is built to have static pressure, with its diameter larger than the piston, thus creating ring tension so that the piston ring is forced against the cylinder wall to help provide a good seal. It must not have too much tension or it will wear out prematurely, but it needs to have enough tension to maintain an adequate seal. The compression rings must be able to seal under all conditions found in the combustion chamber—vacuum during the intake stroke and high pressure during the compression and power strokes. Some compression rings and pistons are designed so that combustion pressure can get behind the compression ring and force it out against the cylinder wall during the power stroke, increasing its sealing effectiveness (**FIGURE 14-13**). This design also allows the compression rings to have a smaller amount of static pressure, which reduces piston ring drag and improves fuel efficiency. It also means that most compression rings have a top and bottom and will not function correctly if installed improperly.

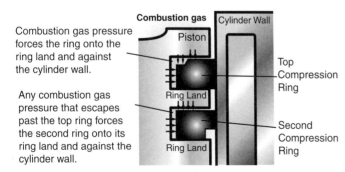

Combustion gas pressure forces the ring onto the ring land and against the cylinder wall.

Any combustion gas pressure that escapes past the top ring forces the second ring onto its ring land and against the cylinder wall.

FIGURE 14-13 Combustion pressure forcing the top compression ring against the cylinder.

Scraper Ring

The **scraper ring** is usually positioned second on the piston, and its main purpose is to scrape the excess oil off the cylinder walls so that it doesn't get burnt in the combustion chamber (**FIGURE 14-14**). Another reason that we want the oil off the cylinder wall is to help transfer the heat to the oil sump and away from the cylinder. The second job of the scraper ring is to help stop blowby of the compression ring so that the crankcase doesn't become over pressurized, which would cause gaskets to fail and the engine to start leaking oil. This ring is designed to remove oil residue from the cylinder walls, so installation on the piston must be correct or the cylinder could have an oil consumption issue that would have to be addressed.

Oil Control Ring

Oil control rings prevent excessive oil from working up into the combustion chambers. The oil control ring is designed to leave a film of lubricating oil less than a thousandth of an inch thick on the cylinder wall. It can be a one-piece ring that depends on its own tension to hold it against the cylinder walls (**FIGURE 14-15**), or it can be a three-piece ring with two side rails and an expander, which provide the tension for the side rails. Both styles have slots or holes in the oil ring and the piston ring groove (**FIGURE 14-16**). These holes allow oil return to the crankcase, and in some pistons they also direct oil to the wrist pin. This movement of oil helps with the cooling process. On modern engines, most oil rings are made of steel. The expander is made of thin steel with a series of crimps or folds in the metal that give it an outward spring force. The expander has a top and a bottom groove that hold the solid side rails and together make up the oil control ring. The side rails depend on the expander to hold them against the cylinder walls.

To fit the piston rings, follow the steps in **SKILL DRILL 14-1**.

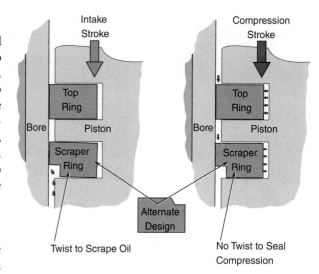

FIGURE 14-14 A scraper ring. Do you see how the ring has an edge to scrape the cylinder wall?

Material

What piston rings are made of depends on the intended application of the engine. Using the wrong piston ring in the wrong type of engine could lead to premature failure, which would then require a rebuild to bring back into service. Matching the type of material to the type of engine will allow for long service life of the engine.

Cast Iron

The cast iron piston ring is a ring that can be used when the engine will not be overused, over-revved, or otherwise abused. These rings are very durable when used in the correct application, but when exposed to an environment that they are not designed to operate in, degradation of the rings will occur.

Ductile Iron

These types of pistons rings are another economical option like cast iron rings; the only major difference is that they are twice as strong as cast iron rings, but with a lot of the same properties. So these rings are used in applications where they are more prone to abuse.

Steel

Steel rings are roughly twice as strong as ductile iron rings but are not compatible with cast iron cylinder walls and have to be coated to survive in a cast iron engine. The steel is harder than the cast iron, causing it to destroy the cylinder wall over time. These rings can take more abuse than the iron variants discussed above.

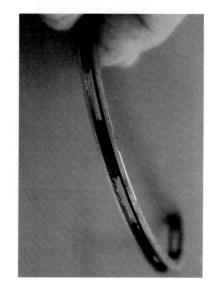

FIGURE 14-15 This is a one piece oil control ring, it has holes in it that align with the holes in the piston skirt to direct oil back to the crankcase.

FIGURE 14-16 This is a three piece oil control ring that has a top and bottom ring and an expander in the middle that allows oil to drain through the piston back to the crankcase.

SKILL DRILL 14-1 Fitting the Piston Rings

1. Install the expander ring and scraper rails. Check that your piston rings are in order and hold the rod and piston assembly in a vise. The ring kit should have a label stating what each ring in the package is.

2. The first ring to go on is the oil expander ring, which slips into the bottom groove. Make sure the ends of the expander ring do not overlap. Now install the first of the oil scraper rails, which go above and below the oil expander ring. Start it about 45 degrees to one side of the expander gap, and slide it in between the roof of the groove and the top of the expander ring. When the edge of the ring is in, slowly work it clockwise around the piston. Slow down when you get to the other side of the piston. The edge of the ring could scratch the side of the piston, so grasp it firmly, and carefully pull it slightly away from the piston; then drop the end of it in place above the expander ring. Start the other scraper rail about 45 degrees to the other side of the expander gap, and slide it into the bottom slot. Work this ring around in the opposite direction, guiding it past the top scraper and into the bottom groove as you go. Pull it away slightly at the end, and drop it into its groove. Double-check that the expander ring gap is not overlapped. If it is, use two paper clips or picks to pull the rings apart until they click into alignment with the rails. It is important to rotate the rings now and make sure nothing is stuck or crooked.

3. Install the piston rings. The packaging or instruction sheet should tell you which compression rings are which. Find the ring for the lower groove first. Look closely at the ring. There is usually a label on one side of the ring, such as a dot, a pip mark, a "T," or some other marking. The marked side of the ring should face up. Hold the ring expander with one hand, and steady the ring with the other. Expand it only enough to get the ring to slip down past the first ring groove and into its place in the second groove at the 3 o'clock position. It should rotate freely. Using the same technique as earlier, expand the top compression ring just enough, with the top mark facing up, and lower the ring into its place at the 9 o'clock position. Lubricate the upper bearing halves with oil or assembly lube. Repeat the process for the rest of the pistons in the tray.

Continued

4. Inspect the installation of the piston rings to make sure that the gaps are 45 degrees away from one another so that compression will not be directed to the crankcase.

5. Oil the whole assembly, and label the piston face with the cylinder that the piston belongs in so that when you assemble the engine, the piston will move in the right cylinder.

Chrome-Coated Rings

The chrome-coated ring can be used for the increased wear resistance that chrome offers. This ring has a high resistance to scuffing and, in the correct application, is preferred over other rings.

Ceramic-Coated Rings

The ceramic-coated ring is one that has a higher wear resistance than chrome-coated rings and it is very resistant to extreme temperatures. These rings are usually higher in cost than the other types but offer increased durability. Again, match the ring with the application.

Design

The design of the piston ring is dependent on the use of the engine, the amount of pressure built up in the combustion chamber, and the environment that the piston ring is going to be operating in. The wrong design could lead to engine failure and cause the engine to require overhaul to return it to service.

Barrel-Cut Rings

The barrel-cut ring is tapered out from the bottom and the top into a flat surface, which, if looked at from a cross-sectional view, looks like a barrel. This type of ring aids in sealing the cylinder and allows room for the excess oil buildup to dissipate so that it will not cause an issue with the sealing of the ring.

Normal-Cut Rings

The normal-cut ring is sometimes referred to as the rectangular ring, which is usually utilized as the top piston ring in many gasoline and diesel engines. This is a very common ring that is used in standard power applications.

Angle-Cut Rings

The angle-cut ring can have an angle on the top edge or the bottom edge, which creates a torsional tension that makes the ring seat without the high pressures that the conventional rings require to seat in the cylinder. This allows the ring to start working more quickly than the conventional ring that needs the pressure buildup to create the sealing effect.

Step-Cut Rings

The step-cut piston ring is one that has interlocking ring lands where the gap would be on a conventional piston ring. The usage for this ring would be an application that has a higher pressure combustion chamber than normal; they are usually used for blown or turbocharged applications.

Oversize

Oversized piston rings are used when the engine cylinders have been bored out to a larger diameter to clean up the imperfections in the cylinder walls. The oversized ring fits the oversized piston, which is usually 0.010" or more larger than the stock bore on the engine.

K14005 Knowledge of different types of connecting rods.

S14002 Fit pistons to connecting rods with full floating pins.

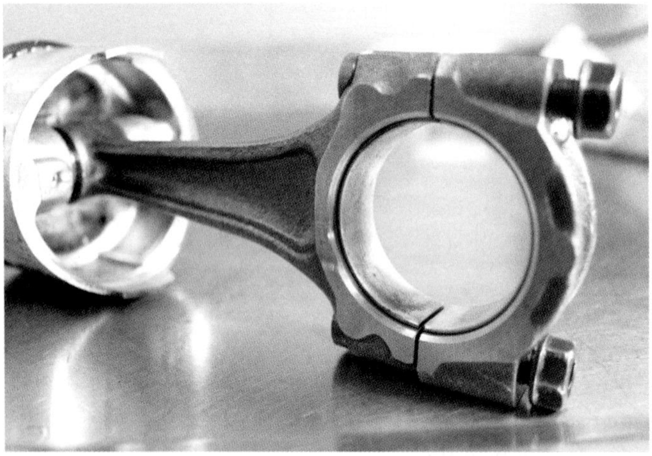

FIGURE 14-17 Connecting rod.

▶ Connecting Rods

The connecting rod connects the piston to the crankshaft. It has a small end that houses the piston pin and connects it to the piston assembly. The middle of the rod, called the beam area, transmits the power flow to the bottom of the rod. At the bottom, or big, end, the connecting rod houses the bearing inserts and attaches firmly around the crankshaft (**FIGURE 14-17**).

In order for the connecting rod to fit over the crankshaft rod journal, the big end is split in half; the bottom half is removable and is called the **rod cap**. The big end of the connecting rod is connected to the crankshaft rod journal; the rod cap bolts or nuts are then torqued (using manufacturer specifications) in place, using a torque wrench. The crankshaft rod journal is an area machined to the highest quality. It contains an oil hole for lubrication of the rod bearings. A thin layer of oil coats the surface, and a bearing insert rides on top of the film of oil.

The crankshaft rod throw (distance from the center of the crankshaft main journals to the center of the rod journals) determines the stroke of the piston. As the crankshaft rotates, the crankshaft journal rotates on bearing inserts inside the big end of the connecting rod and is part of the **rotating assembly**. The connecting rod transfers the reciprocating motion and force of the piston to the rotating crankshaft.

The big end of the rod is where the rod bearings are inserted. There is a notch in the connecting rod and a notch in the rod cap. The rod bearings have tangs on the end; these tangs are inserted in the notch of the rod and the rod cap. The tang in the bearing shell of the rod cap butts up against the parting surface of the rod. The tang in the rod butts up against the rod cap. When the rod cap is torqued into place, the tangs are able to prevent the rod bearing halves from spinning inside the big end of the rod. Some connecting rods and rod bearings have a hole that sprays oil out to lubricate the cylinder wall, wrist pin, and camshaft when the hole lines up with the lubricating hole in the rod journal. When installing the rod bearings, the lubricating hole in the connecting rod must line up to the hole in the bearing shell.

Types of Connecting Rods

Most stock connecting rods are shaped like an I-beam down the length of the connecting rod, but some aftermarket performance connecting rods have an H shape down the length of the connecting rod. The H-shaped rod is the stronger of the two. Most connecting rods have extra metal on each end (balance pads) for balancing. There are four types of connecting rods: cast, forged, aluminum, and powdered metal. Regardless of how the connecting rod is manufactured, when the rod cap is taken off, it must go back on the same connecting rod; it is not interchangeable. It must also be reinstalled in the exact orientation. The best process to make sure the caps and connecting rods do not get mixed up is to mark them close to the parting line.

S14003 Mark connecting rod caps to keep them with the main body.

Materials

In the manufacturing of connecting rods, most are made using a metal casting process wherein molten metal is poured into a mold. Down the center of the connecting rod mold, there is an imperfection in the shape of a line separating one-half of the rod from the other. This mold line is referred to as a casting line and can be used to identify whether a rod was created by the metal casting process. The cast rod is the most common connecting rod style. Rods manufactured by this process are inexpensive, yet strong enough to meet the requirements for most small truck, passenger car, and small engine applications.

The other method for manufacturing connecting rods is through a forging process. In this process, metal is hammered by large presses into the rod shape. The hammering squeezes the molecular structure of the metal tightly, creating an extremely strong, durable rod. These rods are referred to as forged connecting rods. Forged rods are much stronger than cast rods and are usually used in high-performance applications. However, because the process is more labor intensive, forged rods are more costly to manufacture, resulting in a higher price for the buyer. To identify this type of rod, look on the side of the rod beam for a wide flat line where the rod was forged.

The aluminum rod is used in some drag race cars. It is lighter and wider than cast or forged rods. The extra width strengthens the rod, enabling it to withstand the pressures and forces applied to the connecting rod and crankshaft assembly during the short, intense duration of a drag race. Frequent replacement of aluminum connecting rods is necessary because of their lack of durability. They are not appropriate for endurance race cars, aircraft, or general-purpose vehicles.

The powdered metal rod is the most recent technology. The rod starts with a precise amount of powdered metal, which includes iron, copper, carbon, and other agents. The powder is placed in a die and forged (pressed) under great pressure; then it is put through a sintering process, where the rod is heated up until it almost melts. Sintering, a process used in metal fabrication, uses high temperatures, ranging from about 2000°F to 2500°F (1093°C to 1371°C), to melt several powdered metals into one high-quality, metallurgically bonded metal alloy. It is an old process that provides excellent surface finish and allows for the creation of hard-to-make parts. Additionally, the end alloy is stronger than the original individual metals. Some of the benefits are that the rod is lighter than the typical cast and forged rod and that approximately 40% less metal is used, compared to a standard forged rod. The powdered metal rod meets or exceeds the tensile and yield strength of forged rods, and the cost is considerably less.

The powdered metal rod is then fracture split at the big end, giving more adhesion at the parting line of the two halves of the connecting rod assembly (**FIGURE 14-18**) than the machined cap and rod. This is also a time saver, eliminating the machining involved on the parting line between the rod and the rod cap. With the fracture-split design, the rod cap is a precision fit on the rod, and the rod bolt is not relied upon to align the cap to the rod. The fracture-split connecting rod is a superior rod to the machined-cap type, as the metal breaks at the weakest point and is more uniform in molecular structure than the cut type. This type of design is being utilized in a large number of applications and is not unique to this type of rod.

FIGURE 14-18 Mating surfaces of a powdered metal fracture-split rod.

► Wrap-Up

Ready for Review

► The piston and connecting rod assemblies are the main components of the engine, and they convert the chemical energy into mechanical energy to create a motorized vehicle.

► The piston fits in the cylinder like a close-fitting, movable plug. The clearance between the piston and the cylinder wall is typically within a few thousandths of an inch, and on some current model engines, it can be less than a thousandth of an inch.

► The three main types of pistons available for automotive use are cast, hypereutectic, and forged.

► The cast piston is the entry-level model that is usually utilized in stock applications that are not boosted, as these types of pistons will work for a naturally aspirated engine.

► A performance may need a hypereutectic piston, which has more silicon content, creating a harder piston that resists abuse better than a cast piston does. The problem with these pistons is that they are brittle when used out of their specification range.

► The forged piston is used with boosted applications, where durability and heat are required to make the engine last.

► All pistons expand as they heat up. Because there is more metal near the wrist pin, this area tends to expand more.

► To allow for thermal expansion, many pistons are machined into a slightly oval shape, a process called cam grinding, and the piston is called a cam-ground piston. As an oval piston heats up to operating temperature, it expands and becomes round.

► The shape of the top of the piston depends on the shape of its combustion chamber and its compression ratio.

► Combustion chambers vary in shape, depending on the manufacturer and type of engine for which it is intended. The top of the piston forms the bottom of the engine's combustion chamber.

► The compression ratio is the difference between the volume in the combustion chamber above the piston when the piston is at bottom dead center (BDC) and the volume of the combustion chamber above the piston when the piston is at top dead center (TDC).

► The compression ratio can be changed by using a piston with a different head design or a cylinder head with a different chamber size. This is because the sizes of the piston head and chamber affect the ratio between the volume at BDC and the volume at TDC within the combustion chamber.

► There are two processes in manufacturing pistons: forging and casting.

► The forged piston is the stronger and more costly of the two. In forging a piston, metal molecules are compressed into a denser area. This makes the piston stronger and more desirable for diesel engines and racing applications.

► There are two versions of the cast piston: cast aluminum with steel struts and cast aluminum with 16% to 19% silicon, which is called a hypereutectic piston.

► Forced induction engines require a special piston to handle the increased cylinder pressures that are a result of the intake pressurization. Forged aluminum alloy types are used.

► Gasoline direct injection (GDI) engine pistons are designed with a particular dish or dome to direct the fuel to the proper place in the cylinder so that complete combustion can occur.

► The most popular piston coating is a black moly, a molybdenum disulfide coating on the piston skirt that helps reduce friction between the piston skirt area and the cylinder wall.

► The ceramic coating on a piston prevents the piston metal from absorbing heat quickly, which allows the piston to operate at a lower temperature and withstand greater combustion temperatures without deforming.

► The piston pin (wrist pin) is made of steel and is hollow in the center to reduce weight, thereby reducing the engine's reciprocating mass; it can be a floating pin type or a press-fit pin.

► With the floating pin design, the piston pin floats in both the piston and the rod, with the piston pin being held in place by snap rings on each side of the piston.

► Some floating pin pistons use a direction snap ring, which means they must be installed with the correct side facing the wrist pin. Otherwise, the snap ring can work its way out of its groove and score the cylinder wall, destroying the engine.

► You install one snap ring on one side of the piston, then lubricate the pin area of the piston, the connecting rod, and the pin. Next, slide the piston pin in place, and secure the pin with the other snap ring.

► With the press-fit pin design, the piston is held in place by a wrist pin that is pressed into the connecting rod in an interference fit with the wrist pin to lock the pin firmly in place.

► A special tool is used to remove and install the press-fit piston pin.

► Most engines have semi-floating wrist pins.

► The semi-floating pin moves freely in the piston bore but is press fit in the connecting rod bore. The preferred method for installing the wrist pin is to use a rod heater.

► Each piston has a major thrust face and a minor thrust face. The side of the piston that is forced into the cylinder wall on the power stroke is the major thrust face. The side of the piston that is forced into the cylinder wall on the compression stroke is the minor thrust face.

► Most piston pin bores are not centered in the piston. They are set slightly off-center of the piston. Having the pin offset preloads the piston toward the minor thrust side of the piston.

- Piston slap causes an audible noise that is most noticeable when the pistons are cold and at their smallest diameter. Piston slap also increases piston/cylinder wear.
- Piston slap occurs as the piston pivots on the pin near top dead center (TDC) when the piston is forced to the thrust side of the cylinder at the top of the power stroke.
- Offsetting the wrist pin in the piston reduces piston slap.
- Compression ratio relates to how tightly the air-fuel mixture is compressed in the combustion chamber.
- The tighter the air-fuel mixture, the more power that can be extracted from a given amount of air and fuel.
- Increased compression ratios increase compression pressures, thereby increasing the temperature of the mixture within the combustion chamber as it is being compressed. If the mixture gets too hot, it will ignite by itself from the heat, an event known as preignition, which occurs at the beginning of combustion.
- Detonation is a second ignition wave that occurs at the end of the combustion, which is usually caused by low-octane fuel or advanced timing. It makes the cylinder walls vibrate, producing a pinging noise from a localized pressure.
- Piston rings are thin, metallic, C-shaped rings set into grooves, located around the piston skirt, that fill the space between the piston and the cylinder wall. Generally, three to four rings are used per piston.
- The first two rings are called compression rings and are designed to seal and create a close fit between the piston and the cylinder wall.
- The other rings, called oil control rings, are specially designed to hold a small amount of lubrication oil to lubricate the piston and cylinder walls.
- The most common piston arrangement has two thin compression ring grooves and one larger oil ring groove; they are known collectively as piston ring grooves.
- The sides of the piston ring grooves, called ring lands, support the piston rings. The piston ring grooves are located between the top of the piston and the piston pin.
- The width and depth of the piston ring groove dictate the width and depth of the piston rings that should be used.
- Piston rings are not a complete circle; they are split and must have a specified piston ring end gap.
- The ring gap allows the piston rings to be expanded so they can fit over the ring lands when the rings are being installed on the piston.
- The ring gap also allows the piston rings to expand when they heat up as the engine is operating.
- A small ring gap should almost close when the engine is up to full operating temperature, but should not close entirely.
- Insufficient end gap results in the compression ring binding, breaking, twisting, or scoring the cylinder walls when the compression ring expands as the engine warms up.
- Excessive ring gap causes a loss of compression pressure through the gap, which leads to excessive blowby and lost efficiency.

- You must measure the piston ring end gap to make sure the gap is within the specified tolerances.
- The piston ring end gaps should be staggered around the piston when the piston rings are installed. Staggering prevents a straight path for the compression or gases to escape. If the path is too straight and smooth, the speed of gas escape is far too rapid, increasing the blowby gases.
- There must also be side clearance between the compression rings and the ring lands. The clearance prevents the piston ring from becoming stuck in the groove when it expands due to combustion heat.
- The piston ring must also have back clearance inside the piston groove to accommodate heat expansion of the piston.
- The oil scraper ring is positioned second on the piston; its main purpose is to scrape the excess oil off the cylinder walls so that it doesn't get burnt in the combustion chamber.
- The second job of the scraper ring is to stop blowby of the compression ring so that the crankcase doesn't become over-pressurized, which would cause gaskets to fail and the engine to start leaking oil.
- Oil control rings prevent excessive oil from working up into the combustion chambers. The oil control ring is designed to leave a film of lubricating oil less than a thousandth of an inch thick on the cylinder wall.
- Oil control rings can be a one-piece ring that depends on its own tension to hold it against the cylinder walls, or a three-piece ring with two side rails and an expander, which provide the tension for the side rails. Both styles have slots or holes in the oil ring and the piston ring groove.
- The cast iron piston ring can be used when the engine will not be overused, over-revved, or otherwise abused.
- Ductile Iron pistons rings are an economical option like cast iron rings; the only major difference is that they are twice as strong as cast iron rings, but with a lot of the same properties.
- Steel rings are twice as strong as ductile iron rings but are not compatible with cast iron cylinder walls and have to be coated to survive in a cast iron engine.
- The chrome-coated ring can be used for the increased wear resistance that chrome offers and has a high resistance to scuffing.
- The ceramic-coated ring is one that has a higher wear resistance than chrome coated rings and it is very resistant to extreme temperatures and offer increased durability.
- The barrel-cut ring is tapered out from the bottom and the top into a flat surface, which, if looked at from a cross-sectional view, looks like a barrel and aids in sealing the cylinder.
- The normal-cut ring is sometimes referred to as a rectangular ring and is usually utilized as the top piston ring in many gasoline and diesel engines.

▶ The angle-cut ring can have an angle on the top edge or the bottom edge that creates a torsional tension that makes the ring seat without the high pressures that conventional rings need to seat in the cylinder.

▶ The step-cut piston ring is one that has interlocking ring lands where the gap would be on a conventional piston ring. The usage for this ring is for an application that has a higher-pressure combustion chamber than normal, like a turbocharged engine.

▶ Oversized piston rings are used when the engine cylinders have been bored out to a larger diameter to clean up the imperfections in the cylinder walls.

▶ The connecting rod connects the piston to the crankshaft. It has a small end that houses the piston pin and connects it to the piston assembly.

▶ The middle of the connecting rod, called the beam area, transmits the power flow to the bottom of the rod. At the bottom, or big end, the connecting rod houses the bearing inserts and attaches firmly around the crankshaft.

▶ In order for the connecting rod to fit over the crankshaft rod journal, the big end is split in half; the bottom half is removable and is called the rod cap.

▶ The connecting rod's big end is connected to the crankshaft rod journal; the rod cap bolts or nuts are then torqued (using manufacturer specifications) in place using a torque wrench.

▶ The connecting rod transfers the reciprocating motion and force of the piston to the rotating crankshaft.

▶ Most stock connecting rods are shaped like an "I" beam down the length of the connecting rod.

▶ Some aftermarket performance connecting rods have an H shape down the length of the connecting rod. The H-shaped rod is the stronger of the two.

▶ Most connecting rods have extra metal on each end (balance pads) for balancing.

▶ There are four types of connecting rods: cast, forged, aluminum, and powdered metal. The cap must go back on the same connecting rod; caps are not interchangeable. They must also be reinstalled in the exact orientation.

▶ The best practice to make sure the caps and connecting rods do not get mixed up is to mark them close to the parting line.

▶ Some connecting rods are cast, and some are forged.

▶ Forged rods are much stronger than cast rods; they are usually used in high-performance applications and are usually marked.

▶ The aluminum rod is used in some drag race cars. It is lighter and wider than cast or forged rods. The extra width strengthens the rod, enabling it to withstand the pressures and forces applied to the connecting rod and crankshaft assembly during the short, intense duration of a drag race.

▶ The powdered metal rod starts with a precise amount of powdered metal, which includes iron, copper, carbon, and other agents. The powder is placed in a die and forged (pressed) under great pressure and then put through a sintering process.

Key Terms

bottom dead center (BDC) The very bottom of an engine stroke, where the piston can do no further down.

cast piston The entry-level piston that is created from aluminum that meets the needs of most vehicles requirements.

compression ring The top ring on a piston and the main one that seals the combustion chamber.

floating pin Type of piston pin that is held in by two circlips on the sides of the piston and is completely removable for servicing.

forced induction An application that has a positive pressure adder to the engine such as a turbocharger or a supercharger. It forces extra air into the cylinder.

forged piston Piston utilized in a positive pressure environment and created out of a forging that is molecularly stronger than a cast or hypereutectic piston.

gasoline direct injection (GDI) Type of engine that has the fuel injected directly into the cylinder, which then uses the heat of increased pressure and a spark to ignite the air-fuel mixture.

hypereutectic piston Type of piston that is one step above a cast piston and has a higher level of silicon content, which creates a stronger piston that is comparably priced to a cast piston.

oil control ring Piston ring that is usually perforated to allow oil drainback to the crankcase as the scraper ring scrapes the cylinder wall.

piston rings Rings installed around the circumference of the piston and that contact the cylinder wall, thus providing sealing for the cylinder as the piston moves in the bore.

piston ring grooves Areas machined out of the piston that are where the piston rings are installed.

pressed-fit pin Type of piston pin used in cheaper applications and installed when the small end of the connecting rod is heated up so that it expands, and then the pin is installed, and finally the rod is allowed to cool, creating an interference fit for the pin.

ring gap The distance between the two ends of one piston ring. This is a critical measurement because if the gap is too big, blowby will result, and if it is too small, damage to the ring will occur.

ring lands The sides of the grooves that support the ring when it is installed on the piston.

rod cap The piece of the connecting rod that is removable so that it can be installed on the crankshaft.

rotating assembly Consists of the crankshaft, connecting rods, and pistons—all the major components that rotate in the cylinder block.

scraper ring The ring usually below the compression ring, whose main function is to scrape the cylinder wall so that the oil can be directed toward the crankcase.

top dead center (TDC) The very top of the stroke of the engine in a cylinder, where the piston cannot move any higher.

Review Questions

1. Which type of piston is used in diesel engines and racing car engines?
   a. Forged piston
   b. Hypereutectic piston
   c. Cast piston
   d. Cam ground piston

2. All of the following can be used in the piston for controlling heat and expansion, *except:*
   a. steel struts or ribs.
   b. piston rings in a complete circle.
   c. horizontal slots cut in skirt.
   d. vertical slots cut in skirt.

3. Which of the following piston rings helps to stop blowby of compression ring?
   a. Forged ring
   b. Scraper ring
   c. Oil control ring
   d. Oil ring

4. Which of the following materials is used in the making of the first two piston rings?
   a. Molybdenum
   b. Ceramic
   c. Chromium
   d. Cast iron

5. Choose the correct statement with respect to the purpose of compression rings:
   a. They scrape excessive oil from the walls of the cylinder.
   b. They hold a small amount of oil for lubrication between the cylinder and the piston.
   c. These rings act as a seal during power strokes.
   d. They are typically lubricated by oil rings.

6. The type of piston head depends on the:
   a. bottom dead center.
   b. valve relief areas.
   c. compression ratio.
   d. valve train designs.

7. All of the following statements regarding pistons are true, *except:*
   a. Cast pistons are more bulky and are used in naturally aspirated engines.
   b. Hypereutectic pistons are used in racing applications.
   c. Forged pistons are used in diesel car applications.
   d. Hypereutectic pistons have very small clearance between the piston and the block cylinder.

8. Aluminum rods are not used in any of the following, *except:*
   a. endurance race cars.
   b. aircraft.
   c. general-purpose vehicles.
   d. drag race cars.

9. Which of the following are manufactured by the sintering process?
   a. Pistons
   b. Connecting rods
   c. Compression rings
   d. Piston pins

10. All of the following statements are true regarding piston pins, *except:*
    a. The wrist pin is installed by press fit.
    b. The piston pin is made of steel and is full of metal.
    c. The semi-floating pin is press fit in the connecting rod bore.
    d. The fully floating pin is a slide fit in the connecting rod bore.

ASE Technician A/Technician B Style Questions

1. Technician A says that a GDI engine has the fuel injected into the exhaust manifold. Technician B says that a piston is used to transfer the combustion gases to the connecting rod to create mechanical force. Who is correct?
   a. Tech A
   b. Tech B
   c. Both A and B
   d. Neither A nor B

2. Technician A says that a press-fit piston pin can be driven out with an air hammer so that it can be replaced. Technician B states that a qualified person should be the only person to remove and install press fit in piston pins. Who is correct?
   a. Tech A
   b. Tech B
   c. Both A and B
   d. Neither A nor B

3. Technician A says that compression rings are located at the top of the piston to seal the combustion chamber. Technician B states that when installing piston rings, the technician must be careful as they can break easily. Who is correct?
   a. Tech A
   b. Tech B
   c. Both A and B
   d. Neither A nor B

4. Technician A says that when you are installing the piston rings, you must know which way is up on the ring, or failure could result. Technician B states that pistons come pre-installed with piston rings. Who is correct?
   a. Tech A
   b. Tech B
   c. Both A and B
   d. Neither A nor B

5. Technician A says when you are replacing the connecting rods in an engine, you must make sure that they all are different so that they can offset one another. Technician B states that the pistons must not weigh the same or an out-of-balance vibration will be felt. Who is correct?
   a. Tech A
   b. Tech B
   c. Both A and B
   d. Neither A nor B

6. Technician A states that when removing a connecting rod, you must keep the cap in the same direction that it came

off the rod. Technician B says mixing up the caps from the different connecting rods is okay. Who is correct?
a. Tech A
b. Tech B
c. Both Tech A and B
d. Neither A nor B

7. Technician A says that the rotating assembly consists of the connecting rods, crankshaft, camshaft, and the oil pan. Technician B says that the rotating assembly consists of the crankshaft, connecting rods, and pistons. Who is correct?
a. Tech A
b. Tech B
c. Both A and B
d. Neither A nor B

8. Technician A says that the oil control ring scrapes oil off the cylinder wall. Technician B says that the compression ring is the top ring on the piston. Who is correct?
a. Tech A
b. Tech B
c. Both A and B
d. Neither A nor B

9. Technician A says that the higher the compression ratio, the more potential for power from the engine. Technician B says that forced induction engines utilized forged pistons. Who is correct?
a. Tech A
b. Tech B
c. Both A and B
d. Neither A nor B

10. Technician A says that pistons do not start out as round in the cylinder block; they are machined to an oval. Technician B says that to help with reassembly, the technician should lay out the parts on a table. Who is correct?
a. Tech A
b. Tech B
c. Both A and B
d. Neither A nor B

CHAPTER 15

Camshafts, Valvetrains, and Balance Shafts

You Are the Automotive Technician

The customer has a 1999 Chevy Camaro and wants to install a high-performance camshaft in the small block 350 in the vehicle. You, as the technician, have been asked what needs to be done to install this camshaft in this engine. What is the first thing you must find out before you decide on a performance camshaft for this vehicle?

1. What is the environment this vehicle will be used in?
2. Should we change the camshaft?
3. What type of camshaft should be utilized in this vehicle application?

K15001 Knowledge of what a camshaft does in an engine.

▶ Introduction

The camshaft, balance shafts, and the valvetrain are the heart of any engine, as they all are required for the engine to operate in the manner that is was designed for. A simple change of valvetrain or camshaft components can have a drastic change in the ability of the engine to perform. When the technician is diagnosing the engine, he or she must be able to verify the proper operation of the valvetrain components so that the engine will perform as desired by the customer. Throughout this chapter, we talk about the different areas of the valvetrain, balance shafts, and camshafts so that you have a better understanding of these components.

▶ Camshaft

The camshaft provides the motion to open and close each of the valves. The camshaft is a shaft with offset eccentrics, called cam lobes (**FIGURE 15-1**). The cam lobe determines when each valve opens, how far it opens, and how long it stays open. The profile of the cam lobe determines these functions. The base circle takes up about half of the entire profile. When the lifter is on the base circle, the valve is closed. The nose is the highest point of the cam lobe and determines how far the valve opens. The difference between the base circle is called lobe lift. The opening ramp is what opens the valve. The opening ramp starts at the base circle and ends at the nose. The closing ramp is the opposite of the opening ramp and allows the valve to close. It starts at the nose and ends at the base circle.

Camshafts are ground for specific applications and may or may not be symmetrical, meaning that the opening and closing ramps may or may not be identical. Also, different camshaft profiles create different engine operating characteristics.

FIGURE 15-1 The camshaft is used to open the valves at the correct time to support the combustion process.

Removal and Installation

Removing the camshaft depends on how the engine is configured, as the procedure for these two different configurations are slightly different. On an overhead valve system, the rocker arms must be removed, then the pushrods and the lifters, and then the timing chains, in order to remove the camshaft. In an overhead camshaft configuration, the technician must take off the timing chain or timing belt and then detorque the camshaft bearing caps, and finally remove the camshaft. Consult the OEM's service information for proper procedures for removal and installation.

How to Measure a Camshaft

N15001 Inspect and/or measure camshaft for runout, journal wear, and lobe wear.

N15002 Inspect camshaft bearing surface for wear, damage, out-of-round, and alignment; determine needed action.

K15002 Knowledge of how to measure a camshaft.

S15001 Inspect and/or measure the camshaft for runout, journal wear, and lobe wear.

S15002 Inspect camshaft bearing surface for wear, damage, out-of-round, and alignment.

When measuring a camshaft, the technician must visually inspect the camshaft to see if there are any imperfections or deformities before beginning to measure anything. The first measurement that the technician must make is to measure the bearing journals to see if they are within specification (**FIGURE 15-2**). Using a micrometer, to the technician takes three measurements on the camshaft main journals to determine if the main journals are out of round. If they are out of round the camshaft will have to be replaced. After the technician has determined that the main journals are acceptable, the lobes must be measured to determine if there is wear on any of them. The lobe is measured from the bottom to the top of to see if it is within specification; if it is not, the camshaft must be replaced (**FIGURE 15-3**). Once all of those measurements are completed and it is within specification, the camshaft can be reused in the engine.

To measure out a camshaft round and lobe, follow the steps in **SKILL DRILL 15-1**.

Lobe Lift

Lift refers to how far the cam lobe will *lift* the lifter, cam follower, or bucket lifter. The greater the lift, the further the valve opens, and the easier it is for air to enter the cylinder.

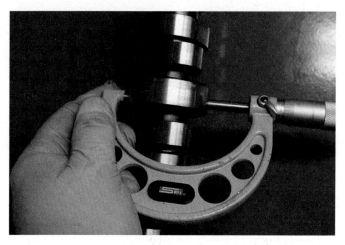

FIGURE 15-2 The technician must measure the bearing journal on the camshaft to determine whether it is out of round or otherwise damaged before it is reinstalled in the engine.

FIGURE 15-3 Measuring the camshaft lobe allows the technician to determine whether the lobe is damaged and require replacement.

SKILL DRILL 15-1 Measuring Out-of-Round and Lobe

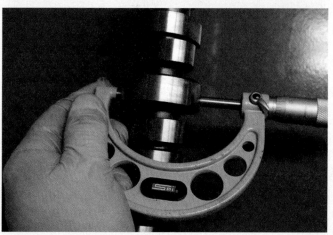

1. Take the camshaft and lay it in the V blocks so that it is secure.

2. Using your outside micrometer, measure a main journal in one location. Record the measurement for verification with service information.

3. Pick two other spots, and repeat measuring. Subtract the smaller number from the larger one to determine how out-of-round the main camshaft journal is. Then compare to service specifications to evaluate if it is acceptable or not.

Continued

4. Go to a lobe for the intake or exhaust, and measure the tall portion first.

5. Measure the base circle or the shorter portion.

6. Now subtract the smaller number from the bigger number, and that is your lobe lift.

7. Compare information with the OEM specifications to see if the camshaft is serviceable.

Journal Diameter	47.655-46.858 mm
Bearing Inside Diameter 1 and 4	46.970-46.934 mm
Bearing Inside Diameter 2 and 3	46.977-46.942 mm
Bearing-to-Journal Clearance	0.041-0.119 mm
Intake Maximum Lobe Lift	6.56 mm
Exhaust Maximum Lobe Lift	6.56 mm

The lobe lift is calculated from measuring the base circle of the camshaft lobe and the actual lobe of the camshaft. Subtracting the two numbers gives the actual lobe lift from that lobe of the camshaft (**FIGURE 15-4**). However, the greater the lift, the faster the valve has to move from closed to open, and the harder the valve springs have to work at closing the valve.

Duration

Duration refers to how long the valve is held open. The longer it is held open, the more time there is for air to enter the cylinder. Higher-duration camshafts are usually used in engines that operate at higher rpm. One other important term is **lobe separation angle**, which refers to how far the intake lobe is offset from the exhaust lobe. The wider the separation, the better the camshaft is for building power at higher rpm. Narrowing the separation builds power at lower rpm.

Valve Overlap

Valve overlap is the portion of time that both valves are open during the four-stroke event cycle. This is directly related to how the engine is going to be used, as the more overlap you have, the worse the idle of the engine becomes (**FIGURE 15-5**). When picking the correct camshaft for the application, the technician must understand what the engine will be used for, which vehicle it will be used in, running gear ratios, vehicle weight, transmission type, torque converter stall speed, and the emissions requirements for that vehicle year. Once all this information is determined, the technician can now pick the correct overlap to match this set of criteria so that the vehicle will operate correctly.

Different Grinds for Performance or Economy

Based on the use of the engine, the technician may pick a different grind for the camshaft. The quickest way to increase the horsepower or torque on an engine is to change the camshaft as it controls the amount of air-fuel mixture as well as how quickly the exhaust gases can escape the cylinder. The more lift a camshaft has, the more open the valve is once it actuates the lifter. The duration is how long the valve is open, which means that on a performance grind it keeps the valve open longer so that more air can flow in and more exhaust can flow out. The technician must pick the correct camshaft for the correct application or the engine will not operate like it should in the environment that is going to be used in.

Honda VTEC

Honda VTEC is Variable Valve Timing and Lift Electronic Control; it works by allowing the valves to open with a different rocker arm once the system is actuated (**FIGURE 15-6**). As the engine runs down the road, the driver calls for more acceleration, so he or she pushes the gas pedal to the floor. When the PCM sees this input, it actuates a solenoid that allows oil flow to flow to a pin between the three rocker arms on the intake valves (**FIGURE 15-7**). It locks the two outer arms to the center arm, which then causes the valves to be open on a different lobe, which has a more aggressive lift than the regular lobes. This allows for virtually two different camshafts for the intake

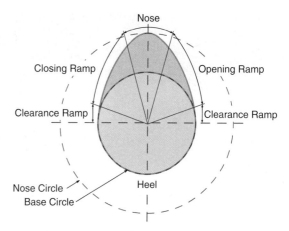

FIGURE 15-4 The different aspects of the camshaft lobe, which you are measuring to see whether it is in specification.

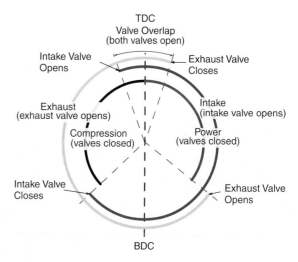

FIGURE 15-5 Valve overlap is when the intake and exhaust valves are opened at the same time. The amount of time both are open is called the valve overlap.

K15003 Knowledge of how a multi-grind camshaft operates.

FIGURE 15-6 A VTEC operational assembly installed on a cylinder head. These components are used to change the operation of the engine to a more performance version.

FIGURE 15-7 The VTEC system uses three rocker arms to operate. The outer two rocker arms operate normally; once the VTEC is activated, a pin moves from one of the rocker arms and locks all three together to force the rockers to run off the middle lobe of the camshaft.

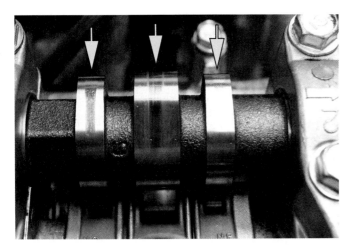

FIGURE 15-8 As you can tell by the arrows, the camshaft has three intake lobes, which is part of the VTEC system. When the VTEC is engaged the rocker arm rides on the middle intake lobe that is a more aggressive grind than the two outside lobes. This allows for the engine to have two different camshaft grinds on one camshaft.

K15004 Knowledge of valvetrain components.

FIGURE 15-9 The balance shaft is utilized in the cylinder block to help reduce vibration created by the combustion process. It just spins timed to the crankshaft so that the weights can offset the vibrations that are created by the operation of the engine.

N15003 Inspect valve lifters; determine needed action.

K15005 Knowledge of how lifters, followers, and lash adjusters operate.

S15003 Install the camshaft in heads with bucket-style lifters.

so that you can get economy and performance from the same engine (**FIGURE 15-8**). The PCM controls the operation of this system, which means that everything in the fuel management, ignition management, and mechanical engine must be operating correctly for this system to function as designed. One of the major problems this system has is if the engine has low or no oil in the oiling system, it will not operate and may cause engine damage. If poor oil quality is used in this engine, it could clog passages and damage components. The first step in diagnosing this system is to check the level and quality of oil in the engine.

▶ Valvetrain Components

The **valvetrain** is responsible for moving air and fuel through the engine. This means that all of the valvetrain components must be opened and closed at precise times. In fact, the optimum points in the cycle that the valves open and close change with engine revolutions per minute (rpm) and load. Newer engines have valvetrains that are computer controlled and can adjust valve timing while the engine is operated.

The term "valvetrain" incorporates all of the parts between the drive of the camshaft and the valves. Valvetrain design is determined by the manufacturer, so valvetrains come in a variety of configurations. The following sections familiarize you with each of the components and layout.

Balance Shafts

The **balance shaft** is utilized to take vibrations out of the rotational mass in an engine's rotating assembly (**FIGURE 15-9**) by rotating a weighted shaft in an engine block and carefully timing it to the engine results in offsetting vibrations. This virtually eliminates the vibrations that the design of the engine creates. Because the balance shaft is offsetting the vibrations caused by the rotating assembly, it must be exactly timed to the events or it will become another vibration that a technician must diagnosis. At the same time the bearings for the balance shaft can have an effect on oil pressure if they are out of specification. Because this shaft is timed to the engine, if it fails it can cause the timing to be off, perhaps meaning that the engine will not operate.

Lifters/Followers/Last Adjusters

There are two types of lifters: solid and hydraulic. **Hydraulic valve lifters** are constructed as a centrally located plunger inside a hollow cylindrical body. Engine oil fills the inside of the lifter body, pushing the plunger up until all the play in the valvetrain is removed. Because they are self-adjusting, these lifters can automatically accommodate changes caused by part wear or temperature fluctuations. Hydraulic lifters are more frequently used in today's engines because they are quieter and require no periodic maintenance.

Solid valve lifters are constructed as a hollow cast iron cylinder, capped on both ends. They function by simply transferring the action of the cam lobe to the pushrod. Because there is no means for changing the length of the solid lifter, as seen in the oil-filled plunger action of the hydraulic lifter, they are not able to self-adjust to changes caused by wear or thermal conditions. As a result, all adjustments must be performed manually. These types of lifters require frequent valve adjustments and are typically noisier than their hydraulic counterparts. An advantage of the solid lifter is that it can be made lighter than a hydraulic lifter, so it can be used at higher engine rpm without contributing to valve float.

The valve lifters can be located in four different places: on the engine block, on the cylinder head, on the rocker arms, and between the cam and the valve tip (bucket style) (**FIGURE 15-10**). Both solid and hydraulic lifters can be of either the **flat tappet** or the **roller tip** design. The flat tappet style has a nearly flat surface that rides directly on the camshaft lobe. The lifter face-to-camshaft lobe contact is one of the highest load areas in the engine. Using a roller tip lifter reduces the friction on the camshaft lobe. Instead of sliding on the camshaft lobe as a flat tappet does, the roller rolls along the lobe with less friction. Because the roller must remain in rolling contact with the cam lobe, the lifter must incorporate a method of preventing it from rotating in the lifter bore. This can be accomplished by connecting two adjacent lifters together with a pivoting link, or it could use a pin on the side of the lifter that rides in a groove in the lifter bore.

In most OHC engines, you will find no rocker arms. Instead, these engines use **camshaft followers** (**FIGURE 15-11**). A camshaft follower performs the same basic function as a rocker arm: It opens a valve. The camshaft follower has a pivot on one end and a slider or roller near the center that directly contacts the camshaft lobe. As the camshaft turns, the roller rolls over the surface of the camshaft. The lobes push the followers away, transmitting the movement to the valve and pushing it down (open).

If the camshaft is located on top of and centered over the valves, the engine will use **bucket-style lifters** (**FIGURE 15-12**). These lifters have a lifter assembly that is mounted on top of the valve and hollowed out, like a bucket. The hollow portion is placed upside down over the top of the valve stem and provides a wear surface between the camshaft and the valve stem. Bucket-style lifters perform the same job as all lifters: They transmit movement from the cam lobe to the tip of the valve. Bucket-style lifters may be hydraulic or mechanical. To adjust the valve clearance in the mechanical lifter, you must change the wafer installed on the top of the bucket. Some technicians refer to wafers as spacers or pucks. These wafers are replaced to obtain the proper valve clearance between the camshaft and the valve stem. They come in different thicknesses to achieve the correct valve clearance. Hydraulic bucket lifters are self-adjusting in the same manner as a standard hydraulic lifter and therefore do not require periodic maintenance.

What Does a Lifter Do?

A lifter transfers force from the camshaft to the pushrod or to the valve spring so that the rotational force can be used to make a valve open. The lifter is not used to close the valve, as the spring is utilized to do that. Another feature of the lifter is that it can be used to take up any excess clearance between the pushrod and the rocker arm and is the main component on a nonadjustable valvetrain. The hydraulic lifter is utilized on many production engines so that as the components wear, the lift automatically takes up the clearance by utilizing oil pressure to adjust the height of the lifter.

Types of Lifters

Solid, Hydraulic, Flat Tappet, Roller

A solid flat tappet lifter has no internal moving parts and is used on an adjustable valvetrain that can change to take up for wear (**FIGURE 15-13**). Solid flat tappet lifters were used in older vehicles as they are very reliable, but they require a lot of regular maintenance to adjust the lash out of the valvetrain. The next invention was the hydraulic flat tappet lifter, which is very similar to the solid flat tappet lifter except that it is oil fed and automatically takes up the excess lash as the components wear (**FIGURE 15-14**). These lifters were designed to create an engine that requires less maintenance so that it can operate at peak efficiency indefinitely. The final version of the lifter is a roller hydraulic lifter that is

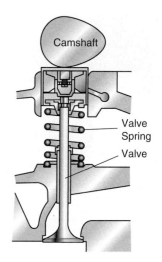

FIGURE 15-10 Engine lifter in between the cam and the valve tip (bucket style).

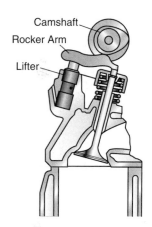

FIGURE 15-11 Engine lifter in the cylinder head.

FIGURE 15-12 This bucket style lifter sits on top of the valve spring and then has the rocker arm push on the outside of it. There is a hydraulic piston embedded within the lifter to take up any slack that is created from where the valve tip or bucket has worn.

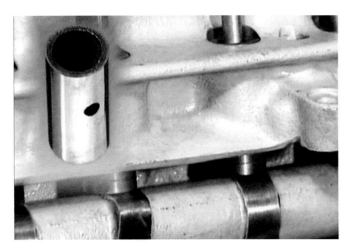

FIGURE 15-13 A solid lifter used on an adjustable valvetrain where the application calls for something that will not fail under extreme rpm.

FIGURE 15-14 A hydraulic lifter that is used on production engines to create a self-adjusting valvetrain that requires minimal upkeep. The hydraulic lifter also takes up any space that is created from wear on the engine.

found in most vehicles today (**FIGURE 15-15**). These lifters combine the best of both worlds: They use a roller bearing so that there is less friction between the lifter and the camshaft and the lift is hydraulic so that it can adjust to wear that occurs on the push rod or the rocker arm tip.

How to Replace Lifters

Replacing lifters on most vehicles requires the technician to remove the lower intake to access the valley of the engine and the valve covers. Once both of those components have been removed, the technician can loosen up the rocker arms, remove the pushrods, and then pull out the lifters from the lifter bores. This procedure varies some from application to application; for instance, on a Chevy Vortec small block V8 you must remove the cylinder heads to access the lifters. Always consult the OEM service information so that you are able to remove these components correctly, efficiently, and safely.

Lash Adjusters

A lash adjuster is usually utilized on an overhead cam engine. These adjusters control the wear that happens between the camshaft lobe and the valve stem tip or rocker arm (**FIGURE 15-16**). They are usually located in between the camshaft and the valve stem or

FIGURE 15-15 A roller hydraulic lifter that is a combination of a hydraulic lifter and a roller lifter. This lifter minimizes friction by using a roller and also minimizes clearance in the valvetrain by utilizing the hydraulic feature to create a maintenance-free design.

FIGURE 15-16 A lash adjuster is used to take up slack in the valvetrain and keep the rocker arm taut to the valve stem.

rocker arm. They are similar to a hydraulic lifter, oil fed and fully adjustable so that as the engine wears, the clearance between the components does not get too extreme.

Rocker Arms

The **rocker arm** pivots inward near the middle, which results in a change of the direction of movement. The camshaft lobe pushes up, and as the rocker arm is pushed up on one end, the other end pushes the valve down to open. Rocker arms can be used on OHV or OHC engines. In OHV engines, each valve has one lifter, one pushrod, one rocker arm, and one lobe on the camshaft, dedicated to its opening and closing. In OHC engines, each valve has one rocker arm and one lobe on the camshaft. The rocker arm comes in different rocker arm ratios, depending on the engine design. The ratio refers to the amount of movement on the valve side of the rocker arm in comparison with that on the opposite side. For example, a 1.5:1 rocker arm will move a valve 1.5 times the lift and speed of the camshaft lobe. The most common ratios are 1.5:1, 1.6:1, and 1.7:1.

Rocker arm ratios allow manufacturers to use smaller lift camshafts. That is, a camshaft with smaller lobes than needed to generate a specified amount of lift can be used because the rocker arm ratio magnifies the camshaft's lift. There are different styles of rocker arms, including stamped, cast, and forged. Stamped rocker arms are "stamped" from a piece of metal. They are not a high-strength or high-horsepower rocker arm and are intended for regular passenger vehicles. Cast rocker arms are cast in a die with molten metal. Metal alloys can be used, making cast, forged, or billet rocker arms that are more durable than their non-alloy counterparts. These rocker arms are generally used in sports cars and other high-performance vehicles. Forged rocker arms use localized pressing forces to form a rocker arm from steel or a steel alloy. The forging process enables the metal to withstand extreme pressure, heat, and wear. These rocker arms are used in high-torque, high-horsepower applications such as race cars and hot rods.

In the case of canted valves used in hemispherical-shaped and some wedge-shaped combustion chambers, the rocker arms may be individually mounted to the cylinder head. In OHC engines, typically the intake valves are on one side of the cylinder head, and the exhaust valves are on the other side of the head, with the camshaft sitting between them. Rocker arms would then be positioned between the camshaft and the valves on each side of the camshaft.

With the push for increased fuel efficiency, many manufacturers use roller rocker arms on their engines. Roller rocker arms use rolling pivots at both ends and the center of the rocker arm. The rolling action at the pivot points reduces friction as well as wear on the rocker arm. The reduced friction gives a small increase in fuel efficiency and performance.

K15006 Knowledge of rocker arms and their usage.

Shaft-Mounted Rocker Arms

Shaft-mounted rocker arms are mounted on a cylindrical shaft that allows oil pressure to reach each individual rocker arm (**FIGURE 15-17**). The rocker arms usually slide onto the shaft and usually have a spring to locate them in the correct position so that the pushrod can line up. This type of rockers is very durable, as the shaft gives the rocker arm a wide area to ride on. As well, the shaft is bolted to the cylinder head instead of the rocker arm, further taking stress off the rocker arm.

Pedestal-Mounted Rocker Arms

The pedestal-mounted rocker arms have an individual pedestal for each rocker arm, which allows for a more isolated rocker arm (**FIGURE 15-18**). This type of rocker arm allows for precise placement of the rocker arm to line up with the valve, no matter where the valve is located in the cylinder head. The design of the cylinder head and valve placement can be more aggressive, as the design can take advantage of a better placement of the different components.

FIGURE 15-17 Shaft-mounted rocker arms have a shaft that runs through all the rockers arms and usually has oil pressure running through the shaft to lubricate the rocker arms and valve springs.

Adjustable/Nonadjustable Rocker Arms

Two types of valvetrains that are available the adjustable and the nonadjustable type. The adjustable type allows the technician to adjust the free play of the rocker arm before it actuates the valve. Over time, the lash will have to be readjusted as the rocker and the valve tip wear, causing increased rocker arm free play. The nonadjustable valvetrain is one in which hydraulic lifters take up the wear so that adjustment is not necessary to maintain the valve lash. This type of valvetrain is the most common one in today's vehicles, as the manufacturers are trying the make the engines virtually maintenance free. There are exceptions to this, however; Honda and others still uses an adjustable valvetrain so that the engine can be dialed, in no matter how much wear happens to the engine.

Performance

For performance applications, the reduction of friction, increased speed, and extra lift are all of the ways that a rocker arm can increase performance. By using a roller rocker arm, the friction between the rocker arm and the valve tip is reduced, increasing the life of both components. Along with reducing the friction at the valve tip, the performance rockers use roller bearings at the fulcrum to increase speed and reduce resistance to movement (**FIGURE 15-19**). Extending the rocker arm leverage by making it long increases the lift of the valve, thus increasing the air-fuel mixture that is allowed into the combustion chamber. A word of caution when using performance rocker arms: Make sure that you are not opening the valve so far that it makes contact with the piston. When contact with the piston occurs, it leads to breakage of engine components as well as causing the engine to create a misfire or become inoperable.

FIGURE 15-18 A pedestal-mounted rocker system allows for each rocker arm to be mounted individually on its own mount so that it can be situated where necessary to accommodate the intake and exhaust runners in the cylinder head.

FIGURE 15-19 A performance rocker arm has a roller tip to minimize friction and usually has an increased ratio to increase the performance of the engine.

▶ Wrap-Up

Ready for Review

▶ The camshaft, balance shafts, and the valvetrain are the heart of any engine, as they are all required for the engine to operate in the manner that is was designed for maximum engine breathing.

▶ The camshaft provides the motion to open and close each of the valves. The camshaft is a shaft with offset eccentrics, called cam lobes.

▶ The cam lobe determines when each valve opens, how far it opens, and how long it stays open.

▶ The profile of the cam lobe determines these functions.

▶ The camshaft base circle takes up about half of the entire profile. When the lifter is on the base circle, the valve is closed.

▶ The camshaft nose is the highest point of the cam lobe and determines how far the valve opens. The difference between the base circle is called lobe lift.

- The camshaft opening ramp is what opens the valve. The opening ramp starts at the base circle and ends at the nose.
- The camshaft closing ramp is the opposite of the opening ramp and allows the valve to close. It starts at the nose and ends at the base circle.
- On an overhead valve system the rocker arms must be removed, then the pushrods must be removed, then the lifters, and then the timing chains to remove the camshaft.
- On an overhead camshaft configuration, the technician must take off the timing chain or timing belt, then detorque the camshaft bearing caps, and remove the camshaft.
- Always consult the service information for proper procedures for removal and installation.
- When measuring a camshaft, the technician must visually inspect the camshaft, to see whether there are any imperfections or deformities, before beginning to measure anything
- The first measurement that the technician must make is measuring the bearing journals to see whether they are within specification
- When using a micrometer, you need to take three measurements on the camshaft main journals to determine whether the main journals are out of round. If they are out of round, the camshaft will have to be replaced.
- You also check the camshaft lobes for wear by measuring the lobes from the bottom to the top of the lobe to see whether it is within specification; if it is not, you must replace the camshaft.
- Lobe lift refers to how far the cam lobe will lift the lifter, cam follower, or bucket lifter.
- The greater the lift, the further the valve opens, and the easier it is for air to enter the cylinder.
- The lobe lift is calculated from measuring the base circle of the camshaft lobe, and the actual lobe of the camshaft. Subtracting the two numbers, you get your actual lobe lift from that lobe of the camshaft.
- Duration refers to how long the valve is held open. The longer it is held open, the more time there is for air to enter the cylinder.
- Higher-duration camshafts are usually used in engines that operate at higher rpm.
- Lobe separation angle refers to how far the intake lobe is offset from the exhaust lobe. The wider the separation, the better the camshaft is for building power at higher rpm. Narrowing the separation builds power at lower rpm.
- Valve overlap is the portion of time that both valves are open during the four-stroke event cycle. This is directly related to how the engine is going to be used as the more overlap you have, the worse the idle of the engine becomes.
- The quickest way to increase the horsepower or torque on an engine is to change the camshaft as it controls the amount of fuel-air mixture as well as how quickly the exhaust gases can escape the cylinder. The more lift a camshaft has, the more open the valve is once it actuates the lifter.

- The valvetrain is responsible for moving air and fuel through the engine, which means that all of the valvetrain components must be opened and closed at precise times.
- Newer engines have valvetrains that are computer controlled and can adjust valve timing while the engine is operated.
- The term "valvetrain" incorporates all of the parts between the drive of the camshaft and the valves.
- The balance shaft is utilized to take out vibrations out of the rotational mass in an engine's rotating assembly by rotating a weighted shaft in an engine block and carefully timing it to the engine results in offsetting vibrations.
- There are two types of lifters: solid and hydraulic.
- Hydraulic valve lifters are constructed as a centrally located plunger inside a hollow cylindrical body. Engine oil fills the inside of the lifter body, pushing the plunger up until all the play in the valvetrain is removed. Because they are self-adjusting, these lifters can accommodate changes caused by part wear or temperature fluctuations.
- Solid valve lifters are constructed as a hollow cast iron cylinder, capped on both ends. They function by simply transferring the action of the cam lobe to the pushrod.
- Solid valve lifters require periodic manual adjustments.
- Solid and hydraulic lifters can be of either the flat tappet or the roller tip design.
- The flat tappet style has a nearly flat surface that rides directly on the camshaft lobe. The lifter face-to-camshaft lobe contact is one of the highest load areas in the engine.
- The roller tip lifter reduces the friction on the camshaft lobe. Instead of sliding on the camshaft lobe as a flat tappet does, the roller rolls along the lobe with less friction.
- The roller tip lifter must remain in rolling contact with the cam lobe, so it must use a method of preventing it from rotating in the lifter bore, which is done by connecting two adjacent lifters together with a pivoting link, or it could use a pin on the side of the lifter that rides in a groove in the lifter bore.
- OHC (overhead camshaft) uses camshaft followers, which performs the same basic function as a rocker arm.
- The camshaft follower has a pivot on one end and a slider or roller near the center that directly contacts the camshaft lobe. As the camshaft turns, the roller rolls over the surface of the camshaft. The lobes push the followers away, transmitting the movement to the valve and pushing it down (open).
- If the camshaft is located on top of and centered over the valves, the engine will use bucket-style lifters.
- Bucket-style lifters have a lifter assembly that is mounted on top of the valve and are hollowed out, like a bucket. The hollow portion is placed upside down over the top of the valve stem and provides a wear surface between the camshaft and the valve stem.
- To adjust the valve clearance in the mechanical lifter, you must change the wafer installed on the top of the bucket. Some technicians refer to wafers as spacers or pucks.
- A lifter transfer force from the camshaft to the pushrod or to the valve spring so that the rotational force can be used to make a valve open and can take up any clearance in the valvetrain.

- ▶ The lifter is not used to close the valve, as the spring is utilized to do that.
- ▶ Replacing lifters on an OHV (overhead valve) engine requires you to remove the lower intake to access the valley of the engine and the valve covers. Once they have removed both of those components, they can loosen up the rocker arms, remove the pushrods, and then pull out the lifters from the lifter bores.
- ▶ A lash adjuster on an overhead cam engine controls the wear that happens between the camshaft lobe and the valve stem tip or rocker arm and located in between the camshaft and the valve stem or rocker arm.
- ▶ The rocker arm pivots inward near the middle, which results in a change of the direction of movement. The camshaft lobe pushes up, and as the rocker arm is pushed up on one end, the other end pushes the valve down to open.
- ▶ Rocker arms can be used on OHV or OHC engines.
- ▶ There are different styles of rocker arms, including stamped, cast, or forged. Stamped rocker arms are "stamped" from a piece of metal. They are not a high-strength or high-horsepower rocker arm and are intended for regular passenger vehicles.
- ▶ Cast rocker arms are cast in a die with molten metal.
- ▶ Many manufacturers use roller rocker arms on their engines. Roller rocker arms use rolling pivots at both ends and the center of the rocker arm. The rolling action at the pivot points reduces friction as well as wear on the rocker arm.
- ▶ Shaft-mounted rocker arms are mounted on a cylindrical shaft that allows oil pressure to reach each individual rocker arm. The rocker arms usually slid onto the shaft and usually have a spring to locate them in the correct position so that the pushrod can line up.
- ▶ The pedestal-mounted rocker arms have an individual pedestal for each rocker arm which allows for a more isolated rocker arm and allows for precise placement of the rocker arm to line up with the valve.
- ▶ There are two types of valvetrains that are available the adjustable and the nonadjustable type.
- ▶ The adjustable valvetrain allows you to adjust the free play of the rocker arm before it actuates the valve. Over time the lash will need to be readjusted as the rocker and the valve tip wears causing increased rocker arm free play.
- ▶ The nonadjustable valvetrain is one that has the hydraulic lifters take up the wear so that adjustment is not necessary to maintain the valve lash.
- ▶ A word of caution when using performance rocker arms, make sure that you are not opening the valve so far that it makes contact with the piston. When contact with the piston occurs it causes breakage of engine components as well as causing the engine to create a misfire or become inoperable.

Key Terms

balance shaft A spinning counterweighted shaft designed to take out vibrations caused by the engine operating. These are timed to the valve events, which means if the timing is off, this shaft could cause increased vibration.

bucket-style lifters Lifters encasing the valve spring and having direct contact with the camshaft lobe. Sometimes these are hydraulic so that any wear will be automatically taken care of. On some applications you must shim these if a wear condition presents itself.

camshaft followers Operates similarly to the rocker arm as it pivots and opens the valve. It is located directly on the camshaft, with usually a pivot point adjacent to the camshaft so that the direct force of the lobe is transferred to the follower.

flat tappet Lifter that has a flat surface on the bottom that rides directly on the camshaft lobe.

hydraulic valve lifter Lifters that have a plunger inside a hollow cylindrical body, which oil fills, pushing the plunger up to the pushrod until all the play is removed. This setup is auto-adjusting, so there is no adjustment, but only replacement.

lobe separation angle How far the intake lobe is offset from the exhaust lobe. This determines how quickly the valves open.

rocker arm Component that, as the camshaft lobe pushes up, is pushed up on one end so that the other end pushes the valve down to open.

roller tip Designed to reduce friction and increase durability on a lifter. A hardened roller installed on the bottom of the lifter makes contact with the camshaft.

solid valve lifter Constructed as a hollow cast iron cylinder, capped on both ends. It wears over time, and the valve lash will have to be adjusted as it wears, as solid valve lifters are not self-adjusting.

valve overlap The portion of time that both valves are open at the same time.

valvetrain Consists of the rocker arms, push rods, lifters, camshaft, and the valves.

Review Questions

1. Which of the following determines when each valve opens, how far it opens, and how long it stays open?
   - **a.** Profile of the cam lobe
   - **b.** Base circle
   - **c.** Closing ramp
   - **d.** Length of the nose
2. The ease of air entry into the cylinder is determined by:
   - **a.** lobe separation angle.
   - **b.** valve overlap.
   - **c.** lobe lift.
   - **d.** duration of the lift.
3. "Lobe separation angle" in a cam shaft refers to:
   - **a.** how far the cam lobe lifts the cam follower.
   - **b.** how long the valve is held open.
   - **c.** the portion of time that both valves are open.
   - **d.** how far the intake lobe is offset from the exhaust lobe.
4. The camshaft should be replaced:
   - **a.** every year.
   - **b.** when the lobes have any wear on them.
   - **c.** when the main journal is round in shape.
   - **d.** if the micrometer readings of the main journal in three spots are matching with each other.

5. Which of the following tools helps in deciding whether the camshaft should be replaced?
   a. Micrometer
   b. Screw gauge
   c. Taper testing machine
   d. Vernier calipers

6. All of the following are taken into consideration while selecting the camshaft with the correct valve overlap, *except:*
   a. transmission type.
   b. type of the stroke of engine.
   c. running gear ratios.
   d. vehicle emissions requirements.

7. All of the following statements regarding the operation of a multi-grind camshaft are true, *except:*
   a. The locking of the two outer arms with the center arm causes valves to open on a different lobe.
   b. The PCM actuates a solenoid which in turn allows oil flow.
   c. Fuel economy and performance are reduced when using multi-grind camshafts.
   d. Engine damage can be caused when this is operated on No/low oil.

8. Choose the correct statement regarding the operation of the valve train and its components:
   a. The valve train is independent of engine rpm.
   b. Balance shafts control the valve timing.
   c. Lifters are used to cut down on the vibrations in the engine.
   d. The valve train is responsible for moving air and fuel through the engine.

9. Choose the correct statement regarding the operation of hydraulic valve lifters.
   a. They operate by transferring the action to the push rod.
   b. They operate by lifting the plunger with the help of engine oil.
   c. They are used in engines with high RPM.
   d. They are light in weight.

10. Which of the following lifters has very less operational friction, less maintenance, and can adjust to wear?
   a. Solid tappet lifter
   b. Hydraulic tappet lifter
   c. Round tappet lifter
   d. Hydraulic-roller tappet lifter

ASE Technician A/Technician B Style Questions

1. Technician A states that the purpose of a pedestal-mounted rocker arm is to increase the number of rocker arms in the engine. Technician B says that shaft-mounted rocker arms are more durable than pedestal-mounted rocker arms. Who is correct?
   a. Tech A
   b. Tech B
   c. Both A and B
   d. Neither A nor B

2. Technician A states that a rocker arm multiplies the force that is transferred to it. Technician B says that a bad lobe on a camshaft can be repaired. Who is correct?
   a. Tech A
   b. Tech B
   c. Both A and B
   d. Neither A nor B

3. Technician A states that on an adjustable valvetrain, periodic adjustment of the valve lash is required for optimal performance. Technician B says that OHC engines do not have adjustable valvetrains. Who is correct?
   a. Tech A
   b. Tech B
   c. Both A and B
   d. Neither A nor B

4. Technician A states that a balance shaft can be eliminated from the engine if it fails. Technician B says that balance shafts have to be timed to the engine. Who is correct?
   a. Tech A
   b. Tech B
   c. Both A and B
   d. Neither A nor B

5. Technician A says that valve overlap is where the valves run into one another. Technician B states that duration is the amount of time combustion takes to occur. Who is correct?
   a. Tech A
   b. Tech B
   c. Both A and B
   d. Neither A nor B

6. Technician A says that a camshaft should be measured on the main journals for out-of-round. Technician B says that a camshaft should be measured on the lobe journals to see if it is within specification. Who is correct?
   a. Tech A
   b. Tech B
   c. Both A and B
   d. Neither A nor B

7. Technician A says that camshafts are interchangeable, so they can be used on multiple engines. Technician B states that camshafts should be selected for the particular application of the intended use. Who is correct?
   a. Tech A
   b. Tech B
   c. Both A and B
   d. Neither A nor B

8. Technician A states that the main camshaft only opens the intake valves. Technician B says that a change in the camshaft to a different profile will cause the engine to act very different. Who is correct?
   a. Tech A
   b. Tech B
   c. Both A and B
   d. Neither A nor B

9. Technician A states that lobe lift is what lifts the lifter or the follower to continue valve actuation. Technician B states that lift multiplication happens at the rocker arm and not the lifter. Who is correct?
   a. Tech A
   b. Tech B
   c. Both A and B
   d. Neither A nor B

10. Technician A says that all the valvetrain components are designed to work with the specific camshaft that they came with. Technician B says that you should not mix and match valvetrain components. Who is correct?
   a. Tech A
   b. Tech B
   c. Both A and B
   d. Neither A nor B

CHAPTER 16

Timing Chains, VVT, Timing Belt, and Cylinder Deactivation

NATEF Tasks

- **N16001** Inspect and replace camshaft and drive belt/chain; includes checking drive gear wear and backlash, end play, sprocket and chain wear, overhead cam drive sprocket(s), drive belt(s), belt tension, tensioners, camshaft reluctor ring/tone-wheel, and valve timing components; verify correct camshaft timing.

Knowledge Objectives

After reading this chapter, you will have:

- **K16001** Knowledge of camshaft operation in relation to the crankshaft.
- **K16002** Knowledge of timing chain-driven engines.
- **K16003** Knowledge of timing belt-driven engines.
- **K16004** Knowledge of the consequences of a timing chain or timing belt failure.

- **K16005** Knowledge of timing gear-driven engines.
- **K16006** Knowledge of variable valve timing camshafts.
- **K16007** Knowledge of cylinder deactivation systems.

Skills Objectives

- **S16001** Inspect the timing chain for wear.
- **S16002** Inspect the timing belt for wear.
- **S16003** Inspect the variable valve timing operation.

- **S16004** Inspect the cylinder deactivation system for proper operation.

You Are the Automotive Technician

A customer comes in with a complaint that the multiple displacement system is not operating correctly, and a check engine light is on. This is a regular customer who trusts what you recommend but is known for not maintaining his vehicle until there is a problem. What is the first thing that you check when you get the vehicle in your service bay?

1. Tire pressure
2. Engine oil level
3. Check engine light
4. Air cleaner

▶ Introduction

The way that the camshaft is operated on an internal combustion engine is dependent on the design and intended usage of the engine. Most camshafts are operated by either a timing chain, timing gears, or a timing belt that times the camshaft to the crankshaft so that combustion events can take place at the proper time. Late-model vehicles are utilizing a more precise control of the combustion events by changing the timing as the engine is running or deactivating cylinders to increase mileage and performance. Throughout this chapter, each type of system will be explained so that the reader can understand how it works, why it is done, and how to diagnosis it.

▶ Timing Chain

A **timing chain** is very similar to a bicycle chain, as it is usually a single or double row chain that connects the crankshaft with the camshafts so that they are rotating in unison. The chain usually runs on a set of sprockets, guides, and tensors so that the tension on it is kept tight as it rotates in the engine (**FIGURE 16-1**). The chain is used as a more durable alternative to the timing belt and with proper care should not require replacement through the life of the engine. The precision of the timing chain is very reliable for the longevity of the engine, but these chains are very susceptible to lack of maintenance just like every other system on the vehicle.

Where Is the Timing Chain Located?

The timing chain can be located in either the front of the back of the engine, as the design of the engine dictates where the timing chain can operate. The key to location of the timing chain is the location of the camshaft, the cylinder head, and the pistons in the cylinder block, as well as whether other items have to be driven off the timing chain. For example, Ford 4.0 SOHC has four timing chains; one chain drives the oil pump/balance shaft, and one drives the jackshaft, which is what drives the chains that drive both of the camshafts located in each cylinder head (**FIGURE 16-2**). The passenger side cylinder head camshaft is driven off the jackshaft at the back of the engine, which requires engine removal to service the chain and sprockets.

What Does It Take to Replace?

Replacing the timing chain in an engine is straightforward, but accessing the timing chain can be very challenging on some vehicles. Depending on the application, it may require that the intake manifold, valve covers, timing cover, and accessory drive be removed, and engine fluids drained (**FIGURE 16-3**). Once the chains have been replaced, the technician must clean all of the parts that have been removed, reinstall them, and verify that everything is correct. Checking and double-checking timing before the

FIGURE 16-1 This camshaft is driven by a timing chain. The chain is similar to a bicycle chain and usually uses tensioners to keep the chain tight on the sprockets.

FIGURE 16-2 The timing chain drive on an OHC engine has multiple guides, rubbing blocks, and tensioners that keep the chain tight on the sprockets.

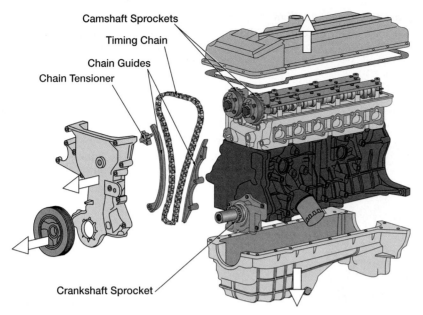

Camshaft Sprockets
Timing Chain
Chain Guides
Chain Tensioner
Crankshaft Sprocket

FIGURE 16-3 This is a view of all the components in a timing chain drive engine.

technician reassembles the engine saves the technician unnecessary problems. The technician must look up the procedure for the particular vehicle being working on, as it varies from engine to engine.

How Is Tension Maintained?

The tension in timing chains is maintained by a combination of spring and oil pressure at particular points on the chain. To take up the slack in the timing chain guides, shoes and tensioners are utilized to keep the timing chain tight against the sprockets that drive the components in the engine (**FIGURE 16-4**). With oil-fed tensioners, a lack of maintaining oil in the engine can cause the timing chain to lose tension and jump out of time. This tension is critical to the operation of the camshafts in the engine; without that precision of the timing chain, the engine would not be as efficient.

Typical Replacement Intervals

The typical timing chain doesn't need to be replaced as it is supposed to be a lifetime component. Nevertheless, lack of maintenance of modern automobiles means that this is not usually the case. Lack of oil or the lack of using quality oil causes the timing chain guides and tensioners to fail, making the chain jump and require replacement. If the maintenance is kept up, the timing chain should last the life of the vehicle and not cause any problems. Make sure to check the service information on procedures and maintenance schedules.

Special Alignment Tools

The precise control of the fuel mileage and power features of the timing chain setup may necessitate special alignment tools to position the camshafts with the crankshaft (**FIGURE 16-5**). The **phasers** on the camshaft allow the camshaft to adjust, either advancing or retarding; because of this the camshafts must be aligned independently of the phasers. Some engines require

FIGURE 16-4 The timing chain tensioner has a small spring in it to set the chain and keep it taught when the engine is not running, once the engine is running the oil-fed tensioner gets a steady flow of oil to maintain tension on the timing chain so that it doesn't jump a tooth on the sprocket.

FIGURE 16-5 Setting up the timing components usually requires special tools to align the timing marks before initial engine starting.

bars, pins, and holders to align the camshaft, camshaft phaser, and or sprockets with the crankshaft. Prior to removing the timing chain, the technician must look through the service information to see what special equipment is required for reassembly.

K16003 Knowledge of timing belt-driven engines.

S16002 Inspect the timing belt for wear.

▶ Timing Belt

The **timing belt** is used on some vehicles to operate the camshaft and keep it in time with the crankshaft (**FIGURE 16-6**). The timing belt offers a quiet operation, as there are fewer metallic parts to make noise, and the ability for the belt to conform to the design of the engine. The timing belt is a cheaper alternative than a timing chain because the design is simpler and lighter weight to increase the fuel economy. The problem with the timing belt is that it must be changed on a regular basis for fear of it breaking and subsequently causing other issues.

Where Is It Located?

Unlike a timing chain, the timing belt must be located where the camshafts can line up in perfect alignment with the crankshaft. This means that the belt is located on the front of the engine, usually behind a plastic or metal cover so that it is somewhat easy to access (**FIGURE 16-7**). The belt is made to be serviced, so the location is made accessible to make this easy.

FIGURE 16-6 Timing belts are used in applications to decrease the noise and reduce costs of production. Timing belts do need regular maintenance as they will need to be changed periodically.

What Is It Made Of?

The timing belt is made of a reinforce rubber substrate that gives the belt its flexibility and rigidity so that it can withstand the abuses that happen within an engine (**FIGURE 16-8**). Even with the extra reinforcement, the timing belt still wears out over time and will have to be replaced. The design of the teeth on the timing belt allow for positive engagement with the sprockets as well as quiet operation when the engine is running. The teeth, however, are also weak points in the timing belt and can cause failure of the belt if they are damaged by a sprocket or outside influence.

How Is Tension Maintained?

Tension on a timing belt is maintained by one of two types of tensioners: either a **hydraulic tensioner** or a **spring-loaded tensioner**. In the hydraulic type, a hydraulic cylinder with hydraulic fluid under pressure presses against the tensioner pulley in the timing setup (**FIGURE 16-9**). The spring-loaded or mechanical tensioner utilizes a spring to move the

FIGURE 16-7 Engines with timing belts have a cover that keeps debris and other things out of the moving components which could cause the timing belt to fail.

FIGURE 16-8 A timing belt is made out of many layers of rubber, Kevlar, and other reinforcing material to help make it last as long as possible.

FIGURE 16-9 A hydraulic tensioner for a timing belt is a self-contained unit that has a metered orifice inside it to slow the movement of fluid to maintain tension on the tensioner.

FIGURE 16-10 The mechanical tensioner uses spring pressure to maintain pressure on the timing belt so that the belt will not jump teeth on the sprockets.

tensioner against the belt while keeping tension on the belt (**FIGURE 16-10**). If the tensioner fails, it could cause the timing belt to jump teeth, potentially causing the engine to bend valves.

Typical Replacement Intervals

It is recommended to replace the timing belt between 60,000 and 100,000 miles, depending on the application. The range is very large because some manufactures utilize different belt material, which enables the belt to be in service for a longer period of time. The best course of action is to consult the original equipment manufacturer (OEM) service information to determine the recommended mileage for replacing the timing belt on the vehicle that you are working on.

Special Alignment Tools

As with the timing chain, you may need special timing tools to hold the camshaft and crankshaft so that you can set the timing belt to the proper location (**FIGURE 16-11**). With variable valve

FIGURE 16-11 Like the timing chain, the timing belt on some engines requires special holding tools to hold the camshaft and crankshaft in place so that the timing belt can be installed correctly.

timing on the modern internal combustion engine, the camshafts can be in any number of locations, so the special tools will place it in the correct position so the timing chain can be installed.

What Happens If the Timing Chain or Timing Belt Breaks?

What happens when the timing chain breaks depends on whether or not the engine is an interference engine or a non-interference engine. In an interference engine the valves may bend when the timing chain or belt breaks: Because the clearance between the valves and pistons is so close, if this happens, it is a catastrophic event (**FIGURE 16-12**). However, this is not always the case, as the chain or belt could fail at the exact moment that the valves were closed, in which case not a single thing would break. The best way to approach this situation is to verify that the valves are not stuck by removing the valve cover if it is convenient to do so; if it is not, then there is a 50/50 chance of successful engine operation after the belt or chain is replaced.

A non-interference engine is one that has clearance between the valves and the pistons, so contact is not an issue. These types of engines are not affected by a timing chain or belt break, as the worst case would be that the engine would not run. Some engines are designated a non-interference or an interference engine in the service information, but not every engine is designated as such.

K16004 Knowledge of the consequences of a timing chain or timing belt failure.

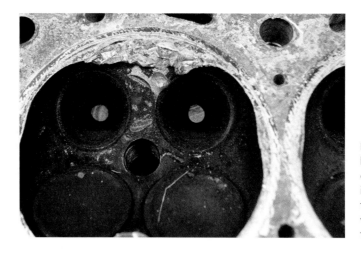

FIGURE 16-12 This is what happens when a timing belt or timing chain fails. In an interference engine application the valves will come in contact with the piston when the timing is off.

▶ Timing Gears

K16005 Knowledge of timing gear-driven engines.

In some older engines, the camshaft is run by a set of **timing gears** instead of a belt or a chain. The timing gears allow for a longer life of the timing components because they do not wear out as quickly as the timing chain, which allows for a service life that is indefinite. The issue with timing gears is the noise that is generated by the meshing of the two gears, causing the engine to be noisier than the timing chain counterpart. The manufacturers have tried to combat the noise issue with using helical cut gears to quiet down the noise and have also utilized a fiber gear setup so that you do not have metal on metal. The issue with the fiber gears is that the fiber wears out, causing the gear to fail and require replacement.

Operation

Typical timing gear utilization requires the crankshaft to operate normally and rotate clockwise; at the same time this causes the camshaft to rotate counterclockwise. The reverse rotation of the camshaft requires that the lobes be cut backwards on the camshaft so that the valve operation will remain correct for the crankshaft. A way around this issue is to use another gear as an intermediate gear that allows the camshaft to turn in the correct direction so that the grind on the camshaft is the same as it should be in a timing chain-driven engine.

▶ Variable Valve Timing (VVT)

K16006 Knowledge of variable valve timing camshafts.

S16003 Inspect the variable valve timing operation.

We can see from the previous section that the ability to control the advance and retard of the cam timing is a huge benefit to engine performance. Retarded timing provides greater engine efficiency when large amounts of air are flowing into the engine at higher rpm. Advanced timing is useful when the engine needs high torque during lower engine rpm operations. In past applications, an engine designer would have to decide which valve timing best served the operating range of the engine and then design the camshaft for that purpose. For optimum engine performance in a vehicle used both for commuting and for rallying or racing, what if an electronic module could manage optimum valve timing for such widely differing engine demands? Well, today's automobiles do almost that by using electronically controlled, hydraulically assisted variable valve timing while the engine is operating. Twin camshafts are advanced or retarded through the use of cam phasers or actuators. The phaser typically takes the place of the standard cam gear or pulley and uses oil pressure from the engine oil pump to move (some advance, some retard) the camshafts when commanded by the powertrain control module (PCM).

One type of actuator or phaser uses a **splined phaser** and a return spring (**FIGURE 16-13**). When oil pressure pushes against the gear mechanism, the cam rotates and advances. When oil pressure is released, the return spring brings the cam back to the fully retarded position. At rest, these types of actuators may be either fully retarded or

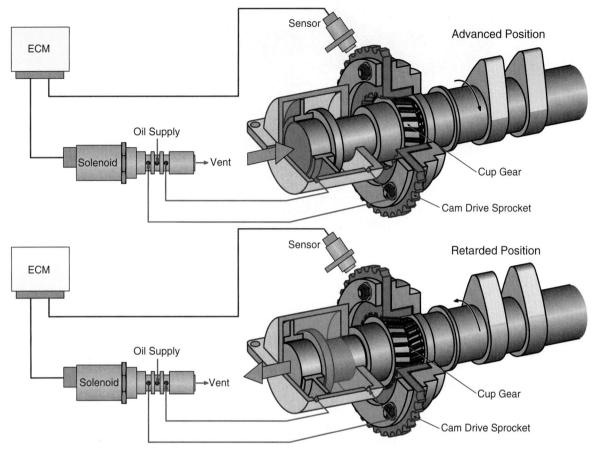

Advanced Position

Sensor

ECM

Oil Supply

Solenoid → Vent

Cup Gear

Cam Drive Sprocket

Retarded Position

Sensor

ECM

Oil Supply

Solenoid → Vent

Cup Gear

Cam Drive Sprocket

FIGURE 16-13 A screw type phaser moves a spherically cut gear in and out to control the movement of the camshaft within the cam sprocket.

fully advanced. The other type of actuator used is the **vane-type phaser** (**FIGURE 16-14**). This phaser uses vanes similar to those used in a vane-type oil pump to move the camshaft. Oil pressure moves into the phaser and pushes on one side of the vane to advance the cam timing. When oil pressure is switched to the other side of the vane, the camshaft is retarded. Cam timing is adjusted according to what the PCM requires based on its input sensors. If oil pressure is held constant, the cam phaser will likewise hold cam timing constant. The cam phaser uses a mechanical stop to limit maximum valve timing advance or retard. Cam phasers can be used on any camshaft arrangement, such as cam-in-block or OHC engines. If the cam is a single cam with exhaust and intake lobes, then both intake and exhaust will be affected by rotating the camshaft to the advanced or retarded position. In a DOHC engine, some engine designers use a phaser on the exhaust camshaft only. The phaser used with this type of engine is not intended for increased engine power, but rather for better exhaust gas recirculation. If the exhaust valve is held open later in the exhaust stroke, then it will also hang open later into the intake stroke, which can result in exhaust gases being pulled back into the engine. The exhaust gases pulled back into the engine dilute the incoming air–fuel mixture with an inert gas to help reduce oxides of nitrogen emissions. Because inert gas does not react chemically, it cools the combustion chamber to reduce oxides of nitrogen, or NOx. Controlling NOx in this way allows for the elimination of the exhaust gas recirculation (EGR) valve on some vehicles. In other DOHC engines, the phaser can be installed only on the intake camshaft for greater engine power, or it can be installed on both the intake and the exhaust camshafts. The newest cam phaser in use relies on an electric motor–driven phaser to vary the cam timing; this type of phaser is more accurate, as it does not rely on the oil being a consistent viscosity or squeaky clean. Variable cam timing is controlled by the PCM.

FIGURE 16-14 A vane phaser has metal vanes that trap oil in compartments to cause the camshaft to advance when they are filled with oil pressure.

Several inputs are used to ensure that the ECM is able to control the timing accurately. These are the same inputs used by the PCM to control fuel delivery and ignition system timing. The PCM also must know oil temperature to ensure that the oil viscosity is not too thick or thin. Based on input from an oil temperature sensor, the PCM either allows or disables variable valve timing; the viscosity of the oil must be correct for accurate valve timing. The PCM must know the amount of engine load to determine the need for an advance or retard of cam timing. To calculate engine load, the PCM primarily uses the following inputs:

- Mass airflow sensor or manifold absolute pressure sensor
- Throttle position sensor
- Intake air temperature sensor
- Engine coolant temperature sensor
- Crankshaft position sensor

The PCM relies on feedback to ensure that the cams are rotating as commanded; the cam position sensor (CMP) is used for this function. The output of the PCM is delivered to the cam timing solenoid. The cam solenoid allows oil pressure to move into the cam phaser. The solenoid is turned on and off with a pulse-width modulation (PWM) signal. PWM is the variable rapid (in milliseconds) time-based on/off switching of a DC signal. The longer the solenoid device is turned off, the less it opens; the longer it is turned on, the more it opens. In this way, the solenoid can regulate the amount, and direction, of oil flow to the cam phaser to alter camshaft/valve timing.

BMW VANOS System

BMW has named their VVT system VANOS, which is a German abbreviation of variable Nockenwqellen Steuerung. This system works similar to other variable valve timing systems as it adjusts the camshaft position of the intake camshaft on a single VANOS system. This system appears in the 1992 model year on some BMW vehicles. Through the development of variable valve timing, the Double VANOS system came along in 1996, controlling both the intake and exhaust camshafts. The current models are equipped with Double VANOS and Valvetronic, which changes how much the valve opens, meaning the PCM can infinitely control everything on the valvetrain.

Toyota VVTi System

VVTi is Variable Valve Timing with intelligence®. This system is similar to the Double VANOS above, as it controls the timing of the events by rotating the camshafts. The camshafts on this type of system are the same conventional type of camshafts that are rotated by oil pressure to change the timing of the valve events. There are multiple different versions of this system, from Dual VVTi to VVTiE, to VVTLi and Valvematic. The first version was introduced in 1995 and has been getting redefined since then.

Nissan CVTC System

CVTC is Continuous Variable Valve Timing® and is utilized in Nissan vehicles. This system takes into account all of the other mentioned sensors above to create the best possible combustion event environment so that it burns at optimal power. This system works on the fly constantly adjusting the timing to meet with the driver's demands. It also utilizes a progressive intake manifold that adds space as the driver requires more power.

Mercedes Benz CamTronic® System

The CamTronic system is used to increase fuel mileage in the Mercedes vehicles as well as help with decreasing emissions. This system uses a movable camshaft and an electronic solenoid that operates the system. When advance or retardation is required, the solenoid pushes a pin out, and it moves the hollow shell of the camshaft, thus changing the grind that operates the valve events. When the PCM determines it needs to retard the timing, the solenoid actuates again and moves the camshaft tube the other way.

Oil Requirements

Like most automotive engines, the fluid requirements are designated by the OEMs and should be followed strictly. When a variable valve timing engine does not follow the requirements, the system could fail, necessitating a lot of repair work to fix. Lack of regular maintenance will end up causing the passages and components in this system to gum up with sludge, requiring teardown to clean and replace components. Always refer to manufacturer specifications for the requirements of individual engines as it varies per application.

Wear Specifications

As the valve timings systems wear, the technician should be able to see how far the camshaft is turning through monitoring the advance or retard degrees on the scan tool. This function gives the technician the ability to verify whether the system is working correctly; the timing belt or chain is stretched; and all the solenoids are operating correctly. As with other engine internal parts, the technician must verify the basics before he or she moves on to a more complicated diagnostic routine. Oil level is a major issue with these types of systems, so the oil must be up, and it must be of a quality that meets the manufacturer's requirements.

How Variable Valve Timing Affects Economy and Power

The ability to change the timing to match the environment that the engine is operating in so that the engine is operating at peak efficiency creates a better running engine. This is a problem in a conventional engine as once the camshaft is picked, it cannot change or adapt to the use of the engine. Allowing the camshaft to adapt to the needs of the driver makes the engine infinitely variable and ensures that it is operating at optimum efficiency at all times. With increased efficiency of the engine comes the ability to increase the performance of the engine. Doing more with less allows the engine to operate at the optimal duration and ignition advance in any given situation.

What Controls Variable Valve Timing

VVT is controlled by the PCM, which moderates the use of VVT by utilizing the different sensors available for inputs so that it can monitor the engine as it is running in order to adjust timing as needed (**FIGURE 16-15**). By allowing the PCM to adjust all of these timing parameters, VVT can utilize the proper combination dictated by the engine properties while the engine is operating in a real-world situation.

▶ Cylinder Deactivation

Cylinder deactivation is a strategy that has been employed by some OE manufacturers to turn their V8 engines in to smaller V4 engines as the engine is operating. Making the engine smaller increases the fuel mileage but also allows for V8 mode when necessary to enable the driver to utilize the increased horsepower. The systems discussed here are

K16007 Knowledge of cylinder deactivation systems.

S16004 Inspect the cylinder deactivation system for proper operation.

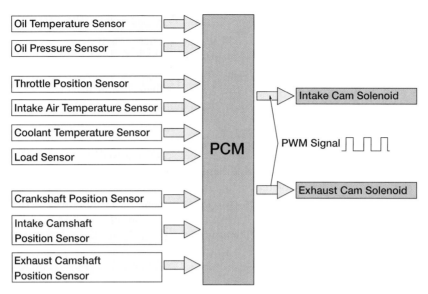

FIGURE 16-15 In a cylinder deactivation system the PCM utilizes the sensor inputs of the engine to monitor and adjust the deactivation of engine cylinders. All of these inputs help the PCM decide when to deactivate and when to reactivate cylinders.

FIGURE 16-16 The Chrysler MDS system and the Chevrolet DOD system use oil pressure to collapse lifters and "turn off" cylinders so that the engine is only using the amount of power that it needs without wasting energy and fuel. These systems help with fuel economy as well as helping the engine last for a longer period of time. This image is a Chevy 5.3 liter LOMA assembly.

very similar, and this is not an exhaustive list. Please consult OEM service information for more instruction on vehicle-specific systems.

Multiple Displacement Systems Explanation

The basics of multiple displacement systems are very simple. When in active mode, the system shuts down oil flow to the lifter on a particular cylinders valve lifters so that they collapse and not open the intake and exhaust valves (**FIGURE 16-16**). At the same time, when the valves are closed, the PCM shuts down the spark and injector to the corresponding cylinder so that the cylinder becomes inert. When the cylinder is inert, it does not compress air, does not ignite fuel, and is not a major drag on the engine. These systems have a lot of intricate parts that depend on the maintenance of the engine. Poor maintenance or part failure causes these systems to shut down, and the engine will remain in normal operational mode so that the engine can be driven.

► Wrap-Up

Ready for Review

- ► Most camshafts are operated by either a timing chain, timing gears, or timing belt, which times the camshaft to crankshaft so that combustion events can take place at the proper time.
- ► Late model engines use a more precise control of the combustion events by changing the timing as the engine is running or deactivating cylinders to increase mileage and performance.

- ► A timing chain is very similar to a bicycle chain as it is usually a single or double row chain that connects the crankshaft with the camshafts so that they are rotating in unison.
- ► The timing chain can be located in either the front of the back of the engine. The key to location of the timing chain is the location of the camshaft, location of the cylinder head, location of pistons in the cylinder block, and whether other items need to be driven off the timing chain.

- Checking and double-checking timing before reassembling the engine can save the technician unnecessary problems.
- You must look up the engine timing procedure for the particular vehicle that you are working on as it varies from engine to engine.
- Timing chain tension is maintained by a combination of spring and oil pressure at particular points on the chain. To take up the slack in the timing chain guides, shoes and tensioners are utilized to keep the timing chain tight against the sprockets that drive the components in the engine.
- The typical timing chain doesn't have to be replaced as it is supposed to be a lifetime component.
- Lack of engine oil or the lack of using quality oil can cause the timing chain guides and tensioners to fail, causing the chain to jump and require replacement.
- Make sure to check the service information on procedures and maintenance schedules.
- Cam phasers on the camshaft allow the camshaft to adjust either advancing or retarding; because of this, the camshafts must be aligned independently of the phasers.
- Some engines require bars, pins, and holders to align the camshaft, camshaft phaser, and/or sprockets with the crankshaft.
- Before removing the timing chain, the technician must look through the service information to see what special equipment is required for reassembly.
- The timing belt is used on some engines and offers quiet operation, as there are fewer metallic parts to make noise; it also enables the belt to conform to the design of the engine.
- A timing belt is less expensive, simpler, and lighter in weight than a timing chain, to increase the fuel economy.
- The problem with timing belts is that they must be changed on a regular basis or else you risk its breaking and causing other issues when it does finally break.
- The design of the timing belt teeth allow for positive engagement with the sprockets as well as quiet operation as the engine is running. The teeth are also weak points in the timing belt and can cause the failure of the belt if they are damaged by a sprocket or outside influence.
- Tension on a timing belt is maintained by one of two types of tensioners, either a hydraulic tensioner or a spring-loaded tensioner.
- The hydraulic type timing belt tensioner has a hydraulic cylinder that has hydraulic fluid under pressure pressing against the tensioner pulley in the timing setup.
- The spring-loaded or mechanical timing belt tensioner utilizes a spring to move the tensioner against the belt, keeping tension on the belt.
- If the timing belt tensioner fails, it could cause the timing belt to jump teeth, potentially causing the engine to bend valves.
- It is recommended that the timing belt be replaced between 60,000 and 100,000 miles, depending on the application.

- Like the timing chain, the timing belt may require special timing tools to hold the camshaft and crankshaft so that it can be set to the proper location.
- If the timing chain breaks, what happens depends on whether it is an interference engine or noninterference engine.
- In an interference engine, the valves bend when the timing chain or belt breaks, as the clearance between the valves and pistons is so close that if something fails, it is a catastrophic event.
- In non-interference or freewheeling engines, there is enough clearance between the valves and the pistons so that contact is not an issue, and they are not damaged by a timing chain or belt break as the worst case would be that the engine would not run.
- Some engines are designated as non-interference or interference engines in the service information.
- Some engines drive the camshaft by using a set of timing gears instead of a belt or a chain.
- Timing gears allow for a longer life of the timing components as they do not wear out as quickly as the timing chain, which allows for a service life that is indefinite.
- Timing gears can be noisy; this is caused by the meshing of the two gears, making the engine noisier than the timing chain counterpart.
- Retarded timing provides greater engine efficiency when large amounts of air are flowing into the engine at higher rpm.
- Advanced timing is useful when the engine needs high torque during lower engine rpm operations.
- Twin camshafts are advanced or retarded through the use of cam phasers or actuators.
- The phaser typically takes the place of the standard cam gear or pulley and uses oil pressure from the engine oil pump to move (some advance, some retard) the camshafts when commanded by the powertrain control module (PCM).
- A splined phaser uses a return spring. When oil pressure pushes against the gear mechanism, the cam rotates and advances the timing. When oil pressure is released, the return spring brings the cam back to the fully retarded position. At rest, these types of actuators may be either fully retarded or fully advanced.
- Vane-type phasers use vanes similar to what is used in a vane-type oil pump to move the camshaft. Oil pressure moves into the phaser and pushes on one side of the vane to advance the cam timing. When oil pressure is switched to the other side of the vane, the camshaft is retarded.
- Cam timing is adjusted according to what the PCM desires based on its input sensors.
- Cam phasers can be used on any camshaft arrangement, cam-in-block, or OHC engines. If the cam is a single cam with exhaust and intake lobes, then both intake and exhaust will be affected by rotating the camshaft to the advanced or retarded position.
- In a DOHC engine, some engines use a phaser on the exhaust camshaft only. The phaser used with this type of engine is not intended for increased engine power, but rather for better exhaust gas recirculation.

▶ Other DOHC engines have a phaser installed only on the intake camshaft for greater engine power, or it can be installed on both the intake and the exhaust camshafts.

▶ The newest cam phaser in use relies on an electric motor–driven phaser to vary the cam timing; this type of phaser is more accurate, as it does not rely on the oil being a consistent viscosity or squeaky clean.

▶ Variable cam timing is controlled by the PCM.

▶ The PCM must know the amount of engine load to determine the need for an advance or retard of cam timing. To calculate engine load, the PCM primarily uses the following inputs:

- Mass airflow sensor or manifold absolute pressure sensor
- Throttle position sensor
- Intake air temperature sensor
- Engine coolant temperature sensor
- Crankshaft position sensor

▶ BMW has named their VVT system VANOS. This system works similarly to other variable valve timing systems, as it adjusts the camshaft position of the intake camshaft on a single VANOS system.

▶ The Toyota VVTi system is Variable Valve Timing with intelligence. This system is similar to the Double VANOS, as it controls the timing of the events by rotating the camshafts. The camshafts on this type of system are the same conventional type of camshafts that are rotated by oil pressure to change the timing of the valve events.

▶ The Nissan CVTC system is a Continuous Variable Valve Timing system. It takes into account all of the input sensors to create the best possible combustion event environment so that it burns at optimal power.

▶ Mercedes Benz CamTronic system is used to increase fuel mileage in the Mercedes vehicles as well as help with decreasing emissions. This system uses a movable camshaft and an electronic solenoid that operates the system. When advance or retardation is required, the solenoid pushes a pin out, which moves the hollow shell of the camshaft, changing the grind that operates the valve events.

▶ The PCM controls variable valve timing, moderating its use by utilizing the different sensors that are available for inputs, thus enabling it to monitor the engine as it is running and adjust timing as needed.

▶ Cylinder deactivation is a strategy that has been employed to turn V8 engines into smaller V4 engines as the engine is operating.

▶ Cylinder deactivation or multiple displacement systems work as follows: When in active mode, the system shuts down oil flow to the lifter on a particular cylinders valve lifters so that they collapse and do not open the intake and exhaust valves. At the same time, when the valves are closed, the PCM shuts down the spark and injector to the corresponding cylinder so that the cylinder becomes inert. When the cylinder is inert, it does not compress air, does not ignite fuel, and is not a major drag on the engine.

Key Terms

cylinder deactivation System that disables multiple cylinders on an engine so fuel mileage is increased while the engine is operating in an environment that doesn't require all the available power.

hydraulic tensioner Type of tensioner that is operated by hydraulic fluid through a metered orifice inside the tensioner. These are also oil fed from the engine on some applications.

phasers Sprockets that are attached to the end of the camshaft that allow for the advancing or retarding of the camshaft for use in variable valve timing. These are usually an assembly that must be installed as one piece.

splined phaser A type of phaser that has the gear teeth cut at an angle so that as the collar is pushed out, the inner gear, which is connected to the camshaft, rotates, thus rotating the camshaft. A splined phaser is oil fed, so the oil must be up to the recommended level.

spring-loaded tensioner Type of tensioner that is operated by a spring to keep the tension on the timing belt.

timing belt A major timing component that links the crankshaft with the camshaft. Unlike a timing chain, the belt must be changed periodically. During operation of the engine, the belt allows for quiet running of the timing component.

timing chain A key timing component that links the crankshaft with the camshaft and makes sure they turn at the same time so that the valve events happen as scheduled. It is a chain that is either single or double row.

timing gears Timing components in some older engines that are utilized by gear-to-gear contact. Timing is kept because the gears are constantly meshed.

vane-type phaser This type of phaser operates with a set of paddles inside the assembly. When oil pressure is applied to one side of the paddles, it rotates the camshaft inside the phaser; to reverse the rotation, it applies oil pressure to the opposite side of the paddles.

Review Questions

1. All of the following can be used to time the camshaft to the crankshaft, *except* the:
   a. timing shaft.
   b. timing chain.
   c. timing gear.
   d. timing belt.
2. The tension in a timing chain is maintained by:
   a. shortening its length periodically.
   b. combination of spring and oil pressure at particular points on the chain.
   c. ensuring the chain does not get lubricated.
   d. sprockets that drive the engine.
3. Which of the following timing components offers a quiet operation and is a cheaper alternative?
   a. Timing shaft
   b. Timing chain

c. Timing gear

d. Timing belt

4. What can potentially cause the engine to bend the valves when a timing belt is used?

a. Timing chain jumping the sprocket teeth

b. Extreme tension in the belt

c. Failure of the tensioner

d. More oil in the belt

5. Choose the correct statement with respect to the consequences of a timing belt or a timing chain failure:

a. Valves may bend when the timing chain or belt breaks in an interference engine.

b. Valves don't bend in an interference engine because of clearance between the piston and the valves.

c. A non-interference engine will function smoothly even if the timing belt or timing chain fails.

d. In a non-interference engine the valves may bend due to very less clearance between the piston and the valves.

6. With proper maintenance, the timing chain:

a. may need replacement during every service.

b. may need replacement after a long drive.

c. may not need replacement in the lifetime of the vehicle.

d. may need replacement every two years when heavily used in stop-and-go traffic.

7. The PCM to determine the need for an advance or retard of cam timing uses inputs from all of the following, *except*:

a. wheel speed sensor.

b. throttle position sensor.

c. manifold absolute pressure sensor.

d. engine coolant temperature sensor.

8. Cylinder deactivation:

a. increases fuel mileage.

b. decreases emissions.

c. decreases engine wear.

d. stops the engine.

9. All of the following statements are true, *except*:

a. The ability to control the advance and retard of the cam timing is a huge benefit to engine performance.

b. Retarded timing provides greater engine efficiency when large amounts of air are flowing into the engine at higher rpm.

c. Advanced timing is useful when the engine needs high torque during lower engine rpm operations.

d. The electronic module could manage optimum valve timing in vehicles used for commuting but not for racing.

10. Which of the following variable valve timing systems helps in the reduction of emissions?

a. Toyota VVTi system

b. Mercedes Benz CamTronic

c. BMW VANOS system

d. Nissan CVTC system

ASE Technician A/Technician B Style Questions

1. Technician A says that cylinder deactivation is a system that deactivates the crankshaft in the engine. Technician B states that a vane phaser must have oil pressure to operate properly. Who is correct?

a. Tech A

b. Tech B

c. Both A and B

d. Neither A nor B

2. Technician A states that a timing chain could require special tools to align the timing marks for installation. Technician B says that variable valve timing is more about fuel economy, and not power. Who is correct?

a. Tech A

b. Tech B

c. Both A and B

d. Neither A nor B

3. Technician A says that a bad electronic coolant temperature sensor could cause the VVT not to operate correctly. Technician B states that a check engine light could disable the VVT system. Who is correct?

a. Tech A

b. Tech B

c. Both A and B

d. Neither A nor B

4. Technician A states that as the timing belt stretches, the technician may be able to see this on the scan tool when it looks at the degrees the engine is advancing. Technician B says that a thicker oil is better when it comes to VVT systems. Who is correct?

a. Tech A

b. Tech B

c. Both A and B

d. Neither A nor B

5. Technician A says that a timing chain should not have to be replaced unless it has been abused. Technician B states that the BMW VANOS system started in the 1985 model year. Who is correct?

a. Tech A

b. Tech B

c. Both A and B

d. Neither A nor B

6. Technician A says that when a timing belt or chain breaks, the chances of the piston bending the valves is very high. Technician B says that in a non-interference engine there should be maximum damage to the valves. Who is correct?

a. Tech A

b. Tech B

c. Both A and B

d. Neither A nor B

7. Technician A says that specialty tools hold the crankshaft and camshafts for belt or chain installation. Technician B states that eyeballing the sprockets is the proper way

of aligning the camshafts with the crankshaft. Who is correct?
a. Tech A
b. Tech B
c. Both A and B
d. Neither A nor B

8. Technician A states that on a timing chain engine, the tension is maintained by rubber banding. Technician B says that tension on a timing belt is maintained by a spring-loaded tensioner or a hydraulic tensioner. Who is correct?
a. Tech A
b. Tech B
c. Both A and B
d. Neither A nor B

9. Technician A says that there can be only one timing chain on any particular engine. Technician B states that the location of the camshafts dictates where the timing chain has to be located. Who is correct?
a. Tech A
b. Tech B
c. Both A and B
d. Neither A nor B

10. Technician A says that a timing belt must be replaced at specific intervals to decrease the chance of internal engine damage. Technician B says that the timing belt is a non-serviceable part that shouldn't need to be replaced. Who is correct?
a. Tech A
b. Tech B
c. Both A and B
d. Neither A nor B

CHAPTER 17

Cylinder Head Design and Service

NATEF Tasks

- **N17001** Remove cylinder head; inspect gasket condition; install cylinder head and gasket; tighten according to manufacturer's specifications and procedures.
- **N17002** Clean and visually inspect a cylinder head for cracks; check gasket surface areas for warpage and surface finish; check passage condition.
- **N17003** Inspect valve guides for wear; check valve stem-to-guide clearance; determine needed action.
- **N17004** Inspect valves and valve seats; determine needed action.
- **N17005** Inspect valve springs for squareness and free height comparison; determine needed action.

- **N17006** Check valve spring assembled height and valve stem height; determine needed action.
- **N17007** Inspect pushrods, rocker arms, rocker arm pivots, and shafts for wear, bending, cracks, looseness, and blocked oil passages (orifices); determine needed action.
- **N17008** Adjust valves (mechanical or hydraulic lifters).
- **N17009** Replace valve stem seals on an assembled engine; inspect valve spring retainers, locks/keepers, and valve lock/keeper grooves; determine needed action.

Knowledge Objectives

After reading this chapter, you will have:

- **K17001** Knowledge of the use of cylinder heads on an engine.
- **K17002** Knowledge of cylinder head components.
- **K17003** Knowledge of cylinder head design and the purpose of the design.
- **K17004** Knowledge of gasket usage and application.
- **K17005** Knowledge of cylinder head repair and servicing.

- **K17006** Knowledge of how to remove the cylinder head.
- **K17007** Knowledge of inspecting the valves and seats.
- **K17008** Knowledge of how the pushrods and rocker arms operate.
- **K17009** Knowledge of valve and seat service.

Skills Objectives

- **S17001** Remove a cylinder head.
- **S17002** Clean and inspect a cylinder head.
- **S17003** Inspect valves and valve seats.
- **S17004** Inspect valve guides for wear and check valve stem-to-guide clearance.

- **S17005** Inspect valve springs.
- **S17006** Reassemble a cylinder head.
- **S17007** Inspect pushrods and rocker arms.

You Are the Automotive Technician

You have diagnosed a blown head gasket on a customer's 2010 Shelby GT500, which is run regularly on the local road racetrack. Because of the stresses from racing and because the vehicle is nearing 75,000 miles, she would like you to disassemble, clean, and inspect the cylinder heads while you have them off, to see whether they need to be rebuilt. She agrees with your suggestion to have them checked for flatness and cracks. She is considering a high-performance camshaft, which she has been told would create more power. But she is confused by the terms "duration," "lift," and "lobe separation," and asks if you could explain them to her so she can decide which camshaft to use.

1. What do the terms "duration," "lift," and "lobe separation" mean?
2. How are heads checked for cracks?
3. What two locations are checked for flatness on heads equipped with overhead cams?

▶ Introduction

The modern internal combustion engine consists of many parts that were present in the original engines of a century ago. Over time, the form and efficiency of these parts have changed significantly, though their basic function has not. The cylinder head, in particular, is an example of what many years of improvement on a solid design can yield. Today's cylinder heads are more durable and efficient than any of their past counterparts. In this chapter, the modern cylinder head is explored, including the theory behind its many designs and its role in the combustion process.

The cylinder head relates to the entire engine assembly by providing the "end cap" for the combustion chamber. It provides a means for admitting air and fuel to the combustion chamber and exhausting gases after combustion. The cylinder head is also an integral part of the engine cooling system; it allows coolant to flow around the top of the combustion chamber, removing excess heat and preventing overheating of the engine.

The camshaft works with the cylinder head and **valves** to regulate the flow of the air-fuel mixture into, and the exhaust gases out of, the combustion chamber by opening and closing the valves at the proper times. The camshaft may be located either in the cylinder head or adjacent to it in the cylinder block. Each location has its own pros and cons. Engines with a camshaft located in the block have been around for decades and therefore are inexpensive to continue manufacturing. But they do not allow for varying valve timing, which is used to reduce emissions and increase engine efficiency. Engines with camshafts in the cylinder head are usually bulkier and require a more complicated drive system, so they are usually more expensive. Nonetheless, overhead camshafts make the engine more efficient and powerful, so they are used in more and more engines.

▶ Cylinder Heads (Gasoline Engines)

K17001 Knowledge of the use of cylinder heads on an engine.

There are five events in the operation of any internal combustion engine: intake of the air-fuel mixture, compression of the air-fuel mixture, ignition of the air-fuel mixture, a power stroke triggered by combustion of the air-fuel mixture, and the exhaust of burned gases from the combustion chamber. The **cylinder head** is integral to each of these steps. It controls the entry of the air-fuel mixture through the intake valve, allows compression of the air-fuel mixture by capping the top of the cylinder, contains a spark plug that ignites the air-fuel mixture, forces the pistons down the cylinder in a power stroke by not allowing the expanding gases to escape, and contains an exhaust valve to release the burned gases from the cylinder once the piston reaches the bottom of the cylinder. Because of the vital roles that the cylinder head plays, cylinder head design has a prime influence on the engine's efficiency and power output.

The cylinder head forms the top of the **combustion chamber**, the area of the engine in which the air-fuel mixture is ignited and combustion occurs. To withstand the very high combustion pressures, the cylinder head must be firmly clamped to the engine block with head bolts or studs. The **head gasket** is a thin metal sheet, often made of layers of different materials, with holes cut to accommodate the piston openings and passageways for oil and coolant. It is installed between the head surface and the block surface to seal the cylinder head assembly to the engine block (**FIGURE 17-1**). The head gasket keeps combustion pressure, coolant, and oil inside their proper areas. The cylinder head also distributes air and fuel into the engine's cylinders.

Cylinder heads can be made of cast iron or aluminum alloy (**FIGURE 17-2**). In today's vehicles, most cylinder heads are made of aluminum alloy because of its light weight. The lighter cylinder heads help reduce the vehicle's overall weight, which helps increase fuel economy. Aluminum also conducts heat away from the combustion chamber more rapidly than cast iron. Thus, with an aluminum-alloy head, the heat of combustion can be conducted to the coolant faster, reducing the chance

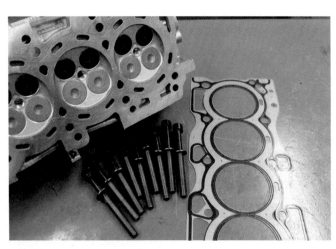

FIGURE 17-1 A cylinder head with head gasket and head bolts.

of localized hot spots. At the same time, engine efficiency is reduced when heat is removed too quickly from the combustion chamber, so aluminum cylinder heads may be designed with smaller water jackets to prevent them from overcooling the engine.

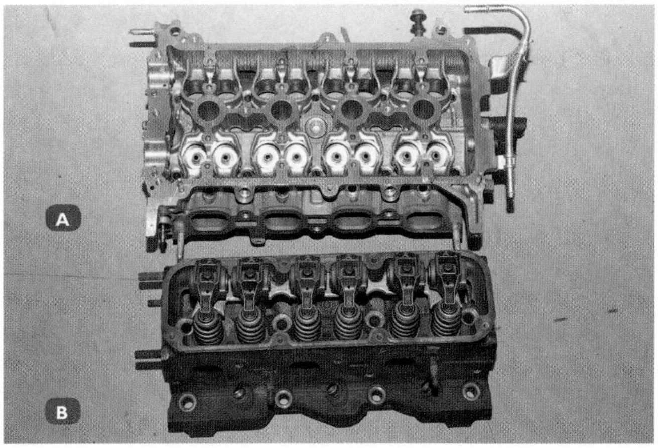

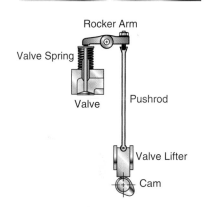

FIGURE 17-2 Cylinder heads. **A.** Aluminum. **B.** Cast iron.

Overhead Valve Engine

In an **overhead valve (OHV) engine**, the valves are positioned in the cylinder head assembly, directly over the top of the piston (**FIGURE 17-3**). The valves are operated by a camshaft that is located in the cylinder block. They transmit valve lifting force through lifters, pushrods, and rocker arms. This is a relatively simple design that is inexpensive to build.

Overhead Cam Engine

In the **overhead cam (OHC) engine**, the camshaft is housed inside the cylinder head and directly actuates the valves, using either cam followers or rocker arms (**FIGURE 17-4**). This system is more complicated than the OHV engine due to the need for a more extensive cam drive as well as the need for enhanced oiling at the top of the engine for the camshaft, lifters, and followers.

Single Overhead Cam Engine

The single overhead cam engine (SOHC) contains one camshaft per cylinder head (**FIGURE 17-5**). The camshaft operates both the intake and exhaust valves, usually driven off a timing belt or chain. In most cases it actuates the valves through a bucket lifter or a rocker that has a lash adjuster to keep it against the camshaft. This design eliminates a lot of the parts that could be part of the valvetrain, which gives the engine the ability to operate faster than a pushrod-designed engine.

Dual Overhead Cam Engine

The **dual overhead cam (DOHC) engine** contains two camshafts per cylinder head (**FIGURE 17-6**). Typically, one camshaft operates the **intake valves**, and the other operates the **exhaust valves**. In most cases, the camshaft sits right on top of the valves and operates the valves directly through a bucket lifter, with no rocker arms or cam followers. This design makes adjusting and servicing the valves more difficult because the camshaft usually needs to be removed to gain access. Offsetting the camshaft and using rocker arms or followers allow easier access.

SAFETY TIP

When lifting heavy cylinder heads, you probably lean over the fender or front of the vehicle, which puts a large amount of strain on your lower back. Always get help when lifting cylinder heads and other heavy components.

FIGURE 17-3 Overhead valve (OHV) engine.

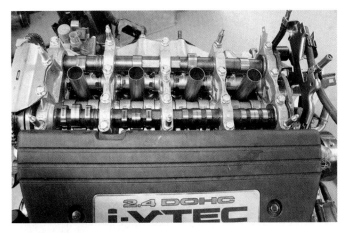

FIGURE 17-4 An overhead camshaft engine (OHC) has the camshafts mounted in the cylinder heads.

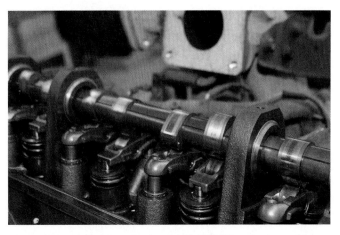

FIGURE 17-5 A single overhead camshaft (SOHC) engine has only one camshaft mounted to the cylinder head. This includes V-engines as they still only have one camshaft per cylinder head and they are an SOHC engine.

K17002 Knowledge of cylinder head components.

Cylinder Head Components

The cylinder head is composed of many distinct parts. At its core is the bare cylinder head casting, the name given to the base on which all other parts are attached. Other parts of the cylinder head are listed here:

- **Intake valves**—The air-fuel mixture enters the combustion chamber through these valves.
- **Exhaust valves**—The exhaust gases exit the combustion chamber through these valves.
- **Valve keepers**—These devices keep a valve spring's retainer attached to the valve while in the cylinder head.
- **Valve retainer**—This thick, washer-shaped piece of metal with a tapered center hole is fitted over the top of the valve stem and holds the top of the valve spring to keep pressure on the valves.
- **Valve springs**—These coil springs return valves to their fully closed positions, and hold them closed, after being opened.
- **Oil seals**—These seals keep oil from leaking past a rotating camshaft.
- **Valve stem seals**—These seals allow only enough oil past them to lubricate the valve guide.
- **Rocker arm**—This lever actuates a valve by pivoting near the center and pushing on the tip of the valve stem to open it.
- **Plugs** (e.g., galley, coolant)—Much like seals, plugs are used to block off passages where oil and coolant flow, and are primarily used to block holes created in the original casting and machining of the head.
- **Camshaft** (only fitted in the cylinder heads of OHC and DOHC engines)—This device provides the force to open the valves.

Valve Arrangement

The arrangement of the valves in the cylinder head is dependent on a few things: the design of the cylinder head, the size of the combustion chamber, the layout of the camshaft and lift assemblies, and the location of the intake and exhaust manifolds. Along with the design of the physical cylinder head, the intended use of the engine has a big impact on the valve size, as the flow requirements of the engine vary greatly depending on the intended use of the engine.

Valves

The valve in the cylinder head is the component that opens and closes the combustion chamber to allow air-fuel mixture to enter or the exhaust to exit (**FIGURE 17-7**). The valve

FIGURE 17-6 A dual overhead camshaft (DOHC) engine has two camshaft mounted to the cylinder head. This includes V-engines as they still only have two camshafts per cylinder head.

FIGURE 17-7 The engine valves are mounted to the cylinder head and seal the combustion chamber from other parts of the engine.

is made out of a high-strength steel that allows for many years of reliable service. The face of the valve seats in the cylinder head and is ground to an interference fit with the valve seat in the cylinder head to complete the seal. When rebuilding the cylinder head, attention must be paid to each valve, as they must all be checked and, if required, remachined to complete a proper cylinder head rebuild. A lot of specialty valves are sodium filled, made of exotic materials, and multiple different sizes, so when one is being replaced, the technician must refer back to the manufacturer's specifications to make sure that the correct valve is being used.

Valve Springs, Retainers, Rotators, and Keepers

The valve is retained in the cylinder head by a trio of components, springs, retainers, and valve keepers. The spring provides the force that closes the valve when the camshaft allows it to close; the spring is kept in its place by the retainer that is locked onto the valve by the keeper. Each one of these components plays a vital role in closing the valve and keeping it closed so that the combustion chamber is sealed, and the power is utilized on pushing the piston down to create motion (**FIGURE 17-8**). The rotator is utilized on the exhaust valve to help keep it cool by rotating it every time it opens and to help keep the carbon buildup on the exhaust valve seat from becoming excessive, causing the valve to stay open.

Valve Seats

The valve seats are the areas where the valve sits in the cylinder head when it is fully closed. The seats are what seals the combustion chamber before the explosion event happens to create the power used to propel the engine. The valve and seat are cut to an interference angle so that when the valve is on the seat, nothing can leak past the valve (**FIGURE 17-9**). Valve seats used to be integral to the cylinder head, but with the advent of unleaded fuel and aluminum cylinder heads, a hardened insert has been created so that it can be serviced when it is worn out of specification.

Valve Guides

Valve guides are holes that are either drilled or pressed into the cylinder head that the valve stem rides in as it is opened and closed. These metal tubes are made of cast iron or a bronze alloy, which allows for the wear resistance and thermal expansion that will work for the particular cylinder head material (**FIGURE 17-10**). Older cylinder heads have the valve guides integrated into the cylinder head and cannot be replaced, but

FIGURE 17-8 The valve spring assembly has multiple pieces: valve spring, retainer, and two keepers to hold it all together.

FIGURE 17-9 A. Valve seats installed in the cylinder head. **B.** A valve seat is replaceable if it becomes damaged in the cylinder head.

FIGURE 17-10 Valve guides control the lateral movement and give it a hole to operate in without destroying the cylinder head. **A.** This is the valve guide as it is installed in the cylinder head. **B.** This is the valve guide pressed out of the cylinder head.

FIGURE 17-11 Different types of valve seals: umbrella seal, posi lock seal, positive seal, and O-ring type.

only remachined. Newer cylinder heads and especially aluminum cylinder heads have pressed-in valve guides that can be replaced when one is worn out of specification. The guides must be inspected every time the cylinder head is off, to verify that they are in serviceable condition.

Valve Seals

The valve seals keep the oil in the cylinder head and out of the combustion chamber. Without these seals, the engine would burn as much oil as it does gasoline. There are many different types of valve seals, but the most recent type used in the automotive engine is the posi lock, or positive stop, valve seal, which is much enhanced over the valve seals of the past (**FIGURE 17-11**). As with any other seal, as time passes, the seals become brittle, allowing oil to seep past them and requiring replacement to stop the leakage. These seals should be replaced every time the cylinder head is rebuilt.

Cylinder Head Design

K17003 Knowledge of cylinder head design and the purpose of the design.

The combustion chamber is located inside the engine, where fuel and air are compressed by the piston and then ignited by the spark plug. The combustion chamber is generally formed into the cylinder head during the casting process. The movable floor of the combustion chamber is formed by the top of the piston. The overall efficiency of the combustion chamber is determined by its design, including its shape, the positioning of the valves, the location of the spark plug, the placement of the water jackets near the combustion chambers, and the shape of the top of the piston. Some engines use two spark plugs per combustion chamber, but this is uncommon.

Today's cylinder heads are designed to help improve the swirl and turbulence of the air-fuel mixture. This prevents fuel droplets from settling on the surfaces of the combustion chamber and cylinder walls, as well as reduces emissions. In the cylinder head, swirl is initially created by the shape and angle of the **intake port**, which allows entry of the air-fuel mixture from the intake manifold and throttle body into the combustion chamber. Turbulence is increased in the quench, or **squish, area**, which is the area between the piston head at top dead center and the cylinder head. Its name comes from the squishing of the air-fuel mixture into a small "charge." The piston squeezes the air-fuel mixture and forces it with great speed out of the squish area. This creates turbulence, which helps to thoroughly mix the heavier fuel and lighter air.

Hemispherical Combustion Chamber

The **hemispherical cylinder head** has been around since approximately 1901. Several early designs were by the Belgian carmaker Pipe in 1905. In the early 1960s, Chrysler Corporation trademarked the name Hemi, which is perhaps the most widely known hemispherical combustion chamber engine created.

A hemispherical, or pent-roof, combustion chamber has the intake valve on one side of the chamber and the exhaust valve on the other (**FIGURE 17-12**). This design provides good cross-flow of the gases and is known as a cross-flow cylinder head. The air-fuel mixture enters on one side, and exhaust gases exit out the other side. Positioning the valves with the spark plug just off center of the combustion chamber leaves more room for relatively large valves and ports, which helps the engine breathe.

With the spark plug located near the center of the chamber, the air-fuel mixture starts to burn at the plug and then continues burning outward in all directions. This moving flame front is called **flame propagation**. With the hemispherical design, the flame front, or front edge of the burning air-fuel mixture, has less distance to travel than in some other designs, which gives rapid and effective combustion.

One of the drawbacks of the original hemispherical combustion chamber engine was that it required a complex valvetrain design that included two rocker arm shafts per head, with uneven rocker arm lengths. In later engines, manufacturers overcame this complex valvetrain design by using either the OHC design or the DOHC design. Thus, the benefits of the hemispherical combustion chamber were combined with the benefits of the OHC and DOHC cylinder heads. In today's DOHC engines, it is very common to see multi-valve, hemispherical cylinder heads. The addition of multiple intake and/or exhaust valves on the cylinder increases engine efficiency. The faster air and fuel can be moved into the combustion chamber and exhaust gases can be moved out of the combustion chamber, the more air and fuel the engine can burn. This concept is similar to having a room full of people and trying to evacuate them with just one door versus multiple doors: The more doors, the faster the flow. This increased flow increases engine power output.

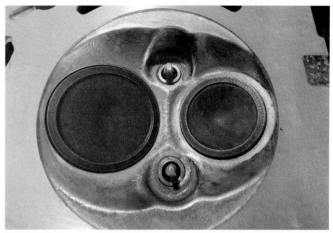

FIGURE 17-12 A hemispherical combustion chamber has the valves on opposite sides of the cylinder; it is half of a sphere.

Wedge

The **wedge combustion chamber** tapers away from the spark plug, which is at the thick end of the wedge. The valves are typically arranged in a straight line positioned along the tapered angle, which puts them at an angle to the top of the piston (**FIGURE 17-13**). The wedge design has a smaller combustion chamber surface area than the other types of cylinder heads, and that a smaller boundary area where fuel cannot burn as easily, which lowers hydrocarbon (unburned fuel) emissions.

Because the flame is directed toward the small end of the wedge, damage caused by detonation is reduced. This wedge design speeds up the velocity of the flame front. If the velocity of the flame front is not fast enough, the pressure building up in the combustion chamber causes the remaining gases to spontaneously ignite, which is called detonation. Detonation creates a second flame front that collides with the first flame front. A very intense pressure wave and audible detonation or pinging sound can be heard. Extreme detonation can damage the engine by concentrating high temperatures and pressures, which can melt a hole in the top of the piston.

Bath Tub

The **bathtub combustion chamber** is oval shaped like an inverted antique bathtub (**FIGURE 17-14**). The valves are mounted vertically and are side by side, making the valvetrain simple in its

FIGURE 17-13 Modern wedge combustion chamber.

FIGURE 17-14 Oval (bathtub) combustion chambers.

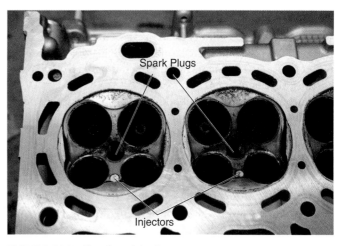

FIGURE 17-15 Gas direct injections.

design. On some of the newer designs, the surface of the head overlaps the piston and forms two squish areas: a large area near the spark plug and a smaller one on the opposite side.

Gas Direct Injection Cylinder Head

The latest cylinder head design is the **gasoline direct injection (GDI) cylinder head**. GDI refers to gasoline injected directly into the combustion chamber just above the piston (**FIGURE 17-15**). Instead of mixing the air-fuel in the intake manifold, it mixes in the combustion chamber. Some GDI systems spray fuel into the combustion chamber during the intake stroke and use the fuel to actually cool the incoming air, which increases its density and resistance to detonation. Other GDI systems have the ability to spray fuel not only on the intake stroke but also near the top of the compression stroke, thus preventing detonation and allowing a lean air-fuel mixture to be burned by concentrating the sprayed fuel very close to the spark plug. The computer has control of the amount and timing of the injection sequence. It varies based on a variety of engine conditions, such as engine load, speed, and temperature. With the GDI cylinder head design, some manufacturers have been able to remove the throttle plate and control engine speed and power by controlling the fuel by itself. This reduces the engine's pumping losses of trying to pull air past the throttle plate. Overall, GDI can improve fuel economy up to about 35% and reduce emissions, especially carbon dioxide.

Intake and Exhaust Ports

The size of intake and **exhaust ports** in the cylinder head can impact engine output by affecting the speed of the air flowing through them. It takes a certain amount of speed to maintain good turbulence and air-fuel mixing. If airflow is too slow, fuel will fall out of the air. If airflow is too fast, the air will be restricted, which reduces the total amount of air-fuel mixture that can enter the combustion chamber.

The use of smaller intake and exhaust ports allows the engine to develop more torque at low engine speeds. By comparison, larger intake and exhaust ports allow greater airflow during the engine's high-speed operation, giving the engine more torque at higher engine speeds. Engines with smaller ported heads, meaning a cylinder head with smaller ports, work well in applications such as four-wheel drive vehicles, which are typically operated at lower engine speeds on trails. Larger port heads work well in engines that operate at high speeds and loads such as in circle-track racing.

Gaskets

Gaskets form a seal by being compressed between stationary parts where liquid or gases could pass. Gaskets are generally designed to be single use and therefore cannot be reused. They can be made of soft materials such as cork, rubber, and paper. They can also be made of soft alloys and metals such as brass, copper, aluminum, and stainless steel. Such materials may be used individually, or in some cases as blends, to produce the required functional material.

▶ **TECHNICIAN TIP**

It has always been said that the intake valve is larger than the exhaust valve. When we had only one intake valve and one exhaust valve per cylinder, that was an accurate statement. Now, with multi-valve heads, that is not always the case. In many three-valve and five-valve engines, the extra valve is an intake valve. In these situations, because there are more intake valves than exhaust valves, the intake valves might be smaller. Therefore, be careful when identifying the valves; these newer multivalve designs might trip you up.

N17001 Remove cylinder head; inspect gasket condition; install cylinder head and gasket; tighten according to manufacturer's specifications and procedures.

K17004 Knowledge of gasket usage and application.

With the increasingly hostile environment that gaskets are required to seal, and with the reduction in the use of asbestos, enhanced gasket materials have been developed. One of the few ways to make engines run cleaner is to raise the temperature at which they operate. Today's cleaner engines typically run 30–40°F hotter than their counterparts of 30 years ago. Thus, the gaskets used in modern engines have to be made of more robust materials, such as vulcanized rubber or EPDM (ethylene propylene diene monomer [M-class] rubber).

Modern gasket manufacturers are producing improved material combinations such as nitrile-cork blends to deal with the extreme demands placed on modern engines, such as higher temperatures, higher compression, longer engine service life, and longer manufacturer warranties. Such combinations can better deal with these issues while maintaining compressibility and minimizing wicking.

Some gasket materials are designed to swell once they are put into service, and increase sealing ability. For instance, when oil inside a valve cover penetrates the edge of the gasket material, it may be designed to swell by approximately 30%. This swelling effect increases the sealing pressure between the head and the valve cover sealing surfaces and helps to seal potential leaks.

Choosing which material and design to use depends on the substance to be sealed (i.e., oil, fuel, exhaust gases), the pressures and temperatures involved (i.e., combustion gases, coolant), and the materials the mating surfaces to be sealed are made of (i.e., what materials the gasket will seal against—aluminum, plastic, cast iron, etc.). The best way to determine which gasket material is appropriate for an engine is to refer to the manufacturer's service information.

Head Gaskets

The head gaskets seal and contain the pressures of combustion within the engine, between the cylinder head and the engine block. They also seal oil passages between the engine block and the cylinder head. Finally, head gaskets control the flow of coolant between the engine block and the cylinder head.

Some high-temperature head gaskets are called anisotropic in nature, meaning that the gasket is designed to conduct heat laterally to transfer heat from the combustion chamber to the coolant faster. These gaskets are normally constructed with a steel core. Special facing materials are added to both sides of the gasket core to provide a comprehensive seal under varying expansion conditions.

On some engines, the thickness of the head gasket provides or adjusts the proper clearances between the piston and the cylinder head. The service information (or repair information) for a vehicle will specify how to select the proper thickness of gasket and why that thickness is needed. Sometimes it is as simple as looking for a mark denoting the thickness of the old gasket and using that to order the new gasket.

Other head gaskets incorporate stainless steel **fire rings** to help contain heat and pressure within the cylinder. Fire rings are steel rings built into the cylinder head gasket. The rings provide extra sealing on the top of the cylinder to help seal in the high-combustion pressures (hence the name "fire ring"). For high-performance use, such as in race cars, some engine builders use soft metal O-rings, which fit in shallow grooves cut in the head around the cylinders and passageways, to seal the compression and fluids. The O-rings are crushed in place when the head bolts are torqued into place. This is a very effective but expensive way to seal the heads.

For many late-model vehicles, the preferred head gasket is a **multilayer steel (MLS) head gasket** (**FIGURE 17-16**). These gaskets offer a wide range of benefits, such as strategically placed sealing beads that help eliminate leak paths, extra strong layers that provide superior combustion sealing, and a stainless steel material that maintains its shape despite thermal expansion and

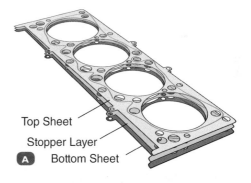

Top Sheet
Stopper Layer
A　Bottom Sheet

B

FIGURE 17-16 Multilayer steel (MLS) head gasket.

scrubbing between the engine block and the cylinder head. Many MLS and other head gaskets have an added silicone-based outer coating on both sides of the side material layers to provide additional cold sealing ability during start-up and warm-up.

Seals

Gaskets cannot be used around a rotating part, such as where the camshaft protrudes through the front of the cylinder head, because they would quickly wear out and leak. To seal the rotating parts of an engine, oil seals are needed. Oil seals are round seals made of rubber or a rubber-type compound of silicone, EPDM, or another durable, flexible material, placed in a metal housing. These seals are typically driven into a machined bore around a rotating part. A metal spring, called a garter spring, is wrapped circularly around the inside of the seal and applies a small, constant pressure to keep the lip in contact with the rotating part it is sealing. The most widely used seal for rotating parts is the lip-type dynamic oil seal. This seal is a precisely shaped, dynamic rubber lip. Like other oil seals, the lip-type dynamic oil seal also uses a garter spring to help keep the lip of the seal in contact with the shaft.

A similar sealing principle is used to seal the valve stem to prevent oil from entering the engine combustion chamber. Like the oil seals, the valve stem seal is pressed onto the valve guide. It allows the valve to be wiped almost clean of oil on its opening trip, keeping a minimum amount of oil pulled down between the valve stem and the guide for lubrication purposes.

Stationary and slowly rotating or sliding shafts can also be sealed by using O-rings, a simple sealing device consisting of a rounded ring of rubber or plastic. O-rings are typically used to seal a joint against high pressure or the circumference of a rotating shaft from high- or low-pressure fluid leakage. The O-ring is inserted around the part to be sealed and held in place by an external housing. The O-ring seals the two surfaces. In many cases, the housing supplies the force to keep the ring in direct contact with the shaft. O-rings are generally effective at sealing high pressures where the differential speed between the opposing surfaces is minimal. In contrast, a lip seal is effective at sealing low pressures, but the differential speed between the opposing surfaces can be substantial. As the lip-type seal wears, the garter spring holds tension on the seal, keeping it against the part it is sealing. The O-ring seal has no mechanism for self-adjustment. Once worn, its sealing ability is compromised.

Sealants

Sealants are used to seal two surfaces that are in stationary contact with each other, such as between a gasket and the sealing surface of the part being sealed, or between two mating surfaces without a gasket between them. Different sealants are used for various applications, and there are applications in which sealants are not to be used as well. For example, sealants are almost never applied to head gaskets.

To aid in gasket sealing, there are many different brands and types of sealants. One of the most popular types is **room temperature vulcanizing (RTV) silicone**. This adhesive is able to set, or "vulcanize," at room temperature (**FIGURE 17-17**). When RTV is applied, it has the consistency of a gel, and as it sets, it becomes rubbery. RTV should only be applied thick enough to fill the gaps with a small amount. If too much is used, it will squeeze out from between the surfaces and form large globs of material on the inside of the engine that can break off and plug up the oil pump screen, starving the engine of oil. Another caution when using RTV silicone is to make sure you use oxygen sensor–safe RTV on engines equipped with oxygen sensors. Regular RTV gases will be drawn through the PCV system and burned in the combustion chamber. The resulting burned silicone gases will then coat the surface of the oxygen sensor, rendering it inoperative.

Some technicians prefer a nonhardening gasket sealant so that the sealant will "give" when the metal parts expand and contract under normal heating and cooling cycles. Additionally, this type of sealant is very forgiving with gasket surfaces that are less than perfect (e.g., scratched, nickel pitted). Gasoline-proof hardening

FIGURE 17-17 Room temperature vulcanizing (RTV) silicone material being applied.

sealants are also available, but they have little to no give once dry and are only used in extreme situations such as to help hold a cracked component together when a new component is not available. Always follow the manufacturer's recommendations for application.

A variety of different chemicals are available to hold gaskets in place and aid in sealing. The most popular adhesive to hold a gasket in place is a form of contact cement that comes in an aerosol can. Contact cement is capable of adhering to many different surfaces, including felt, cork, metal, paper, rubber, and asbestos gaskets. In an automotive application, contact cement has been used on valve cover gaskets, fuel pump gaskets, and intake and exhaust manifold gaskets. However, adhesive sealants are not typically used on most newer-model vehicles. Before using any sealant, check the vehicle manufacturer's service information to be sure the product can be used with your application.

▶ Cylinder Head Service

Cylinder Head Repair

Cracks in the cylinder head are a serious but relatively common problem because of its lightweight construction. The main cause of cylinder head cracks is thermal stress. When metal is heated, it expands. Although cylinder heads are designed to withstand a certain amount of expansion, and their retaining bolts or studs a certain amount of stretch, the elevation in engine operating temperatures due to faults in the cooling system can push a cylinder head and retainers beyond their design limits. Over time, expansion and contraction can cause the metal to deform, resulting in cracks forming. Depending on the location of the crack, coolant, oil, or combustion gases may leak out of the cylinder head into the surrounding engine parts. Pressure testing the cylinder block and heads is a reliable method for identifying hard-to-see cracks.

The presence of a crack does not automatically condemn the cylinder head to the scrap bin. In some cases, repair methods have proven successful and less costly than replacement. Small cracks can be fixed by pinning (also known as cold repair), a process of drilling holes in a crack and installing overlapping pins to fill it that are then peened over to seal and blend the surface. Although pinning sounds simple enough, it should only be performed by a highly trained machinist, preferably an ASE-certified master machinist. Furnace welding can also be used to repair cylinder head cracks. This process involves heating the cylinder head to extreme temperatures (about 1300°F [704°C]) and welding iron into the crack with an acetylene torch. This process requires even more skill than pinning and should not be attempted by anyone who is not an expert.

Heat stress and pressure stress can also cause the head to warp so that the sealing surface is no longer perfectly flat. Resurfacing the cylinder head restores a perfectly flat and specified surface finish to the head for placement of a new gasket. Resurfacing is best performed by milling the surface but can also be performed by grinding with the proper head-surfacing machine. The resurfacing process must be precise, with no more material removed than is necessary to clean up the surface, and is best left to a skilled machinist.

If you are dealing with an OHC head, then two surfaces must be in alignment—the head surface and the camshaft journal bores. If the head surface is warped, it is likely that the camshaft bore is also warped. Because the camshaft is straight, if the camshaft bore is warped, the camshaft will bind in the journal bearings. This means that a warped OHC head should be straightened so that the journal bore is aligned, before the head surface is machined. Straightening a head is usually performed by bolting a head down to a straightening plate with shims placed between the head and the plate so that the head is under tension. Then the head is heated up to not more than 500°F (260°C) and allowed to cool slowly. The head is again checked for flatness, and if it is flat, the head surface and camshaft journals can then be machined.

Damaged valves and valve seats can sometimes be reconditioned and reused rather than replaced. However, the price of new valves has dropped significantly over the years, making replacement the more common option for newer vehicles. For older vehicles for which replacement parts are not readily available, reconditioning is necessary. Reconditioning involves cleaning, fault detection, and machining. The process requires special equipment and a skilled and knowledgeable machinist.

N17002 Clean and visually inspect a cylinder head for cracks; check gasket surface areas for warpage and surface finish; check passage condition.

K17005 Knowledge of cylinder head repair and servicing.

Applied Science

AS-93: Metallurgy: The technician can explain the critical need for metals of different hardnesses in automotive parts.

A typical automotive application of metals with different hardnesses is the relationship between crankshaft journals and crankshaft bearings in engines. Crankshafts are typically manufactured from cast iron or steel and are frequently surface hardened to provide a hard surface for bearing contact, providing resistance to wear. Crankshaft bearings are surfaced with soft materials, typically babbitt, copper-lead, or aluminum alloys.

In normal running, a pressurized film of oil is maintained between the crankshaft and the bearing. Two essential properties are achieved through the use of soft surface materials—embeddability and conformability. Embeddability refers to the ability of the soft surface to absorb foreign materials forced between the crankshaft and the bearing, helping to prevent crankshaft wear. Conformability allows the bearing surface to move or shift to conform to a worn or damaged crankshaft journal.

K17006 Knowledge of how to remove the cylinder head.

S17001 Remove a cylinder head.

S17002 Clean and inspect a cylinder head.

▶ TECHNICIAN TIP

It is always a good idea to measure and record the installed valve height for at least one exhaust valve and one intake valve. This specification can be hard to locate for some vehicles. Because hydraulic lifters can only compensate approximately 0.060" to 0.080", knowing the installed height will be invaluable.

Removing Cylinder Heads

Removing a cylinder head is considered a major task and is usually time intensive; therefore, cylinder head removal is done only after extensive testing and with a certainty that the problem lies in the cylinder head itself, its associated parts, or a part requiring removal of the cylinder head to access it (such as a piston). Once the diagnosis has been made, you need to follow the steps as listed in the service information for the vehicle you are working on, because every engine is different. In fact, some manufacturers require that their head bolts be loosened in a specified pattern in specified steps and at certain temperatures. Failure to follow the manufacturer's instructions can lead to damage to the head.

To remove a cylinder head, follow the steps in **SKILL DRILL 17-1**.

Cleaning, Disassembling, and Inspecting a Cylinder Head

The cylinder head must be cleaned after removal, to make the inspection and repair process more efficient. You cannot have a good repair on a cylinder head if there are chunks of sludge and grime concealing damage or constantly falling into the area where you are working. Cleaning the cylinder head usually involves mechanically cleaning it with a scraping device such as a gasket scraper. If so, most aluminum heads must be scraped with a nonmetallic tool such as a plastic or nylon scraper made for the job. In most cases, the head must also be chemically cleaned in a spray tank, hot tank, cold tank, ultrasonic cleaner, or specially designed oven once it has been disassembled.

Follow the equipment manufacturer's recommendations when using a particular type of cleaner.

To clean and inspect a cylinder head, follow the steps in **SKILL DRILL 17-2**.

SKILL DRILL 17-1 Removing a Cylinder Head

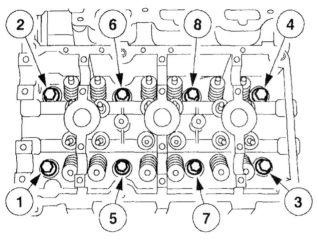

1. Research the procedure for removing the cylinder head(s) in the appropriate service information. Determine whether the head bolts are torque-to-yield (TTY) bolts. If so, you will need to discard them and replace them with new TTY bolts upon reassembly unless the service information directs you to measure and reuse them if in specification. Determine whether the head bolts need to be loosened in a specified sequence.

G01360709

Continued

2. Before the heads come off, make sure you put an identifying mark on at least one of them so that you know which head goes on which side of the block. Follow the specified procedure to remove all of the head bolts, and set them aside.

3. If you are dealing with a head gasket that is stuck to the head and block surface, reinstall two corner head bolts three or four turns in their respective holes. When you break the seal of the head gasket, these bolts will stop the head from falling off.

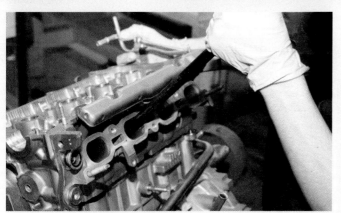

4. If the engine is mounted on an engine stand, double-check that the safety pin is in your engine stand so the weight of the engine does not shift when you try to loosen the heads. Insert a pry bar or a long breaker bar handle into one of the intake port openings of the head, and give it a firm push. You don't want to damage the inside of the intake port, so don't push too hard.

5. Remove the safety bolts from the head. Put a few fingers in one of the intake ports and your other hand in an exhaust port to get a good grip before carefully lifting it. Cast iron cylinder heads are very heavy, especially if you have a big engine, so get some help lifting, if you need it.

Continued

6. Inspect the cylinder head visually for any unusual conditions. Crusty flakes inside the combustion chamber are burned oil, which is a good indication of worn valve guides or piston rings. Engine symptoms can often be diagnosed by looking at the sealing surfaces of the head, block, and old gaskets, which sometimes stick to the head or block.

7. Inspect the block deck where the cylinder head gasket seals for pitting, warpage, or scarring so that you can see whether the cylinder block can be reused.

SKILL DRILL 17-2 Cleaning and Inspecting a Cylinder Head

1. Place your cylinder head in a cylinder head–holding fixture. These fixtures are usually designed to hold the cylinder head off the work bench, allowing you to gain access for valve removal.

2. Tap the valve retainers lightly with a hammer and socket to break the valve keepers loose from the retainers.

Continued

3. Use a valve spring compressor to compress the valve spring on each valve (one at a time), and remove the valve keepers.

4. After the keepers are removed, the valve can be taken off; make sure all parts are kept in the order of the way they came off. That way, if they are going to be reused, their wear patterns will match.

5. All parts you take off the cylinder head should go into a cylinder head disassembly board or small, labeled bins, to help you keep track of what valve and spring goes where for later installation. When in doubt, write it down and label it!

6. Clean the gasket mating surfaces. On a cast iron head, cleaning is usually done with a flexible abrasive pad or by hand with a gasket scraper. If it is an aluminum head, use only plastic or nylon gasket scrapers. Refer to the service information to ensure the proper procedure is being used to clean all gasket mating surfaces.

Continued

7. Using a straightedge, measure the cylinder head warpage by setting the straightedge on the surface you are checking. See if you can slide a 0.001" (0.0254 mm) feeler gauge under the straightedge. If you can't, then keep checking the surface in various places to ensure the same reading across the cylinder head. If you can slide a 0.001" feeler gauge underneath the straightedge, then you need to find out how big the deformation (warpage) is. Keep going up in value—0.002" (0.051 mm), 0.003" (0.0762 mm)—until the feeler will no longer fit underneath the straightedge. The last feeler blade that will go under it is the reading. Compare the reading to the service information warpage limit. Typical allowed warpage is 0.003" or less.

8. Clean the cylinder head in an approved manner. This could be with a spray wash cabinet, hot tank, cold tank, ultrasonic cleaner, or high-temperature oven. Be aware that aluminum heads cannot generally be cleaned in a hot tank or high-temperature oven. Follow the manufacturer's recommended procedure for thoroughly cleaning the head.

9. If the head is made of cast iron, you can locate small cracks with a magnaflux tool. The magnaflux process involves placing a strong electromagnet across each part of the head surface at 90-degree offsets and lightly dusting the head with a magnetic powder. If there is a crack present, the powder will adhere to the crack because the crack creates a north and south magnetic field at that point, and the powder sticks to it.

10. If the head is made of aluminum, the magnaflux process cannot be used because the metal is nonferrous. Spray or wipe a penetrating die over the surface to be checked, followed by a light coat of developer. Once the developer dries, any cracks should show up as colored lines.

Continued

11. Pressure checking can be used on both cast iron and aluminum heads, but is usually available only at well-equipped machine shops. The cooling system passages are blocked off and filled with compressed air. They are then either immersed in water and inspected for leaks or sprayed with a soapy solution and inspected for bubbles.

Inspecting Valves and Valve Seats

Valves and valve seats must operate in very hostile conditions, so they have to be inspected closely whenever the cylinder head is removed from the engine. Valves can burn or warp, which leads to misfire issues. The valve tip can also become worn from lack of lubrication, leading to a ticking sound, and the valve stems can wear in the area that moves inside the valve stem, leading to burning of engine oil. When valves are removed from the cylinder head, the valves and seats should be inspected visually for cracks, burn marks, signs of leaks, and damage to the valve face, stem, and tip. If any of these issues are found, the valve must be replaced, and the seat will have to be either replaced or repaired, depending on the damage. If there are no apparent issues, then the valves and seats should be measured and compared to specifications.

The valve stem diameter should be measured in the area that rides in the valve guide with a micrometer and compared to specifications. Some valves come with a tapered valve stem where the stem closest to the head end of the valve is slightly narrower to allow for expansion of the stem on today's hotter-running engines. The margin of the valve must be measured with a machinist's rule to make sure it is within specifications. The valve seat width also has to be measured and compared to specifications.

To inspect valves and valve seats and determine any necessary actions, follow the steps in **SKILL DRILL 17-3**.

N17003 Inspect valve guides for wear; check valve stem-to-guide clearance; determine needed action.

N17004 Inspect valves and valve seats; determine needed action.

K17007 Knowledge of inspecting the valves and seats.

S17003 Inspect valves and valve seats.

▶ **TECHNICIAN TIP**

The valve margin gets thinner as the valve face is cut or surfaced during a valve job. If it is too thin, the valve will burn in a short time. Always measure the margin and compare it to specifications before reusing it.

SKILL DRILL 17-3 Inspecting Valves and Valve Seats

1. Visually inspect each valve for signs of burning, warpage, and excessive face, stem, and tip wear. If found, replace the valves with new ones.

Continued

2. Visually inspect each valve seat for signs of burning, leakage, or excessive wear. If found, the seat must be machined or replaced.

3. Using a micrometer, measure each valve stem diameter in three places where the valve rides in the valve guide, and average your answers.

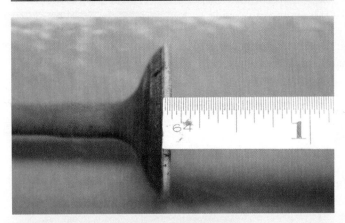

4. Measure the valve margin with a machinist's rule, and record your readings.

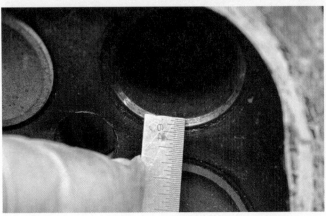

5. Measure the width of the valve seats, and record your readings.

Continued

Application	Specification
Intake Valves	
Face Angle	46°
Face Runout (Maximum)	.0015" (.038 mm)
Head Diameter	1.396-1.399" (35.47-35.53 mm)
Minimum Margin	.010" (.25 mm)
Length	4.227" (107.29 mm)
Tip-To-Groove Distance	.1346" (3.420 mm)
Stem Diameter	.2331-.2339" (5.921-5.941 mm)
Installed Height	.9787-1.002" (24.86-25.62 mm)

6. Compare all readings to the specifications, and determine any needed actions.

Valve Stem Height

The valve stem height must be measured before any machine work is completed to the cylinder head. This measurement must be documented and compared to the installed height once machining has been completed so that the technician can select the right shim to put under the valve spring to return the spring to the correct seat pressure on the valve in order to keep it closed. As the machinist machines the seats and the valve, the valve becomes deeper in the cylinder head, which means the pressure on the valve when the spring is at rest is less than it was before, as the height of the valve stem has become taller. The tension must be returned to specification, or there is a possibility that the valve will not close properly or quickly enough to not cause a misfire (**FIGURE 17-18**).

Inspecting Valve Guides and Valve Stem-to-Guide Clearance

Valves and valve guides are subject to high temperatures and pressures that tend to wear their sides. If they wear much at all, oil can be pulled down the valve stem and burned in the combustion chamber of exhaust. If the wear continues, the valve can move around in the guide so far that the head of the valve does not close properly and catches on the top of the valve seat. This causes the valve to leak and leads to intermittent misfires in that cylinder.

FIGURE 17-18 The technician is measuring the valve installed height so that they can return the height to the same measurement after machining on the cylinder head.

S17004 Inspect valve guides for wear and check valve stem-to-guide clearance.

Valves and guides can be measured in two ways: with a micrometer or with a dial indicator. If using a micrometer, a ball gauge is used to measure the top, center, and bottom of the valve guide. The ball gauge is placed in the valve guide in each of those positions and expanded until both sides of the gauge touch the inside of the guide. It is then removed from the guide, measured with a micrometer, and recorded. The center reading is then subtracted from the ends to determine how much the guide is tapered. The smallest reading (usually the center reading) is used to determine the overall size of the guide. The valve stem is also measured and recorded. If the valve stem is within specifications, then the difference between the valve guide and the valve stem is the valve-to-guide clearance, and all of the readings can be compared to the manufacturer's specifications.

A dial indicator is used with the valve installed in the valve guide. The dial indicator is mounted on the head and placed against the side of the valve stem near the top of the valve. With the valve at its normally open height, rock the head of the valve stem back and forth, observing the movement on the dial indicator, and compare to specifications.

To inspect valve guides for wear, check valve stem-to-guide clearance, and determine any necessary actions, using a micrometer, follow the steps in **SKILL DRILL 17-4**.

To inspect valve guides for wear using a dial indicator, follow the steps in **SKILL DRILL 17-5**.

SKILL DRILL 17-4 Inspecting Valve Guides for Wear

1. Clean the guide with solvent and a valve guide brush if not already cleaned.

2. Insert the ball gauge into the top of the guide, and expand it until it touches both sides with a slight amount of drag.

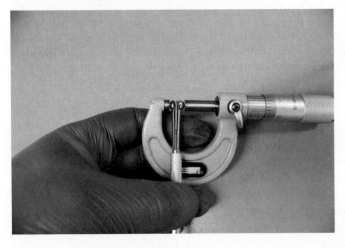

3. Carefully pull the ball gauge out of the guide without disturbing the setting, and measure it with a micrometer. Record your reading.

4. Repeat this procedure on the center portion of the valve guide, and record your reading.

5. Repeat this procedure on the bottom portion of the valve guide, and record your reading.

Continued

6. Measure the valve stem diameter at the top, center, and bottom of the wear area, and record your readings.

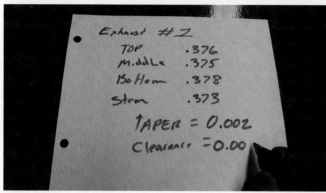

7. Calculate the taper and valve clearance; compare all of the readings to specifications, and determine any necessary actions.

SKILL DRILL 17-5 Inspecting Valve Guides for Wear, Using a Dial Indicator

1. Verify that the valve guide is clean. Reinstall the valve in the guide at the fully open length.

2. Set the dial indicator so it can measure the side-to-side movement of the head of the valve.

Continued

3. Move the valve side to side and measure the movement with the dial indicator. Record your reading.

Application	Specification
Intake Valves	
Face Angle	46°
Face Runout (Maximum)	.0015" (.038 mm)
Head Diameter	1.396–1.399" (35.47–35.53 mm)
Minimum Margin	.010" (.25 mm)
Length	4.227" (107.29 mm)
Tip-To-Groove Distance	.1346" (3.420 mm)
Stem Diameter	.2331–.2339" (5.921–5.941 mm)
Installed Height [1]	.9787–1.002" (24.86–25.62 mm)

4. Compare to specifications, and determine any necessary actions.

Inspecting Valve Springs

Using the correct size and strength of valve spring is critical to engine operation. Valve springs must be able to quickly and firmly force the valves closed. It is important to always measure the valve springs and confirm that they meet the specifications before installing them. The three key steps in testing a valve spring are (1) checking for squareness, (2) measuring spring height, and (3) measuring the installed pressure. Checking for squareness is a test to ensure that the spring is not damaged and can compress and load the valve evenly. Measuring spring height is simply checking that the spring is indeed the correct height and has not fatigued. A valve with uneven pressure or the incorrect installed pressure will cause the valve to wear the valve stem and guide due to the side-to-side pulling force exerted by the "bent" spring.

Reassembling a Cylinder Head

Once all work on the valves, springs, and head is completed, the cylinder head must be cleaned again and then reassembled. The following is a generic version of cylinder head reassembly and is not meant to supersede any manufacturer's cylinder head reassembly instructions. You should always check for the most current information on the vehicle you are working on through the manufacturer's recommended service information.

To reassemble a cylinder head, follow the steps in **SKILL DRILL 17-6**.

Inspecting Pushrods and Rocker Arms

Because pushrods and rocker arms operate under large sliding forces, they tend to experience wear over time and have to be inspected at each point of contact. On pushrods, that means each end. The balls or sockets typically lose their roundedness and become slightly

N17005 Inspect valve springs for squareness and free height comparison; determine needed action.

N17006 Check valve spring assembled height and valve stem height; determine needed action.

S17005 Inspect valve springs.

S17006 Reassemble a cylinder head.

SKILL DRILL 17-6 Reassembling a Cylinder Head

1. Ensure that all parts and passageways have been cleaned, checked for defects, and replaced if necessary. If any defects are found, correct them before continuing.

2. Dip the valve stem that is about to be installed in clean engine oil, or use the appropriate assembly lubrication. This provides initial start-up lubrication.

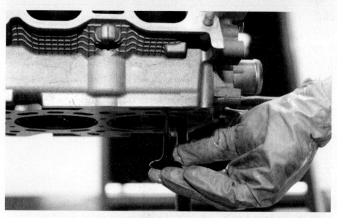

3. Insert the corresponding valve into the valve guide, and place the protective sleeve over the grooves near the end of the valve stem. The sleeve will protect the seal from being cut by the keeper grooves as it passes over them.

4. Dip the valve seal in clean engine oil, and install it down over the exposed top of the valve guide assembly, using an installer if necessary. Be careful! Valve seals can differ in size from intake to exhaust, so be sure you are putting the valve seal on the correct valve. (*Note:* O-ring valve seals are put on after the spring and retainer are compressed, but before the keepers are installed.)

Continued

5. Remove the protective sleeve, and place the valve spring and retainer down over the installed valve.

6. Compress the valve spring and retainer with the valve spring compressor, and install the valve keepers. Be sure the keepers are locked into their groove before releasing pressure on the valve spring compressor!

7. Repeat this process for the installation of the remaining valves.

N17007 Inspect pushrods, rocker arms, rocker arm pivots, and shafts for wear, bending, cracks, looseness, and blocked oil passages (orifices); determine needed action.

N17008 Adjust valves (mechanical or hydraulic lifters).

K17008 Knowledge of how the pushrods and rocker arms operate.

S17007 Inspect pushrods and rocker arms.

pointy. Also, there is typically a small flat spot on the top of the pushrod. If the pushrod is worn, the flat spot will be smaller than it should be, or worn off altogether. Pushrods also have to be perfectly straight; otherwise, they are subject to bending, which would render them inoperative. Rolling them on a piece of glass or perfectly flat surface plate will indicate if they are bent.

Rocker arms have three potential wear surfaces to inspect: the pushrod end, the valve end, and the pivot. The pushrod end of the rocker arm mates with the end of the pushrod, so they usually wear similarly. The valve end of the rocker arm can also wear, creating a groove in the face. The pivot can mate to a ball-shaped pivot, a T-shaped pivot, or a pivot shaft. Look at both the pivot and the mating surface on the rocker arm to see if there is excessive wear. If any of the three surfaces of the rocker arm are excessively worn, the rocker arm and pivot will have to be replaced.

To inspect pushrods, rocker arms, and rocker arm pivots and shafts for wear, bending, cracks, looseness, and blocked oil passages (orifices), and to determine any necessary actions, follow the steps in **SKILL DRILL 17-7**.

Inspecting Flatness of Cylinder Head Deck/Tools Used

When inspecting the flatness of a cylinder head, the technician must first clean the cylinder head mating surface with a Roloc™ bristle disc or something similar so that all of the gasket material is removed from the cylinder head. Once you have the surface clean, you can then use a true bar to see whether the surface of the cylinder head is warped. If the cylinder head is warped, then it will have to be machined to create a true surface in order for the head gasket to seal properly.

Installing the Overhead Camshaft (OHC) and Dual Overhead Camshafts (DOHC)

Now that the valves are installed, it may or may not be time to install the camshaft(s) and valve actuators. In some engine designs, the camshaft(s) prevents access to tighten the head bolts; therefore, the camshaft(s) have to be installed after the head has been properly torqued into place on the block. In other engines, the camshaft and valve actuators can be installed while the head is off the engine, without interfering with torquing the head bolts. Always check the manufacturer's procedure to know when to install the camshaft(s).

SKILL DRILL 17-7 Inspecting Pushrods, Rocker Arms, and Rocker Arm Pivots and Shafts

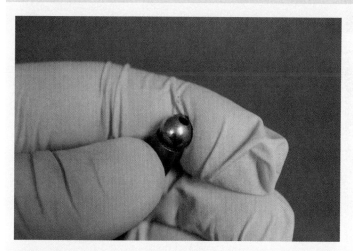

1. Visually inspect the ends of the pushrods for excessive wear. If the pushrod is hollow, blow compressed air through it to verify that it is not plugged.

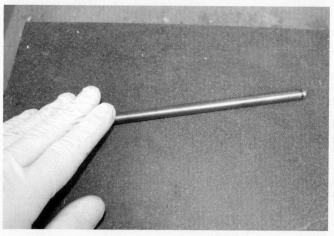

2. Roll each pushrod on a piece of glass or surface plate to check if it is bent. If the pushrods are hollow, check that they are clear by blowing compressed air through them.

Continued

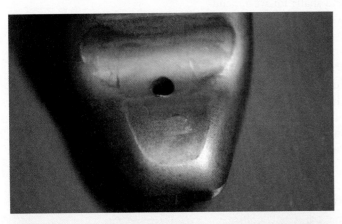

3. Visually inspect the valve end of the rocker arms for excessive wear or damage.

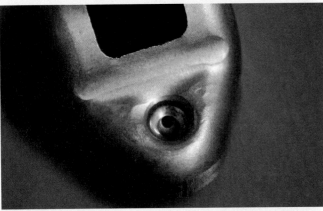

4. Visually inspect the pushrod end of the rocker arms for excessive wear or damage. If they are equipped with an oil passage, blow compressed air through them to check that they are not plugged.

5. Visually inspect the center pivot surface of the rocker arms for wear or damage.

6. Visually inspect the pivots or rocker arm shafts for wear or damage. If the rocker arm shafts are equipped with oil passages, blow compressed air through them to check that they are not plugged.

▶ Valve and Seat Service

Valve Reconditioning

Valve reconditioning requires that the valve be removed from the cylinder head, inspected for straightness, and then placed in a valve grinding machine so that the valve head angles can be ground to the proper angle to create an interference fit with the valve seat in the cylinder head (**FIGURE 17-19**). This step in the process is what creates the seal between the valve and the valve seat so that the combustion chamber is sealed.

Valve Guide Reconditioning

Once it is determined that the valve guide is worn, the machinist must decide whether the valve guide is replaceable or if it is integral to the cylinder head. If the guide is replaceable, then the old guide must be pressed out and the new one pressed in (**FIGURE 17-20**). Once the valve guide is pressed in, it must be trimmed to the proper length so that it will not interfere with the valve spring being compressed. If the valve guide is integral to the cylinder head, the machinist can knurl the valve guide to decrease the clearance between the valve and the guide, bringing it back into specification (**FIGURE 17-21**).

Valve Seat Reconditioning

The valve seat must be reconditioned when the valve is resurfaced so that the angles on both create the seal required to keep the combustion pressures inside the chamber. To recondition a valve seat, the machinist mounts the cylinder head in a valve cutting machine, which lines up the valve guide with where it cuts the seat so that the valve is in the proper location on the valve seat (**FIGURE 17-22**). The machine can then be programmed to cut the three angles that create the required seal between the valve and seat. The key to this procedure is setting up the machine correctly to cut the seal true to the valve guide, which will be the center of the valve.

Valve Stem Seal Replacement

Valve stem seal replacement requires the disassembly of the valve springs and retainers so that the technician can access the valve stem seals for replacement. This job usually involves removing the cylinder head, so the technician can access the underside of the valve to compress the valve spring in order to remove the retainer (**FIGURE 17-23**). The main purpose of replacing these seals is to stop oil seepage into the combustion chamber through one of the valves. This should be standard procedure when replacing the cylinder head gasket on a high-mileage engine and should not be overlooked.

N17009 Replace valve stem seals on an assembled engine; inspect valve spring retainers, locks/keepers, and valve lock/keeper grooves; determine needed action.

K17009 Knowledge of valve and seat service.

▶ TECHNICIAN TIP

In most cylinder heads, intake valves are larger than exhaust valves. In a naturally aspirated engine, the engine relies totally on atmospheric pressure to push air into the cylinder. A drop in pressure occurs as the piston moves down the cylinder during the intake stroke. Atmospheric pressure is pushing air and gas through the intake manifold, filling the void where the piston was. The average atmospheric pressure at sea level is 14.7 pounds per square inch (psi), or 101 kilopascals (kPa). The exhaust valves are smaller because removing the exhaust gas is a much easier task due to the piston creating pressure as it moves up the cylinder. The exhaust gases are actually pushed out by the piston, which creates a greater force than atmospheric pressure pushing air into the cylinder.

▶ TECHNICIAN TIP

Up until the early 1970s, gasoline contained tetraethyl lead, which was used to inexpensively boost the octane. Lead also lubricated the valve seats by providing a cushioning effect, which allowed the valve seats to be machined into the base cast iron material and still give good life. However, when the installation of catalytic converters was mandated for emission control purposes in the mid-70s, lead could not be used in fuel anymore, as lead would contaminate and kill the converter. This situation required the use of hardened valve seats to resist wearing out quickly.

FIGURE 17-19 Valve resurfacing is done in a machine that rotates the valve while the technician is guiding it into the grinding wheel to clean up the surface.

FIGURE 17-20 Most valve guides in today's engines are pressed in so they can be replaced once they are out of specification.

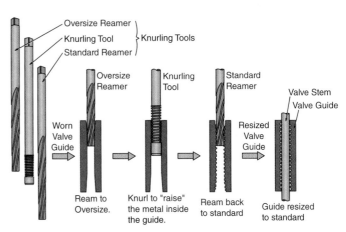

FIGURE 17-21 Older engine, usually with cast iron heads, have the valve guides integrated into the cylinder head, which means they are not removable. To repair these guides, the machinist must knurl the guide with a tool to raise the metal within the guide to make the hole smaller.

FIGURE 17-22 Instead of using a grinding wheel to grind the valve seats into the shape desired, the machinist uses a valve seat cutting machine to machine the valve seat to the desired angles.

FIGURE 17-23 Once the valve assembly is in final assembly the valve seal is installed so that the cylinder head is ready to be installed on the engine.

▶ Wrap-Up

Ready for Review

▶ The cylinder head provides the "end cap" of the combustion chamber and a means for admitting air and fuel to the combustion chamber and exhausting gases after combustion.

▶ The cylinder head is also an integral part of the engine cooling system; it allows coolant to flow around the top of the combustion chamber, removing excess heat and preventing overheating of the engine.

▶ The camshaft works with the cylinder head and valves to regulate the flow of the air-fuel mixture into, and the exhaust gases out of, the combustion chamber by opening and closing the valves at the proper times. The camshaft may be located either in the cylinder head or adjacent to it in the cylinder block.

▶ There are five events in the operation of any internal combustion engine: intake of the air-fuel mixture, compression of the air-fuel mixture, ignition of the air-fuel mixture, a power stroke triggered by combustion of the air-fuel mixture, and the exhaust of burned gases from the combustion chamber.

▶ The head gasket is a thin metal sheet, often made of layers of different materials, with holes cut to accommodate the piston openings and passageways for oil and coolant. It is

- installed between the head surface and the block surface to seal the cylinder head assembly to the engine block.
- In an overhead valve (OHV) engine, the valves are positioned in the cylinder head assembly, directly over the top of the piston. The valves are operated by a camshaft that is located in the cylinder block. They transmit valve lifting force through lifters, pushrods, and rocker arms.
- The dual overhead cam (DOHC) engine contains two camshafts per cylinder head. Typically, one camshaft operates the intake valves and the other operates the exhaust valves. In most cases, the camshaft sits right on top of the valves and operates the valves directly through a bucket lifter, with no rocker arms or cam followers.
- Valve keepers keep a valve spring's retainer attached to the valve while in the cylinder head.
- Valve retainers are thick, washer-shaped pieces of metal with a tapered center hole is fitted over the top of the valve stem and holds the top of the valve spring to keep pressure on the valves.
- Valve springs return valves to their fully closed positions, and hold them closed, after being opened.
- Oil seals keep oil from leaking past a rotating camshaft.
- Valve stem seals allow only enough oil past them to lubricate the valve guide.
- Rocker arms actuate the valves by pivoting near the center and pushing on the tip of the valve stem to open it.
- Plugs are used to block off passages where oil and coolant flow and are primarily used to block holes used in the original casting and machining of the head.
- The valve seats are the areas that the valve sits in the cylinder head when it is fully closed. The seats seal the combustion chamber before the explosion event happens to create the power that is used to propel the engine.
- Valve guides are holes that are either drilled or pressed into the cylinder head that the valve stem rides in as it is opened and closed.
- The combustion chamber is located inside the engine where fuel and air are compressed by the piston and then ignited by the spark plug and is generally formed into the cylinder head during the casting process.
- A cylinder head function is to improve the swirl and turbulence of the air-fuel mixture. This prevents fuel droplets from settling on the surfaces of the combustion chamber and cylinder walls, as well as reducing emissions.
- Swirl is initially created by the shape and angle of the intake port, which allows entry of the air-fuel mixture from the intake manifold and throttle body into the combustion chamber.
- Turbulence is increased in the quench or squish area, which is the area between the piston head at top dead center and the cylinder head.
- A hemispherical or pent-roof combustion chamber has the intake valve on one side of the chamber and the exhaust valve on the other, and provides good cross-flow of the gases and is known as a cross-flow cylinder head.
- Flame propagation (moving flame front) takes place with the spark plug located near the center of the chamber, the air-fuel mixture starts to burn at the plug and then continues burning outward in all directions.
- The wedge combustion chamber tapers away from the spark plug, which is at the thick end of the wedge. The valves are typically arranged in a straight line positioned along the tapered angle, which puts them at an angle to the top of the piston.
- The bathtub combustion chamber is oval shaped, like an inverted antique bathtub. The valves are mounted vertically and are side by side, making the valvetrain simple in its design.
- Gasoline direct injection (GDI) cylinder head refers to gasoline injected directly into the combustion chamber just above the piston. Instead of mixing the fuel-air in the intake manifold, it mixes in the combustion chamber like a diesel engine without spontaneous combustion.
- The size of intake and exhaust ports in the cylinder head can affect engine output by affecting the speed of the air flowing through them. It takes a certain amount of speed to maintain good turbulence and air-fuel mixing.
- If airflow is too slow, fuel will fall out of the air. If airflow is too fast, the air will be restricted, which reduces the total amount of air-fuel mixture that can enter the combustion chamber. Changing the valve sizes is used to later output and emissions.
- Gaskets form a seal by being compressed between stationary parts where liquid or gases could pass. They are designed to be single use and cannot be reused. They can be made of soft materials such as cork, rubber, and paper or soft alloys and metals such as brass, copper, aluminum, and stainless steel.
- The head gasket seal and contain the pressures of combustion within the engine, between the cylinder head and the engine block. They also seal oil passages between the engine block and the cylinder head and control the flow of coolant between the engine block and the cylinder head.
- Stainless steel fire rings are used on some head gaskets to help contain heat and pressure within the cylinder. Fire rings are steel rings built into the cylinder head gasket.
- The preferred head gasket is a multilayer steel (MLS) head gasket.
- The most widely used seal for rotating parts is the lip-type dynamic oil seal, which is a precisely shaped, dynamic rubber lip.
- The valve stem seal is pressed onto the valve guide. It allows the valve to be wiped almost clean of oil on its opening trip, keeping a minimum amount of oil pulled down between the valve stem and the guide for lubrication purposes.
- One of the most popular liquid sealants is room temperature vulcanizing (RTV) silicone. This adhesive is able to set or "vulcanize" at room temperature. When RTV is applied, it has the consistency of a gel, and as it sets, it becomes rubbery. You are essentially gluing the two parts together with RTV.

- The main cause of cylinder head cracks is thermal stress.
- Cracks in the cylinder head are a serious problem that is relatively common because of its lightweight construction.
- Pressure testing the cylinder block and heads is a reliable method for identifying hard-to-see cracks.
- If the head is made of cast iron, you can locate small cracks with a Magnaflux tool. The Magnaflux process involves placing a strong electromagnet across each part of the head surface at 90-degree offsets and lightly dusting the head with a magnetic powder. If there is a crack present, the powder will adhere to the crack because the crack creates a north and south magnetic field at that point, and the powder sticks to it.
- Small cracks can be fixed by pinning, which is a process of drilling holes in a crack and installing overlapping pins to fill it that are then peened over to seal and blend the surface, and should only be performed by a highly trained machinist, preferably an ASE-certified master machinist.
- Furnace welding can also be used to repair cylinder head cracks which involves heating the cylinder head to extreme temperatures (about 1300°F [704°C]) and welding iron into the crack with an acetylene torch.
- Resurfacing the cylinder head restores a perfectly flat and specified surface finish to the head for placement of a new gasket and is best performed by milling the surface but can also be performed by grinding with the proper head-surfacing machine. The resurfacing process must be precise.
- You should follow the steps as listed in the service information when removing any cylinder head.
- The cylinder head must be cleaned after removal to make the inspection and repair process more efficient.
- Aluminum heads must be scraped with a nonmetallic tool such as a plastic or nylon scraper made for the job.
- When valves are removed from the cylinder head, the valves and seats should be inspected visually for cracks, burn marks, signs of leaks, and damage to the valve face, stem, and tip. If any of these issues are found, the valve will need to be replaced and the seat will need to be either replaced or repaired.
- The valves should be measured according to the service information.
- The valve stem height must be measured before any machine work is completed to the cylinder head. This measurement must be compared to the installed height once machining has been completed so you can select the right shim to put under the valve spring to return the spring to the correct seat pressure on the valve to keep it closed.
- Valves and guides can be measured with a micrometer or with a dial indicator. If using a micrometer, a ball gauge is used to measure the top, center, and bottom of the valve guide. The ball gauge is placed in the valve guide in each of those positions and expanded until both sides of the gauge touch the inside of the guide. It is then removed from the guide, measured with a micrometer, and recorded. The center reading is then subtracted from the ends to determine how much the guide is tapered. The smallest reading (usually the center reading) is used to determine the overall size of the guide.
- A dial indicator is mounted on the head and placed against the side of the valve stem near the top of the valve. With the valve at its normally open height, rock the head of the valve stem back and forth, observing the movement.
- The three key steps in testing a valve spring are (1) checking for squareness, (2) measuring spring height, and (3) measuring the installed pressure.
- On pushrods, that means each end. The balls or sockets typically lose their roundness and become slightly pointy. Also, there is typically a small flat spot on the top of the pushrod. If the pushrod is worn, the flat spot will be smaller than it should be or worn off altogether. Pushrods also have to be perfectly straight; otherwise, they are subject to bending, which would render them inoperative. Rolling them on a piece of glass or perfectly flat surface plate indicates whether they are bent.
- When inspecting the flatness of a cylinder head, the technician must first clean the cylinder head mating surface, then use a true bar to see if the surface of the cylinder head is warped. If the cylinder head is warped, then machining will need to be done.
- Always check the manufacturer's procedure to know when to install the camshaft(s).
- Valve reconditioning requires that the valve be removed from the cylinder head, inspected for straightness, and then placed in a valve grinding machine so that the valve head angles can be ground to the proper angle to create an interference fit with the valve seat in the cylinder head.
- If the guide is replaceable, then the old guide must be pressed out and the new one pressed in. Once the valve guide is pressed in, it must be trimmed to the proper length so that it will not interfere with the valve spring being compressed.
- If the valve guide is integral to the cylinder head, the machinist can knurl the valve guide to decrease the clearance between the valve and the guide bringing it back into specification.
- The valve seat must be reconditioned when the valve is resurfaced so that the angles create solid seal.
- To recondition a valve seat, the machinist mounts the cylinder head in a valve cutting machine, which lines up the valve guide with where it cuts the seat so that the valve is in the proper location on the valve seat. The machine can then be programmed to cut the three angles that are required to create the seal that is required between the valve and seat.

Key Terms

bath tub combustion chamber This type of combustion chamber is oval in shape, has the valves in a straight line, and is the same size throughout the chamber.

camshaft Only fitted in the cylinder heads of OHC and DOHC engines. This device provides the force to open the valves.

combustion chamber The area of the engine in which the air-fuel mixture is ignited and combustion occurs.

cylinder head The component that seals the cylinder of the combustion chamber where the explosion happens and creates motion that is converted into mechanical motion.

dual overhead cam (DOHC) engine Engine containing two camshafts per cylinder head.

exhaust ports Direct exhaust gases to the exhaust manifold from the exhaust valve. They are cast into the cylinder head.

exhaust valves Valve that allows burnt exhaust fumes to enter the exhaust system; they then exit the vehicle through the tail pipe.

fire rings Part of the head gasket and usually made out of steel. They offer support around the cylinder opening to help contain the explosion that occurs in the cylinder each time the spark plug fires.

flame propagation The moving flame front within the combustion chamber.

gasket Forms a seal between two components when it is compressed between them.

gasoline direct injection cylinder head Type of cylinder head that has a spark plug and an injector directly in the combustion chamber. This is very similar to the diesel cylinder head, which makes for a very efficient design, as the piston is only compressing air until the last moment when it injects fuel into the cylinder.

head gasket Metal or composite gasket that seals the cylinder to the cylinder head, which creates the combustion chamber.

hemispherical cylinder head Type of combustion chamber design comprising a half sphere, which locates the valves opposite of each other, creating an even flame distribution.

intake port The passage in the cylinder head that feeds the intake valve. It is connected to the intake manifold and is cast into the cylinder head.

intake valves Allows the air or air-fuel mixture into the cylinder to be combusted.

multilayer steel (MLS) head gasket Type of head gasket made out of multiple layers of thin sheet metal that conforms to the surfaces present on the engine block and cylinder head.

oil seals Keep oil from leaking past a rotating camshaft.

overhead cam (OHC) engine Engine for which the camshaft is housed in the cylinder head.

overhead valve (OHV) engine Engine with valves positioned in the cylinder head assembly, directly over the top of the piston.

plugs (e.g., galley, coolant) Much like seals, used to block off passages where oil and coolant flow, primarily to block holes used in the original casting and machining of the head.

room temperature vulcanizing (RTV) silicone Type of sealant made of a semi-solid material that is pliable until exposed to oxygen for an extended period of time. At that point, it becomes a rubber-like material that conforms to the two components it is exposed to.

squish area The area in a combustion chamber that is between the piston at TDC and the cylinder head

valve The valve is the component that seals the exhaust and intake systems from the combustion chamber. This is like a door that opens and closes letting in the fuel air mixture into the cylinder or letting out the exhaust gas.

valve keepers Keep a valve spring's retainer attached to the valve while in the cylinder head.

valve retainer Thick, washer-shaped piece of metal with a tapered center hole that is fitted over the top of the valve stem and holds the top of the valve spring to keep pressure on the valves.

valve springs Coil springs that return valves to their fully closed positions, and hold them closed, after being opened.

valve stem seals Allow only enough oil past them to lubricate the valve guide.

wedge combustion chamber A combustion chamber that tapers away from the spark plug and where the valves are in a straight line in the cylinder head.

Review Questions

1. The smaller water jackets in aluminum cylinder heads:
    a. reduce the heat generated by combustion.
    b. increase the chance of localized hot spots.
    c. prevent them from overcooling the engine.
    d. prevent them from overheating the engine.
2. As the camshaft rotates, the lifter rises and transfers the motion to the:
    a. camshaft lobe.
    b. pushrod.
    c. rocker arm.
    d. tappet.
3. Which of these are primarily used to block holes used in the original casting and machining of the head?
    a. Valve springs
    b. Cam seals
    c. Valve stem seals
    d. Plugs
4. The technician observes that the valves are arranged in a straight line positioned along the tapered angle. This arrangement is typical in which of the following cylinder head designs?
    a. Wedge combustion chamber
    b. Oval combustion chamber
    c. Hemispherical combustion chamber
    d. Gas direct injection cylinder head
5. Which component in the valve train assembly controls the opening and closing of valves?
    a. Camshaft lobe
    b. Valve keeper

c. Valve spring
d. Valve retainers

6. Which of these affects the amount of pressure the spring exerts on the valve train?
   a. Valve spring open pressure
   b. Valve spring closed pressure
   c. Valve spring length
   d. Valve spring thickness

7. Which of the following is a simple sealing device consisting of a rounded ring of rubber or plastic, used to seal components?
   a. Garter spring
   b. Lip-type dynamic oil seal
   c. O-rings
   d. Multilayer steel (MLS) head gasket

8. All of the statements below are true, *except*:
   a. Cylinder head gaskets can be repaired and reused.
   b. Most cylinder head problems can be repaired by a cylinder head machinist.
   c. If the engine is overheating due to a head gasket problem, then a cylinder leakage test detection test should be performed.
   d. The cylinder head is subject to a variety of problems that can affect engine function.

9. All of the statements below are true, *except*:
   a. The timing of the valves is controlled by the physical shape and position of the cam lobes on the cam shaft.
   b. Racing engines are designed to minimize the effect of the column inertia encountered at higher rpm.
   c. Valve timing is critical to the proper operation of the ICE.
   d. On variable valve timing engines, the valve timing can be modified to provide the best operating conditions.

10. When the valve stem clearance is excessive, there is:
    a. no wear on the valve stem.
    b. more oil passing through the guide.
    c. less smoke emission from the exhaust pipe.
    d. less oil consumption.

ASE Technician A/Technician B Style Questions

1. Technician A states that a DOHC engine has one camshaft in the cylinder head and the other in the engine block. Technician B says that the intake valve is used for allowing air-fuel mixture to enter the combustion chamber. Who is correct?
   a. Tech A
   b. Tech B
   c. Both A and B
   d. Neither A nor B

2. Technician A says that one of the reasons that a hemispherical combustion chamber is desirable is because of the cross-flow properties created by the valve location in the cylinder head. Technician B states that the intake port is located in the exhaust manifold. Who is correct?
   a. Tech A
   b. Tech B
   c. Both A and B
   d. Neither A nor B

3. Tech A says that a GDI engine is very similar to a compression ignition engine, as it compresses air alone. Technician B states that valve springs hold the engine valves shut. Who is correct?
   a. Tech A
   b. Tech B
   c. Both A and B
   d. Neither A nor B

4. Technician A says that a gasket can be made of many different materials. Technician B says that using RTV sealant is a common gasket on components. Who is correct?
   a. Tech A
   b. Tech B
   c. Both A and B
   d. Neither A nor B

5. Technician A states that an OHV engine has the camshaft located in the engine block. Technician B says that the technician must measure the camshaft to determine if one of the lobes is bad. Who is correct?
   a. Tech A
   b. Tech B
   c. Both A and B
   d. Neither A nor B

6. Technician A states that using an MLS head gasket allows for removal of some pieces to create the clearance necessary to prevent interference. Technician B states that gaskets are the reason that the fluids stay in the cylinder head and block. Who is correct?
   a. Tech A
   b. Tech B
   c. Both A and B
   d. Neither A nor B

7. Technician A states that fire rings embedded into the head gasket help support the gaskets as the explosions happen within the cylinder. Technician B says that valve stem seal replacement should be done every time the cylinder head comes off the vehicle. Who is correct?
   a. Tech A
   b. Tech B
   c. Both A and B
   d. Neither A nor B

8. Technician A says that valve guide replacement must be performed by the service advisor if valves are in need of being repaired. Technician B states that an engine machinist performs much of the recondition of major engine components. Who is correct?
   a. Tech A
   b. Tech B
   c. Both A and B
   d. Neither A nor B

9. Technician A says that anytime a cylinder head is removed for a cylinder block, the surface must be checked for flatness before reinstallation, or a failure could occur. Technician B states that cylinder block machining can be done with a drill and bit. Who is correct?
   a. Tech A
   b. Tech B
   c. Both A and B
   d. Neither A nor B

10. Technician A says that pushrods should be checked for straightness and cracks before they are reused. Technician B says that rocker arms in an engine are under heavy stress, which means they should be inspected for deformities before they are reinstalled. Who is correct?
   a. Tech A
   b. Tech B
   c. Both A and B
   d. Neither A nor B

CHAPTER 18

Intake and Exhaust Systems Design

NATEF Tasks

There are no NATEF Tasks for this chapter.

Knowledge Objectives

After reading this chapter, you will have:

- **K18001** Knowledge of the intake and exhaust system design.
- **K18002** Knowledge of what an air filter does.
- **K18003** Knowledge of what an intake gasket does for the integrity of the engine.

- **K18004** Knowledge of what are the components of the exhaust system.
- **K18005** Knowledge of the operation of a catalytic converter.
- **K18006** Knowledge of the importance of the exhaust manifold.

Skills Objectives

There are no Skills Objectives for this chapter.

You Are the Automotive Technician

A customer comes into the dealership complaining that her 12-year-old Ford Mustang doesn't idle as well as it should and the malfunction indicator lamp (MIL) is illuminated. You scan it for codes and notice that it has a P0131 (Circuit Low Voltage B1S1), a P0171 (Fuel Trim Lean B1), and a P0300 (Engine Misfire) detected. As an apprentice technician, you refer to the Ford Motor Company's service information to look up the process for diagnosing the codes. You notice that there could be several things that cause those codes, including a vacuum leak, weak oxygen sensor, and dirty fuel injectors. You decide to start by looking for a vacuum leak because you hear what sounds like a leak when the vehicle is running.

1. What are the different ways of locating a vacuum leak?
2. What are the possible places that a vacuum leak can occur?
3. How does a vacuum leak affect a vehicle equipped with a mass airflow sensor?

K18001 Knowledge of the intake and exhaust system design.

▶ Introduction

The intake and exhaust systems are critical parts of the internal combustion engine. The intake system ensures that clean, dry air is supplied to the engine, which is then mixed with fuel and burned in the combustion chamber, creating the thermal expansion that pushes the pistons down the cylinder. Clean, dry air is essential for proper combustion and a long-lasting engine, as dirt would get between the close-moving parts and cause premature engine wear. In fact, it takes only a tablespoon or two of dirt entering the engine through the intake system to ruin an engine. The intake system must provide a sealed passageway to the combustion chambers to ensure that no contaminants leak into the system and that no air is allowed to bypass the airflow sensor, which could create a drivability problem. The intake system also controls the amount of air entering the engine, by use of a throttle plate, which is how engine revolutions per minute (rpm) and power are controlled. The exhaust system provides a path for the burned exhaust gases to safely exit the engine and travel out the rear of the vehicle. It also provides a method of reducing the noise from the power pulses and includes components that help reduce the harmful emissions in the exhaust stream. Getting rid of exhaust gases is just as important as getting air into the engine. If exhaust gases cannot leave the engine easily, then air will not be able to enter the engine easily. An efficient, free-flowing exhaust system will assist the engine in creating maximum power with minimal emissions. In this chapter, we explore the operation, diagnosis, and testing of the components in both the intake and the exhaust systems.

▶ Air Intake System

The air intake system allows outside air to be drawn into the engine to increase the combustion process. Without the intake system the combustion process would not happen causing the engine to not run. The design of the intake system is one that allows for maximum airflow to the engine while keeping the noise to a minimum so that the driver of the vehicle is not disturbed by the noise of rushing air into the engine.

Air Filter Design

K18002 Knowledge of what an air filter does.

The **air cleaner** filters the incoming air. In past designs, the air cleaner housing was made of stamped metal and housed a round air filter. Most air cleaners are now made of plastic and can vary in shape from square to round. The air cleaner element or filter may be manufactured from pleated paper or from oil-impregnated cloth or felt; in much older vehicles, it was manufactured in an oil bath configuration.

Another function of the air cleaner is to muffle the noise of the intake pulses and the incoming air, which travels at high speeds. The air cleaner can also act as a flame arrester. A lot of air passes through the intake system into the engine. In a gasoline engine, the air-fuel mixture by weight is about 15 parts air to 1 part fuel. By volume, that's 10,000 times more air than fuel. When an engine consumes 10 gallons of gas, the air filter will have filtered 100,000 gallons of air. The air-fuel mixture enters the engine, so the air has to be clean. Any abrasives that enter the engine can quickly cause wear and damage. An air cleaner on a multipoint electronic fuel-injected engine usually has a different shape from that on a carbureted engine, but it serves the same purpose.

In many vehicles, the air cleaner is mounted where it can obtain cool, clean air. The air from the air cleaner is then carried to the throttle body by a long, flexible duct. Inside the air cleaner, a filter element filters the air and reduces noise. Many electronically fuel-injected systems have an airflow sensor after the air cleaner element, which accurately measures all air entering the engine and adjusts the air-fuel mixture accordingly; it is essential that there be no air leaks after the airflow sensor, as leaks will upset the air-fuel mixture. It is interesting to note that a mass airflow (MAF) sensor can measure air entering the engine down to tenths of a gram per second.

On most heavy-duty diesel engines and a few gasoline engines, the air cleaner assembly uses an air filter indicator to tell the operator whether the filter has to be cleaned or replaced (**FIGURE 18-1**). The indicator typically has a red band that shows whether the filter is restricted. Some indicators lock in place, even when the engine is stopped, and others indicate filter condition only when the engine is running. The indicator is mounted between the air cleaner and the engine. When the air filter creates enough of a restriction, the vacuum produced in the intake tube causes the indicator to display the warning. These indicators are a quick way to determine whether the air filter needs to be serviced.

Some heavy-duty air cleaners also incorporate a cyclone-type pre-cleaner, which is mounted directly onto the air cleaner unit (**FIGURE 18-2**). The cyclone system uses angled vanes that give the incoming air a swirling motion. Centrifugal force throws the heavier dirt particles outward, and they collect in a bowl at the bottom of the cleaner, where they can be removed manually. An efficient cyclone pre-cleaner can remove up to 90% of particles before they reach the main filter element, greatly extending its life.

One type of air cleaner system is the long-life filtration system that is currently used on the Ford Focus. This air cleaner assembly is a non-serviceable unit that is designed to last 150,000 miles (240,000 km) or more. It is made to also capture any hydrocarbons being released from the throttle body and then allow them to be pulled back into the engine as air flows across the filter. The filter element is made of specially designed foam. This filter can be serviced only by replacement of the entire assembly.

Intake System Design

The **intake manifold** is usually a cast-iron, aluminum, or plastic part with several tubular branches. In a carbureted engine, the intake manifold directs the air-fuel mixture into the engine. The cross-sectional area of each tube has to be kept small to maintain the high air speeds that improve vaporization. At the same time, intake manifold tube size should not be too small, because that restricts the airflow to the engine at higher speeds.

Intake Runner Design

The intake manifold has several tubular branches and carries air and/or air-fuel mixture from the air cleaner to the cylinder head. In carbureted engines and in throttle body injection systems, the intake manifold directs the air-fuel mixture into the engine. On many engines, the intake manifold has a mounting for the throttle body and a flange that bolts it onto the cylinder head. The cross-sectional area of each tube has to be kept small to maintain the high air speeds that improve speed and turbulence. Yet, it cannot be too small because that would restrict the airflow to the engine at higher engine speeds. Cylinder heads that have intake

FIGURE 18-1 Air cleaner with filter service indicator.

FIGURE 18-2 Cyclone-type pre-cleaner.

Applied Science

AS-39: Carriers/Insulators: The technician can demonstrate an understanding of how sound generated in one place can be carried to other parts of the auto body or engine through metal and materials. Sound travels through steel approximately 17 times faster than through the air. This is because the molecules in steel are closer together. Sound is produced when an object vibrates. Vibrations can pass from molecule to molecule quickly in materials such as steel.

When a vehicle has a bad wheel bearing that is producing a rumbling sound, it is often difficult to tell which of the four wheels the noise is coming from. In this case, you might try driving the vehicle alongside a

building or a concrete block wall. Sound waves travel in all directions from their source. Some of them will strike the wall, and the noise will be reflected back toward the vehicle. A greater proportion of the sound waves will strike the wall when it is near the side of the vehicle with the faulty wheel bearing, meaning more sound waves will be reflected toward the vehicle. Thus, if the noise is louder when the passenger side is near the wall, the technician will know the faulty bearing is on the passenger side. A mechanic's stethoscope can also be used to locate sounds on vehicles. The tip of the metal probe can be used to trace the sound to the source of the problem. There are also electronic devices that can be used to locate sounds on vehicles.

FIGURE 18-3 Cross-flow head.

K18003 Knowledge of what an intake gasket does for the integrity of the engine.

K18004 Knowledge of what are the components of the exhaust system.

and exhaust manifolds on opposite sides of the engine are known as cross-flow heads. That means the intake manifold is on one side, and the exhaust manifold is on the other (**FIGURE 18-3**). This design tends to produce more power because the flow of air moves more easily across the head rather than coming in and then turning back out the same side. Most modern engines are set up with a cross-flow cylinder head. The cross-flow head contains individual branches or ports to carry air and fuel into the combustion chamber. In past designs, two cylinders could share an intake port, but this design did not allow for free flow and was replaced with individual ports to allow for more power.

Intake Gaskets R&R

The **intake gaskets** are what seals the intake to the cylinder heads on an engine and often have to be replaced because of leakage. The steps to remove and reinstall an intake with new gaskets differ based on the vehicle that the procedure is being done on.

1. Drain the coolant so that the coolant will not mix with the engine oil when the manifold is removed.
2. Disconnect the electrical connectors and the linkage to the throttle body.
3. Remove the coolant and vacuum hoses that are attached to the manifold.
4. Detorque the manifold by going in reverse of the tightening procedure so that the manifold is not accidentally warped when the bolts are taken out.
5. Check the manifold for warpage, as warpage is one of the major issues that allow the gaskets to leak.
6. Reverse the removal procedure to reinstall (**FIGURE 18-4**).

▶ Exhaust System

The exhaust system is made up of several components that work together to perform four main functions: remove exhaust gases from the engine, quiet the exhaust noise, ensure that poisonous exhaust gases do not enter the passenger compartment, and reduce harmful emissions in the exhaust stream (**FIGURE 18-5**). Exhaust flow is described as follows: Burned gases exit the cylinder through the exhaust port and pass into the exhaust manifold. The first pipe is usually called the engine pipe or down pipe. The down pipe is connected to

FIGURE 18-4 An intake manifold used to direct the air into the engine. The fuel injectors, sensors, and throttle body are bolted to this component so that they are then apart of the engine assembly. The manifolds can be made out of aluminum, plastic, or cast iron.

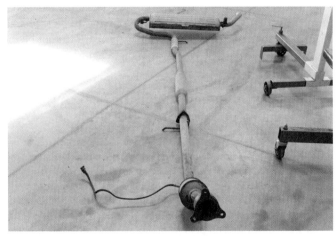

FIGURE 18-5 The exhaust system prevents harmful exhaust gases from entering the passenger compartment, reduces the noise of combustion, removes exhaust gases from the engine, and reduces harmful emissions in the exhaust stream.

the outlet of the manifold, which carries the exhaust gases to the catalytic converter. Catalytic converters were introduced in vehicles in the mid-1970s and were designed to reduce exhaust emissions. The exhaust exits the converter and continues on through an intermediate pipe to the muffler, which reduces exhaust noise. Exhaust gases are then either passed through a resonator or simply discharged to the atmosphere through a tailpipe, usually at the rear, to the side, or above the vehicle.

During engine operation, each time an exhaust valve opens, a pulse of hot exhaust gases is forced into the exhaust manifold. These hot gases produce a lot of noise, some of it at very high frequency. Even while quieting the exhaust noise, the exhaust system can be designed to enhance engine operation and efficiency. In fact, a well-designed system can improve drivability and performance.

Exhaust Manifold

The **exhaust manifold** is bolted to the engine's cylinder head. It also usually provides a mounting place near its outlet for the oxygen sensor, as it is advantageous to position the sensor as close to the cylinders as possible. This position helps it warm up faster during a cold start. The exhaust manifold can be a one-piece or a two-piece construction and is usually made from either cast iron or stainless steel. Due to the extreme temperatures generated at the exhaust manifold, heat shields can be installed to protect other vehicle components from heat damage.

On many current vehicles, the exhaust manifold is often replaced with a header. The **header** is an exhaust manifold made of mandrel-formed steel tubes that are of equal lengths and join at a common collector. Mandrel forming is the use of a special pipe-bending tool to ensure that piping bends in a smooth arc and will not collapse, which would create a partial restriction. The equal length of the pipes ensures that the exhaust pulses create a more equal airflow out of each cylinder. Exhaust manifolds can be restricting, forcing the pistons to work harder to push the exhaust gases out. A header is freer flowing, allowing gases to leave the engine quickly (**FIGURE 18-6**).

The headers also provide a scavenging effect to help remove exhaust gases from the cylinders. The outgoing pulse from one cylinder is timed to arrive at the junction at exactly the right time to help draw out the pulse from another cylinder. This setup is called tuned exhaust, and the lengths of the header tubes determine the rpm range they are tuned to. Tuned exhaust is widely used on high-performance vehicles and race cars. Performance gains can be realized by ensuring that exhaust gases flow freely so that the engine can pull air in and push exhaust out efficiently. When a Formula One car is produced, extreme attention is given to exhaust tuning to ensure that the exhaust will flow correctly, resulting in the maximum power for the engine.

Mufflers

The function of a vehicle's **muffler** is to minimize the sounds coming from the exhaust system (**FIGURE 18-7**). These sounds originate from the combustion process within the engine. Exhaust noise becomes an issue as vehicle systems become generally quieter and as the number of vehicles on our roads increases.

To understand the operation of modern exhaust noise reduction systems, it is helpful to understand what sound is. We sense sound with our eardrum, located within the ear. The eardrum is made to move by variations in air pressure. Variations in air pressure can be created when a force is placed upon an object. An example is clapping your hands. As the two hands collide,

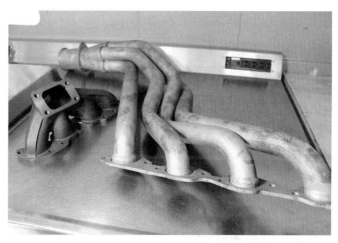

FIGURE 18-6 An exhaust manifold is typically made of cast iron, and a header is made of steel tubing of equal length.

FIGURE 18-7 A muffler used on a vehicle to quiet the engine operation so that it will meet sound standards and will not hurt the human ear.

they push the air surrounding them away. The moving air creates a wave of air pressure, or a sound wave. This sound wave moves your eardrum, which is interpreted as sound by your brain.

The engine produces noise, as each combustion process is a rapid burning of air and fuel—a controlled explosion. These explosions create a great deal of noise if they are not absorbed or canceled. Noise absorption refers to putting a sound material around a perforated pipe that the exhaust gases flow through. This is similar to placing noise-absorbing materials inside the walls of a house to make the rooms quieter. Noise cancellation is a system that prevents the sound waves from leaving the exhaust system by canceling them out inside the muffler. These systems create gas pressures that are equal in force, but opposite in direction to the noise source. These generated pressures are known as anti-noise. Any remaining sound is referred to as residual noise. The muffler is designed to quiet the noises of combustion without restricting exhaust flow to the point of adversely affecting performance. The goal is to produce a vehicle that is smooth and quiet as well as powerful. A muffler may use a dissipative technique, which is sound absorption; or a noise-canceling technique; or both. Exhaust noise can be reduced by various means, including baffles and chambers, variable-flow exhaust, and electronic mufflers.

Exhaust Pipes

The engine pipe, or down pipe, is attached to the exhaust manifold and connects to the catalytic converter. The engine pipe is usually made of a nickel chromium material, which resists rust and corrosion to ensure it is long lasting. Some exhaust down pipes may also use stainless steel to ensure long life. The engine pipe may be attached to the exhaust manifold by spring-loaded bolts that allow the exhaust to move slightly as the engine moves in its mounts. Some engine pipes also have flexible connectors that allow flexing of the engine pipe as the engine moves in its mounts (**FIGURE 18-8**).

Flex Pipes

There may be a flexible connection between the engine pipe and an intermediate pipe. The flexible connector is used close to the gap. Its main functions are to allow engine movement and to reduce vibration without passing it along the exhaust—especially in front-wheel drive vehicles (**FIGURE 18-9**). The flexible connector also helps with the alignment of the pipes as the engine moves under load.

Clamps, Brackets, and Hangers

The exhaust components are supported along the length of the vehicle by brackets suspended from the underbody. The supports are usually rubber mounted and help isolate the vibrations of the exhaust from the main body of the vehicle. Rubber is preferred because of its natural dampening effect (**FIGURE 18-10**).

FIGURE 18-8 The exhaust piping connects the exhaust components to the engine and evacuates the fumes to outside the vehicle.

Applied Science

AS-38: Amplification: The technician can explain to a customer how sound can be amplified in a vehicle due to resonant cavities and other physical characteristics of the vehicle.

The noise level of a vehicle plays an important role in the overall satisfaction rating by the owner. A quiet vehicle is expected by the majority of vehicle owners. Some vehicle owners prefer the sound of a high-performance vehicle, in which case the noise level is not as much of a concern. Air intake and exhaust systems can be manufactured and modified for a variety of different sounds. Back in 1863, physicist Herman Von Helmholtz did many studies regarding air-dampening devices. He discovered a resonator that uses the principle of sound waves

colliding, resulting in the concept of canceling noise. The resonator can be used in the exhaust system to assist the muffler in further reducing noise. The resonator can also be used in the induction system. The benefit is the ability to muffle airflow noise. The Helmholtz resonator is basically a simple device consisting of a cavity with one or more short narrow tubes. For each application, the device must be precisely tuned. For the air induction system, the resonator is installed between the air filter and the engine inlet. The design of the Helmholtz resonator creates a sound frequency that cancels out some of the engine noise. On some vehicles, a vacuum-activated valve disables the effects of the resonator at certain rpm.

FIGURE 18-9 The flexible connector is used to allow the pipe to flex as the engine moves.

FIGURE 18-10 The exhaust is supported by rubber mounts that ensure that vibration is not felt by the driver.

Heat Shields

Heat shields are usually placed around some portions of the exhaust system to help shield the body of the vehicle from the increased temperatures that the exhaust system puts out (**FIGURE 18-11**). These shields help make the floorboards of the passenger compartment cool so that the carpet and people's feet stay at a temperature that is tolerable. Without the shields on the exhaust, the floorboards could become very hot, causing the carpet to melt and possibly starting a fire inside the vehicle.

Catalytic Converters

A **catalytic converter** is used to convert unacceptable exhaust pollutants, such as carbon monoxide, hydrocarbons, and oxides of nitrogen, into less dangerous substances. Three-way converters convert oxides of nitrogen back into nitrogen and oxygen, and the hydrocarbons and carbon monoxide to water and carbon dioxide. Older two-way catalytic converters converted hydrocarbons and carbon monoxide to water and carbon dioxide, but were not able to convert the oxides of nitrogen. A catalytic converter fits in line with the exhaust system. It is located close to the exhaust manifold so that it can reach its operating temperature as soon as possible (**FIGURE 18-12**). Some manufacturers install a catalytic converter in the base of the exhaust manifold and another one downstream before the muffler. Catalytic

K18005 Knowledge of the operation of a catalytic converter.

FIGURE 18-11 The heat shields on an exhaust system are used to deflect heat away from the vehicle so components will not melt or catch fire.

FIGURE 18-12 The catalytic converter is located after the engine pipe and before the muffler. It changes harmful gases into nonharmful gases to be released to the atmosphere.

converters can become contaminated by lead and silicone. Leaded fuel must not be used in an engine with a catalytic converter because lead will coat the catalyst and prevent it from doing its job. Some types of silicone sealer will also coat the catalyst. Once coated, the converter will most likely have to be replaced.

The catalytic converter operates by beginning and then maintaining a chemical reaction in the exhaust gases. It usually creates heat as it is converting the harmful gases to less harmful ones, so it can get extremely hot. Because of this, it has a heat shield to prevent heat from radiating to bodywork and other parts. The catalytic converter is covered in greater detail in the Engine Performance book.

Exhaust Gaskets

Exhaust components are sometimes bolted together. If they are, a gasket may be required to seal them. Exhaust gaskets can be found between the engine cylinder head and the exhaust manifold, the engine pipe and the catalytic converter, and possibly the catalytic converter and the muffler. The exhaust is extremely hot, so the gaskets must withstand the temperatures without burning (**FIGURE 18-13**). Exhaust gaskets can be multilayered high-temperature alloys that are formed with graphite or mica to provide a good seal as exhaust components move with expansion and contraction. Donut gaskets are another type of exhaust gasket. They use spiral wound steel and filler material, which is shaped into a round design, that, when installed in ball-shaped pipe, provides a seal while allowing the pipes to be joined even if they are slightly out of line. Some of these gaskets also allow for slight movement of the engine.

Exhaust Manifold R&R

K18006 Knowledge of the importance of the exhaust manifold.

Removing and reinstalling an exhaust manifold is a procedure that most technicians will accomplish many times throughout their career. The procedure for each vehicle differs slightly, but in the end, the exhaust manifold is removed. The first step is to make sure that the engine is cold so that you will not get burnt. If you try to remove this manifold with the engine hot, be prepared to deal with temperatures above 1500ªF (816ºC). Besides dealing with high temperatures, removing a hot manifold could cause the manifold to become warped, so the manifold must be detorqued in order to minimize the possibility of it warping. After the manifold is removed from the engine, you must inspect it to verify that it is still in serviceable condition. If any damage is found, the manifold must be replaced or reconditioned to be reused. Manifolds are made of cast iron or tubular steel, which means they are thermal cycled every time the engine is warmed up. This constant molecular change of the metal can cause it to fail over a period of time (**FIGURE 18-14**).

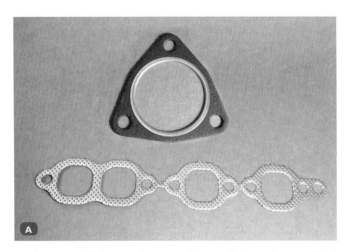

FIGURE 18-13 Exhaust gaskets come in many forms and are used in the extreme temperature of the exhaust system. **A.** These gaskets are used to seal the exhaust manifold to the engine and the exhaust manifold to the downpipe. **B.** This is an exhaust donut that is used to allow for minor variations in the angle of the downpipe to the manifold.

FIGURE 18-14 When the exhaust manifold is overheated or cooled too quickly it may cause it to crack which could lead to noise and drivability problems for the vehicle.

▶ Wrap-Up

Ready for Review

- ▶ The air intake system allows outside air to be drawn into the engine to increase the combustion process. Without the intake system, the combustion process would not happen, thereby causing the engine not to run.
- ▶ The air cleaner filters the incoming air. In past designs, the air cleaner housing was made of stamped metal and housed a round air filter.
- ▶ In a gasoline engine, the air-fuel mixture, by weight, is about 15 parts air to 1 part fuel. By volume, that's 10,000 times more air than fuel. When an engine consumes 10 gallons of gas, the air filter will have filtered 100,000 gallons of air.
- ▶ The intake manifold is usually a cast-iron, aluminum, or plastic part with several tubular branches. The cross-sectional area of each tube needs to be kept small to maintain the high air speed that improves vaporization.
- ▶ Cylinder heads that have intake and exhaust manifolds on opposite sides of the engine are known as cross-flow heads with intake manifold is on one side and the exhaust manifold is on the other, which produces more power because the flow of air moves more easily across the head.
- ▶ The intake gaskets are what seals the intake to the cylinder heads on an engine and often need replacement for leakage.
- ▶ The steps to remove and reinstall an intake with new gaskets differ based on the vehicle that the procedure is being done on.
- ▶ The exhaust system is made up of components that work together to perform four main functions: remove exhaust gases from the engine, quiet the exhaust noise, to ensure that poisonous exhaust gases do not enter the passenger compartment.

- ▶ Each time an exhaust valve opens, a pulse of hot exhaust gases is forced into the exhaust manifold. These hot gases produce a lot of noise, some of it at very high frequency so a muffler is need to reduce the noise.
- ▶ The exhaust manifold is bolted to the engine's cylinder head and provides a mounting place near its outlet for the oxygen sensor.
- ▶ On many current vehicles, the exhaust manifold is often replaced with a header. The header is an exhaust manifold made of mandrel-formed steel tubes that are of equal lengths and join at a common collector.
- ▶ The function of a vehicle's muffler is to minimize the sounds coming from the exhaust system.
- ▶ Engine sounds originate from the combustion process within the engine.
- ▶ Exhaust noise becomes an issue as vehicle systems become generally quieter and as the number of vehicles on our roads increases.
- ▶ The engine pipe, or down pipe, is attached to the exhaust manifold and connects to the catalytic converter and is usually made of a nickel chromium material, which resists rust and corrosion to ensure it is long lasting.
- ▶ The exhaust components are supported along the length of the vehicle by brackets suspended from the underbody and these supports are rubber mounted and help isolate the vibrations of the exhaust from the main body of the vehicle.
- ▶ Heat shields are usually placed around some portions of the exhaust system to help shield the body of the vehicle from the increased temperatures that the exhaust system puts out.

▶ A catalytic converter is used to convert unacceptable exhaust pollutants, such as carbon monoxide, hydrocarbons, and oxides of nitrogen into less dangerous substances.

▶ Three-way catalytic converters convert oxides of nitrogen back into nitrogen and oxygen, and the hydrocarbons and carbon monoxide to water and carbon dioxide.

▶ Exhaust components are sometimes bolted together. If they are, they may need to have a gasket to seal them.

▶ Exhaust gaskets can be found between the engine cylinder head and the exhaust manifold, the engine pipe and the catalytic converter, and possibly the catalytic converter and the muffler.

▶ Removing and reinstalling an exhaust manifold will differ slightly, but in the end, the exhaust manifold will be removed.

Key Terms

air cleaner   Filters the incoming air to remove the contaminants that attempt to enter the engine from the outside.

catalytic converter   Changes the exhaust gases that come out of the engine into more acceptable gases as they react with the catalyst inside the converter.

exhaust manifold   Connects the cylinder head to the rest of the exhaust system so that fumes can be directed away from the vehicle so they will not affect the driver.

header   Version of an exhaust manifold, made of tubular bent steel, that increases exhaust velocity, thus increasing performance of the engine.

intake manifold   Directs the airflow that goes through the throttle body to the individual intake valves that support combustion inside the cylinders.

intake gasket   Seals the manifold to the cylinder head; usually made out of plastic, rubber, or paper.

muffler   Component put on an exhaust system to muffle the noise created by the engine.

Review Questions

1. The intake system does all of the following, *except*:
   a. preventing carbon dioxide from entering the engine.
   b. ensuring that clean, dry air is supplied to the engine.
   c. providing a sealed passageway to the combustion chambers.
   d. controlling the amount of air entering the engine.

2. Choose the correct statement with respect to the exhaust system:
   a. It recycles the burned exhaust gases.
   b. It blocks the air rushing into the engine.
   c. It helps reduce the harmful emissions in the exhaust stream.
   d. It does not affect engine power.

3. Which of the following is one of the functions of an air cleaner?
   a. Preventing harmful gases from entering the passenger compartment
   b. Muffling the noise of the intake pulses

   c. Restricting the airflow to the engine at higher speeds
   d. Reducing the noise of combustion

4. In cross-flow heads:
   a. the design produces lesser power.
   b. the intake and exhaust manifolds are on the opposite sides of the engine.
   c. air and fuel are carried on the same branch.
   d. the intake and exhaust manifolds are adjacent to each other.

5. When reinstalling an intake with new gaskets:
   a. the coolant should be drained.
   b. the vacuum hoses need not be removed.
   c. the linkage to the throttle body need not be disconnected.
   d. the electrical connectors need not be disconnected.

6. Which of the following components in the exhaust system helps in the reduction of exhaust emissions?
   a. Manifold
   b. Catalytic convertor
   c. Muffler
   d. Resonator

7. Which of these is attached to the exhaust manifold and connects to the catalytic converter?
   a. Exhaust gasket
   b. Heat shield
   c. Exhaust pipe
   d. Flex pipe

8. A catalytic converter converts all of the following gases into less harmful gases, *except*:
   a. carbon monoxide.
   b. hydrocarbons.
   c. oxides of nitrogen.
   d. sulfur oxides.

9. Exhaust gaskets may be made of all of the below materials, *except*:
   a. graphite.
   b. mica.
   c. spiral wound steel.
   d. ceramic.

10. The first step in the removal and repair of an exhaust manifold is:
    a. removal of bolts.
    b. to make sure the engine is cold enough to operate.
    c. to inspect the manifold.
    d. to check whether the manifold is warped.

ASE Technician A/Technician B Style Questions

1. Technician A says that the intake manifold is an integral part of the ability of the engine to operate. Technician B states that an exhaust manifold can be made out of cast iron or tubular steel. Who is correct?
   a. Tech A
   b. Tech B
   c. Both A and B
   d. Neither A nor B

2. Technician A states that the design of the intake manifold is contingent on the use of the engine. Technician B says that the exhaust manifold is a single-use item. Who is correct?
   a. Tech A
   b. Tech B
   c. Both A and B
   d. Neither A nor B
3. Technician A states that an air filter must be replaced when you can no longer see light through it. Technician B says that the use of an exhaust header helps with the performance of the engine. Who is correct?
   a. Tech A
   b. Tech B
   c. Both A and B
   d. Neither A nor B
4. Technician A says that the intake manifold is a universal to any engine. Technician B states exhaust manifolds are very heavy, which means that they absorb a lot of the engine heat. Who is correct?
   a. Tech A
   b. Tech B
   c. Both A and B
   d. Neither A nor B
5. Technician A states that a plastic intake utilizes an O-ring gasket for sealing. Technician B says that an aluminum intake must be planed to make sure that the mating surfaces are flat for gasket sealing. Who is correct?
   a. Tech A
   b. Tech B
   c. Both A and B
   d. Neither A nor B
6. Technician A says that the vehicle dictates the design of the intake manifold, as the clearance issues must be designed into the intake. Technician B says that a broken flex pipe will not cause an exhaust noise. Who is correct?
   a. Tech A
   b. Tech B
   c. Both A and B
   d. Neither A nor B

7. Technician A says that a catalytic converter is a major emission piece that must be replaced if it fails. Technician B says that exhaust pipes are sized from the factory to increase power and fuel economy. Who is correct?
   a. Tech A
   b. Tech B
   c. Both A and B
   d. Neither A nor B
8. Technician A says that changing the intake to something that is more performance oriented could cause the emission systems to fail. Technician B says that as an ASE technician, you cannot remove a muffler. Who is correct?
   a. Tech A
   b. Tech B
   c. Both A and B
   d. Neither A nor B
9. Technician A says that using headers will void the emission requirements that are put in place by the federal government. Technician B says that there is a fine for removing a catalytic converter from a vehicle without replacing it. Who is correct?
   a. Tech A
   b. Tech B
   c. Both A and B
   d. Neither A nor B
10. Technician A states that inspecting the exhaust system should be part of a vehicle service. Technician B says that with increased focus on emissions, the design of catalytic converters is becoming more complex. Who is correct?
    a. Tech A
    b. Tech B
    c. Both A and B
    d. Neither A nor B

CHAPTER 19

Supercharging and Turbocharging Theory

NATEF Tasks

There are no NATEF Tasks for this chapter.

Knowledge Objectives

After reading this chapter, you will have:
- **K19001** Knowledge of positive pressure intake systems.
- **K19002** Knowledge of turbocharger usage.
- **K19003** Knowledge of supercharger usage.

Skills Objectives

There are no Skills Objectives for this chapter.

You Are the Automotive Technician

A 2002 Pontiac Grand Prix GTP comes into the repair shop for a noise in the engine. Under the hood the noise appears to be coming from the supercharger on the top of the engine. The technician has noticed that the engine is also running badly like it is unable to breathe. What is the first step the technician must do?

1. Determine the source of the top engine noise.
2. Verify the serpentine belt is installed correctly.
3. Check the engine fluids to see if they are to the full mark.

K19001 Knowledge of positive pressure intake systems.

▶ Introduction

The primary components of the automotive intake system are the air cleaner, intake ducting to the throttle body, and the intake manifold. The intake manifold is bolted to the cylinder head. Its construction and design depend on the engine for which it is created. The intake manifold directs airflow into each cylinder (**FIGURE 19-1**), and when restricted by the throttle plate, it provides a source of vacuum for systems such as the power brake system. On some applications the power assist for the braking system is hydro boost, electric, or powered by an engine driven vacuum pump. The intake manifold creates a mounting place for a throttle body assembly. In throttle body injection, one or two fuel injectors, which are mounted in the top of the throttle body, spray fuel down into the intake manifold. In a port fuel–injected engine, a throttle body is bolted to the opening of the intake manifold, and the injectors are mounted in the intake manifold near the intake valves (**FIGURE 19-2**). The throttle body controls airflow with a butterfly valve or valves, also called throttle valves. The throttle valves are opened and closed either by a throttle cable or, if the engine uses an electronic throttle control, by an electric motor that opens and closes the throttle plates. Attached to the throttle body is a throttle position sensor, which provides throttle position information to the engine computer. The air induction system consists of the following components: an air cleaner and housing, solid and flexible-duct tubing, connectors, and sometimes a mass airflow sensor. The air induction system draws in ambient air through a filter from the environment, or it is pushed through the system by a turbocharger or supercharger (**FIGURE 19-3**). The inlet opening of the induction system may be located in various positions under the hood, usually near an opening where ambient/cool air can enter the system.

Forced induction used on an engine helps to overcome the limitations on the ability of the cylinder heads, intake, and exhaust manifolds to breath naturally. Creating a positive pressure environment allows for more possibility of power to be made because of the more efficient use of space within the engine. A normal engine runs about 60–80 percent efficient, with forced induction it is closer to 100% if not higher, creating more efficiency increases power and fuel mileage.

▶ Forced Induction

One way to improve engine output is to increase the amount of the air-fuel mixture that is burned in the cylinder (increasing volumetric efficiency). Volumetric efficiency can be boosted most effectively by what is called forced induction. Forced induction increases air pressure in the intake manifold above atmospheric pressure. Thus, an engine using forced induction can have a

FIGURE 19-1 The intake manifold.

FIGURE 19-2 A. Throttle body injection. **B.** Port fuel injection.

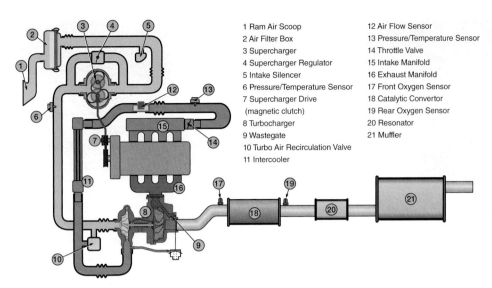

1 Ram Air Scoop
2 Air Filter Box
3 Supercharger
4 Supercharger Regulator
5 Intake Silencer
6 Pressure/Temperature Sensor
7 Supercharger Drive
   (magnetic clutch)
8 Turbocharger
9 Wastegate
10 Turbo Air Recirculation Valve
11 Intercooler

12 Air Flow Sensor
13 Pressure/Temperature Sensor
14 Throttle Valve
15 Intake Manifold
16 Exhaust Manifold
17 Front Oxygen Sensor
18 Catalytic Convertor
19 Rear Oxygen Sensor
20 Resonator
21 Muffler

FIGURE 19-3 In the above drawing, the turbocharger and the supercharger are heavily integrated with the entire engine operation system. So the technician must take into account these extra requirements when repairing the vehicle.

volumetric efficiency well above 100% (**FIGURE 19-4**). One way to achieve forced induction is by using a **turbocharger**, which uses energy that is created from the hot exhaust gases that are coming out of the combustion chamber still expanding which is creating turbulence within the exhaust manifold, that turbulence is what spins the turbine wheel on a turbocharger. The turbine is connected to one end of a shaft, and a compressor is connected to the other. The more exhaust gases the engine produces, the faster the turbocharger spins and the more air is compressed and forced into the engine. Another way to achieve forced induction is to use a supercharger, which is turned by the crankshaft, compresses the air, and forces it into the engine. The faster the engine turns, the more air is moved by the supercharger.

Turbocharger Usage and Description (Also Boost Control)

A turbocharger is a forced induction system that uses kinetic energy from the exhaust gases to increase the intake pressure. Like superchargers, turbochargers increase the amount of airflow into the engine, but they have a negative effect on the flow of air out of the engine. This means that for maximum power output, valves, cam timing, and exhaust system design are more important in turbocharged systems than in supercharged systems. The turbocharger uses exhaust gases to turn a turbine wheel. A shaft connects the turbine to a centrifugal compressor (**FIGURE 19-5**), which compresses the air and forces it under pressure into the intake manifold. Because the turbine is turned by exhaust gases, it runs at very high temperatures. It, along with the compressor, can rotate at well over 100,000 rpm. The turbocharger must have a good supply of clean oil to lubricate the bearings and carry excess heat away from the turbocharger. Some engines also supply coolant to the turbocharger body to improve cooling (**FIGURE 19-6**).

Higher engine speeds mean increased exhaust gas volume, and that makes the turbocharger spin faster and force more air into the cylinders, which can damage the engine if pressure is allowed to get too high. When pressure increases in an engine, so does cylinder temperature. As the temperature increases, the possibility of detonation also increases, as the gasoline will ignite

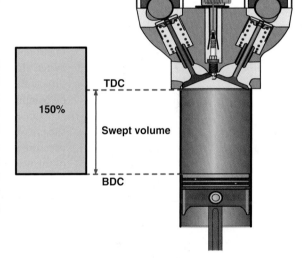

FIGURE 19-4 Volumetric efficiency of a forced induction engine.

K19002 Knowledge of turbocharger usage.

FIGURE 19-5 The turbocharger compresses air to feed to the intake and is run by exhaust gases.

FIGURE 19-6 Some turbochargers are cooled by engine coolant so that the bearing will not overheat, causing it to fail.

FIGURE 19-7 The turbocharger wastegate actuator controls the amount of boost pressure going to the intake manifold.

before the piston reaches the proper position in the cylinder. To control this risk of detonation, a device called a **wastegate** is installed on the exhaust inlet of the turbocharger. When air pressure in the intake manifold reaches a preset level, the wastegate automatically directs the exhaust gases so they bypass the turbine (**FIGURE 19-7**). The wastegate can also be computer controlled to reduce intake air pressure in the case of detonation or knocking.

On a mechanically operated wastegate, the spring pressure in the diaphragm controls the pressure at which the wastegate valve opens. The wastegate actuator is a spring-loaded pressure diaphragm that moves when air pushes against it. The air moves into the chamber of the wastegate actuator and presses on the diaphragm, overcoming the spring force. This causes the control linkage to push the wastegate open, allowing exhaust gases to bypass the turbine wheel, which reduces the boost pressure. This process happens over and over again, and as pressure drops, the wastegate closes and allows exhaust to flow to the turbine wheel again. The wastegate actuator gets pressure from a line connected to the intake manifold. The wastegate can be computer controlled by a **boost solenoid** that delays the intake pressure from reaching the wastegate actuator. The computer receives information from the manifold absolute pressure sensor, which tells how much pressure is in the intake manifold. A pressure relief valve may also be installed so that if the wastegate should fail, it can prevent an abnormal rise in manifold pressure. This relief valve is also known as a **blow-off valve**. A blow-off valve works against spring pressure, and as boost pressure rises above a predetermined amount, the pressure pushes the valve against the spring pressure and opens it, allowing excess pressure to "blow off" into the atmosphere.

FIGURE 19-8 The blow-off valve is a spring-loaded valve that releases excessive pressure in the air intake tube going to the intake manifold.

The blow-off valve may also vent the pressure to the air cleaner box to reduce the turbocharger pressure release noise. The blow-off valve is located between the compressor wheel and the throttle body. It is also used to ensure that when the throttle is abruptly shut, pressure does not rise excessively between the throttle body and the turbocharger compressor wheel (**FIGURE 19-8**). If pressure rises excessively, **compressor surge** will occur. Compressor surge is when manifold pressure rises above normal and works against the spinning exhaust turbine wheel, slowing it considerably. The pressure wave can then flow backward out of the compressor, creating a fluttering noise and continued pressure waves. Compressor surge, which is recognizable by a rapid fluttering sound, can be damaging to the compressor wheel, AS the pressure wave backing up forces the wheel to slow.

Because the turbocharger uses the energy of the exhaust gases, there is a short delay between when a driver opens the throttle and when maximum power is available. This delay is called turbo lag, and on larger engines it can be quite noticeable if the turbocharger is not sized correctly. Because a turbocharger recycles heat energy that would otherwise be lost, a turbocharged engine can increase an engine's efficiency and fuel economy—as long as the vehicle is being driven conservatively. However, even though a turbocharger may seem to be offering additional energy for nothing, it can introduce problems of its own. The extra heat and power it generates can put an extra load on the engine's cooling and lubrication systems. This is why most turbocharged vehicles have shorter service intervals for oil changes than non-turbocharged vehicles.

As the air passes through the turbocharger, it heats up. Hot air is less dense than cool air, so it tries to expand again, and some of the benefits of compressing it are lost. To stop this expansion and improve efficiency, some engines use an intercooler to cool the compressed air. The intercooler fits between the turbocharger and the engine and typically uses outside air to cool the compressed air, but on some applications, it may use the engine's cooling system to cool the compressed air. When the turbocharger housing is large, boost pressure is higher at high speed, but lag is worse for lower exhaust flow when the engine is at lower rpm. When the housing is small, boost pressure is high at lower speeds, but a restriction occurs in the exhaust system at high rpm. To combat turbo lag and avoid creating a restriction, there are several designs that have been made. The first is the twin scroll turbocharger, which uses two passageways into the turbine housing from the exhaust manifold. One passageway is controlled by a flap that can be closed to accelerate the exhaust flow, thus making the turbocharger smaller allowing the turbocharger to operate at a higher boost with lower engine speeds.

Another way to improve the turbo lag issue is to use twin turbochargers. Many manufacturers use two small turbochargers (one on each bank of a v-type engine) that can spin up more quickly, thereby creating boost sooner. The turbo lag is decreased as boost is created at a lower engine speed, and yet additional boost is created at a higher speed because there are two turbochargers to deal with the total exhaust flow.

The final way to create boost pressure without lag is to use a **variable-geometry turbocharger (VGT)**. The variable geometry turbocharger uses a set of movable vanes or fingers that change the flow of exhaust gases through the turbine housing. Under low exhaust speed, the fingers are positioned so that the exhaust gases spin the turbine faster, creating boost. Under high rpm, the speed of the exhaust gases is very high; therefore, the fingers are moved so they do not overspeed the turbine while also not restricting the exhaust flow and creating backup of exhaust, which would lower power. This type of turbocharger offers the best of both worlds. Currently it is used on a variety of engines including diesel and production gasoline engines from a host of different manufactures.

Another new development in turbocharger technology is used on the BMW engine. The engine design uses reverse flow cylinder heads. The center of the V-type engine, which normally was for intake, is now for the exhaust passages. Exhaust leaves the head and moves into the twin turbochargers, one per engine bank. The intake manifold is now on the outside of the head. The different positioning of the turbochargers keeps exhaust temperatures high and produces more turbine speed, which increases the efficiency of the turbocharger. The catalytic converter also gets up to temperature faster, reducing emissions.

The Ford Powerstroke 6.7-liter engine utilizes a variable geometry dual turbocharger setup with a wastegate integrated. This layout allows for the precise control that a VGT turbocharger can provide with the added protection of a wastegate-controlled turbocharger. This type of turbocharger has two compressor wheels that are back to back, which create a more even and powerful intake charge. Couple this turbocharger with the redesigned exhaust manifold locations and a water-to-air intercooler, it creates a potent, reliable package that fits in a small space. Usage of turbochargers is growing within the automotive segment as the need for increasing fuel economy, decreasing engine size, and the demand of more horsepower so that vehicles will be able to operate with a lower impact on the environment.

Turbocharger Engine Requirements

The mechanical engine requirements are very different than a non-turbocharged engine because of the increased demands the engine will be subjected to. The type of crankshaft, camshaft, pistons, oiling and cooling systems all have to be more robust than a non-boosted engine. Like an engine designed for a particular application, a turbocharged engine must be able to handle the extra stress that is put on it from the boosted application. A turbocharged engine requires the use of larger cooling systems, lower compression pistons, so when rebuilding or repairing a turbocharged engine, the technician must take into account the added requirements when replacing parts in the engine.

Turbocharger Failure Diagnosis and Repair/Prelube for Installation

Turbocharger failure happens for a variety of reasons, from lack of oil pressure to bearing failure; you must diagnose what has caused the turbocharger to fail before you fix it or the engine. The engine and turbocharger could fail from debris getting ingested into the turbocharger, dirt in the oil, overheating, lack of oil pressure and mechanical fatigue. Once the technician has determined and corrected the problem, the new turbocharger can be installed. And once the new turbocharger is installed, the technician can prelube the system so that it will not start up without lubrication. Consult the service information for the proper procedure to prelube the engine.

Supercharger Usage and Description (Also Boost Control)

K19003 Knowledge of supercharger usage.

Power is produced when a mixture of air and fuel is burned inside an engine cylinder. If more air is forced into the cylinder, then more fuel can be burned and more power produced with each power stroke. A **supercharger** compresses the air in the intake system above atmospheric pressure, which increases the density of the air entering the engine. Naturally aspirated engines operate with uncompressed air at atmospheric pressure, 14.7 psi (101 kPa). But a supercharger boosts that pressure another 6 psi (41.4 kPa) or higher. In a supercharged system, there is a greater air mass flow rate—that is, a higher density and speed of airflow. On the way into the engine, air pressure is increased by the compressor, and more fuel is added, which creates more pressure and power. The increased pressure causes the exhaust gases to exit much more rapidly, making the timing and exhaust sizing less important. Also, any residual gases will have less of an effect on the airflow entering the combustion chamber, as the supercharger boosts the manifold pressure substantially. Although some of the extra power produced must be used to drive the supercharger, the net result is more total power from the crankshaft. The supercharger may include a **bypass valve** system that allows the supercharger to "idle" when "high power" is not required, releasing the pressure back to the supercharger inlet and allowing the engine to run without boost. The bypass valve can be mounted remotely or directly onto the intake port (**FIGURE 19-9**). It allows air to move back past the compressor portion of the supercharger, keeping boost pressure low.

Several types of superchargers are manufactured for use on vehicles. The oldest version is the roots-style supercharger, which uses lobes to move air. This type of supercharger does not compress air at the lobes, but rather pushes air around the sides of the housing and into the intake. It stacks air against the intake valves to build boost pressure as the lobes come together and to prevent air from leaking back between them. Another version of the supercharger is the twin-screw type. The twin-screw supercharger compresses air between the screws and forces it into the intake. This compressor design is very efficient but very expensive. Many aftermarket high-performance superchargers are

FIGURE 19-9 The supercharger compresses air to feed to the intake and is run by the engine crankshaft.

centrifugal. This supercharger shaft is turned by a drive belt from the crankshaft and spins a compressor wheel, similar to what is used in the turbocharger. The supercharger shaft is connected by a set of gears to create a higher speed of the compressor. Because compressing air heats it up, a heat exchanger can be located between it and the intake manifold. The heat exchanger is like a radiator that the air flows through to cool it before it enters the engine.

Supercharger Engine Requirements

The engine requirements of a supercharged engine are very similar to a turbocharged engine except that the supercharger usually isn't lubricated or utilizes the engine's cooling system. The supercharger is a self-contained unit, as it contains its own lubrication, and it is cooled by the air passes through it. The engine drives the supercharger with a belt, which means that it doesn't have the same temperature problems that a turbocharger setup encounters, so the systems that are in place to support it are less likely to have heat issues.

Supercharger Failure Diagnosis and Repair

As with any engine failure, if the technician does not find the problem that destroyed the engine before he or she replaces the broken parts, then it is likely going to fail again (**FIGURE 19-10**). Diagnosing the problems that caused the supercharger to fail take place before it is replaced. If the failure is internal to the supercharger unit, then the unit must be replaced, as rebuilding is not recommended. When the technician goes through the engine to rebuild it, he or she must keep in mind that the supercharger puts a heavy load on the engine, so that it is able to handle the increased pressures. Special attention must be paid to the assembly process to ensure everything is within the factory specifications so the engine will be able to live a long life. For more information on the use of supercharging in automotive applications, please see the Engine Performance book.

FIGURE 19-10 When a supercharger bearing fails, it usually destroys the supercharger because the tolerances are so tight that any movement within the superchargers causes severe damage to the components.

▶ Wrap-Up

Ready for Review

▶ The primary components of the intake system are the intake manifold, the throttle body, and the air induction system.

▶ A turbocharger uses energy that is normally wasted through the exhaust. Exhaust gases enter a turbine and make it spin. The turbine is connected to one end of a shaft, and a compressor is connected to the other. The more exhaust gases the engine produces, the faster the turbocharger spins and the more air is compressed and forced into the engine.

▶ Higher engine speeds mean increased exhaust gas volume, and that makes the turbocharger spin faster and force more air into the cylinders, which can damage the engine if allowed to get too high.

▶ A turbocharger is a forced induction system that uses wasted kinetic energy from the exhaust gases to increase the intake pressure.

▶ A supercharger is turned by the crankshaft, compresses the air, and forces it into the engine. The faster the engine turns, the more air is moved by the supercharger.

▶ When pressure increases in an engine, so does cylinder temperature. As the temperature increases, the possibility of detonation also increases, because the gasoline will ignite before the piston reaches the proper position in the cylinder. To control this risk of detonation, a device called a wastegate is installed on the exhaust inlet of the turbocharger.

▶ The wastegate can be computer controlled by a boost solenoid that delays the intake pressure from reaching the wastegate actuator. The computer receives information from the manifold absolute pressure sensor, which tells how much pressure is in the intake manifold.

▶ A pressure relief valve, called a blow-off valve, may also be installed so that if the wastegate fails, the blow-off valve will prevent an abnormal rise in manifold pressure.

- A blow-off valve works against spring pressure, and as boost pressure rises above a predetermined amount, the pressure pushes the valve against the spring pressure and opens it, allowing excess pressure to "blow off" into the atmosphere.
- If pressure rises excessively, compressor surge will occur. Compressor surge is when manifold pressure rises above normal and works against the spinning exhaust turbine wheel, slowing it considerably. The pressure wave can then flow backward out of the compressor, creating a fluttering noise and continued pressure waves.
- Because the turbocharger uses the energy of the exhaust gases, there is a short delay between when a driver opens the throttle and when maximum power is available. This delay is called turbo lag.
- Turbochargers have to be cooled to keep the charge dense, so special lubrication and cooling systems are used.
- Some engines use an intercooler to cool the compressed air. It fits between the turbocharger and the engine and uses outside air to cool the compressed air.
- When the turbocharger housing is large, boost pressure is higher at high speed, but lag is worse for a given exhaust flow.
- When the housing is small, boost pressure is high at lower speeds, but a restriction occurs in the exhaust system at high rpm.
- To combat turbo lag and avoid creating a restriction, several designs have been made. The first is the twin scroll turbocharger, which uses two passageways into the turbine housing from the exhaust manifold. One passageway is controlled by a flap that can be closed to accelerate the exhaust flow, making the turbocharger operate at a higher boost at low engine speeds.
- Another way to improve the turbo lag issue is to use twin turbochargers.
- The final way to create boost pressure without lag is to use a variable-geometry turbocharger (VGT).
- The variable geometry turbocharger uses a set of movable vanes or fingers that change the flow of exhaust gases through the turbine housing.
- A new development in turbocharger technology design uses reverse flow cylinder heads. The center of the V-type engine, which normally was for intake, is now for the exhaust passages. Exhaust leaves the head and moves into the twin turbochargers, one per engine bank. The intake manifold is now on the outside of the head; this system keeps exhaust temperatures high and produces more turbine speed, which increases the efficiency of the turbocharger.
- Turbocharger failure can occur for a number of reasons, from lack of oil pressure to bearing failure. You must diagnose what has caused the turbocharger to fail before you fix it or the engine.
- A supercharger compresses the air in the intake system to above atmospheric pressure, which increases the density of the air entering the engine.
- The supercharger may include a bypass valve system that allows the supercharger to "idle" when "high power" is not required, releasing the pressure back to the supercharger inlet and allowing the engine to run without boost.
- The engine requirements for a supercharged engine are very similar to those for a turbocharged engine except that the supercharger usually isn't lubricated or utilizes the engine's cooling system.
- The supercharger is a self-contained unit with its own lubrication, and it is cooled by the air that is passed through it.
- The engine is driving the supercharger with a belt.
- Before replacing a supercharger, the technician must diagnose the problems that caused it to fail.

Key Terms

blow-off valve Allows for excess pressure that is built up in the intake track to exit the intake after the pressure overcomes the spring pressure on this valve.

boost solenoid Electronic control feature that allows the PCM to control the wastegate by either an electronic solenoid or by utilizing this to control the vacuum to the wastegate.

bypass valve Used on a supercharger application to bypass the supercharger in order to limit the amount of boost it creates.

compressor surge Occurs when manifold pressure rises above normal and works against the spinning exhaust turbine wheel, slowing it considerably.

supercharger Component that uses external power to turn the compressor wheel to compress the air as it enters the intake system track. The supercharger is usually driven by a belt off the crankshaft.

turbocharger Forced induction unit that uses exhaust gas pressure to compress intake air so that more air can be pushed into the cylinders, thus creating more power.

variable geometry turbocharger (VGT) Type of turbocharger that is adjustable by directing exhaust gases toward or away from the exhaust impeller. This is a common way to control the turbocharger more precisely in order to match the requirements of the engine.

wastegate Allows for exhaust to bypass the turbocharger impeller so that the turbocharger will not overspeed,

Review Questions

1. Which of the following components directs airflow into each cylinder?
   a. Intake manifold
   b. Throttle body
   c. Air induction system
   d. Turbocharger
2. What does forced induction achieve?
   a. It increases air pressure in the intake manifold above atmospheric pressure.
   b. It decreases the volume of air in the intake manifold.

c. It forces exhaust gases out of the system.

d. It decreases air pressure in the intake manifold below atmospheric pressure.

3. The turbocharger increases pressure in the intake manifold using:

   a. a coolant.

   b. atmospheric air.

   c. heated air.

   d. exhaust gases.

4. A wastegate inside a turbocharger:

   a. decreases intake air pressure when the possibility of detonation increases.

   b. supplies clean oil to lubricate the bearings.

   c. carries excess heat away from the turbocharger.

   d. supplies coolant to the turbocharger body.

5. Which of the following components delays the intake pressure from reaching the wastegate actuator?

   a. Blow-off valve

   b. Boost solenoid

   c. Diaphragm

   d. Compressor surge

6. All of the following statements with respect to the blow-off valve are true, *except*:

   a. It may also vent the pressure to the air cleaner box to reduce the turbocharger pressure release noise.

   b. It is located in the air intake tubing connected to the intake manifold.

   c. It ensures that pressure does not rise excessively between the throttle body and the turbocharger compressor.

   d. It works within the spring diaphragm pressure of a turbocharger.

7. Most turbocharged vehicles have shorter service intervals for oil changes than non-turbocharged vehicles because:

   a. Turbocharged vehicles contain many delicate parts.

   b. Turbocharged systems put an extra load on the engine's cooling and lubrication systems.

   c. The additional energy they produce will decrease over time without regular service.

   d. Turbochargers need to be replaced regularly.

8. All of the following statements with respect to a supercharger are true, *except*:

   a. It compresses the air in the intake system to above atmospheric pressure.

   b. It allows a greater air mass flow rate inside the engine.

   c. It creates more pressure and power for the engine.

   d. It may include a bypass valve system that allows the supercharger to idle when high power is not required.

9. Which of the following types of superchargers is similar to a turbocharger and uses a heat exchanger in it?

   a. Roots style

   b. Centrifugal

   c. Twin-screw type

   d. Lobes type

10. Choose the correct statement:

   a. A supercharger is a self-contained unit.

   b. A supercharger fails at higher temperatures.

c. A supercharger unit can be rebuilt in case of internal failure.

d. A supercharger uses the engine lubrication system to cool itself.

ASE Technician A/Technician B Style Questions

1. Technician A says that a stuck boost solenoid could cause the wastegate to remain open. Technician B states that the wastegate is used to control the mph at which the engine operates. Who is correct?

   a. Tech A

   b. Tech B

   c. Both A and B

   d. Neither A nor B

2. Technician A says that a blow-off valve is the only way to control the amount of boost the turbocharger makes. Technician B says that a forced induction engine has different types of pistons to handle the excess pressures. Who is correct?

   a. Tech A

   b. Tech B

   c. Both A and B

   d. Neither A nor B

3. Technician A says that a blow-off valve on a turbocharged application is similar to a blowby valve on a supercharged application. Technician B states that a supercharger uses exhaust gases to produce power from it. Who is correct?

   a. Tech A

   b. Tech B

   c. Both A and B

   d. Neither A nor B

4. Technician A says that higher-strength materials are used in a base engine for a forced induction engine application because of the increased pressures apparent on the engine. Technician B states that using substandard components could lead to failure. Who is correct?

   a. Tech A

   b. Tech B

   c. Both A and B

   d. Neither A nor B

5. Technician A says that a supercharger application may have two different belt drive systems for the engine. Technician B states that using a turbocharger could require the owner of the vehicle to do more maintenance than a regular engine would. Who is correct?

   a. Tech A

   b. Tech B

   c. Both A and B

   d. Neither A nor B

6. Technician A states that the base compression ratio of a forced induction engine is higher than a non–forced induction engine. Technician B states that a supercharged engine operates better with an intercooler. Who is correct?

   a. Tech A

   b. Tech B

c. Both A and B
d. Neither A nor B

7. Technician A says that the power benefits of a supercharger outweigh the amount of power they consume to operate. Technician B says that a turbocharger uses waste energy to create power, which means it is virtually free power. Who is correct?
   a. Tech A
   b. Tech B
   c. Both A and B
   d. Neither A nor B

8. Technician A says that turbocharger usage allows for a more efficient engine combination. Technician B says the downside to using a turbocharger on an engine is the complexity of the installation process. Who is correct?
   a. Tech A
   b. Tech B
   c. Both A and B
   d. Neither A nor B

9. Technician A says using a supercharger on an engine requires a different engine PCM to handle the extra outputs needed for operation. Technician B says that a turbocharger is self-sufficient on a fuel-injected engine and requires no modifications. Who is correct?
   a. Tech A
   b. Tech B
   c. Both A and B
   d. Neither A nor B

10. Technician A states that a turbocharger must have its oil changed on a regular basis. Technician B states that a supercharger has a closed oiling system that must be serviced on a regular basis. Who is correct?
    a. Tech A
    b. Tech B
    c. Both A and B
    d. Neither A nor B

CHAPTER 20

Engine Machining

NATEF Tasks

There are no NATEF Tasks for this chapter.

Knowledge Objectives

After reading this chapter, you will have:

- **K20001** Knowledge of cylinder block machining practices.
- **K20002** Knowledge of the cylinder bore boring.
- **K20003** Knowledge of why you machine the crankshaft when rebuilding an engine.
- **K20004** Knowledge of the process of connecting rods reconditioning.

- **K20005** Knowledge of why machining of the cylinder head is necessary.
- **K20006** Knowledge of the cylinder head straightening process.
- **K20007** Knowledge of valve grinding and installing seat inserts.

Skills Objectives

There are no Skills Objectives for this chapter.

You Are the Automotive Technician

You are an ASE-certified engine machinist at the local machine shop. A customer wants to know about the machining processes your shop can handle. The Boss 429 spun a main bearing and wore a few thousandths of an inch off the number 3 crankshaft main bearing journal as well as the main bearing saddle in the block. He wants to know what the options are for repairing those issues. He also said the cylinder bores are worn 0.015–0.016" oversize and would like to know how much larger you would have to bore it.

1. How can the crankshaft be saved, even though it is worn badly?
2. What process would you use to repair the worn main bearing saddle in the block?
3. To what size would you most likely bore the cylinders out? What also then must be replaced?

FIGURE 20-1 The machined surface of a metal cylinder head or cylinder bore is not flat like you think. Microscopically the surface has small fissures that hold oil and helps seal against the component they are mated to.

K20001 Knowledge of cylinder block machining practices.

▶ Introduction

In the past 20 years, the field of automotive technology has changed dramatically. More often than not, the vehicle manufacturer takes failed parts back for analysis and sends the technician brand new parts. For example, if a connecting rod failed and caused catastrophic engine damage, the manufacturer would ask for the engine back for a complete analysis of why it failed. The technician's responsibility would be to replace the broken engine with a newly supplied unit.

If the vehicle is not under warranty, it is still usually less expensive to replace most engine assemblies than to tear down and repair them. Typically, once the engine is replaced, the broken engine is sent to the parts store from which the new engine was purchased for a "core return." The parts store sends the broken engine back to the manufacturer to have it professionally rebuilt and all worn parts replaced or remachined (**FIGURE 20-1**).

The automotive technician of today does not necessarily need to know how to proficiently perform each of the procedures listed in this chapter, but he or she does need to know that these processes exist and understand what is possible to repair and what is not. The ability to recognize failures of engines that are beyond repair will help the technician to know whether it is more cost effective for the customer to replace rather than repair.

▶ Cylinder Block

The cylinder block is the backbone for any good engine rebuild because it houses all the internal and external components that make the engine operate. You must be working with a good foundation to create a reliable engine that runs well. Without this vital component, you will not be able to assembly a reliable engine; care must be taken when inspecting, machining, and assembling this component.

Engine Machining

Engine machining is done any time the tolerances of an engine component must be adjusted by adding or removing material. Typically, this process is performed by taking precise measurements and comparing those measurements to a set of factory specifications that are found in service information for that particular vehicle (**FIGURE 20-2**). Engine machining is performed when an engine exhibits a problem and the technician determines that problem is coming from a component of the engine

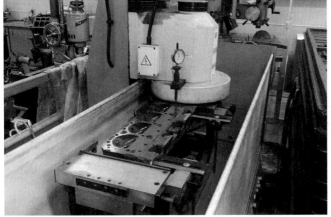

FIGURE 20-2 The decking machine ensures that the deck of the cylinder block is perfectly flat so that the head gasket and cylinder head will seal correctly.

Applied Math

AM-39: Equal/Not Equal: The technician can distinguish when a measurement is not equal to the manufacturer's specifications or tolerances.

When assessing an engine's machining requirements for reconditioning, one of the most important requirements is to measure the cylinder bores to determine if boring, or in more extreme cases, sleeving, is required. Cylinder bores are first inspected for obvious damage, and then they are measured for wear, out-of-round, and taper.

Using an accurate cylinder bore gauge, measurements are taken at the upper, middle, and lower sections of the bore in two directions, along and across the block. The nominal amount of bore wear is calculated by taking the maximum and minimum of the six numbers and calculating the difference between them.

If the factory bore measurement is 78 mm (3.079"), with a specified wear limit of 0.15 mm (0.006"), and the difference between a bore's taper measurements is 0.19 mm (0.007"), the block must be rebored and fitted with oversized pistons. If measured wear is below the specified limit, 0.10 mm (0.004") in this example, the engine could be reassembled with the original pistons, assuming no other damage.

that is not within specifications. For example, a customer complains of a noise when the engine is started up cold. Due to the tone and frequency of the noise and the fact that the volume of the noise goes away as the engine warms up, the technician diagnoses the noise as excessive piston-to-cylinder wall clearance, which is called piston slap. The technician disassembles the engine, checks the piston-to-cylinder wall clearance, and finds that the pistons have excessive clearance. The pistons are replaced, and the cylinder walls are bored oversize to accommodate the larger pistons. The engine is reassembled, and the technician verifies the repair by testing the vehicle on a cold start-up.

Most technicians and shop owners in today's competitive market have chosen to sublet, or send out, all of their machining work to a machine shop. The main task of machine shops is to restore engine parts to factory specifications. The amount of money it takes to purchase the equipment necessary to perform these machining functions makes it financially unwise for most automotive shop owners to purchase these tools and train their employees on them when those employees will use the tools only once in a while. It is best to leave machining to the Automotive Service Excellence (ASE) Master Certified Machinist professionals.

Engine Cylinder Block and Cylinder Head Mating Surface Composition

Surface roughness refers to the irregularities found in the surface texture, which are the result of the machining process employed to refinish the surface. **Surface roughness average (Ra)** is a measure of how rough a surface is at the microscopic level and is rated as the arithmetic average of the surface valleys and peaks. For precise and consistent results, surface finish should be a specified range or maximum level of Ra. The Ra is the measurement used to classify how rough a certain mating surface is (**FIGURE 20-3**). A 30 Ra finish is smoother than a 60 Ra finish. Today's cylinder heads are much lighter and less rigid and use a multilayered steel (MLS) gasket; as a result, the surface must be smoother than it was in the past. A cast iron head must be no rougher than 60 to 100 Ra, and an aluminum cylinder must be approximately 30 Ra. The surface must be smooth enough for initial cold seal when starting the engine, and the gasket requires a certain amount of support so the gases from the combustion chamber cannot distort the head gasket. If the surface is too rough (too much bite), and the cylinder head is aluminum and the block cast iron, then sideways shearing from the aluminum cylinder head during expansion and contraction will occur, causing the gasket to fail.

The engine block can be resurfaced by a surface grinder, using a stone wheel or a broach-style surfacer, applying a cubic boron nitride (CBN) cutter for cast iron and a polycrystalline diamond (PCD) cutter for aluminum. This procedure is performed because the cylinder head and the engine cylinder block must be perfectly flat at the mating surface where they are bolted together. If they are not perfectly flat, leaks or ruptures will quickly occur. The desired surface finish for today's engines that use MLS gaskets can be lower than a 30 Ra finish. Always check the manufacturer's specifications. The desired procedure in surfacing the **engine block's deck** (the portion of the engine cylinder block on which the

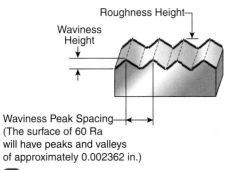

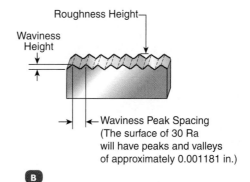

FIGURE 20-3 Surface roughness. **A.** 60 Ra. **B.** 30 Ra.

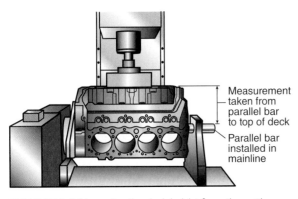

FIGURE 20-4 Measuring the deck height from the setting fixture.

Measurement taken from parallel bar to top of deck

Parallel bar installed in mainline

head gasket lies and to which the cylinder head is bolted) is to surface the engine block parallel to the centerline where the crankshaft is installed. Surfacing the engine block this way makes the deck height on each cylinder the same, which is important to ensure that all pistons have the exact same amount of space between the cylinder head and the cylinder block in order to maintain equal compression values. Several different types of equipment are available for resurfacing the engine block, differing mainly in the cutting bit type. For aluminum cylinder heads or blocks, you need a PCD cutting bit. In refinishing cast iron cylinder heads or blocks, a CBN cutting surface is needed. Each metal has different characteristics and thus requires different tooling and cutting speeds. To check the engine block, measure the distance from where the bearing insert is installed on the main journal to the top of the engine block on each end of the deck surface. Some surface machines use a precision bar that runs through the main journals, and the measurements and settings are taken from the precision bar (**FIGURE 20-4**). The computer numerical control (CNC) machine is a tool that uses computer programs to automatically execute a series of machining operations. These programs are usually completely computer automated, requiring little input from the operator. With some of the newer CNC-style machines, the measurements are taken from the top of the engine block dowel pinhole, where the engine block dowel pins are fixed. These pins are guides that allow exact alignment of the cylinder head and cylinder head gasket when reassembling the engine assembly. During the machining process, the engine block dowel pins are removed, and the dowel pinholes (which are precision-drilled holes) are used as depth markers. There are usually two or more of these holes in an engine block deck surface. The machinist measures the depth of each hole to determine exactly how much metal to take off to make the holes the exact same depth. In this process, the engine block surface is resurfaced to be completely flat and true.

Boring the Cylinder Block

K20002 Knowledge of the cylinder bore boring.

If the cylinders are damaged, have too much **taper** (meaning they are smaller in diameter at one end), or are out of round, then they should be rebored and honed to fit oversized pistons (**FIGURE 20-5**). Oversized pistons have to be used following boring because the boring process enlarges the cylinder walls, leaving the original piston too small to be effectively reused. In some cases, the **cylinder bore** might be damaged beyond boring, worn beyond the limits for an oversized piston, or cracked. To repair the cylinder, it must be bored out (machined) and a cylinder sleeve installed to fill the extra space created in the boring process. Dry cylinder sleeves require the cylinder to be bored out and the sleeve to have an interference fit of approximately 0.002" to 0.0025" (0.05 to 0.06 mm). Dry cylinder sleeves are pressed into the existing bore and do not come into contact with an engine coolant passage. Wet cylinder sleeves are installed and do come into contact with engine coolant. Using sleeves allows you to use pistons the same size as the original ones, restoring the factory bore dimensions.

Boring the engine cylinders to a larger size requires a boring machine. Those typically used by engine machine shops are semiautomated. The semiautomatic machine cuts the engine block cylinders to their new oversized dimensions. To start, the engine block must be correctly mounted underneath the cutting bit. The machinist tells the boring machine what engine is being bored and performs preliminary adjustments to the machine, such as inserting the correct cutting bit for the application to be serviced. After all preliminary setup steps are completed, the machine centers itself in the first bore and begins the cutting process. After the first bore is finished, the machine automatically moves to the next cylinder bore, centers itself, and begins the boring process all over again.

FIGURE 20-5 To bore a cylinder block, the block is fixed to a jig in a cylinder boring machine so that when the bore is being machined, it will be perpendicular to the centerline of the main journals.

When boring the cylinder for a dry sleeve with no top lip, you must bore the cylinder wall so it has a lip on the bottom. This is done by not running the boring bar all the way through the cylinder, so the cylinder sleeve cannot slip in the cylinder bore.

If the cylinder can be bored oversize, usually the cylinder is bored for the first oversized piston available that will fit in the now slightly enlarged cylinder space. For example, if the cylinder is supposed to be 4.000" and the cylinder measures 4.016" at the top and 4.009" at the bottom, the machinist will bore out the cylinder to 4.030" because oversized pistons only come in a few assorted sizes. The most common sizes of oversized pistons available are 0.02" (0.51 mm), 0.03" (0.76 mm), 0.04" (1.0 mm), and 0.06" (1.5 mm). Before boring begins, the exact diameter of the new pistons must be determined in order to know how much material to leave in the cylinders to hone out for final clearance. Be sure to refer to the manufacturer's specifications to see how large a particular engine can be bored oversize. A boring bar is another name for a boring machine used for boring cylinders. It usually includes fingers for centering it in the cylinder. There are three styles of boring bars: the portable boring bar, which can be mounted to the top of the engine cylinder block or to a boring machine stand; the semiautomated boring bar machine; and the CNC-style boring machine.

All boring bars fracture the surface as they cut the material away from the cylinder walls, so there must be enough material left to hone and get past these fractures in the metal. The boring machine simply cuts away metal with a sharp bit, leaving microscopic hills and valleys that must be ground down to prevent premature cylinder wear. This grinding is done with a cylinder hone. Typically, the portable boring bar has to leave more material to hone out, approximately 0.005" (0.13 mm), whereas the more rigid machines with the optional cutters and spindle speeds must only hone out 0.0015" to 0.002" (0.04 to 0.05 mm) to get past the fractured metal. The portable boring bar should not be used on modern thinner-walled engine blocks, as cylinder distortion can take place from the weight of the boring bar bolted to the engine block. The weight of the boring bar is enough to flex the cylinders and change the cylinder dimensions, resulting in incorrect dimensions when the boring job is finished.

The boring process leaves a corkscrew pattern on the walls of the cylinder. If left like this, the cylinder rings would catch and tear on the lands of the corkscrew. Hone stones are used to sand down and file away the cylinder walls, leaving a unidirectional finish also known as a **crosshatch pattern**. This pattern appears as a series of big Xs etched into the walls and is much smoother than the corkscrew left by the boring process. Most hones are self-tensioning, which alleviates the need for the technician to determine the amount of tension needed. The crosshatch pattern is made at either a standard 45- or 60-degree angle (**FIGURE 20-6**). Refer to the manufacturer's specifications for the engine you are working on. A good crosshatch helps to trap the oil and retain it in the cylinder bores where it is needed. Achieving the desired crosshatch is a matter of adjusting the speed for stroking the cylinder hone. As the cylinder hone is moved up and down inside the cylinder, it is also moving in a circle driven by an electric drill. This up-and-down circular motion allows the hone stones to make slanted streaks on the cylinder walls. These slanted streaks make the crosshatched pattern after a number of up-and-down cycles. For a 45-degree pattern, move the stones at a normal pace, which is (depending on cylinder size and depth) about half a second in the down direction and half a second in the up direction. If a more aggressive or steeper-angled X pattern is required, the process must be sped up. It is not an exact science except when an actual cylinder hone machine is doing the work. The faster or more rapid the hone is stroked in the cylinder, the higher the angle of the crosshatch becomes. If the angle gets too high, then oil will run down the cylinder wall and not provide enough lubricant to the rings and pistons, causing scoring and leading to low compression. If the angle gets too steep, then too much oil will be held on the cylinder walls, and the oil will be burned.

Torque Plate

A **torque plate** is approximately 2" (51 mm) thick and bolted in place where the cylinder head is fastened on the engine block (**FIGURE 20-7**). When the cylinder head is torqued, it exerts force around the cylinder wall and can change the machined

Typical Crosshatch Pattern

FIGURE 20-6 The proper crosshatching pattern ensures that the piston rings seat properly and oil burning doesn't occur.

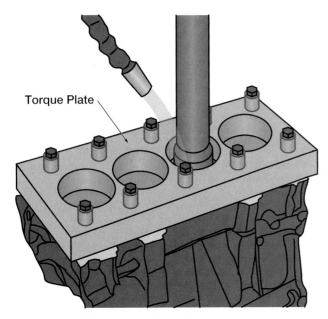

FIGURE 20-7 Using a torque plate when boring a cylinder simulates the cylinder head being bolted onto the cylinder block. This causes the block to be under the same type of stress it will be under once the cylinder head is bolted and the engine is in operation.

dimensions, especially on lighter-weight engine blocks. To eliminate this problem, a torque plate is installed that simulates the cylinder head torqued in place. Now, when the cylinder is honed, it stays true to the dimensions. The torque plate is used in performance machine shops and is also being used more often on the new style of engines that have lightweight blocks made of thinner aluminum or cast iron, which are more prone to cylinder shifting. Some cylinders can distort as much as 0.0015" (0.04 mm) when the cylinder head is bolted down. One high-performance industry, NASCAR, has even gone to the trouble of not only using a torque plate but also using hot water through the block to ensure that the cylinder bores are the size they will be at full temperature. This process is known as hot honing. The use of hot honing is not cost effective for the typical engine, as the machine is very expensive to purchase and operate.

Honing Cylinders

After the boring process, a rigid hone is used for the process of smoothing out the cylinder walls, the final step in refinishing the cylinder. A crosshatched pattern allows the proper amount of oil to stay on the cylinder walls so the piston rings seat into them, and ensures a proper seal so as to not lose compression or burn oil (**FIGURE 20-8**).

Honing is typically performed by a honing machine, which consists of three or more elongated smooth stones attached to an arbor. This assembly is inserted inside a finished/bored cylinder and is spun (either by a computer-controlled honing machine or by a machine operated by a machinist) until the proper surface texture and final bore size of the cylinder are reached.

Several options can be considered before **honing**. If there are no imperfections or grooves, and the cylinder walls have only to be deglazed, a ball hone is used. If the cylinder was bored oversize, then the cylinders have to be honed to final size with a rigid hone. A ball hone consists of a metal center rod with various other metal rods branching out from it, similar to branches on a tree. Stone balls are attached to the ends of these metal rods. When this assembly is inserted into the cylinder, spun with an electric drill, and moved up and down, the abrasive stones wear the "glazing" off the cylinder walls, giving them a neat new crosshatched pattern (**FIGURE 20-9**). Glazing refers to the

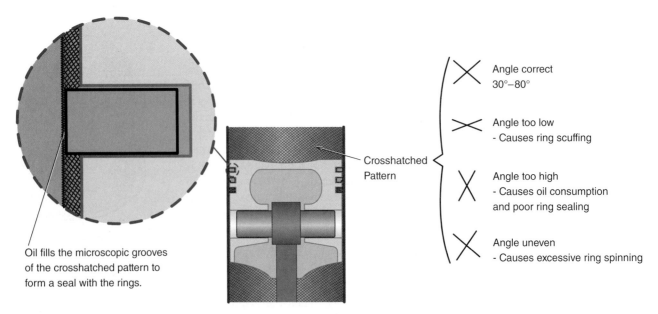

Oil fills the microscopic grooves of the crosshatched pattern to form a seal with the rings.

Crosshatched Pattern

Angle correct
30°–80°

Angle too low
- Causes ring scuffing

Angle too high
- Causes oil consumption and poor ring sealing

Angle uneven
- Causes excessive ring spinning

FIGURE 20-8 The cylinder wall is an integral part of the piston rings sealing the combustion chamber.

FIGURE 20-9 Before and after pictures of honing a cylinder. Without the honing process, the cylinder bore would not hold oil, and the piston rings would not seat correctly.

finish produced when the crosshatch scratches have been worn away, leaving the cylinder smooth and shiny and unable to retain oil. This condition reduces compression, as oil helps the rings to seal, and can also result in oil moving past the rings and burning in the combustion chamber. The honing process with a ball hone is done only if the cylinder does not need to be bored and is in good shape in regard to taper and wear. The ball hone does not restore cylinder size; it simply reapplies the crosshatching. Producing the correct pattern takes practice in order to get just the right speed of the stone moving up and down in the cylinder in relation to the spinning speed.

Once the cylinders are at the proper dimension and have the correct crosshatch pattern, it is time to clean and lubricate them. First, clean the cylinder walls with solvent; then scrub them with warm, soapy water and a stiff brush to remove any metal and stone particles. Next, take a clean lint-free rag and pour some clean oil on it. Rub the oil into the cylinder walls. If any discoloration appears, rewash the cylinders and recheck them with a clean, oiled rag. When no dirt or discoloration occurs, the cylinders are ready for the next step in the rebuilding process.

To hone a cylinder head, follow the steps in **SKILL DRILL 20-1**.

SKILL DRILL 20-1 Honing a Cylinder Head

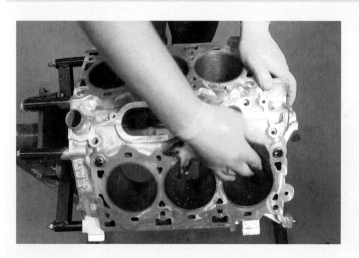

1. Clean the cylinder block with soap and water.

Continued

2. Attach the hone to an electric drill.

3. Dip the hone in a soapy water solution.

4. Insert the wet hone into the cylinder, and start the drill while moving the drill up and down in the cylinder.

5. Continue honing until a crosshatch pattern appears on the cylinder wall.

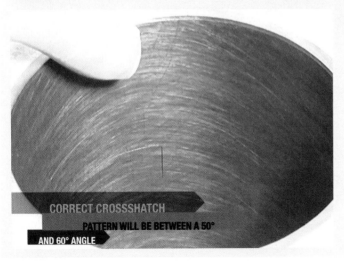

CORRECT CROSSHATCH
PATTERN WILL BE BETWEEN A 50°
AND 60° ANGLE

Continued

6. Continue to other cylinders until all the cylinders are completed.

7. Wash the entire block with hot soapy water to remove any shavings.

Main Bearing Bores

Premature bearing failure and crankshaft failure can occur with an out-of-line main bearing bore. Proper bore alignment must be ensured between all the main bearing bores. The bore alignment can be checked for straightness by using a straightedge with a feeler gauge. The engine main bearing bores can become misaligned due to the stresses released over time from the initial casting process. Over time, engine blocks can distort with temperature changes, and the bearing bores can become misaligned. Engine bearings will be excessively worn, particularly the center bearing because of the bore shift. Checking that the main crankshaft bores are concentric and perfectly circular ensures that they are not out of round or egg shaped. Just like engine block cylinders, these bores can wear into an oblong or egg-shaped hole, which can damage the crankshaft. Out-of-round is checked with a bore gauge tool.

To correct a bore alignment issue, the engine block has to be line bored or line honed. In this process, the main journals must be made smaller. This is done by removing the main caps and cutting the mating surface down (**FIGURE 20-10**). The amount of metal to be removed from the main cap is usually 0.003" to 0.005" (0.076 to 0.13 mm). After all of the main caps are cut, the engine block mating surface is cleaned to remove dust or debris. The main caps are torqued back into place; the line hone or line bore machine is set up; and the original main bearing bore size is cut. Cutting the main bearing bores ensures that the bores line up properly and stop the bearing wear problem (**FIGURE 20-11**).

FIGURE 20-10 Cutting main caps.

FIGURE 20-11 Line honing a mainline.

The manufacturer's specifications for the main bearing bore must be followed when line honing to ensure that the proper oil clearance is established between the bearing and the crankshaft main journal when main bearings are installed. Main bearing oil clearance can be found by measuring the crankshaft main journal size and subtracting this measurement from the inside diameter of the main bearing inserts with the bearings installed and the main bearing caps torqued. If the crankshaft measurements are near the large size of the specifications, then the main bearing bores should be resized to the large size of the factory specifications. If the crankshaft measurements are closer to the small size of the factory specifications, then the main bearing bores should be resized to the small size of the factory specifications.

The proper oil clearance must be maintained to ensure proper oil pressure of the engine and to ensure that the correct amount of lubricant can reach all the engine bearings. Oil clearance can also be quickly checked before engine assembly through the use of Plastigage. Plastigage is a thin, calibrated piece of soft plastic string that is laid on the main bearing journal of the crankshaft and squished between the journal and the bearing. The main bearing cap is torqued down so that the Plastigage is squished, and the Plastigage is then removed. The width of the squeezed Plastigage is compared to a chart to determine the amount of bearing clearance (**FIGURE 20-12**). The wider the Plastigage, the smaller the bearing clearance.

To check clearance on the main bearings using Plastigage, follow the steps in **SKILL DRILL 20-2**.

▶ Crankshaft and Rods

The crankshaft and connecting rods are the heart of the internal combustion engine as they convert the chemical energy into mechanical energy that we can then utilize to propel the vehicle (**FIGURE 20-13**). Because these components are changing direction with every rotation, they are made of high cast or forged steel, which is able to stand up to the abuse that they are operating under (**FIGURE 20-14**). When it is time to rebuild this engine, you must make sure that these components are within service specifications or they will end up causing failures inside the engine, requiring more repair. Careful inspection will result in a component that is usable, and not replacing these expensive pieces, you will save the customer money.

Crankshaft Grinding and Polishing

The **crankshaft journals** have to be inspected for scratches, pits, cracks, and grooves when rebuilding the engine. The bearings need a true, clean surface to run on, or they will be torn up on the very first running of the engine. When imperfections cannot be polished out to 0.0005" (0.013 mm) or less, the crankshaft has to

▶ **TECHNICIAN TIP**

Whenever the crankshaft centerline is refinished, the centerline of the crankshaft moves slightly upward. If the centerline moves too far, then cam timing issues can occur or the compression ratio can be increased slightly. So always make sure that only a minimal amount of material is removed during line boring.

K20003 Knowledge of why you machine the crankshaft when rebuilding an engine.

FIGURE 20-12 Using Plastigage to check oil clearance. If the width of the Plastigage doesn't match the band on the chart, move to the next band.

SKILL DRILL 20-2 Using Plastigage to Check Bearing Clearance

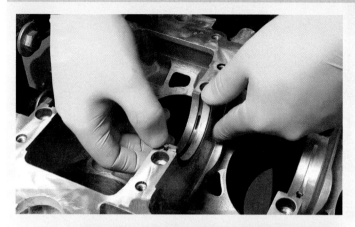

1. Insert the bearings into the main bearing journals on the cylinder block.

2. Insert the bearings into the main bearing caps.

3. Clean the crankshaft with a dry towel, making sure not to leave any residue on the crankshaft.

4. Lay the crankshaft into the cylinder block main bearings.

Continued

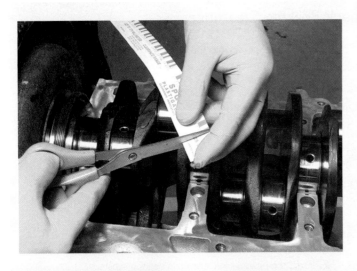

5. Cut the Plastigage into strips the width of the main bearings.

6. Remove the cover from the Plastigage, and install the clay strip perpendicular to the bearing cap on the crankshaft.

7. Do not spin the crankshaft!

8. Install the main bearing caps and torque to spec in the proper sequence.

Continued

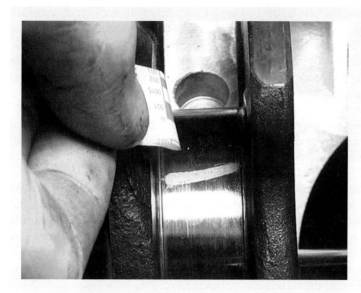

9. Detorque the main bearing caps, and compare the flattened clay to the gauge on the wrapper of the Plastigage.

Crankshaft	
Main bearing journal diameter	62.968-62.992 mm (2.467-2.479 in)
Main bearing journal maximum taper	0.008 mm (0.0003 in)
Main bearing journal maximum out-of-round	0.006 mm (0.0002 in)
Main bearing journal-to-cylinder block clearance	0.024-0.072 mm (0.0009-0.003 in)
Connecting rod journal diameter	49.969-49.991 mm (1.967-1.968 in)
Connecting rod journal maximum taper	0.008 mm (0.0003 in)
Connecting rod journal maximum out-of-round	0.006 mm (0.0002 in)
Crankshaft maximum end play	0.135-0.255 mm (0.005-0.010 in)

10. Compare your readings to the specifications for the crankshaft found in the service information.

be reground. Regrinding involves placing the crankshaft in a lathe set for metal cutting. The lathe spins the crankshaft while a special bit shaves or grinds the metal away.

Most crankshafts are induction hardened. This process hardens the metal by raising the temperature of the part with heat or magnetic fields and then suddenly cooling it in water, oil, or another chemical. Using the induction hardening method allows the crankshaft to be reground on the mains and rod bearing journals without having to redo the hardening process, which is important because the hardening will be as deep as 0.080" (2.03 mm). Some heavy-duty and performance cranks use nitriding. Nitriding is the

FIGURE 20-13 A connecting rod used to connect the piston to the crankshaft. It can be made of steel or aluminum to withstand the abuse it will undergo inside the engine.

FIGURE 20-14 The crankshaft is the backbone of the rotating assembly. It converts the vertical motion into rotational motion so that the vehicle can move.

process of slowly heating the crankshaft in a sealed container with the oxygen removed. Nitrogen is introduced and penetrates the surface. Nitriding produces a harder, more durable surface than induction hardening but only penetrates approximately 0.02" (0.51 mm). The crankshaft will have to be rehardened if the mains or rod journals need to be reground. Heating and hardening cause the crankshaft to grow, which the machinist must take into account when performing the initial metal removal before hardening.

Crankshafts are usually ground to 0.010" (0.25 mm), 0.020" (0.51 mm), or 0.030" (0.76 mm) undersize, meaning they are ground slightly smaller than their original size. When choosing a crankshaft main or rod journal bearing, it must match the amount of material that was removed during grinding. For example, a crankshaft ground to 0.010" undersize must match up to a 0.010" undersize bearing, usually marked ".010 US" on the back of the bearing shell. The undersize bearing is actually thicker to make up for the smaller crankshaft bearing. The crankshaft main and rod journals can be ground to different sizes, but all rod journals must be cut to the same size (**FIGURE 20-15**). Likewise, all the main journals must be the same size as one another. For example, the crankshaft could be a 0.010/0.020, which equals 0.010" rods and 0.02" mains. During the grinding process of the crankshaft, the fillet area of the crankshaft (the area where the rod bearing journal or main bearing journal meets the crankshaft) should be radial or tapered, radiating from the crankshaft and fanning outward, up along the crankshaft counterweight. The radius is important because it helps strengthen the crankshaft. The whole "fillet" process gets rid of sharp edges, which are stress points between the crankshaft journals and the counterweights inside the engine (**FIGURE 20-16**). If a crankshaft is going to break, it will usually break on a sharp edge or corner. These fillet areas help to alleviate those stressed areas.

When a crankshaft cannot be restored because the grooves are too deep, or a bearing has spun on the journal, then it is common practice to use spray welding or submerged arc welding. Spray welding adds materials to the journal by melting and spraying molten metal onto the crankshaft journal surface so that there is material that can be ground. Submerged arc welding uses a steady stream of flux to protect the molten metal from oxygen as the filler material melts and binds to the crank surface. Crankshafts are usually ground the opposite direction of the crank's rotation and then polished the same direction of the crank's rotation to counteract the corkscrew effect of grinding.

The oil passage holes in the crankshaft have to be chamfered before polishing the journals. Chamfering is cutting into the top of the oil passage hole (which is usually right in the center of the bearing's operating surface on the crankshaft journals) with a chamfering tool or drill bit. This process takes that sharp edge at the top of the oil hole and makes it more like a 45-degree angle, which allows the edge not to dig into the bearing the way a 90-degree edge would. It also alleviates the 90-degree edge stress point on the crankshaft. Crankshaft

FIGURE 20-15 To machine the crankshaft journals, a special machine is required to smooth out the rough and out-of-round areas of the journals so they will not tear up the new bearings being installed in the engine.

FIGURE 20-16 Machining the fillets on the crankshaft helps keep the stress risers from causing issues once the engine is reassembled.

polishing must be performed by a specialist called a crankshaft polisher. The crankshaft polishing machine rotates the crankshaft slowly, and a polishing belt slides over the journals to clean up the surface. The polishing belt is usually 320 grit or finer.

Connecting Rods

Before any machining of connecting rods can be performed, the pistons must be removed. When the connecting rods are disassembled from the piston, they must be checked for straightness as well; they must also be examined to see if they are cracked or twisted. If the rods are the full-floating style, then the snap rings can be removed from the piston, and the pins can be worked out of the piston and rod. If the rods are the semi-floating style, then the piston pins will have to be pressed out of the piston and rod with a small hydraulic press (**FIGURE 20-17**).

K20004 Knowledge of the process of connecting rods reconditioning.

Rod—Big End

The big end of the connecting rod is made up of two halves. Each mating half can have either machined surfaces or, in the case of powdered metal connecting rods, **fracture split** surfaces, which are identified by the ragged finish of the parting surfaces on the big end (**FIGURE 20-18**). The ragged fracture line ensures better rod cap alignment on assembly because the fractured surfaces fit together in perfect alignment. The connecting rod's big end needs to be checked for roundness. This measurement is just as important as measuring the roundness of the crankshaft main bearing journals and main bearing bores. Any time the old rod bolts are removed and new bolts are installed, the size of the "big end bore" may become distorted due to the press-fit of the bolts. Accordingly, the size of the big end of the connecting rod should be rechecked and adjusted if necessary.

To resize the connecting rod's big end, the bolts are removed (**FIGURE 20-19**), and the cap and rod mating surfaces are ground approximately 0.0015" to 0.0025" (0.038 to 0.14 mm). Then the rod cap is bolted back onto the rod and the bore machined back to the proper size. The challenge with powdered metal rods is that because the fractured surface is critical to their alignment, they cannot tolerate having those surfaces ground smooth. Thus, they cannot be resized unless bearing inserts of a larger outside diameter are available for that particular engine.

Once the rod mating surfaces have been machined lightly and bolted back together, either a rod honing machine or a rod boring machine can be used for resizing. A rod honing machine removes metal by honing the big end of a connecting rod. This is accomplished by attaching various hone stones to an arbor and spinning inside the big end of the connecting rod bore. A machinist will

FIGURE 20-17 The piston/connecting rod assembly pieces that must be assembled before the piston is installed into the engine.

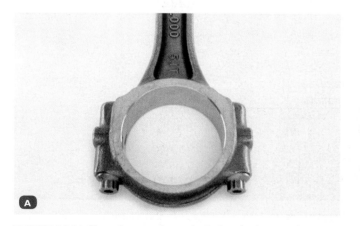

FIGURE 20-18 Big end connecting rods. **A.** Standard connecting rod with machined faces. **B.** Powdered metal with fracture split faces.

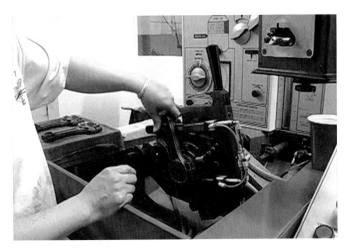

FIGURE 20-19 Resizing the connecting rod big end will ensure that it is perfectly round and will not cause the bearing to fail prematurely.

FIGURE 20-20 A connecting rod with a full floating pin assembly.

K20005 Knowledge of why machining of the cylinder head is necessary.

frequently measure the size of the connecting rod to ensure that it is not oversized during this process. A rod boring machine cuts material away with a cutting bit and resizes the big end portion of the connecting rod assembly. The big end of the connecting rod must be resized to factory specifications to achieve the proper amount of bearing crush. Bearing crush is the additional height that is purposely manufactured into each bearing half to ensure complete contact of the bearing back with the housing bore when the engine is assembled and the main and rod bearing caps are torqued. This torque process actually "squeezes" the bearings, causing them to maintain just the right amount of oil clearance for the engine crankshaft to spin smoothly within them.

Rod—Small End

Connecting rods may have pressed-in wrist pins or, in some engines, a floating wrist pin. The pressed-in wrist pin can be either press fit into the piston pin boss or press fit into the small end of the connecting rod. With the floating type of wrist pin, the pin can turn in both the piston pin bosses and the small end of the connecting rod (**FIGURE 20-20**). The wrist pin is typically held in place with a snap ring on each side of the piston pin boss. Some floating wrist pin designs use a bushing or bearing on the small end of the connecting rod. A small hydraulic press is used to press the bushing out of the rod and install a new one.

When removing and installing pressed-in pins, be sure to use the proper piston support tool, or piston damage will result (**FIGURE 20-21**). Some manufacturers require the bushing to be burnished (rubbed until smooth or glossy) when installed. A rod honing machine or rod boring machine can be used for this procedure.

▶ Head

The cylinder head is one of the most abused pieces on the internal combustion engine as it is supposed to control combustion, cool the cylinder, and control intake and exhaust, as well as not fail under the extreme temperature changes that it cycles through (**FIGURE 20-22**). Without the robustness of the materials that are utilized in this component, the entire engine could not operate, and combustion could not be controlled. When rebuilding an engine, you must take special care to examine

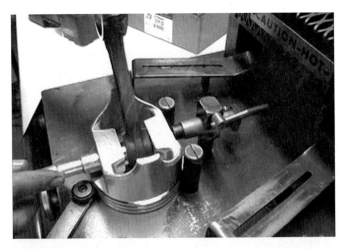

FIGURE 20-21 Pressed fit piston pin installation.

FIGURE 20-22 A four-valve cylinder head is becoming more common on later-model engines.

Applied Math

AM-11: Decimals: The technician can multiply decimal numbers to determine conformance with the manufacturer's specifications.

During the overhaul of a V-6 engine, it is discovered that the cylinders are worn beyond manufacturer's specifications. The technician determines that the cylinders must be bored 0.060" (1.52 mm) oversize. The current displacement of the engine is 231 cubic inches (3.79 liters). Our task is to use a formula to determine the new cubic inch displacement of the engine.

The bore of the engine is 3.860" (98.04 mm) after it was enlarged, and the stroke is 3.4" (86.36 mm). For the first step, we calculate the cubic inch displacement of one cylinder, and then multiply by six cylinders. The volume of a cylinder is determined by multiplication of pi (3.14) × radius squared × length of stroke. In our scenario, this is 3.14 × 3.725" (2403 mm) = 11.69 in.² (7542 square mm) × 3.4" (86.36 mm) = 39.768 in.³ (0.651 liters).

This is the volume or cubic inch displacement of one cylinder. When multiplied by six cylinders, we have a "new" displacement of 239 in.² (3.9 liters). This new displacement is the result of boring the cylinders and installing new pistons, which are 0.060" (1.52 mm) oversize. Now each cylinder will meet manufacturer's specifications because excessive cylinder taper and out-of-round conditions have been resolved. This engine should give many miles of satisfactory service regarding the pistons and block assembly.

the cylinder head, checking all of the specifications and verifying the operational viability of this component so that you are able to reuse it in the engine.

Cylinder Head Straightening

It is necessary to resurface the cylinder head when the cylinder head surface either is warped (not perfectly flat) or has pitting or some type of corrosive metal displacement that would compromise the sealing capability of the cylinder head to cylinder head gasket and engine block. Cylinder head resurfacing is typically performed when the cylinder head has been removed for some type of service (**FIGURE 20-23**). The repair technician measures the straightness of the cylinder head deck surface with a calibrated straightedge and finds it to be warped beyond the manufacturer's allowable specifications, or the technician notices that there is excessive pitting (typically found around coolant passages).

The cylinder head surface is critical because of the combustion pressures, water passages, and sometimes oil passages. The cylinder head must be flat and resurfaced to the proper Ra. A surface roughness Ra is rated as the arithmetic average of the surface valleys and peaks. The cylinder head warps much more easily than the engine block because of its design; it does not have the same supporting structure. A precision ground straightedge and feeler gauge are used to determine flatness (**FIGURE 20-24**).

When checking the cylinder head for flatness, lay the calibrated straightedge parallel with the combustion chambers across the already-cleaned cylinder head deck surface. Starting at the top of the cylinder head, try to fit a 0.001" (0.025 mm) feeler gauge under any part of the mating surface between the calibrated straightedge and the cylinder head.

K20006 Knowledge of the cylinder head straightening process.

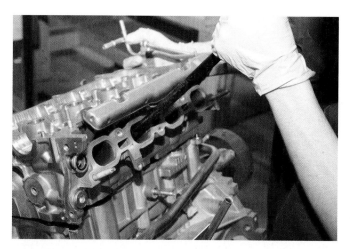

FIGURE 20-23 Cylinder head service is usually required when a catastrophic engine event has happened.

FIGURE 20-24 The deck of the cylinder head. The cylinder head gasket seals on this surface, which means it must be flat to have the best seal possible.

FIGURE 20-25 This machine resurfaces the cylinder head when it is determined that the cylinder head is no longer true.

This process is repeated 5 to 10 times at various places—5 or so times with the straightedge parallel to the combustion chambers and another 5 or so times with the straightedge running at a 90-degree angle to the combustion chambers. Also be sure to cross the straightedge from one side to the other, making an X across the head with the two measurements. This approach will show any twisting of the head from end to end. Before surfacing the cylinder head, check the manufacturer's cylinder head thickness specifications to make sure the cylinder head has enough material to be resurfaced. If the cylinder head is warped more than 0.003" (0.076 mm), it is recommended the cylinder head be surfaced; always check the manufacturer's specifications. The cylinder head can be surfaced by a surface grinder using a stone wheel or a broach-style surfacer using a CBN cutter for cast iron or a PCD for aluminum (**FIGURE 20-25**). A cylinder head with overhead cams usually cannot be machined as much as an adjustable pushrod engine, as the timing chain or timing belt tension would be affected. Again, refer to specifications before machining.

To check flatness on a cylinder head with a feeler gauge and true bar, follow the steps in **SKILL DRILL 20-3**.

SKILL DRILL 20-3 Checking Flatness on a Cylinder Head with a Feeler Gauge and True Bar

1. The cylinder head must be clean and free of gasket material.

2. Lay the cylinder head upside down on a cylinder head holder or on a bench.

Continued

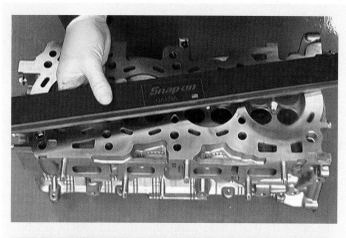

3. Obtain a 0.003" feeler gauge and a true bar so that you can measure warpage on the cylinder head deck.

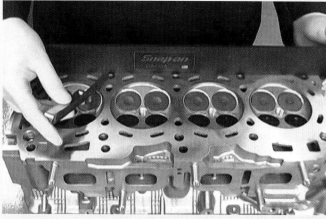

4. Lay the true bar on the machined edge across the cylinder head. Hold the bar with one hand and use the other to try to install the feeler gauge in multiple locations.

5. Repeat this process in multiple different locations on the cylinder head, making sure to crisscross the cylinder head and paying close attention to the water inlets on the deck.

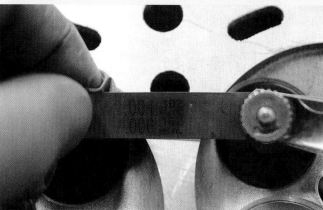

6. If in some area a 0.003" feeler gauge slips in easily, you may need to increase the feeler gauge size to determine the true amount of warpage.

Continued

NOTE: The straightedge used must be flat within 0.0051 mm (0.0002 in) per foot of tool length.

61. Support the cylinder head on a bench with the head gasket side up. Inspect all areas of the deck face with a straightedge and feeler gauge. The cylinder head must not have depressions deeper than 0.0254 mm (0.001 in) across a 38.1 mm (1.5 in) square area, or scratches more than 0.0254 mm (0.001 in) deep.
62. Remove the power steering/engine support bracket.

7. Consult service information to see how much warpage is acceptable.

Overhead Cam Bearings

Overhead cam engines have camshafts that typically ride directly in bores in the cylinder head. There might be no removable bearings. The cam rides right on the machined aluminum and is lubricated by a thin coating of oil that is fed to the surface through an oil galley or hole. Oil pressure must make its way up from the bottom of the engine to the top of the cylinder head to lubricate the camshaft. If oil pressure falls, then the camshaft lacks lubrication and can score the camshaft bores in the cylinder head. This is a problem because if the surface is damaged, there are no bearings to replace.

Another potential problem occurs if the engine has overheated and the cylinder head is warped; in this case, the cam bores can become misaligned, just as the main bearing bores for the crankshaft can become misaligned. If the cam bores are misaligned enough, it can cause the camshaft to bind up and possibly break. When machining a head surface for a warpage concern, do not forget to check the cam bore alignment. To do so, use a straightedge designed for this purpose, or use a straight camshaft and make sure it turns freely in the bores. If the cam bores are misaligned, then the head most likely will have to be straightened. A machine shop can do this using heat and pressure to pull the head back into line. Once the head is straight, the cam bores can be rechecked. If the head has removable cam bearing caps (**FIGURE 20-26**), then the bore can be machined in a process similar to line boring of the main bearing journals. Simply cut a small amount of metal off the bottoms of the cam bore caps, and remachine the bore back to its original specification. If the bore has one-piece cam towers, then the machinist may have to see whether a camshaft with oversized cam journals can be purchased for the engine. Oversized cam journals can sometimes be found for an engine in 0.015" or 0.03" (0.38 or 0.76 mm) sizes. This means that the original bore size will have to be machined 0.015" to 0.03" larger.

Another possible option is to find replacement bearing shells or inserts made by some aftermarket companies to repair the cam bore. These bearing inserts work similarly to a standard camshaft bearing. The last repair option would be to either spray weld the cam journals to a larger size, or weld the cam bores and remachine to the proper size. This process is very costly and would be done only when a replacement head is not easily found.

Valve Grinding

If the valves are in reusable condition, both the valve face and the valve tip will have to be ground. If the engine uses adjustable valves, then both surfaces can be ground at this time.

> ▶ **TECHNICIAN TIP**
>
> If an overhead cam head is warped, the cam bearing bores should be checked for straightness before surfacing the head. If the cam bores are not straight, then surfacing the head will leave the cam journals out of line when the head is bolted onto the block. This causes binding of the cam in the bearings. If the cam journals are not in line, then the head will have to be straightened before resurfacing.

K20007 Knowledge of valve grinding and installing seat inserts.

FIGURE 20-26 A dual overhead camshaft cylinder head with removable camshaft bearing caps.

If the engine uses nonadjustable valves, then the tips will have to be ground after the valve face and valve seat have been ground so that the installed valve height can be adjusted by grinding the valve tip to the proper length. The installed valve height is measured before the valve is disassembled from the cylinder head and will allow the technician to setup the valve to be in the same location after machining.

The valve stem must be within factory specifications, which is why the valve stems and margins should have been checked previously. There are multiple styles of valve grinding benches or valve refacing benches; follow the manufacturer's specific procedures. The valve stem end is first chamfered so that when inserted in the collet that holds the valve (**FIGURE 20-27**), it is held centered. The valve grinding machine can be set up to grind the valves at any angle, typically specified by the manufacturer. Always check the specifications and set the machine to the proper valve face angle. When the machine is turned on, the valve rotates in one direction and the grinding stone rotates in the other. The valve is slowly fed into the grinding stone, not taking too much off at a time, while making sure the face of the valve moves across the face of the grinding stone from side to side until the valve face is refinished and true (**FIGURE 20-28**). Face angles on the valves must be different than the angles on the seat so that they will seal once the valve is closed. Usually the face angles on an intake valve are 30–45 nominal degrees and exhaust valves are 45 degrees. This provides and interference fit with the seat so that the valve will seal on the seat when it is closed. When grinding the valves, make sure not to remove any more metal than necessary to avoid making the margin thinner. This margin, if allowed to become too thin, can cause the edge of the valve to burn or melt because the thinner metal cannot dissipate the heat as well. The smaller the valve margin, the hotter the edge of the valve becomes, and the harder it is to dissipate the heat to other parts of the cylinder head. That is why the thickness of the valve margin is important.

Valve Guides

Before grinding the valve seats, the valve guides must be checked and repaired to ensure they are within factory specifications. The valves and valve stems must also be checked to verify that they are reusable. If the valves are worn beyond specifications, they have to be replaced. If the valve guides are worn, they must be repaired. There are different procedures to repair valve guides in an integral cylinder head (non-replaceable guide) or a non-integral cylinder head (replaceable guides). Each procedure will be described next.

For the integral cylinder head (non-replaceable guide), there are three methods of repairing the valve guides:

1. Knurling the cylinder head using a diamond knurl, a tool offered by Sunnen Products. Knurling is when a bit with a spiral groove (unique to the cylinder head that is being worked on due to its specific diameter) is threaded through or run through the valve guide. This tool leaves behind raised ridges on either side of the groove and effectively shrinks the size of the valve guide due to these raised ridges (**FIGURE 20-29**). This process takes the current material and squeezes it out, closer to the area where the valve stem rides. The knurled guide is then reamed so that it is back within specifications. Reaming removes a small amount of the material displaced by the knurling tool. The knurling process is not used by most reputable machine shops anymore because it is typically considered a "quick fix" and would typically only last for 20,000 to 40,000 miles. Knurled guides do not stand up to the same abuse and wear and tear that an insert or liner would typically stand up to.

FIGURE 20-27 Grinding the valve.

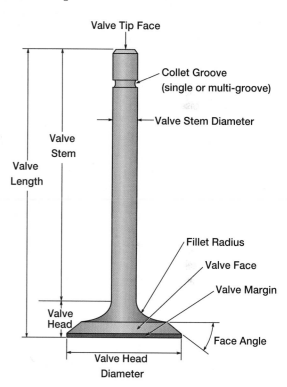

FIGURE 20-28 An engine valve with the different areas labeled for identification.

FIGURE 20-29 A knurled valve guide is where the metal in the integral valve guide is curled up in order to shrink the diameter of the guide so that the valve is not loose in it.

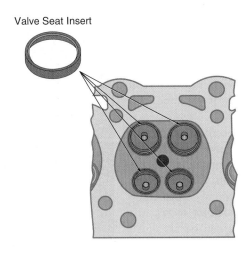

Valve Seat Insert

FIGURE 20-30 A reamed valve guide is machined to accept an oversize valve guide to replace the damaged original one.

2. Reaming the guide oversize and using a valve with an oversized valve stem. Valves with oversized stems are usually very expensive and may not be available for all engines (**FIGURE 20-30**).
3. Installing a thin-walled bronze liner. The valve guide is reamed out on a piece of equipment called a hydraulic valve guide installer, and an oversized thin-walled bronze liner is installed and is burnished to size (**FIGURE 20-31**).

Hardened Seat Inserts

Hardened seats are valve seats that have been heat treated to make them more robust and capable of withstanding the severe demands of today's engines and fuels. Hardened valve seats are used to prevent valve seat regression (**FIGURE 20-32**). Regression refers to the valve actually sitting farther up inside the cylinder head due to the missing material that has been worn away from the valve seat over the life of the vehicle (**FIGURE 20-33**). Hardened seats are also necessary in aluminum heads, as the aluminum is relatively soft.

Installing hardened seats is also a common practice on early cast iron heads that have seats that were not induction hardened from the factory. Starting in the 1920s, lead was added to gasoline as an antiknock additive. It also proved to be an antiwear additive for valve seats. The lead acts as a chemical buffer, keeping the hot valves from "microwelding" themselves to the seat. After lead was taken out of gas, if the exhaust valve seat was not

FIGURE 20-31 A thin wall bronze valve guide.

FIGURE 20-32 A hardened valve seat installed in a cylinder head. As you can tell, the seat itself is separate from the cylinder head and is pressed in, which makes for a serviceable valve seat.

induction hardened or a hardened seat insert was not installed, the valve seat would deteriorate and fail. This would result in the valve being sunk into the head, quickly causing valve seat failure.

Valve seats can be of the integral type or the replaceable type. Integral valve seats are used in some cast iron heads by induction hardening the valve seat area. Replaceable valve seats can come in many different materials—nickel alloy, chrome alloy, cobalt alloy, stainless steel, or even cast iron. Valve seats intended for compressed natural gas (CNG) or propane engines may be made of tungsten steel with additives blended for lubricating qualities. Check with the manufacturer to determine which hardened seat they recommend. Depending on which fuels are being used, different seats will be recommended.

If the head uses replaceable valve seats, the seats will have to be removed by either prying, heating the head in a cylinder head oven, or even welding the seat, which will cause the seat to contract when the weld cools. Integral valve seats must be machined out of the head at the machine shop, so that new seats with an interference fit can be pressed into their place.

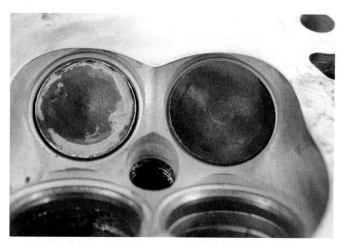

FIGURE 20-33 This is what happens when you use unleaded fuel with older nonhardened valve seats. The integral seats in this cylinder head have sunken into the cylinder head, which will cause running and compression issues.

▶ Wrap-Up

Ready for Review

- ▶ The cylinder block is the backbone for any good engine rebuild because it houses all the internal and external components that make the engine operate.
- ▶ Engine machining is done any time the tolerances of an engine component must be adjusted by adding or removing material after taking precise measurements and comparing those measurements to a set of factory specifications found in the service information.
- ▶ Engine machining is performed when an engine exhibits a problem and the technician determines that problem is coming from a component of the engine that is not operating within specifications.
- ▶ Most technicians and shop owners in today's competitive market have chosen to sublet, or send out, all of their machining work to a machine shop.
- ▶ The main task of machine shops is to restore engine parts to factory specifications.
- ▶ Surface roughness average (Ra) is a measure of how rough a surface is at the microscopic level and is rated as the arithmetic average of the surface valleys and peaks.
- ▶ The surface finish should be a specified range or maximum level of Ra and a measurement mating surface roughness.
- ▶ The engine block can be resurfaced by a surface grinder, using a stone wheel or a broach-style surfacer, and applying a cubic boron nitride (CBN) cutter for cast iron and a polycrystalline diamond (PCD) cutter for aluminum.
- ▶ The desired procedure in surfacing the engine block's deck is to surface the engine block parallel to the mainline where the crankshaft is installed.

- ▶ The computer numerical control (CNC) machine is a tool that uses computer programs to automatically execute a series of machining operations.
- ▶ If cylinders have too much taper or are out of round, they should be rebored and honed to fit oversized pistons.
- ▶ If the cylinder bore is damaged beyond boring, worn beyond the limits for an oversized piston, or cracked, it must be bored out (machined) and a cylinder sleeve installed to fill the extra space created in the boring process.
- ▶ Dry cylinder sleeves require the cylinder to be bored out and the sleeve to have an interference fit of approximately 0.002" to 0.0025" (0.05 to 0.06 mm).
- ▶ Dry cylinder sleeves are pressed into the existing bore.
- ▶ Boring an engine increases its displacement slightly. To calculate an engine's displacement, you must find the swept volume of the cylinder, based on the bore and stroke dimensions.
- ▶ The swept volume formula is bore squared, multiplied by stroke, multiplied by 0.785, multiplied by the number of cylinders.
- ▶ Boring of the engine cylinders to a larger size requires the use of a boring machine.
- ▶ The most common sizes of oversized pistons available are 0.02" (0.51 mm), 0.03" (0.76 mm), 0.04" (1.0 mm), and 0.06" (1.5 mm).
- ▶ The boring process leaves a corkscrew pattern on the walls of the cylinder. If left like this, the cylinder rings would catch and tear on the lands of the corkscrew.
- ▶ Hone stones are used to sand down and file away the cylinder walls, leaving a unidirectional finish also known as a crosshatch pattern.

- This crosshatch pattern appears as a series of big Xs etched into the walls and is much smoother than the corkscrew left by the boring process.
- Most hones are self-tensioning, which alleviates the need for the technician to determine the amount of tension needed.
- The crosshatch pattern is made at either a standard 45- or 60-degree angle.
- A crosshatched pattern allows the proper amount of oil to stay on the cylinder walls, which allows the piston rings to seat into the cylinder walls.
- When the cylinder head is torqued, it exerts force around the cylinder wall and can change the machined dimensions, especially on lighter-weight engine blocks. To eliminate this problem, a torque plate is installed that simulates the cylinder head torqued in place.
- The torque plate is approximately 2" (51 mm) thick and bolted in place where the cylinder head is fastened on the engine block.
- If there are no imperfections or grooves, and the cylinder walls need only to be deglazed, a ball hone will be used.
- A ball hone consists of a metal center rod with various other metal rods branching out from it, similar to branches on a tree.
- If the cylinder was bored oversize, then the cylinders will have to be honed to final size with a rigid hone.
- After the boring process, a rigid hone is used for the smoothing-out process of the cylinder walls and is performed as the final step in refinishing the cylinder.
- Premature bearing failure and crankshaft failure can occur with an out-of-line main bearing bore.
- Proper bore alignment must be ensured between all the main bearing bores.
- The bore alignment can be checked for straightness by using a straightedge with a feeler gauge.
- Checking that the main crankshaft bores are concentric and perfectly circular ensures that they are not out of round or egg shaped.
- Main bearing bores can wear into an oblong or egg-shaped hole and are checked with a bore gauge tool.
- To correct a bore alignment issue, the engine block has to be line bored or line honed.
- In the line boring process, you first make the bore smaller by removing the main caps and then cutting the mating surface down 0.003" to 0.005" (0.076 to 0.13 mm).
- After cutting the main cap mating surface, main caps are torqued back into place; the line hone or line bore machine is set up; and the original main bearing bore size is cut.
- Cutting the main bearing bores ensures that the bores line up properly and stop the bearing wear problem.
- The proper oil clearance must be maintained to ensure proper oil pressure of the engine and to ensure that the proper amount of lubricant can reach all the engine bearings.

- Oil clearance can also be quickly checked before engine assembly through the use of Plastigage.
- Plastigage is a thin, calibrated piece of soft plastic string that is laid on the main bearing journal of the crankshaft and squished between the journal and the bearing.
- The main bearing cap is torqued down so that the Plastigage is squished, and the Plastigage is then removed.
- The width of the squeezed Plastigage is compared to a chart to determine the amount of bearing clearance.
- The wider the Plastigage, the smaller the bearing clearance.
- The crankshaft and connecting rods are the heart of the internal combustion engine, as they convert the chemical energy into mechanical energy that we can then utilize to propel the vehicle.
- The crankshaft journals need to be inspected for scratches, pits, cracks, and grooves when rebuilding the engine.
- When imperfections cannot be polished out to 0.0005" (0.013 mm) or less, the crankshaft needs to be reground.
- Regrinding a crankshaft involves placing the crankshaft in a lathe set for metal cutting. The lathe spins the crankshaft while a special bit shaves or grinds the metal away.
- Nitriding is a crankshaft journal hardening process of slowly heating the crankshaft in a sealed container with the oxygen removed.
- Crankshafts are usually ground to 0.01" (0.25 mm), 0.02" (0.51 mm), or 0.03" (0.76 mm) undersize, meaning they are ground slightly smaller than their original size.
- When choosing a crankshaft main or rod journal bearing, it must match the amount of material that was removed during grinding. For example, a crankshaft ground to 0.01" undersize must match up to a 0.010" undersize bearing, usually marked ".010 US" on the back of the bearing shell.
- The undersize bearing is actually thicker to make up for the smaller crankshaft bearing.
- Undersize means the journal is smaller, where the actual bearing insert is thicker.
- The radius is important because it helps strengthen the crankshaft. The whole "fillet" process gets rid of sharp edges, which are stress points inside the engine.
- If a crankshaft is going to break, it will usually break on a sharp edge or corner. These fillet areas help to alleviate those stressed areas.
- When a crankshaft cannot be restored because the grooves are too deep, or a bearing has spun on the journal, then it is a common practice to use spray welding or submerged arc welding.
- Spray welding adds materials to the journal by melting and spraying molten metal onto the crankshaft journal surface so that there is material that can be ground.
- The oil passage holes in the crankshaft need to be chamfered before polishing the journals.
- Chamfering is cutting into the top of the oil passage hole (which is usually right in the center of the bearing's oper-

ating surface on the crankshaft journals) with a chamfering tool or drill bit.

▶ The big end of the connecting rod is made up of two halves. Each mating half can have either machined surfaces or, in the case of powdered metal connecting rods, fracture split surfaces, which are identified by the ragged finish of the parting surfaces on the big end.

▶ To resize the connecting rod's big end, the bolts are removed, and the cap and rod mating surfaces are ground approximately 0.0015" to 0.0025" (0.038 to 0.14 mm). Then the rod cap is bolted back onto the rod and the bore machined back to the proper size.

▶ The pressed-in wrist pin can be either press fit into the piston pin boss or press fit into the small end of the connecting rod. With the floating type of wrist pin, the pin can turn in both the piston pin bosses and the small end of the connecting rod.

▶ When removing and installing pressed-in pins, be sure to use the proper piston support tool or piston damage will result.

▶ Some manufacturers require the bushing to be burnished (rubbed until smooth or glossy) when installed.

▶ When rebuilding an engine you must take special care to examine the cylinder head, checking all of the important measurements.

▶ If an engine with an aluminum head and overhead cam has overheated and the cylinder head is warped, the cam bores can become misaligned and can cause the camshaft to bind up and possibly break. When machining this type of head surface for a warpage concern, do not forget to check the cam bore alignment.

▶ If the valves are in reusable condition, both the valve face and the valve tip will have to be ground.

▶ The valve stem end is first chamfered so that when inserted in the collet that holds the valve it is held centered.

▶ The valve grinding machine can be set up to grind the valves at any angle, typically specified by the manufacturer. Always check the specifications, and set the machine to the proper valve face angle.

▶ Before grinding the valve seats, the valve guides must be checked and repaired to ensure they are within factory specifications.

▶ The valves and valve stems must also be checked to verify that they are reusable. If the valves are worn beyond specifications, they should be replaced.

▶ For the integral cylinder head (nonreplaceable guide), there are four methods of repairing the valve guides: knurling, reaming the guide oversize and using a valve with an oversized valve stem, installing a thin-walled bronze liner, or installing a thick-walled guide.

▶ Hardened seats are valve seats that have been heat treated to make them capable of withstanding the severe demands.

▶ Hardened valve seats are used to prevent valve seat regression, which is the valve actually sitting farther up inside

the cylinder head due to the missing material that has been worn away from the valve seat.

▶ Valve seats can be of the integral type or the replaceable type.

▶ To install a hardened seat, a head shop is needed and the proper cutter must be used.

▶ It is necessary to resurface the cylinder head when the cylinder head surface is warped; this is done when the straightness of the cylinder head deck surface with a calibrated straightedge is warped beyond the manufacturer's allowable specifications.

▶ A precision ground straightedge and feeler gauge are used to determine head flatness and warpage.

Key Terms

crankshaft journal The part of the crankshaft where the connecting rod attaches or, in the main journal condition, where the crankshaft spins in the engine block.

crosshatch pattern The design of Xs at a 60-degree angle created when honing the cylinder bore.

cylinder bore The diameter of the hole that the piston moves in; it is one of the main components that is included in the size of the engine.

engine block's deck The portion of the engine cylinder block on which the head gasket lies and to which the cylinder head is bolted.

fracture split Type of connecting rod cap that has been broken, instead of cut, so that it will fit perfectly when screwed together.

hardened seat Valve seats that have been heat treated to make them more robust and capable of withstanding the severe demands of today's engines and fuels

honing The procedure that finishes the boring process and gives the bore a finish that will retain oil to lubricate the piston.

surface roughness average (Ra) A measure of how rough a surface is at the microscopic level. It is rated as the arithmetic average of the surface valleys and peaks.

taper The extent to which one the one end of the cylinder is smaller than the other end; it is measured to show the wear in the cylinder.

torque plate Used to simulate the distortion of a torqued cylinder head on the cylinder block so that when the block is bored out, it will stay round when the cylinder head is torqued down.

Review Questions

1. When resurfacing an engine block surface, the machinist determines exactly how much metal to take off by measuring the:
   a. depth of the dowel pinholes.
   b. surface roughness of the cylinder head.
   c. height of the dowel pins.
   d. deck height.

2. Choose the correct statement:
   a. A good crosshatch does not allow oil to be trapped on the surface of the cylinder walls.
   b. The desired pattern can be achieved by adjusting the speed and stroke of the cylinder hone.
   c. If a steeper-angled X pattern is needed, move the stones at a normal pace.
   d. If the angle gets too flat, it leads to low compression.

3. The ball hone:
   a. restores cylinder size.
   b. simply reapplies the crosshatching.
   c. is done when there is considerable wear and tear.
   d. does not remove glazing.

4. All of following are done when correcting a bore alignment issue, *except*:
   a. The main journals must first be made smaller.
   b. The engine block mating surface is cleaned to remove dust or debris.
   c. The engine block has to be line bored or line honed.
   d. The main caps should not be cut.

5. During crankshaft grinding:
   a. the main and rod journals can be ground to different sizes.
   b. the rod journals can be cut to different sizes.
   c. the main journals can be cut to different sizes.
   d. the crankshaft is ground slightly bigger than its original size.

6. A small crack in a cylinder head can be fixed by:
   a. furnace welding.
   b. milling the surface.
   c. pinning.
   d. sealing.

7. Which of these can be used to check for internal cracks?
   a. Magnaflux testing using dry method
   b. Dye checking
   c. Pressure testing
   d. Magnaflux testing using wet method

8. If the cam bores are misaligned, the issue can be fixed by all of the below methods *except* by:
   a. machining the bore in a process similar to line boring of the main bearing journals.
   b. finding replacement bearing shells or inserts.
   c. welding the cam bores and remachining them to the proper size.
   d. simply increasing the bore size.

9. During valve grinding
   a. The valve and grinding stone rotate in the opposite directions.
   b. The grinding stone moves side to side.
   c. The valve and grinding stone rotate in the same direction.
   d. The valve is held in place and does not move.

10. Knurling is:
    a. reaming the guide oversize and using a valve with an oversized valve stem.
    b. when a bit with a spiral groove is threaded through or run through the valve guide.

c. installing a thin-walled aluminum liner.
d. installing a thick-walled guide that is made of aluminum.

ASE Technician A/Technician B Style Questions

1. Technician A says that honing an engine cylinder must create a crosshatch pattern of 60 degrees. Technician B states that cylinder blocks do not need to go to the machine shop to be repaired. Who is correct?
   a. Tech A
   b. Tech B
   c. Both A and B
   d. Neither A nor B

2. Technician A says that cylinder taper must be corrected before reassembly of the engine. Technician B says that a fractured connecting rod cap is stronger than a cut cap. Who is correct?
   a. Tech A
   b. Tech B
   c. Both A and B
   d. Neither A nor B

3. Technician A says that machining may be required to straighten the cylinder head. Technician B states that a cylinder head must be checked for straightness so that it can be corrected if it is not. Who is correct?
   a. Tech A
   b. Tech B
   c. Both A and B
   d. Neither A nor B

4. Technician A says that hardened valve seats came about when the industry converted to unleaded fuel. Technician B states that valve guides must be longer than required so that they wear correctly. Who is correct?
   a. Tech A
   b. Tech B
   c. Both A and B
   d. Neither A nor B

5. Technician A says that pressed-in valve guides are easily replaced with new ones. Technician B states that knurling is used to repair integral valve guides. Who is correct?
   a. Tech A
   b. Tech B
   c. Both A and B
   d. Neither A nor B

6. Technician A states that if valves are to be reused, they should be resurfaced to seat correctly. Technician B states that overhead camshafts typically ride directly in the bores of the cylinder head. Who is correct?
   a. Tech A
   b. Tech B
   c. Both A and B
   d. Neither A nor B

7. Technician A says that a pressed-fit wrist pin is easily installed with the retaining circlips. Technician B says

that a full floating wrist pin must be pressed in. Who is correct?

a. Tech A
b. Tech B
c. Both A and B
d. Neither A nor B

8. Technician A says that the crankshaft is the main component that converts the vertical motion into rotational motion to the transmission. Technician B says the connecting rod does not help with the conversion process of vertical motion into rotational motion. Who is correct?

a. Tech A
b. Tech B
c. Both A and B
d. Neither A nor B

9. Technician A says that the main bearing bores must be checked for alignment with one another before we put the crankshaft into the engine block. Technician B says using a torque plate helps to condition the cylinder block to the stresses that it will be under when the cylinder head is installed. Who is correct?

a. Tech A
b. Tech B
c. Both A and B
d. Neither A nor B

10. Technician A states that the cylinder bore must be checked for straightness. Technician B states that cylinder taper must be corrected before the piston is installed. Who is correct?

a. Tech A
b. Tech B
c. Both A and B
d. Neither A nor B

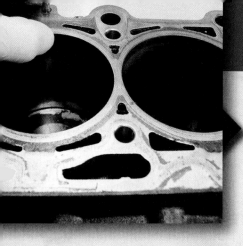

CHAPTER 21

Engine Cleaning and Crack Detection

Knowledge Objectives

After reading this chapter, you will have:

- **K21001** Knowledge of how to clean and inspect the engine once it is disassembled.
- **K21002** Knowledge of what to inspect on the gasket surfaces once the engine is cleaned.

- **K21003** Knowledge of what crack detection procedures are used on what types of components.
- **K21004** Knowledge of component crack repair procedures.

Skills Objectives

There are no Skills Objectives for this chapter.

You Are the Automotive Technician

When rebuilding an engine for the 2012 Ford Mustang, you notice that there is a small crack that goes through one of the bolt holes on the cylinder block's deck. This area is away from the cylinder and is not near a cooling passage. What should be done about this before reassembly?

1. Apply the sealant before installation.
2. Alert your supervisor and the owner of the vehicle and let them make the decision.
3. Install the cylinder head and hope it works.

K21001 Knowledge of how to clean and inspect the engine once it is disassembled.

▶ Introduction

Throughout this chapter, we talk about the different ways to fix and clean engine components so that they can be reassembled into a working engine. The chapter explores the different ways of cleaning the engine, how to examine the engine components, and ways to fix cracks in those components. As always, this is a broad overview, and you should consult your machinist for the services that are available to you to ascertain whether the machinist is able to do all of these processes.

▶ Engine Cleaning and Examination

Engine cleaning is a major part of rebuilding an engine because it shows the condition of the engine components so that they can be evaluated to decide whether they can be reused. This part of the evaluation process determines what components have to be replaced, so that the technician does not spend time conditioning pieces only to find that they must be thrown away. Making these decisions is the start to the cleaning process and should not be overlooked.

Chemical Cleaning

Chemical cleaning is a very environmentally unfriendly way to clean engine components as it uses caustic solutions that do not work well with the environment (**FIGURE 21-1**). The chemical cleaning process is one where the components are dipped in a chemical bath that eats away the dirt, grease, and other materials that are on the engine components. This process does usually remove all of the debris from the components, but at a cost to the environment. Heating up the chemical solution will help with the removal of the debris on the engine components.

High-Pressure Steam Cleaning

High-pressure steam cleaning is very similar to the steam cleaning process that happens in a dishwasher; heated water is sprayed under high pressure at the engine components so that it loosens up the debris on the components (**FIGURE 21-2**). Steam cleaning is much better than chemical cleaning because there is no use of caustic chemicals—only hot water, soap, and pressure. Because water is a compound that is a solution for a lot of materials found on Earth, it is the perfect medium for debris removal.

Mechanical Cleaning

Mechanical cleaning is just as it sounds: It requires a technician with a wire brush and other cleaning equipment working on the engine components to make them clean again

FIGURE 21-1 Using a heated chemical solution in the engine components helps to loosen up the grease and oil deposited on the components and increases the effectiveness of the solution.

FIGURE 21-2 High-pressure steam cleaning is used with a soap solution to clean the components. Shooting the water under pressure against the components allows easy removal of debris.

FIGURE 21-3 The most effective cleaning procedure is for the technician to use a wire brush to physically clean the components, navigating carefully around the fragile pieces.

FIGURE 21-4 A thermal oven heats up the material to a very hot temperature, so everything on it bakes off, resulting in bare components. This should only be done to cast iron and steel components because there are issues with other materials being heated to such a high degree.

(**FIGURE 21-3**). This step usually happens before any other cleaning takes place because the large pieces of dirt and grime must be removed before parts are put into a machine to continue cleaning. If the components were put into a machine without removing the debris, the large pieces of gunk would end up hurting the machine or diluting the solution that is used to clean the components. This initial cleaning should happen before you take the engine apart; that way you will be able to clean the areas that are going to be visible once the engine is completed. Spending the necessary time to complete this step allows for a better end product.

Thermal Cleaning

In **thermal cleaning** the engine components are heated in an oven to above 500 degrees in order to burn off any residue or material on them (**FIGURE 21-4**). This process has been used in a large number of machine shops throughout the years, as it utilizes no caustic solutions. The only major downside is that it takes seven to eight hours to complete this process because it takes that long for the material to burn off. The amount of energy and the fumes from this process could be looked at as another downside, although most shops have put ventilation and personal protection devices in place to mitigate issues with the fumes.

Ultrasonic Cleaning

Once the major debris has been removed and the machining processes are complete, before the engine is assembled it is usually run through an **ultrasonic cleaner** to remove any residue or small machining material (**FIGURE 21-5**). This process does not remove any major grease or oil, but only the small deposits. Ultrasonic uses sound waves to loosen up the material that is lying inside the engine so that it goes into the solution in the ultrasonic cleaner. This solution is somewhat caustic, which amplifies the sound waves and helps eat away the loose material.

FIGURE 21-5 Using sound waves to clean sensitive components cleans the smallest orifices easily and decreases the possibility of damage.

Thread Chasing

Once the engine block and components are returned to the customer, the customer or technician must chase each bolt hole so that when they are torquing bolts into the engine, they will not be influenced by the threads in each hole (**FIGURE 21-6**). This is a very simple process that can be accomplished with a set of thread chasers and some

FIGURE 21-6 Inspecting and repairing any threads that are damaged prior to installation of the component helps the technician avoid problems when the time comes to install the component.

FIGURE 21-7 The gasket surface must be inspected for loose debris, pitting, or other features that do not allow the new gasket to seal correctly when it is installed.

time. Doing this work now will make later work easier because every bolt will go in without issue, and the torque values will be correct when the components are torqued to the cylinder block and head.

Gasket Surface Inspection

K21002 Knowledge of what to inspect on the gasket surfaces once the engine is cleaned.

Once all surfaces are clean, the technician must inspect the gasket surface on all the components that use a gasket to seal them to the block (**FIGURE 21-7**). Inspection of the gasket surface allows the technician to see if the components will create a good seal against the block so that there will be no leaks. If the surface of the component has pitting or is not flat, steps must be taken to flatten the surface or get rid of the pitting so that the gasket has a clean surface to seal on. On components that have a channel for an O-ring type of seal, the channel must be inspected for straightness, no debris in the channel, and completeness, which means that it is not missing any piece of the channel.

▶ Crack Detection and Repair

K21003 Knowledge of what crack detection procedures are used on what types of components.

Component cracking is a major reason for engine failure. This means that when the rebuild is done, the components must all be checked for this type of failure, as cracks are sometimes not visible to the naked eye. A competent machine shop should be able to examine the components and tell you whether they can be reused or must be replaced. Throughout this section, we expose you to different aspects of crack detection and repair so that when you are talking to the machine shop, you understand what will be done to the components that you are bringing to the shop.

Magnafluxing

If a cylinder head is made of cast iron, then the ferrous metal—which includes any metal that has an iron compound in its makeup or that is magnetic—in the cylinder head can be tested using a dry or wet method. The dry method, magnafluxing, consists of using an iron dusting powder that is available in different colors. After applying the powder, a permanent magnet or electromagnet creates a magnetic field that causes a high concentration of magnetic flux at the surface cracks, which attract the iron powder (**FIGURE 21-8**). The machinist will notice a nice solid line of powder sticking to the cracked area because north and south magnetic poles will be created along the crack.

The wet method uses a liquid iron and fluorescent dye mixture along with an electromagnet to pull the dye into any cracks, where a black light illuminates it. The wet method

FIGURE 21-8 Magnafluxing a cast iron cylinder head with cracks.

FIGURE 21-9 Using the pressure checking method to check the cylinder head for cracks is an easy way to verify where there are issues.

is used with the wet fluorescent particle bath inspection systems, which is a different type of unit that has integral magnetic field generators.

Pressure Testing

Pressure testing is normally used on aluminum cylinder heads because the magnaflux process cannot be used. There are two different styles of pressure testers. In the first, a plate is cut out for the combustion chamber areas and used to seal off the water jackets, except for one where air pressure is injected (**FIGURE 21-9**). The cylinder head is checked for leaks by submerging it in water or by using a soapy water formula that is sprayed all over the cylinder head with a squirt bottle. The technician looks for bubbles, which result from an air leak. In the other type of pressure tester, the cylinder head is placed on a pressure-testing bench. The bench is usually made of softer rubber, which acts as the seal around the bottom of the cylinder head. Pressure is then introduced into the combustion chamber via the spark plug hole, and the machinist notes whether any pressure is lost or if a hissing or leaking noise is heard coming from around the valves or any part of the casting.

FIGURE 21-10 When inspecting the cylinder head, the technician must look for cracks, damaged bolt hole threads, and any other areas that need attention before the cylinder head is put into service.

Dye Penetrant Testing

Dye penetrant testing is done on cylinder heads that do not contain ferrous material, so they do not allow the magnafluxing to operate correctly. In the dye penetrant process, an oil infused with a colored dye or fluorescent dye is sprayed onto the component; once the oil seeps into the crack, the dye stains it, which allows the machinist to see where the crack is. This type of crack detection can be utilized on any type of material but is usually used on aluminum.

Visual Inspection

When the machinist is evaluating the components on the bench, a simple visual inspection can be a great way to save a lot of time and money for the customer. Most major issues with engine components are visible to the naked eye if the machinist just evaluates the pieces as they lie (**FIGURE 21-10**). Along with the machinist, the technician who disassembled the engine can evaluate the serviceability of the components before sending them to the machine shop, thus saving time and money for the customer.

Crack Repair

K21004 Knowledge of component crack repair procedures.

One of the most popular ways to fix a crack, other than welding the crack in, is pinning. A hole is drilled at each end of the crack and then in multiple places overlapping the crack. Pins are driven into the holes so that they fill in the area that was just drilled. Once all the pins are in they are peened over with an air hammer to flatten them. If the crack is on the deck surface, resurfacing will allow the head to be reused once the rest of the machine work is complete. This process uses no heat, so the metal does not warp or become disoriented in any way.

Crack Welding

Crack welding is used when the crack is in an easy place to deal with, and the welder is confident that there will not be issues with internal water jacket problems when the welding is done. Cast iron welding requires a talented individual who is able to control the heat in the piece so that it the cast iron will not warp or melt (**FIGURE 21-11**). With aluminum, TIG welding is a process that must be controlled just as much as the cast iron process, but it is even more delicate because if the welder stays in one position too long, the casting will melt through, causing another hole that will have to be filled (**FIGURE 21-12**). Welding is done on castings that have enough material to sustain the weld and survive the experience. Many later model engine components are built with very tight tolerances that do not allow for machining of the engine parts or repair, which means they are throwaways.

FIGURE 21-11 When welding on a cast iron cylinder head, you must use the correct welder, material, and process so that the welding will last.

FIGURE 21-12 When TIGing aluminum the welder must continue to move when applying filler because if they stay in one location too long they will burn through the material causing more damage than was previously there.

► Wrap-Up

Ready for Review

- ▶ Engine cleaning is a major part of rebuilding the engine; an inspection will show the condition of the engine components so that they can be evaluated as to whether they can be reused.
- ▶ Chemical cleaning is a very environmentally unfriendly way to clean engine components because it uses caustic solutions that do not work well with the environment.

- ▶ The chemical cleaning process is one where the components are dipped in a chemical bath that eats away the dirt, grease, and other materials that are on the engine components.
- ▶ Steam cleaning is very similar to the steam cleaning that happens in a dishwasher: heated water is sprayed under high pressure at the engine components to loosen up debris.
- ▶ The use of steam cleaning is much better than using chemical cleaning as there is no use of caustic chemicals—just some hot water and pressure.

- Mechanical cleaning requires a technician with a wire brush and other cleaning equipment working on the engine components to make them clean again, and it happens before any other cleaning in order to remove large pieces of dirt and grime.

- Thermal cleaning heats up the components in an oven to above 500 degrees in order to burn off any residue or material that is on the engine components; this method utilizes no caustic solutions and takes seven to eight hours to complete.

- Ultrasonic cleaning removes any residue or small machining material by using sound waves to loosen up the material that is lying inside the engine so that it goes into the solution that is in the ultrasonic cleaner.

- Once all of the surfaces are clean, the technician must inspect the gasket surface on all the components that use a gasket to seal it to the block.

- Inspecting the gasket surface allows the technician to see whether the components will create a good seal against the block so that there will be no leaks.

- Crack checking is done using a dry or wet method.

- The dry method, magnafluxing, consists of using an iron dusting powder that is available in different colors. After applying the powder, a permanent magnet or electromagnet creates a magnetic field that causes a high concentration of magnetic flux at the surface cracks, which attract the iron powder when applied.

- The wet method uses a liquid iron and fluorescent dye mixture. It is used along with an electromagnet to pull the dye into any cracks and then a black light is used to illuminate the dye.

- Dye penetrant testing is done on cylinder heads that do not have ferrous material. This process uses an oil that is sprayed onto the component that is infused with a colored dye or fluorescent dye, once the oil seeps into the crack the dye stains it which allows the machinist to see where the crack is.

- Pressure testing for crack is normally used on aluminum cylinder heads since the magnaflux process cannot be used.

- There are two different styles of pressure testers. In the first, a plate is cut out for the combustion chamber areas and used to seal off the water jackets, except for one where air pressure is injected, it is placed in a water tanks and you look for bubbles.

- When the machinist is evaluating the components that are on their bench, a simple visual inspection is a great way to save a lot of time and money for the customer.

- One of the most popular ways to fix a crack other than welding the crack in is pinning the crack. A hole is drilled at each end of the crack and then in multiple places overlapping the crack. A pin is driven into each of the holes to fill in the area that was just drilled.

- Crack welding is utilized when the crack is in an easily accessible place and the welder is confident that he or she

will not have issues with internal water jacket problems when the welding is done.

Key Terms

chemical cleaning Process where components are dipped into a bath of caustic chemicals that eat away the dirt and grease. This process works well but creates a lot of environmentally unfriendly by-products.

dye penetrant testing Process in which dye is sprayed all over the component and is allowed to seep into the crevices, illuminating the cracks.

high-pressure steam cleaning Process in which the component is put into a machine that produces steam from heating up water. The component is then sprayed with the hot water in order to dissolve the dirt and grease so it comes right off.

mechanical cleaning Process in which the technician physically scrapes and cleans the components.

pressure testing Process used on components that do not have iron in their molecular makeup. The component is sealed up, and air pressure is used to pressurize the cavities; then the component is put into a tank of water so that the machinist can see where the bubbles are escaping from the component.

thermal cleaning Process in which the components are heated in an oven, burning off the grease and dirt.

ultrasonic cleaner Machine that uses sound waves to vibrate any small, loose particles out of the components before the components are reinstalled in the engine.

Review Questions

1. Which of the following cleaning processes should take place before any other cleaning process on the engine?
   a. Chemical cleaning
   b. Steam cleaning
   c. Mechanical cleaning
   d. Thermal cleaning

2. Which of the following cleaning processes is only used to clean and remove any residue or small machining material and is environmentally friendly?
   a. Ultrasonic cleaning
   b. Steam cleaning
   c. Thermal cleaning
   d. Chemical cleaning

3. Which of the following cleaning processes produces environmentally unfriendly by-products?
   a. Ultrasonic cleaning
   b. Chemical cleaning
   c. Thermal cleaning
   d. Steam cleaning

4. Choose the correct crack testing procedure to be used on cylinder heads that do not contain ferrous material:
   a. Dry magnafluxing
   b. Wet magnafluxing
   c. Pressure testing
   d. Dye penetrant testing

5. On components that have a channel for an O-ring type of seal, the channel must be inspected for all of the following, *except*:
   a. straightness.
   b. debris in the channel.
   c. completeness.
   d. flaking.
6. Which of the following methods is used for detection of fine cracks in both non-ferrous and ferrous metals including aluminum?
   a. Dry magnaflux testing
   b. Wet magnaflux testing
   c. NDT
   d. Dye checking
7. All of the following statements with respect to pressure testing of aluminum cylinder heads are true, *except*:
   a. The cylinder head is checked for leaks using a soapy water formula sprayed on it.
   b. An air leak results in bubbles when submerged.
   c. Pressure testing is normally used on aluminum cylinder heads because the magnaflux process cannot be used.
   d. Pressure testing can only be done with the help of water or a soapy water formula.
8. Which of the following tests done on aluminum cylinder heads utilizes fluorescent penetrant dye?
   a. Pressure test
   b. Magnafluxing
   c. Dye penetrant testing
   d. Dye check method
9. All of the following statements with respect to the pinning process of crack repair are true, *except*:
   a. Resurfacing allows the head to be reused once the rest of the machine work is complete.
   b. The process uses no heat, so the metal does not warp or become disoriented in any way.
   c. Holes are also drilled in between the cracks so as to be filled with pins.
   d. Once all pins are in, they are peened over with an air hammer to flatten them.
10. Choose the correct statement with respect to crack welding:
   a. Crack welding is done when the crack is in a critical or non-approachable area.
   b. Cast welding can easily be done by a novice.
   c. Crack welding of aluminum is easier than that of ferrous metals.
   d. Welding is done on castings that have enough material to sustain the weld and survive the experience.

ASE Technician A/Technician B Style Questions

1. Technician A says that the machinist picks the method that should be used to check out a set of cylinder heads that were dropped off for inspection. Technician B says that the technician tells the machinist which method to use to check a set of cylinder heads. Who is correct?
   a. Tech A
   b. Tech B
   c. Both A and B
   d. Neither A nor B
2. Technician A states that aluminum cylinder heads can be magnafluxed to look for cracks. Technician B says that pressure checking and magnafluxing can be used on the cylinder blocks also. Who is correct?
   a. Tech A
   b. Tech B
   c. Both A and B
   d. Neither A nor B
3. Technician A says that thermal cleaning can cost the machine shop more money than cold tank cleaning. Technician B states that ultrasonic cleaning is for fine particle removal. Who is correct?
   a. Tech A
   b. Tech B
   c. Both A and B
   d. Neither A nor B
4. Technician A says when evaluating a crack to be repaired, the owner of the component must understand the costs involved with this procedure. Technician B says that every crack can be repaired. Who is correct?
   a. Tech A
   b. Tech B
   c. Both A and B
   d. Neither A nor B
5. Technician A says that a thorough visual inspection should precede any machine work. Technician B states that the technician may be able to spot the problem area before taking it to the machine shop. Who is correct?
   a. Tech A
   b. Tech B
   c. Both A and B
   d. Neither A nor B
6. Technician A states that pressure checking is mainly for cast iron components. Technician B says that using dye penetrant to find cracks works for components that do not have iron in them. Who is correct?
   a. Tech A
   b. Tech B
   c. Both A and B
   d. Neither A nor B
7. Technician A says that the gasket surface must be inspected for flatness and to make sure that there is no pitting in the metal. Technician B says that machining the surface can sometimes refresh the surface to be serviceable again. Who is correct?
   a. Tech A
   b. Tech B
   c. Both A and B
   d. Neither A nor B
8. Technician A says that when rebuilding an engine, all the bolt holes must have the threads chased so that there isn't a problem with assembly. Technician B states that the technician will not need to reuse any of the bolts when reassembling the engine. Who is correct?
   a. Tech A
   b. Tech B

c. Both A and B

d. Neither A nor B

9. Technician A states that the ultrasonic cleaner is for heavy grease and dirt residues. Technician B says that the ultrasonic cleaner is utilized on the final rinse of the components. Who is correct?

a. Tech A

b. Tech B

c. Both A and B

d. Neither A nor B

10. Technician A says that even though the engine components are sent to the machinist, some mechanical cleaning must still be performed before assembly. Technician B says that soap and water are the best way to clean the components before final assembly. Who is correct?

a. Tech A

b. Tech B

c. Both A and B

d. Neither A nor B

CHAPTER 22

Gaskets, Seals, and Sealants

NATEF Tasks

- **N22001** Install engine covers using gaskets, seals, and sealers as required.

Knowledge Objectives

After reading this chapter, you will have:

- **K22001** Knowledge of how components are sealed in an engine to prevent leakage.
- **K22002** Knowledge of how gaskets are removed and installed on an engine.

- **K22003** Knowledge of how seals work in an engine.
- **K22004** Knowledge of how sealers work in an engine.
- **K22005** Knowledge of the usage of thread locker and sealants.

Skills Objectives

- **S22001** Install gaskets properly.

- **S22002** Use RTV sealant.

You Are the Automotive Technician

The service information for the 2008 Cadillac CTS states that the oil pan gasket is just a 1/8" bead of RTV sealant. You, as the technician, must prepare the surface and apply the sealant to the oil pan before installation. What is the first step of this process?

1. Applying the sealant before installation.
2. Cleaning the surface with a gasket scraper or a Roloc disc.
3. Installing the oil pan and then applying the sealer.

▶ Introduction

K22001 Knowledge of how components are sealed in an engine to prevent leakage.

Gaskets, seals, and sealants are a vital component to an automotive engine as they are the pieces that keep the fluids in the engine and dirt out. Without these parts, the engine would not be able to operate, and the vehicle would not run. Throughout this chapter we dive into the different types of sealants, gaskets, seals, and preparation of surfaces for great gasket adhesion.

▶ Gaskets, Seals, and Sealants

Seals and gaskets are used to keep fluids and gases from mixing inside the engine, from leaking out, and to keep dirt and moisture from getting in. Because the terms "seal" and "gasket" both refer to parts that do similar jobs, there is some crossover in design or usage, and we will highlight these points as they arise. This chapter will discuss gasket handling, removal and installation. We will also address the selection and use of sealants with—or instead of—gaskets and seals. Additionally, we look at seal design and handling as well as examine some leak detection techniques.

Gaskets

The term **gasket** is most frequently used to describe a sealing element that is clamped between two flat components where there is no expected movement between the parts. Even the most finely machined surface still has small peaks and valleys that are not perceived either visually or by touch (**FIGURE 22-1**). This means that when parts are assembled together, there is an imperfect fit between the mating surfaces. Gaskets are designed to take up the space between parts and prevent fluids or gases from passing through the minute gaps between the pieces. Once a gasket has been compressed, filling in these gaps, it may not suitably change shape a second time. Reinstalling used gaskets will cause a leak.

FIGURE 22-1 Most metal surfaces that gaskets seal on are not truly flat. Metal has small peaks and valleys where it is machined, which requires a gasket to smooth out the imperfections on those sealing surfaces.

What Are Gaskets Made Of?

Gaskets may be made from many materials such as cork, paper, felt, metal, and rubber. These are sometimes referred to as cut gaskets as they are cut to the shape of the part they are used to seal. Gasket shapes can range from a simple donut-shaped drain plug gasket to a complex profile with multiple holes. Some specialized gaskets, such as head gaskets, are manufactured from multiple layers of different materials. Careful handling of any gasket is important to prevent it from being damaged during installation; this is especially true of layered gaskets. If a layered gasket is bent, it must not be used. Damage inside the gasket may not be visible, but the weakened portion will fail in service.

Gaskets Removal and Installation

N22001 Install engine covers using gaskets, seals, and sealers as required.

K22002 Knowledge of how gaskets are removed and installed on an engine.

Before parts may be reassembled, all of the old gasket must be removed to permit the new gasket to seal properly. Removing gaskets must be done with care. Although sometimes gaskets, especially metal gaskets or sealing washers, may easily break cleanly from the surfaces, in many cases heat, sealants, and gasket coatings may cause the gasket surface to become baked onto one or both components. In these cases, the gasket must be carefully scraped from the surface without causing scratches or gouges on the sealing surface. When working with cast iron, it is permissible to use a sharp metal gasket scraper: steel and brass scrapers are available. Most manufacturers recommend aluminum surfaces be scraped with plastic scrapers or a **Roloc™ bristle disc**, and hardwood blocks are also used (**FIGURE 22-2**). Abrasives such as emery cloth may be used to carefully remove stubborn deposits and clean the surfaces overall, but care must be taken to maintain the flatness of the sealing surface. This is especially true if using power-driven

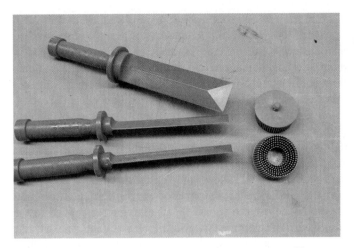

FIGURE 22-2 A Roloc bristle disc is similar to a Scotch-Brite™ pad, as it removes material with the course makeup of the disc. A plastic scraper will not gouge or damage the sealing surface of the component.

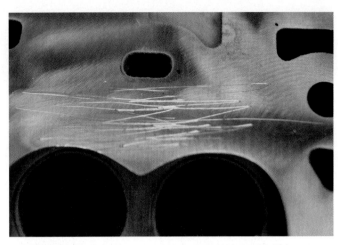

FIGURE 22-3 When the gasket surface has been damaged by a technician using the wrong tool or too much force, it will become damaged. The damaged surface will not seal, thus requiring replacement of the component.

abrasive discs, known commonly as "cookies." Many engine rebuilders do not recommend them as they can quickly round over the surface at holes and shoulders, reducing the effectiveness of gaskets. Bristle brush–type discs are often considered less aggressive; they can be used with care on aluminum parts and do not leave fine abrasive dust behind. If you are using any power tools to remove gaskets, work carefully to prevent component damage (**FIGURE 22-3**).

Chemical release agents can soften the most difficult-to-remove gaskets. In some cases, they are recommended on aluminum components to reduce the opportunity for damage during gasket scraping. However, use care in selecting the gasket remover; some are not suitable for non-ferrous parts. Additionally gasket removers of any design will also remove paint so protect the engine paint and vehicle finish from overspray. Follow the remover's recommendations for personal protective equipment while using (**FIGURE 22-4**). After removing the gasket materials, clean with alcohol, brake and parts cleaner, or other suitable degreaser to remove any traces of oil or coolant from the parts. Although it is not strictly part of the gasket removing process, in preparation for reassembly ensure any threaded holes are clean and dry, and chase the threads as required. Blow out any blind holes to prevent debris or liquids from interfering with assembly torque or causing component damage. If you are in doubt as to the integrity of either or both of the parts, use a straightedge to check for flatness before reassembly.

Gaskets—Checking and Installing

Before replacing the gasket, check the new part for damage. Gaskets should be packaged flat and should not have been distorted. Multilayer gaskets such as head gaskets that have been bent should not be used, even if they appear otherwise undamaged. If layers concealed below the surfaces have been compromised, premature failure will occur. It is wise to match up the gasket with the surface to ensure the gasket is correct and you determine the orientation. Head and manifold gaskets in particular may be directional, and though the bolt pattern may be the same regardless of gasket orientation, passageways may be blocked if they are installed incorrectly. Head gaskets may specify the top surface with the word "Top" or "Up" (**FIGURE 22-5**). A mistake here could create a costly comeback. Also, check the manufacturer recommendations around the use of sealers with flat gaskets. Do not be tempted to add additional sealant where it is not recommended. Some gaskets have special coatings or vulcanized sealing rings that will be rendered ineffective by use of sealants. Also determine if the manufacturer specifies using lubricant, sealant, or thread locker on the fastener threads.

FIGURE 22-4 Using a chemical gasket remover starts to dissolve the gasket material so that it can be easily removed by the technician.

S22001 Install gaskets properly.

FIGURE 22-5 When installing a head gasket, look for a marking that denotes the installation direction; mis-installation can cause the engine to overheat, requiring a rebuild right after replacement.

To install a gasket, follow the steps in **SKILL DRILL 22-1**.

Once everything is in place, torque the fasteners to manufacturer's specifications. Often it is advisable to torque in multiple steps, being careful not to displace the gasket. Some thicker, soft gaskets such as cork will deform and crack if they are over-tightened. Torquing these gaskets may be challenging as they compress, and sometimes click-type wrenches may not indicate the proper torque has been achieved. Note that if torque-angle tightening is required, it is wise to mark the heads of the fasteners after the initial torque is reached and the fasteners are double-checked. This will allow you to visually see that all heads have been turned the specified number of degrees. Torque distribution plates may be used to spread the clamping force applied to the gasket across a larger area, away from the bolt holes, on parts like valve covers. Rubber gaskets may incorporate metal sleeves that limit the compression of the soft gasket material to prevent leaks and allow the fastener torque to be achieved easily.

Seals

K22003 Knowledge of how seals work in an engine.

The term **seal** is usually associated with shafts and may involve movement. Sometimes the term "dynamic" is added to seals where the shaft moves, and seals used with stationary components are referred to as static seals. Here we examine dynamic shaft seal and then

SKILL DRILL 22-1 Installing a Gasket

1. Clean and degrease each surface with a shop towel and alcohol or brake and parts cleaner.

2. Determine gasket orientation by placing the gasket on one of the sealing surfaces.

Continued

3. Use some compatible grease, sealer, or some fasteners to hold the gasket in place while you place the part on the engine.

4. Finger-tighten the fasteners and then torque to specification.

FIGURE 22-6 A lip seal has an edge that forms the lip, which contacts the shaft and allows for circular movement while keeping the liquid behind it.

FIGURE 22-7 A garter spring installed on a lip seal helps keep the seal in constant contact with the shaft.

discuss some variations. **FIGURE 22-6** shows a cutaway diagram of what is referred to as a lip seal. Typically lip seals consist of a metal case to which is vulcanized a sealing "lip." The lip of the seal is designed to ride in contact with a polished surface of a shaft to prevent fluids or gas from escaping, and bar the entry of moisture or dirt. Some seals use the tension of the sealing material alone to hold the lip against the shaft, but most use a garter spring to maintain tension (**FIGURE 22-7**). Most seal construction is similar, even though appearances

FIGURE 22-8 To increase the possibility of sealing the seal to the component, a rubber coating encases the seal so that it seals in the bore where the seal resides.

may differ. For example, some seals may have a rubber coating around the metal case and incorporate a dust lip outside the seal (**FIGURE 22-8**).

Seals like the front and rear main seals of engines or camshaft seals are used to prevent oil leakage between rotating shafts and their respective stationary bosses in the engine block. Valve stem seals (**FIGURE 22-9**) are similar in design, except the garter spring is outside the seal lip. In this case, the valve stem is the polished sealing surface, so the seal works on a surface that reciprocates through the seal lips. The seal lip must face the correct direction in order to be effective. Normally, this is with the hollow of the case installed toward the fluid being retained. Some seals separate two fluids from each other. These are called double lip seals. Even though there are two sealing lips, there is also a specific orientation that must be observed during installation (**FIGURE 22-10**).

Seal Removal

Like gaskets, seals are normally replaced if they are disturbed. Before attempting to remove a seal, first clean the area around the seal case, and measure how deeply it is set into the fixed case; you need to install the new seal to the same depth. Removing seals can be a challenge. Seal pulling tools (**FIGURE 22-11**) can be used where there is no shaft installed; the tools are placed in the opening of the seal to lever against the seal case. Replacing a seal with a shaft in place is difficult because there is limited space between the shaft and the seal case. In some cases, special tools are available—or required—to pull such seals. If a special tool is not required, drilling a small hole in the metal case and installing a self-tapping screw is a common way to remove seals. When the screw is installed, it can be pulled with a slide hammer to remove the seal.

FIGURE 22-9 A valve stem posi lock seal has a spring metal band on the outside of the seal keeping it in constant contact with the valve stem. This lock also helps the seal keep its shape.

FIGURE 22-10 A double lip seal is a seal that has two lips, so if something gets by the inner lip, the outer lip has a chance to stop it.

Regardless of the method you employ to remove seals, take great care not to score or deform the fixed housing the seal is driven into. Also, ensure you do not scratch the shaft sealing surfaces. Damage to either the housing or the shaft will prevent the seal from doing its job and cause an expensive comeback. When you remove the seal, carefully clean the seal bore in the housing. Look for any scratches or nicks that can cause leaks. The surface has to be polished or the housing replaced if there is any damage. Likewise, the shaft has to be checked. On rotating shafts, it is common to find the seal lips have cut a groove into the sealing surface of the shaft. If the seal is reinstalled in the same position, the lips may not be able to prevent the new seal from leaking on this uneven surface. There are a few methods that can be used to correct the seal groove. If the groove is very shallow, polishing the surface with emery and then crocus cloth can remove the groove and allow the seal to run on a smooth, true surface. For deeper grooves, thin steel sleeves with an inner diameter that matches the shaft may be installed. These can be pressed on, or held to the shaft with an anaerobic adhesive. In extreme cases, where the shaft is badly damaged, welding and regrinding the shaft can restore clearance and surface finish. Sometimes, part replacement may be the only option.

FIGURE 22-11 Some seals are hard to remove and require a seal puller that grabs the seal and pulls it out with force.

Seal Installation

Once you ensure the sealing surface and case are clean and free from damage, you can install the seal. In some applications, special installation tools are required to prevent seal or component damage. If no special tools are required, choose a seal driver that has the right diameter. Ideally the seal driver should contact the outer edge of the seal, where it is strongest (**FIGURE 22-12**). If you are driving over a shaft, you need to ensure that the inside diameter and depth is sufficient to clear the shaft. Manufacturers sometimes specify pre-installation treatment of the seal case. Sometimes application of lubrication or sealer is specified for the outer diameter of the case. Follow the service information instructions. Normally the sealing lips should be lubricated to prevent premature wear on startup. Especially in the case of driving a seal into a bore without the sealing shaft in place, a small amount of compatible grease can be added inside the case to prevent the garter spring from being jarred free while driving the seal into the housing. This is not necessary when the seal is being installed over its shaft, as the shaft will hold tension on the spring, and it won't tend to dislodge.

When installing the seal over a shaft, take care to ease the seal lip over the edge of the shaft. In some cases, plastic sleeves can be used to gently expand the lips as the seal is moved into the case (**FIGURE 22-13**). Once the seal is in place over the shaft or seal guide, drive it

FIGURE 22-12 The proper way to install a seal is to use a seal installer. The installer will install the seal straight without damaging the casing or the rubber seal.

FIGURE 22-13 Some seals require a sleeve to peel back the lips so that the seal slides onto the shaft without resistance. Without the sleeve, some seals tear, causing a leak.

Two-Piece Main Seals

Older engines may have used a rear main seal packing rather than a lip seal. These are sometimes colloquially called a "rope seal" or wick seal. One piece of packing was worked into a groove in the web of the rear main bearing cap with a dowel or socket, and the ends trimmed. A second piece was likewise worked into a corresponding groove in the block behind the main bearing bore. When the main cap was installed, the two packing pieces made a reasonable seal against the principle end of the crankshaft and the block and bearing cap. Originally these seals were made of asbestos. Due to the health hazards associated with asbestos, engine gasket kits for engines that would have used rope seals include Viton® rubber or similar material seals instead. When installing two-piece rubber seals, the ends of the seals are offset so that the parting surface is located away from the cap mating surface, improving sealing. RTV is sometimes applied to the edge of the seal as well (**FIGURE 22-14**).

squarely into the bore with the seal driver to the depth specified in the service manual or measured at time of removal. If the seal case cocks or bends during installation, it is not recommended to try to straighten it. The deformed case will compromise the ability of the seal, and it will likely leak.

Static Seals

The most common seals that are used on round components that do not move are called O-rings. O-rings were probably originally named because of their characteristic hollow circle or "O" shape. The cross section of the O-ring is normally also round, but square-cut O-rings are also available (**FIGURE 22-15**). O-rings are usually used to seal a tube into a bore. Examples of this can be a coolant pipe into a water pump, or a dipstick tube sealed against its bore in the block. Port fuel injectors usually use an O-ring to seal fuel into the rail to injector connection, and engine vacuum at injector to manifold connection. The tube and bore are sized for a generous slip fit, and the O-ring takes up the space between the two. The O-ring is fitted into a groove on one of the two mating parts, called a gland. When the joint is static, the gland is usually located on the tube but can be a recess in the bore.

Replacing O-rings is not a difficult task, but there are some things to keep in mind. First, as with other gaskets and seals, reusing O-rings is not recommended. Frequently the rubber becomes hard and brittle in service, so cutting the O-ring off is often easier than trying to stretch it over the gland. Take care not to nick or scratch the sealing surface (**FIGURE 22-16**). Inspect the bore for corrosion where the O-ring has to sit. Polish out any imperfections that may prevent the new O-ring from sealing. Usually the O-rings are lubricated prior to installation. To prevent contamination of the system, the O-rings can usually be lubricated with the fluid they seal or a grease or oil that is compatible with the fluid being sealed. Oil or silicone grease can be used for vacuum sealing O-rings to ease installation. Some O-ring materials are not very tolerant of petroleum products. These can soften and swell, resulting in leaks. Follow the service information recommendations.

When installing the O-rings, avoid twisting them over the gland. It usually takes a small amount of effort to install the part with the O-ring on it into the bore, as the seal is compressed and expands into the gland. Push the parts together squarely to prevent the O-ring from twisting out of the gland or being cut on the edge of the bore.

O-rings can also be used as a gasket where a flanged part is mated to a flat piece, or between two flat pieces. In some applications the gasket is a formed O-ring with a shape that is not the traditional "O" shape, but often is still referred to as an O-ring or O-ring gasket (**FIGURE 22-17**). Where O-ring gaskets are used between two flat components, one of the two usually incorporates a gland profiled to accept the gasket. Just like O-rings on tubes,

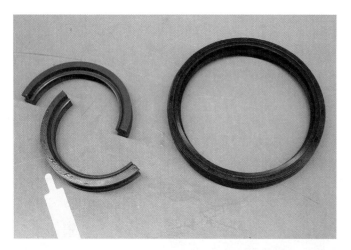

FIGURE 22-14 Older rear main seals consist of a two-piece seal that separates at the rear main cap. Later automotive developments have created a one-piece seal that helped with eliminating possible areas of leakage where the seals come together.

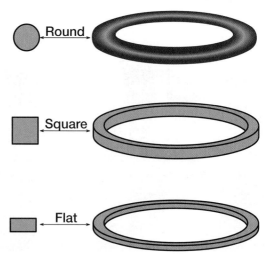

FIGURE 22-15 Not all O-rings are round; some are square cut. When replacing an O-ring, you must replace it with the correct type or it may leak.

FIGURE 22-16 Newer types of engine components have a machined groove in the component that the O-ring type of gasket is to be located. Using a rubber O-ring type of gasket reduces leaks and limits gasket surface damage due to over-scrapping.

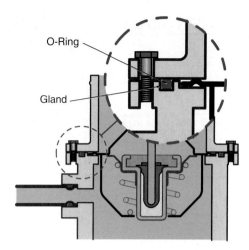

FIGURE 22-17 When the O-ring is compressed between the components, it flattens a little to fill the space in between the two components so that fluid will not escape.

the gasket compresses and fills the gland, and the tension of the rubber provides a positive seal between the two pieces.

Sealing Grommets

A common type of rubber seal that surrounds studs on parts like valve covers is a grommet. Basically a rubber cone with a flat base and a heavy washer to distribute the force of the nut, the cone wedges into the valve cover bore and compresses the center hole around the stud to create a leakproof seal (**FIGURE 22-18**). If a component's gasket is being replaced, it is good practice to replace the grommets at that time, as the gasket and grommets work in unison to create a sealed environment. This is one the most frequently overlooked areas that many technicians ignore.

What Sealants Do in the Automotive Engine

To augment the wide variety of gaskets and seals, a number of chemicals are also used to aid in engine sealing (**FIGURE 22-19**). These can be broken into three major groups: gasket treatment materials, gasket replacement materials, and thread treatment materials. Again, in some cases there is some overlap among materials in these groups.

K22004 Knowledge of how sealers work in an engine.

FIGURE 22-18 To help seal the valve covers, grommets are used to seal the bolts as they go through the valve cover.

FIGURE 22-19 Using the correct sealant for the proper application is crucial to the longevity of the repair. Consult the product service information so that the proper sealant is used.

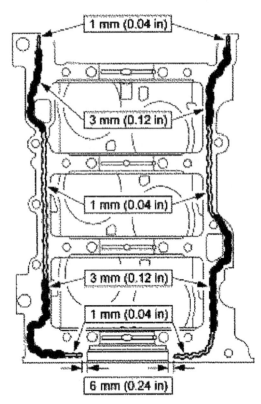

FIGURE 22-20 A form-in-place gasket (FIPG) is created from room temperature vulcanization (RTV) sealant. This sealant is a semi-liquid until it is exposed to air, then it starts to cure and eventually becomes a rubbery substance. The benefit of this type of sealant is its ability to conform to the various metal consistencies, thereby creating a better seal than a conventional gasket.

S22002 Use RTV sealant.

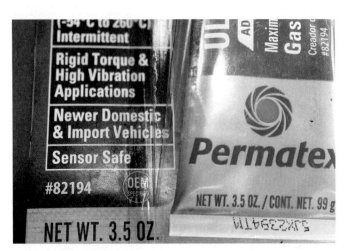

FIGURE 22-21 Most RTV sealant is O_2 sensor safe; look for this logo on the tube of sealant before you utilize it on the engine.

Gasket Treatments

Gasket treatments are hardening or non-hardening sealers that can be applied to gaskets—normally cut paper, cork, or other soft material—to enhance their sealing ability. Hardening treatments, sometimes referred to as gasket shellac, are applied and allowed to dry before installing the gasket. This reduces the permeability of the gasket. Non-hardening sealers also can be used to improve gasket performance, and are usually applied and installed wet. These products are an excellent choice when the gasket must adhere to a component in an installation. When the carrier evaporates, non-hardening sealers maintain a tacky viscous consistency. In some cases, they are specified as a coating for the metal case of a lip seal, or in some circumstances to seal close-fitting machined parts without any additional gasket material.

Gasket Replacement

Sometimes manufacturers forgo the use of premade gaskets altogether in production and rely on **formed-in-place gaskets (FIPGs)** created by applying a sealant to one of the mating surfaces before assembly. There are two main types of FIPG: **room temperature vulcanizing (RTV)** silicone and **anaerobic sealer**.

The most common automotive gasket replacement material is RTV silicone. RTV is sometimes used in addition to gaskets in specific places where it is difficult for the gasket alone to seal, such as the vertical transition surfaces of engine oil pan rails at the bearing caps or to fill the gap between the individual parts of a multipiece intake manifold gasket (**FIGURE 22-20**). RTV is sometimes substituted for a gasket if one is not available. The consistency of RTV allows it to fill considerable gaps and can be used between stamped and machined surfaces without difficulty. There are numerous types of RTV silicone. Many of these specify the best purpose for each formulation, based on either the fluid it is designed to seal or the temperatures it can be exposed to. One manufacturer has FIPG formulations specified as engine, water pump, and transmission. Some RTV formulations can tolerate temperatures high enough to be used to replace or enhance exhaust gaskets. Some RTV releases silicates when curing and can poison exhaust gas oxygen sensors or ratio sensors. When choosing an RTV, it is advisable to select a product that is rated "sensor safe" (**FIGURE 22-21**). The RTV sensor compatibility will be marked clearly on the packaging or published in the RTV technical reference material provided by the RTV manufacturer.

Another type of FIPG is the anaerobic sealer. Anaerobic sealers are used to seal between machined surfaces like engine case halves or flanges. These may permit small amounts of movement such as that caused when mating materials with different expansion and contraction rates. Some manufacturers also state that their sealants can be used to substitute for O-rings.

Removing FIPG

When using FIPG materials, all of the old sealant must be carefully removed. Most of the sealer can be removed carefully by scraping with a sharp razor blade or plastic scraper. Careful cleaning with an open abrasive like a scouring pad can be sparingly used to remove finer remnants. Abrasive papers will often clog and be ineffective with RTV. Use solvent to wash the parts completely to remove any traces of abrasive and dislodged gasket materials. Blow the parts dry, and then clean with alcohol or brake cleaner to remove any oily residues. Some FIPG manufacturers provide a primer that must be applied for their sealer to be effective.

Applying the fresh FIPG should be done according to the OEM recommendations if available. The gasket is applied as a bead: The size of the bead is controlled by cutting the tip of the container to the appropriate diameter. Applying too much sealer is the most common error, especially with RTV gasket materials. When the parts are assembled, the sealer is forced out between the mating surfaces of the two parts. This can leave a large amount of sealer inside the two components, which can break free and be carried around by the oil or coolant inside the engine, where it can block passages and cause issues such as oil starvation or localized overheating (**FIGURE 22-22**).

When using RTV silicone, the components should be assembled and fasteners torqued promptly after installing the sealer because the RTV will begin to cure as it is exposed to the air. If it partially cures before assembly, it may "skin" over or harden in some places and not properly adhere to the mating surfaces, resulting in a leak. Working time for RTV is usually around 10 minutes. If the RTV starts to set before you assemble the components, remove all of the new RTV and reapply.

To properly use an RTV, follow the steps in **SKILL DRILL 22-2**.

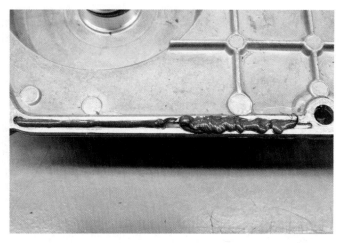

FIGURE 22-22 When using RTV, you must use the proper amount or the excess can become lodged in moving components, causing failure.

SKILL DRILL 22-2 Using an RTV

1. With the old sealant removed, wipe the sealing surfaces with a shop towel dampened with alcohol or brake and parts cleaner to remove any oil or dirt.

2. Cut the application tip to achieve the correct bead size.

Continued

3. Apply an even bead of RTV to one of the sealing surfaces, following the manufacturer's guidelines as to where the RTV should be placed.

4. Install the component and fasteners.

5. Torque the fasteners to specification, in the given sequence if applicable.

6. Observe the product information sheets regarding cure time for the sealant.

Anaerobic sealers remain uncured until the items are assembled and the supply of air is removed. In some cases, this makes them a desirable choice if there is an option between the RTV and Anaerobic materials, and assembly may take a longer period of time.

Additionally, once assembled, the FIPG must be allowed to cure before the components are placed into service. Setup time varies between FIPG products. In the case of one OEM, the recommendation is not to expose the fresh sealant to engine oil for at least 30 minutes after assembly, and the engine should not be run until the sealant has cured for three hours. The instructions for the sealant you are working with will specify the working time and curing characteristics of that product.

Thread Locker and Sealants

Thread treatments fall into two categories: **threadlockers** and **thread sealants**. Thread-locker is usually described in terms of both its "strength" or permanence, and the diameter of fastener it will suit (**FIGURE 22-23**). Although there are inconsistencies between brands regarding the color of the thread locking compound and its relative permanence, for best results it is always best to match the product to application, based on the manufacturer product data sheet. Before reusing fasteners with thread locking compound, the old compound should be fully removed. Usually it chips off fairly easily, and both internal and external threads can be cleaned with thread chasers. Acetone usually acts to dissolve any stubborn thread locking compound. Fasteners and bores should be clean, dry, and oil free before assembly. Most thread lockers are anaerobic in composition, so can be applied without rushing. It is important to note that thread locking fluids do not need to be applied generously; usually a drop or two is sufficient to hold the fastener. Once fasteners are torqued and checked, do not disturb them once the thread locker is set. The instructions accompanying the thread locker you are using will lay out the cure times and when the components can be placed into service.

Thread sealants are particularly important where tapered threads—known as pipe threads—are used as a fluid seal (**FIGURE 22-24**). Oil pressure senders and switches, and temperature senders or sensors are examples of components that must thread into the engine block or housings without leaking. In some cases, sealant is specified for threaded core plugs with straight threads and metal gaskets as well. Flare nuts, compression fittings, and O-ring connections should not require sealant under normal conditions. Although new parts may come with sealant already installed from the factory, if you are re-installing old parts as part of an engine repair, you will need to seal the threads. If the service information does not specify a sealant or that sealant is no longer available, you will need to choose a suitable product. Dedicated thread sealants are usually rated by pressure, temperature, and size of the pipe fitting that product will serve. Sometimes anaerobic sealant or gasket

K22005 Knowledge of the usage of thread locker and sealants.

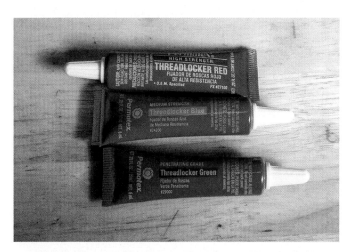

FIGURE 22-23 Keeping bolts in their installed location can be done with a thread locker. The blue type is used so that the bolt can be removed at a later date; the red type is a more permanent type that requires more work to remove.

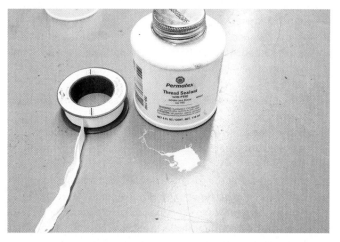

FIGURE 22-24 Teflon tape and paste is used to help seal the threads on bolts or fittings that are meant to carry fluid.

treatment is used for sealing pipe connections, or where threaded fasteners protrude into a cavity that is filled with oil or coolant, such as oil pan or water pump fasteners on some engines.

For many oil and temperature senders, the case is used as an electrical connection for a gauge, light, or computer. It is important to confirm you will have continuity between the sender and the receiving component. Usually, if the sealant is still liquid when the tapered pipe fitting is tightened, the sealant is displaced as the threads come into contact, and the metal-to-metal contact provides sufficient path for current to flow. When using thread sealant, the old sealant must be completely removed and both surfaces clean and dry. Thread sealant is applied around the fastener or pipe fitting to be sealed, and the component is installed. Like thread locker, once the component is installed and the sealant has cured, do not disturb it.

▶ Wrap-Up

Ready for Review

- Gaskets, seals, and sealants keep the fluids in the engine and dirt out.
- The term "gasket" is used to describe a sealing element that is clamped between two flat components where there is no expected movement between the parts.
- Even the most finely machined surface still has small peaks and valleys that are not perceived to us either visually or by touch.
- Gaskets may be made from many materials such as cork, paper, felt, metal, and rubber. These are sometimes referred to as cut gaskets as they are cut to the shape of the part they are used to seal.
- Careful handling of any gasket is important to prevent it from being damaged during installation; this is especially true of layered gaskets. If a layered gasket is bent, it must not be used.
- Before parts may be reassembled, all of the old gasket must be removed to permit the new gasket to seal properly.
- Most manufacturers recommend aluminum surfaces be scraped with plastic scrapers or a Roloc bristle disc, and hardwood blocks are also used.
- Abrasives such as emery cloth may be used to carefully remove stubborn deposits and clean the surfaces overall, but care must be taken to maintain the flatness of the sealing surface.
- When using power tools to remove gaskets, work carefully to prevent component damage.
- Follow the remover's recommendations for personal protective equipment while using chemical gasket-removing agents.
- After removing the gasket materials, clean with alcohol, brake and parts cleaner, or another suitable degreaser to remove any traces of oil or coolant from the parts.
- Use a straightedge and feeler gauge to check for flatness between flat surfaces where a gasket will be used.
- Multilayer gaskets such as head gaskets that have been bent should not be used, even if they appear otherwise undamaged.

- Head gaskets may specify the top surface with the word "Top" or "Up."
- Once everything is in place, torque the fasteners to manufacturer's specifications.
- Torque in multiple steps, being careful not to displace the gasket.
- Some thicker, soft gaskets such as cork will deform and crack if they are over-tightened.
- If torque-angle tightening is required, mark the heads of the fasteners after the initial torque is reached and the fasteners are double-checked.
- Torque distribution plates may be used to spread the clamping force applied to the gasket across a larger area, away from the bolt holes, on parts like valve covers.
- The term "seal" is usually associated with shafts and may involve movement.
- The term "dynamic" is added to seals where the shaft moves.
- Seals used with stationary components are referred to as static seals.
- The seal lip must face the correct direction in order to be effective.
- You want to install the new seal to the same depth.
- Seal pulling tools can be used where there is no shaft installed; the tools are placed in the opening of the seal to lever against the seal case.
- When removing remove seals, take great care not to score or deform the fixed housing the seal is driven into.
- When you remove the seal, carefully clean the seal bore in the housing. Look for any scratches or nicks that can cause leaks.
- In some applications, special installation tools are required to prevent seal or component damage.
- If no special tools are required for seal installation, choose a seal driver that is of the right diameter.
- Manufacturers sometimes specify pre-installation treatment of the seal case.
- Sometimes application of lubrication or sealer is specified for the outer diameter of the case.

- Always follow the service information instructions for seal replacement.
- When installing the seal over a shaft, take care to ease the seal lip over the edge of the shaft.
- Plastic sleeves can be used to gently expand the lips as the seal is moved into the case.
- Some rear main seals are called a "rope seal" or wick seal. One piece of packing was worked into a groove in the web of the rear main bearing cap and the ends trimmed. A second piece is worked into a corresponding groove in the block behind the main bearing bore, and the cap is torqued in place.
- The most common seals that are used on round components that do not move are called O-rings.
- Reusing O-rings is not recommended.
- Take care not to nick or scratch the sealing surface, and inspect the bore for corrosion where the O-ring has to sit. Polish out any imperfections that may prevent the new O-ring from sealing. Usually the O-rings are lubricated.
- When installing the O-rings, avoid twisting them over the gland.
- A rubber seal that surrounds studs on parts like valve covers is a grommet, which is a rubber cone with a flat base and heavy washer to distribute the force of the nut. The cone wedges into the valve cover bore and compresses the center hole around the stud to create a leakproof seal.
- Gasket treatments are hardening or nonhardening sealers that can be applied to gaskets—normally cut paper, cork, or other soft material—to enhance their sealing ability.
- Hardening treatments, sometimes referred to as gasket shellac, are applied and allowed to dry before installing the gasket, and they are not permeable.
- In some cases, manufacturers forgo the use of pre-made gaskets altogether in production, instead relying on formed-in-place gaskets (FIPG) created by applying a sealant to one of the mating surfaces before assembly.
- There are two main types of formed-in-place gaskets: room temperature vulcanizing (RTV) silicone and anaerobic sealer.
- The most common automotive gasket replacement material is RTV silicone.
- RTV is sometimes used in addition to gaskets in specific places where it is difficult for the gasket alone to seal, such as the vertical transition surfaces of engine oil pan rails at the bearing caps or to fill the gap between the individual parts of a multipiece intake manifold gasket.
- RTV is sometimes substituted for a gasket if one is not available. When using RTV, the curing or skin over time is critical because you are actually gluing the two parts together.
- When using FIPG materials, all of the old sealant must be carefully removed. Most of the sealer can be removed carefully by scraping with a sharp razor blade, plastic scraper, or by limited use of a Scotch-Brite pad.
- Abrasive papers will often clog and be ineffective with RTV.
- Use solvent to wash the parts completely in order to remove any traces of abrasive and dislodged gasket materials.
- Some FIPG manufacturers provide a primer that must be applied in order for their sealer to be effective.
- Anaerobic sealers seal in the absence of air and will remain uncured until the items are assembled and the supply of air is removed.
- Thread treatments fall into two categories: thread lockers and thread sealants.
- Thread locker is usually described in terms of both its "strength" or permanence, and the diameter of fastener it will suit.
- Thread sealants are important where tapered threads—known as pipe threads—are used as a fluid seal, like oil pressure senders and switches, and for temperature senders or sensors that must thread into the engine block or housings without leaking.
- Thread sealants are used on head bolts that go into a coolant passage.

Key Terms

anaerobic sealer Used to seal between two machined surfaces and does not need oxygen to cure.

formed in place gasket (FIPG) Type of gasket that is a sealant that takes the place of a conventional gasket and hardens once it is exposed to oxygen.

gasket A sealing element that is clamped between two flat components where there is no expected movement. This piece helps take up the peaks and valleys in each components finish.

Roloc™ bristle disc Type of tool that is a buffing disc that has plastic bristles that gently remove the material on the component without harming the surface.

room temperature vulcanization (RTV) Type of FIPG that is a paste when it comes out the container and then hardens into a rubbery compound when oxygen cures it.

seal A component that can either be stationary or moving and that usually wraps around a shaft and keeps the fluid on one side of it.

threadlocker This compound seals the threads of a bolt to the threads of the component so that it will not be allowed to move once installed.

Review Questions

1. Gaskets and seals in an engine serve all of the following functions, *except*:
   a. keeping fluids and gases from mixing.
   b. preventing fluids from leaking out.
   c. preventing dust and moisture from getting in.
   d. maintaining engine temperature.
2. Head gaskets are made of:
   a. paper.
   b. cork.
   c. different materials.
   d. plastic.

3. Which of the following are used to remove gaskets from aluminum surfaces?
   a. Steel scrapers
   b. Brass scrapers
   c. Plastic scrapers
   d. Aluminum scrapers
4. After removal of gaskets from the surface, which of the following can be used to remove residual oil or coolant?
   a. Water
   b. Chemical release agents
   c. Degreaser
   d. Rag
5. Which of the following seals separate two fluids from each other?
   a. Lip seal
   b. Valve stem seal
   c. Rear main engine seal
   d. Double lip seal
6. All of the following methods can be used to correct a seal groove, *except*:
   a. polishing the surface with emery and then crocus cloth.
   b. installing thin steel sleeves with an inner diameter that matches the shaft.
   c. welding and regrinding the shaft can restore clearance and surface finish.
   d. machining to make the grooves deeper so that steel sleeves can be installed.
7. Choose the correct statement:
   a. Reusing O-rings after thorough cleaning is recommended.
   b. O-rings should not be lubricated prior to installation.
   c. Oil or silicone grease can be used for vacuum sealing O-rings to ease installation.
   d. All O-ring materials are very tolerant of petroleum products.
8. Why are hardening treatments, sometimes referred to as gasket shellac, applied and allowed to dry before installing the gasket?
   a. To decrease the permeability of the gasket
   b. To increase the durability of the gasket
   c. To increase the elasticity of the gasket
   d. To decrease the temperature sensitivity of the gasket
9. Choose the correct statement:
   a. A single type of RTV can be used for all purposes.
   b. Some RTV releases silicates when curing and can poison exhaust gas oxygen sensors or ratio sensors.
   c. RTV can never substitute for a gasket if one is not available.
   d. RTV cannot be used between stamped and machined surfaces
10. All of the following statements with respect to thread lockers are true, *except*:
   a. Acetone usually acts to dissolve any stubborn thread locking compound.
   b. Thread locking fluids should be applied generously.

c. Most thread lockers are anaerobic in composition, so can be applied without rushing.
d. Fasteners and bores should be clean, dry, and oil free before assembly.

ASE Technician A/Technician B Style Questions

1. Technician A says that when you are installing a seal into a component, you must make sure that it is straight in the bore of it could leak. Technician B states that once you install a bolt with thread locker on it, you can take it out as many times as you want, and the compound will still work. Who is correct?
   a. Tech A
   b. Tech B
   c. Both A and B
   d. Neither A nor B
2. Technician A states that when you are using an FIPG, the surface of the components do not have to be clean or debris free. Technician B says that gaskets are used because no surface is perfectly straight without imperfections. Who is correct?
   a. Tech A
   b. Tech B
   c. Both A and B
   d. Neither A nor B
3. Technician A says that anaerobic sealant needs oxygen to cure and seal. Technician B states that RTV must be heated up to cure, and if it is not, it will not cure at room temperature. Who is correct?
   a. Tech A
   b. Tech B
   c. Both A and B
   d. Neither A nor B
4. Technician A says that using a seal installer will lead to a properly installed seal so that it will not leak. Technician B states that using a hammer with a chisel will not install the seal correctly and may lead to leakage. Who is correct?
   a. Tech A
   b. Tech B
   c. Both A and B
   d. Neither A nor B
5. Technician A states that when selecting an O-ring it must be the correct one for the application, the right size and shape or it will potentially fail. Technician B says that there is only one type of O-ring. Who is correct?
   a. Tech A
   b. Tech B
   c. Both A and B
   d. Neither A nor B
6. Technician A states that when removing a seal the technician must be careful of the bore the seal sits in. Technician B says that a seal must have a tight fit in the component bore of it will leak around the seal. Who is correct?
   a. Tech A
   b. Tech B

c. Both A and B

d. Neither A nor B

7. Technician A states that a good practice is checking the gasket to the component before installation. Technician B says that parts stores do not sell the wrong parts for the application. Who is correct?

a. Tech A

b. Tech B

c. Both A and B

d. Neither A nor B

8. Technician A says that a gasket can be made out of any material that will conform to the components that it is being used between. Technician B states that certain O-rings must be used for the fluids that they are sealing against or failure could result. Who is correct?

a. Tech A

b. Tech B

c. Both A and B

d. Neither A nor B

9. Technician A states that using the improper gasket could cause the engine to overheat. Technician B says that the technician should put whatever gaskets they have been handed without asking questions. Who is correct?

a. Tech A

b. Tech B

c. Both A and B

d. Neither A nor B

10. Technician A says that some engines do not use cover gaskets as they are sealed using RTV. Technician B states the use of rubber style of gaskets on newer vehicles is becoming common place as they do not leak as much as paper gaskets. Who is correct?

a. Tech A

b. Tech B

c. Both A and B

d. Neither A nor B

CHAPTER 23

Balancing and Blueprinting

NATEF Tasks

There are no NATEF Tasks for this chapter.

Knowledge Objectives

After reading this chapter, you will have:

- **K23001** Knowledge of the purpose of engine balancing.
- **K23002** Knowledge of who performs the balancing procedures.
- **K23003** Knowledge of the purpose of engine blueprinting.
- **K23004** Knowledge of what is involved in blueprinting a cylinder head.
- **K23005** Knowledge of what is involved in blueprinting an engine.

Skills Objectives

There are no Skills Objectives for this chapter.

You Are the Automotive Technician

A customer comes into your service facility and states he wants a custom high-performance engine built for his 1969 Camaro. What topics should you talk with him about first before moving on into the engine build?

1. What type of performance does he expect from this engine?
2. What color will the engine be?
3. What type of internal components should be installed in this engine?

K23001 Knowledge of the purpose of engine balancing.

▶ Introduction

Balancing and blueprinting an engine allows the engine to live a long life in a vehicle. The technician must understand what is happening here so that if they have to change a component they will know if they need to do some balancing before they install the component. These procedures need to be recommended to customers that have a need for the increased precision in the engines.

▶ Engine Balancing

Although **blueprinting** ensures that there is consistent combustion pressure on the crankshaft between cylinders, the balancing process focuses on the actual masses of internal engine components. This process is necessary for the engine to produce the type of power that it is designed to produce. Taking out the production problems, flaws, and matching the components to one another will allow for a better running engine. The high rpm potential for an internal combustion engine requires special attention to the rotating mass within the engine. If something that is spinning at 7000 rpm doesn't have an exact opposite to offset the force that is being created, it may cause issues with vibrations and possibly component failure.

Who Does Balancing?

K23002 Knowledge of who performs the balancing procedures.

Engine balance is as important for "daily driver" engines as it is for high-performance or race engines. You may find as you repair engines that engine manufacturers offer different weight classes of connecting rods and pistons. This is because engine imbalance in a street application can cause customer dissatisfaction due to noise vibration and harshness, or NVH, complaints. Understanding the principles of engine balance and knowing that there are corrective measures for imbalance can assist you in building engines for general use as well as for performance or racing purposes.

The primary targets of engine balancing are the piston assemblies and crankshaft. These provide the largest reciprocating and rotational masses in the engine, respectively. A slight imbalance is acceptable for most street engines, but when looking at spinning the engine at higher speed, such as in a race engine, small imbalances can set up tremendous forces in the engine. Luxury car manufacturers also hold tight balance specifications to reduce NVH in their vehicles. To reduce undesirable harmonics in the engine, these must be balanced.

A professional balancing act requires all of the components be completely machined and fitted before balancing. If balancing used engine parts, it is essential that the parts are spotlessly clean and dry, with no dirt, oil, or grease on them (**FIGURE 23-1**). To balance the reciprocating components, piston, piston pin, connecting rod, bearing and ring set are weighed. The lightest pieces are identified, and other parts are machined to reduce weight so that each assembly is within 0.5 gram of the lightest component. It is important to work slowly and carefully during this process, as removing too much material from any component will create a new lightest part, requiring you to start the process again. Care also must be taken to ensure that the integrity and strength of components are not compromised.

The piston, piston pin, and ring set may be measured together (**FIGURE 23-2**). The pin and ring set cannot be adjusted, so the piston is machined to reduce the mass of the assembly to within 0.5 gram of the lightest set. Pistons may have balancing pads built at the bottom of the piston pin bosses for this purpose. Material can be cut away by turning in a lathe or by machining the balancing pads with an end mill.

Connecting rods must also be balanced within 0.5 gram. Rod balancing creates an interesting situation. Although the

FIGURE 23-1 Picking a machine shop should include considering the image that it is trying to portray. A clean machine shop is one that is worth doing business with because it shows an attention to detail.

FIGURE 23-2 Make sure that the entire rotating assembly is weighed so that all components are within specification of one another and whole assembly is balanced.

FIGURE 23-3 Balancing each connecting rod allows the machinist to weight match each one so that when all the rods are spinning on the crankshaft, they will not cause any unnecessary vibrations.

overall weight can simply be reduced in the heavier rods, the best result is achieved by matching the mass of each end of the rod. This is because the small end bore can be considered a reciprocating mass in the engine, whereas the big end is considered more of a rotational mass.

To balance the rods, the big end bore is placed on a pivot, the small end placed on a scale. The lightest weight is identified, and that rod set aside (**FIGURE 23-3**). Using a belt sander, the small ends of the remaining rods are lightened until the rod masses are equal. The entire rods are then weighted, and again the lightest rod is identified and set aside. The remaining rods have metal removed from the caps on the belt sander. Once each rod is within 0.5 gram of the lightest rod, the rod work is complete.

Once the piston and rod assemblies are matched, the crankshaft must be balanced in two planes. The first is around the axis of rotation, or the centerline of the crankshaft. The second is along the length of the crankshaft. Balance around the center of rotation is referred to as static balance. A statically balanced crankshaft set on knife-edge supports or bearings will not roll from any position. Sometimes the term "kinetic imbalance" is used, as most crankshaft balancers spin the crankshaft to make the measurement. Static imbalance results in the heavy spot being thrown outward as the crankshaft spins, causing the centerline of the crankshaft to shift with every rotation.

If the heavy spot is on one end of the crankshaft, this is referred to as dynamic imbalance. The tendency is for the crankshaft to flex as the heavy spot tries to come to the centerline of the crankshaft, perpendicular to the axis of rotation. The crankshaft is placed on a computerized balancing fixture, on special rollers that contain vibration sensors. A position sensor, called an encoder, is placed on the crankshaft. The encoder is used to identify where the heavy spots are located in relation to the TDC point of the crankshaft. Typically the TDC point is entered as the machine is programmed, and the encoder can indicate within 0.5 degree of crank rotation.

V-shaped engines require special assemblies, called bob weights, to be prepared and attached to the crankshaft. Bob weights have small washers, like tiny barbell weights, which can be placed on the clamping fixtures to simulate the mass of the rod and piston assemblies. The amount of weight in each assembly is calculated based on the geometry of the engine, the mass of the reciprocating weight, and a so-called "oil allowance." The oil allowance is a factor that simulates the weight of engine oil adhering to the rod/piston assembly. The mass of the bob weight is a percentage of the total reciprocating mass; the percentage varies with engine design. Although there are publications that provide the numbers required to calculate the bob weight mass manually, most crankshaft balancer computers will calculate the weight for you.

FIGURE 23-4 When balancing a crankshaft, the machinist uses a balancing machine to read the various vibrations so that they can be counteracted with weight in order to balance the crankshaft.

Crankshafts are the internally or externally balanced type. The internally balanced crankshafts are measured without harmonic balancer, flywheel, or flexplate installed. External balancing includes the balancer and flywheel or flexplate. The specified balancing may be based on engine design. Fully counterweighted engines are internally balanced. In some larger displacement engines, the available space for counterweights may be limited; therefore, these engines count on the flywheel and harmonic balancer to aid in balancing the crankshaft. If the engine design is externally balanced, the crankshaft must be balanced with the dampener and flywheel installed.

When the crankshaft is spun, the sensors in the balancing machine identify the imbalance location (**FIGURE 23-4**). Usually, material is removed from the heavy portion of the counterweights of the crankshaft by drilling; this is easier than welding on additional material. Crankshafts are balanced in two planes: in rotation and end to end. Rotational balancing is referred to as static balancing. Balancing the principle and power take-off ends is referred to as dynamic balancing.

Normally balance is corrected by drilling lightening holes into the counterweights. A drill head is often fitted to the machine to permit this process to be carried out without dismounting the crank assembly. Occasionally, it may be desirable to add a small amount of weight to one counterweight or another rather than drill more material out. In these cases, plugs made with higher specific gravity metals can be installed. The counterweight is drilled and the plug pressed into place. These so-called heavy metal plugs can also be used to correct crankshaft balance if a bit too much material is removed from a counterweight. The plugs often are fitted with splines to aid in holding them in place, and the bore can be peened over once the plugs are installed.

Tools Used

Balancing an engine's rotating assembly requires a small scale and balancing machine. The balancing machine uses the inputs from the machinist, weighing each individual part and the crankshaft spinning harmonics to determine where weight needs to be added and removed. Along with the big equipment, the machinist must have access to various drills, grinders, and welders to accomplish the needed addition and removal of material to get the crank balanced.

K23003 Knowledge of the purpose of engine blueprinting.

▶ Engine Blueprinting

Blueprinting is a means of ensuring that the conversion of power from combustion is balanced in the engine. Different-sized combustion chambers in a cylinder head, for example, result in slightly different compression ratios (**FIGURE 23-5**). Variation from cylinder to cylinder can result in harmonics being set up in the engine, especially at higher speed, which can be harmful to the engine and shorten engine life. By building "on spec," variations are reduced.

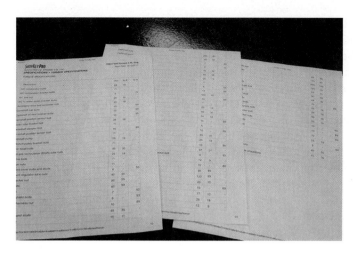

FIGURE 23-5 When blueprinting an engine, the builder must keep track of all its measurements so that if something breaks, he or she will know what type of component needs to be replaced. Also, when the measurements of the engine are known, the technician can see changes different areas of the engine are modified.

What Is Blueprinting?

Blueprinting involves much more machining and matching of components than a stock engine build. With a clear idea of what the intended end use of the engine will be, parts can be selected and matched. Some factors that are taken into consideration include the weight of vehicle; whether the car is intended for race or street; and the fuel the engine will burn. Maximum rpm, transmission selection, final drive ratio, and tire size may also be taken into consideration, either as engine design factors or as items that need to be matched to the engine once it is built. If the engine is to be installed in a race car, the class and style of racing may have restrictions on the work performed. If you are unsure of the rules, it is important to discuss with the client the application and clearly outline the work you are commissioned to perform.

Once the selected parts are in hand, the final fitting and machining is performed to achieve uniform breathing and compression ratio in each bore. Final assemblies are put together, checked, and disassembled numerous times to ensure that the engine is held to the specifications laid out in the contract with the customer.

Cylinder Head and Camshaft

Cylinder heads, valves, and camshafts are the heart of the engine breathing. The shape and size of the combustion chamber directly affect the compression ratio. Many shops "flow" the heads. Port size and shape affect cylinder filling, so for the smoothest running, most balanced engine, it is important to size these so that each cylinder is able to flow uniform volumes of intake and exhaust.

K23004 Knowledge of what is involved in blueprinting a cylinder head.

Flow testing the heads also allows the engine shop to match the camshaft so that the lift and duration of the camshaft can achieve the greatest cylinder filling. If a given head achieves maximum flow at 0.500" lift, for example, a camshaft with greater lift will not improve breathing and can introduce problems with valve to piston clearance or valve float. A cam with 0.500" lift will give the best performance possible with that head. If the intake and exhaust ports are rough, porting and polishing may take place. Removing any flashing, sharp edges, and smoothing the passageways for gases into and out of the cylinder head contribute to good flow (**FIGURE 23-6**). Following any polishing, the heads should be flowed to ensure that gases flow through each port equally.

Combustion chamber sizing may be tested next. Head specifications may provide a combustion chamber volume rating, but manufacturing tolerances mean that variations between cylinders may be present. The shape of the combustion chamber

FIGURE 23-6 Porting a cylinder head occurs when a technician uses a polisher to smooth the intake and exhaust ports so that air will flow in and out of the cylinder head with ease.

FIGURE 23-7 To correctly measure the combustion chamber, the cylinder head chamber must be measured to see the volume it holds. Using a burette to measure the amount of fluid that you deposit into the combustion chamber will allow you to calculate the total compression ratio of the engine.

K23005 Knowledge of what is involved in blueprinting an engine.

prevents easy measurement and calculation of the volume. To perform the measurement, a technique referred to as "pouring" or "cc-ing" the chamber can be implemented (**FIGURE 23-7**). In preparation to pour the heads, the valves and a spark plug should all be installed in each combustion chamber. A plate of clear plastic is prepared that completely covers the combustion chamber area. Drill a small hole in the plate so that the hole is near the combustion chamber wall when placed over the chamber. This hole should be no larger than 0.250". A thin layer of grease is applied to the cylinder head surface around the combustion chamber. Next, the plate is pressed into the grease and slightly elevated so that the hole is in the highest portion of the head. The grease provides a temporary seal between the cylinder head and the plastic plate.

The most accurate method of pouring a head is to use a burette—a measuring container used by chemists. These are often available from industrial supply stores. Burettes are a highly accurate graduated cylinder with a tap in the bottom. The valve allows precise metering of fluids. Syringes can also be used in a pinch, but are not as accurate as the burette. Fill the burette with thin oil, such as automatic transmission fluid or light engine oil, until the meniscus of the oil is at the zero line. Place the burette nozzle over the hole in the plastic plate, and open the valve. Allow the oil to flow into the hole in a gentle stream to prevent aeration or air bubbles from being trapped in the combustion chamber. Stop when the oil reaches the hole in the plate flush with the cylinder head surface; do not fill the hole in the plastic plate. You can now directly read the volume of the first combustion chamber. Document this volume by writing it down; do not trust your memory.

Repeat these steps for each combustion chamber. Once you have the variation between cylinders, you may have to increase the size of smaller chambers to match the biggest. Even if the combustion chambers are of equal volume out of the box for a set of cylinder heads, knowing the volume will aid in setting the engine up to the prescribed compression ratio.

Block Preparation

Cylinder block preparation may start by reworking the machining previously applied to the casting. To encourage freedom of the crankshaft rotation, the main bearing bores are line bored. Once the main bearing lines are corrected, main bearings can be select-fit to reduce the oil clearance to minimum specifications. This permits the crankshaft to take greater load without as much fear of oil displacement.

Once the line boring and bearing selection is complete, the deck heights are corrected. On in-line engines, the distance from the centerline of the crankshaft to the deck of the block is measured at the front and rear of the engine. Differences here are adjusted by machining the deck, using the crank main bores as the reference surfaces. In addition to fore and aft variation, the left and right banks of V-shape engines are often slightly asymmetrical, the distance from the centerline of the crankshaft being different from side to side. In order to ensure consistent compression ratio and geometric balance between cylinders, the heads are each decked to the same height.

Cylinder work begins by boring and honing the cylinders to fit new pistons. Especially in high-compression engines, piston ring sealing is critical (**FIGURE 23-8**). To achieve a properly sized and shaped cylinder, the honing tolerance for a high compression ratio is left a few thousandths higher than for a conventional engine build. Torque plates are tightened to the block to simulate the cylinder heads. The torque plates have bores in them to permit the hone to work the cylinder with the plates in place. When installed, the torque plates introduce stresses into the block and cause the cylinder bore to distort. The cylinders are honed to final size with the places attached, providing a perfectly round bore under tension. This means that if they are measured without the torque plates, the bores will be out of round. With the cylinder heads installed, the bores will once again be perfectly round.

Tools Used

Various tools are used in the blueprinting process, from cylinder hones to a cylinder head flow bench, to die grinders with attachments. The tools that are utilized for measurement in blueprinting are very precise instruments and should be taken care of so that damage doesn't hurt any of the internal workings. General automotive repair shop tools are also utilized to carry out some of the modifications that must be performed to make the engine conform to the specifications. Drills, die grinders, and other shaping tools are used to modify the engine components to fit precisely in the engine. Whatever tools you use, you must take your time to make sure that you are taking the required amount of material off and are not taking too much off.

FIGURE 23-8 Honing a cylinder is very important when setting up a freshly machined engine. The hone marks are areas that allow for the cylinder wall to retain oil to lubricate the piston rings so that they will seat on the cylinder wall correctly. Improperly seated rings allow blowby, and engine damage may occur.

▶ Wrap-Up

Ready for Review

▶ Blueprinting ensures that there is consistent combustion pressure on the crankshaft between cylinders; the balancing process focuses on the actual masses of internal engine components.

▶ Engine balancing involves the piston assemblies and crankshaft. These, respectively, provide the largest reciprocating and rotational masses in the engine. A slight imbalance is acceptable for most street engines, but when looking at spinning the engine at higher speed, such as in a race engine, small imbalances can set up tremendous forces in the engine.

▶ A professional balancing requires that all of the components be completely machined and fitted before balancing, and they must be free of any grease.

▶ To balance the reciprocating components, the piston, piston pin, connecting rod, bearing, and ring set are weighed.

▶ The lightest reciprocating components are identified, and other parts are machined to reduce weight so that each assembly is within 0.5 gram of the lightest component.

▶ The piston, piston pin, and ring set may be measured together.

▶ The pin and ring set cannot be adjusted, so the piston is machined to reduce the mass of the assembly to within 0.5 gram of the lightest set.

▶ Pistons may have balancing pads built at the bottom of the piston pin bosses for this purpose. Material can be cut away by turning in a lathe or by machining the balancing pads with an end mill.

▶ Connecting rods must also be balanced within 0.5 gram.

▶ Although the overall rod weight can simply be reduced in the heavier rods, the best result is achieved by matching the mass of each end of the rod. This is because the small end bore can be considered a reciprocating mass in the engine, whereas the big end is considered more a rotational mass.

▶ To balance the rods, the big end bore is placed on a pivot and the small end placed on a scale. The lightest weight is identified and that rod set aside.

▶ A belt sander is used to remove material at the small ends of the rods until the rod masses are equal.

▶ A statically balanced crankshaft set on knife-edge supports or bearings will not roll from any position.

▶ Crankshaft kinetic imbalance is used because most crankshaft balancers spin the crankshaft to make the measurement.

▶ Static imbalance results in the heavy spot being thrown outward as the crankshaft spins, causing the centerline of the crankshaft to shift with every rotation.

▶ If the heavy spot is on one end of the crankshaft, this is referred to as dynamic imbalance.

▶ The crankshaft is balanced on a computerized balancing fixture, where it is placed on special rollers that contain vibration sensors. A position sensor, called an encoder, is used to identify where the heavy spots are located in relation to the TDC point, which is entered as the machine is programmed; the encoder measures within 0.5 degree of crank rotation.

▶ V-shaped engines require bob weights to be prepared and attached to the crankshaft.

▶ Bob weights have small washers, like tiny barbell weights, which can be placed on the clamping fixtures to simulate the mass of the rod and piston assemblies. The weight is calculated based on engine geometry and mass of the reciprocating weight and a so-called "oil allowance."

▶ The oil allowance is a factor that simulates the weight of engine oil adhering to the rod/piston assembly.

▶ The mass of the bob weight is a percentage of the total reciprocating mass; the percentage varies with engine design, and most crankshaft balancer computers calculate the weight for you.

▶ Crankshafts can be either the internally or the externally balanced type.

▶ Internally balanced crankshafts are measured without the harmonic balancer, flywheel, or flexplate installed.

▶ External balancing includes the balancer and flywheel or flexplate.

▶ Engine balance is corrected by drilling lightening holes into the counterweights.

▶ Balancing an engine's rotating assembly requires a small scale and balancing machine.

▶ The balancing machine uses the inputs from the machinist weighing each individual part, and the crankshaft spinning harmonics, to determine where weight has to be added and removed.

▶ Port size and shape affect cylinder filling, called flow testing, so that each cylinder is able to flow uniform volumes of intake and exhaust.

▶ Flow testing the heads also allows the engine shop to match the camshaft so that the lift and duration of the camshaft can achieve the greatest cylinder filling.

▶ If the intake and exhaust ports are rough, porting, and polishing may take place. Removing any flashing and sharp edges, and smoothing the passageways for gases into and out of the cylinder head, contribute to good flow.

▶ Following any polishing, the heads should be flowed to ensure that gases flow through each port equally.

▶ Combustion chamber sizing uses a technique referred to as "pouring" or "cc-ing" the chamber.

▶ Once the line boring and bearing selection is complete, the deck heights are corrected.

▶ Deck height on in-line engines is the distance from the centerline of the crankshaft to the deck of the block and is measured at the front and rear of the engine.

▶ Differences in deck height are adjusted by machining the deck, using the crank main bores as the reference surfaces.

▶ The left and right banks of V-shape engines are often slightly asymmetrical because the distance from the centerline of the crankshaft is different from side to side. In order to ensure consistent compression ratio and geometric balance between cylinders, the heads are each decked to the same height.

▶ Cylinder work begins by boring and honing the cylinders to fit new pistons. Especially in high compression engines, piston ring sealing is critical.

▶ Torque plates are used to achieve a properly sized and shaped cylinder during the honing process.

▶ The torque plates introduce stresses into the block and cause the cylinder bore to distort.

Key Terms

blueprinting The process of measuring every component that will be installed in the engine so that it all fits precisely the same as the original intention of the engine.

engine balance The ability of the rotating assembly to offset the opposite harmonics as it rotates.

Review Questions

1. All of the following statements with respect to balancing and blueprinting are true, *except*:
   a. They ensure that there is a consistent combustion pressure inside the engine.
   b. They are necessary for the engine to produce the type of power that it is designed to produce.
   c. They are essential to ensure the longevity of the engine.
   d. They help the driver to drive without much effort.

2. The primary targets of the engine balancing are:
   a. piston assemblies and crankshaft.
   b. cylinder heads and crankshaft.
   c. valves and camshafts.
   d. combustion chamber and piston assemblies.

3. Which of the following components has reciprocating mass at one end and rotational mass at the another end?
   a. Connecting rod
   b. Piston
   c. Piston pin
   d. Bearing and ring set

4. The amount of weight in each assembly is calculated based on all of the following, *except*:
   a. the geometry of the engine.
   b. the mass of the reciprocating weight.
   c. oil allowance.
   d. the space available for counterweights.

5. What is the purpose of the engine blueprinting?
   a. Ensuring that the conversion of power from combustion is balanced in the engine
   b. To balance the center of gravity for the car
   c. Maintain uniform compression ratios
   d. Ensuring the conversion of chemical energy into mechanical energy

6. What is the function of blueprinting?
   a. Matching the engine build to the type of fuel used
   b. Selecting and matching the parts to the intended end use of the engine
   c. Achieving greater fuel efficiency
   d. Balancing an engine's rotating assembly

7. The most accurate method of pouring a head is to use a:
   a. measuring cup.
   b. pipette.
   c. burette.
   d. beaker.

8. The compression ratio of an engine is directly affected by the:
   a. number of cylinders.
   b. size of the cylinder blocks.
   c. port size and shape.
   d. shape and size of a combustion chamber.

9. Which of the following are used to achieve a properly sized and shaped cylinder during the honing process?
   a. Torque plates
   b. Bob weights
   c. Balancing pads
   d. Belt sanders

10. All of the following statements with respect to blueprinting an engine are true, *except*:
    a. Once the line boring and bearing selection is complete, the deck heights are corrected.
    b. The left and right banks of V-shape engines are often slightly asymmetrical.
    c. Cylinder work begins by boring and honing the cylinders to fit new pistons.
    d. Deck height on in-line engines is measured from centerline of the crankshaft and rear of the engine.

ASE Technician A/Technician B Style Questions

1. Technician A says that when replacing a piston, it doesn't matter which type or size of piston you install in the engine. Technician B says that using the service manual to verify and craft each individual part to the precise specification is the proper way to rebuild an engine. Who is correct?
   a. Tech A
   b. Tech B
   c. Both A and B
   d. Neither A nor B

2. Technician A states that balancing the rotating assembly, the machinist picks the lightest component and matches the rest of the components to it. Technician B says that balancing the engine is done with picking the correct gaskets. Who is correct?
   a. Tech A
   b. Tech B
   c. Both A and B
   d. Neither A nor B

3. Technician A says that a technician can do his or her own balancing with a small scale. Technician B states that normal engines do not need to be balanced at all. Who is correct?
   a. Tech A
   b. Tech B
   c. Both A and B
   d. Neither A nor B

4. Technician A says that blueprinting the engine is done when you make every internal component blue. Technician B says that utilizing OE service information will lead to the best possible outcomes when rebuilding an engine. Who is correct?
   a. Tech A
   b. Tech B
   c. Both A and B
   d. Neither A nor B

5. Technician A states that before final assembly after blueprinting, the cylinder block must be thoroughly cleaned, machined, and remeasured. Technician B states that the components that are replaced are already the correct size and should just be installed. Who is correct?
   a. Tech A
   b. Tech B
   c. Both A and B
   d. Neither A nor B

6. Technician A says that by machining the cylinder head ports, the engine can breathe more easily. Technician B states the faster the engine can intake and exhaust air, the more powerful it will be. Who is correct?
   a. Technician A
   b. Technician B
   c. Both A and B
   d. Neither A nor B

7. Technician A says that when blueprinting an engine, the builder must understand what its intended use is. Technician B states that not all engines are easily blueprinted. Who is correct?
   a. Tech A
   b. Tech B
   c. Both A and B
   d. Neither A nor B

8. Technician A states that flow testing the cylinder heads is a waste of effort. Technician B says that the camshaft must be matched to the cylinder heads on an engine for optimal power. Who is correct?
   a. Tech A
   b. Tech B
   c. Both A and B
   d. Neither A nor B

9. Technician A states that to lighten a crankshaft, metal is removed from the crankshaft counterweights. Technician B says that sometimes weight must be added in a different location to balance out the crankshaft. Who is correct?
   a. Tech A
   b. Tech B
   c. Both A and B
   d. Neither A nor B

10. Technician A states that in a manual transmission vehicle, the clutch plate and pressure plate must be balanced to the assembly also. Technician B says that engine balance is just as important to the daily driver as it is to the high-performance engine. Who is correct?
    a. Tech A
    b. Tech B
    c. Both A and B
    d. Neither A nor B

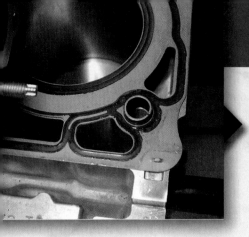

CHAPTER 24
Engine Assembly

NATEF Tasks

- **N24001** Inspect auxiliary shaft(s) (balance, intermediate, idler, counterbalance or silencer); inspect shaft(s) and support bearings for damage and wear; determine needed action; reinstall and time.

- **N24002** Assemble engine block.
- **N24003** Establish camshaft position sensor indexing.

Knowledge Objectives

After reading this chapter, you will have:

- **K24001** Knowledge of how to prepare to assemble an engine.
- **K24002** Knowledge of how to use precision measuring instruments.
- **K24003** Knowledge of how to perform installation checks before final assembly.
- **K24004** Knowledge of the steps for final assembly of the rotating components.
- **K24005** Knowledge of the proper procedures for checking installed parts as the engine gets assembled.

- **K24006** Knowledge of the different types of head bolts so proper application can be achieved.
- **K24007** Knowledge of the reasons for priming an engine.
- **K24008** Knowledge of the assembly of external engine components.
- **K24009** Knowledge of camshaft position sensor installation for engine operation.
- **K24010** Knowledge of timing belt or chain installation.

Skills Objectives

- **S24001** Perform a piston clearance check using a cylinder bore gauge.
- **S24002** Install a crankshaft.
- **S24003** Paint the engine and covers.
- **S24004** Install engine plugs.
- **S24005** Install head bolts.
- **S24006** Install torque-to-yield bolts.

- **S24007** Prime the engine.
- **S24008** Install the intake manifold.
- **S24009** Install the engine accessories.
- **S24010** Index the camshaft position sensor.
- **S24011** Replace the camshaft drive belt or chain.
- **S24012** Install valve stem seals on an assembled engine.

You Are the Automotive Technician

You have successfully disassembled, cleaned, and machined the engine parts and checked all necessary clearances. Prior to the final reassembly of the engine, you performed a temporary test buildup to verify that no additional machining was needed. After assembling the block and heads, you will need to install the timing belt and set the timing for all four camshafts.

1. Why is it important to perform a temporary test buildup of the rotating assembly prior to final assembly?
2. What damage is possible if you install the timing belt or chain with the wrong camshaft timing?
3. How are rod and main bearing clearances measured?

K24001 Knowledge of how to prepare to assemble an engine.

▶ Engine Assembly Preparation

The engine assembly preparation will start with cleaning all of the engine parts so that each part is in the best shape to put onto the engine. Simple steps of organization and cleanliness can make assembling the engine very easy and will help make the engine last a very long time. A clean work area also allows for room to lay out the necessary parts to assembly the engine without conflict and possibility of errors.

Introduction

Engine assembly is a process that must be carried out in a very clean environment and with the utmost attention to detail. Failure to heed this advice or carelessness during this process will result in an engine that may not live for more than a few minutes after being started up. In this chapter, we first perform a test buildup of the engine to measure all of the critical clearances and to make sure all of the parts work together properly. Next, if everything is within specifications, the engine will be carefully disassembled, cleaned once more, and painted so it is ready for final assembly.

Engine Preassembly

Engine preassembly is something that should be taken very seriously as this is where the technician can decide whether the components that have been selected are the correct ones for the application (**FIGURE 24-1**). Throughout this process, the technician evaluates the usage of the different pieces that are designated for this engine. If everything fits correctly, the technician will be able to move on to the next stage in the process.

Crankshaft and Block Preparation

Crankshaft

Like the camshaft, main bearing oil clearance and end play have to be confirmed. Main bearing clearance can be calculated from measurements taken with precision measurement tools or by using Plastigage.

Inspect the crankshaft again to ensure that it has not been nicked or otherwise damaged while in storage. If the crank had been reground or the bearing journals polished, thoroughly wash the crankshaft in solvent to remove any anticorrosion coating from the machine shop. Run a soft bristle rifle brush and solvent through the oil drillings in the journals to ensure that no grinding dust, metal particles, or dirt obstructs oil flow to the main journals or crankpins. Blow the crankshaft dry with compressed air, making sure the solvent is thoroughly cleared out of the oil galleries.

Measure the crankshaft main and crankpin journals with a suitable outside micrometer to confirm they were sized correctly by the machine shop. Confirm at this time that the bearings are also the correct replacement size for the crankshaft (**FIGURE 24-2**). Lay out all of the main bearing caps, bearings, and fasteners on a clean surface. If the engine uses select fit bearings, identify the main bore each bearing ought to be placed. Some engines use different select fit shells in the block and cap to create the correct clearance.

With the engine inverted on the engine stand, start by carefully checking each bearing boss and bore. Wipe each saddle and bearing cap with a dry lint-free cloth to remove any oil or dirt that may have worked its way down while working with the camshaft bearings. After wiping the backs of the first bearing, carefully install it into the appropriate saddle and bearing cap. Be mindful of the oil hole orientation. Ensure the locating tab is properly inserted into the notch in the bearing saddle. Repeat these steps for each subsequent bearing.

FIGURE 24-1 Organization of the engine components before installation allows the engine to be assembled easily with minimal errors.

Handle new bearings carefully. Some bearings have antiscuff coatings designed to aid in protecting the crankshaft during first start. Hold the shells by the edges as much as possible. The shells should snap in to the bores because of bearing spread, and there should be a small protrusion above each saddle and cap, providing bearing crush.

If you choose to measure and calculate the bearing clearance, carefully install the main bearing caps in the proper orientation. If a cradle-style main bearing cap assembly is used, ensure that it is facing in the correct direction. Lightly lubricate the fasteners as outlined in the service manual, and thread them into place. For engines using torque-to-yield fasteners, use the old fasteners for the pre-check. Torque all of the fasteners to specification in the torque sequence as published by the engine maker. Mark torque angle bolts as described earlier in this chapter. Using a **torque angle gauge** or torque angle torque wrench, tighten each fastener the further specified amount. Check that each paint mark is in the new position to ensure that no fasteners were missed.

Once the main bearing caps are installed correctly, measure the bearing ID. As always, use care to avoid damaging the bearing surfaces when measuring. The oil clearance is calculated by subtract the crankshaft main journal measurements you made earlier.

To check crankshaft bearing clearance by using Plastigage, place the clean and dry crankshaft in the saddle. Use care not to knock or bump the crank during installation. For engines using individual bearing caps, take a small piece of Plastigage and place it in the center of one journal. Do not use oil or grease to hold the Plastigage in place as it will soften and provide an inaccurate reading. Place the bearing cap for that journal in place. Confirm orientation of the cap. As mentioned before, if the engine uses torque-to-yield fasteners that are to be replaced, use the old fasteners for this check. Once you install the cap, do not turn the crankshaft or the Plastigage will smear, ruining your measurement.

Torque the fasteners to specification, and then tighten to the specified angle, if required. Remove the cap fasteners, and remove the cap. Compare the deformed Plastigage on the journal with the scale on the side of the paper Plastigage envelope to determine the oil clearance. Note your findings, and carefully remove the Plastigage from the crankshaft with your fingernail. A bit of oil on a clean rag will soften and remove any Plastigage transferred to the bearing cap. Repeat this process for each bearing cap in turn.

Checking the bearing clearance and end play is slightly different for engines using cradle-style main bearing caps (**FIGURE 24-3**). With all of the bearing shells installed, place the clean and dry crank in the block saddle. Place some Plastigage on each crank journal before installing the cradle. Again, using the original fasteners, torque and tighten each fastener to the correct angle, being careful to not turn the crankshaft. Then remove all of the fasteners, using the detorque sequence, and check each bearing clearance.

If the main bearing cradle includes a stiffening section that extends between the block rails and the oil pan, ensure that all surfaces are clean and free of old sealant before measuring the clearances (**FIGURE 24-4**). Once all clearances are verified, reinstall the bearing caps or cradle, and check end float as described in the following section.

FIGURE 24-2 When selecting components for replacement, before installing refer to service information to verify that the component meets the factory specifications.

FIGURE 24-3 Checking end play of a crankshaft is a crucial measurement, because if the crankshaft moves, it may cause other components to fail. Check the factory specifications to see whether the end play is within tolerances.

FIGURE 24-4 When installing components, make sure that they are free from gaskets, sealants, and corrosion so that they will seat correctly when installed.

Thrust Clearances

The crankshaft end play is controlled by the space between the thrust bearings and a precision ground thrust surface on the crankshaft. The **thrust bearings** can be manufactured as part of one of the main bearing shells or as separate replacement parts. The thrust bearing fits into reliefs machined in the saddle and matching cap. Usually the thrust bearings are located in the middle or rearmost bearing.

If the thrust bearings are part of the main bearing shell, the clearance can be checked by measurement and calculation before the crankshaft is installed. Using a telescoping gauge and a micrometer, first measure the distance between the crankshaft thrust bearing surfaces. Next, using a micrometer, measure the thickness of the thrust bearing shell when installed in the block and cap. The difference between these two numbers is the oil clearance.

Thrust clearance can also be measured with the crank installed. The most common method employed with either integral or discrete thrust bearings is to indicate the end float. To perform this method, place some assembly lubricant on the both halves of the main bearings. Be careful not to get any lubricant around the parting surface. You may use a small amount of grease to hold the individual thrust bearings to the block. Once again install the crankshaft in the main bearings, and torque the caps to specification. Set up a dial gauge on the end of the crankshaft. Using a suitable prybar, gently push the crankshaft fore and aft in the block to indicate the crankshaft thrust clearance, and compare to specifications.

Another method of checking thrust clearance with the crankshaft installed is to use feeler gauges between the thrust surface of the crankshaft and the thrust bearings. To perform this measurement, gently pry the crankshaft fully forward. Try increasingly thick feeler gauges between the thrust surfaces until you find a gauge that fits in the gap with a slight drag. The largest gauge that will fit is the oil clearance. You can double-check the clearance by pushing the crankshaft completely rearward and measuring again at the back of the thrust bearing.

If all of the bearing clearances have checked out, the crankshaft is ready for final installation.

Piston, Ring, and Block Clearance Checks

Piston Installed Height

S24001 Perform a piston clearance check using a cylinder bore gauge.

A final piston-related check that may be required on engines where the deck has been machined is **piston installed height**, also referred to as piston-to-deck height. If the piston-to-deck clearance is insufficient, there is a risk of the piston striking the cylinder head during operation.

Measuring piston installed height is particularly critical for diesel engines. Because diesel engines have high compression ratios, the clearance volume of the cylinder is very small. This is especially true in indirect injection engines, where the clearance volume is actually in a pre-chamber.

Confirming piston-to-deck clearance may be required on gasoline engines as well, especially those built for performance. We cover performance-related checks and corrections in the chapter on Blueprinting and Balancing. In most cases clearance between the piston and head with stock parts is not an issue as long as the machining done to true up the surfaces is not in excess of the manufacturer's limits.

This measurement is taken with a depth micrometer or a dial depth gauge. With the piston at TDC, measure down to the head of the piston (**FIGURE 24-5**). Compare the reading with specifications. Repeat the test for each piston.

For any diesel or gasoline engine, piston-to-head clearance lost to material removed during decking of the block and heads is usually compensated for by using a thicker head gasket. To restore original performance, the head gasket should be thicker by the amount removed from both the block and the head. If your measurement shows that the clearances cannot be restored using the thickest head gasket, you will have to consult with your machine shop for options.

To check piston clearance using a cylinder bore gauge, follow the steps in **SKILL DRILL 24-1**.

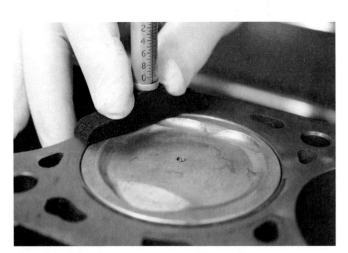

FIGURE 24-5 When changing pistons, the technician should do a piston height check to see whether the piston protrudes from the cylinder block. Too much protrusion will allow the piston to come in contact with the cylinder head, causing damage.

SKILL DRILL 24-1 Checking Piston Clearance Using a Cylinder Bore Gauge

1. Measure each piston according to the repair information, and record the measurement either on a worksheet or on the head of the piston with a felt pen.

2. Set up the cylinder bore gauge, using a specialized fixture or outside micrometer adjusted to the nominal cylinder diameter. When using a micrometer, great care must be taken to ensure the bore gauge is properly zeroed.

3. The cylinder bore gauge indicator must be preloaded to allow measurement in both directions. Set the gauge so the revolution counter is in the middle of travel, and zero the main pointer by turning the face bezel.

4. Install the cylinder bore gauge to the specified depth in the cylinder, and measure parallel to the crankshaft line. Gently rock the bore gauge back and forth. Measure again perpendicular to the crankshaft line.

Continued

5. While rocking the gauge back and forth, the graduation at which the dial indicator "rolls over," or changes direction, is the amount you must add or subtract from the setup diameter. For example, the nominal setup on this cylinder is 3.500". The dial indicator shows +0.035". The diameter is therefore 3.535". Record the largest diameter change for each cylinder.

6. Calculate the cylinder to piston clearance for each cylinder.

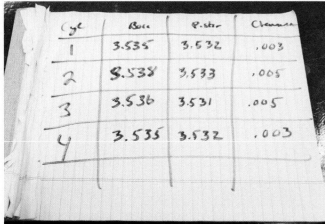

Installing the Piston on the Connecting Rod

There are two different ways to install the piston on the connecting rod, one way is called the press-fit type that is installed by using a heater that heats the small end of the connecting rod, then pressing a piston pin into the correct position, and allowing it to cool to keep the pin in the piston (**FIGURE 24-6**). The second type is the full float type that has the connecting rod machined to allow the installation of a bushing that the piston pin rides in (**FIGURE 24-7**). The piston pin is held in by circlips that snap into the piston. These pins can be removed by taking the circlips out and then removing the piston pin; this type allows for more movement of the piston on the pin, which reduces friction.

K24002 Knowledge of how to use precision measuring instruments.

▶ Temporary Test Buildup

Temporary buildup allows the technician to verify that the parts that he or she has gathered are correct for this buildup. It is better to find out any problems with materials in this stage before you try to assemble it for the final time. Along with putting the engine together, the technician can then start to determine what the finished product will look like and what must be done to do to modify the engine before it is put in the vehicle. Time spent in this phase of the assembly will save the technician time in the final assembly.

Using a Micrometer

Before using a micrometer to measure the crankshaft, it is important to make sure the crankshaft is clean and free of oil and grease. Use the **outside micrometer** to measure each main bearing journal, and record your findings (**FIGURE 24-8**). With all the main caps and bearings installed and torqued (the crankshaft is not installed at this time), use an **inside micrometer** or snap gauge to measure the inside diameter of the main bearing bore (**FIGURE 24-9**). Take

FIGURE 24-6 A press-fit piston pin is pressed into the connecting rod, which doesn't allow it to move. Because the pin doesn't move the piston is forced to stay in line with the connecting rod.

FIGURE 24-7 A full float piston pin is "floating" in the connecting rod and piston. This design reduces friction, and the pin is retained by clips that snap into the piston.

FIGURE 24-8 Measuring crankshaft journals with an outside micrometer.

FIGURE 24-9 Measuring the inside of a main bearing.

care not to damage the bearing surface. This procedure does take some experience, but when performed correctly, it is very accurate.

Once the inside micrometer or snap gauge is set to the correct size, read the inside micrometer or use the outside micrometer to measure the outside of the snap gauge, and record your findings. Subtract the crankshaft main journal readings from the main bearing bore readings, and record your findings. The difference will be in thousandths and ten-thousandths of an inch, giving you the bearing clearance. Check this with the manufacturer's specifications.

Using a Bore Gauge

When using a **bore gauge**, it is important to make sure the crankshaft is clean and free from oil or grease. You need to measure the main journals with an outside micrometer and record your findings. Next, use a bore gauge setting fixture to set the bore gauge according to the crankshaft main journals measurements, and zero the dial. With all the main bearings in place and the main caps torqued to the proper torque setting, use the bore gauge to check your clearance (**FIGURE 24-10**). The reading on the bore

FIGURE 24-10 Checking bearing clearance with a bore gauge.

Using a cylinder bore gauge is often considered a faster and more reliable method of measuring bore diameter, as the gauge is only set up once. However, an error in setting up the gauge will skew all of your readings! Often machinists take a second measurement on the first bore, using an inside mike or telescoping gauge, to verify the bore gauge setup.

K24003 Knowledge of how to perform installation checks before final assembly.

S24002 Install a crankshaft.

gauge is the bearing clearance. Record the clearance, and check the reading against the manufacturer's specifications.

Using Plastigage

Plastigage is an extruded plastic thread that comes in different sizes, depending on the expected clearances to be checked. For main bearings, choose the gauge that is sized for 0.0005" to 0.003" (0.013 to 0.076 mm); it should be green in color. Put a drop of oil on each bearing, and wipe it so that there is a very thin, even layer. It is not a good idea to lay a crankshaft on totally dry bearings. Install the crankshaft into the main journals, making sure you do not turn the crankshaft.

Cut a piece of plastic gauge just short of the width of the bearing, and lay it across the width of the crankshaft main journal. Using the proper main cap, torque the main cap bolts to manufacturer's specifications, making sure the crankshaft does not turn. If the crankshaft turns during this measurement, the gauge strip will smear, giving an inaccurate reading.

After the main cap has been torqued into place, loosen the bolts and take the cap off. The plastic gauge strip will be stuck to the crankshaft journal or the bearing insert. Check the paper that the plastic gauge came in to see which width matches the plastic gauge, and read the chart for the proper bearing clearance. Check your findings against the manufacturer's specifications. Repeat this process for all the main journals, and record your findings.

Installing Main Bearings

Lay out all of the main bearing caps, bearings and fasteners on a clean surface. If the engine uses select fit bearings, identify the main bore where each bearing ought to be placed. Some engines use different select fit shells in the block and cap to create the correct clearance.

With the engine inverted on the engine stand, start by carefully checking each bearing boss and bore. Wipe each saddle and bearing cap with a dry, lint-free cloth to remove any oil or dirt that may have worked its way down while working with the camshaft bearings. After wiping the backs of the first bearing, carefully install it into the appropriate saddle and bearing cap. Be mindful of the oil hole orientation. Ensure the locating tab is properly inserted into the notch in the bearing saddle. Repeat these steps for each subsequent bearing.

Handle new bearings carefully. Some bearings have antiscuff coatings designed to aid in protecting the crankshaft during first start. Hold the shells by the edges as much as possible. The shells should snap in to the bores due to bearing spread, and there should be a small protrusion above each saddle and cap, providing bearing crush.

Checking Main Bearing Clearance

Inspect the crankshaft again to ensure that it has not been nicked or otherwise damaged while in storage. If the crank has been reground or the bearing journals polished, thoroughly wash the crankshaft in solvent to remove any anticorrosion coating from the machine shop. Run a soft bristle rifle brush and solvent through the oil drillings in the journals to ensure that no grinding dust, metal particles, or dirt will obstruct oil flow to the main journals or crankpins. Blow the crankshaft dry with compressed air, ensuring the solvent is thoroughly cleared out of the oil galleries.

Measure the crankshaft main and crankpin journals with a suitable outside micrometer to confirm they were sized correctly by the machine shop. Confirm at this time that the bearings are also the correct replacement size for the crankshaft.

Torque the fasteners to specification, and then tighten to the specified angle, if required. Remove the cap fasteners and the cap. Compare the deformed Plastigage on the journal with the scale on the side of the paper Plastigage envelope to determine the oil clearance. Note your findings, and carefully remove the Plastigage from the crankshaft with your fingernail. A bit of oil on a clean rag will soften and remove any Plastigage transferred to the bearing cap. Repeat this process for each bearing cap in turn.

To test install a crankshaft, follow the steps in **SKILL DRILL 24-2**.

SKILL DRILL 24-2 Installing a Crankshaft

1. If the main journals of the crankshaft were cut undersize, make sure the new main bearing inserts match the undersized journals. Before you open the sealed bearing insert package, double-check the labels to make sure they are the correct type and size.

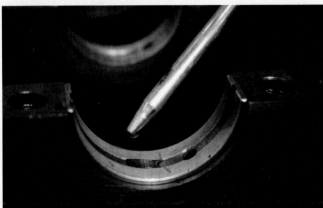

2. Wipe out the saddles of the block and the cap-to-block mating surfaces, being sure there is no debris or lint left behind. Then press the bearings (which have an oil hole) into place by hand. Make sure the tang in the bearing fits into the groove in the bearing saddle. Check that the oil holes in the block line up with the holes in the bearings.

3. Install the bearings in the bearing caps, being careful to line up the bearing tang with the groove in the cap.

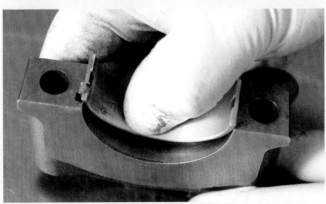

4. Put a drop of oil on each bearing insert, and wipe it so that there is a thin, even layer. Make sure to wipe some oil on the thrust surface of the thrust bearing as well.

Continued

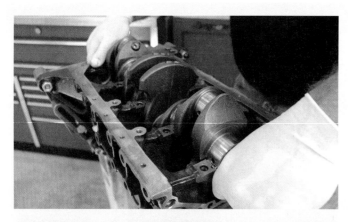

5. Ask for some lifting help if it is needed, and then gently set the crank into the block.

6. Lay a strip of the Plastigage on top of each of the main journals of the crank.

7. Place the main caps in their proper places, following any stampings or markings you made during disassembly.

8. When all the main bearing cap bolts are in and hand tightened, torque them to the manufacturer's specification. It is good practice to tighten the bolts in steps and following the manufacturer's sequence, if given.

Continued

9. Once the bolts are tightened to the correct torque, unscrew them, but again be very careful not to move the crankshaft accidentally. When the bolts are fully unscrewed, lift them up and tap on them gently to loosen the cap.

10. The squashed piece of plastic gauge material should be stuck to the main journal or to the bearing insert in the cap. Hold the measuring strip that came with the gauge next to the squashed plastic. Make sure you are looking at the correct side of the measure; there is usually an inch scale and a metric scale. The number next to the strip that is the closest match to the compressed Plastigage strip will be the size of the main bearing clearance.

11. Put some oil on the bearing inserts in the caps. Refer to the marks that you stamped on the caps to make sure the correct ones go in the correct place. Torque all of the regular main caps first, and leave the cap that has the thrust bearings as the last one.

12. You need to seat the thrust bearing before you torque it. Put a block of wood against the crankshaft, and tap it forward and backward with a hammer. Doing so will ensure that the upper and lower thrust bearing shells are lined up with each other. Now you can torque the cap that has the thrust bearings in it. When all of the caps are torqued, the crank should be very easy to turn by hand. You should not feel any binding or tight spots.

Thrust Bearing and Crankshaft End Play

The crankshaft end play is controlled by the space between the thrust bearings and a precision ground thrust surface on the crankshaft. The thrust bearings can be manufactured as part of one of the main bearing shells or as separate replacement parts. The thrust bearing fits into reliefs machined in the saddle and matching cap. Usually the thrust bearings are located in the middle or rearmost bearing. If the thrust bearings are part of the main bearing shell, the clearance can be checked by measurement and calculation before the crankshaft is installed. Using a telescoping gauge and a micrometer, first measure the distance between

FIGURE 24-11 Checking thrust bearing clearance, using a feeler gauge.

the crankshaft thrust bearing surfaces. Next, using a micrometer, measure the thickness of the thrust bearing shell when installed in the block and cap. The difference between these two numbers is the oil clearance.

Thrust clearance can also be measured with the crank installed. The most common method employed with either integral or discrete thrust bearings is to indicate the end float. To perform this method, place some assembly lubricant on both halves of the main bearings. Be careful not to get any lubricant around the parting surface. You may use a small amount of grease to hold the individual thrust bearings to the block. Once again install the crankshaft in the main bearings and torque the caps to specification. Set up a dial gauge on the end of the crankshaft. Using a suitable prybar, gently push the crankshaft fore and aft in the block to indicate the crankshaft thrust clearance, and compare to specifications.

Another method of checking thrust clearance with the crankshaft installed is to use feeler gauges between the thrust surface of the crankshaft and the thrust bearings. To perform this measurement, gently pry the crankshaft fully forward. Try increasingly thick feeler gauges between the thrust surfaces until you find a gauge that fits in the gap with a slight drag. The largest gauge that will fit is the oil clearance. You can double-check the clearance by pushing the crankshaft completely rearward and measuring again at the back of the thrust bearing (**FIGURE 24-11**). If all of the bearing clearances have checked out, the crankshaft is ready for final installation.

Test Installing the Piston and Rod Assemblies

Connecting rod oil clearance can be measured in the same way as the main clearances; measurement and calculation or Plastigage. The connecting rods also need to be checked for side clearance, but this must be done with the connecting rods installed. When using the measure and calculate technique, the piston does not have to be installed on the connecting rod. If this is the technique that you elect to use, it is recommended to make this check before checking piston clearances. With the pistons installed, there is a greater risk of damaging the pistons than with the Plastigage technique. Moreover, great care must be taken to keep the connecting rod caps aligned properly when torquing the fasteners.

With bearings properly installed in their bores, assemble the rod caps onto the connecting rods. As with the crankshaft bearings, note any oil holes, and ensure that the oil holes in the bearing match the holes in the rod. Be mindful of the marks indicating orientation, especially with fractured rod caps. In order to check the connecting rod clearance with Plastigage, the piston and connecting rod assembly must be assembled. To prevent excessive skirt scuffing and save unneeded handling of the pistons and rods, the piston rings are installed, and the pistons will be installed once only. If for some reason you need to change bearings, it is usually possible to do this without fully removing the piston.

First, clean and dry the rod and cap. Fit the bearings into the rod and cap of each assembly. For select fit bearings, double-check that the correct bearing is placed in the assembly. Install the cap on the rod in the correct orientation, and thread the nuts on the studs, or screw the bolts in a turn or two. This will keep your parts together and prevent unnecessary clutter and confusion. Next, install the piston rings on each piston.

On a clean work surface, lay out the ring set. There are typically three rings on each piston—the upper two compression rings and oil control rings. Examine the rings and service information to understand how the top of each ring is indicated. Instructions are usually also printed on the ring packaging. As discussed in a previous chapter, the shape of each ring contributes to its ability to seal compression and scrape oil only if it is correctly installed. Typically the letter "T," a dot, or other symbol indicates the top of the ring (**FIGURE 24-12**).

Place the first piston and connecting rod assembly in a bench vise. Use soft jaw, and clamp lightly on the connecting rod such that the skirt of the piston rests on top of the jaws.

This will prevent the piston from rocking while you are installing the rings, and makes the job easier. Start installing the rings from the bottom up.

If the oil ring is one piece, using a piston ring expander, gently open the ring so that it can slip over the head of the piston into its groove. For multipiece rings, install the separator first, and then gently thread the side rails into the groove above and below the separator. Position the parting line of the expander to the center of the piston pin. Install the first of the oil scraper rails, which go above and below the oil expander ring. Start it about 45 degrees to one side of the expander gap, and slide it in between the roof of the groove and the top of the expander ring. Start the other scraper rail about 45 degrees to the other side of the expander gap, and slide it into the bottom slot, or according to the published service information.

Install the second compression ring by expanding it gently with the piston ring installer. Expand the ring as much as you need to get it over the piston without dragging the ring over the piston, but no more (**FIGURE 24-13**). Over-expanding the ring can cause it to twist and break. Never try to thread a compression ring on, or try to use your fingers to expand the ring; doing so will break the ring. Be sure to observe the marking for the top of the ring. Complete installation by positioning the first compression ring in the same way.

Once the rings are installed, ensure that they all move freely in their grooves and that there are no segments of the oil control ring package that are overlapped or out of place. Lay the first piston assembly aside, and repeat the steps for each subsequent piston. Take the piston and rod assembly for the first cylinder, and place it in the vise again, as you did for ring installation. Orient the piston rings so that the gaps are in the location specified in the service information. It is critical that the gaps are offset when the piston is installed to prevent combustion gases from simply flowing through the gaps. Offsetting the ring gaps reduces the amount of gases that get past the rings—called blowby—to acceptable levels. The gaps are usually placed just off the wrist pin line, not against the thrust surfaces (**FIGURE 24-14**).

Before the piston and rings can be installed, the rings must be pushed into the grooves in the piston, using a piston ring compressor. Several types of compressor are available (**FIGURE 24-15**). The most common designs use an adjustable band that can be slackened to fit the band over the uncompressed rings. When the band is tightened, the rings are compressed into the grooves.

FIGURE 24-12 Different brands of piston rings have different markings for installation direction. Be sure to read the information that is with the rings so that they are installed in the correct direction, or engine damage could result.

FIGURE 24-13 When installing piston rings, use a ring expander so that uniform pressure is applied to the piston ring, to prevent breakage.

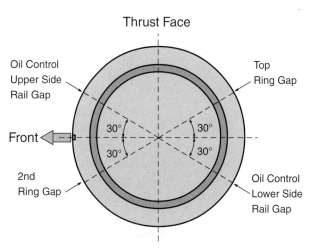

FIGURE 24-14 When positioning the piston rings once they are installed on the piston, make sure the gaps are not in line so that combustion pressure is pushed into the crankcase. Excessive blowby can cause the engine to build up positive pressure in the crankcase.

FIGURE 24-15 Various piston ring compressors are used depending on the application. Choose the correct one for the size of the piston.

FIGURE 24-16 The piston ring compressor may have locating tabs that help with centering it in the cylinder bore.

FIGURE 24-17 When installing the piston into the cylinder, be aware of the location of the connecting rod, piston rings, and the indexing of the piston toward the front of the engine. This occurs during the test install phase, which means we are verifying that everything fits perfectly.

Adjustable ring compressors are convenient because they can be used to fit a variety of piston sizes. Where many engines with a given size of piston are repaired, rigid ring compressors can be used. Rigid compressors are carefully sized tapered sleeves. The sleeve starts at a diameter slightly larger than the uncompressed rings and tapers to the diameter of the piston. The piston is simply pushed through the sleeve into the cylinder. These compressors are very fast to use, but a different sleeve must be purchased for each piston size.

Regardless of the compressor design, be mindful of installing them in the correct direction. Most band-style compressors have small locating tabs that prevent the tool from being drawn into the cylinder with the piston. Usually the tension of the band tool should be greatest near the block when the piston is being installed. If you are in doubt, consult the tool manufacturer's instructions (**FIGURE 24-16**). Wipe the piston ring compressor with a clean shop towel to remove any debris, and then place some clean engine oil or assembly lubricant in the compressor band. Locate the compressor over the rings. Leave a portion of the skirt exposed to locate the piston in the cylinder. When installing the ring compressor, ensure the locating tabs or detents face down. Use care when tightening the compressor, to ensure that all of the rings are compressing into their grooves.

Remove the bearing cap, and set it aside. If the connecting rod has studs and nuts retaining the cap, install commercially available protectors or some lengths of fuel line on the studs. Often called rod protectors, these are really to protect the crankpin from nicks as the pistons are installed.

Test Installing Pistons

Rotate the crankshaft so that the crankpin for cylinder 1 is at bottom dead center (BDC). Carefully wipe the cylinder bore with a clean, dry shop towel, and then with a shop towel dampened with engine oil. Carefully install the piston skirt into the cylinder bore, observing correct orientation (**FIGURE 24-17**). Tap the edges of the ring compressor lightly to seat it against the deck of the block. If it is uneven, a ring could escape, expand, and become broken as you are installing the piston. While holding the compressor firmly against the block, use a piston hammer or hammer handle to gently tap or push the piston through the compressor. If the piston does not tap in easily, stop and check: something is wrong. If you force things, you could damage the new ring set or piston.

Checking Piston-to-Deck Height

A final piston-related check that may be required on engines where the deck has been machined is piston installed height, also referred to as piston-to-deck height. If the piston-to-deck clearance is insufficient, there is a risk of the piston striking the cylinder head during operation.

Measuring piston installed height is particularly critical for diesel engines. Because diesel engines have high compression ratios, the clearance volume of the cylinder is very small. This is especially true if engines using indirect injection engines where the clearance volume is actually in a pre-chamber. Confirming piston-to-deck clearance may be required on gasoline engines as well, especially those built for performance. In most cases, clearance between the piston and head with stock parts is not an issue as long as the machining done to true up the surfaces is not in excess of the manufacturer's limits. This measurement is taken with a depth micrometer or a dial depth gauge. With the piston at TDC, measure down to the head of the piston. **FIGURE 24-18** shows this test being performed. Compare the reading with specifications. Repeat the test for each piston.

For any diesel or gasoline engines, piston-to-head clearance lost to material removed during decking of the block and heads is usually compensated for by using a thicker head gasket. To restore original performance, the head gasket should be thicker by the amount removed from both the block and the head. If your measurement shows that the clearances cannot be restored using the thickest head gasket, you will have to consult with your machine shop for options.

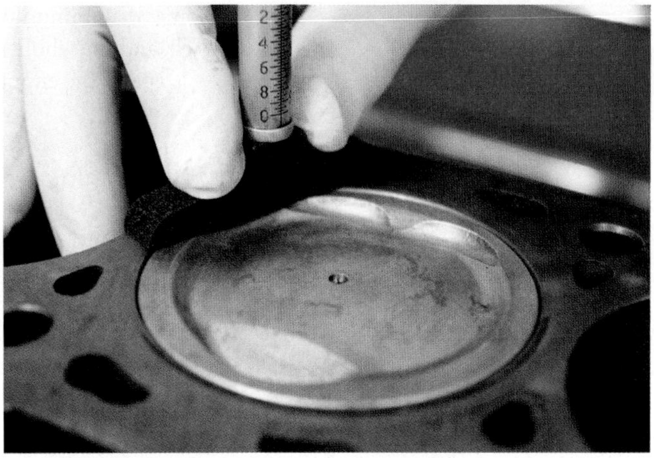

FIGURE 24-18 Checking piston-to-deck height.

Checking Piston-to-Valve Clearance of a Performance Camshaft

If a performance camshaft is used and there is a higher lift and more duration in the cam profile than in a stock camshaft, it is recommended to check piston-to-valve clearance. At the end of the exhaust stroke, as the piston travels to the top of the cylinder (TDC), the exhaust valve is just closing and the intake valve is just beginning to open. There has to be enough clearance so that the pistons do not hit the valves, which would result in bent valves and damaged pistons.

To check this clearance, the crankshaft, piston, and rod must be installed in the block. After installing the piston and rod, temporarily install the cylinder head along with the head gasket and valvetrain. Just remember that if hydraulic lifters are used, they will have to be pumped up first, and lighter test springs should be used in place of the stock valve springs so that the valves will open fully. The clearance can be checked by using one of two methods: the clay method or the dial indicator method. Both methods show you the minimum amount of clearance between the piston and the valve. The clay method gives an imprint of where the valve and piston have an interference issue so that you will be better able to determine how to fly cut the pistons if necessary. The dial indicator method allows you to check the clearance at various positions of the piston.

▶ Final Assembly of the Engine Rotating Components (Short Blocks)

This section of the chapter is where we wrap up the reassembly of the short block of the engine. Attention must be paid to this portion of the engine build as it needs to be completed properly to make sure the engine lives a long life. A mistake here could cause the engine to fail the first time that it is run.

Painting the Engine

From the factory, cast iron engines are painted to protect from rust and corrosion. Although refinishing the engine is not strictly part of an engine overhaul, it does give the whole rebuilding job a professional, finished look. Some engine shops paint the engine as standard practice to demonstrate attention to detail and the quality of their work. Other organizations paint upon request, such as a custom engine build where the owner wishes a specific color.

Repainting is a mandatory part of the rebuild if the cast iron components have been cleaned in a caustic hot tank or with a steam cleaner. During these processes, the original paint is removed. If left unfinished, the cast iron will rust very quickly, and the freshly rebuilt engine will have shoddy appearance. For aesthetic purposes, the various stamped or cast metal covers should also be painted when the block is refinished. The engine can be painted before or after installing the oil gallery and soft plugs. Components can also be painted separately, as long as care is taken to mask any sealing surfaces. This may be done where the client wishes a specific color scheme or does not want certain parts such as

N24001 Inspect auxiliary shaft(s) (balance, intermediate, idler, counterbalance or silencer); inspect shaft(s) and support bearings for damage and wear; determine needed action; reinstall and time.

N24002 Assemble engine block.

K24004 Knowledge of the steps for final assembly of the rotating components.

S24003 Paint the engine and covers.

chrome or aluminum valve covers to be sprayed. Often, the engine is partially assembled as a shell, and the whole unit refinished at the same time.

To paint the engine and covers, follow the steps in **SKILL DRILL 24-3**.

SKILL DRILL 24-3 Painting the Engine and Covers

1. Prepare the engine parts for painting by building an empty shell of the long block, and then paint everything. Install all the bolts you want to have painted, but make sure you tighten at least four bolts for the heads and the intake. You do not need to paint any gaskets or internal parts. The covers will mask off all the big openings, but for all the other holes, use some masking tape and cut around the edges with a razor blade.

2. When the masking is done, wipe all the surfaces to be painted with a degreaser or lacquer thinner to prepare the surface and remove any oil residue. Put some old spark plugs in the heads.

3. In a well-ventilated area and wearing a painter's mask, spray the engine with your chosen color of engine paint. You can also spray a coat or two on any accessories that you want to protect and brighten up with some color.

Installing the Soft Plugs and Oil Gallery Plugs

To help ensure that the engine has no leaks when started up, all the oil gallery plugs and soft plugs have to be installed. The core plugs could actually have been installed before any other work was done on the block, but if you discovered anything during your preassembly checks requiring further machining, they may have to be removed again. The oil pressure switch or sensor can be installed with the gallery plugs.

Make sure all oil galleries are clean and clear of debris. You can check this visually with a flashlight, or blow air through the passageways. Next, apply a small amount of appropriate sealer on the gallery plug's threads, and thread them into the block and head. The soft plugs will need an appropriate sealer applied to the soft plug and the block's sealing edge. Soft plugs are hammered into place in the block and in some heads. To install the engine plugs, follow the steps in **SKILL DRILL 24-4**.

S24004 Install engine plugs.

SKILL DRILL 24-4 Installing Engine Plugs

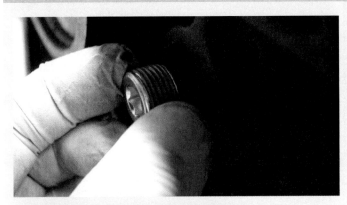

1. Start with the bare block sitting on the floor, with the rear area facing up. The rebuild kit should come with all of the oil gallery and soft plugs included. Any threaded plugs, such as the rear oil gallery plugs, should be coated with a sealer, preferably a liquid Teflon or a similar non-hardening sealer. Do not use Teflon tape; pieces can break off inside and cause an oil system clog. These plugs are usually a tapered pipe thread, so do not over-tighten them.

2. Clean the edges of the water jacket holes before you install the soft plugs.

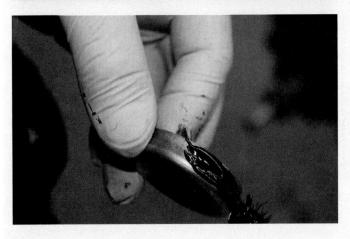

3. Next, coat the soft plug with a non-hardening sealer. Wipe it so that it is thin and even, being careful not to leave any bare spots.

Continued

4. Select a large impact socket that is slightly smaller than the inside diameter of the soft plug. Tap each soft plug in until it is just below the beveled edge of the water jacket opening.

5. Turn the block over so that the front is facing up, and select a punch that is smaller than the inner diameter of the front oil gallery plugs. Wipe a small dab of sealer evenly around each plug and tap it in until it is 1/16" (1.6 mm) below the surface of the block.

6. When the oil gallery plugs are installed, use a chisel to indent the surface of the block around each opening in at least two places. This will keep the plugs from backing out when the oil pressure builds.

7. Turn the block so the soft plug holes are facing up. This way it will be easier to clean and seal the side water jacket holes. Be careful as you tap the plugs in; sometimes they start to go crooked. If one does start to go in at an angle, tap it on the high side, and the plug will straighten out as it goes in. To finish off the water jacket, install the drain plugs while the block is upside down, also with some thread sealer. Put the block back on the engine stand.

8. Check for miscellaneous plugs. Almost every engine has some hidden plug, like an oil gallery plug, in an odd place. Carefully review your disassembly notes and the service information to make sure you do not miss any plugs.

Once all of the core and gallery plugs are installed, it is time to install any final items located inside the oil pan and behind the front cover. If you removed the camshaft from the cam-in-block engine, reinstall it now after lubricating the cam lobes and journals with the specified break-in lubricant or engine assembly lube. For in-block camshafts, install the timing set now. Camshaft timing is covered in detail after head installation, to include overhead camshaft engines.

For engines incorporating a one-piece rear main seal, install it now. You need access to the rear of the block to place the seal. To install the seal, you will probably have to take the block off the stand so that you can access the rear area of the block and drive the new seal into the bore. Be careful not to tear the lip of the seal. Because it is often a large seal, special tools are often recommended. You then need to replace the engine onto the stand.

Many engines use an adapter housing that bolts to the back of the block (**FIGURE 24-19**). The oil pan usually seals over this housing. The rear main seal can be driven in before the adapter is sealed and bolted into place. It may be possible to install the seal and retainer assembly while it is on the block if there is enough clearance between the block and engine stand adapter to place the seal and retainer assembly on the block and torque the fasteners. When installing the seal and retainer, use care not to damage the sealing lips. Lubricate the seal lips well with engine assembly lubricant, and gently encourage the seal over the crankshaft principle end.

FIGURE 24-19 In some rear main seals, an adapter housing is bolted to the back of the cylinder block. When you replace the rear main seal, it is recommended that you replace the gasket on the rear main seal housing.

Installing the Crankshaft

Once the bearing clearances are correct, remove the crankshaft. Apply engine assembly lubricant to the bearing shells in the block, and carefully place the crankshaft in the saddle. Place assembly lubricant on the cap bearing surfaces. Being careful to keep the parting surfaces—between cap and block—completely free of lubricant, install each cap in turn, starting from the center out.

If the engine has a two-piece main seal, install the upper half before lowering the crankshaft into place. Offset the ends of the seal so that one end sits slightly higher than the block surface and the other end slightly lower than the block surface. That way the parting seam on the seal is not exactly lined up with the block surface, which helps prevent leaks. On a neoprene rubber seal, the pointy lip must point toward the inside of the engine. When you press it into place, use the plastic protector shim between the seal and the block to keep the rubber back of the seal from being damaged by the sharp edge of the block. For engines with an older type of rope seal, work the rope into the groove of the block, and then use a large socket to tap it deeper into the groove. Cut off the excess flush with the block, using a razor knife. Put a little oil or assembly lube on the lip of the rope so the seal will not burn out on start-up. Place a dab of silicone sealer on each side of the seal, where the rear cap meets the metal of the block, to prevent oil from leaking from the rear of the block. Spread a little silicone sealer on the ends of neoprene or rope seals as well.

Collect all of the main bearing cap fasteners. Torque-to-yield fasteners should be replaced with new ones for final assembly. Lubricate the bolts as specified in the service literature. Carefully torque each fastener to specification in the torque pattern and stages specified. Sometimes it is advised to bump the crankshaft back and forth to seat the thrust bearing between torque stages. Follow the service information recommendations. To complete the torque angle or torque-to-yield tightening process, mark the fastener heads, and tighten each fastener to the specified angle.

Finally, ensure the crankshaft turns freely in the new bearings. If any binding occurs, stop and correct the trouble before continuing.

Installing Piston Rings

Place the first piston and connecting rod assembly in a bench vise. Use soft jaw, and clamp lightly on the connecting rod such that the skirt of the piston rests on top of the jaws.

▶ **TECHNICIAN TIP**

Some builders squeeze the bearing slightly to prevent the bearing back from being scraped on the sharp edge of the parting surface when installing.

▶ **TECHNICIAN TIP**

Some technicians choose to minimize the chance of damaging the new rings by leaving them off the piston until their checks are finalized. This is often done where there have been significant machining operations performed, or custom parts are being installed and the pistons are likely to be removed and replaced multiple times during the buildup. You may wish to do this for a stock engine where torque-to-yield studs are used, as the studs will have to be knocked out and new ones installed for final assembly. Where torque-to-yield bolts are used, there is no need to remove the rod to change the fasteners.

FIGURE 24-20 When installing the piston ring, you need to use the expander to carefully install the ring on the piston. Start with the coil control ring and work upward.

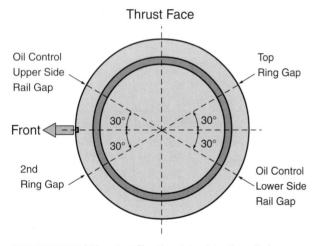

FIGURE 24-21 When installing the piston into the cylinder block, verify that the piston ring gaps are still separate.

This prevents the piston from rocking while you are installing the rings, and makes the job easier. Start installing the rings from the bottom up.

If the oil ring is one piece, using a piston ring expander, gently open the ring so that it can slip over the head of the piston into its groove. For multipiece rings, install the separator first, and then gently thread the side rails into the groove above and below the separator. Position the parting line of the expander to the center of the piston pin. Install the first of the oil scraper rails, which go above and below the oil expander ring. Start it about 45 degrees to one side of the expander gap, and slide it in between the roof of the groove and the top of the expander ring. Start the other scraper rail about 45 degrees to the other side of the expander gap, and slide it into the bottom slot, or according to the published service information.

Install the second compression ring by expanding it gently with the piston ring installer. Expand the ring as much as you need to get it over the piston without dragging the ring over the piston, but no more (**FIGURE 24-20**). Over-expanding the ring can cause it to twist and break. Never try to thread a compression ring on, or try to use your fingers to expand the ring; doing so will break the ring. Be sure to observe the marking for the top of the ring. Complete installation by installing the first compression ring in the same way.

Once the rings are installed, ensure that they all move freely in their grooves and that there are no segments of the oil control ring package that are overlapped or out of place. Lay the first piston assembly aside, and repeat the steps for each subsequent piston.

Take the piston and rod assembly for the first cylinder and place it in the vise again, as you did for ring installation. Orient the piston rings so that the gaps are in the location specified in the service information. It is critical that the gaps are offset when the piston is installed, to prevent combustion gases from simply flowing through the gaps. Offsetting the ring gaps reduces the amount of gases that get past the rings—called blowby—to acceptable levels. The gaps are usually placed just off the wrist pin line, not against the thrust surfaces (**FIGURE 24-21**).

Installing Pistons in the Block

Before the piston and rings can be installed, the rings must be pushed into the grooves in the piston, using a piston ring compressor. Several types of compressor are available. The most common designs use an adjustable band that can be slackened to fit the band over the uncompressed rings. When the band is tightened, the rings are compressed into the grooves. Adjustable ring compressors are convenient because they can be used to fit a variety of piston sizes.

Where many engines with a given size of piston are repaired, rigid ring compressors can be used. Rigid compressors are carefully sized tapered sleeves. The sleeve starts at a diameter slightly larger than the uncompressed rings and tapers to the diameter of the piston. The piston is simply pushed through the sleeve into the cylinder. These compressors are very fast to use, but a different sleeve must be purchased for each piston size.

Regardless of the compressor design, be mindful of installing them in the correct direction. Most band-style compressors have small locating tabs that prevent the tool from being drawn into the cylinder with the piston. Usually the tension of the band tool should be greatest near the block when the piston is being installed. If you are in doubt, consult the tool manufacturer's instructions (**FIGURE 24-22**).

Wipe the piston ring compressor with a clean shop towel to remove any debris, and then place some clean engine oil or assembly lubricant in the compressor band. Locate the compressor over the rings. Leave a portion of the skirt exposed to locate the piston in the cylinder. When installing the ring compressor, ensure the locating tabs or detents face down. Use care when tightening the compressor to ensure that all of the rings are compressing into their grooves.

Remove the bearing cap, and set it aside. If the connecting rod has studs and nuts retaining the cap, install commercially available protectors, or some lengths of fuel line on the studs. Often called rod protectors, these are really to protect the crankpin from nicks as the pistons are installed. Rotate the crankshaft so that the crankpin for cylinder 1 is at BDC. Carefully wipe the cylinder bore with a clean, dry shop towel, and then with a shop towel dampened with engine oil.

Carefully install the piston skirt into the cylinder bore, observing correct orientation. Tap the edges of the ring compressor lightly to seat it against the deck of the block. If it is uneven, a ring could escape, expand, and become broken as you are installing the piston. While holding the compressor firmly against the block, use a piston hammer or hammer handle to gently tap or push the piston through the compressor. If the piston does not tap in easily, stop and check: something is wrong. If you force things, you could damage the new ring set or piston.

FIGURE 24-22 Use the locating tabs to help guide the piston into the cylinder bore correctly. Failure to "square up" the piston may lead to a broken piston ring.

Connecting Rod Side Clearance

Using a feeler gauge, confirm that the side clearance is within specification (**FIGURE 24-23**). Finally, ensure that the crankshaft turns smoothly after piston is installed. As the number of pistons increases, drag will increase, but any binding indicates a problem such as a rod cap installed backwards. Stop and investigate any time the turning resistance becomes excessive. Repeat the steps above for each of the remaining pistons.

K24005 Knowledge of the proper procedures for checking installed parts as the engine gets assembled.

Installing Head Gaskets

Using a shop towel wetted with denatured alcohol or brake and parts cleaner, clean any oil or sealant residue from the cylinder head and block deck. If a cooling passage insert is used in the engine, it must be installed now. If you are using a different thickness head gasket to compensate for machining, confirm the new gasket is the correct thickness. If different gaskets are required for each bank of a V-engine, ensure that you have the correct gasket for the bank you are working on. Check the head gasket for a marking such as "Top" (**FIGURE 24-24**). The gasket may fit on the block and align with bolt holes if installed

FIGURE 24-23 Checking thrust bearing clearance by using a feeler gauge.

FIGURE 24-24 Installing the cylinder head gasket is a crucial part of assembling the engine. If the cylinder head gasket is installed upside down, the engine may overheat or starve for oil on the top end.

upside down, but positioning it incorrectly could obstruct oil or coolant passageways. Place the gasket on the deck and see that all holes in the gasket line up. Head gaskets are normally installed dry. Unless specified by the engine manufacturer, do not use any additional sealer or gasket treatment on the head gasket. The dowels in the block will keep the gasket in position.

Cylinder Head Installation

If you have not done so already, rotate the engine so that the head deck is upright and parallel to the ground. Install the lock pin in the repair stand to keep the engine from spinning upside down. Using a shop towel wetted with denatured alcohol or brake and parts cleaner, clean any oil or sealant residue from the cylinder head and block deck.

If you are using a different thickness head gasket to compensate for machining, confirm the new gasket is the correct thickness. If different gaskets are required for each bank of a V-engine, ensure that you have the correct gasket for the bank you are working on. Check the head gasket for a marking such as "Top." The gasket may fit on the block and align with bolt holes if installed upside down, but positioning it incorrectly could obstruct oil or coolant passageways. Place the gasket on the deck and see that all holes in the gasket line up. Head gaskets are normally installed dry. Unless specified by the engine manufacturer, do not use any additional sealer or gasket treatment on the head gasket. The dowels in the block will keep the gasket in position.

If the engine uses overhead camshafts, it may be necessary to have the camshafts removed to access the cylinder head fasteners. Where the valvetrain utilizes direct acting valves and shims, remove the buckets and shims, and place them in order on a bench when handling the head without the camshafts installed (**FIGURE 24-25**). If you happen to tip the head without the cams in, the shims and buckets can fall out, and each valve clearance will then have to be checked again. In some cases, the rocker arms are installed with or after the head bolts. When installing the rockers, ensure that the rockers are all placed squarely on the valve stem, to prevent the valve from being bent when tightening the rocker shafts in place.

After a final wipe with a clean, dry, lint-free cloth, gently set the head on the head gasket. Use the alignment dowels to guide the head into place (**FIGURE 24-26**). Make sure to set the head down flat and not to slide it on the gasket. Sliding the head on the dowels, which are part of the gasket surface, may scratch the head and cause a sealing problem. Use an assistant or engine crane with heavy heads, if required. Once installed, press lightly on opposite corners to ensure the head is seated flat on the locating dowels. If the head is held up somewhere, threading in the fasteners will damage parts. Some engines require that the timing chain and gear set now be threaded up into position.

FIGURE 24-25 When disassembling the cylinder head, lay the parts out in the order that you took them apart so that reassembly will be easier.

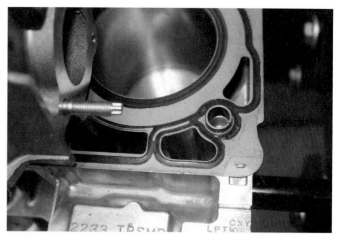

FIGURE 24-26 Align cylinder head on dowel pins.

After lubricating the fasteners as directed by the service information, thread in the head bolts by hand. If you have different sizes of head bolts, make sure the bolts go in the correct holes. Also, remember to use a non-hardening sealer on any bolts that thread through holes that are exposed to oil or coolant. Go through each bolt on both heads, running the bolts down with a ratchet and socket until they are just snug. If standard bolts are used, torque in increments recommended by the manufacturer, in the pattern provided. Remember to always double-check the torque on each fastener.

Where torque-to-yield fasteners are used, remember to torque them to the initial specification, and then recheck. As with the other torque-to-yield fasteners, mark the heads with a paint dot in the 12 o'clock position, and complete the job by turning the fastener the specified number of degrees, using a torque angle gauge. Visually confirm the paint marks have all been relocated to the position, based on the angle. In some cases, fasteners like head bolts require a second angle step. There is no need to repaint the fasteners; just tighten the specified number of degrees in the second step, and confirm the original mark is in the new position for all fasteners.

Some cylinder head assemblies use smaller diameter fasteners to clamp noncombustion portions of the head to the block. These fasteners—usually around 8 mm or 5/6" bolts—are installed and torqued after the primary head bolts are installed and torqued. Once the heads are installed, reinstall the shim and bucket assemblies in their correct location, and install the camshafts, if applicable.

Torquing Head Bolts

After lubricating the fasteners as directed by the service information, thread in the head bolts by hand. If you have different sizes of head bolts, make sure the bolts go in the correct holes. Also, remember to use a non-hardening sealer on any bolts that thread through holes that are exposed to oil or coolant. Go through each bolt on both heads, running the bolts down with a ratchet and socket until they are just snug. If standard bolts are used, torque in increments recommended by the manufacturer, in the pattern provided. Remember to always double-check the torque on each fastener.

Where torque-to-yield fasteners are used, remember to torque them to the initial specification, and then recheck. As with the other torque-to-yield fasteners, mark the heads with a paint dot in the 12 o'clock position, and complete the job by turning the fastener the specified number of degrees, using a torque angle gauge. Visually confirm the paint marks have all been relocated to the position, based on the angle. In some cases, fasteners like head bolts require a second angle step. There is no need to repaint the fasteners; just tighten the specified number of degrees in the second step, and confirm the original mark is in the new position for all fasteners.

Some cylinder head assemblies use smaller diameter fasteners to clamp noncombustion portions of the head to the block. These fasteners—usually around 8 mm or 5/6" bolts—are installed and torqued after the primary head bolts are installed and torqued. Once the heads are installed, reinstall the shim and bucket assemblies in their correct location and install the camshafts, if applicable.

To install the heads follow the steps in **SKILL DRILL 24-5**.

To install torque-to-yield bolts, follow the steps in **SKILL DRILL 24-6**.

Installing Timing Chain and Gears or Timing Belt— OHC Engines

Synchronizing the opening and closing of the valves to piston travel is only possible if the camshaft and crankshaft are installed in the correct relationship. This is referred to as cam timing or valve timing. During the process, you may find you need to move the camshaft or crankshaft to index them together properly. Use care doing this, as you may find that valves and pistons interfere if you need to move either shaft more than a few degrees. If this is the case, you will need to turn each shaft a small amount in order to align the shafts. If you feel resistance, don't force one shaft or the other to go, or you will bend valves.

As you know the camshaft can be connected to the crankshaft with timing gears, timing chains, and timing belts. Where a single camshaft and crankshaft are used, the timing

K24006 Knowledge of the different types of head bolts so proper application can be achieved.

S24005 Install head bolts.

S24006 Install torque-to-yield bolts.

SKILL DRILL 24-5 Installing the Heads

1. Ensure the bolt holes and bolt threads are clean. Use new bolts if they are of the torque-to-yield type. If the head bolts go into holes that have solid bottoms, blow out any debris with compressed air. If specified, oil the threads and the undersides of the heads of the head bolts themselves. Apply some non-hardening sealer to the threads of any bolts that extend into the water jacket.

2. Clean the block deck surface and the decks of the heads with the appropriate cleaner. Install head gaskets. Look for any "this side up" or "front" labels on the head gaskets. Composition gaskets do not require any sealant.

3. On OHC cam engines, make sure the crankshaft is set to the specified position before installing the head.

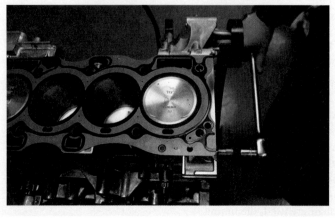

4. On OHC engines, make sure the camshaft is set to the specified position before installing the head. Failure to do so could lead to damaged or bent valves.

Continued

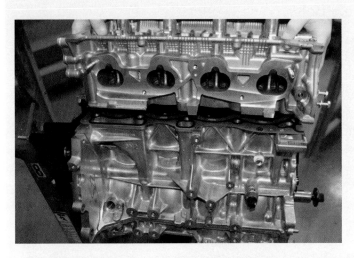

5. Carefully lay the head over the alignment dowels of the block, and start threading in the bolts. If you have a few different sizes of head bolts, make sure the right bolts go in the right places. One general indicator that they are in the correct holes is that each bolt sticks up from its hole the same amount when set in place.

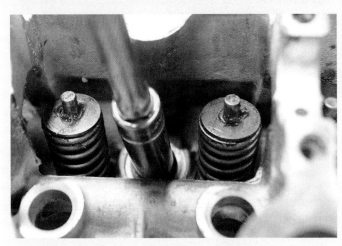

6. Run each bolt down finger tight. Follow the proper tightening procedure to torque down the cylinder head so that you do not warp it.

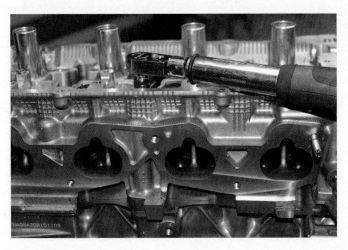

7. If the procedure for tightening the cylinder head is a multiple step process make sure that you are gradually increasing the torque as specified within the service literature. This may require multiple passes on the cylinder head bolts. Once the final pass is completed you have completed the cylinder head bolt installation process.

SKILL DRILL 24-6 Installing Torque-to-Yield Bolts

1. Using the appropriate thread chaser and compressed air, ensure that the threaded holes on the component are clean and dry.

2. Using a clean shop towel dampened with alcohol or brake and parts cleaner, wipe the mating surfaces.

3. Install the gasket, if applicable, and the mating component.

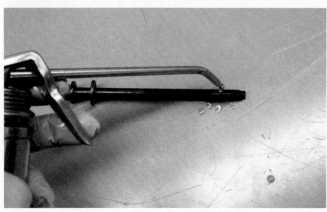

4. Lubricate the fasteners according to the engine maker's specification.

Continued

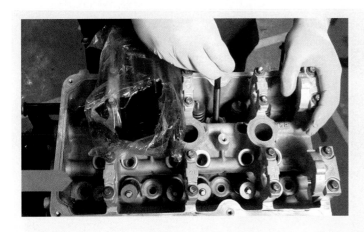

5. Install the bolts and lightly seat them.

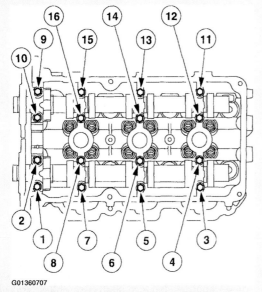

G01360707

6. Using a torque wrench, tighten each fastener to the initial specification in the specified sequence.

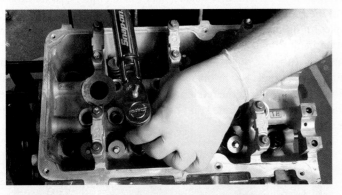

7. Following the same sequence, recheck each fastener torque.

8. Using a paint pen or marker, place a dot at the 12 o'clock position.

Continued

9. Using a torque angle gauge, tighten each fastener the specified number of degrees, following the published tightening sequence. The dot will move to a new position as the fastener is tightened. If multiple passes are required, complete the first angle on all fasteners, and then repeat the process for next step.

10. Confirm the paint marks are all facing the same direction.

system is very simple. **FIGURE 24-27** shows an example of each system. As camshafts, mechanical injection pumps on diesel engines, balance shaft assemblies, and additional cylinder heads are added, the cam timing system can become dramatically more complex. Some engines use multiple timing chains, some driving one bank from a chain on the front of the engine, and the other bank from a chain on the rear.

Installing the timing set is fundamentally the same regardless of the number of components driven by the timing system. Through the use of timing marks, the camshaft and crankshaft are indexed to each other so that the reference cylinder is on compression. Especially with cam in block engines, the timing marks on both sprockets or gears are installed in relation to each other.

FIGURE 24-27 When installing the cylinder head, you must set the timing to factory settings so that the engine will run.

FIGURE 24-28 Chain tensioner in collapsed position.

FIGURE 24-29 Chain links in position on the timing sprocket marks.

Chain Drive

OHC chain drives typically are the roller chain style, which looks a lot like a bicycle chain. Roller chain has a long life, usually lasting the life of the engine, as long as the engine oil is maintained properly. Timing chains need lubrication to operate, so engine oil is usually sprayed onto the chain from the front of the engine block, because of this the timing chain area is usually sealed by a timing cover. OHC engines using timing chains have guides and chain tensioners to keep the chain in place, in addition to two or more sprockets. Refer to the service information for timing mark locations and the specific instructions for installing these.

Chain tensioners are installed with the tensioner in the collapsed position (**FIGURE 24-28**). When installing the chain, you might be directed to count the chain links between the mark on the crank sprocket and the mark on the cam sprocket to get the right timing. Usually the timing links are a different color to make alignment easier. Align the links on the timing chain to the timing marks on both the crank and cam sprockets (**FIGURE 24-29**). Install any chain guides, and then release the chain tensioner to take up the slack in the chain. Before rotating the engine, recheck the timing marks to be sure they are still lined up after the tensioner is released. Always refer to the manufacturer's installation procedures and diagrams.

Belt-Driven Timing Sets

Belt-driven timing sets use a flexible belt to transmit drive from the crankshaft to the camshaft. The belt runs more quietly than a chain and does not require lubrication. But timing belts do wear out and have to be changed periodically, typically between 50,000 and 100,000 miles (80,000 to 160,000 km), depending on the vehicle manufacturer. Because they do not need to be lubricated, they are generally behind a timing belt cover that is not sealed to the front of the engine. The cover acts more as a belt guard and to protect it from dirt and debris.

As with the timing chain type of engine, always refer to current service information for timing mark locations. Install the cogged gears onto the camshaft, if not already installed, being sure not to forget the keys, if equipped. They should have already been aligned when the cylinder head was on the bench, but it is best to double-check for the proper alignment of the timing marks. Be careful not to move the camshaft very much, as the valves could have an interference fit to the pistons. If the camshaft does need to move substantially, turn the crankshaft so it is approximately 20 to 30 degrees before or after TDC. This will pull all of the pistons down from the top of the cylinder so that the valves will not hit the pistons when the cam is turned. With the timing marks aligned (**FIGURE 24-30**), install the timing belt with as much of the slack as possible on the tensioner side of the belt, and then install the belt tensioner (**FIGURE 24-31**). Verify that all timing marks are aligned. Always refer to the manufacturer's installation procedures on timing belts and belt tension.

FIGURE 24-30 Timing marks aligned.

FIGURE 24-31 Timing belt tensioner installed.

Usually no additional sealer or adhesive is recommended on formed rubber gaskets, so you may find it helpful to make some guide studs by using a hacksaw to cut the heads off a few bolts of the correct size and pitch. Using long bolts helps guide parts together. Thread one of your guide studs into one of the bolt holes in each corner of the block. The gasket can be placed over these, and then the pan. Once the other fasteners are installed, you can remove your guide studs. Keep these around for future jobs.

Installing the Oil Pickup Tube and Oil Pump

Next, install the oil pump and or pickup. The oil pump may be located inside the oil pan, on the side of the block, or in the timing cover. It is typically driven by the crankshaft or camshaft. It is recommended that you pack the oil pump with assembly lube. Doing so helps to prime the pump quickly when the engine is first started in order to get the oil moving through the pickup tube and into the oil pump. Be sure to install it to the manufacturer's specifications and torque.

The pickup tube generally includes a strainer that prevents chunks of debris from entering the oil pump. It also is designed to pull oil from the bottom of the oil pan. In many cases, the oil pickup tube is not part of the oil pump. The tube is installed as a separate component. Oil pickup tubes come in three different versions—a screw-in style that screws into the oil pump or engine block, a bolt-on type (**FIGURE 24-32**), and a press-in style. The screw-in style has a pipe thread and requires a non-hardening sealer to ensure that the oil pump does not pull air around the threads. The bolt-on type is bolted onto the pump or block and usually uses a gasket or O-ring for sealing purposes.

The press-in style pickup tube is held in place with an interference fit, but the oil pump needs to be installed first. Be sure to install the oil pump drive gear or shaft before installing the pump, as it cannot be installed later (**FIGURE 24-33**). Once the oil pump is mounted, the pickup tube can be installed. It is usually good practice to adjust the strainer so it is at the proper height inside the bottom of the oil pan. This can be done by installing the pickup tube in the pump just enough so that it is fairly solid but can still twist. Rotate the strainer so that it is obviously going to touch the bottom of the oil pan. Then set the oil pan in place, which will rotate the strainer until the pan contacts both block rails fully. Lift off the oil pan and measure the height of the strainer from the block. Adjust the strainer until it has between 1/4" and 3/8" (6.4 and 9.5 mm) of clearance from the bottom of the pan. Then tap the pickup tube into the oil pump or block until it is firmly in place. Some engine builders tack-weld the pickup assembly to the oil pump to prevent the pickup tube from falling out or loosening up. If you do weld it in place, make sure the pump is removed from the engine when you weld it, and the pump cover is removed from the pump so that there is no chance the welding process will hurt the gears or engine bearings.

Installing the Oil Pan and Timing Cover
Timing Covers

Once you have confirmed the correct timing relationship between crank and camshafts on the engine, it is time to install the remaining timing covers. Often crankshaft and camshaft

FIGURE 24-32 Bolt-on style oil pickup tube.

FIGURE 24-33 Oil pump installed.

position sensors are installed during the cover installation. Some sensors are located behind the timing covers; others may be fitted in the timing cover itself (**FIGURE 24-34**). These should be installed at the appropriate time. They may also require setup with special tools to ensure appropriate clearances are maintained as the sensor pickup is rotated past the sensor body.

Timing chain covers use cut or form-in-place gaskets to create an oil tight seal. The front crankshaft seal is usually pressed into the timing cover as well. If not already installed, place the seal in the timing cover now. Ensure the cover and the mating surface are clean and free of oil. Install the gaskets. Cut gaskets can be held in place with a thin coating of sealer. FIPG should be applied to the cover just before it is installed. Carefully place the cover over the guide pins, where provided, and install the fasteners finger tight. Torque the fasteners in the sequence specified in the repair literature. Timing belt covers also use gaskets—often thin rubber weather seals—to keep water and dirt out of the timing set. Ensure these are in place before installing the cover (**FIGURE 24-35**).

FIGURE 24-34 On some timing covers, mounted sensors read the various speeds of the spinning shafts. These sensors are integral to the operation of the engine.

Oil Pan

With the timing set, covers and rear main seal installed, the oil pan can be fitted. Gasketing a pan can be accomplished with one-piece formed rubber gaskets, multiple-piece cut gaskets, or RTV form-in-place gasket materials.

Start by inverting the engine and locking it in place. Make sure that the sealing surfaces on both the engine and pan are clean and dry by wiping them with a clean cloth moistened with alcohol or brake cleaner. Lay out the gaskets and fasteners with the pan. If different length fasteners are used, make sure you know which holes they are located in. The fasteners should be clean and the threads chased. If any of the fasteners are placed in through holes exposed to oil, they should be coated with non-hardening sealer. If load spreading plates are used, ensure they are installed on the correct fasteners and that their positions on the pan are known.

If the oil pan is made from stamped steel, check the holes to ensure that they have not been deformed. When the fasteners are tightened, the metal is displaced toward the block. Any holes that have evidence of material welling up toward the block can be reconditioned by placing the pan over a large punch held in the vise and tapping the other side of the pan with a hammer. **FIGURE 24-36** shows the process of chasing the pan holes flat. Cast

FIGURE 24-35 Timing belt covers are usually plastic and are meant as a guard against potential interference from external debris.

FIGURE 24-36 When getting ready to install an oil pan, the technician must ensure that the gasket surface is flat. Some steel oil pans are warped when they are removed, which means that the technician must flatten out the gasket surface to ensure a correct seal.

aluminum pans should be checked for nicks and burrs; their holes can be countersunk lightly if required.

With formed rubber or cut gaskets, RTV may be required in the corners where the different gaskets meet, or the gasket must change vertical direction. **FIGURE 24-37** shows RTV being applied to the surfaces, as outlined in the service information. Studs are sometimes used instead of bolts in a few places: this makes holding the gasket in position easier and helps line up the pan with the block. If no studs are used, cork or paper gaskets can be held in position with non-hardening sealer or gasket adhesive.

To install pans with RTV gasket material, lay a properly sized bead of RTV around the sealing surface of the block. Service information will describe the places the RTV should be located. The size of the bead is determined by where you cut the applicator tip. Excess RTV caused by too large a bead being applied will squeeze from between the mating surfaces, both outside and inside the engine block. **FIGURE 24-38** shows an assembly with the correct amount of sealer used. If excessive silicone is used, the ribbon of RTV that is displaced to the inside of the engine may become dislodged. Loose RTV inside the oil pan can be drawn against the oil pickup strainer where it will restrict oil flow to the pump. Smaller pieces may even be drawn through the strainer and become lodged elsewhere in the lubrication system. The shop-made guide studs mentioned above may be helpful in aligning the pan when RTV is used as well.

With the gaskets properly located, or the RTV correctly laid down, the pan is carefully positioned on the block, and some fasteners are started. When tightening oil pan fasteners, use care with cut gaskets, as the soft material may displace or the gasket may crack at the bolt locations. Many formed rubber gaskets incorporate a metal sleeve that permits the gasket to compress when the fasteners are torqued, but limit the amount the pan can be pressed into the gasket. Torque all fasteners and recheck.

Oil Priming (Pre-Oiling) the Engine

To pre-oil the engine, follow the steps in **SKILL DRILL 24-7**.

Once the pre-lubrication is complete, the connecting hose is removed, and the plug or sensor is reinstalled. If a gauge was used to indicate oil pressure while the pre-lubricator was running, remove it and replace the gallery plug.

K24007 Knowledge of the reasons for priming an engine.

S24007 Prime the engine.

▶ **TECHNICIAN TIP**

Low pressure can be an indicator of excessive bearing clearance; but we had checked this earlier, so is not likely to be the cause. However, as mentioned above, sometimes oil is forced through the lubrication system to ensure that all bearing surfaces receive oil without excessive bearing leakage. This may even be done before the engine is torn down as a diagnostic check. Although it is possible to use the engine oil pump for this test, the pickup must be submerged in a container of engine oil. Using an external pump provides a simpler means of investigating concerns about lubrication reaching the entire engine, or to check for excessive oil leakage at bearings.

FIGURE 24-37 Installing an oil pan with an RTV gasket requires a consistent bead to be applied onto the raised portion of the pan so that it seals correctly on the cylinder block.

FIGURE 24-38 When installing too much RTV, the excess squeezes out externally or into the oil pan. When it dries, it could clog up the oil pump pickup, so you need to be careful when applying RTV.

SKILL DRILL 24-7 Pre-Oiling the Engine

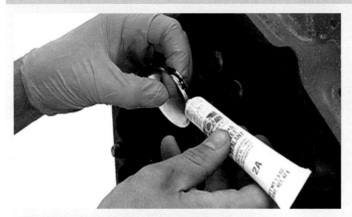

1. Install the rear camshaft plug, if it has not already been done. Cam plugs are usually narrower than water jacket core plugs. Spread a thin layer of non-hardening sealant on the edge of the plug itself. Be careful not to use silicone, and do not put the sealant directly onto the block, as sealant may get into the oil galleries and plug them up. Hammer the plug flush with the opening of the cam bore. The best way to do this is to use a bearing race driver or a similar oversized flat metal object. Tap on the plug until it is flush with the back of the camshaft bore. Then use a large socket to tap the plug in slightly so that it is just inside the sealing lip of the camshaft bore.

2. Install the oil filter. Lubricate the rubber seal of the oil filter with a little engine oil, and thread it on hand tight.

3. Install an oil pressure gauge into one of the ports that lead to the oil gallery.

4. If you have not done so already, install the one-piece rear main seal to finish closing off the oil system.

Continued

5. Fill up the crankcase with the type and quantity of engine oil recommended in the repair manual.

6. If the oil pump is driven by the distributor, put an oil pump primer rod into the distributor hole. The primer rod will engage onto the oil pump drive rod so you can spin the oil pump with a drill from the outside of the engine. The drill should be spinning in the same direction that the distributor rotates when the engine is running. Check the repair information for this information. If you spin it the wrong way, the pump will not show any oil pressure on the gauge. Even at normal drill speeds, the oil gauge should read that it has plenty of pressure. Now run the drill and spin the oil pump for about 30 seconds to a minute.

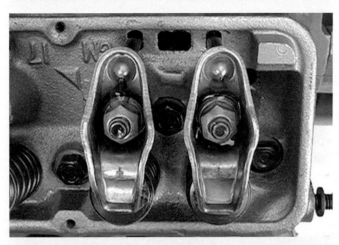

7. When oil pressure builds inside the engine, oil will make it through the galleries and into the crankshaft and the lifters. After oil goes through the lifters, it will move up the pushrods and start to drip out of the holes in the rocker arms. Make sure this happens for each of the rockers. If you run the drill for a minute or two and a few of the rockers do not produce oil, have a helper rotate the crankshaft two full turns while operating the drill. This changes the positions of the lifters and should make it easier for the remaining lifters to produce oil. Because there are no valve covers installed, be aware that oil might spill out of the head when the rockers get full.

8. If the oil pump is driven by the crankshaft, use a pressurized pre-oiler to pressurize the system and verify that oil is getting to all valves.

Continued

9. Once the engine has been pre-oiled, install the valve covers. Rubber-style gaskets should not require any sealant, but may require a gasket adhesive. If you have cork gaskets and want to use some kind of sealer, spray one side of the gasket with a high-tack aerosol gasket sealant. Stick the sealed side to the valve cover so that the gasket stays with the cover. When you place the gaskets, make sure the gaskets contact the edges of the heads on all sides so that you do not have any oil leaks once the engine starts. The valve cover bolts do not have a very high torque rating, so be careful not to torque them beyond specifications.

▶ Assembling External Engine Components
External Engine Components and Accessories

The engine is now ready for installation of the external components, such as the manifolds, sensors, water pump, thermostat, alternator, power steering pump, air-conditioning compressor, or any other component removed during disassembly. Make sure all components are installed in the proper order, as many parts fit behind or over other parts. Also be careful to install and properly tighten all fasteners. You should not have any parts left over that were not replaced with new parts. If you do have leftover parts, determine where they came from.

K24008 Knowledge of the assembly of external engine components.

Installing the Intake Manifold
Intake Manifolds

Some manifolds are two-piece design. In these, the component that attaches to the head and distributes the fresh air to the cylinders is referred to as the manifold; the second portion is referred to as the plenum. The manifold is installed first, and then the plenum is installed onto the manifold (**FIGURE 24-39**). The plenum is usually a large, open chamber through which each runner in the manifold is fed. Sometimes electric or pneumatic operated valves are fitted inside the plenum to modify the airflow path into the manifold based on engine operating conditions. In at least one engine design, a gasoline injection distributor and injectors are located inside the plenum.

S24008 Install the intake manifold.

Intake manifolds are sealed with a variety of gasket options. Cut gaskets are used with many metal manifolds; RTV with others. Plastic manifolds may use formed rubber O-ring–like gaskets. Prepare the surfaces by wiping with a clean cloth dampened with alcohol or brake cleaner to remove any oil or dirt. Ensure all threaded holes are clear, and the fasteners are prepared. If you had shop towels in the intake ports to keep debris out during the other steps, remove these now. Make sure the intake ports in the head are clear.

Multiple piece gaskets are usually installed on V-engines. Usually one paper or composite gasket goes between each head and the intake, and a cork or neoprene gasket is used to seal the intake manifold to the valley of the engine. RTV is usually applied at the junction of the different gasket materials. Where overhead camshafts

FIGURE 24-39 Some intake manifolds are designed as two pieces. The lower portion is made of aluminum, and the upper plenum is made of plastic. Care must be taken when the upper plenum is removed as it is fragile and could break.

FIGURE 24-40 Some overhead camshaft engines do not have any components in the valley, which means they do not need a sealed valley.

FIGURE 24-41 Some intake manifolds only use O-rings as gaskets; this feature allows for fewer vacuum leaks and other leaks.

are used, there may be no valley portion of the gasket because oil should not be present in the space between the cylinder heads (**FIGURE 24-40**).

The manifold to head gaskets often have vulcanized rubber ribs around critical areas such as water jackets. When installing the manifold gasket, ensure that no holes are obstructed. Unless specified, sealants or RTV should not be applied. Applying RTV as a standalone gasket is done as described in the sections for the oil pan and timing cover. As with any other place RTV is incorporated, minimize the amount of silicone squeezed out when the parts are assembled. If O-ring seals are used, there is typically a tab formed to help locate the seal. A small dab of silicone grease—not RTV—also aids in maintaining the position of the gaskets during installation. Do not use RTV with these seals (**FIGURE 24-41**).

After a final cleaning of the sealing surfaces, install the gaskets, and position the manifold on the engine. Check that the manifold is flat against the sealing surface. Run the fasteners in finger tight, and then torque to specification, using the sequence outlined in the service information. Confirm the torque.

To install the intake manifold, follow the steps in **SKILL DRILL 24-8**.

Where the fuel distribution unit and injectors are placed in the plenum, fasten the injector block into position. Place new distribution tube seals in the intake manifold, and carefully clip the nozzle into the appropriate bore. Place a cap on the fuel delivery and return pipes to prevent debris from entering while you continue working (**FIGURE 24-42**).

If the engine is direct gasoline injection, now may be the time to install these injectors. The GDI injectors are usually sealed into the head and fuel rail with O-rings, and the fuel rail fastened to the head, using bolts, in much the same way as the port fuel injectors. New high-pressure rail feed pipes are required in most cases as the pipe has an integral sealing area that deforms when the union is tightened. If the high pressure pump could not be installed when assembling the camshafts in the head, that may now be installed.

SKILL DRILL 24-8 Installing the Intake Manifold

1. Clean the surfaces of the manifold and head with a solvent, such as brake cleaner.

Continued

2. On V-type engines, put some RTV sealant in the four corners where the heads meet the block. Put a thin layer of gasket sealer around the water jacket ports and their mating surfaces on the intake gaskets, if equipped. When the sealer on the gaskets is tacky, line up the bolt holes, and stick the gaskets in place. Then spread some more gasket sealer on the tops of the gaskets, around the water jacket ports. On any engine, if the decks of the heads or the block, or both, were machined, the heads will sit a little bit lower, and the gap between the intake manifold and the block rail will be smaller. Some gasket sets have rubber or cork gaskets that are too thick to allow the intake to seat properly. Such gaskets are not recommended. Instead, to seal the block rail to the intake, run a solid bead of silicone sealer along the front and rear upper rails of the block. Run the bead evenly from gasket to gasket. This is a good idea for many engines, whether the decks have been machined or not, because it usually provides a much better seal.

3. When the block is ready, double-check that everything is in place (including the oil splash guard on the bottom of the intake), and then set the intake manifold in place. Get some help if you think you may need it; cast iron manifolds are very heavy, and it is important to lower it as close to its final position as you can. The aim is to need very little adjustment to align the bolt holes.

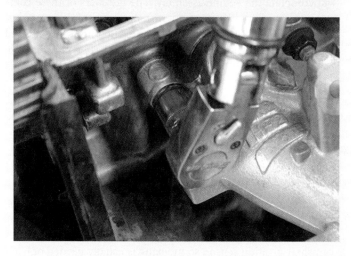

4. On most V-type engines, the intake manifold bolts lead directly into the oil-soaked area under the valve covers. Treat the threads of these bolts with non-hardening sealer to avoid oil leaks. It is sometimes hard to get to the bolts near the plenum of the intake with a socket. In such cases, use the box end of a wrench. The intake bolts usually have a tightening sequence and specified torque similar to the heads, but the sequence usually starts with the middle bolts near the plenum. If you cannot get to all of the bolts with a torque wrench, tighten one of the bolts to the first torque increment, and then put a box-end wrench on the same bolt and feel with your hand how tight it is. Now you can tighten the first few inaccessible bolts for each of the three increments, and you should end up with all of the bolts torqued to a similar rating.

- Port fuel injectors and the fuel rail are installed next. The fuel pressure regulator may also be installed if it is located on the fuel rail. Injector O-rings should be new, and lubricated with fresh engine oil. Usually the best way to install these is to place them in the rail first and then press the injectors into the bores provided in the intake manifold. The rails are then fastened into place. V-engines usually have two rails, which may require a crossover pipe between them to be installed. If banjo fittings are used, replace any metal washers with new ones before installing.

FIGURE 24-42 When you are removing an intake manifold, you have to cap the fuel lines you disconnected so that debris does not get into them.

FIGURE 24-43 Installing the exhaust manifold correctly allows for the emission components to operate efficiently.

S24009 Install the engine accessories.

N24003 Establish camshaft position sensor indexing.

K24009 Knowledge of camshaft position sensor installation for engine operation.

S24010 Index the camshaft position sensor.

Once the injectors are in place, clean the plenum sealing surfaces. Install a new plenum-to-intake manifold gasket, and fasten the plenum to the intake manifold. Torque the fasteners to specification in the sequence provided by the manufacturer. Observe directions to align any variable intake linkage and install any related components. The throttle body with new gasket may be installed as well.

Installing Exhaust Manifolds

Exhaust Manifold

If necessary, chase the threaded holes for the exhaust manifold mounting. It is advisable to use new studs, nuts, and bolts, as previously used fasteners tend to soften and corrode over time. If you are using the old fasteners, thoroughly clean them of corrosion, and chase the threads. All exhaust manifold fasteners should receive a coating of good-quality high-temperature anti-seize compound on the threaded portions. Install the exhaust studs in the block, and tighten with a stud wrench. Ensure proper gasket orientation, install the manifold, and torque the fasteners. Install any heat shields as required. EGR valves and piping may need to be installed with the exhaust manifold. Some manifolds incorporate the catalytic converter or collector pipes that have brackets that bolt onto the block. If these brackets are not installed, the manifold may crack in service (**FIGURE 24-43**).

Installing the Remaining External Components

The remaining external components may include the balancer, exhaust manifolds, sensors, water pump (on some engines), thermostat, alternator, or any number of other components that will complete the engine assembly. The fasteners of these components are often different from one another, so it is easy to get them confused, which can lead to stripped bolt holes or damaged fasteners. This is where organization during disassembly pays off.

Assembling the Accessories

As a last step, various accessories have to be installed on the engine. Depending on the vehicle, these may be installed before or after the engine is installed in the vehicle. Refer to service information for the correct procedure.

To assemble the engine accessories, follow the steps in **SKILL DRILL 24-9**.

Establishing Camshaft Position Sensor Indexing

Camshaft position sensors must be positioned correctly so that they accurately signal the position of the camshaft to the powertrain control module and the ignition module. Any misadjustment of the sensor will cause the fuel system timing to be off. Most newer engines do not have an adjustable camshaft position sensor, so indexing is usually needed only on sensors that can be manually adjusted. The adjustment can typically be made in one of two ways: A special tool can be used to properly align the sensor or a lab scope can be used to compare the camshaft position sensor adjustment to the crankshaft position sensor. If one channel of the lab scope is connected to the camshaft position sensor signal wire and another channel is connected to the crankshaft position sensor signal wire, then when the engine is running, the camshaft position sensor can be adjusted so they align. This is also a great way to measure timing chain or belt stretch on a vehicle with nonadjustable camshaft sensors. The greater the two signals are out of line, the more stretch in the belt or chain.

To establish camshaft position sensor indexing, follow the steps in **SKILL DRILL 24-10**.

SKILL DRILL 24-9 Assembling the Engine Accessories

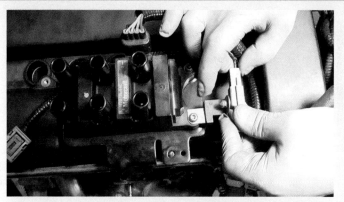

1. Install the miscellaneous accessories. Once again, check your notes from the disassembly. The engine must be brought back to the same state it was in before coming out of the chassis. Replace any sensors, plugs, or brackets. You might even go so far as to reinstall the fuel injection system or the carburetor.

2. Install the flexplate. All engines require the flexplate or flywheel to be torqued back into place. Many engines specify that new bolts be used each time the flywheel is installed; check service information for the engine you are working on. Use a flywheel wrench to keep the crank from moving while you tighten the bolts. Automatic transmission engines only need the flexplate installed for now.

3. For engines with a flywheel and clutch assembly, the clutch pressure plate and disc should be installed. After the flywheel is torqued into place, set the friction disc into a centered position. A clutch alignment tool centers this disc where it needs to be while you fit the pressure plate on and tighten its screws. When the pressure plate is torqued onto the flywheel, the disc is pinched into its proper position so that it will not move. Now pull out the alignment tool and put it away.

4. For most engines, the torque rating for the crankshaft front center bolt is the highest in the entire engine. Make sure you have the crank held still with a flywheel wrench while you tighten this bolt.

5. Decide what else you need to bolt to the engine. Keep in mind that you might still need to roll the engine through a doorway or past some other obstacle to get it to the hoisting location, but the aim is for it to be almost completed assembled, ready for reinstallation in the vehicle.

SKILL DRILL 24-10 Establishing Camshaft Position Sensor Indexing

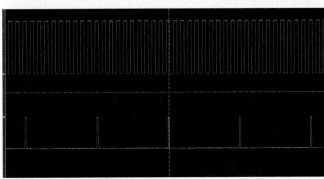

1. Attach a lab scope to the crankshaft position sensor signal wire and the camshaft position sensor signal wire.

2. Start the engine and observe the lab scope. The readings should line up. Adjust the camshaft position sensor, if adjustable, to bring it in line with the crankshaft position sensor.

Inspecting and Replacing Camshaft and Drive Belt or Chain

K24010 Knowledge of timing belt or chain installation.

S24011 Replace the camshaft drive belt or chain.

The camshaft and drive belt or chain assembly make up an important system for the internal combustion engine. They link the valvetrain system to the crankshaft and determine the right time in the engine cycle for the valves to open and close. Because of operational wear, these areas need to be serviced to make sure the engine continues to operate correctly. The system is first inspected through a visual inspection of the parts to check for wear or worn parts that can be seen. Through visual inspection, it can be determined which parts are in need of replacement by following the manufacturer's recommendations in the service information.

To inspect and replace the camshaft and drive belt or chain, follow the steps in **SKILL DRILL 24-11**.

Inspecting and Replacing Valve Stem Seals on an Assembled Engine

S24012 Install valve stem seals on an assembled engine.

It is sometimes necessary to replace the valve stem seals on an assembled engine. This is performed when the engine is in relatively good condition, but the valve seals are causing the engine to burn oil that is getting past the valve seal and valve guides. The seals can be changed once the engine is disassembled far enough to remove the valve springs. Removing the valve springs presents a problem. With the valve springs off, there is nothing to hold the valves from falling down into the cylinders. Thus, compressed air, typically from a cylinder

SKILL DRILL 24-11 Inspecting and Replacing the Camshaft and Drive Belt or Chain

1. Determine all specifications for timing chain or belt tension assembly according to the manufacturer of the engine assembly being serviced. Many manufacturers use the standards that steel timing chains be changed if they have 1/2" (13 mm) of deflection between gears and that timing belts be changed after approximately 60,000 miles (100,000 km) of use. If the manufacturer says to disconnect the battery, keep in mind that memory will be lost in many electrical devices and that they will have to be reset.

2. Remove all fluids from systems that require to be removed during timing chain or belt inspection, according to the manufacturer's service procedures.

3. Remove all systems that cover the timing chain or belt assembly, such as the harmonic balancer, water pump, alternators, and power steering pump. For internal inspection and replacement of the timing chain or belt assembly, follow the manufacturer's service procedures. *Note:* In some operations, the manufacturer will want to replace the water pump or other devices that are operated by the chain or belt assembly.

4. Remove the camshaft timing chain or belt cover. Inspect the metal or nonmetal cover for any wear marks. Replace if worn, according to the manufacturer's specifications. Look for possible causes for the worn cover.

5. With the timing chain or belt cover off and the timing gears and belts or chains in full view, turn the engine over manually to align the timing marks of the crankshaft and camshaft sprockets with the appropriate marks on the block and head.

Timing mark lined up with head surface

Continued

6. Measure distance between the colored links to see if the chain has stretched and is not in specification.

7. Remove the chain or belt following the specified procedure. Use the proper cam holding tool, if specified, to prevent damage to valves.

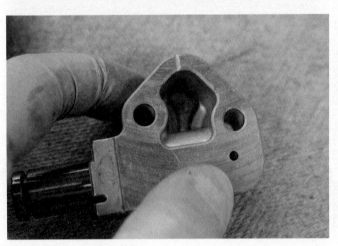

8. If the tensioner is oil operated, check the oil passages to the tensioner for clogs or buildup of dirty sludge, and clean or replace according to the manufacturer's recommendations.

9. Inspect any guide pulleys for smooth rotation on their bearings, and replace if damaged or according to the manufacturer's recommendations. With the chain or belt removed, inspect the cam sprockets visually for wear, cracking, and damage.

Continued

10. Inspect sprockets for backlash and end play, if applicable, on the vehicle being inspected according to the manufacturer's recommendations.

11. On engines with any type of variable valve timing, check components visually for worn and damaged parts on the gears; inspect any oil control devices for leaks; and perform other tests on components according to the manufacturer's recommendations.

12. Reinstall new parts according to the manufacturer's recommendations and specifications. Reassemble the timing chain or belt assembly and adjust, if needed, according to specifications.

13. Turn the crankshaft two complete revolutions by hand, and recheck the timing marks and belt or chain tension.

14. Reassemble all components following the specified procedure sensor, if adjustable, to bring it in line with the crankshaft position sensor.

leakage tester, is used to hold the valves closed while the valve spring is off. Careful work is required around the valve so the pressure seal is not broken and the valve dropped into the cylinder. Once the valve springs are off, the seal can be replaced with a new one. When you do so, use a special sleeve that fits over the valve keeper grooves and protects the seal as it is installed.

To replace valve stem seals on an assembled engine and to inspect valve spring retainers, locks or keepers, and valve lock or keeper grooves, follow the steps in **SKILL DRILL 24-12**.

SKILL DRILL 24-12 Replacing Valve Stem Seals and Inspecting Valve Spring Retainers, Locks/Keepers, and Valve Lock or Keeper Grooves

1. Remove any engine components that are in the way of removing the valve cover(s), and then remove the valve cover(s).

2. Remove the rocker arms or cam followers.

3. Rotate the engine so the cylinder you are working on is at TDC on the compression stroke, and pressurize the cylinder. If the engine rotates, reset it in the proper position.

Continued

4. Use a socket and hammer to tap on the valve retainers. This helps break the keepers loose from the retainer.

- Use a spring compressor to compress the valve spring, and remove the keepers and valve spring assembly. Using a magnet may help to remove the keepers. Do not allow them to fall into the engine, as they may become lost and pose a hazard to the engine.

5. Remove the old valve seal by carefully pulling it off the valve stem. Remove any broken pieces that may be lying in the head.

6. Install the protective sleeve over the valve stem. Lubricate the valve stem with clean engine oil, and install the valve seal into position. The valve stem may have to be pushed onto the valve stem boss.

Continued

7. Reinstall the valve spring and keepers, making sure everything is seated properly.

8. Repeat the process on the other valve(s) on that cylinder. And then repeat the process for the valve seals on the other cylinders. Reassemble the engine, and check for proper operation.

▶ Wrap-Up

Ready for Review

- ▶ Engine assembly is a process that must be carried out in a very clean environment and with the utmost attention to detail.
- ▶ Bearing oil clearance and end play have to be confirmed.
- ▶ Main bearing clearance can be calculated from measurements taken with precision measurement tools or by using Plastigage.
- ▶ With the engine inverted on the engine stand, start by carefully checking each bearing boss and bore.
- ▶ Handle new bearings carefully because some bearings have antiscuff coatings designed to aid in protecting the crankshaft during first start.
- ▶ Hold the shells by the edges as much as possible.
- ▶ The shells should snap into the bores because of bearing spread, and there should be a small protrusion above each saddle and cap, providing bearing crush.
- ▶ Torque all of the fasteners to specification in the torque sequence published by the engine maker.

- ▶ Mark torque angle bolts and use a torque angle gauge or torque angle torque wrench to tighten each fastener the further specified amount.
- ▶ To check crankshaft bearing clearance using Plastigage, place the clean, dry crankshaft in the saddle. Once you install the cap, do not turn the crankshaft, or the Plastigage will smear, ruining your measurement. Torque the can and then remove it and check the clearance.
- ▶ The crankshaft end play is controlled by the space between the thrust bearings and a precision ground thrust surface on the crankshaft.
- ▶ The thrust bearings can be manufactured as part of one of the main bearing shells or as separate replacement parts, and fit into reliefs machined in the saddle and matching cap.
- ▶ Thrust bearings are located in the middle or rearmost bearing.
- ▶ If the thrust bearings are part of the main bearing shell, the clearance can be checked by using a telescoping gauge

- and a micrometer to measure the width of thrust bearing and then subtracting it from the width of the crank journal.
- Thrust clearance can also be measured with the crank installed, using a dial indicator. With the crankshaft installed and main bearings and torqued, set up a dial gauge on the end of the crankshaft, and push the crankshaft fore and aft in the block to indicate the crankshaft thrust clearance; then compare it to specifications.
- You can check thrust clearance with the crankshaft installed is to use feeler gauges between the thrust surface of the crankshaft and the thrust bearings.
- Check piston installed height or piston to deck height. If the piston to deck clearance is insufficient, there is a risk of the piston striking the cylinder head during operation.
- Measuring piston installed height is particularly critical for diesel engines. Since diesel engines have high compression ratios, the clearance volume of the cylinder is very small.
- This piston installed height measurement is taken with a depth micrometer or a dial depth gauge. With the piston at TDC, measure down to the head of the piston and compare the reading with specifications.
- There are two different ways to install the piston on the connecting rod, the press fit and full float.
- Press fit is using a heater that heats the small end of the connecting rod and then pressing in a piston pin into the correct position, then be allowed to cool to keep the pin in the piston.
- The full float fit has the connecting rod machined to allow the installation of a bushing that the piston pin rides in. The piston pin is held in by circlips that snap into the piston.
- Use the outside micrometer to measure each main bearing journal, and record your findings with all the main caps and bearings installed and torqued with crankshaft, then use an inside micrometer or snap gauge to measure the inside diameter of the main bearing bore.
- When using a bore gauge, it is important to make sure the crankshaft is clean and free from oil or grease. Measure the main journals with an outside micrometer and record your findings. Use a bore gauge setting fixture to set the bore gauge according to the crankshaft main journals measurements and zero the dial. With all the main bearings in place and the main caps torqued to the proper torque setting, use the bore gauge and check your clearance. The reading on the bore gauge is the bearing clearance.
- Plastigage™ is an extruded plastic thread that comes in different sizes, depending on the expected clearances to be checked.
- Cut a piece of Plastigage™ just short of the width of the bearing, and lay it across the width of the crankshaft main journal, torque the main cap bolts to specifications, making sure the crankshaft does not turn, loosen the bolts and take the cap off and check the paper that the plastic gauge

- came in to see which width matches the plastic gauge, and read the chart for the proper bearing clearance.
- Carefully check each main bearing boss and bore. Wipe each saddle and bearing cap with a dry lint-free cloth to remove any oil or dirt that may have worked its way down while working with bearings. After wiping the backs of the first bearing, carefully install it into the appropriate saddle and bearing cap and be mindful of the oil hole orientation.
- Inspect the crankshaft and wash the crankshaft in solvent to remove any anticorrosion coating from the machine shop. Run a soft bristle rifle brush and solvent through the oil drillings in the journals to ensure that no grinding dust, metal particles or dirt will obstruct oil flow to the main journals or crankpins. Blow the crankshaft dry with compressed air.
- Measure the crankshaft main and crankpin journals with a suitable outside micrometer to confirm they were sized correctly by the machine shop. Confirm at this time that the bearings are also the correct replacement size for the crankshaft.
- Torque the fasteners to specification and then tighten to the specified angle.
- Measure the thrust bearing clearance.
- Connecting rod oil clearance can be measured in the same way as the main clearances; measurement and calculation or Plastigage.
- The connecting rods also need to be checked for side clearance, but this must be done with the connecting rods installed. When using the measure and calculate technique, the piston does not have to be installed on the connecting rod. If this is the technique that you elect to use, it is recommended to make this check before checking piston clearances.
- With bearings properly installed in their bores, assemble the rod caps onto the connecting rods. As with the crankshaft bearings, note any oil holes and ensure that the oil holes in the bearing match the holes in the rod. Be mindful of the marks indicating orientation especially with fractured rod caps.
- First, clean and dry the rod and cap and fit the bearings into the rod and cap of each assembly. Double-check that the correct bearing is placed in the assembly. Install the cap on the rod in the correct orientation and thread the nuts on the studs, or screw the bolts in a turn or two.
- Using a bare piston install the compression ring in the bore and check the ring gap.
- Assemble the piston rings to the piston according to specifications using a ring expander or special tool.
- Typically the letter 'T', a dot, or other symbol indicates the top of the ring.
- Once the rings are installed, ensure that they all move freely in their grooves, and that there are no segments of the oil control ring package that are overlapped or out of place. Check side groove clearance.
- Orient the piston rings so that the gaps are in the location specified in the service information. It is critical that

the gaps are offset when the piston is installed to prevent combustion gasses from simply flowing through the gaps. Offsetting the ring gaps reduces the amount of gasses that get past the rings—called "blowby"—to acceptable levels.

▶ Wipe the piston ring compressor with a clean shop towel to remove any debris, and then place some clean engine oil or assembly lubricant in the compressor band. Locate the compressor over the rings. Leave a portion of the skirt exposed to locate the piston in the cylinder.

▶ When installing the ring compressor, ensure the locating tabs or detents face down. Use care when tightening the compressor to ensure that all of the rings are compressing into their grooves.

▶ Remove the bearing cap, install available protectors, or some lengths of fuel line on the studs. Often called rod protectors, these are really to protect the crankpin from nicks as the pistons are installed.

▶ Rotate the crankshaft so that the crankpin for Cylinder 1 is at bottom dead center and carefully install the piston skirt into the cylinder bore, observing correct orientation. If it is uneven, a ring could escape, expand, and become broken as you are installing the piston. While holding the compressor firmly against the block use a piston hammer, or hammer handle, to gently tap or push the piston through the compressor. If the piston does not tap in easily, stop and check.

▶ A final piston related check that may be required on engines where the deck has been machined is piston installed height, also referred to as piston to deck height.

▶ If a performance camshaft is used and there is a higher lift and more duration in the cam profile than in a stock camshaft, it is recommended to check piston-to-valve clearance.

▶ Repainting is a mandatory part of the rebuild if the cast iron components have been cleaned in a caustic hot tank or with a steam cleaner.

▶ The core plugs could actually have been installed before any other work was done on the block, but if you discovered anything during your pre-assembly checks requiring further machining, they may have to be removed again.

▶ The oil pressure switch or sensor can be installed with the gallery plugs.

▶ Make sure all oil galleries are clean and clear of debris. You can check this visually with a flashlight, or blow air through the passageways.

▶ Clean any oil or sealant residue from the cylinder head and block deck.

▶ If you are using a different thickness head gasket to compensate for machining, confirm the new gasket is the correct thickness. If different gaskets are required for each bank of a V-engine, ensure that you have the correct gasket for the bank you are working on.

▶ Check the head gasket for a marking such as "Top" and the gasket may fit on the block and align with bolt holes if installed upside down, but obstruct oil or coolant passageways.

▶ Place the gasket on the deck and see that all holes in the gasket line up. Head gaskets are normally installed dry. Unless specified by the engine manufacturer, do not use any additional sealer or gasket treatment on the head gasket. The dowels in the block will keep the gasket in position.

▶ Rotate the engine so that the head deck is upright and parallel to the ground and clean any oil or sealant residue from the cylinder head and block deck.

▶ If the engine uses overhead camshafts, it may be necessary to have the camshafts removed to access the cylinder head fasteners.

▶ After lubricating the fasteners as directed by the service information, thread in the head bolts by hand.

▶ Make sure the head bolts go in the correct holes. Also, remember to use a non-hardening sealer on any bolts that thread into through holes that are exposed to oil or coolant.

▶ Go through each bolt on both heads, running the bolts down with a ratchet and socket until they are just snug. If standard bolts are used, torque in increments recommended by the manufacturer in the pattern provided. Remember to always double-check the torque on each fastener.

▶ Where torque-to-yield fasteners are used, remember to torque them to the initial specification, and re-check. Mark the heads with a paint dot in the 12 o'clock position, and complete the job by turning the fastener the specified number of degrees using a torque angle gauge.

▶ Synchronizing the opening and closing of the valves to piston travel is only possible if the camshaft and crankshaft are installed in the correct relationship. This is referred to as cam timing or valve timing.

▶ Installing the timing set is fundamentally the same regardless of the number of components driven by the timing system. Through the use of timing marks the camshaft and crankshaft are indexed to each other so that the reference cylinder is on compression. Especially with cam in block engines, the timing marks on both sprockets or gears are installed in relation to each other.

▶ Belt-driven timing sets use a flexible belt to transmit drive from the crankshaft to the camshaft. The belt runs more quietly than a chain and does not require lubrication. But timing belts do wear out and need to be changed periodically, typically between 50,000 and 100,000 miles (80,000 to 160,000 km), depending on the vehicle manufacturer.

▶ The oil pump may be located inside the oil pan, on the side of the block, or in the timing cover. It is typically driven by the crankshaft or camshaft. It is recommended that you pack the oil pump with assembly lube.

▶ Crankshaft and camshaft position sensors are located behind the timing covers, while others may be fitted in the timing cover itself and should be installed at the appropriate time and may also require setup with special tools to ensure appropriate clearances are maintained as the sensor pickup is rotated past the sensor body.

- Gasketing a pan can be accomplished with one piece formed rubber gaskets, multiple piece cut gaskets, or RTV form in place gasket materials.
- Pre-lubricate the engine before starting.
- Intake manifolds are sealed with a variety of gasket options. Cut gaskets are used with many metal manifolds; RTV with others. Plastic manifolds may use formed rubber O-ring like gaskets.

Key Terms

bore gauge Used to quickly measure a bore. It is a dial indicator that has an adapter to allow it to measure the inside of a bore to check for taper or out-of-round.

inside micrometer Used to measure the inside of a hole or passage so that it can be determined whether it is serviceable.

outside micrometer Measures the outside dimensions of the component so that it can be compared to the specification to see if it is serviceable.

piston installed height Measurement taken as the engine is being assembly; it tells the technician how far out of the block the piston protrudes. This must be checked because if the piston strikes the cylinder head, there will be catastrophic problems internally in the engine.

Plastigage A plastic thread that is used to check clearance between two different parts. It is put between the components and then torqued to specification. As the component is torqued down, it smashes the plastic, which causes it to flatten out, giving the technician a reading of the clearance between the two components.

thrust bearing Bearing that controls the forward and rearward movement of the crankshaft as it rotates in the engine block.

torque angle gauge Tells the technician the degrees of rotation of the fastener as they are torquing it.

Review Questions

1. All of the below statements are true with respect to a temporary test buildup *except*:
   a. It should always include the piston rings or a rear main seal for the crankshaft.
   b. It will determine if additional machining will be necessary.
   c. It should include the cylinder heads and the valve train.
   d. It will determine if exchange of any parts will be necessary.

2. Which of these should be used to check the bearing clearance with the crankshaft installed?
   a. Micrometer
   b. Bore gauge
   c. Plastigage
   d. Feeler gauge

3. When installing the crankshaft, to prevent oil leak from the rear of the block:
   a. paint the surface in a double coat.
   b. use a dab of silicone sealer.
   c. use plugs to close any openings.
   d. temporarily solder together the parts in the rear of the block.

4. When the piston is installed:
   a. the piston rings must be aligned in their proper positions to minimize blowby gases.
   b. ensure lubricants or oil is not present.
   c. the crankshaft should be positioned so its journal is at top dead center.
   d. hammer the piston hard into the cylinder until you do not feel any resistance.

5. RTV should not be used on:
   a. paper gaskets.
   b. fiber gaskets.
   c. cork gaskets.
   d. neoprene gaskets with multi-sealing edges.

6. When installing the intake manifold:
   a. always tighten the bolts in two steps, one-half of the torque at a time.
   b. treat the threads of the bolts with adhesive to avoid oil leaks.
   c. for bolts near the plenum of the intake, use the box end of a wrench.
   d. use thick rubber or cork gaskets that do not allow the intake to seat properly.

7. All of the following tools are used to check bearing clearances, *except*:
   a. inner micrometer.
   b. bore gauge.
   c. Plastigage.
   d. feeler gauge.

8. All of the following statements with respect to thrust bearing are true, *except*:
   a. The thrust bearings can be manufactured as part of one of the main bearing shells or as separate replacement parts.
   b. The thrust bearing fits into reliefs machined in the saddle and matching cap.
   c. Usually the thrust bearings are located in the foremost bearing.
   d. The thickness of the thrust bearing shell when installed in the block and cap can be measured using a micrometer.

9. When torquing the flywheel back into place, the friction disc can be set in a centered position using a:
   a. flywheel wrench.
   b. clutch alignment tool.
   c. gasket.
   d. ratchet and socket.

10. When replacing valve seals, which of these is used to hold the valves closed while the valve spring is off?
   a. A special sleeve
   b. Compressed air
   c. An adhesive
   d. A wrench

ASE Technician A/Technician B Style Questions

1. Technician A says that reusing torque-to-yield bolts is a good idea when rebuilding an engine. Technician B states that using a torque angle gauge is the proper way to tighten bolts that have a degree-tightening specification. Who is correct?
   a. Tech A
   b. Tech B
   c. Both A and B
   d. Neither A nor B

2. Technician A says that using Plastigage is an easy way of determining bearing clearance when assembling an engine. Technician B says that you shouldn't have to check bearing clearance if everything is new. Who is correct?
   a. Tech A
   b. Tech B
   c. Both A and B
   d. Neither A nor B

3. Technician A says that it is easier to replace valve stem seals while the engine is assembled. Technician B states that replacing the valve stem seals should be done every time the cylinder head is off the engine. Who is correct?
   a. Tech A
   b. Tech B
   c. Both A and B
   d. Neither A nor B

4. Technician A states that indexing the camshaft position sensor should be done after the engine is completely assembled. Technician B says that the timing belt must be inspected every time it is removed and replaced periodically. Who is correct?
   a. Tech A
   b. Tech B
   c. Both A and B
   d. Neither A nor B

5. Technician A says that exhaust manifolds with support brackets attached to them must have those brackets reinstalled, or the manifold may crack. Technician B states that factory support brackets are only installed to help with the assembly line when the vehicle is put together, and they can be discarded. Who is correct?
   a. Tech A
   b. Tech B
   c. Both A and B
   d. Neither A nor B

6. Technician A states that piston rings should be installed with an installer instead of just trying to spread them around the piston. Technician B says that some pistons come with the piston rings already installed. Who is correct?
   a. Tech A
   b. Tech B
   c. Both A and B
   d. Neither A nor B

7. Technician A states that after you assemble the engine, you should pre-prime the oil pump so that the engine doesn't start dry. Technician B says that the oil pump comes pre-primed so there is no need to pre-prime the engine. Who is correct?
   a. Tech A
   b. Tech B
   c. Both A and B
   d. Neither A nor B

8. Technician A says that a timing chain must be installed in the correct position to get the engine to run. Technician B says that a timing belt can be installed in any position, as it will end up in the right place. Who is correct?
   a. Tech A
   b. Tech B
   c. Both A and B
   d. Neither A nor B

9. Technician A states that the technician should verify he or she has the correct head gaskets before deciding to install the cylinder head. Technician B states that the technician should confer with the service information for the proper procedure to install the cylinder head. Who is correct?
   a. Tech A
   b. Tech B
   c. Both A and B
   d. Neither A nor B

10. Technician A says that the technician must test out the thrust bearing clearance before installing the engine into the vehicle. Technician B says that on a manual transmission vehicle, the thrust bearing usually gets more worn. Who is correct?
    a. Tech A
    b. Tech B
    c. Both A and B
    d. Neither A nor B

CHAPTER 25

Engine Installation and Break In

NATEF Tasks

- **N25001** Verify operation of the instrument panel engine warning indicators.

Knowledge Objectives

After reading this chapter, you will be able to:

- **K25001** Determine when the installation will occur in the engine rebuild process.
- **K25002** Determine the usage of engine motor mounts and why they need to be there.
- **K25003** Perform prestart engine checks.
- **K25004** Determine proper procedures for initial engine start-up.
- **K25005** Perform proper initial break-in procedures.

Skills Objectives

- **S25001** The ability to do an engine installation.
- **S25002** The ability to do prechecks.
- **S25003** The ability to do an engine break-in.
- **S25004** The ability to perform an engine timing adjustment.

You Are the Automotive Technician

You have just installed a used engine in this 2010 Chevy Equinox, but it does not start. What is the first step in figuring out what is causing the engine not to start?

1. Check fluid levels.
2. Check engine harness wiring.
3. Check gasoline level in the fuel tank.

K25001 Determine when the installation will occur in the engine rebuild process.

▶ Introduction

Installing an engine in a vehicle is a very precise process that the technician must take very seriously, as many things could happen. Making sure that the engine is correct for the vehicle is the first step, because finding out the engine is wrong after it has been installed will cause more work than there needs to be. This chapter goes over basic items that must be looked at before the engine is installed so that the installation will be successful.

▶ Engine Installation

S25001 The ability to do an engine installation.

Just as in the engine removal process, have assistants help you install the engine. First, organize the work site. Begin by making sure the area is clean and clear of obstructions. To be prepared, arrange the bolts and engine mounts needed to secure the engine so they will be conveniently accessible. Additionally, lay out tools that will be needed for the initial installation of the engine. Time spent organizing the work site will ensure a safe and smooth engine installation.

To reinstall the engine, basically reverse the process used to remove it. However, there are some additional procedures. For vehicles equipped with automatic transmissions, it is a good idea to consider changing the front transmission seal while the torque converter is removed. It only takes a few minutes and will avoid having to remove the transmission again if it were to leak. Also be sure to fill the torque converter with the proper transmission fluid. Lay the torque converter down facing up and pour enough transmission fluid into the torque converter to fill it about halfway (**FIGURE 25-1**). When reinstalling the torque converter, push in and turn the torque converter, making sure it engages into the front pump. You should feel three distinct clunks. If the torque converter is not being replaced, make sure it is engaged into the front pump. When mating the engine up to the transmission, make sure the torque converter does not bind against the flex plate. If it does, remove the engine and reengage the torque converter into the transmission. Some converters have studs that protrude out and are connected with nuts. The converter will have to be rotated to match the holes in the flex plate for the two to mate up (**FIGURE 25-2**).

For vehicles equipped with manual transmissions, the clutch disc needs to be aligned with the clutch pilot hole using a clutch alignment tool (**FIGURE 25-3**). First verify that the correct pilot bearing or bushing is installed in the rear of the crankshaft. Once you know the correct pilot bearing is in place, you can use an alignment tool that has the same splines as the clutch disc and fits snugly in the pilot bearing. Align the clutch disc, and install the pressure plate.

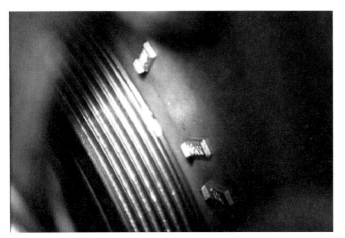

FIGURE 25-1 If the ignition timing is adjustable, make sure it is set close enough to start, and then hook up a timing light to make an adjustment when the engine first starts.

FIGURE 25-2 When installing the engine with an automatic transmission, the torque converter will have to be aligned with the flexplate on the engine so that the torque converter bolts can be installed.

FIGURE 25-3 Installing a clutch on a flywheel must be done with a clutch alignment tool that aligns the clutch with the pilot hole bushing.

When installing a manual transmission to the engine, you sometimes need to turn the splined input shaft to align it with the clutch disc splines. A good way to do this is to leave the transmission in fourth gear and then turn the output shaft. Also, the front of the input shaft has to align with the flywheel pilot bearing or bushing. Make sure the bell housing holes are aligned with the engine's dowel pins, and tighten all of the bell housing bolts evenly.

▶ Engine Motor Mounts

After the transmission is bolted to the engine, the engine must be mounted to the vehicle frame or cradle. To do so, attach the **motor mounts** that connect the engine to the frame or mounting platform (**FIGURE 25-4**). To mount the engine, lower it carefully, aligning the motor mounts (**FIGURE 25-5**). On some vehicles, the exhaust header must be aligned to the exhaust pipe at this time. Tighten the motor mounts when the engine and mounts are in place. Reinstall all parts and components in reverse order of disassembly.

K25002 Determine the usage of engine motor mounts and why they need to be there.

▶ Prestart Engine Checks

Before starting the engine after installation, you need to make several checks, including the following:

K25003 Perform prestart engine checks.

S25002 The ability to do prechecks.

1. Check all fluid levels, especially the engine oil and coolant levels. If a vacuum fill method of filling the cooling system was used, the cooling system will be full. If this method was not used, the system will look full but likely will have air pockets in the system. If there is a vacuum pocket at the thermostat, the air pocket may prevent the thermostat from getting up to temperature and opening, potentially causing the brand new engine to overheat.
2. Check that the battery terminals are connected firmly and the battery is charged.
3. Make sure the fuel is supplied to the injection system by turning the key to the Run position, and check that there are no fuel leaks at the connections and fittings.
4. If the ignition timing is adjustable, make sure it is set close enough to start, and then hook up a timing light to make an adjustment when the engine first starts (**FIGURE 25-6**).
5. Check all of the auxiliary components, such as the air conditioner and the power steering pump, for proper installation and hose routing.
6. Check the serpentine belt and/or other belts and pulleys for proper installation.
7. Determine that electrical connectors and vacuum hoses are properly connected (**FIGURE 25-7**).
8. Connect the exhaust removal hose to the exhaust pipe. Verify that the brake pedal is not spongy.

FIGURE 25-4 After the motor mount is installed in the vehicle, reattach it to the engine.

FIGURE 25-5 Lowering the engine slowly so that the bolt holes on the engine block align with the holes on the motor mount will aid in motor mount reattachment.

FIGURE 25-6 Using a timing light to set ignition timing.

FIGURE 25-7 Making sure that all the electrical connectors are hooked up will allow for a smooth engine startup.

► Engine Start-Up

K25004 Determine proper procedures for initial engine start-up.

Engine start-up after installation is a critical time for engine operation and longevity. It is important to make sure all fluid levels are checked and at the correct level. Keep your eyes and ears open, listening for unusual noises and looking for fluid leaks. Monitor the temperature and oil pressure gauges, and shut the engine down immediately if the gauges indicate overheating or low oil pressure. If the engine is not starting, do not crank the engine excessively, because the starter might be damaged from excessive heat. Also, the lack of proper lubrication from the slow-turning oil pump can cause premature engine damage. Crank the engine for no more than 10 seconds at a time. Some new camshaft break-in procedures require the engine to start immediately and to run at 1200 to 2000 rpm for 20 or 30 minutes to provide proper lubrication and break-in.

► Initial Break-In

N25001 Verify operation of the instrument panel engine warning indicators.

K25005 Perform proper initial break-in procedures.

S25003 The ability to do an engine break-in.

To ensure that the piston rings are seated properly and that the camshaft and other internal components are not damaged, it is important to follow the manufacturer's break-in procedures. If required during the initial engine break-in period, run the engine at high idle (1200–2000 rpm). Observe the temperature and oil pressure gauges (**FIGURE 25-8**). If the engine begins to run hot or the oil pressure drops, shut it off immediately. Also, monitor the engine for external leaks. If any are found, shut the engine down, and repair the leak. Run the engine at fast idle until it reaches and holds normal operating temperature or for the prescribed break-in time, and then shut it down. Check the engine oil and oil level to ensure that there is no evidence of coolant in the oil. If the oil looks milky or the oil level has risen above the full line, there may be an internal coolant leak.

FIGURE 25-8 Observing the oil pressure as the engine is first started will aid in determining if there is a major issue that needs to be addressed before it causes major engine damage.

► Engine Timing Adjustment and Diagnostic Trouble Code Inspection

After starting the engine, you have to determine whether the engine ignition timing is set correctly if it is adjustable. There are almost as many methods of setting the timing as there are vehicle models. Again, you need to consult the appropriate service literature to determine the correct method.

Notice that there are significant differences in timing methods from one decade to another. On vehicles from the 1970s and earlier, the primary method for setting the timing is to adjust the distributor while using a timing light. For 1980s models, you might need to disconnect a computer spark control wire, or ground a particular wire, or disconnect a sensor, and then set the timing by adjusting the distributor while using a timing light. On most vehicles made since the mid-to late 1980s, the computer controls the timing, and you do not need to manually set it other than setting the engine timing initially.

Another important task to complete after you have started the engine is connecting a diagnostic scan tool to the **data link connector (DLC)** and checking for **diagnostic trouble codes (DTCs)**. If you find that a DTC was set during the engine break-in period, diagnose the condition. Once corrected, run the engine until it is fully warm again, and check for any DTCs.

Once the engine is timed properly and the runs without turning on the MIL, and the engine has reached operating temperature with no sign of leaks or other problems, take the vehicle for a test drive. Drive it for 30 minutes without exceeding 50 mph (80 kph) and 2000 rpm. This will allow the piston rings to seat and ensure good seating of other internal components such as cam lobes. Once back at the shop, recheck all of the fluid levels, and look for any leaks. Also check for any loose or missing components. If everything is in working order, clean the vehicle, and return it to the customer.

S25004 The ability to perform an engine timing adjustment.

▶ Wrap-Up

Ready for Review

- ▶ Engine installation process is not a single person process.
- ▶ Always follow service information on installation processes of the engine assembly.
- ▶ When installing a clutch make sure to align the clutch with the pilot bearing with an aligner.
- ▶ The torque converter must be fully installed in the transmission before the engine is installed to prevent damage.
- ▶ Prestart engine checks should be performed before trying to start the engine to prevent damage to the engine.
- ▶ Upon initial break in of the engine properly seating the piston rings is necessary to ensure a long life for the engine.
- ▶ Setting the timing to a should be done as soon as the engine is operational as it is necessary to make the engine operate correctly. This only applies to vehicles with a distributor that is adjustable.
- ▶ After break in recheck the PCM for diagnostic engine codes.

Key Terms

diagnostic link connector (DLC) The port that the technician connects a scanner to in order to interrogate the PCM in the vehicle for information about faults.

diagnostic trouble code (DTC) A failure code that directs the technician to the area where there is a fault.

motor mounts Rubber insulators that connect the engine with the vehicle frame. They isolate the vibrations the engine gives off so that the driver doesn't feel it.

Review Questions

1. Choose the correct statement with respect to reinstalling the engine in vehicles equipped with automatic transmissions:
   a. It is a good idea to consider changing the front transmission seal while the torque converter is removed.
   b. Fill the torque converter to its fullest limit with the proper transmission fluid.
   c. You should feel two distinct clunks when the torque converter engages into the front pump.
   d. When mating the engine up to the transmission, make sure the torque converter binds against the flex plate.

2. All of the following statements with respect to reinstalling the engine in vehicles equipped with manual transmissions are true, *except*:
   a. The clutch disc needs to be aligned with the clutch pilot hole using a clutch alignment tool.
   b. A good way to turn the splined input shaft to align it with the clutch disc splines is to leave the transmission in first gear and then turn the output shaft.
   c. The front of the input shaft has to align with the flywheel pilot bearing or bushing.
   d. Make sure the bell housing holes are aligned with the engine's dowel pins, and tighten all of the bell housing bolts evenly.

3. All of the statements with respect to engine motor mounts are true, *except*:
   a. The engine must be mounted to the frame before the transmission is bolted to the engine.
   b. Motor mounts should be tightened only when the engine and mounts are in place.

c. The parts and components should be installed in the reverse order of disassembly.

d. The exhaust header must be aligned to the exhaust pipe at the time of attaching the motor mount.

4. What needs to be checked for if a vacuum fill method of filling the cooling system was used?

a. Level of the coolant

b. Temperature of the coolant

c. Air pockets in the system

d. Type of coolant

5. If the engine is not starting:

a. crank the engine for 1 minute.

b. do not crank the engine excessively.

c. add some engine oil.

d. increase the fuel level.

6. To provide proper lubrication and break-in, some new camshaft break-in procedures require the engine to start immediately and to run at 1200 to 2000 rpm for:

a. 5–10 minutes.

b. 10–15 minutes.

c. 20–30 minutes.

d. a few seconds after start.

7. Which of the following components is more likely to get damaged due to excessive heating and over-cranking while engine start-up?

a. Oil pump

b. Starter

c. Camshafts

d. Ignition cables

8. An internal cooling leak in the engine can be detected if:

a. the engine begins to run hot.

b. the coolant pressure is high.

c. the oil looks milky.

d. the oil level is low.

9. When you take the vehicle for a test drive after reinstalling the engine, what speed should the vehicle not exceed for the first 30 minutes?

a. 30 mph

b. 40 mph

c. 50 mph

d. 60 mph

10. On most vehicles made since the mid-to late 1980s, the engine ignition timing:

a. is set by adjusting the distributor while using a timing light.

b. is set by disconnecting a computer spark control wire, or grounding a particular wire, or disconnecting a sensor, and then setting the timing by adjusting the distributor while using a timing light.

c. is set using a scan tool.

d. is set by a computer and you do not need to manually set it other than setting the engine timing initially.

ASE Technician A/Technician B Style Questions

1. Technician A says that you should double-check the fluid levels before you start a fresh engine. Technician B states that a check engine light could come on because the technician that installed the engine forgot to plug something in. Who is correct?

a. Tech A

b. Tech B

c. Both A and B

d. Neither A nor B

2. Technician A says that the motor mounts for the engine should be inspected before they are installed in the vehicle. Technician B says that solid motor mounts allow for power transfer to the vehicle. Who is correct?

a. Tech A

b. Tech B

c. Both A and B

d. Neither A nor B

3. Technician A states that the PCM is used to monitor the speed of the air that is passing the vehicle as it drives down the road. Technician B says that the DLC is used to scan the vehicle for trouble codes and other engine-related information. Who is correct?

a. Tech A

b. Tech B

c. Both A and B

d. Neither A nor B

4. Technician A says that when breaking in an engine, the technician should hold the throttle to 1200–2000 rpm. Technician B states that double-checking all the components that were removed is good habit to get into. Who is correct?

a. Tech A

b. Tech B

c. Both A and B

d. Neither A nor B

5. Technician A says that a freshly rebuilt engine should only be installed into a vehicle that has a new transmission. Technician B states that when installing a transmission with the engine, the engine crane should be rated to handle the weight of both of the components. Who is correct?

a. Tech A

b. Tech B

c. Both A and B

d. Neither A nor B

6. Technician A states that before installing the engine, the technician should make sure the area is free from unnecessary obstacles. Technician B says that the engine should be installed with all the fluids in it. Who is correct?

a. Tech A

b. Tech B

c. Both A and B

d. Neither A nor B

7. Technician A says that before the vehicle is given back to the customer, the technician should make sure the indicator lights work properly. Technician B says that the technician should check all the vehicle's fluids to make sure they are in operable range. Who is correct?

a. Tech A

b. Tech B

c. Both A and B

d. Neither A nor B

8. Technician A states that the technician should figure out what destroyed the previous engine before installing a rebuilt one. Technician B says that the customer should be made aware of any potential problems they may have with other parts of the vehicle before he or she leaves. Who is correct?

a. Tech A

b. Tech B

c. Both A and B

d. Neither A nor B

9. Technician A states that a rebuilt engine means that the vehicle is brand new. Technician B says that the rebuilt engine could cause other components to fail because of the increased power. Who is correct?

a. Tech A

b. Tech B

c. Both A and B

d. Neither A nor B

10. Technician A states that while the engine is running, the vehicle's exhaust should be vented to the outside. Technician B says that a new engine means that the exhaust from it is clean enough to breathe. Who is correct?

a. Tech A

b. Tech B

c. Both A and B

d. Neither A nor B

NATEF Tasks

There are no NATEF Tasks for this chapter.

Knowledge Objectives

After reading this chapter, you will be able to:

- **K26001** Knowledge of root cause based diagnosis procedures.
- **K26002** Knowledge of engine failure indications.
- **K26003** Knowledge of engine problem identification.

- **K26004** Knowledge of vehicle serviceability.
- **K26005** Knowledge of cooling system serviceability.
- **K26006** Knowledge of oiling system serviceability.

Skills Objectives

- **S26001** The ability to verify failed components.
- **S26002** The ability to research repair history of a vehicle.

- **S26003** The ability to identify the area that caused the failure of the engine.
- **S26004** The ability to fill out a check sheet.

You Are the Automotive Technician

The 2013 Chevrolet Silverado 2500 6.0 liter has been assigned to you to diagnosis. The engine will not turn over as it appears to be seized up. You notice that it has a large oil leak near the front of the vehicle. What is the first step into repair.

1. Remove the engine and install a rebuilt one.
2. Diagnose why the engine failed by investigating the large oil leak.
3. Recommend replacing the vehicle as the cost will out weight the cost of a new vehicle.

▶ Introduction

This chapter will give the technician some areas to examine when a customer's vehicle comes in to the facility. The technician must be able to ascertain the conditions that may have caused the complaint so that they will be able to repeat the event. Sometimes this is not necessary, as the complaint is very apparent to anyone that operates the vehicle. Communication with the customer is the main source of information on what caused this problem to happen and how they want to proceed to fix the issue.

▶ Engine Failure Diagnosis

Engine failure is one of the largest expenses a person can have on a vehicle as it is the heart of the vehicle. Usually when an engine fails it is because of another system that has failed which has resulted in the engine breakdown. By not fixing the issue that has caused the engine to break, the vehicle will ultimately break again as the conditions are the same as they were before when the failure happened. The **three Cs** should be examined: Concern, Cause, Correction.

What Caused the Engine to Fail?

The first step in any diagnosis should be a customer interview. Done properly, interviews increase customer confidence in the repair process while providing important information to help technicians correctly discover the cause of the problem. During this process, the customer should be reassured that the information being gathered is to assist in the accurate diagnosis of the vehicle and that his or her input is valuable. The technician should avoid using too many technical terms. When asking customers to describe noises, for example, it is helpful to provide them with a list of conditions and examples of the sounds they make.

Using a check sheet to standardize the questions asked is invaluable. You can create your own worksheet for customer interviews and customize it for tests your shop is equipped to perform (Appendices A–D). When designing the check sheet, ensure you leave lots of room for free-form notes, and incorporate lots of open-ended questions—that is, questions that cannot be answered in single words. Check sheets can be developed for any number of situations in engine operation: engine noise, engine performance, misfire, fluid consumption testing, and so forth.

If the customer calls for a service appointment, ask whether he or she has a few minutes to answer some questions about the problem, and run through the interview sheet with the customer right then. If the customer is not able then to spend time on the phone, ask if you can email the worksheet and it can be filled out at a convenient time before the vehicle is brought in. If the customer knows the type of information you need to diagnose the vehicle, he or she will often notice details about the problem in question and be able to give you a more accurate picture of the failure. You should still review the sheet with the customer, as some of the comments may spur additional questions.

Fixing the Problem Before Replacing an Engine

If it is decided that the existing engine will be repaired or reconditioned, the root cause of engine failure must first be determined so it can be corrected. If the engine has worn excessively due to time in service, it may be that no other repairs are required except for engine reconditioning. If premature engine failure has occurred, then before the engine is repaired, the cost of rectifying the underlying issues must be estimated. If the root cause is not fixed, the repaired engine will fail prematurely as well.

Engine failures can occur for numerous reasons:

- Faulty components
- Incorrect previous service or repair
- Operating conditions
- Ingress of contaminants
- Lack of maintenance
- Support system failures
- Hydraulic lock

Clues to the cause of engine failures may be present when examining the vehicle before the engine is removed; others are often found when inspecting bearings, pistons, rings, and cylinders (**FIGURE 26-1**).

Faulty Components

Faulty components do get past inspection processes during manufacture. A familiar example of this is when cam lobes that are incorrectly heat treated they become rounded in engine operation, resulting in loss of performance in one or more cylinders. Although failure due to manufacturing tolerance usually occurs early on in the life of the engine, parts do wear and fail in service as well. For example, timing chains stretch, resulting in valve timing variation, which affects engine performance.

When evaluating failed parts, consider the service life they have provided. If the failed part appears to have given adequate service life, it is plausible that the piece has simply worn out. Replacing worn or damaged components should be sufficient for restoring the engine to service. If the parts seem to have worn prematurely, further investigation is required to ensure that your repair provides the expected longevity. In this case, the faulty component is an intermediate result, and the root cause has to be assessed. Note as well that failures outside of the engine may cause engine damage. An over-pressure torque converter can balloon, causing excessive thrust bearing wear. Remember to consider all possibilities when trying to identify the cause of an engine breakdown.

FIGURE 26-1 Inspecting the systems that contribute to the operation of the engine, without finding the cause of the failure, there is potential for the next engine to fail also.

S26003 The ability to identify the area that caused the failure of the engine.

Previous Repairs

Improperly performed previous repairs can also result in a variety of engine failures. Incorrect machining of engine parts can result in numerous bearing and piston problems. A broken ring land (which can occur on either installation or removal of the pistons), nicked bearing journals, incorrect torque of fasteners, excessive engine sealant, and improper clearances are all examples of problems that may occur. For the purposes of this text we will forgo any discussion on improperly machined parts and assume that the vehicle is coming in with a first-time failure.

The vehicle may not have had recent major repairs, like those listed above, that have suffered failure. Something as simple as a double-gasketed oil filter can cause a loss of oil and oil pressure very rapidly. If operated in those conditions for even brief periods, bearings, pistons, camshafts, and lifters can be scuffed, which can accelerate wear. Allowing dirt into the engine is the most common cause of service-induced failure. Failure to use compressed air to blow sand and debris away from the spark plug area before changing plugs can allow particulates to fall into a spark plug hole while the plugs are being renewed, causing accelerated wear to the cylinder, piston, and rings. Fasteners accidentally dropped into the engine intake can cause catastrophic engine failures.

It is also possible that although repairs were recently carried out to correct the root cause of engine damage, other components damaged by that condition have not been repaired or replaced. For example, an engine may have been experiencing overheating issues for a period of time because of a faulty thermostat. The customer may have had the overheating problem diagnosed and repaired correctly. Perhaps the head gasket has failed because of cylinder head warpage due to overheating. Although it may appear to have come on suddenly, the failure actually relates back to the overheating condition that caused damage to the engine.

Collecting an accurate repair history from the customer before you attempt to diagnose an engine condition is helpful in locating the root cause (**FIGURE 26-2**). Be on the lookout for signs of previous repairs: new parts, disturbed dirt and grease, and components that are markedly cleaner than the rest of the engine or engine bay. Recently cleaned or

S26004 The ability to fill out a check sheet.

FIGURE 26-3 A worn out bearing or crankshaft journal can cause engine failure. This could be caused by lack of maintenance or overloading the engine.

FIGURE 26-2 When evaluating an engine that has failed, the technician must research the history of the repairs on the vehicle as it may give him a direction to go when diagnosing the potential causes of failure.

FIGURE 26-4 A thrust bearing helps minimize the movement of the crankshaft forward and backwards within the engine block. If excessive load is applied in this direction failure of the thrust bearing will happen.

shampooed engines may also indicate recent repairs. If any signs of recent repairs are evident, be sure to make note of these, and ask the customer for information about the repair.

Operating Conditions

Engines subjected to unusually high or sustained loading are prone to earlier failure. This often shows up as high oil consumption initially. Oil mist is churned up in the engine and burned through the PCV system. Bearing wear and piston and ring failures can occur from high load, but these issues are accelerated if the oil level drops appreciably. Lugging the engine results in bearing fatigue and can cause crankshaft breakage (**FIGURE 26-3**). Excessive thrust bearing wear may appear in engines where the clutch is being held for long periods of time such as in stop-and-go traffic or in off-road driving with a four-wheel drive vehicle (**FIGURE 26-4**). Discussing how the vehicle is used and how operating conditions relate to engine failure to the customer is important to ensure he or she understands the nature of the failure. Your machine shop may be able to suggest some options to increase life expectancy of the engine, based on the proposed use.

Lack of Maintenance and Support Systems

Although support systems are often adversely affected by lack of maintenance, not all support system failures are caused by improper care. The following sections address support system issues that can result in engine damage. Addressed here are the air induction, cooling, lubrication, ignition, and fuel systems.

Is the Vehicle in Serviceable Condition?

K26004 Knowledge of vehicle serviceability.

The technician must evaluate the vehicle's viability before telling the customer the cost of repairs. If the repairs entail a cost greater than the value of the vehicle, the technician should advise the customer not to have them made. The technician is expected to make these determinations, so the customer can decide whether to proceed with repairs.

Cooling System Condition

K26005 Knowledge of cooling system serviceability.

The cooling system is responsible for removing excessive combustion heat from the engine. Failure of the cooling system often results in temperature-related engine failures.

The cooling system can also result in mechanical damage to the engine without overheating. Overheating problems can lead to failed head gaskets and warped or cracked heads and manifolds. When overheating occurs, surplus heat of combustion cannot be conducted away from the piston head, and the piston may begin to stick or seize in the cylinder bore. Abnormal combustion such as pre-ignition and detonation can also occur. The result of severe overheating is rapid, profound engine damage (**FIGURE 26-5**).

The potential causes of cooling system failure:

- Plugged radiators
- Collapsed hoses
- Low coolant level
- Faulty pressure caps
- Inoperative or ineffective cooling fans
- Belt driven thermostatic cooling fans permit slipping when the engine is cold it they do not engage when the engine is hot, airflow through the radiator is reduced which causes overheating
- Electric cooling fans work on a thermal switch, a relay, temperature sensors, and/or the PCM which all may fail
- Installing the wrong cooling fan that pushes air through the radiator instead of pulling it through the radiator could be an issue

Any one of these items could cause a poor cooling condition which could result in engine failure and potential failure of a replacement engine.

The cooling system can also contribute to mechanical failure without signs of overheating. Engine coolant contains corrosion inhibitors that become ineffective over time. If not regularly changed according to manufacturer recommendations, internal damage in the cooling system occurs. With cast iron blocks and heads, rust forms and can block coolant passages—especially the fine tubes in radiators and heater cores. This may result in localized hot spots without presenting overheating. The use of incorrect engine coolant is increasingly a concern and cause of engine problems. In the past, generic, green ethylene glycol could be used to fill any cooling system because manufacturers' engine coolant was mostly the same (**FIGURE 26-6**). Currently, there are several different coolant chemistries that are not compatible with each other or with the "universal" green coolant. Diesel engines often have specialized formulations that differ from spark-ignition engines. Using improper coolants can cause components to deteriorate and fail. Usually these failures are related to cavitations or galvanic corrosion (**FIGURE 26-7**).

FIGURE 26-5 Severely overheated components could appear to be discolored, out of shape, and warped beyond repair. If you think the engine has been severely overheated you need to investigate further as to the source of the overheating.

FIGURE 26-6 Mixing coolant with different coolant causes the properties of both coolants to lose their effectiveness. Installing the correct coolant is key to ensuring a long life in the engine.

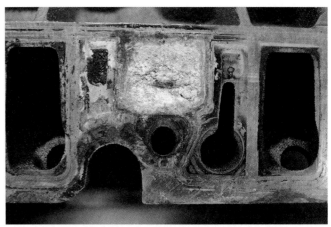

FIGURE 26-7 Galvanic corrosion or cavitation can eat away at the cooling passages and gaskets which then can cause engine failure.

Cavitation occurs when aeration is introduced in a liquid system. When the coolant is in close contact with the hot engine parts, micro-boiling occurs, causing bubbles to form at the surface. When the bubbles break free, a low pressure exists, which tears small particles from the surface. Under normal circumstances, silicates in the coolant coat the metal surfaces with a thin layer. The cavitation removes the silicate layer and does not affect the metal below. New silicates from the coolant replenish this surface. Once the coolant is depleted of additives, the cavitation results in loss of metal.

Galvanic corrosion occurs when dissimilar metals are in contact through a liquid electrolyte. Both processes erode the surface and weaken the metal. Sometimes this is seen as etching around the coolant passages and the fire rings of cylinder head gaskets. If left unchecked, the erosion process results in leaks and porous castings. Leaks occur around gasket surfaces as the openings near the gasket begin to dissolve.

External coolant leaks can result in overheating conditions, but internal coolant leaks can also cause rapid and profound engine wear. Coolant contaminates the lubrication system, accelerating wear throughout the engine. Slight seepage may start off as a minimal problem, but as the condition continues, the detrimental effects on the engine become more severe. Loss of coolant is the first sign to be aware of. If the coolant level is dropping with no external leaks, internal leaks can be suspected. Coolant leaking into the combustion chamber causes white, sweet-smelling exhaust smoke (**FIGURE 26-8**). Spark plugs have a dull white appearance and are void of deposits (**FIGURE 26-9**). Pistons of affected cylinders are often "steam cleaned" by the coolant, giving them a pristine appearance when the cylinder head is removed (**FIGURE 26-10**). The most common point of entry for coolant into the combustion chamber is the cylinder head gasket. Leaking head gaskets can lead to overheating.

In small quantities, coolant leaking into the combustion chamber may not contaminate the oil, but excessive amounts will result in misfires, and liquid coolant will leak past the rings into the crankcase. Coolant can also enter the crankcase by other means. To check for coolant entering the crankcase, start by watching for a rising oil level or change in oil appearance. Coolant-contaminated engine oil often takes on a "chocolate milkshake" appearance (**FIGURE 26-11**). Small amounts of coolant in the oil may not change the appearance because at higher engine temperatures the water in the coolant mixture may evaporate, leaving the glycol component behind. This still

FIGURE 26-8 On a gasoline engine white sweet smoke coming from the exhaust is a sign of burning coolant. Further investigation is needed to ascertain the source of the coolant.

FIGURE 26-9 Clean dull looking spark plugs are a sign of burning coolant.

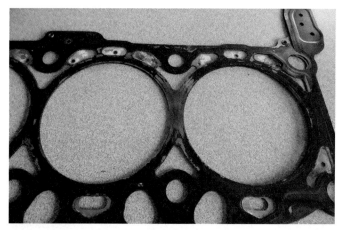

FIGURE 26-10 A failed head gasket can cause coolant to enter the combustion chamber which causes running and overheating issues. A side effect is the "steam cleaning" effect of the coolant in a hot combustion chamber.

FIGURE 26-11 A coolant/oil mixture looks like a chocolate milkshake. This is a sign that oil is getting into the cooling system.

FIGURE 26-12 Lack of oil and oil pressure causes increased engine component failure.

causes problems as glycol is not a good lubricant. More importantly, the glycol "uses up" the dispersant ability of the oil, causing other contaminants.

The coolant causes rapid deterioration of the oil filter, allowing unfiltered coolant/oil slurry to pass through the engine unchecked. Without the aid of the filter, the oil quickly becomes saturated with soot and metallic particles. The increased moisture content in the oil begins to react with combustion byproducts in the blowby gases, forming acids that corrode components. The engine oil begins to thicken and form sludge. The sludge further blocks smaller oil passages and may even block the oil pump pickup, resulting in either local or total engine oil starvation. Bearing, cylinder, and piston ring wear are accelerated (**FIGURE 26-12**). Coolant dilution of the lubricating oil initially results in corrosion etching on bearings, the babbit becoming dark in color. More severe cases show oil starvation wear. Piston and ring wear also display heavy scuffing and seizing when the oil thickens and lubrication becomes compromised.

Oiling System Condition

The lubrication system is designed to separate moving parts, clean and polish components, hold particulates in suspension, prevent corrosion, and cushion components under the pressure of combustion. Lubrication problems fall into three categories: contamination, starvation, and consumption. Next, we explain how each one can cause issues with the engine.

K26006 Knowledge of oiling system serviceability.

Contamination

Dust from the outside air is often present in the engine oil. Modern engine oils are designed to trap these contaminants and carry them to the filter, where they can be removed from suspension. The crankcase should be airtight, with fresh, filtered air only admitted through the PCV system. Any failed seal or gasket that may allow unfiltered air to enter the crankcase will also admit dust and dirt. Cracked or loose PCV hoses also admit unfiltered air. Excessive particulates in the oil due to unfiltered air entering can result in the filter material becoming prematurely loaded. Unfiltered oil will then pass through the filter bypass, carrying contaminants throughout the engine.

In addition to the airborne contaminants mentioned, oil also carries carbon created during combustion, and metallic particles from engine wear, to the filter to be removed. Regularly changing the filter and engine oil is necessary to keep clean, filtered oil circulating through the engine. If the filter is not changed, it will become blocked with contaminants so oil cannot flow through the element. The result is similar to air induction faults that prematurely plug the filter. The bypass opens to allow unfiltered oil to circulate through the engine. The result is bearing wear and journal scoring, valve stem

FIGURE 26-13 Bearings with foreign material embedded in them need to be replaced and not reused.

FIGURE 26-14 Sludge buildup can be from lack of regular maintenance, poor quality of lubricates, and poor engine design.

wear, and piston pin wear. Due to their inherent embeddability, contaminants are stuck in the bearings. Because of the volume and size of particles in the unfiltered oil, the particles cannot be driven into the babbit, but stay partially exposed and in contact with the journals, resulting in scoring (**FIGURE 26-13**).

Piston wear with lubrication contamination is more pronounced toward the skirt and oil control rings; this is because there is a limited amount of oil in the combustion chamber, but the cylinder walls are normally whetted with oil. The skirt usually exhibits scuffing across the entire width of the major and minor thrust surfaces. If the lubrication contamination is due to an air intake problem, note that the compression rings will be worn as well.

Starvation

If oil is prevented from flowing for any reason, a condition referred to as oil starvation occurs. Oil flow is commonly affected by blockages, aeration, or low oil pressure. Lack of oil between moving parts causes rapid, severe wear on parts. Oil starvation can be localized when blockages occur before a single journal or passageway, resulting in damage in that area only. A plugged pickup screen results in oil starvation that affects all moving components in the engine.

Insufficient Maintenance

If not replaced regularly, engine oil also begins to break down, or oxidize. High temperatures and excessive water tend to accelerate the breakdown of engine oil. This results in thickening of the oil to a grease-like sludge that is not easily moved through the lubrication passages, and causes rapid wear on all moving parts (**FIGURE 26-14**). Oil that has become saturated with moisture loses its effectiveness to prevent the acids found in combustion gases from etching bearings and precision surfaces. Rapid bearing wear and corrosion occur unchecked.

Remember that all engines burn small amounts of oil in normal operation. Extending the service interval may cause the oil level to drop below the minimum acceptable level. Problems associated with low oil level are addressed next.

Low Oil Level

Customers who do not check the oil level regularly may not notice the level dropping. Insufficient oil in the engine reduces the ability of the lubrication system to remove heat of friction from the moving components. Additionally, some engines use bleed holes or oil jets to aid in cooling the head of the piston. In these cases, the lubricating oil breaks down, thins excessively, and loses its ability to separate moving parts. Micro-welds and galling forms between moving parts, tearing up burrs, which further accelerate wear.

Running an engine low on oil shortens the oil's service life. Due to the loading of metallic particles, thermal breakdown, and premature saturation of contaminants, the symptoms and results of running an engine low on oil are similar to those found with extended oil change intervals.

If the level of the oil drops too low, the oil pump pickup may not be submerged at all times. When the pickup is not submerged, the oil pump loses the supply of oil, and pressure drops. The pump then needs additional time to prime and begin the flow of oil to the galleries. In this condition, the oil pressure gauge may fluctuate, or the oil light flash. This is a critical condition that results in rapid engine wear. Often, during the customer interview this may be described as an intermittent affair where the oil lamp flickers during certain vehicle maneuvers such as accelerating, braking, or cornering in a single direction. Oil sloshes in the pan away from the pickup in these circumstances, causing momentary loss of pressure.

Aeration

Ironically, an engine that is overfilled with oil can cause oil starvation. This occurs when the crankshaft comes into contact with the oil and whips air into the lubricant. The aerated oil is pumped through the engine, but because the air compresses, pressure is reduced. A cracked oil pickup tube or gasket can also cause air to be drawn into the oil pump, resulting in a slurry of oil and air being distributed to the engine.

Mechanical Induced Pressure Faults

Worn oil pumps, a faulty oil pressure regulator, or severe internal oil leaks can all contribute to low oil pressure. Internal oil leaks cause a loss of oil pressure without a corresponding loss of oil to the outside of the engine. Worn bearings, missing or loose oil gallery plugs, or cracked oil galleries are examples of internal leaks that can prevent the oil pump from building adequate pressure, especially at low rpm.

Piston wear from insufficient lubrication presents a wide wear region on the thrust surfaces of the piston. Deep scoring is usually present on the piston skirt and corresponding cylinder surface, resulting from galling and metal transfer from piston to the cylinder. The appearance may be shiny (**FIGURE 26-15**).

Bearings worn due to insufficient lubrication appear shiny with excessive wear. This is because the journal and bearing maintain contact, without the protective oil film to separate the moving parts. A burnishing action wears away and polishes the bearing surface. In extreme cases, the bearing overheats and galls. Galling causes scratches as material adheres to the crankshaft; overheating discolors the bearing to a dark blue or black (**FIGURE 26-16**).

Oil Consumption

Although oil consumption can cause low oil level problems, it can also be a symptom of engine mechanical issues. Oil in the cylinder during combustion also causes additional problems for the engine. Because it has many considerations, it is treated separately here. The following paragraphs discuss evaluating an engine's oil consumption, followed by potential causes. Then some detrimental results of excessive combustion are identified.

In some extreme cases, it may be clear that the engine consumes oil by the customer description of the problem, the appearance of oil on the spark plugs, or through visual examination of the exhaust for blue-colored smoke (**FIGURE 26-17**). If the engine consumption is not clear-cut, an oil consumption test is recommended. Different manufacturers state specifications, usually in volume of oil consumed in a given mileage.

FIGURE 26-15 Piston skirts in an engine with an oil starvation issue will appear very shiny as they have been polished by the cylinder wall. This requires replacement.

FIGURE 26-16 An overheated bearing can be caused by lack of oil pressure which then causes the bearing to be out of shape.

FIGURE 26-17 Oil fouled spark plugs appear like this and can cause multiple engine performance issues.

Record the exact mileage on the oil consumption worksheet. Ask the customer to drive the vehicle for 1000 miles and then return to you. Tell the customer to check the oil daily, but not to add oil unless the level drops to the lower level line. If it is necessary to add oil, ask the customer to diligently record the mileage and the amount of oil added each time. If the customer has to add oil in 1000 miles, the oil consumption is probably excessive and will present with blue smoke and spark plug fouling. In 1000 miles, you can measure the amount of oil required to fill the oil to the full line on the dipstick, giving you a reading for consumption divided by 1000 miles. If the oil consumption is found to be over specification, finding the cause of the excessive consumption is next. There are only oil that can enter the cylinder: past the valve seals, the piston rings, or the PCV system.

Burning oil in the combustion chamber results in blue-colored exhaust smoke (**FIGURE 26-18**). Valve seal leakage often presents as a brief blue smoke exhaust at first engine start. This is because the oil runs down the valve stems and collects on the valve head or inside the combustion chamber when the engine is turned off. The oil burns at first start, causing the puff of blue smoke. Worn valve guides and restricted oil return holes from the cylinder head can also increase oil consumption past the valve stem seals. Oil bypassing the sealing effect of the piston rings can occur for many reasons. The most obvious is ring and cylinder damage, but carbon formation and bearing clearance can also contribute to oil consumption.

When piston rings and cylinders are worn, oil scraping effectiveness and cylinder sealing decrease. Oil can then be pumped past the rings into the combustion chamber. Blue smoke may be more noticeable under heavy closed throttle deceleration with worn piston rings. Scoring of the cylinder wall due to oil contamination makes this condition more pronounced. It may be valuable to perform both a dry and wet compression test to identify ring and cylinder wear if the compression rings are involved or the cylinder is scored. The same is true for a leakdown test.

Oil carburization due to oil burning or overheating can cause the oil return holes in the piston to become blocked (**FIGURE 26-19**). In this case, the oil scrapers cannot effectively remove the oil film from the cylinder wall. Where methods of positively whetting the cylinder wall are used, such as oil holes in the big end bore of the connecting rod, the effect is more obvious. Where the return of scraped oil is used to lubricate the small end bore of the connecting rod, piston pin, and piston pin bosses, piston pin wear and noise may become a symptom. Oil consumption past the rings may also initiate piston ring sticking, compounding the problems.

Excessive bearing clearance from the main and connecting rod big end bores can flood the wall with more oil than any ring can control. Again, the excessive amounts of oil are permitted to flow into the combustion chamber. Excessive clearances are often associated with engine noises, so are usually not a cause of prolonged oil consumption. Oil mist can also be

FIGURE 26-18 Blue smoke out of the tail pipe is a result of burning oil.

FIGURE 26-19 If you add heat to oil and bake it in an enclosed area it becomes rock hard like carbon. This carbon does not allow oil to pass by and could potentially cause an oil starvation issue.

routed into the engine through the PCV system. This typically occurs during high engine speeds or when the oil level is overfilled. Excessive blowby due to piston land damage or stuck or worn rings can also increase oil consumption through the PCV system. Inspecting crankcase pressure with the engine running and leakdown tests can be used to indicate whether blowby is an issue on the engine you are working on.

A vapor separator is used in most overhead valve engines to limit the effects of oil consumption through the PCV system, but excessive oil mist overwhelms the ability of the oil trap, and oil is drawn into the intake manifold. If the vapor separator drain becomes blocked by oil varnish or carbon, its effectiveness is reduced, and oil consumption can occur. "Smoke" or visible oil mist from the cylinder head cover when the PCV is removed may be a good indicator of PCV consumption.

We have already seen that burning oil reduces oil quantity in the engine, and described some of the detrimental results of low engine level. Likewise, some of the conditions that cause oil burning compound the problem by encouraging further oil consumption, such as when oil burns and causes rings to stick. Oil burning can also contribute to additional engine problems due to increased carbon deposit formations. The decreased clearance volume above the head of the piston artificially raises compression ratio, and can lead to abnormal combustion. This topic is covered in detail in a following section.

As discussed, oil consumption can be identified by a combination of factors, beginning with a dropping oil level with no evidence of external leaks. Spark plugs will have either a whitish ash or a black, oily deposit, and may be contain heavy carbon deposits in some cases. The backs of the intake valves may be heavily coated with a soft, greasy carbon if the oil consumption is through valve guides due to worn stem seals or guides. Heavily coked combustion chambers, piston heads, and compression rings are also indicators that accompany oil consumption.

Accessory Drive Belt Condition

The accessory drive belt operates the various pumps, compressors, and alternators on the engine, which keeps the engine operating correctly, so the belt must be maintained. A visual inspection is one of the easiest ways to verify that it is in operable condition. The technician is looking for cracks, ribs missing, fraying, and other abnormal-looking wear that might cause the belt to fail while the engine is operating. There is a recommended mileage for replacement, which means the technician should consult the service manual.

▶ Wrap-Up

Ready for Review

- ▶ Diagnose the system that failed that caused the engine to fail.
- ▶ Fix the failed system before repairing the vehicle.
- ▶ Research previous repairs on the vehicle before continuing to diagnosis the engine.
- ▶ Verify the cooling system is operational order.
- ▶ Verify the oil system is in operational order.
- ▶ Cavitation happens when micro-bubbles burst next to metallic components which can then cause erosion of the material.
- ▶ Galvanic corrosion happens when the coolant becomes an electrolyte causing it to conduct electricity.
- ▶ Oil starvation can cause engine failure because of lack of oil pressure.
- ▶ Oil aeration is caused when oil is infused with air from an outside source.
- ▶ Oil consumption can be caused by multiple internal components of an engine.
- ▶ Using check sheets helps the technician to remember what the customer stated when they came in to get their vehicle repaired.
- ▶ Accessory drive belt condition should be checked every time the vehicle comes in for service.

Key Terms

cavitation Occurs when aeration is introduced into a liquid system. Introducing excess air into the coolant, causing the coolant to fail at absorbing heat from the engine.

galvanic corrosion Occurs when dissimilar metals come in contact through a liquid electrolyte.

oil carburization Happens when the engine is burning oil, and it becomes a carbon compound that plugs passages in the engine.

three Cs The major issues that happen to a vehicle can be diagnosed when these are answered. Concern: What is the problem? Cause: What caused the system to fail? Correction: What will it take to fix the failed system?

Review Questions

1. All of the following are best practices when conducting an interview, *except*:
   a. Ask closed-ended questions.
   b. Use a check sheet to standardize the questions asked.
   c. Reassure the customer that the information being gathered is to assist in the accurate diagnosis of the vehicle.
   d. Avoid using too many technical terms.

2. Which of the following Cs should be examined during engine diagnosis?
   a. Cause
   b. Cost
   c. Concern
   d. Correction

3. White, sweet-smelling exhaust smoke is usually the result of:
   a. high oil level.
   b. low coolant level.
   c. coolant leaking into the combustion chamber.
   d. severe internal oil leaks.

4. How do bearings worn due to insufficient lubrication appear?
   a. With crosshatches
   b. Rusty
   c. Coated with carbon
   d. Shiny

5. High oil consumption, bearing wear, and piston and ring failures are usually the result of:
   a. faulty components.
   b. improperly performed previous repairs.
   c. unusually high or sustained loading.
   d. lack of maintenance and support systems.

6. Failed head gaskets and warped or cracked heads and manifolds may indicate:
   a. problems in the accessory drive belt.
   b. low oil level.
   c. mechanically induced pressure faults.
   d. problems in the cooling system.

7. In which of these conditions is piston wear more pronounced toward the skirt and oil control rings?
   a. Lubricant contamination
   b. Lubricant starvation
   c. High lubricant consumption
   d. Aeration

8. Oil carburization due to oil burning or overheating can cause all of the following symptoms, *except*:
   a. noise.
   b. green smoke.
   c. piston pin wear.
   d. piston ring sticking.

9. The unfiltered oil passage through the engine will result in all of the following failures, *except*:
   a. bearing wear.
   b. journal scouring.
   c. valve stem wear.
   d. cylinder wall wear.

10. The accessory drive below must be replaced:
   a. during every service.
   b. once in a year.
   c. only when it appears to be damaged.
   d. as recommended in the service manual.

ASE Technician A/Technician B Style Questions

1. Technician A says that when the technician is evaluating a failed engine he or she should start with checking all the fluids. Technician B states that low coolant pressure could cause the engine to lock up due to lack of lubrication. Who is correct?
   a. Tech A
   b. Tech B
   c. Both A and B
   d. Neither A nor B

2. Technician A says that a lean air-fuel mixture could cause the engine to overheat. Technician B states that a leaking radiator could cause the engine to overheat. Who is correct?
   a. Tech A
   b. Tech B
   c. Both A and B
   d. Neither A nor B

3. Technician A states that increased bearing clearance could cause a low oil pressure condition. Technician B says that a bad radiator fan could cause the engine to overheat. Who is correct?
   a. Tech A
   b. Tech B
   c. Both A and B
   d. Neither A nor B

4. Technician A states that an engine should be ran at 5000 rpm to verify that the oil pump is in operation. Technician B says that an engine that has high oil consumption should be evaluated for an internal engine failure. Who is correct?
   a. Tech A
   b. Tech B
   c. Both A and B
   d. Neither A nor B

5. Technician A states that good communication with the service advisor will allow for a timely and complete repair. Technician B says that auto technicians are on their own and should plan to do everything in the repair shop. Who is correct?
   a. Tech A
   b. Tech B

c. Both A and B
d. Neither A nor B

6. Technician A states that using the incorrect oil could cause the engine to burn oil in the combustion chambers. Technician B says that an improperly repaired vehicle could cause the engine to fail after a short time. Who is correct?
   a. Tech A
   b. Tech B
   c. Both A and B
   d. Neither A nor B

7. Technician A says that the technician should ignore the previous repair information when diagnosing the current problem. Technician B says that the repair facility should not be concerned with how the customer is treated. Who is correct?
   a. Tech A
   b. Tech B
   c. Both A and B
   d. Neither A nor B

8. Technician A says that bearing clearance is what maintains oil pressure within the engine. Technician B states that a cylinder leak down test will tell the technician whether the engine has a bent connecting rod. Who is correct?
   a. Tech A
   b. Tech B
   c. Both A and B
   d. Neither A nor B

9. Technician A states that bearing contamination from foreign objects could come from the air cleaner system. Technician B states that a failed head gasket could mix coolant and oil. Who is correct?
   a. Tech A
   b. Tech B
   c. Both A and B
   d. Neither A nor B

10. Technician A says that cavitation could happen in the oil system if the crankcase is overfilled with oil. Technician B says that galvanic corrosion could occur if the engine coolant has not been maintained. Who is correct?
    a. Tech A
    b. Tech B
    c. Both A and B
    d. Neither A nor B

APPENDIX A

Customer Questionnaire—Engine Noises

Engine Noise Diagnosis Customer Questionnaire	
RO	**Date**

How long has the problem existed?

- ❏ < 1 week
- ❏ < 1 month
- ❏ < 3 months
- ❏ > 3 months

Has repair been attempted before?

- ❏ No
- ❏ Yes, by us

RO: _____
TECH: _____

- ❏ Yes, by another garage/someone else

If previous repair:
Date of repair: _____
Repair performed:

_____
_____
_____

CUSTOMER CONCERNS

NOISES

Which of the following terms best describes the noise heard by the customer?

- ❏ Knock
- ❏ Ping
- ❏ Rattle
- ❏ Grinding
- ❏ Hiss
- ❏ Bubbling
- ❏ Other

During what engine temperature(s) is the noise heard or heard loudest/most?

- ❏ All engine temperatures
- ❏ Cold start
- ❏ During warm up
- ❏ Operating temperature

What best describes weather conditions when the noise is heard the loudest/most?

- ❏ Any weather conditions
- ❏ Clear weather
- ❏ Damp weather
- ❏ Rainy weather
- ❏ Snowy weather

Notes: _____
_____
_____
_____
_____
_____
_____

What best describes the vehicle operating conditions where the noise is heard loudest/most?

- ❏ At all times
- ❏ Cold start
- ❏ Cold idle
- ❏ Cold acceleration (normal from a stop)
- ❏ Cold cruise/normal driving
- ❏ Cold high load (passing, climbing hill)
- ❏ Cold deceleration/slowing

Frequency of the noise:

- ❏ Every day
- ❏ Most days
- ❏ Some days
- ❏ Occasionally

Which best describes the noise occurrence:

- ❏ Always there/continuous
- ❏ Comes and goes in a repeatable manner
- ❏ Comes and goes randomly

What best describes the temperature of the days when the noise is heard the loudest/most?

- ❏ Not temperature related
- ❏ Cold
- ❏ Warm
- ❏ Hot

Actual temperature range provided by customer _____ C/F

When was the last maintenance (oil change/inspection) on the vehicle?

_____

Fuel History:
Did the problem begin to occur after a recent fuel up? YES/NO
Do you use the same fuel station every fill-up? YES/NO
What fuel octane do you use?

- ❏ 85
- ❏ 95
- ❏ 105
- ❏ OTHER _____

- ❏ Hot start
- ❏ Hot idle
- ❏ Hot acceleration (normal from a start)
- ❏ Hot cruise/normal driving
- ❏ Hot high load (passing, hill climbing)
- ❏ Hot deceleration/slowing

If cold or hot cruise, what speeds is the noise most pronounced?

_____

APPENDIX B

Customer Noise Descriptors

Noise	Sounds like...
Banging	Slamming a wooden door, gunshot
Bonging	Hitting a large gong
Booming	Distant thunder
Buzzing	Mosquito, electric razor
Chafing	Rubbing dry hands together
Chirping	Bird or cricket calling
Clacking	Train rolling on the tracks
Clanging	Dinner or cow bell
Clapping	Hands clapping
Clashing	Cymbals hitting together
Clattering	Bowling pins falling
Clicking	Operating a ballpoint pen
Clinking	Bottles hitting together
Clunking	Slamming a heavy door
Cracking	Ice cubes cracking in water
Crackling	A fire burning
Creaking	Opening a door with rusty hinges
Croaking	A frog's call
Crunching	Walking on dry snow
Droning	A distant small airplane
Drumming	Fingers nervously tapping a desk
Fluttering	A flag in the wind
Grating	A shovel dragged over pavement
Grinding	Sharpening a tool on a grinder; pepper mill in use
Groaning	Twisting wooden beam on a ship
Growling	A guard dog
Gurgling	Water down a bathtub
Hissing	Leaking tire

Noise	Sounds like...
Hooting	Owl's call
Howling	Wind blowing through an open door
Humming	Electrical transformer
Jingling	Keys on a key ring
Knocking	Knuckles wrapping on a wooden door
Moaning	Blowing a cross an empty bottle
Oil canning	Bending a metal can
Pattering	Raindrops gently hitting a window
Pinging	Dropping pebbles into a tin can
Popping	Cork from a champagne bottle
Pounding	A fist hitting a desk
Rapping	Judges gavel
Rattle	Shaking pebbles in a can
Roaring	The crowd going wild at a sports event; lion's roar
Rumbling	Bowling ball rolling down an alley
Scratching	Rubbing two pieces of paper together
Screeching	Fingernails on a chalkboard
Slapping	Dribbling basketball on a hardwood floor
Squealing	Skidding tires
Tap	A heavy click, striking a desk with the wide side of a ruler
Ticking	Tapping pencil point on a desk
Whining	Distant siren; vacuum cleaner
Whistling	Boiling kettle
Zapping	Electrical shock

APPENDIX C

Engine Performance Customer Questionnaire

Engine Performance Customer Questionnaire	
RO	**Date**

How long has the problem existed?

- ❏ < 1 week
- ❏ < 1 month
- ❏ < 3 months
- ❏ > 3 months

Vehicle was:

- ❏ Driven in
- ❏ Towed in

CUSTOMER CONCERNS

Which of the following terms best describes the customer concern?

- ❏ Performance
- ❏ Noise
- ❏ Smoke
- ❏ Other

MALFUNCTION INDICATOR LAMP

- ❏ Never on
- ❏ Bulb check, then out
- ❏ On occasionally
- ❏ On at all times
- ❏ Flashing

OIL PRESSURE WARNING LAMP

- ❏ Never on
- ❏ Bulb check then out
- ❏ On occasionally
- ❏ On at all times
- ❏ Flashing at idle only
- ❏ Flashing at any engine speed and load

What weather conditions is the problem most pronounced?

- ❏ < 0°C/32°F
- ❏ > 0°C < 20°C
- ❏ > 20°C

- ❏ Dry
- ❏ Rainy
- ❏ Humid
- ❏ Snow

Has repair been attempted before?

- ❏ No
- ❏ Yes, by us

RO:_____

TECH:_____

- ❏ Yes, by another garage/ someone else

Which best describes the frequency of problem?

- ❏ Always there/continuous
- ❏ Comes and goes in a repeatable manner
- ❏ Comes and goes randomly

TEMPERATURE LAMP

- ❏ Never on
- ❏ Bulb check, then out
- ❏ On occasionally
- ❏ On at all times

If vehicle has a gauge, where does the needle stay?

When was the last maintenance (oil change/inspection) on the vehicle?

_____

Fuel History:
Did the problem begin to occur after a recent fuel up? YES/NO
Do you use the same fuel station every fill-up? YES/NO
What fuel octane do you use?

- ❏ 85
- ❏ 95
- ❏ 105
- ❏ OTHER _____

Primary driving conditions

- ❏ City
- ❏ Highway

If previous repair:
Date of repair: _____
Repair performed:

_____
_____
_____

ENGINE PERFORMANCE

Starting Performance

- ❏ Starts normally
- ❏ Starts, long crank time
- ❏ Cranks, no start
- ❏ No crank

ENGINE NOISE

Description

- ❏ Click
- ❏ Clunk
- ❏ Clatter
- ❏ Clacking

- ❏ Knocking
- ❏ Rattle
- ❏ Whine
- ❏ Hiss

ENIGINE SMOKE

Smoke color

- ❏ Blue
- ❏ White
- ❏ Black

(continued)

Idling

- ❏ Normal idle
- ❏ Rough, uneven
- ❏ Stalls, cannot maintain idle
- ❏ Idle very low at all time
- ❏ Idle fast at all time
- ❏ Other

Driveability

- ❏ Normal
- ❏ Poor acceleration
- ❏ Hesitation, stumble from stop
- ❏ Hesitation on acceleration
  when underway
- ❏ Surges/lags at cruise
- ❏ Backfires
- ❏ Misfire/engine stall
- ❏ Stall, won't restart
- ❏ Stalls, restarts OK
- ❏ Top end performance low,
  lacks power

Frequency

- ❏ Always
- ❏ Often
- ❏ Frequently

Temperature noise heard most prominently (check all that apply)

- ❏ Cold
- ❏ During warm up
- ❏ Warm
- ❏ Operating temperature
- ❏ All

Noise heard mostly when (check all that apply)

- ❏ Idle
- ❏ Low speed
- ❏ Cruising speed
- ❏ High speed
- ❏ Acceleration
- ❏ Deceleration
- ❏ Braking
- ❏ Upshifting
- ❏ Downshifting
- ❏ Cranking/starting
- ❏ All
- ❏ Other:

Fuel Consumption

- ❏ Light
- ❏ Normal
- ❏ Excessive
- ❏ Leakage

Fuel octane normally used:

_____

Customer uses same fuel supplier regularly?

- ❏ Yes
- ❏ No

Coolant

Color and condition:

❏ OK ❏ NG

Leakage
❏ YES ❏ NO
❏ UNSURE

Consumption
❏ YES ❏ NO
❏ UNSURE

Oil
Viscosity/Brand

_____

Color and condition:
❏ OK ❏ NG

Leakage
❏ YES ❏ NO
❏ UNSURE

Consumption
❏ YES ❏ NO
❏ UNSURE

APPENDIX D

Engine Performance Technician Worksheet

Date	RO	ID
VIN	Mileage	

BASICS

COOLANT

Level: ❑ OK ❑ Low

Condition ❑ Clean ❑ Contaminated

Color ❑ Green ❑ Yellow ❑ Red ❑ Blue ❑ Pink ❑ Other

Brand (if known)

Strength

Comments

ENGINE OIL

Level ❑ OK ❑ Low ❑ High

Condition ❑ Clean

Contaminated: ❑ Fuel ❑ Dark ❑ Milky ❑ Sludge

Oil Filler Cap ❑ Clean ❑ Milky ❑ Carbon/Varnish ❑ Sludge

Oil Filter ❑ OEM ❑ Name brand aftermarket ❑ Other

VISIBLE SMOKE

❑ YES—Complete this section
❑ NO—go to next section

Condition for smoke:	Smoke Visible:	Smoke Color:
❑ Start up	❑ Engine cold	❑ Blue
❑ Idle	❑ Warm up	❑ Black
❑ Acceleration	❑ Operating temperature	❑ White
❑ Deceleration	❑ All times	
❑ All times		

ABNORMAL NOISE

❑ YES—Complete this section
❑ NO—go to next section

Condition for noise:		Noise heard:	Noise frequency:
❑ Start up	❑ Under load	❑ Engine cold	❑ Regular
❑ Idle	❑ Upshifting	❑ Warm up	❑ Irregular
❑ Acceleration	❑ Downshifting	❑ Operating temperature	❑ Constant
❑ Deceleration	❑ All times	❑ All times	❑ Intermittent

Type of noise		Noise volume:	Noise tempo compared to engine rpm:
❑ Click	❑ Clacking	❑ Slight/soft	❑ Changes with rpm
❑ Clunk	❑ Knocking	❑ Loud	❑ Constant
❑ Clatter	❑ Whine		❑ Slower
	❑ Rattle		❑ Faster
			❑ Same
			❑ Intermittent

Noise tempo compared to engine rpm:	Constant—no change with rpm	Engine conditions:	Location:
❑ Changes with rpm	❑ Slower	❑ Cold	❑ Intake
❑ Slower	❑ Faster	❑ Warm-up	❑ Top end
❑ Faster	❑ Same	❑ Operating	❑ Exhaust
❑ Same	❑ Intermittent	❑ All times	❑ Cylinder
❑ Intermittent			❑ Bottom end

(continued)

Check and record
Daces, Freeze
Frame

TESTS

Compression Test DRY	I 5	2 6	3 7	4 8
Compression Test WET	I 5	2 6	3 7	4 8
Cylinder Leakdown	I 5	2 6	3 7	4 8
Leakdown Location	I 5	2 6	3 7	4 8
Oil Pressure	SPEC		MEASURED	
Coolant pressure test	Pass	Fail	External	Internal

CHAPTER 27

Diesel Engine Theory

NATEF Tasks

There are no NATEF Tasks for this chapter.

Knowledge Objectives

After reading this chapter, you will be able to:

- K27001 Understand what a compression ignition engine is.
- K27002 Explain the different types of diesel engines.
- K27003 Discuss the benefits of diesel engines.
- K27004 Explain the mechanical similarities of diesel and gasoline engines.
- K27005 Understand the fueling system on a diesel engine.
- K27006 Discuss diesel fuel.
- K27007 Explain the usage of forced induction on diesel engines.

- K27008 Talk about the different starting procedures used in a diesel engine compared to gasoline engines.
- K27009 Discuss the differences between a gas and diesel engine.
- K27010 State the emission issues with diesel engines.
- K27011 Understand SCR on a diesel engine.
- K27012 Explain smoke diagnosis on a diesel engine.

Skills Objectives

- S27001 The ability to do a compression test on a diesel engine.

You Are the Automotive Technician

A customer comes into the Mercedes-Benz dealership with his diesel ML350. He explains that he is having difficulty starting his vehicle in cold weather. He informs you of the cetane rating in the fuel he has been using, and you determine that the low rating might be contributing to his problem. You advise him that you will need to complete a more thorough inspection to determine what needs to be repaired. You ask him to wait in the customer lounge during the inspection and tell him you will keep him informed. After using several different time-measured tools and techniques, you determine that the system's timing is not in conformance with the manufacturer's specifications. You return to the lounge and tell the customer that your recommendation is retiming the system to the manufacturer's specifications for a more consistent start-up in cold weather.

1. What is the difference between a low and high cetane number?
2. Why are water traps or separators important in diesel fuel systems?
3. What are three types of lift pumps that are common on light-duty diesel cars and trucks?
4. What are some of the benefits with the latest "clean diesels"?

▶ Introduction

The compression-ignition engine is a fuel-efficient engine that usually runs on diesel fuel but can be easily adapted to alternative fuels such as vegetable-based biodiesel or synthetic fuels. As fuel efficient and powerful as these engines are, they have a reputation for being slow and noisy and for emitting smoke. Fortunately, today's compression-ignition diesel engines use computer controls with advanced engineering and design techniques to all but eliminate the basis for such a reputation. In fact, the modern diesel engine is quiet, efficient, and powerful, with drastically reduced emissions.

▶ Types of Diesel Engines

A variety of fuel delivery systems for diesel engines have been used over the years, with each design operating on different principles. However, to meet strict emission control regulations, older fuel injection systems have given way to electronically controlled fuel systems operating on similar principles. Likewise, engine layout uses both direct and indirect fuel injection designs (**FIGURE 27-1**).

Indirect Injection (IDI)

Indirect injection is another method of injecting fuel. It has been used for years with light-duty diesel vehicles as a means of reducing the characteristic "diesel clatter" caused by the ignition of fuel (discussed in the next section). With indirect injection, fuel is sprayed into a robust and very hot antichamber in the cylinder head, often called a **prechamber** (**FIGURE 27-2**). The advantages of indirect injection are easier starting, a quieter running engine, and better emission control. Prechambers have various and complex designs. Often, they are designed to control the ignition and flame front in order to develop maximum heat energy transfer and complete burning of the fuel with a minimum shock wave. Along with the use of prechambers, various methods of controlling the rate of fuel injection have been used to quiet the ignition of fuel in light-duty (passenger vehicle) diesel engines. These include throttling-type nozzles (injector tips) with variable spray patterns and variable rates of injection, along with various prechamber and piston designs.

Direct Injection (DI)

Direct injection means the fuel is injected directly into the combustion chamber. The advantage of this design is that it produces more power and is a simpler design than indirect injection. The disadvantages typically result in more engine noise, harder starting, and higher emissions. Nonetheless, with electronic engine controls, direct injection is gaining popularity in the small diesel market. With this design, the cylinder head usually has a flat surface, and the combustion chamber is formed in the piston crown (**FIGURE 27-3**). At TDC there is very little clearance between the cylinder head and the top of the piston. In fact, in many designs if you were to remove the cylinder head gasket and replace the head on the block, you would not be able to turn the engine over because there would not be enough clearance between the two surfaces without the thickness of the head gasket present. Modern fuel systems use electronically controlled high-pressure fuel systems that make quiet and smoke-free direct injection possible, and desirable. Through electronic controls, the fuel mixture can be infinitely controlled, producing maximum power with very low emissions.

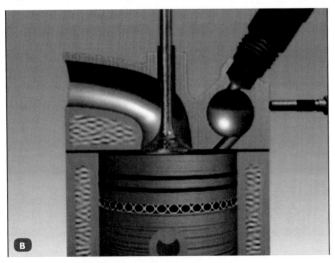

FIGURE 27-1 A. A direct injection designed diesel combustion chamber. Notice the injector is directly in the combustion chamber. **B.** An indirect injection diesel engine cylinder. The fuel is sprayed into the prechamber where it is ignited.

▶ Benefits of Diesels

The benefits of diesel have been known since its inception, but until recently the excess noise and pollution that accompany these benefits have been too costly to validate the viability of it. The modern diesel engine is one that competes with any gasoline engine on the noise and emission requirements so that they can become mainstream, requested engines. In the European market, the diesel doesn't garner the issues that it does in the American market, but the new diesels are made to satisfy what everyone needs and wants from an engine.

Mileage Difference Compared to Gas Engine

A diesel engine is designed to promote increased fuel mileage as compared to that of a gasoline engine. A small amount of fuel is injected into the diesel engine to create motion; an inherent benefit of this reduced fuel usage is an environment that favors increased fuel mileage. The designs of these engines, which are being used increasingly, call for a more robust engine block and cylinder head design to handle the increased pressures. This translates into a bigger engine that may offset the increased efficiency created by the design, but the use of aluminums and other alloy types of materials helps combat the increased engine size in an attempt to regain efficiencies that were lost because of size.

Longevity Difference Compared to Gas Engine

A diesel engine lasts longer than a gasoline engine, in part because the engine doesn't mix the fuel in the cylinder until the last moment before the combustion process happens, which saves wear and tear on the cylinder walls, rings, and pistons. Another even bigger reason is that the diesel engine is built to be more robust than the gasoline engine, so it can take more abuse and last longer (**FIGURE 27-4**).

▶ Mechanical Similarities

The mechanical similarities of the diesel engine to its gasoline counterpart are numerous. The diesel engine still has pistons, connecting rods, crankshaft, camshafts, pushrods, lifters, rocker arms, and valves, but they are usually more robust and can handle the increased stresses on them as the engine operates. The major difference between the two engines is that in a gasoline engine the mixing of the fuel and air happens in the intake port just before it goes into the cylinder, whereas in a diesel engine it happens in the cylinder. GDI engines are discussed later in this chapter, and they have some similarities.

Compression Testing

Compression testing can be accomplished just as it is on the gasoline engine.
To check the compression of a diesel engine, follow the steps in **SKILL DRILL 27-1**.

K27003 Discuss the benefits of diesel engines.

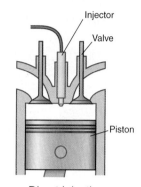
FIGURE 27-2 Indirect injection.   **FIGURE 27-3** Direct injection.

K27004 Explain the mechanical similarities of diesel and gasoline engines.

S27001 The ability to do a compression test on a diesel engine.

© Vereshchagin Dmitry/Shutterstock   © Ed Aldridge/Shutterstock

FIGURE 27-4 As you can tell by the size of the engine blocks, the diesel engine is built more robust than a conventional gasoline engine.

SKILL DRILL 27-1 Compression Checking a Diesel Engine

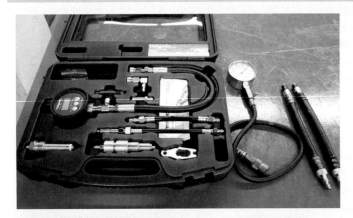

1. First acquire a compression gauge that is rated to handle the increased pressure that a diesel engine produces. This is not the same pressures as a gasoline engine.

2. Remove the glow plug so that you have access to each cylinder.

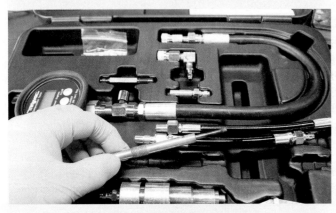

3. Select the proper adapter to screw into the glow plug hole.

4. Screw the adapter into the glow plug hole and attach the gauge.

Continued

ENGINE MECHANICAL - 6.6L (1 OF 5)

[Print]

5. Have someone turn the engine over a minimum of four complete rotations.

6. Record your findings on each cylinder, and compare to OEM service information.

• Bore	103 mm	4.0551 in
• Stroke	99 mm	3.8976 in
• Compression Ratio	16.8:1	
• Engine Compression Test – Minimum	2069 KPa	300 psi
• Idle Speed	680 RPM	
• Firing Order	1-2-7-8-4-5-6-3	

GDI to Diesel Comparison

The **gasoline direct injection** engine is a rather new concept that utilizes the traits of a diesel engine's combustion style with the ease of the spark-fired engine. The GDI engine is set up like a diesel engine with a low-pressure transfer pump, which feeds a high-pressure injection pump. The high-pressure injection pump feeds the high-voltage injectors that are installed directly into the cylinder. Along with the fuel system, the engineers that designed this engine have increased the compression to an 11–14:1 compression ratio, as they are only compressing air. Once the air is compressed in the cylinder and the piston is at TDC, the fuel is injected, and the spark is ignited to create combustion. This leads to a highly efficient engine that has very low emissions, as the combustion burns the air-fuel mixture completely because of the higher pressures that are present. The similarities are many with a diesel engine, other than the spark plug igniting the mixture.

▶ Fuel Systems

Diesel engine fuel injection systems have many different designs. Some technicians think there are only one or two methods of delivering fuel to the diesel engine. In fact, there are several diesel fuel injection system designs, such as the unit injector, plunger pump, distributor pump, and common rail fuel injection systems, to name only a few. Historically, manufacturers like Detroit Diesel, Cummins, and Mack have had completely different fuel injection systems. Considering the various designs mentioned, today's diesel engines extensively use electronic fuel controls with increased fuel delivery pressures designed to meet today's strict emission control standards. Because of their durability and fuel efficiency, diesel engine passenger vehicles have been growing in popularity, particularly in Europe, where diesel vehicles outsold petrol/gasoline vehicles for the first time in 2006, and where the trend toward diesel is still growing. Diesel engines are more robust in construction because they operate with much higher compression ratios—high enough to make the compressed air in the cylinder hot enough to spontaneously ignite the fuel when it is introduced into the combustion chamber. Once the fuel is injected, ignition lag creates the familiar

K27005 Understand the fueling system on a diesel engine.

diesel knock, a loud clattering sound that has generally been tolerated by drivers of heavy goods vehicles, but is less acceptable to the discerning owners of more luxurious passenger vehicles. This lag time is called the **ignition delay period**, which is the time it takes for the fuel to ignite after being injected into the engine.

Injection Systems Common Rail/Distributor Injection
Common Rail Injection Pump

The common rail injection pump operates off of the engine's timing gear to create the needed pressure to operate the engine. A transfer pump feeds the common rail pump with fuel at a low pressure and then the injection pump compresses that fuel to bring that pressure up to the specification to operate the engine. At some points the common rail pump creates pressures exceeding 26,000 psi. The pump feeds a fuel rail similar to a gasoline engine so that each injector has the same amount of fuel and pressure available at any time. The injectors are computer controlled so it is not necessary for the injection pump to be timed to the engine's stroke events. This injection pump's purpose is to continuously produce high fuel pressure for the injectors which makes control of fueling events easier as it is controlled by the ECM. This precision of control allows for increased power, fuel mileage, and decreased emissions.

Distributor-Type Injection Pump

The distributor-type pump uses a vane-type transfer pump to fill the single pumping element. This transfer raises fuel pressure to injection pressure. A distribution system then distributes fuel to each cylinder in the firing order of the engine. The most common type in light automotive use is the Bosch VE pump. Driven from the engine, a drive shaft rotates a plunger and a cam disc. Cams on the face of the disc have as many lobes as cylinders in the engine. A plunger spring holds the cam disc against rollers that rotate on their shafts. The lobes move the plunger to and fro in its barrel, making it rotate and reciprocate at the same time (**FIGURE 27-5**). Its rotation operates the fuel inlet port to the pumping chamber and at the same time distributes pressurized fuel to the correct injector. The reciprocating motion pressurizes the fuel in the pumping chamber. The plunger's pumping action forces fuel through a delivery valve to the injector. The plunger has a central passage, a connecting passage to the distributing slit, and a cross drilling to a control sleeve. As the plunger rotates, each intake slit aligns with the intake port, and the distributing slit with the distributing port. As the plunger rotates, the intake slit moves away from the intake port. At the same time, the cams act on the plunger, causing it to move axially along the barrel, pressurizing the fuel in the pumping chamber. The distributing slit now uncovers the distribution port,

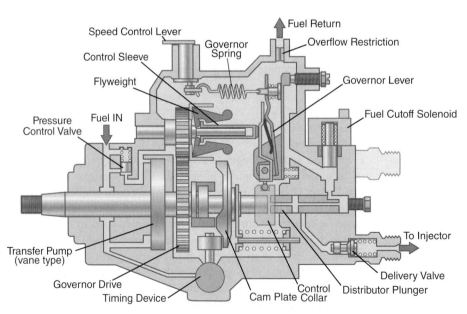

FIGURE 27-5 The internal components of a Bosch VE distributor fuel injection pump.

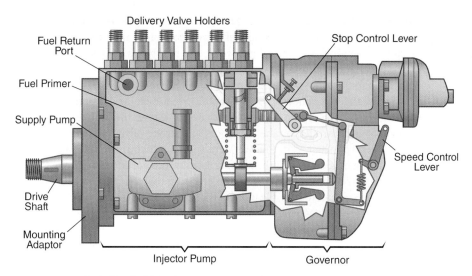

FIGURE 27-6 An in-line fuel injection pump.

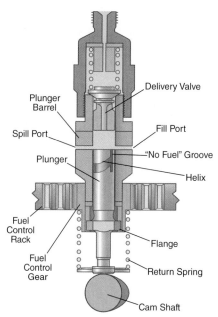

FIGURE 27-7 Fuel injection pumping element.

and the pressurized fuel passes through the delivery valve to the injector. Further rotation of the plunger closes off the distribution port and opens the intake port. At the same time, the plunger spring moves the plunger back along the barrel for the next pumping stroke.

For intake, fuel from the feed pump reaches the open intake port in the barrel. The intake slit aligns with the intake port, and fuel fills the pumping chamber and passages in the plunger. For injection, the plunger rotates to close off the intake port and moves along the barrel to pressurize fuel in the pumping chamber. The distributing slit aligns with the distribution port, where the pressurized fuel forces the delivery valve off its seat and reaches the injector. In this phase, a cutoff port in the plunger is covered by the control sleeve. To end fuel delivery, the plunger's cutoff port moves out of the control sleeve and lets pressurized fuel spill back into the pump housing. This relieves pressure in the pumping chamber, the delivery valve closes, and injection ceases. Metering the fuel is controlled by the effective stroke of the control sleeve, and the effective stroke is determined by the action of the governor sliding the control sleeve along the plunger. Sliding it one way opens the cutoff port earlier and reduces effective stroke. Sliding it the other way delays its opening and increases effective stroke. The governor changes the position of the control sleeve to vary the quantity of fuel delivered, according to throttle position and load. When the ignition is switched off, an electrical solenoid closes off the intake port and stops fuel delivery.

In-Line Injection Pump

Some diesel engines use in-line fuel injection pumps to meter and pressurize the fuel (**FIGURE 27-6**). The basic principle is for a plunger to act on a column of fuel to lift an injector needle off its seat. A pumping element and delivery valve for each cylinder are located inside the pump (**FIGURE 27-7**). The element has a barrel, with a mated plunger inside. Their accurate fit and highly polished finish ensure minimal fuel leakage past them without requiring additional seals. The barrel usually has two holes, or ports, called the inlet, or fill, port and the spill port. The ports are located in the injection pump fuel gallery. The gallery contains filtered fuel from the low-pressure supply system. At the top of the barrel are a delivery valve, a delivery valve holder, and the high-pressure steel pipe to carry fuel to each cylinder (**FIGURE 27-8**). When the fuel pressure rises, the delivery valve is lifted off its seat. When the plunger covers the fill and spill ports, fuel is pressurized and flows to the injector. When injection ceases, the pressure below the delivery valve drops to gallery, or supply, pressure. To meter the fuel, the upper end of the plunger has a vertical groove, extending from its top to an annular groove. The top edge of this annular groove is cut in a helix shape, also called the control edge (**FIGURE 27-9**). Rotating the plunger controls the duration of the stroke for which the spill port is covered. This is called the effective stroke, and it determines how much fuel

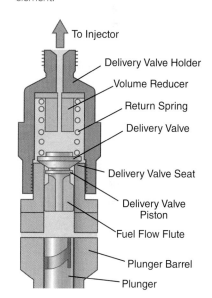

FIGURE 27-8 A delivery valve, delivery valve spring, and delivery valve holder at the top of a plunger barrel.

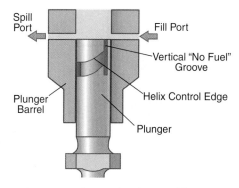

FIGURE 27-9 A pumping plunger with a helical control edge.

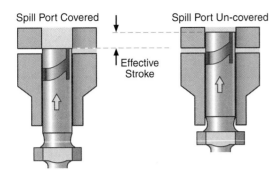

FIGURE 27-10 The effective stroke is the duration of the plunger movement after the spill port is covered.

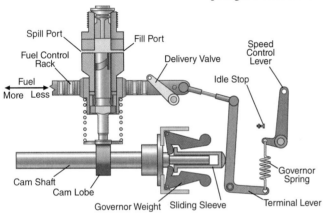

FIGURE 27-11 A typical mechanical governor.

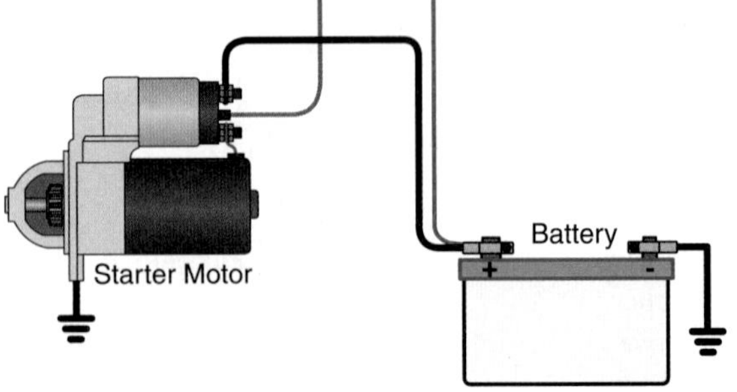

FIGURE 27-12 The pneumatic governor takes advantage of the venturi effect to control fuel delivery.

is delivered to the injector (**FIGURE 27-10**). A short effective stroke means a small amount of fuel is injected. A longer effective stroke lets more fuel be delivered. To stop the engine, the vertical groove on the plunger is aligned with the spill port. This alignment stops pressure in the barrel from rising because the fuel can pass through the groove and exit through the spill port.

The plunger is rotated by a control sleeve, a rack, and a pinion. Moving the rack rotates the pinion, the control sleeve, and then the plunger. The rack's movement is controlled by the governor. The stroke of the plunger is accomplished by a camshaft, cam follower, and spring, which move the plunger in a reciprocating motion. When the plunger is below the ports, fuel from the gallery enters the barrel above the plunger, thus ensuring that the barrel is full of fuel.

As the camshaft rotates, the plunger is pushed past the ports, which traps and pressurizes the fuel. Moving the plunger farther raises the pressure of the fuel. The increased pressure forces the fuel out past the delivery valve, along the fuel line to the injector. Fuel flows to the injector until the control edge of the helix uncovers the spill port. The pressurized fuel above the plunger then moves down the vertical groove, to the annular groove, and into the spill port. The delivery valve prevents fuel from leaking from the pipe back into the element. It reduces pressure in the fuel line to ensure there is no dribbling by the injector. This pressure reduction is accomplished by a relief plunger and a conical face, which is held against its matching seat by the delivery valve spring. The relief plunger on the valve is a close fit inside the bore of the delivery valve seat.

The delivery valve operates as follows: Fuel pressure above the delivery valve forces the valve toward its seat bore, sealing the area above and below the delivery valve. Further movement of the delivery valve toward its seat increases the volume in the injector pipe and reduces the pressure therein. This drop in pressure causes the injector needle to snap shut, helping to prevent fuel dribble from the injector. The conical face of the delivery valve then contacts the seat, further sealing the plunger from the injector pipe.

Mechanical or Pneumatic Governors

Governors on in-line pumps are usually mechanical or pneumatic. The primary job of the governor is to maintain a set engine speed regardless of load. Maintaining the speed is accomplished by balancing governor spring tension with flyweight position. For example, increased governor spring tension increases fuel delivery and engine speed; increased engine speed causes the flyweights to move outward from centrifugal force, reducing fuel delivery and engine speed. A mechanical governor uses rotating flyweights to control movement of the fuel control rack against a spring. Removing the load from the engine lets its speed rise. Centrifugal force pushes out the weights, which push a sleeve against the spring. The force from the spring tries to push the rack to the maximum fuel position. The force on the sleeve from the flyweights acts against the spring to try to push the rack to the minimum fuel position (**FIGURE 27-11**).

For any governor position, the fuel control rack determines the volume of fuel delivered, and therefore engine speed. During idling, the governor prevents the engine from stalling. It also stops it from overspeeding. Thus, mechanical governors in automotive use are called idling and maximum speed governors, because idling speed and maximum speed are all they control. They can also be called limiting speed governors. For other throttle positions, the operator determines the rack position by moving the position of the floating link, which increases or decreases governor spring tension.

A pneumatic governor takes advantage of a principle called the **venturi effect** to control fuel delivery (**FIGURE 27-12**). When air flows through a constricted section of pipe, there is a reduction in pressure. To be clear, when we talk about a pressure lower than atmospheric pressure, we are talking about vacuum. Therefore, vacuum increases as airflow increases through the constriction. The pneumatic governor has a manifold-mounted venturi unit, linked by tubing to a sealed diaphragm assembly on the in-line injection pump housing. This venturi unit has a main venturi and an auxiliary one. A throttle butterfly in the intake manifold controls airflow through the venturi and into the engine.

Here is how it works: When the engine is not running, the diaphragm spring pushes the diaphragm and fuel control rack toward the full-fuel position. With the engine running at idle, the throttle butterfly is almost closing the intake, and air flows through the auxiliary venturi at high velocity. The high airflow produces low pressure, which is transferred through the connecting hose to the sealed chamber on the spring side of the diaphragm. Atmospheric pressure on the pump side now forces the diaphragm and rack toward the no-fuel position. This reduces the effective pump stroke and the amount of fuel injected. Depressing the accelerator allows more air to enter the engine but decreases the air velocity through the auxiliary venturi. Pressure in the sealed chamber rises and allows the spring to move the diaphragm, and control rack, against atmospheric pressure to increase the fuel delivered. The diaphragm position at any given time is determined by the air velocity through the auxiliary venturi, in accordance with engine speed and load. This provides a rack setting that allows the correct quantity of fuel to be injected to match the operating condition.

Diesel Injectors

The injector assembly has several main parts (**FIGURE 27-13**). The nozzle assembly is made up of a needle and body; a pressure spring and spindle hold the needle on the seat in the nozzle body. A nozzle holder, sometimes called the injector body, may allow for mounting the injector on the engine and for some method of adjusting the spring force applied to the needle valve. A cover keeps out dirt and water. The injection pump delivers fuel to the injector.

The fuel passes through a drilling in the nozzle body to a chamber above which the needle valve seats in the nozzle assembly. As fuel pressure in the injector gallery rises, it acts on the tapered shoulder of the needle valve, increasing the pressure until it overcomes the force from the spring and lifts the needle valve from its seat. The highly pressurized fuel enters the engine at a high velocity in an atomized spray. As soon as delivery from the pump stops, pressure under the needle's tapered shoulder drops, and the spring force pushes the needle down on the seat, cutting off the fuel supply to the engine. Some of the fuel is allowed to leak between the nozzle needle and the body to cool and lubricate the injector. This fuel is collected by the return, or leak-off, line and delivered to the fuel tank for later use. Because the return line is a low-pressure fuel line, it is a good place to check for the presence of a good fuel supply, or air in the system.

There are two main types of injector nozzle: hole and pintle (**FIGURE 27-14**). Hole-type nozzles are commonly used in direct injection engines. They can be single hole or multi-hole, and they

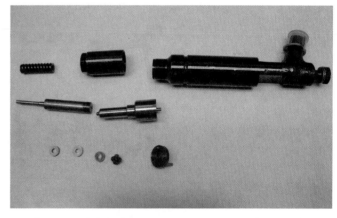

FIGURE 27-13 A fuel injector nozzle assembly—needle and body, pressure spring, and nozzle body.

FIGURE 27-14 A. Hole-type injector nozzle. **B.** Pintle-type injector nozzle.

operate at very high pressures, up to 3000 psi (20,700 kPa). They give a hard spray, which is necessary to penetrate the highly compressed air. The fuel has a high velocity and good atomization, which are desirable characteristics in open combustion chamber engines. In pintle-type nozzles, a pin, or pintle, protrudes through a spray hole. The shape of the pintle determines the shape of the spray and the atomization of the spray pattern. Pintle nozzles open at lower pressures than hole-type nozzles. They are used in indirect injection engines, where the fuel has a comparatively short distance to travel, and the air is not as compressed as in the main chamber.

HEUI

Another popular fuel injection system is the **hydraulically actuated electronically controlled unit injector (HEUI) system** (**FIGURE 27-15**). This diesel fuel injection system operates by drawing fuel from the tank using a tandem high- and low-pressure fuel pump. The pump circulates fuel via the low side of the pump at low pressure through a combination of fuel filter, water separator, and heater bowl. Then, fuel flows back through the high side of the pump at high pressure into the fuel galleries, located in the cylinder head, and through to the injector units. The injectors are controlled by a PCM. The PCM controls the duration of fuel injection pulses based on a range of input variables discussed earlier in the chapter. Once the injector solenoid has been activated, oil from a high-pressure oil pump hydraulically actuates the injectors. In other words, the injectors are operated by hydraulic pressure instead of a cam and mechanical linkage. By varying the oil pressure, injection can be controlled independently of the engine speed, or crankshaft and camshaft position. A solenoid-actuated valve controls the high-pressure oil flow, which is applied to the top of an intensifier piston in the injector. This can increase injection pressures to 18,000 to 24,000 psi (124,000 to 165,000 kPa). The area of the head of the intensifier piston is approximately seven times the area of its plunger. As a result, a 7:1 pressure increase on the fuel beneath the plunger can be achieved.

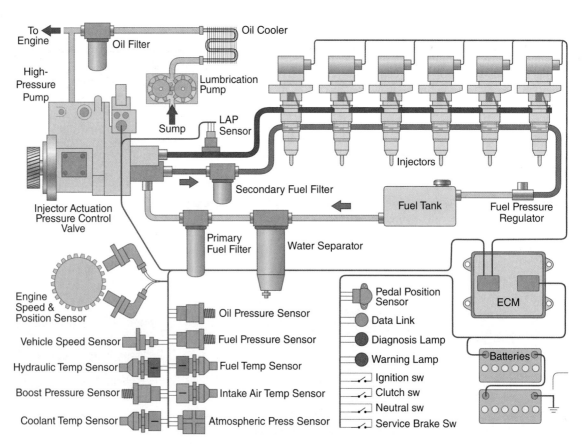

FIGURE 27-15 A hydraulically actuated electronically controlled unit injector (HEUI) fuel injection system.

Piezo Injectors

A **piezo injector** is just like a conventional diesel injector, except it is actuated by a piezo crystal (**FIGURE 27-16**). The crystal expands when power is applied to it. The actuation time of the crystal is five times faster than a typical injector solenoid, which makes this type of injector a better alternative. Because there are no moving parts to actuate the injector, failure of this portion of the component is minimized. The crystal allows fuel to enter the injector, which then overcomes the spring pressure inside the injector and allows fuel flow into the combustion chamber. These types of injectors are used on the high-pressure common rail–type of fuel system.

Fuel Pump

A diesel fuel system consists of a couple different fuel pumps that feed the injection system. The basic layout is that there is a fuel pump that transfers or lifts the fuel to the high-pressure pump that is located on the engine. Depending on the manufacturer of the engine, the location of the transfer or lift pump and the high-pressure pump could be in any number of places.

Transfer Pump

The **lift pump** is a low-pressure pump that supplies fuel to the injection pump, or unit injectors. Often called a transfer or supply pump, the lift pump transfers fuel from the tank to the fuel injection system. In modern vehicles, the tank is mounted below the engine, and the fuel has to be lifted to the level of the engine. Three types of lift pumps are common on light-duty diesel cars and trucks: diaphragm, plunger, and vane.

Diaphragm Lift Pump

The diaphragm lift pump can be mounted on the engine or on the injection pump (**FIGURE 27-17**). It is fitted with inlet and outlet valves, and an eccentric on a camshaft acts on a two-piece rocker arm connected to a diaphragm. Rotating the eccentric causes the rocker arm to pivot on its pin and pull the diaphragm down. This compresses the diaphragm return spring and increases the volume in the pumping chamber above the diaphragm. Atmospheric pressure at the fuel tank forces fuel along the fuel line to open the inlet valve. Fuel flows into the pumping chamber. The eccentric keeps rotating, and the rocker arm is released. The spring exerts force on the diaphragm to pressurize the fuel in the chamber.

This pressure closes the inlet valve and opens the outlet valve, letting fuel be delivered to the injection system. If the system does not need all of the fuel delivered, the pressure in the outlet fuel line rises to the same level as in the pumping chamber. This pressure holds down the diaphragm and keeps the diaphragm return spring compressed. As a result, the split linkage in the rocker arm allows the lever to maintain contact with the eccentric without acting on the diaphragm pull rod; therefore, pumping ceases until the pressure drops and pumping action needs to resume.

Plunger Lift Pump

A second type of lift pump in light vehicle applications is the plunger pump. It is mounted on the in-line injection pump and is driven by a cam inside the in-line injection pump housing. Internally, a spring-loaded cam follower converts the rotary motion of the camshaft into reciprocating motion. The reciprocating motion is transferred to a spring-loaded plunger fitted with close tolerance in a cylindrical bore. It has two spring-loaded check valves, which are called the inlet valve and the outlet valve (**FIGURE 27-18**). As the engine

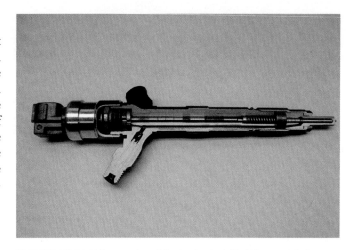

FIGURE 27-16 When a piezo injector is electrified the crystal changes shape and acts as an actuator. The piezo crystal operates 5 time faster than a solenoid.

FIGURE 27-17 A mounted diaphragm–type lift pump.

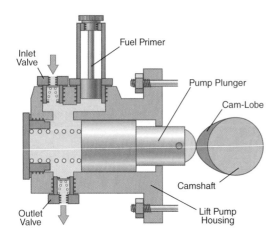

FIGURE 27-18 A plunger-type lift pump.

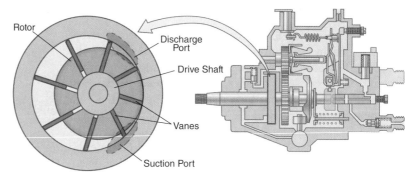

FIGURE 27-19 A vane lift pump in a distributor-type injection pump.

drives the injection pump, the lobe of the camshaft pushes the cam follower into the plunger pump. The cam follower acts directly on the plunger, pushing it toward the end of the cylinder bore. Fuel is displaced from one side of the plunger, through the outlet check valve, to the other side of the plunger. When the cam follower retracts, spring force on the plunger moves the plunger out of the cylindrical bore. Fuel from the fuel tank enters behind the plunger through the inlet check valve. Fuel in front of the plunger is displaced out of the pump to the fuel injection system.

Vane Lift Pump

A vane lift pump is used in distributor-type injection pumps. Also known as a transfer pump, it is mounted on the input shaft and pumps fuel whenever the distributor pump is driven by the engine (**FIGURE 27-19**). It consists of a rotor, mounted off-center in a pump housing. Slots are machined into the rotor to carry vanes. As the rotor rotates, the vanes can move into and out of the slots. The vanes seal on the edges of the rotor slots and the pump housing. Trapped fuel is carried around by the action of the rotor until the leading vane uncovers the outlet port. Because the rotor is offset, as it continues to turn, the volume between the vanes reduces, and fuel is squeezed out of the pump. A pressure relief valve controls the pump's operating pressure.

Priming Pump

Some diesel engines in light vehicle applications have a priming lever, plunger, or diaphragm button on the lift pump. Separating the priming pump for the removal of air from the fuel system is called bleeding, or priming. Air can enter the system during filter replacement or when a fuel line is disconnected. Without a priming pump, the engine would require excessive cranking, which could damage the starter motor and/or discharge the battery. The diaphragm lift pump often has a lever that acts on the diaphragm rocker arm. Moving the priming lever moves the diaphragm down. Releasing the lever allows the diaphragm return spring to force the diaphragm up.

The action of the diaphragm and valves during bleeding is the same for normal operation of the pump. Because distributor-type injection pump systems use an internal vane pump, their fuel supply system incorporates diaphragm-type priming pump, usually located on top of the fuel filter. The diaphragm is connected to an actuating button (**FIGURE 27-20**) and is held in its uppermost position by a diaphragm spring. Reed valves connect the priming pump housing to the filter. Pressing down on the actuating button reduces the volume in the pumping chamber, which forces fuel into the filter element. Releasing the button lets the spring lift the diaphragm, which increases the volume in the pumping chamber. Air pressure in the fuel tank then forces fuel into the pumping chamber. A plunger-type priming pump is often used with plunger lift pumps, which are mounted on in-line

FIGURE 27-20 Diaphragm-type priming pump installed on a filter housing.

fuel injection pumps. It can also be mounted on top of fuel filter housings for distributor-type injector pump systems. The plunger priming pump consists of a plunger and a barrel assembly, mounted on the side of the plunger pump or filter housing. This plunger priming pump uses the valves of the plunger lift pump to direct fuel flow. Plunger pumps mounted on the top of filter housings contain inlet and outlet check valves. Pulling the primer plunger increases chamber volume, which decreases the pressure in the chamber below atmospheric pressure. Fuel in the tank is forced along the fuel lines, through the inlet check valve, and into the pumping chamber. Pushing the plunger into the barrel decreases the volume in the chamber, which forces fuel out through the outlet check valve.

Diesel Fuel

The main factors that affect the performance of diesel fuel are the **cetane** rating of the fuel, the fuel's viscosity, its cloud point, and the extent to which the fuel is contaminated. As mentioned earlier, the cetane number, or rating, expresses ignition quality of diesel fuel and is a comparative measure of the speed with which diesel fuel ignites under compression. The higher the number, the faster the fuel ignites. If the fuel does not burn rapidly after the piston has reached top dead center, then it may not burn completely during the power stroke, in which case it will not deliver the maximum possible power, and unburned fuel may then escape into the atmosphere as black exhaust smoke.

Diesel fuel should have a minimum cetane number of 40 for direct injection diesel engines and 35 for indirect injection diesel engines (**FIGURE 27-21**). Fuels with lower cetane ratings contribute to harder starting, ignition delay, power loss, and decreased fuel economy. Cetane improver additives can improve ignition and reduce white smoke during cold weather start-ups. Diesel fuel's viscosity value measures its resistance to flow. Diesel fuel with viscosity that is either too high or too low can cause serious damage to the engine's injection system. As discussed earlier, the clearances between the fuel injection components are very close. It is so close that improper fuel viscosity will cause a lack of lubrication. As a result, the injection components can be ruined.

The cloud point is the temperature at which fuel turns cloudy. When the fuel temperature drops to the fuel's cloud point, paraffin waxes that occur naturally in diesel fuel crystallize and cling together, making the fuel appear cloudy. This is known as "waxing" and, if not prevented, can clog filters and stop fuel flow to the engine. Clouding can be combated by using fuels with a lower cloud point, providing heat to the tanks, or including a cloud point improver to the fuel. This improver separates the clinging wax particles so they can pass through the fuel filters. Some oil companies produce special winter-grade fuels for cold weather operation.

Diesel fuel is vulnerable to contamination, particularly from water in the tank and from various types of sediment. As the fuel is fed into the system from the bottom of the tank, it is easy for contaminants to enter the system with the fuel. As the fuel in the tank is used, air from the atmosphere enters the tank. Water condenses on the walls of the tank and runs down into the fuel. The water is heavier than the fuel and usually ends up in the bottom of the tank along with sediment such as rust, or scale, or weld slag. Water in the fuel can cause injector seizures and engine failure. It also accelerates component wear. Water traps or separators are very important in diesel fuel systems. Dirt and other debris can clog fuel filters and form deposits, resulting in reduced power and excessive fuel system wear.

Fuel Filters

Diesel fuel filters are very important to the operation of a diesel engine. Because of the close tolerances of the injection system components, the fuel system must be kept exceptionally clean. The system is kept so clean that diesel fuel filters are rated in microns. A micron is 0.000039" (0.001 mm). Currently, some manufacturers specify final fuel filtration down to 3 to 5 microns. To put that in perspective, the diameter of a human hair is typically about 40 to 120 microns. A diesel engine fuel injection system usually has two fuel filters. A primary filter, located between the fuel tank and the supply pump, filters particles to 30 to 50 microns.

K27006 Discuss diesel fuel.

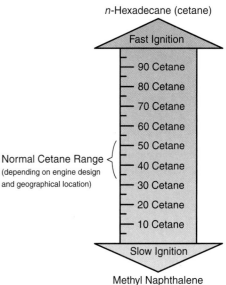

FIGURE 27-21 As you can tell by this image, as the cetane increases the easier the fuel is combusted. Normal ranges at 35-55 depending on environment.

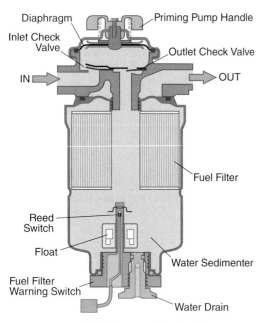

Diaphragm — Priming Pump Handle
Inlet Check Valve
Outlet Check Valve
IN
OUT
Fuel Filter
Reed Switch
Float
Water Sedimenter
Fuel Filter Warning Switch
Water Drain

FIGURE 27-22 A fuel filter combined with a water separator.

A secondary fuel filter, located between the supply pump and the high-pressure fuel injection pumping element, filters particles to 10 to 12 microns. As mentioned, some secondary filters are specified to remove particles down to 3 to 5 microns. Additionally, diesel fuel filters must remove water from the fuel system. This is accomplished with water separators or traps, sometimes called sedimenters (**FIGURE 27-22**). They can be separate units or combined with an impregnated paper element filter. Separate units pass the incoming fuel over an inverted funnel. At the edge of the funnel, the fuel changes direction very quickly. Water and dirt are heavier than fuel, so they are trapped, away from the funnel edge. With gravity, they settle at the base of the trap. The lower housing is usually clear for easy inspection, and it can include a drain plug so sediment can be drained daily.

The most common type of filter material in light diesel vehicles is resin-impregnated paper, pleated to offer a large surface area for the fuel. These filters are considered the most efficient. A fuel filter with the resin-impregnated paper element can be combined with a water separator. When this combined unit is used, the method of fuel flow is determined by the manufacturer. With some filters, fuel flows from outside to inside. In others, it flows from the base to the top, or from top to bottom. Some of the filters use paper elements, with the fuel flow options the same as previously described. In another method, fuel first passes through the paper element to trap abrasive particles. Any water in the fuel is usually in the form of small droplets, which are forced through the paper element. Once through the filter, the small droplets combine into larger droplets and form a sediment layer in the base of the filter. The bowl may be transparent and may contain a drain plug.

Other filter types pass fuel into the separator or sedimenter first and force the larger particles out of suspension by a change in direction. The fuel is then forced through a filtering medium, ready for use. This filter usually contains a disposable element. Often, the base has a drain plug for daily draining of the water from the filter.

Additionally, a water level switch can activate a light on the dash to warn the operator that the chamber may need draining. The switch has a float that is lighter than water but heavier than fuel. In the float is a magnet. As the float rises with the water level in the fuel, the magnet closes a reed switch, which turns on a warning light in the instrument cluster. The operator can then remove the drain plug to drain the water.

Aftermarket Setups

Aftermarket setups for fuel filtration and water separation usually involve running multiple filters that gradually get smaller so that the fuel is filtered to remove any moisture or dirt before it gets to the high-pressure pump. These types of setups work well but are usually timing consuming to set up and require more maintenance than the factor unit. If you run into something like this in the field, you will have to figure out the brand of the components so that you are able to order replacement filters and parts for the units when they fail.

K27007 Explain the usage of forced induction on diesel engines.

▶ Forced Induction

Forced induction has become commonplace on most diesel engines, as it helps make the engine even more efficient that it would normally be (**FIGURE 27-23**). A boosted engine increases power output to a level that allows the engine to do more work than it would usually be able to do. There are many different forced induction setups; we touch on a few here, but this is not an exhaustive list.

Standard Turbocharger

A standard turbocharger is one that is designed operate at a constant flow, with the only variation related to the amount of exhaust that is utilized to spin the impeller in the exhaust system (**FIGURE 27-24**). Once the size is picked for this type of turbo, the engine must operate in all modes with the same-size turbo. This setup causes some turbo lag: because it is designed to operate best when the engine is above 1500 rpm, until the engine reaches that rpm, the turbo must spool up to create enough boost to overcome the natural air pressure.

FIGURE 27-23 Turbocharging a diesel engine is an easy way to increase the power the engine produces.

FIGURE 27-24 A standard turbocharger is one size and operates as such through any load placed on an engine. This will cause some turbo lag at lower RPM.

This is a problem for some people who need instant power to pull the load they are towing, so driver adaptation is required with this style of forced induction.

Variable Geometry Turbochargers

Variable geometry turbochargers are able to change the size of the turbocharger as the engine is running so that it is able to match the size of the turbocharger with the needs of the engine (**FIGURE 27-25**). These types of turbochargers have the ability to change the amount of output by sliding a set of vanes or a slotted wheel to control the amount of exhaust that is being directed to the impeller. When this type of turbochargers is used, the engine is not subject to turbo lag because the turbocharger can adjust to make up for low exhaust gas pressures. These types of turbochargers are very popular in the late-model vehicle market as they allow for a fully adjustable intake charge.

Dual Turbochargers

The dual turbocharger setup on a diesel engine is usually a sequential type that uses the first turbocharger for low speed operation and then the second or both turbochargers for higher rpm operation (**FIGURE 27-26**). The use of the smaller turbocharger in this setup is to help combat turbocharger lag because of the lack of exhaust just off idle. As the engine rpm rises, the larger turbocharger starts to come into effect, creating a dual boost environment. The issues with this type of setup are that the turbochargers must be matched; the engine management software must be able to operate the other components

FIGURE 27-25 A VGT turbocharger is adjustable so that the "size" of the turbocharger can be changed as the needs of the engine are changed through the RPM range.

FIGURE 27-26 An air charge cooler is used to remove heat from the compressed turbocharger air so that it is a more densely packed air charge going into the intake tract.

K27008 Talk about the different starting procedures used in a diesel engine compared to gasoline engines.

that feed off these two turbochargers. Along with providing the extra boost pressure, the extra turbocharger also helps keep the emissions low, which makes for a cleaner, more efficiently running engine.

Air Charge Cooler

The **air charge cooler** is very similar to the radiator on a vehicle, as it uses outside air to cool the gas or fluid that is inside the cooler (**FIGURE 27-26**). As the exhaust spins the turbocharger, the impeller and compressor wheels begin to heat up, which transfers that heat to the air that is being compressed in the turbo. Routing the pressurized air through the charge air cooler allows the compressed air to cool down before it enters the engine. This reduces the temperatures in the combustion chamber, helping to prevent the formation of NOx emissions. A cooler air temperature as the air enters the engine allows the air to absorb more heat from the engine, resulting in a better running engine.

▶ Starting Elements

Starting a compression ignition engine is accomplished by a few different setups that heat up the incoming air to promote ignition. The main component that has been used is a glow plug, which is similar to a spark plug, but it doesn't spark. The engine could utilize an air grid–heating element to heat the air before it enters the cylinder head. In addition to using one or both of the above-mentioned components, the diesel engine starts better in colder weather if the heater that is normally installed is plugged in so that the heating element in the coolant can keep the engine warm.

Glow Plugs

A **glow plug** is a heating element that assists in raising the temperature in the combustion chamber, which makes the engine easier to start in cold weather. The glow plugs are only used for cold, initial starting of the engine. They are needed because a diesel engine is a CI engine, which means it starts solely from the heat of compression (**FIGURE 27-27**). If the engine is cold and the ambient temperature of the air intake to the diesel engine is too low, much of the heat generated by the initial rotations of the engine will be conducted away into the engine block and other components, and into the environment. If that happens, the air-fuel mixture temperature in the cylinder may not be raised sufficiently by engine compression for ignition to occur. Glow plugs preheat the incoming air so that ignition can occur more easily, which assists a cold engine to start more reliably. Once the engine is running, the glow plugs are no longer required. A glow plug consists of a heating element and a resistor-type heating element attached to the end of a plug that penetrates the combustion chamber or precombustion chamber. When the glow plug is activated, current flows through the resistor, causing it to heat up, which then raises the temperature of the incoming air. The glow plugs are activated by turning the key on before cranking a typical modern diesel engine for somewhere between 10 and 20 seconds prior to the engine firing. Older and less-efficient diesel engines, or worn engines, may require much longer preheating times to start the engine. There are a variety of methods for altering the timing and style of the electronic fuel injection process in modern automotive diesel engines to ensure reliable cold starting. Even though glow plugs are fitted, they are rarely used for more than a few seconds. Glow plug resistor elements, also called filaments, must be made of materials that are resistant both to heat and to oxidation.

Maintenance

Maintenance of the glow plug circuit is something that the technician must attend to, or the customer's vehicle may not operate in cold weather. As with other components of the engine, glow plug replacement must be on the maintenance schedule of a customer's

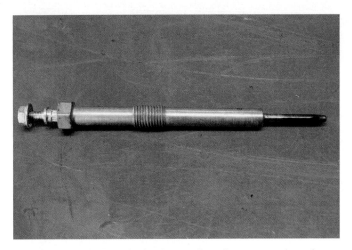

FIGURE 27-27 A glow plug is a large resistor that gets very hot when electricity is applied to it. This is located within the combustion chamber so that it can help get the combustion process get started on an engine that is not running. This is very crucial in a cold weather startup.

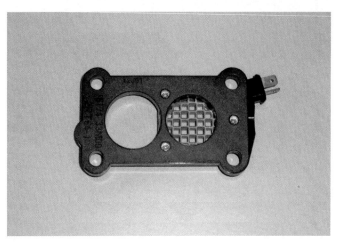

FIGURE 27-28 Later model diesel engines are using a grid heater within the intake tract to help start the vehicle with hotter air. This grid gets very hot and the air picks up the heat as it goes over the grid.

vehicle. Besides replacing the glow plugs, the technician should be checking out the whole system for wiring issues or signs of melted components.

Fuel Heaters

Some diesel engine vehicles are equipped with fuel heaters that heat the fuel in the tank so that when it gets to the injection system, it is already preheated. Because the fuel is preheated within or near the fuel tank, it requires less of the engine's heat, which allows all of the heat to stay in the combustion chamber which promotes complete combustion.

Air Heaters

A popular aid in starting modern diesel engines is an intake air heater, which helps to heat the air before it enters the engine. The air heater is fed 12 volts to heat up so that the incoming air heats up as it goes past the element. These are very simple devices, which can be diagnosed with a multimeter and do not often fail, as they have few parts.

▶ Brief Overview of Differences Between Gas and Diesel

The major difference between a gasoline engine and a diesel engine is that the diesel engine does not have spark plugs to start the combustion process (**FIGURE 27-29**). The technical terms for these two types of engines are a spark-ignition engine and a compression-ignition engine. The diesel engine, being a compression-ignition engine, does not require the use of spark plugs to start the combustion process as the design of the engine and the fuel used means that ignition occurs by just compressing the fuel to create spontaneous combustion. This allows for all the fuel to be burnt, with very little being pushed out to the exhaust system. In the spark-ignition engine, the spark plug starts the combustion process; its major flaw is that the spark plug is situated in a section of the combustion chamber such that the fire may not reach the other side until the event is over. If incomplete combustion occurs the excess fuel is pushed into the exhaust system where it is burnt up in the catalytic converter.

K27009 Discuss the differences between a gas and diesel engine.

CR Different

The compression ratio on a typical gasoline engine is around 8–9:1 so that it can run on conventional 87 octane unleaded fuel. A diesel engine's compression ratio is around 17–24:1 so that it can take advantage of the increased power output with the higher compression. Because you are not compressing fuel, like in a gasoline engine, the diesel engine can run a higher compression ratio without adverse affects on the engine.

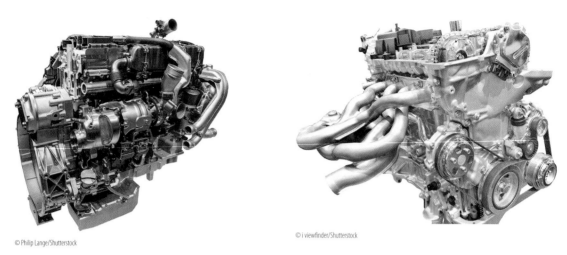

© Philip Lange/Shutterstock

© i viewfinder/Shutterstock

FIGURE 27-29 A gasoline 4-cylinder engine is on the left and a diesel 4-cylinder engine is on the right. The differences are noticeable as the many different components that are required to operate each engine.

Part Size

The physical size of the parts on a diesel engine are such that they are made to be rebuilt, and to last through a lot of abuse. Unlike a gasoline engine, diesels are made to be serviceable, which increases the value of their parts and makes them harder to find. Two technicians may need a crane to lift some components up off the engine, so that they themselves will not get hurt.

▶ Emissions with Diesels

K27010 State the emission issues with diesel engines.

One of the biggest drawbacks to diesel engines is the creation of particulate matter and oxides of nitrogen as a result of combustion. These two major pollutants have prevented the majority of people in the automotive community from adopting diesel engines. As of 2010, the U.S. federal government enacted emission standards to limit the amount of PM and NOx that a diesel engine can put into the atmosphere, which has resulted in manufacturers putting a lot of emission equipment on new vehicles to combat these two pollutants. Throughout this section, we talk about the different devices that are used to lower the amounts of NOx and PM so that the diesel can compete with the gasoline alternatives.

Diesel Particulate Filter (DPF)

Since 2007, all highway diesel engines have been required to have a **diesel particulate filter (DPF)** (**FIGURE 27-30**). Its job is to convert particulate matter, or soot, into ash. Soot can best be described as unburned particles left over from the combustion process, and ash is what is left after the soot has been incinerated. The conversion is accomplished through a catalytic process in the DPF. Often, it takes additional fuel with a spark or high temperatures to complete the process. After time, the ash builds up in the DPF and has to be removed. This service interval is typically 150,000 miles (240,000 km) for an on-road vehicle.

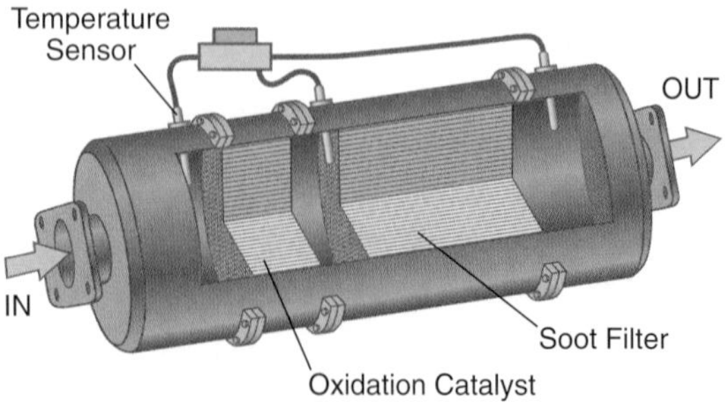

Regeneration

Once the DPF has been loaded up with the particulate matter, there comes a time when we need to rid the DPF of that matter, and that happens when regeneration starts (**FIGURE 27-31**). Regeneration disposes of the particulate matter by burning it into a much finer particles that are easily released into the atmosphere. The engine management computer allows some extra fuel to enter the DPF and then, through heat, causes that fuel to combust, creating a very hot environment that burns up the excess PM. When this happens, the vehicle must have met the parameters to allow regeneration to happen. Throughout the process, the engine management computer is watching the temperatures within the DPF to see that it is working effectively; if it is not, the engine management computer warns the operator by turning on the check engine light.

Temperature
Sensor

OUT

IN

Soot Filter

Oxidation Catalyst

FIGURE 27-30 A diesel particulate filter (DPF).

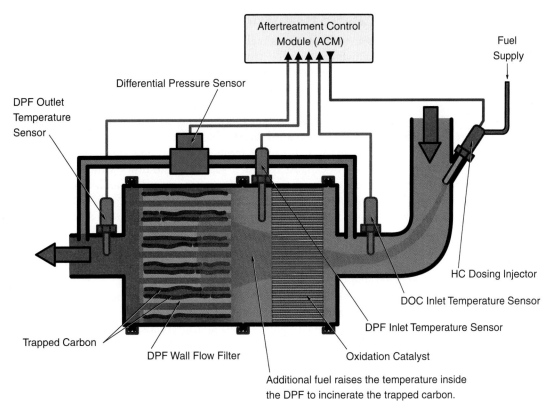

FIGURE 27-31 In regeneration mode diesel fuel is sprayed into the DPF causing it to start on fire to burn off all of the soot that is trapped in the DPF.

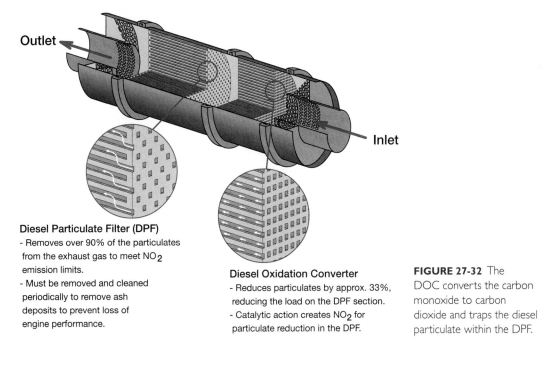

Diesel Particulate Filter (DPF)
- Removes over 90% of the particulates from the exhaust gas to meet NO_2 emission limits.
- Must be removed and cleaned periodically to remove ash deposits to prevent loss of engine performance.

Diesel Oxidation Converter
- Reduces particulates by approx. 33%, reducing the load on the DPF section.
- Catalytic action creates NO_2 for particulate reduction in the DPF.

FIGURE 27-32 The DOC converts the carbon monoxide to carbon dioxide and traps the diesel particulate within the DPF.

Diesel Oxidation Catalyst (DOC)

The **diesel oxidation catalyst (DOC)** promotes the conversion of carbon monoxide, hydrocarbons, and diesel particulates into harmless carbon dioxide and water (**FIGURE 27-32**). This is done through a chemical reaction within the catalyst so that it creates a better output than input. This component, along with the DPF and SCR, helps create a diesel engine that is more efficient, meets the emission standards, and makes the output better for everyone.

Selective Catalytic Reduction (SCR)

K27011 Understand SCR on a diesel engine.

Another clean diesel technology is called **selective catalytic reduction (SCR)** (**FIGURE 27-33**), an active emission control system that injects a liquid reductant, or reducing agent, through a special catalyst into the exhaust stream of a diesel engine. To meet the stringent 2010 diesel emission standards, the manufacturers decided to make this system standard on most on the road diesel engines. The reductant, or reducing agent, is urea, which is a chemical reactant specifically designed for use in SCR systems to reduce nitrogen oxides. Urea is called diesel exhaust fluid (DEF) (**FIGURE 27-34**). DEF is a water-based fluid containing urea that reacts with NOx emissions. When the DEF fluid is sprayed into the hot exhaust system, it vaporizes and flows with the NOx gases over the catalyst, converting the gas into harmless nitrogen and water. It causes a chemical reaction that converts nitrogen oxides into nitrogen, water, and very small amounts of carbon dioxide, which is exhausted through the tailpipe. "Clean diesels" have the ability to completely and efficiently burn fuel within the engine. Additional benefits include quieter engines with a higher horsepower-to-weight ratio. The primary enhancements include improved fuel delivery systems, improved configuration of combustion chambers, and turbocharging.

The SCR system is integrated into the engine management computer, so if the system is disabled or empty, the computer may put the vehicle in reduced power mode. The emission standards are such that the original equipment manufacturers are putting more safe guards on how the vehicle runs with and without DEF. There is no way around beating the SCR system, so you must fix the problems with it and move on.

▶ Diesel Smoke Analysis

K27012 Explain smoke diagnosis on a diesel engine.

The color of diesel smoke is something that the technician can use in figuring out how to repair a vehicle. Knowing the different colors can help the technician direct the repair process to the correct area so that the engine is repaired quickly and correctly the first time.

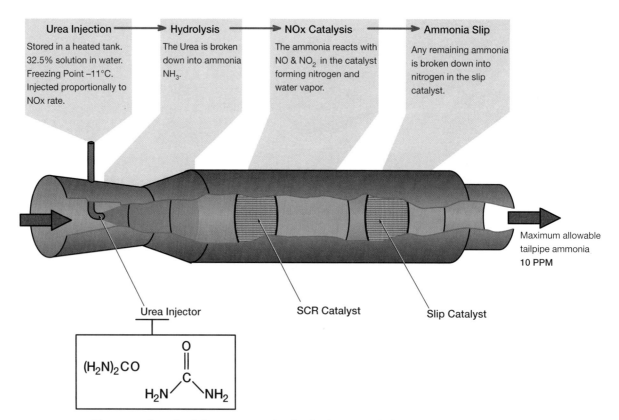

FIGURE 27-33 The conversion of emission process as the diesel exhaust travels through the vehicle's emissions system.

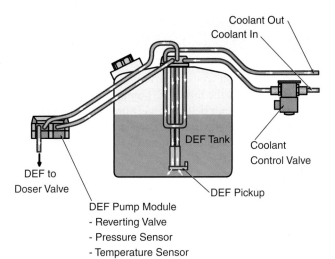

Coolant Out
Coolant In

DEF Tank

Coolant
Control Valve

DEF to
Doser Valve

DEF Pickup

DEF Pump Module
- Reverting Valve
- Pressure Sensor
- Temperature Sensor
- DEF filter

FIGURE 27-34 The Urea or SCR system that is used to help meet the emission standards that became more stringent in 2010.

White Smoke

White smoke could be a result of leaking injectors in the cylinders, low compression on a cylinder, or possibly fuel timing could be out of specification. If this condition occurs on the engine that you are trying to diagnose, you must first go after these areas to see if one of them is not functioning properly.

Gray or Blue Smoke

Gray or blue smoke is a sign that the engine is burning oil for some reason. The source of the oil infiltration could be piston rings, valve seals or head gasket failures, cylinder glazing, or sticking piston rings. These must be diagnosed if the complaint is that the engine produces gray or blue smoke at certain times.

Black Smoke

Black smoke is an indication of excess fuel being blown out into the exhaust, which means that combustion is not completing like it should. This is a sign that the engine is leaking fuel into the exhaust instead of burning it. Poor fuel quality, restricted air cleaner, and incorrect valve clearance could all potentially cause this type of smoke. If you go to an emission testing with an engine that is blowing heavy black smoke, you will most likely fail.

SAFETY TIP

Modern high-pressure fuel injection systems can easily spray fuel into your body. Always wear eye protection, and do not search for a fuel leak by placing your hand on a fuel injection line.

SAFETY TIP

When working around running engines, be alert for unguarded rotating and moving engine components, in case someone failed to reinstall a protective guard or device.

SAFETY TIP

When working on modern diesel engines with high-pressure fuel systems, be sure you have the correct manufacturer's service information for the engine. On some models, residual pressure may exist in the fuel lines even though the engine is not running.

Applied Science

AS-22: Internal/External Combustion: The technician can demonstrate an understanding of how fuel characteristics affect combustion in an automotive engine.

A diesel fuel's cetane number is a measure of the fuel's ignition delay, or the length of time between the start of injection and the first identifiable pressure increase in the cylinder due to combustion. Light vehicle diesel engines, especially modern designs, require high cetane ratings to operate at the required high speeds, as well as to meet current emission standards and noise-level targets. Fuels with low cetane ratings have longer ignition delay periods. Longer ignition delay means more fuel is delivered into the cylinder before ignition, leading to a longer period of uncontrolled combustion and violent pressure and temperature increases in the cylinder. This rapid pressure increase results in shock loadings, commonly known as "diesel knock." Longer periods of uncontrolled combustion also contribute to an increase in harmful exhaust emissions from diesel engines.

► Wrap-Up

Ready for Review

- ► Examples of diesel fuel injection system designs are unit injector, plunger pump, distributor pump, and common rail fuel injection.
- ► A high-pressure fuel injection system injects fuel into the cylinder at precisely the right time with the exact amount of fuel needed.
- ► High injection pressures are needed to overcome the compression and combustion pressures in the combustion chamber.
- ► The cetane number or rating of a diesel fuel expresses ignition quality and defines how easily the fuel will ignite when it is injected into the cylinder.
- ► Factors that affect the performance of diesel fuel are the cetane rating, viscosity, cloud point, and contamination.
- ► Quiet diesel technology has been accomplished through advanced injector design with better spray patterns and injection timing control.
- ► Clean diesel technology, through electronic diesel control (EDC), has produced cleaner, more complete combustion with lower emissions, greater economy, more power, and lower noise levels.
- ► EDC can vary the rate of fuel delivery per cylinder and degree of crankshaft movement.
- ► The shape and depth of the combustion chamber plays an important role in the reduction of particulate matter and nitrogen oxides.
- ► Turbocharging increases volumetric effi ciency (VE).
- ► On-board diagnostics, second generation (OBDII), systems are the industry standard for on-board diagnostics that monitor engine and related component operation.
- ► Biodiesel is a non petroleum-based processed fuel derived from vegetable oils.
- ► Biodiesel is both biodegradable and nontoxic, and has signifi cantly fewer emissions than petroleumbased diesel fuel.
- ► Diesel fuel tanks should be kept full to prevent water condensing on tank surfaces and contaminating the fuel.
- ► Diesel fuel filters are rated in microns; a micron is 0.000039" (0.001 mm).
- ► The lift pump is a low-pressure pump that transfers fuel from the tank to the fuel injection system.
- ► There are three types of lift pumps on light-duty diesel cars and trucks: diaphragm, plunger, and vane.
- ► A priming pump is a separate pump used for removal of air from the fuel system.
- ► An in-line fuel injection pump has a pumping element and delivery valve for each cylinder inside the pump.
- ► The primary job of the governor is to maintain a set engine speed regardless of load.

- ► The most common type of distributor pump in light automotive use is the Bosch VE pump.
- ► A diesel fuel injector delivers highly pressurized fuel in an atomized spray to the combustion chamber.
- ► Glow plugs preheat the incoming air so that ignition can occur more easily.
- ► Cummins and Detroit Diesel engine unit injector fuel delivery systems develop high fuel injection pressure in the injector rather than from a separate pump.
- ► Highly reliable electronic fuel control systems have made diesel engines fast, quiet, and clean.
- ► The common rail system (CRS) uses a separate high-pressure pump to increase the fuel pressure in the accumulator (rail) to 23,200 psi (160,000 kPa).
- ► The hydraulically actuated electronically controlled unit injector (HEUI) diesel injection system operates the injectors by hydraulic pressure instead of a cam and mechanical linkage.

Key Terms

air charge cooler A radiator that helps cool the air that is in the intake track.

cetane The rating of the fuel, the fuel's viscosity, its cloud point, and the extent to which the fuel is contaminated.

direct injection The type of diesel engine that directly injects the fuel into the cylinder, without prechambers.

diesel oxidation catalyst Promotes the conversion of carbon monoxide, hydrocarbons, and diesel particulates into harmless carbon dioxide and water.

diesel particulate filter (DPF) Converts particulate matter, or soot, into ash.

gasoline direct injection (GDI) A gasoline engine that is designed to be very similar to a diesel engine. The injection event happens right in the cylinder, as in a direct injection diesel. These engines have higher compression ratios and a more complete burn process.

glow plug A heating element that helps raise the temperature in the combustion chamber, which makes the engine easier to start in colder weather.

hydraulically actuated electronically controlled unit injector (HEUI) Type of injector that uses an electronic solenoid that is controlled by the PCM to control high-pressure oil, which actuates the injector at the precise time.

ignition delay period The time it takes for the fuel to ignite after being injected into the engine.

indirect injection A method of injecting fuel into a diesel engine that uses a prechamber into which the fuel is injected. The prechamber is a small area where the combustion happens in a diesel engine.

lift pump A low-pressure pump that feeds the high-pressure injection pump driven by the engine.

piezo injector Type of injector that is operated by a piezo crystal that cycles five times faster than a typical injector.

prechamber A component that is pressed into the cylinder head and usually houses the injector and glow plug in a diesel engine. This is the area where the combustion event starts.

selective catalytic reduction (SCR) An active emission control system that injects a liquid reductant, or reducing agent, through a special catalyst into the exhaust stream of a diesel engine. To meet the stringent 2010 diesel emission standards, the manufactures decided to make this system standard on most road diesel engines.

venturi effect Occurs when air flows through a constricted section of pipe and there is a reduction in pressure.

Review Questions

1. The compression-ignition engine runs on all of the following fuels, *except*:
   a. gasoline.
   b. diesel.
   c. vegetable based biodiesel.
   d. synthetic fuels.
2. With indirect injection, fuel is sprayed into a robust and very hot:
   a. combustion chamber.
   b. prechamber.
   c. piston.
   d. cylinder.
3. Direct injection differs from indirect injection in terms of:
   a. easier starting
   b. a quieter running engine
   c. better emission control
   d. more power
4. Compared to gasoline engines, diesel engines:
   a. produce lesser noise.
   b. produce lesser emissions.
   c. have increased fuel mileage.
   d. are smaller.
5. Choose the correct statement:
   a. A gasoline engine lasts longer than a diesel engine.
   b. The gasoline engine is built to be more robust than the diesel engine.
   c. The diesel engine greatly differs from its gasoline counterpart in mechanical aspects.
   d. The diesel and gasoline engines differ in the place where the mixing of air and fuel takes place.
6. The gasoline direct injection engine:
   a. has a gasoline engine's combustion style.
   b. has the ease of the spark-fired engine.
   c. does not burn the air-fuel mixture completely.
   d. has a low compression ratio.
7. The primary job of the governor is to:
   a. maintain a set engine speed regardless of load.
   b. reduce fuel consumption.
   c. prevent coolant contamination.
   d. reduce emissions.
8. A distributor-type injection pump that pumps fuel whenever the distributor pump is driven by the engine is a:
   a. diaphragm lift pump.
   b. plunger lift pump.
   c. vane lift pump.
   d. priming pump.
9. The cetane number, or rating, expresses:
   a. the fuel's viscosity.
   b. the fuel's cloud point.
   c. the extent to which the fuel is contaminated.
   d. the ignition quality of diesel fuel.
10. Which of these might be a result of leaking injectors in the cylinders, low compression on a cylinder, or fuel timing being out of specification?
    a. Gray smoke
    b. White smoke
    c. Blue smoke
    d. Black smoke

ASE Technician A/Technician B Style Questions

1. Technician A states that every diesel engine vehicle must meet the emission standards that changed in 2010. Technician B says that a diesel engine still has spark plugs. Who is correct?
   a. Tech A
   b. Tech B
   c. Both A and B
   d. Neither A nor B
2. Technician A says that DPF means diesel part fixture. Technician B says that only an IDI diesel engine uses a prechamber. Who is correct?
   a. Tech A
   b. Tech B
   c. Both A and B
   d. Neither A nor B
3. Technician A says that diesel engines respond well to turbocharging. Technician B says that the use of the DOC is to lower emissions. Who is correct?
   a. Tech A
   b. Tech B
   c. Both A and B
   d. Neither A nor B
4. Technician A states that a lift pump is to transfer the fuel from the tank to the high-pressure pump on the engine. Technician B says that a HEUI is an electronically controlled oil pressure actuated injector. Who is correct?
   a. Tech A
   b. Tech B
   c. Both A and B
   d. Neither A nor B

5. Technician A says that a glow plug is just for starting the diesel engine. Technician B says that a intake heater grid allows for the coolant to be heated before it enters the engine. Who is correct?
a. Tech A
b. Tech B
c. Both A and B
d. Neither A nor B

6. Technician A states that cetane is an important number for the engine oil that goes into a diesel engine. Technician B says that a diesel engine doesn't have a throttle body. Who is correct?
a. Tech A
b. Tech B
c. Both A and B
d. Neither A nor B

7. Technician A states that the high-pressure injection system could reach 25,000 psi of fuel pressure. Technician B says that the compression ratio of a diesel engine is lower than a conventional gasoline engine. Who is correct?
a. Tech A
b. Tech B
c. Both A and B
d. Neither A nor B

8. Technician A states that a piezo injector uses a crystal to actuate the injection event. Technician B says that the ignition delay period is the amount of time it takes for the fuel to ignite after being injected into the cylinder. Who is correct?
a. Tech A
b. Tech B
c. Both A and B
d. Neither A nor B

9. Technician A says that white smoke coming from the exhaust could be a leaking injector. Technician B states that diesel engines use special oil formulated to withstand the environment they operate in. Who is correct?
a. Tech A
b. Tech B
c. Both A and B
d. Neither A nor B

10. Technician A says that the air charge that comes off the turbocharger gets cooled as it goes through an intercooler. Technician B says that most diesel engines are used in applications that require power and mileage. Who is correct?
a. Tech A
b. Tech B
c. Both A and B
d. Neither A nor B

GLOSSARY

3 Cs A term used to describe the repair documentation process of 1st documenting the customer concern, 2nd documenting the cause of the problem, and 3rd documenting the correction.

aftermarket A company other than the original manufacturer that produces equipment or provides services.

air charge cooler A radiator that helps cool the air that is in the intake track.

air cleaner Filters the incoming air to remove the contaminants that attempt to enter the engine from the outside.

Allen wrench A type of hexagonal drive mechanism for fasteners.

anaerobic sealer Used to seal between two machined surfaces and does not need oxygen to cure.

anti-drainback valve Used to keep the oil filter full of oil once the engine is shut off so that at the next start-up, the engine will not have to wait as long for oil pressure.

antifoaming agents Reduce the effect of oil churning in the crankcase and minimize foaming. Foaming allows air bubbles to form in the engine oil, reducing the lubrication quality of oil and contributing to breakdown of the oil due to oxidation. Because air is compressible, oil with foam reduces the ability of the oil to keep the moving parts separated, causing more wear and friction. The antifoaming additives keep these conditions from occurring.

arc joint pliers Pliers with parallel slip jaws that can increase in size. Also called Channellocks.

Atkinson cycle engine Allows for all four events—intake, compression, power, and exhaust—to happen on one revolution of the engine.

auxiliary coolers Used to cool automatic transmission fluid, power steering fluid, EGR gases, and compressed intake air. Each of these coolers transmits heat to either the cooling system or directly to the atmosphere. Because there is such a wide variety of auxiliary coolers, refer to the manufacturer's service information for how to properly inspect the auxiliary cooler for leaks and proper operation.

aviation snips A scissor-like tool for cutting sheet metal.

baffles Panels constructed in the oil pan to direct the flow of oil regardless of the angle of the engine in relationship to the ground. So if you are driving on a hill, the oil pump will continue to be fully submerged because of the baffles keeping the oil from moving to the low end of the oil pan.

balance shaft A spinning counterweighted shaft designed to take out vibrations caused by the engine operating. These are timed to the valve events, which means if the timing is off, this shaft could cause increased vibration.

ball-peen (engineer's) hammer A hammer that has a head that is rounded on one end and flat on the other; designed to work with metal items.

banded or screw clamp Adjust with a screwdriver.

barrier cream A cream that looks and feels like a moisturizing cream but has a specific formula to provide extra protection from chemicals and oils.

bath tub combustion chamber This type of combustion chamber is oval in shape, has the valves in a straight line, and is the same size throughout the chamber.

bearing crush Indicates a condition in which the bearings are slightly bigger than the journals, which cause them to crush on the ends when the cap is installed and torqued down.

bearing inserts Bearings for the crankshaft and the rod bearings. They come in two pieces and clamp around the components journal.

belt tension gauge Used to check belt tension.

bench vice A device that securely holds material in jaws while it is being worked on.

billet Type of component that is cut out of a large blank instead of being cast into a shape.

blind rivet A rivet that can be installed from its insertion side.

blow-off valve Allows for excess pressure that is built up in the intake track to exit the intake after the pressure overcomes the spring pressure on this valve.

blueprinting The process of measuring every component that will be installed in the engine so that it all fits precisely the same as the original intention of the engine.

bolt A type of threaded fastener with a thread on one end and a hexagonal head on the other.

bolt cutters Strong cutters available in different sizes, designed to cut through non-hardened bolts and other small-stock material.

boost solenoid Electronic control feature that allows the PCM to control the wastegate by either an electronic solenoid or by utilizing this to control the vacuum to the wastegate.

bore gauge Used to quickly measure a bore. It is a dial indicator that has an adapter to allow it to measure the inside of a bore to check for taper or out-of-round.

borescope Used for examining internal passages for evidence of a coolant leak.

bottom dead center (BDC) The very bottom of an engine stroke, where the piston can do no further down.

bottoming tap A thread-cutting tap designed to cut threads to the bottom of a blind hole.

box-end wrench A wrench or spanner with a closed or ring end to grip bolts and nuts.

British thermal units (BTUs) The amount of work needed to raise the temperature of 1 lb of water by 1°F, which equals about 1055 joules.

bucket-style lifters Lifters encasing the valve spring and having direct contact with the camshaft lobe. Sometimes these are hydraulic so that any wear will be automatically taken care of. On some applications you must shim these if a wear condition presents itself.

bypass valve Used on a supercharger application to bypass the supercharger in order to limit the amount of boost it creates.

cam phaser An assembly that allows for the advancement or retardation of the camshaft to adjust valve timing, which increases power and decreases emissions.

camshaft Only fitted in the cylinder heads of OHC and DOHC engines. This device provides the force to open the valves.

camshaft followers Operates similarly to the rocker arm as it pivots and opens the valve. It is located directly on the camshaft, with usually a pivot point adjacent to the camshaft so that the direct force of the lobe is transferred to the follower.

cast piston The entry-level piston that is created from aluminum that meets the needs of most vehicles requirements.

catalytic converter An emission device that helps oxidize the exhaust as it flows out of the engine, to help combat the hazardous fumes that are created by the combustion process.

cause Part of the 3Cs, documenting the cause of the problem. This documentation will go on the repair order, invoice, and service history.

cavitation Occurs when aeration is introduced into a liquid system. Introducing excess air into the coolant, causing the coolant to fail at absorbing heat from the engine.

C-clamp A clamp shaped like the letter C; it comes in various sizes and can clamp various items.

center punch Less sharp than a prick punch, the center punch makes a bigger indentation that centers a drill bit at the point where a hole is required to be drilled.

cetane The rating of the fuel, the fuel's viscosity, its cloud point, and the extent to which the fuel is contaminated.

chemical cleaning Process where components are dipped into a bath of caustic chemicals that eat away the dirt and grease. This process works well but creates a lot of environmentally unfriendly byproducts.

coarse (UNC) Used to describe thread pitch; stands for Unified National Coarse.

cold chisel The most common type of chisel, used to cut cold metals. The cutting end is tempered and hardened so that it is harder than the metals that need to be cut.

combination pliers A type of pliers for cutting, gripping, and bending.

combination wrench A type of wrench that has a box-end wrench on one side and an open end on the other.

combustion chamber The area of the engine in which the air-fuel mixture is ignited and combustion occurs.

compression ratio The column of the cylinder with the piston at bottom dead center as compared to the volume of the cylinder at top dead center, given in a ratio such as 10:1 CR.

compression ring The top ring on a piston and the main one that seals the combustion chamber.

compression test Test that checks the integrity of the cylinder by taking a reading on how much pressure is produced by complete events.

compressor surge Occurs when manifold pressure rises above normal and works against the spinning exhaust turbine wheel, slowing it considerably.

concern Part of the 3Cs, documenting the original concern that the customer came into the shop with. This documentation will go on the repair order, invoice, and service history.

conduction Heat transfer from one solid to another when there is a difference of temperature or of electrical potential without movement of the material.

connecting rod Connects the piston to the crankshaft and is an integral part in converting the chemical energy of the fuel to the mechanical energy needed to rotate the engine.

convection The movement caused within a fluid by the hotter and therefore less dense material to rise and colder material to sink, which results in the transfer of heat.

conventional oil Type of oil that is processed from crude oil to the desired viscosity, after which additives are added to increase wear resistance.

coolant The liquid used to prevent freezing, overheating, and corrosion of the engine.

coolant dye kit Used to aid leak detection by adding dye to coolant and using an ultraviolet light source (black light) to trace to the source of the leak; the dye glows fluorescent when a black light is shined on it.

coolant pH test strips Used to test the acid-to-alkalinity balance of the coolant.

coolant system pressure tester Used to apply pressure to the cooling system to diagnose leakage complaints. Under pressure, coolant may leak internally to the combustion chamber, intake or exhaust system, or the engine lubrication system. It can also leak externally to the outside of the engine.

cooling fan Forces air through the radiator for heat transfer. Cooling fans can be driven by a belt or by an electric motor. The fan can be controlled by viscous fluid or thermostatic sensors, switches, and relays.

cooling system flush machine Used to flush coolant backward through the system; cleaners remove corrosion buildup and old coolant. Most of these machines have their own pump so the vehicle does not have to run to perform the flush.

core plugs Made out of brass or steel; they seal the holes that are left after the casting process. The alternative purpose of these plugs is to help with freeze protection for the cylinder block.

correction Part of the 3Cs, documenting the repair that solved the vehicle fault. This documentation will go on the repair order, invoice, and service history.

corrosion inhibitors Help stop acids that cause corrosion from forming, especially on bearing surfaces. Corrosion due to acid etches into bearing surfaces and causes premature wear of the bearings.

cracked hose Hose that has cracked and will soon start to leak. Verify cracking by a visual inspection.

crank core Is the rough unfinished crankshaft assembly that has just left the foundry area.

crank throws Pieces that make up the stroke of the engine and are where the connecting rods attach to the crankshaft.

crankcase The lower part of the engine block that houses the crankshaft and rotating assembly.

crankshaft The component that transfers force from the connecting rod to the flywheel. This integral piece to the piston engine is the main component that allows the chemical explosion to be converted to mechanical motion that can be utilized to propel the vehicle.

crankshaft journal The part of the crankshaft where the connecting rod attaches or, in the main journal condition, where the crankshaft spins in the engine block.

crescent pump Usually mounted on the front of the cylinder block and straddles the front of the crankshaft. The inner gear is then driven by the crankshaft directly. An external toothed gear meshes with the inner one. Some gear teeth are meshed, but others are separated by the crescent-shaped part of the pump housing. The increasing volume between gear teeth causes pressure to fall, creating a vacuum, and atmospheric pressure pushes oil into the pump. Oil is then carried around between the gears and crescent before being discharged to the outlet port.

cross-arm A description for an arm that is set at right angles or 90 degrees to another component.

cross-cut chisel A type of chisel for metal work that cleans out or cuts key ways.

cross-flow radiator Type of radiator that has the coolant flow from left to right and is more conformable to the low hood designs of today's vehicles.

crosshatch pattern The design of Xs at a 60-degree angle created when honing the cylinder bore.

crude oil Oil that originates from the ground; it is then refined into a usable substance.

curved file A type of file that has a curved surface for filing holes.

cylinder bore The diameter of the hole that the piston moves in; it is one of the main components that is included in the size of the engine.

cylinder deactivation System that disables multiple cylinders on an engine so fuel mileage is increased while the engine is operating in an environment that doesn't require all the available power.

cylinder head The component that seals the cylinder of the combustion chamber where the explosion happens and creates motion that is converted into mechanical motion.

cylinder leakage test Test done by pressuring up the cylinder with compressed air and measuring the amount of air that is leaking past the piston rings, head gasket, or valves.

cylinder power balance test Test that helps the technician realize which cylinders are actually contributing to the running of the engine and those that are weak.

data link connector (DLC) Located near the steering column and allows for a scan tool to interrogate the PCM in a vehicle for information.

dead blow hammer A type of hammer that has a cushioned head to reduce the amount of head bounce.

deck The area that is machined on top of the cylinder block and is a gasket sealing area for the head gaskets. This area must be completely flat and must be checked when the head gaskets have failed.

depth micrometer A measuring device that accurately measures the depth of a hole.

detergents Reduce carbon deposits on parts such as piston rings and valves.

diagnostic link connector (DLC) The port that the technician connects a scanner to in order to interrogate the PCM in the vehicle for information about faults.

diagnostic trouble code (DTC) A monitor code that shows that there is a fault with in the engine management system.

diagonal cutting pliers Cutting pliers for small wire or cable.

dial bore gauge An accurate measuring device for inside bores, usually made with a dial indicator attached to it.

dial indicator An accurate measuring device where measurements are read from a dial and needle.

die Used to cut external threads on a metal shank or bolt.

die stock A handle for securely holding dies to cut threads.

diesel oxidation catalyst Promotes the conversion of carbon monoxide, hydrocarbons, and diesel particulates into harmless carbon dioxide and water.

diesel particulate filter (DPF) Converts particulate matter, or soot, into ash.

dipper Used in a splash lubrication system. This scope, attached to the bottom of the connecting rod, dips into the oil and throws it up on the cylinder wall each revolution.

direct injection The type of diesel engine that directly injects the fuel into the cylinder, without prechambers.

dispersants Collect particles that can block the system; the dispersants separate the particles from one another, and keep them moving. They are removed when the oil is changed.

double flare A seal that is made at the end of metal tubing or pipe.

double insulated Tools or appliances that are designed in such a way that no single failure can result in a dangerous voltage coming into contact with the outer casing of the device.

downflow radiator Type of radiator that has the cooling tubes from top to bottom, so the surface area needed becomes taller than the cross flow radiator, which is why they are used mostly in trucks or vehicles that have a higher hood line.

drift punch A type of punch used to start pushing roll pins to prevent them from spreading.

drill vice A tool with jaws that can be attached to a drill press table for holding material that is to be drilled.

drive belts Provide power to drive the water pump and other accessories on the front of the engine. Four types are used: V-belts, serpentine (also called multi-groove) belts, stretch belts, and toothed belts.

dry sump lubrication system A type of lubricating system with an external reservoir that houses the oil until the pump needs it to pressurize and distribute it through the engine.

dual overhead cam (DOHC) engine Engine containing two camshafts per cylinder head.

dye penetrant testing Process in which dye is sprayed all over the component and is allowed to seep into the crevices, illuminating the cracks.

ear protection Protective gear worn when the sound levels exceed 85 decibels, when working around operating machinery for any period of time, or when the equipment you are using produces loud noise.

elasticity The amount of stretch or give a material has.

engine balance The ability of the rotating assembly to offset the opposite harmonics as it rotates.

engine block's deck The portion of the engine cylinder block on which the head gasket lies and to which the cylinder head is bolted.

engine displacement The size of the engine, given in cubic inches, cubic centimeters, and lifters. It is found by multiplying the piston displacement by the number of cylinders in the engine.

engine hoist A crane that allows for the engine to be removed, usually rated from 3 to 6 tons, to safely lift the heavy engines found in today's vehicles.

engine stand Supports the engine when it is removed from the vehicle so that the technician can disassemble and repair the various components.

engineering and work practice controls Systems and procedures required by OSHA and put in place by employers to protect their employees from hazards.

Environmental Protection Agency (EPA) Federal government agency that deals with issues related to environmental safety.

ethylene glycol An organic material that has properties that do not allow it to freeze until it is below the freezing point of water. It is usually infused with anticorrosive additives and rust inhibitors so that it conditions the materials that it flows through.

European Automobile Manufacturers' Association (ACEA) Creates classifications formulated for engine oils used in European vehicles; these classifications are much more stringent than the API and ILSAC standards.

exhaust gas analyzer Used to detect exhaust gases that are finding their way into the cooling system due to a leaking head gasket or damaged head or block. Be careful not allow liquid coolant to be picked up by the analyzer probe.

exhaust manifold Connects the cylinder head to the rest of the exhaust system so that fumes can be directed away from the vehicle so they will not affect the driver.

exhaust ports Direct exhaust gases to the exhaust manifold from the exhaust valve. They are cast into the cylinder head.

exhaust system The piping and components that direct the flow of exhaust from the engine to out from underneath the vehicle.

exhaust valves Valve that allows burnt exhaust fumes to enter the exhaust system; they then exit the vehicle through the tail pipe.

extreme loading The areas in the engine that are high stress because of the location of the components.

extreme-pressure additives Coat parts with a protective layer so that the oil resists being forced out under heavy load.

fasteners Devices that securely hold items together, such as screws, cotter pins, rivets, and bolts.

feeler gauge A thin blade device for measuring space between two objects.

fine (UNF) Used to describe thread pitch; it stands for Unified National Fine.

finished rivet A rivet after the completion of the riveting process.

fire rings Part of the head gasket and usually made out of steel. They offer support around the cylinder opening to help contain the explosion that occurs in the cylinder each time the spark plug fires.

first aid The immediate care given to an injured or suddenly ill person.

flame propagation The moving flame front within the combustion chamber.

flare nut wrench A type of box-end wrench that has a slot in the box section to allow the wrench to slip through a tube or pipe. Also called a flare tubing wrench.

flat blade screwdriver A type of screwdriver that fits a straight slot in screws.

flat tappet Lifter that has a flat surface on the bottom that rides directly on the camshaft lobe.

flat-nose pliers Pliers that are flat and square at the end of the nose.

flex hone Type of hone that has multiple balls attached to it on the flexible steel end, which allow it to move in the cylinder as it is being honed. This type of hone is the most common in the industry today.

flexplate A circular component that has the starter ring gear attached to it for starting purposes. It also transfers power from the engine to the torque converter on an automatic transmission.

floating pin Type of piston pin that is held in by two circlips on the sides of the piston and is completely removable for servicing.

flywheel A balanced component that has a machined surface where the clutch pressure plate attaches so that power can be transferred from the engine to the manual transmission.

forced induction An application that has a positive pressure adder to the engine such as a turbocharger or a supercharger. It forces extra air into the cylinder.

forcing screw The center screw on a gear, bearing, or pulley puller. Also called a jacking screw.

forged piston Piston utilized in a positive pressure environment and created out of a forging that is molecularly stronger than a cast or hypereutectic piston.

formed in place gasket (FIPG) Type of gasket that is a sealant that takes the place of a conventional gasket and hardens once it is exposed to oxygen.

fracture split Type of connecting rod cap that has been broken, instead of cut, so that it will fit perfectly when screwed together.

freeze frame data Refers to snapshots that are automatically stored in a vehicle's power train control module (PCM) when a fault occurs (only available on model year 1996 and newer).

freeze plug A slang term used to describe the core plugs.

full-flow filters Type of filters that are designed to filter all of the oil before delivering it to the engine.

galvanic corrosion Occurs when dissimilar metals come in contact through a liquid electrolyte.

gas welding goggles Protective gear designed for gas welding; they provide protection against foreign particles entering the eye and are tinted to reduce the glare of the welding flame.

gasket A sealing element that is clamped between two flat components where there is no expected movement. This piece helps take up the peaks and valleys in each components finish.

gasket scraper A broad sharp flat blade to assist in removing gaskets and glue.

gasoline direct injection (GDI) A gasoline engine that is designed to be very similar to a diesel engine. The injection event happens right in the cylinder, as in a direct injection diesel. These engines have higher compression ratios and a more complete burn process.

gasoline direct injection cylinder head Type of cylinder head that has a spark plug and an injector directly in the combustion chamber. This is very similar to the diesel cylinder head, which makes for a very efficient design, as the piston is only compressing air until the last moment when it injects fuel into the cylinder.

gear or worm clamp Adjust with a screwdriver or nut driver.

gear pullers A tool with two or more legs and a cross bar with a center forcing screw to remove gears.

geared oil pump The driving gear meshes with a second gear as both gears turn, and their teeth separate, creating a low-pressure area. Higher atmospheric pressure outside forces the oil up into the inlet, which fills the spaces between the gear teeth. As the gears rotate, they carry oil around the chamber. As the teeth mesh again, oil is forced from the outlet into the oil gallery and toward the oil filter, where it is filtered of any particles.

gelling The thickening of oil to a point that it will not flow through the engine; it becomes close to a solid in extreme cold temperatures.

girdle A subassembly of main caps all attached that attaches to the engine block to retain the crankshaft.

glow plug A heating element that helps raise the temperature in the combustion chamber, which makes the engine easier to start in colder weather.

gravity pouring The process used to pour the molten metal into a mold to create a cylinder block blank.

hard rubber mallet A special-purpose tool with a head made of hard rubber; often used for moving things into place where it is important not to damage the item being moved.

hardened hose Hose that has become brittle and will break and leak. Verify hardening by squeezing the hose and comparing it to a known good hose.

hardened seat Valve seats that have been heat treated to make them more robust and capable of withstanding the severe demands of today's engines and fuels

harmonic balancer Reduces the vibrations from the harmonics of the engine rotating and the explosions that happen inside the engine.

hazardous material Any material that poses an unreasonable risk of damage or injury to persons, property, or the environment if it is not properly controlled during handling, storage, manufacture, processing, packaging, use and disposal, or transportation.

header Version of an exhaust manifold, made of tubular bent steel, that increases exhaust velocity, thus increasing performance of the engine.

head gasket Metal or composite gasket that seals the cylinder to the cylinder head, which creates the combustion chamber.

headgear Protective gear that includes items like hairnets, caps, or hard hats.

heat buildup A dangerous condition that occurs when the glove can no longer absorb or reflect heat, and heat is transferred to the inside of the glove.

heater core A small radiator used to provide heat to the passenger compartment from the hot coolant passing through it. The amount of heat can be controlled by a heater control valve.

heater hoses Connect the water pump and engine to the heater core. They carry heated coolant to the heater core to be used to heat the passenger compartment.

hemispherical cylinder head Type of combustion chamber design comprising a half sphere, which locates the valves opposite of each other, creating an even flame distribution.

high-pressure steam cleaning Process in which the component is put into a machine that produces steam from heating up water. The component is then sprayed with the hot water in order to dissolve the dirt and grease so it comes right off.

hollow punch A punch with a center hollow for cutting circles in thin materials such as gaskets.

honing The procedure that finishes the boring process and gives the bore a finish that will retain oil to lubricate the piston.

hydraulic tensioner Type of tensioner that is operated by hydraulic fluid through a metered orifice inside the tensioner. These are also oil fed from the engine on some applications.

hydraulic valve lifter Lifters that have a plunger inside a hollow cylindrical body, which oil fills, pushing the plunger up to the pushrod until all the play is removed. This setup is auto-adjusting, so there is no adjustment, but only replacement.

hydraulically actuated electronically controlled unit injector (HEUI) Type of injector that uses an electronic solenoid that is controlled by the PCM to control high-pressure oil, which actuates the injector at the precise time.

hydrocracking Refining crude oil with hydrogen, resulting in a base oil that has the higher performance characteristics of synthetic oils.

hydrometer Used to test coolant mixture and freeze protection by testing the specific gravity of the coolant. You must use a hydrometer specifically designed for the antifreeze you are testing.

hypereutectic piston Type of piston that is one step above a cast piston and has a higher level of silicon content, which creates a stronger piston that is comparably priced to a cast piston.

ignition delay period The time it takes for the fuel to ignite after being injected into the engine.

impact driver A tool that is struck with a hammer to provide an impact turning force to remove tight fasteners.

indirect injection A method of injecting fuel into a diesel engine that uses a prechamber into which the fuel is injected. The prechamber is a small area where the combustion happens in a diesel engine.

induction hardened Process done to harden steel by inducting a voltage through the steel to make it heat up, and then quenching it in a coolant.

infrared temperature sensor A noncontact thermometer used to check actual temperatures and variations of temperature throughout the cooling system to help pinpoint faulty parts and system blockages.

inside micrometer A micrometer designed to measure internal diameters.

intake gasket Seals the manifold to the cylinder head; usually made out of plastic, rubber, or paper.

intake manifold Directs the airflow that goes through the throttle body to the individual intake valves that support combustion inside the cylinders.

intake port The passage in the cylinder head that feeds the intake valve. It is connected to the intake manifold and is cast into the cylinder head.

intake valves Allows the air or air-fuel mixture into the cylinder to be combusted.

intermediate tap One of a series of taps designed to cut an internal thread. Also called a plug tap.

intermittent faults A fault or customer concern that you can not detect all of the time and only occurs sometimes.

journal saddles The machined areas in the engine block where the other half of the main bearings sit.

lab scope An electrical instrument used to measure the waveform of an electrical device and create a visual representation of the electrical performance of the component.

lift pump A low-pressure pump that feeds the high-pressure injection pump driven by the engine.

lifter bore The hole in the cylinder block that the lifter rides in. This could have a bushing in it, but most are just machined into the casting.

lobe separation angle How far the intake lobe is offset from the exhaust lobe. This determines how quickly the valves open.

locking pliers A type of pliers where the jaws can be set and locked into position.

lockout/tag-out A safety tag system to ensure that faulty equipment or equipment in the middle of repair is not used.

lost foam process A casting process where foam spacers take up the space in a mold so that when molten metal is poured over them, they will keep their shape until the metal is cooled enough to retain its shape. Once that foam gets hot enough, it dissolves and exits the component.

lubricating oil Oil distilled from crude oil and used as a base stock in the oil that you use in vehicles.

lubrication system Refers to the oil circuit that sends lubrication throughout the engine.

lug wrench A tool designed to remove wheel lugs nuts and commonly shaped like a cross.

magnafluxing The process that uses special fluorescent dye and a magnet to check for cracks in cast iron engine components. This process can only be used on ferrous material.

magnetic pickup tools An extending shaft, often flexible, with a magnet fitted to the end for picking up metal objects.

main bearing caps Keep the crankshaft attached to the cylinder block. This caps house half of the main bearing; the other half is housed in the cylinder block. They can be cross bolted and have either two or four bolts.

main cap girdle Location where all the main bearing caps are attached with a structure so that they combine to become a strong unit.

main journal The journals that support the crankshaft inside the cylinder block are called the main journals.

Mallory metal Metal added to counterweights to balance them; it is 117% heavier than steel.

mandrel The shaft of a pop rivet.

mandrel head The head of the pop rivet that connects to the shaft and causes the rivet body to flare.

measuring tape A thin measuring blade that rolls up and is contained in a spring-loaded dispenser.

mechanical cleaning Process in which the technician physically scrapes and cleans the components.

mechanical fingers Spring-loaded fingers at the end of a flexible shaft that pick up items in tight spaces.

mechanical integrity Determines the strength of the internal components of the engine, which should be the first step to any repair.

micrometer An accurate measuring device for internal and external dimensions. Commonly abbreviated as "mic."

Miller cycle engine The intake valve is left open longer than the typical Otto cycle engine.

motor mounts Rubber insulators that connect the engine with the vehicle frame. They isolate the vibrations the engine gives off so that the driver doesn't feel it.

muffler Component put on an exhaust system to muffle the noise created by the engine.

multilayer steel (MLS) head gasket Type of head gasket made out of multiple layers of thin sheet metal that conforms to the surfaces present on the engine block and cylinder head.

needle-nose pliers Pliers with long tapered jaws for gripping small items and getting into tight spaces.

nippers (pincer pliers) Pliers designed to cut protruding items level with the surface.

nitriding A surface hardening treatment that produces a thin, very hard surface on a steel object.

nut A fastener with a hexagonal head and internal threads for screwing on bolts.

Occupational Safety and Health Administration (OSHA) Government agency created to provide national leadership in occupational safety and health.

offset area The area where the rod journals are located.

offset screwdriver A screwdriver with a 90-degree bend in the shaft for working in tight spaces.

offset vice A vice that allows long objects to be gripped vertically.

oil carburization Happens when the engine is burning oil, and it becomes a carbon compound that plugs passages in the engine.

oil control ring Piston ring that is usually perforated to allow oil drainback to the crankcase as the scraper ring scrapes the cylinder wall.

oil filter wrench A specialized wrench that allows extra leverage to remove an oil filter when it is tight.

oil galleries The passageways that carry oil through the engine. They are either cast or drilled into the engine block and head(s).

oil monitoring systems Monitor engine running conditions to calculate the condition of the oil in the engine. When the condition of the oil falls below the specification, the oil monitoring system alerts the driver to change the oil.

oil pan Located at the bottom of the engine, this component usually covers the crankshaft and rods, commonly where the oil sump is located on a wet sump oil system.

oil pressure relief valve A calibrated spring-loaded valve that allows for pressure bleed-off if the oil pump creates too much pressure.

oil pump A positive pressure pump that produces oil flow within the engine and lubricates the internal moving components.

oil pump pickup tube Attached to the oil pump and fully submerged in the oil pan sump so that it is always submerged in oil. There is usually a strainer attached to it so that no debris can reach the oil pump.

oil seals Keep oil from leaking past a rotating camshaft.

oil slinger Usually attached to the crankshaft and half-submerged in oil, causing it to throw the oil onto the moving parts with every rotation.

oil sump The location of the engine where the oil collects after it runs off the rotating assembly and off the valvetrain.

open-end wrench A wrench with open jaws to allow side entry to a nut or bolt.

original equipment manufacturer (OEM) The company that manufactured the vehicle.

outside micrometer A micrometer designed to measure the external dimensions of items.

overhead cam (OHC) engine Engine for which the camshaft is housed in the cylinder head.

overhead valve (OHV) engine Engine with valves positioned in the cylinder head assembly, directly over the top of the piston.

oxidation inhibitors Stop very hot oil from combining with oxygen in the air to produce a sticky tarlike material that coats parts and clogs the oil galleries and drain-back passages.

parallax error A visual error caused by viewing measurement markers at an incorrect angle.

peening A term used to describe the action of flattening a rivet through a hammering action.

personal protective equipment (PPE) Safety equipment designed to protect the technician, such as safety boots, gloves, clothing, protective eyewear, and hearing protection.

phasers Sprockets that are attached to the end of the camshaft that allow for the advancing or retarding of the camshaft for use in variable valve timing. These are usually an assembly that must be installed as one piece.

Phillips head screwdriver A type of screwdriver that fits a head shaped like a cross in screws.

piezo injector Type of injector that is operated by a piezo crystal that cycles five times faster than a typical injector.

pin punch A type of punch in various sizes with a straight or parallel shaft.

pipe wrench A wrench that grips pipes and can exert a lot of force to turn them. Because the handle pivots slightly, the more pressure put on the handle to turn the wrench, the more the grip tightens.

piston Part of the combustion chamber that is moveable and transfers the combustion energy to the connecting rod, which then creates mechanical energy by rotating the crankshaft.

piston installed height Measurement taken as the engine is being assembly; it tells the technician how far out of the block the piston protrudes. This must be checked because if the piston strikes the cylinder head, there will be catastrophic problems internally in the engine.

piston ring grooves Areas machined out of the piston that are where the piston rings are installed.

piston rings Rings installed around the circumference of the piston and that contact the cylinder wall, thus providing sealing for the cylinder as the piston moves in the bore.

piston slap Term used when the piston hits the cylinder wall, causing a loud noise every revolution; usually caused by excessive clearance between the cylinder wall and the piston.

piston stroke The distance the piston travels from TDC to BDC in the engine block.

Plastigage A plastic thread that is used to check clearance between two different parts. It is put between the components and then torqued to specification. As the component is torqued down, it smashes the plastic, which causes it to flatten out, giving the technician a reading of the clearance between the two components.

pliers A hand tool with gripping jaws.

plugs (e.g., galley, coolant) Much like seals, used to block off passages where oil and coolant flow, primarily to block holes used in the original casting and machining of the head.

policy A guiding principle that sets the shop direction.

polyalphaolefin (PAO) oil An artificially made base stock that is not refined from crude oil.

pop rivet gun A hand tool for installing pop rivets.

pour point depressants Keep oil from forming wax particles under cold-temperature operation.

power The rate or speed at which work is performed.

power control module (PCM) The computer that operates the fuel and ignition systems on later model vehicles.

prechamber A component that is pressed into the cylinder head and usually houses the injector and glow plug in a diesel engine. This is the area where the combustion event starts.

pressed-fit pin Type of piston pin used in cheaper applications and installed when the small end of the connecting rod is heated up so that it expands, and then the pin is installed, and finally the rod is allowed to cool, creating an interference fit for the pin.

pressure or force-fed lubrication system Type of oiling system that has a pump that creates positive pressure to shoot oil throughout the engine's moving parts.

pressure testing Process used on components that do not have iron in their molecular makeup. The component is sealed up, and air pressure is used to pressurize the cavities; then the component is put into a tank of water so that the machinist can see where the bubbles are escaping from the component.

pressure transducer Electrical device that creates an electrical signal based on a pressure input.

prick punch A pinch with a sharp point for accurately marking a point on metal.

procedure A list of the steps required to get the same result each time a task or activity is performed.

propylene glycol An organic material that is taking the place of ethylene glycol as it is nontoxic and still has most of the properties that are needed to use in an automotive application.

pry bar A high-strength carbon steel rod with offsets for levering and prying.

pullers A generic term to describe hand tools that mechanically assist the removal of bearings, gears, pulleys, and other parts.

punches A generic term to describe a high-strength carbon steel shaft with a blunt point for driving. Center and prick punches are exceptions and have a sharp point for marking or making an indentation.

radiation The emission of energy as electromagnetic waves that excite molecules in the objects they come in contact with.

radiator clamp pliers Used to safely remove spring-type radiator clamps.

radiator hoses Used to connect the radiator to the water pump and engine. They are usually made of formed, nylon-reinforced rubber. Some radiator hoses use coiled wire inside them to prevent hose collapse as the cooling system temperature fluctuates.

ratchet A generic term to describe a handle for sockets that allows the user to select direction of rotation. It can turn sockets in restricted areas without the user having to remove the socket from the fastener.

ratcheting box-end wrench A wrench with an inner piece that is able to rotate within the outer housing, allowing it to be repositioned without being removed.

ratcheting screwdriver A screwdriver with a selectable ratchet mechanism built into the handle that allows the screwdriver tip to ratchet as it is being used.

recovery system Uses an overflow tank to catch any coolant that is released from the radiator cap when the coolant heats up.

refractometer Used to test coolant mixture and freeze protection by testing the fluid's ability to bend light. This tester can be used with any type of antifreeze.

reluctor ring A toothed ring that a crankshaft position sensor picks up to reference where the crankshaft is in its revolution. It is sometimes cast into the crankshaft and sometimes attached to the harmonic damper.

repair order The document that is given to the repair technician that details the customer concern and any needed information.

respirator Protective gear used to protect the wearer from inhaling harmful dusts or gases. Respirators range from single-use disposable masks to types that have replaceable cartridges. The correct types of cartridge must be used for the type of contaminant encountered.

ridge reamer Used to remove the ridge that is developed at the top of the cylinder as the piston wears the cylinder, so that the piston can be removed.

ring gap The distance between the two ends of one piston ring. This is a critical measurement because if the gap is too big, blowby will result, and if it is too small, damage to the ring will occur.

ring lands The sides of the grooves that support the ring when it is installed on the piston.

rocker arm Component that, as the camshaft lobe pushes up, is pushed up on one end so that the other end pushes the valve down to open.

rod bearing Supports the connecting rod.

rod cap The piece of the connecting rod that is removable so that it can be installed on the crankshaft.

rod throws The area where the connecting rod is attached to the crankshaft.

roll bar Another type of pry bar, with one end used for prying and the other end for aligning larger holes, such as engine motor mounts.

roller tip Designed to reduce friction and increase durability on a lifter. A hardened roller installed on the bottom of the lifter makes contact with the camshaft.

Roloc™ bristle disc Type of tool that is a buffing disc that has plastic bristles that gently remove the material on the component without harming the surface.

room temperature vulcanizing (RTV) silicone Type of sealant made of a semi-solid material that is pliable until exposed to oxygen for an extended period of time. At that point, it becomes a rubber-like material that conforms to the two components it is exposed to.

rotating assembly Consists of the crankshaft, connecting rods, and pistons—all the major components that rotate in the cylinder block.

rotor housing Houses the rotors in a Wankel/rotary engine. This is the base for the engine, similar to the engine block.

rotor-type oil pump An inner rotor driving an outer one; as they turn, the volume between them increases. The larger volume created between the rotors lowers the pressure at the pump inlet, creating a vacuum. Outside atmospheric pressure, which is higher, forces oil into the pump, and the oil fills the spaces between the rotor lobes. As the lobes of the inner rotor move into the spaces in the outer rotor, oil is squeezed out through the outlet.

running compression test Test done with the engine running to see the compression of a particular cylinder under a load as it looks for a cylinder that is failing once the engine is operating.

safety glasses Safety glasses are protective eye glasses with built-in side shields to help protect your eyes from the front and side. Approved safety glasses should be worn whenever you are in a workshop. They are designed to help protect your eyes from direct impact or debris damage.

safety data sheet (SDS) A sheet that provides information about handling, use, and storage of a material that may be hazardous.

scan tool Used to activate the cooling fan through bidirectional controls for testing; to monitor cooling sensor operation and to command air door actuators when testing low heat complaints; and to read DTCs related to cooling system operation.

scavenge pump Type of pump used in a dry sump oil system to remove the oil from the oil reservoir and pump it through the engine.

scavenging The process that uses a column of moving air to create a low pressure area behind it to assist in removing any remaining gases; this creates a vacuum.

scraper ring The ring usually below the compression ring, whose main function is to scrape the cylinder wall so that the oil can be directed toward the crankcase.

screw extractor A tool for removing broken screws or bolts.

seal A component that can either be stationary or moving and that usually wraps around a shaft and keeps the fluid on one side of it.

second law of thermodynamics The second law of thermodynamics also states that the entropy (measurable coordinates that characterize a system) of an isolated system can only increase over time. It can remain constant in ideal cases where the system is in a steady state (equilibrium) or undergoing a reversible process. There is an upper limit to the efficiency of conversion of heat to work in a heat engine.

selective catalytic reduction (SCR) An active emission control system that injects a liquid reductant, or reducing agent, through a special catalyst into the exhaust stream of a diesel engine. To meet the stringent 2010 diesel emission standards, the manufactures decided to make this system standard on most road diesel engines.

serpentine belt Also called a multi-groove V-belt, with a flat profile that has a number of small V-shaped grooves running lengthwise along the inside of the belt. These grooves are the exact reverse of the grooves in the outer edge of the pulleys; they increase the contact surface area, as well as prevent the belt from slipping off the pulley as it rotates. The serpentine belt is used to drive multiple accessories and to save underhood space forward of the engine. It winds its way around the crankshaft pulley, water pump, alternator, air-conditioning compressor, and tensioner. Most serpentine belts use a spring-loaded tensioner to maintain proper tightness of the belt and prevent it from slipping.

serpentine belt wear gauge Used to check whether the serpentine belt grooves are worn past their specifications.

service advisor The person at a repair facility that is in charge of communicating with the customer.

service history A complete listing of all the servicing and repairs that have been performed on that vehicle.

single flare A sealing system made on the end of metal tubing.

sledgehammer A heavy hammer, usually with two flat faces, that provides a strong blow.

sliding T-handle A handle fitted at 90 degrees to the main body that can be slid from side to side.

snap ring pliers A pair of pliers for installing and removing snap rings or circlips.

socket An enclosed metal tube commonly with 6 or 12 points to remove and install bolts and nuts.

soft hose Hose that has become very weak and is in danger of ballooning or bursting. Verify softening by squeezing the hose and comparing it to a known good hose. Hose clamps come in several forms and require different tools to properly remove or replace. These clamps secure the hose to the component it is connected to. Be sure to follow proper installation instructions to prevent future leaks from this seal.

solid valve lifter Constructed as a hollow cast iron cylinder, capped on both ends. It wears over time, and the valve lash will have to be adjusted as it wears, as solid valve lifters are not self-adjusting.

speed brace A U-shaped socket wrench that allows high-speed operation. Also called a speeder handle.

splash lubrication Type of lubrication system that uses a dipper to throw oil up on the cylinder walls and onto the crankshaft to lubricate the internal components.

splined phaser A type of phaser that has the gear teeth cut at an angle so that as the collar is pushed out, the inner gear, which is connected to the camshaft, rotates, thus rotating the camshaft. A splined phaser is oil fed, so the oil must be up to the recommended level.

split ball gauge A measuring device used to accurately measure small holes.

spring-loaded tensioner Type of tensioner that is operated by a spring to keep the tension on the timing belt.

square file A type of file with a square cross section.

square thread A thread type with square shoulders used to translate rotational to lateral movement.

squish area The area in a combustion chamber that is between the piston at TDC and the cylinder head.

starter motor The electric motor that, in conjunction with the flywheel, rotates the engine over to start the combustion process.

starter teeth The teeth that are a part of the Bendix in the starter and that mesh with the ring gear on the flywheel in order to turn the engine over.

steel hammer A hammer with a head made of hardened steel.

steel rule An accurate measuring ruler made of steel.

straight edge A measuring device generally made of steel to check how flat a surface is.

Strategy-Based Diagnostic Process A systematic process used to diagnose faults in a vehicle.

stretch belt Looks like an ordinary serpentine belt but is found on vehicles without a tensioner. It is made of a special material that allows it to stretch just enough to be installed over the pulleys but then shrink back to its original size, which is shorter than the distance around the pulleys. This stretchiness keeps the belt properly tensioned. Stretch belts require special tools to install and are usually cut off when being removed.

stud A type of threaded fastener with a thread cut on each end rather than having a bolt head on one end.

subframe A removal section of the frame that usually supports the drivetrain and suspension components.

supercharger Component that uses external power to turn the compressor wheel to compress the air as it enters the intake system track. The supercharger is usually driven by a belt off the crankshaft.

surface roughness average (Ra) A measure of how rough a surface is at the microscopic level. It is rated as the arithmetic average of the surface valleys and peaks.

surge tank A pressurized tank that is piped into the cooling system. Coolant constantly moves through it. It is used when the radiator is not the highest part of the cooling system. (Remember, air collects at the highest point in the cooling system.)

swollen hose Hose that has lost its elasticity and is swelling under pressure. It may soon rupture; typically, you will see a bubble protruding from the side of this hose. Replace this hose immediately.

synthetic blend Type of oil that is cheaper than synthetic as it utilizes conventional oil along with synthetic to create an oil that has the best of both worlds.

synthetic oil Artificially made or heavily processed oil that has been engineered with enhanced lubricating properties.

tap A term used to generically describe an internal thread-cutting tool.

tap handle A tool designed to securely hold taps for cutting internal threads.

taper The extent to which one the one end of the cylinder is smaller than the other end; it is measured to show the wear in the cylinder.

taper tap A tap with a tapper; it is usually the first of three taps used when cutting internal threads.

technical service bulletin (TSB) Service notifications and procedures sent out by the manufacturers to dealer groups alerting technicians about common issues with a particular vehicle or group of vehicles.

telescoping gauge A gauge that expands and locks to the internal diameter of bores; a caliper or outside micrometer is used to measure its size.

temperature indicators Provide information to the operator about engine temperature. The temperature gauge indicates engine temperature continuously. A temperature warning indicator comes on only when the engine is overheating, and warns the operator that engine damage will occur if the vehicle is driven much farther.

tensile strength In reference to fasteners, the amount of force it takes before a fastener breaks.

The American Petroleum Institute (API) Sets minimum performance standards for lubricants, including engine oils.

The International Lubricant Standardization and Approval Committee (ILSAC) International body that rates gasoline and engine oils to meet the standards set forth by the manufacturers' requirements.

The Japanese Engine Oil Standards Implementation Panel (JASO) Japanese standards set for the classification of motorcycle engines, both two-stroke and four-stroke, as well as Japanese automotive diesel engines.

The Society of Automotive Engineers (SAE) Body that started out with setting standards that oil manufacturers must meet to qualify for the viscosity rating for that particular grade of oil.

thermal cleaning Process in which the components are heated in an oven, burning off the grease and dirt.

thermometer Used to check the temperature of air exiting the heating ducts.

thermostat Regulates coolant flow to the radiator. It opens at a predetermined temperature to allow coolant flow to the radiator for cooling. It also enables the engine to reach operating temperature more quickly for reduced emissions and wear.

thread file A type of file that cleans clogged or distorted threads on bolts and studs.

thread pitch The coarseness or fineness of a thread as measured by either the threads per inch or the distance from the peak of one thread to the next. Metric fasteners are measured in millimeters.

thread repair A generic term to describe a number of processes that can be used to repair threads.

threaded fasteners Bolts, studs, and nuts designed to secure parts that are under various tension and sheer stresses. These include bolts, studs, and nuts, and are designed to secure vehicle parts under stress.

threadlocker This compound seals the threads of a bolt to the threads of the component so that it will not be allowed to move once installed.

three Cs The major issues that happen to a vehicle can be diagnosed when these are answered. Concern: What is the problem? Cause: What caused the system to fail? Correction: What will it take to fix the failed system?

threshold limit value (TLV) The maximum allowable concentration of a given material in the surrounding air.

thrust bearing Bearing that controls the forward and rearward movement of the crankshaft as it rotates in the engine block.

timing belt A major timing component that links the crankshaft with the camshaft. Unlike a timing chain, the belt must be changed periodically. During operation of the engine, the belt allows for quiet running of the timing component.

timing chain A key timing component that links the crankshaft with the camshaft and makes sure they turn at the same time so that the valve events happen as scheduled. It is a chain that is either single or double row.

timing gears Timing components in some older engines that are utilized by gear-to-gear contact. Timing is kept because the gears are constantly meshed.

timing marks Marks for assembly of the timing components so that the valve events will happen at the correct time in order to support combustion.

tin snips Cutting device for sheet metal, works in a similar fashion to scissors.

toothed belt Has teeth on the inside that are perpendicular to the belt and fit inside the teeth of a gear. Timing belts are always toothed belts to keep the camshaft running exactly half the speed of the crankshaft. To save on labor cost, these belts are generally replaced whenever a water pump replacement is required. And the water pump is generally replaced whenever the timing belt is changed.

torque angle A method of tightening bolts or nuts based on angles of rotation.

torque angle gauge Tells the technician the degrees of rotation of the fastener as they are torquing it.

torque plate Used to simulate the distortion of a torqued cylinder head on the cylinder block so that when the block is bored out, it will stay round when the cylinder head is torqued down.

torque specifications Supplied by manufacturers and describes the amount of twisting force allowable for a fastener or a specification showing the twisting force from an engine crankshaft.

torque Twisting force applied to a shaft, which may or may not result in motion.

torque wrench A tool used to measure the rotational or twisting force applied to fasteners.

torque-to-yield (TTY) bolts Bolts that are tightened using the torque-to-yield method.

torque-to-yield A method of tightening bolts close to their yield point or the point at which they will not return to their original length.

toxic dust Any dust that may contain fine particles that could be harmful to humans or the environment.

triangular file A type of file with three sides so it can get into internal corners.

tube flaring tool A tool that makes a sealing flare on the end of metal tubing.

tubing cutter A hand tool for cutting pipe or tubing squarely.

turbocharger Forced induction unit that uses exhaust gas pressure to compress intake air so that more air can be pushed into the cylinders, thus creating more power.

ultrasonic cleaner Machine that uses sound waves to vibrate any small, loose particles out of the components before the components are reinstalled in the engine.

V blocks Metal blocks with a V-shaped cutout for holding shafts while working on them. Also referred to as vee blocks.

vacuum gauge Measures the negative pressure that is present in the internal combustion engine as the pistons create suction as they move through the Otto cycle.

valve The valve is the component that seals the exhaust and intake systems from the combustion chamber. This is like a door that opens and closes letting in the fuel air mixture into the cylinder or letting out the exhaust gas.

valve keepers Keep a valve spring's retainer attached to the valve while in the cylinder head.

valve overlap The portion of time that both valves are open at the same time.

valve retainer Thick, washer-shaped piece of metal with a tapered center hole that is fitted over the top of the valve stem and holds the top of the valve spring to keep pressure on the valves.

valve springs Coil springs that return valves to their fully closed positions, and hold them closed, after being opened.

valve stem seals Allow only enough oil past them to lubricate the valve guide.

valve timing The relationship between the crankshaft and the valve opening events, which is what allows combustion to happen properly.

valvetrain Consists of the rocker arms, push rods, lifters, camshaft, and the valves.

vane-type phaser This type of phaser operates with a set of paddles inside the assembly. When oil pressure is applied to one side of the paddles, it rotates the camshaft inside the phaser; to reverse the rotation, it applies oil pressure to the opposite side of the paddles.

variable displacement engine An engine that can change the cubic inches of displacement through cylinder deactivation.

variable geometry turbocharger (VGT) Type of turbocharger that is adjustable by directing exhaust gases toward or away from the exhaust impeller. This is a common way to control the turbocharger more precisely in order to match the requirements of the engine.

venturi effect Occurs when air flows through a constricted section of pipe and there is a reduction in pressure.

vernier calipers An accurate measuring device for internal, external, and depth measurements that incorporates fixed and adjustable jaws.

viscosity The measurement of how easily a liquid flows; the most common organization that rates lubricating fluids is SAE.

viscosity index improver An additive that helps to reduce the change in viscosity as the temperature of the oil changes. Viscosity index improvers also keep the engine oil from becoming too thin during hot operation.

voltmeter Used to check for electrical problems such as cooling fan and temperature gauge issues.

volumetric efficiency The measurement of the amount of air-fuel mixture that is drawn into the cylinder as compared to the size of the cylinder.

V-type Has a wedge-shaped interior and sits inside a corresponding groove in the pulley. The sides of the V-belt wedge in the sides of the pulley.

wad punch A type of punch that is hollow for cutting circular shapes in soft materials such as gaskets.

warding file A type of thin, flat file with a tapered end.

wastegate Allows for exhaust to bypass the turbocharger impeller so that the turbocharger will not overspeed,

water jackets Passages surrounding the cylinders and head on the engine where coolant can flow to pick up excess heat. They are sealed by replaceable core plugs.

water pump A pump that is driven by the engine to move coolant through the cooling system so that heat can be extracted from the engine and transferred to the air through radiation.

wedge combustion chamber A combustion chamber that tapers away from the spark plug and where the valves are in a straight line in the cylinder head.

welding helmet Protective gear designed for arc welding; it provides protection against foreign particles entering the eye, and the lens is tinted to reduce the glare of the welding arc.

windage tray Component usually made out of sheet metal or plastic; it prevents the churning of oil by the rotation of the crankshaft.

wire clamp A spring clamp that is not adjustable. It is fitted and removed with special hose clamp pliers, which have grooved jaws.

Woodruff key A piece of steel that has part of the key in a half moon and the other half straight. Used on shafts to spin a gear or component on the shaft.

wrenches A generic term to describe tools that tighten and loosen fasteners with hexagonal heads.

yield point The point at which a bolt is stretched so hard that it will not return to its original length when loosened; it is measured in pounds per square inch of bolt cross section.

INDEX